# 重庆统计年鉴

CHONGQING STATISTICAL YEARBOOK 2023

2023

# 重慶 统计年鉴 2023

CHONGQING STATISTICAL YEARBOOK 2023

重庆市统计局
国家统计局重庆调查总队 编
CHONGQING MUNICIPAL BUREAU OF STATISTICS
NBS SURVEY OFFICE IN CHONGQING

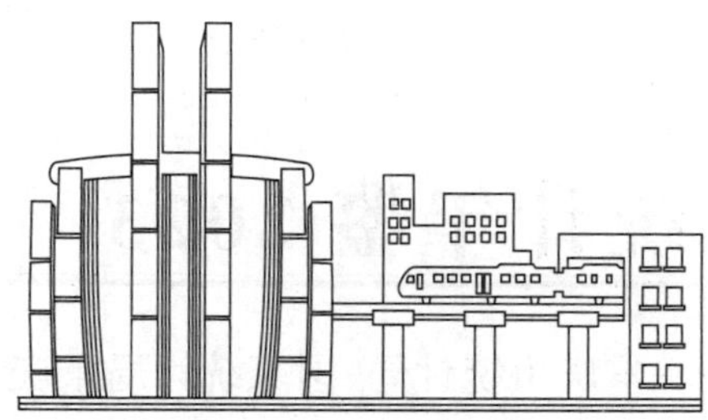

中国统计出版社
China Statistics Press

**图书在版编目（CIP）数据**

重庆统计年鉴. 2023 = Chongqing Statistical Yearbook 2023 : 汉英对照 / 重庆市统计局, 国家统计局重庆调查总队编. -- 北京 : 中国统计出版社, 2023.8
ISBN 978-7-5230-0161-5

Ⅰ. ①重… Ⅱ. ①重… ②国… Ⅲ. ①统计资料－重庆－2023－年鉴－汉、英 Ⅳ. ①C832.719-54

中国国家版本馆 CIP 数据核字（2023）第 133188 号

# 重庆统计年鉴 2023

作　　者 / 重庆市统计局　国家统计局重庆调查总队
责任编辑 / 熊丹书
装帧设计 / 重庆合纪元广告设计有限公司
出版发行 / 中国统计出版社有限公司
地　　址 / 北京市丰台区西三环南路甲 6 号
邮政编码 / 100073
电　　话 / 邮购（010）63376909　书店（010）68783171
网　　址 / http://www.zgtjcbs.com
印　　刷 / 重庆巍承印务有限公司
经　　销 / 新华书店
开　　本 / 890mm × 1240mm 1/16
字　　数 / 1456 千字
印　　张 / 45.5
版　　别 / 2023 年 8 月第 1 版
版　　次 / 2023 年 8 月第 1 次印刷
定　　价 / 430.00 元　Price:430.00yuan(RMB)

本书附同版本 CD-ROM 一张，光盘内容以书面文字为准。
如有印装差错，由本社发行部调换。

《重庆统计年鉴 2023》
编辑委员会



编辑部



**CHONGQING STATISTICAL YEARBOOK 2023**
**EDITORIAL BOARD**



**EDITORIAL DEPARTMENT**

# 编者说明
EDITOR'S NOTES

一、《重庆统计年鉴 2023》是由重庆市统计局和国家统计局重庆调查总队编纂、中国统计出版社公开出版发行的一部全面记录重庆市经济建设和社会发展情况的大型资料性年刊。本书收录了重庆市历史重要年份和2022年经济和社会各方面的统计数据，以及各区县（自治县）主要统计资料。

二、全书共二十二章，包括：1.综合;2.国民经济核算;3.人口与就业;4.固定资产投资;5.能源消费;6.财政;7.人民生活与物价;8.城镇建设;9.资源和环境;10.要素市场;11.农业和农村经济;12.工业;13.建筑业;14.运输和邮电;15.国内贸易;16.对外经济贸易和旅游业;17.金融业;18.教育、科技和文化业;19.卫生、体育和其他社会活动;20.区县;21.三峡工程重庆库区移民;22.基本单位名录库。同时附录一个篇章：全国及各省（自治区、直辖市）主要统计资料。每章前设《简要说明》，介绍本章节的主要内容和资料来源，章末附有《主要统计指标解释》。

三、本年鉴统计资料：大部分数据来自统计年报，部分来自抽样调查。

四、本年鉴所使用的度量衡单位均采用国际统一标准计量单位；各种分类标准均采用国家统一分类标准。

五、本年鉴部分数据的合计数或相对数，由于计量单位取舍不同而产生的计算误差未作机械调整。

六、本年鉴各表的部分指标注解位于该表下方或最后一张续表的下方。

七、符号使用说明：年鉴各表中的“空格”表示该项统计指标数据不足本表最小单位数、数据不详或无该项数据；“#”表示其中的主要项。

八、本年鉴在编辑、翻译过程中得到诸多单位和同志的大力支持，在此深表谢意。限于我们的水平，加之时间仓促，请各界人士在使用资料时如发现错误和不足，恳请批评指正。

Ⅰ. *Chongqing Statistical Yearbook 2023* is a large statistical yearbook compiled by Chongqing Municipal Bureau of Statistics and NBS Survey Office in Chongqing and published by China Statistics Press, which records the economic construction and social development of Chongqing in an all-round way. The yearbook covers the comprehensive data on Chongqing's social and economic development in 2022 and some major years in the history, as well as the major statistics on all the districts and counties (autonomous counties).

Ⅱ. The yearbook contains 22 chapters, namely 1. Comprehensive Statistics;2. National Economic Accounting;3. Population and Employment;4. Investment in Fixed Assets;5. Energy Consumption;6. Government Finance;7. People's Livelihood and Prices;8. Urban Construction;9. Resources and Environment;10. Markets of Key Factors;11. Agriculture and Rural Economy;12. Industry;13. Construction;14. Transport, Postal and Telecommunication Services;15. Domestic Trade;16. Foreign Economic Relations, Trade and Tourism;17. Financial Intermediation;18. Education, Science & Technology and Culture;19. Public Health, Sports and Other Social Activities;20. Districts;21. Resettlement of Chongqing Reservoir Area of Three Gorges Project;22. Statistics on Basic Units. There is also an *Appendix* which covers the main data of the whole nation and other provinces, autonomous regions and municipalities. There is a *Brief Introduction* at the beginning of each chapter, which introduces the main contents of the chapter and the sources of data. The Explanatory Notes on Main Statistical Indicators is provided at the end of each chapter.

Ⅲ. The data in this publication: most of the data are obtained from the annual statistical reports, while some others are obtained from sample surveys.

Ⅳ. The units of measurement used in this yearbook are international standard measurement units; and the basis of classification of this book complies with the national uniform standard.

Ⅴ. The statistical discrepancies of the total values or relative values due to rounding are not adjusted in this yearbook.

Ⅵ. The notes concerning individual indicators are placed at the lower part of the table or the lower part of the last page.

Ⅶ. Notations used in this yearbook: (blank space) indicates that the figure is not large enough to be measured with the smallest unit in the table, or data are unknown, or are not available; " # " indicates a major breakdown of the total.

Ⅷ. We'd like to send our sincere acknowledgement various units and comrades for their vigorous assistances during the edition and translation of this yearbook. Due to our limited ability and the hasty time, faults and shortage are unavoidable. Any criticism or suggestion is appreciated.

# 目 录
CONTENTS

## 第一章 综 合 COMPREHENSIVE STATISTICS
CHAPTER 1



## 第二章 国民经济核算 NATIONAL ECONOMIC ACCOUNTING
CHAPTER 2

# 目　录
CONTENTS



## 第三章 CHAPTER 3　人口与就业　POPULATION AND EMPLOYMENT

# 目 录
CONTENTS

## 第四章 CHAPTER 4 固定资产投资 INVESTMENT IN FIXED ASSETS

## 第五章 CHAPTER 5 能源消费 ENERGY CONSUMPTION

# 目 录
CONTENTS



## 第六章 CHAPTER 6 财 政 GOVERNMENT FINANCE



## 第七章 CHAPTER 7 人民生活与物价 PEOPLE'S LIVING CONDITIONS AND PRICE OF GOODS

# 目 录
CONTENTS

## 第九章 CHAPTER 9 资源和环境 RESOURCES AND ENVIRONMENT

# 目 录

CONTENTS

## 第十章 CHAPTER 10 要素市场 MARKETS OF KEY FACTORS



## 第十一章 CHAPTER 11 农业和农村经济 AGRICULTURE AND RURAL ECONOMY

## 第十二章 CHAPTER 12 工 业 INDUSTRY

# 目 录
CONTENTS



## 第十三章 CHAPTER 13 建筑业 CONSTRUCTION

## 第十四章 运输和邮电 TRANSPORT, POSTAL AND TELECOMMUNICATION SERVICES
CHAPTER 14

# 目　录
CONTENTS



## 第十五章 CHAPTER 15 国内贸易 DOMESTIC TRADE

## 第十六章 对外经济贸易和旅游业 CHAPTER 16 FOREIGN ECONOMICRELATIONS, TRADE AND TOURISM

# 目 录

CONTENTS



## 第十七章 金融业 FINANCIAL STATISTICS

CHAPTER 17

# 目 录
CONTENTS

## 第十八章 教育、科技和文化业 EDUCATION, SCIENCE, TECHNOLOGY AND CULTURE
CHAPTER 18

# 目 录
CONTENTS



## 第十九章 卫生、体育及其他社会活动 CHAPTER 19 PUBLIC HEALTH, SPORTS AND OTHER SOCIAL ACTIVITIES

## 第二十章 区 县 DISTRICTS, COUNTIES
CHAPTER 20

# 目 录
CONTENTS

## 第二十一章 三峡工程重庆库区移民 RESERVOIR AREA OF THREE GORGES PROJECT IN CHONGQING
CHAPTER 21



## 第二十二章 基本单位名录库 STATISTICS ON BASIC UNITS
CHAPTER 22

# 附 录 APPENDIX

# 第一章·综 合

## COMPREHENSIVE STATISTICS

# 简要说明

BRIEF INTRODUCTION

本章主要包括重庆市行政区划、国民经济和社会发展综合资料，由市统计局综合处根据有关部门资料进行整理和编辑。

行政区划资料由市民政局提供。

This chapter mainly covers the data of Chongqing's administrative divisions and national economic and social development. The data of this chapter are sorted and compiled by Division of Comprehensive Statistics, Chongqing Municipal Bureau of Statistics on the basis of the information provided by the relevant departments.

The data of administrative divisions are provided by Chongqing Civil Affairs Bureau.

# 表 1.1 行政区划（2022 年）
## DIVISIONS OF ADMINISTRATIVE AREAS (2022)

单位：个 (unit)

| 地 区 | Region | 行政区划 Divisions of Administrative Areas | | | | 自治组织 Autonomous Organization | |
|---|---|---|---|---|---|---|---|
| | | 镇 Towns | 乡 Townships | 民族乡 Ethnic Township | 街道 Street Communities | 村委会 Village Committees | 社区居委会 Neighborhood Committees |
| **全 市** | **Total** | **625** | **147** | **14** | **245** | **7947** | **3283** |
| 两江新区 | Liang Jiang new Area | | | | 8 | | 55 |
| 高新区 | High tech District | 7 | | | 3 | 61 | 36 |
| 万盛经开区 | Wansheng Economic development District | 8 | | | 2 | 56 | 43 |
| 万州区 | Wanzhou District | 27 | 9 | 2 | 14 | 413 | 197 |
| 黔江区 | Qianjiang District | 18 | 6 | | 6 | 138 | 82 |
| 涪陵区 | Fuling District | 14 | 2 | | 11 | 303 | 120 |
| 渝中区 | Yuzhong District | | | | 11 | | 79 |
| 大渡口区 | Dadukou District | 3 | | | 5 | 32 | 61 |
| 江北区 | Jiangbei District | 3 | | | 9 | 13 | 111 |
| 沙坪坝区 | Shapingba District | 4 | | | 18 | 48 | 112 |
| 九龙坡区 | Jiulongpo District | 4 | | | 9 | 48 | 111 |
| 南岸区 | Nan'an District | 7 | | | 8 | 48 | 103 |
| 北碚区 | Beibei District | 8 | | | 9 | 104 | 86 |
| 渝北区 | Yubei District | 11 | | | 11 | 173 | 183 |
| 巴南区 | Ba'nan District | 14 | | | 9 | 198 | 115 |
| 长寿区 | Changshou District | 12 | | | 7 | 221 | 49 |
| 江津区 | Jiangjin District | 25 | | | 5 | 175 | 126 |
| 合川区 | Hechuan District | 23 | | | 7 | 322 | 97 |
| 永川区 | Yongchuan District | 16 | | | 7 | 207 | 56 |
| 南川区 | Nanchuan District | 29 | 2 | | 3 | 184 | 60 |
| 綦江区（不含万盛） | Qijiang District (excluding Wansheng) | 16 | | | 5 | 302 | 79 |
| 大足区 | Dazu District | 21 | | | 6 | 203 | 106 |
| 璧山区 | Bishan District | 9 | | | 6 | 131 | 60 |
| 铜梁区 | Tongliang District | 23 | | | 5 | 266 | 67 |
| 潼南区 | Tongnan District | 20 | | | 3 | 208 | 96 |
| 荣昌区 | Rongchang District | 15 | | | 6 | 92 | 64 |
| 开州区 | Kaizhou District | 27 | 5 | | 8 | 423 | 112 |
| 梁平区 | Liangping District | 26 | 2 | | 5 | 269 | 74 |
| 武隆区 | Wulong District | 10 | 8 | 4 | 4 | 184 | 30 |
| 城口县 | Chengkou County | 10 | 13 | | 2 | 173 | 31 |
| 丰都县 | Fengdu County | 23 | 5 | | 2 | 260 | 78 |
| 垫江县 | Dianjiang County | 22 | 2 | | 2 | 222 | 79 |
| 忠 县 | Zhongxian County | 19 | 5 | 1 | 4 | 280 | 92 |
| 云阳县 | Yunyang County | 31 | 6 | 1 | 4 | 380 | 98 |
| 奉节县 | Fengjie County | 18 | 7 | 4 | 4 | 314 | 78 |
| 巫山县 | Wushan County | 11 | 11 | 2 | 2 | 301 | 39 |
| 巫溪县 | Wuxi County | 19 | 11 | | 2 | 288 | 41 |
| 石柱土家族自治县 | Shizhu County | 17 | 13 | | 3 | 198 | 44 |
| 秀山土家族苗族自治县 | Xiushan County | 18 | 4 | | 5 | 202 | 66 |
| 酉阳土家族苗族自治县 | Youyang County | 19 | 18 | | 2 | 270 | 8 |
| 彭水苗族土家族自治县 | Pengshui County | 18 | 18 | | 3 | 237 | 59 |

# 表 1.2 国民经济和社会发展总量与速度指标
PRINCIPAL AGGREGATE INDICATORS ON NATIONAL ECONOMIC AND SOCIAL DEVELOPMENT AND GROWTH RATE

| 指　标 | Item | 总量指标 Aggregate Indicators | | |
|---|---|---|---|---|
| | | 1996 | 2000 | 2011 |
| **人口与就业** | **Population and Employment** | | | |
| **人　口(万人)** | **Population (10 000 persons)** | | | |
| 年末常住人口 | Year-end Resident Population | 2875.30 | 2848.82 | 2944.43 |
| #城　镇 | Urban | 848.21 | 1013.88 | 1618.71 |
| 乡　村 | Rural | 2027.09 | 1834.94 | 1325.72 |
| #男　性 | Male | 1465.99 | 1460.57 | 1489.68 |
| 女　性 | Female | 1409.31 | 1388.25 | 1454.75 |
| **就　业(万人)** | **Employment (10 000 persons)** | | | |
| 就业人员数 | Employed Persons | 1719.43 | 1661.16 | 1587.04 |
| #在岗职工人数 | On-post Staff and Workers | 294.63 | 208.87 | 318.73 |
| 城镇登记失业人数 | Registered Unemployment in Urban Areas | 10.95 | 10.15 | 12.96 |
| **宏观经济** | **Macroeconomic Indicators** | | | |
| **国民经济核算(亿元)** | **National Economic Accounting (100 million yuan)** | | | |
| 本市生产总值 | Gross Domestic Product | 1326.40 | 1822.06 | 10161.17 |
| 第一产业 | Primary Industry | 287.56 | 280.45 | 794.14 |
| 第二产业 | Secondary Industry | 575.20 | 774.63 | 4571.26 |
| #工　业 | Industry | 506.83 | 644.04 | 3700.24 |
| 第三产业 | Tertiary Industry | 463.64 | 766.98 | 4795.77 |
| **固定资产投资(亿元)** | **Investment in Fixed Assets (100 million yuan)** | | | |
| 固定资产投资总额 | Total Investment in Fixed Assets | 320.73 | 655.81 | 7685.87 |
| 建设项目 | Construction Projects | 265.11 | 516.18 | 5670.78 |
| 房地产开发 | Real Estate Development | 55.62 | 139.63 | 2015.09 |
| **财　政(亿元)** | **Government Finance (100 million yuan)** | | | |
| 一般公共预算收入 | General Public Budget Revenue | | | |
| 一般公共预算支出 | General Public Budget Expenditure | | | |
| **物价指数(上年=100)** | **Price Indices (preceding year=100)** | | | |
| 居民消费价格指数 | Consumer Price Index | 109.7 | 96.7 | 105.3 |
| 工业生产者出厂价格指数 | Producer Price Indices for Manufactured Goods | 104.1 | 98.6 | 103.8 |
| 工业生产者购进价格指数 | Purchasing Price Indices of Raw Material, Fuel and Power | 106.3 | 105.6 | 105.7 |
| 商品零售价格指数 | Retail Price Index | 106.1 | 95.5 | 104.7 |
| **产　业** | **Industry** | | | |
| **农　业** | **Agriculture** | | | |
| 农林牧渔业总产值(亿元) | Gross Output Value of Farming, Forestry, Animal Husbandry and Fishery (100 million yuan) | 424.99 | 412.63 | 1204.16 |
| #农　业 | Farming | 271.38 | 244.74 | 717.28 |
| 林　业 | Forestry | 11.55 | 10.82 | 38.09 |
| 牧　业 | Animal Husbandry | 131.17 | 141.99 | 398.10 |
| 渔　业 | Fishery | 10.89 | 15.08 | 34.94 |
| 主要农产品产量(万吨) | Output of Major Farm Products (10 000 tons) | | | |
| 粮　食 | Grain | 1172.14 | 1131.21 | 1064.16 |
| 油　料 | Oil-bearing Crops | 23.60 | 31.06 | 45.79 |
| 烟　叶 | Tobacco | 13.24 | 10.41 | 9.36 |

注：1) 本表数据本市生产总值、工业增加值速度指标按可比价计算，其余指标均为自然增长。
2) 2017 年起按营改增试点后新的收入划分办法及新增建设用地土地有偿使用收入等基金列转公共预算，与往年不可比。
3) 为与国家统计口径一致，剔除跨省项目投资和农户投资，2017 年固定资产投资总量数据与往年存在口径差异（下表同）。
4) 2020 年年末常住人口数据用第七次人口普查时点数，第七次全国人口普查后国家对历史年份人口和就业数据进行了修订。

| 总量指标 Aggregate Indicators | | 平均增长速度(%) Average Annual Growth Rate(%) | | | |
|---|---|---|---|---|---|
| 2017 | 2022 | 直辖以来 Since being directly under the Central Government 1997-2022 | 西部大开发以来 Since the Western Development Strategy 2001-2022 | 十八大以来 Since the 18th National Congress 2012-2022 | 近五年 Average growth rate in the past five years 2018-2022 |
| | | | | | |
| 3143.51 | 3213.34 | 0.4 | 0.5 | 0.8 | 0.4 |
| 2043.13 | 2280.32 | 3.9 | 3.8 | 3.2 | 2.2 |
| 1100.38 | 933.02 | -2.9 | -3.0 | -3.1 | -3.2 |
| 1585.31 | 1623.17 | 0.4 | 0.5 | 0.8 | 0.5 |
| 1558.20 | 1590.17 | 0.5 | 0.6 | 0.8 | 0.4 |
| | | | | | |
| 1659.33 | 1644.37 | -0.2 | 0.0 | 0.3 | -0.2 |
| 369.18 | 321.66 | 0.3 | 2.0 | 0.1 | -2.7 |
| 14.26 | 21.88 | 2.7 | 3.6 | 4.9 | 8.9 |
| | | | | | |
| 20066.29 | 29129.03 | 10.7 | 11.0 | 8.6 | 5.4 |
| 1276.09 | 2012.05 | 4.1 | 4.5 | 4.8 | 4.9 |
| 8455.02 | 11693.86 | 12.6 | 13.0 | 8.9 | 4.9 |
| 6202.40 | 8275.99 | 12.7 | 13.2 | 8.8 | 5.1 |
| 10335.18 | 15423.12 | 10.3 | 10.1 | 8.8 | 5.9 |
| | | | | | |
| | | 19.6 | 18.7 | 10.9 | 4.7 |
| | | 18.2 | 18.2 | 12.3 | 8.6 |
| | | 18.0 | 15.7 | 5.1 | -2.7 |
| | | | | | |
| 2252.4 | 2103.4 | | | | |
| 4336.3 | 4892.8 | | | | |
| | | | | | |
| 101.0 | 102.1 | 1.6 | 2.1 | 1.9 | 1.9 |
| 104.1 | 102.3 | | 0.9 | 0.2 | 1.3 |
| 104.4 | 104.4 | | 0.3 | 0.8 | 2.8 |
| 100.8 | 102.5 | 0.6 | 1.2 | 1.4 | 1.8 |
| | | | | | |
| 1902.47 | 3068.45 | 4.2 | 4.7 | 4.9 | 5.3 |
| | | | | | |
| 1165.69 | 1881.78 | 4.0 | 4.5 | 4.7 | 5.1 |
| 85.17 | 176.42 | 6.1 | 8.7 | 10.5 | 11.5 |
| 522.48 | 800.94 | 3.5 | 3.6 | 3.2 | 3.7 |
| 94.81 | 136.99 | 7.9 | 7.5 | 9.0 | 3.4 |
| | | | | | |
| 1079.87 | 1072.84 | -0.3 | -0.2 | 0.1 | -0.1 |
| 62.40 | 70.85 | 4.3 | 3.8 | 4.0 | 2.6 |
| 6.91 | 5.52 | -3.3 | -2.8 | -4.7 | -4.4 |

Note: a) The growth rate of GDP and value-added of industry is calculated on the basis of comparable price, while the other indices are natural growth rate.

b) Due to the change of replacing business tax with VAT under the new revenue division system, and the funds like the revenue from paid use of newly-added construction land have included in public budget since 2017,the data are incomparable with the previous year.

c) According to the NBS's system, the investments of trans-provincial projects and rural households have been removed, so the data of total investment in fixed assets in 2017 are incomparable with the previous years (the same for the tables below).

d) After the 7th national population census, the country revised the population and employment data in historical years.

**表 1.2 续表 1 continued 1**

| 指　标 | Item | 总量指标 Aggregate Indicators 1996 | 2000 | 2011 |
|---|---|---|---|---|
| 茶　叶 | Tea | 1.55 | 1.45 | 2.79 |
| 水　果 | Fruits | 56.62 | 81.68 | 261.16 |
| 猪　肉 | Pork | 114.18 | 122.45 | 138.02 |
| 水产品 | Aquatic Products | 14.07 | 20.03 | 27.56 |
| **工　业（规模以上）** | **Industry (above Designated Size)** | | | |
| 工业总产值（亿元） | Gross Output Value of Industry (100 million yuan) | 730.41 | 962.32 | 11847.06 |
| 主营业务收入（亿元） | Revenue from Principal Business (100 million yuan) | 711.34 | 959.36 | 11382.34 |
| 利税总额（亿元） | Total Pre-tax Profits (100 million yuan) | 48.04 | 85.57 | 1164.30 |
| 产品销售率（%） | Sales as Percentage of Output (%) | 96.5 | 99.1 | 97.4 |
| 全员劳动生产率（元 / 人年） | Overall Labor Productivity (yuan/person-year) | 13546 | 31081 | 213463 |
| 主要工业产品产量 | Output of Major Industrial Products | | | |
| 天然气（亿立方米） | Natural Gas (100 million cu.m) | 26.10 | 38.98 | 62.94 |
| 发电量（亿千瓦时） | Electricity (100 million kwh) | 128.73 | 167.90 | 529.57 |
| 钢　材（万吨） | Steel Products (10 000 tons) | 117.55 | 156.98 | 948.17 |
| 铝　材（万吨） | Aluminum Products (10 000 tons) | 7.36 | 13.98 | 134.45 |
| 微型计算机设备（万台） | Micro-computers (10 000 units) | | | 2547.82 |
| 水　泥（万吨） | Cement (10 000 tons) | 648.76 | 1402.78 | 4935.15 |
| 汽　车（万辆） | Motor Vehicles (10 000 vehicles) | 12.41 | 24.59 | 172.20 |
| #轿　车 | Cars | 1.34 | 4.82 | 93.67 |
| 摩托车（万辆） | Motorcycles (10 000 vehicles) | 177.36 | 191.07 | 879.59 |
| 啤　酒（万千升） | Beer (10 000 kilo liters) | 28.54 | 50.42 | 77.31 |
| 卷　烟（亿支） | Cigarettes (100 million units) | 453.91 | 343.50 | 516.00 |
| **建筑业（资质内）** | **Construction (Grade above)** | | | |
| 建筑业总产值（亿元） | Gross Output Value of Construction (100 million yuan) | 205.30 | 348.66 | 3328.83 |
| 房屋施工面积（万平方米） | Floor Space Under Construction (10 000 sq.m) | 4065 | 6088 | 21976 |
| 房屋竣工面积（万平方米） | Floor Space Completed (10 000 sq.m) | 2277 | 3084 | 8990 |
| **交通运输业** | **Transportation** | | | |
| 客运量（万人） | Passenger Traffic (10 000 persons) | 42370 | 56969 | 141499 |
| 铁　路 | Railway | 972 | 1442 | 2933 |
| 公　路 | Highway | 37410 | 53170 | 136142 |
| 水　运 | Waterway | 3900 | 2240 | 1322 |
| 民　航 | Civil Aviation | 88 | 117 | 1102 |
| 货运量（万吨） | Freight Traffic (10 000 tons) | 24339 | 26852 | 96782 |
| 铁　路 | Railway | 1633 | 1812 | 2191 |
| 公　路 | Highway | 20214 | 23646 | 82818 |
| 水　运 | Waterway | 2491 | 1392 | 11762 |
| 民　航 | Civil Aviation | 1.20 | 2.40 | 11.31 |
| 港口货物吞吐量（万吨） | Cargo Throughput in Coastal Ports (10 000 tons) | 1076 | 2448 | 11606 |

5) 工业总产值的绝对值和指数按现价计算。2018 年同期总产值、主营业务收入、利润总额及产品产量数据根据有关制度规定进行了修订，增速按照可比口径计算。
6) 建筑业 2003 年起的所有数据均不包括劳务分包企业。
7) 从 2000 年起民航货运量按新制度统计，旅客行李不再计入货运。
8) 1996 年起铁路数据按重庆现地域进行了调整（以下各表同）。
9) 2013 年公路、水路数据按部门专项调查作了调整，速度按可比价计算。

| 总量指标 Aggregate Indicators | | 平均增长速度(%) Average Annual Growth Rate(%) | | | |
| --- | --- | --- | --- | --- | --- |
| 2017 | 2022 | 直辖以来 Since being directly under the Central Government 1997-2022 | 西部大开发以来 Since the Western Development Strategy 2001-2022 | 十八大以来 Since the 18th National Congress 2012-2022 | 近五年 Average growth rate in the past five years 2018-2022 |
| 3.88 | 403.38 | 4.8 | 6.1 | 6.1 | 6.5 |
| 5.30 | 593.28 | 9.5 | 9.4 | 8.2 | 8.0 |
| 129.97 | 149.96 | 1.1 | 0.9 | 0.8 | 2.9 |
| | | | | | |
| 21173.21 | 25827.06 | 16.6 | 17.6 | 10.9 | 7.3 |
| 20772.41 | 26417.28 | 16.4 | 18.1 | 11.5 | 7.8 |
| 2474.10 | 2632.51 | 17.5 | 17.8 | 12.3 | 4.2 |
| 98.0 | 97.5 | | | | |
| 318885 | 457817 | 15.7 | 14.5 | 8.0 | 7.5 |
| | | | | | |
| 111.31 | 141.45 | 6.7 | 6.0 | 7.6 | 4.9 |
| 690.51 | 997.84 | 8.2 | 8.4 | 5.9 | 7.6 |
| 917.25 | 1690.59 | 10.8 | 11.4 | 5.4 | 13.0 |
| 188.36 | 238.64 | 14.3 | 13.8 | 5.4 | 4.8 |
| 6619.78 | 8631.92 | | | 11.7 | 5.5 |
| 6370.93 | 5316.55 | 8.4 | 6.2 | 0.7 | -3.6 |
| 299.82 | 209.18 | 11.5 | 10.2 | 1.8 | -6.9 |
| 84.94 | 54.86 | 15.3 | 11.7 | -4.7 | -8.4 |
| 595.69 | 448.88 | 3.6 | 4.0 | -5.9 | -5.5 |
| 78.95 | 80.75 | 4.1 | 2.2 | 0.4 | 0.5 |
| 421.50 | 569.55 | 0.9 | 2.3 | 0.9 | 6.2 |
| | | | | | |
| 7608.00 | 9746.96 | 16.0 | 16.3 | 10.3 | 5.1 |
| 33211 | 34968 | 8.6 | 8.3 | 4.3 | 1.0 |
| 13448 | 11770 | 6.5 | 6.3 | 2.5 | -2.6 |
| | | | | | |
| 63298 | 21149 | -2.6 | -4.4 | -15.9 | -19.7 |
| 6349 | 4824 | 6.4 | 5.6 | 4.6 | -5.3 |
| 53307 | 14432 | -3.6 | -5.8 | -18.5 | -23.0 |
| 866 | 378 | -8.6 | -7.8 | -10.8 | -15.3 |
| 2776 | 1516 | 11.6 | 12.3 | 5.9 | -11.4 |
| 115346 | 135433 | 6.8 | 7.6 | 3.1 | 3.3 |
| 1808 | 1828 | 0.4 | 0.0 | -1.6 | 0.2 |
| 95019 | 111915 | 6.8 | 7.3 | 2.8 | 3.3 |
| 18506 | 21678 | 8.7 | 13.3 | 5.7 | 3.2 |
| 13.00 | 12.00 | 9.3 | 7.6 | 4.2 | -1.6 |
| 19722 | 20655 | 12.0 | 10.2 | 5.4 | 0.9 |

e) The value and index of gross output value of industry are calculated at current price.Since 2018, gross output value, revenue from principal business, total pre-tax profits and output of products are adjusted in accordance with related regulations,and the growth rate are calculated by comparable scope.
f) All the data of construction has not included labor subcontractors since 2003.
g) Since 2000, the cargo turnover of civil aviation has been calculated by the new statistic system, and the luggage of passengers is no longer accounted in.
h) The data of railway has been modified based on the present administrative division of Chongqing since 1996 (the same for the tables below).
i) The data of highway and waterway has been modified according to the specialized survey by the related departments since 2013, and the growth rate is calculated on the basis of comparable price.

**表 1.2 续表 2 continued 2**

| 指　标 | Item | 总量指标 Aggregate Indicators | | |
|---|---|---|---|---|
| | | 1996 | 2000 | 2011 |
| **邮电通信业** | **Postal and Telecommunication Services** | | | |
| 邮电业务收入(亿元) | Business Revenue from Postal and Telecommunication Services (100 million yuan) | 16.73 | 54.44 | 202.39 |
| 本地电话用户(万户) | Local Telephone Subscribers (10 000 subscribers) | 66.50 | 268.43 | 571.25 |
| 移动电话用户(万户) | Mobile Telephone Subscribers (10 000 subscribers) | 9.00 | 160.00 | 1801.19 |
| 固定互联网络用户(万户) | Internet Subscribers (10 000 subscribers) | 0.03 | 10.00 | 326.78 |
| **国内贸易(亿元)** | **Domestic Trade (100 million yuan)** | | | |
| 社会消费品零售总额 | Retail Sales of Consumer Goods | 514.17 | 765.52 | 4384.77 |
| 对外贸易(亿美元) | Foreign Trade (USD 100 million) | | | |
| 进出口总值 | Total Imports and Exports | 15.85 | 17.85 | 292.18 |
| 出　口 | Exports | 5.93 | 9.95 | 198.38 |
| 进　口 | Imports | 9.92 | 7.90 | 93.80 |
| **实际使用外资** | **Realized FDI Value** | | | |
| 实际使用外资(FDI)(亿美元) | Realized FDI Value (USD 100 million) | 2.19 | 2.44 | 58.26 |
| **国际旅游** | **International Tourism** | | | |
| 接待入境旅游者(万人次) | Number of Overseas Visitor Arrival Received (10 000 person-time) | 16.18 | 26.61 | 186.40 |
| 国际旅游收入(万美元) | Foreign Exchange Earnings from International Tourism (USD 10 000) | 7090 | 13837 | 96806 |
| **金融保险业(亿元)** | **Finance and Insurance (100 million yuan)** | | | |
| 金融机构人民币存款年末余额 | Deposit Balance of RMB of Financial Institutions | 846.43 | 1904.71 | 15832.81 |
| #住户存款 | Saving Deposits of Residents | | | |
| 金融机构人民币贷款年末余额 | Loan Balance of RMB of Financial Institutions | 913.93 | 1881.29 | 13001.39 |
| 股票筹资额 | Raised Capital of Shares | 10.41 | 22.63 | 158.02 |
| 保险公司保费收入 | Insurance Premium of Insurance Companies | 12.82 | 27.71 | 311.81 |
| 保险公司赔款及给付 | Indemnity Expenditure and Payment of Insurance Companies | 6.48 | 8.27 | 73.98 |
| **教育、科技、文化** | **Education, Science & Technology and Culture** | | | |
| **教　育** | **Education** | | | |
| 专任教师(万人) | Full-time Teachers (10 000 person) | | | |
| #普通高等学校 | Regular Institutions of Higher Education | 0.94 | 1.04 | 3.31 |
| 普通中学 | Regular Secondary Schools | 6.95 | 8.18 | 11.10 |
| 小　学 | Primary Schools | 11.77 | 11.09 | 11.53 |
| 在校学生数(万人) | Student Enrollment (10 000 persons) | | | |
| #普通高等学校 | Regular Institutions of Higher Education | 7.99 | 13.25 | 61.30 |
| 普通中学 | Regular Secondary Schools | 101.27 | 147.79 | 183.89 |
| 小　学 | Primary Schools | 273.71 | 276.13 | 195.48 |
| 教育经费支出(亿元) | Expenditure on Education (100 million yuan) | | | 497.14 |
| **科　技** | **Science and Technology** | | | |
| 技术市场成交额(亿元) | Transaction Value of Technology Market (100 million yuan)" | 3.43 | 29.66 | 101.08 |

10) 畜牧业数据自 2007 年起根据第三次农业普查数据进行了调整。
11) 2019 年起，水运港口吞吐量调整为交通运输部一套表联网直报数据（不含无营运证码头）。
12) 普通高等学校数据含研究生。
13) 因全国银行业统计制度调整，报表项目归属发生变化，2011 年起"个人存款"口径作了调整。
14) 因国家保险核算制度改变，2011 年起保费收入指标同期不可比。

| 总量指标 Aggregate Indicators | | 平均增长速度(%) Average Annual Growth Rate(%) | | | |
|---|---|---|---|---|---|
| 2017 | 2022 | 直辖以来 Since being directly under the Central Government 1997-2022 | 西部大开发以来 Since the Western Development Strategy 2001-2022 | 十八大以来 Since the 18th National Congress 2012-2022 | 近五年 Average growth rate in the past five years 2018-2022 |
| 350.85 | 507.83 | 14.0 | 10.7 | 8.7 | 7.7 |
| 566.78 | 598.73 | 8.8 | 3.7 | 0.4 | 1.1 |
| 3274.89 | 3962.16 | 26.4 | 15.7 | 7.4 | 3.9 |
| 866.93 | 1660.77 | 52.2 | 26.2 | 15.9 | 13.9 |
| 9769.39 | 13926.08 | 13.5 | 14.1 | 11.1 | 7.3 |
| 666.04 | 1228.30 | 18.2 | 21.2 | 13.9 | 13.0 |
| 425.99 | 790.89 | 20.7 | 22.0 | 13.4 | 13.2 |
| 240.05 | 437.41 | 15.7 | 20.0 | 15.0 | 12.8 |
| 22.20 | 18.57 | 8.6 | 9.7 | -9.9 | -3.5 |
| 358.35 | 6.55 | -3.4 | -6.2 | -26.2 | -55.1 |
| 194759 | 1166 | -6.7 | -10.6 | -33.1 | -64.1 |
| 33718.98 | 48218.18 | 16.8 | 15.8 | 10.7 | 7.4 |
| 14367.38 | 25458.85 | | | | 12.1 |
| 27871.89 | 49365.86 | 16.6 | 16.0 | 12.9 | 12.1 |
| 102.97 | 173.00 | 11.4 | 9.7 | 0.8 | 10.9 |
| 744.75 | 981.09 | 18.2 | 17.6 | 11.0 | 5.7 |
| 256.83 | 342.99 | 16.5 | 18.5 | 15.0 | 6.0 |
| 4.17 | 5.53 | 7.1 | 7.9 | 4.8 | 5.8 |
| 11.56 | 12.98 | 2.4 | 2.1 | 1.4 | 2.3 |
| 12.53 | 13.41 | 0.5 | 0.5 | 1.4 | 1.4 |
| 80.52 | 117.16 | 10.9 | 10.4 | 6.1 | 7.8 |
| 159.22 | 175.07 | 2.1 | 0.8 | -0.4 | 1.9 |
| 209.95 | 203.19 | -2.5 | -1.4 | 0.4 | -0.7 |
| 944.17 | 1320.70 | | | 6.8 | 5.3 |
| 121.69 | 183.86 | 14.0 | 8.8 | -1.7 | -7.1 |

j) Since 2007, the data of poultry eggs has been adjusted in accordance with the 3rd agricultural census.
k) Since 2019, water port throughput has been adjusted to the Ministry of Transport set of tables networking direct reporting data (excluding docks without operating licenses).
l) The data of regular institutions of higher education include postgraduates.
m) Due to the adjustment of national statistic system for banking, the category of items has been changed. The scope of "Saving Deposits of Residents" has been changed since 2011.
n) Due to the change of national insurance accounting system, the insurance premium since 2011 is incomparable with the previous years.

**表 1.2 续表 3 continued 3**

| 指 标 | Item | 总量指标 Aggregate Indicators 1996 | 2000 | 2011 |
|---|---|---|---|---|
| **文 化** | **Culture** | | | |
| 图书出版数量(万册、万张) | Books Published (10 000 copies) | 13023 | 11198 | 15597 |
| 期刊出版数量(万册) | Magazines Published (10 000 copies) | | 3480 | 5183 |
| 报纸出版数量(万份) | Newspaper Published (10 000 copies) | | 48674 | 66057 |
| 电视人口覆盖率(%) | Television Coverage of Population (%) | 78.90 | 93.70 | 98.56 |
| 广播人口覆盖率(%) | Radio Coverage of Population (%) | 86.30 | 89.90 | 98.02 |
| **家庭、生活** | **Family and Living Standards** | | | |
| **家 庭** | **Family** | | | |
| 城镇常住居民平均每户常住人口(人) | Average Permanent Population Per Household of Urban Residents (person) | | | |
| 农村常住居民平均每户常住人口(人) | Average Permanent Population Per Household of Rural Residents (person) | | | |
| **婚 姻** | **Marital Statistics** | | | |
| 内地居民登记结婚对数(万对) | Registered Marriages of Inland Residents (10 000 couples) | 26.44 | 19.02 | 60.78 |
| 内地居民登记离婚对数(万对) | Registered Divorces of Inland Residents (10 000 couples) | 1.68 | 2.07 | 10.54 |
| **居 住** | **Residence** | | | |
| 城镇常住居民人均住房建筑面积 (平方米) | Per Capita Residential Floor Space of Urban Residents (sq.m) | | | |
| 农村常住居民人均住房建筑面积(平方米) | Per Capita Living Space of Rural Residents (sq.m) | | | |
| **工资和收入** | **Wages and Income** | | | |
| 城镇非私营单位在岗职工工资总额(亿元) | Total Wages of On-post Staff and Workers of Urban Non-private Units (100 million yuan) | 145.49 | 173.23 | 1252.21 |
| 城镇非私营单位在岗职工平均工资(元) | Average Wages of On-post Staff and Workers of Urban Non-private Units(yuan) | 5010 | 8020 | 40042 |
| 城镇常住居民人均可支配收入(元) | Per Capita Disposable Income of Urban Residents (yuan) | 5023 | 6152 | 18517 |
| 农村常住居民人均可支配收入(元) | Per Capita Disposable Income of Rural Residents (yuan) | 1479 | 1900 | 6605 |
| **卫 生** | **Public Health** | | | |
| 医院、卫生院(个) | Hospitals and Health Centers (unit) | 2567 | 2250 | 1407 |
| 卫生技术人员(人) | Medical Technical Personnel (person) | 87542 | 88619 | 120169 |
| #执业(助理)医师 | Licensed (Assistant) Doctors | 30733 | 44940 | 49585 |
| 卫生机构床位数(张) | Number of Beds in Health Care Institutions (bed) | 66339 | 65666 | 115657 |
| **市政建设** | **Municipal Construction** | | | |
| 供水总量(万立方米) | Water Supply (10 000 cu.m) | 84548 | 70722 | 107571 |
| 天然气供气总量(万立方米) | Natural Gas Supply (10 000 cu.m) | 111980 | 75257 | 314354 |
| 排水管道长度(公里) | Length of Draining Pipelines (km) | 1857 | 2806 | 11212 |
| 道路长度(公里) | Length of Urban Roads (km) | 2652 | 3299 | 7158 |
| 公园绿地面积(公顷) | Public Green Areas (hectare) | 1104 | 1588 | 23755 |

15) 因人民银行统计指标口径发生变动，2015 年起人民币存贷款余额指标同期不可比。
16) 2002 年起卫生统计指标名称变更，统计口径变化，不可与往年同比；2002 年起卫生技术人员和床位不包括医学院校、卫生学校和计生站；执业(助理)医师 2002 年以前统计口径为"医生"(以下各表同)。2010 年指标卫生技术人员、执业(助理)医师为调整数，均含村卫生室。

| 总量指标 Aggregate Indicators | | 平均增长速度(%) Average Annual Growth Rate(%) | | | |
|---|---|---|---|---|---|
| 2017 | 2022 | 直辖以来 Since being directly under the Central Government 1997-2022 | 西部大开发以来 Since the Western Development Strategy 2001-2022 | 十八大以来 Since the 18th National Congress 2012-2022 | 近五年 Average growth rate in the past five years 2018-2022 |
| | | | 1.1 | 0.3 | -1.2 |
| 13532 | 14370 | | 0.0 | -4.3 | -5.4 |
| 4706 | 3372 | | -2.5 | -7.0 | 3.4 |
| 38600 | 31204 | | | | |
| 99.22 | 99.65 | 0.6 | 0.3 | 0.1 | 0.1 |
| 98.96 | 99.55 | 0.6 | 0.4 | 0.1 | 0.1 |
| 3.13 | 2.99 | | | | |
| 2.99 | 2.86 | | | | |
| 26.54 | 17.40 | -1.4 | 0.0 | -4.8 | -7.6 |
| 13.35 | 7.16 | 5.2 | 5.3 | -3.6 | -12.1 |
| 35.28 | 40.56 | | | | |
| 54.81 | 55.72 | | | | |
| 2668.11 | 3586.11 | 13.1 | 14.8 | 10.0 | 6.1 |
| 73272 | 111424 | 12.7 | 12.7 | 9.8 | 8.7 |
| 32193 | 45509 | 8.8 | 9.5 | 8.5 | 7.2 |
| 12638 | 19313 | 10.4 | 11.1 | 10.2 | 8.9 |
| 1640 | 1667 | | | | |
| 191254 | 253241 | | | | |
| 68419 | 94609 | | | | |
| 206080 | 117336 | | | | |
| 149887.73 | 199584 | 3.4 | 4.8 | 5.8 | 5.9 |
| 491352 | 622711 | 6.8 | 10.1 | 6.4 | 4.9 |
| 17335 | 28773 | 11.1 | 11.2 | 8.9 | 10.7 |
| 10427 | 13923 | 6.6 | 6.8 | 6.2 | 6.0 |
| 27999 | 31758 | 13.8 | 14.6 | 2.7 | 2.6 |

o) Due to the change of the PBoC's statistical indicators, the loan and deposit balance of RMB since 2015 is incomparable with the previous years.

p) Due to the changes of names and statistic scopes of the indicators of public health since 2002, the indicators are not comparable with the data in previous years: since 2002, the medical technical personnel and the number of beds have no longer included the data of medical universities, health schools and family plan service stations; the indicator of licensed (assistant) doctor was formerly "doctor" before 2002 (the same for the tables below). The data of medical technical personnel and licensed (assistant) doctors are adjusted data, with village health stations included.

# 表 1.3 国民经济和社会发展结构指标
## COMPOSITION INDICATORS ON NATIONAL ECONOMIC AND SOCIAL DEVELOPMENT

单位: % (%)

| 指 标 | Item | 1996 | 2000 | 2005 | 2010 | 2018 | 2019 | 2020 | 2021 | 2022 |
|---|---|---|---|---|---|---|---|---|---|---|
| **人口与就业** | **Population and Employment** | | | | | | | | | |
| **人 口** | **Population** | | | | | | | | | |
| 城镇乡村人口结构 | By Urban and Rural Areas | 100.0 | 100.0 | 100.0 | 100.0 | 100.0 | 100.0 | 100.0 | 100.0 | 100.0 |
| 城 镇 | Urban | 29.5 | 35.6 | 45.2 | 53.0 | 66.6 | 68.2 | 69.5 | 70.3 | 71.0 |
| 乡 村 | Rural | 70.5 | 64.4 | 54.8 | 47.0 | 33.4 | 31.8 | 30.5 | 29.7 | 29.0 |
| 性别结构 | By Sex | 100.0 | 100.0 | 100.0 | 100.0 | 100.0 | 100.0 | 100.0 | 100.0 | 100.0 |
| 男 | Male | 51.0 | 51.3 | 50.4 | 50.6 | 50.4 | 50.4 | 50.5 | 50.6 | 50.5 |
| 女 | Female | 49.0 | 48.7 | 49.6 | 49.4 | 49.6 | 49.6 | 49.5 | 49.4 | 49.5 |
| **就 业** | **Employment** | | | | | | | | | |
| 产业结构 | By Industry | 100.0 | 100.0 | 100.0 | 100.0 | 100.0 | 100.0 | 100.0 | 100.0 | 100.0 |
| 第一产业 | Primary Industry | 58.3 | 55.4 | 46.6 | 38.9 | 23.5 | 22.9 | 22.6 | 21.9 | 23.6 |
| 第二产业 | Secondary Industry | 18.6 | 17.5 | 19.4 | 22.7 | 26.6 | 26.0 | 25.1 | 25.6 | 25.2 |
| 第三产业 | Tertiary Industry | 23.1 | 27.1 | 34.0 | 38.4 | 49.9 | 51.1 | 52.3 | 52.5 | 51.2 |
| 登记注册类型结构 | By Status of Registration | 100.0 | 100.0 | 100.0 | 100.0 | 100.0 | 100.0 | 100.0 | 100.0 | 100.0 |
| 国有经济 | State-owned | 11.5 | 9.0 | 8.5 | 8.1 | 6.8 | 6.3 | 6.6 | 6.8 | 7.0 |
| 集体经济 | Collective-owned | 71.5 | 66.8 | 56.5 | 46.1 | 26.2 | 25.3 | 25.0 | 24.3 | 25.9 |
| 私营和个体 | Private and Individuals | 16.3 | 22.0 | 30.0 | 37.4 | 50.6 | 52.6 | 53.2 | 54.5 | 53.4 |
| 其他经济 | Others | 0.7 | 2.2 | 5.0 | 8.4 | 16.4 | 15.8 | 15.2 | 14.4 | 13.7 |
| **宏观经济** | **Macroeconomic Indicators** | | | | | | | | | |
| **国民经济核算** | **National Economic Accounting** | | | | | | | | | |
| 本市生产总值结构 | GDP by Industry | 100.0 | 100.0 | 100.0 | 100.0 | 100.0 | 100.0 | 100.0 | 100.0 | 100.0 |
| 第一产业 | Primary Industry | 21.7 | 15.4 | 13.2 | 8.1 | 6.4 | 6.6 | 7.2 | 6.8 | 6.9 |
| 第二产业 | Secondary Industry | 43.4 | 42.5 | 45.2 | 44.9 | 41.0 | 39.8 | 39.8 | 40.0 | 40.1 |
| #工 业 | Industry | 38.2 | 35.3 | 37.6 | 36.5 | 29.0 | 27.8 | 27.9 | 28.3 | 28.4 |
| 第三产业 | Tertiary Industry | 34.9 | 42.1 | 41.6 | 47.0 | 52.6 | 53.6 | 53.0 | 53.2 | 53.0 |
| **固定资产投资** | **Investment in Fixed Assets** | | | | | | | | | |
| 产业结构 | By Industry | 100.0 | 100.0 | 100.0 | 100.0 | 100.0 | 100.0 | 100.0 | 100.0 | 100.0 |
| 第一产业 | Primary Industry | 0.7 | 1.4 | 2.2 | 3.8 | 1.6 | 1.9 | 2.0 | 2.2 | 2.7 |
| 第二产业 | Secondary Industry | 36.1 | 21.7 | 29.2 | 35.0 | 23.6 | 24.3 | 24.7 | 25.2 | 27.1 |
| 第三产业 | Tertiary Industry | 63.2 | 76.9 | 68.6 | 61.2 | 74.8 | 73.8 | 73.3 | 72.7 | 70.2 |

**表 1.3 续表 1 continued 1**

单位: % (%)

| 指 标 | Item | 1996 | 2000 | 2005 | 2010 | 2018 | 2019 | 2020 | 2021 | 2022 |
|---|---|---|---|---|---|---|---|---|---|---|
| **财 政** | **Government Finance** | | | | | | | | | |
| 一般公共预算收入结构 | General Public Budget Revenue | | | | 100.0 | 100.0 | 100.0 | 100.0 | 100.0 | 100.0 |
| #市 级 | Municipal Level | | | | | 37.9 | 36.2 | 34.5 | 34.9 | 32.3 |
| **产 业** | **Industry** | | | | | | | | | |
| **农 业** | **Agriculture** | | | | | | | | | |
| 农林牧渔业产值结构 | Gross Output Value of Farming, Forestry,Animal Husbandry and Fishery | 100.0 | 100.0 | 100.0 | 100.0 | 100.0 | 100.0 | 100.0 | 100.0 | 100.0 |
| 农 业 | Farming | 63.9 | 59.3 | 54.1 | 61.2 | 63.0 | 59.8 | 58.1 | 59.9 | 61.3 |
| 林 业 | Forestry | 2.7 | 2.6 | 3.0 | 3.1 | 4.9 | 4.8 | 4.6 | 5.7 | 5.7 |
| 牧 业 | Animal Husbandry | 30.9 | 34.4 | 37.7 | 31.5 | 25.3 | 29.1 | 31.7 | 27.4 | 26.1 |
| 渔 业 | Fishery | 2.5 | 3.7 | 3.6 | 2.8 | 4.9 | 4.5 | 3.9 | 4.7 | 4.5 |
| 农 辅 | Agricultural Services | | | 1.6 | 1.4 | 1.9 | 1.8 | 1.7 | 2.3 | 2.4 |
| **工 业** | **Industry** | | | | | | | | | |
| 规模以上工业增加值结构 | Value-added of Industrial Enterprises above Designated Size | 100.0 | 100.0 | 100.0 | 100.0 | 100.0 | 100.0 | 100.0 | 100.0 | 100.0 |
| 轻工业 | Light Industry | 28.9 | 36.1 | 34.2 | 30.1 | 23.9 | 23.9 | 24.1 | 25.0 | 25.0 |
| 重工业 | Heavy Industry | 71.1 | 63.9 | 63.8 | 69.9 | 76.1 | 76.1 | 75.9 | 75.0 | 75.0 |
| **运输业** | **Transportation** | | | | | | | | | |
| 货运量结构 | Freight Traffic | 100.0 | 100.0 | 100.0 | 100.0 | 100.0 | 100.0 | 100.0 | 100.0 | 100.0 |
| 铁 路 | Railway | 6.7 | 6.7 | 4.9 | 2.8 | 1.3 | 1.5 | 1.5 | 1.1 | 1.3 |
| 公 路 | Highway | 83.1 | 88.1 | 85.1 | 85.3 | 83.5 | 79.8 | 82.1 | 84.0 | 82.6 |
| 水 运 | Waterway | 10.2 | 5.2 | 9.9 | 11.9 | 15.2 | 18.7 | 16.3 | 14.9 | 16.0 |
| **国内商业** | **Domestic Trade** | | | | | | | | | |
| 社会消费品零售总额结构 | Retail Sales of Consumer Goods | | | | 100.0 | 100.0 | 100.0 | 100.0 | 100.0 | 100.0 |
| 城 镇 | Urban | | | | 94.5 | 86.8 | 86.7 | 86.4 | 85.8 | 85.5 |
| 乡 村 | Village | | | | 5.5 | 13.2 | 13.3 | 13.6 | 14.2 | 14.5 |
| **对外经济贸易** | **Foreign Economic Relations and Trade** | | | | | | | | | |
| 进出口总值结构 | Imports and Exports | 100.0 | 100.0 | 100.0 | 100.0 | 100.0 | 100.0 | 100.0 | 100.0 | 100.0 |
| 出 口 | Exports | 37.4 | 55.7 | 58.7 | 60.3 | 65.0 | 64.1 | 64.3 | 64.6 | 64.3 |
| 进 口 | Imports | 62.6 | 44.3 | 41.3 | 39.7 | 35.0 | 35.9 | 35.7 | 35.4 | 35.7 |
| **旅 游** | **Tourism** | | | | | | | | | |
| 国际旅游人数结构 | International Tourists | 100.0 | 100.0 | 100.0 | 100.0 | 100.0 | 100.0 | 100.0 | 100.0 | 100.0 |
| #外国人 | Foreigners | 66.9 | 72.5 | 79.8 | 75.9 | 56.7 | 57.1 | 52.3 | 49.5 | 65.3 |
| 港澳台同胞 | Compatriots from Hongkong, Macao and Taiwan | 32.9 | 27.5 | 20.2 | 24.1 | 43.3 | 42.9 | 47.7 | 50.5 | 34.7 |

**表 1.3 续表 2 continued 2**

单位: % (%)

| 指 标 | Item | 1996 | 2000 | 2005 | 2010 | 2018 | 2019 | 2020 | 2021 | 2022 |
|---|---|---|---|---|---|---|---|---|---|---|
| **生活、环境** | **Living Standards and Environment** | | | | | | | | | |
| **生 活** | **Living Standards** | | | | | | | | | |
| 城镇常住居民人均可支配收入结构 | Per Capita Disposable Income of Urban Residents | 100.0 | 100.0 | 100.0 | 100.0 | 100.0 | 100.0 | 100.0 | 100.0 | 100.0 |
| 工资性收入 | Income from Wages and Salaries | 87.8 | 76.5 | 73.9 | 65.8 | 57.5 | 58.3 | 58.4 | 58.4 | 58.4 |
| 经营净收入 | Income from Household Operations | 0.5 | 1.1 | 5.2 | 8.2 | 11.4 | 11.5 | 11.2 | 11.3 | 11.2 |
| 财产净收入 | Income from Properties | 1.0 | 2.4 | 3.5 | 5.7 | 7.3 | 7.2 | 7.1 | 7.1 | 7.2 |
| 转移净收入 | Income from Transfers | 10.7 | 20.0 | 17.4 | 20.3 | 23.9 | 23.0 | 23.3 | 23.2 | 23.3 |
| 农村常住居民人均可支配收入结构 | Per Capita Disposable Income of Rural Residents | 100.0 | 100.0 | 100.0 | 100.0 | 100.0 | 100.0 | 100.0 | 100.0 | 100.0 |
| 工资性收入 | Income from Wages and Salaries | 18.7 | 31.4 | 33.1 | 28.9 | 35.2 | 35.1 | 35.1 | 35.3 | 35.8 |
| 经营净收入 | Income from Household Operations | 69.8 | 62.0 | 57.4 | 43.3 | 34.9 | 34.4 | 34.0 | 33.7 | 32.3 |
| 财产净收入 | Income from Properties | 2.2 | 0.5 | 1.1 | 1.6 | 2.4 | 2.4 | 2.5 | 2.5 | 2.5 |
| 转移净收入 | Income from Transfers | 9.4 | 6.2 | 8.5 | 26.2 | 27.5 | 28.0 | 28.4 | 28.5 | 29.4 |
| **卫 生** | **Public Health** | | | | | | | | | |
| 卫生技术人员结构 | Medical Technical Personnel (person) | 100.0 | 100.0 | 100.0 | 100.0 | 100.0 | 100.0 | 100.0 | 100.0 | 100.0 |
| #执业(助理)医师 | Licensed (Assistant) Doctors | 35.1 | 50.7 | 47.4 | 41.6 | 36.5 | 37.1 | 37.3 | 37.4 | 37.4 |
| 注册护士 | Registered Nurses | 22.0 | 23.4 | 26.5 | 34.7 | 45.5 | 45.9 | 46.0 | 46.2 | 46.3 |
| 卫生机构床位结构 | Beds in Health Care Institutions | | 100.0 | 100.0 | 100.0 | 100.0 | 100.0 | 100.0 | 100.0 | 100.0 |
| #医 院 | Hospitals | | 59.0 | 68.8 | 62.6 | 73.7 | 73.8 | 74.3 | 74.0 | 74.2 |
| **环 境** | **Environment** | | | | | | | | | |
| 治理工业污染资金使用结构 | Uses of Fund in Industrial Pollution Control | | 100.0 | 100.0 | 100.0 | 100.0 | 100.0 | 100.0 | 100.0 | 100.0 |
| 治理废水 | Waste Water Control | | 48.1 | 49.9 | 48.7 | 23.8 | 17.9 | 7.5 | 18.3 | 31.2 |
| 治理废气 | Waste Gas Control | | 41.9 | 42.1 | 35.3 | 44.7 | 53.2 | 60.2 | 49.1 | 56.1 |
| 治理固体废物 | Solid Waste Control | | 3.8 | 2.3 | 4.1 | 1.1 | 1.3 | 28.1 | 14.1 | 1.8 |
| 治理噪声 | Noise Control | | 0.8 | 1.7 | 0.6 | 1.9 | 3.3 | 1.3 | 1.3 | 1.0 |
| 其 他 | Others | | 5.4 | 4.0 | 11.2 | 28.5 | 24.3 | 2.9 | 17.2 | 9.8 |

# 表 1.4 人均主要社会经济活动水平
## PER CAPITA MAIN SOCIAL AND ECONOMIC ACTIVITIES

单位：元 (yuan)

| 指 标 | Item | 1996 | 2000 | 2005 | 2010 | 2018 | 2019 | 2020 | 2021 | 2022 |
|---|---|---|---|---|---|---|---|---|---|---|
| **国民经济核算** | **National Economic Accounting** | | | | | | | | | |
| 本市生产总值 | Gross Domestic Product | 4613 | 6383 | 12335 | 28084 | 68464 | 74337 | 78294 | 87450 | 90663 |
| **主要农产品产量（公斤）** | **Output of Major Farm Products (kg)** | | | | | | | | | |
| 粮 食 | Grain | 389 | 367 | 369 | 350 | 317 | 315 | 317 | 320 | 314 |
| 油 料 | Oil-bearing Crops | 11 | 10 | 13 | 13 | 19 | 19 | 20 | 20 | 21 |
| 猪 肉 | Pork | 38 | 40 | 49 | 42 | 39 | 33 | 32 | 42 | 44 |
| 水产品 | Aquatic Products | 5 | 6 | 8 | 7 | 16 | 16 | 15 | 16 | 16 |
| 水 果 | Fruit | 19 | 27 | 49 | 72 | 127 | 139 | 160 | 162 | 162 |
| **主要工业产品产量（规模以上工业）** | **Output of Major Industrial Products (Industrial Enterprises over Designated Size)** | | | | | | | | | |
| 天然气（立方米） | Natural Gas (cu.m) | 87 | 126 | 181 | 204 | 314 | 324 | 381 | 409 | 414 |
| 发电量（千瓦时） | Electricity (kwh) | 427 | 545 | 741 | 1383 | 2269 | 2229 | 2283 | 2726 | 2923 |
| 钢 材（公斤） | Steel Products (kg) | 39 | 51 | 93 | 212 | 355 | 333 | 384 | 384 | 495 |
| 铝 材（公斤） | Aluminum Products (kg) | 2 | 5 | 12 | 31 | 59 | 62 | 64 | 64 | 70 |
| 水 泥（公斤） | Cement (kg) | 215 | 455 | 665 | 1392 | 1933 | 1977 | 1906 | 1825 | 1557 |
| 啤 酒（升） | Beer (liter) | 9 | 16 | 17 | 23 | 21 | 20 | 19 | 24 | 24 |
| 卷 烟（支） | Cigarettes (unit) | 1507 | 1115 | 1255 | 1517 | 1528 | 1579 | 1634 | 1668 | 1668 |
| **国内商业** | **Domestic Trade** | | | | | | | | | |
| 社会消费品零售总额 | Retail Sales of Consumer Goods | 1788 | 2682 | 4874 | 12239 | 33949 | 36630 | 36854 | 43504 | 43344 |
| **财政、金融** | **Government Finance and Financial Intermediation** | | | | | | | | | |
| 地方一般公共预算收入 | General Public Budget Revenue of Local Government | | | | | 6656 | 6261 | 6135 | 6693 | 6162 |
| 地方一般公共预算支出 | General Public Budget Expenditure of Local Government | | | | | 13341 | 14216 | 14333 | 14160 | 14332 |
| 人均住户存款 | Per Capita of Savings Deposit of RMB | | | | | 46736 | 52377 | 59188 | 65131 | 74576 |
| **职工工资、居民收入** | **Wages and Income** | | | | | | | | | |
| 城镇非私营单位就业人员平均工资 | Average Wages of Employeed Persons of Urban Non-private Economic Units | | 8016 | 16583 | 34727 | 78928 | 86559 | 93816 | 101670 | 107008 |
| 城镇非私营单位在岗职工平均工资 | Average Wages of On-post Staff and Workers of Urban Non-private Economic Units | 5010 | 8020 | 16630 | 35326 | 81764 | 89714 | 98380 | 106966 | 111424 |
| 城镇常住居民人均可支配收入 | Per Capita Disposable Income of Urban Residents | 5023 | 6152 | 9700 | 16032 | 34889 | 37939 | 40006 | 43502 | 45509 |
| 农村常住居民人均可支配收入 | Per Capita Disposable Income of Rural Residents | 1479 | 1900 | 2842 | 5378 | 13781 | 15133 | 16361 | 18100 | 19313 |

注：1）本市人均生产总值、人均社会消费品零售总额按常住人口计算，城镇、农村居民收入为抽样调查数，其他人均指标均按户籍人口计算。
2）畜牧业数据自 2007 年起根据第三次农业普查数据进行了调整。

Note: a) The Per capita GDP and the per capitar is calculated by permanent population; the per capita income of urban and rural residents is the data of sample survey; and other per capita indicators in this table are based on registered population.
b) Since 2007, the data of poultry eggs has been adjusted in accordance with the 3rd agricultural census.

# 表 1.5 平均每天主要社会经济活动
## SELECTED INDICATORS ON AVERAGE DAILY SOCIAL AND ECONOMIC ACTIVITIES

| 指 标 | Item | 1996 | 2000 | 2005 | 2010 | 2018 | 2019 | 2020 | 2021 | 2022 |
|---|---|---|---|---|---|---|---|---|---|---|
| **每天创造的财富** | **Daily Production** | | | | | | | | | |
| 本市生产总值(万元) | Gross Domestic Product (10 000 yuan) | 36340 | 49919 | 94475 | 220966 | 591474 | 646733 | 686067 | 769241 | 798056 |
| 第一产业 | Primary Industry | 7878 | 7684 | 12468 | 17794 | 37772 | 42509 | 49412 | 52655 | 55125 |
| 第二产业 | Secondary Industry | 15759 | 21223 | 42717 | 99291 | 242253 | 257314 | 273139 | 307322 | 320380 |
| #工 业 | Industry | 13886 | 17645 | 35476 | 80699 | 171729 | 179502 | 191528 | 217548 | 226739 |
| 第三产业 | Tertiary Industry | 12702 | 21013 | 39290 | 103881 | 311449 | 346910 | 363516 | 409263 | 422551 |
| 一般公共预算收入(万元) | General Public Budget Revenue (10 000 yuan) | | | | | 62070 | 58491 | 57393 | 62615 | 57628 |
| 粮 食(吨) | Grain (ton) | 32113 | 30992 | 32005 | 31675 | 29571 | 29458 | 29628 | 29941 | 29393 |
| 油 料(吨) | Oil-bearing Crops (ton) | 647 | 851 | 1170 | 1218 | 1745 | 1786 | 1838 | 1876 | 1941 |
| 猪 肉(吨) | Pork (ton) | 3128 | 3355 | 3958 | 3812 | 3621 | 3070 | 2981 | 3891 | 4109 |
| 水产品(吨) | Aquatic Products (ton) | 385 | 549 | 687 | 615 | 1451 | 1484 | 1436 | 1494 | |
| 天然气(万立方米) | Natural Gas (10 000 cu.m) | 715 | 1068 | 1564 | 1849 | 2925 | 3028 | 3563 | 3823 | 3875 |
| 发电量(万千瓦小时) | Electricity (10 000 kwh) | 3527 | 4600 | 6412 | 12513 | 21153 | 20867 | 21348 | 25505 | 27338 |
| 钢 材(吨) | Steel Products (ton) | 3221 | 4301 | 8074 | 19176 | 33114 | 31136 | 35889 | 35903 | 46318 |
| 水 泥(吨) | Cement (ton) | 17774 | 38432 | 57553 | 125974 | 180180 | 185010 | 178225 | 170766 | 145659 |
| 汽 车(辆) | Motor Vehicles (unit) | 340 | 674 | 1155 | 4427 | 4715 | 3789 | 4329 | 5474 | 5731 |
| #轿 车 | Cars | 37 | 132 | 420 | 2333 | 1237 | 727 | 788 | 1084 | 1503 |
| 摩托车(辆) | Motorcycles (unit) | 4859 | 5235 | 11530 | 23267 | 12512 | 11159 | 13399 | 12011 | 12298 |
| **每天消费量** | **Daily Consumption** | | | | | | | | | |
| 一般公共预算支出(万元) | General Public Budget Expenditure (10 000 yuan) | | | | | 124410 | 132813 | 134081 | 132467 | 134048 |
| 社会消费品零售总额(万元) | Total Retail Sales of Consumer Goods (10 000 yuan) | 14087 | 20973 | 37331 | 96300 | 293294 | 318676 | 322937 | 382676 | 381537 |
| **每天其他经济活动** | **Other Daily Economic Activities** | | | | | | | | | |
| 客运量(万人) | Passenger Traffic (10 000 persons) | 116.08 | 156.08 | 165.58 | 347.41 | 174.34 | 174.41 | 109.03 | 96.58 | 57.94 |
| 货运量(万吨) | Freight Traffic (10 000 tons) | 66.68 | 73.57 | 107.40 | 222.97 | 351.33 | 308.95 | 332.57 | 395.22 | 371.05 |
| 港口货物吞吐量(万吨) | Cargo Throughput of Ports (10 000 tons) | 2.95 | 6.71 | 14.39 | 26.49 | 56.01 | 46.92 | 45.20 | 54.26 | 56.59 |
| 邮电业务收入(万元) | Business Revenue from Postal and Telecommunication Services (10 000 yuan) | 458.39 | 1491.42 | 3073.23 | 4906.32 | 10103.81 | 10687.67 | 11358.63 | 12619.08 | 13913.15 |
| 进出口总额(万美元) | Total Imports and Exports (USD 10 000) | 434.36 | 489.17 | 1176.12 | 3404.38 | 21654.83 | 23003.85 | 25801.64 | 33926.83 | 33651.93 |
| 出 口 | Exports | 162.64 | 272.66 | 690.56 | 2051.78 | 14075.92 | 14739.43 | 16583.29 | 21919.55 | 21668.23 |
| 进 口 | Imports | 271.72 | 216.51 | 485.56 | 1352.60 | 7578.91 | 8264.42 | 9218.63 | 12007.28 | 11983.70 |
| 实际使用外资(万美元) | Actual Utilization of Foreign Capital (USD 10 000) | 59.94 | 66.95 | 141.30 | 833.60 | 890.49 | 648.02 | 575.67 | 612.56 | 508.89 |
| 接待入境旅游人数(人次) | Number of Overseas Visitor Arrival Received (person-time) | 443 | 729 | 1435 | 3754 | 10631 | 11270 | 401 | 271 | 179 |

注：2006 年以前工业产品产量为国有及规模以上非国有工业企业数，2007 年起为规模以上工业企业数，2015 年起天然气和发电量为全口径工业企业数据。
Note: The output of industrial products before 2006 is based on the state-owned industrial enterprises and non-state-owned industrial enterprises above designated size; while it is based on the industrial enterprises above designated size since 2007. And the data of natural gas and electricity about the industrial enterprises are those of full coverage since 2015.

# 表 1.6 各部门机构数（2021 – 2022 年）
## GRASSROOTS UNITS IN VARIOUS SECTORS (2021-2022)

单位：个 (unit)

| 指 标 | Item | 2021 | 2022 |
|---|---|---|---|
| **农村基层单位** | **Rural Grassroots Units** | | |
| 乡政府 | Township Governments | 147 | 147 |
| 镇政府 | Town Governments | 625 | 625 |
| 居委会 | Neighborhood Committees | 3273 | 3283 |
| **工 业（规模以上）** | **Industry (above Designated Size)** | **7098** | **7617** |
| #国有及国有控股 | State-owned and State-holding | 540 | 648 |
| **建筑业** | **Construction Enterprises** | **3726** | **3914** |
| **邮政营业网点（处）** | **Number of post business outlets** | **10644** | **11066** |
| **批发零售业和住宿餐饮业（限额以上）** | **Wholesale & Retail and Hotels & Catering Trades above Designated Size** | | |
| 批发业企业 | Wholesale Enterprises | 3321 | 3538 |
| 零售业企业 | Retail Enterprises | 3706 | 4001 |
| 住宿业企业 | Hotels Enterprises | 550 | 604 |
| 餐饮业企业 | Catering Enterprises | 1214 | 1339 |
| **教育事业** | **Education** | | |
| 普通高等学校 | Regular Institutions of Higher Education | 69 | 70 |
| 普通中学 | Regular Secondary Schools | 1123 | 1120 |
| 小 学 | Primary Schools | 2717 | 2637 |
| 幼儿园 | Kindergartens | 5684 | 5667 |
| 特殊教育 | Special Education | 39 | 39 |
| **文化机构数** | **Cultural Institutions** | | |
| #艺术业 | Art Institutions | 1348 | 1257 |
| 文物事业 | Cultural Relic Institutions | 199 | 217 |
| 图书馆事业 | Public Libraries | 43 | 43 |
| 群众文化事业 | Mass Cultural Institutions | 1071 | 1072 |
| **出版、发行事业** | **Publishing and Distribution Establishments** | | |
| 书报刊电子音像出版社 | Publishing Houses | 194 | 194 |
| 出版物和专项印刷厂 | Printing Houses | 95 | 106 |
| 国有书店 | State-owned Book Stores | 44 | 21 |
| **卫生事业** | **Health Care** | | |
| #医院、卫生院 | Hospitals, Health Centers | 1677 | 1667 |
| **社会福利** | **Social Welfare** | | |
| #提供住宿的社会服务机构 | Social Service Institutions with Accommodation | 1202 | 1255 |
| 不提供住宿的社会服务机构 | Social Service Institutions without Accommodation | 17821 | 18043 |

注：国有书店统计口径发生变，与往年不可比。
Note: The statistical scope of state-owned book stores has been changed, so the data are incomparable with the previous year.

# 主要统计指标解释

## ■ 行政区划

指国家对行政区域的划分。根据有关法规规定，我国的行政区域划分如下：(1) 全国分为省、自治区、直辖市；(2) 省、自治区分为自治州、县、自治县、市；(3) 自治州分为县、自治县、市；(4) 县、自治县分为乡、民族乡、镇；(5) 直辖市和较大的市分为区、县；(6) 国家在必要时设立的特别行政区。

## ■ 平均增长速度

平均增长速度表明社会经济现象在一个较长的时期内逐期平均增长变化的程度，它不能根据各个环比增长速度直接求得，但与平均发展速度之间存在着一定的数量关系：平均增长速度 = 平均发展速度 − 1。

平均发展速度是一种根据环比发展速度计算的序时平均数，由于各时期对比的基础不同，所以计算平均发展速度不能采用一般的序时平均数的计算方法，计算方法分为水平法和累计法。水平法，又称几何平均法，即将环比发展速度按连乘法用几何平均数公式计算。累计法，也称方程法，根据一段时期内各年发展水平总和与基期水平的关系，列出方程式计算平均发展速度。水平法着重考虑最后一年所达到的发展水平；累计法着重考虑整个时期累计发展水平的总量。

本《年鉴》内所列的平均增长速度，除固定资产投资用“累计法”计算外，其余均用“水平法”计算。从某年到某年平均增长速度的年份，均不包括基期年在内。如建国四十三年以来的平均增长速度是以 1949 年为基期计算的，则写为 1950-1992 年平均增长速度，其余类推。

## ■ 国民经济行业分类

自 2017 年年报和 2018 年定期报表开始使用新的《国民经济行业分类》（GB/T4754-2017）。该分类是由国家统计局组织修订，原国家质量监督检验检疫总局和中国国家标准化管理委员会于 2017 年 6 月 30 日发布。这次修订是在 2011 年分类标准的基础上，结合我国经济活动特点，参照联合国《全部经济活动的国际标准产业分类》（ISIC/Rev.4）进行的。修订后的《国民经济行业分类》（GB/T4754-2017）共有门类 20 个，大类 97 个，中类 473 个，小类 1382 个。

## ■ 企业登记注册类型

是以在市场监管部门登记注册的各类企业为划分对象，以市场监管部门对企业登记注册的类型为依据，将企业登记注册类型分为内资企业、港澳台商投资企业和外商投资企业三大类。内资企业包括国有企业、集体企业、股份合作企业、联营企业、有限责任公司、股份有限公司、私营企业和其他企业；港澳台商投资企业和外商投资企业分别包括合资经营企业、合作经营企业、独资经营企业和股份有限公司等。

## ■ 国有企业

指企业全部资产归国家所有，并按《中华人民共和国企业法人登记管理条例》规定登记注册的非公司制的经济组织。不包括有限责任公司中的国有独资公司。

## ■ 集体企业

指企业资产归集体所有，并按《中华人民共和国企业法人登记管理条例》规定登记注册的经济组织。

## ■ 股份合作企业

指以合作制为基础，由企业职工共同出资入股，吸收一定比例的社会资产投资组建，实行自主经营，自负盈亏，共同劳动，民主管理，按劳分配与按股分红相结合的一种集体经济组织。

## ■ 联营企业

指两个及两个以上相同或不同所有制性质的企业法人或事业单位法人，按自愿、平等、互利的原则，共同投资组成的经济组织。联营企业包括国有联营企业、

## 主要统计指标解释

集体联营企业、国有与集体联营企业和其他联营企业。

### ■ 有限责任公司

指根据《中华人民共和国公司登记管理条例》规定登记注册，由两个以上、五十个以下的股东共同出资，每个股东以其所认缴的出资额对公司承担有限责任，公司以其全部资产对其债务承担责任的经济组织。有限责任公司包括国有独资公司以及其他有限责任公司。

### ■ 股份有限公司

指根据《中华人民共和国公司登记管理条例》规定登记注册，其全部注册资本由等额股份构成并通过发行股票筹集资本，股东以其认购的股份对公司承担有限责任，公司以其全部资产对其债务承担责任的经济组织。

### ■ 私营企业

指由自然人投资设立或由自然人控股，以雇佣劳动为基础的营利性经济组织。包括按照《公司法》、《合伙企业法》以及《个人独资企业法》规定登记注册的私营独资企业、私营合伙企业、私营有限责任公司、私营股份有限公司和个人独资企业。

### ■ 其他企业

指上述企业之外的其他内资经济组织。

### ■ 与港澳台商合资经营企业

指港澳台地区投资者与内地企业依照原《中华人民共和国中外合资经营企业法》及有关法律的规定，按合同规定的比例投资设立，分享利润、分担风险和亏损的企业。

### ■ 与港澳台商合作经营企业

指港澳台地区投资者与内地企业依照原《中华人民共和国中外合作经营企业法》及有关法律的规定，依照合作合同的约定进行投资或提供条件设立，分配利润、分担风险和亏损的企业。

### ■ 港澳台商独资经营企业

指依照原《中华人民共和国外资企业法》及有关法律的规定，在内地由港澳台地区投资者全额投资设立的企业。

### ■ 港澳台商投资股份有限公司

指根据国家有关规定，经商务部（原外经贸部）批准设立，并且其中港、澳、台商的股本占公司注册资本的比例达25%以上的股份有限公司。凡其中港、澳、台商的股本占公司注册资本的比例小于25%的，属于内资中的股份有限公司。

### ■ 其他港澳台商投资企业

指在中国境内参照原《外国企业或个人在中国境内设立合伙企业管理办法》和《外商投资合伙企业登记管理规定》，依法设立的港、澳、台商投资合伙企业等。

### ■ 中外合资经营企业

指外国企业或外国人与中国内地企业依照原《中华人民共和国中外合资经营企业法》及有关法律的规定，按合同规定的比例投资设立，分享利润和分担风险和亏损的企业。

### ■ 中外合作经营企业

指外国企业或外国人与中国内地企业依照原《中华人民共和国中外合作经营企业法》及有关法律的规定，依照合作合同的约定进行投资或提供条件设立，分配利润、分担风险和亏损的企业。

### ■ 外资企业

指依照原《中华人民共和国外资企业法》及有关法律的规定，在中国内地由外国投资者全额投资设立的企业。

### ■ 外商投资股份有限公司

指根据国家有关规定，经商务部（原外经贸部）批准设立，并且其中外资的股本占公司注册资本的比例达25%以上的股份有限公司。凡其中外资股本占公司注册资本的比例小于25%的，属于内资企业中的股份有限公司。

## 主要统计指标解释

### ■ 其他外商投资企业

指在中国境内依照原《外国企业或个人在中国境内设立合伙企业管理办法》和《外商投资合伙企业登记管理规定》，依法设立的外商投资合伙企业等。

# Explanatory Notes on Main Statistical Indicators

## Divisions of Administrative Areas

Refer to the division of administrative areas by the State. The relative laws define the administrative division as follows: 1) the whole country is divided into provinces, autonomous regions and municipalities directly under the Central Government; 2) provinces and autonomous regions are further divided into autonomous prefectures, counties, autonomous counties and cities; 3) autonomous prefectures are further divided into counties, autonomous counties and cities; 4) counties and autonomous counties are further divided into townships, ethnic townships and towns; 5) municipalities directly under the Central Government and large cities are divided into districts and counties, 6) the State shall, when necessary, establish special administrative regions.

## Average Annual Growth Rate

Shows the average growth rate of social and economic development during a longer period. It can not be directly calculated by chain based growth rate. The relation is:

*Average growth rate = average speed of development – 1*

Average speed of development is the time series average of speed which is obtained through chain-based calculation. Because the reference bases during the different periods are different, average speed of development can not be calculated by the general method. Level approach and accumulative approach for calculating average speed of development rate are applied. The "level approach", or geometric average approach, is derived by the formula of geometric average of the chain-based speeds of development by continuous multiplication. The other is called the "accumulative approach" or the "equation" method, which is derived by the summation of the actual figure of each year in the interval divided by the figure in the base year. The level approach focuses on the level of the last year, while the accumulative approach emphasizes the aggregate development for the entire duration.

The average annual growth rates listed in the Yearbook are calculated by the level approach except for the growth rate of investment in fixed assets. The base year is not listed in the duration for which average annual growth rates are computed. For instance, the average annual growth rate of the 43 years since 1949 is shown as the average annual growth rate of 1950-1992 without showing the base year 1949.

## Industrial Classification of the National Economy

The new Industrial Classification of the National Economy (GB/T 4754-2017) is introduced starting from the compilation of 2017 annual statistics and 2018 monthly or quarterly statistics. The revision, based on the 2011 classification, was organized by the National Bureau of Statistics taking into consideration of the characteristics of economic activities in China and the International Standards of the Industrial Classification of All Economic Activities (ISIC/Rev.4) of the United Nations. The new Classification was promulgated by the former National Administration of Quality Supervision, Inspection and Quarantine and the Standardization Administration of the People's Republic of China on June 30, 2017. The revised version of the Industrial Classification of the National Economy (GB/T 4754-2017) is composed of 20 sections, 97 divisions, 473 groups and 1382 classes.

## Registration Status of Enterprises (units)

Enterprises are classified into 3 categories, namely enterprises with domestic investment, enterprises with investment from Hong Kong, Macao and Taiwan, and enterprises with foreign investment, according to the registration status of an enterprise in market supervision administration. Domestic-invested enterprises include state-owned enterprises, collective-owned enterprises, cooperative enterprises, joint ownership enterprises, limited liability corporations, share-holding corporations Ltd., private enterprises and other enterprises. Included in the enterprises with investment from Hong Kong, Macao and Taiwan and enterprises with foreign investment are joint-venture enterprises, cooperative enterprises, sole-proprietorship enterprises and share-holding corporations Ltd.

## State-owned Enterprises

Refer to non-corporation economic units where the entire

assets are owned by the state and which have been registered in accordance with the Regulation of the People's Republic of China on the Management of Registration of Corporate Enterprises. Not included from this category are state sole-proprietorship corporations in the limited liability corporations.

## Collective-owned Enterprises

Refer to economic units where the assets are owned collectively and which have been registered in accordance with the Regulation of the People's Republic of China on the Management of Registration of Corporate Enterprises.

## Cooperative Enterprises

Refer to a form of collective economic units (enterprises) where capitals come mainly from employees as their shares, with certain proportion of capital from the outside, where production is organized on the basis of independent operation, independent accounting for profits and losses, joint work, democratic management, and a distribution system that integrates remuneration according to work with dividend according to capital share.

## Joint Ownership Enterprises

Refer to economic units established by two or more corporate enterprises or corporate institutions of the same or different ownership, through joint investment on the basis of voluntary participation, equality, and mutual benefits. They include state joint ownership enterprises; collective joint ownership enterprises; joint state-collective enterprises; and other joint ownership enterprises.

## Limited Liability Corporations

Refer to economic units established with investment from 2-50 investors and registered in accordance with the Regulation of the People's Republic of China on the Management of Registration of Corporations, each investor bearing limited liability to the corporation depending on its share of investment, and the corporation bearing liability to its debt to the maximum of its total assets. Limited liability corporations include state sole-proprietorship corporations and other limited liability corporations.

## Share-holding Corporations Ltd.

Refer to economic units registered in accordance with the Regulation of the People's Republic of China on the Management of Registration of Corporations, with total registered capital divided into equal shares and additional capitals raised through issuing stocks. Each investor bears limited liability to the corporation depending on the holding of shares, and the corporation bears liability to its debt to the maximum of its total assets.

## Private Enterprises

Refer to profit-making economic units invested and established by natural persons, or controlled by natural persons, using employed labour. Included in this category are private sole-proprietorship enterprise, private partnership enterprise, private limited liability companies, private limited-liability company by shares and individual sole-proprietorship enterprise registered in accordance with the Company Law, the Law on Partnership Business and the Law on Individual Proprietorship Enterprises.

## Other Domestic-Invested Enterprises

Refer to domestic-invested economic units other than those mentioned above.

## Joint Venture Enterprises with Hong Kong, Macao and Taiwan

Are enterprises jointly established by investors from Hong Kong, Macao and Taiwan with enterprises in the mainland of China in accordance with the former Law of the People's Republic of China on Sino-foreign Equity Joint Ventures and other relevant laws, where the establishment of the investment and the sharing of profits, taking risks and loss are stipulated in joint venture contracts.

## Cooperative Enterprises with Hong Kong, Macao and Taiwan

Established by investors from Hong Kong, Macao and Taiwan with enterprises in the mainland of China in accordance with the former Law of the People's Republic of China on Sino-foreign Contractual Joint Venture and other relevant laws, where the investment or provision of facilities and the sharing of profits and risks are stipulated under cooperative contracts.

EXPLANATORY NOTES TO MAJOR STATISTICAL INDICATORS

## Sole-proprietorship Enterprises with Investment from Hong Kong, Macao and Taiwan

Refer to enterprises established in the mainland of China with exclusive investment from investors from Hong Kong, Macao and Taiwan in accordance with the former Law of the People's Republic of China on Enterprises with Foreign Investment and other relevant laws.

## Share-holding Corporations Ltd. with Investment from Hong Kong, Macao and Taiwan

Refer to share-holding corporations Ltd. established with the approval from the Ministry of Commerce (the former Ministry of Foreign Trade and Economic Relations) in line with relevant state regulations, where the share of investment from Hong Kong, Macao or Taiwan businessmen exceeds 25% of the total registered capital of the corporation. In case the share of investment from Hong Kong, Macao or Taiwan is less than 25% of the total registered capital, the enterprise is to be classified as domestic-invested share-holding corporation Ltd.

## Other Enterprises with Funds From Hong Kong, Macao and Taiwan

Refer to partnership enterprises with investments from Hong Kong, Macao and Taiwan established within the territory of China in accordance with former Administrative Measures on the Establishment of Partnership Enterprises in China by Foreign Enterprises or Foreign Individuals and Regulations for the Administration of the Registration of Foreign-invested Partnership Enterprises.

## Joint Venture Enterprises with Foreign Investment

Refer to enterprises jointly established by foreign enterprises or foreigners with enterprises in the mainland of China in accordance with the former Law of the People's Republic of China on Sino-foreign Equity Joint Ventures and other relevant laws, where the sharing of investment, profits and risks and loss are stipulated in contracts.

## Cooperative Enterprises with Foreign Investment

Refer to enterprises jointly established by foreign enterprises or foreigners with enterprises in the mainland of China in accordance with the former Law of the People's Republic of China on Sino-foreign Contractual Joint Venture and other relevant laws, where the investment or provision of facilities and the sharing of profits and taking risks and loss are stipulated in cooperative contracts.

## Sole-proprietorship Enterprises with Foreign Investment

Refer to enterprises established in the mainland of China with exclusive investment from foreign investors in accordance with the former Law of the People's Republic of China on Enterprises with Foreign Investment and other relevant laws.

## Share-holding Corporations Ltd. with Foreign Investment

Refer to share-holding corporations Ltd. established with the approval from the Ministry of Commerce (the former Ministry of Foreign Trade and Economic Relations) in line with relevant state regulations, where the share of investment from foreign investors exceeds 25% of the total registered capital of the corporation. In case the share of foreign investment is less than 25% of the total registered capital, the enterprise is to be classified as domestic-invested share-holding corporation Ltd.

## Other Enterprises with Foreign Funds

Refer to partnership enterprises established within the territory of China in accordance with former Administrative Measures on the Establishment of Partnership Enterprises in China by Foreign Enterprises or Foreign Individuals and Regulations for the Administration of the Registration of Foreign-invested Partnership Enterprises.

# 第二章·国民经济核算

NATIONAL ECONOMIC ACCOUNTING

# 简要说明

## BRIEF INTRODUCTION

本章本市生产总值资料包括各年度地区生产总值的绝对值、构成和指数，三次产业贡献率，三次产业拉动力等数据。

本章资料由市统计局国民经济核算处提供。

The data of Gross Domestic Product (GDP) in this chapter includes the values, composition and indices of GDP in all the years, the share of the contributions of the growth of three strata of industry to the increase of the GDP, the contribution of the three strata of industry to GDP growth.

All the data in this chapter are provided by Division of National Economic Accounting, Chongqing Municipal Bureau of Statistics.

# 表 2.1 地区生产总值（1949 － 1978 年）
GROSS DOMESTIC PRODUCT (1949-1978)

单位：亿元 (100 million yuan)

| 年 份<br>Year | 本 市<br>生产总值<br>Gross Domestic Product | 第一产业<br>Primary Industry | 第二产业<br>Secondary Industry | | |
|---|---|---|---|---|---|
| | | | | 工 业<br>Industry | 建筑业<br>Construction |
| 1949 | 13.89 | 9.74 | 2.71 | 2.50 | 0.21 |
| 1950 | 15.02 | 10.23 | 3.00 | 2.77 | 0.23 |
| 1951 | 15.97 | 10.72 | 3.37 | 3.11 | 0.26 |
| 1952 | 17.97 | 11.86 | 3.94 | 3.59 | 0.35 |
| 1953 | 21.26 | 13.57 | 5.63 | 4.96 | 0.67 |
| 1954 | 22.79 | 13.89 | 6.52 | 6.00 | 0.52 |
| 1955 | 23.32 | 13.86 | 7.04 | 6.61 | 0.43 |
| 1956 | 26.37 | 15.01 | 8.33 | 7.70 | 0.63 |
| 1957 | 26.56 | 13.12 | 10.03 | 9.45 | 0.58 |
| 1958 | 34.81 | 15.43 | 14.53 | 13.52 | 1.01 |
| 1959 | 38.03 | 12.02 | 20.40 | 18.90 | 1.50 |
| 1960 | 38.82 | 11.10 | 21.38 | 19.89 | 1.49 |
| 1961 | 28.96 | 10.35 | 12.52 | 11.90 | 0.62 |
| 1962 | 25.12 | 9.92 | 9.67 | 9.42 | 0.25 |
| 1963 | 27.92 | 12.08 | 10.30 | 9.91 | 0.39 |
| 1964 | 32.58 | 13.37 | 13.07 | 12.49 | 0.58 |
| 1965 | 38.29 | 16.21 | 15.79 | 14.74 | 1.05 |
| 1966 | 39.61 | 16.18 | 17.75 | 16.52 | 1.23 |
| 1967 | 34.70 | 15.21 | 13.76 | 12.96 | 0.80 |
| 1968 | 28.25 | 15.18 | 7.81 | 7.41 | 0.40 |
| 1969 | 32.79 | 14.75 | 11.96 | 11.23 | 0.73 |
| 1970 | 39.96 | 15.96 | 17.41 | 16.10 | 1.31 |
| 1971 | 45.97 | 16.71 | 22.18 | 20.81 | 1.37 |
| 1972 | 45.37 | 16.67 | 20.82 | 19.67 | 1.15 |
| 1973 | 46.32 | 18.14 | 19.66 | 18.24 | 1.42 |
| 1974 | 45.70 | 18.43 | 18.00 | 16.85 | 1.15 |
| 1975 | 53.37 | 18.81 | 24.00 | 22.49 | 1.51 |
| 1976 | 53.43 | 19.07 | 23.44 | 22.00 | 1.44 |
| 1977 | 60.22 | 21.74 | 26.99 | 24.98 | 2.01 |
| 1978 | 71.70 | 24.81 | 34.46 | 31.53 | 2.93 |

**表 2.1 续表 continued**

单位：亿元 (100 million yuan)

| 年 份<br>Year | 第三产业<br>Tertiary Industry | 批发和零售业<br>Wholesale and Retail Trades | 交通运输、仓储及邮政业<br>Transport, Storage, Post | 住宿和餐饮业<br>Hotels and Catering Services | 金融业<br>Financial Intermediation | 房地产业<br>Real Estate | 其 他<br>Others | 本市人均生产总值（元）<br>Per Capita GDP (yuan) |
|---|---|---|---|---|---|---|---|---|
| 1949 | 1.44 | 0.44 | 0.61 | 0.26 | 0.03 | 0.02 | 0.08 | 87 |
| 1950 | 1.79 | 0.50 | 0.70 | 0.28 | 0.06 | 0.05 | 0.20 | 91 |
| 1951 | 1.88 | 0.56 | 0.74 | 0.29 | 0.09 | 0.07 | 0.13 | 94 |
| 1952 | 2.17 | 0.64 | 0.83 | 0.31 | 0.06 | 0.08 | 0.25 | 103 |
| 1953 | 2.06 | 0.65 | 0.78 | 0.32 | 0.07 | 0.09 | 0.15 | 120 |
| 1954 | 2.38 | 0.70 | 0.87 | 0.34 | 0.10 | 0.11 | 0.26 | 124 |
| 1955 | 2.42 | 0.69 | 0.88 | 0.37 | 0.10 | 0.13 | 0.25 | 125 |
| 1956 | 3.03 | 0.81 | 1.08 | 0.44 | 0.13 | 0.14 | 0.43 | 135 |
| 1957 | 3.41 | 0.97 | 1.23 | 0.44 | 0.14 | 0.15 | 0.48 | 131 |
| 1958 | 4.85 | 1.53 | 1.75 | 0.46 | 0.21 | 0.14 | 0.76 | 170 |
| 1959 | 5.61 | 1.81 | 2.04 | 0.52 | 0.34 | 0.17 | 0.73 | 185 |
| 1960 | 6.34 | 1.82 | 2.04 | 0.53 | 0.57 | 0.16 | 1.22 | 193 |
| 1961 | 6.09 | 1.54 | 1.82 | 0.53 | 0.57 | 0.18 | 1.45 | 154 |
| 1962 | 5.53 | 1.23 | 1.61 | 0.66 | 0.46 | 0.18 | 1.39 | 139 |
| 1963 | 5.54 | 1.21 | 1.47 | 0.58 | 0.35 | 0.19 | 1.74 | 151 |
| 1964 | 6.14 | 1.52 | 1.70 | 0.52 | 0.58 | 0.18 | 1.64 | 169 |
| 1965 | 6.29 | 1.55 | 1.71 | 0.52 | 0.86 | 0.21 | 1.44 | 191 |
| 1966 | 5.68 | 1.33 | 1.41 | 0.50 | 0.35 | 0.22 | 1.87 | 191 |
| 1967 | 5.73 | 1.44 | 1.35 | 0.48 | 0.41 | 0.25 | 1.80 | 164 |
| 1968 | 5.26 | 1.18 | 1.22 | 0.46 | 0.56 | 0.30 | 1.54 | 131 |
| 1969 | 6.08 | 1.40 | 1.37 | 0.49 | 0.72 | 0.36 | 1.74 | 147 |
| 1970 | 6.59 | 1.52 | 1.41 | 0.50 | 0.85 | 0.40 | 1.91 | 172 |
| 1971 | 7.08 | 1.56 | 1.47 | 0.60 | 1.09 | 0.45 | 1.91 | 192 |
| 1972 | 7.88 | 1.72 | 1.61 | 0.66 | 0.96 | 0.52 | 2.41 | 185 |
| 1973 | 8.52 | 1.79 | 1.76 | 0.66 | 1.06 | 0.55 | 2.70 | 183 |
| 1974 | 9.27 | 1.81 | 1.83 | 0.64 | 1.23 | 0.62 | 3.14 | 177 |
| 1975 | 10.56 | 2.02 | 2.04 | 0.69 | 1.45 | 0.71 | 3.65 | 201 |
| 1976 | 10.92 | 2.04 | 1.94 | 0.67 | 1.59 | 0.78 | 3.90 | 199 |
| 1977 | 11.49 | 2.21 | 2.11 | 0.69 | 1.90 | 0.87 | 3.71 | 221 |
| 1978 | 12.43 | 2.34 | 2.38 | 0.78 | 2.00 | 0.88 | 4.05 | 287 |

注：本表人均生产总值按户籍人口计算。
Note: The per capita GDP hereof is calculated by registered population.

# 表 2.2 地区生产总值构成(1949 – 1978 年)
## COMPOSITION OF GROSS DOMESTIC PRODUCT (1949-1978)

单位: % (%)

| 年 份 Year | 本 市 生产总值 Gross Domestic Product | 第一产业 Primary Industry | 第二产业 Secondary Industry | | |
|---|---|---|---|---|---|
| | | | | 工 业 Industry | 建筑业 Construction |
| 1949 | 100.0 | 70.1 | 19.5 | 18.0 | 1.5 |
| 1950 | 100.0 | 68.1 | 20.0 | 18.4 | 1.6 |
| 1951 | 100.0 | 67.1 | 21.1 | 19.5 | 1.6 |
| 1952 | 100.0 | 66.0 | 21.9 | 20.0 | 1.9 |
| 1953 | 100.0 | 63.8 | 26.5 | 23.3 | 3.2 |
| 1954 | 100.0 | 60.9 | 28.6 | 26.3 | 2.3 |
| 1955 | 100.0 | 59.4 | 30.2 | 28.3 | 1.9 |
| 1956 | 100.0 | 56.9 | 31.6 | 29.2 | 2.4 |
| 1957 | 100.0 | 49.4 | 37.8 | 35.6 | 2.2 |
| 1958 | 100.0 | 44.3 | 41.7 | 38.8 | 2.9 |
| 1959 | 100.0 | 31.6 | 53.6 | 49.7 | 3.9 |
| 1960 | 100.0 | 28.6 | 55.1 | 51.2 | 3.9 |
| 1961 | 100.0 | 35.7 | 43.2 | 41.1 | 2.1 |
| 1962 | 100.0 | 39.5 | 38.5 | 37.5 | 1.0 |
| 1963 | 100.0 | 43.3 | 36.9 | 35.5 | 1.4 |
| 1964 | 100.0 | 41.0 | 40.1 | 38.3 | 1.8 |
| 1965 | 100.0 | 42.3 | 41.2 | 38.5 | 2.7 |
| 1966 | 100.0 | 40.8 | 44.8 | 41.7 | 3.1 |
| 1967 | 100.0 | 43.8 | 39.7 | 37.3 | 2.4 |
| 1968 | 100.0 | 53.7 | 27.6 | 26.2 | 1.4 |
| 1969 | 100.0 | 45.0 | 36.5 | 34.2 | 2.3 |
| 1970 | 100.0 | 39.9 | 43.6 | 40.3 | 3.3 |
| 1971 | 100.0 | 36.3 | 48.2 | 45.3 | 2.9 |
| 1972 | 100.0 | 36.7 | 45.9 | 43.4 | 2.5 |
| 1973 | 100.0 | 39.2 | 42.4 | 39.4 | 3.0 |
| 1974 | 100.0 | 40.3 | 39.4 | 36.9 | 2.5 |
| 1975 | 100.0 | 35.2 | 45.0 | 42.1 | 2.9 |
| 1976 | 100.0 | 35.7 | 43.9 | 41.2 | 2.7 |
| 1977 | 100.0 | 36.1 | 44.8 | 41.5 | 3.3 |
| 1978 | 100.0 | 34.6 | 48.1 | 44.0 | 4.1 |

**表 2.2 续表 continued**

单位: % (%)

| 年 份<br>Year | 第三产业<br>Tertiary Industry | 批发和零售业<br>Wholesale and Retail Trades | 交通运输、仓储及邮政业<br>Transport, Storage, Post | 住宿和餐饮业<br>Hotels and Catering Services | 金融业<br>Financial Intermediation | 房地产业<br>Real Estate | 其 他<br>Others |
|---|---|---|---|---|---|---|---|
| 1949 | 10.4 | 3.2 | 4.4 | 1.9 | 0.2 | 0.1 | 0.6 |
| 1950 | 11.9 | 3.3 | 4.7 | 1.9 | 0.4 | 0.3 | 1.3 |
| 1951 | 11.8 | 3.5 | 4.6 | 1.8 | 0.6 | 0.4 | 0.9 |
| 1952 | 12.1 | 3.6 | 4.6 | 1.7 | 0.3 | 0.4 | 1.5 |
| 1953 | 9.7 | 3.1 | 3.7 | 1.5 | 0.3 | 0.4 | 0.7 |
| 1954 | 10.5 | 3.1 | 3.8 | 1.5 | 0.4 | 0.5 | 1.2 |
| 1955 | 10.4 | 3.0 | 3.8 | 1.6 | 0.4 | 0.6 | 1.0 |
| 1956 | 11.5 | 3.1 | 4.1 | 1.7 | 0.5 | 0.5 | 1.6 |
| 1957 | 12.8 | 3.7 | 4.6 | 1.7 | 0.5 | 0.6 | 1.7 |
| 1958 | 14.0 | 4.4 | 5.0 | 1.3 | 0.6 | 0.4 | 2.3 |
| 1959 | 14.8 | 4.8 | 5.4 | 1.4 | 0.9 | 0.4 | 1.9 |
| 1960 | 16.3 | 4.7 | 5.3 | 1.4 | 1.5 | 0.4 | 3.0 |
| 1961 | 21.1 | 5.3 | 6.3 | 1.8 | 2.0 | 0.6 | 5.1 |
| 1962 | 22.0 | 4.9 | 6.4 | 2.6 | 1.8 | 0.7 | 5.6 |
| 1963 | 19.8 | 4.3 | 5.3 | 2.1 | 1.3 | 0.7 | 6.1 |
| 1964 | 18.9 | 4.7 | 5.2 | 1.6 | 1.8 | 0.6 | 5.0 |
| 1965 | 16.5 | 4.0 | 4.5 | 1.4 | 2.2 | 0.5 | 3.9 |
| 1966 | 14.4 | 3.4 | 3.6 | 1.3 | 0.9 | 0.6 | 4.6 |
| 1967 | 16.5 | 4.1 | 3.9 | 1.4 | 1.2 | 0.7 | 5.2 |
| 1968 | 18.7 | 4.2 | 4.3 | 1.6 | 2.0 | 1.1 | 5.5 |
| 1969 | 18.5 | 4.3 | 4.2 | 1.5 | 2.2 | 1.1 | 5.2 |
| 1970 | 16.5 | 3.8 | 3.5 | 1.3 | 2.1 | 1.0 | 4.8 |
| 1971 | 15.5 | 3.4 | 3.2 | 1.3 | 2.4 | 1.0 | 4.2 |
| 1972 | 17.4 | 3.8 | 3.5 | 1.5 | 2.1 | 1.1 | 5.4 |
| 1973 | 18.4 | 3.9 | 3.8 | 1.4 | 2.3 | 1.2 | 5.8 |
| 1974 | 20.3 | 4.0 | 4.0 | 1.4 | 2.7 | 1.4 | 6.8 |
| 1975 | 19.8 | 3.8 | 3.8 | 1.3 | 2.7 | 1.3 | 6.9 |
| 1976 | 20.4 | 3.8 | 3.6 | 1.3 | 3.0 | 1.5 | 7.2 |
| 1977 | 19.1 | 3.7 | 3.5 | 1.1 | 3.2 | 1.4 | 6.2 |
| 1978 | 17.3 | 3.3 | 3.3 | 1.1 | 2.8 | 1.2 | 5.6 |

# 表 2.3 地区生产总值指数（1949 － 1978 年）（上年 =100）
## INDICES OF GROSS DOMESTIC PRODUCT (1949-1978) (PRECEDING YEAR =100)

| 年份 Year | 本市生产总值 Gross Domestic Product | 第一产业 Primary Industry | 第二产业 Secondary Industry | | |
|---|---|---|---|---|---|
| | | | | 工业 Industry | 建筑业 Construction |
| 1949 | 100.0 | 100.0 | 100.0 | 100.0 | 100.0 |
| 1950 | 105.7 | 103.0 | 112.5 | 112.0 | 118.2 |
| 1951 | 103.4 | 104.0 | 110.9 | 111.2 | 107.7 |
| 1952 | 109.3 | 107.0 | 115.4 | 113.7 | 135.7 |
| 1953 | 111.2 | 103.4 | 134.8 | 130.6 | 177.1 |
| 1954 | 110.6 | 106.0 | 120.2 | 125.2 | 82.3 |
| 1955 | 102.7 | 100.2 | 109.6 | 111.9 | 82.4 |
| 1956 | 113.5 | 105.1 | 127.3 | 125.4 | 157.1 |
| 1957 | 102.3 | 97.4 | 108.4 | 110.4 | 83.3 |
| 1958 | 118.9 | 100.7 | 137.2 | 135.4 | 165.5 |
| 1959 | 97.4 | 67.8 | 123.9 | 123.4 | 130.2 |
| 1960 | 111.0 | 74.7 | 132.8 | 133.3 | 127.2 |
| 1961 | 64.8 | 83.7 | 57.9 | 59.2 | 41.5 |
| 1962 | 100.0 | 135.4 | 83.7 | 85.7 | 45.5 |
| 1963 | 114.9 | 124.0 | 109.3 | 108.1 | 153.3 |
| 1964 | 115.0 | 106.1 | 124.0 | 123.2 | 143.5 |
| 1965 | 114.5 | 109.7 | 121.9 | 119.0 | 184.8 |
| 1966 | 105.9 | 101.8 | 113.5 | 113.1 | 118.0 |
| 1967 | 90.2 | 99.4 | 82.9 | 83.9 | 70.8 |
| 1968 | 84.4 | 106.4 | 66.2 | 66.7 | 57.8 |
| 1969 | 112.1 | 91.4 | 136.0 | 134.5 | 164.4 |
| 1970 | 120.7 | 102.5 | 138.6 | 136.5 | 170.1 |
| 1971 | 111.9 | 100.4 | 125.2 | 127.1 | 102.3 |
| 1972 | 100.1 | 101.6 | 95.3 | 95.9 | 85.1 |
| 1973 | 103.2 | 109.5 | 96.2 | 94.4 | 127.2 |
| 1974 | 101.6 | 101.6 | 98.6 | 99.5 | 87.6 |
| 1975 | 111.8 | 92.8 | 130.1 | 130.2 | 128.3 |
| 1976 | 95.1 | 98.5 | 89.2 | 89.4 | 86.5 |
| 1977 | 120.0 | 111.7 | 133.5 | 131.6 | 162.4 |
| 1978 | 117.1 | 109.8 | 125.9 | 124.6 | 141.5 |

注：本表按可比价格计算（下表同）。
Note: The indices hereof are calculated at constant prices (the same below).

**表 2.3 续表 continued**

| 年 份 Year | 第三产业 Tertiary Industry | 批发和零售业 Wholesale and Retail Trades | 交通运输、仓储及邮政业 Transport, Storage, Post | 住宿和餐饮业 Hotels and Catering Services | 金融业 Financial Intermediation | 房地产业 Real Estate | 其 他 Others | 本市人均生产总值 Per Capita GDP |
|---|---|---|---|---|---|---|---|---|
| 1949 | 100.0 | 100.0 | 100.0 | 100.0 | 100.0 | 100.0 | 100.0 | 100.0 |
| 1950 | 118.6 | 105.6 | 127.6 | 107.4 | 197.3 | 250.4 | 102.5 | 102.2 |
| 1951 | 94.9 | 98.7 | 93.2 | 103.4 | 148.0 | 140.2 | 9.0 | 100.5 |
| 1952 | 120.1 | 116.0 | 113.0 | 106.7 | 65.9 | 114.5 | 380.3 | 106.3 |
| 1953 | 111.5 | 121.9 | 106.0 | 103.2 | 116.7 | 112.5 | 112.0 | 109.5 |
| 1954 | 112.4 | 109.0 | 113.6 | 106.3 | 142.9 | 122.2 | 114.3 | 109.1 |
| 1955 | 98.5 | 98.8 | 95.0 | 105.9 | 100.0 | 118.2 | 93.8 | 100.7 |
| 1956 | 118.3 | 114.3 | 115.8 | 119.4 | 130.0 | 115.4 | 133.3 | 109.1 |
| 1957 | 106.0 | 103.1 | 108.2 | 100.0 | 107.7 | 106.7 | 112.5 | 98.3 |
| 1958 | 134.9 | 138.1 | 137.4 | 104.5 | 142.9 | 93.3 | 160.4 | 118.6 |
| 1959 | 103.3 | 103.7 | 95.3 | 110.9 | 120.0 | 107.1 | 110.4 | 98.1 |
| 1960 | 101.1 | 102.9 | 90.1 | 102.0 | 125.0 | 93.3 | 112.9 | 113.4 |
| 1961 | 70.8 | 66.4 | 72.4 | 100.0 | 86.7 | 114.3 | 47.9 | 68.2 |
| 1962 | 105.0 | 95.8 | 96.2 | 123.1 | 103.8 | 100.0 | 126.1 | 102.8 |
| 1963 | 112.6 | 113.2 | 107.9 | 93.8 | 96.3 | 106.3 | 150.0 | 112.7 |
| 1964 | 109.0 | 98.1 | 104.6 | 90.0 | 173.1 | 94.1 | 124.1 | 110.8 |
| 1965 | 100.5 | 109.9 | 98.2 | 100.0 | 153.3 | 118.8 | 69.4 | 111.2 |
| 1966 | 85.2 | 102.7 | 92.0 | 94.4 | 40.6 | 84.2 | 84.0 | 102.8 |
| 1967 | 102.9 | 102.6 | 101.0 | 102.0 | 117.9 | 118.8 | 96.8 | 87.6 |
| 1968 | 101.6 | 87.2 | 98.1 | 96.2 | 136.4 | 126.3 | 113.1 | 81.9 |
| 1969 | 105.6 | 111.8 | 114.7 | 102.0 | 104.4 | 104.2 | 87.0 | 109.3 |
| 1970 | 101.9 | 104.4 | 106.8 | 102.0 | 102.1 | 104.0 | 86.7 | 117.2 |
| 1971 | 104.7 | 104.6 | 102.8 | 118.0 | 120.0 | 112.5 | 94.2 | 108.2 |
| 1972 | 111.9 | 112.6 | 112.4 | 108.5 | 111.8 | 113.3 | 111.7 | 97.3 |
| 1973 | 108.8 | 102.2 | 108.0 | 100.0 | 107.9 | 105.9 | 119.4 | 100.6 |
| 1974 | 108.9 | 101.6 | 110.2 | 96.9 | 115.4 | 113.0 | 112.5 | 99.1 |
| 1975 | 109.9 | 109.7 | 105.2 | 106.5 | 113.4 | 109.8 | 112.6 | 109.0 |
| 1976 | 104.4 | 100.5 | 106.4 | 100.0 | 109.9 | 109.0 | 102.6 | 94.0 |
| 1977 | 103.7 | 107.3 | 107.8 | 103.0 | 113.0 | 111.0 | 91.7 | 118.9 |
| 1978 | 105.1 | 103.6 | 101.7 | 116.2 | 103.5 | 100.0 | 108.7 | 117.2 |

注：本表人均生产总值按户籍人口计算。
Note: The per capita GDP hereof is calculated by registered population.

# 表 2.4 地区生产总值指数(1949 － 1978 年)(1949 年 =100)
## INDICES OF GROSS DOMESTIC PRODUCT (1949-1978) (1949=100)

| 年份<br>Year | 本市生产总值<br>Gross Domestic Product | 第一产业<br>Primary Industry | 第二产业<br>Secondary Industry | 工业<br>Industry | 建筑业<br>Construction |
|---|---|---|---|---|---|
| 1949 | 100.0 | 100.0 | 100.0 | 100.0 | 100.0 |
| 1950 | 105.7 | 103.0 | 112.5 | 112.0 | 118.2 |
| 1951 | 109.3 | 107.1 | 124.8 | 124.5 | 127.3 |
| 1952 | 119.5 | 114.6 | 144.0 | 141.6 | 172.7 |
| 1953 | 132.9 | 118.5 | 194.1 | 184.9 | 305.9 |
| 1954 | 147.0 | 125.6 | 233.3 | 231.5 | 251.8 |
| 1955 | 151.0 | 125.9 | 255.7 | 259.0 | 207.5 |
| 1956 | 171.4 | 132.3 | 325.5 | 324.8 | 326.0 |
| 1957 | 175.3 | 128.9 | 352.8 | 358.6 | 271.6 |
| 1958 | 208.4 | 129.8 | 484.0 | 485.5 | 449.5 |
| 1959 | 203.0 | 88.0 | 599.7 | 599.1 | 585.2 |
| 1960 | 225.3 | 65.7 | 796.4 | 798.6 | 744.4 |
| 1961 | 146.0 | 55.0 | 461.1 | 472.8 | 308.9 |
| 1962 | 146.0 | 74.5 | 385.9 | 405.2 | 140.5 |
| 1963 | 167.8 | 92.4 | 421.8 | 438.0 | 215.4 |
| 1964 | 193.0 | 98.0 | 523.0 | 539.6 | 309.1 |
| 1965 | 221.0 | 107.5 | 637.5 | 642.1 | 571.2 |
| 1966 | 234.0 | 109.4 | 723.6 | 726.2 | 674.0 |
| 1967 | 211.1 | 108.7 | 599.9 | 609.3 | 477.2 |
| 1968 | 178.2 | 115.7 | 397.1 | 406.4 | 275.8 |
| 1969 | 199.8 | 105.7 | 540.1 | 546.6 | 453.4 |
| 1970 | 241.2 | 108.3 | 748.6 | 746.1 | 771.2 |
| 1971 | 269.9 | 108.7 | 937.2 | 948.3 | 788.9 |
| 1972 | 270.2 | 110.4 | 893.2 | 909.4 | 671.4 |
| 1973 | 278.8 | 120.9 | 859.3 | 858.5 | 854.0 |
| 1974 | 283.3 | 122.8 | 847.3 | 854.2 | 748.1 |
| 1975 | 316.7 | 114.0 | 1102.3 | 1112.2 | 959.8 |
| 1976 | 301.2 | 112.3 | 983.3 | 994.3 | 830.2 |
| 1977 | 361.4 | 125.4 | 1312.7 | 1308.5 | 1348.2 |
| 1978 | 423.2 | 137.7 | 1652.7 | 1630.4 | 1907.7 |

注：本表按可比价格计算（下表同）。
Note: The indices hereof are calculated at constant prices (the same below).

表 2.4 续表 continued

| 年份 Year | 第三产业 Tertiary Industry | 批发和零售业 Wholesale and Retail Trades | 交通运输、仓储及邮政业 Transport, Storage, Post | 住宿和餐饮业 Hotels and Catering Services | 金融业 Financial Intermediation | 房地产业 Real Estate | 其他 Others | 本市人均生产总值 Per Capita GDP |
|---|---|---|---|---|---|---|---|---|
| 1949 | 100.0 | 100.0 | 100.0 | 100.0 | 100.0 | 100.0 | 100.0 | 100.0 |
| 1950 | 118.6 | 105.6 | 127.6 | 107.4 | 197.3 | 250.4 | 102.5 | 102.2 |
| 1951 | 112.6 | 104.2 | 118.9 | 111.1 | 292.0 | 351.1 | 9.2 | 102.7 |
| 1952 | 135.2 | 120.9 | 134.4 | 118.5 | 192.4 | 402.0 | 35.0 | 109.2 |
| 1953 | 150.7 | 147.4 | 142.5 | 122.3 | 224.5 | 452.3 | 39.2 | 119.6 |
| 1954 | 169.4 | 160.7 | 161.9 | 130.0 | 320.8 | 552.7 | 44.8 | 130.5 |
| 1955 | 166.9 | 158.8 | 153.8 | 137.7 | 320.8 | 653.3 | 42.0 | 131.4 |
| 1956 | 197.4 | 181.5 | 178.1 | 164.4 | 417.0 | 753.9 | 56.0 | 143.4 |
| 1957 | 209.2 | 187.1 | 192.7 | 164.4 | 449.1 | 804.4 | 63.0 | 141.0 |
| 1958 | 282.2 | 258.4 | 264.8 | 171.8 | 641.8 | 750.5 | 101.1 | 167.2 |
| 1959 | 291.5 | 268.0 | 252.4 | 190.5 | 770.2 | 803.8 | 111.6 | 164.0 |
| 1960 | 294.7 | 275.8 | 227.4 | 194.3 | 962.8 | 749.9 | 126.0 | 186.0 |
| 1961 | 208.6 | 183.1 | 164.6 | 194.3 | 834.7 | 857.1 | 60.4 | 126.9 |
| 1962 | 219.0 | 175.4 | 158.3 | 239.2 | 866.4 | 857.1 | 76.2 | 130.5 |
| 1963 | 246.6 | 198.6 | 170.8 | 224.4 | 834.3 | 911.1 | 114.3 | 147.1 |
| 1964 | 268.8 | 194.8 | 178.7 | 202.0 | 1444.2 | 857.3 | 141.8 | 163.0 |
| 1965 | 270.1 | 214.1 | 175.5 | 202.0 | 2214.0 | 1018.5 | 98.4 | 181.3 |
| 1966 | 230.1 | 219.9 | 161.5 | 190.7 | 898.9 | 857.6 | 82.7 | 186.4 |
| 1967 | 236.8 | 225.6 | 163.1 | 194.5 | 1059.8 | 1018.8 | 80.1 | 163.3 |
| 1968 | 240.6 | 196.7 | 160.0 | 187.1 | 1445.6 | 1286.7 | 90.6 | 133.7 |
| 1969 | 254.1 | 219.9 | 183.5 | 190.8 | 1509.2 | 1340.7 | 78.8 | 146.1 |
| 1970 | 258.9 | 229.6 | 196.0 | 194.6 | 1540.9 | 1394.3 | 68.3 | 171.2 |
| 1971 | 271.1 | 240.2 | 201.5 | 229.6 | 1849.1 | 1568.6 | 64.3 | 185.2 |
| 1972 | 303.4 | 270.5 | 226.5 | 249.1 | 2067.3 | 1777.2 | 71.8 | 180.2 |
| 1973 | 330.1 | 276.5 | 244.6 | 249.1 | 2230.6 | 1882.1 | 85.7 | 181.3 |
| 1974 | 359.5 | 280.9 | 269.5 | 241.4 | 2574.1 | 2126.8 | 96.4 | 179.7 |
| 1975 | 395.1 | 308.1 | 283.5 | 257.1 | 2919.0 | 2335.2 | 108.5 | 195.9 |
| 1976 | 412.5 | 309.6 | 301.6 | 257.1 | 3208.0 | 2545.4 | 111.3 | 184.1 |
| 1977 | 427.8 | 332.2 | 325.1 | 264.8 | 3625.0 | 2825.4 | 102.1 | 218.9 |
| 1978 | 449.6 | 344.2 | 330.6 | 307.7 | 3751.9 | 2825.4 | 111.0 | 256.6 |

注：本表人均地区生产总值按户籍人口计算。
Note: The per capita GDP hereof is calculated by registered population.

# 表 2.5 地区生产总值(1978 – 2022 年)
GROSS DOMESTIC PRODUCT (1978-2022)

单位: 亿元 (100 million yuan)

| 年 份 Year | 本 市 生产总值 Gross Domestic Product | 第一产业 Primary Industry | 第二产业 Secondary Industry | 工 业 Industry | 建筑业 Construction | 第三产业 Tertiary Industry |
|---|---|---|---|---|---|---|
| 1978 | 71.70 | 24.81 | 34.46 | 31.53 | 2.93 | 12.43 |
| 1979 | 80.98 | 28.79 | 38.21 | 35.00 | 3.21 | 13.98 |
| 1980 | 90.68 | 32.57 | 42.42 | 38.89 | 3.53 | 15.69 |
| 1981 | 97.20 | 36.32 | 43.69 | 40.07 | 3.62 | 17.19 |
| 1982 | 108.08 | 40.62 | 47.14 | 43.26 | 3.88 | 20.32 |
| 1983 | 120.01 | 45.44 | 50.56 | 46.20 | 4.36 | 24.01 |
| 1984 | 141.64 | 50.66 | 60.63 | 55.46 | 5.17 | 30.35 |
| 1985 | 164.32 | 53.73 | 73.49 | 66.16 | 7.33 | 37.10 |
| 1986 | 184.60 | 60.06 | 81.38 | 72.52 | 8.86 | 43.16 |
| 1987 | 206.73 | 62.69 | 90.77 | 79.66 | 11.11 | 53.27 |
| 1988 | 261.27 | 75.00 | 117.61 | 104.79 | 12.82 | 68.66 |
| 1989 | 303.75 | 81.99 | 135.84 | 123.86 | 11.98 | 85.92 |
| 1990 | 327.75 | 100.40 | 135.62 | 117.60 | 18.02 | 91.73 |
| 1991 | 374.63 | 109.49 | 154.28 | 135.35 | 18.93 | 110.86 |
| 1992 | 462.47 | 117.28 | 195.10 | 171.96 | 23.14 | 150.09 |
| 1993 | 611.05 | 141.99 | 273.64 | 242.29 | 31.35 | 195.42 |
| 1994 | 838.14 | 196.19 | 379.43 | 341.74 | 37.69 | 262.52 |
| 1995 | 1130.60 | 264.19 | 497.13 | 439.66 | 57.47 | 369.28 |
| 1996 | 1326.40 | 287.56 | 575.20 | 506.83 | 68.37 | 463.64 |
| 1997 | 1525.26 | 307.21 | 658.77 | 574.18 | 84.59 | 559.28 |
| 1998 | 1622.42 | 300.89 | 685.83 | 581.69 | 104.14 | 635.70 |
| 1999 | 1687.81 | 286.16 | 709.74 | 597.94 | 111.80 | 691.91 |
| 2000 | 1822.06 | 280.45 | 774.63 | 644.04 | 130.59 | 766.98 |
| 2001 | 2014.59 | 290.10 | 859.92 | 707.59 | 152.33 | 864.57 |
| 2002 | 2279.80 | 312.57 | 981.32 | 802.97 | 178.35 | 985.91 |
| 2003 | 2615.57 | 332.86 | 1164.12 | 953.06 | 211.06 | 1118.59 |
| 2004 | 3059.54 | 420.43 | 1392.55 | 1146.43 | 246.12 | 1246.56 |
| 2005 | 3448.35 | 455.08 | 1559.17 | 1294.86 | 264.31 | 1434.10 |
| 2006 | 3900.26 | 379.68 | 1873.42 | 1573.06 | 300.36 | 1647.16 |
| 2007 | 4770.72 | 469.43 | 2237.30 | 1862.32 | 374.98 | 2063.99 |
| 2008 | 5899.49 | 555.05 | 2651.79 | 2188.63 | 463.16 | 2692.65 |
| 2009 | 6651.22 | 581.05 | 3016.81 | 2470.84 | 545.97 | 3053.36 |
| 2010 | 8065.26 | 649.48 | 3624.12 | 2945.51 | 678.61 | 3791.66 |
| 2011 | 10161.17 | 794.14 | 4571.26 | 3700.24 | 871.02 | 4795.77 |
| 2012 | 11595.37 | 879.67 | 5308.14 | 4291.40 | 1016.74 | 5407.56 |
| 2013 | 13027.60 | 941.24 | 5988.62 | 4775.67 | 1212.95 | 6097.74 |
| 2014 | 14623.78 | 990.75 | 6774.58 | 5369.87 | 1404.71 | 6858.45 |
| 2015 | 16040.54 | 1067.72 | 7208.01 | 5621.47 | 1586.54 | 7764.81 |
| 2016 | 18023.04 | 1236.98 | 7765.38 | 5896.16 | 1869.22 | 9020.68 |
| 2017 | 20066.29 | 1276.09 | 8455.02 | 6202.38 | 2252.64 | 10335.18 |
| 2018 | 21588.80 | 1378.68 | 8842.23 | 6268.10 | 2574.13 | 11367.89 |
| 2019 | 23605.77 | 1551.59 | 9391.96 | 6551.84 | 2840.12 | 12662.22 |
| 2020 | 25041.43 | 1803.54 | 9969.55 | 6990.77 | 2978.78 | 13268.34 |
| 2021 | 28077.28 | 1921.91 | 11217.26 | 7940.52 | 3276.74 | 14938.11 |
| 2022 | 29129.03 | 2012.05 | 11693.86 | 8275.99 | 3417.87 | 15423.12 |

**表 2.5 续表 continued**

单位：亿元 (100 million yuan)

| 年 份 Year | 批发和零售业 Wholesale and Retail Trades | 交通运输、仓储及邮政业 Transportation, Storage, Postal Services | 住宿和餐饮业 Hotels and Catering Services | 金融业 Financial Intermediation | 房地产业 Real Estate | 其 他 Other | 本市人均生产总值（元） Per Capita GDP (yuan) |
|---|---|---|---|---|---|---|---|
| 1978 | 2.34 | 2.38 | 0.78 | 2.00 | 0.88 | 4.05 | 287 |
| 1979 | 2.59 | 2.69 | 0.92 | 2.21 | 0.99 | 4.58 | 321 |
| 1980 | 2.90 | 3.08 | 1.02 | 2.46 | 1.11 | 5.12 | 357 |
| 1981 | 3.22 | 3.39 | 1.07 | 2.73 | 1.12 | 5.66 | 379 |
| 1982 | 3.89 | 4.18 | 1.11 | 2.99 | 1.28 | 6.87 | 419 |
| 1983 | 4.49 | 5.94 | 1.24 | 3.83 | 1.44 | 7.07 | 461 |
| 1984 | 5.73 | 6.50 | 1.52 | 6.63 | 1.81 | 8.16 | 542 |
| 1985 | 8.90 | 6.97 | 1.80 | 7.40 | 2.09 | 9.94 | 624 |
| 1986 | 10.08 | 6.59 | 2.17 | 8.71 | 2.64 | 12.97 | 694 |
| 1987 | 12.30 | 6.82 | 2.71 | 14.91 | 3.59 | 12.94 | 766 |
| 1988 | 17.10 | 8.67 | 3.29 | 17.92 | 4.47 | 17.21 | 958 |
| 1989 | 21.61 | 12.18 | 3.89 | 24.78 | 4.95 | 18.51 | 1103 |
| 1990 | 17.19 | 11.93 | 5.41 | 26.21 | 5.73 | 25.26 | 1181 |
| 1991 | 20.45 | 12.30 | 6.35 | 31.61 | 7.27 | 32.88 | 1340 |
| 1992 | 33.43 | 21.43 | 7.23 | 40.20 | 7.39 | 40.41 | 1645 |
| 1993 | 50.54 | 22.43 | 9.37 | 52.71 | 9.28 | 51.09 | 2165 |
| 1994 | 66.24 | 27.04 | 12.78 | 74.54 | 11.29 | 70.63 | 2951 |
| 1995 | 88.15 | 46.37 | 19.01 | 97.16 | 17.95 | 100.64 | 3957 |
| 1996 | 114.28 | 62.04 | 23.47 | 103.07 | 26.12 | 134.66 | 4613 |
| 1997 | 136.50 | 79.11 | 30.93 | 115.52 | 33.96 | 163.26 | 5306 |
| 1998 | 150.06 | 84.59 | 31.70 | 125.41 | 47.16 | 196.78 | 5649 |
| 1999 | 160.36 | 91.36 | 33.65 | 118.84 | 53.43 | 234.27 | 5890 |
| 2000 | 173.54 | 97.64 | 35.96 | 117.07 | 69.39 | 273.38 | 6383 |
| 2001 | 190.63 | 123.25 | 38.50 | 124.19 | 81.46 | 306.54 | 7096 |
| 2002 | 210.32 | 145.09 | 42.40 | 132.53 | 97.06 | 358.51 | 8079 |
| 2003 | 234.00 | 159.52 | 47.16 | 144.69 | 122.68 | 410.54 | 9311 |
| 2004 | 249.80 | 189.20 | 57.68 | 161.96 | 130.78 | 457.14 | 10934 |
| 2005 | 267.11 | 223.63 | 66.53 | 186.55 | 138.57 | 551.71 | 12335 |
| 2006 | 306.23 | 263.31 | 77.21 | 214.77 | 154.25 | 631.39 | 13915 |
| 2007 | 389.15 | 285.18 | 101.58 | 236.33 | 208.66 | 843.09 | 16966 |
| 2008 | 487.32 | 367.33 | 136.11 | 312.44 | 203.74 | 1185.71 | 20865 |
| 2009 | 560.61 | 416.74 | 160.47 | 397.79 | 241.30 | 1276.45 | 23346 |
| 2010 | 713.26 | 489.08 | 183.09 | 538.85 | 312.56 | 1554.82 | 28084 |
| 2011 | 857.95 | 580.22 | 214.20 | 767.98 | 453.30 | 1922.12 | 34864 |
| 2012 | 960.16 | 591.23 | 236.26 | 927.39 | 631.69 | 2060.83 | 39178 |
| 2013 | 1171.49 | 642.61 | 291.11 | 1070.32 | 778.18 | 2144.03 | 43528 |
| 2014 | 1311.17 | 680.87 | 321.92 | 1210.01 | 869.31 | 2465.17 | 48307 |
| 2015 | 1462.21 | 726.11 | 356.16 | 1387.18 | 918.97 | 2914.18 | 52476 |
| 2016 | 1703.43 | 777.15 | 391.99 | 1593.99 | 1067.93 | 3486.19 | 58327 |
| 2017 | 1955.06 | 827.97 | 426.01 | 1737.64 | 1276.56 | 4111.94 | 64176 |
| 2018 | 2024.60 | 899.38 | 458.25 | 1875.97 | 1336.72 | 4772.97 | 68464 |
| 2019 | 2192.06 | 977.14 | 501.98 | 2087.95 | 1502.50 | 5400.59 | 74337 |
| 2020 | 2332.57 | 944.04 | 468.44 | 2220.80 | 1578.67 | 5723.82 | 78294 |
| 2021 | 2695.69 | 1087.98 | 561.06 | 2404.53 | 1750.89 | 6437.96 | 87450 |
| 2022 | 2816.74 | 1083.96 | 567.71 | 2491.02 | 1668.59 | 6795.10 | 90663 |

注：本表人均地区生产总值按常住人口计算。
Note: The per capita GDP hereof is calculated by registered population.

# 表 2.6 地区生产总值构成（1978 – 2022 年）
COMPOSITION OF GROSS DOMESTIC PRODUCT (1978-2022)

单位：% (%)

| 年 份<br>Year | 本 市<br>生产总值<br>Gross Domestic Product | 第一产业<br>Primary Industry | 第二产业<br>Secondary Industry | 工 业<br>Industry | 建筑业<br>Construction | 第三产业<br>Tertiary Industry |
|---|---|---|---|---|---|---|
| 1978 | 100.0 | 34.6 | 48.1 | 44.0 | 4.1 | 17.3 |
| 1979 | 100.0 | 35.6 | 47.2 | 43.2 | 4.0 | 17.2 |
| 1980 | 100.0 | 35.9 | 46.8 | 42.9 | 3.9 | 17.3 |
| 1981 | 100.0 | 37.4 | 44.9 | 41.2 | 3.7 | 17.7 |
| 1982 | 100.0 | 37.6 | 43.6 | 40.0 | 3.6 | 18.8 |
| 1983 | 100.0 | 37.9 | 42.1 | 38.5 | 3.6 | 20.0 |
| 1984 | 100.0 | 35.8 | 42.8 | 39.2 | 3.6 | 21.4 |
| 1985 | 100.0 | 32.7 | 44.7 | 40.3 | 4.4 | 22.6 |
| 1986 | 100.0 | 32.5 | 44.1 | 39.3 | 4.8 | 23.4 |
| 1987 | 100.0 | 30.3 | 43.9 | 38.5 | 5.4 | 25.8 |
| 1988 | 100.0 | 28.7 | 45.0 | 40.1 | 4.9 | 26.3 |
| 1989 | 100.0 | 27.0 | 44.7 | 40.8 | 3.9 | 28.3 |
| 1990 | 100.0 | 30.6 | 41.4 | 35.9 | 5.5 | 28.0 |
| 1991 | 100.0 | 29.2 | 41.2 | 36.1 | 5.1 | 29.6 |
| 1992 | 100.0 | 25.4 | 42.2 | 37.2 | 5.0 | 32.4 |
| 1993 | 100.0 | 23.2 | 44.8 | 39.7 | 5.1 | 32.0 |
| 1994 | 100.0 | 23.4 | 45.3 | 40.8 | 4.5 | 31.3 |
| 1995 | 100.0 | 23.4 | 44.0 | 38.9 | 5.1 | 32.6 |
| 1996 | 100.0 | 21.7 | 43.4 | 38.2 | 5.2 | 34.9 |
| 1997 | 100.0 | 20.1 | 43.2 | 37.6 | 5.6 | 36.7 |
| 1998 | 100.0 | 18.5 | 42.3 | 35.9 | 6.4 | 39.2 |
| 1999 | 100.0 | 17.0 | 42.1 | 35.4 | 6.7 | 40.9 |
| 2000 | 100.0 | 15.4 | 42.5 | 35.3 | 7.2 | 42.1 |
| 2001 | 100.0 | 14.4 | 42.7 | 35.1 | 7.6 | 42.9 |
| 2002 | 100.0 | 13.7 | 43.0 | 35.2 | 7.8 | 43.3 |
| 2003 | 100.0 | 12.7 | 44.5 | 36.4 | 8.1 | 42.8 |
| 2004 | 100.0 | 13.7 | 45.5 | 37.5 | 8.0 | 40.8 |
| 2005 | 100.0 | 13.2 | 45.2 | 37.6 | 7.6 | 41.6 |
| 2006 | 100.0 | 9.7 | 48.0 | 40.3 | 7.7 | 42.3 |
| 2007 | 100.0 | 9.8 | 46.9 | 39.0 | 7.9 | 43.3 |
| 2008 | 100.0 | 9.4 | 44.9 | 37.1 | 7.8 | 45.7 |
| 2009 | 100.0 | 8.7 | 45.4 | 37.1 | 8.3 | 45.9 |
| 2010 | 100.0 | 8.1 | 44.9 | 36.5 | 8.4 | 47.0 |
| 2011 | 100.0 | 7.8 | 45.0 | 36.4 | 8.6 | 47.2 |
| 2012 | 100.0 | 7.6 | 45.8 | 37.0 | 8.8 | 46.6 |
| 2013 | 100.0 | 7.2 | 46.0 | 36.7 | 9.3 | 46.8 |
| 2014 | 100.0 | 6.8 | 46.3 | 36.7 | 9.6 | 46.9 |
| 2015 | 100.0 | 6.7 | 44.9 | 35.0 | 9.9 | 48.4 |
| 2016 | 100.0 | 6.9 | 43.1 | 32.7 | 10.4 | 50.0 |
| 2017 | 100.0 | 6.4 | 42.1 | 30.9 | 11.2 | 51.5 |
| 2018 | 100.0 | 6.4 | 41.0 | 29.0 | 12.0 | 52.6 |
| 2019 | 100.0 | 6.6 | 39.8 | 27.8 | 12.0 | 53.6 |
| 2020 | 100.0 | 7.2 | 39.8 | 27.9 | 11.9 | 53.0 |
| 2021 | 100.0 | 6.8 | 40.0 | 28.3 | 11.7 | 53.2 |
| 2022 | 100.0 | 6.9 | 40.1 | 28.4 | 11.7 | 53.0 |

**表 2.6 续表 continued** 单位: % (%)

| 年 份<br>Year | 批发和零售业<br>Wholesale and Retail Trades | 交通运输、仓储及邮政业<br>Transport, Storage, Post | 住宿和餐饮业<br>Hotels and Catering Services | 金融业<br>Financial Intermediation | 房地产业<br>Real Estate | 其 他<br>Others |
|---|---|---|---|---|---|---|
| 1978 | 3.3 | 3.3 | 1.1 | 2.8 | 1.2 | 5.6 |
| 1979 | 3.2 | 3.3 | 1.1 | 2.7 | 1.2 | 5.7 |
| 1980 | 3.2 | 3.4 | 1.1 | 2.7 | 1.2 | 5.7 |
| 1981 | 3.3 | 3.5 | 1.1 | 2.8 | 1.2 | 5.8 |
| 1982 | 3.6 | 3.9 | 1.0 | 2.8 | 1.2 | 6.3 |
| 1983 | 3.7 | 4.9 | 1.0 | 3.2 | 1.2 | 6.0 |
| 1984 | 4.0 | 4.6 | 1.1 | 4.7 | 1.3 | 5.7 |
| 1985 | 5.4 | 4.2 | 1.1 | 4.5 | 1.3 | 6.1 |
| 1986 | 5.5 | 3.6 | 1.2 | 4.7 | 1.4 | 7.0 |
| 1987 | 5.9 | 3.3 | 1.3 | 7.2 | 1.7 | 6.4 |
| 1988 | 6.5 | 3.3 | 1.3 | 6.9 | 1.7 | 6.6 |
| 1989 | 7.1 | 4.0 | 1.3 | 8.2 | 1.6 | 6.1 |
| 1990 | 5.2 | 3.6 | 1.7 | 8.0 | 1.7 | 7.8 |
| 1991 | 5.5 | 3.3 | 1.7 | 8.4 | 1.9 | 8.8 |
| 1992 | 7.2 | 4.6 | 1.6 | 8.7 | 1.6 | 8.7 |
| 1993 | 8.3 | 3.7 | 1.5 | 8.6 | 1.5 | 8.4 |
| 1994 | 7.9 | 3.2 | 1.5 | 8.9 | 1.3 | 8.5 |
| 1995 | 7.8 | 4.1 | 1.7 | 8.6 | 1.6 | 8.8 |
| 1996 | 8.6 | 4.7 | 1.8 | 7.8 | 2.0 | 10.0 |
| 1997 | 8.9 | 5.2 | 2.0 | 7.6 | 2.2 | 10.8 |
| 1998 | 9.2 | 5.2 | 2.0 | 7.7 | 2.9 | 12.2 |
| 1999 | 9.5 | 5.4 | 2.0 | 7.0 | 3.2 | 13.8 |
| 2000 | 9.5 | 5.4 | 2.0 | 6.4 | 3.8 | 15.0 |
| 2001 | 9.5 | 6.1 | 1.9 | 6.2 | 4.0 | 15.2 |
| 2002 | 9.2 | 6.4 | 1.9 | 5.8 | 4.3 | 15.7 |
| 2003 | 8.9 | 6.1 | 1.8 | 5.5 | 4.7 | 15.8 |
| 2004 | 8.2 | 6.2 | 1.9 | 5.3 | 4.3 | 14.9 |
| 2005 | 7.7 | 6.5 | 1.9 | 5.4 | 4.0 | 16.1 |
| 2006 | 7.9 | 6.8 | 2.0 | 5.5 | 4.0 | 16.1 |
| 2007 | 8.2 | 6.0 | 2.1 | 5.0 | 4.4 | 17.6 |
| 2008 | 8.3 | 6.2 | 2.3 | 5.3 | 3.5 | 20.1 |
| 2009 | 8.4 | 6.3 | 2.4 | 6.0 | 3.6 | 19.2 |
| 2010 | 8.8 | 6.1 | 2.3 | 6.7 | 3.9 | 19.2 |
| 2011 | 8.4 | 5.7 | 2.1 | 7.6 | 4.5 | 18.9 |
| 2012 | 8.3 | 5.1 | 2.0 | 8.0 | 5.4 | 17.8 |
| 2013 | 9.0 | 4.9 | 2.2 | 8.2 | 6.0 | 16.5 |
| 2014 | 9.0 | 4.7 | 2.2 | 8.3 | 5.9 | 16.8 |
| 2015 | 9.1 | 4.5 | 2.2 | 8.6 | 5.7 | 18.3 |
| 2016 | 9.5 | 4.3 | 2.2 | 8.8 | 5.9 | 19.3 |
| 2017 | 9.7 | 4.1 | 2.1 | 8.7 | 6.4 | 20.5 |
| 2018 | 9.4 | 4.2 | 2.1 | 8.7 | 6.2 | 22.0 |
| 2019 | 9.3 | 4.1 | 2.1 | 8.8 | 6.4 | 22.9 |
| 2020 | 9.3 | 3.8 | 1.9 | 8.9 | 6.3 | 22.8 |
| 2021 | 9.6 | 3.9 | 2.0 | 8.6 | 6.2 | 22.9 |
| 2022 | 9.7 | 3.7 | 1.9 | 8.6 | 5.7 | 23.4 |

# 表 2.7 地区生产总值指数（1978 － 2022 年）（上年 =100）
INDICES OF GROSS DOMESTIC PRODUCT (1978-2022) (PRECEDING YEAR=100)

| 年份 Year | 本市生产总值 Gross Domestic Product | 第一产业 Primary Industry | 第二产业 Secondary Industry | 工业 Industry | 建筑业 Construction | 第三产业 Tertiary Industry |
|---|---|---|---|---|---|---|
| 1978 | 117.1 | 109.8 | 125.9 | 124.6 | 141.5 | 105.1 |
| 1979 | 111.1 | 109.1 | 112.0 | 112.0 | 111.7 | 112.1 |
| 1980 | 107.7 | 104.3 | 108.8 | 108.7 | 109.9 | 109.8 |
| 1981 | 106.2 | 105.8 | 105.0 | 104.7 | 108.2 | 110.3 |
| 1982 | 108.9 | 107.5 | 107.4 | 107.4 | 107.1 | 115.7 |
| 1983 | 110.3 | 107.3 | 109.9 | 109.7 | 111.7 | 117.2 |
| 1984 | 115.9 | 106.5 | 120.6 | 120.7 | 119.7 | 121.3 |
| 1985 | 108.6 | 109.3 | 106.5 | 105.1 | 121.9 | 112.4 |
| 1986 | 108.6 | 110.3 | 106.5 | 105.5 | 115.9 | 110.4 |
| 1987 | 105.3 | 96.7 | 108.2 | 106.9 | 119.3 | 111.9 |
| 1988 | 109.5 | 103.5 | 113.2 | 114.1 | 106.2 | 109.8 |
| 1989 | 104.9 | 104.6 | 102.7 | 104.1 | 91.5 | 109.6 |
| 1990 | 107.0 | 107.8 | 107.8 | 103.8 | 144.2 | 104.8 |
| 1991 | 109.2 | 106.7 | 109.5 | 110.9 | 100.2 | 111.5 |
| 1992 | 116.5 | 101.8 | 121.8 | 122.2 | 118.7 | 124.2 |
| 1993 | 115.6 | 105.0 | 122.1 | 122.5 | 118.8 | 115.5 |
| 1994 | 113.5 | 102.9 | 116.3 | 117.6 | 105.8 | 117.6 |
| 1995 | 112.3 | 104.5 | 114.1 | 114.0 | 114.3 | 115.0 |
| 1996 | 111.4 | 104.8 | 112.1 | 112.2 | 111.3 | 114.5 |
| 1997 | 111.2 | 103.2 | 112.3 | 111.6 | 118.5 | 114.1 |
| 1998 | 108.6 | 102.1 | 107.2 | 105.2 | 122.8 | 114.0 |
| 1999 | 107.8 | 100.4 | 110.5 | 110.9 | 107.7 | 107.6 |
| 2000 | 108.7 | 101.4 | 110.7 | 110.7 | 110.7 | 109.1 |
| 2001 | 109.2 | 102.1 | 112.0 | 111.4 | 114.7 | 109.0 |
| 2002 | 110.5 | 104.2 | 114.1 | 114.0 | 114.7 | 108.9 |
| 2003 | 111.7 | 104.4 | 116.4 | 116.7 | 115.1 | 109.0 |
| 2004 | 112.5 | 104.8 | 116.9 | 117.4 | 114.9 | 109.8 |
| 2005 | 111.8 | 104.5 | 113.4 | 114.6 | 107.3 | 112.1 |
| 2006 | 112.5 | 94.2 | 117.2 | 118.3 | 111.9 | 113.2 |
| 2007 | 116.0 | 109.5 | 121.0 | 122.5 | 113.4 | 112.1 |
| 2008 | 114.6 | 106.7 | 118.3 | 119.9 | 109.2 | 112.2 |
| 2009 | 115.1 | 105.4 | 118.1 | 117.7 | 121.2 | 113.6 |
| 2010 | 117.2 | 106.1 | 122.7 | 122.9 | 121.4 | 112.4 |
| 2011 | 116.4 | 105.1 | 121.0 | 121.3 | 119.6 | 114.0 |
| 2012 | 113.6 | 105.4 | 116.6 | 117.2 | 113.9 | 111.9 |
| 2013 | 112.3 | 104.7 | 112.9 | 112.5 | 114.9 | 112.8 |
| 2014 | 110.9 | 104.4 | 112.7 | 112.4 | 114.2 | 109.9 |
| 2015 | 111.0 | 104.8 | 111.2 | 110.4 | 114.7 | 111.6 |
| 2016 | 110.7 | 104.7 | 111.3 | 110.3 | 114.8 | 111.0 |
| 2017 | 109.3 | 104.0 | 109.3 | 109.4 | 109.0 | 110.0 |
| 2018 | 106.0 | 104.4 | 103.0 | 101.1 | 109.5 | 109.0 |
| 2019 | 106.3 | 103.6 | 106.4 | 106.4 | 106.6 | 106.4 |
| 2020 | 103.9 | 104.6 | 104.8 | 105.3 | 103.3 | 102.9 |
| 2021 | 108.4 | 107.8 | 107.2 | 109.8 | 101.3 | 109.5 |
| 2022 | 102.6 | 104.0 | 103.3 | 102.9 | 104.0 | 101.9 |

注：1) 本表按可比价格计算（下表同）。
2) 本表人均生产总值按常住人口计算。
Note: a) The indices hereof are calculated at constant prices (the same below).
b) The per capita GDP hereof is calculated by registered population.

**表 2.7 续表 continued**

| 年 份<br>Year | 批发和零售业<br>Wholesale and Retail Trades | 交通运输、仓储及邮政业<br>Transport, Storage, Post | 住宿和餐饮业<br>Hotels and Catering Services | 金融业<br>Financial Intermediation | 房地产业<br>Real Estate | 其 他<br>Others | 本市人均生产总值<br>Per Capita GDP |
|---|---|---|---|---|---|---|---|
| 1978 | 103.6 | 101.7 | 116.2 | 103.5 | 100.0 | 108.7 | 117.2 |
| 1979 | 110.5 | 109.2 | 115.2 | 111.6 | 111.1 | 115.1 | 110.4 |
| 1980 | 106.3 | 103.5 | 113.2 | 107.4 | 106.7 | 118.4 | 107.1 |
| 1981 | 108.6 | 105.8 | 106.9 | 109.8 | 99.1 | 117.2 | 105.4 |
| 1982 | 115.2 | 117.2 | 107.3 | 108.1 | 111.8 | 120.8 | 108.0 |
| 1983 | 115.2 | 131.2 | 106.8 | 130.1 | 121.1 | 106.8 | 109.5 |
| 1984 | 123.9 | 111.6 | 124.0 | 139.5 | 122.8 | 116.7 | 115.5 |
| 1985 | 137.3 | 96.8 | 117.4 | 103.0 | 105.5 | 113.7 | 108.0 |
| 1986 | 106.6 | 99.8 | 117.6 | 111.9 | 118.7 | 115.1 | 107.5 |
| 1987 | 110.0 | 108.3 | 114.5 | 128.3 | 121.4 | 103.8 | 103.9 |
| 1988 | 122.8 | 106.0 | 119.2 | 104.0 | 105.8 | 105.7 | 108.2 |
| 1989 | 108.2 | 116.6 | 112.7 | 113.3 | 100.0 | 106.4 | 104.0 |
| 1990 | 83.5 | 104.1 | 133.4 | 108.6 | 116.7 | 110.2 | 106.1 |
| 1991 | 108.5 | 102.4 | 116.6 | 113.9 | 117.3 | 112.9 | 108.4 |
| 1992 | 142.3 | 133.5 | 116.3 | 120.4 | 96.4 | 120.6 | 115.9 |
| 1993 | 138.5 | 102.8 | 124.4 | 109.3 | 109.4 | 109.5 | 115.2 |
| 1994 | 104.1 | 109.1 | 133.3 | 115.3 | 102.8 | 135.9 | 112.8 |
| 1995 | 111.2 | 123.1 | 137.0 | 116.5 | 114.5 | 108.5 | 111.6 |
| 1996 | 115.9 | 115.6 | 120.3 | 104.0 | 131.5 | 118.7 | 110.7 |
| 1997 | 113.5 | 114.7 | 126.3 | 109.6 | 124.5 | 112.6 | 111.3 |
| 1998 | 115.0 | 104.1 | 104.4 | 110.4 | 122.4 | 121.9 | 108.7 |
| 1999 | 108.3 | 101.9 | 108.2 | 89.7 | 110.2 | 121.5 | 108.0 |
| 2000 | 112.2 | 104.0 | 108.1 | 101.8 | 111.6 | 112.4 | 109.1 |
| 2001 | 108.9 | 116.2 | 106.2 | 101.5 | 112.6 | 109.2 | 109.8 |
| 2002 | 110.1 | 105.2 | 109.5 | 107.9 | 113.8 | 108.6 | 111.2 |
| 2003 | 109.3 | 104.8 | 110.1 | 107.9 | 116.1 | 108.7 | 112.2 |
| 2004 | 110.8 | 114.6 | 118.0 | 105.9 | 103.7 | 109.7 | 112.9 |
| 2005 | 114.0 | 112.4 | 113.7 | 109.9 | 109.8 | 111.9 | 111.9 |
| 2006 | 111.4 | 120.3 | 115.2 | 112.4 | 107.7 | 112.5 | 112.2 |
| 2007 | 112.3 | 112.5 | 112.0 | 109.7 | 116.8 | 111.4 | 115.6 |
| 2008 | 116.9 | 113.7 | 113.0 | 112.9 | 89.1 | 114.7 | 114.0 |
| 2009 | 119.9 | 103.3 | 115.6 | 131.2 | 120.3 | 107.6 | 114.2 |
| 2010 | 117.5 | 113.8 | 101.4 | 119.8 | 107.3 | 108.5 | 116.3 |
| 2011 | 114.6 | 114.1 | 110.6 | 105.7 | 110.6 | 117.6 | 114.7 |
| 2012 | 112.6 | 109.2 | 107.7 | 120.6 | 111.5 | 110.2 | 111.9 |
| 2013 | 110.3 | 110.8 | 108.2 | 116.5 | 111.4 | 113.9 | 111.1 |
| 2014 | 109.1 | 107.4 | 107.5 | 112.3 | 107.6 | 110.8 | 109.6 |
| 2015 | 109.2 | 108.7 | 109.1 | 115.4 | 105.5 | 113.5 | 109.9 |
| 2016 | 107.9 | 105.8 | 107.7 | 110.3 | 107.5 | 115.6 | 109.5 |
| 2017 | 107.6 | 108.7 | 108.4 | 108.1 | 104.1 | 114.2 | 108.0 |
| 2018 | 105.9 | 106.5 | 105.3 | 106.9 | 100.6 | 114.4 | 105.1 |
| 2019 | 106.6 | 106.9 | 107.5 | 108.0 | 102.7 | 106.3 | 105.5 |
| 2020 | 102.8 | 99.8 | 93.9 | 103.9 | 100.5 | 104.6 | 103.1 |
| 2021 | 113.3 | 111.1 | 114.7 | 102.1 | 104.5 | 111.4 | 108.0 |
| 2022 | 102.0 | 99.1 | 100.9 | 102.4 | 94.8 | 104.0 | 102.5 |

注：1) 本表按可比价格计算（下表同）。
2) 本表人均生产总值按常住人口计算。
Note: a) The indices hereof are calculated at constant prices (the same below).
b) The per capita GDP hereof is calculated by registered population.

# 表 2.8 地区生产总值指数（1978 – 2022 年）（1978 年 =100）
INDICES OF GROSS DOMESTIC PRODUCT (1978-2022) (1978=100)

| 年份<br>Year | 本市生产总值<br>Gross Domestic Product | 第一产业<br>Primary Industry | 第二产业<br>Secondary Industry | 工业<br>Industry | 建筑业<br>Construction | 第三产业<br>Tertiary Industry |
|---|---|---|---|---|---|---|
| 1978 | 100.0 | 100.0 | 100.0 | 100.0 | 100.0 | 100.0 |
| 1979 | 111.1 | 109.1 | 112.0 | 112.0 | 111.7 | 112.1 |
| 1980 | 119.7 | 113.8 | 121.9 | 121.7 | 122.8 | 123.1 |
| 1981 | 127.1 | 120.4 | 128.0 | 127.4 | 132.9 | 135.8 |
| 1982 | 138.4 | 129.4 | 137.5 | 136.8 | 142.3 | 157.1 |
| 1983 | 152.7 | 138.8 | 151.1 | 150.1 | 158.9 | 184.1 |
| 1984 | 177.0 | 147.8 | 182.2 | 181.2 | 190.2 | 223.3 |
| 1985 | 192.2 | 161.5 | 194.0 | 190.4 | 231.9 | 251.0 |
| 1986 | 208.7 | 178.1 | 206.6 | 200.9 | 268.8 | 277.1 |
| 1987 | 219.8 | 172.2 | 223.5 | 214.8 | 320.7 | 310.1 |
| 1988 | 240.7 | 178.2 | 253.0 | 245.1 | 340.6 | 340.5 |
| 1989 | 252.5 | 186.4 | 259.8 | 255.1 | 311.6 | 373.2 |
| 1990 | 270.2 | 200.9 | 280.1 | 264.8 | 449.3 | 391.1 |
| 1991 | 295.1 | 214.4 | 306.7 | 293.7 | 450.2 | 436.1 |
| 1992 | 343.8 | 218.3 | 373.6 | 358.9 | 534.4 | 541.6 |
| 1993 | 397.4 | 229.2 | 456.2 | 439.7 | 634.9 | 625.5 |
| 1994 | 451.0 | 235.8 | 530.6 | 517.1 | 671.7 | 735.6 |
| 1995 | 506.5 | 246.4 | 605.4 | 589.5 | 767.8 | 845.9 |
| 1996 | 564.2 | 258.2 | 678.7 | 661.4 | 854.6 | 968.6 |
| 1997 | 627.4 | 266.5 | 762.2 | 738.1 | 1012.7 | 1105.2 |
| 1998 | 681.4 | 272.1 | 817.1 | 776.5 | 1243.6 | 1259.9 |
| 1999 | 734.5 | 273.2 | 902.9 | 861.1 | 1339.4 | 1355.7 |
| 2000 | 798.4 | 277.0 | 999.5 | 953.2 | 1482.7 | 1479.1 |
| 2001 | 871.9 | 282.8 | 1119.4 | 1061.9 | 1700.7 | 1612.2 |
| 2002 | 963.4 | 294.7 | 1277.2 | 1210.6 | 1950.7 | 1755.7 |
| 2003 | 1076.1 | 307.7 | 1486.7 | 1412.8 | 2245.3 | 1913.7 |
| 2004 | 1210.6 | 322.5 | 1738.0 | 1658.6 | 2579.8 | 2101.2 |
| 2005 | 1353.5 | 337.0 | 1970.9 | 1900.8 | 2768.1 | 2355.4 |
| 2006 | 1522.7 | 317.5 | 2309.9 | 2248.6 | 3097.5 | 2666.3 |
| 2007 | 1766.3 | 347.7 | 2795.0 | 2754.5 | 3512.6 | 2988.9 |
| 2008 | 2024.2 | 371.0 | 3306.5 | 3302.6 | 3835.8 | 3353.5 |
| 2009 | 2329.9 | 391.0 | 3905.0 | 3887.2 | 4649.0 | 3809.6 |
| 2010 | 2730.6 | 414.9 | 4791.4 | 4777.4 | 5643.9 | 4282.0 |
| 2011 | 3178.4 | 436.1 | 5797.6 | 5795.0 | 6750.1 | 4881.5 |
| 2012 | 3610.7 | 459.6 | 6760.0 | 6791.7 | 7688.4 | 5462.4 |
| 2013 | 4054.8 | 481.2 | 7632.0 | 7640.7 | 8834.0 | 6161.6 |
| 2014 | 4496.8 | 502.4 | 8601.3 | 8588.1 | 10088.4 | 6771.6 |
| 2015 | 4991.4 | 526.5 | 9564.6 | 9481.3 | 11571.4 | 7557.1 |
| 2016 | 5525.5 | 551.2 | 10645.4 | 10457.9 | 13284.0 | 8388.4 |
| 2017 | 6039.4 | 573.2 | 11635.4 | 11440.9 | 14479.6 | 9227.2 |
| 2018 | 6401.8 | 598.4 | 11984.5 | 11566.7 | 15855.2 | 10057.6 |
| 2019 | 6805.1 | 619.9 | 12751.5 | 12307.0 | 16901.6 | 10701.3 |
| 2020 | 7070.5 | 648.4 | 13363.6 | 12959.3 | 17459.4 | 11011.6 |
| 2021 | 7664.4 | 699.0 | 14325.8 | 14229.3 | 17686.4 | 12057.7 |
| 2022 | 7863.7 | 727.0 | 14798.6 | 14641.9 | 18393.9 | 12286.8 |

注：1) 本表按可比价格计算（下表同）。
2) 本表人均生产总值按常住人口计算。
Note: a) The indices hereof are calculated at constant prices (the same below).
b) The per capita GDP hereof is calculated by registered population.

**表 2.8 续表 continued**

| 年 份 Year | 批发和零售业 Wholesale and Retail Trades | 交通运输、仓储及邮政业 Transport, Storage, Post | 住宿和餐饮业 Hotels and Catering Services | 金融业 Financial Intermediation | 房地产业 Real Estate | 其 他 Others | 本市人均生产总值 Per Capita GDP |
|---|---|---|---|---|---|---|---|
| 1978 | 100.0 | 100.0 | 100.0 | 100.0 | 100.0 | 100.0 | 100.0 |
| 1979 | 110.5 | 109.2 | 115.2 | 111.6 | 111.1 | 115.1 | 110.4 |
| 1980 | 117.5 | 113.0 | 130.4 | 119.9 | 118.5 | 136.3 | 118.2 |
| 1981 | 127.6 | 119.6 | 139.4 | 131.7 | 117.4 | 159.7 | 124.6 |
| 1982 | 147.0 | 140.2 | 149.6 | 142.4 | 131.3 | 192.9 | 134.6 |
| 1983 | 169.3 | 183.9 | 159.8 | 185.3 | 159.0 | 206.0 | 147.4 |
| 1984 | 209.8 | 205.2 | 198.2 | 258.5 | 195.3 | 240.4 | 170.2 |
| 1985 | 288.1 | 198.6 | 232.7 | 266.3 | 206.0 | 273.3 | 183.8 |
| 1986 | 307.1 | 198.2 | 273.7 | 298.0 | 244.5 | 314.6 | 197.6 |
| 1987 | 337.8 | 214.7 | 313.4 | 382.3 | 296.8 | 326.6 | 205.3 |
| 1988 | 414.8 | 227.6 | 373.6 | 397.6 | 314.0 | 345.2 | 222.1 |
| 1989 | 448.8 | 265.4 | 421.0 | 450.5 | 314.0 | 367.3 | 231.0 |
| 1990 | 374.7 | 276.3 | 561.6 | 489.2 | 366.4 | 404.8 | 245.1 |
| 1991 | 406.5 | 282.9 | 654.8 | 557.2 | 429.8 | 457.0 | 265.7 |
| 1992 | 578.4 | 377.7 | 761.5 | 670.9 | 414.3 | 551.1 | 307.9 |
| 1993 | 801.1 | 388.3 | 947.3 | 733.3 | 453.2 | 603.5 | 354.7 |
| 1994 | 833.9 | 423.6 | 1262.8 | 845.5 | 465.9 | 820.2 | 400.1 |
| 1995 | 927.3 | 521.5 | 1730.0 | 985.0 | 533.5 | 889.9 | 446.5 |
| 1996 | 1074.7 | 602.9 | 2081.2 | 1024.4 | 701.6 | 1056.3 | 494.3 |
| 1997 | 1219.8 | 691.5 | 2628.6 | 1122.7 | 873.5 | 1189.4 | 550.2 |
| 1998 | 1402.8 | 719.9 | 2744.3 | 1239.5 | 1069.2 | 1449.9 | 598.1 |
| 1999 | 1519.2 | 733.6 | 2969.3 | 1111.8 | 1178.3 | 1761.6 | 645.9 |
| 2000 | 1704.5 | 762.9 | 3209.8 | 1131.8 | 1315.0 | 1980.0 | 704.7 |
| 2001 | 1856.2 | 886.5 | 3408.8 | 1148.8 | 1480.7 | 2162.2 | 773.8 |
| 2002 | 2043.7 | 932.6 | 3732.6 | 1239.6 | 1685.0 | 2348.1 | 860.5 |
| 2003 | 2233.8 | 977.4 | 4109.6 | 1337.5 | 1956.3 | 2552.4 | 965.5 |
| 2004 | 2475.1 | 1120.1 | 4849.3 | 1416.4 | 2028.7 | 2800.0 | 1090.0 |
| 2005 | 2821.6 | 1259.0 | 5513.7 | 1556.6 | 2227.5 | 3133.2 | 1219.7 |
| 2006 | 3143.3 | 1514.6 | 6351.8 | 1749.6 | 2399.0 | 3524.9 | 1368.5 |
| 2007 | 3529.9 | 1703.9 | 7114.0 | 1919.3 | 2802.0 | 3926.7 | 1582.0 |
| 2008 | 4126.5 | 1937.3 | 8038.8 | 2166.9 | 2496.6 | 4503.9 | 1803.5 |
| 2009 | 4947.7 | 2001.2 | 9292.9 | 2843.0 | 3003.4 | 4846.2 | 2059.6 |
| 2010 | 5813.5 | 2277.4 | 9423.0 | 3405.9 | 3222.6 | 5258.1 | 2395.3 |
| 2011 | 6662.3 | 2598.5 | 10421.8 | 3600.0 | 3564.2 | 6183.5 | 2747.4 |
| 2012 | 7501.7 | 2837.6 | 11224.3 | 4341.6 | 3974.1 | 6814.2 | 3074.3 |
| 2013 | 8274.4 | 3144.1 | 12144.7 | 5058.0 | 4427.1 | 7761.4 | 3415.5 |
| 2014 | 9027.4 | 3376.8 | 13055.6 | 5680.1 | 4763.6 | 8599.6 | 3743.4 |
| 2015 | 9857.9 | 3670.6 | 14243.7 | 6554.8 | 5025.6 | 9760.5 | 4114.0 |
| 2016 | 10636.7 | 3883.5 | 15340.5 | 7229.9 | 5402.5 | 11283.1 | 4504.8 |
| 2017 | 11445.1 | 4221.4 | 16629.1 | 7815.5 | 5624.0 | 12885.3 | 4865.2 |
| 2018 | 12120.4 | 4495.8 | 17510.4 | 8354.8 | 5657.7 | 14740.8 | 5113.3 |
| 2019 | 12920.3 | 4806.0 | 18823.7 | 9023.2 | 5810.5 | 15669.5 | 5394.5 |
| 2020 | 13282.1 | 4796.4 | 17675.5 | 9375.1 | 5839.6 | 16390.3 | 5561.7 |
| 2021 | 15048.6 | 5328.8 | 20273.8 | 9572.0 | 6102.4 | 18258.8 | 6006.6 |
| 2022 | 15349.6 | 5280.8 | 20456.3 | 9801.7 | 5785.1 | 18989.2 | 6156.8 |

注：1) 本表按可比价格计算（下表同）。
2) 本表人均生产总值按常住人口计算。

Note: a) The indices hereof are calculated at constant prices (the same below).
b) The per capita GDP hereof is calculated by registered population.

# 表 2.9 三次产业贡献率（1996 – 2022 年）
SHARE OF THE CONTRIBUTIONS OF THE GROWTH OF THREE STRATA OF INDUSTRY TO THE INCREASE OF THE GDP(1996-2022)

单位：% (%)

| 年 份 Year | 本 市 生产总值 Gross Domestic Product | 第一产业 Primary Industry | 第二产业 Secondary Industry | #工 业 Industry | 第三产业 Tertiary Industry |
|---|---|---|---|---|---|
| 1996 | 100.0 | 8.4 | 50.5 | 45.5 | 41.1 |
| 1997 | 100.0 | 5.4 | 52.8 | 44.6 | 41.8 |
| 1998 | 100.0 | 4.3 | 40.3 | 26.1 | 55.4 |
| 1999 | 100.0 | 0.8 | 64.3 | 58.4 | 34.9 |
| 2000 | 100.0 | 2.5 | 60.2 | 52.8 | 37.3 |
| 2001 | 100.0 | 3.5 | 55.3 | 43.9 | 41.2 |
| 2002 | 100.0 | 5.7 | 58.7 | 48.2 | 35.6 |
| 2003 | 100.0 | 5.1 | 63.1 | 53.0 | 31.8 |
| 2004 | 100.0 | 4.8 | 63.6 | 54.0 | 31.6 |
| 2005 | 100.0 | 4.5 | 55.2 | 50.1 | 40.3 |
| 2006 | 100.0 | -6.1 | 62.3 | 55.0 | 43.8 |
| 2007 | 100.0 | 6.6 | 61.9 | 55.5 | 31.5 |
| 2008 | 100.0 | 4.8 | 61.5 | 56.8 | 33.7 |
| 2009 | 100.0 | 3.5 | 61.0 | 51.0 | 35.5 |
| 2010 | 100.0 | 3.2 | 68.8 | 59.5 | 28.0 |
| 2011 | 100.0 | 2.5 | 57.4 | 47.4 | 40.1 |
| 2012 | 100.0 | 2.9 | 56.9 | 48.1 | 40.2 |
| 2013 | 100.0 | 2.6 | 50.4 | 39.9 | 47.0 |
| 2014 | 100.0 | 2.5 | 56.1 | 44.6 | 41.4 |
| 2015 | 100.0 | 2.6 | 49.9 | 37.7 | 47.5 |
| 2016 | 100.0 | 2.9 | 47.5 | 33.7 | 49.6 |
| 2017 | 100.0 | 2.7 | 45.2 | 35.3 | 52.1 |
| 2018 | 100.0 | 4.4 | 22.6 | 6.4 | 73.0 |
| 2019 | 100.0 | 3.4 | 45.3 | 34.1 | 51.3 |
| 2020 | 100.0 | 6.9 | 55.2 | 46.2 | 37.9 |
| 2021 | 100.0 | 6.6 | 34.1 | 32.2 | 59.3 |
| 2022 | 100.0 | 11.1 | 49.7 | 32.3 | 39.2 |

# 表 2.10 三次产业拉动力（1996 – 2022 年）
## CONTRIBUTION OF THE THREE STRATA OF INDUSTRY TO GDP GROWTH (1996-2022)

单位：% (%)

| 年 份 Year | 本 市 生产总值 Gross Domestic Product | 第一产业 Primary Industry | 第二产业 Secondary Industry | #工 业 Industry | 第三产业 Tertiary Industry |
|---|---|---|---|---|---|
| 1996 | 11.4 | 1.0 | 5.8 | 5.2 | 4.6 |
| 1997 | 11.2 | 0.6 | 5.9 | 5.0 | 4.7 |
| 1998 | 8.6 | 0.4 | 3.5 | 2.2 | 4.7 |
| 1999 | 7.8 | 0.1 | 5.0 | 4.6 | 2.7 |
| 2000 | 8.7 | 0.2 | 5.2 | 4.6 | 3.3 |
| 2001 | 9.2 | 0.3 | 5.1 | 4.0 | 3.8 |
| 2002 | 10.5 | 0.6 | 6.2 | 5.1 | 3.7 |
| 2003 | 11.7 | 0.6 | 7.4 | 6.2 | 3.7 |
| 2004 | 12.5 | 0.6 | 8.0 | 6.8 | 3.9 |
| 2005 | 11.8 | 0.5 | 6.5 | 5.9 | 4.8 |
| 2006 | 12.5 | -0.8 | 7.8 | 6.9 | 5.5 |
| 2007 | 16.0 | 1.1 | 9.9 | 8.9 | 5.0 |
| 2008 | 14.6 | 0.7 | 9.0 | 8.3 | 4.9 |
| 2009 | 15.1 | 0.5 | 9.2 | 7.7 | 5.4 |
| 2010 | 17.2 | 0.6 | 11.8 | 10.2 | 4.8 |
| 2011 | 16.4 | 0.4 | 9.4 | 7.8 | 6.6 |
| 2012 | 13.6 | 0.4 | 7.7 | 6.5 | 5.5 |
| 2013 | 12.3 | 0.3 | 6.2 | 4.9 | 5.8 |
| 2014 | 10.9 | 0.3 | 6.1 | 4.9 | 4.5 |
| 2015 | 11.0 | 0.3 | 5.5 | 4.1 | 5.2 |
| 2016 | 10.7 | 0.3 | 5.1 | 3.6 | 5.3 |
| 2017 | 9.3 | 0.3 | 4.2 | 3.3 | 4.8 |
| 2018 | 6.0 | 0.3 | 1.4 | 0.4 | 4.3 |
| 2019 | 6.3 | 0.2 | 2.9 | 2.1 | 3.2 |
| 2020 | 3.9 | 0.3 | 2.2 | 1.8 | 1.4 |
| 2021 | 8.4 | 0.6 | 2.9 | 2.7 | 4.9 |
| 2022 | 2.6 | 0.3 | 1.3 | 0.8 | 1.0 |

# 表 2.11 分经济类型地区生产总值(1996 – 2022 年)
GROSS DOMESTIC PRODUCT BY STATUS OF REGISTRATION (1996-2022)

单位: 亿元 (100 million yuan)

| 年 份<br>Year | 本市生产总值<br>Gross Domestic Product | 国有经济<br>State-owned Economy | 民营经济<br>Private Economy | 外商港澳台经济<br>Economy Funded by HK, Macao, Taiwan & Foreign | 生产总值构成<br>Composition of Gross Domestic Product | 国有经济<br>State-owned Economy |
|---|---|---|---|---|---|---|
| 1996 | 1326.40 | 586.05 | 699.68 | 40.67 | 100.0 | 44.2 |
| 1997 | 1525.26 | 677.26 | 790.89 | 57.11 | 100.0 | 44.4 |
| 1998 | 1622.42 | 623.86 | 942.85 | 55.71 | 100.0 | 38.5 |
| 1999 | 1687.81 | 664.11 | 959.42 | 64.28 | 100.0 | 39.3 |
| 2000 | 1822.06 | 738.03 | 1011.41 | 72.62 | 100.0 | 40.5 |
| 2001 | 2014.59 | 807.10 | 1123.62 | 83.87 | 100.0 | 40.1 |
| 2002 | 2279.80 | 1016.08 | 1127.43 | 136.29 | 100.0 | 44.6 |
| 2003 | 2615.57 | 1104.30 | 1300.39 | 210.88 | 100.0 | 42.2 |
| 2004 | 3059.54 | 1184.19 | 1690.13 | 185.22 | 100.0 | 38.7 |
| 2005 | 3448.35 | 1263.85 | 1952.67 | 231.83 | 100.0 | 36.7 |
| 2006 | 3900.26 | 1404.29 | 2166.21 | 329.76 | 100.0 | 36.0 |
| 2007 | 4770.72 | 1700.52 | 2621.94 | 448.26 | 100.0 | 35.6 |
| 2008 | 5899.49 | 1959.82 | 3374.55 | 565.12 | 100.0 | 33.2 |
| 2009 | 6651.22 | 2139.54 | 3812.28 | 699.40 | 100.0 | 32.2 |
| 2010 | 8065.26 | 2527.90 | 4567.73 | 969.63 | 100.0 | 31.3 |
| 2011 | 10161.17 | 3082.59 | 5837.55 | 1241.03 | 100.0 | 30.3 |
| 2012 | 11595.37 | 3460.38 | 6679.06 | 1455.93 | 100.0 | 29.8 |
| 2013 | 13027.60 | 3987.86 | 7498.81 | 1540.93 | 100.0 | 30.6 |
| 2014 | 14623.78 | 4548.68 | 8386.53 | 1688.57 | 100.0 | 31.1 |
| 2015 | 16040.54 | 4954.42 | 9334.46 | 1751.66 | 100.0 | 30.9 |
| 2016 | 18023.04 | 5588.54 | 10545.62 | 1888.88 | 100.0 | 31.0 |
| 2017 | 20066.29 | 6333.80 | 11753.63 | 1978.86 | 100.0 | 31.6 |
| 2018 | 21588.80 | 6757.29 | 12758.98 | 2072.53 | 100.0 | 31.3 |
| 2019 | 23605.77 | 7351.39 | 14045.22 | 2209.16 | 100.0 | 31.1 |
| 2020 | 25041.43 | 8036.64 | 14782.89 | 2221.90 | 100.0 | 32.1 |
| 2021 | 28077.28 | 9059.60 | 16737.81 | 2279.87 | 100.0 | 32.3 |
| 2022 | 29129.03 | 9611.46 | 17404.40 | 2113.17 | 100.0 | 33.0 |

**表 2.11 续表 continued**

单位：% (%)

| 年 份 Year | 民营经济 Private Economy | 外商港澳台经济 Economy Funded by HK, Macao, Taiwan & Foreign | 生产总值指数（上年 =100）Indices of Gross Domestic Product (Preceding Year=100) | 国有经济 State-owned Economy | 民营经济 Private Economy | 外商港澳台经济 Economy Funded by HK, Macao, Taiwan & Foreign |
|---|---|---|---|---|---|---|
| 1996 | 52.8 | 3.0 | 111.4 | 104.8 | 117.7 | 115.1 |
| 1997 | 51.9 | 3.7 | 111.2 | 109.6 | 111.2 | 136.3 |
| 1998 | 58.1 | 3.4 | 108.6 | 90.6 | 124.2 | 100.1 |
| 1999 | 56.8 | 3.9 | 107.8 | 108.7 | 107.5 | 120.1 |
| 2000 | 55.5 | 4.0 | 108.7 | 111.1 | 108.3 | 114.3 |
| 2001 | 55.8 | 4.1 | 109.2 | 107.4 | 112.1 | 114.5 |
| 2002 | 49.5 | 5.9 | 110.5 | 127.8 | 103.2 | 159.3 |
| 2003 | 49.7 | 8.1 | 111.7 | 105.0 | 113.4 | 151.3 |
| 2004 | 55.2 | 6.1 | 112.5 | 105.5 | 123.1 | 83.0 |
| 2005 | 56.6 | 6.7 | 111.8 | 108.9 | 113.4 | 122.5 |
| 2006 | 55.5 | 8.5 | 112.5 | 111.2 | 111.4 | 142.2 |
| 2007 | 55.0 | 9.4 | 116.0 | 110.0 | 117.5 | 132.1 |
| 2008 | 57.2 | 9.6 | 114.6 | 109.1 | 120.0 | 116.9 |
| 2009 | 57.3 | 10.5 | 115.1 | 111.3 | 115.1 | 126.4 |
| 2010 | 56.6 | 12.1 | 117.2 | 114.7 | 115.8 | 133.9 |
| 2011 | 57.4 | 12.3 | 116.4 | 109.5 | 118.4 | 123.0 |
| 2012 | 57.6 | 12.6 | 113.6 | 107.5 | 113.7 | 126.5 |
| 2013 | 57.6 | 11.8 | 112.3 | 111.8 | 114.3 | 105.3 |
| 2014 | 57.3 | 11.6 | 110.9 | 110.3 | 111.4 | 109.9 |
| 2015 | 58.2 | 10.9 | 111.0 | 110.9 | 112.0 | 106.1 |
| 2016 | 58.5 | 10.5 | 110.7 | 110.7 | 111.8 | 104.4 |
| 2017 | 58.6 | 9.8 | 109.3 | 109.2 | 109.8 | 107.4 |
| 2018 | 59.1 | 9.6 | 106.0 | 105.9 | 106.1 | 106.2 |
| 2019 | 59.5 | 9.4 | 106.3 | 104.7 | 107.2 | 105.7 |
| 2020 | 59.0 | 8.9 | 103.9 | 104.4 | 103.8 | 102.3 |
| 2021 | 59.6 | 8.1 | 108.4 | 108.7 | 109.4 | 99.0 |
| 2022 | 59.7 | 7.3 | 102.6 | 104.6 | 103.0 | 91.9 |

# 表 2.12 支出法地区生产总值(1996-2021 年)
## GROSS DOMESTIC PRODUCT BY EXPENDITURE APPROACH (1996-2021)

单位: 亿元、% (100 million yuan,%)

| 年份 Year | 本市生产总值 Gross Domestic Product | 最终消费支出 Final Consumption Expenditures | 居民消费支出 Household Consumption Expenditures | 城镇居民 Urban Household | 农村居民 Rural Household | 政府消费支出 Government Consumption Expenditures |
|---|---|---|---|---|---|---|
| 1996 | 1326.40 | 752.07 | 614.44 | 358.22 | 256.22 | 137.63 |
| 1997 | 1525.26 | 841.94 | 682.81 | 336.63 | 346.18 | 159.13 |
| 1998 | 1622.42 | 879.35 | 694.69 | 366.80 | 327.89 | 184.66 |
| 1999 | 1687.81 | 943.49 | 736.87 | 425.91 | 310.96 | 206.62 |
| 2000 | 1822.06 | 1014.89 | 785.52 | 482.31 | 303.21 | 229.37 |
| 2001 | 2014.59 | 1101.98 | 849.63 | 537.82 | 311.81 | 252.35 |
| 2002 | 2279.80 | 1256.17 | 923.28 | 621.37 | 301.91 | 332.89 |
| 2003 | 2615.57 | 1420.25 | 1032.52 | 738.25 | 294.27 | 387.73 |
| 2004 | 3059.54 | 1578.72 | 1168.25 | 858.66 | 309.59 | 410.47 |
| 2005 | 3448.35 | 1758.66 | 1299.65 | 956.54 | 343.11 | 459.01 |
| 2006 | 3900.26 | 2004.73 | 1481.50 | 1127.42 | 354.08 | 523.23 |
| 2007 | 4770.72 | 2466.46 | 1839.98 | 1427.82 | 412.16 | 626.48 |
| 2008 | 5899.49 | 2914.35 | 2182.85 | 1709.17 | 473.68 | 731.50 |
| 2009 | 6651.22 | 3272.40 | 2451.03 | 1965.73 | 485.30 | 821.37 |
| 2010 | 8065.26 | 3847.13 | 2823.79 | 2318.33 | 505.46 | 1023.34 |
| 2011 | 10161.17 | 4663.98 | 3456.01 | 2837.38 | 618.63 | 1207.97 |
| 2012 | 11595.37 | 5426.63 | 4037.41 | 3290.49 | 746.92 | 1389.22 |
| 2013 | 13027.60 | 6122.97 | 4610.60 | 3776.08 | 834.52 | 1512.37 |
| 2014 | 14623.78 | 6873.18 | 5230.49 | 4289.00 | 941.49 | 1642.69 |
| 2015 | 16040.54 | 7571.13 | 5723.77 | 4716.39 | 1007.38 | 1847.36 |
| 2016 | 18023.04 | 8578.97 | 6477.12 | 5369.53 | 1107.59 | 2101.85 |
| 2017 | 20066.29 | 9591.69 | 7251.32 | 6033.10 | 1218.22 | 2340.37 |
| 2018 | 21588.80 | 10365.38 | 7875.34 | 6576.50 | 1298.84 | 2490.04 |
| 2019 | 23605.77 | 11401.59 | 8676.61 | 7262.32 | 1414.29 | 2724.98 |
| 2020 | 25041.43 | 11744.47 | 8955.07 | 7428.47 | 1526.60 | 2789.40 |
| 2021 | 28077.28 | 13168.24 | 10345.59 | 8568.40 | 1777.19 | 2822.65 |

**表 2.12 续表 continued** 单位：亿元、% (100 million yuan,%)

| 年份 Year | 资本形成总额 Gross Capital Formation | 固定资本形成总额 Gross Fixed Capital Formation | 存货变动 Change in Inventories | 货物和服务净流出 Net Exports of Goods and Services | 最终消费率 (%) Final Consumption Rate(%) | 资本形成率 (%) Gross Capital Rate(%) |
|---|---|---|---|---|---|---|
| 1996 | 423.12 | 319.03 | 104.09 | 151.21 | 56.7 | 31.9 |
| 1997 | 549.09 | 399.74 | 149.35 | 134.23 | 55.2 | 36.0 |
| 1998 | 616.52 | 523.43 | 93.09 | 126.55 | 54.2 | 38.0 |
| 1999 | 609.30 | 568.48 | 40.82 | 135.02 | 55.9 | 36.1 |
| 2000 | 712.43 | 638.34 | 74.09 | 94.74 | 55.7 | 39.1 |
| 2001 | 848.14 | 765.87 | 82.27 | 64.47 | 54.7 | 42.1 |
| 2002 | 1025.91 | 937.68 | 88.23 | -2.28 | 55.1 | 45.0 |
| 2003 | 1360.10 | 1248.57 | 111.53 | -164.78 | 54.3 | 52.0 |
| 2004 | 1685.81 | 1535.77 | 150.04 | -204.99 | 51.6 | 55.1 |
| 2005 | 1958.66 | 1862.69 | 95.97 | -268.97 | 51.0 | 56.8 |
| 2006 | 2234.85 | 2145.46 | 89.39 | -339.32 | 51.4 | 57.3 |
| 2007 | 2747.93 | 2624.27 | 123.66 | -443.67 | 51.7 | 57.6 |
| 2008 | 3321.41 | 3138.73 | 182.68 | -336.27 | 49.4 | 56.3 |
| 2009 | 3917.57 | 3729.53 | 188.04 | -538.75 | 49.2 | 58.9 |
| 2010 | 4685.92 | 4484.43 | 201.49 | -467.79 | 47.7 | 58.1 |
| 2011 | 5883.32 | 5636.22 | 247.10 | -386.13 | 45.9 | 57.9 |
| 2012 | 6493.41 | 6188.22 | 305.19 | -324.67 | 46.8 | 56.0 |
| 2013 | 7178.21 | 6833.66 | 344.55 | -273.58 | 47.0 | 55.1 |
| 2014 | 8013.83 | 7637.18 | 376.65 | -263.23 | 47.0 | 54.8 |
| 2015 | 8693.97 | 8294.05 | 399.92 | -224.56 | 47.2 | 54.2 |
| 2016 | 9696.40 | 9250.37 | 446.03 | -252.33 | 47.6 | 53.8 |
| 2017 | 10715.40 | 10222.49 | 492.91 | -240.80 | 47.8 | 53.4 |
| 2018 | 11463.12 | 10947.26 | 515.86 | -239.70 | 48.0 | 53.1 |
| 2019 | 12440.24 | 11892.87 | 547.37 | -236.06 | 48.3 | 52.7 |
| 2020 | 13522.37 | 12938.50 | 583.87 | -225.41 | 46.9 | 54.0 |
| 2021 | 15133.65 | 14482.76 | 650.89 | -224.61 | 46.9 | 53.9 |

重/庆/统/计/年/鉴

# 主要统计指标解释

## 国内（地区）生产总值（GDP）

是按市场价格计算的一个国家（或地区）所有常住单位在一定时期内生产活动的最终成果。国内（地区）生产总值有三种表现形态，即价值形态、收入形态和产品形态。从价值形态看，它是所有常住单位在一定时期内所生产的全部货物和服务价值超过同期中间投入的全部非固定资产货物和服务价值的差额，即所有常住单位的增加值之和；从收入形态看，它是所有常住单位在一定时期内所创造并分配给常住单位和非常住单位的初次收入之和；从产品形态看，它是所有常住单位在一定时期内最终使用的货物和服务价值与货物和服务净出口（净流出）价值之和。在实际核算中，国内（地区）生产总值的三种表现形态表现为三种计算方法，即生产法、收入法和支出法。三种方法分别从不同的方面反映国内（地区）生产总值及其构成。

## 三次产业

三次产业的划分是世界上较为常用的产业结构分类，但各国的划分不尽一致。根据国家统计局2018年修订的《三次产业划分规定》（国统设管函〔2018〕74号），我国的三次产业按照如下标准界定：

第一产业是指农、林、牧、渔业（不含农、林、牧、渔专业及辅助性活动）。

第二产业是指采矿业（不含开采专业及辅助性活动），制造业（不含金属制品、机械和设备修理业），电力、热力、燃气及水生产和供应业，建筑业。

第三产业即服务业，是指除第一产业、第二产业以外的其他行业。

## 支出法国内（地区）生产总值

是从最终使用的角度反映一个国家（或地区）一定时期内生产活动最终成果的一种方法，包括最终消费支出、资本形成总额及货物和服务净出口（净流出）三部分。计算公式为：

支出法国内（地区）生产总值＝最终消费支出＋资本形成总额＋货物和服务净出口（净流出）

## 最终消费支出

指常住单位为满足物质、文化和精神生活的需要，从本国经济领土和国外购买的货物和服务的支出。它不包括非常住单位在本国经济领土内的消费支出。最终消费支出分为居民消费支出和政府消费支出。

（1）居民消费支出：指常住住户在一定时期内对于货物和服务的全部最终消费支出。居民消费支出除了直接以货币形式购买的货物和服务的消费支出外，还包括以其他方式获得的货物和服务的消费支出，后者称为虚拟消费支出。居民虚拟消费支出主要包括：单位以实物报酬及实物转移的形式提供给劳动者的货物和服务；住户生产用于自身消费的货物（如自产自用的农产品），以及纳入生产核算范围并用于自身消费的服务（如住户的自有住房服务）；银行和保险机构提供的间接计算的金融服务。

（2）政府消费支出：指政府部门为全社会提供的公共服务的消费支出和免费或以较低的价格向居民住户提供的货物和服务的净支出，前者等于政府服务的产出价值减去政府单位所获得的经营收入的价值，后者等于政府部门免费或以较低价格向居民住户提供的货物和服务的市场价值减去向住户收取的价值。

## 资本形成总额

指常住单位在一定时期内获得的减去处置的固定资产和存货的净额，包括固定资产形成总额和存货变动。

（1）固定资本形成总额　指常住单位在一定时期内获得的固定资产减处置的固定资产的价值总额。固定资产是通过生产活动生产出来的，且其使用年限在一年以上、单位价值在规定标准以上的资产，不包括自然资产、耐用消费品、小型工器具。固定资本形成总额包括住宅、其他建筑和构筑物、机器和设备、培育性生物资源、知识产权产品（研发支出、矿藏的勘探、计算机软件）的价值获得减处置。

（2）存货变动　指常住单位在一定时期内存货实物量变动的市场价值，即期末价值减期初价值的差额，

## 主要统计指标解释

再扣除当期由于价格变动而产生的持有收益。存货变动可以是正值，也可以是负值，正值表示存货上升，负值表示存货下降。存货包括生产单位购进的原材料、燃料和储备物资等存货，以及生产单位生产的产成品、在制品和半成品等存货。

### ■ 货物和服务净出口（净流出）

指一个国家（地区）货物和服务出口（流出）减货物和服务进口（流入）的差额。出口（流出）包括常住单位向非常住单位出售或无偿转让的各种货物和服务的价值；进口（流入）包括常住单位从非常住单位购买或无偿得到的各种货物和服务的价值。

### ■ 产业部门贡献率

是各产业部门增加值可比价增量与国内生产总值可比价增量之比。

### ■ 产业部门拉动力

拉动力是指总的经济增长率中带动的百分点数，产业部门拉动力是指在GDP增长中各产业部门拉动的百分点数。其计算公式为：

拉动力（%）= 贡献率（%）× GDP 增长率（%）

# Explanatory Notes on Main Statistical Indicators

## Gross Domestic Product (GDP)

Refers to the final products at market prices produced by all resident units in a country (or a region) during a certain period of time. Gross domestic product is expressed in three different perspectives value added, income, and products respectively. The form of value added refers to the total value of all products and services produced by all resident units during a certain period of time minus total value of intimidate input of materials and services of the nature of non-fixed assets or the summation of the value added of all resident units; the form of income includes all the income created by all resident units and distributed primarily to all resident and non-resident units; the form of products refers to all final goods and services of final use by all resident units plus the value of net exports of goods and services. In the practice of national accounting, gross domestic product is calculated with three approaches, i.e. product approach, income approach and expenditure approach, which reflect gross domestic product and its composition from different aspects.

## Three Strata of Industry

Classification of economic activities into three strata of industry is a common practice in the world, although the grouping varies to some extent from country to country. According to the "Regulations on the Division of the Three Industries" revised by the National Bureau of Statistics in 2018 (Guo Tong Jian Guan Han 〔2018〕 No. 74), economic activities are categorized into the following three strata of industry:

Primary industry refers to agriculture, forestry, animal husbandry and fishery industries (not including services in support of agriculture, forestry, animal husbandry, fishing professions and auxiliary activities).

Secondary industry refers to mining and quarrying (not including support mining professional and auxiliary activities), manufacturing (not including repair service of metal products, machinery and equipment), production and supply of electricity, heat, gas and water, and construction.

## GDP by Expenditure Approach

Refers to the method of measuring the final results of production activities of a country (region) during a given period from the perspective of final uses. It includes final consumption expenditure, gross capital formation and net export (net outflow) of goods and services. The formula for computation is.:

GDP by expenditure approach = final consumption expenditure + gross capital formation + net export(net outflow) of goods and services

## Final Consumption Expenditure

Refers to the total expenditure of resident units on final consumption of goods and services from domestic economic territory and abroad to meet the requirements of material, cultural and spiritual life. It excludes the expenditure of non-resident units on consumption in the economic territory of the country. The final consumption expenditure is broken down into household consumption expenditure and government consumption expenditure.

(I) Gross Fixed Capital Formation refers to the value of acquisitions less those disposals of fixed assets during a given period. Fixed assets are the assets produced through production activities with unit value above a specified amount and which could be used for over one year. Natural assets, consumer durables, small instruments are not included. Gross Fixed Capital Formation includes the value of housing, other buildings and structure, equipment and machinery, breeding biological resources, intellectual property right product (expenditure for R&D, the prospecting of minerals and the acquisition of computer software) minus the disposal of them.

(II) Changes in Inventories refers to the market

value of the change in the physical volume of inventory of resident units during a given period, i.e. the difference between the values at the beginning and at the end of the period minus the gains due to the change in prices. The changes in inventories can have a positive or a negative value. A positive value indicates an increase in inventory while a negative value indicates a decrease in inventory. The inventory includes raw materials, fuels and reserve materials purchased by the production units as well as the inventory of finished products, semi-finished products and work-in-progress.

## □ Gross Capital Formation

Refers to the fixed assets acquired less disposals and the net value of inventory, thus including gross fixed capital formation and changes in inventories.

(I) Gross fixed capital formation refer to the value of fixed assets purchased, transferred in by the resident units and those produced and used by themselves deducting the value of fixed assets sold and transferred out. It can by classified into total tangible assets formation and total intangible assets formation. The total tangible assets formation include the value of the construction projects, installation projects completed and the equipment, apparatus and instruments purchased as well as the value of land improved, the value of draught animals, breeding stock, milk, wool and recreational animals and the newly increased economic forest in a certain period. The total intangible assets formation includes the prospecting of minerals, the acquisition of computer software, the originals of recreational works and works of literature and arts minus the disposal of them.

(II) Changes in Inventories refers to the market value of the change in the physical volume of inventory of resident units during a given period, i.e. the difference between the values at the beginning and the end of the period minus the gains due to the change in prices. The changes in inventories can have a positive or a negative value. A positive value indicates an increase in inventory while a negative value indicates a decrease in inventory. The inventory includes raw materials, fuels and reserve materials purchased by the production units as well as the inventory of finished products, semi-finished products and work-in-progress.

## □ Net Export of Goods and Services

Refers to the exports(outflow) of goods and services subtracting the imports(inflow) of goods and services of a country (region). Exports(outflow) include the value of various goods and services sold or gratuitously transferred by resident units to non-resident units. Imports(inflow) include the value of various goods and services purchased or gratuitously acquired resident units from non-resident units.

## □ Share of the Contributions of the Industry

Refers to the proportion of the increment of the value-added of each industry to the increase of GDP.

## □ Contribution of the Industry

Contribution is the driven percentage points to GDP growth. Contribution of the industry is the driven percentage points of each industry to GDP growth. Its calculation formula is:

contribution ( %) = share of contribution (%) × GDP growth rate (%)

# 第三章·人口与就业

# POPULATION AND EMPLOYMENT

# 简要说明

## BRIEF INTRODUCTION

本章内容主要包括全市的户籍人口、常住人口、第五、六、七次人口普查的主要数据，以及计划生育、就业、工资等情况，由市统计局人口和就业处整理编辑。

户籍统计人口资料由市公安局提供；计划生育资料由市卫生健康委员会提供；失业资料由市人力资源和社会保障局提供；常住人口、人口普查主要数据、就业和工资资料由市统计局人口就业处提供。

第七次全国人口普查后国家对历史年份人口和就业数据进行了修订。

The data in this chapter include the basic statistics on the registered population, resident population and the main indicators in 5th 6th and 7th population censuses, as well as the statistics on family planning, employment and wages. All the data are prepared and compiled by Division of Population and Employment Statistics, Chongqing Municipal Bureau of Statistics.

The data on registered population are provided by Chongqing Municipal Public Security Bureau; the data on family planning are provided by Health Commission of Chongqing; the data on unemployment are provided by Chongqing Municipal Human Resources and Social Security Bureau and the main indicators of resident population, population censuses, employment and wages are provided by Division of Population and Employment Statistics, Chongqing Municipal Bureau of Statistics.

After the 7th national population census, the country revised the population and employment data in historical years.

# 表 3.1 主要年份总户数、总人口(户籍统计)
## TOTAL HOUSEHOLDS AND TOTAL POPULATION IN MAJOR YEARS (HOUSEHOLD REGISTRATION)

单位：万人 (10 000 persons)

| 年 份<br>Year | 总户数<br>(万户)<br>Total Number of Households<br>(10 000 households) | 总人口<br>Total Population | 按性别分<br>By Sex | | 按城乡分<br>By Residence | |
|---|---|---|---|---|---|---|
| | | | 男<br>Male | 女<br>Female | 乡 村<br>Rural | 城 镇<br>Urban |
| 1952 | 401.93 | 1782.54 | 931.95 | 850.58 | | |
| 1957 | 433.34 | 1992.20 | 1031.65 | 960.55 | 1670.09 | 322.11 |
| 1962 | 442.01 | 1797.19 | 916.99 | 880.20 | 1528.95 | 268.24 |
| 1965 | 455.55 | 1974.89 | 1010.19 | 964.70 | 1685.08 | 289.81 |
| 1970 | 518.02 | 2289.64 | 1173.57 | 1116.07 | 1989.66 | 299.98 |
| 1975 | 579.36 | 2592.59 | 1332.89 | 1259.70 | 2280.39 | 312.20 |
| 1978 | 601.07 | 2635.56 | 1357.98 | 1277.58 | 2304.66 | 330.90 |
| 1980 | 610.19 | 2664.79 | 1376.22 | 1288.57 | 2291.51 | 373.28 |
| 1985 | 684.46 | 2768.26 | 1437.35 | 1330.91 | 2310.89 | 457.37 |
| 1986 | 716.53 | 2807.60 | 1458.75 | 1348.85 | 2343.23 | 464.37 |
| 1987 | 751.96 | 2845.14 | 1478.88 | 1366.26 | 2370.06 | 475.08 |
| 1988 | 784.83 | 2873.34 | 1494.20 | 1379.14 | 2390.36 | 482.98 |
| 1989 | 812.65 | 2897.01 | 1507.74 | 1389.27 | 2405.25 | 491.76 |
| 1990 | 833.78 | 2920.90 | 1520.83 | 1400.07 | 2427.92 | 492.98 |
| 1991 | 844.66 | 2938.99 | 1531.11 | 1407.88 | 2439.61 | 499.38 |
| 1992 | 849.77 | 2950.78 | 1538.46 | 1412.32 | 2438.94 | 511.84 |
| 1993 | 855.75 | 2964.92 | 1546.50 | 1418.42 | 2438.27 | 526.65 |
| 1994 | 870.20 | 2985.59 | 1558.05 | 1427.54 | 2440.41 | 545.18 |
| 1995 | 879.35 | 3001.77 | 1566.86 | 1434.91 | 2442.33 | 559.44 |
| 1996 | 888.56 | 3022.77 | 1577.97 | 1444.80 | 2445.65 | 577.12 |
| 1997 | 897.78 | 3042.92 | 1588.10 | 1454.82 | 2448.34 | 594.58 |
| 1998 | 907.17 | 3059.69 | 1596.88 | 1462.81 | 2445.66 | 614.03 |
| 1999 | 922.73 | 3072.34 | 1602.42 | 1469.92 | 2437.18 | 635.16 |
| 2000 | 938.87 | 3091.09 | 1611.68 | 1479.41 | 2430.20 | 660.89 |
| 2001 | 950.56 | 3097.91 | 1614.91 | 1483.00 | 2408.39 | 689.52 |
| 2002 | 961.69 | 3113.83 | 1623.13 | 1490.70 | 2392.38 | 721.45 |
| 2003 | 977.01 | 3130.10 | 1631.66 | 1498.44 | 2376.18 | 753.92 |
| 2004 | 988.59 | 3144.23 | 1637.18 | 1507.05 | 2358.40 | 785.83 |
| 2005 | 1010.41 | 3169.16 | 1649.26 | 1519.90 | 2351.88 | 817.28 |
| 2006 | 1030.66 | 3198.87 | 1662.77 | 1536.10 | 2353.44 | 845.43 |
| 2007 | 1056.97 | 3235.32 | 1681.10 | 1554.22 | 2358.35 | 876.97 |
| 2008 | 1080.15 | 3257.05 | 1690.56 | 1566.49 | 2349.67 | 907.38 |
| 2009 | 1110.70 | 3275.61 | 1697.69 | 1577.92 | 2326.92 | 948.69 |
| 2010 | 1154.83 | 3303.45 | 1709.03 | 1594.42 | 2196.45 | 1107.00 |
| 2011 | 1205.20 | 3329.81 | 1720.53 | 1609.28 | 2052.17 | 1277.64 |
| 2012 | 1220.64 | 3343.44 | 1725.87 | 1617.57 | 2026.19 | 1317.25 |
| 2013 | 1236.78 | 3358.42 | 1731.82 | 1626.60 | 2014.37 | 1344.05 |
| 2014 | 1248.67 | 3375.20 | 1738.87 | 1636.33 | 2003.08 | 1372.12 |
| 2015 | 1254.54 | 3371.84 | 1736.49 | 1635.35 | 1980.82 | 1391.02 |
| 2016 | 1260.88 | 3392.11 | 1745.24 | 1646.87 | 1776.60 | 1615.51 |
| 2017 | 1260.93 | 3389.82 | 1741.13 | 1648.69 | 1753.01 | 1636.81 |
| 2018 | 1269.58 | 3403.64 | 1745.88 | 1657.76 | 1747.92 | 1655.72 |
| 2019 | 1277.26 | 3416.29 | 1750.74 | 1665.55 | 1738.50 | 1677.79 |
| 2020 | 1277.53 | 3412.71 | 1746.13 | 1666.58 | 1731.44 | 1681.27 |
| 2021 | 1285.38 | 3414.66 | 1745.79 | 1668.87 | 1722.04 | 1692.62 |
| 2022 | 1292.06 | 3413.80 | 1743.92 | 1669.88 | 1703.09 | 1710.71 |

注：2016 年开始户籍人口取消农业与非农业划分，改用乡村与城镇进行划分。
Note: The agriculture and non-agriculture population of household registration from 2016 adopted the classification of urban and rural population.

# 表 3.2 主要年份人口自然变动（户籍统计）
POPULATION NATURAL DYNAMICS IN MAJOR YEARS (HOUSEHOLD REGISTRATION)

单位：万人、‰ (10 000 persons, ‰)

| 年 份 Year | 出 生 Birth | | 死 亡 Death | | 自然增长 Natural Growth | |
|---|---|---|---|---|---|---|
| | 人 口 Population | 出生率 Birth Rate | 人 口 Population | 死亡率 Death Rate | 人 口 Population | 自然增长率 Natural Growth Rate |
| 1957 | 59.00 | 29.88 | 23.65 | 11.98 | 35.35 | 17.90 |
| 1962 | 43.72 | 24.36 | 27.87 | 15.53 | 15.85 | 8.83 |
| 1965 | 74.01 | 38.03 | 21.43 | 11.01 | 52.58 | 27.02 |
| 1970 | 87.78 | 38.99 | 22.11 | 9.82 | 65.67 | 29.17 |
| 1975 | 72.03 | 28.06 | 21.33 | 8.31 | 50.70 | 19.75 |
| 1978 | 26.09 | 9.91 | 17.18 | 6.52 | 8.91 | 3.39 |
| 1980 | 29.68 | 11.16 | 17.19 | 6.46 | 12.49 | 4.70 |
| 1985 | 36.13 | 13.10 | 18.76 | 6.80 | 17.37 | 6.30 |
| 1986 | 54.47 | 19.54 | 18.36 | 6.59 | 36.11 | 12.95 |
| 1987 | 48.72 | 17.24 | 18.42 | 6.52 | 30.30 | 10.72 |
| 1988 | 38.58 | 13.49 | 19.43 | 6.79 | 19.15 | 6.70 |
| 1989 | 39.79 | 13.79 | 19.99 | 6.93 | 19.80 | 6.86 |
| 1990 | 42.53 | 14.62 | 19.59 | 6.73 | 22.94 | 7.89 |
| 1991 | 37.61 | 12.83 | 19.20 | 6.55 | 18.41 | 6.28 |
| 1992 | 35.62 | 12.09 | 20.89 | 7.09 | 14.73 | 5.00 |
| 1993 | 35.75 | 12.09 | 20.23 | 6.84 | 15.52 | 5.25 |
| 1994 | 40.05 | 13.46 | 19.95 | 6.70 | 20.10 | 6.76 |
| 1995 | 39.39 | 13.16 | 21.45 | 7.17 | 17.94 | 5.99 |
| 1996 | 41.06 | 13.63 | 21.62 | 7.18 | 19.44 | 6.45 |
| 1997 | 36.99 | 12.20 | 20.95 | 6.91 | 16.04 | 5.29 |
| 1998 | 35.51 | 11.64 | 21.64 | 7.09 | 13.87 | 4.55 |
| 1999 | 30.68 | 10.01 | 20.68 | 6.74 | 10.00 | 3.27 |
| 2000 | 35.22 | 11.43 | 24.59 | 7.98 | 10.63 | 3.45 |
| 2001 | 26.26 | 8.48 | 18.76 | 6.06 | 7.50 | 2.42 |
| 2002 | 28.65 | 9.20 | 18.07 | 5.80 | 10.58 | 3.40 |
| 2003 | 30.00 | 9.61 | 18.05 | 5.78 | 11.95 | 3.83 |
| 2004 | 33.72 | 10.74 | 23.44 | 7.47 | 10.28 | 3.27 |
| 2005 | 30.66 | 9.71 | 13.88 | 4.40 | 16.78 | 5.31 |
| 2006 | 36.57 | 11.49 | 14.89 | 4.68 | 21.68 | 6.81 |
| 2007 | 44.66 | 13.88 | 16.56 | 5.15 | 28.10 | 8.73 |
| 2008 | 43.26 | 13.33 | 24.56 | 7.57 | 18.70 | 5.76 |
| 2009 | 40.82 | 12.50 | 26.13 | 8.00 | 14.69 | 4.50 |
| 2010 | 62.83 | 19.10 | 38.97 | 11.85 | 23.86 | 7.25 |
| 2011 | 41.27 | 12.44 | 19.55 | 5.90 | 21.72 | 6.54 |
| 2012 | 36.76 | 11.02 | 23.83 | 7.14 | 12.93 | 3.88 |
| 2013 | 35.81 | 10.69 | 20.17 | 6.02 | 15.64 | 4.67 |
| 2014 | 39.74 | 11.80 | 22.55 | 6.70 | 17.19 | 5.10 |
| 2015 | 37.34 | 11.07 | 23.82 | 7.06 | 13.52 | 4.01 |
| 2016 | 38.08 | 11.26 | 18.59 | 5.50 | 19.49 | 5.76 |
| 2017 | 41.09 | 12.12 | 44.79 | 13.21 | -3.70 | -1.09 |
| 2018 | 35.90 | 10.57 | 24.44 | 7.19 | 11.47 | 3.38 |
| 2019 | 33.38 | 9.79 | 23.84 | 6.99 | 9.54 | 2.80 |
| 2020 | 28.70 | 8.41 | 33.57 | 9.83 | -4.87 | -1.42 |
| 2021 | 22.92 | 6.71 | 23.92 | 7.01 | -1.00 | -0.30 |
| 2022 | 20.84 | 6.10 | 24.37 | 7.14 | -3.53 | -1.04 |

# 表 3.3 常住人口及城镇化率（1996 － 2022 年）
RESIDENT POPULATION AND URBANIZATION RATE (1996-2022)

单位：万人 (10 000 persons)

| 年份<br>Year | 常住人口<br>Resident Population | 城镇<br>Urban | 乡村<br>Rural | 城镇化率 (%)<br>Urbanization Rate (%) |
|---|---|---|---|---|
| 1996 | 2875.30 | 848.21 | 2027.09 | 29.5 |
| 1997 | 2873.36 | 890.74 | 1982.62 | 31.0 |
| 1998 | 2870.75 | 935.86 | 1934.89 | 32.6 |
| 1999 | 2860.37 | 981.11 | 1879.26 | 34.3 |
| 2000 | 2848.82 | 1013.88 | 1834.94 | 35.6 |
| 2001 | 2829.21 | 1058.12 | 1771.09 | 37.4 |
| 2002 | 2814.83 | 1123.12 | 1691.71 | 39.9 |
| 2003 | 2803.19 | 1174.55 | 1628.64 | 41.9 |
| 2004 | 2793.32 | 1215.42 | 1577.90 | 43.5 |
| 2005 | 2798.00 | 1265.95 | 1532.05 | 45.2 |
| 2006 | 2808.00 | 1311.29 | 1496.71 | 46.7 |
| 2007 | 2816.00 | 1361.35 | 1454.65 | 48.3 |
| 2008 | 2839.00 | 1419.09 | 1419.91 | 50.0 |
| 2009 | 2859.00 | 1474.92 | 1384.08 | 51.6 |
| 2010 | 2884.62 | 1529.55 | 1355.07 | 53.0 |
| 2011 | 2944.43 | 1618.71 | 1325.72 | 55.0 |
| 2012 | 2974.88 | 1685.12 | 1289.76 | 56.6 |
| 2013 | 3011.03 | 1755.27 | 1255.76 | 58.3 |
| 2014 | 3043.48 | 1818.32 | 1225.16 | 59.7 |
| 2015 | 3070.02 | 1887.29 | 1182.73 | 61.5 |
| 2016 | 3109.96 | 1969.69 | 1140.27 | 63.3 |
| 2017 | 3143.51 | 2043.13 | 1100.38 | 65.0 |
| 2018 | 3163.14 | 2106.81 | 1056.33 | 66.6 |
| 2019 | 3187.84 | 2175.23 | 1012.61 | 68.2 |
| 2020 | 3208.93 | 2229.08 | 979.85 | 69.5 |
| 2021 | 3212.43 | 2259.13 | 953.30 | 70.3 |
| 2022 | 3213.34 | 2280.32 | 933.02 | 71.0 |

## 表 3.4 常住人口自然变动情况（1997 － 2022 年）
NATURAL CHANGE OF RESIDENT POPULATION (1997-2022)

单位：万人、‰ (10 000 persons, ‰)

| 年 份 | 出生人口 | 出生率 | 死亡人口 | 死亡率 | 自然增长人口 | 自然增长率 |
|---|---|---|---|---|---|---|
| 1997 | 39.09 | 13.60 | 21.16 | 7.36 | 17.93 | 6.24 |
| 1998 | 37.88 | 13.19 | 22.06 | 7.68 | 15.82 | 5.51 |
| 1999 | 34.10 | 11.90 | 19.89 | 6.94 | 14.21 | 4.96 |
| 2000 | 28.57 | 10.01 | 19.24 | 6.74 | 9.33 | 3.27 |
| 2001 | 27.54 | 9.70 | 19.59 | 6.90 | 7.95 | 2.80 |
| 2002 | 26.41 | 9.36 | 17.16 | 6.08 | 9.25 | 3.28 |
| 2003 | 27.78 | 9.89 | 20.22 | 7.20 | 7.56 | 2.69 |
| 2004 | 26.44 | 9.45 | 18.47 | 6.60 | 7.97 | 2.85 |
| 2005 | 26.28 | 9.40 | 17.89 | 6.40 | 8.39 | 3.00 |
| 2006 | 27.75 | 9.90 | 18.22 | 6.50 | 9.53 | 3.40 |
| 2007 | 28.40 | 10.10 | 17.72 | 6.30 | 10.68 | 3.80 |
| 2008 | 28.56 | 10.10 | 17.81 | 6.30 | 10.75 | 3.80 |
| 2009 | 28.21 | 9.90 | 17.66 | 6.20 | 10.55 | 3.70 |
| 2010 | 26.33 | 9.17 | 18.38 | 6.40 | 7.95 | 2.77 |
| 2011 | 28.80 | 9.88 | 19.56 | 6.71 | 9.24 | 3.17 |
| 2012 | 32.14 | 10.86 | 20.30 | 6.86 | 11.84 | 4.00 |
| 2013 | 31.04 | 10.37 | 20.26 | 6.77 | 10.78 | 3.60 |
| 2014 | 32.30 | 10.67 | 21.34 | 7.05 | 10.96 | 3.62 |
| 2015 | 33.78 | 11.05 | 21.98 | 7.19 | 11.80 | 3.86 |
| 2016 | 36.37 | 11.77 | 22.37 | 7.24 | 14.00 | 4.53 |
| 2017 | 34.96 | 11.18 | 22.73 | 7.27 | 12.23 | 3.91 |
| 2018 | 34.75 | 11.02 | 23.78 | 7.54 | 10.97 | 3.48 |
| 2019 | 33.28 | 10.48 | 24.04 | 7.57 | 9.24 | 2.91 |
| 2020 | 23.88 | 7.47 | 24.63 | 7.70 | -0.75 | -0.23 |
| 2021 | 20.83 | 6.49 | 25.81 | 8.04 | -4.98 | -1.55 |
| 2022 | 19.20 | 5.98 | 26.00 | 8.09 | -6.80 | -2.11 |

## 表 3.5 人口变动情况抽样调查(2022 年)
## POPULATION CHANGE SAMPLING SURVEY (2022)

单位:万人 (10 000 persons)

| 项 目 | Item | 2022 |
|---|---|---|
| 常住人口 | Resident Population | 3213.34 |
| #城 镇 | #Urban | 2280.32 |
| 乡 村 | Rural | 933.02 |
| #男 性 | #Male | 1623.17 |
| 女 性 | Female | 1590.17 |
| #0-14 岁 | #Aged 0-14 | 468.24 |
| 15-59 岁 | Aged 15-59 | 2032.99 |
| 15 岁 | Aged 15 | 40.81 |
| 60 岁及以上 | Aged 60 and Over | 712.11 |
| 65 岁及以上 | Aged 65 and Over | 588.16 |
| 流出人口 | Population Outside Residential Area | 1543.29 |
| #流出至市外 | #Outside Chongqing | 403.53 |
| 市外流入人口 | Population from Other Areas to Chongqing | 221.45 |
| 城镇化率(%) | Urbanization Rate (%) | 70.96 |
| 出生人口 | Births | 19.20 |
| 出生率(‰) | Birth Rate (‰) | 5.98 |
| 死亡人口 | Deaths | 26.00 |
| 死亡率(‰) | Death Rate (‰) | 8.09 |
| 自然增长人口 | Natural Growth | -6.80 |
| 自然增长率(‰) | Natural Growth Rate (‰) | -2.11 |

# 表 3.6 第五次人口普查基本情况
## BASIC STATISTICS ON THE 5TH NATIONAL POPULATION CENSUS

| 指　标 | Item | 2000 |
|---|---|---|
| **总人口（万人）** | **Total Population (10 000 persons)** | **2848.82** |
| 男 | Male | 1460.57 |
| 女 | Female | 1388.25 |
| 性别比（女 =100） | Sex Ratio (female=100) | 105.21 |
| **家庭户户数（万户）** | **Family Households (10 000 households)** | **923.4** |
| **家庭户规模（人 / 户）** | **Average Family Household Size (person/household)** | **3.02** |
| **各年龄组人口（万人）** | **Population by Age Group (10 000 persons)** | |
| 0-14 岁 | Aged 0-14 | 665.20 |
| 15-59 岁 | Aged 15-59 | 1810.73 |
| 15 岁 | Aged 15 | 37.78 |
| 60 岁及以上 | Aged 60 and Over | 372.89 |
| 65 岁及以上 | Aged 65 and Over | 251.84 |
| **预期寿命（岁）** | **Life Expectancy (years old)** | **71.73** |
| 男 | Male | 69.84 |
| 女 | Female | 73.89 |
| **城乡人口（万人）** | **Population by Residence (10 000 persons)** | |
| 城镇人口 | Urban Population | 1013.88 |
| 乡村人口 | Rural Population | 1834.94 |
| **民族人口（万人，%）** | **Population by Ethnicity (10 000 persons, %)** | |
| 汉　族 | Han | 2664.50 |
| 占总人口比重 | Percentage to Total Population | 93.5 |
| 少数民族 | Ethnic Minorities | 184.32 |
| 占总人口比重 | Percentage to Total Population | 6.5 |
| **每十万人拥有的各种受教育程度人口（人）** | **Population with Various Education Attainment Per 100 000 Population (person)** | |
| 大专及以上 | Junior College and Above | 3154 |
| 高中和中专 | Senior Secondary/Secondary Technical School | 8815 |
| 初　中 | Junior Secondary School | 27190 |
| 小　学 | Primary School | 42863 |
| **文盲人口及文盲率** | **Illiterate Population and Illiterate Rate** | |
| 文盲人口（万人） | Illiterate Population (10 000 persons) | 212.24 |
| 文盲率（%） | Illiterate Rate (%) | 7.45 |

注：此表为常住人口推算数据。
Note:The data in the table above are calculated on the basis of resident population.

## 表 3.7 第六次人口普查基本情况
BASIC STATISTICS ON THE 6TH NATIONAL POPULATION CENSUS

| 指　标 | Item | 2010 |
|---|---|---|
| **总人口（万人）** | **Total Population (10 000 persons)** | **2884.62** |
| 男 | Male | 1460.89 |
| 女 | Female | 1423.73 |
| 性别比（女 =100） | Sex Ratio (female=100) | 102.61 |
| **家庭户户数（万户）** | **Family Households (10 000 households)** | **1000.10** |
| **家庭户规模（人 / 户）** | **Average Family Household Size (person/household)** | **2.70** |
| **各年龄组人口（万人）** | **Population by Age Group (10 000 persons)** | |
| 0-14 岁 | Aged 0-14 | 490.34 |
| 15-59 岁 | Aged 15-59 | 1891.84 |
| 15 岁 | Aged 15 | 47.19 |
| 60 岁及以上 | Aged 60 and Over | 502.44 |
| 65 岁及以上 | Aged 65 and Over | 338.15 |
| **预期寿命（岁）** | **Life Expectancy (years old)** | 75.70 |
| 男 | Male | 73.16 |
| 女 | Female | 78.60 |
| **城乡人口（万人）** | **Population by Residence (10 000 persons)** | |
| 城镇人口 | Urban Population | 1529.55 |
| 乡村人口 | Rural Population | 1355.07 |
| **民族人口（万人，%）** | **Population by Ethnicity (10 000 persons, %)** | |
| 汉　族 | Han | 2690.91 |
| 占总人口比重 | Percentage to Total Population | 93.3 |
| 少数民族 | Ethnic Minorities | 193.71 |
| 占总人口比重 | Percentage to Total Population | 6.7 |
| **每十万人拥有的各种受教育程度人口（人）** | **Population with Various Education Attainment Per 100 000 Population (person)** | |
| 大专及以上 | Junior College and Above | 8478 |
| 高中和中专 | Senior Secondary/Secondary Technical School | 13223 |
| 初　中 | Junior Secondary School | 33441 |
| 小　学 | Primary School | 33653 |
| **文盲人口及文盲率** | **Illiterate Population and Illiterate Rate** | |
| 文盲人口（万人） | Illiterate Population (10 000 persons) | 121.52 |
| 文盲率（%） | Illiterate Rate (%) | 4.21 |

# 表 3.8 第七次人口普查基本情况
BASIC STATISTICS ON THE 7TH NATIONAL POPULATION CENSUSES

| 指　标 | Item | 2020 |
|---|---|---|
| **总人口(万人)** | **Total Population (10 000 persons)** | **3205.42** |
| 男 | Male | 1620.21 |
| 女 | Female | 1585.21 |
| 性别比(女=100) | Sex Ratio (female=100) | 102.21 |
| **家庭户户数(万户)** | **Family Households (10 000 households)** | **1204.02** |
| **家庭户规模(人/户)** | **Average Family Household Size (person/household)** | **2.45** |
| **各年龄组人口(万人)** | **Population by Age Group (10 000 persons)** | |
| 0-14 岁 | Aged 0-14 | 509.84 |
| 15-59 岁 | Aged 15-59 | 1994.54 |
| 15 岁 | Aged 15 | 36.19 |
| 60 岁及以上 | Aged 60 and Over | 701.04 |
| 65 岁及以上 | Aged 65 and Over | 547.36 |
| **预期寿命(岁)** | **Life Expectancy (years old)** | 78.56 |
| 男 | Male | 75.86 |
| 女 | Female | 81.64 |
| **城乡人口(万人)** | **Population by Residence (10 000 persons)** | |
| 城镇人口 | Urban Population | 2226.41 |
| 乡村人口 | Rural Population | 979.01 |
| **民族人口(万人,%)** | **Population by Ethnicity (10 000 persons, %)** | |
| 汉　族 | Han | 2988.34 |
| 占总人口比重 | Percentage to Total Population | 93.23 |
| 少数民族 | Ethnic Minorities | 217.08 |
| 占总人口比重 | Percentage to Total Population | 6.77 |
| **每十万人拥有的各种受教育程度人口(人)** | **Population with Various Education Attainment Per 100 000 Population (person)** | |
| 大专及以上 | Junior College and Above | 15412 |
| 高中和中专 | Senior Secondary/Secondary Technical School | 15956 |
| 初　中 | Junior Secondary School | 30582 |
| 小　学 | Primary School | 29894 |
| **文盲人口及文盲率** | **Illiterate Population and Illiterate Rate** | |
| 文盲人口(万人) | Illiterate Population (10 000 persons) | 52.12 |
| 文盲率(%) | Illiterate Rate (%) | 1.63 |

## 表 3.9 七次人口普查主要指标
MAIN INDICATORS OF SEVEN POPULATION CENSUSES

单位：万人、%（10 000 persons, %）

| 普查时间 | Census Time | 总人口 Total Population 合 计 Total | 男 Male | 女 Female | 性别比（女=100） Sex Ratio (female=100) | 年平均增长率 Annual Average Growth Rate |
|---|---|---|---|---|---|---|
| 第一次人口普查（1953 年 7 月 1 日） | First Population Census (July 1, 1953) | 1766.39 | 924.56 | 841.83 | 109.83 | |
| 第二次人口普查（1964 年 7 月 1 日） | Second Population Census (July 1, 1964) | 1889.17 | 969.02 | 920.15 | 105.31 | 0.61 |
| 第三次人口普查（1982 年 7 月 1 日） | Third Population Census (July 1, 1982) | 2705.89 | 1402.46 | 1303.43 | 107.60 | 2.02 |
| 第四次人口普查（1990 年 7 月 1 日） | Fourth Population Census (July 1, 1990) | 2886.62 | 1499.83 | 1386.79 | 108.15 | 0.81 |
| 第五次人口普查（2000 年 11 月 1 日） | Fifth Population Census (November 1, 2000) | 2848.82 | 1460.57 | 1388.25 | 105.21 | -0.13 |
| 第六次人口普查（2010 年 11 月 1 日） | Sixth Population Census (November 1，2010) | 2884.62 | 1460.89 | 1423.73 | 102.61 | 0.12 |
| 第七次人口普查（2020 年 11 月 1 日） | Seventh Population Census (November 1，2020) | 3205.42 | 1620.21 | 1585.21 | 102.21 | 1.06 |

## 表 3.10 人口年龄结构和抚养比（1982 − 2022 年）
AGE COMPOSITION AND DEPENDENCY RATIO OF POPULATION (1982-2022)

单位：万人（10 000 persons）

| 年 份 Year | 总人口（年末） Total Population (year-end) | 0-14 岁 Aged 0-14 人口数 Population | 0-14 岁 比重(%) Proportion | 15-64 岁 Aged 15-64 人口数 Population | 15-64 岁 比重(%) Proportion | 65 岁及以上 Aged 65 and over 人口数 Population | 65 岁及以上 比重(%) Proportion | 总抚养比(%) Gross Dependency Ratio(%) | 少儿抚养比(%) Children Dependency Ratio(%) | 老年抚养比(%) Old Dependency Ratio(%) |
|---|---|---|---|---|---|---|---|---|---|---|
| 1982 | 2705.89 | 901.31 | 33.31 | 1676.02 | 61.94 | 128.56 | 4.75 | 61.45 | 53.78 | 7.67 |
| 1990 | 2886.62 | 626.27 | 21.70 | 2092.06 | 72.47 | 168.29 | 5.83 | 37.98 | 29.94 | 8.04 |
| 2000 | 2848.82 | 665.20 | 23.35 | 1931.78 | 67.81 | 251.84 | 8.84 | 47.47 | 34.43 | 13.04 |
| 2001 | 2829.21 | 643.93 | 22.76 | 1925.56 | 68.06 | 259.72 | 9.18 | 46.93 | 33.44 | 13.49 |
| 2002 | 2814.83 | 624.05 | 22.17 | 1922.81 | 68.31 | 267.97 | 9.52 | 46.40 | 32.46 | 13.94 |
| 2003 | 2803.19 | 615.58 | 21.96 | 1894.40 | 67.58 | 293.21 | 10.46 | 47.97 | 32.49 | 15.48 |
| 2004 | 2793.32 | 592.19 | 21.20 | 1896.66 | 67.90 | 304.47 | 10.90 | 47.27 | 31.22 | 16.05 |
| 2005 | 2798.00 | 576.39 | 20.60 | 1913.83 | 68.40 | 307.78 | 11.00 | 46.20 | 30.12 | 16.08 |
| 2006 | 2808.00 | 561.60 | 20.00 | 1934.71 | 68.90 | 311.69 | 11.10 | 45.14 | 29.03 | 16.11 |
| 2007 | 2816.00 | 543.49 | 19.30 | 1957.12 | 69.50 | 315.39 | 11.20 | 43.89 | 27.77 | 16.12 |
| 2008 | 2839.00 | 546.22 | 19.24 | 1973.39 | 69.51 | 319.39 | 11.25 | 43.86 | 27.68 | 16.18 |
| 2009 | 2859.00 | 544.93 | 19.06 | 1988.72 | 69.56 | 325.35 | 11.38 | 43.76 | 27.40 | 16.36 |
| 2010 | 2884.62 | 490.34 | 17.00 | 2056.13 | 71.28 | 338.15 | 11.72 | 40.30 | 23.85 | 16.45 |
| 2011 | 2944.43 | 502.68 | 17.07 | 2085.26 | 70.82 | 356.49 | 12.11 | 41.21 | 24.11 | 17.10 |
| 2012 | 2974.88 | 502.43 | 16.89 | 2097.34 | 70.50 | 375.11 | 12.61 | 41.84 | 23.96 | 17.88 |
| 2013 | 3011.03 | 499.51 | 16.59 | 2120.40 | 70.42 | 391.12 | 12.99 | 42.01 | 23.56 | 18.45 |
| 2014 | 3043.48 | 506.24 | 16.63 | 2126.24 | 69.86 | 411.00 | 13.51 | 43.14 | 23.81 | 19.33 |
| 2015 | 3070.02 | 510.08 | 16.62 | 2130.11 | 69.38 | 429.83 | 14.00 | 44.13 | 23.95 | 20.18 |
| 2016 | 3109.96 | 518.89 | 16.68 | 2140.73 | 68.84 | 450.34 | 14.48 | 45.28 | 24.24 | 21.04 |
| 2017 | 3143.51 | 525.19 | 16.71 | 2142.36 | 68.15 | 475.96 | 15.14 | 46.73 | 24.51 | 22.22 |
| 2018 | 3163.14 | 524.42 | 16.58 | 2137.29 | 67.57 | 501.43 | 15.85 | 48.00 | 24.54 | 23.46 |
| 2019 | 3187.84 | 520.10 | 16.31 | 2141.85 | 67.19 | 525.89 | 16.50 | 48.83 | 24.28 | 24.55 |
| 2020 | 3208.93 | 510.40 | 15.90 | 2150.57 | 67.02 | 547.96 | 17.08 | 49.21 | 23.73 | 25.48 |
| 2021 | 3212.43 | 491.18 | 15.29 | 2151.04 | 66.96 | 570.21 | 17.75 | 49.34 | 22.83 | 26.51 |
| 2022 | 3213.34 | 468.24 | 14.57 | 2156.94 | 67.13 | 588.16 | 18.30 | 48.98 | 21.71 | 27.27 |

# 表 3.11 就业人员基本情况（1985 – 2022 年）
## BASIC STATISTICS ON EMPLOYMENT (1985-2022)

| 年 份<br>Year | 就业人员总计<br>Total Number of Employed Persons | #城 镇<br>Urban Areas | 按经济类型分 By Ownership<br>国 有<br>State-owned | 集 体<br>Collective-owned | 私营和个体<br>Private and Individuals | 其 他<br>Others |
|---|---|---|---|---|---|---|
| 1985 | 1432.03 | 269.37 | | | | |
| 1986 | 1469.13 | 275.35 | | | | |
| 1987 | 1507.33 | 282.39 | | | | |
| 1988 | 1512.49 | 288.70 | | | | |
| 1989 | 1540.03 | 291.29 | | | | |
| 1990 | 1569.34 | 296.92 | | | | |
| 1991 | 1620.67 | 307.87 | | | | |
| 1992 | 1662.58 | 313.51 | | | | |
| 1993 | 1658.95 | 310.05 | | | | |
| 1994 | 1729.55 | 326.75 | | | | |
| 1995 | 1709.26 | 347.06 | | | | |
| 1996 | 1719.43 | 463.98 | 198.16 | 1228.60 | 280.24 | 12.43 |
| 1997 | 1715.40 | 483.74 | 189.07 | 1201.03 | 307.29 | 18.01 |
| 1998 | 1710.97 | 505.22 | 175.52 | 1176.65 | 334.24 | 24.56 |
| 1999 | 1699.06 | 518.40 | 161.15 | 1151.98 | 354.15 | 31.78 |
| 2000 | 1661.16 | 528.97 | 149.28 | 1109.96 | 365.86 | 36.06 |
| 2001 | 1616.08 | 539.80 | 136.63 | 1058.10 | 379.86 | 41.49 |
| 2002 | 1551.77 | 549.17 | 130.66 | 975.92 | 395.96 | 49.23 |
| 2003 | 1499.99 | 560.28 | 125.88 | 903.90 | 412.41 | 57.80 |
| 2004 | 1471.34 | 573.97 | 124.72 | 854.48 | 425.18 | 66.96 |
| 2005 | 1456.30 | 589.27 | 123.50 | 822.48 | 437.72 | 72.60 |
| 2006 | 1454.77 | 602.99 | 123.90 | 789.42 | 457.52 | 83.93 |
| 2007 | 1468.87 | 631.65 | 115.79 | 765.19 | 484.88 | 103.01 |
| 2008 | 1492.43 | 665.74 | 119.83 | 746.54 | 514.89 | 111.17 |
| 2009 | 1513.00 | 696.82 | 119.79 | 727.99 | 546.66 | 118.56 |
| 2010 | 1551.03 | 743.30 | 125.29 | 714.65 | 580.79 | 130.30 |
| 2011 | 1587.04 | 787.70 | 131.00 | 678.00 | 599.85 | 178.19 |
| 2012 | 1605.89 | 835.70 | 128.53 | 642.62 | 620.54 | 214.20 |
| 2013 | 1618.69 | 869.50 | 121.22 | 605.86 | 650.90 | 240.71 |
| 2014 | 1632.12 | 902.35 | 114.87 | 575.50 | 687.01 | 254.74 |
| 2015 | 1647.41 | 935.50 | 119.55 | 536.66 | 703.95 | 287.25 |
| 2016 | 1658.32 | 976.13 | 119.37 | 500.15 | 754.03 | 284.77 |
| 2017 | 1659.33 | 1004.52 | 118.32 | 468.20 | 792.10 | 280.71 |
| 2018 | 1663.23 | 1032.46 | 112.65 | 435.35 | 842.27 | 272.96 |
| 2019 | 1668.16 | 1068.58 | 105.78 | 421.50 | 877.01 | 263.87 |
| 2020 | 1676.01 | 1100.12 | 111.16 | 418.32 | 891.25 | 255.28 |
| 2021 | 1668.27 | 1108.23 | 114.16 | 405.60 | 908.78 | 239.73 |
| 2022 | 1644.37 | 1087.42 | 115.18 | 425.75 | 877.27 | 226.17 |

单位：万人 (10 000 persons)

| 按产业分 By Sector | | | 分产业比重(%) Composition by Sector | | |
|---|---|---|---|---|---|
| 第一产业 Primary Industry | 第二产业 Secondary Industry | 第三产业 Tertiary Industry | 第一产业 Primary Industry | 第二产业 Secondary Industry | 第三产业 Tertiary Industry |
| 1042.22 | 223.37 | 166.44 | 72.8 | 15.6 | 11.6 |
| 1048.32 | 241.66 | 179.15 | 71.4 | 16.4 | 12.2 |
| 1064.06 | 258.93 | 184.34 | 70.6 | 17.2 | 12.2 |
| 1056.49 | 262.83 | 193.17 | 69.8 | 17.4 | 12.8 |
| 1082.41 | 263.81 | 193.81 | 70.3 | 17.1 | 12.6 |
| 1103.04 | 263.86 | 202.44 | 70.3 | 16.8 | 12.9 |
| 1130.47 | 275.72 | 214.48 | 69.8 | 17.0 | 13.2 |
| 1118.59 | 277.77 | 266.22 | 67.3 | 16.7 | 16.0 |
| 1088.70 | 287.88 | 282.37 | 65.6 | 17.4 | 17.0 |
| 1062.90 | 301.13 | 365.52 | 61.5 | 17.4 | 21.1 |
| 1018.30 | 310.88 | 380.08 | 59.6 | 18.2 | 22.2 |
| 1001.89 | 320.31 | 397.23 | 58.3 | 18.6 | 23.1 |
| 989.07 | 313.77 | 412.56 | 57.6 | 18.3 | 24.1 |
| 979.48 | 303.18 | 428.31 | 57.3 | 17.7 | 25.0 |
| 959.71 | 296.12 | 443.23 | 56.5 | 17.4 | 26.1 |
| 920.92 | 290.23 | 450.01 | 55.4 | 17.5 | 27.1 |
| 870.52 | 287.31 | 458.25 | 53.9 | 17.8 | 28.3 |
| 801.04 | 285.09 | 465.64 | 51.6 | 18.4 | 30.0 |
| 742.90 | 280.83 | 476.26 | 49.5 | 18.7 | 31.8 |
| 704.22 | 280.73 | 486.39 | 47.8 | 19.1 | 33.1 |
| 678.32 | 283.08 | 494.90 | 46.6 | 19.4 | 34.0 |
| 664.35 | 286.46 | 503.96 | 45.7 | 19.7 | 34.6 |
| 658.52 | 294.43 | 515.92 | 44.8 | 20.1 | 35.1 |
| 652.19 | 307.66 | 532.58 | 43.7 | 20.6 | 35.7 |
| 638.08 | 326.04 | 548.88 | 42.2 | 21.5 | 36.3 |
| 603.85 | 351.86 | 595.32 | 38.9 | 22.7 | 38.4 |
| 568.95 | 390.80 | 627.29 | 35.9 | 24.6 | 39.5 |
| 531.18 | 422.73 | 651.98 | 33.1 | 26.3 | 40.6 |
| 495.08 | 452.21 | 671.40 | 30.6 | 27.9 | 41.5 |
| 463.78 | 464.48 | 703.86 | 28.4 | 28.5 | 43.1 |
| 440.30 | 473.70 | 733.41 | 26.7 | 28.8 | 44.5 |
| 419.19 | 476.66 | 762.47 | 25.3 | 28.7 | 46.0 |
| 402.91 | 461.68 | 794.74 | 24.3 | 27.8 | 47.9 |
| 390.62 | 442.56 | 830.05 | 23.5 | 26.6 | 49.9 |
| 381.48 | 434.06 | 852.62 | 22.9 | 26.0 | 51.1 |
| 378.00 | 421.00 | 877.01 | 22.6 | 25.1 | 52.3 |
| 366.16 | 426.83 | 875.28 | 21.9 | 25.6 | 52.5 |
| 388.51 | 414.42 | 841.44 | 23.6 | 25.2 | 51.2 |

# 表 3.12 就业人员年末数（1999 － 2022 年）
## NUMBER OF EMPLOYED PERSONS AT YEAR-END (1999-2022)

| 指 标 | Item | 1999 | 2000 | 2001 | 2002 | 2003 | 2004 | 2005 | 2006 | 2007 |
|---|---|---|---|---|---|---|---|---|---|---|
| **就业人员总计** | **Total Number of Employed Persons** | **1699.06** | **1661.16** | **1616.08** | **1551.77** | **1499.99** | **1471.34** | **1456.30** | **1454.77** | **1468.87** |
| 城 镇 | Urban | 518.40 | 528.97 | 539.80 | 549.17 | 560.28 | 573.97 | 589.27 | 602.99 | 631.65 |
| 乡 村 | Rural | 1180.66 | 1132.19 | 1076.28 | 1002.60 | 939.71 | 897.37 | 867.03 | 851.78 | 837.22 |
| **按经济类型分** | **By Ownership** | | | | | | | | | |
| 国有经济 | State-owned | 161.15 | 149.28 | 136.63 | 130.66 | 125.88 | 124.72 | 123.50 | 123.90 | 115.79 |
| 集体经济 | Collective-owned | 1151.98 | 1109.96 | 1058.10 | 975.92 | 903.90 | 854.48 | 822.48 | 789.42 | 765.19 |
| 私 营 | Private | 66.43 | 74.92 | 84.44 | 95.22 | 105.95 | 112.91 | 118.48 | 130.28 | 151.49 |
| 个 体 | Individual | 287.72 | 290.94 | 295.42 | 300.74 | 306.46 | 312.27 | 319.24 | 327.24 | 333.39 |
| 其他经济 | Others | 31.78 | 36.06 | 41.49 | 49.23 | 57.80 | 66.96 | 72.60 | 83.93 | 103.01 |
| #联 营 | Joint Ownership | 0.63 | 0.86 | 4.11 | 4.93 | 5.78 | 6.84 | 5.57 | 4.62 | 2.03 |
| 股份制 | Shareholding | 10.95 | 11.49 | 13.21 | 15.55 | 15.72 | 16.71 | 14.84 | 12.86 | 16.47 |
| 外商投资 | Foreign-funded | 2.42 | 2.74 | 2.86 | 2.91 | 3.23 | 4.16 | 4.86 | 5.01 | 7.06 |
| 港澳台投资 | With Funds from Hong Kong, Macao and Taiwan | 2.50 | 2.44 | 2.66 | 2.25 | 2.55 | 2.33 | 2.32 | 2.33 | 2.80 |
| **按行业分** | **Grouped By Sector** | | | | | | | | | |
| 第一产业 | Primary Industry | 959.71 | 920.92 | 870.52 | 801.04 | 742.90 | 704.22 | 678.32 | 664.35 | 658.52 |
| 第二产业 | Secondary Industry | 296.12 | 290.23 | 287.31 | 285.09 | 280.83 | 280.73 | 283.08 | 286.46 | 294.43 |
| 采矿业 | Mining | 17.89 | 16.59 | 15.72 | 15.14 | 14.00 | 14.14 | 14.66 | 14.77 | 16.83 |
| 制造业 | Manufacturing | 160.07 | 156.02 | 152.59 | 149.91 | 146.38 | 144.23 | 144.46 | 145.72 | 148.33 |
| 电力、热力、燃气及水生产和供应业 | Electric Power, Heat, Gas and Water Production and Supply | 6.18 | 6.20 | 6.22 | 6.26 | 6.27 | 6.32 | 6.52 | 6.85 | 7.14 |
| 建筑业 | Construction | 111.98 | 111.42 | 112.78 | 113.78 | 114.18 | 116.04 | 117.44 | 119.12 | 122.13 |
| 第三产业 | Tertiary Industry | 443.23 | 450.01 | 458.25 | 465.64 | 476.26 | 486.39 | 494.90 | 503.96 | 515.92 |
| 批发与零售业 | Wholesale and Retail Trades | 113.05 | 115.65 | 117.43 | 118.87 | 120.03 | 121.16 | 122.88 | 125.63 | 125.33 |
| 交通运输、仓储及邮政业 | Transport, Storage and Post | 40.02 | 40.23 | 40.93 | 41.02 | 42.11 | 43.25 | 44.29 | 45.05 | 46.17 |
| 住宿和餐饮业 | Hotels and Catering Services | 70.18 | 70.52 | 71.14 | 72.03 | 73.36 | 74.27 | 75.40 | 77.22 | 78.76 |
| 信息传输、软件和信息技术服务业 | Information Transmission, Software and Information Technology | 5.60 | 5.91 | 6.03 | 6.14 | 6.34 | 6.58 | 7.03 | 7.39 | 8.09 |
| 金融业 | Financial Intermediation | 6.38 | 6.41 | 6.46 | 6.53 | 6.61 | 6.65 | 6.76 | 6.90 | 8.03 |
| 房地产业 | Real Estate | 4.88 | 5.03 | 5.11 | 5.22 | 5.45 | 6.11 | 6.83 | 7.74 | 10.77 |
| 租赁与商务服务业 | Leasing and Business Services | 16.09 | 16.34 | 16.95 | 17.53 | 18.23 | 19.33 | 19.97 | 19.97 | 21.41 |
| 科学研究、技术服务业 | Scientific Research and Technical Services | 7.58 | 7.71 | 7.96 | 8.15 | 8.25 | 8.35 | 8.39 | 8.43 | 8.57 |
| 水利、环境和公共设施管理业 | Management of Water Conservancy, Environment and Public Facilities | 5.26 | 5.31 | 5.40 | 5.50 | 5.56 | 5.71 | 5.76 | 5.94 | 6.19 |
| 居民服务、修理和其他服务业 | Services to Households, Repair and Other Services | 108.75 | 110.16 | 112.59 | 115.05 | 118.23 | 122.36 | 124.75 | 126.15 | 126.62 |
| 教 育 | Education | 29.79 | 30.59 | 31.69 | 32.09 | 33.33 | 33.68 | 33.91 | 34.20 | 35.01 |
| 卫生和社会工作 | Health and Social Work | 12.98 | 13.00 | 13.08 | 13.18 | 13.41 | 13.50 | 13.51 | 13.65 | 13.94 |
| 文化、体育与娱乐业 | Culture, Sports and Entertainment | 2.73 | 2.74 | 2.79 | 2.84 | 2.88 | 2.94 | 2.96 | 3.05 | 3.44 |
| 公共管理、社会保障和社会组织 | Public Management, Social Security and Social Organization | 19.94 | 20.41 | 20.69 | 21.49 | 22.47 | 22.50 | 22.46 | 22.64 | 23.59 |

单位：万人 (10 000 persons)

| 2008 | 2009 | 2010 | 2011 | 2012 | 2013 | 2014 | 2015 | 2016 | 2017 | 2018 | 2019 | 2020 | 2021 | 2022 |
|---|---|---|---|---|---|---|---|---|---|---|---|---|---|---|
| **1492.43** | **1513.00** | **1551.03** | **1587.04** | **1605.89** | **1618.69** | **1632.12** | **1647.41** | **1658.32** | **1659.33** | **1663.23** | **1668.16** | **1676.01** | **1668.27** | **1644.37** |
| 665.74 | 696.82 | 743.30 | 787.70 | 835.70 | 869.50 | 902.35 | 935.50 | 976.13 | 1004.52 | 1032.46 | 1068.58 | 1100.12 | 1108.23 | 1087.42 |
| 826.69 | 816.18 | 807.73 | 799.34 | 770.19 | 749.19 | 729.77 | 711.91 | 682.19 | 654.81 | 630.77 | 599.58 | 575.89 | 560.04 | 556.95 |
| 119.83 | 119.79 | 125.29 | 131.00 | 128.53 | 121.22 | 114.87 | 119.55 | 119.37 | 118.32 | 112.65 | 105.78 | 111.16 | 114.16 | 115.18 |
| 746.54 | 727.99 | 714.65 | 678.00 | 642.62 | 605.86 | 575.50 | 536.66 | 500.15 | 468.20 | 435.35 | 421.50 | 418.32 | 405.60 | 425.75 |
| 175.00 | 203.50 | 230.10 | 240.87 | 252.18 | 268.64 | 288.53 | 295.88 | 319.13 | 346.10 | 381.24 | 405.02 | 406.25 | 415.10 | 391.97 |
| 339.89 | 343.16 | 350.69 | 358.98 | 368.36 | 382.26 | 398.48 | 408.07 | 434.90 | 446.00 | 461.03 | 471.99 | 485.00 | 493.68 | 485.30 |
| 111.17 | 118.56 | 130.30 | 178.19 | 214.20 | 240.71 | 254.74 | 287.25 | 284.77 | 280.71 | 272.96 | 263.87 | 255.28 | 239.73 | 226.17 |
| 1.95 | 2.56 | 2.36 | 1.55 | 1.60 | 0.41 | 0.50 | 0.38 | 0.33 | 0.27 | 0.21 | 0.08 | 0.11 | 0.15 | 0.26 |
| 21.04 | 22.48 | 24.91 | 30.00 | 36.15 | 34.43 | 39.58 | 38.54 | 38.03 | 40.14 | 38.49 | 42.62 | 49.12 | 44.33 | 40.75 |
| 7.33 | 8.47 | 9.43 | 13.14 | 13.98 | 19.56 | 22.48 | 22.38 | 21.34 | 20.93 | 21.04 | 18.14 | 19.99 | 20.11 | 19.31 |
| 2.40 | 3.89 | 5.20 | 14.55 | 16.67 | 17.95 | 17.46 | 15.80 | 16.85 | 16.07 | 14.29 | 14.81 | 15.50 | 15.37 | 13.51 |
| 652.19 | 638.08 | 603.85 | 568.95 | 531.18 | 495.08 | 463.78 | 440.30 | 419.19 | 402.91 | 390.62 | 381.48 | 378.00 | 366.16 | 388.51 |
| 307.66 | 326.04 | 351.86 | 390.80 | 422.73 | 452.21 | 464.48 | 473.70 | 476.66 | 461.68 | 442.56 | 434.06 | 421.00 | 426.83 | 414.42 |
| 19.77 | 22.24 | 24.84 | 28.11 | 30.63 | 30.86 | 30.57 | 26.79 | 19.88 | 10.87 | 8.34 | 8.32 | 7.65 | 4.16 | 3.53 |
| 152.11 | 159.37 | 168.67 | 190.51 | 206.49 | 216.36 | 224.97 | 236.13 | 247.09 | 238.92 | 227.13 | 221.59 | 216.24 | 222.61 | 218.79 |
| 7.43 | 7.91 | 8.20 | 8.54 | 9.41 | 8.93 | 9.51 | 9.24 | 9.63 | 10.39 | 9.77 | 9.75 | 9.65 | 9.81 | 9.76 |
| 128.35 | 136.52 | 150.15 | 163.64 | 176.20 | 196.06 | 199.43 | 201.54 | 200.06 | 201.50 | 197.32 | 194.40 | 187.46 | 190.25 | 182.34 |
| 532.58 | 548.88 | 595.32 | 627.29 | 651.98 | 671.40 | 703.86 | 733.41 | 762.47 | 794.74 | 830.05 | 852.62 | 877.01 | 875.28 | 841.44 |
| 128.42 | 134.05 | 166.71 | 179.52 | 182.73 | 184.73 | 197.40 | 212.77 | 217.36 | 227.35 | 242.89 | 249.71 | 257.66 | 260.39 | 250.33 |
| 47.25 | 48.42 | 50.12 | 53.49 | 56.88 | 61.27 | 64.93 | 67.03 | 69.45 | 73.17 | 72.10 | 72.38 | 73.45 | 73.53 | 70.91 |
| 80.28 | 82.64 | 85.07 | 88.22 | 91.19 | 92.94 | 94.64 | 94.82 | 98.68 | 102.22 | 105.45 | 106.92 | 109.25 | 107.45 | 100.82 |
| 8.58 | 8.85 | 9.34 | 10.57 | 12.34 | 13.98 | 15.31 | 16.31 | 17.64 | 18.89 | 20.21 | 23.24 | 24.15 | 24.37 | 24.98 |
| 9.09 | 9.74 | 10.85 | 12.34 | 14.09 | 14.37 | 15.02 | 17.19 | 19.91 | 21.02 | 24.21 | 26.50 | 28.90 | 23.59 | 22.12 |
| 13.28 | 12.69 | 14.66 | 16.83 | 19.63 | 24.69 | 28.06 | 28.52 | 29.57 | 32.84 | 34.20 | 35.21 | 38.00 | 37.53 | 35.96 |
| 22.50 | 23.41 | 24.63 | 26.31 | 28.20 | 31.34 | 32.72 | 34.99 | 40.64 | 44.31 | 50.12 | 52.48 | 55.68 | 56.33 | 55.75 |
| 8.75 | 8.93 | 9.05 | 9.44 | 10.51 | 11.64 | 12.59 | 13.36 | 15.28 | 16.71 | 17.32 | 17.97 | 18.56 | 18.86 | 18.53 |
| 6.44 | 6.78 | 7.03 | 7.45 | 8.13 | 8.52 | 9.18 | 10.53 | 11.53 | 12.26 | 12.32 | 12.96 | 13.87 | 14.02 | 12.84 |
| 129.21 | 131.76 | 133.00 | 133.87 | 133.43 | 125.51 | 124.66 | 122.66 | 122.82 | 122.38 | 123.44 | 122.59 | 122.44 | 122.67 | 114.13 |
| 36.02 | 36.91 | 38.17 | 39.88 | 41.74 | 44.48 | 47.05 | 48.23 | 49.52 | 50.05 | 50.91 | 52.78 | 54.62 | 55.98 | 55.62 |
| 14.55 | 15.38 | 16.10 | 17.42 | 18.95 | 21.67 | 23.75 | 25.42 | 27.55 | 29.65 | 30.02 | 30.89 | 31.25 | 32.76 | 33.12 |
| 3.88 | 4.08 | 4.30 | 4.64 | 5.22 | 5.97 | 6.36 | 6.96 | 7.61 | 8.31 | 9.12 | 9.75 | 9.89 | 9.85 | 8.69 |
| 24.33 | 25.24 | 26.29 | 27.31 | 28.94 | 30.29 | 32.19 | 34.62 | 34.91 | 35.58 | 37.74 | 39.24 | 39.29 | 37.95 | 37.64 |

# 表 3.13 城镇就业人员年末数（2021 – 2022 年）
## NUMBER OF EMPLOYED PERSONS IN URBAN UNITS AT YEAR-END (2021-2022)

单位：万人 (10 000 persons)

| 指 标 | Item | 2021 | 2022 |
|---|---|---|---|
| **就业人员总计** | **Total Number of Employed Persons** | **1108.23** | **1087.42** |
| **按经济类型分** | **By Ownership** | | |
| 国有经济 | State-owned | 114.16 | 115.18 |
| 集体经济 | Collective-owned | 9.03 | 9.25 |
| 私 营 | Private | 378.29 | 371.83 |
| 个 体 | Individual | 367.02 | 364.99 |
| 其他经济 | Others | 239.73 | 226.17 |
| #联 营 | Joint Ownership | 0.15 | 0.26 |
| 股份制 | Shareholding | 44.33 | 40.75 |
| 外商投资 | Foreign-funded | 20.11 | 19.31 |
| 港澳台投资 | With Funds from Hong Kong, Macao and Taiwan | 15.37 | 13.51 |
| **按行业分** | **Grouped By Sector** | | |
| 第一产业 | Primary Industry | 34.22 | 45.86 |
| 第二产业 | Secondary Industry | 417.26 | 407.53 |
| 采矿业 | Mining | 3.81 | 3.19 |
| 制造业 | Manufacturing | 217.68 | 215.23 |
| 电力、热力、燃气及水生产和供应业 | Electric Power, Heat, Gas and Water Production and Supply | 9.81 | 9.76 |
| 建筑业 | Construction | 185.96 | 179.35 |
| 第三产业 | Tertiary Industry | 656.75 | 634.03 |
| 批发与零售业 | Wholesale and Retail Trades | 165.01 | 159.75 |
| 交通运输、仓储及邮政业 | Transport, Storage and Post | 52.32 | 50.88 |
| 住宿和餐饮业 | Hotels and Catering Services | 74.38 | 69.85 |
| 信息传输、软件和信息技术服务业 | Information Transmission, Software and Information Technology | 24.15 | 24.68 |
| 金融业 | Financial Intermediation | 23.29 | 21.92 |
| 房地产业 | Real Estate | 36.84 | 35.34 |
| 租赁与商务服务业 | Leasing and Business Services | 38.86 | 38.29 |
| 科学研究、技术服务业 | Scientific Research and Technical Services | 16.73 | 16.42 |
| 水利、环境和公共设施管理业 | Management of Water Conservancy, Environment and Public Facilities | 11.27 | 10.37 |
| 居民服务、修理和其他服务业 | Services to Households, Repair and Other Services | 90.74 | 84.35 |
| 教 育 | Education | 50.91 | 50.65 |
| 卫生和社会工作 | Health and Social Work | 30.14 | 30.64 |
| 文化、体育与娱乐业 | Culture, Sports and Entertainment | 9.21 | 8.22 |
| 公共管理、社会保障和社会组织 | Public Management, Social Security and Social Organization | 32.90 | 32.67 |

# 表 3.14 主要年份城镇非私营单位在岗职工人数
## NUMBER OF ON-POST STAFF AND WORKERS OF URBAN NON-PRIVATE UNITS IN MAJOR YEARS

单位：万人 (10 000 persons)

| 年 份 Year | 合 计 Total | 按产业分 By Three Strata of Industry | | | 按经济类型分 By Status of Registration | | |
|---|---|---|---|---|---|---|---|
| | | 第一产业 Primary Industry | 第二产业 Secondary Industry | 第三产业 Tertiary Industry | 国 有 State-owned | 集 体 Collective--owned | 其 他 Others |
| 1949 | 5.34 | | | | 5.34 | | |
| 1952 | 47.62 | | | | 47.62 | | |
| 1957 | 71.19 | | | | 71.19 | | |
| 1962 | 80.79 | | | | 80.79 | | |
| 1965 | 91.96 | | | | 91.96 | | |
| 1970 | 109.98 | | | | 109.98 | | |
| 1975 | 127.99 | | | | 127.99 | | |
| 1978 | 154.44 | | | | 154.44 | | |
| 1980 | 220.06 | | | | 162.97 | 57.09 | |
| 1985 | 257.63 | 4.80 | 144.90 | 107.93 | 186.74 | 70.81 | 0.08 |
| 1986 | 264.01 | 4.79 | 151.13 | 108.09 | 191.47 | 72.43 | 0.11 |
| 1987 | 270.46 | 5.39 | 153.80 | 111.27 | 196.79 | 73.36 | 0.31 |
| 1988 | 277.70 | 5.45 | 157.28 | 114.97 | 201.88 | 75.42 | 0.40 |
| 1989 | 280.69 | 5.66 | 158.65 | 116.38 | 205.98 | 74.01 | 0.70 |
| 1990 | 285.68 | 5.68 | 159.47 | 120.53 | 209.61 | 75.16 | 0.91 |
| 1991 | 293.59 | 5.68 | 163.94 | 123.97 | 215.78 | 76.58 | 1.23 |
| 1992 | 297.07 | 5.46 | 165.35 | 126.26 | 218.41 | 76.94 | 1.72 |
| 1993 | 290.02 | 4.16 | 164.74 | 121.12 | 215.05 | 70.79 | 4.18 |
| 1994 | 293.23 | 4.24 | 162.90 | 126.09 | 212.02 | 71.03 | 10.18 |
| 1995 | 294.25 | 4.35 | 160.58 | 129.32 | 212.34 | 69.85 | 12.06 |
| 1996 | 294.63 | 4.43 | 159.37 | 130.83 | 214.01 | 67.47 | 13.15 |
| 1997 | 289.29 | 4.13 | 153.73 | 131.43 | 211.13 | 61.64 | 16.52 |
| 1998 | 236.61 | 3.83 | 115.89 | 116.89 | 172.24 | 40.91 | 23.46 |
| 1999 | 222.34 | 3.58 | 106.07 | 112.69 | 158.64 | 35.54 | 28.16 |
| 2000 | 208.87 | 3.43 | 96.01 | 109.43 | 146.91 | 29.74 | 32.22 |
| 2001 | 201.23 | 2.94 | 91.73 | 106.56 | 134.79 | 23.77 | 42.67 |
| 2002 | 199.93 | 2.64 | 92.63 | 104.66 | 128.41 | 20.82 | 50.70 |
| 2003 | 204.99 | 2.46 | 97.56 | 104.97 | 121.27 | 18.94 | 64.78 |
| 2004 | 208.04 | 2.35 | 100.50 | 105.19 | 120.85 | 16.85 | 70.34 |
| 2005 | 209.66 | 2.14 | 101.00 | 106.52 | 120.09 | 13.66 | 75.91 |
| 2006 | 212.97 | 2.12 | 102.22 | 108.63 | 120.37 | 12.22 | 80.38 |
| 2007 | 220.84 | 1.80 | 104.87 | 114.17 | 112.55 | 10.63 | 97.66 |
| 2008 | 229.59 | 1.80 | 108.92 | 118.87 | 115.19 | 10.23 | 104.17 |
| 2009 | 234.90 | 1.68 | 111.88 | 121.34 | 114.32 | 9.88 | 110.70 |
| 2010 | 250.22 | 1.79 | 121.20 | 127.23 | 118.76 | 10.26 | 121.20 |
| 2011 | 318.73 | 1.52 | 172.03 | 145.18 | 125.42 | 10.46 | 182.85 |
| 2012 | 334.37 | 1.26 | 176.74 | 156.37 | 123.45 | 9.47 | 201.45 |
| 2013 | 375.36 | 1.07 | 194.49 | 179.80 | 114.74 | 8.47 | 252.15 |
| 2014 | 386.76 | 1.15 | 196.08 | 189.53 | 112.47 | 8.43 | 265.86 |
| 2015 | 385.08 | 1.15 | 190.33 | 193.60 | 113.47 | 7.88 | 263.73 |
| 2016 | 379.66 | 1.07 | 183.99 | 194.60 | 113.49 | 7.93 | 258.24 |
| 2017 | 369.18 | 1.13 | 171.76 | 196.29 | 112.83 | 6.56 | 249.79 |
| 2018 | 356.61 | 0.77 | 158.58 | 197.26 | 106.20 | 4.94 | 245.47 |
| 2019 | 342.07 | 0.59 | 134.87 | 206.61 | 100.88 | 4.54 | 236.65 |
| 2020 | 336.50 | 0.37 | 133.11 | 203.02 | 106.22 | 4.23 | 226.05 |
| 2021 | 329.90 | 0.41 | 127.29 | 202.20 | 109.65 | 4.07 | 216.18 |
| 2022 | 321.66 | 0.39 | 120.91 | 200.36 | 111.06 | 3.71 | 206.89 |

注：“城镇非私营单位”与原“城镇经济单位”口径相同（以下各表同）。
Note: The scope of "urban economic units" is identical to the former "urban non-private units"(the same for the tables below).

# 表 3.15 主要年份城镇非私营单位在岗职工工资总额
## TOTAL WAGE BILL OF ON-POST STAFF AND WORKERS OF URBAN NON-PRIVATE UNITS IN MAJOR YEARS

单位：万元 (10 000 yuan)

| 年份 Year | 合计 Total | 按产业分 By Three Strata of Industry | | | 按经济类型分 By Status of Registration | | |
|---|---|---|---|---|---|---|---|
| | | 第一产业 Primary Industry | 第二产业 Secondary Industry | 第三产业 Tertiary Industry | 国有 State-owned | 集体 Collective--owned | 其他 Others |
| 1949 | 1368 | | | | 1368 | | |
| 1952 | 18577 | | | | 18577 | | |
| 1957 | 37710 | | | | 37710 | | |
| 1962 | 45532 | | | | 45532 | | |
| 1965 | 51159 | | | | 51159 | | |
| 1970 | 60866 | | | | 60866 | | |
| 1975 | 74645 | | | | 74645 | | |
| 1978 | 91615 | | | | 91615 | | |
| 1980 | 159426 | | | | 125305 | 34121 | |
| 1985 | 259688 | 4528 | 149468 | 105692 | 195684 | 63939 | 65 |
| 1986 | 300882 | 4960 | 177126 | 118796 | 233311 | 67396 | 175 |
| 1987 | 349808 | 5802 | 206458 | 137548 | 271210 | 78190 | 408 |
| 1988 | 435140 | 6771 | 256248 | 172121 | 340494 | 94048 | 598 |
| 1989 | 497553 | 7713 | 294228 | 195612 | 392179 | 104065 | 1309 |
| 1990 | 573310 | 8232 | 335056 | 230022 | 454776 | 116718 | 1816 |
| 1991 | 637968 | 9313 | 373271 | 255384 | 501204 | 134105 | 2659 |
| 1992 | 728780 | 10757 | 415886 | 302137 | 577638 | 146315 | 4827 |
| 1993 | 831520 | 8623 | 489684 | 333213 | 664939 | 152705 | 13876 |
| 1994 | 1144546 | 12990 | 618503 | 513053 | 902585 | 190980 | 50981 |
| 1995 | 1309344 | 15878 | 715405 | 578061 | 1016056 | 222720 | 70568 |
| 1996 | 1454905 | 18116 | 782060 | 654729 | 1132834 | 237510 | 84561 |
| 1997 | 1580484 | 17286 | 828011 | 735187 | 1225441 | 244245 | 110798 |
| 1998 | 1588049 | 18478 | 815904 | 753667 | 1223697 | 201028 | 163324 |
| 1999 | 1606804 | 19304 | 760591 | 826909 | 1207329 | 184757 | 214718 |
| 2000 | 1732318 | 20606 | 777295 | 934417 | 1290215 | 176693 | 265410 |
| 2001 | 1941508 | 21510 | 833110 | 1086888 | 1381940 | 158228 | 401340 |
| 2002 | 2196175 | 21857 | 921105 | 1253213 | 1520518 | 159655 | 516002 |
| 2003 | 2535070 | 22059 | 1104724 | 1408287 | 1661336 | 160049 | 713685 |
| 2004 | 2939800 | 23358 | 1291498 | 1624944 | 1904154 | 164332 | 871314 |
| 2005 | 3458237 | 23019 | 1503886 | 1931332 | 2224886 | 157943 | 1075408 |
| 2006 | 4034057 | 26173 | 1757357 | 2250527 | 2542465 | 165315 | 1326277 |
| 2007 | 4998743 | 27226 | 2111205 | 2860312 | 2814125 | 160900 | 2023718 |
| 2008 | 6137760 | 30232 | 2592679 | 3514849 | 3390954 | 177772 | 2569034 |
| 2009 | 7161387 | 31720 | 2989883 | 4139784 | 3855720 | 198908 | 3106759 |
| 2010 | 8629547 | 37250 | 3690436 | 4901861 | 4435431 | 242086 | 3952030 |
| 2011 | 12522120 | 48280 | 5980962 | 6492878 | 5534535 | 291274 | 6696311 |
| 2012 | 14791899 | 42564 | 6739973 | 8009362 | 6278652 | 280113 | 8233134 |
| 2013 | 18702874 | 37727 | 8741241 | 9923906 | 6475086 | 293061 | 11934727 |
| 2014 | 21584168 | 44340 | 9680243 | 11859585 | 7357033 | 341168 | 13885967 |
| 2015 | 23738675 | 47745 | 10266335 | 13424595 | 8419348 | 347442 | 14971885 |
| 2016 | 25242283 | 51015 | 10480632 | 14710636 | 9219990 | 400104 | 15622189 |
| 2017 | 26681112 | 61493 | 10267372 | 16352247 | 10422552 | 363646 | 15894914 |
| 2018 | 29037895 | 40636 | 10551564 | 18445695 | 11342620 | 290052 | 17405223 |
| 2019 | 30296886 | 36353 | 9378081 | 20882452 | 11439852 | 282898 | 18574136 |
| 2020 | 32510819 | 24209 | 9642323 | 22844287 | 13005960 | 294819 | 19210040 |
| 2021 | 34711850 | 30792 | 10214390 | 24466668 | 14401194 | 292060 | 20018596 |
| 2022 | 35861102 | 31620 | 10537327 | 25292155 | 15161308 | 274773 | 20425021 |

# 表 3.16 主要年份城镇非私营单位在岗职工平均工资
AVERAGE WAGE OF ON-POST STAFF AND WORKERS OF URBAN NON-PRIVATE UNITS IN MAJOR YEARS

单位：元 (yuan)

| 年 份 Year | 平均工资 Average Wages | 按产业分 By Three Strata of Industry | | | 按经济类型分 By Status of Registration | | |
|---|---|---|---|---|---|---|---|
| | | 第一产业 Primary Industry | 第二产业 Secondary Industry | 第三产业 Tertiary Industry | 国 有 State-owned | 集 体 Collective--owned | 其 他 Others |
| 1949 | 284 | | | | 284 | | |
| 1952 | 330 | | | | 330 | | |
| 1957 | 535 | | | | 535 | | |
| 1962 | 448 | | | | 448 | | |
| 1965 | 588 | | | | 588 | | |
| 1970 | 581 | | | | 581 | | |
| 1975 | 588 | | | | 588 | | |
| 1978 | 632 | | | | 632 | | |
| 1980 | 737 | | | | 783 | 606 | |
| 1985 | 1038 | | | | 1110 | 930 | 861 |
| 1986 | 1154 | 1034 | 1197 | 1100 | 1234 | 941 | 1842 |
| 1987 | 1309 | 1140 | 1354 | 1254 | 1397 | 1073 | 1943 |
| 1988 | 1588 | 1249 | 1647 | 1522 | 1708 | 1264 | 1685 |
| 1989 | 1782 | 1388 | 1863 | 1691 | 1923 | 1393 | 2380 |
| 1990 | 2025 | 1452 | 2106 | 1942 | 2189 | 1565 | 2256 |
| 1991 | 2203 | 1640 | 2308 | 2089 | 2356 | 1768 | 2485 |
| 1992 | 2468 | 1931 | 2526 | 2415 | 2661 | 1906 | 3273 |
| 1993 | 2833 | 1793 | 2967 | 2694 | 3068 | 2067 | 4704 |
| 1994 | 3925 | 3093 | 3776 | 4151 | 4227 | 2693 | 7100 |
| 1995 | 4508 | 3657 | 4423 | 4527 | 4789 | 3162 | 6346 |
| 1996 | 5010 | 4127 | 4889 | 5033 | 5352 | 3603 | 6607 |
| 1997 | 5502 | 4188 | 5412 | 5649 | 5828 | 4016 | 6845 |
| 1998 | 6433 | 4713 | 6529 | 6394 | 6732 | 4891 | 6907 |
| 1999 | 7182 | 5296 | 7184 | 7240 | 7541 | 5200 | 7641 |
| 2000 | 8020 | 5884 | 7704 | 8372 | 7431 | 4534 | 7450 |
| 2001 | 9523 | 6521 | 8925 | 10053 | 10035 | 6614 | 9503 |
| 2002 | 10960 | 7587 | 9905 | 11905 | 11745 | 7601 | 10339 |
| 2003 | 12440 | 8877 | 11425 | 13462 | 13616 | 8552 | 11316 |
| 2004 | 14357 | 9871 | 13125 | 15624 | 15847 | 9839 | 12831 |
| 2005 | 16630 | 10676 | 14962 | 18345 | 18614 | 11614 | 14373 |
| 2006 | 19215 | 12279 | 17434 | 21031 | 21402 | 13522 | 16805 |
| 2007 | 23098 | 14852 | 20703 | 25401 | 25365 | 15149 | 21336 |
| 2008 | 26985 | 16571 | 24134 | 29736 | 29761 | 17444 | 24864 |
| 2009 | 30965 | 18864 | 27445 | 34313 | 34023 | 20337 | 28723 |
| 2010 | 35326 | 20894 | 31555 | 39043 | 38075 | 24205 | 33552 |
| 2011 | 40042 | 31868 | 35592 | 45353 | 44585 | 28490 | 37543 |
| 2012 | 45392 | 34585 | 39477 | 52038 | 51675 | 30626 | 42173 |
| 2013 | 51015 | 36006 | 46476 | 55913 | 57271 | 34852 | 48684 |
| 2014 | 56852 | 38346 | 50471 | 63520 | 65794 | 40514 | 53527 |
| 2015 | 62091 | 41460 | 54308 | 69872 | 74665 | 44318 | 57206 |
| 2016 | 67386 | 48055 | 58018 | 76267 | 81867 | 51450 | 61458 |
| 2017 | 73272 | 55424 | 60911 | 84087 | 92964 | 56240 | 64730 |
| 2018 | 81764 | 53119 | 66592 | 94146 | 107300 | 59601 | 71167 |
| 2019 | 89714 | 61595 | 70859 | 101982 | 114570 | 63376 | 79583 |
| 2020 | 98380 | 66407 | 74672 | 113672 | 124131 | 70592 | 86724 |
| 2021 | 106966 | 75182 | 82381 | 122263 | 132577 | 72529 | 94489 |
| 2022 | 111424 | 81896 | 87028 | 126224 | 137768 | 75564 | 98123 |

## 表 3.17 城镇非私营单位在岗职工人数（2021 – 2022 年）
NUMBER OF ON-POST STAFF AND WORKERS IN NON-PRIVATE UNITS (2021-2022)

单位：万人 (10 000 persons)

| 指 标 | Item | 合 计 Total | | #国 有 State-owned | | #集 体 Collective-owned | |
|---|---|---|---|---|---|---|---|
| | | 2021 | 2022 | 2021 | 2022 | 2021 | 2022 |
| **总 计** | **Total** | **329.90** | **321.66** | **109.65** | **111.06** | **4.07** | **3.71** |
| **按机构类型分** | **By Type of Institutions** | | | | | | |
| 企 业 | Corporations | 230.70 | 222.67 | 12.27 | 13.66 | 2.83 | 2.62 |
| 机关和事业 | Agencies and Institutions | 97.81 | 97.75 | 96.71 | 96.77 | 1.10 | 0.97 |
| 民间非营利组织和其他 | NGO and Other Organizations | 1.39 | 1.24 | 0.67 | 0.63 | 0.14 | 0.12 |
| **按行业分** | **By Sector** | | | | | | |
| 第一产业 | Primary Industry | 0.41 | 0.39 | 0.18 | 0.16 | 0.02 | 0.03 |
| 第二产业 | Secondary Industry | 127.29 | 120.91 | 2.41 | 2.99 | 2.30 | 2.11 |
| 采矿业 | Mining | 0.70 | 0.63 | 0.17 | 0.04 | 0.04 | 0.02 |
| 制造业 | Manufacturing | 64.88 | 63.56 | 0.94 | 0.77 | 0.35 | 0.31 |
| 电力、热力、燃气及水生产和供应业 | Electric Power, Heat, Gas and Water Production and Supply | 6.29 | 6.28 | 0.46 | 0.34 | 0.10 | 0.08 |
| 建筑业 | Construction | 55.42 | 50.44 | 0.84 | 1.84 | 1.81 | 1.70 |
| 第三产业 | Tertiary Industry | 202.20 | 200.36 | 107.06 | 107.91 | 1.75 | 1.57 |
| 批发与零售业 | Wholesale and Retail Trades | 17.42 | 15.36 | 0.93 | 0.99 | 0.10 | 0.08 |
| 交通运输、仓储及邮政业 | Transport, Storage and Post | 20.56 | 19.56 | 3.10 | 2.71 | 0.10 | 0.10 |
| 住宿和餐饮业 | Hotels and Catering Services | 3.81 | 3.34 | 0.11 | 0.13 | 0.08 | 0.07 |
| 信息传输、软件和信息技术服务业 | Information Transmission, Software and Information Technology | 5.63 | 6.10 | 1.30 | 1.39 | | |
| 金融业 | Financial Intermediation | 14.12 | 13.57 | 0.38 | 0.42 | | |
| 房地产业 | Real Estate | 15.05 | 14.36 | 0.20 | 0.24 | 0.05 | 0.04 |
| 租赁与商务服务业 | Leasing and Business Services | 12.29 | 13.78 | 1.03 | 1.48 | 0.06 | 0.06 |
| 科学研究、技术服务业 | Scientific Research and Technical Services | 7.84 | 7.99 | 3.32 | 2.99 | 0.04 | 0.04 |
| 水利、环境和公共设施管理业 | Management of Water Conservancy, Environment and Public Facilities | 3.60 | 3.74 | 1.19 | 1.23 | 0.01 | |
| 居民服务、修理和其他服务业 | Services to Households, Repair and Other Services | 0.81 | 0.91 | 0.24 | 0.30 | 0.04 | 0.03 |
| 教 育 | Education | 40.09 | 40.90 | 37.87 | 38.63 | 0.50 | 0.47 |
| 卫生和社会工作 | Health and Social Work | 21.69 | 21.77 | 19.55 | 19.70 | 0.60 | 0.57 |
| 文化、体育与娱乐业 | Culture, Sports and Entertainment | 2.58 | 2.45 | 1.30 | 1.28 | 0.01 | 0.01 |
| 公共管理、社会保障和社会组织 | Public Management, Social Security and Social Organization | 36.71 | 36.53 | 36.54 | 36.42 | 0.16 | 0.10 |

# 表 3.18 城镇非私营单位在岗职工工资总额（2021 − 2022 年）
TOTAL WAGE BILL OF ON-POST STAFF AND WORKERS OF URBAN NON-PRIVATE UNITS (2021-2022)

单位: 万元 (10 000 yuan)

| 指 标 | Item | 合 计 Total | | #国 有 State-owned | | #集 体 Collective-owned | |
|---|---|---|---|---|---|---|---|
| | | 2021 | 2022 | 2021 | 2022 | 2021 | 2022 |
| **总 计** | **Total** | **34711850** | **35861102** | **14401194** | **15161308** | **292060** | **274773** |
| **按机构类型分** | **By Type of Institutions** | | | | | | |
| 企 业 | Corporations | 21692919 | 22318677 | 1582294 | 1780705 | 157944 | 150058 |
| 机关和事业 | Agencies and Institutions | 12888586 | 13442373 | 12762528 | 13326767 | 125857 | 115216 |
| 民间非营利组织和其他 | NGO and Other Organizations | 130345 | 100052 | 56372 | 53836 | 8259 | 9499 |
| **按行业分** | **By Sector** | | | | | | |
| 第一产业 | Primary Industry | 30792 | 31620 | 17403 | 17920 | 759 | 971 |
| 第二产业 | Secondary Industry | 10214390 | 10537327 | 232728 | 298037 | 130380 | 123387 |
| 采矿业 | Mining | 74801 | 67546 | 17032 | 4159 | 2659 | 1411 |
| 制造业 | Manufacturing | 5781170 | 6240943 | 97606 | 85556 | 19458 | 16631 |
| 电力、热力、燃气及水生产和供应业 | Electric Power, Heat, Gas and Water Production and Supply | 693695 | 751517 | 60736 | 32657 | 4477 | 3676 |
| 建筑业 | Construction | 3664724 | 3477321 | 57354 | 175665 | 103786 | 101669 |
| 第三产业 | Tertiary Industry | 24466668 | 25292155 | 14151063 | 14845351 | 160921 | 150415 |
| 批发与零售业 | Wholesale and Retail Trades | 1496554 | 1445830 | 163688 | 176686 | 4990 | 4336 |
| 交通运输、仓储及邮政业 | Transport, Storage and Post | 2038125 | 1992956 | 388358 | 346738 | 4890 | 4608 |
| 住宿和餐饮业 | Hotels and Catering Services | 188773 | 174175 | 6193 | 7695 | 2867 | 2612 |
| 信息传输、软件和信息技术服务业 | Information Transmission, Software and Information Technology | 904575 | 1015609 | 254980 | 302703 | 81 | 94 |
| 金融业 | Financial Intermediation | 3018711 | 3001957 | 62601 | 64396 | | |
| 房地产业 | Real Estate | 1288164 | 1268748 | 24293 | 31900 | 2448 | 1913 |
| 租赁与商务服务业 | Leasing and Business Services | 827866 | 972629 | 67680 | 110251 | 4130 | 3881 |
| 科学研究、技术服务业 | Scientific Research and Technical Services | 1177679 | 1209339 | 468198 | 433325 | 4092 | 4104 |
| 水利、环境和公共设施管理业 | Management of Water Conservancy, Environment and Public Facilities | 314253 | 335814 | 102860 | 106741 | 696 | 393 |
| 居民服务、修理和其他服务业 | Services to Households, Repair and Other Services | 52224 | 59196 | 20316 | 25199 | 2408 | 1320 |
| 教 育 | Education | 5280138 | 5654895 | 5056652 | 5430686 | 53092 | 49763 |
| 卫生和社会工作 | Health and Social Work | 3104573 | 3232444 | 2880516 | 2997913 | 62934 | 62994 |
| 文化、体育与娱乐业 | Culture, Sports and Entertainment | 250922 | 253039 | 147294 | 148663 | 1752 | 1448 |
| 公共管理、社会保障和社会组织 | Public Management, Social Security and Social Organization | 4524111 | 4675524 | 4507434 | 4662455 | 16541 | 12949 |

# 表 3.19 城镇非私营单位就业人员平均工资(2021－2022 年)
AVERAGE WAGE OF EMPLOYED PERSONS OF URBAN NON-PRIVATE ECONOMIC UNITS (2021-2022)

单位：元 (yuan)

| 指 标 | Item | 就业人员平均工资 Average Wage of Employed Persons | | #在岗职工平均工资 Average Wage of On-Post Employees | | #国 有 State-owned | | #集 体 Collective-owned | |
|---|---|---|---|---|---|---|---|---|---|
| | | 2021 | 2022 | 2021 | 2022 | 2021 | 2022 | 2021 | 2022 |
| **总 计** | **Total** | **101670** | **107008** | **106966** | **111424** | **132577** | **137768** | **72529** | **75564** |
| **按机构类型分** | **By Type of Institutions** | | | | | | | | |
| 企 业 | Corporations | 90770 | 95636 | 95927 | 99841 | 131233 | 133912 | 56397 | 58573 |
| 机关和事业 | Agencies and Institutions | 129302 | 135033 | 132855 | 138412 | 133048 | 138598 | 115800 | 119912 |
| 民间非营利组织和其他 | NGO and Other Organizations | 92039 | 80922 | 95757 | 84763 | 87574 | 90131 | 59259 | 83650 |
| **按行业分** | **By Sector** | | | | | | | | |
| 第一产业 | Primary Industry | 73140 | 78421 | 75182 | 81896 | 98621 | 109605 | 38156 | 36536 |
| 第二产业 | Secondary Industry | 80684 | 85252 | 82381 | 87028 | 95492 | 105035 | 57376 | 60012 |
| 采矿业 | Mining | 96743 | 98536 | 102404 | 106371 | 106954 | 126410 | 74904 | 73848 |
| 制造业 | Manufacturing | 89966 | 95981 | 90586 | 96622 | 98871 | 113484 | 56536 | 54303 |
| 电力、热力、燃气及水生产和供应业 | Electric Power, Heat, Gas and Water Production and Supply | 110863 | 118261 | 111067 | 118790 | 132628 | 98125 | 45959 | 48978 |
| 建筑业 | Construction | 67918 | 69105 | 68894 | 70209 | 68872 | 102257 | 57809 | 61409 |
| 第三产业 | Tertiary Industry | 114809 | 120289 | 122263 | 126224 | 133486 | 138679 | 92774 | 96812 |
| 批发与零售业 | Wholesale and Retail Trades | 87988 | 91094 | 88724 | 91679 | 173905 | 177270 | 48450 | 51707 |
| 交通运输、仓储及邮政业 | Transport, Storage and Post | 97665 | 100274 | 99327 | 101696 | 127680 | 131248 | 49893 | 49455 |
| 住宿和餐饮业 | Hotels and Catering Services | 48566 | 49054 | 49872 | 50000 | 52934 | 59212 | 37883 | 37433 |
| 信息传输、软件和信息技术服务业 | Information Transmission, Software and Information Technology | 155067 | 166375 | 155584 | 166760 | 207707 | 228214 | 50688 | 42773 |
| 金融业 | Financial Intermediation | 129860 | 150097 | 214646 | 222475 | 168275 | 152076 | | |
| 房地产业 | Real Estate | 87315 | 84809 | 87967 | 85628 | 124292 | 133729 | 48091 | 51409 |
| 租赁与商务服务业 | Leasing and Business Services | 66893 | 70473 | 68560 | 71732 | 67455 | 76614 | 74405 | 62700 |
| 科学研究、技术服务业 | Scientific Research and Technical Services | 149205 | 147217 | 151885 | 151616 | 142208 | 144124 | 99796 | 98549 |
| 水利、环境和公共设施管理业 | Management of Water Conservancy, Environment and Public Facilities | 86319 | 86427 | 87824 | 88352 | 87099 | 85375 | 96625 | 98275 |
| 居民服务、修理和其他服务业 | Services to Households, Repair and Other Services | 65841 | 69402 | 67199 | 69904 | 87944 | 94879 | 56170 | 47833 |
| 教 育 | Education | 127699 | 134999 | 132818 | 139495 | 134674 | 141725 | 107594 | 108195 |
| 卫生和社会工作 | Health and Social Work | 143140 | 148341 | 145058 | 150647 | 149571 | 154601 | 106269 | 112625 |
| 文化、体育与娱乐业 | Culture, Sports and Entertainment | 93912 | 99017 | 95940 | 101203 | 113357 | 116228 | 126029 | 114332 |
| 公共管理、社会保障和社会组织 | Public Management, Social Security and Social Organization | 121249 | 125707 | 124068 | 128290 | 124160 | 128297 | 103900 | 128985 |

# 表 3.20 城镇非私营单位就业人员工资总额(2021－2022 年)
## TOTAL WAGE BILL OF EMPLOYMENT OF URBAN NON-PRIVATE UNITS (2021-2022)

单位:万元 (10 000 yuan)

| 指　标 | Item | 合　计 Total | | #国　有 State-owned | | #集　体 Collective-owned | |
|---|---|---|---|---|---|---|---|
| | | 2021 | 2022 | 2021 | 2022 | 2021 | 2022 |
| **总　计** | **Total** | **36314425** | **37219493** | **14595352** | **15370380** | **300353** | **286016** |
| **按机构类型分** | **By Type of Institutions** | | | | | | |
| 企　业 | Corporations | 23123220 | 23495525 | 1608054 | 1812222 | 162776 | 158253 |
| 机关和事业 | Agencies and Institutions | 13058223 | 13620977 | 12929199 | 13502755 | 128822 | 117794 |
| 民间非营利组织和其他 | NGO and Other Organizations | 132982 | 102991 | 58099 | 55403 | 8755 | 9969 |
| **按行业分** | **By Sector** | | | | | | |
| 第一产业 | Primary Industry | 31912 | 33024 | 17486 | 18025 | 823 | 1076 |
| 第二产业 | Secondary Industry | 11053056 | 11196925 | 237898 | 304109 | 132741 | 125362 |
| 采矿业 | Mining | 81946 | 74001 | 17032 | 4161 | 2659 | 1411 |
| 制造业 | Manufacturing | 5923532 | 6368386 | 98122 | 85916 | 20355 | 17213 |
| 电力、热力、燃气及水生产和供应业 | Electric Power, Heat, Gas and Water Production and Supply | 704130 | 758785 | 61167 | 33326 | 4714 | 3782 |
| 建筑业 | Construction | 4343448 | 3995753 | 61577 | 180706 | 105013 | 102956 |
| 第三产业 | Tertiary Industry | 25229457 | 25989544 | 14339968 | 15048246 | 166789 | 159578 |
| 批发与零售业 | Wholesale and Retail Trades | 1511621 | 1458040 | 165815 | 178401 | 5188 | 4496 |
| 交通运输、仓储及邮政业 | Transport, Storage and Post | 2061649 | 2013095 | 393541 | 352753 | 5248 | 4915 |
| 住宿和餐饮业 | Hotels and Catering Services | 194797 | 179414 | 6249 | 8242 | 3524 | 3126 |
| 信息传输、软件和信息技术服务业 | Information Transmission, Software and Information Technology | 909730 | 1018441 | 255175 | 302979 | 81 | 98 |
| 金融业 | Financial Intermediation | 3459042 | 3353185 | 62774 | 64494 | | |
| 房地产业 | Real Estate | 1310532 | 1313533 | 25303 | 33337 | 2538 | 2007 |
| 租赁与商务服务业 | Leasing and Business Services | 862265 | 1005177 | 71813 | 118375 | 5079 | 4782 |
| 科学研究、技术服务业 | Scientific Research and Technical Services | 1201849 | 1235406 | 473411 | 439095 | 4110 | 4117 |
| 水利、环境和公共设施管理业 | Management of Water Conservancy, Environment and Public Facilities | 321700 | 343764 | 106730 | 111119 | 698 | 393 |
| 居民服务、修理和其他服务业 | Services to Households, Repair and Other Services | 54591 | 61320 | 20944 | 25725 | 2431 | 1337 |
| 教　育 | Education | 5359553 | 5731365 | 5129017 | 5497201 | 54387 | 54817 |
| 卫生和社会工作 | Health and Social Work | 3154976 | 3291807 | 2925284 | 3051171 | 65051 | 64808 |
| 文化、体育与娱乐业 | Culture, Sports and Entertainment | 256334 | 258201 | 149880 | 151887 | 1804 | 1500 |
| 公共管理、社会保障和社会组织 | Public Management, Social Security and Social Organization | 4570818 | 4726796 | 4554032 | 4713467 | 16650 | 13182 |

# 表 3.21 城镇登记失业人数(1985－2022 年)
## NUMBER OF REGISTERED UNEMPLOYED PERSONS IN URBAN AREAS (1985-2022)

单位：万人、% (10 000 persons, %)

| 年 份<br>Year | 登记失业人数<br>Registered Unemployed Persons | 其 中 of which<br>#女 性<br>Female | 按失业时间分 By Unemployment Period<br>6 个月以上<br>Over 6 Months | <br>6 个月以下<br>Less than 6 Months | 登记失业率<br>Registered Unemployment Rate |
|---|---|---|---|---|---|
| 1985 | 6.46 | | | | 2.3 |
| 1986 | 6.00 | | | | 2.1 |
| 1987 | 6.29 | | | | 2.2 |
| 1988 | 6.25 | | | | 2.1 |
| 1989 | 8.43 | | | | 2.8 |
| 1990 | 8.81 | | | | 2.9 |
| 1991 | 9.42 | | | | 3.0 |
| 1992 | 10.01 | | | | 3.1 |
| 1993 | 10.23 | | | | 3.2 |
| 1994 | 10.80 | | | | 3.2 |
| 1995 | 10.47 | | | | 2.9 |
| 1996 | 10.95 | | | | 3.0 |
| 1997 | 10.85 | 6.18 | 6.92 | 3.93 | 3.5 |
| 1998 | 10.10 | 5.71 | 6.46 | 3.64 | 3.5 |
| 1999 | 10.08 | 5.48 | 6.15 | 3.93 | 3.5 |
| 2000 | 10.15 | 5.26 | 5.30 | 4.85 | 3.5 |
| 2001 | 13.72 | 7.24 | 7.72 | 6.00 | 3.9 |
| 2002 | 16.18 | 7.70 | 7.79 | 8.39 | 4.1 |
| 2003 | 16.16 | 8.20 | 8.62 | 7.54 | 4.1 |
| 2004 | 16.76 | 8.19 | 9.44 | 7.32 | 4.1 |
| 2005 | 16.89 | 8.27 | 9.67 | 7.22 | 4.1 |
| 2006 | 15.41 | 8.12 | 8.98 | 6.43 | 4.0 |
| 2007 | 14.13 | 7.60 | 8.01 | 6.12 | 4.0 |
| 2008 | 13.02 | 6.94 | 6.27 | 6.75 | 4.0 |
| 2009 | 13.44 | 6.55 | 6.02 | 7.42 | 4.0 |
| 2010 | 13.02 | 6.20 | 4.06 | 8.96 | 3.9 |
| 2011 | 12.96 | 7.01 | 3.34 | 9.62 | 3.5 |
| 2012 | 12.43 | 5.93 | 1.25 | 11.18 | 3.3 |
| 2013 | 12.07 | 6.44 | 1.07 | 11.00 | 3.4 |
| 2014 | 13.42 | 6.87 | 0.62 | 12.80 | 3.5 |
| 2015 | 14.26 | 7.55 | 0.81 | 13.45 | 3.6 |
| 2016 | 15.68 | 8.12 | 0.93 | 14.75 | 3.7 |
| 2017 | 14.26 | 7.07 | 0.77 | 13.49 | 3.4 |
| 2018 | 13.09 | 7.09 | 0.78 | 12.31 | 3.3 |
| 2019 | 17.46 | 8.09 | 0.39 | 17.07 | 2.6 |
| 2020 | 26.71 | 15.17 | 3.81 | 22.90 | 4.5 |
| 2021 | 18.91 | 10.01 | 8.39 | 10.52 | 2.9 |
| 2022 | 21.88 | 11.57 | 11.98 | 9.90 | 3.3 |

# 表 3.22 城镇私营单位就业人员平均工资（2021－2022 年）
## AVERAGE WAGE OF EMPLOYED PERSONS OF URBAN PRIVATE UNITS (2021-2022)

单位：元 (yuan)

| 指 标 | Item | 就业人员平均工资 Average Wage of Employed Persons | |
|---|---|---|---|
| | | 2021 | 2022 |
| **总 计** | **Total** | **59307** | **60380** |
| **按行业分** | **By Sector** | | |
| 第一产业 | Primary Industry | 38185 | 37942 |
| 第二产业 | Secondary Industry | 61684 | 63207 |
| 采矿业 | Mining | 61782 | 66264 |
| 制造业 | Manufacturing | 63753 | 67890 |
| 电力、热力、燃气及水生产和供应业 | Electric Power, Heat, Gas and Water Production and Supply | 58211 | 63261 |
| 建筑业 | Construction | 59494 | 58019 |
| 第三产业 | Tertiary Industry | 57700 | 58438 |
| 批发与零售业 | Wholesale and Retail Trades | 53924 | 55074 |
| 交通运输、仓储及邮政业 | Transport, Storage and Post | 59128 | 58789 |
| 住宿和餐饮业 | Hotels and Catering Services | 43101 | 42913 |
| 信息传输、软件和信息技术服务业 | Information Transmission, Software and Information Technology | 79590 | 83343 |
| 金融业 | Financial Intermediation | 110758 | 120353 |
| 房地产业 | Real Estate | 62536 | 60695 |
| 租赁与商务服务业 | Leasing and Business Services | 57880 | 55998 |
| 科学研究、技术服务业 | Scientific Research and Technical Services | 69688 | 70067 |
| 水利、环境和公共设施管理业 | Management of Water Conservancy, Environment and Public Facilities | 42418 | 44712 |
| 居民服务、修理和其他服务业 | Services to Households, Repair and Other Services | 43644 | 43976 |
| 教 育 | Education | 54061 | 56429 |
| 卫生和社会工作 | Health and Social Work | 73077 | 77343 |
| 文化、体育与娱乐业 | Culture, Sports and Entertainment | 50926 | 48549 |
| 公共管理、社会保障和社会组织 | Public Management, Social Security and Social Organization | | |

# 主要统计指标解释

## 人口数

指一定时点、一定地区范围内的有生命的个人的总和。年度统计的年末人口数是指每年 12 月 31 日 24 时的人口数。

## 出生率（又称粗出生率）

指在一定时期内（通常为一年）一定地区内出生人数与同期内平均人数（或期中人数）之比，一般用千分率表示。本资料中的出生率指年出生率。计算公式为:

出生率 = 年出生人数 / 年平均人数 ×1000‰

式中：出生人数是指活产婴儿，即胎儿脱离母体时（不管怀孕月数）有过呼吸或其他生命现象。年平均人数是年初、年底人口数的平均数，也可用年中人口数代替。

## 死亡率（又称粗死亡率）

指在一定时期内（通常为一年）一定地区的死亡人数与同期平均人数（或期中人数）之比，一般用千分率表示。本资料中的死亡率指年死亡率。计算公式为:

死亡率 = 年死亡人数 / 年平均人数 ×1000‰

## 人口自然增长率

指在一定时期内（通常为一年）人口自然增加数（出生人数减死亡人数）与该时期内平均人数（或期中人数）之比，一般用千分率表示。计算公式为：

人口自然增长率 =( 本年出生人数 - 本年死亡人数 )/ 年平均人数 ×1000‰ = 人口出生率 - 人口死亡率

## 总抚养比

也称总负担系数。指人口总体中非劳动年龄人口数与劳动年龄人口数之比。通常用百分比表示。说明每 100 名劳动年龄人口大致要负担多少名非劳动年龄人口。用于从人口角度反映人口与经济发展的基本关系。计算公式为：

$$GDR = \frac{P_{0\sim14} + P_{65^+}}{P_{15\sim64}} \times 100\%$$

其中：GDR 为总抚养比；

$P_{0\sim14}$ 为 0 ~ 14 岁少年儿童人口数；

$P65_+$ 为 65 岁及 65 岁以上的老年人口数；

$P_{15\sim64}$ 为 15 ~ 64 岁人口数。

## 老年人口抚养比

也称老年人口抚养系数。指某一人口中老年人口数与劳动年龄人口数之比。通常用百分比表示。用以表明每 100 名劳动年龄人口要负担多少名老年人。老年人口抚养比是从经济角度反映人口老化社会后果的指标之一。计算公式为：

$$ODR = \frac{P_{65^+}}{P_{15-64}} \times 100\%$$

其中：ODR 为老年人口抚养比；

$P_{65+}$ 为 65 岁及 65 岁以上的老年人口数；

$P_{15\sim64}$ 为 15 ~ 64 岁人口数。

## 少年儿童抚养比

也称少年儿童抚养系数。指某一人口中少年儿童人口数与劳动年龄人口数之比。通常用百分比表示。以反映每 100 名劳动年龄人口要负担多少名少年儿童。计算公式为：

$$CDR = \frac{P_{0\sim14}}{P_{15\sim64}} \times 100\%$$

其中：CDR 为少年儿童抚养比；

$P_{0\sim14}$ 为 0 ~ 14 岁少年儿童人口数；

$P_{15\sim64}$ 为 15 ~ 64 岁人口数。

## 常住人口

常住人口包括：（1）居住本乡镇街道，户口在本乡镇街道或户口在本乡镇街道，但人离开本乡镇街道不满半年的人；（2）居住本乡镇街道，离开户口登记地半年以上的人；（3）居住本乡镇街道，户口待定的人；（4）原住本乡镇街道，现在国外工作学习的人。

## 主要统计指标解释

### 文盲人口

文盲人口是指15岁及以上不识字或识字很少的人口。

### 文盲率

文盲率是指文盲人口占常住人口比重。

### 城镇人口和乡村人口

城镇人口是指居住在城镇范围内的全部常住人口；乡村人口是除上述人口以外的全部人口。

历年城乡人口数据是按照当时国家《统计上划分城乡的规定》计算。

### 就业人员

指在一定年龄以上，有劳动能力，为取得劳动报酬或经营收入而从事一定社会劳动的人员。具体指年满16周岁，为取得报酬或经营利润，在调查周内从事了1小时（含1小时）以上劳动的人员；或由于学习、休假等原因在调查周内暂时处于未工作状态，但有工作单位或场所的人员；或由于临时停工放假、单位不景气放假等原因在调查周内暂时处于未工作状态，但不满三个月的人员。

### 在岗职工

指在本单位工作且与本单位签订劳动合同，并由单位支付各项工资和社会保险、住房公积金的人员，以及上述人员中由于学习、病伤、产假等原因暂未工作仍由单位支付工资的人员。在岗职工还包括：

(1) 应订立劳动合同而未订立劳动合同人员（如使用的农村户籍人员）；

(2) 处于试用期人员；

(3) 编制外招用的人员，如临时人员；

(4) 派往外单位工作，但工资仍由本单位发放的人员（如挂职锻炼、外派工作等情况）。

### 国有单位

指资产归国家所有的经济组织。包括按《中华人民共和国企业法人登记管理条例》规定登记注册的非公司制的经济组织，以及中央、地方各级国家机关、事业单位和社会团体。

### 集体单位

指生产资料归集体所有，并按《中华人民共和国企业法人登记管理条例》规定登记注册的经济组织。

### 工资总额

指根据《关于工资总额组成的规定》(1990年1月1日国家统计局发布的一号令）进行修订，本单位在报告期内（季度或年度）直接支付给本单位全部就业人员的劳动报酬总额。包括计时工资、计件工资、奖金、津贴和补贴、加班加点工资、特殊情况下支付的工资，是在岗职工工资总额、劳务派遣人员工资总额和其他就业人员工资总额之和。

工资总额是税前工资，包括单位从个人工资中直接为其代扣或代缴的房费、水费、电费、住房公积金和社会保险基金个人缴纳部分等。

工资总额不论是计入成本的还是不计入成本的，不论是以货币形式支付的还是以实物形式支付的，均应列入工资总额的计算范围。

### 平均工资

指单位就业人员在一定时期内平均每人所得的工资额。它表明一定时期工资收入的高低程度，是反映就业人员工资水平的主要指标。计算公式为：

平均工资＝报告期就业人员工资总额／报告期就业人员平均人数

### 城镇登记失业人员

指有非农业户口，在一定的劳动年龄内(16周岁至退休年龄），有劳动能力，无业而要求就业，并在当地劳动保障部门进行失业登记的人员。

### 城镇登记失业率

城镇登记失业人员与城镇单位就业人员（扣除使用的农村劳动力、聘用的离退休人员、港澳台及外方人员）、城镇单位中的不在岗职工、城镇私营业主、个体户主、城镇私营企业和个体就业人员、城镇登记失业人员之和的比。

# Explanatory Notes on Main Statistical Indicators

## Total population

Refers to the total number of people alive at a certain point of time within a given area.The annual statistics on total population is taken at midnight, the 3lst of December.

## Birth Rate (or Crude Birth Rate)

Refers to the ratio of the number of births to the average population during a certain period of time (usually a year), which is often expressed in ‰. Birth rate in the chapter refers to annual birth rate. The following formula is used:

Birth Rate = Number of Births / Average Number of Population × 1000‰

Number of Births refers to live births, i.e. the births when babies had showed any vital phenomena regardless of the length of pregnancy.

Annual Average Number of Population is the average of the number of population at the beginning of the year and that at the end of the year. Sometimes it is substituted for with the mid-year population.

## Death Rate (or Crude Death Rate)

Refers to the ratio of the number of deaths to the average population (or mid-year population) during a certain period of time (usually a year), which is often expressed in ‰. Death rate in the chapter refers to annual death rate. The following formula is used:

Death Rate = Number of Deaths / Annual Average Number of Population × 1000‰

## Natural Growth Rate of Population

Refers to the ratio of natural increase in population (number of births minus number of deaths) in a certain period of time (usually a year) to average population (or mid-year population) of the same period, which is often expressed in ‰. The following formulas are applied:

Natural Growth of Population = Number of Births - Number of Deaths / Average number of Population × 1000‰

Natural Growth Rate of Population = Birth Rate - Death Rate

## Gross Dependency Ratio

Also called gross dependency coefficient, refers to the ratio of non-working-age population to the working-age population, express in %. Describing in general the number of non-working-age population that every 100 people at working ages will take care of, this indicator reflects the basic relation between population and economic development from the demographic perspective. The gross dependency ratio is calculated with the following formula:

$$GDR = \frac{P_{0\sim14} + P_{65^+}}{P_{15\sim64}} \times 100\%$$

Where: GDR is the gross dependency ratio,

P0-14 is the population of children aged 0-14,

P65+ is the elderly population aged 65 and over, and

P15-64 is the population aged 15-64.

## Old Dependency Ratio

Also called old dependency coefficient, refers to the ratio of the elderly population to the working-age population, express in %. It describes the number of the elderly population that every 100 people at working ages will take care of. Old dependency ratio is one of the indicators reflecting the social implication of population aging from the economic perspective. The old dependency ratio is calculated with the following formula:

$$ODR = \frac{P_{65^+}}{P_{15\sim64}} \times 100\%$$

Where: ODR is the old dependency ratio,

P65+ is the elderly population aged 65 and over, and

P15-64 is the population aged 15-64.

## Children Dependency Ratio

Also called children dependency coefficient, refers to the ratio of the children population to the working-age population, express in %. It describes the number of children population that every 100 people at working ages will take care of. The children dependency ratio is calculated with the following formula:

EXPLANATORY NOTES TO MAJOR STATISTICAL INDICATORS

$$CDR = \frac{P_{0\sim14}}{P_{15\sim64}} \times 100\%$$

Where: CDR is the children dependency ratio,
P0-14 is the children population aged 0-14, and
P15-64 is the population aged 15-64.

## Resident Population

Resident Population includes the following: 1) population who reside in this township or town (sub-district) with residence registered in this area, or population who have residence registered in this township or town (sub-district) but have been away from this area for less than half a year; 2) population having actually resided in this township or town (sub-district) for over half a year with residence registered in other area; 3) population residing in this townships or towns (sub-district) with residence not registered; 4) population with residence registered in this township or town (sub-district) who work or study abroad.

## The Illiterate Population

Refers to those over 15 years of age who have inability to read or write, or can read or write only a few words.

## Illiteracy Rate

Refers to the percentage of the illiterate population in the total Resident Population.

## Urban Population and Rural Population

Urban population refers to all people residing in cities and towns, while rural population refers to population other than urban population.

Statistics on urban and rural population over the years are compiled in line with the regulations of statistical classification on urban and rural population stipulated by the government, which were in effect at different times.

## Employed Persons

Refers to persons above a specified age who had labour capacity and performed some social work for compensation or business gains. Specifically, it refers to persons, aged 16 and over, who performed some work for compensation or business gains for one hour or more during the reference period; or persons who do not work for the reasons of study or on holiday, but had work units or sites during the reference period; or persons temporary absence from a job for disorganization or suspension of work, recession, etc. but not exceeding three months during the reference period.

## Employed Staff and Workers

Refer to persons who signed labor contracts with working units and working units would pay wages, social insurance and housing funds for them. Persons who have their work posts but are temporarily absent from work for reasons of study or on sick, injury or maternal leave and still receive wages from their working units are also included. Employed staff and workers also include:

1) Persons who should have signed the labor contracts but not (like people with rural household registration);

2) Employees on probation;

3) Employees beyond the staffing quota, for example, temporary employees;

4) Employees who are sent to other working units but still obtain wages from their original units (situations like on-the-job placement, expatriated assignment, etc.).

## State-owned Units

Refer to economic units whose assets are owned by the state. Included are non-corporation units registered according to Regulation of the People's Republic of China on the Registration of Enterprises and Corporations, state organs, institutions and social organizations at the central and local levels.

## Collective Units

Refer to economic units registered according to Regulation of the People's Republic of China on the Registration of Enterprises and Corporations where the means of production are collectively owned.

## Total Wage Bill

It is revised according to the "Provision of Composition of Total Wages" (Order No.1 by National Bureau of Statistics on January, 1st, ,1990), total wage bill refers to the total remuneration payment to all employed persons in various units during the reporting period (by quarter or by year), including hourly-paid wages, piece-rate wages, bonuses, allowance and subsidies, overtime wages and wages paid under special circumstances. It equals to the sum of total wages of employed staff and workers, dispatch labors and other employed persons.

Total wage bill is pre-tax wages, including the room charges, utility bills, housing funds and social insurance paid or withheld by employee's units.

Total wage bill, whether or not included in cost, whether or not paid in money or in kind, shall be included in the calculation of total wage.

## Average Wage

Refers to the average per capita wage during a certain period of time for employed persons. It shows the general level of wage income during a certain period of time, one major indicator to reflect the wage level. It is calculated as follows:

*Average Earning of Employees=Total Wage Bill of Employed Persons at Reference Time/Average Number of Persons Employed at Reference Time.*

## Registered Unemployed Persons in Urban Areas

Refer to the persons with non-agricultural household registration at certain working ages (16 years old to retirement age), who are capable of working, unemployed and willing to work, and have been registered at the local employment service agencies to apply for a job.

## Registered Unemployment Rate in Urban Areas

Refers to the ratio of the number of the registered unemployed persons to the sum of the number of persons employed in various units (minus the employed rural labour force, re-employed retirees, and Hong Kong, Macao, Taiwan or foreign employees), laid-off staff and workers in urban units, owners of private enterprises in urban areas, owners of self-employed individuals in urban areas, employees of private enterprises in urban areas, employee of self-employed individuals in urban areas, and the registered unemployed persons in urban areas.

# 第四章·固定资产投资

## INVESTMENT IN FIXED ASSETS

# 简要说明

## BRIEF INTRODUCTION

本章内容主要包括全社会固定资产投资、建设项目投资、房地产开发和商品房销售情况，由市统计局固定资产投资处整理提供。

The data in this chapter cover the total investment in fixed assets, investment in construction, real estate development, sales of commercialized buildings. All the data are prepared and provided by Division of Statistics of Investment in Fixed Assets, Chongqing Municipal Bureau of Statistics.

# 表 4.1 全社会固定资产投资增长情况(1997-2022 年)
## GROWTH RATE OF TOTAL INVESTMENT IN FIXED ASSETS (1997-2022)

单位:%(%)

| 年 份<br>Year | 固定资产投资<br>Investment in Fixed Assets | 固定资产投资按投资领域分<br>Fixed asset investment (divided by investment field) | | |
|---|---|---|---|---|
| | | 基础设施投资<br>Infrastructure | 工业投资<br>Industrial Investment | 房地产开发投资<br>Real Estate Development |
| 1997 | 15.7 | 45.5 | 8.3 | 21.4 |
| 1998 | 34.3 | 103.9 | 10.9 | 44.1 |
| 1999 | 13.0 | 15.8 | -12.4 | 15.6 |
| 2000 | 16.5 | 15.7 | 17.1 | 24.1 |
| 2001 | 22.3 | 22.9 | 1.5 | 40.8 |
| 2002 | 24.2 | 22.7 | 31.1 | 25.0 |
| 2003 | 27.5 | 28.1 | 46.5 | 33.3 |
| 2004 | 27.8 | 20.0 | 51.8 | 23.5 |
| 2005 | 23.7 | 22.2 | 41.8 | 27.8 |
| 2006 | 22.2 | 27.6 | 30.2 | 21.6 |
| 2007 | 28.9 | 16.6 | 44.0 | 35.0 |
| 2008 | 28.0 | 20.8 | 30.0 | 16.6 |
| 2009 | 31.5 | 28.3 | 30.2 | 25.0 |
| 2010 | 30.4 | 23.9 | 24.6 | 30.8 |
| 2011 | 31.0 | 21.4 | 33.4 | 24.4 |
| 2012 | 22.0 | 24.8 | 21.1 | 24.5 |
| 2013 | 19.5 | 23.2 | 15.2 | 20.1 |
| 2014 | 18.0 | 14.3 | 18.0 | 20.5 |
| 2015 | 17.1 | 28.6 | 19.8 | 3.3 |
| 2016 | 12.1 | 30.0 | 13.5 | -0.7 |
| 2017 | 9.5 | 15.8 | 8.9 | 6.8 |
| 2018 | 7.0 | 11.5 | 7.3 | 6.8 |
| 2019 | 5.7 | -0.7 | 8.8 | 4.5 |
| 2020 | 3.9 | 9.6 | 5.8 | -2.0 |
| 2021 | 6.1 | 7.4 | 9.1 | 0.1 |
| 2022 | 0.7 | 9.0 | 10.4 | -20.4 |

注:1)2018 年开始,国家统计局规定各省市固定资产投资统计只发布增速数据。
2)除特殊注明外,4-1 至 4-16 表中数据均为固定资产投资(不含农户)口径。
Note:a)Since 2018, National Bureau of Statistics stipulated that the fixed asset investment statistics of all provinces and cities only release growth rate data.
b) Unless otherwise specified, data in Tables 4-1 to 4-16 refer to Investment in Fixed Assets (excluding rural household).

## 表 4.2 主要年份民间固定资产投资增长情况（2012-2022 年）
## GROWTH RATE OF NON-GOVERNMENTAL INVESTMENT IN FIXED ASSETS (2012-2022)

单位：%（%）

| 年 份<br>Year | 民间投资增速<br>Non-governmental Investment in Fixed Assets | 占固定资产投资比重<br>As Percentage of Total Investment |
|---|---|---|
| 2012 | 25.9 | 45.1 |
| 2013 | 27.7 | 46.1 |
| 2014 | 27.1 | 49.6 |
| 2015 | 17.9 | 49.9 |
| 2016 | 11.0 | 51.0 |
| 2017 | 13.5 | 54.6 |
| 2018 | 12.8 | 54.9 |
| 2019 | 3.3 | 53.6 |
| 2020 | 1.1 | 52.2 |
| 2021 | 9.3 | 53.8 |
| 2022 | -8.4 | 47.0 |

## 表 4.3 全社会固定资产投资资金来源（2021-2022 年）
## SOURCES OF FUNDS FOR INVESTMENT IN FIXED ASSETS (2021-2022)

单位：亿元 (100 million yuan)

| 指 标 | Item | 2021 | 2022 |
|---|---|---|---|
| **本年资金来源合计** | **Total Investment from All Sources in Current Year** | **14784.71** | **14037.56** |
| 上年末结余资金 | Balance of the Previous Year | 2231.45 | 2315.40 |
| 本年资金来源小计 | Subtotal of Funds Invested in This Year | 12553.25 | 11722.16 |
| 国家预算内资金 | State Budgetary Appropriation | 670.21 | 979.56 |
| 国内贷款 | Domestic Loans | 1658.85 | 1658.93 |
| 债 券 | Bonds | 87.49 | 105.77 |
| 利用外资 | Foreign Investment | 51.70 | 54.20 |
| 自筹资金 | Self-raised Funds | 5470.10 | 5995.12 |
| 其他资金来源 | Others | 4614.90 | 2928.58 |

注：2019 年起固定资产投资项目到位资金统计范围由计划总投资 500 万元及以上调整为 5000 万元及以上项目（以下相关表同）。
Note: Since 2019, the statistic scope of the actual funds for investment in fixed assets is adjusted from 5 million above yuan planned investment to 50 million and above planned total investment.

# 表 4.4 全社会固定资产投资构成（2021－2022 年）
## COMPOSITION OF TOTAL INVESTMENT IN FIXED ASSETS (2021-2022)

| 指　标 | Item | 构　成（%）Structure (%) | |
|---|---|---|---|
| | | 2021 | 2022 |
| **投资总额（万元）** | **Total Investment (10 000 yuan)** | **100.0** | **100.0** |
| **按隶属关系分** | **By Jurisdiction of Administration** | | |
| 中央项目 | Central Investment | 6.3 | 7.1 |
| 地方项目（包括无隶属关系的） | Local Investment (including non-governmental investment) | 93.7 | 92.9 |
| **按登记注册类型分** | **By Status of Registration** | | |
| 内　资 | Domestic-funded | 95.7 | 95.9 |
| #国　有 | State-owned | 9.5 | 11.1 |
| 集　体 | Collective-owned | 0.2 | 0.4 |
| 股份合作企业 | Cooperative Enterprise | 0.03 | 0.04 |
| 联　营 | Joint | 0.01 | 0.05 |
| 有限责任公司 | Limited Liability | 41.8 | 44.2 |
| 股份有限公司 | Share-holding | 2.1 | 1.8 |
| 私　营 | Private | 40.5 | 36.9 |
| 其　他 | Others | 1.5 | 1.4 |
| 港澳台投资经济 | Funds from Hong Kong, Macao and Taiwan | 2.8 | 2.7 |
| 外商投资经济 | Foreign-funded | 1.5 | 1.4 |
| **按构成分** | **By Use of Funds** | | |
| 建筑工程 | Construction | 61.8 | 65.5 |
| 安装工程 | Installation | 7.9 | 8.6 |
| 设备工具器具购置 | Purchase of Equipment and Instruments | 10.0 | 12.5 |
| 其他费用 | Others | 20.4 | 13.4 |

# 表 4.5 各行业按构成分固定资产投资比上年增长情况（2022 年）
## GROWTH RATE OF TOTAL INVESTMENT IN FIXED ASSETS OVER PRECEDING YEAR BY COMPOSITION OF INVESTMENT (2022)

单位：%（%）

| 指　标 | Item | 全部投资 Total Investment in Fixed Assets | 建筑安装工程投资 Constructions and Installations | 设备工器具购置 Purchase of Equipments and Instruments | 其他费用 Other Expenses |
|---|---|---|---|---|---|
| **总　计** | **Total** | **0.7** | **6.0** | **-5.4** | **-14.4** |
| 第一产业 | Primary Industry | 19.9 | 22.8 | 13.3 | -8.4 |
| 第二产业 | Secondary Industry | 11.0 | 18.1 | -8.8 | 24.1 |
| 工　业 | Industry | 10.4 | 18.2 | -8.9 | 24.1 |
| 采矿业 | Mining | 13.2 | 9.8 | 11.9 | 112.9 |
| 制造业 | Manufacturing | 8.8 | 19.2 | -11.1 | 12.7 |
| 电力、热力、燃气及水的生产和供应业 | Production and Supply of Electricity, Heat, Gas & Water | 23.3 | 16.0 | 23.8 | 58.6 |
| 建筑业 | Construction | 1.8 | -3.2 | 105.1 | |
| 第三产业 | Tertiary Industry | -3.4 | 1.7 | 5.7 | -17.9 |
| 批发与零售业 | Wholesale and Retail Trades | -5.4 | 11.4 | -31.8 | -54.6 |
| 交通运输、仓储及邮政业 | Transport, Storage and Post | 4.4 | 5.3 | 33.0 | -2.4 |
| 住宿和餐饮业 | Hotels and Catering Services | -1.1 | 14.3 | -31.8 | -77.0 |
| 信息传输、计算机服务和软件业 | Information Transmission, Computer Services and Software | 33.2 | 76.7 | 4.1 | -53.8 |
| 金融业 | Financial Intermediation | -95.5 | -94.8 | | |
| 房地产业 | Real Estate | -20.4 | -14.7 | -7.5 | -31.9 |
| 租赁与商务服务业 | Leasing and Business Services | 40.8 | 44.9 | -37.3 | 51.1 |
| 科学研究、技术服务与地质勘查业 | Scientific Research, Technical Services and Geological Prospecting | 144.8 | 143.6 | 60.9 | 250.6 |
| 水利、环境和公共设施管理业 | Management of Water Conservancy, Environment and Public Facilities | 13.5 | 9.3 | -19.4 | 36.4 |
| 居民服务和其他服务业 | Services to Households and Other Services | 33.0 | 29.8 | 106.3 | 23.9 |
| 教　育 | Education | 14.8 | 19.4 | 35.0 | -9.8 |
| 卫生、社会保障和社会福利业 | Health, Social Security and Social Welfare | 21.8 | 36.4 | 13.2 | -40.5 |
| 文化、体育与娱乐业 | Culture, Sports and Entertainment | 45.9 | 54.9 | 74.1 | -25.9 |
| 公共管理与社会组织 | Public Management and Social Organizations | -31.4 | -39.3 | -50.7 | 65.0 |

# 表 4.6 各行业按建设性质分固定资产投资比上年增长情况(2022 年)
GROWTH RATE OF TOTAL INVESTMENT IN FIXED ASSETS OVER PRECEDING YEAR BY SECTOR AND TYPE OF CONSTRUCTION (2022)

单位: % (%)

| 指 标 | Item | 全部投资 Total Investment in Fixed Assets | #新 建 New Construction | 扩 建 Expansion | 改建和技术改造 Reconstruction and Technical Transformation |
|---|---|---|---|---|---|
| **总 计** | **Total** | **0.7** | **1.2** | **5.4** | **-4.7** |
| 第一产业 | Primary Industry | 19.9 | 15.1 | 39.4 | -7.3 |
| 第二产业 | Secondary Industry | 11.0 | 7.0 | 28.1 | 8.7 |
| 工 业 | Industry | 10.4 | 7.0 | 28.1 | 8.7 |
| 采矿业 | Mining | 13.2 | 50.9 | -25.5 | 104.6 |
| 制造业 | Manufacturing | 8.8 | 2.7 | 50.3 | 7.4 |
| 电力、热力、燃气及水的生产和供应业 | Production and Supply of Electricity, Heat, Gas & Water | 23.3 | 26.4 | 32.1 | -0.2 |
| 建筑业 | Construction | 1.8 | -1.3 | | |
| 第三产业 | Tertiary Industry | -3.4 | -1.4 | -21.0 | -15.5 |
| 批发与零售业 | Wholesale and Retail Trades | -5.4 | -2.6 | 45.4 | -20.3 |
| 交通运输、仓储及邮政业 | Transport, Storage and Post | 4.4 | 7.0 | 2.9 | -31.6 |
| 住宿和餐饮业 | Hotels and Catering Services | -1.1 | 2.6 | -49.4 | -32.0 |
| 信息传输、计算机服务和软件业 | Information Transmission, Computer Services and Software | 33.2 | 51.8 | -32.9 | 408.6 |
| 金融业 | Financial Intermediation | -95.5 | -96.8 | | -86.8 |
| 房地产业 | Real Estate | -20.4 | -20.0 | 12.7 | -17.6 |
| 租赁与商务服务业 | Leasing and Business Services | 40.8 | 48.6 | -10.7 | -51.0 |
| 科学研究、技术服务与地质勘查业 | Scientific Research, Technical Services and Geological Prospecting | 144.8 | 146.3 | 562.4 | 32.3 |
| 水利、环境和公共设施管理业 | Management of Water Conservancy, Environment and Public Facilities | 13.5 | 13.7 | -13.0 | 23.1 |
| 居民服务和其他服务业 | Services to Households and Other Services | 33.0 | 37.1 | 350.9 | -67.0 |
| 教 育 | Education | 14.8 | 12.4 | 71.5 | -31.0 |
| 卫生、社会保障和社会福利业 | Health, Social Security and Social Welfare | 21.8 | 25.5 | -60.2 | 209.5 |
| 文化、体育与娱乐业 | Culture, Sports and Entertainment | 45.9 | 50.2 | 77.7 | -5.2 |
| 公共管理与社会组织 | Public Management and Social Organizations | -31.4 | -38.9 | -75.4 | -10.0 |

# 表 4.7 各行业按登记注册类型分固定资产投资比上年增长情况（2022 年）

## GROWTH RATE OF TOTAL INVESTMENT IN FIXED ASSETS OVER PRECEDING YEAR BY SECTOR AND REGISTRATION STATUS (2022)

单位：%（%）

| 指 标 | Item | 全部投资 Total Investment in Fixed Assets | #内 资 Domestic Funded | 港澳台投资 Funds from Hong Kong,Macao and Taiwan | 外商投资 Foreign Funded |
|---|---|---|---|---|---|
| **总 计** | **Total** | **0.7** | **1.1** | **-5.6** | **-10.6** |
| 第一产业 | Primary Industry | 19.9 | 19.9 | | |
| 第二产业 | Secondary Industry | 11.0 | 10.5 | 29.2 | -14.7 |
| 工 业 | Industry | 10.4 | 10.5 | 29.2 | -14.7 |
| 采矿业 | Mining | 13.2 | 13.0 | | |
| 制造业 | Manufacturing | 8.8 | 9.0 | 25.0 | -12.8 |
| 电力、热力、燃气及水的生产和供应业 | Production and Supply of Electricity, Heat, Gas & Water | 23.3 | 22.5 | 132.2 | -71.4 |
| 建筑业 | Construction | 1.8 | 1.8 | | |
| 第三产业 | Tertiary Industry | -3.4 | -2.8 | -29.7 | -65.3 |
| 批发与零售业 | Wholesale and Retail Trades | -5.4 | -6.4 | | 44.8 |
| 交通运输、仓储及邮政业 | Transport, Storage and Post | 4.4 | 4.9 | -42.9 | -31.5 |
| 住宿和餐饮业 | Hotels and Catering Services | -1.1 | -0.6 | -18.8 | -13.3 |
| 信息传输、计算机服务和软件业 | Information Transmission, Computer Services and Software | 33.2 | 54.8 | 14.9 | -83.3 |
| 金融业 | Financial Intermediation | -95.5 | -95.5 | | |
| 房地产业 | Real Estate | -20.4 | -26.8 | -24.8 | 19.6 |
| 租赁与商务服务业 | Leasing and Business Services | 40.8 | 40.4 | -71.0 | 200.0 |
| 科学研究、技术服务与地质勘查业 | Scientific Research, Technical Services and Geological Prospecting | 144.8 | 144.5 | | |
| 水利、环境和公共设施管理业 | Management of Water Conservancy, Environment and Public Facilities | 13.5 | 13.6 | -33.0 | |
| 居民服务和其他服务业 | Services to Households and Other Services | 33.0 | 34.5 | -80.9 | |
| 教 育 | Education | 14.8 | 14.9 | -24.5 | |
| 卫生、社会保障和社会福利业 | Health, Social Security and Social Welfare | 21.8 | 22.1 | | 27.3 |
| 文化、体育与娱乐业 | Culture, Sports and Entertainment | 45.9 | 45.9 | | |
| 公共管理与社会组织 | Public Management and Social Organizations | -31.4 | -31.4 | | |

## 表 4.8 各行业实际到位资金比上年增长情况(2022 年)
GROWTH RATE OF ACTUAL FUNDS AVAILABLE FOR INVESTMENT OVER PRECEDING YEAR BY SECTOR (2022)

单位:%(%)

| 指 标 | Item | 本年实际到位资金 Actual Funds Available for Investment | 国家预算资金 State Budget | 国内贷款 Domestic Loans |
|---|---|---|---|---|
| **总 计** | **Total** | **-6.6** | **46.2** | **0.0** |
| 第一产业 | Primary Industry | 25.3 | 36.4 | -0.6 |
| 第二产业 | Secondary Industry | 10.3 | 23.8 | 67.3 |
| 工 业 | Industry | 10.3 | 23.8 | 67.3 |
| 采矿业 | Mining | 16.6 | 636.3 | 0.4 |
| 制造业 | Manufacturing | 8.0 | 108.7 | 73.4 |
| 电力、热力、燃气及水的生产和供应业 | Production and Supply of Electricity, Heat, Gas & Water | 31.1 | -19.0 | 81.1 |
| 建筑业 | Construction | 6.9 | | |
| 第三产业 | Tertiary Industry | -11.8 | 46.8 | -8.4 |
| 批发与零售业 | Wholesale and Retail Trades | -3.3 | 824.7 | -26.0 |
| 交通运输、仓储及邮政业 | Transport, Storage and Post | 30.5 | 45.3 | 3.9 |
| 住宿和餐饮业 | Hotels and Catering Services | 15.1 | -88.0 | 57.4 |
| 信息传输、计算机服务和软件业 | Information Transmission, Computer Services and Software | 51.1 | -5.1 | 339.7 |
| 金融业 | Financial Intermediation | -97.3 | | |
| 房地产业 | Real Estate | -41.9 | | -34.4 |
| 租赁与商务服务业 | Leasing and Business Services | 42.1 | -10.0 | -64.1 |
| 科学研究、技术服务与地质勘查业 | Scientific Research, Technical Services and Geological Prospecting | 152.8 | 112.4 | 174.1 |
| 水利、环境和公共设施管理业 | Management of Water Conservancy, Environment and Public Facilities | 29.8 | 64.5 | 3.1 |
| 居民服务和其他服务业 | Services to Households and Other Services | 57.1 | 69.1 | -60.7 |
| 教 育 | Education | 28.8 | 5.3 | 80.5 |
| 卫生、社会保障和社会福利业 | Health, Social Security and Social Welfare | 28.3 | 19.2 | -8.7 |
| 文化、体育与娱乐业 | Culture, Sports and Entertainment | 72.9 | 61.2 | 103.7 |
| 公共管理与社会组织 | Public Management and Social Organizations | -14.9 | -34.0 | 3.1 |

**表 4.8 续表 continued**

单位：%（%）

| 指　标 | Item | 利用外资<br>Foreign Investment | 自筹资金<br>Self-raised Funds | 其他资金<br>Other Funds |
|---|---|---|---|---|
| **总　计** | **Total** | **4.8** | **9.6** | **-36.5** |
| 第一产业 | Primary Industry | | 26.8 | 50.1 |
| 第二产业 | Secondary Industry | -25.9 | 5.5 | 20.6 |
| 工　业 | Industry | -25.9 | 5.5 | 20.7 |
| 采矿业 | Mining | | 15.6 | 63.1 |
| 制造业 | Manufacturing | -34.3 | 3.8 | 24.2 |
| 电力、热力、燃气及水的生产和供应业 | Production and Supply of Electricity, Heat, Gas & Water | 1171.7 | 28.0 | 4.0 |
| 建筑业 | Construction | | 11.0 | |
| 第三产业 | Tertiary Industry | 300.6 | 12.9 | -43.6 |
| 批发与零售业 | Wholesale and Retail Trades | | 0.8 | -46.3 |
| 交通运输、仓储及邮政业 | Transport, Storage and Post | 763.9 | 32.4 | 79.7 |
| 住宿和餐饮业 | Hotels and Catering Services | | 29.3 | -68.7 |
| 信息传输、计算机服务和软件业 | Information Transmission, Computer Services and Software | | 31.2 | -63.2 |
| 金融业 | Financial Intermediation | | -97.7 | -97.1 |
| 房地产业 | Real Estate | 1872.3 | -11.1 | -46.5 |
| 租赁与商务服务业 | Leasing and Business Services | -31.7 | 35.8 | 225.3 |
| 科学研究、技术服务与地质勘查业 | Scientific Research, Technical Services and Geological Prospecting | | 139.1 | 78.6 |
| 水利、环境和公共设施管理业 | Management of Water Conservancy, Environment and Public Facilities | -46.8 | 19.9 | 45.7 |
| 居民服务和其他服务业 | Services to Households and Other Services | | 137.3 | -23.2 |
| 教　育 | Education | 33.3 | 46.2 | -11.3 |
| 卫生、社会保障和社会福利业 | Health, Social Security and Social Welfare | | 25.1 | 49.4 |
| 文化、体育与娱乐业 | Culture, Sports and Entertainment | -37.1 | 60.9 | 191.2 |
| 公共管理与社会组织 | Public Management and Social Organizations | | -8.1 | 19.5 |

注：房地产业中其他资金包含定金及预收款、个人按揭贷款。
Note: The data of rural households is excluded herein.

# 表 4.9 按行业分建设项目投资和建设总规模比上年增长情况（2022 年）
## CHANGE IN INVESTMENT IN CONSTRUCTION PROJECTS AND TOTAL CONSTRUCTION INVESTMENT SIZE BY SECTOR COMPARED WITH THE LAST YEAR (2022)

单位：%（%）

| 指 标 | Item | 建设总规模 Total Investment in Construction | 在建总规模 Total Investment in Projects under Construction | 在建净规模 Net Investment in Projects under Construction | 投资额 Investment |
|---|---|---|---|---|---|
| **总 计** | **Total** | **9.6** | **9.7** | **4.4** | **12.1** |
| 第一产业 | Primary Industry | 15.0 | 21.2 | 91.4 | 19.9 |
| 第二产业 | Secondary Industry | 8.9 | 13.0 | 19.2 | 11.0 |
| 工 业 | Industry | 8.9 | 13.0 | 19.2 | 10.4 |
| 采矿业 | Mining | 5.8 | 27.0 | 13.8 | 13.2 |
| 制造业 | Manufacturing | 8.9 | 10.7 | 8.2 | 8.8 |
| 电力、热力、燃气及水的生产和供应业 | Production and Supply of Electricity, Heat, Gas & Water | 10.0 | 26.4 | 184.6 | 23.3 |
| 建筑业 | Construction | -23.1 | -1.4 | 69.8 | 1.8 |
| 第三产业 | Tertiary Industry | 9.8 | 7.9 | -1.4 | 12.4 |
| 批发与零售业 | Wholesale and Retail Trades | -2.1 | -11.6 | -20.1 | -5.4 |
| 交通运输、仓储及邮政业 | Transport, Storage and Post | 2.7 | -0.2 | -15.2 | 4.4 |
| 住宿和餐饮业 | Hotels and Catering Services | -8.8 | -17.5 | -39.4 | -1.1 |
| 信息传输、计算机服务和软件业 | Information Transmission, Computer Services and Software | 36.7 | 46.1 | 65.5 | 33.2 |
| 金融业 | Financial Intermediation | -92.7 | -72.7 | -91.8 | -95.5 |
| 房地产业 | Real Estate | 21.8 | 26.0 | 27.6 | 18.5 |
| 租赁与商务服务业 | Leasing and Business Services | 17.8 | 35.8 | 55.4 | 40.8 |
| 科学研究、技术服务与地质勘查业 | Scientific Research, Technical Services and Geological Prospecting | 101.2 | 108.5 | 114.1 | 144.8 |
| 水利、环境和公共设施管理业 | Management of Water Conservancy, Environment and Public Facilities | 11.1 | 8.4 | -1.0 | 13.5 |
| 居民服务和其他服务业 | Services to Households and Other Services | 54.7 | 84.4 | 90.8 | 33.0 |
| 教 育 | Education | 19.3 | 21.6 | 8.2 | 14.8 |
| 卫生、社会保障和社会福利业 | Health, Social Security and Social Welfare | 13.2 | 14.4 | 6.0 | 21.8 |
| 文化、体育与娱乐业 | Culture, Sports and Entertainment | 56.5 | 66.2 | 123.9 | 45.9 |
| 公共管理与社会组织 | Public Management and Social Organizations | -3.6 | -20.4 | -18.7 | -31.4 |

注：本表数据不包含房地产开发投资项目。
Note: The data of rural households is excluded herein.

# 表 4.10 按行业分建设项目施工、投产项目个数（2022 年）
## NUMBER OF CONSTRUCTION PROJECTS UNDER CONSTRUCTION AND PUT INTO USE BY SECTOR (2022)

| 指　标 | Item | 施工项目（个）Number of Projects under Construction (unit) | #新开工 New Projects | 全部建成投产项目（个）Number of Projects Completed & Put into Use (unit) | 项目建成投产率(%) Rate of Projects Completed & Put into Use (%) |
|---|---|---|---|---|---|
| **总　计** | **Total** | **16182** | **7728** | **7791** | **48.1** |
| 第一产业 | Primary Industry | 1283 | 810 | 692 | 53.9 |
| 第二产业 | Secondary Industry | 6027 | 2795 | 2947 | 48.9 |
| 工　业 | Industry | 6019 | 2792 | 2947 | 49.0 |
| 采矿业 | Mining | 197 | 105 | 84 | 42.6 |
| 制造业 | Manufacturing | 5326 | 2486 | 2667 | 50.0 |
| 电力、热力、燃气及水的生产和供应业 | Production and Supply of Electricity, Heat, Gas & Water | 496 | 201 | 196 | 39.5 |
| 建筑业 | Construction | 8 | 3 | | |
| 第三产业 | Tertiary Industry | 8872 | 4123 | 4152 | 46.8 |
| 批发与零售业 | Wholesale and Retail Trades | 1596 | 671 | 669 | 41.9 |
| 交通运输、仓储及邮政业 | Transport, Storage and Post | 277 | 113 | 135 | 48.7 |
| 住宿和餐饮业 | Hotels and Catering Services | 263 | 127 | 130 | 49.4 |
| 信息传输、计算机服务和软件业 | Information Transmission, Computer Services and Software | 183 | 94 | 91 | 49.7 |
| 金融业 | Financial Intermediation | 3 | 2 | 2 | 66.7 |
| 房地产业 | Real Estate | 256 | 95 | 91 | 35.5 |
| 租赁与商务服务业 | Leasing and Business Services | 163 | 68 | 70 | 42.9 |
| 科学研究、技术服务与地质勘查业 | Scientific Research, Technical Services and Geological Prospecting | 131 | 65 | 35 | 26.7 |
| 水利、环境和公共设施管理业 | Management of Water Conservancy, Environment and Public Facilities | 3937 | 1850 | 1894 | 48.1 |
| 居民服务和其他服务业 | Services to Households and Other Services | 57 | 31 | 28 | 49.1 |
| 教　育 | Education | 482 | 185 | 197 | 40.9 |
| 卫生、社会保障和社会福利业 | Health, Social Security and Social Welfare | 346 | 133 | 161 | 46.5 |
| 文化、体育与娱乐业 | Culture, Sports and Entertainment | 833 | 511 | 453 | 54.4 |
| 公共管理与社会组织 | Public Management and Social Organizations | 125 | 51 | 65 | 52.0 |

## 表 4.11 工业投资按行业分构成（2021 − 2022 年）
## INDUSTRIAL INVESTMENT BY SECTOR (2021-2022)

单位：%（%）

| 指　标 | Item | 2021 | 2022 |
|---|---|---|---|
| 合　计 | **Total** | **100.0** | **100.0** |
| 采矿业 | Mining | 5.3 | 5.9 |
| 煤炭开采和洗选业 | Mining and Washing of Coal | 0.1 | 0.0 |
| 石油和天然气开采业 | Extraction of Petroleum and Natural Gas | 2.7 | 3.4 |
| 黑色金属矿采选业 | Mining and Processing of Ferrous Metal Ores | 0.1 | 0.0 |
| 有色金属矿采选业 | Mining and Processing of Non-ferrous Metal Ores | | 0.0 |
| 非金属矿采选业 | Mining and Processing of Non-metal Ores | 1.3 | 1.6 |
| 开采辅助活动 | Support Activities for Mining | 1.2 | 0.7 |
| 其他采矿业 | Mining of Other Ores | | 0.2 |
| 制造业 | Manufacturing | 85.5 | 83.4 |
| 农副食品加工业 | Processing of Food from Agricultural Products | 3.4 | 4.7 |
| 食品制造业 | Manufacture of Foods | 2.5 | 1.7 |
| 酒、饮料和精制茶制造业 | Manufacture of Liquor, Beverages and Refined Tea | 0.9 | 1.1 |
| 烟草制品业 | Manufacture of Tobacco | 0.1 | 0.1 |
| 纺织业 | Manufacture of Textile | 0.2 | 0.3 |
| 纺织服装、服饰业 | Manufacture of Textile, Wearing Apparel and Accessories | 0.4 | 0.7 |
| 皮革、毛皮、羽毛及其制品和制鞋业 | Manufacture of Leather, Fur, Feather and Related Products and Footwear | 0.2 | 0.2 |
| 木材加工和木、竹、藤、棕、草制品业 | Processing of Timber, Manufacture of Wood, Bamboo, Rattan, Palm and Straw Products | 0.9 | 1.0 |
| 家具制造业 | Manufacture of Furniture | 1.7 | 1.3 |
| 造纸及纸制品业 | Manufacture of Paper and Paper Products | 1.4 | 1.2 |
| 印刷和记录媒介复制业 | Printing and Reproduction of Recording Media | 0.7 | 0.8 |
| 文教、工美、体育和娱乐用品制造业 | Manufacture of Articles for Culture, Education, Arts and Crafts, Sport and Entertainment Activities | 0.7 | 0.9 |
| 石油加工、炼焦及核燃料加工业 | Processing of Petroleum, Coking and Processing of Nuclear Fuel | 0.2 | 0.1 |
| 化学原料及化学制品制造业 | Manufacture of Raw Chemical Materials and Chemical Products | 3.8 | 4.5 |
| 医药制造业 | Manufacture of Medicines | 3.6 | 3.7 |
| 化学纤维制造业 | Manufacture of Chemical Fibres | 0.4 | 0.7 |
| 橡胶和塑料制品业 | Manufacture of Rubber and Plastics Products | 2.9 | 2.8 |
| 非金属矿物制品业 | Manufacture of Non-metallic Mineral Products | 5.9 | 6.5 |
| 黑色金属冶炼和压延加工业 | Smelting and Pressing of Ferrous Metals | 1.6 | 1.1 |
| 有色金属冶炼和压延加工业 | Smelting and Pressing of Non-ferrous Metals | 4.7 | 1.7 |
| 金属制品业 | Manufacture of Metal Products | 3.6 | 3.0 |
| 通用设备制造业 | Manufacture of General Purpose Machinery | 4.1 | 3.4 |
| 专用设备制造业 | Manufacture of Special Purpose Machinery | 5.7 | 4.1 |
| 汽车制造业 | Manufacture of Automobiles | 9.7 | 11.3 |
| 铁路、船舶、航空航天和其他运输设备制造业 | Manufacture of Railway, Ship, Aerospace and Other Transport Equipment | 1.9 | 2.1 |
| 电气机械和器材制造业 | Manufacture of Electrical Machinery and Apparatus | 5.3 | 6.7 |
| 计算机、通信和其他电子设备制造业 | Manufacture of Computers, Communication and Other Electronic Equipment | 16.6 | 15.2 |
| 仪器仪表制造业 | Manufacture of Measuring Instruments and Machinery | 0.5 | 1.1 |
| 其他制造业 | Other Manufacture | 0.7 | 0.7 |
| 废弃资源综合利用业 | Utilization of Waste Resources | 0.9 | 0.8 |
| 金属制品、机械和设备修理业 | Repair Service of Metal Products, Machinery and Equipment | | 0.0 |
| 电力、热力、燃气及水生产和供应业 | Production and Supply of Electricity, Heat, Gas and Water | 9.2 | 10.7 |
| 电力、热力生产和供应业 | Production and Supply of Electric Power and Heat Power | 5.9 | 7.1 |
| 燃气生产和供应业 | Production and Supply of Gas | 1.0 | 1.5 |
| 水的生产和供应业 | Production and Supply of Water | 2.3 | 2.1 |

# 表 4.12 建设项目投资比上年增长情况(2021-2022 年)
GROWTH RATE OF INVESTMENT IN CONSTRUCTION PROJECTS COMPARED WITH THE LAST YEAR (2021-2022)

单位: % (%)

| 指 标 | Item | 2021 | 2022 |
|---|---|---|---|
| **投资总额** | **Total Investment (10 000 yuan)** | **9.6** | **12.1** |
| **按隶属关系分** | **By Jurisdiction of Administration** | | |
| 中央项目 | Central Investment | 12.3 | 3.1 |
| 地方项目 | Local Investment | 9.4 | 12.9 |
| **按构成分** | **By Use of Funds** | | |
| 建筑工程 | Construction | 8.9 | 15.0 |
| 安装工程 | Installation | 36.8 | 23.1 |
| 设备、工具、器具购置 | Purchase of Equipments and Instruments | 1.9 | -5.3 |
| 其他费用 | Others | 8.9 | 10.2 |
| **按建设性质分** | **By Type of Construction** | | |
| #新 建 | New Construction Projects | 8.7 | 12.6 |
| 扩 建 | Expansion | 3.5 | 16.8 |
| 改建和技术改造 | Reconstruction and Technical Transformation | 16.1 | 6.7 |
| **按国民经济行业分** | **By Sector** | | |
| 第一产业 | Primary Industry | 15.7 | 19.9 |
| 第二产业 | Secondary Industry | 8.0 | 11.0 |
| #工 业 | Industry | 9.1 | 10.4 |
| 第三产业 | Tertiary Industry | 10.4 | 12.4 |
| **新增固定资产(万元)** | **Newly Increased Fixed Assets (10 000 yuan)** | **40.6** | **11.7** |
| **建设项目(个)** | **Construction Projects (unit)** | | |
| 施工项目 | Projects under Construction | 4.8 | 6.2 |
| 本年投产项目 | Projects Completed in This Year | 5.7 | 2.5 |

## 表 4.13 按行业分的建设项目投资个数和规模（2022 年）
## NUMBER AND SCALE OF INVESTMENT IN CONSTRUCTION PROJECTS BY SECTOR (2022)

单位：万元 (10 000 yuan)

| 行 业 | Sector | 施工项目个数（个）<br>Number of In-process Project (unit) | 计 划 总投资<br>Planned Total Investment |
|---|---|---|---|
| **总 计** | **Total** | **16182** | **424213228** |
| 第一产业 | Primary Industry | 1283 | 8940268 |
| 第二产业 | Secondary Industry | 6027 | 138163788 |
| 工 业 | Industry | 6019 | 137956762 |
| 采矿业 | Mining | 197 | 4930773 |
| 制造业 | Manufacturing | 5326 | 119543038 |
| 电力、热力、燃气及水的生产和供应业 | Production and Supply of Electricity, Heat, Gas & Water | 496 | 13482951 |
| 建筑业 | Construction | 8 | 207026 |
| 第三产业 | Tertiary Industry | 8872 | 277109172 |
| 批发与零售业 | Wholesale and Retail Trades | 263 | 6032402 |
| 交通运输、仓储及邮政业 | Transport, Storage and Post | 1596 | 126425195 |
| 住宿和餐饮业 | Hotels and Catering Services | 183 | 1380281 |
| 信息传输、计算机服务和软件业 | Information Transmission, Computer Services and Software | 277 | 7523092 |
| 金融业 | Financial Intermediation | 3 | 17465 |
| 房地产业 | Real Estate | 256 | 9385842 |
| 租赁与商务服务业 | Leasing and Business Services | 163 | 5580111 |
| 科学研究、技术服务与地质勘查业 | Scientific Research, Technical Services and Geological Prospecting | 131 | 3821723 |
| 水利、环境和公共设施管理业 | Management of Water Conservancy, Environment and Public Facilities | 3937 | 82803465 |
| 居民服务和其他服务业 | Services to Households and Other Services | 57 | 437379 |
| 教 育 | Education | 482 | 10273772 |
| 卫生、社会保障和社会福利业 | Health, Social Security and Social Welfare | 346 | 8354645 |
| 文化、体育与娱乐业 | Culture, Sports and Entertainment | 833 | 12105362 |
| 公共管理、社会保障和社会组织 | Public Management, Social Security and Social Organizations | 125 | 1085281 |

注：该表数据中不含农户投资。
Note: The data of rural households is excluded herein.

# 表 4.14 基础设施建设投资构成（2021－2022 年）
## COMPOSITION OF INVESTMENT IN INFRASTRUCTURE CONSTRUCTION (2021-2022)

单位：%（%）

| 指　标 | Item | 2021 | 2022 |
|---|---|---|---|
| 合　计 | **Total** | **100.0** | **100.0** |
| 电力、热力、燃气及水的生产和供应业 | Production and Supply of Electricity, Heat, Gas and Water | 7.9 | 8.7 |
| #电力、热力的生产和供应业 | Production and Supply of Electric Power and Heat Power | 5.0 | 5.7 |
| 燃气生产和供应业 | Production and Supply of Gas | 0.8 | 1.3 |
| 水的生产和供应业 | Production and Supply of Water | 2.0 | 1.7 |
| 交通运输及邮政业 | Transport, Storage and Post | 47.8 | 46.1 |
| #交通运输业 | Transport | 47.6 | 45.9 |
| #城市公共交通业 | City Public Transport | 8.1 | 9.1 |
| 邮政业 | Post | 0.2 | 0.2 |
| 电信和其他信息传输服务业 | Telecommunications and Other Information Transmission Services | 2.7 | 2.3 |
| 水利、环境和公共设施管理业 | Management of Water Conservancy, Environment and Public Facilities | 41.6 | 42.9 |
| #水利管理业 | Management of Water Conservancy | 5.4 | 6.3 |
| 生态保护和环境治理业 | Ecology Protection and Environment Control | 3.0 | 3.3 |
| 公共设施管理业 | Management of Public Facilities | 33.2 | 33.3 |

# 表 4.15 房地产开发基本情况(1990 － 2022 年)
## BASIC STATISTICS ON REAL ESTATE DEVELOPMENT (1990-2022)

单位：万平方米 ( 10 000 sq.m )

| 年 份 Year | 企业数 (个) Number of Enterprises (unit) | 从业人员 (人) Number of Employed Persons (person) | 本年土地购置面积 Land Space Purchased This Year | 本年完成投资总额 (万元) Investment Completed This Year (10 000 yuan) | #住 宅 Residential Buildings | 资金来源 (万元) Sources of Funds (10 000 yuan) | 房屋施工面 积 Floor Space of Buildings under Construction | #住 宅 Residential Buildings |
|---|---|---|---|---|---|---|---|---|
| 1990 | | | | 17503 | 10600 | 17568 | 107.80 | 65.48 |
| 1991 | | | | 19185 | 14040 | 18042 | 112.57 | 83.54 |
| 1992 | | | | 33868 | 21239 | 33148 | 160.91 | 94.56 |
| 1993 | | | | 123151 | 66833 | 107210 | 437.73 | 293.03 |
| 1994 | | | | 279089 | 196411 | 377959 | 650.71 | 394.43 |
| 1995 | | | | 468845 | 252085 | 612121 | 1267.96 | 810.36 |
| 1996 | 635 | 22512 | 588.65 | 556185 | 259881 | 836655 | 1424.35 | 855.64 |
| 1997 | 622 | 24911 | 259.49 | 675022 | 282592 | 1060761 | 1652.32 | 904.18 |
| 1998 | 991 | 50088 | 521.48 | 973014 | 440889 | 1391253 | 2058.35 | 1223.66 |
| 1999 | 1073 | 50526 | 624.53 | 1125135 | 523357 | 1504042 | 2103.76 | 1285.41 |
| 2000 | 1339 | 63925 | 619.21 | 1396327 | 728125 | 1784950 | 2833.42 | 1896.18 |
| 2001 | 1474 | 78961 | 870.34 | 1966684 | 1107126 | 2373982 | 3653.71 | 2508.30 |
| 2002 | 1559 | 76582 | 1320.26 | 2459130 | 1306998 | 3148171 | 4414.96 | 3081.57 |
| 2003 | 1597 | 54148 | 1637.19 | 3278881 | 1774341 | 4793499 | 5287.80 | 3747.34 |
| 2004 | 1828 | 70711 | 1137.61 | 4050791 | 2171303 | 6220133 | 6247.86 | 4544.54 |
| 2005 | 1862 | 70563 | 1385.40 | 5177291 | 3004026 | 8819371 | 7487.36 | 5514.75 |
| 2006 | 1936 | 70094 | 1467.69 | 6296300 | 3767847 | 9985438 | 8864.37 | 6655.00 |
| 2007 | 2039 | 87606 | 1737.74 | 8498966 | 5218209 | 15546697 | 10578.84 | 8179.29 |
| 2008 | 2280 | 86094 | 1164.41 | 9909970 | 6195250 | 15595559 | 11639.27 | 9166.21 |
| 2009 | 2359 | 87818 | 1227.79 | 12389125 | 7890183 | 22026661 | 13052.60 | 10338.12 |
| 2010 | 2391 | 86602 | 1354.93 | 16202571 | 10914854 | 34393672 | 17138.50 | 13744.78 |
| 2011 | 2453 | 94535 | 1664.55 | 20150883 | 14384457 | 44332807 | 20397.24 | 15923.84 |
| 2012 | 2552 | 89482 | 2183.07 | 25083500 | 17067687 | 51082969 | 22009.03 | 16997.85 |
| 2013 | 2594 | 93207 | 1896.65 | 30127838 | 20442392 | 58468351 | 26251.89 | 19248.95 |
| 2014 | 2695 | 94579 | 1864.59 | 36302331 | 24513660 | 67627353 | 28623.93 | 20294.49 |
| 2015 | 2585 | 95326 | 1626.77 | 37512812 | 23904910 | 66028296 | 28985.67 | 19390.32 |
| 2016 | 2467 | 98199 | 959.00 | 37259452 | 23199701 | 63546787 | 27363.39 | 17932.69 |
| 2017 | 2316 | 103130 | 1112.22 | 39800837 | 26328813 | 75021329 | 25960.99 | 16747.92 |
| 2018 | 2250 | 101326 | 1260.92 | 42487612 | 30126477 | 84089315 | 27226.56 | 17859.42 |
| 2019 | 2226 | 100845 | 641.58 | 44393034 | 32467657 | 80275546 | 27986.64 | 18466.12 |
| 2020 | 2278 | 101727 | 812.95 | 43519565 | 31890503 | 75973485 | 27368.16 | 18241.78 |
| 2021 | 2323 | 95596 | 694.50 | 43549551 | 32881139 | 57237673 | 26893.17 | 17709.78 |
| 2022 | 2208 | 82939 | 256.74 | 32168663 | 24110429 | 32321349 | 22646.90 | 14984.24 |

**表 4.15 续表 continued**

单位: 万平方米 ( 10 000 sq.m )

| 年 份 Year | 房屋新开工面 积 Floor Space of Buildings Started This Year | #住 宅 Residential Buildings | 房屋竣工面 积 Floor Space of Buildings Completed | #住 宅 Residential Buildings | 商品房销售面积 Floor Space of Commercialized Buildings Sold | #住 宅 Residential Buildings | 商品房销售额（万元） Sales of Commercialized Buildings (10 000 yuan) | #住 宅 Residential Buildings |
|---|---|---|---|---|---|---|---|---|
| 1990 | | | 46.16 | 34.16 | 23.29 | | 17648 | |
| 1991 | | | 37.33 | 28.61 | 27.48 | | 20007 | |
| 1992 | | | 45.90 | 30.48 | 32.87 | | 29583 | |
| 1993 | | | 81.05 | 66.01 | 37.39 | | 42221 | |
| 1994 | | | 141.27 | 115.05 | 46.32 | | 55336 | |
| 1995 | | | 258.25 | 208.70 | 114.61 | | 116657 | |
| 1996 | 348.68 | 220.54 | 351.76 | 275.62 | 166.21 | 142.98 | 189856 | 145507 |
| 1997 | 470.34 | 299.69 | 459.92 | 358.36 | 260.78 | 215.33 | 313111 | 222376 |
| 1998 | 914.23 | 596.44 | 600.04 | 422.61 | 416.82 | 359.73 | 554786 | 417609 |
| 1999 | 847.51 | 608.43 | 619.56 | 438.56 | 429.98 | 364.56 | 591992 | 393569 |
| 2000 | 1290.05 | 969.26 | 849.42 | 622.08 | 579.96 | 491.09 | 783709 | 528698 |
| 2001 | 1661.19 | 1259.38 | 1020.63 | 738.41 | 746.05 | 635.04 | 1076534 | 719196 |
| 2002 | 1709.47 | 1277.55 | 1390.73 | 1033.60 | 1016.58 | 870.41 | 1581505 | 1111929 |
| 2003 | 2098.24 | 1580.04 | 1676.97 | 1231.75 | 1316.83 | 1132.95 | 2102260 | 1499915 |
| 2004 | 2191.00 | 1692.00 | 1585.98 | 1227.66 | 1329.32 | 1157.95 | 2327978 | 1817280 |
| 2005 | 2335.00 | 1825.00 | 2209.82 | 1713.55 | 2017.66 | 1792.41 | 4307679 | 3406768 |
| 2006 | 2709.28 | 2176.75 | 2224.84 | 1700.05 | 2228.46 | 2011.70 | 5056850 | 4186980 |
| 2007 | 3555.87 | 2903.82 | 2253.07 | 1769.19 | 3552.92 | 3310.13 | 9673125 | 8567327 |
| 2008 | 3508.62 | 2857.70 | 2367.94 | 1951.35 | 2872.19 | 2669.93 | 8000006 | 7048198 |
| 2009 | 3813.68 | 2989.72 | 2907.05 | 2384.51 | 4002.89 | 3771.22 | 13777615 | 12317053 |
| 2010 | 6312.64 | 5268.76 | 2626.59 | 2179.81 | 4314.39 | 3986.31 | 18469396 | 16106444 |
| 2011 | 6824.36 | 5214.42 | 3424.33 | 2826.78 | 4533.50 | 4063.42 | 21460860 | 18254119 |
| 2012 | 5813.48 | 4345.14 | 3990.63 | 3386.35 | 4522.40 | 4105.11 | 22973464 | 19724206 |
| 2013 | 7641.63 | 5387.60 | 3804.36 | 2867.45 | 4817.56 | 4359.19 | 26827626 | 22835658 |
| 2014 | 6254.04 | 4275.96 | 3717.78 | 2771.55 | 5100.39 | 4423.68 | 28149910 | 22532816 |
| 2015 | 5810.85 | 3668.92 | 4630.29 | 3185.90 | 5381.37 | 4477.71 | 29522124 | 22444311 |
| 2016 | 4875.16 | 2998.92 | 4421.30 | 3084.00 | 6257.15 | 5105.46 | 34319972 | 26356415 |
| 2017 | 5680.04 | 3759.63 | 5055.73 | 3316.37 | 6711.00 | 5452.65 | 45578543 | 36015634 |
| 2018 | 7386.16 | 5145.20 | 4083.45 | 2784.64 | 6536.25 | 5424.76 | 52727000 | 44428692 |
| 2019 | 6725.40 | 4593.17 | 5069.17 | 3400.08 | 6104.68 | 5149.08 | 51294213 | 44577816 |
| 2020 | 5947.70 | 4106.57 | 3774.33 | 2585.26 | 6143.47 | 4814.49 | 50713443 | 42931808 |
| 2021 | 4873.36 | 3231.19 | 4196.21 | 2724.39 | 6197.71 | 4945.42 | 53912555 | 47860626 |
| 2022 | 2222.44 | 1537.53 | 2792.57 | 1914.99 | 4142.92 | 2723.02 | 29548733 | 23216880 |

# 表 4.16 房地产开发主要指标（2021－2022 年）
MAIN INDICATORS OF REAL ESTATE DEVELOPMENT (2021-2022)

| 指 标 | Item | 2021 | 2022 |
|---|---|---|---|
| **企业个数（个）** | **Number of Enterprises (unit)** | **2323** | **2208** |
| 内资企业 | Domestic Funded | 2243 | 2109 |
| #国 有 | State-owned | 24 | 33 |
| 有限责任 | Limited Liability | 497 | 443 |
| 私 营 | Private | 1579 | 1496 |
| 港、澳、台投资企业 | Enterprises with Funds from Hong Kong, Macao and Taiwan | 70 | 65 |
| 外商投资企业 | Foreign-funded | 36 | 36 |
| **从业人员（人）** | **Number of Employees (person)** | **95915** | **82939** |
| 内资企业 | Domestic Funded | 91785 | 78726 |
| #国 有 | State-owned | 778 | 1029 |
| 有限责任 | Limited Liability | 20026 | 15903 |
| 私 营 | Private | 64000 | 54654 |
| 港、澳、台投资企业 | Enterprises with Funds from Hong Kong, Macao and Taiwan | 2843 | 2357 |
| 外商投资企业 | Foreign-Funded | 1287 | 1856 |
| **土地开发及购置（万平方米）** | **Land Development and Purchase (10 000 sq.m)** | | |
| 本年土地购置面积 | Land Space Purchased in This Year | 694.50 | 256.74 |
| **本年完成投资总额（万元）** | **Investment Completed in This Year (10 000 yuan)** | **43549551** | **32168663** |
| 按工程用途分 | By Purpose of Projects | | |
| 住 宅 | Residential Buildings | 32881139 | 24110429 |
| 办公楼 | Office Buildings | 808829 | 603682 |
| 商业营业用房 | Buildings for Commercial Use | 4130713 | 3203248 |
| 其 他 | Others | 5728870 | 4251304 |
| **资金来源（万元）** | **Total Funds by Source (10 000 yuan)** | **57237673** | **32321349** |
| #国内贷款 | Domestic Loans | 6399559 | 4166411 |
| 利用外资 | Foreign Investment | 195 | 3846 |
| 自筹资金 | Self-raised Fund | 12594991 | 10784918 |
| **房屋建筑面积（万平方米）** | **Floor Space of Buildings (10 000 sq.m)** | | |
| 施工面积 | Floor Space under Construction | 26893.17 | 22646.90 |
| #住 宅 | Residential Buildings | 17709.78 | 14984.24 |
| 竣工面积 | Floor Space Completed | 4196.21 | 2792.57 |
| #住 宅 | Residential Buildings | 2724.39 | 1914.99 |
| 本年新开工面积 | Floor Space Started in This Year | 4873.36 | 2222.44 |
| #住 宅 | Residential Buildings | 3231.19 | 1537.53 |
| **商品房销售** | **Sales of Commercialized Buildings** | | |
| 商品房销售面积（万平方米） | Floor Space of Commercialized Buildings Sold (10 000 sq.m) | 6197.71 | 4142.92 |
| #住 宅 | Residential Buildings | 4945.42 | 2723.02 |
| 商品房销售额（万元） | Total Sales of Commercialized Buildings (10 000 yuan) | 53912555 | 29548733 |
| #住 宅 | Residential Buildings | 47860626 | 23216880 |
| **实收资本合计（万元）** | **Total Capital Hold (10 000 yuan)** | **35988993** | **37145254** |
| **资产负债率（%）** | **Ratio of Liabilities to Assets (%)** | **75.5** | **74.5** |
| **房地产开发经营情况（万元）** | **Real Estate Development and Operation (10 000 yuan)** | | |
| 主营业务收入 | Revenue from Major Business | 40273277 | 28394828 |
| #土地转让收入 | Land Transferred | 178638 | 394774 |

## 表 4.17 商品房施工、竣工和销售面积情况（2021 – 2022 年）
## FLOOR SPACE OF COMMERCIALIZED BUILDINGS UNDER CONSTRUCTION, COMPLETED AND SOLD (2021-2022)

单位：万平方米 (10 000 sq.m)

| 指 标 | Item | 2021 | 2022 |
|---|---|---|---|
| **商品房施工面积** | **Floor Space of Commercialized Buildings under Construction** | **26893.17** | **22646.90** |
| #主城九区 | 9 Central Urban Districts | 14297.99 | 12307.49 |
| #住 宅 | Residential Buildings | 17709.78 | 14984.24 |
| 办公楼 | Office Buildings | 738.76 | 538.01 |
| 商业营业用房 | Buildings for Commercial Use | 2900.18 | 2432.86 |
| **商品房竣工面积** | **Floor Space of Commercialized Buildings Completed** | **4196.21** | **2792.57** |
| #主城九区 | 9 Central Urban Districts | 2046.99 | 1498.68 |
| #住 宅 | Residential Buildings | 2724.39 | 1914.99 |
| 办公楼 | Office Buildings | 141.53 | 44.09 |
| 商业营业用房 | Buildings for Commercial Use | 398.93 | 238.55 |
| **商品房销售面积** | **Floor Space of Commercialized Buildings Sold** | **6197.71** | **4142.92** |
| #主城九区 | 9 Central Urban Districts | 3070.83 | 1940.41 |
| #住 宅 | Residential Buildings | 4945.42 | 2723.02 |
| 办公楼 | Office Buildings | 110.45 | 102.83 |
| 商业营业用房 | Buildings for Commercial Use | 371.87 | 336.28 |

## 表 4.18 房地产开发企业资产负债情况(2021 - 2022 年)
## ASSETS AND LIABILITIES OF ENTERPRISES FOR REAL ESTATE DEVELOPMENT (2021-2022)

单位：万元 (10 000 yuan)

| 指　标 | Item | 2021 | 2022 |
|---|---|---|---|
| 实收资本合计 | Total Capital Held | 35988993 | 37145254 |
| 资产总计 | Total Assets | 328898034 | 323045187 |
| 累计折旧 | Total Depreciation | 1147168 | 1162931 |
| #本年折旧 | Depreciation This Year | 197709 | 198102 |
| 负债总计 | Total Liabilities | 248430128 | 240819816 |
| 所有者权益 | Owners' Equity | 80467906 | 82225372 |
| 资产负债率(%) | Assets Liability Ratio (%) | 75.5 | 74.5 |

## 表 4.19 房地产开发企业经营情况(2021 - 2022 年)
## OPERATING STATISTICS ON ENTERPRISES FOR REAL ESTATE DEVELOPMENT (2021-2022)

单位：万元 (10 000 yuan)

| 指　标 | Item | 2021 | 2022 |
|---|---|---|---|
| 主营业务收入 | Revenue from Major Business | 40273277 | 28394828 |
| 土地转让收入 | Land Transferred | 178638 | 394774 |
| 商品房屋销售收入 | Commercialized Buildings Sold | 38238793 | 26395020 |
| 自持物业收入 | Self-holding properties | 716479 | 705841 |
| 其他收入 | Others | 1139368 | 899194 |
| 应交增值税 | VAT payable | 1790631 | 1912855 |
| 利润总额 | Total Profits | 4284003 | 3434477 |

注：2017 年度，主营业务收入构成项中的"房屋出租收入"调整为"自持物业收入"的其中项。
Note: In 2017, the item of houses leased revenue has been adjusted to self-holding properties revenue.

# 主要统计指标解释

## 全社会固定资产投资

是以货币形式表现的在一定时期内全社会建造和购置固定资产的工作量以及与此有关的费用的总称。该指标是反映固定资产投资规模、结构和发展速度的综合性指标，又是观察工程进度和考核投资效果的重要依据。全社会固定资产投资按登记注册类型可分为国有、集体、联营、股份制、私营和个体、港澳台商、外商、其他等。

## 固定资产投资（不含农户）

指城镇和农村各种登记注册类型的企业、事业、行政单位及城镇个体户进行的计划总投资 500 万元及 500 万元以上的建设项目投资和房地产开发投资，包含原口径的城镇固定资产投资加上农村企事业组织项目投资，该口径自 2011 年起开始使用。

## 建设项目

指各种登记注册类型的企业、事业、行政单位及个体户进行的计划总投资（或实际需要总投资）500 万元及 500 万元以上的建设项目。（2010 年及以前为 50 万元及 50 万元以上的建设项目，2011 年开始为 500 万元及 500 万元以上的建设项目）

## 房地产开发投资

指各种登记注册类型的房地产开发公司、商品房建设公司及其他房地产开发法人单位和附属于其他法人单位实际从事房地产开发或经营的活动单位统一开发的包括统代建、拆迁还建的住宅、厂房、仓库、饭店、宾馆、度假村、写字楼、办公楼等房屋建筑物和配套的服务设施，土地开发工程（如道路、给水、排水、供电、供热、通讯、平整场地等基础设施工程）的投资；不包括单纯的土地交易活动。

## 建设规模

指建设项目或工程设计文件中规定的全部设计能力（或工程效益）。包括已经建成投产和尚未建成投产的工程的生产能力（或工程效益）。

## 本年施工规模

指报告期内施工的单项工程（或更新改造项目）的设计能力（或工程效益），包括报告期以前已开工跨入本年继续施工的工程的设计能力和报告期新开工工程的设计能力。也包括报告期内建成投产或报告期施工后又停缓建的单项工程设计能力。不包括在报告期以前建成投产或已经停、缓建的工程，以及报告期内尚未正式开工的工程的设计能力。

## 新增固定资产

是指已经完成建造和购置过程，并已交付生产或使用单位的固定资产的价值，包括已经建成投入生产或交付使用的工程投资和达到固定资产标准的设备、工具、器具的投资及有关应摊入的费用。该指标是表示固定资产投资成果的价值指标，也是反映建设进度，计算固定资产投资效果的重要指标。

## 固定资产投资按构成分

(1) 建筑工程 指各种房屋、建筑物的建造工程，又称建筑工作量。这部分投资额必须兴工动料，通过施工活动才能实现，是固定资产投资额的重要组成部分。

(2) 安装工程 指各种设备、装置的安装工程，又称安装工作量。

在安装工程中，不包括被安装设备本身价值。

(3) 设备工具器具购置 指报告期内购置或自制的，达到固定资产标准的设备、工具、器具的价值。新建单位及扩建单位的新建车间，按照设计或计划要求购置或自制的全部设备、工具、器具，不论是否达到固定资产标准均计入“设备工具器具购置”中。

(4) 其他费用 指在固定资产建造和购置过程中发生的，除建筑安装工程和设备、工器具购置投资完成额以外的应当分摊计入固定资产投资的费用，不指经营

## 主要统计指标解释

中财务上的其他费用。

### 固定资产投资的实际到位资金

根据固定资产投资的资金来源不同，分为国家预算资金、国内贷款、利用外资、自筹资金和其他资金。

(1) 国家预算资金 国家预算包括一般预算、政府性基金预算、国有资本经营预算和社保基金预算。各类预算中用于固定资产投资的资金全部作为国家预算资金填报，其中一般预算中用于固定资产投资的部分包括基建投资、车购税、灾后恢复重建基金和其他财政投资。各级政府债券也应归入国家预算资金。

(2) 国内贷款 指报告期固定资产项目投资单位向银行及非银行金融机构借入用于固定资产投资的各种国内借款，包括银行利用自有资金及吸收存款发放的贷款、上级主管部门拨入的国内贷款、国家专项贷款（包括煤代油贷款、劳改煤矿专项贷款等），地方财政专项资金安排的贷款、国内储备贷款、周转贷款等。

(3) 利用外资 指报告期收到的境外（包括外国及港澳台地区）资金（包括设备、材料、技术在内）。包括对外借款（外国政府贷款、国际金融组织贷款、出口信贷、外国银行商业贷款、对外发行债券和股票）、外商直接投资、外商其他投资（包括利用外商投资收益在国内进行固定资产再投资活动的资金）。不包括我国自有外汇资金（国家外汇、地方外汇、留成外汇、调剂外汇和国内银行自有资金发放的外汇贷款等）。各类外资按报告期末的外汇牌价（中间价）折成人民币计算。

(4) 自筹资金 指固定资产投资单位在报告期收到的，由各企事业单位筹集用于固定资产投资的资金，包括各类企事业单位的自有资金和从其他单位筹集的用于固定资产投资的资金，但不包括各类财政性资金、从各类金融机构借入资金和国外资金。

(5) 其他资金 指在报告期收到的除以上各种资金之外的用于固定资产投资的资金，包括社会集资、个人资金、无偿捐赠的资金及其他单位拨入的资金等。

### 固定资产投资按建设性质分

按整个建设项目情况来确定。建设项目的性质一般分为新建、扩建、改建和技术改造、单纯建造生活设施、迁建、恢复、单纯购置。房地产开发单位、农户投资不划分建设性质。

(1) 新建 指从无到有“平地起家”开始建设的项目。现有企业、事业、行政单位投资的项目一般不属于新建。但如有的单位原有基础很小，经过建设后新增的固定资产价值超过该企业、事业、行政单位原有固定资产价值（原值）三倍以上的，也应作为新建。

(2) 扩建 指在厂内或其他地点，为扩大原有产品的生产能力（或效益）或增加新的产品生产能力，而增建的生产车间（或主要工程）、分厂、独立的生产线等项目。行政、事业单位在原单位增建业务性用房（如学校增建教学用房、医院增建门诊部、病房等）也作为扩建。

现有企、事业单位为扩大原有主要产品生产能力或增加新的产品生产能力，增建一个或几个主要生产车间（或主要工程）、分厂，同时进行一些更新改造工程的，也应作为扩建。

(3) 改建和技术改造 指现有企业、事业单位对原有设施进行技术改造或更新（包括相应配套的辅助性生产、生活福利设施）的建设项目。改建项目包括现有企业、事业单位为适应市场变化的需要，而改变企业的主要产品种类（如军工企业转民用产品等）的建设项目，原有产品生产作业线由于各工序（车间）之间能力不平衡，为填平补齐充分发挥原有生产能力而增建不增加本企业主要产品设计能力的车间的建设项目。技术改造是指企业、事业单位在现有基础上，用先进的技术代替落后的技术，用先进的工艺和装备代替落后的工艺和装备，以改变企业落后的技术经济面貌，实现以内涵为主的扩大再生产，达到提高产品质量、促进产品更新换代、节约能源、降低消耗、扩大生产规模、全面提高社会经济效益的目的。技术改造具体包括以下内容：机器设备和工具的更新改造；生产工艺改革、节约能源和原材料的改造；厂房建筑和公共设施的改造；保护环境进行的“三废”治理改造；劳动条件和生产环境的改造等。

### 本年新增生产能力（或工程效益）

指在本年度内按照新增生产能力（或工程效益）的计算条件和标准，实际建成投入生产或交付使用的生产能力（或工程效益）。

# 主要统计指标解释

## 施工项目个数

是指本年正式进行过建筑或安装施工活动的建设项目个数。包括本年新开工项目，以前年度开工跨入本年继续施工项目，本年全部建成投产项目、以前年度全部停缓建在本年恢复施工的项目，本年进行过施工又在本年内全部停缓建的项目。施工项目个数可以反映一定时期固定资产投资的实际规模，与同期全部建成投产项目个数相比，可以从建设速度的角度反映固定资产投资的效果。

## 本年投产项目个数

指报告期内按设计文件规定建成主体工程和相应配套的辅助设施，形成生产能力或工程效益，经过验收合格，并且已正式投入生产或交付使用的建设项目。

## 本年房屋施工面积

指报告期内施工的全部房屋建筑面积。包括本期新开工的面积和上期开工跨入本期继续施工的房屋面积，以及上期已停建在本期复工的房屋面积。本期竣工和本期施工后又停缓建的房屋，其建筑面积仍计入本期施工房屋面积中。

## 本年房屋竣工面积

指在报告期内房屋建筑按照设计要求已全部完工，达到住人和使用条件，经验收鉴定合格（或达到竣工验收标准），可正式移交使用的各栋房屋建筑面积的总和。

## 本年竣工房屋价值

指在报告期内竣工房屋本身的建造价值。竣工房屋价值按房屋设计和预算规定的内容计算。竣工房屋本身的基础、结构、房屋、装修以及水、电、卫等附属工程的建造价值，也包括作为房屋建筑组成部分而列入房屋建筑工程预算内的设备（如电梯、通风设备等）的购置和安装费用。不包括厂房内的工艺设备、工艺管线的购置和安装，工艺设备基础的建造，室外的水、暖、电、卫、道路工程、挡土墙等环境工程的费用，办公及生活用家具的购置等费用，购置土地的费用，迁移补偿费和场地平整的费用等。

## 商品房销售面积

指报告期内出售商品房屋的合同总面积（即双方签署的正式买卖合同中所确定的建筑面积）。由现房销售建筑面积和期房销售建筑面积两部分组成。

（1）现房销售面积：是指在报告期内正式签订买卖合同、已经竣工达到入住条件的商品房屋建筑面积。包括以一次性付款方式和分期付款方式销售的现房建筑面积。

（2）期房销售面积：是指在报告期内正式签订买卖合同、正在建设尚未竣工交付使用的商品房屋建筑面积。包括以一次性付款方式和分期付款方式销售的商品房屋建筑面积。期房销售建筑面积竣工后不再结转为现房销售建筑面积。

## 完成开发土地面积

指报告期内对土地进行开发并已完成七通一平等前期开发工程，具备进行房屋建筑物施工或达到出让条件的土地面积。

## 本年购置土地面积

指在本年内通过各种方式获得土地使用权的土地面积。

固定资产投资按国民经济行业分　指根据其从事的社会经济活动性质对各类单位进行的分类。应根据建设项目建成投产后的主要产品种类或主要用途及社会经济活动种类来划分，不能根据项目单位本身的行业类别来划分。如果项目投产后有几种产品，应根据主要产品来确定行业类别。一般情况下，一个建设项目只能属于一种国民经济行业。

## 固定资产投资按隶属关系分

是按建设单位或企业、事业、行政单位的主管上级机关确定的。

(1)中央　是指中共中央、人大常委会和国务院各部、委、局、总公司以及直属机构直接领导的建设项目和企业、事业、行政单位。这些单位的固定资产投资计划由国务院各部门直接编制和下达，统一组织或委托下级实施。包括有中央垂直管理的部门（如国家统计局各级调查队）和中央直属企业、事业单位（如工商银行、中国电信、中国石油）等。

## 主要统计指标解释

(2) 地方 是由省（自治区、直辖市）、地（区、市、州、盟）、县（区、市、旗）三级政府及业务主管部门直接领导和管理的建设项目、企业、事业、行政单位。地方项目还包括不隶属以上各级政府及主管部门的建设项目和企业、事业单位，如外商投资企业和无主管部门的企业等。

### ■ 项目建成投产率

指一定时期内全部建成投产项目个数与同期施工项目个数的比率。该指标从建设单位建设速度的角度反映投资效果。

# Explanatory Notes on Main Statistical Indicators

## Total Investment in Fixed Assets in the Whole Country

Refers to the volume of activities in construction and purchases of fixed assets of the whole country and related fees, expressed in monetary terms during the reference period. It is a comprehensive indicator which shows the size, structure and growth of the investment in fixed assets, providing a basis for observing the progress of construction projects and evaluating results of investment. Total investment in fixed assets in the whole country includes, by type of ownership, the investment by State-owned units, collective-owned units, joint ownership units, share-holding units, private units, individuals as well as investments by entrepreneurs from Hong Kong, Macao and Taiwan, foreign investors and others.

## Investment in Fixed Assets (Excluding Rural Households)

Refers to the investment in construction projects with a total planned investment of 5 million yuan and over by enterprises of various ownerships, institutions, administrative units and urban self-employed individuals, and the investment in real estate development in both urban and rural areas. Since 2011, it covers the urban investment in fixed assets under the previous statistical coverage plus project investments by rural enterprises and institutions.

## Investment of Construction

Refers to construction projects involving a total planned(or required)investment of 5,000,000 yuan and over by enterprises of various types of ownership, institutions, administrative units and individuals investment in real estate development, and private investment.

## Investment in Real Estate Development

Refers to investment by real estate development companies, commercialized buildings construction companies and other real estate development units of various types of ownership in the construction of buildings, such as residential buildings, factory buildings, warehouses, hotels, guesthouses, holiday villages, office buildings, and the complementary service facilities and land development projects, such as roads, water supply, water drainage, power supply, heating supply, telecommunications, land leveling and other infrastructural projects. It does not include activities in pure land transactions.

## Construction Scale

Refers to the total designed production capacity (project efficiency) of the construction projects in accordance with the design document, including those have been put into operation and those that have not been completed.

## Scale of Projects under Construction in Current Year

Refers to the designed production capacity (project efficiency) of a single project (or renovation project) under construction in the reference period, including the designed production capacity of projects that have been started previously and still under construction in the current year, the newly started projects, and projects that have been completed and put into operation in the reference period or those have been started but suspended or postponed in the reference period. Projects that have been completed and put into operation, suspended or postponed before the reference period, and projects that have not been officially started in the reference period are not included.

## Newly Increased Fixed Assets

Refer to the value of fixed assets that has completed the construction and purchase, and has been delivered to the production or owner units, including investment in projects that have been completed and put into operation in current year and the investment in equipment, tools and appliance that meet the standard of fixed assets and fees that should be apportioned. This is an indicator that demonstrates the results of investment in fixed assets in monetary terms, and an important indicator to reflect the speed of construction and to calculate the efficiency of investment.

## Investment in Fixed Assets by Structure

(1) Construction refers to the construction of houses and

EXPLANATORY NOTES TO
MAJOR STATISTICAL INDICATORS

buildings, also known as work volume of construction. This part of investment can only be achieved through construction activities, it is the major component of the total investment in fixed assets.

(2) Installation refers to the installation of various kinds of equipment and instruments, also known as work volume of installation.

The value of equipment installed itself is not included in the value of installation projects.

(3) Purchase of equipment and instruments refers to the total value of equipment, tools, and instruments purchased or self-produced which come up to the cut-off point for fixed assets during the reference period. Equipment, tools and instruments purchased or self-produced for new workshops by newly established or expanded units are categorized as "purchase of equipment and instruments" no matter whether they come up to the cut-off point for fixed assets.

(4) Other expenses refer to expenses arising during the construction or purchase of fixed assets other than those expenses on construction, installation and purchase of equipment and instruments. Other financial expenses arising in operation are not included.

## Actual Funds in Place for Investment in Fixed Assets

Are categorized as funds from the State budget, domestic loans, foreign investment, self-raised funds, and others, depending on the sources of investment.

(1) Fund from the State budget: State budget consists of general budget, government fund budget, operation budget of state-owned assets and social security fund budget. Funds for investment in fixed assets from various budgets are reported as fund from the state budget, of which, the general budget utilized on fixed assets investment includes investment on infrastructure construction, vehicle purchase tax, post-disaster restoration and reconstruction funds and other financial investment. Government bonds at all levels should also be included.

(2) Domestic loans refer to loans of various forms borrowed by investing units from banks and non-bank financial institutions during the reference period for the purpose of investment in fixed assets, including loans issued by banks from their self-owned funds and deposit, loans appropriated by higher responsible authorities, special loans by government (including loan for substituting petroleum with coal, special loans for reform-through-labour coal mines), loans arranged by local government from special funds, domestic reserve loan, and revolving loan, etc.

(3) Foreign investment refers to overseas (including foreign countries, Hong Kong, Macao and Taiwan) funds received during the reference period (covering equipment, materials and technology), including foreign borrowings (loans from foreign governments and international financial institutions, export credit, commercial loans from foreign banks, issue of bonds and stocks overseas), foreign direct investment and other foreign investments (including funds from foreign direct investment income that are reinvested in fixed assets domestically). Excluded from this category is capital in foreign exchanges owned by China (foreign exchanges owned by the central and local governments, foreign exchanges retained by enterprises, foreign exchanges by enterprises through the regulating mechanism, loans in foreign exchanges issued by the Bank of China with its own fund, etc.). In calculating the utilization of foreign capital, foreign currencies are converted into RMB applying the exchange rate (central parity rate) at the end of the reference period.

(4) Self-raised funds refer to funds for investment in fixed assets received during the reference period by investing units, including investment in fixed assets using own funds of various enterprises and institutions or funds raised from other units other than financial funds, funds borrowed from financial institutions and overseas funds.

(5) Others refer to funds for investment in fixed assets received from sources other than those listed above, including funds raised from individuals and through donations, and funds transferred from other units.

## Investment in Fixed Assets By Type of Construction

Construction projects in general can be classified, by the type of construction, into new construction, expansion, reconstruction and technical transformation, purely construction of living facilities, moving, restoration and purely purchasing. However, investment by type of construction is not applied to investment by real-estate development units and investment by rural households.

(1) New construction in general refers to construction projects, which start from scratch. The existing projects invested by enterprises, institutions and administrative agencies cannot be classified as new construction. In case the size of the existing unit is quite small, and the value of newly added fixed assets is more than three times of the original value, the expansion will be considered as new construction.

(2) Expansion refers to projects of construction of new production workshop, branch factory or independent

production line within a factory or in other locations, for the purpose of increasing the production capacity (or improving efficiency) or adding new production capacity. Newly constructed accommodation for the operation of institutions and administrative organizations (such as newly constructed buildings for teaching in schools, buildings for clinics or wards in hospitals, etc.) are also classified as expansion.

Also included in expansion are investments by existing enterprises or institutions in building major production line(s) or branch factory (ies) along with some work on innovation, for the purpose of expanding the production capacity of original products or producing new products.

(3) Reconstruction and technical transformation refers to construction projects by existing enterprises or institutions in innovation or technical transformation of the old facilities (including auxiliary production equipment and welfare facilities). Also considered as reconstruction is the construction of new workshops by the existing enterprises or institutions to change the variety of products to meet the market demand (such as the production of civil products by defence industries), or to bring the designed production capacity into full play through a more balanced production process on production lines. Technical transformation refers to replacement of old technology or equipment by new technology or equipment, in order to expand the reproduction through improvement of technology contents in production, to improve product quality, to promote new products, to save energy, to reduce consumption, to expand the production scale and to improve overall social-economic efficiency. Contents of technical transformation include: updating of machinery, equipment and tools; reforming production process by using energy or materials saving technology; construction of factory workshops and transformation of public facilities; treatment transformation of "three wastes" (waste gas, waste water and industrial residue) aiming at environmental protection; improvement of working conditions and environment, etc.

## The Newly Increased Production Capacity (project efficiency) of Current Year

Refers to the production capacity (project efficiency) that has been completed and put into operation in current year according to the calculation conditions and standards on newly increased production capacity (project efficiency).

## Number of Projects under Construction

Refers to number of all projects with actual construction or installation activities in current year, including newly started projects, projects started previously and extended into the current year, projects completed and put into operation in current year, projects suspended previously and resumed in current year, and projects started this year but suspended or postponed in current year. The number of projects under construction can reflect the actual size of investment in fixed assets during a given period, and when compared with the number of projects completed and put into use during the same period, it demonstrates the results of investment in fixed assets from the angle of the speed of the construction.

## Number of Projects Put into Use This Year

Refer to projects have completed the main construction and correspondent auxiliary facilities in accordance with the design documents, resulting in forming production capacity (efficiency) and have been checked and accepted after relevant tests, and have been formally delivered for use.

## Floor Space under Construction in this Year

Refers to total floor space of all buildings under construction during the reference period, including floor space of newly started buildings during the reference period, floor space of construction extended from the previous period to the current period, and floor space of construction suspended during the previous period and resumed in the current period. Floor space of construction completed in the current period, and floor space of construction started and then suspended in the current period are also included in the floor space under construction of the current year.

## Floor Space of Buildings Completed in this Year

Refers to the floor space of all buildings completed in the reference period, which have been appraised and accepted (or come up to the designed standards) and have been transferred to the owners for use.

## Value of Buildings Completed in this Year

Refers to the intrinsic construction value of buildings completed in the reference period. It is figured by the rules of buildings design and budget, which not only includes the construction value of foundations, structure, furnishings,

EXPLANATORY NOTES TO MAJOR STATISTICAL INDICATORS

subsidiary projects such as water, electricity, toilet, etc. but also includes purchase and installation expenditures of facilities (such as lift, ventilation, etc.) listed into buildings budget as component of building construction. It excludes the purchase and installation of technical facilities, leads and lines in factories, construction of technical facilities' basis, expenditures of environment projects such as water, eructate, electricity, toilet, road projects, wall fended to earth outside, purchase of furniture in office or house, purchase of lands, as well as expenditures of move compensation and land leveling etc.

## Floor Space of Commercial Buildings Actually Sold

Refers to the total contracted floor space of commercial buildings actually sold in reporting period(the floor space provided in the formal contract),which consists of the floor space of the sold completed buildings and the floor space of the sold forward-delivery buildings.

(I) Floor Space of Sold Completed Buildings refers to the floor space of the completed commercial buildings prepared for occupancy with the formally signed sales contract in the reporting period, including the floor space of the completed buildings purchased by one-off payment and by installment.

(II) Floor Space of Sold Forward-Delivery Buildings refers to the floor space of the uncompleted commercial buildings still under construction with the formally signed sales contract in the reporting period, including the floor space of the commercial buildings purchased by one-off payment and by installment. The floor space of sold forward-delivery buildings,after completion,will not be carried forward into the floor space of sold completed buildings.

## Developed Land Area Completed

Refers to the land area of land development and prophase development projects completed, which can carry out construction or remise.

## Purchased Land Area in Current Year

Refers to the land area accessible by various means in current year.

Investment in fixed assets by sector refers to the classification of investment by the nature of social economic activities the investing units are engaged in. The classification of construction projects by sector is determined by the major products or the purpose of the projects when they are put into production or use, and by the nature of their social economic activities, instead of being determined by industrial classification of the project enterprises. The project will be classified according to major product if there are several kinds of products yielded. In general, one project can only be classified into one sector.

## Investment in Fixed Assets by Jurisdiction of Management

Refers to the classification of investment by the competent authorities under which investment is made by construction units, enterprises, institutions or administrative units.

(1) Central investment refers to the investment in projects or by enterprises, institutions or administrative units which are under the direct leadership and management of the State Council and of the national commissions, ministries, agencies and State-owned large corporations. Various ministries and departments of the State Council prepare and implement plans through unified organization or lower-level commissions, which include departments direct under central government (i.e. survey offices at all level of the National Bureau of Statistics) and enterprises and institutions directly under central government (like the Industrial and Commercial Bank of China, China Telecom and China National Petroleum Corporation).

(2) Local investment refers to the investment in projects or by enterprises, institutions or administrative units which are under the direct leadership and management of competent departments and governments at the level of province (autonomous regions and municipalities directly under the Central Government), prefecture (prefectures, cities and leagues) and county (districts, cities and banners). Also included are projects by foreign-invested enterprises and enterprises without competent managing authorities.

## Rate of Construction Projects Completed and Put into Use

Refers to the ratio of the number of construction projects completed and put into use in a certain period of time to the number of projects under construction in the same period. This reflects the investment efficiency from the perspective of the speed of projects construction.

# 第五章 · 能源消费

ENERGY CONSUMPTION

# 简要说明

## BRIEF INTRODUCTION

本章主要内容包括能源消费及品种构成，能源消费弹性系数，平均每万元GDP能源消费量及日均能源消费量，综合能源平衡表，按工业行业分的能源消费量和工业产值综合能耗。

本章资料由市统计局能源资源统计处根据有关资料和调查结果编制。

The data in this chapter mainly cover energy consumption and its composition, the elasticity ratio of energy consumption, average energy consumption per 10,000 yuan of GDP, average daily energy consumption, overall energy balance sheet, energy consumption by industrial sector and comprehensive energy consumption per unit output value.

This chapter is compiled by Division of Energy Resources Statistics, Chongqing Municipal Bureau of Statistics on the basis of the related materials and the results of surveys.

# 表 5.1 主要年份能源消费总量
TOTAL CONSUMPTION OF ENERGY IN MAJOR YEARS

单位：万吨标准煤 (10 000 tons of SCE)

| 年份<br>Year | 能源消费总量<br>Total Consumption of Energy | 煤炭<br>Coal | 天然气<br>Natural Gas | 油料<br>Oil | 一次电力及其他能源<br>Primary Electricity and Other Energy |
|---|---|---|---|---|---|
| 1949 | 78.71 | 76.36 | | 1.77 | 0.58 |
| 1952 | 133.44 | 129.29 | | 2.94 | 1.20 |
| 1957 | 226.36 | 212.81 | 2.93 | 6.01 | 4.61 |
| 1962 | 408.86 | 368.46 | 15.62 | 12.20 | 12.58 |
| 1965 | 294.29 | 253.19 | 16.87 | 8.45 | 15.78 |
| 1970 | 403.02 | 325.98 | 43.03 | 12.05 | 21.96 |
| 1975 | 558.92 | 441.18 | 67.44 | 18.87 | 31.42 |
| 1978 | 763.19 | 604.12 | 89.15 | 27.64 | 42.28 |
| 1980 | 845.92 | 645.95 | 110.79 | 34.79 | 54.40 |
| 1981 | 861.98 | 657.73 | 118.29 | 29.04 | 56.92 |
| 1982 | 901.48 | 681.49 | 118.98 | 41.46 | 59.57 |
| 1983 | 952.74 | 719.36 | 127.22 | 43.82 | 62.34 |
| 1984 | 996.03 | 748.83 | 130.43 | 51.54 | 65.23 |
| 1985 | 1065.48 | 805.25 | 138.04 | 53.93 | 68.26 |
| 1986 | 1091.00 | 805.64 | 148.81 | 64.89 | 71.66 |
| 1987 | 1197.87 | 889.42 | 167.89 | 65.33 | 75.22 |
| 1988 | 1298.74 | 993.10 | 157.69 | 68.98 | 78.96 |
| 1989 | 1343.61 | 1025.17 | 163.38 | 72.16 | 82.89 |
| 1990 | 1301.67 | 970.51 | 168.60 | 75.53 | 87.02 |
| 1991 | 1337.69 | 988.47 | 169.13 | 82.94 | 97.15 |
| 1992 | 1374.12 | 1006.75 | 170.22 | 88.70 | 108.46 |
| 1993 | 1411.75 | 1025.38 | 172.42 | 92.87 | 121.09 |
| 1994 | 1456.27 | 1044.34 | 186.02 | 90.72 | 135.18 |
| 1995 | 1525.10 | 1064.15 | 221.75 | 88.29 | 150.91 |
| 1996 | 1605.93 | 1130.64 | 223.89 | 83.59 | 167.81 |
| 1997 | 1742.43 | 1187.85 | 242.72 | 124.85 | 187.00 |
| 1998 | 1819.10 | 1195.96 | 250.02 | 157.60 | 215.52 |
| 1999 | 1955.53 | 1283.61 | 264.51 | 168.52 | 238.90 |
| 2000 | 2069.17 | 1373.08 | 267.96 | 173.52 | 254.61 |
| 2001 | 2208.95 | 1459.45 | 276.81 | 176.98 | 295.71 |
| 2002 | 2422.98 | 1655.55 | 284.84 | 183.54 | 299.06 |
| 2003 | 2693.21 | 1893.74 | 299.64 | 189.52 | 310.32 |
| 2004 | 2891.06 | 1892.59 | 346.34 | 326.12 | 326.01 |
| 2005 | 3027.40 | 1944.56 | 405.24 | 353.49 | 324.11 |
| 2006 | 3339.78 | 2192.60 | 457.18 | 402.63 | 287.36 |
| 2007 | 3869.50 | 2322.58 | 496.90 | 471.30 | 578.72 |
| 2008 | 4039.65 | 2430.96 | 556.50 | 515.46 | 536.74 |
| 2009 | 4398.56 | 2667.99 | 564.67 | 531.92 | 633.96 |
| 2010 | 4987.34 | 2964.56 | 645.85 | 636.16 | 740.77 |
| 2011 | 5516.15 | 3533.55 | 705.35 | 782.81 | 494.44 |
| 2012 | 5834.84 | 3563.96 | 810.10 | 801.63 | 659.15 |
| 2013 | 6225.92 | 3935.09 | 823.92 | 889.18 | 577.72 |
| 2014 | 6603.61 | 3983.97 | 937.46 | 887.81 | 794.37 |
| 2015 | 6924.77 | 3994.40 | 1008.76 | 999.15 | 922.46 |
| 2016 | 7099.71 | 3830.26 | 1019.61 | 1084.27 | 1165.57 |
| 2017 | 7251.59 | 3899.16 | 1087.18 | 1139.04 | 1126.20 |
| 2018 | 7452.72 | 4050.94 | 1323.39 | 1347.72 | 730.66 |
| 2019 | 7687.25 | 4062.09 | 1376.68 | 1433.92 | 814.56 |
| 2020 | 7621.87 | 3930.98 | 1397.16 | 1404.82 | 888.92 |
| 2021 | 8046.31 | 3983.30 | 1756.70 | 1406.51 | 899.80 |
| 2022 | 8022.76 | 4070.77 | 1271.63 | 1754.90 | 925.48 |

注：本表各年能源品种均已折合为按当量值计算的吨标准煤。
Note: All sorts of energy consumption has been converted into tons of SCE calculated in equivalent value. The historical data in table 5-6,table 5-7, table 5-8 and the table above are corrected in accordance with the 4th China Economic Census.

# 表 5.2 规模以上工业按行业分能源消费量（2022 年）
## ENERGY CONSUMPTION OF ENTERPRISES ABOVE DESIGNATED SIZE BY SECTOR (2022)

| 行　业 | Sector | 原　煤（吨）<br>Coal (ton) | 焦　炭（吨）<br>Coke (ton) |
|---|---|---|---|
| **工业消费总量** | **Total Industry Consumption** | **42846817** | **3632571** |
| **采矿业** | **Mining** | **2319702** | **4325** |
| 煤炭开采和洗选业 | Mining and Washing of Coal | 1896004 | |
| 石油和天然气开采业 | Extraction of Petroleum and Natural Gas | | |
| 黑色金属矿采选业 | Mining and Processing of Ferrous Metal Ores | | |
| 有色金属矿采选业 | Mining and Processing of Non-ferrous Metal Ores | | |
| 非金属矿采选业 | Mining and Processing of Non-metal Ores | 423699 | 4325 |
| 开采专业及辅助性活动 | Support Activities for Mining | | |
| 其他采矿业 | Mining of Other Ores | | |
| **制造业** | **Manufacturing** | **15903867** | **3628246** |
| 农副食品加工业 | Processing of Food from Agricultural Products | 17366 | |
| 食品制造业 | Manufacture of Foods | 94977 | |
| 酒、饮料和精茶制造业 | Manufacture of Liquor, Beverages and Refined Tea | 2750 | |
| 烟草制品业 | Manufacture of Tobacco | | |
| 纺织业 | Manufacture of Textile | 15 | |
| 纺织服装、服饰业 | Manufacture of Textile, Wearing Apparel and Accessories | | |
| 皮革、毛皮、羽毛及其制品和制鞋业 | Manufacture of Leather, Fur, Feather and Related Products and Footwear | 6916 | |
| 木材加工及木、竹、藤、棕、草制品业 | Processing of Timber, Manufacture of Wood, Bamboo, Rattan, Palm and Straw Products | 9465 | |
| 家具制造业 | Manufacture of Furniture | | |
| 造纸及纸制品业 | Manufacture of Paper and Paper Products | 1563571 | |
| 印刷和记录媒介复制业 | Printing and Reproduction of Recording Media | 817 | |
| 文教体育用品制造业 | Manufacture of Articles for Culture, Education, Arts and Crafts, Sport and Entertainment Activities | | |
| 石油、煤炭及其他燃料加工业 | Processing of Petroleum, Coal and Other Fuels | | |

| 汽　油(吨) Gasoline (ton) | 煤　油(吨) Kerosene (ton) | 柴　油(吨) Diesel Oil (ton) | 天然气(万立方米) Natural Gas(10 000 cu.m) | 电　力(万千瓦时) Electricity(10 000 kw.h) |
|---|---|---|---|---|
| **41303** | **948** | **178876** | **895089** | **7157870** |
| **428** | | **25078** | **61614** | **119264** |
| 12 | | 302 | 740 | 1003 |
| 295 | | 93 | 60873 | 43734 |
| | | | | |
| 25 | | 44 | | 105 |
| 96 | | 24639 | | 74422 |
| | | | | |
| | | | | |
| **36480** | **947** | **146373** | **705084** | **5877070** |
| 1932 | | 1370 | 10917 | 74527 |
| 1184 | | 1259 | 7619 | 41135 |
| 485 | | 452 | 4783 | 22887 |
| 48 | | 40 | 924 | 6923 |
| 49 | | 56 | 2980 | 17433 |
| 217 | | 105 | 412 | 5191 |
| 356 | | 155 | 71 | 6010 |
| 158 | | 388 | 246 | 27105 |
| 366 | | 428 | 65 | 14694 |
| 209 | | 3477 | 10949 | 266934 |
| 531 | | 998 | 1228 | 28100 |
| 111 | | 34 | 256 | 5612 |
| 5 | | 5 | 348 | 2254 |

表 5.2 续表 continued

| 行 业 | Sector | 原 煤(吨) Coal (ton) | 焦 炭(吨) Coke (ton) |
|---|---|---|---|
| 化学原料及化学制品制造业 | Manufacture of Raw Chemical Materials and Chemical Products | 4432443 | 111630 |
| 医药制造业 | Manufacture of Medicines | 4463 | |
| 化学纤维制造业 | Manufacture of Chemical Fibres | | |
| 橡胶和塑料制品业 | Manufacture of Rubber and Plastics | 58759 | |
| 非金属矿物制品业 | Manufacture of Non-metallic Mineral Products | 5971553 | 23001 |
| 黑色金属冶炼及压延加工业 | Smelting and Pressing of Ferrous Metals | 1532582 | 3485030 |
| 有色金属冶炼及压延加工业 | Smelting and Pressing of Non-ferrous Metals | 2189120 | 5531 |
| 金属制品业 | Manufacture of Metal Products | 1035 | |
| 通用设备制造业 | Manufacture of General Purpose Machinery | 1897 | 3034 |
| 专用设备制造业 | Manufacture of Special Purpose Machinery | | |
| 汽车制造业 | Manufacture of Automobiles | 298 | 20 |
| 铁路、船舶、航空航天和其他运输设备制造业 | Manufacture of Railway, Ship, Aerospace and Other Transport Equipment | | |
| 电气机械和器材制造业 | Manufacture of Electrical Machinery and Equipment | 8 | |
| 计算机、通信和其他电子设备制造业 | Manufacture of Computers, Communication and Other Electronic Equipments | 126 | |
| 仪器仪表制造业 | Manufacture of Measuring Instruments and Machinery | | |
| 其他制造业 | Other Manufacture | | |
| 废弃资源综合利用业 | Utilization of Waste Resources | 15706 | |
| 金属制品、机械和设备修理业 | Repair of Metal Products, Machinery and Equipment | | |
| **电力、燃气及水的生产和供应业** | **Electric Power, Gas and Water Production and Supply** | **24623248** | |
| 电力、热力生产和供应业 | Production and Supply of Electric Power and Heat Power | 24623248 | |
| 燃气生产和供应业 | Production and Supply of Gas | | |
| 水的生产和供应业 | Production and Supply of Water | | |

| 汽　油(吨)<br>Gasoline (ton) | 煤　油(吨)<br>Kerosene (ton) | 柴　油(吨)<br>Diesel Oil (ton) | 天然气(万立方米)<br>Natural Gas(10 000 cu.m) | 电　力(万千瓦时)<br>Electricity(10 000 kw.h) |
|---|---|---|---|---|
| 1253 | 35 | 5411 | 426291 | 806701 |
| 972 | | 654 | 13769 | 80320 |
| 12 | | 10 | 3073 | 37723 |
| 1309 | 1 | 3144 | 5632 | 129254 |
| 1467 | 148 | 97341 | 90919 | 843284 |
| 249 | | 615 | 12813 | 750686 |
| 322 | 14 | 1879 | 56264 | 1045796 |
| 1768 | 29 | 1840 | 6810 | 131881 |
| 3545 | 246 | 6344 | 3008 | 115103 |
| 1302 | 6 | 2091 | 1063 | 39443 |
| 10447 | 62 | 9725 | 22804 | 503616 |
| 3782 | 334 | 3510 | 7606 | 128042 |
| 2754 | | 1355 | 4442 | 140303 |
| 1124 | 66 | 1083 | 9213 | 573780 |
| 391 | 5 | 239 | 65 | 11894 |
| 1 | | 2 | | 1251 |
| 67 | | 2275 | 515 | 18794 |
| 62 | | 87 | | 396 |
| **4395** | | **7426** | **128392** | **1161536** |
| 3596 | | 6844 | 59931 | 977887 |
| 496 | | 332 | 68306 | 28833 |
| 302 | | 250 | 155 | 154815 |

# 表 5.3 规模以上工业企业产值综合能耗（2022 年）
# COMPREHENSIVE ENERGY CONSUMPTION OF INDUSTRIAL ENTERPRISES ABOVE DESIGNATED SIZE PER UNIT OUTPUT VALUE (2022)

| 行业 | Sector | 综合能源消费量（吨标准煤）Comprehensive Energy Consumption (ton of SCE) | 产值能耗（吨标准煤/万元）Energy Consumption per Unit Output Value (ton of SCE/10 000 yuan) |
|---|---|---|---|
| **工业消费总量** | **Total Industry Consumption** | **46507803** | **0.17** |
| **采矿业** | **Mining** | **988321** | **0.30** |
| 煤炭开采和洗选业 | Mining and Washing of Coal | 81001 | 0.20 |
| 石油和天然气开采业 | Extraction of Petroleum and Natural Gas | 487017 | 0.31 |
| 黑色金属矿采选业 | Mining and Processing of Ferrous Metal Ores | | |
| 有色金属矿采选业 | Mining and Processing of Non-ferrous Metal Ores | 230 | 0.11 |
| 非金属矿采选业 | Mining and Processing of Non-metal Ores | 420073 | 0.31 |
| 开采专业及辅助性活动 | Support Activities for Mining | | |
| 其他采矿业 | Mining of Other Ores | | |
| **制造业** | **Manufacturing** | **32001803** | **0.13** |
| 农副食品加工业 | Processing of Food from Agricultural Products | 255526 | 0.02 |
| 食品制造业 | Manufacture of Foods | 229671 | 0.07 |
| 酒、饮料和精茶制造业 | Manufacture of Liquor, Beverages and Refined Tea | 92567 | 0.04 |
| 烟草制品业 | Manufacture of Tobacco | 19390 | 0.01 |
| 纺织业 | Manufacture of Textile | 58814 | 0.10 |
| 纺织服装、服饰业 | Manufacture of Textile, Wearing Apparel and Accessories | 12302 | 0.02 |
| 皮革、毛皮、羽毛及其制品和制鞋业 | Manufacture of Leather, Fur, Feather and Related Products and Footwear | 15089 | 0.02 |
| 木材加工及木、竹、藤、棕、草制品业 | Processing of Timber, Manufacture of Wood, Bamboo, Rattan, Palm and Straw Products | 44001 | 0.02 |
| 家具制造业 | Manufacture of Furniture | 23132 | 0.02 |
| 造纸及纸制品业 | Manufacture of Paper and Paper Products | 1290758 | 0.28 |
| 印刷和记录媒介复制业 | Printing and Reproduction of Recording Media | 52911 | 0.02 |
| 文教体育用品制造业 | Manufacture of Articles for Culture, Education, Arts and Crafts, Sport and Entertainment Activities | 10167 | 0.01 |
| 石油、煤炭及其他燃料加工业 | Processing of Petroleum, Coal and Other Fuels | 9505 | 0.02 |

**表 5.3 续表 continued**

| 行 业 | Sector | 综合能源消费量（吨标准煤）Comprehensive Energy Consumption (ton of SCE) | 产值能耗（吨标准煤／万元）Energy Consumption per Unit Output Value (ton of SCE/10 000 yuan) |
|---|---|---|---|
| 化学原料及化学制品制造业 | Manufacture of Raw Chemical Materials and Chemical Products | 9450331 | 0.82 |
| 医药制造业 | Manufacture of Medicines | 318289 | 0.05 |
| 化学纤维制造业 | Manufacture of Chemical Fibres | 156229 | 0.16 |
| 橡胶和塑料制品业 | Manufacture of Rubber and Plastics | 287590 | 0.05 |
| 非金属矿物制品业 | Manufacture of Non-metallic Mineral Products | 7607377 | 0.52 |
| 黑色金属冶炼及压延加工业 | Smelting and Pressing of Ferrous Metals | 5714123 | 0.47 |
| 有色金属冶炼及压延加工业 | Smelting and Pressing of Non-ferrous Metals | 3490779 | 0.23 |
| 金属制品业 | Manufacture of Metal Products | 257461 | 0.04 |
| 通用设备制造业 | Manufacture of General Purpose Machinery | 201269 | 0.02 |
| 专用设备制造业 | Manufacture of Special Purpose Machinery | 67244 | 0.01 |
| 汽车制造业 | Manufacture of Automobiles | 938420 | 0.02 |
| 铁路、船舶、航空航天和其他运输设备制造业 | Manufacture of Railway, Ship, Aerospace and Other Transport Equipment | 271581 | 0.03 |
| 电气机械和器材制造业 | Manufacture of Electrical Machinery and Equipment | 235862 | 0.02 |
| 计算机、通信和其他电子设备制造业 | Manufacture of Computers, Communication and Other Electronic Equipments | 827279 | 0.01 |
| 仪器仪表制造业 | Manufacture of Measuring Instruments and Machinery | 16400 | 0.01 |
| 其他制造业 | Other Manufacture | 1543 | 0.03 |
| 废弃资源综合利用业 | Utilization of Waste Resources | 45488 | 0.06 |
| 金属制品、机械和设备修理业 | Repair of Metal Products, Machinery and Equipment | 707 | 0.01 |
| **电力、燃气及水的生产和供应业** | **Electric Power, Gas and Water Production and Supply** | **13517679** | **0.83** |
| 电力、热力生产和供应业 | Production and Supply of Electric Power and Heat Power | 13091808 | 1.11 |
| 燃气生产和供应业 | Production and Supply of Gas | 209511 | 0.06 |
| 水的生产和供应业 | Production and Supply of Water | 216360 | 0.25 |

# 表 5.4 规模以上工业按行业分用水情况（2022 年）
## WATER CONSUMPTION OF ENTERPRISES ABOVE DESIGNATED SIZE BY SECTOR (2022)

单位：万立方米 (10000 cu.m)

| 行　业 | Sector | 取水量 Water Consumption | | | 外供水量 Water Supply from Outside | | |
|---|---|---|---|---|---|---|---|
| | | 报告期 Reporting Period | 上年同期 Period of Previous Year | 同比增长 (%) Up YOY (%) | 报告期 Reporting Period | 上年同期 Period of Previous Year | 同比增长 (%) Up YOY (%) |
| **总 计** | **Total** | **285283.47** | **286161.25** | **-0.3** | **202213.87** | **200385.96** | **0.9** |
| **采矿业** | **Mining** | **1294.21** | **3160.70** | **-59.1** | **0.43** | **1.01** | **-57.1** |
| 煤炭开采和洗选业 | Mining and Washing of Coal | 35.72 | 1688.80 | -97.9 | | | |
| 石油和天然气开采业 | Extraction of Petroleum and Natural Gas | 410.87 | 495.30 | -17.0 | | | |
| 黑色金属矿采选业 | Mining and Processing of Ferrous Metal Ores | 0.00 | 2.11 | -100.0 | | | |
| 有色金属矿采选业 | Mining and Processing of Non-ferrous Metal Ores | 0.68 | 0.58 | 16.7 | | | |
| 非金属矿采选业 | Mining and Processing of Non-metal Ores | 846.93 | 973.91 | -13.0 | 0.43 | 1.01 | -57.1 |
| 开采专业及辅助性活动 | Support Activities for Mining | | | | | | |
| 其他采矿业 | Mining for Other Ores | | | | | | |
| **制造业** | **Manufacturing** | **45575.72** | **45088.28** | **1.1** | **2567.02** | **2298.73** | **11.7** |
| 农副食品加工业 | Processing of Food from Agricultural Products | 1347.24 | 1313.32 | 2.6 | | | |
| 食品制造业 | Manufacture of Foods | 1025.29 | 959.93 | 6.8 | | | |
| 酒、饮料和精制茶制造业 | Manufacture of Liquor, Beverage and Refined Tea | 806.71 | 825.39 | -2.3 | 63.59 | 47.27 | 34.5 |
| 烟草制品业 | Manufacture of Tobacco | 61.89 | 54.45 | 13.7 | | | |
| 纺织业 | Manufacture of Textile | 200.80 | 214.36 | -6.3 | | | |
| 纺织服装、服饰业 | Manufacture of Textile, Wearing Apparel and Accessories | 87.63 | 78.67 | 11.4 | | | |
| 皮革、毛皮、羽毛(绒)及其制品和制鞋业 | Manufacture of Leather, Fur, Feather and Related Products and Footwear | 47.89 | 50.60 | -5.3 | 0.24 | 0.24 | 0.0 |
| 木材加工及木、竹、藤、棕、草制品业 | Processing of Timber Manufacture of Wood, Bamboo, Rattan, Palm and Straw Products | 81.38 | 84.13 | -3.3 | | | |
| 家具制造业 | Manufacture of Furniture | 68.32 | 71.63 | -4.6 | 0.11 | 0.00 | |
| 造纸及纸制品业 | Manufacture of Paper and Paper Products | 5545.82 | 5801.01 | -4.4 | | | |
| 印刷和记录媒介复制业 | Printing and Reproduction of Recording Media | 130.00 | 126.71 | 2.6 | | | |
| 文教、工美、体育和娱乐用品制造业 | Manufacture of Articles for Culture, Education, Arts and Crafts, Sport and Entertainment Activities | 37.46 | 34.18 | 9.6 | | | |
| 石油、煤炭及其他燃料加工业 | Processing of Petroleum, Coal and Other Fuels | 36.29 | 75.13 | -51.7 | | | |

**表 5.4 续表 continued**

单位：万立方米（10 000 cu.m）

| 行 业 | Sector | 取水量 Water Consumption 报告期 Reporting Period | 上年同期 Period of Previous Year | 同比增长（%） Up YOY (%) | 外供水量 Water Supply from Outside 报告期 Reporting Period | 上年同期 Period of Previous Year | 同比增长（%） Up YOY (%) |
|---|---|---|---|---|---|---|---|
| 化学原料及化学制品制造业 | Manufacture of Raw Chemical Materials and Chemical Products | 11840.76 | 11065.65 | 7.0 | 257.87 | 239.81 | 7.5 |
| 医药制造业 | Manufacture of Medicines | 1184.04 | 1139.75 | 3.9 | 5.63 | 5.18 | 8.7 |
| 化学纤维制造业 | Manufacture of Chemical Fibres | 190.46 | 169.23 | 12.5 | | | |
| 橡胶和塑料制品业 | Manufacture of Rubber and Plastics | 439.75 | 449.41 | -2.2 | | | |
| 非金属矿物制品业 | Manufacture of Non-metallic Mineral Products | 4492.66 | 4729.78 | -5.0 | 21.98 | 21.12 | 4.1 |
| 黑色金属冶炼及压延加工业 | Smelting and Pressing of Ferrous Metals | 3857.03 | 3984.99 | -3.2 | | | |
| 有色金属冶炼及压延加工业 | Smelting and Pressing of Non-ferrous Metals | 3939.34 | 3913.22 | 0.7 | 2213.35 | 1978.72 | 11.9 |
| 金属制品业 | Manufacture of Metal Products | 516.91 | 572.86 | -9.8 | 0.08 | 0.08 | 2.6 |
| 通用设备制造业 | Manufacture of General Purpose Machinery | 511.13 | 549.28 | -6.9 | 0.06 | 4.70 | -98.8 |
| 专用设备制造业 | Manufacture of Special Purpose Machinery | 319.93 | 323.06 | -1.0 | | | |
| 汽车制造业 | Manufacture of Automobiles | 2460.23 | 2396.47 | 2.7 | 1.06 | 0.65 | 63.8 |
| 铁路、船舶、航空航天和其他运输设备制造业 | Manufacture of Railway, Ship, Aerospace and Other Transport Equipment | 903.56 | 1001.74 | -9.8 | | | |
| 电气机械和器材制造业 | Manufacture of Electrical Machinery and Equipment | 766.09 | 603.03 | 27.0 | | | |
| 计算机、通信和其他电子设备制造业 | Manufacture of Computers, Communication and Other Electronic Equipments | 4494.95 | 4321.28 | 4.0 | 3.06 | 0.99 | 209.3 |
| 仪器仪表制造业 | Manufacture of Measuring Instruments and Machinery | 81.56 | 79.90 | 2.1 | | | |
| 其他制造业 | Other Manufacture | 1.79 | 1.38 | 29.3 | | | |
| 废弃资源综合利用业 | Utilization of Waste Resources | 95.47 | 94.11 | 1.4 | | | |
| 金属制品、机械和设备修理业 | Repair of Metal Products, Machinery and Equipment | 3.33 | 3.62 | -8.2 | | | |
| **电力、燃气及水的生产和供应业** | **Electric Power, Gas and Water Production and Supply** | **238413.54** | **237912.27** | **0.2** | **199646.41** | **198086.22** | **0.8** |
| 电力、热力生产和供应业 | Production and Supply of Electric Power and Heat Power | 21541.27 | 19773.24 | 8.9 | 4725.47 | 4218.07 | 12.0 |
| 燃气生产和供应业 | Production and Supply of Gas | 312.42 | 282.47 | 10.6 | | | |
| 水的生产和供应业 | Production and Supply of Water | 216559.85 | 217856.56 | -0.6 | 194920.94 | 193868.14 | 0.5 |

## 表 5.5 能源消费弹性系数（1985 － 2022 年）
## ELASTICITY RATIO OF ENERGY CONSUMPTION (1985-2022)

| 年 份<br>Year | 能源消费比上年增长 %<br>Growth Rate of Energy Consumption over Preceding Year (%) | 本市生产总值比上年增长 %<br>Growth Rate of GDP over Preceding Year (%) | 能源消费弹性系数<br>Elasticity Ratio of Energy Consumption |
|---|---|---|---|
| 1985 | 7.0 | 8.6 | 0.81 |
| 1986 | 2.4 | 8.6 | 0.28 |
| 1987 | 9.8 | 5.3 | 1.85 |
| 1988 | 8.4 | 9.5 | 0.89 |
| 1989 | 3.5 | 4.9 | 0.71 |
| 1990 | -3.1 | 7.0 | -0.45 |
| 1991 | 2.8 | 9.2 | 0.30 |
| 1992 | 2.7 | 16.5 | 0.17 |
| 1993 | 2.7 | 15.6 | 0.18 |
| 1994 | 3.2 | 13.5 | 0.23 |
| 1995 | 4.7 | 12.3 | 0.38 |
| 1996 | 5.3 | 11.4 | 0.46 |
| 1997 | 8.5 | 11.2 | 0.76 |
| 1998 | 4.4 | 8.6 | 0.51 |
| 1999 | 7.5 | 7.8 | 0.96 |
| 2000 | 5.8 | 8.7 | 0.67 |
| 2001 | 6.8 | 9.2 | 0.73 |
| 2002 | 9.7 | 10.5 | 0.92 |
| 2003 | 11.2 | 11.7 | 0.95 |
| 2004 | 9.9 | 12.4 | 0.80 |
| 2005 | 8.8 | 11.7 | 0.75 |
| 2006 | 9.3 | 12.4 | 0.75 |
| 2007 | 12.9 | 15.9 | 0.81 |
| 2008 | 6.9 | 14.5 | 0.48 |
| 2009 | 9.1 | 14.9 | 0.61 |
| 2010 | 11.8 | 17.1 | 0.69 |
| 2011 | 11.9 | 16.4 | 0.73 |
| 2012 | 5.5 | 13.6 | 0.40 |
| 2013 | 6.5 | 12.3 | 0.53 |
| 2014 | 6.8 | 10.9 | 0.62 |
| 2015 | 4.0 | 11.0 | 0.36 |
| 2016 | 3.0 | 10.7 | 0.28 |
| 2017 | 3.7 | 9.3 | 0.40 |
| 2018 | 3.4 | 6.0 | 0.57 |
| 2019 | 3.9 | 6.3 | 0.62 |
| 2020 | -0.2 | 3.9 | -0.04 |
| 2021 | 4.5 | 8.3 | 0.54 |
| 2022 | -0.2 | 2.6 | -0.08 |

注：本市能源消费增长速度按等价值计算；生产总值增长速度按可比价格计算。
Note:The growth rate of energy consumption is calculated at equivalent value, while the growth rate of GDP is calculated at comparable prices.

## 表 5.6 平均每万元本市生产总值能源消费量（2021 － 2022 年）
## AVERAGE ENERGY CONSUMPTION PER 10 000 YUAN OF GDP (2021-2022)

| 品 种 | Type | 2021 | 2022 |
|---|---|---|---|
| **单位生产总值能源消费量（吨标煤 / 万元）** | **Energy Consumption per Unit of GDP (ton of SCE/10 000 yuan)** | **0.342** | **0.332** |
| 煤 炭 | Coal | 0.147 | 0.146 |
| 天然气 | Natural Gas | 0.065 | 0.046 |
| 油 料 | Oil | 0.052 | 0.063 |
| 一次电力及其他能源 | Primary Electricity and Other Energy | 0.078 | 0.077 |

注：本表 GDP 按 2020 年价计算；能源品种均已折合为按等价值计算的吨标准煤。
Note: The GDP hereof is calculated at 2020 price, and each type of energy has been converted into tons of SCE calculated in equivalent value.

## 表 5.7 平均每天主要能源消费量（2021 － 2022 年）
## AVERAGE DAILY ENERGY CONSUMPTION (2021-2022)

| 品 种 | Type | 2021 | 2022 |
|---|---|---|---|
| **每天能源消费量（万吨标煤 / 天）** | **Average Daily Energy Consumption (10 000 tons of SCE/day)** | **25.40** | **25.35** |
| 煤 炭 | Coal | 10.91 | 11.15 |
| 天然气 | Natural Gas | 3.85 | 3.48 |
| 油 料 | Oil | 4.81 | 4.81 |
| 一次电力及其他能源 | Primary Electricity and Other Energy | 5.82 | 5.90 |

注：本表能源品种均已折合为按等价值计算的吨标准煤。
Note: All sorts of energy in the table has been converted into tons of SCE calculated in equivalent value.

## 表 5.8 综合能源平衡表（2021 － 2022 年）
## OVERALL ENERGY BALANCE SHEET (2021-2022)

单位：万吨标准煤 (10 000 tons of SCE)

| 项 目 | Item | 2021 | | 2022 | |
|---|---|---|---|---|---|
| | | 按当量值计算 Equivalent Weight | 按等价值计算 Equivalent Value | 按当量值计算 Equivalent Weight | 按等价值计算 Equivalent Value |
| **可供消费的能源总量** | **Total Energy Available for Consumption** | **8057.23** | **9282.28** | **8022.76** | **9252.32** |
| #一次能源生产量 | Primary Energy Output | 2237.27 | 2813.57 | 2179.55 | 2639.24 |
| 调进量 | Imports | 8006.12 | 8833.20 | 7761.14 | 8587.70 |
| 调出量(-) | Exports (-) | -1991.92 | -2170.25 | -2007.17 | -2063.86 |
| **能源消费总量** | **Total Energy Consumption** | **8046.31** | **9271.36** | **8022.76** | **9252.32** |
| 终端消费 | End-use Consumption | 6943.39 | 9326.38 | 6733.91 | 9291.63 |
| 第一产业 | Primary Industry | 114.09 | 125.82 | 115.85 | 131.28 |
| 第二产业 | Secondary Industry | 4368.36 | 5729.23 | 4222.89 | 5999.58 |
| 第三产业 | Tertiary Industry | 1497.87 | 2067.76 | 1358.77 | 1977.62 |
| 生活消费 | Household Consumption | 963.07 | 1403.57 | 1036.40 | 1583.14 |
| 城 镇 | Urban | 735.63 | 1028.89 | 800.32 | 1181.49 |
| 乡 村 | Rural | 227.44 | 374.68 | 236.08 | 401.65 |
| 加工转换投入(-)产出(+)量 | Input (-) and Output (+) during the Process of Energy Conversion | -1031.76 | 233.74 | -1214.04 | 216.32 |
| 损失量 | Energy Losses | 71.16 | 178.72 | 74.82 | 177.01 |

## 表 5.9 电力平衡表（2021 – 2022 年）
ELECTRICITY BALANCE SHEET (2021-2022)

单位：亿千瓦小时 (100 million kwh)

| 项　目 | Item | 2021 | 2022 |
|---|---|---|---|
| **可供量** | **Total Energy Available for Consumption** | **1340.65** | **1404.29** |
| 生产量 | Output | 991.43 | 997.84 |
| 水　电 | Hydropower | 282.78 | 203.11 |
| 火　电 | Thermal Power | 681.21 | 755.15 |
| 核　电 | Nuclear Power | | |
| 风电及其他发电 | Wind Power and Other Power | 27.44 | 39.58 |
| 外省（区、市）调入量 | Imports | 445.21 | 436.38 |
| 本省（区、市）调出量（–） | Exports (-) | -95.99 | -29.93 |
| **消费量** | **Total Energy Consumption** | **1340.65** | **1404.29** |
| 在消费量中： | Consumption by Sector | | |
| 农、林、牧、渔、水利业 | Agriculture, Forestry, Animal Husbandry, Fishery and Water Conservancy | 6.31 | 8.15 |
| 工　业 | Industry | 762.05 | 752.27 |
| 建筑业 | Construction | 28.40 | 28.50 |
| 交通运输、仓储和邮政业 | Transport, Storage and Post | 35.77 | 37.38 |
| 批发、零售业和住宿、餐饮业 | Wholesale and Retail Trades, Hotels and Catering Services | 92.17 | 98.37 |
| 其他行业 | Other Sectors | 178.83 | 190.97 |
| 生活消费 | Household Consumption | 237.12 | 288.65 |
| 在消费量中： | Consumption by Usage | | |
| 终端消费 | End-use Consumption | 1282.75 | 1350.34 |
| #工　业 | Industry | 704.15 | 698.32 |
| 输配电损失量 | Losses in Transmission | 57.90 | 53.95 |

重/庆/统/计/年/鉴

# 主要统计指标解释

## ■ 能源消费总量

指一定地域内，国民经济各行业和居民家庭在一定时期内消费的各种能源的总和。包括：原煤、原油、天然气、水能、核能、风能、太阳能、地热能、生物质能等一次能源；一次能源通过加工转换产生的洗煤、焦炭、煤气、电力、热力、成品油等二次能源和同时产生的其他产品；其他化石能源、可再生能源和新能源。其中水能、风能、太阳能、地热能、生物质能等可再生能源，是指人们通过一定技术手段获得的，并作为商品能源使用的部分。在核算过程中，一次能源、二次能源消费不能重复计算。能源消费总量分为终端能源消费量、能源加工转换损失量和能源损失量三部分。

(1) 终端能源消费量：指一定时期内，全国生产和生活消费的各种能源在扣除了用于加工转换二次能源消费量和损失量以后的数量。

(2) 能源加工转换损失量：指一定时期内，全国投入加工转换的各种能源数量之和与产出各种能源产品之和的差额。该指标是观察能源在加工转换过程中损失量变化的指标。

(3) 能源损失量：指一定时期内，能源在输送、分配、储存过程中发生的损失和由客观原因造成的各种损失量，不包括各种气体能源放空、放散量。

## ■ 能源消费弹性系数

反映能源消费增长速度与国民经济增长速度之间关系的指标。计算公式为：

$$能源消费弹性系数=\frac{能源消费量年平均增长速度}{国民经济年平均增长速度}$$

## ■ 单位国内生产总值能耗

指一定时期内，一个国家或地区每生产一个单位的国内生产总值所消费的能源。计算公式为：

$$单位国内生产总值能耗=\frac{能源消费总量}{国内生产总值}$$

## ■ 单位国内生产总值电耗

指一定时期内，一个国家或地区每生产一个单位的国内生产总值所消费的电力。计算公式为：

$$单位国内生产总值电耗=\frac{全社会用电量}{国内生产总值}$$

# Explanatory Notes on Main Statistical Indicators

## Total Energy Consumption

Refers to the total consumption of energy of various kinds by the production sectors of the economy and the households in a given period of time. It includes the primary kinds of energy such as coal, crude oil, natural gas, hydro-power, nuclear power, wind power, solar power, geothermal power and bio-energy; the secondary kinds of energy and their products which are transformed from the primary energy such as washed coal, coke, coal gas, electricity, heating, and petroleum products; and other kinds of fossil energy, renewable energy and new energy. The renewable energy, including hydro-power, wind power, solar power, geothermal power and bio-energy, refers to the part attained with some given technical means and used for commercial purposes. Total energy consumption can be divided into three parts: end-use energy consumption; loss during the process of energy conversion; and energy loss.

(1) End-use Energy Consumption: It refers to the total energy consumption by the production sectors and the households in the country (region) in a given period of time. It does not include the consumption during the conversion of primary energy into secondary energy and the loss in the process of energy conversion.

(2) Loss During the Process of Energy Conversion: It refers to the total input of various kinds of energy for conversion, minus the total output of various kinds of energy in the country in a given period of time. It is an indicator to show the loss that occurs during the process of energy conversion.

(3) Energy Loss: It refers to the total of the loss of energy during the course of energy transport, distribution and storage and the loss caused by any objective reason in a given period of time. The loss of various kinds of gas due to gas discharges and stocktaking is not included.

## Elasticity Ratio of Energy Consumption

Is an indicator to show the relationship between the growth rate of energy consumption and the growth rate of the national economy. The formula is:

Elasticity ratio of energy consumption=

$$\frac{\text{Average Annual Growth Rate of Energy Consumption}}{\text{Average Annual Growth Rate of National Economy}}$$

## Energy Consumption per Unit of GDP

Refers to the energy consumption per unit of Gross Domestic Product in a country or the Gross Regional Product in a region in the same reference period. The formula is:

Energy Consumption per Unit of GDP=

$$\frac{\text{Total Energy Consumption}}{\text{Gross Domestic Product}}$$

## Electricity Consumption per Unit of GDP

Refers to the electricity consumption per unit of Gross Domestic Product in a country or the Gross Regional Product in a region in the same reference period. The formula is:

Electricity Consumption per Unit of GDP=

$$\frac{\text{Total Electricity Consumption}}{\text{Gross Domestic Product}}$$

# 第六章·财 政

GOVERNMENT FINANCE

# 简要说明

## BRIEF INTRODUCTION

本章资料包括全市财政收入和支出情况、税收收入情况，由市统计局综合处分别根据市财政局、市税务局的有关资料整理编辑。

The data in this chapter include the revenue and expenditure of the municipal government, and the revenue from taxation. The data is sorted and compiled by Division of Comprehensive Statistics of Chongqing Municipal Bureau of Statistics on the basis of the materials from Chongqing Municipal Bureau of Finance, Chongqing Municipal Taxation Bureau.

# 表 6.1 财政收入及支出(1994 – 2022 年)
GOVERNMENT REVENUE AND EXPENDITURE (1994-2022)

单位：万元 (10 000 yuan)

| 年 份<br>Year | 财政收入<br>Government Revenue | #地方财政一般预算收入<br>General Budgetary Revenue of Local Government | 基金预算收入<br>Budgetary Revenue from Funds | #中央两税(四税)收入<br>Revenue from the 2 (4) Taxes of Central Government | #地方财政一般预算收入<br>General Budgetary Revenue of Local Government | 基金预算支出<br>Budgetary Expenditure for Funds |
|---|---|---|---|---|---|---|
| 1994 | 716172 | 366325 | | 349847 | 560818 | |
| 1995 | 837748 | 460052 | | 377696 | 662235 | |
| 1996 | 942682 | 549412 | | 393270 | 794216 | |
| 1997 | 1180555 | 593060 | 152236 | 435259 | 1010110 | 141517 |
| 1998 | 1338867 | 711287 | 146759 | 480821 | 1257608 | 101866 |
| 1999 | 1402935 | 767341 | 131571 | 504023 | 1502365 | 121320 |
| 2000 | 1632353 | 872442 | 172128 | 587783 | 1876433 | 148173 |
| 2001 | 1961761 | 1061243 | 202847 | 697671 | 2375486 | 180044 |
| 2002 | 2694610 | 1260674 | 317977 | 991425 | 3058591 | 392083 |
| 2003 | 3412781 | 1615618 | 453697 | 1205457 | 3415775 | 497789 |
| 2004 | 4629591 | 2006241 | 1018198 | 1435206 | 3957233 | 893988 |
| 2005 | 5811921 | 2568072 | 1381552 | 1656599 | 4873543 | 1379973 |
| 2006 | 7421702 | 3177165 | 2117414 | 1944772 | 5942543 | 2259393 |
| 2007 | 10572948 | 4427000 | 3458604 | 2491920 | 7683886 | 3339659 |
| 2008 | 12901828 | 5775738 | 3857654 | 3023634 | 10160112 | 4325469 |
| 2009 | 15353975 | 6818189 | 4838943 | 3403122 | 13180913 | 4879759 |
| 2010 | 29751187 | 10182938 | 9722944 | 4687841 | 17691065 | 9776826 |
| 2011 | 35236522 | 14883336 | 14205767 | 5607771 | 25702404 | 13896341 |

**表 6.1 续表 continued**

单位：万元 (10 000 yuan)

| 年 份 Year | 财政收入 Government Revenue | #地方公共财政预算收入 Public Budgetary Revenue of Local Government | 政府性基金预算收入 Budgetary Revenue from Governmental Funds | 国有资本经营预算收入 State-owned Capital Operational Budgetary Revenue | #中央四税收入 Revenue from the 4 Taxes of Central Government | #地方公共财政预算支出 Public Budgetary Expenditure of Local Government | 政府性基金预算支出 Budgetary Expenditure from Governmental Funds | 国有资本经营预算支出 State-owned Capital Operational Budgetary Expenditure |
|---|---|---|---|---|---|---|---|---|
| 2012 | 37268412 | 14658509 | 14808929 | 1911999 | 5888975 | 27177878 | 15114916 | 1131344 |
| 2013 | 41055563 | 16932438 | 16698044 | 659489 | 6765592 | 30622848 | 17353191 | 646773 |

注：财政收入 2002 年前为地方财政收入与中央两税（增值税和消费税）之和，2002 年起为地方财政收入、中央四税收入和其他中央收入之和。其中其他中央收入不含关税，自 2003 年起包含车辆购置税（以下各表同）。2012 年同期数已按公共财政预算口径作相应调整。

Note: Government revenue before 2002 is the sum of revenue of local government and revenue from the 2 taxes of Central Government (value-added tax and consumption tax), whereas it has been the sum of revenue of local government, revenue from the 4 taxes of Central Government and other revenue of Central Government since 2002. Other revenue of Central Government does not include tariff, while vehicle purchasing tax has been included since 2003 (the same applies to the following tables). The data of 2012 has been adjusted in accordance with the statistic scope of public financial budget.

| 年 份 Year | #地方一般公共预算收入 Public Budgetary Revenue of Local Government | 基金预算收入 Budgetary Revenue from Governmental Funds | 国有资本经营预算收入 State-owned Capital Operational Budgetary Revenue | #中央四税收入 Revenue from the 4 Taxes of Central Government | #地方公共财政预算支出 Public Budgetary Expenditure of Local Government | 政府性基金预算支出 Budgetary Expenditure from Governmental Funds | 国有资本经营预算支出 State-owned Capital Operational Budgetary Expenditure |
|---|---|---|---|---|---|---|---|
| 2013 | 16868717 | 16726787 | 659489 | 6765586 | 30589372 | 17353191 | 646772 |
| 2014 | 19220159 | 18412843 | 680138 | 7767125 | 33043884 | 18600130 | 663118 |
| 2015 | 21548276 | 16642130 | 905730 | 8759172 | 37919973 | 17531573 | 748848 |

| 年 份 Year | #地方一般公共预算收入 Public Budgetary Revenue of Local Government | 基金预算收入 Budgetary Revenue from Governmental Funds | 国有资本经营预算收入 State-owned Capital Operational Budgetary Revenue | 一般公共预算支出 General Public Budget Expenditure | 政府性基金预算支出 Budgetary Expenditure from Governmental Funds | 国有资本经营预算支出 State-owned Capital Operational Budgetary Expenditure |
|---|---|---|---|---|---|---|
| 2015 | 20806250 | 16443229 | 905730 | 38138156 | 17313390 | 748848 |
| 2016 | 22279117 | 14973130 | 904940 | 40018090 | 17381158 | 727387 |
| 2017 | 22523788 | 22511136 | 1267342 | 43362800 | 21822878 | 988242 |
| 2018 | 22655421 | 23162545 | 1052203 | 45409487 | 26777294 | 521548 |
| 2019 | 21349326 | 22479326 | 1317955 | 48476795 | 24192717 | 462001 |
| 2020 | 20948541 | 24578576 | 985213 | 48939461 | 31326457 | 523321 |
| 2021 | 22854533 | 23579430 | 1039975 | 48350551 | 29530244 | 404356 |
| 2022 | 21034234 | 17539493 | 993504 | 48927688 | 29552129 | 282294 |

注：2017 年起按营改增试点后新的收入划分办法及新增建设用地土地有偿使用收入等基金列转公共预算，与往年不可比。

Note: Due to the change of replacing business tax with VAT under the new revenue division system, and the funds like the revenue from paid use of newly-added construction land have included in public budget since 2017, the data are incomparable with the previous year.

# 表 6.2 财政收入(2021－2022 年)
GOVERNMENT REVENUE (2021-2022)

单位: 万元 (10 000 yuan)

| 项　目 | Item | 2021 | 2022 |
|---|---|---|---|
| **一般公共预算收入** | **General Public Budget Revenue** | **22854533** | **21034234** |
| #市　级 | Municipal Level | 7984790 | 6803200 |
| 税收收入 | Total Tax Revenue | 15434039 | 12709388 |
| 增值税 | Value-added Tax | 5736845 | 3941747 |
| 企业所得税 | Corporate Income Tax | 2683794 | 2461816 |
| 个人所得税 | Individual Income Tax | 786592 | 798205 |
| 资源税 | Resource Tax | 132487 | 127313 |
| 城市维护建设税 | City Maintenance and Construction Tax | 998573 | 878881 |
| 房产税 | House Property Tax | 861091 | 938774 |
| 印花税 | Stamp Tax | 342587 | 347953 |
| 城镇土地使用税 | Urban Land Use Tax | 854153 | 814916 |
| 土地增值税 | Land Appreciation Tax | 708607 | 867587 |
| 车船税 | Tax on Vehicles and Boat Operation | 177571 | 184445 |
| 耕地占用税 | Farm Land Occupation Tax | 226898 | 276723 |
| 契　税 | Deed Tax | 1860867 | 972955 |
| 烟叶税 | Tobacco Leaf Tax | 25271 | 29027 |
| 环境保护税 | Environment Protection Tax | 31460 | 35891 |
| 其他税收收入 | Other Tax Revenue | 7243 | 33155 |
| 非税收入 | Total Non-tax Revenue | 7420494 | 8324846 |
| 专项收入 | Special Program Receipts | 1728658 | 1443334 |
| 行政性收费收入 | Charge of Administrative and Institutional Units | 777415 | 717132 |
| 罚没收入 | Penalty Receipts | 553195 | 470119 |
| 国有资源(资产)有偿使用收入 | Revenue from Use of State-owned Resources (assets) | 3304122 | 4934452 |
| 政府住房基金收入 | Revenue from Government Funds for Housing | 764226 | 490945 |
| 其他收入 | Other Revenue | 292878 | 268864 |
| **基金预算收入** | **Budgetary Revenue of Funds** | **23579430** | **17539493** |
| 国有土地使用权出让收入 | Transferring Fee of Use Rights of State-owned Land | 20436661 | 15618617 |
| **国有资本经营预算收入** | **State-owned Capital Operational Budgetary Revenue** | **1039975** | **993504** |

# 表 6.3 财政支出（2021 – 2022 年）
## GOVERNMENT EXPENDITURE (2021-2022)

单位：万元 (10 000 yuan)

| 项　目 | Item | 2021 | 2022 |
|---|---|---|---|
| **一般公共预算支出** | **General Public Budget Expenditure** | **48350551** | **48927688** |
| #市　级 | Municipal Level | 16251454 | 16096891 |
| 一般公共服务支出 | Expenditure for General Public Services | 3576062 | 3410871 |
| 外交支出 | Expenditure for Foreign Affairs | 4080 | 1376 |
| 国防支出 | Expenditure for National Defense | 66276 | 51998 |
| 公共安全支出 | Expenditure for Public Security | 2732005 | 2617823 |
| 教育支出 | Expenditure for Education | 7949530 | 8221685 |
| 科学技术支出 | Expenditure for Science and Technology | 926407 | 988878 |
| 文化旅游体育与传媒支出 | Expenditure for Cultural tourism, sports and media | 642286 | 610468 |
| 社会保障和就业支出 | Expenditure for Social Security and Employment Effort | 10195768 | 10227881 |
| 卫生健康支出 | Expenditure for Health | 4277183 | 4848674 |
| 节能环保支出 | Expenditure for Environment Protection | 1637451 | 1759820 |
| 城乡社区支出 | Expenditure for Urban and Rural Community Affairs | 4356389 | 3844667 |
| 农林水支出 | Expenditure for Agriculture, Forestry and Water Conservancy | 4062587 | 3938467 |
| 交通运输支出 | Expenditure for Transportation | 2774391 | 2904198 |
| 资源勘探信息等支出 | Expenditure for Affairs of Exploration, Power and Information | 1320217 | 1533315 |
| 商业服务业等支出 | Expenditure for Affairs of Commerce and Services | 321478 | 303592 |
| 金融支出 | Expenditure for Finance | 157954 | 60416 |
| 援助其他地区支出 | Expenditure for Other Regional Assistance | 14846 | 14171 |
| 自然资源海洋气象等支出 | Expenditure for Marine Meteorology of natural resources | 456053 | 519805 |
| 住房保障支出 | Expenditure for Affairs of Housing Security | 1280879 | 1450150 |
| 粮油物资储备支出 | Expenditure for Affairs of Management of Grain & Oil Resources | 208947 | 155699 |
| 灾害防治及应急管理支出 | Expenditure for Disaster prevention and emergency management | 423947 | 387996 |
| 债务付息及发行费用支出 | Expenditure for Interest Payment on Debts and Issuing Debts | 942842 | 1041323 |
| 其他支出 | Other Expenditure | 22973 | 34415 |
| **政府性基金预算支出** | **Governmental Fund Budgetary Expenditure** | **29530244** | **29552129** |
| **国有资本经营预算支出** | **State-owned Capital Operational Budgetary Expenditure** | **404356** | **282294** |

# 表 6.4 税收收入(2021 - 2022 年)
TAXES (2021-2022)

单位: 万元 (10 000 yuan)

| 项 目 | Item | 2021 | 2022 |
|---|---|---|---|
| 税收收入合计 | Total Revenue from Taxation | 30426301 | 26183430 |
| 中央级 | Central Government | 15239908 | 13422496 |
| 重庆市级 | Chongqing Municipal Government | 5058474 | 3993146 |
| 区县级 | District and County Governments | 10127919 | 8767788 |
| **按税种分** | **By Tax Category** | | |
| 增值税 | Value-added Tax | 12542341 | 9563485 |
| 其中: 国内增值税 | Domestic Value-added Tax | 11064392 | 8026777 |
| 消费税 | Consumption Tax | 2150695 | 2467570 |
| 其中: 国内消费税 | Domestic Consumption Tax | 2093608 | 2430797 |
| 企业所得税 | Corporate Income Tax | 6747607 | 6140563 |
| 个人所得税 | Individual Income Tax | 1989080 | 2024751 |
| 资源税 | Resource Tax | 132486 | 127312 |
| 城市维护建设税 | City Maintenance and Construction Tax | 998748 | 878906 |
| 房产税 | House Property Tax | 861092 | 938773 |
| 印花税 | Stamp Tax | 342587 | 347953 |
| 城镇土地使用税 | Urban Land Use Tax | 854151 | 814915 |
| 土地增值税 | Land Appreciation Tax | 708606 | 867588 |
| 车船税 | Tax on Vehicles and Boat Operation | 177570 | 184441 |
| 车辆购置税 | Vehicle Purchasing Tax | 762356 | 446258 |
| 烟叶税 | Tobacco Leaf Tax | 25271 | 29027 |
| 耕地占用税 | Farm Land Occupation Tax | 226899 | 276723 |
| 契 税 | Deed Tax | 1860867 | 972962 |
| 环境保护税 | Environment Protection Tax | 31462 | 35893 |
| 其他税收 | Other Tax | 14483 | 66310 |
| **按行业分** | **By Sector** | | |
| 第一产业 | Primary Industry | 24553 | 26866 |
| 第二产业 | Secondary Industry | 12146412 | 11803062 |
| 工 业 | Industry | 9634119 | 9714709 |
| 建筑业 | Construction | 2512293 | 2088353 |
| 第三产业 | Tertiary Industry | 18255336 | 14353502 |
| 交通运输仓储及邮政业 | Transport, Storage and Post | 381306 | -409623 |
| 批发和零售业 | Wholesale and Retail Trades | 3965103 | 3918847 |
| 金融业 | Financial Intermediation | 3811472 | 3717623 |
| 信息传输、计算机服务和软件业 | Information Transmission, Computer Services and Software | 683742 | 665096 |
| 住宿和餐饮业 | Hotel and Catering Services | 63652 | 40004 |
| 文化、体育和娱乐业 | Culture, Sports and Entertainment | 135146 | 125543 |
| 租赁和商务服务业 | Leasing and Business Services | 1404289 | 1451715 |
| 房地产业 | Real Estate | 5832849 | 3143731 |
| 其他行业 | Other Trades | 1977777 | 1700566 |

注: 税收收入含海关代征。
Note: Tax revenue includes customs collection.

# 表 6.5 按企业类型分的税收收入（2022 年）
## TAX REVENUE BY REGISTRATION STATUS (2022)

| 项 目 | Item | 合 计<br>Total | 内资企业 Domestic-funded<br>国有企业<br>State-owned | <br>集体企业<br>Collective-owned | <br>股份合作企业<br>Cooperative |
|---|---|---|---|---|---|
| **总 计** | **Total** | **26183430** | **2350781** | **29185** | **10601** |
| 国内增值税 | Domestic Value-added Tax | 8026777 | 634022 | 12570 | 6067 |
| 国内消费税 | Domestic Consumption Tax | 2430797 | 487951 | 5 | 2 |
| 企业所得税 | Corporate Income Tax | 6140563 | 271700 | 5628 | 820 |
| 个人所得税 | Individual Income Tax | 2024751 | 45859 | 1407 | 972 |
| 资源税 | Resource Tax | 127312 | 43838 | 343 | 2 |
| 城市维护建设税 | City Maintenance and Construction Tax | 878906 | 66293 | 738 | 408 |
| 房产税 | House Property Tax | 938773 | 37088 | 2036 | 609 |
| 印花税 | Stamp Tax | 347953 | 9957 | 153 | 147 |
| 城镇土地使用税 | Urban Land Use Tax | 814915 | 29532 | 922 | 465 |
| 土地增值税 | Land Appreciation Tax | 867588 | 49525 | 4844 | 99 |
| 车船税 | Tax on Vehicles and Boat Operation | 184441 | 162 | 14 | 873 |
| 车辆购置税 | Vehicle Purchasing Tax | 446258 | 765 | 70 | 37 |
| 耕地占用税 | Farm Land Occupation Tax | 276723 | 16922 | 41 | |
| 契 税 | Deed Tax | 972962 | 25977 | 176 | 87 |
| 环境保护税 | Environment Protection Tax | 35893 | 1118 | 39 | 13 |
| 其他税收 | Other Tax | 1668818 | 630072 | 199 | |

单位：万元 (10 000 yuan)

| 内资企业 Domestic-funded | | | | | 港澳台投资企业 Enterprises with Funds from Hong Kong, Macao and Taiwan | 外商投资企业 Foreign-funded Enterprises | 个体经营 Self-employed | 非企业单位 Non-enterprise unit |
|---|---|---|---|---|---|---|---|---|
| 联营企业 Joint Ownership | 有限责任公司 Limited Liability Corporations | 股份有限公司 Share-holding Corporations Ltd. | 私营企业 Private | 其他企业 Other | | | | |
| **4294** | **7068097** | **4237727** | **6908517** | **9015** | **1122562** | **2495304** | **183766** | **1763581** |
| 2595 | 1095847 | 2112765 | 3172708 | 2779 | 278556 | 466706 | 127118 | 115044 |
| | 1400936 | 232728 | 49356 | 1 | 110123 | 147106 | 2589 | |
| 650 | 1953869 | 1112431 | 1702624 | 1567 | 426470 | 645506 | | 19298 |
| 288 | 328501 | 287594 | 628214 | 2424 | 46715 | 87947 | 46538 | 548292 |
| | 31608 | 17932 | 30314 | 1 | 513 | 1338 | 999 | 424 |
| 173 | 290802 | 159380 | 259404 | 159 | 40187 | 51191 | 4635 | 5536 |
| 81 | 449851 | 83338 | 206813 | 482 | 59523 | 47560 | 322 | 51070 |
| 290 | 117041 | 43260 | 127198 | 518 | 12614 | 23249 | 325 | 13201 |
| 125 | 473110 | 39256 | 209285 | 810 | 24204 | 30316 | 315 | 6575 |
| 92 | 304522 | 55669 | 256578 | 106 | 87865 | 26789 | 90 | 81409 |
| | 125748 | 53762 | 3186 | | 16 | 565 | | 115 |
| | 11225 | 1083 | 53525 | 54 | 642 | 713 | 497 | 377647 |
| | 182260 | 3266 | 25666 | 72 | 1285 | | 55 | 47156 |
| | 253526 | 10851 | 169185 | 31 | 6789 | 8560 | 189 | 497591 |
| | 13670 | 5276 | 13167 | 7 | 1311 | 1081 | 87 | 124 |
| | 35581 | 19136 | 1294 | 4 | 25749 | 956677 | 7 | 99 |

重/庆/统/计/年/鉴

# 主要统计指标解释

## 一般公共预算收入

指国家财政参与社会产品分配所取得的收入，是实现国家职能的财力保证。主要包括：（1）各项税收：包括增值税、企业所得税、个人所得税、资源税、城市维护建设税、房产税、印花税、城镇土地使用税、土地增值税、车船税、耕地占用税、契税、烟叶税、环境保护税、其他税收收入；（2）非税收入：包括专项收入、行政事业性收费、罚没收入、国有资本经营收入、国有资源（资产）有偿使用收入和其他收入。财政收入按现行分税制财政体制划分为中央本级收入和地方本级收入。

## 一般公共预算支出

指国家财政将筹集起来的资金进行分配使用，以满足经济建设和各项事业的需要。主要包括：一般公共服务、外交、国防、公共安全、教育、科学技术、文化旅游体育与传媒、社会保障和就业、卫生健康支出、节能环保、城乡社区、农林水、交通运输、资源勘探信息等、商业服务业等、金融、援助其他地区、国土海洋气象等、住房保障、粮油物资储备、债务付息、债务发行费用等方面的支出。财政支出根据政府在经济和社会活动中的不同职权，划分为中央财政支出和地方财政支出。

## 中央一般公共预算收入和地方一般公共预算收入

属于中央一般公共预算的收入包括关税，进口货物增值税和消费税，出口货物退增值税和消费税，国内消费税，铁道部门、各银行总行、各保险公司总公司等集中缴纳的城市维护建设税，增值税 50% 部分，纳入共享范围的企业所得税 60% 部分，未纳入共享范围的中央企业所得税、中央企业上交的利润，个人所得税 60% 部分，车辆购置税，船舶吨税，证券交易印花税，海洋石油资源税，中央非税收入等。属于地方一般公共预算的收入包括城市维护建设税（不含铁道部门、各银行总行、各保险公司总公司集中缴纳的部分），房产税，城镇土地使用税，土地增值税，车船税，耕地占用税，契税，烟叶税，印花税（不含证券交易印花税），增值税 50% 部分，纳入共享范围的企业所得税 40% 部分，个人所得税 40% 部分，海洋石油资源税以外的其他资源税，地方非税收入等。

## 中央一般公共预算支出和地方一般公共预算支出

指根据政府在经济和社会活动中的不同职责，划分中央和地方政府的责权，按照政府的责权划分确定的支出。中央一般公共预算支出包括一般公共服务，外交支出，国防支出，公共安全支出，以及中央政府调整国民经济结构、协调地区发展、实施宏观调控的支出等。地方一般公共预算支出包括一般公共服务，公共安全支出，地方统筹的各项社会事业支出等。

# Explanatory Notes on Main Statistical Indicators

## General Public Budget Revenue

Refers to income for the government finance through participating in the distribution of social products. It is the financial guarantee to ensure government functioning. The government revenue includes the following main items: (1) Various tax revenues including domestic value added tax (VAT), Value-added tax,corporate income tax,individual income tax,resource tax,city maintenance and construction tax,house property tax,samp tax,urban land use tax,land Appreciation tax,tax on vehicles and boat operation,farm land occupation tax,deed tax,tobacco leaf tax,environment protection tax,other tax revenue. (2) Non-tax revenue, including special program receipts, charge of administrative and institutional units, penalty receipts, operating income from government capital, income from use of state-owned resources (assets) and others non-tax receipts.

## General Public Budget Expenditure

Refers to the distribution and use of the funds which the government finance has raised, so as to meet the needs of economic construction and various undertakings. It includes the following main items: expenditure for general public services, expenditure for foreign affairs, expenditure for national defence expenditure for public security, expenditure for education, expenditure for science and technology, expenditure for cultural tourism, sports and media, expenditure for social safety net and employment effort, expenditure for health, expenditure for energy conservation and environment protection, expenditure for urban and rural community affairs, expenditure for agriculture, forestry and water conservancy, expenditure for transportation, expenditure for resource exploration and information, expenditure for affairs of commerce and services, expenditure for finance, aid to other regions, expenditure for land, ocean and weather, expenditure for housing security, expenditure for grain & oil reserves, interest payment for public debts, expenditure for issuing debts. General public budget expenditure is divided into general public budget expenditure of central government and general public budget expenditure of local government according to the different functions of the governments played in economic and social activities,

## General Public Budget Revenue of the Central Government and the Local Governments

The general public budget revenue of the Central Government includes tariff, VAT and consumption tax from imports, VAT and consumption tax rebate for exports, domestic consumption tax, city maintenance and construct tax from the Ministry of Railways, head offices of banks, head offices of insurance company, which are handed over to the government in a centralized way, 50% of the value added tax, 60% the share part of the corporate income tax, unshared part of corporate income tax of the central enterprises, profit handed in by the central enterprises, 60% of individual income tax, vehicle purchase tax, ship tonnage tax, stamp tax on securities transactions, resource tax on the offshore petroleum resources. The general public budget revenue of the local governments includes city maintenance and construct tax (excluding the part of the Ministry of Railways, head offices of banks, head offices of insurance company, which are handed over to the government in a centralized way), house property tax, urban land use tax, land appreciation tax, tax on vehicles and boat operation, farm land occupation tax, deed tax, and tobacco leaf tax, stamp tax (not including stamp tax on security exchange), 50% of the value added tax, 40% the share part of the corporate income tax, 40% of individual income tax, resource tax other than the tax on offshore petroleum resources, local non-tax revenue, etc.

## General Public Budget Expenditure of the Central Government and Local Governments

According to the different functions of the Central Government and local governments in economic and social activities, the rights of administration are demarcated between those of the Central Government and those of local governments; and the classification of the expenditure between the Central Government and local governments are made on the basis of the classification of the rights administration between them. The general public budget expenditure of the Central Government includes the expenditure for general public services, expenditure for foreign affairs, expenditure for public security, and the general public budget expenditure of the Central Government for adjusting the national economic structure; coordinating the development among different regions; and exercising macroeconomic regulation. The general public budget expenditure of the local governments includes mainly the expenditure for general public services, expenditure for public security, and expenditures for social development which are planed by local governments, etc.

# 第七章・人民生活与物价

# PEOPLE'S LIVING CONDITIONS AND PRICE OF GOODS

# 简要说明

## BRIEF INTRODUCTION

本章资料反映全市城乡居民生活状况，主要内容包括城乡居民家庭基本情况、恩格尔系数、住户存款、年收入支出及其构成、主要商品购买数量、耐用消费品的拥有量，以及居民消费价格指数、商品零售价格指数、工业生产者价格指数、固定资产投资价格指数、住宅销售价格指数等。居民住户调查资料是抽样调查汇总的结果，价格调查是一种非全面调查，采用重点调查和典型调查相结合的方法。

城镇常住居民和农村常住居民生活状况和价格调查的数据来源于国家统计局重庆调查总队。城乡居民物质生活情况和居民储蓄由市统计局综合处整理编辑。

The data in this chapter present the living conditions of the urban and rural households in Chongqing, including basic conditions of urban and rural households, Engle's coefficient, saving deposits, annual income & expenditure and their compositions, purchases of major commodities, possession of durable consumer goods, as well as consumer price indices, retail price indices, purchasing price index, price indices of investment in fixed assets and price index of residential real estate sales, etc. The data of urban and rural households are the results of sample survey, while price survey is an incomplete survey, where the main unit survey and typical survey are combined.

The data about the living conditions of urban and rural residents and price survey are provided by NBS Survey Office in Chongqing. The data of material & cultural life and saving deposits of urban & rural residents are sorted and compiled by Division of Comprehensive Statistics, Chongqing Municipal Bureau of Statistics.

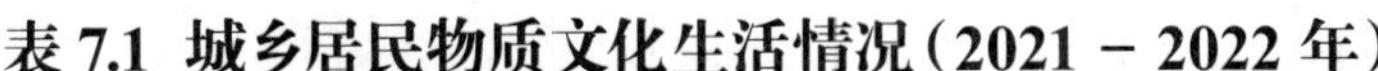

## 表 7.1 城乡居民物质文化生活情况（2021 – 2022 年）
## MATERIAL AND CULTURAL LIFE OF URBAN & RURAL RESIDENTS (2021-2022)

| 指　标 | Item | 2021 | 2022 |
|---|---|---|---|
| **就　业** | **Employment** | | |
| 每一城镇常住劳动力负担人数（人） | Number of Dependents per Urban Employee (person) | 1.32 | 1.32 |
| 每一农村常住劳动力负担人数（人） | Number of Dependents per Rural Laborer (person) | 1.39 | 1.42 |
| **收入和支出** | **Income and Expenditure** | | |
| 城镇非私营单位在岗职工平均工资（元） | Annual Average Wage of On-Post Staff and Workers of Urban Non-private Units (yuan) | 106966 | 111424 |
| 城镇常住居民人均可支配收入（元） | Annual per Capita Disposable Income of Urban Households (yuan) | 43502 | 45509 |
| 农民常住居民人均可支配收入（元） | Annual per Capita Net Income of Rural Households (yuan) | 18100 | 19313 |
| 城镇常住居民人均消费性支出（元） | Annual per Capita Consumption Expenditure of Urban Households(yuan) | 29850 | 30574 |
| 农村常住居民人均生活消费支出（元） | Annual per Capita Living Expenditure of Rural Households (yuan) | 16096 | 16727 |
| 城镇常住居民家庭恩格尔系数（%） | Engle's Coefficient of Urban Households (%) | 32.0 | 33.0 |
| 农村常住居民家庭恩格尔系数（%） | Engle's Coefficient of Rural Households (%) | 36.6 | 36.5 |
| 人均住户存款（元） | Per Capita Saving Deposits of Residents (yuan) | 65131 | |
| **住　房** | **Housing** | | |
| 城镇常住居民人均住房建筑面积（平方米） | Per Capita Residential Floor Space of Urban Residents (sq.m) | 40.31 | 40.56 |
| 农村常住居民人均住房建筑面积（平方米） | Per Capita Living Space of Rural Residents (sq.m) | 55.46 | 55.72 |
| **城市公用事业** | **City Public Utilities** | | |
| 人均道路面积（平方米） | Per Capita Area of Paved Roads (sq.m) | 15.34 | 16.08 |
| 用水普及率（%） | Percentage of Population with Access to Tap Water (%) | 96.50 | 98.67 |
| 燃气普及率（%） | Percentage of Population with Access to Gas (%) | 98.15 | 98.74 |
| 人均公园绿地面积（平方米） | Per Capita Public Green Land(sq.m) | 16.33 | 17.35 |
| **教　育** | **Education** | | |
| 学龄儿童入学率（%） | Enrollment Ratio of School-Aged Children (%) | 99.93 | 99.99 |
| 每万人口中在校大学生（人） | Number of Undergraduates Per 10 000 Population (person) | 360 | 384 |
| **文　化** | **Culture** | | |
| 每百户城镇常住家庭拥有彩色电视机（台） | Number of Color TV Sets Per 100 Urban Households (unit) | 124.61 | 125.47 |
| 每百户农村常住家庭拥有彩色电视机（台） | Number of Color TV Sets Per 100 Rural Households (unit) | 115.89 | 110.44 |
| 广播人口覆盖率（%） | Rate of Radio Broadcast Coverage of the Population (%) | 99.49 | 99.55 |
| 电视人口覆盖率（%） | Rate of TV Coverage of the Population (%) | 99.56 | 99.65 |
| **卫　生** | **Public Health** | | |
| 每万人拥有医院、卫生院病床（张） | Number of Beds of Hospitals and Health Centers Per 10 000 Population (bed) | 59 | 72 |
| 每万人拥有执业（助理）医师（人） | Number of Licensed (Assistant) Doctors Per 10 000 Population (person) | 29 | 29 |

# 表 7.2 个人储蓄存款年末余额（1980 － 2022 年）
## YEAR-END SAVINGS DEPOSIT OF RMB OF HOUSEHOLDS (1980-2022)

| 年 份<br>Year | 个人储蓄存款<br>年末余额（亿元）<br>Year-end Savings Deposit of RMB of Households (100 million yuan) | 定 期<br>Time Deposits | 活 期<br>Demand Deposits | 人均个人储蓄<br>存款余额（元）<br>Per Capita Balance of Savings Deposit of RMB (yuan) |
|---|---|---|---|---|
| 1980 | 6.22 | | 23 | 23 |
| 1981 | 8.35 | | 31 | 31 |
| 1982 | 10.56 | | 39 | 39 |
| 1983 | 13.34 | | 49 | 49 |
| 1984 | 18.39 | | 67 | 67 |
| 1985 | 25.41 | | 92 | 92 |
| 1986 | 34.79 | | 124 | 124 |
| 1987 | 44.46 | | 156 | 156 |
| 1988 | 50.50 | 40.65 | 9.85 | 176 |
| 1989 | 68.17 | 55.75 | 12.42 | 235 |
| 1990 | 92.17 | 77.63 | 14.54 | 316 |
| 1991 | 121.95 | 103.36 | 18.59 | 415 |
| 1992 | 154.45 | 128.64 | 25.81 | 523 |
| 1993 | 198.05 | 160.51 | 37.54 | 668 |
| 1994 | 285.40 | 231.23 | 54.17 | 956 |
| 1995 | 401.45 | 331.09 | 70.36 | 1337 |
| 1996 | 500.71 | 403.84 | 96.87 | 1656 |
| 1997 | 580.67 | 454.04 | 126.63 | 1908 |
| 1998 | 724.54 | 552.72 | 171.82 | 2368 |
| 1999 | 909.10 | 672.96 | 236.14 | 2959 |
| 2000 | 1085.36 | 774.38 | 310.98 | 3511 |
| 2001 | 1317.17 | 929.37 | 387.80 | 4252 |
| 2002 | 1595.01 | 1082.90 | 512.11 | 5122 |
| 2003 | 1896.56 | 1265.52 | 631.04 | 6059 |
| 2004 | 2189.73 | 1469.99 | 719.74 | 6964 |
| 2005 | 2545.85 | 1740.13 | 805.72 | 8033 |
| 2006 | 2949.05 | 1999.88 | 949.17 | 9219 |
| 2007 | 3228.15 | 2099.55 | 1128.60 | 9978 |
| 2008 | 3988.96 | 2640.70 | 1348.26 | 12247 |
| 2009 | 4908.68 | 3060.01 | 1848.67 | 14986 |
| 2010 | 5839.66 | 3475.19 | 2364.47 | 17677 |
| 2011 | 6990.25 | 4106.17 | 2708.61 | 20993 |
| 2012 | 8361.64 | 4996.24 | 3166.45 | 25009 |
| 2013 | 9622.31 | 5735.53 | 3693.17 | 28651 |
| 2014 | 10774.12 | 6422.07 | 3845.29 | 31921 |

| 年 份<br>Year | 住户存款<br>Savings Deposit of RMB of Households | 其 中 of which | | 人均住户存款<br>Per Capita Saving Deposits of RMB of Residents (yuan) |
|---|---|---|---|---|
| | | 定期及其他存款<br>Time Deposits and Other Deposits | 活 期<br>Demand Deposits | |
| 2015 | 12207.28 | 7968.14 | 4239.15 | 36204 |
| 2016 | 13399.44 | 8639.07 | 4760.37 | 39502 |
| 2017 | 14367.38 | 9383.75 | 4983.63 | 42384 |
| 2018 | 15907.23 | 10654.17 | 5253.06 | 46736 |
| 2019 | 17938.33 | 12257.97 | 5680.36 | 52280 |
| 2020 | 20209.77 | 13932.02 | 6277.75 | 59188 |
| 2021 | 22239.89 | 15610.14 | 6629.76 | 65131 |
| 2022 | 25458.85 | 18211.49 | 7247.35 | 74576 |

注：因人民银行统计口径调整，2015 年前起取消个人储蓄存款统计项，新建立了住户存款项目，下设活期存款、定期及其他存款两个分项。

Note: Due to the changes of the PBoC's statistical indicators, two sub-items including demand deposits, time deposits and other deposits were built under the item of savings deposit of RMB of households since 2015.

# 表 7.3 城乡居民家庭人均收入及恩格尔系数（1978－2012 年）

## PER CAPITA ANNUAL INCOME AND ENGLE'S COEFFICIENT OF URBAN AND RURAL HOUSEHOLDS (1978-2012)

| 年 份<br>Year | 城镇常住居民人均可支配收入<br>Per Capita Annual Disposable Income of Permanent Urban Residents | | 农村常住居民人均可支配收入<br>Per Capita Annual Disposable Income of Permanent Rural Residents | | 城镇居民家庭恩格尔系数（%）<br>Engle's Coefficient of Urban Households (%) | 农村居民家庭恩格尔系数（%）<br>Engle's Coefficient of Rural Households (%) |
|---|---|---|---|---|---|---|
| | 绝对数（元）<br>Value (yuan) | 指 数（1979=100）<br>Index（1979=100） | 绝对数（元）<br>Value (yuan) | 指 数（1978=100）<br>Index（1978=100） | | |
| 1978 | | | 126 | 100.0 | | 74.0 |
| 1979 | 355 | 100.0 | 150 | 119.2 | 61.9 | 72.9 |
| 1980 | 412 | 116.1 | 163 | 129.6 | 52.8 | 68.1 |
| 1981 | 481 | 135.6 | 229 | 181.9 | 58.1 | 65.6 |
| 1982 | 505 | 142.5 | 237 | 187.8 | 59.4 | 65.6 |
| 1983 | 536 | 151.1 | 278 | 220.4 | 61.3 | 66.9 |
| 1984 | 616 | 173.9 | 311 | 246.5 | 60.0 | 67.9 |
| 1985 | 762 | 215.1 | 325 | 258.1 | 51.8 | 63.9 |
| 1986 | 984 | 277.6 | 359 | 284.8 | 50.4 | 63.4 |
| 1987 | 1109 | 312.8 | 386 | 306.2 | 51.0 | 62.2 |
| 1988 | 1278 | 360.5 | 458 | 363.1 | 49.9 | 60.5 |
| 1989 | 1449 | 408.7 | 510 | 404.8 | 55.5 | 61.6 |
| 1990 | 1691 | 477.0 | 587 | 465.6 | 52.7 | 63.6 |
| 1991 | 1892 | 533.7 | 629 | 499.1 | 51.2 | 63.8 |
| 1992 | 2195 | 619.3 | 677 | 537.6 | 52.4 | 62.8 |
| 1993 | 2781 | 784.4 | 748 | 593.7 | 51.3 | 61.3 |
| 1994 | 3634 | 1025.2 | 1018 | 808.1 | 51.4 | 63.5 |
| 1995 | 4375 | 1234.2 | 1270 | 1008.2 | 48.7 | 64.7 |
| 1996 | 5023 | 1416.9 | 1479 | 1173.8 | 50.2 | 63.2 |
| 1997 | 5302 | 1495.6 | 1692 | 1343.0 | 46.7 | 65.8 |
| 1998 | 5431 | 1532.1 | 1804 | 1431.3 | 45.6 | 61.3 |
| 1999 | 5818 | 1641.3 | 1841 | 1460.7 | 42.6 | 60.3 |
| 2000 | 6152 | 1735.5 | 1900 | 1508.1 | 41.6 | 52.6 |
| 2001 | 6544 | 1846.1 | 1982 | 1573.1 | 39.9 | 52.7 |
| 2002 | 7000 | 1974.7 | 2112 | 1676.3 | 36.8 | 53.9 |
| 2003 | 7773 | 2192.7 | 2233 | 1772.4 | 36.2 | 50.1 |
| 2004 | 8793 | 2480.3 | 2536 | 2012.2 | 35.4 | 53.3 |
| 2005 | 9700 | 2736.2 | 2842 | 2255.1 | 33.8 | 49.5 |
| 2006 | 10878 | 3068.7 | 2911 | 2310.1 | 33.4 | 48.8 |
| 2007 | 11758 | 3316.8 | 3560 | 2825.5 | 33.9 | 50.9 |
| 2008 | 13321 | 3757.8 | 4193 | 3327.5 | 35.6 | 49.2 |
| 2009 | 14502 | 4090.9 | 4557 | 3616.8 | 33.6 | 44.4 |
| 2010 | 16032 | 4522.4 | 5378 | 4268.2 | 33.0 | 42.9 |
| 2011 | 18517 | 5223.4 | 6605 | 5241.9 | 34.5 | 41.5 |
| 2012 | 21003 | 5924.6 | 7526 | 5972.2 | 36.7 | 38.9 |

注：改革开放以来，城乡住户调查经历了多次变革，现根据国家统计局住户办统一制定的方法对 1998 年以后的城乡住户调查数据按现行口径进行了技术性处理，从而导致本表中所列部分数据与历史数据存在一定差别。

Note: Since 1978, the methodology on the Integrated Urban and Rural Household Survey on Income and Expenditures and Living Conditions has been changed several times. The data on the living conditions of urban and rural residents after 1998 have been adjusted according to the NBS' s latest rules, so partial data in this table are different from the historical data.

## 表 7.4 居民人均收支及恩格尔系数（2013 – 2022 年）
## PER CAPITA RESIDENTS INCOME AND EXPENDITURE AND ENGLE COEFFICIENT (2013-2022)

| 年份 Year | 居民人均可支配收入（元）Per Capita Annual Disposable Income (yuan) | | | 居民人均消费支出（元）Per Capita Annual Living Expenditure (yuan) | | | 恩格尔系数(%) Engle Coefficient (%) | | |
|---|---|---|---|---|---|---|---|---|---|
| | 全体居民 Total | 城镇常住居民 Permanent Urban Residents | 农村常住居民 Permanent Rural Residents | 全体居民 Total | 城镇常住居民 Permanent Urban Residents | 农村常住居民 Permanent Rural Residents | 全体居民 Total | 城镇常住居民 Permanent Urban Residents | 农村常住居民 Permanent Rural Residents |
| 2013 | 16569 | 23058 | 8493 | 12600 | 17124 | 6971 | 35.8 | 35.0 | 38.1 |
| 2014 | 18352 | 25147 | 9490 | 13811 | 18279 | 7983 | 36.0 | 34.5 | 40.5 |
| 2015 | 20110 | 27239 | 10505 | 15140 | 19742 | 8938 | 35.2 | 33.6 | 40.0 |
| 2016 | 22034 | 29610 | 11549 | 16385 | 21031 | 9954 | 34.3 | 32.7 | 38.7 |
| 2017 | 24153 | 32193 | 12638 | 17898 | 22759 | 10936 | 33.2 | 32.1 | 36.5 |
| 2018 | 26386 | 34889 | 13781 | 19248 | 24154 | 11977 | 32.3 | 31.5 | 34.9 |
| 2019 | 28920 | 37939 | 15133 | 20774 | 25785 | 13112 | 32.1 | 31.2 | 34.9 |
| 2020 | 30824 | 40006 | 16361 | 21678 | 26464 | 14140 | 33.6 | 32.6 | 36.7 |
| 2021 | 33803 | 43502 | 18100 | 24598 | 29850 | 16096 | 33.2 | 32.0 | 36.6 |
| 2022 | 35666 | 45509 | 19313 | 25371 | 30574 | 16727 | 33.9 | 33.0 | 36.5 |

## 表 7.5 居民家庭基本情况（2021 – 2022 年）
## BASIC CONDITIONS OF RESIDENT HOUSEHOLDS (2021-2022)

| 指 标 | Item | 2021 | 2022 |
|---|---|---|---|
| **平均每户常住人口（人）** | **Average Permanent Population Per Household (person)** | | |
| 全体居民 | Total Residents | 2.97 | 2.94 |
| 城镇常住居民 | Permanent Urban Residents | 3.02 | 2.99 |
| 农村常住居民 | Permanent Rural Residents | 2.89 | 2.86 |
| **平均每户常住劳动力（人）** | **Average Number of Full/Semi Permanent Laborers Per Household (person)** | | |
| 全体居民 | Total Residents | 2.20 | 2.17 |
| 城镇常住居民 | Permanent Urban Residents | 2.29 | 2.28 |
| 农村常住居民 | Permanent Rural Residents | 2.07 | 2.01 |
| **平均每户常住成员从业人数（人）** | **Average Number of Permanent Employed Persons Per Household (person)** | | |
| 全体居民 | Total Residents | 1.62 | 1.59 |
| 城镇常住居民 | Permanent Urban Residents | 1.51 | 1.48 |
| 农村常住居民 | Permanent Rural Residents | 1.79 | 1.77 |
| **平均每人住房建筑面积（平方米）** | **Per Capita Residential Floor Space (sq.m)** | | |
| 全体居民 | Total Residents | 46.10 | 46.26 |
| 城镇常住居民 | Permanent Urban Residents | 40.31 | 40.56 |
| 农村常住居民 | Permanent Rural Residents | 55.46 | 55.72 |

注：从 2012 年四季度起，国家统计局对分别进行的城乡住户调查实施了一体化改革，统一了城乡居民收入指标名称、分类和统计标准，建立了城乡统一的一体化住户调查制度（即《住户收支与生活状况调查》），本年鉴所载 2013 年以来城乡住户收支与生活状况有关指标及数据资料均取自一体化改革后的住户调查。

Note: Starting from the 4th quarter of 2012, the NBS carried out the integrated reform on the urban and rural household survey, unified the index titles, categories and statistical standards of urban and rural residents income, and established the integrated urban and rural household survey system (Household Income & Expenditure and Living Conditions Survey). The indices and data concerning the urban and rural households income & expenditure and living conditions from 2013 herein are collected from the household survey after the integrated reform.

## 表 7.6 全体居民人均可支配收入与现金可支配收入情况(2021 – 2022 年)
## PER CAPITA ANNUAL DISPOSABLE INCOME AND CASH DISPOSABLE INCOME OF HOUSEHOLDS (2021-2022)

单位: 元 (yuan)

| 指 标 | Item | 2021 | 2022 |
|---|---|---|---|
| **可支配收入** | **Per Capita Annual Disposable Income** | **33803** | **35666** |
| 工资性收入 | Income from Wages and Salaries | 18138 | 19178 |
| 经营净收入 | Income from Household Operations | 5358 | 5525 |
| 第一产业 | Primary Industry | 2009 | 1931 |
| 第二产业 | Secondary Industry | 282 | 308 |
| 第三产业 | Tertiary Industry | 3067 | 3287 |
| 财产净收入 | Income from Properties | 2090 | 2217 |
| 转移净收入 | Income from Transfers | 8217 | 8746 |
| **#现金可支配收入** | **Per Capita Cash Disposable Income** | **31610** | **33219** |
| 现金工资性收入 | Income from Wages and Salaries | 18028 | 19046 |
| 现金经营净收入 | Income from Household Operations | 5002 | 5022 |
| 第一产业 | Primary Industry | 1338 | 1238 |
| 第二产业 | Secondary Industry | 300 | 327 |
| 第三产业 | Tertiary Industry | 3364 | 3457 |
| 现金财产净收入 | Income from Properties | 907 | 962 |
| 现金转移净收入 | Income from Transfers | 7673 | 8190 |

## 表 7.7 全体居民人均消费性支出情况（2021－2022 年）
## PER CAPITA ANNUAL CONSUMPTION EXPENDITURE OF HOUSEHOLDS (2021-2022)

单位：元 (yuan)

| 指　标 | Item | 2021 | 2022 |
|---|---|---|---|
| **消费支出** | **Per Capita Annual Consumption Expenditure** | **24598** | **25371** |
| 食品烟酒 | Food, Tobacco and Liquor | 8154 | 8600 |
| 衣　着 | Clothing | 1708 | 1698 |
| 居　住 | Residence | 4490 | 4783 |
| 生活消费及服务 | Household Facilities, Articles and Services | 1683 | 1657 |
| 交通通信 | Transport and Communications | 3050 | 3078 |
| 教育文化娱乐 | Education, Culture and recreation | 2601 | 2585 |
| 医疗保健 | Health Care and Medical Services | 2326 | 2351 |
| 其他用品和服务 | Other Goods and Services | 585 | 620 |

## 表 7.8 全体居民人均收支构成情况（2021 – 2022 年）
## COMPOSITION OF PER CAPITA CASH INCOME AND CASH EXPENDITURE OF HOUSEHOLDS (2021-2022)

单位：% (%)

| 指　标 | Item | 2021 | 2022 |
|---|---|---|---|
| **可支配收入（可支配收入 =100)** | **Composition of Per Capita Annual Disposable Income** | **100.0** | **100.0** |
| 工资性收入 | Income from Wages and Salaries | 53.6 | 53.8 |
| 经营净收入 | Income from Household Operations | 15.9 | 15.5 |
| 财产净收入 | Income from Properties | 6.2 | 6.2 |
| 转移净收入 | Income from Transfers | 24.3 | 24.5 |
| **消费支出（消费支出 =100）** | **Composition of Per Capita Annual Consumption Expenditure** | **100.0** | **100.0** |
| 食品烟酒 | Food, Liquor and Tobacco | 33.2 | 33.9 |
| 衣　着 | Clothing | 6.9 | 6.7 |
| 居　住 | Garments | 18.3 | 18.9 |
| 生活用品及服务 | Household Facilities, Articles and Services | 6.8 | 6.5 |
| 交通通信 | Transport, Post and Communication Services | 12.4 | 12.1 |
| 教育文化娱乐 | Educational, Cultural and Recreational Services | 10.6 | 10.2 |
| 医疗保健 | Medicine and Medical Service | 9.5 | 9.3 |
| 其他用品及服务 | Miscellaneous Commodities Services | 2.3 | 2.4 |

# 表 7.9 全体居民家庭人均主要食品消费量（2021－2022 年）
## PER CAPITA CONSUMPTION OF MAJOR FOODS BY HOUSEHOLDS (2021-2022)

单位：千克 (kg)

| 指 标 | Item | 2021 | 2022 |
|---|---|---|---|
| 粮 食（原粮） | Grain (Unprocessed) | 161.02 | 158.24 |
| 蔬菜及菜制品 | Vegetables and Processed Products | 147.38 | 147.35 |
| 肉 类 | Meat, Poultry and Related Products | 46.85 | 52.96 |
| 猪 肉 | Pork | 39.64 | 45.82 |
| 牛 肉 | Beef | 2.32 | 2.67 |
| 羊 肉 | Mutton | 0.70 | 0.66 |
| 其他肉类及制品 | Poultry | 4.19 | 3.82 |
| 蛋类及蛋制品 | Eggs and Processed Products | 14.16 | 14.68 |
| 奶和奶制品 | Milk and Dairy Products | 17.45 | 15.72 |
| 水产品 | Aquatic Products | 14.88 | 15.03 |
| 油脂类 | Edible Oil | 16.25 | 15.53 |
| 鲜瓜果 | Fruits | 49.48 | 53.10 |

注：由于 2022 年收支报表制度改革，仅统计鲜瓜果消费量，不再统计干鲜水果类消费量。
Note: Due to the reform of the income and expenditure reporting system in 2022, only the consumption of fresh melons and fruits will be counted, and the consumption of dry and fresh fruits will no longer be counted.

## 表 7.10 全体居民家庭平均每百户年末耐用消费品拥有量（2021－2022 年）
NUMBER OF DURABLE CONSUMER GOODS OWNED PER 100 HOUSEHOLDS AT YEAR-END (2021-2022)

| 指 标 | Item | 2021 | 2022 |
|---|---|---|---|
| 家用汽车（辆） | Automobile (unit) | 31.81 | 32.87 |
| 摩托车（辆） | Motorcycle (unit) | 25.02 | 23.40 |
| 洗衣机（台） | Washing Machine (unit) | 99.28 | 99.44 |
| 电冰箱（柜）(台） | Refrigerator (unit) | 104.79 | 105.31 |
| 微波炉（台） | Microwave Oven (unit) | 50.03 | 50.95 |
| 彩色电视机（台） | Color TV Set (unit) | 121.19 | 119.67 |
| 空 调（台） | Air Conditioner (unit) | 176.62 | 180.88 |
| 热水器（台） | Water Heater (unit) | 96.61 | 97.09 |
| 排油烟机（台） | Exhaust Fan (unit) | 63.44 | 64.60 |
| 移动电话（部） | Mobile Telephone (set) | 261.69 | 262.11 |
| 计算机（台） | Computer (unit) | 53.92 | 54.19 |
| 健身器材（套） | Fitness Equipment (unit) | 7.97 | 7.33 |

## 表 7.11 城镇常住居民人均可支配收入与现金可支配收入情况（2021 – 2022 年）
## PER CAPITA ANNUAL DISPOSABLE INCOME AND CASH DISPOSABLE INCOME OF URBAN HOUSEHOLDS (2021-2022)

单位：元 (yuan)

| 指　标 | Item | 2021 | 2022 |
|---|---|---|---|
| **可支配收入** | **Per Capita Annual Disposable Income** | **43502** | **45509** |
| 工资性收入 | Income from Wages and Salaries | 25396 | 26556 |
| 经营净收入 | Income from Household Operations | 4894 | 5098 |
| 第一产业 | Primary Industry | 434 | 408 |
| 第二产业 | Secondary Industry | 373 | 397 |
| 第三产业 | Tertiary Industry | 4086 | 4293 |
| 财产净收入 | Income from Properties | 3106 | 3265 |
| 转移净收入 | Income from Transfers | 10107 | 10591 |
| **#现金可支配收入** | **Per Capita Cash Disposable Income** | **41073** | **42738** |
| 现金工资性收入 | Income from Wages and Salaries | 25240 | 26375 |
| 现金经营净收入 | Income from Household Operations | 5240 | 5224 |
| 第一产业 | Primary Industry | 339 | 302 |
| 第二产业 | Secondary Industry | 396 | 423 |
| 第三产业 | Tertiary Industry | 4505 | 4499 |
| 现金财产净收入 | Income from Properties | 1192 | 1254 |
| 现金转移净收入 | Income from Transfers | 9401 | 9885 |

## 表 7.12 城镇常住居民人均消费性支出情况（2021 - 2022 年）
PER CAPITA ANNUAL CONSUMPTION EXPENDITURE OF URBAN HOUSEHOLDS (2021-2022)

单位: 元 (yuan)

| 指 标 | Item | 2021 | 2022 |
|---|---|---|---|
| **消费支出** | **Per Capita Annual Consumption Expenditure** | **29850** | **30574** |
| 食品烟酒 | Food, Tobacco and Liquor | 9557 | 10101 |
| 衣 着 | Clothing | 2215 | 2191 |
| 居 住 | Residence | 5467 | 5842 |
| 生活消费及服务 | Household Facilities, Articles and Services | 2125 | 2030 |
| 交通通信 | Transport and Communication | 3796 | 3745 |
| 教育文化娱乐 | Education, Culture and recreation | 3241 | 3140 |
| 医疗保健 | Health Care and Medical Services | 2662 | 2698 |
| 其他用品和服务 | Other Goods and Services | 787 | 827 |

## 表 7.13 城镇常住居民人均收支构成情况（2021 - 2022 年）
## COMPOSITION OF PER CAPITA CASH INCOME AND CASH EXPENDITURE OF URBAN HOUSEHOLDS (2021-2022)

单位：% (%)

| 指　标 | Item | 2021 | 2022 |
|---|---|---|---|
| **可支配收入** | **Composition of Per Capita Annual Disposable Income** | **100.0** | **100.0** |
| 工资性收入 | Income from Wages and Salaries | 58.4 | 58.4 |
| 经营净收入 | Income from Household Operations | 11.3 | 11.2 |
| 财产净收入 | Income from Properties | 7.1 | 7.2 |
| 转移净收入 | Income from Transfers | 23.2 | 23.3 |
| **消费支出** | **Composition of Per Capita Annual Consumption Expenditure** | **100.0** | **100.0** |
| 食品烟酒 | Food, Liquor and Tobacco | 32.0 | 33.0 |
| 衣　着 | Clothing | 7.4 | 7.2 |
| 居　住 | Garments | 18.3 | 19.1 |
| 生活用品及服务 | Household Facilities, Articles and Services | 7.1 | 6.6 |
| 交通通信 | Transport, Post and Communication Services | 12.7 | 12.2 |
| 教育文化娱乐 | Educational, Cultural and Recreational Services | 10.9 | 10.3 |
| 医疗保健 | Medicine and Medical Service | 8.9 | 8.8 |
| 其他用品及服务 | Miscellaneous Commodities Services | 2.7 | 2.7 |

## 表 7.14 城镇常住居民家庭人均主要食品消费量（2021－2022 年）
## PER CAPITA CONSUMPTION OF MAJOR FOODS BY URBAN HOUSEHOLDS (2021-2022)

单位：千克 (kg)

| 指 标 | Item | 2021 | 2022 |
|---|---|---|---|
| 粮 食 ( 原粮 ) | Grain (Unprocessed) | 138.05 | 133.01 |
| 蔬菜及菜制品 | Vegetables and Processed Products | 146.62 | 153.41 |
| 肉 类 | Meat, Poultry and Related Products | 48.92 | 54.97 |
| 猪 肉 | Pork | 39.24 | 45.55 |
| 牛 肉 | Beef | 3.17 | 3.67 |
| 羊 肉 | Mutton | 0.90 | 0.77 |
| 其他肉类及制品 | Poultry | 5.62 | 4.98 |
| 蛋类及蛋制品 | Eggs and Processed Products | 13.31 | 14.67 |
| 奶和奶制品 | Milk and Dairy Products | 21.68 | 19.05 |
| 水产品 | Aquatic Products | 16.45 | 16.60 |
| 油脂类 | Edible Oil | 16.60 | 15.79 |
| 鲜瓜果 | Fruits | 56.61 | 59.97 |

注：由于 2022 年收支报表制度改革，仅统计鲜瓜果消费量，不再统计干鲜水果类消费量。
Note: Due to the reform of the income and expenditure reporting system in 2022, only the consumption of fresh melons and fruits will be counted, and the consumption of dry and fresh fruits will no longer be counted.

# 表 7.15 城镇常住居民家庭平均每百户年末耐用消费品拥有量（2021 – 2022 年）
## NUMBER OF DURABLE CONSUMER GOODS OWNED PER 100 URBAN HOUSEHOLDS AT YEAR-END (2021-2022)

| 指 标 | Item | 2021 | 2022 |
|---|---|---|---|
| 家用汽车（辆） | Automobile (unit) | 38.99 | 40.20 |
| 摩托车（辆） | Motorcycle (unit) | 16.75 | 15.75 |
| 洗衣机（台） | Washing Machine (unit) | 100.87 | 100.86 |
| 电冰箱（柜）(台） | Refrigerator (unit) | 103.36 | 103.12 |
| 微波炉（台） | Microwave Oven (unit) | 69.59 | 70.34 |
| 彩色电视机（台） | Color TV Set (unit) | 124.61 | 125.47 |
| 空 调（台） | Air Conditioner (unit) | 231.38 | 232.66 |
| 热水器（台） | Water Heater (unit) | 103.21 | 103.48 |
| 排油烟机（台） | Exhaust Fan (unit) | 88.08 | 88.16 |
| 移动电话（部） | Mobile Telephone (set) | 262.25 | 263.59 |
| 计算机（台） | Computer (unit) | 73.12 | 71.85 |
| 健身器材（套） | Fitness Equipment (unit) | 12.13 | 11.04 |

## 表 7.16 农村常住居民人均可支配收入与现金可支配收入情况（2021－2022 年）
## PER CAPITA ANNUAL DISPOSABLE INCOME AND CASH DISPOSABLE INCOME OF RURAL HOUSEHOLDS (2021-2022)

单位：元 (yuan)

| 指　标 | Item | 2021 | 2022 |
|---|---|---|---|
| **可支配收入** | **Per Capita Annual Disposable Income** | **18100** | **19313** |
| 工资性收入 | Income from Wages and Salaries | 6386 | 6921 |
| 经营净收入 | Income from Household Operations | 6110 | 6235 |
| 第一产业 | Primary Industry | 4557 | 4461 |
| 第二产业 | Secondary Industry | 135 | 159 |
| 第三产业 | Tertiary Industry | 1417 | 1615 |
| 财产净收入 | Income from Properties | 446 | 476 |
| 转移净收入 | Income from Transfers | 5157 | 5681 |
| **#现金可支配收入** | **Per Capita Cash Disposable Income** | **16290** | **17405** |
| 现金工资性收入 | Income from Wages and Salaries | 6352 | 6868 |
| 现金经营净收入 | Income from Household Operations | 4617 | 4686 |
| 第一产业 | Primary Industry | 2954 | 2793 |
| 第二产业 | Secondary Industry | 144 | 167 |
| 第三产业 | Tertiary Industry | 1518 | 1726 |
| 现金财产净收入 | Income from Properties | 446 | 476 |
| 现金转移净收入 | Income from Transfers | 4875 | 5375 |

## 表 7.17 农村常住居民人均消费性支出情况（2021 – 2022 年）
## PER CAPITA ANNUAL CONSUMPTION EXPENDITURE OF RURAL HOUSEHOLDS (2021-2022)

单位: 元 (yuan)

| 指　标 | Item | 2021 | 2022 |
|---|---|---|---|
| **消费支出** | **Per Capita Annual Consumption Expenditure** | **16096** | **16727** |
| 食品烟酒 | Food, Tobacco and Liquor | 5884 | 6106 |
| 衣　着 | Clothing | 888 | 880 |
| 居　住 | Residence | 2909 | 3023 |
| 生活消费及服务 | Household Facilities, Articles and Services | 965 | 1036 |
| 交通通信 | Transport and Communication | 1842 | 1970 |
| 教育文化娱乐 | Education, Culture and recreation | 1566 | 1663 |
| 医疗保健 | Health Care and Medical Services | 1782 | 1773 |
| 其他用品和服务 | Other Goods and Services | 259 | 276 |

## 表 7.18 农村常住居民人均收支构成情况（2021 － 2022 年）
## COMPOSITION OF PER CAPITA CASH INCOME AND CASH EXPENDITURE OF RURAL HOUSEHOLDS (2021-2022)

单位：% (%)

| 指　标 | Item | 2021 | 2022 |
|---|---|---|---|
| **可支配收入** | **Composition of Per Capita Annual Disposable Income** | **100.0** | **100.0** |
| 工资性收入 | Income from Wages and Salaries | 35.3 | 35.8 |
| 经营净收入 | Income from Household Operations | 33.7 | 32.3 |
| 财产净收入 | Income from Properties | 2.5 | 2.5 |
| 转移净收入 | Income from Transfers | 28.5 | 29.4 |
| **消费支出** | **Composition of Per Capita Annual Consumption Expenditure** | **100.0** | **100.0** |
| 食品烟酒 | Food, Liquor and Tobacco | 36.6 | 36.5 |
| 衣　着 | Clothing | 5.5 | 5.3 |
| 居　住 | Garments | 18.1 | 18.1 |
| 生活用品及服务 | Household Facilities, Articles and Services | 6.0 | 6.2 |
| 交通通信 | Transport, Post and Communication Services | 11.4 | 11.8 |
| 教育文化娱乐 | Educational, Cultural and Recreational Services | 9.7 | 9.9 |
| 医疗保健 | Medicine and Medical Service | 11.1 | 10.6 |
| 其他用品及服务 | Miscellaneous Commodities Services | 1.6 | 1.7 |

## 表 7.19 农村常住居民家庭人均主要食品消费量（2021－2022 年）
## PER CAPITA CONSUMPTION OF MAJOR FOODS BY RURAL HOUSEHOLDS (2021-2022)

单位：千克 (kg)

| 指　标 | Item | 2021 | 2022 |
|---|---|---|---|
| 粮 食(原粮) | Grain (Unprocessed) | 198.20 | 200.14 |
| 蔬菜及菜制品 | Vegetables and Processed Products | 148.61 | 137.26 |
| 肉 类 | Meat, Poultry and Related Products | 43.51 | 49.63 |
| 猪　肉 | Pork | 40.29 | 46.26 |
| 牛　肉 | Beef | 0.94 | 0.99 |
| 羊　肉 | Mutton | 0.39 | 0.48 |
| 其他肉类及制品 | Poultry | 1.89 | 1.90 |
| 蛋类及蛋制品 | Eggs and Processed Products | 15.54 | 14.68 |
| 奶和奶制品 | Milk and Dairy Products | 10.61 | 10.17 |
| 水产品 | Aquatic Products | 12.33 | 12.43 |
| 油脂类 | Edible Oil | 15.68 | 15.11 |
| 鲜瓜果 | Fruits | 37.94 | 41.68 |

注：由于 2022 年收支报表制度改革，仅统计鲜瓜果消费量，不再统计干鲜水果类消费量。
Note: Due to the reform of the income and expenditure reporting system in 2022, only the consumption of fresh melons and fruits will be counted, and the consumption of dry and fresh fruits will no longer be counted.

## 表 7.20 农村常住居民家庭平均每百户年末耐用消费品拥有量 (2021－2022 年)
## NUMBER OF DURABLE CONSUMER GOODS OWNED PER 100 RURAL HOUSEHOLDS AT YEAR-END (2021-2022)

| 指　标 | Item | 2021 | 2022 |
|---|---|---|---|
| 家用汽车(辆) | Automobile (unit) | 20.70 | 21.23 |
| 摩托车(辆) | Motorcycle (unit) | 37.84 | 35.55 |
| 洗衣机(台) | Washing Machine (unit) | 96.83 | 97.19 |
| 电冰箱(柜)(台) | Refrigerator (unit) | 107.01 | 108.79 |
| 微波炉(台) | Microwave Oven (unit) | 19.73 | 20.12 |
| 彩色电视机(台) | Color TV Set (unit) | 115.89 | 110.44 |
| 空　调(台) | Air Conditioner (unit) | 91.78 | 98.59 |
| 热水器(台) | Water Heater (unit) | 86.39 | 86.94 |
| 排油烟机(台) | Exhaust Fan (unit) | 25.26 | 27.15 |
| 移动电话(部) | Mobile Telephone (set) | 260.81 | 259.77 |
| 计算机(台) | Computer (unit) | 24.16 | 26.11 |
| 健身器材(套) | Fitness Equipment (unit) | 1.52 | 1.43 |

# 表 7.21 主要年份居民消费价格指数和商品零售价格指数
## CONSUMER PRICE INDICES AND GENERAL RETAIL PRICE INDICES IN MAJOR YEARS

| 年份<br>Year | 以1950年为100<br>1950=100 | | 以1978年为100<br>1978=100 | | 以上年为100<br>Preceding Year=100 | |
|---|---|---|---|---|---|---|
| | 居民消费价格指数<br>Consumer Price Index | 商品零售价格指数<br>Retail Price Index | 居民消费价格指数<br>Consumer Price Index | 商品零售价格指数<br>Retail Price Index | 居民消费价格指数<br>Consumer Price Index | 商品零售价格指数<br>Retail Price Index |
| 1952 | 106.1 | 108.7 | | | 97.3 | 97.2 |
| 1957 | 114.0 | 116.5 | | | 104.6 | 103.9 |
| 1962 | 145.8 | 158.1 | | | 95.2 | 95.0 |
| 1965 | 125.1 | 133.1 | | | 98.0 | 98.2 |
| 1970 | 129.2 | 137.9 | | | 99.6 | 99.5 |
| 1975 | 131.2 | 140.2 | | | 100.3 | 100.3 |
| 1978 | 135.4 | 145.1 | 100.0 | 100.0 | 102.9 | 103.2 |
| 1980 | 148.3 | 160.1 | 109.5 | 110.3 | 107.9 | 108.6 |
| 1985 | 179.4 | 191.7 | 132.4 | 132.0 | 109.9 | 110.0 |
| 1986 | 186.9 | 199.8 | 138.0 | 137.5 | 104.2 | 104.2 |
| 1987 | 205.2 | 220.8 | 151.5 | 151.9 | 109.8 | 110.5 |
| 1988 | 251.8 | 272.2 | 185.9 | 187.3 | 122.7 | 123.3 |
| 1989 | 294.9 | 317.1 | 217.7 | 218.2 | 117.1 | 116.5 |
| 1990 | 299.0 | 317.4 | 220.7 | 218.4 | 101.4 | 100.1 |
| 1991 | 319.9 | 336.8 | 236.1 | 231.7 | 107.0 | 106.1 |
| 1992 | 355.7 | 369.8 | 262.5 | 254.4 | 111.2 | 109.8 |
| 1993 | 422.2 | 430.1 | 311.6 | 295.9 | 118.7 | 116.3 |
| 1994 | 547.6 | 544.1 | 404.1 | 374.3 | 129.7 | 126.5 |
| 1995 | 653.8 | 632.8 | 482.5 | 435.3 | 119.4 | 116.3 |
| 1996 | 717.2 | 671.4 | 529.3 | 461.9 | 109.7 | 106.1 |
| 1997 | 741.2 | 682.6 | 546.8 | 470.4 | 103.3 | 101.7 |
| 1998 | 714.5 | 645.1 | 527.1 | 444.5 | 96.4 | 94.5 |
| 1999 | 709.5 | 622.5 | 523.4 | 428.9 | 99.3 | 96.5 |
| 2000 | 686.1 | 594.5 | 506.1 | 409.6 | 96.7 | 95.5 |
| 2001 | 697.8 | 588.6 | 514.7 | 405.5 | 101.7 | 99.0 |
| 2002 | 695.0 | 582.1 | 512.6 | 401.0 | 99.6 | 98.9 |
| 2003 | 699.2 | 579.2 | 515.7 | 399.0 | 100.6 | 99.5 |
| 2004 | 725.1 | 587.3 | 534.8 | 404.6 | 103.7 | 101.4 |
| 2005 | 730.9 | 579.7 | 539.1 | 399.3 | 100.8 | 98.7 |
| 2006 | 748.4 | 589.0 | 552.0 | 405.7 | 102.4 | 101.6 |
| 2007 | 783.6 | 610.8 | 577.9 | 420.7 | 104.7 | 103.7 |
| 2008 | 827.5 | 641.3 | 610.3 | 441.7 | 105.6 | 105.0 |
| 2009 | 814.3 | 624.0 | 600.5 | 429.8 | 98.4 | 97.3 |
| 2010 | 840.3 | 634.6 | 619.8 | 437.1 | 103.2 | 101.7 |
| 2011 | 884.9 | 664.2 | 652.6 | 457.4 | 105.3 | 104.7 |
| 2012 | 907.7 | 674.7 | 669.5 | 464.7 | 102.6 | 101.6 |
| 2013 | 931.8 | 687.0 | 687.2 | 473.2 | 102.7 | 101.8 |
| 2014 | 948.2 | 693.0 | 699.3 | 477.3 | 101.8 | 100.9 |
| 2015 | 960.1 | 694.4 | 708.1 | 478.3 | 101.3 | 100.2 |
| 2016 | 977.3 | 703.3 | 720.8 | 484.4 | 101.8 | 101.3 |
| 2017 | 987.1 | 709.2 | 728.0 | 488.5 | 101.0 | 100.8 |
| 2018 | 1007.3 | 717.6 | 742.9 | 494.2 | 102.0 | 101.2 |
| 2019 | 1034.5 | 729.0 | 763.0 | 502.1 | 102.7 | 101.6 |
| 2020 | 1058.3 | 745.1 | 780.5 | 513.2 | 102.3 | 102.2 |
| 2021 | 1061.5 | 755.5 | 782.9 | 520.4 | 100.3 | 101.4 |
| 2022 | 1084.0 | 774.7 | 799.5 | 533.6 | 102.1 | 102.5 |

# 表 7.22 居民消费价格分类指数（2021 - 2022 年）
CONSUMER PRICE INDICES BY CATEGORY (2021-2022)

上年 =100 (preceding year=100)

| 项 目 | Item | 2021 | 2022 |
|---|---|---|---|
| **居民消费价格指数** | **Consumer Price Index** | **100.3** | **102.1** |
| 食品烟酒 | Food, Tobacco and Liquor | 97.8 | 103.9 |
| 食 品 | Food | 95.6 | 105.3 |
| 粮 食 | Grain | 98.5 | 101.7 |
| 薯 类 | Tubers | 101.5 | 109.7 |
| 豆 类 | Beans | 107.5 | 106.3 |
| 食用油 | Oil | 106.6 | 106.1 |
| 菜及食用菌 | Vegetables | 101.2 | 107.3 |
| #鲜 菜 | Fresh Vegetables | 101.2 | 106.8 |
| 畜肉类 | Livestock Meat | 78.1 | 99.8 |
| 禽肉类 | Poultry | 94.0 | 110.5 |
| 水产品 | Aquatic Products | 107.6 | 101.8 |
| 蛋 类 | Eggs | 109.7 | 108.9 |
| 奶 类 | Dairy Products | 98.8 | 101.4 |
| 干鲜瓜果类 | Dried and Fresh Melons and Fruits | 99.9 | 114.4 |
| #鲜 果 | Fresh Fruits | 100.5 | 117.4 |
| 糖果糕点类 | Confectionery and Cakes | 104.0 | 102.9 |
| 调味品 | Flavoring | 101.9 | 107.1 |
| 其他食品类 | Other Foods | 96.3 | 103.3 |
| 茶及饮料 | Tea and Beverages | 100.1 | 103.0 |
| 烟 酒 | Tobacco and Liquor | 100.2 | 100.3 |
| 卷 烟 | Tobacco | 101.6 | 100.9 |
| 酒 类 | Liquor | 97.5 | 99.2 |
| 在外餐饮 | Dining Out | 102.1 | 101.8 |
| 衣 着 | Clothing | 101.4 | 100.0 |
| #服 装 | Garments | 101.4 | 100.0 |
| 居 住 | Residence | 100.4 | 99.9 |
| 生活用品及服务 | Living Goods and Service | 100.7 | 101.4 |
| #家庭服务 | Family Services | 102.7 | 102.2 |
| 交通通信 | Transportation and Communications | 104.7 | 105.5 |
| 交 通 | Transportation | 106.0 | 108.3 |
| 通 信 | Telecommunication | 101.5 | 98.1 |
| 教育文化娱乐 | Education, Culture and Recreation | 101.7 | 101.6 |
| #教 育 | Education | 101.9 | 101.9 |
| 医疗保健 | Health Care | 99.6 | 99.7 |
| 药品及医疗器具 | Medicine and Medical Equipment | 98.8 | 99.2 |
| 医疗服务 | Medical Services | 100.1 | 100.0 |
| 其他用品及服务 | Other Articles and Service | 97.3 | 100.6 |

# 表 7.23 商品零售价格分类指数（2021 – 2022 年）
## RETAIL PRICE INDICES BY CATEGORY (2021-2022)

上年 =100 (preceding year = 100)

| 项　目 | Item | 2021 | 2022 |
|---|---|---|---|
| **商品零售价格总指数** | **General Retail Price Index** | **101.4** | **102.5** |
| 食　品 | Food | 97.6 | 104.3 |
| 饮料、烟酒 | Beverages, Tobacco and Liquor | 100.1 | 100.8 |
| 服装、鞋帽 | Garments, Shoes and Hats | 101.4 | 100.0 |
| 纺织品 | Textiles | 99.4 | 99.9 |
| 家用电器及音像器材 | Household Appliances and Video Materials | 103.2 | 100.5 |
| 文化办公用品 | Cultural and Office Appliances | 101.0 | 99.7 |
| 日用品 | Articles for Daily Use | 99.6 | 101.1 |
| 体育娱乐用品 | Sports and Recreation Articles | 99.9 | 100.1 |
| 交通、通信用品 | Transportation and Communication Articles | 101.1 | 98.2 |
| 家　具 | Furniture | 101.4 | 100.7 |
| 化妆品 | Cosmetics | 98.4 | 102.9 |
| 金银饰品 | Gold, Silver and Jewelry | 96.1 | 102.2 |
| 中西药品及医疗保健用品 | Traditional Chinese & Western Medicines and Health Care Articles | 98.8 | 99.2 |
| 书报杂志及电子出版物 | Books, Newspaper, Magazines and Electronic Publications | 101.7 | 109.2 |
| 燃　料 | Fuels | 110.5 | 114.0 |
| 建筑材料及五金电料 | Building Materials and Hardware | 101.9 | 103.9 |

# 表 7.24 农产品生产价格指数 (2004 － 2022 年)
## PRODUCER PRICE INDICES FOR AGRICULTURAL PRODUCTS (2004-2022)

上年 =100 (preceding year = 100)

| 指 标 | Item | 2004 | 2005 | 2006 | 2007 | 2008 | 2009 | 2010 | 2011 | 2012 | 2013 | 2014 | 2015 | 2016 | 2017 | 2018 | 2019 | 2020 | 2021 | 2022 |
|---|---|---|---|---|---|---|---|---|---|---|---|---|---|---|---|---|---|---|---|---|
| **合 计** | **Total** | **125.5** | **100.0** | **93.6** | **121.8** | **120.4** | **89.0** | **103.2** | **120.2** | **104.6** | **103.0** | **100.2** | **102.4** | **109.8** | **96.8** | **99.7** | **112.1** | **113.6** | **98.4** | **98.7** |
| **农业产品** | **Farm Products** | **120.3** | **102.2** | **100.4** | **108.6** | **108.9** | **104.2** | **109.1** | **113.8** | **106.0** | **103.1** | **102.6** | **100.6** | **104.4** | **102.8** | **106.3** | **102.1** | **105.8** | **105.0** | **103.2** |
| #谷 物 | Cereal | 139.6 | 101.3 | 97.3 | 108.2 | 108.5 | 100.4 | 108.4 | 114.4 | 108.0 | 102.5 | 100.3 | 102.6 | 99.8 | 100.8 | 101.8 | 99.5 | 102.6 | 113.4 | 100.8 |
| #小 麦 | Wheat | 131.6 | 102.7 | 95.1 | 103.9 | 106.4 | 103.5 | 104.3 | 110.6 | 112.0 | | | | | | | | | | |
| 稻 谷 | Rice | 141.5 | 101.2 | 97.8 | 108.2 | 109.2 | 100.8 | 106.8 | 116.2 | 107.1 | 101.7 | 99.4 | 103.7 | 103.8 | 102.4 | 100.3 | 99.6 | 100.1 | 107.1 | 100.4 |
| 玉 米 | Corn | 130.4 | 101.7 | 94.9 | 109.0 | 106.2 | 97.9 | 113.4 | 111.4 | 109.4 | 104.4 | 102.6 | 100.4 | 92.0 | 97.8 | 104.9 | 99.4 | 107.8 | 131.9 | 101.5 |
| 大 豆 | Beans | 122.1 | 97.4 | 100.0 | 107.9 | 115.4 | 98.9 | 106.6 | 111.5 | 105.8 | 102.8 | 104.4 | 102.4 | 96.7 | 100.0 | 101.8 | 102.5 | 103.0 | 106.8 | 104.3 |
| 油 料 | Oil-bearing Crops | 123.2 | 93.1 | 102.8 | 120.1 | 118.9 | 80.3 | 108.8 | 109.0 | 105.7 | 106.8 | 101.2 | 107.7 | 98.1 | 103.7 | 102.2 | 98.8 | 107.7 | 99.4 | 109.8 |
| 蔬 菜 | Vegetables | 106.0 | 103.8 | 102.5 | 109.8 | 106.6 | 110.5 | 107.9 | 111.1 | 108.7 | 103.7 | 104.2 | 98.0 | 110.7 | 103.0 | 109.0 | 100.3 | 112.8 | 102.9 | 101.3 |
| 水果及坚 果 | Fruits and Nuts | 103.0 | 103.4 | 101.3 | 104.5 | 109.2 | 107.0 | 111.2 | 119.5 | 93.8 | 108.0 | 104.8 | 108.2 | 102.1 | 116.2 | 98.1 | 104.9 | 96.3 | 103.1 | 102.8 |
| **饲养动物及其产品** | **Animal Husbandry Products** | **128.8** | **98.8** | **89.8** | **128.8** | **126.1** | **80.8** | **98.4** | **126.6** | **103.3** | **102.9** | **97.6** | **104.4** | **114.8** | **91.3** | **94.6** | **97.2** | **130.5** | **83.3** | **92.5** |
| #活 猪 | Pig | 131.2 | 97.5 | 86.9 | 132.2 | 127.2 | 77.1 | 94.4 | 134.5 | 101.8 | 101.7 | 92.9 | 105.3 | 122.3 | 84.8 | 89.1 | 155.5 | 151.6 | 63.9 | 87.2 |
| 牛 | Cattle and Buffaloes | 101.7 | 103.9 | 101.6 | 120.6 | 116.0 | 104.2 | 103.4 | 107.6 | 104.9 | 109.3 | 110.1 | 99.7 | 99.3 | 99.5 | 102.7 | 112.7 | 113.4 | 103.0 | 99.3 |
| 羊 | Sheep and Goats | 111.1 | 102.8 | 101.2 | 108.0 | 128.9 | 100.7 | 100.0 | 116.6 | 115.7 | 110.4 | 107.9 | 95.0 | 87.3 | 97.8 | 126.2 | 124.5 | 109.4 | 102.5 | 99.9 |
| 活家禽 | Poultry | 117.2 | 104.3 | 100.2 | 116.2 | 111.7 | 102.8 | 105.6 | 111.8 | 107.1 | 105.3 | 106.8 | 102.3 | 100.6 | 108.4 | 103.6 | 106.1 | 97.9 | 104.0 | 101.6 |
| 禽 蛋 | Eggs | 111.9 | 103.9 | 98.9 | 110.1 | 112.1 | 101.9 | 104.2 | 105.6 | 104.7 | 104.4 | 104.2 | 105.4 | 100.3 | 100.5 | 104.4 | 102.0 | 89.6 | 100.5 | 110.3 |
| **渔业产品** | **Fishery Products** | **107.8** | **105.7** | **101.7** | **105.9** | **110.3** | **104.7** | **102.2** | **108.2** | **108.1** | **102.0** | **104.7** | **101.2** | **104.2** | **104.1** | **99.7** | **101.4** | **106.6** | **122.2** | **95.6** |
| 养 殖淡水鱼 | Bred Freshwater Fish | | | | | | | | 108.6 | 108.2 | 102.0 | 101.8 | 101.2 | 104.2 | 104.1 | 99.7 | 101.4 | 106.6 | 122.2 | 95.6 |
| 捕 捞淡水鱼 | Fished Freshwater Fish | | | | | | | | 110.5 | 104.1 | | 107.0 | | | | | | | | |

注：根据新《农业产值和价格综合统计报表制度》，原“肉禽（毛重）”指标替换为“活家禽”，原“淡水鱼”指标替换为“养殖淡水鱼”和“捕捞淡水鱼”。2011 年起采用新指标指数，2010 年及以前采用旧指标指数。

Note: In accordance with the "Comprehensive Statistic Reporting Rules for Agriculture Output and Price", the former "poultry (gross weight)" is replaced by "poultry", while the former "freshwater fish" is replaced by "bred freshwater fish" and "fished freshwater fish". The new indices are used since 2011 while the old indices are used for the data before 2010.

## 表 7.25 工业生产者购进价格指数（2021－2022 年）
## PURCHASING PRICE INDICES FOR INDUSTRIAL PRODUCERS (2021-2022)

上年 =100 (preceding year=100)

| 指 标 | Item | 2021 | 2022 |
|---|---|---|---|
| **工业生产者购进价格指数** | **Purchasing Price Indices of Raw Material, Fuel and Power** | **107.2** | **104.4** |
| 燃料、动力类 | Fuel and Power | 104.4 | 117.6 |
| 黑色金属材料类 | Ferrous Metals | 115.7 | 100.6 |
| 有色金属材料类 | Nonferrous Metals | 125.0 | 106.1 |
| 化工原料类 | Raw Chemical Materials | 116.0 | 105.8 |
| 木材及纸浆类 | Timber and Paper Pulp | 105.4 | 105.9 |
| 建筑材料类及非金属矿类 | Building Materials and Non-metal Minerals | 110.1 | 100.5 |
| 其他工业原材料及半成品类 | Other Industrial Raw Materials and Semi-products | 102.3 | 101.5 |
| 农副产品类 | Agricultural Products | 102.9 | 103.6 |
| 纺织原料类 | Textile Materials | 100.5 | 102.9 |

## 表 7.26 工业生产者出厂价格指数（2021－2022 年）
## PRODUCER PRICE INDICES FOR INDUSTRIAL PRODUCTS BY CATEGORY (2021-2022)

上年 =100 (preceding year=100)

| 指 标 | Item | 2021 | 2022 |
|---|---|---|---|
| **工业生产者出厂价格指数** | **Producer Price Index for Industrial Products** | **103.2** | **102.3** |
| 生产资料 | Means of Production | 104.4 | 102.7 |
| 采 掘 | Mining and Quarrying | 102.1 | 101.9 |
| 原材料 | Raw Materials | 111.0 | 104.7 |
| 加 工 | Processing | 103.4 | 102.4 |
| 生活资料 | Consumer Goods | 100.2 | 101.4 |
| 食 品 | Food | 101.7 | 101.5 |
| 衣 着 | Clothing | 98.3 | 100.5 |
| 一般日用品 | Articles for Daily Use | 99.7 | 102.3 |
| 耐用消费品 | Durable Consumer Goods | 99.8 | 101.1 |

# 表 7.27 按工业行业分工业生产者出厂价格指数（2021 – 2022 年）
## PRODUCER PRICE INDICES FOR INDUSTRIAL PRODUCTS BY SECTOR (2021-2022)

上年 =100 (preceding year=100)

| 行 业 | Sector | 2021 | 2022 |
|---|---|---|---|
| **工业生产者出厂价格指数** | **Producer Price Index for Industrial Products** | **103.2** | **102.3** |
| 煤炭开采和洗选业 | Mining and Washing of Coal | 103.3 | 101.4 |
| 石油和天然气开采业 | Extraction of Petroleum and Natural Gas | 106.3 | 109.8 |
| 黑色金属矿采选业 | Mining and Processing of Ferrous Metal Ores | 104.9 | 100.2 |
| 有色金属矿采选业 | Mining and Processing of Non-ferrous Metal Ores | 114.4 | 104.7 |
| 非金属矿采选业 | Mining and Processing of Non-metal Ores | 97.0 | 95.2 |
| 农副食品加工业 | Processing of Food from Agricultural Products | 105.0 | 102.8 |
| 食品制造业 | Manufacture of Foods | 100.4 | 102.0 |
| 酒、饮料和精制茶制造业 | Manufacture of Liquor, Beverages and Refined Tea | 102.8 | 100.6 |
| 烟草制品业 | Manufacture of Tobacco | 100.0 | 100.0 |
| 纺织业 | Manufacture of Textile | 102.5 | 102.7 |
| 纺织服装、服饰业 | Manufacture of Textile, Wearing Apparel and Accessories | 98.7 | 101.7 |
| 皮革、毛皮、羽毛及其制品和制鞋业 | Manufacture of Leather, Fur, Feather and Related Products and Footwear | 98.2 | 99.9 |
| 木材加工和木、竹、藤、棕、草制品业 | Processing of Timber, Manufacture of Wood, Bamboo, Rattan, Palm and Straw Products | 102.7 | 104.9 |
| 家具制造业 | Manufacture of Furniture | 102.8 | 101.4 |
| 造纸和纸制品业 | Manufacture of Paper and Paper Products | 104.3 | 99.6 |
| 印刷和记录媒介复制业 | Printing and Reproduction of Recording Media | 96.6 | 101.9 |
| 文教、工美、体育和娱乐用品制造业 | Manufacture of Articles of Culture, Education, Arts and Crafts, Sport and Entertainment Activities | 100.9 | 100.0 |
| 石油、煤炭及其他燃料加工业 | Processing of Petroleum, Coking and Other Fuels | 100.9 | 104.4 |
| 化学原料和化学制品制造业 | Manufacture of Raw Chemical Materials and Chemical Products | 118.8 | 109.0 |
| 医药制造业 | Manufacture of Medicines | 99.4 | 102.8 |
| 化学纤维制造业 | Manufacture of Chemical Fibers | 121.1 | 60.6 |
| 橡胶和塑料制品业 | Manufacture of Rubber and Plastics | 100.8 | 102.2 |
| 非金属矿物制品业 | Manufacture of Non-metallic Mineral Products | 103.3 | 100.8 |
| 黑色金属冶炼和压延加工业 | Smelting and Pressing of Ferrous Metals | 125.8 | 106.7 |
| 有色金属冶炼和压延加工业 | Smelting and Pressing of Non-ferrous Metals | 123.1 | 105.4 |
| 金属制品业 | Manufacture of Metal Products | 104.4 | 100.3 |
| 通用设备制造业 | Manufacture of General Purpose Machinery | 101.2 | 101.1 |
| 专用设备制造业 | Manufacture of Special Purpose Machinery | 99.9 | 100.7 |
| 汽车制造业 | Manufacture of Automobiles | 100.0 | 100.3 |
| 铁路、船舶、航空航天和其他运输设备制造业 | Manufacture of Railway, Ship, Aerospace and Other Transport Equipments | 102.5 | 100.9 |
| 电气机械和器材制造业 | Manufacture of Electrical Machinery and Apparatus | 104.4 | 101.8 |
| 计算机、通信和其他电子设备制造业 | Manufacture of Computers, Communication and Other Electronic Equipment | 98.8 | 102.7 |
| 仪器仪表制造业 | Manufacture of Measuring Instrument and Machinery | 97.4 | 100.4 |
| 其他制造业 | Other Manufacture | 100.2 | 100.8 |
| 废弃资源综合利用业 | Utilization of Waste Resources | 105.8 | 98.4 |
| 金属制品、机械和设备修理业 | Repair Service of Metal Products, Machinery and Equipment | 100.4 | 101.2 |
| 电力、热力生产和供应业 | Production and Supply of Electric Power and Heat Power | 101.1 | 103.9 |
| 燃气生产和供应业 | Production and Supply of Gas | 103.1 | 109.0 |
| 水的生产和供应业 | Production and Supply of Water | 100.5 | 101.3 |

# 表 7.28 住宅销售价格指数（1998 – 2022 年）
## SALES PRICE INDICES OF HOUSES (1998-2022)

上年 =100 (preceding year=100)

| 年 份<br>Year | 新建商品住宅<br>Newly-built Commercial Housing | 二手住宅<br>Second-hand Houses |
|---|---|---|
| 1998 | 105.6 | |
| 1999 | 102.8 | |
| 2000 | 102.5 | |
| 2001 | 102.5 | |
| 2002 | 102.9 | |
| 2003 | 108.5 | |
| 2004 | 114.7 | |
| 2005 | 107.0 | 106.1 |
| 2006 | 103.2 | 101.9 |
| 2007 | 108.0 | 104.5 |
| 2008 | 107.2 | 103.8 |
| 2009 | 101.3 | 103.7 |
| 2010 | 110.8 | 107.4 |
| 2011 | 104.1 | 100.6 |
| 2012 | 99.2 | 99.6 |
| 2013 | 106.7 | 102.6 |
| 2014 | 102.2 | 100.9 |
| 2015 | 95.0 | 97.1 |
| 2016 | 103.6 | 103.9 |
| 2017 | 110.6 | 107.7 |
| 2018 | 108.9 | 107.9 |
| 2019 | 110.9 | 106.3 |
| 2020 | 105.5 | 99.0 |
| 2021 | 107.4 | 103.9 |
| 2022 | 103.8 | 100.7 |

注：2017 年及以前为新建住宅数据，2018 年起变更为新建商品住宅数据
Note: The data of the year before 2017 are newly-built housing. Since 2018, the data are replaced by newly-built commercial housing.

重/庆/统/计/年/鉴

# 主要统计指标解释

## 城乡居民储蓄存款余额

指某一时点城乡居民存入银行及农村信用社的储蓄金额，包括城镇居民储蓄存款和农民个人储蓄存款，不包括居民的手存现金和工矿企业、部队、机关、团体等单位存款。

## 恩格尔系数

指食品烟酒支出金额在消费性总支出金额中所占的比例。计算公式为：

$$恩格尔系数=\frac{食品烟酒支出总额}{消费性支出总额}\times 100\%$$

## 住户收支与生活状况调查指标解释

从2012年四季度起，国家统计局对分别进行的城乡住户调查实施了一体化改革，规范了城乡划分范围，统一了城乡居民收入指标名称、分类和统计标准，建立了城乡统一的一体化住户调查，并据此采集全国居民有关数据。

### （一）居民可支配收入

居民可支配收入指居民可用于最终消费支出和储蓄的总和，即居民可用于自由支配的收入。既包括现金收入，也包括实物收入。按照收入的来源，可支配收入包含四项，分别为：工资性收入、经营净收入、财产净收入和转移净收入。

**工资性收入** 指就业人员通过各种途径得到的全部劳动报酬和各种福利，包括受雇于单位或个人、从事各种自由职业、兼职和零星劳动得到的全部劳动报酬和福利。

**经营净收入** 指住户或住户成员从事生产经营活动所获得的净收入，是全部经营收入中扣除经营费用、生产性固定资产折旧和生产税之后得到的净收入。计算公式为：

经营净收入＝经营收入－经营费用－生产性固定资产折旧－生产税

**财产净收入** 指住户或住户成员将其所拥有的金融资产、住房等非金融资产和自然资源交由其他机构单位、住户或个人支配而获得的回报并扣除相关的费用之后得到的净收入。财产净收入包括利息净收入、红利收入、储蓄性保险净收益、转让承包土地经营权租金净收入、出租房屋净收入、出租其他资产净收入和自有住房折算净租金等。财产净收入不包括转让资产所有权的溢价所得。

转移净收入 计算公式为：

转移净收入＝转移性收入－转移性支出

**转移性收入** 指国家、单位、社会团体对住户的各种经常性转移支付和住户之间的经常性收入转移。包括养老金或退休金、社会救济和补助、政策性生产补贴、政策性生活补贴、经常性捐赠和赔偿、报销医疗费、住户之间的赡养收入，本住户非常住成员寄回带回的收入等。转移性收入不包括住户之间的实物馈赠。

**转移性支出** 指调查户对国家、单位、住户或个人的经常性或义务性转移支付。包括缴纳的税款、各项社会保障支出、赡养支出、经常性捐赠和赔偿支出以及其他经常转移支出等。

### （二）居民消费支出

居民消费支出是指居民用于满足家庭日常生活消费需要的全部支出，既包括现金消费支出，也包括实物消费支出。消费支出可划分为食品烟酒、衣着、居住、生活用品及服务、交通通信、教育文化娱乐、医疗保健以及其他用品及服务八大类。

**食品烟酒** 指用于各种食品和烟草、酒类的支出。

**衣着** 指与居民穿着有关的支出，包括服装、服装材料、鞋类、其他衣类及配件、衣着相关加工服务的支出。

**居住** 指与居住有关的支出，包括房租、水、电、燃料、物业管理等方面的支出，也包括自有住房折算租金。

**生活用品及服务** 指家庭及个人的各类生活品及家庭服务。包括家具及室内装饰品、家用器具、家用纺织品、家庭日用杂品、个人用品和家庭服务。

**交通通信** 指用于交通和通信工具及相关的各种服务费、维修费和车辆保险等支出。

**教育文化娱乐** 指用于教育、文化和娱乐方面的支出。

**医疗保健** 指用于医疗和保健的药品、用品和服务的总费用。包括医疗器具及药品，以及医疗服务。

**其他用品及服务** 指无法直接归入上述各类支出的其他用品与服务支出。

# 主要统计指标解释

## 2012 年及以前的分城镇和农村住户调查指标解释

2012 年及以前年份，中国的住户调查一直分城乡分别开展。由于分别调查，农村与城镇居民收入、支出等指标的统计口径有所不同，数据也不完全可比，城镇调查城镇居民可支配收入，农村调查农村居民纯收入。城镇居民收入与支出数据，指现金收入或现金支出，不包括实物收支；其中，计算城镇居民人均可支配收入和消费支出时，不包括自有住房折算租金，也不包括购建房支出。农村居民收入与支出数据，分为总收支和现金收支，即农村居民的总收支部分包括了自产自用的实物收支；其中，计算农村居民人均纯收入和消费支出时，也不包括自有住房折算租金，但农村居民居住消费支出中，包括了购建房支出。

为了保持历史数据的可比，本年鉴中 2012 年及以前年份的数据和指标解释仍保持了原城镇住户调查和农村住户调查方案的原貌。

### （一）城镇住户调查

**城镇家庭人口** 指居住在一起，经济上合在一起共同生活的家庭成员。凡计算为家庭人口的成员其全部收支都包括在本家庭中。

**城镇居民家庭可支配收入** 指家庭成员得到可用于最终消费支出和其他非义务性支出以及储蓄的总和，即居民家庭可以用来自由支配的收入。它是家庭总收入扣除交纳的个人所得税、个人交纳的社会保障支出以及记账补贴后的收入。计算公式为：

城镇居民家庭可支配收入 = 家庭总收入 – 交纳个人所得税 – 个人交纳的社会保障支出 – 记账补贴

### （二）农村住户调查

**农村住户** 指农村常住户。农村常住户指长期（一年以上）居住在乡镇（不包括城关镇）行政管理区域内的住户，以及长期居住在城关镇所辖行政村范围内的农村住户。户口不在本地而在本地居住一年及以上的住户也包括在本地农村常住户范围内；有本地户口，但举家外出谋生一年以上的住户，无论是否保留承包耕地都不包括在本地农村住户范围内。

**农村居民家庭纯收入** 指农村住户当年从各个来源得到的总收入相应地扣除所发生的费用后的收入总和。计算公式为：

农村居民家庭纯收入 = 总收入 – 家庭经营费用支出 – 税费支出 – 生产性固定资产折旧 – 赠送农村内部亲友

纯收入主要用于再生产投入和当年生活消费支出，也可用于储蓄和各种非义务性支出。“农民人均纯收入”是按人口平均的纯收入水平，反映的是一个地区农村居民的平均收入水平。

**居民消费价格指数** 居民消费价格指数是度量一组代表性消费商品及服务项目价格水平随着时间而变动的相对数，反映居民家庭购买的消费品及服务价格水平的变动情况。它是宏观经济分析和决策、价格总水平监测和调控以及国民经济核算的重要指标。其按年度计算的变动率通常被用来作为反映通货膨胀（或紧缩）程度的指标。

**商品零售价格指数** 商品的零售价格是商品在流通过程中最后一个环节的价格，是工业、商业、餐饮业和其他零售企业向城乡居民、机关团体出售生活消费品和办公用品的价格。通过系统地调查、搜集和整理市场商品零售价格资料，编制商品零售价格指数，以此反映市场商品零售价格的变动趋势和变动程度。其目的在于掌握商品价格的变动趋势，为国家宏观调控和国民经济核算提供参考依据。

**农产品生产价格指数** 是反映一定时期内，农产品生产者出售农产品价格水平变动趋势及幅度的相对数。该指数可以客观反映全国农产品生产价格水平和结构变动情况，满足农业与国民经济核算需求。其中某代表品生产价格指数是通过对全部有出售该产品行为的调查单位的个体指数进行几何平均求得的，类价格指数是通过对其所属的类（或代表品）的价格指数进行加权平均求得的。季度累计价格指数的计算方法与分季指数的计算方法相同。

**工业生产者价格** 是反映工业产品价格变化趋势和变动幅度的统计指标，是工业品价格在不同时间和空间条件下平均变动的相对数。工业生产者价格包括工业品第一次出售时的出厂价格和企业作为中间投入的原材料、燃料、动力购进价格，是进行国民经济核算和经济管理的重要依据。

**固定资产投资价格指数** 是反映全社会及各类工程固定资产投资中涉及的各类投资品和取费项目价格的变动趋势和变动幅度的相对数。编制固定资产投资价格指数可以消除按现价计算的固定资产投资指标中的价格变动因素。

**住宅销售价格指数** 是综合反映住宅商品价格水平总体变化趋势和变化幅度的相对数。中国住宅销售价格指数由 70 个大中城市的新建住宅销售价格指数和二手住宅销售价格指数组成。

# Explanatory Notes on Main Statistical Indicators

## Saving Deposits of Urban and Rural Residents

Refer to the total value of savings deposits of urban and rural households in banks and rural credit cooperatives at a given point of time, including the saving deposits of urban residents and the saving deposits of rural residents. The cash in hand by residents and the deposits of organizations such as enterprises, military units, government agencies, institutions, etc. are not included.

## Engel Coefficient

Refers to the percentage of expenditure on food, cigarette and alcohol in the total consumption expenditure, using the following formula:

Engel Coefficient =

$$\frac{\text{expenditure on food, cigarette and alcohol}}{\text{total consumption expenditure}} \times 100\%$$

## Households Survey on Income and Expenditures and Living Conditions

Since the fourth quarter of 2012, the NBS has launched its reform on the hous-ehold survey programme, to form an integrated survey, instead of the two separate urban and rural household surveys. The reform regulates the division of urban and rural areas, integrates the concepts, classifications and standards, conducts the integrated household survey, and collects household data in the whole country thereafter.

### 1. Disposable Income of Households

**Disposable Income of Households** refers to the income of households for purpose of final expenditure and savings. It includes income both in cash and in kind. By sources of income, disposable income includes four categories: income from wages and salaries, net business income, net income from properties and net income from transfer.

**Income from Wages and Salaries** refers to remuneration of labour and salaries from all kinds of sources, including those employed by other units or individuals, freelance work, part-time jobs, and sporadic labour.

**Net Business Income** refers to net income earned by households and their members engaged in production and business activities. It refers to the net income of operating revenue minus operating costs, depreciation of productive fixed assets, and production tax. The formula is:

Net Business Income=Operating Revenue-Operating Costs-Depreciation of Productive Fixed Assets-Production Tax

**Net Income from Properties** refers to the net income received as returns by households or members of financial assets, non-financial assets such as housing, to other institutions, households or individuals, and minus relevant costs. Net income from properties includes net income of interest, bonus income, net income of saving insurance, net income of rents of transferring management right of contract land, income of renting housing, income of renting other assets, net converted rents of self-owned housing. Net income from properties do not include premium of transferring ownership of assets.

Net Income from Transfer The formula is:

Net Income from Transfer=Income from Transfers-Expenditure from Transfer

**Income from Transfer** refers to the regular transfer from country, institutions, social communities to households and between households. It includes old-age and retirement pension, regular donation and compensation, applying for medical fees, supporting income between households, income from non-usual-residing members of households, etc. Income from transfer do not include presents in kinds between households.

**Expenditure from Transfer** refers to regular or deontic transfer from households to country, institutions, households or individuals. It includes taxes paid, expenditure of all kinds of social security, supporting expenditure, regular donation and compensation and other regular transfer expenditure, etc.

### 2. Consumption Expenditure of Households

**Consumption Expenditure of Households** refers to all expenditure of households for living expenditure to satisfy family daily living. It includes expenditure in cash and in kind. It includes eight categories: food, tobacco and liquor; clothing; residence; household facilities, articles and services; transport and communications; education, cultural and recreational activities; health care and medical services, and miscellaneous goods and services.

**Food, Tobacco and Liquor** refers to expenditure for food, tobacco and liquor of all kinds.

**Clothing** refers to expenditure related to clothing, including clothes, clothing materials, footwear, other clothing and accessories, processing services related to clothing.

**Residence** refers to expenditure related to residence, including housing rents, water, electricity, fuel, property management, and including converted self-owned housing rents.

**Household Facilities, Articles and Services** refers to expenditure for family and individual articles for living purpose and family services. It includes furniture and interior decoration, home appliances, home textiles, household miscellaneous daily articles, personal articles, and family services.

**Transport and Communications** refers to expenditure for transport and communication and related services, maintenance and repairs, and vehicle insurance.

**Education, Cultural and Recreational Activities** refers to expenditure on education, cultural and recreational activities.

**Health Care and Medical Services** refers to expenditure on drugs, supplies and services of medical and health care. It includes medical appliances and drugs, and medical services.

**Miscellaneous Goods and Services** refers to expenditure of all kinds of expenditure of other articles and services that can't be divided into the category above.

## Explanatory on Indicators before 2012

Prior to 2012, household surveys in China were conducted separately in urban and rural areas. Statistical coverage of indicators of household income and expenditure of urban and rural households were different, data were not comparable completely. Disposable income was surveyed in urban households, and net income was surveyed in rural households. Income and expenditure of urban households refer to that in cash, not including physical payments; Among which, when calculating per capita disposable income and consumption, self-owned housing conversion rental is not included, and expenditure of purchasing housing is not included either. Income and expenditure of rural households are divided into that of total and in cash, that is, total income and expenditure include self occupied physical payments; Among which, when computing per capita net income and expenditure of rural households, self-owned housing conversion rental is not included, but purchasing of housing is included in consumption expenditure of rural households.

For comparable reason, data prior to 2012 in this yearbook were still original urban households and rural households survey.

### 1. Urban Household Survey

**Population of Urban Households** refer to members of households living and sharing economically together in the urban areas. All the income and expenditure of all the members of such households are included in the income and expenditure of the household.

**Disposable Income of Urban Households** refers to the actual income at the disposal of members of the households which can be used for final consumption, other non-compulsory expenditure and savings. This equals to total income minus income tax, personal contribution to social security and subsidy for keeping diaries in being a sample household. The following formula is used:

Disposable Income of Urban Households=Total Household Income - Income Tax - Personal Contribution to Social Security - Subsidy for Keeping Diaries for A Sampled Household

### 2. Rural Household Survey

**Rural Households** refer to usual resident households in rural areas. Usual resident households in rural areas are households residing on a long term basis(for more than one year) in the areas under the administration of township governments (not including county towns), and in the areas under the administration of villages in county towns. Households residing in the current addresses for over one year with their household registration in other places are still considered as resident households of the locality. For households with their household registration in one place but all members of the households having moved away to make a living in another place for over one year, they will not be included in the rural households of the area where they are registered, irrespective of whether they still keep their contracted land.

**Net Income of Rural Households** refers to the total income of rural households from all sources minus all corresponding expenses. The formula for calculation is as follows:

Net income of rural households = total income - household operation expenses - taxes and fees-depreciation of fixed assets for production - gifts to rural relatives.

Net income is mainly used as input for reinvestment in production and as consumption expenditure of the year, and also used for savings and non-compulsory expenses of various forms. "Per capita net income of farmers" is the level of net income averaged by population, reflecting the average income level of rural population in a given area.

**Consumer Price Index** reflects the relative change in prices of consumer goods and services in a certain period of time, Formation of consumer price index aims to study the impact of consumer price changes on the actual living cost of urban

EXPLANATORY NOTES TO MAJOR STATISTICAL INDICATORS

and rural residents and to provide scientific basis for central government and relevant departments in drawing up consumer up consumer policy, price policy, wage policy and monetary policy and in accounting the nation economy. It is also a key index reflecting the fluctuation of inflation.

**Retail Price Index** refers to the prices at which industrial, commercial, catering and other retail enterprises sell daily consumer goods and products for office use to urban and rural residents and institutions and social organizations. It reflects the general change in prices of retail commodities in a certain period of time. Formation of retail price index aims to keep abreast of price fluctuation of retail commodities and provide the reference basis for the central government in working out economic policies.

**Producer Price Indices for Farm Products** reflect the trend and degree of changes in producers' prices received by farmers when they sell farm products during a given period. These indices depict the change in the level and structure of producer prices for farm products of the country and meet the needs of agricultural statistics and national accounts statistics. The producer price index for a given product is calculated as the geometrical mean of individual indices for all surveyed units which sell such product, and the indices for a product category is obtained as the weighted mean of price indices for all products in the category. Method for calculating accumulative quarterly indices is the same as for calculating the individual quarterly indices.

**Producer Price** is a statistic index reflecting the fluctuation tendency and extent of the price of manufactured goods. It is a relative ratio of the average price fluctuation of manufactured goods in different times and places. This index includes the factory price of the manufactured goods at the first sale and the price of the raw materials, fuel and power purchased by the enterprises as intermediate input, which is an important basis for national economic accounting and economic administration.

**Price Indices of Investment in Fixed Assets** is a relative ratio reflecting the trend and degree of changes in prices of investment goods and charging projects in fixed assets of various engineering projects during a given period. This indicator is used to remove the factor of price change in the aggregates of investment at current prices.

**Price Index of Residential Real Estate Sales** is a relative ratio reflecting the general trend and variation degrees of the sales price of the residential real estate. This index of China is composed of the sales price of residential real estate and the sales price of second-hand residential real estate in 70 medium-large cities.

# 第八章 · 城镇建设

URBAN CONSTRUCTION

# 简要说明
## BRIEF INTRODUCTION

本章资料反映全市城镇建设的基本情况。

城镇建设资料主要包括城镇建设用地、基础设施水平、市政设施、园林绿化、供水供气、公共交通、基础设施建设投资等，由市统计局固定资产投资处根据市住房和城乡建设委员会、市规划和自然资源局资料整理提供。

The data in this chapter show the basic conditions of urban construction in Chongqing.

The statistics on urban construction mainly include the data of land for urban construction, urban infrastructure, municipal infrastructure, parks and green areas, tap water and gas supply, public traffic, investment in infrastructure construction. The data concerned are provided by Commission of Housing and Urban-Rural Development of Chongqing and Bureau of Planning and Natural Resources of Chongqing, and sorted and compiled by Division of Statistics of Investment in Fixed Assets, Chongqing Municipal Bureau of Statistics.

## 表 8.1 城市建设用地（2022 年）
## LAND FOR URBAN CONSTRUCTION (2022)

单位：平方公里 (sq.km)

| 项　目 | Item | 全　市 Total | #区合计 Total of Districts |
|---|---|---|---|
| **建成区面积** | **Built-up Area** | **1831.72** | **1640.80** |
| **建设用地面积** | **Land for Urban Construction** | **1698.47** | **1525.59** |
| 居住用地 | Land for Residence | 528.85 | 464.97 |
| 公共管理与公共服务用地 | Land for Public Management and Public Services | 157.99 | 141.33 |
| 商业服务业设施用地 | Land for Commercialized Service Facilities | 95.24 | 85.95 |
| 工业用地 | Land for Industry | 352.62 | 333.46 |
| 物流仓储用地 | Land for Logistics and Warehousing | 39.33 | 36.84 |
| 道路与交通设施用地 | Land for Road and Traffic Facilities | 337.83 | 308.96 |
| 公用设施用地 | Land for Public Facilities | 35.69 | 29.56 |
| 绿化与广场用地 | Land for Greening and Squares | 150.92 | 124.52 |

注："区合计"数为 26 个市辖区合计（下表同）。
Note:"Total of Districts" refers to the total data of 26 municipal districts (the same below).

## 表 8.2 城市基础设施水平（2021 － 2022 年）
## STATISTICS ON URBAN INFRASTRUCTURE (2021-2022)

| 项　目 | Item | 全　市 Total | | #区合计 Total of Districts | |
|---|---|---|---|---|---|
| | | 2021 | 2022 | 2021 | 2022 |
| 人均日生活用水量（升） | Per Capita Daily Water Consumption (liter) | 172.11 | 175.54 | 178.52 | 180.77 |
| 用水普及率 (%) | Water Coverage Rate (%) | 96.50 | 98.67 | 96.26 | 98.57 |
| 燃气普及率 (%) | Gas Coverage Rate (%) | 98.15 | 98.74 | 98.19 | 98.82 |
| 人均道路面积（平方米） | Per Capita Road Surface Area (sq.m) | 15.34 | 16.08 | 15.95 | 16.64 |
| 污水处理厂集中处理率 (%) | Rate of Intensive Treatment by Wastewater Treatment Plant (%) | 98.66 | 98.26 | 98.57 | 98.06 |
| 人均公园绿地面积（平方米） | Per Capita Area of Public Green Land (sq.m) | 16.33 | 17.35 | 16.67 | 17.11 |
| 建成区绿地率 (%) | Green Space Rate of Built District (%) | 39.24 | 41.21 | 39.33 | 41.33 |
| 建成区绿化覆盖率 (%) | Green Coverage Rate of Built District (%) | 42.53 | 44.47 | 42.56 | 44.56 |

注：人均数为户籍人口口径。
Note: The data of average population refers to registration statistics.

## 表 8.3 城市市政设施(2021 – 2022 年)
## MUNICIPAL INFRASTRUCTURE (2021-2022)

| 项　目 | Item | 全　市 Total | | #区合计 Total of Districts | |
|---|---|---|---|---|---|
| | | 2021 | 2022 | 2021 | 2022 |
| 道路长度(公里) | Length of Paved Roads (km) | 13573 | 13923 | 12246 | 12531 |
| 道路面积(万平方米) | Area of Paved Roads (10 000 sq.m) | 28699 | 29445 | 26320 | 26922 |
| #人行道 | Sidewalk | 8665 | 8873 | 7944 | 8112 |
| 桥梁数(座) | Number of Bridges (unit) | 2799 | 3065 | 2506 | 2754 |
| #立交桥 | Overpass | 337 | 377 | 328 | 366 |
| 路灯盏数(盏) | Number of Street Lights (unit) | 1028730 | 1053678 | 899107 | 921464 |
| 排水管道长度(公里) | Length of Drainpipes (km) | 27729 | 28773 | 24604 | 25504 |
| #污水管道 | Sewage Pipes | 13600 | 14213 | 11852 | 12368 |
| 污水年排放量(万立方米) | Annual Discharged Volume of Wastewater (10 000 cu.m) | 164514 | 169936 | 150294 | 155510 |
| 污水处理厂处理总量(万立方米) | Total Volume of Wastewater Treated by Wastewater Treatment Plant (10 000 cu.m) | 162306 | 166987 | 148151 | 152498 |

## 表 8.4 城市园林绿化(2021 – 2022 年)
## PARKS AND GREEN LAND IN URBAN AREA (2021-2022)

| 项　目 | Item | 全　市 Total | | #区合计 Total of Districts | |
|---|---|---|---|---|---|
| | | 2021 | 2022 | 2021 | 2022 |
| 绿化覆盖面积(公顷) | Green Covered Area (hectare) | 94950 | 98592 | 82291 | 85446 |
| #建成区 | Built District | 78008 | 81495 | 70035 | 73114 |
| 园林绿地面积(公顷) | Area of Public Green Land (hectare) | 84559 | 88184 | 73383 | 76584 |
| #建成区 | Built District | 71974 | 75488 | 71974 | 67814 |
| 公园绿地面积(公顷) | Area of Parks and Green Land (hectare) | 30561 | 31758 | 27504 | 28514 |
| 公园个数(个) | Number of Parks and Zoos (unit) | 679 | 746 | 536 | 594 |
| 公园面积(公顷) | Area of Parks and Zoos (hectare) | 18420 | 19213 | 16192 | 16671 |

## 表 8.5 城市供水及供气情况（2021 － 2022 年）
BASIC STATISTICS ON TAP WATER AND GAS SUPPLY IN URBAN AREA (2021-2022)

| 项 目 | Item | 全 市 Total | | #区合计 Total of Districts | |
|---|---|---|---|---|---|
| | | 2021 | 2022 | 2021 | 2022 |
| **城市供水** | **Tap Water Supply in Urban Area** | | | | |
| 年末供水综合生产能力（万立方米 / 日） | Production Capacity of Tap Water Supply at Year-end (10 000 cu.m/day) | 847 | 872 | 770 | 794 |
| 年末供水管道长度（公里） | Length of Water Supply Pipelines at Year-end (km) | 28091 | 29341 | 25393 | 26938 |
| 供水总量（万立方米） | Total Volume of Water Supply (10 000 cu.m) | 193100 | 199584 | 177845 | 183613 |
| #生产运营用水 | For Production Use | 41106 | 40407 | 39302 | 38598 |
| 公共服务用水 | For Public Services | 27077 | 27167 | 25696 | 25701 |
| 居民家庭用水 | For Residential Use | 85993 | 88175 | 77428 | 79155 |
| 其他用水 | Others | 9788 | 13175 | 8700 | 12317 |
| 用水户数（户） | Households with Access to Tap Water (household) | 8297630 | 8922079 | 7400356 | 7977509 |
| #家庭用户 | Residential Households | 7481027 | 8209193 | 6694377 | 7383998 |
| 用水人口（万人） | Number of Residents with Access to Tap Water (10 000 persons) | 1806 | 1807 | 1588 | 1594 |
| **城市供气** | **Gas Supply in Urban Area** | | | | |
| 天然气供气总量（万立方米） | Total Volume of Natural Gas Supply (10 000 cu.m) | 609100 | 622711 | 579515 | 591130 |
| #家庭用量 | For Residential Use | 260501 | 254458 | 241321 | 234303 |
| 天然气用气户数（户） | Households with Access to Natural Gas (household) | 8762805 | 9015616 | 7959230 | 8186553 |
| #家庭用户 | Residential Households | 8383340 | 8701732 | 7603435 | 7891512 |
| 天然气用气人口（万人） | Population with Access to Natural Gas (10 000 persons) | 1762 | 1746 | 1568 | 1557 |
| 天然气汽车加气站（个） | Number of CNG Stations for Motor Vehicles (unit) | 129 | 133 | 114 | 117 |
| 液化石油气供气总量（吨） | Total Volume of Liquefied Petroleum Gas Supply (ton) | 77225 | 63512 | 64141 | 50826 |
| #家庭用量 | For Residential Use | 46962 | 36701 | 36607 | 26708 |
| 液化石油气用气户数（户） | Households with Access to Liquefied Petroleum Gas (household) | 284368 | 247718 | 190072 | 158353 |
| #家庭用户 | Residential Households | 213982 | 188946 | 130364 | 110090 |
| 液化石油气用气人口（万人） | Population with Access to Liquefied Petroleum Gas (10 000 persons) | 74 | 61 | 52 | 42 |

## 表 8.6 城市公共交通情况（2021 － 2022 年）
BASIC STATISTICS ON PUBLIC TRANSPORTATION IN URBAN AREA (2021-2022)

| 指　标 | Item | 2021 | 2022 |
|---|---|---|---|
| **公共汽车** | **Public Vehicles** | | |
| 年末营运线路网长度（公里） | Year-end Length of Public Transport Network under Operation (km) | 29159 | 30161 |
| 公共汽车（辆） | Number of Public Vehicles (unit) | 15023 | 15131 |
| #天然气燃料车 | CNG Vehicles | 6281 | 5168 |
| 客运量（万人次） | Passenger Volume (10 000 person-times) | 221052 | 183298 |
| **轻　轨** | **Light Rail Transits** | | |
| 通车里程（公里） | Length of Light Rail Transits under Operation (km) | 370 | 435 |
| 车辆数（辆） | Number of Vehicles (unit) | 2248 | 2682 |
| 客运量（万人次） | Passengers Traffic (10 000 person-times) | 109709 | 91109 |
| **出租汽车** | **Taxis** | | |
| 车辆数（辆） | Number of Vehicles (unit) | 24478 | 24679 |
| 客运量（万人次） | Passenger Traffic (10 000 persons) | 73532 | 72447 |

## 表 8.7 公用事业和市政建设投资额（2021-2022 年）
INVESTMENT IN PUBLIC UTILITIES AND MUNICIPAL CONSTRUCTION (2021-2022)

单位：万元 (10 000 yuan)

| 指　标 | Item | 2021 | 2022 |
|---|---|---|---|
| **公用事业** | **Public Utilities** | | |
| 供　水 | Tap Water Supply | 260158 | 208404 |
| 燃　气 | Gas Supply | 37034 | 37322 |
| 轨道交通 | Rail Transit | 3147403 | 2624382 |
| **市政建设** | **Municipal Construction** | | |
| 园林绿化 | Parks and Green Land | 726081 | 1121690 |
| 市容环境卫生 | City Appearance and Environmental Sanitation | 411931 | 177442 |

# 主要统计指标解释

## ■ 供水综合生产能力

指按供水设施取水、净化、送水、出厂输水干管等环节设计能力计算的综合生产能力。包括在原设计能力基础上，经挖、革、改增加的生产能力。计算时，以四个环节中最薄弱的环节为主确定能力。

## ■ 供水管道长度

指从送水泵至用户水表之间所有管道的长度。不包括新安装尚未使用、水厂内以及用户建筑物内的管道。

## ■ 城市供水总量

指报告期供水企业（单位）供出的全部水量。包括有效供水量和漏损水量。

## ■ 生活用水

包括公共服务用水和居民家庭用水。公共服务用水指为城区社会公共生活服务的用水。包括行政事业单位、部队营区和公共设施服务、批发零售业、住宿餐饮业以及社会服务业等单位的用水。居民家庭用水指城市范围内所有居民家庭的日常生活用水。包括城市居民、农民家庭、公共供水站用水。

## ■ 用水普及率

指报告期末城区用水人口数与城市人口总数的比率。计算公式：

$$用水普及率=\frac{城区用水人口（含暂住人口）}{城区人口+城区暂住人口}\times 100\%$$

## ■ 城市供气总量

指报告期燃气企业（单位）向用户供应的燃气数量。包括销售量和损失量。

## ■ 燃气普及率

指报告期末城区使用燃气的城市人口数与城市人口总数的比率。其中燃气包括人工煤气、天然气、液化石油气三种。计算公式为：

$$燃气普及率=\frac{城区用气人口（含暂住人口）}{城区人口+城区暂住人口}\times 100\%$$

## ■ 道路长度

指道路长度和与道路相通的桥梁、隧道的长度，按车行道中心线计算。

## ■ 道路面积

为车行道与人行道面积之和。

## ■ 城市桥梁

指为跨越天然或人工障碍物而修建的构筑物。包括跨河桥、立交桥、人行天桥以及人行地下通道等。

## ■ 城市排水管道长度

指所有排水总管、干管、支管、检查井及连接井进出口等长度之和。

## ■ 年末公共交通车辆运营数

指年末城市用于公共交通运营业务的全部车辆数。新购、新制和调入的运营车辆，自投入之日起开始计算；调出、报废和调作他用的运营车辆，自上级主管机关批准之日起不再计入。

## ■ 城市绿地面积

指报告期末用作园林和绿化的各种绿地面积。包括公园绿地、生产绿地、防护绿地、附属绿地和其他绿地的面积。

## ■ 公园绿地

城市中向公众开放的、以游憩为主要功能，有一定的游憩设施和服务设施，同时兼有健全生态、美化景观、防灾减灾等综合作用的绿化用地。包括综合公园、社区公园、专类公园、带状公园和街旁绿地。其中综合公园、专类公园和带状公园面积之和为公园面积。

# 主要统计指标解释

## ■ 生产用水

指在城区范围内生产、运营的农、林、牧、渔业、工业、建筑业、交通运输业等单位在生产、运营过程中的用水。

## ■ 人工煤气生产能力

指报告期末人工燃气生产厂制气、净化、输送等环节的综合生产能力，不包括备用设备能力。一般按设计能力计算，当实际生产能力大于设计能力时，应按实际测定的生产能力计算。测定时应以制气、净化、输送三个环节中最薄弱的环节为主。

## ■ 供气管道长度

指报告期末从气源厂压缩机的出口或门站出口至各类用户引入管之间的全部已经通气、投入使用的管道长度。不包括煤气生产厂、输配站、液化气储存站、灌瓶站、储配站、气化站、混气站、供应站等厂(站)内的管道。

## ■ 城市供热能力

指供热企业(单位)向城市热用户输送热能的设计能力。

## ■ 城市供热总量

指在报告期供热企业(单位)向城市热用户输送全部蒸汽和热水的总热量。

## ■ 城市供热管道长度

指从各类热源到热用户建筑物接入口之间的全部蒸汽和热水的管道长度。不包括各类热源厂内部的管道长度。

## ■ 城市污水日处理能力

指污水处理厂(或污水处理装置)每昼夜处理污水量的设计能力。

## ■ 清扫保洁面积

指报告期末对城市道路和公共场所(主要包括城市行车道、人行道、车行隧道、人行过街地下通道、道路附属绿地、地铁站、高架路、人行过街天桥、立交桥、广场、停车场及其他设施等)进行清扫保洁的面积。一天清扫保洁多次的，按清扫保洁面积最大的一次计算。

## ■ 市容环卫专用车辆设备

指用于环境卫生作业、监察的专用车辆和设备，包括用于道路清扫、冲洗、洒水、除雪、垃圾粪便清运、市容监察以及与其配套使用的车辆和设备。

## ■ 每万人拥有公共交通车辆

指按城市人口计算的每万人平均拥有的公共交通车辆标台数。计算公式：

$$每万人拥有公共交通车辆=\frac{公共交通运营车标台数}{城区人口+城区暂住人口}$$

# Explanatory Notes on Main Statistical Indicators

## Production Capacity of Water Supply

Refers to the designed comprehensive production capacity of water facilities, covering the 4 links of water collection, purification, conveyance, and outflow through trunk pipelines. Increase capacity through transformation and innovation projects is included as well. The capacity is determined mainly on the weakest of the above-mentioned 4 links.

## Length of Water Supply Pipelines

Refers to the total length of all the pipelines between the water pumps and the user water meters, excluding pipelines newly installed but not used yet, pipeline in the water factory, and pipeline in the user's buildings.

## Total Volume of Urban Water Supply

Refers to the total volume of water supplied by water-works (units) during the reference period, including both the effective water supply and loss during the water supply.

## Consumption of Water for Living Use

It includes Consumption of Water for Public Service Use and Consumption of Water for Households Use. Consumption of Water for Public Service Use refers to water consumption for public service in the urban areas. It includes water consumption of administrative institutions, army camps, public facilities, wholesale and retail, accommodation and catering industry and social service industry, etc. Consumption of Water for Households Use refers to consumption of water for daily life of all households in cities, including households of urban residents and farmers, and public water supply stations.

## Coverage Rate of Urban Population with Access to Tap Water

Refers to the ratio of the urban population with access to tap water to the total urban population at the end of reference period. The formula is:

Coverage of Urban Population with Access to Tap Water =

$$\frac{\text{Urban Population with Access to Tap Water}}{\text{Urban Population}} \times 100\%$$

## Volume of Gas Supply

Refers to the total volume of gas provided to users by gas-producing enterprises (units) during the reporting period, including the volume sold and the volume lost.

## Coverage Rate of Urban Population with Access to Gas

Refers to the ratio of the urban population with access to gas to the total urban population at the end of the reference period. Gas here includes artificial coal gas, natural gas and liquefied petroleum gas. The formula is:

Coverage Rate of Urban Population with Access to Gas =

$$\frac{\text{Urban Population with Access to Gas}}{\text{Urban Population}} \times 100\%$$

## Length of Paved Roads

Refers to the length of roads with paved surface including bridges and tunnels connected with roads. Length of the roads is measured by the central lines.

## Area of Roads

Is the summed of carriageway and sidewalk.

## Urban Bridges

Refer to bridges built to cross over natural or man-made barriers, including bridges over rivers, overpasses for traffic and for pedestrians, underpasses for pedestrians, etc.

### Length of Urban Sewage Pipes

Refers to the total length of general drainage, trunks, branch and inspection wells, connection wells, inlets and outlets, etc.

### Number of Vehicles under Operation at Year-end

Refers to the total number of vehicles under operation by public transport enterprises (units) at the end of the year, based on the records of operational vehicles by the enterprises (units).

### Area of Urban Green Land

Refers to the total area occupied for green projects at the end of the reference period, including park green land, production green land, protection green land, green land attached to institutions, and other green areas.

### Park Green Area

Refers to green areas open to the public for amusement and rest with the facilities of amusement, rest and services. Its function includes perfecting ecology, beautifying landscape, and preventing and reducing disaster. Park green areas include comprehensive park, community park, theme park, linear park and roadside green space. Total areas of comprehensive park, topic park and belt-shaped is the area of park.

### Consumption of Water for Production and Operation Use

Refers to water consumption in the process of production and operation by production and operation units of agriculture, forestry, animal husbandry, fisheries, industry, construction industry, and transportation industry, etc. in urban areas.

### Production Capacity of Gaswork Gas

Refers to the overall production capacity of the urban gasworks in gas generation, purification and delivery at the end of the reference period, excluding capacity of the reserved facilities. In general, it is determined by the designed capacity, and when actual production capacity is larger than the designed capacity, the capacity is determined by the actual measurement on the weakest segment in the production, purification and delivery.

### Length of Gas Pipelines

Refers to the total length of pipelines in use between the outlet of the compressor of gas-work or outlet of gas stations and the leading pipe of users, excluding pipelines within gasworks, delivery stations, LPG storage stations, refilling stations, gas-mixing stations and supply stations.

### Heating Capacity in Urban Areas

Refers to the designed capacity of heating enterprises (units) in supplying heating energy to urban users during the reference period.

### Quantity of Heat Supplied in Urban Areas

Refers to the total quantity of heat from steam and hot water supplied to urban users by heating enterprises (units) during the reference period.

### Length of Urban Heating Pipelines

Refers to the total length of steam or hot water pipelines for sources of heat to the leading pipelines of the buildings of the users, excluding internal pipelines in heat generating enterprises.

### Daily Disposal Capacity of Urban Sewage

Refers to the designed 24-hour capacity of sewage disposal by the sewage treatment works or facilities.

### Road Area Cleaned

Refers to the area which are regularly cleaned, as at the end of the reference period, at urban roads and public places (mainly including urban roadways, pedestrian walkways, vehicular tunnels, pedestrian underpasses, underground railway stations, lifted roads, pedestrians walk bridges, overpasses, plazas, parking lots and other facilities). If there are several times of cleaning in a day at a location, the area of that time of cleaning with the largest area cleaned will be taken.

EXPLANATORY NOTES TO MAJOR STATISTICAL INDICATORS

## □ Vehicles and Facilities Dedicated to Urban Cleanliness and Environmental Sanitation

Refer to vehicles and facilities dedicated for use in the operation, management and monitoring of environmental hygiene work. They include vehicles for road cleaning, washing, showering, ice removal, disposal of garbage and human wastes, cleanliness monitoring and related activities.

## □ Public Transportation Vehicles per 10000 Population

Refers to the number of public transportation vehicles, calculated by urban population, per 10000 population in the city district. The formula for calculation is:

$$\text{Public Transportation Vehicles} = \frac{\text{Number of Public Transportation Vehicles}}{\text{City District Population}}$$

# 第九章・资源和环境

# RESOURCES AND ENVIRONMENT

# 简要说明

BRIEF INTRODUCTION

资源主要内容包括自然资源、自然地理、气象状况。自然资源中土地、矿产资源数据由市规划和自然资源局提供，林木资源数据由市林业局提供，水资源数据由市水利局提供。气象状况由市气象局提供。

自然地理、气象综合资料，由市统计局综合处根据有关部门资料进行整理和编辑。环境主要内容包括工业废水、废气、固体废物的排放处理和利用，工业污染治理投资，生活污染物排放等，由市统计局能源资源统计处根据市生态环境局、市水利局、市林业局等部门的资料整理提供。

表9-5、9-6、9-7、9-8、9-10、9-11数据为初步数据。

The scope of resources mainly covers natural resources, natural geography and climate. The data of land and mineral resources in natural resources are provided by Chongqing Municipal Bureau of Planning and Natural Resources; the data of forest resources are provided by Chongqing Forestry Administration; the data of water resources are provided by Chongqing Water Resources Bureau; and the data of climate are provided by Chongqing Meteorological Bureau.

The data of natural environment and climate are provided by the departments concerned and sorted and compiled by Division of Comprehensive Statistics of Municipal Bureau of Statistics. The statistics of environment mainly includes the discharge, treatment and utilization of industrial waste water, waste gas and solid wastes, the investment in industrial pollution treatment and the discharge of domestic pollutants, which are provided by Chongqing Ecology and Environment Bureau, Ministry of Water Resources of Chongqing and Chongqing Forestry Administration, and sorted and compiled by Division of Energy Resources Statistics, Municipal Bureau of Statistics.

The data in Tables 9-5, 9-6, 9-7, 9-8, 9-10, and 9-11 are preliminary data.

# 表 9.1 自然资源（2021 – 2022 年）
NATURAL RESOURCES (2021-2022)

| 项 目 | Item | 2021 | 2022 |
|---|---|---|---|
| **林木资源** | **Forest Resources** | | |
| 新造林面积（万公顷） | Area of Afforested Land (10 000 hectares) | 13.19 | 13.35 |
| 森林覆盖率（%） | Forest Coverage Rate (%) | 54.5 | 55.0 |
| **水资源（当年量）** | **Water Resources (current quantity)** | | |
| 降水深（毫米） | Precipitation (mm) | 1404.3 | 945.2 |
| 地表径流量（亿立方米） | Surface Runoff (100 million cu.m) | 750.78 | 373.46 |
| 地下水量（亿立方米） | Groundwater Resources (100 million cu.m) | 129.39 | 82.64 |

# 表 9.2 自然地理（2022 年）
NATURAL ENVIRONMENT (2022)

**位置**：重庆位于北纬 28 度 10 分 -32 度 13 分，东经 105 度 11 分 -110 度 11 分之间，地处较为发达的东部地区和资源丰富的西部地区的结合部，东邻湖北、湖南，南靠贵州，西接四川，北连陕西，是长江上游最大的经济中心、西南工商业重镇和水陆交通枢纽。1997 年 3 月 14 日，第八届全国人民代表大会第五次会议通过了设立重庆直辖市的决议，与北京、天津、上海同为四大直辖市。

**面积**：重庆辖区面积 8.24 万平方公里，南北长 450 公里，东西宽 470 公里。2021 年全市共辖 26 个区：万州区、黔江区、涪陵区、渝中区、大渡口区、江北区、沙坪坝区、九龙坡区、南岸区、北碚区、渝北区、巴南区、长寿区、江津区、合川区、永川区、南川区、綦江区、大足区、璧山区、铜梁区、潼南区、荣昌区、开州区、梁平区和武隆区；12 个县（自治县）：城口县、丰都县、垫江县、忠县、云阳县、奉节县、巫山县、巫溪县、石柱县土家族自治县、秀山土家族苗族自治县、酉阳土家族苗族自治县、彭水苗族土家族自治县。

**地势**：重庆地势由南北向长江河谷逐级降低，西北部和中部以丘陵、低山为主，东南部靠大巴山和武陵山两座大山脉。

**河流**：主要河流有长江、嘉陵江、乌江、涪江、綦江、大宁河等。

**气候**：重庆属中亚热带湿润季风气候区，具有夏热冬暖，光热同季，无霜期长，雨量充沛，湿润多阴等特点。重庆年平均气温 17.4℃。重庆降水充沛，年降水量普遍在 1000 ～ 1300mm。

## Location:

Chongqing is located at 28° 10' ~ 32° 13' north latitude and 105° 11' ~ 110° 11' east longitude. As a joint between the eastern areas with developed economy and the western areas with rich resources, with Hubei and Hunan on its east, Guizhou on its south, Sichuan on its west and Shaanxi on its north, Chongqing is the largest economic center in the upper reaches of the Yangtze River, an important industrial and commercial city in the southwest and a hub of land and water communications. On March 14, 1997, the resolution to establish Chongqing Municipality was passed on the 5th Session of the 8th National People' s Congress, and Chongqing became the fourth municipality directly under the Central Government after Beijing, Tianjin and Shanghai.

## Area:

Chongqing covers an area of 82,400 square kilometers, stretching 450 kilometers from north to south and 470 kilometers from east to west. In 2021, Chongqing has 26 districts, namely Wanzhou, Qianjiang, Fuling, Yuzhong, Dadukou, Jiangbei, Shapingba, Jiulongpo, Nan'an, Beibei, Yubei, Banan, Changshou, Jiangjin, Hechuan, Yongchuan, Nanchuan, Qijiang, Dazu, Bishan, Tongliang, Tongnan, Rongchang, Kaizhou, Liangping, Wulong and 12 counties, namely Chengkou, Fengdu, Dianjiang, Zhongxian, Yunyang, Fengjie, Wushan, Wuxi, Shizhu Tujia Autonomous County, Xiushan Tujia Autonomous County, Youyang Tujia Autonomous County and Pengshui Miao Autonomous County.

## Topography:

The altitude of Chongqing declines gradually from the north and the south to the valley of the Yangtze River. There are mainly hills and low mountains in the northwest and central areas of Chongqing, while the two large mountains of Daba and Wuling are in the southeast of Chongqing.

## River:

The rivers stretching through Chongqing mainly include Yangtze River, Jialing River, Wujiang River, Fujiang River, Qijiang River and Daning River.

## Climate:

Chongqing has a humid subtropical monsoon climate, hot in summer and warm in winter with the rainy season coinciding with the hot season. It has the characteristics of long frost-free period, plenty of rainfall and a lot of humid and cloudy days. The annual average temperature of Chongqing is 17.4℃ .Chongqing has abundant precipitation, with annual precipitation of 1000-1300mm.

# 表 9.3 气象基本情况（1951 – 2022 年）
BASIC STATISTICS ON CLIMATE (1951-2022)

| 年 份<br>Year | 降水量<br>（毫米）<br>Precipitation<br>(mm) | 平均气温<br>（摄氏度）<br>Average<br>Temperature<br>(℃) | 日照时数<br>（时）<br>Sunshine<br>Hours<br>(hour) | 平均相对湿度<br>（%）<br>Average<br>Relative<br>Humidity (%) | 平均风速<br>（米 / 秒）<br>Average<br>Wind Speed<br>(m/s) | 平均气压<br>（百帕）<br>Average<br>Air Pressure<br>(100 pa) |
|---|---|---|---|---|---|---|
| 1951 | 1043.4 | 18.4 | | 81 | 1.0 | |
| 1952 | 1227.9 | 18.5 | 1198.6 | 81 | 1.0 | |
| 1953 | 852.1 | 18.8 | 1245.6 | 80 | 0.9 | |
| 1954 | 1112.8 | 17.9 | 1061.2 | 81 | 0.9 | 981.2 |
| 1955 | 927.4 | 18.2 | 1388.6 | 77 | 0.8 | 982.0 |
| 1956 | 1497.4 | 18.2 | 1433.2 | 76 | 1.4 | 982.8 |
| 1957 | 1171.9 | 17.9 | 1094.2 | 80 | 1.3 | 983.3 |
| 1958 | 740.7 | 18.6 | 1260.7 | 77 | 1.4 | 983.3 |
| 1959 | 915.7 | 18.7 | 1378.3 | 76 | 1.4 | 983.0 |
| 1960 | 1026.0 | 18.4 | 1102.0 | 78 | 1.4 | 983.5 |
| 1961 | 787.7 | 18.7 | 1338.8 | 77 | 1.5 | 982.8 |
| 1962 | 1210.4 | 18.0 | 1323.9 | 80 | 1.4 | 983.3 |
| 1963 | 1072.8 | 18.9 | 1370.4 | 77 | 1.4 | 982.4 |
| 1964 | 1031.6 | 18.2 | 1170.4 | 80 | 1.5 | 982.9 |
| 1965 | 1318.9 | 18.1 | 1009.5 | 81 | 1.4 | 983.4 |
| 1966 | 958.9 | 18.6 | 1278.9 | 78 | 1.4 | 982.7 |
| 1967 | 1046.0 | 18.1 | 1216.3 | 79 | 1.4 | 983.4 |
| 1968 | 1384.5 | 17.7 | 1054.6 | 82 | 1.2 | 983.5 |
| 1969 | 1080.5 | 18.6 | 1357.1 | 76 | 1.2 | 982.8 |
| 1970 | 1097.5 | 18.1 | 1197.9 | 79 | 1.1 | 983.5 |
| 1971 | 854.3 | 18.6 | 1370.6 | 76 | 1.3 | 983.4 |
| 1972 | 1171.8 | 18.4 | 1284.1 | 78 | 1.3 | 982.9 |
| 1973 | 1092.3 | 18.9 | 1349.4 | 78 | 1.3 | 983.2 |
| 1974 | 1258.0 | 17.8 | 1068.3 | 79 | 1.3 | 983.0 |
| 1975 | 1025.4 | 18.5 | 1202.5 | 78 | 1.2 | 982.9 |
| 1976 | 1044.9 | 17.7 | 1129.2 | 79 | 1.1 | 983.5 |
| 1977 | 1151.2 | 18.1 | 1234.8 | 79 | 1.1 | 984.0 |
| 1978 | 1057.2 | 18.8 | 1495.7 | 77 | 1.2 | 983.5 |
| 1979 | 1160.0 | 18.4 | 1222.2 | 80 | 1.1 | 983.4 |
| 1980 | 1062.6 | 18.2 | 1071.8 | 79 | 1.4 | 983.6 |
| 1981 | 1157.9 | 18.1 | 1188.0 | 79 | 1.4 | 983.5 |
| 1982 | 1185.2 | 17.7 | 992.3 | 81 | 1.1 | 983.6 |
| 1983 | 1138.1 | 18.1 | 954.4 | 80 | 0.9 | 983.9 |

注：此表为重庆市区资料。
Note: the table above shows the data of the downtown area of Chongqing.

**表 9.3 续表 continued**

| 年 份<br>Year | 降水量（毫米）<br>Precipitation (mm) | 平均气温（摄氏度）<br>Average Temperature (℃) | 日照时数（时）<br>Sunshine Hours (hour) | 平均相对湿度（%）<br>Average Relative Humidity (%) | 平均风速（米/秒）<br>Average Wind Speed (m/s) | 平均气压（百帕）<br>Average Air Pressure (100 pa) |
|---|---|---|---|---|---|---|
| 1984 | 1035.1 | 17.8 | 1028.7 | 79 | 1.1 | 983.1 |
| 1985 | 1004.0 | 17.9 | 997.1 | 79 | 1.3 | 983.3 |
| 1986 | 1141.4 | 17.8 | 946.1 | 80 | 1.3 | 984.2 |
| 1987 | 910.2 | 18.6 | 946.3 | 78 | 1.2 | 983.4 |
| 1988 | 1254.0 | 18.0 | 840.6 | 80 | 1.1 | 983.6 |
| 1989 | 1137.4 | 17.7 | 855.0 | 81 | 1.0 | 983.8 |
| 1990 | 956.7 | 18.7 | 1083.7 | 79 | 1.2 | 983.2 |
| 1991 | 1180.6 | 18.2 | 874.8 | 81 | 1.1 | 983.5 |
| 1992 | 987.4 | 18.1 | 975.0 | 78 | 1.6 | 984.0 |
| 1993 | 1164.3 | 17.8 | 894.6 | 81 | 1.5 | 984.0 |
| 1994 | 982.5 | 18.7 | 1063.8 | 80 | 1.4 | 983.2 |
| 1995 | 923.5 | 18.3 | 993.6 | 79 | 1.3 | 983.7 |
| 1996 | 1398.3 | 17.7 | 899.4 | 81 | 1.3 | 983.6 |
| 1997 | 898.8 | 18.5 | 943.0 | 79 | 1.4 | 983.8 |
| 1998 | 1508.0 | 19.2 | 941.9 | 79 | 1.5 | 983.0 |
| 1999 | 1305.6 | 18.5 | 833.6 | 81 | 1.5 | 983.2 |
| 2000 | 1010.9 | 18.2 | 961.1 | 80 | 1.4 | 983.0 |
| 2001 | 814.8 | 18.8 | 1050.4 | 78 | 1.6 | 983.3 |
| 2002 | 1430.6 | 18.8 | 1117.1 | 80 | 1.6 | 983.3 |
| 2003 | 1025.0 | 18.9 | 875.7 | 80 | 1.6 | 983.2 |
| 2004 | 1182.1 | 18.4 | 974.7 | 78 | 1.3 | 984.0 |
| 2005 | 1019.8 | 18.6 | 903.9 | 77 | 1.4 | 982.5 |
| 2006 | 839.6 | 19.2 | 1114.3 | 75 | 1.4 | 982.9 |
| 2007 | 1439.2 | 19.0 | 856.2 | 81 | 1.3 | 983.3 |
| 2008 | 985.3 | 18.6 | 703.8 | 82 | 1.3 | 983.9 |
| 2009 | 1198.9 | 19.0 | 943.9 | 80 | 1.4 | 982.8 |
| 2010 | 1044.7 | 18.7 | 910.6 | 78 | 1.3 | 983.0 |
| 2011 | 992.8 | 17.7 | 1270.2 | 74 | 1.2 | 971.1 |
| 2012 | 1104.4 | 18.3 | 812.0 | 72 | 1.4 | 982.7 |
| 2013 | 1026.9 | 19.9 | 1187.5 | 71 | 1.4 | 982.6 |
| 2014 | 1452.5 | 18.6 | 598.4 | 79 | 1.3 | 983.6 |
| 2015 | 1448.7 | 19.6 | 1129.8 | 75 | 1.4 | 983.3 |
| 2016 | 1345.8 | 18.5 | 1150.5 | 79.5 | 1.6 | 971.0 |
| 2017 | 1196.2 | 18.4 | 1049.3 | 78.5 | 1.6 | 971.4 |
| 2018 | 1128.2 | 18.3 | 1141.5 | 78.2 | 1.7 | 970.7 |
| 2019 | 1333.8 | 18.2 | 1107.0 | 79.4 | 1.6 | 970.8 |
| 2020 | 1181.4 | 19.2 | 1012.2 | 75.6 | 1.3 | 983.3 |
| 2021 | 1287.0 | 18.0 | 1066.0 | 79.0 | 2.0 | 971.0 |
| 2022 | 1036.0 | 20.0 | 1422.0 | 73.0 | 2.0 | 970.0 |

## 表 9.4 全年气象情况（2022 年）
STATISTICS ON THE CLIMATE OF THE CURRENT YEAR (2022)

| 月 份<br>Month | 降水量<br>（毫米）<br>Precipitation<br>(mm) | 平均气温<br>（摄氏度）<br>Average<br>Temperature<br>(℃) | 日照时数<br>（时）<br>Sunshine<br>Hours<br>(hour) | 平均相对湿度<br>（%）<br>Average<br>Relative<br>Humidity (%) | 平均风速<br>（米 / 秒）<br>Average<br>Wind Speed<br>(m/s) | 平均气压<br>（百帕）<br>Average<br>Air Pressure<br>(100 pa) | 雨日数<br>（天）<br>Days of<br>Rain<br>(day) |
|---|---|---|---|---|---|---|---|
| 全 年<br>Total | 1036.0 | 20.0 | 1422.0 | 73.0 | 2.0 | 970.0 | 120.0 |
| 1 | 19.0 | 9.0 | 42.0 | 82.0 | 1.0 | 977.0 | 10.0 |
| 2 | 23.0 | 8.0 | 53.0 | 73.0 | 2.0 | 979.0 | 10.0 |
| 3 | 90.0 | 18.0 | 134.0 | 72.0 | 2.0 | 969.0 | 9.0 |
| 4 | 114.0 | 19.0 | 137.0 | 74.0 | 2.0 | 971.0 | 15.0 |
| 5 | 256.0 | 21.0 | 130.0 | 77.0 | 2.0 | 968.0 | 16.0 |
| 6 | 246.0 | 26.0 | 94.0 | 79.0 | 2.0 | 961.0 | 11.0 |
| 7 | 68.0 | 31.0 | 244.0 | 62.0 | 2.0 | 960.0 | 6.0 |
| 8 | 23.0 | 34.0 | 291.0 | 47.0 | 3.0 | 960.0 | 5.0 |
| 9 | 115.0 | 24.0 | 108.0 | 77.0 | 2.0 | 970.0 | 13.0 |
| 10 | 31.0 | 19.0 | 101.0 | 73.0 | 2.0 | 976.0 | 9.0 |
| 11 | 17.0 | 16.0 | 61.0 | 80.0 | 2.0 | 973.0 | 7.0 |
| 12 | 34.0 | 8.0 | 26.0 | 81.0 | 1.0 | 981.0 | 11.0 |

# 表 9.5 环境保护情况（2021 – 2022 年）
## ENVIRONMENTAL PROTECTION (2021-2022)

| 项　目 | Item | 2021 | 2022 |
|---|---|---|---|
| 环保投资（亿元） | Investment in Environmental Protection (100 million yuan) | 956.5 | 1100.2 |
| 水资源总量（亿立方米） | Total Water Resources (100 million cu.m) | 750.8 | 373.5 |
| 用水总量（亿立方米） | Total Use of Water (100 million cu.m) | 72.1 | 68.8 |
| 生活污水排放量（万吨） | Discharged Volume of Domestic Sewage (10 000 tons) | 120741 | 121165 |
| 化学需氧量排放量（万吨） | Discharged Volume of COD (10 000 tons) | 33.8 | 32.6 |
| 二氧化硫排放量（万吨） | Discharged Volume of $SO_2$ (10 000 tons) | 5.1 | 4.6 |
| #生活二氧化硫排放量（万吨） | Discharged Volume of $SO_2$ from Daily Life (10 000 tons) | 0.9 | 0.9 |
| 饮用水源水质达标率（%） | Rate of Drinking Water Sources up to Standard (%) | 100.0 | 100.0 |
| 工业污染治理施工项目数（个） | On-going Projects of Industrial Pollution Treatment (unit) | 54 | 26 |
| 工业污染治理项目完成投资（万元） | Completed Investment in Projects of Industrial Pollution Treatment (10 000 yuan) | 20656.9 | 55782.2 |
| 工业污染治理竣工项目数（个） | Completed Projects of Industrial Pollution Treatment (unit) | 24 | 23 |
| 工业固体废物综合利用率（%） | Rate of Industrial Solid Wastes Comprehensively Utilized (%) | 93.54 | 94.19 |
| 森林覆盖率 (%) | Forest Coverage (%) | 54.50 | 55.04 |
| 自然保护区数（个） | Number of Nature Reserves (unit) | 58 | 58 |
| 自然保护区面积（万公顷） | Area of Nature Reserves (10 000 hectares) | 80.4 | 80.4 |
| 保护区面积占土地总面积比重（%） | Percentage of Nature Reserves to Total Land Area (%) | 9.8 | 9.8 |
| 城市区域环境噪声平均值（分贝） | Average Urban Environmental Noise (db) | 52.5 | 52.5 |
| 城市道路交通噪声（分贝） | Urban Road Traffic Noise (db) | 64.4 | 64.8 |
| 全市大气可吸入颗粒物年均浓度（毫克 / 立方米） | Annual Average Concentration of $PM_{10}$ in Chongqing (mg/cu.m) | 0.054 | 0.048 |
| 全市大气二氧化硫年均浓度（毫克 / 立方米） | Annual Average Concentration of $SO_2$ in Chongqing (mg/cu.m) | 0.009 | 0.010 |
| 全市大气二氧化氮年均浓度（毫克 / 立方米） | Annual Average Concentration of $NO_2$ in Chongqing (mg/cu.m) | 0.032 | 0.029 |
| 全市环境空气质量优良天数比例（%） | Proportion of High Air Quality Days in Chongqing (%) | 89.3 | 91.0 |

# 表 9.6 工业"三废"排放处理及综合利用情况(1995－2022 年)
DISCHARGE, TREATMENT AND COMPREHENSIVE UTILIZATION OF WASTE GAS, WASTE WATER AND SOLID WASTES (1995-2022)

| 年 份<br>Year | 工业废水排放总量(万吨)<br>Total Volume of Industrial Waste Water Discharged (10 000 tons) | 工业废气(万吨) Industrial Waste Gas (10 000 tons)<br>工业废气排放总量(亿标立方米)<br>Total Volume of Industrial Waste Gas Discharged (100 million cu.m) | 工业二氧化硫 排放量<br>Volume of $SO_2$ Discharged | 工业烟(粉)尘 排放量<br>Volume of Industrial Dusts and Fume Discharged |
|---|---|---|---|---|
| 1995 | 95590 | 1979.00 | 71.45 | 22.39 |
| 1996 | 93889 | 1697.00 | 72.16 | 22.36 |
| 1997 | 101324 | 1794.00 | 71.43 | 33.18 |
| 1998 | 93997 | 1712.76 | 73.64 | 28.65 |
| 1999 | 90220 | 1839.33 | 75.88 | 26.44 |
| 2000 | 84344 | 1907.90 | 66.42 | 22.01 |
| 2001 | 81214 | 1856.24 | 56.94 | 21.41 |
| 2002 | 79872 | 1978.89 | 55.18 | 20.31 |
| 2003 | 81973 | 2276.94 | 59.97 | 22.23 |
| 2004 | 83031 | 3540.86 | 64.11 | 21.98 |
| 2005 | 84885 | 3654.55 | 68.32 | 21.28 |
| 2006 | 85866 | 5066.96 | 71.08 | 20.01 |
| 2007 | 69003 | 7616.62 | 68.31 | 18.23 |
| 2008 | 67027 | 7350.73 | 62.72 | 15.33 |
| 2009 | 65684 | 12586.52 | 58.61 | 10.77 |
| 2010 | 45180 | 10943.13 | 57.27 | 8.36 |
| 2011 | 33954 | 9121.07 | 53.13 | 17.12 |
| 2012 | 30611 | 8359.88 | 50.98 | 16.61 |
| 2013 | 33450 | 9532.44 | 49.44 | 17.98 |
| 2014 | 34968 | 9289.60 | 47.48 | 21.47 |
| 2015 | 35524 | 9928.07 | 42.68 | 19.64 |
| 2016 | 27837 | 12161.24 | 11.14 | 15.67 |
| 2017 | 21301 | 9596.76 | 10.49 | 14.91 |
| 2018 | 28387 | 11443.77 | 8.58 | 15.40 |
| 2019 | 29760 | 11805.18 | 6.89 | 14.96 |
| 2020 | 21491 | 13037.67 | 4.70 | 5.91 |
| 2021 | 16268 | 12983.59 | 4.17 | 4.62 |
| 2022 | 15720 | 13507.34 | 3.69 | 3.76 |

| 年 份<br>Year | 工业固体废物(万吨) Industrial Solid Wastes (10 000 tons)<br>产生量<br>Produced Volume | 排放量<br>Discharged Volume | 处置量<br>Treated Volume | 综合利用量<br>Comprehensively Utilized Volume | 综合利用率(%)<br>Rate of Comprehensive Utilization (%) |
|---|---|---|---|---|---|
| 1995 | 1092 | 230 | 68.34 | 467.79 | 50.37 |
| 1996 | 1174 | 229 | 61.06 | 510.06 | 58.10 |
| 1997 | 1279 | 273 | 49.16 | 623.00 | 54.27 |
| 1998 | 1368 | 229 | 43.75 | 597.00 | 61.78 |
| 1999 | 1512 | 291 | 42.40 | 655.47 | 64.32 |
| 2000 | 1305 | 238 | 37.64 | 626.01 | 71.00 |
| 2001 | 1300 | 168 | 87.85 | 881.64 | 65.30 |
| 2002 | 1348 | 160 | 68.78 | 960.95 | 68.20 |
| 2003 | 1336 | 142 | 73.54 | 967.98 | 68.43 |
| 2004 | 1489 | 118 | 62.09 | 1093.35 | 70.93 |
| 2005 | 1777 | 184 | 122.41 | 1329.39 | 72.07 |
| 2006 | 1815 | 133 | 123.99 | 1367.71 | 73.70 |
| 2007 | 2087 | 138 | 162.73 | 1623.36 | 76.71 |
| 2008 | 2311 | 149 | 73.24 | 1850.57 | 79.07 |
| 2009 | 2552 | 150 | 126.68 | 2076.74 | 79.80 |
| 2010 | 2869 | 134 | 155.20 | 2348.27 | 80.40 |
| 2011 | 3346 | 24 | 561.89 | 2590.56 | 76.86 |
| 2012 | 3164 | 5 | 487.18 | 2606.19 | 81.56 |
| 2013 | 3208 | 11 | 428.35 | 2728.19 | 84.01 |
| 2014 | 3105 | 7 | 422.44 | 2670.15 | 84.19 |
| 2015 | 2828 | 7 | 382.71 | 2423.85 | 84.45 |
| 2016 | 2579 | 1 | | 2257.57 | 85.59 |
| 2017 | 2564 | 1 | | 2322.87 | 90.25 |
| 2018 | 2731 | 1 | | 2319.73 | 82.72 |
| 2019 | 2802 | | | 2509.21 | 86.10 |
| 2020 | 2356 | | | 2456.90 | 93.95 |
| 2021 | 2364 | | | 2253.33 | 93.54 |
| 2022 | 2564 | | | 2438.22 | 94.19 |

注：因统计口径变化，调整了 2016 年以来的数据。
Note: Due to statistical standard changes, the data since 2016 has been adjusted.

# 表 9.7 重点调查工业废气排放及处理情况（2022 年）
## WASTE GAS DISCHARGE AND TREATMENT BY THE INDUSTRIAL ENTERPRISES UNDER MAJOR SURVEY (2022)

| 行 业 | Sector | 汇总工业企业数（个）Number of Industrial Enterprises (unit) | 废气治理设施数（套）Number of Facilities for Waste Gas Treatment (set) |
|---|---|---|---|
| **总 计** | **Total** | **2708** | **5222** |
| **农、林、牧、渔专业及辅助性活动** | **Services of Farming, Forestry, Animal Husbandry and Fishery** | | |
| 农、林、牧、渔专业及辅助性活动 | Services of Farming, Forestry, Animal Husbandry and Fishery | 1 | |
| **采矿业** | **Mining and Quarrying** | | |
| 煤炭开采和洗选业 | Mining and Washing of Coal | 2 | 1 |
| 石油和天然气开采业 | Extraction of Petroleum and Natural Gas | 14 | 4 |
| 黑色金属矿采选业 | Mining and Processing of Ferrous Metal Ores | | |
| 非金属矿采选业 | Mining and Processing of Nonmetal Ores | 32 | 107 |
| **制造业** | **Manufacturing** | | |
| 农副食品加工业 | Processing of Food from Agricultural Products | 275 | 118 |
| 食品制造业 | Manufacture of Foods | 68 | 38 |
| 酒、饮料和精制茶制造业 | Liquor, Beverage and Refined Tea | 101 | 43 |
| 烟草制品业 | Manufacture of Tobacco | 4 | 2 |
| 纺织业 | Manufacture of Textile | 18 | 9 |
| 纺织服装、服饰业 | Textile and Garments | 2 | |
| 皮革、毛皮、羽毛及其制品和制鞋业 | Manufacture of Leather, Fur, Feather and Related Products and Footwear | 15 | 20 |
| 木材加工和木、竹、藤、棕、草制品业 | Processing of Timber, Manufacture of Wood, Bamboo,Rattan, Palm and Straw Products | 27 | 85 |
| 家具制造业 | Manufacture of Furniture | 32 | 65 |
| 造纸及纸制品业 | Manufacture of Paper and Paper Products | 37 | 51 |
| 印刷和记录媒介复制业 | Printing, Reproduction of Recording Media | 48 | 54 |
| 文教、工美、体育和娱乐用品制造业 | Manufacture of Culture, Education, Handicraft, Fine Arts, Sports and Entertainment Articles | 1 | 2 |
| 石油、煤炭及其他燃料加工业 | Processing of Petroleum, Coal and other Fuels | 5 | 15 |
| 化学原料及化学制品制造业 | Manufacture of Raw Chemical Materials and Chemical Products | 174 | 435 |
| 医药制造业 | Manufacture of Medicines | 86 | 188 |
| 化学纤维制造业 | Manufacture of Chemical Fibers | 4 | 10 |
| 橡胶和塑料制品业 | Manufacture of Rubber and Plastics | 87 | 182 |
| 非金属矿物制品业 | Manufacture of Non-metallic Mineral Products | 614 | 1321 |
| 黑色金属冶炼及压延加工业 | Smelting and Pressing of Ferrous Metals | 26 | 75 |
| 有色金属冶炼及压延加工业 | Smelting and Pressing of Nonferrous Metals | 67 | 125 |
| 金属制品业 | Manufacture of Metal Products | 259 | 390 |
| 通用设备制造业 | Manufacture of General Purpose Machinery | 101 | 211 |
| 专用设备制造业 | Manufacture of Special Purpose Machinery | 21 | 27 |
| 汽车制造业 | Manufacture of Motor Vehicles | 238 | 647 |
| 铁路、船舶、航空航天和其他运输设备制造业 | Manufacture of Railway, Ship, Aviation and Other Transporting Equipment | 84 | 232 |
| 电气机械和器材制造业 | Manufacture of Electrical Machinery and Equipment | 40 | 192 |
| 计算机、通信和其他电子设备制造业 | Manufacture of Communication Equipment, Computers and Other Electronic Equipment | 89 | 339 |
| 仪器仪表制造业 | Manufacture of Measuring Instruments and Machinery | 7 | 21 |
| 其他制造业 | Other Manufacture | 9 | 40 |
| 废弃资源综合利用业 | Comprehensive Utilization of Waste Resources | 45 | 38 |
| 金属制品、机械和设备修理业 | Repair of Metal Products, Machinery and Equipment | 3 | 11 |
| **电力、热力、燃气及水生产和供应业** | **Production and Supply of Electric Power,Gas and Water** | | |
| 电力、热力的生产和供应业 | Production and Supply of Electric Power and Heat Power | 39 | 119 |
| 燃气生产和供应业 | Production and Supply of Gas | 3 | 4 |
| 水的生产和供应业 | Production and Supply of Water | 30 | 1 |

| 工业废气排放总量（亿标立方米）Total Volume of Industrial Waste Gas Discharged (100 million cu.m) | 工业二氧化硫产生量（吨）Volume of Sulfur Dioxide Produced (ton) | 工业二氧化硫排放量（吨）Volume of Sulphur Dioxide Discharged (ton) | 工业烟（粉）尘产生量（吨）Volume of Fume and Dust Produced (ton) | 工业烟（粉）尘排放量（吨）Volume of Fume and Dust Discharged ( ton) |
|---|---|---|---|---|
| **13500.93** | **968079.74** | **36858.54** | **15129954.59** | **37565.25** |
| 0.02 | | | | |
| | | | 361.80 | 72.36 |
| 25.01 | 1126.22 | 333.95 | 2.47 | 2.47 |
| 49.55 | 0.08 | 0.04 | 17169.25 | 361.87 |
| 30.83 | 86.32 | 50.27 | 176.22 | 59.43 |
| 84.26 | 7228.42 | 592.93 | 122570.31 | 69.97 |
| 16.45 | 29.60 | 24.77 | 53.45 | 22.34 |
| 1.09 | 0.50 | 0.49 | 555.07 | 555.05 |
| 12.41 | 2.28 | 2.28 | 3.57 | 3.57 |
| 0.03 | 0.01 | 0.01 | | |
| 3.11 | 0.42 | 0.42 | 101.17 | 15.43 |
| 44.51 | 41.63 | 41.63 | 642.96 | 87.47 |
| 42.80 | | | 112.38 | 34.58 |
| 180.28 | 22251.67 | 850.90 | 202091.29 | 170.33 |
| 62.93 | 0.23 | 0.23 | 3.97 | 0.77 |
| 4.80 | | | | |
| 4.18 | 1.21 | 1.21 | 5.98 | 0.60 |
| 1056.90 | 59130.55 | 3335.29 | 853610.77 | 2633.77 |
| 691.14 | 12.77 | 7.14 | 74.96 | 7.96 |
| 11.34 | 442.13 | 82.71 | 902.98 | 3.85 |
| 154.31 | 1082.31 | 98.03 | 14864.84 | 72.25 |
| 2634.42 | 47239.92 | 11881.28 | 7421770.84 | 23610.24 |
| 2415.61 | 185047.00 | 5297.09 | 449220.47 | 3982.45 |
| 1032.69 | 86344.49 | 5437.54 | 609578.62 | 796.66 |
| 255.41 | 40.56 | 8.98 | 1552.59 | 168.97 |
| 76.97 | 1.15 | 0.98 | 920.57 | 128.35 |
| 19.69 | 0.49 | 0.49 | 112.74 | 23.44 |
| 951.78 | 75.55 | 29.16 | 2342.39 | 287.72 |
| 145.87 | 3.30 | 2.14 | 899.14 | 274.48 |
| 86.74 | 3.15 | 2.28 | 113.16 | 22.80 |
| 588.66 | 6.55 | 6.51 | 418.97 | 55.74 |
| 5.41 | 0.07 | 0.07 | 0.56 | 0.27 |
| 13.67 | 0.20 | 0.20 | 154.18 | 4.96 |
| 14.10 | 49.71 | 21.11 | 3107.25 | 64.32 |
| 0.09 | 0.37 | 0.11 | 0.12 | 0.01 |
| 2783.71 | 557830.06 | 8747.55 | 5426459.51 | 3970.74 |
| 0.05 | 0.76 | 0.76 | 0.03 | 0.03 |
| 0.09 | 0.07 | 0.01 | | |

# 表 9.8 重点调查工业固体废物产生及处理利用情况（2022 年）
## GENERATION, TREATMENT AND UTILIZATION OF SOLID WASTES OF THE INDUSTRIAL ENTERPRISES UNDER MAJOR SURVEY (2022)

| 行 业 | Sector | 企业数（个）Number of Enterprises (unit) |
|---|---|---|
| **总 计** | **Total** | **2708** |
| **农、林、牧、渔专业及辅助性活动** | **Services of Farming, Forestry, Animal Husbandry and Fishery** | |
| 农、林、牧、渔专业及辅助性活动 | Services of Farming, Forestry, Animal Husbandry and Fishery | 1 |
| **采矿业** | **Mining and Quarrying** | |
| 煤炭开采和洗选业 | Mining and Washing of Coal | 2 |
| 石油和天然气开采业 | Extraction of Petroleum and Natural Gas | 14 |
| 黑色金属矿采选业 | Mining and Processing of Ferrous Metal Ores | |
| 非金属矿采选业 | Mining and Processing of Nonmetal Ores | 32 |
| **制造业** | **Manufacturing** | |
| 农副食品加工业 | Processing of Food from Agricultural Products | 275 |
| 食品制造业 | Manufacture of Foods | 68 |
| 酒、饮料和精制茶制造业 | Liquor, Beverage and Refined Tea | 101 |
| 烟草制品业 | Manufacture of Tobacco | 4 |
| 纺织业 | Manufacture of Textile | 18 |
| 纺织服装、服饰业 | Textile and Garments | 2 |
| 皮革、毛皮、羽毛及其制品和制鞋业 | Manufacture of Leather, Fur, Feather and Related Products and Footwear | 15 |
| 木材加工和木、竹、藤、棕、草制品业 | Processing of Timber, Manufacture of Wood, Bamboo, Rattan, Palm and Straw Products | 27 |
| 家具制造业 | Manufacture of Furniture | 32 |
| 造纸及纸制品业 | Manufacture of Paper and Paper Products | 37 |
| 印刷和记录媒介复制业 | Printing, Reproduction of Recording Media | 48 |
| 文教、工美、体育和娱乐用品制造业 | Manufacture of Culture, Education, Handicraft, Fine Arts, Sports and Entertainment Articles | 1 |
| 石油、煤炭及其他燃料加工业 | Processing of Petroleum, Coal and other Fuels | 5 |
| 化学原料及化学制品制造业 | Manufacture of Raw Chemical Materials and Chemical Products | 174 |
| 医药制造业 | Manufacture of Medicines | 86 |
| 化学纤维制造业 | Manufacture of Chemical Fibers | 4 |
| 橡胶和塑料制品业 | Manufacture of Rubber and Plastics | 87 |
| 非金属矿物制品业 | Manufacture of Non-metallic Mineral Products | 614 |
| 黑色金属冶炼及压延加工业 | Smelting and Pressing of Ferrous Metals | 26 |
| 有色金属冶炼及压延加工业 | Smelting and Pressing of Nonferrous Metals | 67 |
| 金属制品业 | Manufacture of Metal Products | 259 |
| 通用设备制造业 | Manufacture of General Purpose Machinery | 101 |
| 专用设备制造业 | Manufacture of Special Purpose Machinery | 21 |
| 汽车制造业 | Manufacture of Motor Vehicles | 238 |
| 铁路、船舶、航空航天和其他运输设备制造业 | Manufacture of Railway, Ship, Aviation and Other Transporting Equipment | 84 |
| 电气机械和器材制造业 | Manufacture of Electrical Machinery and Equipment | 40 |
| 计算机、通信和其他电子设备制造业 | Manufacture of Communication Equipment, Computers and Other Electronic Equipment | 89 |
| 仪器仪表制造业 | Manufacture of Measuring Instruments and Machinery | 7 |
| 其他制造业 | Other Manufacture | 9 |
| 废弃资源综合利用业 | Comprehensive Utilization of Waste Resources | 45 |
| 金属制品、机械和设备修理业 | Repair of Metal Products, Machinery and Equipment | 3 |
| **电力、热力、燃气及水生产和供应业** | **Production and Supply of Electric Power and Heat Power** | |
| 电力、热力的生产和供应业 | Production and Supply of Electric Power and Heat Power | 39 |
| 燃气生产和供应业 | Production and Supply of Gas | 3 |
| 水的生产和供应业 | Production and Supply of Water | 30 |

| 工业固体废物产生量（万吨） Volume of Industrial Solid Waste Produced (10 000 tons) | #危险废物产生量 Volume of Hazardous Wastes Produced | 工业固体废物综合利用处置量（万吨） Volume of Industrial Solid Wastes Comprehensively Utilized (10 000 tons) | 工业固体废物贮存量（万吨） Volume of Industrial Solid Wastes in Stock (10 000 tons) | 工业固体废物倾倒丢弃量（万吨） Volume of Industrial Solid Waste Dumped (10 000 tons) |
|---|---|---|---|---|
| **2563.30** | **100.80** | **2437.70** | **152.95** | **0.007** |
| | | | | |
| 18.81 | | 18.81 | | |
| 23.35 | 8.58 | 23.35 | 0.64 | |
| | | | | |
| 6.16 | | 6.16 | | |
| | | | | |
| 9.79 | 0.01 | 9.79 | | |
| 15.22 | 0.01 | 15.22 | | |
| 11.63 | 0.01 | 11.78 | | |
| 0.70 | | 0.70 | | |
| 0.42 | | 0.43 | | |
| | | | | |
| 0.04 | | 0.04 | | |
| 0.17 | 0.01 | 0.18 | | |
| | | | | |
| 1.47 | 0.04 | 1.42 | 0.05 | |
| 87.31 | 0.26 | 86.93 | 0.62 | |
| 0.95 | 0.08 | 0.95 | 0.01 | |
| 0.01 | 0.01 | 0.01 | | |
| | | | | |
| 0.08 | 0.04 | 0.08 | | |
| 269.17 | 31.65 | 272.39 | 9.65 | |
| 9.17 | 2.11 | 9.20 | 0.09 | |
| 1.82 | 0.55 | 1.84 | 0.03 | |
| 3.32 | 0.24 | 3.32 | 0.04 | |
| 44.46 | 0.17 | 44.71 | 0.18 | |
| 584.47 | 15.50 | 578.62 | 14.23 | |
| 440.39 | 7.78 | 360.92 | 81.26 | |
| 9.99 | 3.28 | 10.09 | 0.13 | |
| 5.17 | 0.72 | 5.18 | 0.02 | 0.007 |
| 0.68 | 0.02 | 0.67 | 0.02 | |
| 44.41 | 6.10 | 44.38 | 0.24 | |
| 3.64 | 0.48 | 3.66 | 0.03 | |
| | | | | |
| 6.40 | 0.59 | 6.34 | 0.13 | |
| 28.81 | 8.73 | 28.84 | 0.20 | |
| | | | | |
| 0.29 | 0.02 | 0.29 | | |
| 0.45 | 0.10 | 0.45 | | |
| 10.75 | 1.42 | 9.96 | 1.34 | |
| 0.09 | 0.04 | 0.09 | | |
| | | | | |
| 922.38 | 12.25 | 879.61 | 44.05 | |
| | | | | |
| 0.64 | | 0.64 | | |
| 0.67 | | 0.67 | | |

# 表 9.9 重点调查工业废水排放及处理情况（2022 年）
## WASTE WATER DISCHARGE AND TREATMENT BY THE INDUSTRIAL ENTERPRISES UNDER MAJOR SURVEY (2022)

| 行业 | Sector | 企业数（个） Number of Enterprises (unit) | 工业废水排放总量（万吨） Total Volume of Waste Water Discharged (10 000 tons) | 废水治理设施数（套） Number of Facilities for Waste Water Control (set) |
|---|---|---|---|---|
| **总计** | **Total** | **2708** | **15686.81** | **1438** |
| **农、林、牧、渔专业及辅助性活动** | **Services of Farming, Forestry, Animal Husbandry and Fishery** | | | |
| 农、林、牧、渔专业及辅助性活动 | Services of Farming, Forestry, Animal Husbandry and Fishery | 1 | 0.40 | |
| **采矿业** | **Mining and Quarrying** | | | |
| 煤炭开采和洗选业 | Mining and Washing of Coal | 2 | | 2 |
| 石油和天然气开采业 | Extraction of Petroleum and Natural Gas | 14 | 35.18 | 7 |
| 黑色金属矿采选业 | Mining and Processing of Ferrous Metal Ores | | | |
| 非金属矿采选业 | Mining and Processing of Nonmetal Ores | 32 | 0.75 | 19 |
| **制造业** | **Manufacturing** | | | |
| 农副食品加工业 | Processing of Food from Agricultural Products | 275 | 802.38 | 200 |
| 食品制造业 | Manufacture of Foods | 68 | 487.45 | 51 |
| 酒、饮料和精制茶制造业 | Liquor, Beverage and Refined Tea | 101 | 208.01 | 60 |
| 烟草制品业 | Manufacture of Tobacco | 4 | 8.82 | 2 |
| 纺织业 | Manufacture of Textile | 18 | 102.24 | 12 |
| 纺织服装、服饰业 | Textile and Garments | 2 | 1.98 | 1 |
| 皮革、毛皮、羽毛及其制品和制鞋业 | Manufacture of Leather, Fur, Feather and Related Products and Footwear | 15 | 1.64 | 2 |
| 木材加工和木、竹、藤、棕、草制品业 | Processing of Timber, Manufacture of Wood, Bamboo, Rattan, Palm and Straw Products | 27 | 6.16 | 9 |
| 家具制造业 | Manufacture of Furniture | 32 | 8.46 | 10 |
| 造纸及纸制品业 | Manufacture of Paper and Paper Products | 37 | 3561.02 | 26 |
| 印刷和记录媒介复制业 | Printing, Reproduction of Recording Media | 48 | 8.52 | 12 |
| 文教、工美、体育和娱乐用品制造业 | Manufacture of Culture, Education, Handicraft, Fine Arts, Sports and Entertainment Articles | 1 | | |
| 石油、煤炭及其他燃料加工业 | Processing of Petroleum, Coal and other Fuels | 5 | 3.90 | 3 |
| 化学原料及化学制品制造业 | Manufacture of Raw Chemical Materials and Chemical Products | 174 | 2700.68 | 108 |
| 医药制造业 | Manufacture of Medicines | 86 | 544.57 | 77 |
| 化学纤维制造业 | Manufacture of Chemical Fibers | 4 | 26.60 | 2 |
| 橡胶和塑料制品业 | Manufacture of Rubber and Plastics | 87 | 73.34 | 26 |
| 非金属矿物制品业 | Manufacture of Non-metallic Mineral Products | 614 | 427.17 | 47 |
| 黑色金属冶炼及压延加工业 | Smelting and Pressing of Ferrous Metals | 26 | 822.80 | 13 |
| 有色金属冶炼及压延加工业 | Smelting and Pressing of Nonferrous Metals | 67 | 58.55 | 33 |
| 金属制品业 | Manufacture of Metal Products | 259 | 371.83 | 156 |
| 通用设备制造业 | Manufacture of General Purpose Machinery | 101 | 164.49 | 84 |
| 专用设备制造业 | Manufacture of Special Purpose Machinery | 21 | 28.38 | 12 |
| 汽车制造业 | Manufacture of Motor Vehicles | 238 | 756.74 | 183 |
| 铁路、船舶、航空航天和其他运输设备制造业 | Manufacture of Railway, Ship, Aviation and Other Transporting Equipment | 84 | 208.36 | 83 |
| 电气机械和器材制造业 | Manufacture of Electrical Machinery and Equipment | 40 | 80.68 | 38 |
| 计算机、通信和其他电子设备制造业 | Manufacture of Communication Equipment, Computers and Other Electronic Equipment | 89 | 2369.89 | 82 |
| 仪器仪表制造业 | Manufacture of Measuring Instruments and Machinery | 7 | 16.93 | 7 |
| 其他制造业 | Other Manufacture | 9 | 22.89 | 6 |
| 废弃资源综合利用业 | Comprehensive Utilization of Waste Resources | 45 | 12.67 | 20 |
| 金属制品、机械和设备修理业 | Repair of Metal Products, Machinery and Equipment | 3 | 7.45 | 2 |
| **电力、热力、燃气及水生产和供应业** | **Production and Supply of Electric Power and Heat Power** | | | |
| 电力、热力的生产和供应业 | Production and Supply of Electric Power and Heat Power | 39 | 250.90 | 29 |
| 燃气生产和供应业 | Production and Supply of Gas | 3 | 3.79 | 2 |
| 水的生产和供应业 | Production and Supply of Water | 30 | 1501.18 | 12 |

## 表 9.10 工业污染治理项目及投资情况（2021－2022 年）
INDUSTRIAL POLLUTION TREATMENT PROJECTS AND INVESTMENT (2021-2022)

| 项　目 | Item | 2021 | 2022 |
|---|---|---|---|
| **企业数（个）** | **Number of Enterprises (unit)** | **52** | **33** |
| **施工项目数（个）** | **Number of Projects under Construction (unit)** | **54** | **26** |
| 治理废水 | Treatment of Waste Water | 7 | 4 |
| 治理废气 | Treatment of Waste Gas | 34 | 19 |
| 治理固体废物 | Treatment of Solid Wastes | 2 | 1 |
| 治理噪声 | Treatment of Noise Pollution | | |
| 治理其他 | Treatment of Other Pollution | 11 | 2 |
| **资金来源合计（万元）** | **Total Funds (10 000 yuan)** | **20656.88** | **55782.15** |
| 排污费补助 | Pollution Discharge Fees Subsidy | | |
| 政府其他补助 | Other Government Subsidy | 940.29 | 412.26 |
| 企业自筹 | Self-raised Fund | 19716.59 | 55369.90 |
| **资金使用合计（万元）** | **Total Expenditures (10 000 yuan)** | **20656.88** | **55782.15** |
| 治理废水 | Treatment of Waste Water | 2545.94 | 412.80 |
| 治理废气 | Treatment of Waste Gas | 16735.22 | 55314.35 |
| 治理固体废物 | Treatment of Solid Wastes | 115.67 | 30.00 |
| 治理噪声 | Treatment of Noise Pollution | | |
| 治理其他 | Treatment of Other Pollution | 1260.05 | 25.00 |
| **本年竣工项目数（个）** | **Number of Projects Completed in Current Year (unit)** | **24** | **23** |
| **当年竣工项目新增设计处理利用“三废”能力** | **Newly Added Designed Capacity of the Projects Completed in Current Year for the Treatment and Utilization of "Three Wastes"** | | |
| 废　水（吨 / 日） | Waste Water (ton/day) | 6589 | 62346 |
| 废　气（万标立方米 / 时） | Waste Gas (10 000 cu.m/hour) | 304.71 | 355.69 |
| 固体废物（吨 / 日） | Solid Wastes (ton/day) | | |

## 表 9.11 生活污染物排放情况（2021－2022 年）
DISCHARGE OF DOMESTIC POLLUTANTS (2021-2022)

| 项　目 | Item | 2021 | 2022 |
|---|---|---|---|
| 生活污水排放量（万吨） | Volume of Domestic Waste Water Discharged (10 000 tons) | 120741 | 121165 |
| 生活污水中化学需氧量排放量（吨） | Volume of COD Emission in Domestic Waste Water (ton) | 33846 | 37016 |
| 生活二氧化硫排放量（吨） | Volume of Sulphur Dioxide Emission from Daily Life (ton) | 8856 | 9077 |
| 生活烟尘排放量（吨） | Volume of Soot Emission from Daily Life (ton) | 10909 | 11231 |

重/庆/统/计/年/鉴

# 主要统计指标解释

## 自然资源

指人类可以直接从自然界获得，并用于生产和生活的物质资源。自然资源一般可以分成可再生资源和非再生资源两大类。可再生资源指在较短时间内可以再生、可以循环利用的资源，包括土地资源、水资源、气候资源、生物资源和海洋资源等。非再生资源指在使用后不能再生的资源，包括矿产资源和地热能源。

## 土地资源

土地指陆地的表层部分，它主要由岩石、岩石的风化物和土壤构成。土地资源按利用类型可以分为农用地、建筑用地和未利用地。农用地包括耕地、园地、林地、牧草地和水面。建筑用地包括居民点及工矿用地、交通用地和水利设施用地。未利用地指农用地和建筑用地以外的土地，包括滩涂、荒漠、戈壁、冰川和石山等。

## 耕地

指种植农作物的土地，包括熟地，新开发、复垦、整理地，休闲地（含轮歇地、轮作地）；以种植农作物（含蔬菜）为主，间有零星果树、桑树或其他树木的土地；平均每年能保证收获一季的已垦滩地和海涂。耕地中包括南方宽度＜1.0米，北方宽度＜2.0米固定的沟、渠、路和地坎（埂）；临时种植药材、草皮、花卉、苗木等的耕地，以及其他临时改变用途的耕地。

## 林地

指生长乔木、竹类、灌木的土地，及沿海生长红树林的土地。包括迹地，不包括居民点内部的绿化林木用地，铁路、公路征地范围内的林木，以及河流、沟渠的护堤林。

## 牧草地

指生长草本植物为主的土地。

## 森林资源

指森林、林木、林地以及依托森林、林木、林地生存的野生动物、植物和微生物。林木指树木和竹子。森林指以乔木为主体的植物群落，是集生的乔木及与共同作用的植物、动物、微生物和土壤、气候等的总体。

## 活立木总蓄积量

指一定范围内土地上全部树木蓄积的总量，包括森林蓄积、疏林蓄积、散生木蓄积和四旁（村旁、路旁、水旁、宅旁）树蓄积。

## 森林面积

指由乔木树种构成，郁闭度0.2以上（含0.2）的林地或冠幅宽度10米以上的林带的面积，即有林地面积。森林面积包括天然起源和人工起源的针叶林面积、阔叶林面积、针阔混交林面积和竹林面积，不包括灌木林地面积和疏林地面积。

## 森林蓄积量

指一定森林面积上存在着的林木树干部分的总材积。它是反映一个国家或地区森林资源总规模和水平的基本指标之一，也是反映森林资源的丰富程度、衡量森林生态环境优劣的重要依据。

## 森林覆盖率

以行政区域为单位的森林面积占区域土地总面积的百分比。计算公式为：

$$森林覆盖率=\frac{森林面积}{土地总面积}\times 100\%$$

## 水资源总量

指当地降水形成的地表和地下产水总量，即地表径流量与降水入渗补给量之和。

## 地表水资源量

指河流、湖泊以及冰川等地表水体中可以逐年更新的动态水量，即天然河川径流量。

## 地下水资源量

指地下饱和含水层逐年更新的动态水量，即降水

## 主要统计指标解释

和地表水入渗对地下水的补给量。

### 地表水与地下水重复计算量

指地表水和地下水相互转化的部分，即天然河川径流量中的地下水排泄量和地下水补给量中来源于地表水的入渗补给量。

### 供水总量

指各种水源为用水户提供的包括输水损失在内的毛水量。

### 地表水源供水量

指地表水体工程的取水量，按蓄、引、提、调四种形式统计。从水库、塘坝中引水或提水，均属蓄水工程供水量；从河道或湖泊中自流引水的，无论有闸或无闸，均属引水工程供水量；利用扬水站从河道或湖泊中直接取水的，属提水工程供水量；跨流域调水指水资源一级区或独立流域之间的跨流域调配水量，不包括在蓄、引、提水量中。

### 地下水源供水量

指水井工程的开采量，按浅层淡水、深层承压水和微咸水分别统计。城市地下水源供水量包括自来水厂的开采量和工矿企业自备井的开采量。

### 径流

指大气降水扣除损耗外，从地表和地下向流域出口断面汇集的水流。径流可分为地表径流、地下径流和壤中流。地表径流指沿地表向河流、湖泊、沼泽、海洋等汇集的水流；地下径流指沿潜水层或隔水层间的含水层，向河流、湖泊、沼泽、海洋等汇集的地下水水流。

### 径流量

指在一定时段内通过河流某一过水断面的水量，用以反映一个国家或地区水资源的丰歉程度。计算公式为：

径流量 = 降水量 – 蒸发量

### 矿产资源

矿产指由地质作用形成，具有利用价值的，呈固态、液态、气态的自然资源，是社会生产发展的重要物质基础。目前我国已发现矿种有 170 多种，按其特点和用途，可分为能源矿产（如煤炭、石油、天然气、地热）、金属矿产（如铁矿、锰矿、铜矿、铅矿、铝土矿）、非金属矿产（如金刚石、石灰石、黏土）和水气矿产（如地下水、矿泉水、二氧化碳气）四大类。其中：金属矿产按其物质成分和性质又可分为：黑色金属矿产、有色金属矿产、贵金属矿产、稀有金属矿产、稀土金属矿产、分散元素金属矿产六类。

### 矿产基础储量

基础储量是查明矿产资源的一部分。它能满足现行采矿和生产所需的指标要求，是控制的、探明的并通过可行性或预可行性研究认为属于经济的、边界经济的部分，用未扣除设计、采矿损失的数量表示。

### 气候

指地球与大气之间长期能量交换与质量交换所形成的一种自然环境状态，它是多种因素综合作用的结果。气候既是人类生活和生产的环境要素之一，又是供给人类生活和生产的重要资源。气温、降水、湿度等气象要素的多年平均值是用来描述一个地区气候状况的主要参数，而各种气象要素某年、某月的平均值（或总量）则可以反映出该时期天气气候状况的重要特征。

### 平均气温

气温指空气的温度，我国一般以摄氏度为单位表示。气象观测的温度表是放在离地面约 1.5 米处通风良好的百叶箱里测量的，因此，通常说的气温指的是离地面 1.5 米处百叶箱中的温度。计算方法：月平均气温是将全月各日的平均气温相加，除以该月的天数而得。年平均气温是将 12 个月的月平均气温累加后除以 12 而得。

### 年平均相对湿度

指空气中实际水气压与当时气温下的饱和水气压之比。其统计方法与气温相同。

### 降水量

指从天空降落到地面的液态或固态（经融化后）水，未经蒸发、渗透、流失而在地面上积聚的深度。其统计计算方法为：

月降水量是将全月各日的降水量累加而得。

年降水量是将 12 个月的月降水量累加而得。

# 主要统计指标解释

## 全年日照时数

指太阳实际照射地面的时数，通常以小时为单位表示。其统计方法与降水量相同。

## 化学需氧量 (COD) 排放量

为工业废水中 COD 排放量与生活污水中 COD 排放量之和。化学需氧量指用化学氧化剂氧化水中有机污染物时所需的氧量。一般利用化学氧化剂将废水中可氧化的物质（有机物、亚硝酸盐、亚铁盐、硫化物等）氧化分解，然后根据残留的氧化剂的量计算出氧的消耗量，来表示废水中有机物的含量，反映水体有机物污染程度。COD 值越高，表示水中有机污染物污染越重。

## 二氧化硫排放量

指报告期内工业 $SO_2$ 排放量与生活 $SO_2$ 排放量之和。

## 工业废水排放量

指经过企业厂区所有排放口排到企业外部的工业废水量。包括生产废水、外排的直接冷却水、超标排放的矿井地下水和与工业废水混排的厂区生活污水，不包括外排的间接冷却水（清污不分流的间接冷却水应计算在内）。

## 工业废水排放达标量

指报告期内废水中各项污染物指标都达到国家或地方排放标准的外排工业废水量，包括未经处理外排达标的，经废水处理设施处理后达标排放的，以及经污水处理厂处理后达标排放的。

## 工业废气排放量

指报告期内企业厂区内燃料燃烧和生产工艺过程中产生的各种排入空气的含有污染物的气体的总量，以标准状态（273K，101325Pa）计算。测算公式为：

工业废气排放量 = 燃料燃烧过程中废气排放量 + 生产工艺过程中废气排放量

## 工业二氧化硫排放量

指报告期内企业在燃料燃烧和生产工艺过程中排入大气的 $SO_2$ 总量，计算公式为：

工业 $SO_2$ 排放量 = 燃料燃烧过程中 $SO_2$ 排放量 + 生产工艺过程中 $SO_2$ 排放量

## 工业烟尘排放量

指企业厂区内的燃料燃烧过程中产生的烟气中夹带的颗粒物排放量。

## 工业粉尘排放量

指企业在生产工艺过程中排放的能在空气中悬浮一定时间的固体颗粒物排放量。如钢铁企业的耐火材料粉尘、焦化企业的筛焦系统粉尘、烧结机的粉尘、石灰窑的粉尘、建材企业的水泥粉尘等。不包括电厂排入大气的烟尘。

## 一般工业固体废物产生量

指未被列入《国家危险废物名录》或者根据国家规定的危险废物鉴别标准（GB5085）、固体废物浸出毒性浸出方法（GB5086）及固体废物浸出毒性测定方法（GB / T 15555）鉴别方法判定不具有危险特性的工业固体废物。计算公式是：

一般工业固体废物产生量 =（一般工业固体废物综合利用量 – 其中：综合利用往年贮存量）+ 一般工业固体废物贮存量 +（一般工业固体废物处置量 – 其中：处置往年贮存量）+ 一般工业固体废物倾倒丢弃量

## 一般工业固体废物综合利用量

指报告期内企业通过回收、加工、循环、交换等方式，从固体废物中提取或者使其转化为可以利用的资源、能源和其他原材料的固体废物量（包括当年利用的往年工业固体废物累计贮存量）。如用作农业肥料、生产建筑材料、筑路等。综合利用量由原产生固体废物的单位统计。

## 一般工业固体废物处置量

指报告期内企业将工业固体废物焚烧和用其他改变工业固体废物的物理、化学、生物特性的方法，达到减少或者消除其危险成分的活动，或者将工业固体废物最终置于符合环境保护规定要求的填埋场的活动中，所消纳固体废物的量。

## 主要统计指标解释

### ■ 一般工业固体废物贮存量

指报告期内企业以综合利用或处置为目的，将固体废物暂时贮存或堆存在专设的贮存设施或专设的集中堆存场所内的量。专设的固体废物贮存场所或贮存设施必须有防扩散、防流失、防渗漏、防止污染大气、水体的措施。

### ■ 一般工业固体废物倾倒丢弃量

指报告期内企业将所产生的固体废物倾倒或者丢弃到固体废物污染防治设施、场所以外的量。

### ■ “三废”综合利用产品产值

指报告期内利用“三废”（废液、废气、废渣）作为主要原料生产的产品产值（现行价），已经销售或准备销售的应计算产品产值，留作生产上自用的不应计算产品产值。

### ■ 城镇生活污水排放量

指城镇居民每年排放的生活污水。用人均系数法测算。测算公式为：

城镇生活污水排放量 = 城镇生活污水排放系数 × 市镇非农业人口 ×365

### ■ 生活及其他烟尘排放量

指除工业生产活动以外的所有社会、经济活动及公共设施的经营活动中燃烧所排放的烟尘纯重量。以生活及其他煤炭消费量为基础进行测算。

### ■ 人工林面积

指由人工播种、植苗或扦插造林形成的生长稳定，(一般造林 3-5 年后或飞机播种 5-7 年后) 每公顷保存株数大于或等于造林设计植树株数 80% 或郁闭度 0.20 以上 (含 0.20) 的林分面积。

# Explanatory Notes on Main Statistical Indicators

## Natural Resources

Refer to material resources that could be obtained from the nature by human being and used for production and living. Natural resources in general can be classified as renewable resources and non-renewable resources. Renewable resources refer to resources that could be renewed and recycled during a relatively short period of time, including land resource, water resource, climate resource, biology resource and marine resource. Non-renewable resources include resources that could not be renewed, such as minerals and geothermal resource.

## Land Resource

Refers to the surface of the earth, consisting of mainly rocks and its weathering and earth. Land resource can be classified, by its utilization, as land for agriculture, land for construction and unused land. Land for agriculture included cultivated land, plantation land, forestland, grassland and waters. Land for construction includes land for residential purpose, for manufacturing and mining, for transportation and for water-conservancy projects. Unused land refers to land other than land for agriculture and construction, including beaches, deserts, Gobi glaciers and rock mountains.

## Cultivated Land

Refers to land mainly for the regular cultivation of farm crops (including vegetables), with some fruit trees, mulberry trees and others, covers cultivated land, newly-developed land, reclaimed land, consolidated land, fallow, beach land that can guarantee one harvest per year on average. It also covers fixed ditch, canal, road and sill (ridge) with width less than 1 meter in the South and 2 meters in the North, lands planted temporarily with herbs, grass, flowers and nursery stocks, and other cultivated land with temporary change of use.

## Forestland

Refers to land for planting arbor, bamboo, bush shrub and land in coastal zones for planting mangrove. It includes slash, but not the green belts in residential area, forests requested for railway and highway, and the dike protection forest around rivers and ditches.

## Pastureland

Refers to land mainly for the growth of herbs.

## Forest Resource

Refers to forests, trees, forestland and wild animals, plants and microorganism that live on forest and trees. Trees include trees and bamboo. Forest refers to the population of clusters of trees and other plants, animals and microorganism as well as the earth and climate that have interactions with the trees.

## Total Standing Stock Volume

Refers to the total stock volume of trees growing in land, including trees in forest, tress in sparse forest, scattered trees and trees planted by the side of villages, farm houses and along roads and rivers.

## Forest Area

Refers to the area of forest where trees and bamboo grow with canopy density above 0.2, including land of natural woods and planted woods, but excluding bush land and thin forest land. It reflects the total areas of afforestation.

## Stock Volume of Forest

Refers to total stock volume of wood growing in forest area, which shows the total size and level of forest resources of a country or a region. It is also an important indicator illustrating the richness of forest resource and

EXPLANATORY NOTES TO MAJOR STATISTICAL INDICATORS

the status of forest ecological environment.

## Forest Coverage Rate

Taking the administrative jurisdiction as the unit, the percentage of area of afforested land to the area of total land. The formula for calculating forest coverage rate is as follows:

$$\text{Forestry Coverage Rate} = \frac{\text{Area of Afforested Land}}{\text{Area of Total Land}} \times 100\%$$

## Total Water Resources

Refers to total volume of surface water and groundwater and is measured as run-off for surface water and replenishment of groundwater with rainfall in local area.

## Surface Water Resources

Refers to total volume of year by year renewable dynamic resources which exist in rivers, lakes, glaciers and other surface water and are the natural run-off of rivers.

## Groundwater Resources

Refers to total volume of year by year renewable dynamic resources which exist in saturation acquifers of groundwater and are measured as replenishment of groundwater with rainfall and surface water.

## Duplicated Measurement between Surface Water and Groundwater

Refers to mutual exchange between surface water and groundwater, i.e. run-off of rivers includes some depletion into groundwater while groundwater includes some replenishment from surface water.

## Water Supply

Refers to gross water of various sources supplied to consumers, including losses during distribution.

## Surface Water Supply

Refers to withdrawals by surface water supply system, broken down with storage, flow, pumping and transfer. Supply from storage projects includes withdrawals from reservoirs; supply from flow includes withdrawals from rivers and lakes with natural flows no matter if there are locks or not; supply from pumping projects includes withdrawals from rivers or lakes with pumping stations; and supply from transfer refers to water supplies transferred from first-level regions of water resources or independent river drainage areas to others, and should not be covered under supplies of storage, flow and pumping.

## Groundwater Supply

Refers to withdrawals from supplying wells, broken down with shallow layer freshwater, deep layer freshwater and slightly brackish water. Groundwater supply for urban areas includes water mining by both waterworks and own wells of enterprises.

## Runoff

Refers to the water gathered at the way out of the cross section of drainage area either from the surface or underground after deducting the wastage of the precipitation. Runoff can be divided into surface runoff, underground runoff and within soil runoff. Surface runoff refers to water flow to the rivers, lakes, swamps, and seas on the surface of the earth. Underground runoff refers to water flow to rivers, swamps, and seas through the water-bearing stratum of confined layer or unconfined layer.

## Volume of Runoff

Refers to the total volume of water running through a certain cross section of a river during a certain period of time, reflecting the water resource condition in a country or a region. The formula for calculating volume or runoff is as follows: Runoff=Precipitation-Evaporation

EXPLANATORY NOTES TO MAJOR STATISTICAL INDICATORS

## Mineral Resources

Refer to useful minerals, with solid state, liquid state, gaseity, due to the geological process. Minerals are important natural resources, and important material base for social development. At present, there are more than 170 types of minerals discovered in China. They can be categorized into four groups: energy producing minerals (including coal, petroleum, natural gas and terrestrial heat), metallic minerals (including iron, manganese, copper, lead and bauxite), non metallic minerals (including diamond, limestone and clay), and water/gas related minerals (including ground water, mineral water and carbon dioxide). Metallic minerals can be further classified as ferrous, non-ferrous, noble metal, rare metal, rare earth metal and dispersed metals.

## Ensured Mineral Reserves

Refer to the actual mineral reserves, which equal to the proven mineral reserves (including industrial reserves and prospective reserves) minus extracted parts and underground losses.

## Climate

Refers to the natural environmental status formed by the long-time exchange of energy and mass between the earth and the atmosphere, and is the result of interaction of many factors. Climate is both one of the environment factors and also the important resources for the living and production activities of the human being. The average values across several years of meteorological factors such as temperature, rainfall and humidity are used as important parameters to describe the climate of a region, while the average values (or total values) of a given year of month of meteorological factors reflect the key characteristics of climate for that period of time.

## Average Temperature

Refers to the air temperature. China uses centigrade as the unit. The thermometry used for weather observation is put in a breezy shutter, which is 1.5 meters high from the ground. Therefore, the commonly used temperature refers to the temperature in the breezy shutter 1.5 meters away from the ground. The calculation method is as follows:

Monthly average temperature is the summation of average daily temperature of one month divided by the actual days of that particular month.

Annual average temperature is the summation of monthly average of a year divided by 12 months.

## Average Annual Relative Humidity

Refers to the ratio of actual water vapor pressure to the saturation water vapor pressure under the current temperature. The calculation method is the same as that of temperature.

## Volume of Precipitation

Refers to the deepness of liquid state of solid state (thawed) water falling from the sky to the ground that has not been evaporated, infiltrated or run off. The calculation method is as follows:

Monthly precipitation is the summation of daily precipitation of a month.

Annual precipitation is the summation of 12 months' precipitation of a year.

## Annual Sunshine Hours

Refer to the actual hours of sun irradiating the earth, usually expressed in hours. The calculation method is the same as that of the precipitation.

## COD Emission

Refers to the total volume of COD emitted from industrial activities and life activities. COD refers to the amount of oxygen required when chemical oxidants are used to oxidize organic pollutants in water. Chemical oxidants are used to oxidize possible material in water, such as organic material, nitrite, ferrous salt, sulfide and so on. Then according to residual amount of oxidants to calculate consumption of oxygen, it is said that how much organic pollutants are in water. A higher value of COD corresponds to more serious pollution by organic pollutants.

EXPLANATORY NOTES TO MAJOR STATISTICAL INDICATORS

### $SO_2$ Emission

Refer to the total volume of $SO_2$ emitted from industrial activities and life activities within a given period of time.

### Volume of Industrial Waste Water Discharged

Refers to the volume of industrial waste water discharged, through all outlets, to the outside of industrial enterprises, including waste water produced, direct - cooling water, underground water from mines that does not meet the standard of discharge, and the domestic sewage mixed up with industrial waste water when discharged, but excluding discharged indirect - cooling water.

### Volume of Waste Water up to the Standard for Discharge

Refers to the volume of discharged industrial wastewater that, with or without treatment, has come up to the national or local standards for discharge.

### Industrial Waste Air Emission

Refers to discharge into atmosphere of waste air containing pollutants generated from fuel burning and production process in enterprises within a given period of time. It is calculated at standard status (273K, 101325Pa) as:

Industrial waste air emission = emission through fuel burning + emission through production process

### Industrial $SO_2$ Emission

Refers to volume of sulphur dioxide emission from fuel burning and production process in premises of enterprises for a given period of time. Its calculation formula is:

Industrial $SO_2$ Emission = $SO_2$ Emission from fuel burning + $SO_2$ Emission from production process

### Industrial Soot Emission

Refers to volume of soot in smoke emitted in process of fuel burning in premises of enterprises.

### Industrial Dust Emission

Refers to volume of dust emitted by production process of enterprises and suspended in the air for a given period of time, including dust from refractory material of iron and steel works, dust from coke-screening systems and sintering machines of coke plants, dust from lime kilns and dust from cement production in building material enterprises, but excluding soot and dust emitted from power plants.

### Common Industrial Solid Wastes Produced

Refers to the industrial solid wastes that are not listed in the《National Catalogue of Hazardous Wastes》, or not regarded as hazardous according to the national hazardous waste identification standards (GB5085), solid waste-Extraction procedure for leaching toxicity (GB5086) and solid waste-Extraction procedure for leaching toxicity (GB/T 15555). The calculation formula is as followed:

Common Industrial Solid Wastes Produced = (common industrial solid wastes utilized – the proportion of utilized stock of previous years) + common industrial solid waste stock + (common industrial solid wastes disposed – the proportion of disposed stock of previous years) + common industrial solid wastes discharged.

### Common Industrial Solid Wastes Comprehensively Utilized

Refers to volume of solid wastes from which useful materials can be extracted or which can be converted into usable resources, energy or other materials by means of reclamation, processing, recycling and exchange (including utilizing in the year the stocks of industrial solid wastes of the previous year) during the report period, e.g. being used as agricultural fertilizers, building materials or as material for paving road. Examples of such utilizations include fertilizers, building materials and road materials. The information shall be collected by the producing units of the wastes.

## Common Industrial Solid Wastes Disposed

Refers to the quantity of industrial solid wastes which are burnt or specially disposed using other methods to alter the physical, chemical and biological properties and thus to reduce or eliminate the hazard, or placed ultimately in the sites meeting the requirements for environmental protection during the report period.

## Stock of Common Industrial Solid Wastes

Refers to the volume of solid wastes placed in special facilities or special sites by enterprises for purposes of utilization or disposal during the report period. The sites or facilities should take measures against dispersion, loss, seepage, and air and water contamination.

## Common Industrial Solid Wastes Discharged

Refers to the volume of industrial solid wastes dumped or discharged by producing enterprises to disposal facilities or to other sites.

## Output Value of Products Made from Utilization of Waste Gas, Waste Water and Industrial Solid Wastes

Refers to the value of products (calculated at current prices) made by industrial enterprises using recovered waste water, waste gas or solid wastes as main raw materials. Only the value of the products, which have been sold or are ready, to be sold should be included. The value of the products, which will be used in the production of the enterprises, should not be included.

## Urban Consumption Waste Water Discharge

Refers to annual discharge of consumption waste water by urban households. Its calculation formula is:

Discharge = Discharge of Consumption Wastewater by Urban Households × Urban Non-agricultural Population × 365

## Soot Emission by Consumption and Others

Refers to net volume of soot emitted by fuel burning from all social and economic activities and operation of public facilities other than industrial activities. It is calculated on the basis of coal consumption by households and others.

## Area of Man-made Forests

Refer to the area of stable growing forests, planted manually or by airplanes, with a survival rate of 80% or higher of the designed number of trees per hectare, or with a canopy density of 0.20 degree or above after 3-5 years of manual planting or 5-7 years of airplane planting.

# 第十章·要素市场

## MARKETS OF KEY FACTORS

# 简要说明

## BRIEF INTRODUCTION

本章资料中的国有土地使用权出让与划拨、城市房产市场交易情况由市统计局固定资产投资处根据市规划和自然资源局、市住房和城乡建设委员会资料整理提供，亿元以上商品市场由市统计局贸易外经处提供，技术市场由市统计局社会科技处根据市科学技术局资料整理提供，人才市场、劳动力市场和证券市场情况由市统计局综合处根据市人力资源和社会保障局和重庆证监局资料整理编辑。

货币流通、保险业务和有价证券的相关资料详见第十七章金融。

The data on transaction and allotment of the right to use the state-owned land and the real estate markets in urban areas are sorted and compiled by Division of Statistics of Investment in Fixed Assets, Chongqing Municipal Bureau of Statistics on the basis of the data provided by Commission of Housing and Urban-Rural Development of Chongqing and Bureau of Planning and Natural Resources, of Chongqing,; the data of the transaction of the commodity markets with transaction value over 100 million yuan are provided by Division of Trade and External Economic Relations Statistics, Chongqing Municipal Bureau of Statistics; the data of transactions of technology exchanges are provided by Division of Social and Technology Statistics, Chongqing Municipal Bureau of Statistics on the basis of the data from Chongqing Science and Technology Bureau; the data of the human resource markets, labor force markets and securities markets are sorted and compiled by Division of Comprehensive Statistics, Chongqing Municipal Bureau of Statistics on the basis of the data from Chongqing Municipal Human Resources and Social Security Bureau and China Securities Regulatory Commission Chongqing Bureau.

See Chapter 17 Financial Intermediation for the data on currency, insurance and securities.

## 表 10.1 国有土地使用权出让与划拨情况（2021 – 2022 年）
TRANSACTIONS AND ALLOTMENT OF THE RIGHT TO USE THE STATE-OWNED LAND (2021-2022)

| 指　标 | Item | 2021 | 2022 |
|---|---|---|---|
| **土地使用权出让** | **Transaction of Right to Use State-owned Land** | | |
| 地　块（宗） | Land Parcel (parcel) | 1265 | 884 |
| 面　积（公顷） | Land Area (hectare) | 5411 | 4121 |
| 出让价款（亿元） | Value of Transaction (100 million yuan) | 1929 | 815 |
| **土地使用权划拨** | **Allotment of Right to Use State-owned Land** | | |
| 地　块（宗） | Land Parcel (parcel) | 1156 | 1643 |
| 面　积（公顷） | Land Area (hectare) | 7564 | 12042 |

## 表 10.2 城市房产市场交易情况（2021 – 2022 年）
REAL ESTATE MARKETS IN URBAN AREA (2021-2022)

| 指　标 | Item | 2021 | 2022 |
|---|---|---|---|
| **房产转让** | **Housing Transactions** | | |
| **成交面积（万平方米）** | **Area of Transactions (10 000 sq.m)** | **4733.25** | **2639.25** |
| #住　宅 | Residential Buildings | 3738.13 | 1711.16 |
| 商品房（新建） | Commercialized Buildings | 2970.78 | 1522.82 |
| 存量房（二手房） | Buildings in Stock | 1762.48 | 1116.43 |
| **成交金额（亿元）** | **Total Value of Transactions (100 million yuan)** | **4713.46** | **2196.86** |
| #住　宅 | Residential Buildings | 4186.77 | 1774.68 |
| 商品房 | Commercialized Buildings | 3430.72 | 1374.93 |
| 存量房 | Buildings in Stock | 1282.75 | 821.92 |

注：本表为主城九区的数据。
Note: The table above shows the data of the 9 urban districts.

## 表 10.3 亿元以上商品市场交易情况（2021－2022 年）
## TRANSACTIONS OF COMMODITY MARKETS WITH TRANSACTION VALUE OVER 100 MILLION YUAN (2021-2022)

| 指 标 | Item | 年末出租摊位数量（个）Number of Rent Stands at Year-end (unit) | | 总成交额（万元）Total Volume of Transactions (10 000 yuan) | |
|---|---|---|---|---|---|
| | | 2021 | 2022 | 2021 | 2022 |
| **合 计** | **Total** | **84659** | **81730** | **34310253** | **33123240** |
| 粮油、食品类 | Grain, Oil and Food | 21992 | 21750 | 9229836 | 10812003 |
| 饮料类 | Beverages | 1087 | 1012 | 91851 | 83457 |
| 烟酒类 | Tobacco and Liquor | 584 | 560 | 73406 | 68082 |
| 服装鞋帽、针、纺织品类 | Clothing, Shoes, Hats and Textiles | 16208 | 15851 | 3962096 | 3307342 |
| 化妆品类 | Cosmetics | 406 | 373 | 50094 | 39110 |
| 金银珠宝类 | Gold,Silver and Jewelry | 19 | 151 | 995 | 4194 |
| 日用品类 | Articles for Daily Use | 2859 | 2595 | 749030 | 699843 |
| 五金电料类 | Hardwear and Electrical Materials | 6193 | 6394 | 1214474 | 1249065 |
| 体育、娱乐用品类 | Sports and Entertainment Articles | 252 | 247 | 66833 | 45512 |
| 书报杂志类 | Newspapers and Magazines | 6 | 6 | 210 | 211 |
| 电子出版物及音像制品类 | E-journal and Video Products | 27 | 27 | 3870 | 3620 |
| 家用电器和音像制品类 | Household Electric Appliances and Video Products | 1049 | 965 | 269098 | 241354 |
| 中西药品类 | Traditional Chinese and Western Medicines | 142 | 140 | 23313 | 24670 |
| 文化办公用品类 | Cultural and Office Articles | 622 | 611 | 40167 | 37479 |
| 家具类 | Furniture | 3518 | 3281 | 1073037 | 1001900 |
| 通信器材类 | Communication Appliances | 893 | 810 | 236955 | 574911 |
| 煤炭及制品类 | Coal and Related Products | 4 | 4 | 607 | 629 |
| 木材及制品类 | Wood and Wooden Products | 181 | 183 | 18454 | 17352 |
| 化工材料及制品类 | Chemical Materials and Products | 5 | 5 | 792 | 786 |
| 金属材料类 | Metal Materials | 4547 | 4538 | 8345875 | 7268829 |
| 建筑及装潢材料类 | Building and Decoration Materials | 12951 | 12740 | 2228029 | 1951186 |
| 机电产品及设备类 | Mechanical and Electrical Products | 3006 | 2471 | 1401823 | 1114702 |
| 汽车类 | Automobiles | 4955 | 4776 | 4519877 | 3919796 |
| 种子饲料类 | Seeds and Feedstuff | 361 | 37 | 15170 | 4867 |
| 棉麻类 | Cotton and Hemp | 5 | 4 | 961 | 759 |
| 其他类 | Others | 2787 | 2199 | 693400 | 651581 |

## 表 10.4 技术市场交易情况(2022 年)
TRANSACTIONS OF TECHNOLOGY EXCHANGES (2022)

单位:项、万元 (item, 10 000 yuan)

| 指　标 | Item | 技术买方 Purchases of Technology | | 技术卖方 Sales of Technology | |
|---|---|---|---|---|---|
| | | 项 数 Number | 金 额 Value | 项 数 Number | 金 额 Value |
| **总　计** | **Total** | **6919** | **6304852.70** | **6919** | **6304852.70** |
| #企业法人 | Corporations | 5054 | 5900034.10 | 3565 | 6126757.60 |
| 事业法人 | Public Institutions | 733 | 81029.20 | 3296 | 150078.80 |
| 机关法人 | Governments | 1042 | 283345.60 | 1 | 88.60 |
| 其他组织 | Other Organizations | 23 | 634.80 | 5 | 10740.20 |
| 社团法人 | Association Corporations | 22 | 37458.40 | 1 | 2500.00 |
| 自然人 | Natural Persons | 45 | 2350.80 | 51 | 14687.60 |

## 表 10.5 全市人力资源情况(2021－2022 年)
HUMAN RESOURCES OF THE WHOLE CITY (2021-2022)

| 指　标 | Item | 2021 | 2022 |
|---|---|---|---|
| 人力资源服务机构(个) | Human Resource Service Agencies (unit) | 3169 | 2846 |
| 公共就业服务机构 | Public Employment Service Agencies | 39 | 41 |
| 国有性质的服务企业 | State-owned Service Corporations | 127 | 89 |
| 民营性质的服务企业 | Private Service Corporations | 2982 | 2701 |
| 外资性质的服务企业 | Foreign-funded Service Corporations | 4 | 6 |
| 港资性质的服务企业 | Service Corporations with Investment from Hong Kong | 5 | 3 |
| 民办非企业等其他性质的服务机构 | Other Private Non-corporate Service Corporations | 7 | 3 |
| 设立固定招聘场所个数 | Number of fixed recruitment places | 24 | 297 |
| 举办招聘会次数(次) | Number of Job Fairs (time) | 3894 | 4347 |
| 参加招聘会求职人员人数(人) | Persons Participating in Job Fairs (person) | 1469793 | 1125572 |
| 参加招聘会用人单位(个) | Enterprises Participating in Job Fairs (unit) | 77657 | 75309 |
| 现存档案总量(万份) | Total Amount of Current Archives (10 000 copies) | 321 | 349 |
| 当年流动人员职称评定(人) | Number of Exchanged Persons Evaluated for Professional Titles in Current Year (person) | 8275 | 9414 |

# 表 10.6 证券市场基本情况（2021－2022 年）
## GENERAL STATISTICS ON SECURITIES MARKETS (2021-2022)

| 指　标 | Item | 2021 | 2022 |
|---|---|---|---|
| 境内上市公司总计（个） | Number of Listed Companies in Mainland (unit) | 63 | 70 |
| 上交所（个） | Shanghai Stock Exchange (unit) | 31 | 34 |
| 深交所（个） | Shenzhen Stock Exchange (unit) | 30 | 32 |
| 北交所（个） | Beijing Stock Exchange (unit) | 2 | 4 |
| #仅发 A 股公司 | A Shares Only | 58 | 65 |
| #仅发 B 股公司 | B Shares Only | 1 | 1 |
| #同时发 A、B 股公司 | A & B Shares | 1 | 1 |
| #同时发 A、H 股公司 | A & H Shares | 3 | 3 |
| 股票市价总值（亿元） | Total Market Capitalization (100 million yuan) | 11368 | 9347 |
| #股票流通市值 | Negotiable Market Capitalization (100 million yuan) | 9005 | 7530 |
| 总股本（亿股） | Total Shares of Stocks Issued (100 million shares) | 960 | 1010 |
| #流通股本 | Negotiable Shares (100 million shares) | 818 | 854 |
| 股票筹资额（亿元） | Raised Capital (100 million yuan) | 173 | 173 |
| A 股 | A Shares | 173 | 173 |
| B 股 | B Shares | | |
| 证券市场募集资金（亿元） | Raised Funds in Securities Market (100 million yuan) | 1821 | 1854 |
| #通过发行、配售股票筹集资金 | Funds-raised from Issuing and Placing Stocks | 173 | 173 |
| #通过全国股转系统筹集资金 | Funds-raised from National Equities Transfer System | 1 | 5 |
| #发行公司信用类债券筹集资金 | Funds-raised from Issuing Companies' Debentures | 1236 | 982 |
| #交易所资产支持证券 | Stock Supported by Exchange Assets | 412 | 695 |
| 证券公司总部（个） | Securities Head Offices (unit) | 1 | 1 |
| 证券分公司（个） | Securities Branch Offices (unit) | 49 | 53 |
| 证券营业部（个） | Securities Business Departments (unit) | 208 | 200 |
| 投资者开户数（万户） | Number of Investors' Accounts (10000 accounts) | 1178 | 1113 |

# 第十一章·农业和农村经济

# AGRICULTURE AND RURAL ECONOMY

# 简要说明

## BRIEF INTRODUCTION

本章反映全市农业生产和农村经济的基本情况，内容主要包括农村基本情况、农业生产条件与生产情况、农作物播种面积、农林牧渔产品产量、农林牧渔业产值、农业商品产值和商品率等方面的统计资料。

本章资料由国家统计局重庆调查总队根据市农委、市林业局、市水利局和调查总队等资料整理提供。

The data in this chapter show the basic conditions of agricultural production and rural economy, including basic statistics on rural areas, basic conditions of agricultural production, sown area of farm crops, output of farming, forestry, animal husbandry and fishery products, gross output value of farming, forestry, animal husbandry and fishery, output value of agricultural commodities and rate of commercialization, and township-owned enterprises.

The data in this chapter are provided by Chongqing Agriculture Commission, Municipal Bureau of Forestry, Municipal Bureau of Water Conservancy and NBS Survey Office in Chongqing, and sorted and compiled by NBS Survey Office in Chongqing.

# 表 11.1 主要年份农业生产条件
CONDITIONS OF AGRICULTURAL PRODUCTION IN MAJOR YEARS

| 年 份<br>Year | 有效灌溉面积（万公顷）<br>Irrigated Area (10 000 hectares) | 农用机械总动力（万千瓦）<br>Total Agricultural Machinery Power (10 000 kw) | 农用化肥施用量（折纯）（万吨）<br>Consumption of Chemical Fertilizers (net) (10 000 tons) | 农膜使用量（万吨）<br>Consumption of Farm Plastic Film (10 000 tons) | 农药使用量（万吨）<br>Consumption of Chemical Pesticides (10 000 tons) |
|---|---|---|---|---|---|
| 2001 | 63.19 | 628 | 72.58 | 1.94 | 1.91 |
| 2002 | 64.12 | 666 | 73.37 | 2.53 | 1.93 |
| 2003 | 64.97 | 696 | 71.59 | 2.42 | 1.95 |
| 2004 | 61.68 | 728 | 77.02 | 2.68 | 1.95 |
| 2005 | 61.81 | 776 | 79.20 | 2.75 | 1.95 |
| 2006 | 62.13 | 820 | 80.54 | 2.82 | 1.96 |
| 2007 | 63.37 | 860 | 84.32 | 3.01 | 2.04 |
| 2008 | 65.89 | 903 | 88.14 | 3.09 | 2.10 |
| 2009 | 67.20 | 967 | 91.17 | 3.47 | 2.20 |
| 2010 | 68.53 | 1071 | 91.82 | 3.66 | 2.10 |
| 2011 | 69.29 | 1141 | 95.58 | 3.93 | 2.03 |
| 2012 | 70.30 | 1162 | 96.02 | 4.09 | 1.95 |
| 2013 | 67.52 | 1199 | 96.64 | 4.29 | 1.84 |
| 2014 | 67.73 | 1243 | 97.26 | 4.38 | 1.84 |
| 2015 | 68.72 | 1300 | 97.73 | 4.52 | 1.82 |
| 2016 | 69.06 | 1319 | 96.16 | 4.53 | 1.76 |
| 2017 | 69.43 | 1353 | 95.46 | 4.55 | 1.75 |
| 2018 | 69.69 | 1428 | 93.17 | 4.46 | 1.72 |
| 2019 | 69.77 | 1465 | 91.08 | 4.26 | 1.65 |
| 2020 | 69.83 | 1498 | 89.83 | 4.17 | 1.62 |
| 2021 | 66.53 | 1532 | 89.05 | 4.12 | 1.60 |
| 2022 | 67.65 | 1566 | 88.74 | 4.08 | 1.60 |

# 表 11.2 农作物播种面积（1978 － 2022 年）
## SOWN AREA OF FARM CORPS (1978-2022)

单位：公顷 (hectare)

| 年 份 Year | 农作物总播种面积 Total Sown Area | #粮 食 Grain | #稻 谷 Rice | #油 料 Oil-bearing Crops | #油菜籽 Rapeseeds | #蔬 菜 Vegetables | #烟 叶 Tobacco |
|---|---|---|---|---|---|---|---|
| 1978 | 3498061 | 3177221 | 849243 | 92351 | 71374 | 95954 | 26582 |
| 1980 | 3345304 | 3048196 | 828317 | 116577 | 89369 | 78400 | 10416 |
| 1985 | 3214717 | 2748498 | 820140 | 176866 | 137367 | 140569 | 30956 |
| 1986 | 3232433 | 2710205 | 819858 | 183859 | 143792 | 159811 | 40897 |
| 1987 | 3241258 | 2697509 | 807797 | 180579 | 143292 | 160867 | 41729 |
| 1988 | 3287399 | 2727164 | 821305 | 185171 | 150612 | 171444 | 54056 |
| 1989 | 3381959 | 2788700 | 836231 | 188593 | 154505 | 177979 | 75726 |
| 1990 | 3438950 | 2847370 | 821986 | 203171 | 168751 | 183873 | 66607 |
| 1991 | 3526637 | 2889404 | 816684 | 224412 | 188989 | 197049 | 70859 |
| 1992 | 3522037 | 2874889 | 819262 | 215622 | 179402 | 200686 | 81258 |
| 1993 | 3513064 | 2870480 | 804560 | 184964 | 147692 | 222621 | 82461 |
| 1994 | 3493884 | 2877837 | 800342 | 174643 | 135505 | 225902 | 54997 |
| 1995 | 3526684 | 2876853 | 799482 | 201550 | 162572 | 236283 | 58939 |
| 1996 | 3585745 | 2889834 | 802279 | 202483 | 159584 | 257106 | 77657 |
| 1997 | 3605420 | 2881902 | 797955 | 191800 | 152222 | 267203 | 99482 |
| 1998 | 3614446 | 2900656 | 794636 | 192330 | 148896 | 290397 | 56603 |
| 1999 | 3592496 | 2862143 | 788576 | 197151 | 151801 | 301389 | 63969 |
| 2000 | 3590815 | 2773404 | 776636 | 226384 | 173185 | 327094 | 70775 |
| 2001 | 3555871 | 2714600 | 763964 | 225046 | 167911 | 366330 | 55210 |
| 2002 | 3464566 | 2606866 | 757195 | 236325 | 173930 | 359674 | 56012 |
| 2003 | 3307179 | 2410369 | 738486 | 236724 | 176836 | 386990 | 57237 |
| 2004 | 3435957 | 2516507 | 749300 | 244129 | 173815 | 390237 | 52995 |
| 2005 | 3444733 | 2501263 | 747949 | 252421 | 187333 | 399970 | 51508 |
| 2006 | 3073880 | 2155500 | 672300 | 187290 | 133680 | 417414 | 48879 |
| 2007 | 3104939 | 2148543 | 644265 | 192920 | 135370 | 432906 | 43553 |
| 2008 | 3109135 | 2131012 | 658847 | 215531 | 150170 | 481563 | 47749 |
| 2009 | 3110741 | 2111605 | 661205 | 237025 | 173643 | 552233 | 52579 |
| 2010 | 3129847 | 2097420 | 658084 | 254993 | 191847 | 589093 | 42733 |
| 2011 | 3225774 | 2089469 | 656816 | 257096 | 196200 | 618631 | 46165 |
| 2012 | 3320301 | 2085011 | 654772 | 271016 | 204557 | 652660 | 49989 |
| 2013 | 3318492 | 2059450 | 652372 | 283508 | 215603 | 681707 | 49323 |
| 2014 | 3288585 | 2034685 | 650782 | 299963 | 232581 | 708068 | 45964 |
| 2015 | 3311315 | 2020951 | 647088 | 309315 | 242458 | 731667 | 45829 |
| 2016 | 3333052 | 2039069 | 660909 | 310441 | 236856 | 714671 | 43451 |
| 2017 | 3339556 | 2030710 | 658941 | 318516 | 244284 | 727170 | 34904 |
| 2018 | 3348490 | 2017846 | 656446 | 325072 | 250151 | 739183 | 32402 |
| 2019 | 3345743 | 1999278 | 655137 | 329946 | 254990 | 753222 | 29840 |
| 2020 | 3372541 | 2003058 | 657266 | 333870 | 258258 | 772028 | 27365 |
| 2021 | 3409256 | 2013191 | 658905 | 337983 | 261497 | 791378 | 26988 |
| 2022 | 3479024 | 2046710 | 659186 | 346713 | 269719 | 812024 | 28401 |

# 表 11.3 主要年份农林牧渔产品产量
OUTPUT OF FARMING, FORESTRY, ANIMAL HUSBANDRY AND FISHERY IN MAJOR YEARS

| 年 份<br>Year | 粮 食（万吨）<br>Grain (10 000 tons) | #稻 谷<br>Rice | #豆 类<br>Beans | 油 料（万吨）<br>Oil-bearing Crops (10 000 tons) | #油菜籽<br>Rapeseeds | 麻 类（吨）<br>Vegetables (ton) | 甘 蔗（万吨）<br>Tobacco (10 000 tons) |
|---|---|---|---|---|---|---|---|
| 1949 | 402.68 | 246.57 | | 0.90 | | 1416 | 8.78 |
| 1952 | 470.97 | 281.33 | | 3.19 | | 1889 | 10.61 |
| 1957 | 596.55 | 316.39 | | 5.13 | | 1811 | 6.86 |
| 1962 | 378.23 | 191.26 | | 1.40 | | 598 | 1.04 |
| 1965 | 566.17 | 293.32 | | 3.87 | | 1048 | 14.47 |
| 1970 | 564.37 | 307.80 | | 2.68 | | 666 | 9.00 |
| 1975 | 603.72 | 325.84 | | 4.13 | | 632 | 24.87 |
| 1978 | 814.71 | 345.07 | 29.07 | 7.71 | 6.03 | 1659 | 31.20 |
| 1980 | 835.43 | 341.59 | 22.20 | 11.57 | 9.28 | 6172 | 36.64 |
| 1985 | 948.97 | 461.73 | 22.26 | 18.12 | 13.63 | 25787 | 30.24 |
| 1986 | 1004.92 | 493.41 | 25.02 | 20.91 | 15.85 | 21719 | 31.42 |
| 1987 | 1004.51 | 499.56 | 22.34 | 20.89 | 16.14 | 35995 | 29.43 |
| 1988 | 958.02 | 503.00 | 20.53 | 19.25 | 14.94 | 31013 | 29.32 |
| 1989 | 1044.88 | 541.81 | 17.25 | 18.78 | 14.38 | 18932 | 24.41 |
| 1990 | 1085.07 | 550.40 | 19.93 | 22.02 | 17.74 | 12707 | 20.55 |
| 1991 | 1115.28 | 535.90 | 21.53 | 26.92 | 22.81 | 11487 | 26.07 |
| 1992 | 1050.24 | 509.07 | 18.48 | 25.18 | 21.40 | 9716 | 14.33 |
| 1993 | 1052.72 | 479.90 | 21.90 | 21.70 | 17.22 | 9257 | 12.30 |
| 1994 | 1134.10 | 523.13 | 25.94 | 19.26 | 15.31 | 11471 | 9.39 |
| 1995 | 1153.68 | 532.63 | 30.38 | 25.12 | 20.54 | 11092 | 8.76 |
| 1996 | 1172.14 | 542.64 | 20.10 | 23.60 | 18.66 | 10898 | 8.27 |
| 1997 | 1184.63 | 552.44 | 21.90 | 23.34 | 18.34 | 11175 | 8.08 |
| 1998 | 1155.36 | 519.38 | 22.17 | 25.11 | 19.03 | 7541 | 7.28 |
| 1999 | 1143.05 | 533.01 | 21.93 | 24.09 | 17.33 | 6826 | 7.59 |
| 2000 | 1131.21 | 525.43 | 24.60 | 31.06 | 22.61 | 8406 | 9.06 |
| 2001 | 1035.35 | 466.45 | 23.32 | 29.96 | 21.91 | 8857 | 10.08 |
| 2002 | 1082.15 | 484.42 | 27.78 | 35.04 | 25.84 | 12139 | 12.06 |
| 2003 | 1087.20 | 494.29 | 32.21 | 38.27 | 28.51 | 9620 | 11.35 |
| 2004 | 1144.57 | 509.55 | 38.11 | 41.75 | 30.99 | 10209 | 11.77 |
| 2005 | 1168.19 | 521.43 | 42.16 | 42.71 | 31.81 | 12362 | 11.46 |
| 2006 | 808.40 | 344.90 | 29.24 | 28.94 | 23.47 | 11846 | 10.16 |
| 2007 | 1064.07 | 485.13 | 33.79 | 30.58 | 23.05 | 15210 | 11.17 |
| 2008 | 1112.17 | 517.26 | 34.72 | 35.07 | 26.22 | 16695 | 11.00 |
| 2009 | 1083.78 | 495.70 | 36.69 | 39.97 | 30.38 | 15557 | 11.28 |
| 2010 | 1080.63 | 499.16 | 38.06 | 43.81 | 33.38 | 14606 | 11.29 |
| 2011 | 1064.16 | 475.36 | 38.61 | 45.79 | 34.07 | 12897 | 11.31 |
| 2012 | 1060.51 | 475.36 | 39.32 | 49.16 | 36.34 | 10137 | 11.29 |
| 2013 | 1055.15 | 477.16 | 39.20 | 52.00 | 38.40 | 9461 | 10.30 |
| 2014 | 1043.89 | 475.46 | 39.03 | 55.46 | 41.84 | 9046 | 9.62 |
| 2015 | 1051.05 | 476.56 | 39.58 | 58.12 | 44.19 | 8460 | 9.05 |
| 2016 | 1078.20 | 487.58 | 39.54 | 60.85 | 46.24 | 7434 | 8.91 |
| 2017 | 1079.88 | 486.99 | 40.22 | 62.40 | 47.43 | 6957 | 8.79 |
| 2018 | 1079.34 | 486.92 | 40.86 | 63.70 | 48.60 | 6450 | 9.10 |
| 2019 | 1075.20 | 487.00 | 40.90 | 65.20 | 49.90 | 3819 | 8.10 |
| 2020 | 1081.42 | 489.19 | 41.48 | 67.07 | 51.37 | 3659 | 8.17 |
| 2021 | 1092.84 | 493.05 | 42.15 | 68.48 | 52.46 | 3182 | 8.28 |
| 2022 | 1072.84 | 485.24 | 43.45 | 70.85 | 54.73 | 3008 | 8.32 |

**表 11.3 续表 1 continued 1**

| 年 份<br>Year | 烟 叶<br>（吨）<br>Tobacco<br>(ton) | 蔬 菜<br>（万吨）<br>Vegetables<br>(10 000 tons) | 茶 叶<br>（吨）<br>Tea<br>(ton) | 蚕 茧<br>（吨）<br>Silkworm Cocoons<br>(ton) | 水 果<br>（万吨）<br>Fruits<br>(10 000 tons) | 禽 蛋<br>（万吨）<br>Poultry Eggs<br>(10 000 tons) |
|---|---|---|---|---|---|---|
| 1949 | 8535 | | 916 | 761 | 6.02 | |
| 1952 | 9238 | | 1059 | 1236 | 7.75 | |
| 1957 | 8247 | | 1914 | 1588 | 7.14 | |
| 1962 | 2566 | | 1981 | 1325 | 8.80 | |
| 1965 | 4654 | | 2369 | 2306 | 6.83 | |
| 1970 | 1667 | | 2927 | 6608 | 4.54 | |
| 1975 | 8146 | | 4884 | 10477 | 7.12 | |
| 1978 | 22528 | 243.95 | 8004 | 15404 | 7.91 | 4.46 |
| 1980 | 8098 | 229.86 | 9217 | 25751 | 15.69 | 5.51 |
| 1985 | 36239 | 390.86 | 16172 | 33130 | 24.70 | 8.77 |
| 1986 | 46724 | 421.94 | 16893 | 32693 | 28.61 | 9.44 |
| 1987 | 44992 | 439.00 | 18267 | 35755 | 29.57 | 9.98 |
| 1988 | 68928 | 460.93 | 18676 | 41748 | 20.50 | 10.17 |
| 1989 | 62093 | 469.31 | 18568 | 42063 | 37.19 | 11.24 |
| 1990 | 74393 | 499.61 | 18103 | 43502 | 35.08 | 12.01 |
| 1991 | 98156 | 533.00 | 18264 | 47757 | 40.75 | 12.94 |
| 1992 | 124705 | 541.38 | 17178 | 50686 | 41.38 | 14.61 |
| 1993 | 113208 | 558.23 | 19522 | 54505 | 56.85 | 15.71 |
| 1994 | 68904 | 569.83 | 21920 | 57408 | 52.87 | 17.32 |
| 1995 | 77981 | 593.91 | 17452 | 27000 | 59.29 | 19.18 |
| 1996 | 132355 | 637.03 | 15536 | 27402 | 56.62 | 20.85 |
| 1997 | 164736 | 668.44 | 14996 | 28072 | 60.72 | 23.50 |
| 1998 | 79970 | 711.30 | 15299 | 29226 | 74.10 | 24.46 |
| 1999 | 95653 | 737.11 | 14441 | 24177 | 71.70 | 26.29 |
| 2000 | 104082 | 775.42 | 14526 | 29098 | 81.68 | 27.89 |
| 2001 | 80064 | 779.96 | 14142 | 32396 | 82.61 | 29.79 |
| 2002 | 87052 | 833.84 | 14093 | 33856 | 113.41 | 31.58 |
| 2003 | 86048 | 840.17 | 14320 | 27802 | 128.59 | 35.36 |
| 2004 | 85036 | 863.57 | 16064 | 29376 | 137.22 | 36.55 |
| 2005 | 90173 | 890.47 | 16545 | 31092 | 154.63 | 39.15 |
| 2006 | 91945 | 888.76 | 17087 | 27488 | 145.74 | 30.30 |
| 2007 | 71513 | 908.56 | 18672 | 29196 | 161.06 | 31.69 |
| 2008 | 85513 | 1029.32 | 24406 | 24388 | 178.54 | 31.86 |
| 2009 | 99900 | 1062.06 | 22406 | 19464 | 198.77 | 33.95 |
| 2010 | 81030 | 1154.80 | 25086 | 20321 | 225.09 | 34.47 |
| 2011 | 93608 | 1385.96 | 27761 | 20118 | 249.16 | 33.99 |
| 2012 | 102908 | 1508.36 | 31259 | 20594 | 280.31 | 35.69 |
| 2013 | 96604 | 1544.82 | 34139 | 18161 | 311.87 | 35.92 |
| 2014 | 84391 | 1629.96 | 33712 | 17714 | 342.97 | 37.06 |
| 2015 | 86759 | 1707.86 | 35014 | 17681 | 372.28 | 38.16 |
| 2016 | 83921 | 1795.49 | 36636 | 16320 | 369.24 | 39.10 |
| 2017 | 69053 | 1862.63 | 38752 | 13996 | 403.38 | 40.31 |
| 2018 | 62441 | 1932.73 | 41994 | 13545 | 431.27 | 41.46 |
| 2019 | 58516 | 2008.80 | 44807 | 12471 | 476.40 | 43.52 |
| 2020 | 52676 | 2092.57 | 48052 | 11563 | 514.82 | 45.72 |
| 2021 | 53192 | 2184.33 | 50834 | 11928 | 553.18 | 47.87 |
| 2022 | 55235 | 2272.36 | 53027 | 11452 | 593.28 | 50.50 |

**表 11.3 续表 2 continued 2**

| 年 份<br>Year | 水产品<br>（吨）<br>Aquatic Products (ton) | 肉猪出栏头数<br>（万头）<br>Number of Slaughtered Fattened Hogs (10 000 heads) | 猪年末头数<br>（万头）<br>Number of Hogs at Year End (10 000 heads) | 猪 肉<br>（万吨）<br>Output of Pork (10 000 tons) |
|---|---|---|---|---|
| 1949 | 3576 | 174.70 | | |
| 1952 | 4119 | 254.80 | | |
| 1957 | 6515 | 345.10 | | |
| 1962 | 3791 | 76.90 | | |
| 1965 | 6964 | 421.50 | | |
| 1970 | 7649 | 414.50 | | |
| 1975 | 10797 | 489.90 | | |
| 1978 | 14362 | 542.70 | 914.98 | 37.38 |
| 1980 | 17734 | 797.63 | 1165.05 | 55.92 |
| 1985 | 42838 | 1140.06 | 1353.02 | 79.96 |
| 1986 | 47805 | 1190.22 | 1377.37 | 83.15 |
| 1987 | 51854 | 1243.78 | 1418.69 | 86.89 |
| 1988 | 58419 | 1345.77 | 1448.48 | 94.02 |
| 1989 | 65707 | 1375.38 | 1471.66 | 96.09 |
| 1990 | 65482 | 1375.79 | 1429.13 | 96.12 |
| 1991 | 71813 | 1429.45 | 1440.56 | 99.87 |
| 1992 | 74459 | 1469.47 | 1444.16 | 102.66 |
| 1993 | 89227 | 1492.99 | 1438.96 | 104.30 |
| 1994 | 103492 | 1555.69 | 1476.05 | 108.48 |
| 1995 | 121289 | 1610.14 | 1489.55 | 112.27 |
| 1996 | 140656 | 1637.51 | 1477.06 | 114.18 |
| 1997 | 160692 | 1699.74 | 1475.25 | 119.66 |
| 1998 | 178607 | 1720.14 | 1492.95 | 121.61 |
| 1999 | 191313 | 1703.19 | 1512.18 | 120.61 |
| 2000 | 200345 | 1724.96 | 1509.91 | 122.45 |
| 2001 | 196967 | 1746.85 | 1533.03 | 124.87 |
| 2002 | 211568 | 1781.69 | 1548.89 | 127.48 |
| 2003 | 224893 | 1828.49 | 1583.03 | 131.82 |
| 2004 | 239255 | 1909.32 | 1640.75 | 136.43 |
| 2005 | 250568 | 2006.39 | 1708.80 | 144.46 |
| 2006 | 226129 | 1732.70 | 1377.40 | 124.80 |
| 2007 | 255372 | 1757.17 | 1402.12 | 128.40 |
| 2008 | 190600 | 1843.67 | 1521.09 | 136.58 |
| 2009 | 203900 | 1916.65 | 1534.86 | 140.20 |
| 2010 | 224300 | 1895.65 | 1468.86 | 139.13 |
| 2011 | 275600 | 1877.63 | 1431.37 | 138.02 |
| 2012 | 330720 | 1877.56 | 1395.56 | 138.00 |
| 2013 | 385000 | 1898.60 | 1355.28 | 139.79 |
| 2014 | 443409 | 1912.11 | 1319.05 | 140.94 |
| 2015 | 480863 | 1857.09 | 1270.56 | 136.79 |
| 2016 | 508427 | 1767.74 | 1204.71 | 130.62 |
| 2017 | 515130 | 1751.11 | 1191.61 | 129.97 |
| 2018 | 529581 | 1758.22 | 1167.19 | 132.16 |
| 2019 | 541717 | 1480.42 | 921.62 | 112.07 |
| 2020 | 523976 | 1434.53 | 1082.90 | 108.82 |
| 2021 | 545343 | 1806.86 | 1179.83 | 142.01 |
| 2022 | 566303 | 1904.43 | 1197.14 | 149.96 |

注：1. 蚕茧和禽蛋数据自 2007 年起根据第三次农业普查数据进行了调整。
2. 本表中除水产品外，其余数据从 2007 年起已根据第三次农业普查数据重新进行了调整。

Note: a) Since 2007, the data of poultry eggs and Silkworm Cocoons has been adjusted in accordance with the 3rd agricultural census.
b) Except the data of aquatic products, the other data in this table have been adjusted according to the Third National Agricultural Census since 2007.

# 表 11.4 主要年份农林牧渔业总产值
## GROSS OUTPUT VALUE OF FARMING, FORESTRY, ANIMAL HUSBANDRY AND FISHERY IN MAJOR YEARS

单位：万元 (10 000 yuan)

| 年 份 Year | 农林牧渔业总产值 Gross Output Value | 农 业 Farming | 林 业 Forestry | 牧 业 Animal Husbandry | 渔 业 Fishery | 农林牧渔专业及辅助性活动 Professional and Support Activities for Agriculture,Forestry,Animal Husbandry and Fishery |
|---|---|---|---|---|---|---|
| 1949 | 142123 | 111424 | 3837 | 26293 | 568 | |
| 1952 | 186367 | 140707 | 6523 | 38205 | 932 | |
| 1957 | 240351 | 176658 | 10816 | 51916 | 961 | |
| 1962 | 153506 | 120349 | 4605 | 28245 | 307 | |
| 1965 | 165688 | 122775 | 5799 | 36617 | 497 | |
| 1970 | 269234 | 192504 | 11128 | 64604 | 998 | |
| 1975 | 295062 | 210016 | 18048 | 65660 | 1338 | |
| 1978 | 357616 | 262881 | 17236 | 75731 | 1768 | |
| 1980 | 417925 | 296840 | 16160 | 102514 | 2411 | |
| 1985 | 739003 | 477570 | 43546 | 208842 | 9044 | |
| 1986 | 801998 | 516990 | 42045 | 231097 | 11867 | |
| 1987 | 902072 | 564063 | 40932 | 282816 | 14262 | |
| 1988 | 1104369 | 641751 | 49662 | 393394 | 19561 | |
| 1989 | 1243819 | 706771 | 49328 | 463300 | 24420 | |
| 1990 | 1460003 | 858133 | 55308 | 518757 | 27805 | |
| 1991 | 1595286 | 938353 | 60038 | 565193 | 31702 | |
| 1992 | 1713839 | 995009 | 70992 | 612498 | 35340 | |
| 1993 | 2073607 | 1197742 | 77531 | 749776 | 48558 | |
| 1994 | 2831816 | 1552652 | 86981 | 1127394 | 64789 | |
| 1995 | 3778259 | 2278927 | 106732 | 1304229 | 88371 | |
| 1996 | 4249903 | 2713807 | 115493 | 1311666 | 108937 | |
| 1997 | 4393508 | 2678892 | 117313 | 1468914 | 128389 | |
| 1998 | 4288839 | 2549365 | 150929 | 1444758 | 143787 | |
| 1999 | 4168780 | 2496237 | 115588 | 1409527 | 147428 | |
| 2000 | 4126272 | 2447376 | 108236 | 1419910 | 150750 | |
| 2001 | 4311666 | 2503968 | 112044 | 1544041 | 151613 | |
| 2002 | 4609755 | 2640760 | 135143 | 1661965 | 171887 | |
| 2003 | 4885655 | 2701156 | 145824 | 1776384 | 183251 | 79040 |
| 2004 | 6127723 | 3329516 | 184814 | 2309374 | 212464 | 91555 |
| 2005 | 6621943 | 3583035 | 199704 | 2494965 | 237959 | 106280 |
| 2006 | 5752428 | 3230078 | 223069 | 2042194 | 159087 | 98000 |
| 2007 | 7116736 | 4051452 | 178527 | 2598315 | 184442 | 104000 |
| 2008 | 8517434 | 4640022 | 217986 | 3335134 | 211481 | 112811 |
| 2009 | 8861491 | 5177597 | 258084 | 3058737 | 242699 | 124374 |
| 2010 | 9804523 | 6000252 | 304021 | 3091828 | 272083 | 136339 |
| 2011 | 12041572 | 7172773 | 380907 | 3980989 | 349432 | 157471 |
| 2012 | 13273378 | 8011808 | 434776 | 4198356 | 449928 | 178510 |
| 2013 | 14182742 | 8555035 | 480200 | 4410107 | 538200 | 199200 |
| 2014 | 14857775 | 9064316 | 535593 | 4386190 | 649279 | 222398 |
| 2015 | 16090494 | 9630283 | 604358 | 4844533 | 749120 | 262200 |
| 2016 | 18516019 | 11238339 | 734330 | 5386888 | 853222 | 303240 |
| 2017 | 19024671 | 11656934 | 851673 | 5224787 | 948077 | 343200 |
| 2018 | 20524064 | 12926761 | 1011375 | 5200547 | 1003935 | 381446 |
| 2019 | 23378062 | 13974860 | 1131166 | 6795173 | 1052978 | 423885 |
| 2020 | 27490502 | 15961325 | 1260364 | 8718522 | 1073122 | 477169 |
| 2021 | 29356489 | 17598909 | 1681325 | 8041545 | 1381704 | 653006 |
| 2022 | 30684459 | 18817834 | 1764195 | 8009449 | 1369934 | 723047 |

注：1) 按照国民经济行业分类标准（GB/T4754-2002），从 2003 年起增加了农林牧渔服务业（下表同）。
2) 2006 年以来为第二次农普衔接数。从 2007 年起，因口径变化，对农业和林业总产值进行了调整。

Note: a)According to the national standard of industry classification (GB/T4754-2002), the gross output value has included agricultural services since 2003 (the same below).
b)The numbers after 2006 are the coordination numbers of the Second National Agricultural Census. The total output value of agriculture and forestry has been modified since 2007 due to the change of statistical scope.

# 表 11.5 主要年份农林牧渔业总产值指数（上年 =100）
GROSS OUTPUT VALUE INDICES OF FARMING, FORESTRY, ANIMAL HUSBANDRY AND FISHERY IN MAJOR YEARS (PRECEDING YEAR=100)

| 年 份<br>Year | 农林牧渔业总产值<br>Gross Output Value | 农 业<br>Farming | 林 业<br>Forestry | 牧 业<br>Animal Husbandry | 渔 业<br>Fishery | 农林牧渔专业及辅助性活动<br>Professional and Support Activities for Agriculture,Forestry,Animal Husbandry and Fishery |
|---|---|---|---|---|---|---|
| 1952 | 119.9 | 116.8 | 123.7 | 135.7 | 111.2 | |
| 1957 | 129.0 | 126.7 | 144.5 | 133.4 | 156.4 | |
| 1962 | 63.9 | 69.9 | 58.0 | 39.4 | 49.5 | |
| 1965 | 151.1 | 137.2 | 125.4 | 275.5 | 194.9 | |
| 1970 | 101.5 | 100.3 | 88.5 | 109.7 | 107.3 | |
| 1975 | 108.2 | 110.6 | 129.7 | 94.6 | 134.0 | |
| 1978 | 123.2 | 126.7 | 119.1 | 109.7 | 121.2 | |
| 1980 | 115.3 | 105.9 | 99.6 | 165.8 | 121.0 | |
| 1985 | 144.1 | 130.9 | 210.2 | 169.8 | 292.2 | |
| 1986 | 105.8 | 106.3 | 83.9 | 109.3 | 119.4 | |
| 1987 | 102.7 | 102.1 | 89.0 | 106.3 | 110.3 | |
| 1988 | 101.8 | 97.3 | 99.1 | 111.7 | 115.2 | |
| 1989 | 106.4 | 108.4 | 99.9 | 103.0 | 111.0 | |
| 1990 | 102.7 | 101.1 | 96.4 | 106.4 | 106.8 | |
| 1991 | 106.2 | 105.3 | 102.1 | 108.2 | 113.9 | |
| 1992 | 101.9 | 98.7 | 110.4 | 107.3 | 100.9 | |
| 1993 | 104.1 | 103.4 | 104.8 | 104.6 | 120.8 | |
| 1994 | 105.6 | 103.5 | 101.8 | 109.0 | 115.4 | |
| 1995 | 106.3 | 105.1 | 106.7 | 107.7 | 116.8 | |
| 1996 | 102.8 | 101.8 | 101.3 | 103.6 | 116.2 | |
| 1997 | 103.3 | 102.0 | 95.8 | 105.4 | 115.7 | |
| 1998 | 102.4 | 101.5 | 117.2 | 101.6 | 112.4 | |
| 1999 | 99.8 | 100.7 | 75.7 | 100.4 | 108.5 | |
| 2000 | 101.0 | 100.3 | 86.6 | 102.9 | 104.5 | |
| 2001 | 102.1 | 100.3 | 109.7 | 104.1 | 101.9 | |
| 2002 | 101.7 | 99.7 | 102.3 | 104.2 | 105.6 | |
| 2003 | 104.6 | 103.5 | 119.6 | 104.8 | 106.8 | |
| 2004 | 105.7 | 105.5 | 108.8 | 104.9 | 108.4 | 116.5 |
| 2005 | 105.2 | 103.9 | 100.8 | 106.9 | 106.0 | 113.3 |
| 2006 | 96.8 | 94.9 | 99.9 | 99.6 | 89.0 | 105.7 |
| 2007 | 109.5 | 114.8 | 105.1 | 101.6 | 110.2 | 106.0 |
| 2008 | 107.1 | 107.7 | 104.5 | 106.7 | 104.0 | 104.3 |
| 2009 | 106.4 | 106.8 | 106.6 | 105.7 | 108.8 | 104.8 |
| 2010 | 105.9 | 106.7 | 110.2 | 103.8 | 110.0 | 104.4 |
| 2011 | 104.9 | 105.2 | 111.0 | 102.5 | 118.4 | 105.0 |
| 2012 | 105.1 | 105.1 | 109.9 | 103.4 | 120.0 | 104.0 |
| 2013 | 104.6 | 104.3 | 108.0 | 103.5 | 117.0 | 105.3 |
| 2014 | 104.4 | 103.9 | 108.0 | 103.5 | 115.2 | 105.3 |
| 2015 | 104.6 | 104.6 | 109.3 | 102.5 | 114.0 | 109.4 |
| 2016 | 104.6 | 104.4 | 111.4 | 103.0 | 110.2 | 109.8 |
| 2017 | 103.7 | 104.3 | 111.7 | 100.6 | 107.4 | 110.1 |
| 2018 | 104.8 | 105.3 | 114.2 | 101.6 | 106.3 | 109.0 |
| 2019 | 102.9 | 105.5 | 110.8 | 94.0 | 102.8 | 108.4 |
| 2020 | 105.0 | 105.9 | 109.9 | 102.7 | 99.2 | 109.3 |
| 2021 | 109.2 | 104.9 | 116.0 | 116.4 | 105.1 | 115.0 |
| 2022 | 104.6 | 103.9 | 106.6 | 105.2 | 103.7 | 109.7 |

注：本表指数按可比价计算；其中 1952 年以 1949 年为 100。
Note: Indices of this table are calculated at constant prices. The index of 1952 is calculated with the index of 1949 equal to 100.

## 表 11.6 农林牧渔业总产值（2021－2022 年）
## GROSS OUTPUT VALUE OF FARMING, FORESTRY,ANIMAL HUSBANDRY AND FISHERY (2021-2022)

单位：万元 (10 000 yuan)

| 指标 | Item | 农林牧渔业总产值 Gross Output Value 2021 | 2022 | 指数 上年=100 Index Preceding Year=100 |
|---|---|---|---|---|
| **总计** | **Total** | **29356489** | **30684459** | **104.6** |
| 农业 | Farming | 17598909 | 18817834 | 103.9 |
| 谷物及其他作物 | Cereal and Other Crops | 4171212 | 4278199 | 101.8 |
| #谷物 | Cereal | 2591423 | 2595097 | |
| 豆类 | Beans | 229553 | 246769 | |
| 油料 | Oil-bearing Crops | 438996 | 498883 | |
| 烟草 | Tobacco | 135910 | 148864 | |
| 蔬菜园艺作物 | Vegetables and Gardening | 7902077 | 8404186 | 103.6 |
| #蔬菜（含菜用瓜） | Vegetables (including Melons as Vegetables) | 7320550 | 7807783 | |
| 花卉 | Flowers | 138896 | 133537 | |
| 水果、坚果、饮料和香料作物 | Fruits, Nuts, Drinks and Spices | 3822651 | 4162279 | 106.1 |
| #水果、坚果（含果用瓜） | Fruits and Nuts (including Melons as Fruits) | 3499522 | 3803916 | |
| 茶及其他饮料 | Tea and Other Drinks | 198353 | 215243 | |
| #茶 | Tea | 198353 | 206913 | |
| 中药材 | Traditional Chinese Medical Materials | 1702969 | 1973170 | 105.6 |
| 林业 | Forestry | 1681325 | 1764195 | 106.6 |
| 林木的培育和种植 | Forest Cultivation | 1485937 | 1552492 | 106.5 |
| #造林 | Afforestation | 863176 | 958399 | |
| 竹木采运 | Bamboo Felling and Transportation | 71598 | 132713 | 101.9 |
| 林产品 | Forest Products | 123790 | 141136 | 110.8 |
| 牧业 | Animal Husbandry | 8041545 | 8009449 | 105.2 |
| 牲畜饲养 | Livestock Raising | 1110194 | 1128269 | 102.2 |
| #牛 | Cattle | 623687 | 644871 | |
| 奶产品 | Milk Products | 15375 | 15975 | |
| 猪的饲养 | Hog Raising | 4390707 | 4134373 | 106.1 |
| 家禽饲养 | Poultry Raising | 2023642 | 2144673 | 104.2 |
| #禽蛋 | Poultry Eggs | 507340 | 592826 | |
| 其他畜牧业 | Others | 517003 | 602133 | 107.8 |
| #蚕茧 | Silkworm Cocoons | 43000 | 41302 | |
| 渔业 | Fishery | 1381704 | 1369934 | 103.7 |
| #内陆水域水产品 | Aquatic Products in Inland Water Areas | 1381704 | 1369934 | 103.7 |
| #养殖 | By Breeding | 1325937 | 1369934 | |
| #鱼类 | Fish | 1292818 | 1261873 | |
| 农林牧渔专业及辅助性活动 | Professional and Support Activities for Agriculture,Forestry,Animal Husbandry and Fishery | 653006 | 723047 | 109.7 |

注：本表数据绝对值按现价计算，中类指标指数按可比价计算，部分指标数据较上年变化较大系核算方法变化所致。
Note: The absolute figures in this table are calculated at current prices whereas the indices are calculated at constant prices.

# 表 11.7 农业生产条件(2021－2022 年)
## CONDITIONS OF AGRICULTURAL PRODUCTION (2021-2022)

| 指 标 | Item | 2021 | 2022 |
|---|---|---|---|
| **农业机械化情况** | **Agricultural Mechanization** | | |
| 农业机械总动力(万千瓦) | Total Agricultural Machinery Power (10 000 kw) | 1532 | 1566 |
| **农业主要能源及物耗** | **Main Agricultural Energy and Material Consumption** | | |
| 有效灌溉面积(万公顷) | Irrigated Area (10 000 hectare) | 66.53 | 67.65 |
| 化肥施用量(折纯量)(万吨) | Consumption of Chemical Fertilizer (net) (10 000 tons) | 89.05 | 88.74 |
| #氮　肥 | Nitrogenous Fertilizer | 42.56 | 42.12 |
| 磷　肥 | Phosphate Fertilizer | 15.46 | 15.35 |
| 钾　肥 | Potash Fertilizer | 5.16 | 5.16 |
| 复合肥 | Compound Fertilizer | 25.87 | 26.12 |
| 农用塑料薄膜使用量(万吨) | Consumption of Farm Plastic Film (10 000 tons) | 4.12 | 4.08 |
| #地膜使用量 | Consumption of Farm Plastic Film | 2.23 | 2.21 |
| 地膜覆盖面积(公顷) | Area Covered by Farm Plastic Film (hectare) | 231221 | 229279 |
| 农用柴油使用量(万吨) | Consumption of Diesel Oil (10 000 tons) | 21.25 | 21.27 |
| 农药使用量(万吨) | Consumption of Chemical Pesticides (10 000 tons) | 1.60 | 1.60 |

# 表 11.8 主要农作物播种面积及产量（2021 － 2022 年）
## SOWN AREA AND OUTPUT OF MAJOR FARM CROPS (2021-2022)

| 指 标 | Item | 播种面积（公顷）Sown Area (hectare) | | 总产量（吨）Total Output (ton) | | 单位产量（公斤/公顷）Yield Per Unit (kg/ha) | |
|---|---|---|---|---|---|---|---|
| | | 2021 | 2022 | 2021 | 2022 | 2021 | 2022 |
| **粮 食** | **Grain** | **2013191** | **2046710** | **10928403** | **10728378** | **5428** | **5242** |
| 谷 物 | Cereal | 1142658 | 1149885 | 7613831 | 7563913 | 6663 | 6578 |
| 稻 谷 | Rice | 658905 | 659186 | 4930492 | 4852410 | 7483 | 7361 |
| #中 稻 | Middle Rice | 658905 | 659186 | 4930492 | 4852410 | 7483 | 7361 |
| 小 麦 | Wheat | 18683 | 18853 | 61493 | 62780 | 3291 | 3330 |
| 玉 米 | Corn | 443766 | 447785 | 2545582 | 2563711 | 5736 | 5725 |
| 高 粱 | Sorghum | 16963 | 18724 | 67317 | 73805 | 3968 | 3942 |
| 其他谷物 | Other Cereal | 4341 | 5338 | 8947 | 11207 | 2061 | 2100 |
| 豆 类 | Beans | 203946 | 212433 | 421485 | 434472 | 2067 | 2045 |
| #大 豆 | Soybean | 99446 | 107384 | 205622 | 215894 | 2068 | 2010 |
| 薯 类 | Tubers | 666587 | 684393 | 2893087 | 2729993 | 4340 | 3989 |
| #马铃薯 | Potato | 328375 | 347868 | 1197953 | 1265972 | 3648 | 3639 |
| **油 料** | **Oil-bearing Crops** | **337983** | **346713** | **684791** | **708492** | **2026** | **2043** |
| #花 生 | Peanut | 63548 | 64267 | 142836 | 144196 | 2248 | 2244 |
| 油菜籽 | Rapeseed | 261497 | 269719 | 524582 | 547281 | 2006 | 2029 |
| 芝 麻 | Sesame Seed | 4118 | 4006 | 5017 | 4740 | 1218 | 1183 |
| **麻 类** | **Fiber Crops** | **1792** | **1657** | **3182** | **3008** | **1776** | **1815** |
| #苎 麻 | Ramie | 1784 | 1649 | 3166 | 2994 | 1775 | 1815 |
| 黄红麻 | Jute and Ambary Hemp | 6 | 6 | 14 | 13 | 2333 | 2294 |
| **糖 料（甘蔗）** | **Sugar Crops (sugarcane)** | **1863** | **1857** | **82802** | **83243** | **44445** | **44824** |
| **烟 叶** | **Tobacco** | **26988** | **28401** | **53192** | **55235** | **1971** | **1945** |
| #烤 烟 | Flue-cured Tobacco | 22075 | 23970 | 41490 | 44822 | 1880 | 1870 |
| **蔬菜、瓜果** | **Vegetables and Melons** | **818430** | **839535** | **22460466** | **23356054** | **27443** | **27820** |
| #蔬 菜（含菜用瓜） | Vegetables (including Melons as Vegetables) | 791378 | 812024 | 21843320 | 22723637 | 27602 | 27984 |

## 表 11.9 林牧渔业生产情况（2021－2022 年）
OUTPUT OF FORESTRY, ANIMAL HUSBANDRY AND FISHERY (2021-2022)

| 指 标 | Item | 2021 | 2022 |
|---|---|---|---|
| **林 业（公顷）** | **Forestry (hectare)** | | |
| 当年造林面积 | Increased Forest Area in Current Year | 131871 | 133463 |
| **牧 业** | **Animal Husbandry** | | |
| 年末生猪存栏头数（万头） | Number of Hogs (year-end, 10 000 heads) | 1179.83 | 1197.14 |
| 年内出栏肥猪头数（万头） | Number of Slaughtered Fattened Hogs (10 000 heads) | 1806.86 | 1904.43 |
| 年内出栏家禽（万只） | Number of Slaughtered Poultry (10 000 heads) | 24077.59 | 24238.85 |
| **渔 业（万亩）** | **Fishery (10 000 mu)** | | |
| 水产品养殖面积 | Cultured Areas of Aquatic Products | 126.53 | 127.88 |
| #池 塘 | Ponds | 74.55 | 74.78 |
| 水 库 | Reservoirs | 51.83 | 52.95 |

## 表 11.10 林牧渔业主要产品产量（2021－2022 年）
OUTPUT OF THE MAJOR PRODUCTS OF FORESTRY, ANIMAL HUSBANDRY AND FISHERY (2021-2022)

单位：吨 (ton)

| 指 标 | Item | 2021 | 2022 |
|---|---|---|---|
| 水 果 | Fruits | 5531813 | 5932844 |
| #柑 橘 | Citrus | 3378229 | 3635601 |
| 猪 肉 | Pork | 1420122 | 1499649 |
| 禽 肉 | Meat of Poultry | 367396 | 370785 |
| 蜂 蜜 | Honey | 22099 | 22272 |
| 水产品 | Aquatic Products | 545343 | 566303 |
| #养 殖 | Cultured Aquatic Products | 545343 | 566303 |
| 年末实有茶园面积（公顷） | Area of Tea Plantations (year-end) (hectare) | 54322 | 55705 |
| #本年采摘面积 | Picked Area in Current Year | 39970 | 41827 |
| 年末果园面积（公顷） | Area of Orchards (year-end) (hectare) | 355117 | 366183 |
| #梨 园 | Pear | 24476 | 24036 |
| #柑 橘 | Citrus | 225215 | 230878 |

# 主要统计指标解释

## 农林牧渔业总产值

指以货币表现的农、林、牧、渔业全部产品和对农林牧渔业生产活动进行的各种支持性服务活动的价值总量，它反映一定时期内农林牧渔业生产总规模和总成果。1993年以前农林牧渔业总产值包括农、林、牧、副、渔五业，从1993年起取消副业，将野生动物的捕猎划入牧业，野生植物采集和农民家庭兼营商品性工业划归农业。从2003年起，执行新的国民经济行业分类标准，农林牧渔业总产值中包括了农、林、牧、渔及农林牧渔服务业产值，2018年以后农林牧渔服务业产值改称农林牧渔专业及辅助性活动产值。农业中取消了家庭兼营商品性工业产值，将野生林产品的采集划归林业。第一、二、三次农业普查以后，根据农业普查结果，对农业、牧业、渔业产值进行了修订。2010年执行《统计用产品分类目录》，对2009年的农业、林业产值做了相应调整。

农林牧渔业总产值采用“产品法”进行计算，通常是按农、林、牧、渔业产品及其副产品的产量分别乘以各自单位产品价格求得；少数生产周期较长，当年没有产品或产品产量不易统计的，则采用间接方法匡算其产值；然后将四业产品产值及农林牧渔专业及辅助性活动产值相加即为农林牧渔业总产值。

## 粮食产量

指日历年度内生产的全部粮食数量。按收获季节包括夏收粮食、早稻和秋收粮食，按作物品种包括谷物、豆类和薯类。其产量计算方法：谷物按脱粒后的原粮计算，豆类按去豆荚后的干豆计算；薯类(包括甘薯和马铃薯，不包括芋头和木薯)1964年以前按每4公斤鲜薯折1公斤粮食计算，从1964年开始改为按5公斤鲜薯折1公斤粮食计算；城市郊区作为蔬菜的薯类(如马铃薯等)按鲜品计算，并且不作粮食统计。1989年以前全国粮食产量数据主要靠全面报表取得，1989年开始使用抽样调查数据。

## 油料产量

指全部油料作物的生产量。包括花生、油菜籽、芝麻、向日葵籽、胡麻籽（亚麻籽）和其他油料。不包括大豆、木本油料和野生油料。花生以带壳干花生计算。

## 水产品产量

指渔业（捕捞和养殖）生产活动的最终有效成果，包括全部海水和淡水鱼类、甲壳类（虾、蟹）、贝类、头足类、藻类和其他类渔业产品的最终产量。水产品产量是通过各级渔业主管部门逐级上报取得数据。1995年及以前，贝类中牡蛎按鲜肉计算；蚶、蛤、蛙按5斤鲜品折1斤计算。1996年以后则统一按鲜品计算。

## 猪、牛、羊、禽肉产量

指当年出栏并已屠宰、除去头蹄下水后带骨肉(即胴体重)的重量。1996年以前为全面统计并逐级上报数据。1996年第一次农业普查以后，根据普查结果，对畜牧业主要年报数据进行了修正。1999年，国家统计局在部分地区开展了猪、牛、羊、禽等主要畜禽品种的抽样调查，并用抽样数据作为国家定案数据使用。未开展抽样调查的地区，仍使用各级统计部门逐级上报数据。2008年，建立了主要畜禽监测调查制度，猪、牛、羊、禽等主要畜禽数据均以抽样调查数为法定数据。

## 期初(末)畜禽存栏头(只)数

指报告期初(末)饲养的大牲畜、猪、羊、家禽等畜禽的数量。数据上报方式及数据调整情况同猪、牛、羊、禽肉产量。

## 农作物播种面积

指日历年度内收获农作物在全部土地（耕地或非耕地）上的播种或移植面积。凡是本年内收获的农作物，无论是本年还是上年播种，都算为播种面积，但不包括本年播种，下年收获的农作物面积。

## 耕地灌溉面积

指具有一定的水源，地块比较平整，灌溉工程或设备已经配套，在一般年景下能够进行正常灌溉的耕地面积。在一般情况下，耕地灌溉面积应等于灌溉工

## 主要统计指标解释

程或设备已经配套，能够进行正常灌溉的水田和水浇地面积之和。它是反映我国农田水利建设的重要指标。

### ■ 农用化肥施用量

指本年内实际用于农业生产的化肥数量，包括氮肥、磷肥、钾肥和复合肥。化肥施用量要求按折纯量计算数量。折纯量是指把氮肥、磷肥、钾肥分别按含氮、含五氧化二磷、含氧化钾的百分之百成分进行折算后的数量。复合肥按其所含主要成分折算。公式为：

折纯量＝实物量 × 某种化肥有效成分含量的百分比

### ■ 农业机械总动力

指全部农业机械动力的额定功率之和。农业机械是指用于种植业、畜牧业、渔业、农产品初加工、农用运输和农田基本建设等活动的机械及设备。农机总动力按使用能源不同分为以下四部分：

柴油发动机动力：指全部柴油发动机额定功率之和；

汽油发动机动力：指全部汽油发动机额定功率之和；

电动机动力：指全部电动机（含潜水电泵的电动机）额定功率之和；

其他机械动力：指采用柴油、汽油、电力之外的其他能源，如水力、风力、煤炭、太阳能等动力机械功率之和。

# Explanatory Notes on Main Statistical Indicators

## Gross Output Value of Agriculture, Forestry, Animal Husbandry and Fishery

refers to the total value of products (expressed in monetary terms) of agriculture, forestry, animal husbandry and fishery, and total value of services in support of agriculture, forestry, animal husbandry and fishery activities. It reflects the total scale and results of agricultural production during a given period. Before 1993, the gross output value of agriculture, forestry, animal husbandry and fishery included agriculture, forestry, animal husbandry, sideline and fishery. Since 1993, the subdivision of sideline occupations has been cancelled, and the hunting of wild animals has been classified into animal husbandry, and the gathering of wild plants and commodity industry run by rural household have been included in farming. A new industrial classification of economic activities was introduced in 2003. Under the new classification, the gross output value of agriculture included the value of farming, forestry, animal husbandry, and fishery, and included value of services to agriculture, forestry, animal husbandry and fishery. In 2018, the output value of services to agriculture, forestry, animal husbandry and fishery was renamed the output value of professional and support activities in agriculture, forestry, animal husbandry and fishery, value of industrial output by rural households is not included in agriculture. According to the result of the first, second and third agriculture census, efforts were made to adjust the output value of agriculture, animal husbandry and fishery output. In line with the Classification of Products for Statistical Purposes implemented in 2010, relevant revisions were made on the output value of agriculture and forestry in 2009.

Gross output value of agriculture is calculated by product method, and is obtained by multiplying the output of each product or by-product by its price, resulting in the output value of each single item. For a small number of products, annual output of which is not available or difficult to get due to the long production (growing) process involved, the output value is estimated through an indirect approach. The sum of output values of all products of agriculture, forestry, animal husbandry and fishery and professional and support activities in agriculture, forestry, animal husbandry and fishery is then equal to the gross output value of agriculture.

## Grain Output

refers to the total output of grains produced within a calendar year. It includes summer crops, early rice and autumn crops by harvest seasons; and covers cereals, beans and tubers by type of crops. Output of cereals cover husked grain only. Output of beans refers to dry beans without pods. The output of tubers (sweet potatoes and potatoes, not including taros and cassava) are converted with the ratio of 4:1, i.e. 4 kilograms of fresh tubers were equivalent to 1 kilogram of grain before 1964. Since 1964 the ratio has been changed to 5:1. Tubers consumed as vegetables (such as potatoes) in cities and suburbs are calculated as fresh vegetables and their output is not included in the output of grain. Data on grain production before 1989 were obtained through the comprehensive statistical reporting system. Since 1989, data from sample surveys are used.

## Output of Oil-bearing Crops

refers to the total production of oil-bearing crops of various kinds, including peanuts (dry, in shell), rapeseeds, sesame, sunflower seeds, flax seeds, and other oil-bearing crops. Soybeans, oil-bearing woody plants, and wild oil-bearing crops are not included.

## Output of Aquatic Products

refers to final output actually yielded from fishing production (fishery and breeding), including all output of marine and freshwater fish, crustaceans (shrimps, crabs), shellfish, cephalopod, seaweed and other fishery

EXPLANATORY NOTES TO
MAJOR STATISTICAL INDICATORS

products. Data on output of aquatic products are reported by fishery agencies level by level. Before 1995, among the shellfish, oyster was counted as fresh meat; and 5 kilograms of ark shell, clams and frogs were equivalent to 1 kilogram of fresh aquatic products; they have all been counted as fresh aquatic products since 1996.

### □ Output of Pork, Beef, Mutton and Poultry

refers to the meat of slaughtered hogs, cattle, sheep and goats with head, feet, and offal taken away. Before 1996, data were obtained through bottom-up comprehensive reporting system. The first agricultural census of China in 1996 revealed some discrepancy between the production of animal products from the annual reports and that from the census. Efforts were made to adjust the output value of animal husbandry to make the figures from the annual reports consistent with the census data. Since 1999, the NBS conducted sample surveys in selected regions for the major animal husbandry products, such as hogs, cattle, sheep and goats and fowls, and the data from sample surveys are used as finalized national data. Production of other regions which are not covered by the sample survey is still reported by statistical agencies level by level. A monitoring and survey program was set up in 2008 on main livestock, and data on the main livestock such as hog, cattle, sheep and poultry from the sample survey became the official data.

### □ Number of Livestock or Poultry in Stock at Beginning/End of Period

refers to the total number of large animals, pigs, sheep, fowls, etc. raised at the beginning/end of the reference period. Data reporting system and data adjustment are the same as that in the output of pork, beef, mutton and poultry.

### □ Sown Area of Crops

refers to area of all land (cultivated or non-cultivated area) sown or transplanted with crops that are harvested within the calendar year. All crops harvested within the year are counted as sown area, regardless of being sown in this year or the previous year. Crops sown this year but will be harvested in the coming year are excluded.

### □ Irrigated Area of Cultivated Land

refers to area of land that are effectively irrigated, i.e. relatively level land, where there are water sources or complete sets of irrigation facilities to lift and move adequate water for irrigation purpose under normal conditions. Under normal situations, irrigated area of cultivated land is the sum of watered fields and irrigated fields where irrigation systems or equipment have been installed for regular irrigation purpose. It is an important indicator to reflect the farmland water conservancy construction in China.

### □ Consumption of Chemical Fertilizers in Agriculture

refers to the quantity of chemical fertilizers applied in agriculture in the year, including nitrogenous fertilizer, phosphate fertilizer, potash fertilizer, and compound fertilizer. The consumption of chemical fertilizers is calculated in terms of volume of effective components by means of converting the gross weight of the respective fertilizers into weight containing effective component (e.g. nitrogen content in nitrogenous fertilizer, phosphorous pentoxide contents in phosphate fertilizer, and potassium oxide contents in potash fertilizer). Compound fertilizer is converted in regard to its major components. The formula is:

Volume of effective component= physical quantity× effective component of certain chemical fertilizer (%)

### □ Total Power of Agricultural Machinery

refers to the total rated capacity of all agricultural machinery. Agricultural machinery refers to the machines and equipment which are used for activities of farming, animal husbandry, fishery, primary processing of agricultural products, agricultural transport and infrastructure construction of farmland. Total power of agricultural machinery is classified into 4 groups according to the energy used:

Diesel engine power refers to the total rated capacity of all diesel engines.

Gasoline engine power refers to the total rated

capacity of all gasoline engines.

Electric motor power refers to the total rated capacity of all electric motors (include submersible pump motors).

Other mechanical powers refer to the total mechanical capacity of machinery using other forms of energy apart from diesel, gasoline and electricity, such as hydro power, wind power, coal and solar energy.

Data are mainly from Ministry of Agriculture and Rural Affairs.

# 第十二章·工　业

## INDUSTRY

# 简要说明

## BRIEF INTRODUCTION

本章资料主要包括工业企业主要指标，规模以上（即指年主营业务收入2000万元及以上）工业企业单位数、主要经济指标和效益指标，国有控股工业企业的主要经济指标和效益指标，私营工业企业的主要经济指标和效益指标，内资工业企业的主要经济指标和效益指标，外商投资和港澳台投资企业的主要经济指标和效益指标，大中型工业企业的主要经济指标和效益指标，主要工业产品产量以及占全国当年产量的比重。本章资料由市统计局工业处整理提供。

The data in this chapter cover the main indicators of industrial enterprises; the number, main economic indicators and benefit indicators of enterprises above designated size (enterprises with annual revenue from principal business 20 million yuan and above); the main economic indicators and benefit indicators of state-holding industrial enterprises, private industrial enterprises, domestic-funded industrial enterprises, industrial enterprises with Hong Kong, Macao, Taiwan and foreign funds and large and medium-sized industrial enterprises; the output of major industrial products and their percentage to nation total in this year. The data in this chapter are sorted and provided by Division of Industry Statistics, Chongqing Municipal Bureau of Statistics.

# 表 12.1 工业企业主要指标（1978 – 2022 年）
## MAJOR INDICATORS OF INDUSTRIAL ENTERPRISES (1978-2022)

单位：万元 (10 000 yuan)

| 年 份<br>Year | 单位数<br>（个）<br>Number of Enterprises<br>(unit) | 从业人员平均人数<br>（人）<br>Average Employment<br>(person) | 工业总产值<br>Industrial Gross Output Value | |
|---|---|---|---|---|
| | | | 绝对值<br>Value | 指 数<br>（上年 =100）<br>Index Preceding Year=100 |
| 1978 | 8037 | 951217 | 643444 | 100.0 |
| 1980 | 10963 | 998963 | 772307 | 104.6 |
| 1985 | 9924 | 1251649 | 1408126 | 117.2 |
| 1986 | 12454 | 1473491 | 1604215 | 104.1 |
| 1987 | 11556 | 1511086 | 1921043 | 112.4 |
| 1988 | 11303 | 1552189 | 2529674 | 116.1 |
| 1989 | 10976 | 1587712 | 2991130 | 102.4 |
| 1990 | 10763 | 1610473 | 2993490 | 100.7 |
| 1991 | 10780 | 1652984 | 3424558 | 111.8 |
| 1992 | 9693 | 1662144 | 4191279 | 116.3 |
| 1993 | 9083 | 1752822 | 5847377 | 118.2 |
| 1994 | 9713 | 1692108 | 7185418 | 115.4 |
| 1995 | 11474 | 1724173 | 7651109 | 115.2 |
| 1996 | 2332 | 1474400 | 7304148 | |
| 1997 | 2210 | 1428600 | 7947952 | 114.4 |
| 1998 | 2000 | 1164200 | 7667894 | 100.7 |
| 1999 | 1975 | 1004400 | 8585525 | 118.9 |
| 2000 | 2040 | 907900 | 9623226 | 113.6 |
| 2001 | 2054 | 841900 | 10728325 | 115.5 |
| 2002 | 2072 | 820103 | 12283741 | 119.8 |
| 2003 | 2243 | 843341 | 15889928 | 126.7 |
| 2004 | 2634 | 900546 | 21427261 | 129.9 |
| 2005 | 2946 | 924204 | 25258684 | 118.6 |
| 2006 | 3214 | 968440 | 32142340 | 127.4 |
| 2007 | 3942 | 1082675 | 43632489 | 133.6 |
| 2008 | 6119 | 1321310 | 57558984 | 129.3 |
| 2009 | 6412 | 1372758 | 67729015 | 115.2 |
| 2010 | 7130 | 1465587 | 91435532 | 128.4 |
| 2011 | 4778 | 1457566 | 118470581 | 128.2 |
| 2012 | 4985 | 1549702 | 130951235 | 118.0 |
| 2013 | 5559 | 1694189 | 157854080 | 114.5 |
| 2014 | 6158 | 1771250 | 187823331 | 114.6 |
| 2015 | 6608 | 1819621 | 214000118 | 112.4 |
| 2016 | 6782 | 1852580 | 239065803 | 110.2 |
| 2017 | 6684 | 1690124 | 211732144 | 114.4 |
| 2018 | 6437 | 1578325 | 206470086 | 102.9 |
| 2019 | 6694 | 1513645 | 212956473 | 106.8 |
| 2020 | 6938 | 1521512 | 227955096 | 106.7 |
| 2021 | 7314 | 1533890 | 264935390 | 115.8 |
| 2022 | 7617 | 1541951 | 258270588 | 104.7 |

注：1）本表统计口径 1996 年以前为全部独立核算工业企业，1996-2006 年为全部国有及规模以上（即年主营业务收入在 500 万元及以上）非国有工业企业，2007 年为规模以上（即年主营业务收入在 500 万元及以上）工业企业 ,2011 年为规模以上（即年主营业务收入在 2000 万元及以上）工业企业（下表同）。
2）工业总产值的绝对值按现价计算。由于工业统计制度变更，工业总产值指数 2003 年及以前按可比价计算，2004 年起按现价计算。
3）2018 年同期总产值、主营业务收入、利润总额及产品产量数据根据有关制度规定进行了修订，增速按照可比口径计算。

Note: a) The statistic scope of this table is all the industrial enterprises with independent accounting system before 1996, is all the state-owned industrial enterprises and non-state-owned industrial enterprises over designated size (with annual revenue from principal business 5 million yuan and above) from 1996 to 2006, and is the industrial enterprises over designated size (with annual revenue from principal business 5 million yuan and above) in 2007 and is the industrial enterprises over designated size (with annual revenue from principal business 20 million yuan and above) in 2011 (the same below).
b) Gross output value of industry are calculated at current prices. As industry statistic system has been changed, the index of industrial gross output value in 2003 and previous years is calculated at constant prices, while the index is calculated at current prices since 2004.
c) Since 2018, gross output value, revenue from principal business, total pre-tax profits and output of products are adjusted in accordance with related regulations, and the growth rate are calculated by comparable scope.

**表 12.1 续表 continued**

单位：万元 (10 000 yuan)

| 年 份<br>Year | 年末固定资产<br>Year-end Fixed Assets | | 流动资产合计<br>Total Circulating Assets | 主营业务收入<br>Revenue from Principal Business | 利税总额<br>Total Pre-tax Profits | 利润总额<br>Total Profits |
|---|---|---|---|---|---|---|
| | 原 值<br>Original Value | 净 值<br>Net Value | | | | |
| 1978 | 706016 | 475301 | 298093 | 595593 | 119300 | |
| 1980 | 823370 | 540178 | 329897 | 708120 | 146213 | |
| 1985 | 1339800 | 923111 | 604983 | 1449426 | 260677 | |
| 1986 | 1445859 | 970019 | 743986 | 1559353 | 225749 | |
| 1987 | 1635303 | 1135872 | 908572 | 1897962 | 251220 | |
| 1988 | 1830786 | 1254850 | 1062157 | 2472560 | 358610 | |
| 1989 | 2063326 | 1405200 | 1441939 | 2734475 | 365348 | |
| 1990 | 2314886 | 1490850 | 1942657 | 2782262 | 253309 | |
| 1991 | 2585930 | 1647544 | 2418353 | 3338105 | 291455 | |
| 1992 | 2947902 | 1784094 | 2852708 | 4167995 | 365134 | |
| 1993 | 3424857 | 2106423 | 3484050 | 6124846 | 551046 | |
| 1994 | 4953046 | 2967592 | 4631636 | 6294911 | 573144 | |
| 1995 | 7307273 | 4057468 | 5702467 | 7524836 | 580345 | |
| 1996 | 7708153 | 5398622 | 5749079 | 7113430 | 480449 | -49429 |
| 1997 | 8578673 | 5952377 | 6959065 | 7981695 | 460736 | -116702 |
| 1998 | 9866758 | 6940364 | 7202796 | 7809127 | 393220 | -193078 |
| 1999 | 10840971 | 7604150 | 7733524 | 8546131 | 572648 | -67491 |
| 2000 | 11515782 | 7848443 | 8157646 | 9593576 | 855670 | 156449 |
| 2001 | 12056356 | 7958216 | 8874861 | 10732455 | 1016889 | 238170 |
| 2002 | 12730167 | 8282507 | 9228472 | 12357157 | 1320260 | 405426 |
| 2003 | 13424490 | 8576299 | 10305605 | 15950727 | 1910901 | 859689 |
| 2004 | 14970250 | 9738481 | 11641381 | 21088433 | 2420163 | 1155898 |
| 2005 | 16779752 | 11001178 | 13571979 | 25151726 | 2564825 | 1155912 |
| 2006 | 20266728 | 13551444 | 15484263 | 32008042 | 3192103 | 1557631 |
| 2007 | 24067348 | 16421036 | 18541937 | 42629860 | 5025623 | 2405387 |
| 2008 | 30254424 | 20829025 | 24807777 | 56676087 | 6017115 | 3086786 |
| 2009 | 34109428 | 22757818 | 28630140 | 66247114 | 7105030 | 3560249 |
| 2010 | 44634155 | 29639590 | 36084780 | 90390303 | 10118841 | 5185939 |
| 2011 | 50234507 | 30341715 | 45089210 | 113823442 | 11643029 | 6603471 |
| 2012 | 58315944 | 36101279 | 53572842 | 128803222 | 12244123 | 6453886 |
| 2013 | 72786258 | 46301592 | 62293267 | 155817793 | 17342546 | 9076025 |
| 2014 | 85835043 | 54276237 | 71747271 | 186886282 | 22189470 | 12296456 |
| 2015 | 103933391 | 65401572 | 80949784 | 209022428 | 24492098 | 14118589 |
| 2016 | 122053328 | 80001548 | 92379294 | 234670318 | 27647239 | 16483625 |
| 2017 | 115697854 | 72411733 | 92886887 | 207724101 | 24741003 | 15018747 |
| 2018 | 119512666 | 69263522 | 94867527 | 202320580 | 22285896 | 13310598 |
| 2019 | 123535800 | 70277571 | 103132661 | 210472464 | 20489730 | 12103190 |
| 2020 | 131337615 | 68817146 | 117530672 | 224927871 | 22634701 | 15065319 |
| 2021 | 138128570 | 69860124 | 135039402 | 268302513 | 29419650 | 21337946 |
| 2022 | 150123053 | 76165962 | 146531965 | 264172780 | 26325140 | 18296766 |

# 表 12.2 主要工业产品产量（1978 – 2022 年）
## OUTPUT OF MAJOR INDUSTRIAL PRODUCTS (1978-2022)

| 年 份<br>Year | 天然气<br>（亿立方米）<br>Natural Gas<br>(100 million cum) | 发电量<br>（亿千瓦时）<br>Electricity<br>(100 million kwh) | 钢 材<br>（万吨）<br>Steel Products<br>(10 000 tons) | 铝 材<br>（万吨）<br>Aluminum Products<br>(10 000 tons) | 水 泥<br>（万吨）<br>Cement<br>(10 000 tons) | 汽 车<br>（万辆）<br>Motor Vehicles<br>(10 000 units) | #轿 车<br>（万辆）<br>Cars<br>(10 000 units) | 摩托车<br>（万辆）<br>Motorcycles<br>(10 000 units) |
|---|---|---|---|---|---|---|---|---|
| 1978 | 0.09 | 29.60 | 73.09 | 1.47 | 96.14 | 0.16 | | |
| 1980 | 15.78 | 33.32 | 76.52 | 2.27 | 129.10 | 0.23 | | 0.27 |
| 1985 | 24.47 | 36.67 | 86.35 | 4.50 | 262.78 | 0.89 | | 47.18 |
| 1986 | 25.88 | 41.96 | 94.99 | 4.55 | 269.20 | 0.61 | | 31.94 |
| 1987 | 28.39 | 54.73 | 111.36 | 5.00 | 308.29 | 0.90 | | 27.14 |
| 1988 | 29.44 | 66.38 | 121.06 | 5.01 | 353.43 | 1.66 | | 44.47 |
| 1989 | 31.96 | 72.64 | 102.59 | 4.99 | 345.39 | 2.02 | | 36.85 |
| 1990 | 34.59 | 73.75 | 109.61 | 3.97 | 351.85 | 2.18 | | 38.22 |
| 1991 | 35.86 | 84.05 | 105.67 | 5.51 | 428.56 | 3.04 | | 48.48 |
| 1992 | 36.44 | 91.95 | 112.24 | 5.55 | 517.31 | 4.56 | | 69.37 |
| 1993 | 37.14 | 118.41 | 162.74 | 5.79 | 562.32 | 6.82 | | 120.38 |
| 1994 | 41.87 | 124.36 | 130.74 | 6.19 | 642.62 | 8.77 | | 170.23 |
| 1995 | 45.00 | 127.62 | 120.68 | 5.93 | 820.57 | 11.47 | | 220.17 |
| 1996 | 26.10 | 128.73 | 117.55 | 7.36 | 648.76 | 12.41 | 1.34 | 177.36 |
| 1997 | 30.69 | 139.88 | 116.08 | 9.31 | 862.10 | 16.07 | 2.89 | 177.04 |
| 1998 | 33.24 | 158.67 | 131.01 | 10.62 | 1173.59 | 15.74 | 3.56 | 126.90 |
| 1999 | 34.74 | 158.27 | 135.10 | 12.11 | 1197.60 | 21.85 | 4.46 | 174.93 |
| 2000 | 38.98 | 167.90 | 156.98 | 13.98 | 1402.78 | 24.59 | 4.82 | 191.07 |
| 2001 | 41.88 | 170.41 | 161.42 | 16.82 | 1511.18 | 24.38 | 4.31 | 253.53 |
| 2002 | 45.41 | 184.75 | 201.48 | 19.94 | 1679.52 | 33.13 | 6.78 | 323.42 |
| 2003 | 47.29 | 188.64 | 235.24 | 21.60 | 1927.00 | 40.45 | 12.06 | 441.32 |
| 2004 | 51.57 | 232.82 | 288.10 | 26.23 | 1906.23 | 42.89 | 15.73 | 473.07 |
| 2005 | 57.09 | 234.03 | 294.70 | 39.36 | 2100.69 | 42.15 | 15.33 | 420.84 |
| 2006 | 70.88 | 275.44 | 382.87 | 66.41 | 2533.84 | 51.99 | 26.30 | 534.60 |
| 2007 | 71.11 | 325.22 | 436.57 | 81.13 | 2819.92 | 70.80 | 41.80 | 638.25 |
| 2008 | 79.50 | 396.64 | 487.20 | 79.76 | 3230.51 | 76.64 | 40.72 | 774.90 |
| 2009 | 75.70 | 428.26 | 477.44 | 75.15 | 3610.99 | 118.65 | 63.30 | 761.74 |
| 2010 | 67.48 | 456.71 | 699.91 | 102.79 | 4598.04 | 161.58 | 85.17 | 849.23 |
| 2011 | 62.94 | 529.57 | 948.17 | 134.45 | 4935.15 | 172.20 | 93.67 | 879.59 |
| 2012 | 55.76 | 536.53 | 1150.22 | 94.41 | 5499.59 | 184.46 | 102.40 | 877.51 |
| 2013 | 50.91 | 586.13 | 1290.55 | 109.79 | 6120.40 | 215.06 | 108.14 | 810.94 |
| 2014 | 48.05 | 644.50 | 1323.45 | 133.41 | 6666.61 | 262.89 | 111.32 | 844.62 |
| 2015 | 69.31 | 644.64 | 1411.46 | 171.37 | 6798.83 | 304.51 | 108.79 | 841.64 |
| 2016 | 96.45 | 670.81 | 1234.22 | 216.18 | 6781.59 | 315.62 | 97.95 | 787.66 |
| 2017 | 111.31 | 690.51 | 917.25 | 188.36 | 6370.93 | 299.82 | 84.94 | 595.69 |
| 2018 | 106.76 | 772.07 | 1208.65 | 197.78 | 6577.01 | 172.07 | 45.17 | 456.66 |
| 2019 | 110.53 | 761.65 | 1136.45 | 211.50 | 6752.88 | 138.30 | 26.52 | 407.30 |
| 2020 | 130.04 | 779.20 | 1309.95 | 219.61 | 6505.23 | 158.00 | 28.78 | 489.05 |
| 2021 | 139.55 | 930.94 | 1310.46 | 217.72 | 6232.94 | 199.80 | 39.57 | 438.39 |
| 2022 | 141.45 | 997.84 | 1690.59 | 238.64 | 5316.55 | 209.18 | 54.86 | 448.88 |

**表 12.2 续表 continued**

| 年 份 Year | 微型计算机设备（万台） Computers (10 000 sets) | 打印机（万台） Marking Machine (10 000 sets) | 移动通信手持机（手机）（万台） Mobile Telephones (10 000 sets) | 维纶纤维（万吨） PVA Fiber (10 000 tons) | 硫 酸（万吨） Sulphuric Acid (10 000 tons) | 啤 酒（万千升） Beer (10 000 kiloliters) | 卷 烟（亿支） Cigarettes (100 million pieces) | 农用化肥（万吨） Chemical Fertilizer (10 000 tons) |
|---|---|---|---|---|---|---|---|---|
| 1978 | | | | | 12.76 | | 87.70 | 20.23 |
| 1980 | | | | | 15.85 | | 115.75 | 13.10 |
| 1985 | | | | | 15.09 | 3.47 | 246.70 | 15.23 |
| 1986 | | | | | 20.86 | 4.16 | 314.90 | 17.28 |
| 1987 | | | | | 23.25 | 5.18 | 346.95 | 21.70 |
| 1988 | | | | | 25.31 | 6.26 | 355.65 | 21.55 |
| 1989 | | | | | 27.33 | 5.90 | 356.20 | 21.60 |
| 1990 | | | | | 25.24 | 5.91 | 357.85 | 24.58 |
| 1991 | | | | | 33.10 | 6.67 | 368.85 | 28.24 |
| 1992 | | | | | 34.28 | 7.74 | 439.10 | 28.86 |
| 1993 | | | | | 25.96 | 15.61 | 437.10 | 31.73 |
| 1994 | | | | | 25.31 | 16.69 | 430.65 | 35.59 |
| 1995 | | | | | 48.84 | 18.89 | 502.25 | 54.37 |
| 1996 | | | | 1.71 | 51.29 | 28.54 | 453.91 | 78.97 |
| 1997 | | | | 1.23 | 52.00 | 40.05 | 507.38 | 66.07 |
| 1998 | | | | 0.90 | 59.47 | 50.66 | 369.35 | 73.40 |
| 1999 | | | | 0.63 | 61.83 | 50.81 | 482.85 | 74.27 |
| 2000 | | | | 0.77 | 50.65 | 50.42 | 343.50 | 72.26 |
| 2001 | | | | 1.03 | 65.77 | 39.91 | 338.50 | 77.57 |
| 2002 | | | | 1.11 | 85.64 | 41.36 | 343.80 | 82.53 |
| 2003 | | | | 1.18 | 99.18 | 44.42 | 387.50 | 89.97 |
| 2004 | | | | 1.30 | 135.51 | 46.21 | 386.32 | 104.22 |
| 2005 | | | | 1.56 | 150.08 | 53.87 | 396.08 | 121.89 |
| 2006 | | | | 1.52 | 190.44 | 64.73 | 406.00 | 127.82 |
| 2007 | | | | 1.57 | 223.78 | 76.49 | 426.00 | 154.20 |
| 2008 | | | | 1.47 | 172.31 | 68.01 | 451.00 | 127.06 |
| 2009 | | | 374.93 | 1.23 | 202.29 | 72.77 | 476.00 | 152.00 |
| 2010 | 193.43 | | 650.26 | 1.26 | 222.00 | 75.20 | 501.00 | 181.49 |
| 2011 | 2547.82 | | 592.48 | 1.55 | 176.76 | 77.31 | 516.00 | 169.52 |
| 2012 | 4160.88 | 901.35 | 1095.76 | 1.41 | 221.54 | 77.23 | 551.00 | 206.63 |
| 2013 | 5593.34 | 1943.69 | 3695.78 | 1.79 | 209.35 | 80.04 | 571.00 | 204.33 |
| 2014 | 6446.78 | 1616.29 | 9418.24 | 1.62 | 202.83 | 73.72 | 576.00 | 213.99 |
| 2015 | 6180.79 | 1447.71 | 17605.08 | 1.34 | 204.16 | 76.71 | 546.50 | 214.85 |
| 2016 | 6764.65 | 1374.62 | 28708.36 | 1.83 | 193.66 | 76.09 | 440.40 | 177.44 |
| 2017 | 6619.78 | 1450.93 | 23732.52 | 2.05 | 185.64 | 78.95 | 421.50 | 145.95 |
| 2018 | 6987.52 | 1589.48 | 18424.48 | 1.98 | 171.04 | 70.61 | 520.00 | 147.16 |
| 2019 | 7614.25 | 1365.83 | 17431.86 | 1.18 | 161.39 | 67.17 | 539.50 | 81.62 |
| 2020 | 9130.26 | 513.12 | 13450.47 | 0.89 | 59.36 | 65.54 | 557.50 | 162.90 |
| 2021 | 10730.36 | 114.43 | 11158.33 | 1.26 | 66.38 | 80.40 | 569.52 | 158.91 |
| 2022 | 8631.92 | 102.43 | 7448.51 | 0.88 | 93.46 | 80.75 | 569.55 | 166.16 |

# 表 12.3 工业企业经济效益指标（1992－2022 年）
## INDICATORS ON ECONOMIC BENEFIT OF INDUSTRIAL ENTERPRISES (1992-2022)

单位：% (%)

| 年 份<br>Year | 经济效益综合指数<br>Comprehensive Index of Economic Benefits | 总资产贡献率<br>Ratio of Total Assets to Industrial Output Value | 资本保值增值率<br>Ratio of Assets Appreciation YOY | 资产负债率<br>Asset-Liability Ratio |
|---|---|---|---|---|
| 1992 | 76.2 | | | |
| 1993 | 84.6 | | | |
| 1994 | 83.9 | | | |
| 1995 | 73.0 | | | |
| 1996 | 63.8 | 2.8 | 125.7 | 68.6 |
| 1997 | 60.3 | 2.7 | 113.9 | 68.4 |
| 1998 | 57.3 | 5.0 | 103.0 | 68.3 |
| 1999 | 67.7 | 5.5 | 101.4 | 67.1 |
| 2000 | 87.1 | 6.3 | 112.1 | 64.8 |
| 2001 | 95.2 | 6.9 | 108.3 | 62.7 |
| 2002 | 109.8 | 7.8 | 120.7 | 61.3 |
| 2003 | 129.7 | 9.9 | 115.8 | 60.8 |
| 2004 | 140.9 | 10.6 | 120.2 | 60.8 |
| 2005 | 139.4 | 10.0 | 116.2 | 59.7 |
| 2006 | 153.7 | 10.5 | 114.4 | 59.8 |
| 2007 | 187.7 | 12.6 | 118.2 | 59.7 |
| 2008 | 204.0 | 12.2 | 117.6 | 60.0 |
| 2009 | 204.4 | 12.1 | 114.6 | 60.3 |
| 2010 | 226.0 | 13.6 | 125.0 | 60.3 |
| 2011 | 244.1 | 13.7 | 120.5 | 60.7 |
| 2012 | 262.5 | 12.6 | 121.1 | 63.0 |
| 2013 | 254.1 | 14.2 | 118.0 | 63.8 |
| 2014 | 284.9 | 15.4 | 115.8 | 62.4 |
| 2015 | | 14.9 | 112.5 | 61.9 |
| 2016 | | 14.7 | 112.7 | 61.2 |
| 2017 | | 13.4 | 114.2 | 58.8 |
| 2018 | | 11.9 | 106.5 | 57.1 |
| 2019 | | 10.3 | 107.8 | 56.3 |
| 2020 | | 10.3 | 107.7 | 56.4 |
| 2021 | | 11.9 | 109.6 | 55.8 |
| 2022 | | 9.9 | 107.1 | 57.0 |

**表 12.3 续表 continued**

单位：% (%)

| 年 份<br>Year | 流动资产周转率（次）<br>Turnover Ratio of Circulating Assets (time) | 成本费用利润率<br>Ratio of Profits to Cost | 全员劳动生产率（元/人年）<br>Overall Labor Productivity (yuan/person-year) | 产品销售率<br>Sales as Percentage of Output |
|---|---|---|---|---|
| 1992 | 1.4 | 3.2 | 7296 | 97.0 |
| 1993 | 1.6 | 3.1 | 10758 | 97.1 |
| 1994 | 1.4 | 2.7 | 12638 | 96.4 |
| 1995 | 1.2 | 0.7 | 11804 | 96.3 |
| 1996 | 1.3 | -1.2 | 13546 | 96.5 |
| 1997 | 1.2 | -1.8 | 14972 | 95.6 |
| 1998 | 1.1 | -2.4 | 16690 | 97.2 |
| 1999 | 1.1 | -1.1 | 23385 | 97.5 |
| 2000 | 1.2 | 1.7 | 31081 | 99.1 |
| 2001 | 1.2 | 2.3 | 37750 | 97.9 |
| 2002 | 1.3 | 3.4 | 46464 | 98.1 |
| 2003 | 1.5 | 5.7 | 55957 | 97.8 |
| 2004 | 1.8 | 5.8 | 66148 | 99.9 |
| 2005 | 1.9 | 4.9 | 77511 | 98.8 |
| 2006 | 2.1 | 5.2 | 87750 | 98.4 |
| 2007 | 2.3 | 6.1 | 127993 | 97.1 |
| 2008 | 2.4 | 5.8 | 156167 | 98.0 |
| 2009 | 2.3 | 5.8 | 159484 | 98.3 |
| 2010 | 2.5 | 6.1 | 183031 | 98.1 |
| 2011 | 2.6 | 6.0 | 213463 | 97.4 |
| 2012 | 2.4 | 5.4 | 223843 | 97.8 |
| 2013 | 2.5 | 6.2 | 230218 | 98.0 |
| 2014 | 2.7 | 7.0 | 270083 | 98.2 |
| 2015 | 2.6 | 7.2 | 297050 | 97.9 |
| 2016 | 2.6 | 7.5 | 300204 | 98.3 |
| 2017 | 2.3 | 7.7 | 318885 | 98.0 |
| 2018 | 2.2 | 7.0 | 330180 | 98.2 |
| 2019 | 2.1 | 6.2 | 351562 | 97.6 |
| 2020 | 2.0 | 7.2 | 370814 | 97.6 |
| 2021 | 2.0 | 8.6 | 418826 | 98.9 |
| 2022 | 1.9 | 7.5 | 457818 | 97.5 |

注：1）经济效益综合指数 1997 年前由资金利税率、增加值率、流动资产周转率、成本费用利润率、全员劳动生产率、产品销售率等六项指标构成，从 1997 年起由总资产贡献率、资本保值增值率、资产负债率、流动资产周转率、成本费用利润率、全员劳动生产率、产品销售率等七项指标构成。

2）由于部分指标无法取得，因此 2008 年资本保值增值率、全员劳动生产率采用 2008 年 12 月快报数代替，其余指标均取自 2008 年经济普查数。

Note: a) Comprehensive index of economic benefits before 1997 are composed of 6 items, namely ratio of pretax profits to total industrial assets, ratio of value-added to gross industrial output value, turnover ratio of circulating assets, ratio of profits to cost, overall labor productivity and sales as percentage of output, and since 1997 are composed of 7 items, namely ratio of total assets to industrial output value, ratio of ssets appreciation YOY, asset-liability ratio, turnover ratio of circulating assets, ratio of profits to cost, overall labor productivity and sales as percentage of output.

b) Because some of the indices are not available, the index of industrial gross output value, value-added of industry and its index in 2008 are replaced by the accumulated value in December 2008, and other indices are the data from the census of economy in 2008.

# 表 12.4 规模以上工业企业单位数（2021 － 2022 年）
## NUMBER OF INDUSTRIAL ENTERPRISES ABOVE DESIGNATED SIZE (2021-2022)

单位：个 (unit)

| 指　标 | Item | 2021 | 2022 |
|---|---|---|---|
| **总　计** | **Total** | **7314** | **7617** |
| #国有控股企业 | State-holding Enterprises | 616 | 648 |
| #亏损企业 | Loss-generating Enterprises | 819 | 1317 |
| **按登记注册类型分** | **By Status of Registration** | | |
| 内资企业 | Domestic-funded Enterprises | 6889 | 7197 |
| 国有企业 | State-owned Enterprises | 64 | 69 |
| 集体企业 | Collective-owned Enterprises | 13 | 12 |
| 股份合作企业 | Cooperative Share Holding Enterprises | 11 | 8 |
| 国有联营 | State Joint Ownership Enterprises | 1 | 1 |
| 集体联营 | Collective Joint Ownership Enterprises | | 1 |
| 国有与集体联营 | Joint State-Collective Enterprises | | |
| 其他联营 | Other Joint Ownership Enterprises | | |
| 国有独资公司 | Solely State-funded Corporations | 148 | 150 |
| 其他有限责任公司 | Other Limited Liability Corporations | 752 | 741 |
| 股份有限公司 | Share-holding Corporations Ltd. | 94 | 90 |
| 私营独资 | Solely Private-funded Enterprises | 140 | 136 |
| 私营合作 | Cooperative Private Enterprises | 15 | 14 |
| 私营有限责任公司 | Private Limited Liability Corporations | 5426 | 5744 |
| 私营股份有限公司 | Private Share-holding Corporations Ltd. | 223 | 230 |
| 其他内资 | Other Enterprises | 2 | 1 |
| 港澳台商投资企业 | Enterprises Funded by Hong Kong, Macao and Taiwan | 129 | 125 |
| 合资经营 | Joint-ventures | 47 | 44 |
| 合作经营 | Cooperative Enterprises | | |
| 独　资 | Enterprises with Sole Investment | 76 | 76 |
| 投资股份有限公司 | Share-holding Corporations Ltd. | 4 | 4 |
| 其　他 | Others | 2 | 1 |
| 外商投资企业 | Foreign-funded Enterprises | 296 | 295 |
| 中外合资经营 | Joint-ventures | 133 | 125 |
| 中外合作经营 | Cooperative Enterprises | 5 | 5 |
| 外资企业 | Enterprises with Sole Investment | 149 | 153 |
| 外商投资股份有限公司 | Share-holding Corporations Ltd. | 6 | 5 |
| 其　他 | Others | 3 | 7 |
| **按轻重工业分** | **By Light and Heavy Industries** | | |
| 轻工业 | Light Industry | 2145 | 2250 |
| 重工业 | Heavy Industry | 5169 | 5367 |
| **按企业规模分** | **By Size** | | |
| 大型企业 | Large | 173 | 179 |
| 中型企业 | Medium | 882 | 832 |
| 小型微型企业 | Small&Mini | 6259 | 6606 |

## 表 12.5 规模以上工业企业主要产品产量占全国的比重（2022 年）
OUTPUT OF MAJOR INDUSTRIAL PRODUCTS OF INDUSTRIA ENTERPRISES ABOVE DESIGNATED SIZED AS PERCENTAGE OF NATION TOTAL (2022)

| 产 品 | Products | 全 国<br>Nation Total | 重 庆<br>Chongqing | 重庆占全国比重（%）<br>Chongqing as % of Nation Total |
|---|---|---|---|---|
| 布（亿米） | Cloth (100 million m) | 367.50 | 2.83 | 0.8 |
| 原 盐（万吨） | Salt (10 000 tons) | 4986.40 | 196.18 | 3.9 |
| 卷 烟（亿支） | Cigarettes (100 million pieces) | 24321.50 | 569.55 | 2.3 |
| 白 酒（万千升） | Liquor (10 000 kiloliters) | 671.20 | 11.50 | 1.7 |
| 啤 酒（万千升） | Beer (10 000 kiloliters) | 3568.70 | 80.75 | 2.3 |
| 饮 料（万吨） | Soft Beverage (10 000 tons) | 18140.80 | 203.41 | 1.1 |
| 乳制品（万吨） | Dairy Products (10 000 tons) | 3117.70 | 25.03 | 0.8 |
| 发电量（亿千瓦小时） | Electricity (100 million kwh) | 83886.30 | 997.84 | 1.2 |
| 天然气（亿立方米） | Natural Gas (100 million cu.m) | 2177.90 | 141.45 | 6.5 |
| 生 铁（万吨） | Pig Iron (10 000 tons) | 86382.80 | 723.00 | 0.8 |
| 粗 钢（万吨） | Crude Steel (10 000 tons) | 101300.30 | 975.10 | 1.0 |
| 钢 材（万吨） | Steel Products (10 000 tons) | 134033.50 | 1690.59 | 1.3 |
| 铝 材（万吨） | Aluminum Products (10 000 tons) | 6221.60 | 238.64 | 3.8 |
| 水 泥（万吨） | Cement (10 000 tons) | 211794.90 | 5316.55 | 2.5 |
| 硫 酸（万吨） | Sulphuric Acid (10 000 tons) | 9504.60 | 93.46 | 1.0 |
| 纯 碱（万吨） | Soda Ash (10 000 tons) | 2920.20 | 120.89 | 4.1 |
| 烧 碱（万吨） | Caustic Soda (10 000 tons) | 3980.50 | 36.99 | 0.9 |
| 农用化学肥料（万吨） | Chemical Fertilizer (10 000 tons) | 5471.90 | 166.16 | 3.0 |
| 中成药（万吨） | Traditional Chinese Medicine (10 000 tons) | 227.70 | 7.53 | 3.3 |
| 汽 车（万辆） | Motor Vehicles (10 000 units) | 2747.60 | 209.18 | 7.6 |
| #轿 车 | Cars | 1046.80 | 54.86 | 5.2 |
| 微型计算机设备（万台） | Microcomputers (10 000 sets) | 43418.20 | 8631.92 | 19.9 |
| 移动通信手持机（手机）(万台) | Mobile Telephone (10 000 sets) | 156080.00 | 7448.51 | 4.8 |

# 表 12.6 规模以上工业企业主要经济指标（2022 年）
# MAIN ECONOMIC INDICATORS OF INDUSTRIAL ENTERPRISES ABOVE DESIGNATED SIZE (2022)

| 指　标 | Item | 单位数（个）Number of Enterprises (unit) |
|---|---|---|
| **总　计** | **Total** | **7617** |
| **按登记注册类型分** | **By Status of Registration** | |
| 内资企业 | Domestic-funded Enterprises | 7197 |
| #国有企业 | State-owned | 69 |
| 集体企业 | Collective-owned | 12 |
| 港澳台投资企业 | Funded by Hong Kong, Macao and Taiwan | 125 |
| 外商投资企业 | Foreign-funded | 295 |
| **按轻、重工业分** | **By Light and Heavy Industries** | |
| 轻工业 | Light Industry | 2250 |
| 重工业 | Heavy Industry | 5367 |
| **按企业规模分** | **By Size** | |
| 大型企业 | Large | 179 |
| 中型企业 | Medium | 844 |
| 小型微型企业 | Small&Mini | 6594 |
| **按行业分** | **By Sector** | |
| 煤炭开采和洗选业 | Mining and Washing of Coal | 18 |
| 石油和天然气开采业 | Extraction of Petroleum and Natural Gas | 6 |
| 黑色金属矿采选业 | Mining and Processing of Ferrous Metal Ores | |
| 有色金属矿采选业 | Mining and Processing of Non-ferrous Metal Ores | 1 |
| 非金属矿采选业 | Mining and Processing of Non-metal Ores | 142 |
| 开采辅助活动 | Support Activities for Mining | |
| 其他采矿业 | Mining of Other Ores | |
| 农副食品加工业 | Processing of Food from Agricultural Products | 510 |
| 食品制造业 | Manufacture of Foods | 204 |
| 酒、饮料和精制茶制造业 | Manufacture of Liquor, Beverages and Refined Tea | 79 |
| 烟草制品业 | Manufacture of Tobacco | 3 |
| 纺织业 | Manufacture of Textile | 58 |
| 纺织服装、服饰业 | Manufacture of Textile Wearing Apparel and Accessories | 62 |
| 皮革、毛皮、羽毛及其制品和制鞋业 | Manufacture of Leather, Fur, Feather and Related Products and Footwear | 58 |
| 木材加工和木、竹、藤、棕、草制品业 | Processing of Timber, Manufacture of Wood, Bamboo, Rattan, Palm and Straw Products | 99 |
| 家具制造业 | Manufacture of Furniture | 98 |
| 造纸及纸制品业 | Manufacture of Paper and Paper Products | 131 |
| 印刷和记录媒介复制业 | Printing and Reproduction of Recording Media | 121 |
| 文教、工美、体育和娱乐用品制造业 | Manufacture of Articles for Culture, Education, Arts and Crafts, Sport and Entertainment Activities | 69 |
| 石油、煤炭及其他燃料加工业 | Processing of Petroleum, Coking and Processing of Nuclear Fuel | 17 |
| 化学原料和化学制品制造业 | Manufacture of Raw Chemical Materials and Chemical Products | 246 |
| 医药制造业 | Manufacture of Medicines | 173 |
| 化学纤维制造业 | Manufacture of Chemical Fibres | 10 |
| 橡胶和塑料制品业 | Manufacture of Rubber and Plastics Products | 339 |
| 非金属矿物制品业 | Manufacture of Non-metallic Mineral Products | 783 |
| 黑色金属冶炼和压延加工业 | Smelting and Pressing of Ferrous Metals | 80 |
| 有色金属冶炼和压延加工业 | Smelting and Pressing of Non-ferrous Metals | 152 |
| 金属制品业 | Manufacture of Metal Products | 416 |
| 通用设备制造业 | Manufacture of General Purpose Machinery | 435 |
| 专用设备制造业 | Manufacture of Special Purpose Machinery | 314 |
| 汽车制造业 | Manufacture of Automobiles | 1125 |
| 铁路、船舶、航空航天和其他运输设备制造业 | Manufacture of Railway, Ship, Aerospace and Other Transport Equipment | 483 |
| 电气机械及器材制造业 | Manufacture of Electrical Machinery and Apparatus | 332 |
| 计算机、通信和其他电子设备制造业 | Manufacture of Computers, Communication and Other Electronic Equipment | 548 |
| 仪器仪表制造业 | Manufacture of Measuring Instruments and Machinery | 105 |
| 其他制造业 | Other Manufacture | 17 |
| 废弃资源综合利用业 | Utilization of Waste Resources | 55 |
| 金属制品、机械和设备修理业 | Repair Service of Metal Products, Machinery and Equipment | 11 |
| 电力、热力的生产和供应业 | Production and Supply of Electric Power and Heat Power | 118 |
| 燃气生产和供应业 | Production and Supply of Gas | 110 |
| 水的生产和供应业 | Production and Supply of Water | 89 |

单位：万元 (10 000 yuan)

| 从业人员平均人数（万人）<br>Average Employment<br>(10 000 persons) | 工业总产值<br>Gross Industrial Output Value | 实收资本<br>Paid-in Capital | #国家资本<br>State Capital | #外商资本<br>Foreign Capital |
|---|---|---|---|---|
| **154.20** | **258270587.5** | **52775447.0** | **11091790.3** | **3494739.5** |
| 131.18 | 202686069.1 | 44415763.0 | 10227493.5 | 345754.2 |
| 2.00 | 2551717.0 | 1725645.3 | 658247.3 | |
| 0.16 | 109210.1 | 6719.5 | | |
| 9.71 | 26530904.2 | 3735750.4 | 200862.0 | 349350.4 |
| 13.31 | 29053614.2 | 4623933.6 | 663434.8 | 2799634.9 |
| 37.64 | 48325514.1 | 7005953.7 | 434942.7 | 383235.8 |
| 116.56 | 209945073.4 | 45769493.3 | 10656847.6 | 3111503.7 |
| 48.36 | 115564593.2 | 20742235.3 | 4867592.9 | 1505543.3 |
| 44.91 | 61392085.3 | 12164582.2 | 2923714.7 | 711237.7 |
| 60.92 | 81313909.0 | 19868629.5 | 3300482.7 | 1277958.5 |
| 0.09 | 385303.6 | 79967.2 | 56639.2 | |
| 0.19 | 1582912.1 | 1293131.3 | 34141.6 | |
| | 2110.7 | 30.0 | | |
| 1.02 | 1058168.6 | 1292170.2 | 50242.1 | |
| 5.38 | 9554561.6 | 791869.3 | 38656.7 | 25868.4 |
| 3.14 | 3119083.9 | 330612.1 | 9657.6 | 11487.6 |
| 1.47 | 1611158.6 | 602465.5 | 6336.2 | 183228.5 |
| 0.40 | 2294202.0 | 264386.0 | 264186.0 | |
| 0.74 | 486390.0 | 64102.0 | 5700.0 | |
| 1.08 | 532177.0 | 70842.2 | 337.0 | 1407.1 |
| 1.18 | 623962.5 | 51911.3 | 22100.0 | |
| 1.13 | 1458011.7 | 123633.0 | | |
| 1.19 | 819949.5 | 98172.5 | 200.0 | 100.0 |
| 2.02 | 4259165.4 | 1247929.0 | 3000.0 | 28155.8 |
| 2.01 | 1889338.4 | 274882.2 | 6159.6 | 10248.5 |
| 1.07 | 550470.9 | 62340.4 | | |
| 0.17 | 557313.9 | 99069.3 | 29618.2 | |
| 4.31 | 10793129.2 | 2862606.3 | 703931.9 | 394230.4 |
| 4.45 | 5983985.1 | 1270837.3 | 36061.0 | 5831.3 |
| 0.42 | 985939.9 | 101358.9 | 5703.0 | |
| 4.23 | 4885097.4 | 933310.9 | 57465.6 | 190976.2 |
| 10.16 | 12859240.3 | 3198041.2 | 421020.7 | 67564.2 |
| 1.72 | 11555630.4 | 1277847.4 | 5500.0 | 61937.7 |
| 2.74 | 13680850.2 | 1681845.6 | 410835.7 | 47041.9 |
| 5.76 | 6212615.2 | 863990.2 | 86455.6 | 17257.0 |
| 7.57 | 8402363.9 | 1994970.8 | 243355.3 | 209771.5 |
| 4.92 | 6385440.5 | 1187072.0 | 477995.1 | 33542.6 |
| 29.46 | 43691078.0 | 7051233.6 | 859595.0 | 962291.9 |
| 9.77 | 9027145.7 | 1403031.2 | 269003.1 | 24368.2 |
| 8.41 | 13066022.4 | 1676240.4 | 255636.4 | 121109.9 |
| 27.64 | 59460694.4 | 9827611.3 | 424191.9 | 882925.9 |
| 2.31 | 2225911.2 | 673321.7 | 171145.8 | 67345.7 |
| 1.25 | 1118106.7 | 333161.9 | 25155.5 | |
| 0.42 | 865200.8 | 129623.3 | 1590.8 | 1301.4 |
| 0.30 | 103158.7 | 36074.3 | 800.0 | |
| 3.55 | 11846840.3 | 6937815.8 | 4883776.1 | 111747.8 |
| 1.16 | 3472300.2 | 641766.4 | 167306.4 | 35000.0 |
| 1.33 | 865556.6 | 1946173.0 | 1058291.2 | |

**表 12.6 续表 1 continued 1**

| 指 标 | Item | 资 产<br>Total Assets |
|---|---|---|
| **总 计** | **Total** | **275353626.9** |
| **按登记注册类型分** | **By Status of Registration** | |
| 内资企业 | Domestic-funded Enterprises | 234540784.1 |
| #国有企业 | State-owned | 6857431.3 |
| 集体企业 | Collective-owned | 69400.1 |
| 港澳台投资企业 | Funded by Hong Kong, Macao and Taiwan | 18150377.2 |
| 外商投资企业 | Foreign-funded | 22662465.6 |
| **按轻、重工业分** | **By Light and Heavy Industries** | |
| 轻工业 | Light Industry | 46873444.0 |
| 重工业 | Heavy Industry | 228480182.9 |
| **按企业规模分** | **By Size** | |
| 大型企业 | Large | 117634686.1 |
| 中型企业 | Medium | 65403470.5 |
| 小型微型企业 | Small&Mini | 92315470.3 |
| **按行业分** | **By Sector** | |
| 煤炭开采和洗选业 | Mining and Washing of Coal | 446541.6 |
| 石油和天然气开采业 | Extraction of Petroleum and Natural Gas | 4025928.5 |
| 黑色金属矿采选业 | Mining and Processing of Ferrous Metal Ores | |
| 有色金属矿采选业 | Mining and Processing of Non-ferrous Metal Ores | 2011.7 |
| 非金属矿采选业 | Mining and Processing of Non-metal Ores | 1774205.6 |
| 开采辅助活动 | Support Activities for Mining | |
| 其他采矿业 | Mining of Other Ores | |
| 农副食品加工业 | Processing of Food from Agricultural Products | 6036177.3 |
| 食品制造业 | Manufacture of Foods | 2468631.1 |
| 酒、饮料和精制茶制造业 | Manufacture of Liquor, Beverages and Refined Tea | 2383896.1 |
| 烟草制品业 | Manufacture of Tobacco | 1754579.8 |
| 纺织业 | Manufacture of Textile | 441272.9 |
| 纺织服装、服饰业 | Manufacture of Textile Wearing Apparel and Accessories | 278486.1 |
| 皮革、毛皮、羽毛及其制品和制鞋业 | Manufacture of Leather, Fur, Feather and Related Products and Footwear | 374569.6 |
| 木材加工和木、竹、藤、棕、草制品业 | Processing of Timber, Manufacture of Wood, Bamboo, Rattan, Palm and Straw Products | 843443.6 |
| 家具制造业 | Manufacture of Furniture | 740615.8 |
| 造纸及纸制品业 | Manufacture of Paper and Paper Products | 3816534.0 |
| 印刷和记录媒介复制业 | Printing and Reproduction of Recording Media | 1660420.8 |
| 文教、工美、体育和娱乐用品制造业 | Manufacture of Articles for Culture, Education, Arts and Crafts, Sport and Entertainment Activities | 474540.4 |
| 石油、煤炭及其他燃料加工业 | Processing of Petroleum, Coking and Processing of Nuclear Fuel | 549789.9 |
| 化学原料和化学制品制造业 | Manufacture of Raw Chemical Materials and Chemical Products | 11411486.6 |
| 医药制造业 | Manufacture of Medicines | 7926073.1 |
| 化学纤维制造业 | Manufacture of Chemical Fibres | 1114847.1 |
| 橡胶和塑料制品业 | Manufacture of Rubber and Plastics Products | 4112705.7 |
| 非金属矿物制品业 | Manufacture of Non-metallic Mineral Products | 17272850.7 |
| 黑色金属冶炼和压延加工业 | Smelting and Pressing of Ferrous Metals | 6375416.2 |
| 有色金属冶炼和压延加工业 | Smelting and Pressing of Non-ferrous Metals | 10931346.9 |
| 金属制品业 | Manufacture of Metal Products | 5440465.8 |
| 通用设备制造业 | Manufacture of General Purpose Machinery | 9950235.9 |
| 专用设备制造业 | Manufacture of Special Purpose Machinery | 6982355.8 |
| 汽车制造业 | Manufacture of Automobiles | 51980631.5 |
| 铁路、船舶、航空航天和其他运输设备制造业 | Manufacture of Railway, Ship, Aerospace and Other Transport Equipment | 9133477.6 |
| 电气机械及器材制造业 | Manufacture of Electrical Machinery and Apparatus | 17804279.6 |
| 计算机、通信和其他电子设备制造业 | Manufacture of Computers, Communication and Other Electronic Equipment | 44092875.9 |
| 仪器仪表制造业 | Manufacture of Measuring Instruments and Machinery | 3283555.5 |
| 其他制造业 | Other Manufacture | 2137783.7 |
| 废弃资源综合利用业 | Utilization of Waste Resources | 684005.8 |
| 金属制品、机械和设备修理业 | Repair Service of Metal Products, Machinery and Equipment | 121859.7 |
| 电力、热力的生产和供应业 | Production and Supply of Electric Power and Heat Power | 24673337.4 |
| 燃气生产和供应业 | Production and Supply of Gas | 3541430.5 |
| 水的生产和供应业 | Production and Supply of Water | 8310961.1 |

单位：万元 (10 000 yuan)

| #流动资产 Circulating Assets | 固定资产 Fixed Assets 原 值 Original Value | 净 值 Net Value | 负 债 Total Liabilities | #流动负债 Total Circulating Liabilities |
|---|---|---|---|---|
| **146531965.4** | **150123053.4** | **76165962.1** | **157061970.4** | **123592701.6** |
| 120680747.4 | 127568891.6 | 65317817.3 | 131500791.8 | 102563308.2 |
| 3026916.4 | 3174911.0 | 2018857.0 | 4071886.1 | 2213658.7 |
| 43457.9 | 27053.2 | 16623.1 | 45714.6 | 43260.2 |
| 11899989.8 | 8118354.5 | 4178771.4 | 11291139.1 | 9223070.0 |
| 13951228.2 | 14435807.3 | 6669373.4 | 14270039.5 | 11806323.4 |
| 27325546.6 | 21265091.6 | 10888765.1 | 24102860.7 | 20343282.9 |
| 119206418.8 | 128857961.8 | 65277197.0 | 132959109.7 | 103249418.7 |
| 68522775.8 | 58468822.9 | 28967271.0 | 69118337.5 | 58229064.4 |
| 33839317.1 | 36930188.2 | 17797398.1 | 37147047.7 | 28788195.2 |
| 44169872.5 | 54724042.3 | 29401102.7 | 50796585.2 | 36575442.0 |
| 161824.4 | 293509.8 | 243191.1 | 204730.5 | 144309.2 |
| 484062.6 | 6311551.5 | 2720457.5 | 1108758.0 | 997738.1 |
| 1693.1 | 1031.2 | 313.4 | 1613.1 | |
| 730752.4 | 619227.0 | 341620.2 | 1031113.3 | 766358.2 |
| 3201101.5 | 2900201.0 | 1443346.1 | 2683840.5 | 2209450.4 |
| 1279651.0 | 1471881.2 | 734621.5 | 1193278.2 | 903130.9 |
| 1195942.1 | 976552.7 | 442908.0 | 1178457.6 | 1058476.9 |
| 1443835.0 | 580826.5 | 162577.8 | 467858.1 | 466991.8 |
| 180890.6 | 275311.8 | 158525.8 | 217415.8 | 174532.1 |
| 189141.7 | 110187.4 | 54069.6 | 129839.1 | 96594.1 |
| 234461.0 | 180152.5 | 96563.9 | 181594.5 | 148089.6 |
| 278883.3 | 919415.8 | 377273.5 | 448416.4 | 225816.6 |
| 317810.4 | 509498.2 | 226818.8 | 368723.6 | 242390.6 |
| 1656405.0 | 2853155.0 | 1593050.6 | 1585067.4 | 1042897.8 |
| 814015.2 | 1139976.8 | 516649.0 | 862406.9 | 695651.1 |
| 220900.0 | 295565.3 | 132196.7 | 196575.2 | 129952.7 |
| 281968.7 | 366936.8 | 98557.9 | 413380.6 | 227764.8 |
| 4944347.7 | 8271894.5 | 4109557.5 | 5524421.0 | 4612154.5 |
| 4309136.5 | 3559361.7 | 1749168.1 | 3333963.4 | 2740374.7 |
| 585263.8 | 518989.2 | 351316.2 | 510513.5 | 463158.7 |
| 1833877.4 | 3268441.8 | 1477981.4 | 2019296.3 | 1519306.0 |
| 8828739.0 | 9264337.9 | 4972269.3 | 10047539.0 | 8054850.0 |
| 2448406.0 | 4463500.3 | 3090023.2 | 3557972.4 | 2709968.4 |
| 5611855.9 | 6869243.6 | 4054740.0 | 7049784.5 | 5421627.7 |
| 3104012.8 | 2780007.1 | 1347583.4 | 3120730.9 | 2490193.1 |
| 5892410.0 | 4217148.8 | 2199540.5 | 5070033.8 | 4111875.5 |
| 4337069.9 | 2292231.7 | 1227830.3 | 3545144.1 | 2991113.4 |
| 34165894.0 | 22409812.4 | 9767754.1 | 33250022.3 | 28329255.6 |
| 5707748.1 | 4504219.0 | 1740691.8 | 5281442.8 | 4158742.7 |
| 13239074.4 | 3911906.8 | 2234863.5 | 12659263.1 | 11448849.1 |
| 26255144.2 | 16758238.0 | 8907467.6 | 26022016.1 | 21328401.6 |
| 2327287.7 | 632709.2 | 351175.3 | 1784192.3 | 1563284.0 |
| 1197604.2 | 1087458.4 | 644587.2 | 1105673.3 | 1006028.5 |
| 352357.8 | 335958.1 | 226945.8 | 322568.4 | 247062.0 |
| 101086.7 | 30405.7 | 14540.0 | 68275.3 | 65986.0 |
| 4725318.3 | 29297611.6 | 14666694.0 | 14929977.5 | 8185069.2 |
| 1487686.7 | 1777291.7 | 1086603.9 | 1896812.8 | 1247633.4 |
| 2404306.3 | 4067305.4 | 2601887.6 | 3689258.8 | 1367622.6 |

**表 12.6 续表 2 continued 2**

| 指　标 | Item | 所有者权益<br>Creditors' Equity |
|---|---|---|
| **总　计** | **Total** | **118304217.7** |
| **按登记注册类型分** | **By Status of Registration** | |
| 内资企业 | Domestic-funded Enterprises | 103052555.1 |
| #国有企业 | State-owned | 2785544.1 |
| 集体企业 | Collective-owned | 23685.4 |
| 港澳台投资企业 | Funded by Hong Kong, Macao and Taiwan | 6859237.6 |
| 外商投资企业 | Foreign-funded | 8392425.0 |
| **按轻、重工业分** | **By Light and Heavy Industries** | |
| 轻工业 | Light Industry | 22769707.5 |
| 重工业 | Heavy Industry | 95534510.2 |
| **按企业规模分** | **By Size** | |
| 大型企业 | Large | 48529814.5 |
| 中型企业 | Medium | 28256419.4 |
| 小型微型企业 | Small&Mini | 41517983.8 |
| **按行业分** | **By Sector** | |
| 煤炭开采和洗选业 | Mining and Washing of Coal | 241811.1 |
| 石油和天然气开采业 | Extraction of Petroleum and Natural Gas | 2917170.6 |
| 黑色金属矿采选业 | Mining and Processing of Ferrous Metal Ores | |
| 有色金属矿采选业 | Mining and Processing of Non-ferrous Metal Ores | 398.6 |
| 非金属矿采选业 | Mining and Processing of Non-metal Ores | 743091.7 |
| 开采辅助活动 | Support Activities for Mining | |
| 其他采矿业 | Mining of Other Ores | |
| 农副食品加工业 | Processing of Food from Agricultural Products | 3352334.4 |
| 食品制造业 | Manufacture of Foods | 1275352.6 |
| 酒、饮料和精制茶制造业 | Manufacture of Liquor, Beverages and Refined Tea | 1205438.1 |
| 烟草制品业 | Manufacture of Tobacco | 1286721.7 |
| 纺织业 | Manufacture of Textile | 223856.9 |
| 纺织服装、服饰业 | Manufacture of Textile Wearing Apparel and Accessories | 148647.1 |
| 皮革、毛皮、羽毛及其制品和制鞋业 | Manufacture of Leather, Fur, Feather and Related Products and Footwear | 192974.9 |
| 木材加工和木、竹、藤、棕、草制品业 | Processing of Timber, Manufacture of Wood, Bamboo, Rattan, Palm and Straw Products | 395028.0 |
| 家具制造业 | Manufacture of Furniture | 371890.7 |
| 造纸及纸制品业 | Manufacture of Paper and Paper Products | 2231466.8 |
| 印刷和记录媒介复制业 | Printing and Reproduction of Recording Media | 797147.1 |
| 文教、工美、体育和娱乐用品制造业 | Manufacture of Articles for Culture, Education, Arts and Crafts, Sport and Entertainment Activities | 277964.6 |
| 石油、煤炭及其他燃料加工业 | Processing of Petroleum, Coking and Processing of Nuclear Fuel | 136409.2 |
| 化学原料和化学制品制造业 | Manufacture of Raw Chemical Materials and Chemical Products | 5887063.4 |
| 医药制造业 | Manufacture of Medicines | 4592109.8 |
| 化学纤维制造业 | Manufacture of Chemical Fibres | 604333.5 |
| 橡胶和塑料制品业 | Manufacture of Rubber and Plastics Products | 2093407.1 |
| 非金属矿物制品业 | Manufacture of Non-metallic Mineral Products | 7225304.6 |
| 黑色金属冶炼和压延加工业 | Smelting and Pressing of Ferrous Metals | 2817443.4 |
| 有色金属冶炼和压延加工业 | Smelting and Pressing of Non-ferrous Metals | 3881562.1 |
| 金属制品业 | Manufacture of Metal Products | 2319732.6 |
| 通用设备制造业 | Manufacture of General Purpose Machinery | 4880199.2 |
| 专用设备制造业 | Manufacture of Special Purpose Machinery | 3437210.8 |
| 汽车制造业 | Manufacture of Automobiles | 18744070.7 |
| 铁路、船舶、航空航天和其他运输设备制造业 | Manufacture of Railway, Ship, Aerospace and Other Transport Equipment | 3852033.5 |
| 电气机械及器材制造业 | Manufacture of Electrical Machinery and Apparatus | 5145015.6 |
| 计算机、通信和其他电子设备制造业 | Manufacture of Computers, Communication and Other Electronic Equipment | 18070857.9 |
| 仪器仪表制造业 | Manufacture of Measuring Instruments and Machinery | 1499363.3 |
| 其他制造业 | Other Manufacture | 1032110.6 |
| 废弃资源综合利用业 | Utilization of Waste Resources | 361436.9 |
| 金属制品、机械和设备修理业 | Repair Service of Metal Products, Machinery and Equipment | 53584.1 |
| 电力、热力的生产和供应业 | Production and Supply of Electric Power and Heat Power | 9743358.9 |
| 燃气生产和供应业 | Production and Supply of Gas | 1644615.7 |
| 水的生产和供应业 | Production and Supply of Water | 4621699.9 |

单位：万元 (10 000 yuan)

| 营业收入<br>Revenue | 营业成本<br>Cost | 税金及附加<br>Tax and Extra Charges | 本年应交增值税<br>VAT Payable | 利润总额<br>Total After-tax Profits | 利税总额<br>Total Pre-tax Profits | 应付职工薪酬<br>Total Wages |
|---|---|---|---|---|---|---|
| **271752779.5** | **229521448.5** | **3299789.8** | **4728584.8** | **18296765.5** | **26325140.1** | **19486456.0** |
| 214397873.3 | 177712737.8 | 2889332.4 | 4101034.5 | 16105309.5 | 23095676.4 | 16501132.4 |
| 2672658.7 | 2242008.2 | 20536.1 | 62358.6 | 137012.4 | 219907.1 | 368507.6 |
| 86619.3 | 69543.0 | 743.0 | 5779.0 | 6184.0 | 12706.0 | 14006.4 |
| 27095461.5 | 24971934.3 | 167636.2 | 277199.0 | 1090643.6 | 1535478.8 | 1281344.0 |
| 30259444.7 | 26836776.4 | 242821.2 | 350351.3 | 1100812.4 | 1693984.9 | 1703979.6 |
| 50234467.6 | 38916133.3 | 1682267.1 | 1285622.5 | 4678211.2 | 7646100.8 | 4304737.3 |
| 221518311.9 | 190605315.2 | 1617522.7 | 3442962.3 | 13618554.3 | 18679039.3 | 15181718.7 |
| 124467993.5 | 108466730.8 | 2287754.3 | 1808004.6 | 6010231.2 | 10105990.1 | 7296068.1 |
| 62186339.1 | 50523316.9 | 452408.6 | 1196243.2 | 5748472.7 | 7397124.5 | 5478915.3 |
| 85098446.9 | 70531400.8 | 559626.9 | 1724337.0 | 6538061.6 | 8822025.5 | 6711472.6 |
| 407436.4 | 332767.1 | 1635.4 | 4110.6 | 50914.9 | 56660.9 | 11905.6 |
| 1571363.9 | 961819.7 | 54568.3 | 66921.1 | 465356.3 | 586845.7 | 47835.1 |
| 2026.6 | 1387.9 | 72.0 | 195.1 | 198.3 | 465.4 | 233.4 |
| 1007818.8 | 738983.8 | 33987.9 | 33642.5 | 91229.6 | 158860.0 | 83610.9 |
| 9700893.9 | 8432032.7 | 37585.9 | 137291.0 | 617485.1 | 792362.0 | 558317.4 |
| 3258416.0 | 2578918.8 | 20434.8 | 87137.5 | 272459.2 | 380031.5 | 328048.5 |
| 1877518.8 | 1246494.5 | 127162.3 | 42305.0 | 381081.8 | 550549.1 | 176968.7 |
| 2350018.5 |  | 1285491.8 | 211199.4 | 220050.3 | 1716741.5 | 143988.8 |
| 457271.3 | 383433.8 | 3516.0 | 7729.7 | 30217.8 | 41463.5 | 56461.7 |
| 513226.5 | 386738.5 | 1665.0 | 10654.2 | 35122.1 | 47441.3 | 96000.7 |
| 604970.8 | 517296.4 | 2796.0 | 10891.0 | 45141.7 | 58828.7 | 93837.3 |
| 1420727.4 | 1175421.2 | 4497.6 | 14003.3 | 104401.3 | 122902.2 | 160297.5 |
| 798102.5 | 624641.9 | 6813.7 | 20479.3 | 66736.8 | 94029.8 | 118557.2 |
| 4162354.1 | 3620087.3 | 23136.4 | 89115.3 | 211331.1 | 323582.8 | 269740.5 |
| 1890213.0 | 1506748.9 | 13546.6 | 35141.2 | 186894.8 | 235582.6 | 236026.9 |
| 531262.4 | 412549.3 | 5053.0 | 19719.2 | 60788.1 | 85560.3 | 89752.5 |
| 499618.4 | 408159.7 | 11516.2 | 13486.7 | 43804.9 | 68807.8 | 49190.0 |
| 11055303.3 | 8518758.6 | 66302.6 | 300018.8 | 1539225.6 | 1905547.0 | 693949.3 |
| 5683433.9 | 3284696.1 | 49276.8 | 230009.9 | 772344.7 | 1051631.4 | 650825.6 |
| 896746.9 | 770050.4 | 3226.4 | 14881.0 | 71723.0 | 89830.4 | 56424.0 |
| 4847166.6 | 3945243.4 | 47979.4 | 94817.7 | 409336.6 | 552133.7 | 428940.5 |
| 12974915.3 | 10474422.9 | 105419.7 | 336656.7 | 1058909.9 | 1500986.3 | 1158116.8 |
| 11409862.4 | 9773340.3 | 29577.5 | 48427.2 | 954334.8 | 1032339.5 | 307072.4 |
| 17160090.9 | 14939359.9 | 62171.6 | 163912.1 | 1228481.4 | 1454565.1 | 454795.7 |
| 6659326.1 | 5647289.9 | 34623.1 | 119350.0 | 466065.0 | 620038.1 | 726346.4 |
| 8470634.3 | 6899998.8 | 51112.8 | 183198.3 | 664692.4 | 899003.5 | 861964.6 |
| 6145367.2 | 4566479.6 | 44073.5 | 158255.5 | 765083.6 | 967412.6 | 634513.6 |
| 49353128.7 | 41791614.8 | 798714.3 | 1071998.8 | 1882942.6 | 3753655.7 | 3764075.6 |
| 8603508.7 | 7321608.8 | 56611.8 | 183345.4 | 582130.3 | 822087.5 | 1050610.9 |
| 16170094.5 | 14215325.8 | 59192.4 | 243315.5 | 1106872.6 | 1409380.5 | 953757.1 |
| 60503468.1 | 55400642.2 | 146512.8 | 319369.6 | 2602810.5 | 3068692.9 | 3205472.6 |
| 2266619.9 | 1694885.0 | 14832.3 | 75710.4 | 196146.9 | 286689.6 | 347930.8 |
| 1148838.6 | 991764.8 | 5701.8 | 18385.6 | 57105.4 | 81192.8 | 247861.1 |
| 850229.2 | 696044.5 | 3574.1 | 18557.7 | 89738.0 | 111869.8 | 64771.4 |
| 103074.7 | 89364.4 | 622.8 | 4663.8 | 1686.1 | 6972.7 | 42887.1 |
| 11694425.9 | 10507719.4 | 62140.2 | 271967.5 | 491933.4 | 826041.1 | 878604.7 |
| 3623069.2 | 3180421.2 | 10921.2 | 42913.9 | 341965.7 | 395800.8 | 205877.3 |
| 1080235.8 | 794000.4 | 13723.8 | 24807.3 | 130022.9 | 168554.0 | 230885.8 |

# 表 12.7 规模以上工业企业经济效益指标（2022 年）
## INDICATORS ON ECONOMIC BENEFIT OF INDUSTRIAL ENTERPRISES ABOVE DESIGNATED SIZE (2022)

| 指 标 | Item | 总资产贡献率 Ratio of Total Assets to Industrial Output Value |
|---|---|---|
| **总 计** | **Total** | **9.9** |
| **按登记注册类型分** | **By Status of Registration** | |
| 内资企业 | Domestic-funded Enterprises | 10.2 |
| #国有企业 | State-owned | 4.0 |
| 集体企业 | Collective-owned | 18.7 |
| 港澳台投资企业 | Funded by Hong Kong, Macao and Taiwan | 8.7 |
| 外商投资企业 | Foreign-funded | 7.6 |
| **按轻、重工业分** | **By Light and Heavy Industries** | |
| 轻工业 | Light Industry | 16.6 |
| 重工业 | Heavy Industry | 8.5 |
| **按企业规模分** | **By Size** | |
| 大型企业 | Large | 8.7 |
| 中型企业 | Medium | 11.8 |
| 小型微型企业 | Small&Mini | 10.2 |
| **按行业分** | **By Sector** | |
| 煤炭开采和洗选业 | Mining and Washing of Coal | 14.7 |
| 石油和天然气开采业 | Extraction of Petroleum and Natural Gas | 15.1 |
| 黑色金属矿采选业 | Mining and Processing of Ferrous Metal Ores | |
| 有色金属矿采选业 | Mining and Processing of Non-ferrous Metal Ores | 23.3 |
| 非金属矿采选业 | Mining and Processing of Non-metal Ores | 9.3 |
| 开采辅助活动 | Support Activities for Mining | |
| 其他采矿业 | Mining of Other Ores | |
| 农副食品加工业 | Processing of Food from Agricultural Products | 13.4 |
| 食品制造业 | Manufacture of Foods | 15.8 |
| 酒、饮料和精制茶制造业 | Manufacture of Liquor, Beverages and Refined Tea | 23.1 |
| 烟草制品业 | Manufacture of Tobacco | 97.3 |
| 纺织业 | Manufacture of Textile | 10.5 |
| 纺织服装、服饰业 | Manufacture of Textile Wearing Apparel and Accessories | 17.5 |
| 皮革、毛皮、羽毛及其制品和制鞋业 | Manufacture of Leather, Fur, Feather and Related Products and Footwear | 16.2 |
| 木材加工和木、竹、藤、棕、草制品业 | Processing of Timber, Manufacture of Wood, Bamboo, Rattan, Palm and Straw Products | 15.1 |
| 家具制造业 | Manufacture of Furniture | 13.4 |
| 造纸及纸制品业 | Manufacture of Paper and Paper Products | 8.9 |
| 印刷和记录媒介复制业 | Printing and Reproduction of Recording Media | 14.7 |
| 文教、工美、体育和娱乐用品制造业 | Manufacture of Articles for Culture, Education, Arts and Crafts, Sport and Entertainment Activities | 18.3 |
| 石油、煤炭及其他燃料加工业 | Processing of Petroleum, Coking and Processing of Nuclear Fuel | 12.9 |
| 化学原料和化学制品制造业 | Manufacture of Raw Chemical Materials and Chemical Products | 17.3 |
| 医药制造业 | Manufacture of Medicines | 13.6 |
| 化学纤维制造业 | Manufacture of Chemical Fibres | 7.5 |
| 橡胶和塑料制品业 | Manufacture of Rubber and Plastics Products | 14.0 |
| 非金属矿物制品业 | Manufacture of Non-metallic Mineral Products | 9.4 |
| 黑色金属冶炼和压延加工业 | Smelting and Pressing of Ferrous Metals | 16.9 |
| 有色金属冶炼和压延加工业 | Smelting and Pressing of Non-ferrous Metals | 14.2 |
| 金属制品业 | Manufacture of Metal Products | 11.8 |
| 通用设备制造业 | Manufacture of General Purpose Machinery | 9.3 |
| 专用设备制造业 | Manufacture of Special Purpose Machinery | 14.0 |
| 汽车制造业 | Manufacture of Automobiles | 7.3 |
| 铁路、船舶、航空航天和其他运输设备制造业 | Manufacture of Railway, Ship, Aerospace and Other Transport Equipment | 9.1 |
| 电气机械及器材制造业 | Manufacture of Electrical Machinery and Apparatus | 8.1 |
| 计算机、通信和其他电子设备制造业 | Manufacture of Computers, Communication and Other Electronic Equipment | 7.0 |
| 仪器仪表制造业 | Manufacture of Measuring Instruments and Machinery | 8.8 |
| 其他制造业 | Other Manufacture | 3.7 |
| 废弃资源综合利用业 | Utilization of Waste Resources | 16.9 |
| 金属制品、机械和设备修理业 | Repair Service of Metal Products, Machinery and Equipment | 5.8 |
| 电力、热力的生产和供应业 | Production and Supply of Electric Power and Heat Power | 4.6 |
| 燃气生产和供应业 | Production and Supply of Gas | 11.7 |
| 水的生产和供应业 | Production and Supply of Water | 2.3 |

单位: % (%)

| 资本保值增值率 Ratio of Assets Appreciation YOY | 资产负债率 Asset-Liability Ratio | 流动资产周转率(次) Turnover Ratio of Circulating Assets (time) | 成本费用利润率 Ratio of Profits to Cost | 产品销售率 Sales as Percentage of Output |
|---|---|---|---|---|
| **107.1** | **57.0** | **1.9** | **7.5** | **97.5** |
| | | | | |
| 108.2 | 56.1 | 1.8 | 8.5 | 97.1 |
| 119.5 | 59.4 | 0.9 | 5.5 | 97.4 |
| 103.7 | 65.9 | 2.0 | 7.9 | 95.8 |
| 106.2 | 62.2 | 2.3 | 4.2 | 98.8 |
| 96.6 | 63.0 | 2.2 | 3.9 | 99.1 |
| | | | | |
| 106.0 | 51.4 | 1.8 | 10.8 | 98.4 |
| 107.4 | 58.2 | 1.9 | 6.8 | 97.2 |
| | | | | |
| 106.2 | 58.8 | 1.8 | 5.3 | 98.3 |
| 109.1 | 56.8 | 1.8 | 10.6 | 96.1 |
| 106.7 | 55.0 | 1.9 | 8.6 | 97.4 |
| | | | | |
| 443.5 | 45.9 | 2.5 | 14.3 | 99.7 |
| 119.5 | 27.5 | 3.3 | 42.9 | 99.7 |
| | | | | |
| 66.7 | 80.2 | 1.2 | 11.5 | 96.0 |
| 107.3 | 58.1 | 1.4 | 10.5 | 97.8 |
| | | | | |
| 100.8 | 44.5 | 3.0 | 6.9 | 96.9 |
| 103.3 | 48.3 | 2.6 | 9.4 | 98.1 |
| 94.7 | 49.4 | 1.6 | 25.0 | 96.1 |
| 109.3 | 26.7 | 1.6 | 27.1 | 100.0 |
| 153.0 | 49.3 | 2.5 | 7.3 | 96.6 |
| 97.7 | 46.6 | 2.7 | 7.6 | 95.6 |
| 95.2 | 48.5 | 2.6 | 8.3 | 96.6 |
| 93.3 | 53.2 | 5.1 | 8.3 | 98.7 |
| | | | | |
| 99.0 | 49.8 | 2.5 | 9.3 | 95.0 |
| 110.3 | 41.5 | 2.5 | 5.5 | 96.3 |
| 98.3 | 51.9 | 2.3 | 11.3 | 98.5 |
| 99.4 | 41.4 | 2.4 | 13.4 | 96.3 |
| | | | | |
| 96.1 | 75.2 | 1.8 | 10.1 | 82.3 |
| 105.7 | 48.4 | 2.2 | 16.6 | 96.4 |
| 102.1 | 42.1 | 1.3 | 16.6 | 93.6 |
| 86.7 | 45.8 | 1.5 | 9.1 | 90.9 |
| 121.7 | 49.1 | 2.6 | 9.5 | 97.0 |
| 104.2 | 58.2 | 1.5 | 9.2 | 94.5 |
| 95.8 | 55.8 | 4.7 | 9.6 | 99.0 |
| 120.2 | 64.5 | 3.1 | 8.0 | 96.6 |
| 107.8 | 57.4 | 2.2 | 7.8 | 98.3 |
| 105.3 | 51.0 | 1.4 | 8.8 | 98.6 |
| 131.5 | 50.8 | 1.4 | 15.1 | 97.0 |
| 105.0 | 64.0 | 1.4 | 4.2 | 97.5 |
| 109.8 | 57.8 | 1.5 | 7.5 | 96.0 |
| 110.5 | 71.1 | 1.2 | 7.5 | 105.1 |
| 107.7 | 59.0 | 2.3 | 4.6 | 96.8 |
| | | | | |
| 108.2 | 54.3 | 1.0 | 9.9 | 98.0 |
| 133.7 | 51.7 | 1.0 | 5.2 | 93.4 |
| 120.9 | 47.2 | 2.4 | 12.1 | 95.8 |
| 102.0 | 56.0 | 1.0 | 1.7 | 99.8 |
| 104.7 | 60.5 | 2.5 | 4.4 | 99.8 |
| 110.8 | 53.6 | 2.4 | 10.3 | 98.7 |
| 107.4 | 44.4 | 0.5 | 13.5 | 98.2 |

表 12.7 续表 continued

| 指 标 | Item | 销售利润率 Rate of Return on Sale |
|---|---|---|
| **总 计** | **Total** | **6.7** |
| **按登记注册类型分** | **By Status of Registration** | |
| 内资企业 | Domestic-funded Enterprises | 7.5 |
| #国有企业 | State-owned | 5.1 |
| 集体企业 | Collective-owned | 7.1 |
| 港澳台投资企业 | Funded by Hong Kong, Macao and Taiwan | 4.0 |
| 外商投资企业 | Foreign-funded | 3.6 |
| **按轻、重工业分** | **By Light and Heavy Industries** | |
| 轻工业 | Light Industry | 9.3 |
| 重工业 | Heavy Industry | 6.2 |
| **按企业规模分** | **By Size** | |
| 大型企业 | Large | 4.8 |
| 中型企业 | Medium | 9.2 |
| 小型微型企业 | Small&Mini | 7.7 |
| **按行业分** | **By Sector** | |
| 煤炭开采和洗选业 | Mining and Washing of Coal | 12.5 |
| 石油和天然气开采业 | Extraction of Petroleum and Natural Gas | 29.6 |
| 黑色金属矿采选业 | Mining and Processing of Ferrous Metal Ores | |
| 有色金属矿采选业 | Mining and Processing of Non-ferrous Metal Ores | 9.8 |
| 非金属矿采选业 | Mining and Processing of Non-metal Ores | 9.1 |
| 开采辅助活动 | Support Activities for Mining | |
| 其他采矿业 | Mining of Other Ores | |
| 农副食品加工业 | Processing of Food from Agricultural Products | 6.4 |
| 食品制造业 | Manufacture of Foods | 8.4 |
| 酒、饮料和精制茶制造业 | Manufacture of Liquor, Beverages and Refined Tea | 20.3 |
| 烟草制品业 | Manufacture of Tobacco | 9.4 |
| 纺织业 | Manufacture of Textile | 6.6 |
| 纺织服装、服饰业 | Manufacture of Textile Wearing Apparel and Accessories | 6.8 |
| 皮革、毛皮、羽毛及其制品和制鞋业 | Manufacture of Leather, Fur, Feather and Related Products and Footwear | 7.5 |
| 木材加工和木、竹、藤、棕、草制品业 | Processing of Timber, Manufacture of Wood, Bamboo, Rattan, Palm and Straw Products | 7.4 |
| 家具制造业 | Manufacture of Furniture | 8.4 |
| 造纸及纸制品业 | Manufacture of Paper and Paper Products | 5.1 |
| 印刷和记录媒介复制业 | Printing and Reproduction of Recording Media | 9.9 |
| 文教、工美、体育和娱乐用品制造业 | Manufacture of Articles for Culture, Education, Arts and Crafts, Sport and Entertainment Activities | 11.4 |
| 石油、煤炭及其他燃料加工业 | Processing of Petroleum, Coking and Processing of Nuclear Fuel | 8.8 |
| 化学原料和化学制品制造业 | Manufacture of Raw Chemical Materials and Chemical Products | 13.9 |
| 医药制造业 | Manufacture of Medicines | 13.6 |
| 化学纤维制造业 | Manufacture of Chemical Fibres | 8.0 |
| 橡胶和塑料制品业 | Manufacture of Rubber and Plastics Products | 8.4 |
| 非金属矿物制品业 | Manufacture of Non-metallic Mineral Products | 8.2 |
| 黑色金属冶炼和压延加工业 | Smelting and Pressing of Ferrous Metals | 8.4 |
| 有色金属冶炼和压延加工业 | Smelting and Pressing of Non-ferrous Metals | 7.2 |
| 金属制品业 | Manufacture of Metal Products | 7.0 |
| 通用设备制造业 | Manufacture of General Purpose Machinery | 7.9 |
| 专用设备制造业 | Manufacture of Special Purpose Machinery | 12.5 |
| 汽车制造业 | Manufacture of Automobiles | 3.8 |
| 铁路、船舶、航空航天和其他运输设备制造业 | Manufacture of Railway, Ship, Aerospace and Other Transport Equipment | 6.8 |
| 电气机械及器材制造业 | Manufacture of Electrical Machinery and Apparatus | 6.9 |
| 计算机、通信和其他电子设备制造业 | Manufacture of Computers, Communication and Other Electronic Equipment | 4.3 |
| 仪器仪表制造业 | Manufacture of Measuring Instruments and Machinery | 8.7 |
| 其他制造业 | Other Manufacture | 5.0 |
| 废弃资源综合利用业 | Utilization of Waste Resources | 10.6 |
| 金属制品、机械和设备修理业 | Repair Service of Metal Products, Machinery and Equipment | 1.6 |
| 电力、热力的生产和供应业 | Production and Supply of Electric Power and Heat Power | 4.2 |
| 燃气生产和供应业 | Production and Supply of Gas | 9.4 |
| 水的生产和供应业 | Production and Supply of Water | 12.0 |

单位: % (%)

| 流动比率 Current Ratio | 速动比率 Quick Ratio | 产权比率 Equity Ratio | 人均实现利税（元） Per Capita Pre-tax Profits (yuan) | 从业人员人均工资（元） Per Capita Wages of Employees (yuan) |
|---|---|---|---|---|
| **1.2** | **1.0** | **1.3** | **170726** | **126375** |
| 1.2 | 1.0 | 1.3 | 176062 | 125791 |
| 1.4 | 1.1 | 1.5 | 110174 | 184623 |
| 1.0 | 0.8 | 1.9 | 78919 | 86996 |
| 1.3 | 1.1 | 1.7 | 158134 | 131961 |
| 1.2 | 1.0 | 1.7 | 127310 | 128061 |
| 1.3 | 1.1 | 1.1 | 203148 | 114372 |
| 1.2 | 1.0 | 1.4 | 160257 | 130251 |
| 1.2 | 1.0 | 1.4 | 208978 | 150873 |
| 1.2 | 0.9 | 1.3 | 164703 | 121992 |
| 1.2 | 1.0 | 1.2 | 144801 | 110160 |
| 1.1 | 1.1 | 0.9 | 651275 | 136846 |
| 0.5 | 0.5 | 0.4 | 3024978 | 246573 |
| | | 4.1 | 116350 | 58350 |
| 1.0 | 0.9 | 1.4 | 156512 | 82375 |
| 1.5 | 1.1 | 0.8 | 147361 | 103834 |
| 1.4 | 1.1 | 0.9 | 120991 | 104441 |
| 1.1 | 0.9 | 1.0 | 374269 | 120305 |
| 3.1 | 1.4 | 0.4 | 4324286 | 362692 |
| 1.0 | 0.5 | 1.0 | 55731 | 75889 |
| 2.0 | 1.1 | 0.9 | 43846 | 88725 |
| 1.6 | 1.1 | 0.9 | 49728 | 79321 |
| 1.2 | 0.8 | 1.1 | 108475 | 141481 |
| 1.3 | 0.9 | 1.0 | 79216 | 99880 |
| 1.6 | 1.2 | 0.7 | 160031 | 133403 |
| 1.2 | 1.0 | 1.1 | 117498 | 117719 |
| 1.7 | 1.1 | 0.7 | 79814 | 83724 |
| 1.2 | 0.8 | 3.0 | 402385 | 287661 |
| 1.1 | 0.9 | 0.9 | 441917 | 160934 |
| 1.6 | 1.3 | 0.7 | 236109 | 146122 |
| 1.3 | 1.1 | 0.8 | 211366 | 132762 |
| 1.2 | 0.9 | 1.0 | 130497 | 101380 |
| 1.1 | 1.0 | 1.4 | 147793 | 114033 |
| 0.9 | 0.7 | 1.3 | 600547 | 178634 |
| 1.0 | 0.8 | 1.8 | 531639 | 166226 |
| 1.3 | 1.0 | 1.4 | 107571 | 126014 |
| 1.4 | 1.2 | 1.0 | 118759 | 113866 |
| 1.5 | 1.2 | 1.0 | 196749 | 129045 |
| 1.2 | 1.0 | 1.8 | 127398 | 127752 |
| 1.4 | 1.1 | 1.4 | 84127 | 107512 |
| 1.2 | 1.0 | 2.5 | 167584 | 113408 |
| 1.2 | 1.0 | 1.4 | 111016 | 115964 |
| 1.5 | 1.2 | 1.2 | 124108 | 150619 |
| 1.2 | 1.0 | 1.1 | 64747 | 197656 |
| 1.4 | 1.2 | 0.9 | 264468 | 153124 |
| 1.5 | 1.2 | 1.3 | 22937 | 141076 |
| 0.6 | 0.6 | 1.5 | 232557 | 247355 |
| 1.2 | 1.2 | 1.2 | 340620 | 177175 |
| 1.8 | 1.7 | 0.8 | 126352 | 173078 |

# 表 12.8 国有控股工业企业主要经济指标(2022 年)
MAIN ECONOMIC INDICATORS OF STATE-HOLDING INDUSTRIAL ENTERPRISES (2022)

| 指 标 | Item | 单位数(个) Number of Enterprises (unit) |
|---|---|---|
| **总 计** | **Total** | **648** |
| **按登记注册类型分** | **By Status of Registration** | |
| 内资企业 | Domestic-funded Enterprises | 611 |
| #国有企业 | State-owned | 69 |
| 集体企业 | Collective-owned | |
| 港澳台投资企业 | Funded by Hong Kong, Macao and Taiwan | 7 |
| 外商投资企业 | Foreign-funded | 30 |
| **按轻、重工业分** | **By Light and Heavy Industries** | |
| 轻工业 | Light Industry | 81 |
| 重工业 | Heavy Industry | 567 |
| **按企业规模分** | **By Size** | |
| 大型企业 | Large | 50 |
| 中型企业 | Medium | 139 |
| 小型微型企业 | Small&Mini | 459 |
| **按行业分** | **By Sector** | |
| 煤炭开采和洗选业 | Mining and Washing of Coal | 2 |
| 石油和天然气开采业 | Extraction of Petroleum and Natural Gas | 5 |
| 黑色金属矿采选业 | Mining and Processing of Ferrous Metal Ores | |
| 有色金属矿采选业 | Mining and Processing of Non-ferrous Metal Ores | |
| 非金属矿采选业 | Mining and Processing of Non-metal Ores | 7 |
| 开采辅助活动 | Support Activities for Mining | |
| 其他采矿业 | Mining of Other Ores | |
| 农副食品加工业 | Processing of Food from Agricultural Products | 16 |
| 食品制造业 | Manufacture of Foods | 9 |
| 酒、饮料和精制茶制造业 | Manufacture of Liquor, Beverages and Refined Tea | 4 |
| 烟草制品业 | Manufacture of Tobacco | 3 |
| 纺织业 | Manufacture of Textile | 2 |
| 纺织服装、服饰业 | Manufacture of Textile Wearing Apparel and Accessories | 1 |
| 皮革、毛皮、羽毛及其制品和制鞋业 | Manufacture of Leather, Fur, Feather and Related Products and Footwear | 2 |
| 木材加工和木、竹、藤、棕、草制品业 | Processing of Timber, Manufacture of Wood, Bamboo, Rattan, Palm and Straw Products | |
| 家具制造业 | Manufacture of Furniture | |
| 造纸及纸制品业 | Manufacture of Paper and Paper Products | 2 |
| 印刷和记录媒介复制业 | Printing and Reproduction of Recording Media | 5 |
| 文教、工美、体育和娱乐用品制造业 | Manufacture of Articles for Culture, Education, Arts and Crafts, Sport and Entertainment Activities | |
| 石油、煤炭及其他燃料加工业 | Processing of Petroleum, Coking and Processing of Nuclear Fuel | 2 |
| 化学原料和化学制品制造业 | Manufacture of Raw Chemical Materials and Chemical Products | 37 |
| 医药制造业 | Manufacture of Medicines | 19 |
| 化学纤维制造业 | Manufacture of Chemical Fibres | |
| 橡胶和塑料制品业 | Manufacture of Rubber and Plastics Products | 10 |
| 非金属矿物制品业 | Manufacture of Non-metallic Mineral Products | 46 |
| 黑色金属冶炼和压延加工业 | Smelting and Pressing of Ferrous Metals | 3 |
| 有色金属冶炼和压延加工业 | Smelting and Pressing of Non-ferrous Metals | 22 |
| 金属制品业 | Manufacture of Metal Products | 21 |
| 通用设备制造业 | Manufacture of General Purpose Machinery | 32 |
| 专用设备制造业 | Manufacture of Special Purpose Machinery | 18 |
| 汽车制造业 | Manufacture of Automobiles | 70 |
| 铁路、船舶、航空航天和其他运输设备制造业 | Manufacture of Railway, Ship, Aerospace and Other Transport Equipment | 21 |
| 电气机械及器材制造业 | Manufacture of Electrical Machinery and Apparatus | 18 |
| 计算机、通信和其他电子设备制造业 | Manufacture of Computers, Communication and Other Electronic Equipment | 22 |
| 仪器仪表制造业 | Manufacture of Measuring Instruments and Machinery | 21 |
| 其他制造业 | Other Manufacture | 7 |
| 废弃资源综合利用业 | Utilization of Waste Resources | 3 |
| 金属制品、机械和设备修理业 | Repair Service of Metal Products, Machinery and Equipment | 1 |
| 电力、热力的生产和供应业 | Production and Supply of Electric Power and Heat Power | 102 |
| 燃气生产和供应业 | Production and Supply of Gas | 40 |
| 水的生产和供应业 | Production and Supply of Water | 75 |

单位：万元 (10 000 yuan)

| 从业人员平均人数（万人）<br>Average Employment<br>(10 000 persons) | 工业总产值<br>Gross Output Value | 实收资本<br>Paid-in Capital | #国家资本<br>State Capital | #外商资本<br>Foreign Capital |
|---|---|---|---|---|
| **30.26** | **68261300.5** | **26993420.5** | **10402197.9** | **663997.7** |
| 27.78 | 62415336.1 | 25585531.8 | 9947502.3 | 282345.6 |
| 2.00 | 2551717.0 | 1725645.3 | 658247.3 | |
| 0.47 | 710146.0 | 357955.1 | 156021.6 | 59812.7 |
| 2.01 | 5135818.4 | 1049933.6 | 298674.0 | 321839.4 |
| 3.06 | 5916404.1 | 1065059.7 | 408379.0 | 8990.4 |
| 27.20 | 62344896.4 | 25928360.8 | 9993818.9 | 655007.3 |
| 17.05 | 39192430.3 | 13615131.3 | 4593783.3 | 453539.6 |
| 7.88 | 14612151.8 | 5474376.2 | 2781895.1 | 41513.5 |
| 5.33 | 14456718.4 | 7903913.0 | 3026519.5 | 168944.6 |
| 0.04 | 174279.1 | 56639.2 | 56639.2 | |
| 0.19 | 1558967.8 | 1292931.3 | 34141.6 | |
| 0.24 | 150694.4 | 82141.5 | 44441.5 | |
| 0.56 | 1097673.3 | 167855.3 | 35572.3 | |
| 0.33 | 397179.6 | 57873.0 | 9657.6 | 7500.0 |
| 0.05 | 36832.1 | 21310.3 | 6072.6 | |
| 0.40 | 2294202.0 | 264386.0 | 264186.0 | |
| 0.01 | 6243.2 | 8000.0 | 5700.0 | |
| 0.01 | 8047.7 | 4000.0 | | |
| 0.08 | 39257.2 | 22100.0 | 22100.0 | |
| 0.04 | 39559.7 | 15950.0 | 3000.0 | |
| 0.24 | 151529.1 | 50145.5 | 6159.6 | |
| 0.06 | 219082.6 | 29618.2 | 29618.2 | |
| 1.59 | 3708708.8 | 1315283.3 | 633969.8 | 15885.1 |
| 1.07 | 1314003.2 | 298864.0 | 31677.8 | |
| 0.21 | 488022.0 | 106609.2 | 55903.1 | 7490.4 |
| 1.23 | 2043882.7 | 966815.9 | 356270.7 | 3723.2 |
| 0.68 | 3937377.9 | 962360.2 | 5500.0 | 61937.7 |
| 0.98 | 6913069.6 | 1052583.5 | 405033.7 | 0.0 |
| 0.76 | 841012.3 | 254690.4 | 81455.6 | 5358.2 |
| 1.23 | 1328788.3 | 750288.9 | 128588.8 | 25280.0 |
| 0.71 | 945896.5 | 528708.9 | 474248.2 | 14893.8 |
| 7.47 | 16457010.9 | 2979381.5 | 798764.5 | 319361.3 |
| 1.21 | 1393782.9 | 597050.8 | 267424.2 | 18996.2 |
| 0.47 | 982013.8 | 403403.0 | 231413.6 | |
| 2.68 | 4452664.6 | 4877453.9 | 166785.3 | |
| 1.20 | 1277434.5 | 496432.8 | 171145.8 | 57020.0 |
| 1.18 | 1082820.7 | 327354.4 | 25155.5 | |
| 0.02 | 24088.3 | 13553.8 | | |
| 0.0039 | 2468.6 | 800.0 | 800.0 | |
| 3.45 | 11755766.7 | 6803708.4 | 4850777.1 | 91551.8 |
| 0.67 | 2413040.5 | 420737.4 | 163034.4 | 35000.0 |
| 1.20 | 725899.9 | 1764389.9 | 1036961.2 | |

**表 12.8 续表 1 continued 1**

| 指 标 | Item | 资 产 Total Assets |
|---|---|---|
| **总 计** | **Total** | **116029158.2** |
| **按登记注册类型分** | **By Status of Registration** | |
| 内资企业 | Domestic-funded Enterprises | 109806714.5 |
| #国有企业 | State-owned | 6857431.3 |
| 集体企业 | Collective-owned | |
| 港澳台投资企业 | Funded by Hong Kong, Macao and Taiwan | 1339697.3 |
| 外商投资企业 | Foreign-funded | 4882746.4 |
| **按轻、重工业分** | **By Light and Heavy Industries** | |
| 轻工业 | Light Industry | 5787102.9 |
| 重工业 | Heavy Industry | 110242055.3 |
| **按企业规模分** | **By Size** | |
| 大型企业 | Large | 59741621.8 |
| 中型企业 | Medium | 24051872.3 |
| 小型微型企业 | Small&Mini | 32235664.1 |
| **按行业分** | **By Sector** | |
| 煤炭开采和洗选业 | Mining and Washing of Coal | 163672.4 |
| 石油和天然气开采业 | Extraction of Petroleum and Natural Gas | 4008051.5 |
| 黑色金属矿采选业 | Mining and Processing of Ferrous Metal Ores | |
| 有色金属矿采选业 | Mining and Processing of Non-ferrous Metal Ores | |
| 非金属矿采选业 | Mining and Processing of Non-metal Ores | 411050.8 |
| 开采辅助活动 | Support Activities for Mining | |
| 其他采矿业 | Mining of Other Ores | |
| 农副食品加工业 | Processing of Food from Agricultural Products | 1251420.7 |
| 食品制造业 | Manufacture of Foods | 313825.8 |
| 酒、饮料和精制茶制造业 | Manufacture of Liquor, Beverages and Refined Tea | 56703.8 |
| 烟草制品业 | Manufacture of Tobacco | 1754579.8 |
| 纺织业 | Manufacture of Textile | 23872.3 |
| 纺织服装、服饰业 | Manufacture of Textile Wearing Apparel and Accessories | 9636.6 |
| 皮革、毛皮、羽毛及其制品和制鞋业 | Manufacture of Leather, Fur, Feather and Related Products and Footwear | 66291.6 |
| 木材加工和木、竹、藤、棕、草制品业 | Processing of Timber, Manufacture of Wood, Bamboo, Rattan, Palm and Straw Products | |
| 家具制造业 | Manufacture of Furniture | |
| 造纸及纸制品业 | Manufacture of Paper and Paper Products | 48867.4 |
| 印刷和记录媒介复制业 | Printing and Reproduction of Recording Media | 227204.4 |
| 文教、工美、体育和娱乐用品制造业 | Manufacture of Articles for Culture, Education, Arts and Crafts, Sport and Entertainment Activities | |
| 石油、煤炭及其他燃料加工业 | Processing of Petroleum, Coking and Processing of Nuclear Fuel | 130464.8 |
| 化学原料和化学制品制造业 | Manufacture of Raw Chemical Materials and Chemical Products | 4942056.2 |
| 医药制造业 | Manufacture of Medicines | 1557014.3 |
| 化学纤维制造业 | Manufacture of Chemical Fibres | |
| 橡胶和塑料制品业 | Manufacture of Rubber and Plastics Products | 336825.4 |
| 非金属矿物制品业 | Manufacture of Non-metallic Mineral Products | 4028726.3 |
| 黑色金属冶炼和压延加工业 | Smelting and Pressing of Ferrous Metals | 4082028.6 |
| 有色金属冶炼和压延加工业 | Smelting and Pressing of Non-ferrous Metals | 7350058.2 |
| 金属制品业 | Manufacture of Metal Products | 1270239.2 |
| 通用设备制造业 | Manufacture of General Purpose Machinery | 3333646.2 |
| 专用设备制造业 | Manufacture of Special Purpose Machinery | 2186880.1 |
| 汽车制造业 | Manufacture of Automobiles | 23288021.9 |
| 铁路、船舶、航空航天和其他运输设备制造业 | Manufacture of Railway, Ship, Aerospace and Other Transport Equipment | 1637219.6 |
| 电气机械及器材制造业 | Manufacture of Electrical Machinery and Apparatus | 3740005.7 |
| 计算机、通信和其他电子设备制造业 | Manufacture of Computers, Communication and Other Electronic Equipment | 11565964.7 |
| 仪器仪表制造业 | Manufacture of Measuring Instruments and Machinery | 2143161.3 |
| 其他制造业 | Other Manufacture | 2091519.9 |
| 废弃资源综合利用业 | Utilization of Waste Resources | 31851.2 |
| 金属制品、机械和设备修理业 | Repair Service of Metal Products, Machinery and Equipment | 1758.9 |
| 电力、热力的生产和供应业 | Production and Supply of Electric Power and Heat Power | 24105922.2 |
| 燃气生产和供应业 | Production and Supply of Gas | 2288948.8 |
| 水的生产和供应业 | Production and Supply of Water | 7581667.6 |

单位：万元 (10 000 yuan)

| | 固定资产 Fixed Assets | | 负 债 | |
|---|---|---|---|---|
| #流动资产 Circulating Assets | 原 值 Original Value | 净 值 Net Value | Total Liabilities | #流动负债 Total Circulating Liabilities |
| **51110359.9** | **76578220.8** | **38016923.0** | **65023828.1** | **46968415.2** |
| 48664196.2 | 70037203.2 | 35110508.7 | 60561178.9 | 43938642.5 |
| 3026916.4 | 3174911.0 | 2018857.0 | 4071886.1 | 2213658.7 |
| 386408.7 | 831781.8 | 350224.3 | 738965.9 | 587396.0 |
| 2059755.0 | 5709235.8 | 2556190.0 | 3723683.3 | 2442376.7 |
| 3809914.5 | 2396477.2 | 1050672.6 | 2469839.4 | 2206518.1 |
| 47300445.4 | 74181743.6 | 36966250.4 | 62553988.7 | 44761897.1 |
| 27236373.1 | 37763343.7 | 18131174.1 | 30964987.9 | 23855142.5 |
| 12851016.3 | 14077635.5 | 6073030.7 | 15899961.2 | 12370607.6 |
| 11022970.5 | 24737241.6 | 13812718.2 | 18158879.0 | 10742665.1 |
| 120512.4 | 50210.4 | 33496.1 | 132744.0 | 106629.5 |
| 475464.9 | 6300536.3 | 2712346.1 | 1094054.5 | 983034.6 |
| 158615.7 | 141309.7 | 60420.6 | 191810.2 | 84342.9 |
| 814762.3 | 366925.5 | 234706.1 | 293095.7 | 230846.9 |
| 178169.2 | 181198.1 | 77526.4 | 174397.1 | 152460.9 |
| 33200.4 | 41842.5 | 12348.0 | 15853.1 | 14831.9 |
| 1443835.0 | 580826.5 | 162577.8 | 467858.1 | 466991.8 |
| 4581.4 | 21727.7 | 18442.5 | 22742.9 | 22076.7 |
| 7712.4 | 3008.9 | 1048.0 | 4042.5 | 4042.5 |
| 42731.8 | 20850.1 | 11555.5 | 35030.5 | 28645.1 |
| 25860.3 | 30928.5 | 18355.7 | 17743.5 | 17743.5 |
| 161203.8 | 168061.6 | 42478.2 | 114612.7 | 113019.8 |
| 55563.8 | 88028.3 | 45871.4 | 52620.5 | 25700.1 |
| 1861799.8 | 4086161.2 | 1681206.7 | 2826563.3 | 2405824.5 |
| 821040.8 | 718230.4 | 396623.5 | 1089825.8 | 944577.5 |
| 212951.1 | 284273.3 | 16766.1 | 239337.2 | 225612.0 |
| 1826715.4 | 2725200.8 | 1582743.8 | 2763330.0 | 2320534.4 |
| 973060.7 | 3384612.9 | 2591845.5 | 1912467.6 | 1389743.0 |
| 3511760.1 | 5375886.5 | 3132577.0 | 4828817.8 | 3681283.7 |
| 913769.5 | 545325.6 | 213807.0 | 813227.0 | 679027.2 |
| 2180857.8 | 1147297.5 | 679230.0 | 1880282.0 | 1577819.9 |
| 1765444.3 | 510261.8 | 215609.0 | 1325014.3 | 1208063.0 |
| 15387167.3 | 10123154.7 | 4207010.2 | 15235983.7 | 12438542.1 |
| 1027054.5 | 1294507.1 | 396416.3 | 1044320.2 | 887371.0 |
| 2961164.3 | 318600.2 | 193867.3 | 2873768.0 | 2449928.5 |
| 3695992.0 | 3127580.5 | 1220383.9 | 3999683.9 | 2404643.8 |
| 1523265.6 | 353120.6 | 198548.5 | 1196260.5 | 1016833.6 |
| 1177219.2 | 1054233.9 | 624564.1 | 1089669.0 | 991342.4 |
| 8865.5 | 25536.9 | 13097.0 | 7577.6 | 3289.7 |
| 1653.9 | 278.1 | 87.9 | 708.9 | 708.9 |
| 4572590.2 | 28975113.2 | 14450960.8 | 14560785.2 | 8010437.0 |
| 893191.9 | 1203102.3 | 698862.7 | 1227026.2 | 773277.6 |
| 2272582.6 | 3330289.2 | 2071543.3 | 3492574.6 | 1309189.2 |

**表 12.8 续表 2 continued 2**

| 指　标 | Item | 所有者权益 Creditors' Equity |
|---|---|---|
| **总　计** | **Total** | **51018791.3** |
| **按登记注册类型分** | **By Status of Registration** | |
| 内资企业 | Domestic-funded Enterprises | 49258997.2 |
| #国有企业 | State-owned | 2785544.1 |
| 集体企业 | Collective-owned | |
| 港澳台投资企业 | Funded by Hong Kong, Macao and Taiwan | 600731.2 |
| 外商投资企业 | Foreign-funded | 1159062.9 |
| **按轻、重工业分** | **By Light and Heavy Industries** | |
| 轻工业 | Light Industry | 3317262.8 |
| 重工业 | Heavy Industry | 47701528.5 |
| **按企业规模分** | **By Size** | |
| 大型企业 | Large | 28790100.4 |
| 中型企业 | Medium | 8151910.2 |
| 小型微型企业 | Small&Mini | 14076780.7 |
| **按行业分** | **By Sector** | |
| 煤炭开采和洗选业 | Mining and Washing of Coal | 30928.4 |
| 石油和天然气开采业 | Extraction of Petroleum and Natural Gas | 2913997.1 |
| 黑色金属矿采选业 | Mining and Processing of Ferrous Metal Ores | |
| 有色金属矿采选业 | Mining and Processing of Non-ferrous Metal Ores | |
| 非金属矿采选业 | Mining and Processing of Non-metal Ores | 219240.6 |
| 开采辅助活动 | Support Activities for Mining | |
| 其他采矿业 | Mining of Other Ores | |
| 农副食品加工业 | Processing of Food from Agricultural Products | 958324.5 |
| 食品制造业 | Manufacture of Foods | 139428.6 |
| 酒、饮料和精制茶制造业 | Manufacture of Liquor, Beverages and Refined Tea | 40850.6 |
| 烟草制品业 | Manufacture of Tobacco | 1286721.7 |
| 纺织业 | Manufacture of Textile | 1129.4 |
| 纺织服装、服饰业 | Manufacture of Textile Wearing Apparel and Accessories | 5594.0 |
| 皮革、毛皮、羽毛及其制品和制鞋业 | Manufacture of Leather, Fur, Feather and Related Products and Footwear | 31261.1 |
| 木材加工和木、竹、藤、棕、草制品业 | Processing of Timber, Manufacture of Wood, Bamboo, Rattan, Palm and Straw Products | |
| 家具制造业 | Manufacture of Furniture | |
| 造纸及纸制品业 | Manufacture of Paper and Paper Products | 31123.9 |
| 印刷和记录媒介复制业 | Printing and Reproduction of Recording Media | 112591.7 |
| 文教、工美、体育和娱乐用品制造业 | Manufacture of Articles for Culture, Education, Arts and Crafts, Sport and Entertainment Activities | |
| 石油、煤炭及其他燃料加工业 | Processing of Petroleum, Coking and Processing of Nuclear Fuel | 77844.2 |
| 化学原料和化学制品制造业 | Manufacture of Raw Chemical Materials and Chemical Products | 2115492.5 |
| 医药制造业 | Manufacture of Medicines | 467188.6 |
| 化学纤维制造业 | Manufacture of Chemical Fibres | |
| 橡胶和塑料制品业 | Manufacture of Rubber and Plastics Products | 97488.1 |
| 非金属矿物制品业 | Manufacture of Non-metallic Mineral Products | 1265396.5 |
| 黑色金属冶炼和压延加工业 | Smelting and Pressing of Ferrous Metals | 2169561.0 |
| 有色金属冶炼和压延加工业 | Smelting and Pressing of Non-ferrous Metals | 2521240.3 |
| 金属制品业 | Manufacture of Metal Products | 457011.9 |
| 通用设备制造业 | Manufacture of General Purpose Machinery | 1453363.7 |
| 专用设备制造业 | Manufacture of Special Purpose Machinery | 861865.6 |
| 汽车制造业 | Manufacture of Automobiles | 8065505.3 |
| 铁路、船舶、航空航天和其他运输设备制造业 | Manufacture of Railway, Ship, Aerospace and Other Transport Equipment | 592899.4 |
| 电气机械及器材制造业 | Manufacture of Electrical Machinery and Apparatus | 866237.7 |
| 计算机、通信和其他电子设备制造业 | Manufacture of Computers, Communication and Other Electronic Equipment | 7566280.7 |
| 仪器仪表制造业 | Manufacture of Measuring Instruments and Machinery | 946900.6 |
| 其他制造业 | Other Manufacture | 1001851.0 |
| 废弃资源综合利用业 | Utilization of Waste Resources | 24273.6 |
| 金属制品、机械和设备修理业 | Repair Service of Metal Products, Machinery and Equipment | 1050.0 |
| 电力、热力的生产和供应业 | Production and Supply of Electric Power and Heat Power | 9545136.0 |
| 燃气生产和供应业 | Production and Supply of Gas | 1061922.2 |
| 水的生产和供应业 | Production and Supply of Water | 4089090.8 |

单位：万元 (10 000 yuan)

| 营业收入<br>Revenue | 营业成本<br>Cost | 税金及附加<br>Tax and Extra Charges | 利润总额<br>Total After-tax Profits | 利税总额<br>Total Pre-tax Profits | 应付职工薪酬<br>Total Wages |
|---|---|---|---|---|---|
| **78683490.0** | **65196297.4** | **2144416.0** | **4133566.9** | **8051094.8** | **5701571.4** |
| 72043469.3 | 59725296.3 | 1986255.6 | 4247761.0 | 7861606.0 | 5260685.7 |
| 2672658.7 | 2242008.2 | 20536.1 | 137012.4 | 219907.1 | 368507.6 |
| 797102.6 | 745378.2 | 4413.3 | 24105.7 | 51845.7 | 76891.2 |
| 5842918.1 | 4725622.9 | 153747.1 | -138299.8 | 137643.1 | 363994.5 |
| 6026155.3 | 3270053.9 | 1321834.7 | 532162.3 | 2185433.8 | 537297.1 |
| 72657334.7 | 61926243.5 | 822581.3 | 3601404.6 | 5865661.0 | 5164274.3 |
| 44510990.1 | 36527383.5 | 1891251.3 | 1429849.7 | 4417697.2 | 3426296.8 |
| 16002310.9 | 13157723.5 | 104188.9 | 1277533.8 | 1721039.3 | 1335382.3 |
| 18170189.0 | 15511190.4 | 148975.8 | 1426183.4 | 1912358.3 | 939892.3 |
| 178033.7 | 140340.7 | 887.1 | 27118.9 | 29633.6 | 3744.2 |
| 1547000.9 | 941796.0 | 54562.9 | 461253.7 | 582737.7 | 47616.4 |
| 141986.5 | 114157.2 | 3797.2 | 9206.0 | 16727.7 | 14428.9 |
| 1043569.9 | 878663.7 | 5186.2 | 120916.9 | 137161.2 | 58121.0 |
| 534219.4 | 450339.3 | 3489.1 | 10832.3 | 23270.2 | 55613.2 |
| 28015.9 | 18545.0 | 286.3 | 1478.7 | 3090.8 | 6026.6 |
| 2350018.5 | 690935.8 | 1285491.8 | 220050.3 | 1716741.5 | 143988.8 |
| 13750.7 | 12925.1 | 76.1 | -1778.7 | -1629.1 | 1705.6 |
| 5592.1 | 3754.8 | 65.5 | 71.8 | 421.8 | 1221.2 |
| 31284.6 | 26848.3 | 574.0 | 496.2 | 2101.1 | 7504.8 |
| 36282.3 | 31260.3 | 219.3 | 1333.3 | 2371.2 | 4509.6 |
| 161041.3 | 135775.0 | 1357.6 | 15779.0 | 19039.6 | 42391.3 |
| 231306.8 | 184119.0 | 4887.1 | 20598.8 | 30866.8 | 27535.6 |
| 4075563.4 | 3133482.8 | 28332.0 | 568343.3 | 737114.7 | 313715.4 |
| 1201062.4 | 563934.0 | 15748.2 | 82631.1 | 183534.4 | 175876.0 |
| 522587.9 | 417183.1 | 7338.8 | 61892.3 | 73397.0 | 25980.6 |
| 2531512.8 | 2140192.9 | 20416.0 | 159516.4 | 228139.1 | 217420.3 |
| 3988824.3 | 3676984.9 | 14164.0 | -96803.1 | -66634.3 | 149561.2 |
| 10422066.8 | 9118635.2 | 39345.4 | 764962.6 | 859828.7 | 189719.8 |
| 1048017.8 | 935533.0 | 3365.3 | 50560.0 | 68357.6 | 139202.9 |
| 1347460.2 | 1060287.3 | 12695.7 | 95488.9 | 152242.1 | 180321.6 |
| 904719.2 | 774245.2 | 5638.3 | 33100.1 | 57313.3 | 113034.5 |
| 21250758.5 | 17989432.7 | 492971.8 | -107546.6 | 939561.8 | 1407373.7 |
| 1164496.5 | 980262.7 | 9508.5 | 56558.5 | 93004.0 | 213809.6 |
| 1900607.2 | 1780804.2 | 3085.2 | 37985.7 | 53384.7 | 100053.9 |
| 4475159.8 | 3591111.1 | 35298.1 | 579186.9 | 666977.1 | 363286.8 |
| 1303158.7 | 970069.3 | 9092.4 | 111159.0 | 167786.1 | 221472.5 |
| 1115243.5 | 963656.4 | 5568.1 | 56313.5 | 79631.0 | 242842.6 |
| 25719.0 | 21279.6 | 348.9 | 193.8 | 2395.3 | 4667.1 |
| 2468.6 | 2260.3 | 13.1 | 87.1 | 212.4 | 524.1 |
| 11602611.5 | 10443522.1 | 61402.3 | 480305.7 | 810208.6 | 865828.8 |
| 2564386.5 | 2323057.9 | 7198.5 | 197962.1 | 234363.3 | 152265.5 |
| 934962.8 | 680902.5 | 12005.2 | 114312.4 | 147743.8 | 210207.3 |

# 表 12.9 国有控股工业企业经济效益指标(2022 年)
## INDICATORS ON ECONOMIC BENEFIT OF STATE-HOLDING INDUSTRIAL ENTERPRISES (2022)

| 指　标 | Item | 总资产贡献率 Ratio of Total Assets to Industrial Output Value |
|---|---|---|
| **总　计** | **Total** | **7.3** |
| **按轻、重工业分** | **By Light and Heavy Industries** | |
| 轻工业 | Light Industry | 37.7 |
| 重工业 | Heavy Industry | 5.8 |
| **按企业规模分** | **By Size** | |
| 大型企业 | Large | 7.5 |
| 中型企业 | Medium | 7.8 |
| 小型微型企业 | Small&Mini | 6.7 |
| **按行业分** | **By Sector** | |
| 煤炭开采和洗选业 | Mining and Washing of Coal | 23.5 |
| 石油和天然气开采业 | Extraction of Petroleum and Natural Gas | 15.1 |
| 黑色金属矿采选业 | Mining and Processing of Ferrous Metal Ores | |
| 有色金属矿采选业 | Mining and Processing of Non-Ferrous Metal Ores | |
| 非金属矿采选业 | Mining and Processing of Nonmetal Ores | 4.5 |
| 开采辅助活动 | Mining Support Activities | |
| 其他采矿业 | Mining of Other Ores | |
| 农副食品加工业 | Processing of Food from Agricultural Products | 10.3 |
| 食品制造业 | Manufacture of Foods | 7.9 |
| 酒、饮料和精制茶制造业 | Liquor, Beverage and Refined Tea | 5.5 |
| 烟草制品业 | Manufacture of Tobacco | 97.3 |
| 纺织业 | Manufacture of Textile | -2.6 |
| 纺织服装、服饰业 | Manufacture of Textile Wearing Apparel, Footwear and Caps | 4.4 |
| 皮革、毛皮、羽毛及其制品和制鞋业 | Manufacture of Leather, Fur, Feather and Related Products and Footwear | 4.0 |
| 木材加工和木、竹、藤、棕、草制品业 | Processing of Timber, Manufacture of Wood, Bamboo, Rattan, Palm and Straw Products | |
| 家具制造业 | Manufacture of Furniture | |
| 造纸和纸制品业 | Manufacture of Paper and Paper Products | 5.6 |
| 印刷和记录媒介复制业 | Printing, Reproduction of Recording Media | 8.4 |
| 文教、工美、体育和娱乐用品制造业 | Manufacture of Culture, Education, Handicraft, Fine Arts, Sports and Entertainment Articles | |
| 石油加工、炼焦和核燃料加工业 | Processing of Petroleum, Coking, Processing of Nuclear Fuel | 24.6 |
| 化学原料和化学制品制造业 | Manufacture of Raw Chemical Materials and Chemical Products | 15.5 |
| 医药制造业 | Manufacture of Medicines | 12.4 |
| 化学纤维制造业 | Manufacture of Chemical Fibers | 0.0 |
| 橡胶和塑料制品业 | Manufacture of Rubber and Plastics | 22.5 |
| 非金属矿物制品业 | Manufacture of Non-metallic Mineral Products | 6.9 |
| 黑色金属冶炼和压延加工业 | Smelting and Pressing of Ferrous Metals | -1.0 |
| 有色金属冶炼和压延加工业 | Smelting and Pressing of Nonferrous Metals | 12.6 |
| 金属制品业 | Manufacture of Metal Products | 5.5 |
| 通用设备制造业 | Manufacture of General Purpose Machinery | 4.9 |
| 专用设备制造业 | Manufacture of Special Purpose Machinery | 2.5 |
| 汽车制造业 | Manufacture of Motor Vehicles | 3.8 |
| 铁路、船舶、航空航天和其他运输设备制造业 | Manufacture of Railway, Ship, Aviation and Other Transporting Equipment | 5.8 |
| 电气机械和器材制造业 | Manufacture of Electrical Machinery and Equipment | 1.6 |
| 计算机、通信和其他电子设备制造业 | Manufacture of Communication Equipment, Computers and Other Electronic Equipment | 5.7 |
| 仪器仪表制造业 | Manufacture of Measuring Instruments and Machinery for Cultural Activity and Office Work | 7.8 |
| 其他制造业 | Other Manufacture | 3.8 |
| 废弃资源综合利用业 | Comprehensive Utilization of Waste Resources | 7.5 |
| 金属制品、机械和设备修理业 | Repair of Metal Products, Machinery and Equipment | 11.9 |
| 电力、热力生产和供应业 | Production and Supply of Electric Power and Heat Power | 4.6 |
| 燃气生产和供应业 | Production and Supply of Gas | 10.7 |
| 水的生产和供应业 | Production and Supply of Water | 2.2 |

单位: % (%)

| 资本保值增值率 Ratio of Assets Appreciation YOY | 资 产负债率 Asset-Liability Ratio | 流动资产周转率(次) Turnover Ratio of Circulating Assets (time) | 成本费用利润率 Ratio of Profits to Cost | 产品销售率 Sales as Percentage of Output |
|---|---|---|---|---|
| **105.8** | **56.0** | **1.5** | **5.9** | **98.5** |
| | | | | |
| 100.5 | 42.7 | 1.6 | 12.9 | 98.5 |
| 106.3 | 56.7 | 1.5 | 5.5 | 98.5 |
| | | | | |
| 103.6 | 51.8 | 1.6 | 3.6 | 98.8 |
| 109.2 | 66.1 | 1.3 | 9.0 | 98.3 |
| 107.8 | 56.3 | 1.7 | 8.6 | 98.2 |
| | | | | |
| 0.0 | 81.1 | 1.5 | 17.8 | 99.5 |
| 119.4 | 27.3 | 3.3 | 43.3 | 99.8 |
| | | | | |
| 100.9 | 46.7 | 0.9 | 7.3 | 99.8 |
| | | | | |
| 108.4 | 23.4 | 1.3 | 12.9 | 96.2 |
| 100.1 | 55.6 | 3.0 | 2.1 | 97.2 |
| 89.9 | 28.0 | 0.8 | 5.7 | 69.3 |
| 109.4 | 26.7 | 1.6 | 27.1 | 100.0 |
| | 95.3 | 3.0 | -11.9 | |
| 101.8 | 42.0 | 0.7 | 1.2 | 100.0 |
| 110.6 | 52.8 | 0.7 | 1.6 | 88.5 |
| | | | | |
| 108.0 | 36.3 | 1.4 | 3.9 | 87.6 |
| 89.7 | 50.4 | 1.0 | 10.6 | 98.7 |
| | | | | |
| 108.5 | 40.3 | 4.2 | 10.3 | 93.5 |
| 111.3 | 57.2 | 2.2 | 16.5 | 97.6 |
| 64.2 | 70.0 | 1.5 | 7.6 | 97.2 |
| 0.0 | 0.0 | 0.0 | 0.0 | 0.0 |
| 227.4 | 71.1 | 2.5 | 14.2 | 99.5 |
| 105.4 | 68.6 | 1.4 | 6.9 | 94.8 |
| 96.2 | 46.9 | 4.1 | -2.6 | 99.7 |
| 111.2 | 65.7 | 3.0 | 8.1 | 98.5 |
| 108.9 | 64.0 | 1.2 | 5.2 | 107.7 |
| 93.3 | 56.4 | 0.6 | 8.0 | 99.8 |
| 140.2 | 60.6 | 0.5 | 3.9 | 93.5 |
| 101.0 | 65.4 | 1.4 | -0.6 | 97.6 |
| 102.5 | 63.8 | 1.1 | 5.3 | 97.9 |
| 109.2 | 76.8 | 0.6 | 2.1 | 98.8 |
| 107.9 | 34.6 | 1.2 | 15.5 | 98.5 |
| 109.4 | 55.8 | 0.9 | 9.7 | 99.6 |
| | 52.1 | 1.0 | 5.3 | |
| 95.3 | 23.8 | 2.9 | 0.8 | 100.0 |
| 83.3 | 40.3 | 1.5 | 3.7 | 95.0 |
| 104.7 | 60.4 | 2.5 | 4.4 | 99.8 |
| 107.2 | 53.6 | 2.9 | 8.3 | 100.0 |
| 108.8 | 46.1 | 0.4 | 13.7 | 98.2 |

**表 12.9 续表 continued**

| 指 标 | Item | 销售利润率 Rate of Return on Sale |
|---|---|---|
| **总 计** | **Total** | **5.3** |
| **按轻、重工业分** | **By Light and Heavy Industries** | |
| 轻工业 | Light Industry | 8.8 |
| 重工业 | Heavy Industry | 5.0 |
| **按企业规模分** | **By Size** | |
| 大型企业 | Large | 3.2 |
| 中型企业 | Medium | 8.0 |
| 小型微型企业 | Small&Mini | 7.9 |
| **按行业分** | **By Sector** | |
| 煤炭开采和洗选业 | Mining and Washing of Coal | 15.2 |
| 石油和天然气开采业 | Extraction of Petroleum and Natural Gas | 29.8 |
| 黑色金属矿采选业 | Mining and Processing of Ferrous Metal Ores | |
| 有色金属矿采选业 | Mining and Processing of Non-Ferrous Metal Ores | |
| 非金属矿采选业 | Mining and Processing of Nonmetal Ores | 6.5 |
| 开采辅助活动 | Mining Support Activities | 0.0 |
| 其他采矿业 | Mining of Other Ores | 0.0 |
| 农副食品加工业 | Processing of Food from Agricultural Products | 11.6 |
| 食品制造业 | Manufacture of Foods | 2.0 |
| 酒、饮料和精制茶制造业 | Liquor, Beverage and Refined Tea | 5.3 |
| 烟草制品业 | Manufacture of Tobacco | 9.4 |
| 纺织业 | Manufacture of Textile | -12.9 |
| 纺织服装、服饰业 | Manufacture of Textile Wearing Apparel, Footwear and Caps | 1.3 |
| 皮革、毛皮、羽毛及其制品和制鞋业 | Manufacture of Leather, Fur, Feather and Related Products and Footwear | 1.6 |
| 木材加工和木、竹、藤、棕、草制品业 | Processing of Timber, Manufacture of Wood, Bamboo, Rattan, Palm and Straw Products | |
| 家具制造业 | Manufacture of Furniture | |
| 造纸和纸制品业 | Manufacture of Paper and Paper Products | 3.7 |
| 印刷和记录媒介复制业 | Printing, Reproduction of Recording Media | 9.8 |
| 文教、工美、体育和娱乐用品制造业 | Manufacture of Culture, Education, Handicraft, Fine Arts, Sports and Entertainment Articles | |
| 石油加工、炼焦和核燃料加工业 | Processing of Petroleum, Coking, Processing of Nuclear Fuel | 8.9 |
| 化学原料和化学制品制造业 | Manufacture of Raw Chemical Materials and Chemical Products | 14.0 |
| 医药制造业 | Manufacture of Medicines | 6.9 |
| 化学纤维制造业 | Manufacture of Chemical Fibers | |
| 橡胶和塑料制品业 | Manufacture of Rubber and Plastics | 11.8 |
| 非金属矿物制品业 | Manufacture of Non-metallic Mineral Products | 6.3 |
| 黑色金属冶炼和压延加工业 | Smelting and Pressing of Ferrous Metals | -2.4 |
| 有色金属冶炼和压延加工业 | Smelting and Pressing of Nonferrous Metals | 7.3 |
| 金属制品业 | Manufacture of Metal Products | 4.8 |
| 通用设备制造业 | Manufacture of General Purpose Machinery | 7.1 |
| 专用设备制造业 | Manufacture of Special Purpose Machinery | 3.7 |
| 汽车制造业 | Manufacture of Motor Vehicles | -0.5 |
| 铁路、船舶、航空航天和其他运输设备制造业 | Manufacture of Railway, Ship, Aviation and Other Transporting Equipment | 4.9 |
| 电气机械和器材制造业 | Manufacture of Electrical Machinery and Equipment | 2.0 |
| 计算机、通信和其他电子设备制造业 | Manufacture of Communication Equipment, Computers and Other Electronic Equipment | 12.9 |
| 仪器仪表制造业 | Manufacture of Measuring Instruments and Machinery for Cultural Activity and Office Work | 8.5 |
| 其他制造业 | Other Manufacture | 5.1 |
| 废弃资源综合利用业 | Comprehensive Utilization of Waste Resources | 0.8 |
| 金属制品、机械和设备修理业 | Repair of Metal Products, Machinery and Equipment | 3.5 |
| 电力、热力生产和供应业 | Production and Supply of Electric Power and Heat Power | 4.1 |
| 燃气生产和供应业 | Production and Supply of Gas | 7.7 |
| 水的生产和供应业 | Production and Supply of Water | 12.2 |

单位：% (%)

| 流动比率<br>Current Ratio | 速动比率<br>Quick Ratio | 产权比率<br>Equity Ratio | 人均实现利税（元）<br>Per Capita Pre-tax Profits (yuan) | 从业人员人均工资（元）<br>Per Capita Wages of Employees (yuan) |
|---|---|---|---|---|
| **1.1** | **0.9** | **1.3** | **266073** | **188426** |
| | | | | |
| 1.7 | 1.2 | 0.7 | 714895 | 175760 |
| 1.1 | 0.9 | 1.3 | 215633 | 189849 |
| | | | | |
| 1.1 | 1.0 | 1.1 | 259133 | 200979 |
| 1.0 | 0.9 | 2.0 | 218295 | 169379 |
| 1.0 | 0.9 | 1.3 | 358993 | 176439 |
| | | | | |
| 1.1 | 1.1 | 4.3 | 740840 | 93605 |
| 0.5 | 0.5 | 0.4 | 3019366 | 246717 |
| | | | | |
| 1.9 | 1.7 | 0.9 | 70284 | 60626 |
| | | | | |
| 3.5 | 3.1 | 0.3 | 245369 | 103973 |
| 1.2 | 0.8 | 1.3 | 69671 | 166507 |
| 2.2 | 2.0 | 0.4 | 61816 | 120532 |
| 3.1 | 1.4 | 0.4 | 4324286 | 362692 |
| 0.2 | 0.2 | 20.1 | -108607 | 113707 |
| 1.9 | 1.7 | 0.7 | 52725 | 152650 |
| 1.5 | 1.1 | 1.1 | 27287 | 97465 |
| | | | | |
| 1.5 | 0.6 | 0.6 | 62400 | 118674 |
| 1.4 | 1.1 | 1.0 | 78031 | 173735 |
| | | | | |
| 2.2 | 0.5 | 0.7 | 541523 | 483081 |
| 0.8 | 0.7 | 1.3 | 463303 | 197181 |
| 0.9 | 0.7 | 2.3 | 171688 | 164524 |
| | | | | |
| 0.9 | 0.7 | 2.5 | 349510 | 123717 |
| 0.8 | 0.7 | 2.2 | 185932 | 177197 |
| 0.7 | 0.5 | 0.9 | -97848 | 219620 |
| 1.0 | 0.7 | 1.9 | 880070 | 194186 |
| 1.4 | 1.1 | 1.8 | 90420 | 184131 |
| 1.4 | 1.2 | 1.3 | 123774 | 146603 |
| 1.5 | 1.2 | 1.5 | 81180 | 160106 |
| 1.2 | 1.1 | 1.9 | 125761 | 188378 |
| 1.2 | 0.9 | 1.8 | 76863 | 176702 |
| 1.2 | 1.0 | 3.3 | 113343 | 212429 |
| 1.5 | 1.3 | 0.5 | 248779 | 135504 |
| 1.5 | 1.2 | 1.3 | 139242 | 183795 |
| 1.2 | 1.0 | 1.1 | 67656 | 206323 |
| 2.7 | 2.6 | 0.3 | 95812 | 186684 |
| 2.3 | 2.3 | 0.7 | 53100 | 131025 |
| 0.6 | 0.5 | 1.5 | 234775 | 250892 |
| 1.2 | 1.1 | 1.2 | 350319 | 227602 |
| 1.7 | 1.7 | 0.9 | 123325 | 175465 |

# 表 12.10 私营工业企业主要经济指标(2022 年)
## MAIN ECONOMIC INDICATORS OF PRIVATE INDUSTRIAL ENTERPRISES (2022)

| 指 标 | Item | 单位数(个) Number of Enterprises (unit) |
|---|---|---|
| **总 计** | **Total** | **6124** |
| **按登记注册类型分** | **By Status of Registration** | |
| 私营独资企业 | Solely Private-funded Enterprises | 136 |
| 私营合伙企业 | Private Partnership Enterprises | 14 |
| 私营有限责任公司 | Private Limited Liability Companies | 5744 |
| 私营股份有限公司 | Private Share-holding Companies | 230 |
| **按轻、重工业分** | **By Light and Heavy Industries** | |
| 轻工业 | Light Industry | 1952 |
| 重工业 | Heavy Industry | 4172 |
| **按企业规模分** | **By Size** | |
| 大型企业 | Large | 58 |
| 中型企业 | Medium | 544 |
| 小型微型企业 | Small&Mini | 5522 |
| **按行业分** | **By Sector** | |
| 煤炭开采和洗选业 | Mining and Washing of Coal | 16 |
| 石油和天然气开采业 | Extraction of Petroleum and Natural Gas | 1 |
| 黑色金属矿采选业 | Mining and Processing of Ferrous Metal Ores | |
| 有色金属矿采选业 | Mining and Processing of Non-Ferrous Metal Ores | |
| 非金属矿采选业 | Mining and Processing of Nonmetal Ores | 126 |
| 开采辅助活动 | Mining Support Activities | |
| 其他采矿业 | Mining of Other Ores | |
| 农副食品加工业 | Processing of Food from Agricultural Products | 465 |
| 食品制造业 | Manufacture of Foods | 181 |
| 酒、饮料和精制茶制造业 | Liquor, Beverage and Refined Tea | 58 |
| 烟草制品业 | Manufacture of Tobacco | |
| 纺织业 | Manufacture of Textile | 48 |
| 纺织服装、鞋、帽制造业 | Manufacture of Textile Wearing Apparel, Footwear and Caps | 54 |
| 皮革、毛皮、羽毛(绒)及其制品业 | Manufacture of Leather, Fur, Feather and Related Products | 54 |
| 木材加工及木竹藤棕草制品业 | Processing of Timber, Manufacture of Wood, Bamboo, Rattan, Palm and Straw Products | 93 |
| 家具制造业 | Manufacture of Furniture | 93 |
| 造纸及纸制品业 | Manufacture of Paper and Paper Products | 107 |
| 印刷业、记录媒介的复制 | Printing, Reproduction of Recording Media | 96 |
| 文教、工美、体育和娱乐用品制造业 | Manufacture of Culture, Education, Handicraft, Fine Arts, Sports and Entertainment Articles | 63 |
| 石油加工、炼焦及核燃料加工业 | Processing of Petroleum, Coking, Processing of Nuclear Fuel | 15 |
| 化学原料及化学制品制造业 | Manufacture of Raw Chemical Materials and Chemical Products | 171 |
| 医药制造业 | Manufacture of Medicines | 131 |
| 化学纤维制造业 | Manufacture of Chemical Fibers | 9 |
| 橡胶和塑料制品业 | Manufacture of Rubber and Plastics | 309 |
| 非金属矿物制品业 | Manufacture of Non-metallic Mineral Products | 671 |
| 黑色金属冶炼及压延加工业 | Smelting and Pressing of Ferrous Metals | 71 |
| 有色金属冶炼及压延加工业 | Smelting and Pressing of Nonferrous Metals | 117 |
| 金属制品业 | Manufacture of Metal Products | 364 |
| 通用设备制造业 | Manufacture of General Purpose Machinery | 356 |
| 专用设备制造业 | Manufacture of Special Purpose Machinery | 264 |
| 汽车制造业 | Manufacture of Motor Vehicles | 861 |
| 铁路、船舶、航空航天和其他运输设备制造业 | Manufacture of Railway, Ship, Aviation and Other Transporting Equipment | 433 |
| 电气机械及器材制造业 | Manufacture of Electrical Machinery and Equipment | 282 |
| 通信设备、计算机及其他电子设备制造业 | Manufacture of Communication Equipment, Computers and Other Electronic Equipment | 405 |
| 仪器仪表及文化、办公用机械制造业 | Manufacture of Measuring Instruments and Machinery for Cultural Activity and Office Work | 67 |
| 其他制造业 | Other Manufacture | 10 |
| 废弃资源综合利用业 | Comprehensive Utilization of Waste Resources | 46 |
| 金属制品、机械和设备修理业 | Repair of Metal Products, Machinery and Equipment | 9 |
| 电力、热力的生产和供应业 | Production and Supply of Electric Power and Heat Power | 9 |
| 燃气生产和供应业 | Production and Supply of Gas | 61 |
| 水的生产和供应业 | Production and Supply of Water | 8 |

单位：万元 (10 000 yuan)

| 从业人员平均人数（万人） Average Employment (10 000 persons) | 工业总产值 Gross Output Value | 实收资本 Paid-in Capital | #国家资本 State Capital | #外商资本 Foreign Capital |
|---|---|---|---|---|
| **90.15** | **115662020.9** | **15613978.2** | **247279.6** | **3410.0** |
| 1.25 | 1297659.9 | 71276.7 | | |
| 0.12 | 86555.1 | 7135.8 | | |
| 82.16 | 105837416.0 | 13741856.3 | 244805.1 | 3410.0 |
| 6.63 | 8440389.9 | 1793709.4 | 2474.5 | |
| 28.13 | 31382408.5 | 3556608.1 | 12971.4 | 1230.0 |
| 62.02 | 84279612.4 | 12057370.1 | 234308.2 | 2180.0 |
| 13.02 | 24588875.7 | 2586321.7 | 151743.0 | 2000.0 |
| 28.33 | 36029258.8 | 4227213.4 | 9415.0 | |
| 48.80 | 55043886.4 | 8800443.1 | 86121.6 | 1410.0 |
| 0.05 | 211024.5 | 23328.0 | | |
| 0.0012 | 23944.3 | 200.0 | | |
| 0.72 | 865022.2 | 1207503.7 | 5600.6 | |
| 4.33 | 6618462.6 | 548262.1 | 655.1 | |
| 2.47 | 2258545.9 | 244143.7 | 0.0 | |
| 0.79 | 897521.5 | 297862.5 | 263.6 | |
| 0.39 | 218156.9 | 36964.0 | | |
| 0.98 | 440058.0 | 59284.1 | 4.0 | |
| 1.07 | 575072.4 | 27511.3 | | |
| 1.01 | 1268784.3 | 114673.5 | | |
| 1.11 | 751703.9 | 97428.3 | 200.0 | |
| 1.15 | 1809481.4 | 117458.2 | | |
| 1.39 | 1350277.6 | 159493.7 | | |
| 0.71 | 393045.0 | 34326.9 | | |
| 0.11 | 338231.3 | 69451.1 | | |
| 1.83 | 3982389.8 | 596736.4 | 10350.0 | |
| 2.65 | 3185622.8 | 603393.1 | 4383.2 | |
| 0.40 | 943169.1 | 85358.9 | 5703.0 | |
| 3.53 | 3865391.0 | 555691.3 | 1562.5 | 1230.0 |
| 7.65 | 9031720.8 | 1736788.9 | 42700.0 | |
| 0.92 | 7118457.7 | 278857.2 | | |
| 1.42 | 5233892.0 | 402571.5 | 1240.0 | |
| 4.50 | 4785028.5 | 509335.3 | | |
| 4.90 | 5048440.3 | 734210.8 | 400.0 | |
| 3.60 | 4910738.2 | 480775.1 | 746.9 | |
| 15.22 | 15839585.3 | 2272161.7 | 23218.0 | 2180.0 |
| 7.87 | 7105387.4 | 746918.9 | 1578.9 | |
| 6.24 | 9098939.4 | 1019826.9 | 1122.0 | |
| 11.30 | 15242400.0 | 2044210.2 | 133340.0 | |
| 0.75 | 509781.1 | 84153.6 | | |
| 0.08 | 35286.0 | 5807.5 | | |
| 0.31 | 791413.6 | 83497.2 | 1590.8 | |
| 0.19 | 57984.6 | 26952.3 | | |
| 0.07 | 30577.4 | 81357.2 | 8849.0 | |
| 0.38 | 780142.6 | 196239.0 | 3472.0 | |
| 0.05 | 46341.5 | 31244.1 | 300.0 | |

**表 12.10 续表 1 continued 1**

| 指 标 | Item | #流动资产 Circulating Assets |
|---|---|---|
| **总 计** | **Total** | **54532320.4** |
| **按登记注册类型分** | **By Status of Registration** | |
| 私营独资企业 | Solely Private-funded Enterprises | 363701.9 |
| 私营合伙企业 | Private Partnership Enterprises | 16410.6 |
| 私营有限责任公司 | Private Limited Liability Companies | 47730332.1 |
| 私营股份有限公司 | Private Share-holding Companies | 6421875.8 |
| **按轻、重工业分** | **By Light and Heavy Industries** | |
| 轻工业 | Light Industry | 15131986.6 |
| 重工业 | Heavy Industry | 39400333.8 |
| **按企业规模分** | **By Size** | |
| 大型企业 | Large | 15070195.6 |
| 中型企业 | Medium | 14041868.9 |
| 小型微型企业 | Small&Mini | 25420255.9 |
| **按行业分** | **By Sector** | |
| 煤炭开采和洗选业 | Mining and Washing of Coal | 41312.0 |
| 石油和天然气开采业 | Extraction of Petroleum and Natural Gas | 8597.7 |
| 黑色金属矿采选业 | Mining and Processing of Ferrous Metal Ores | |
| 有色金属矿采选业 | Mining and Processing of Non-Ferrous Metal Ores | |
| 非金属矿采选业 | Mining and Processing of Nonmetal Ores | 560159.3 |
| 开采辅助活动 | Mining Support Activities | |
| 其他采矿业 | Mining of Other Ores | |
| 农副食品加工业 | Processing of Food from Agricultural Products | 1691587.4 |
| 食品制造业 | Manufacture of Foods | 792996.8 |
| 酒、饮料和精制茶制造业 | Liquor, Beverage and Refined Tea | 395334.9 |
| 烟草制品业 | Manufacture of Tobacco | |
| 纺织业 | Manufacture of Textile | 124798.9 |
| 纺织服装、鞋、帽制造业 | Manufacture of Textile Wearing Apparel, Footwear and Caps | 161228.6 |
| 皮革、毛皮、羽毛(绒)及其制品业 | Manufacture of Leather, Fur, Feather and Related Products | 183794.2 |
| 木材加工及木竹藤棕草制品业 | Processing of Timber, Manufacture of Wood, Bamboo, Rattan, Palm and Straw Products | 217274.7 |
| 家具制造业 | Manufacture of Furniture | 289546.7 |
| 造纸及纸制品业 | Manufacture of Paper and Paper Products | 446957.9 |
| 印刷业、记录媒介的复制 | Printing, Reproduction of Recording Media | 457391.7 |
| 文教、工美、体育和娱乐用品制造业 | Manufacture of Culture, Education, Handicraft, Fine Arts, Sports and Entertainment Articles | 136454.8 |
| 石油加工、炼焦及核燃料加工业 | Processing of Petroleum, Coking, Processing of Nuclear Fuel | 226404.9 |
| 化学原料及化学制品制造业 | Manufacture of Raw Chemical Materials and Chemical Products | 1484913.7 |
| 医药制造业 | Manufacture of Medicines | 2201595.8 |
| 化学纤维制造业 | Manufacture of Chemical Fibers | 574562.4 |
| 橡胶和塑料制品业 | Manufacture of Rubber and Plastics | 1393506.3 |
| 非金属矿物制品业 | Manufacture of Non-metallic Mineral Products | 5648006.5 |
| 黑色金属冶炼及压延加工业 | Smelting and Pressing of Ferrous Metals | 1329476.5 |
| 有色金属冶炼及压延加工业 | Smelting and Pressing of Nonferrous Metals | 1498686.5 |
| 金属制品业 | Manufacture of Metal Products | 1876716.2 |
| 通用设备制造业 | Manufacture of General Purpose Machinery | 2380059.7 |
| 专用设备制造业 | Manufacture of Special Purpose Machinery | 2110605.2 |
| 汽车制造业 | Manufacture of Motor Vehicles | 9864586.3 |
| 铁路、船舶、航空航天和其他运输设备制造业 | Manufacture of Railway, Ship, Aviation and Other Transporting Equipment | 4137598.8 |
| 电气机械及器材制造业 | Manufacture of Electrical Machinery and Equipment | 6590003.2 |
| 通信设备、计算机及其他电子设备制造业 | Manufacture of Communication Equipment, Computers and Other Electronic Equipment | 6314908.9 |
| 仪器仪表及文化、办公用机械制造业 | Manufacture of Measuring Instruments and Machinery for Cultural Activity and Office Work | 365713.9 |
| 其他制造业 | Other Manufacture | 20385.0 |
| 废弃资源综合利用业 | Comprehensive Utilization of Waste Resources | 266774.1 |
| 金属制品、机械和设备修理业 | Repair of Metal Products, Machinery and Equipment | 72943.3 |
| 电力、热力的生产和供应业 | Production and Supply of Electric Power and Heat Power | 112474.0 |
| 燃气生产和供应业 | Production and Supply of Gas | 524730.3 |
| 水的生产和供应业 | Production and Supply of Water | 30233.3 |

单位：万元 (10 000 yuan)

| 固定资产 Fixed Assets | | 负 债 | 其 中 of which |
|---|---|---|---|
| 原 值 Original Value | 净 值 Net Value | Total Liabilities | #流动负债 Total Circulating Liabilities |
| **47050946.4** | **25064873.5** | **55340645.0** | **45184593.3** |
| 535935.9 | 286515.2 | 432645.8 | 354236.2 |
| 63422.8 | 47382.9 | 18561.6 | 15007.5 |
| 42519056.7 | 22578882.4 | 50237802.9 | 41148052.1 |
| 3932531.0 | 2152093.0 | 4651634.7 | 3667297.5 |
| 12751846.3 | 7011100.9 | 14520786.0 | 11889522.6 |
| 34299100.1 | 18053772.6 | 40819859.0 | 33295070.7 |
| 7753235.5 | 4134290.2 | 13986308.9 | 12975512.9 |
| 16025703.2 | 8769904.5 | 15465865.4 | 11573153.2 |
| 23272007.7 | 12160488.5 | 25888470.7 | 20635927.2 |
| 243299.4 | 209695.0 | 71986.5 | 37679.7 |
| 11015.2 | 8111.4 | 14703.5 | 14703.5 |
| 454692.5 | 263431.8 | 808161.4 | 655206.4 |
| 2177191.2 | 1007433.4 | 1765208.6 | 1409569.0 |
| 1068804.4 | 566798.1 | 793836.1 | 576020.4 |
| 399858.1 | 221019.2 | 356414.2 | 264390.8 |
| 118444.1 | 47178.2 | 110232.8 | 88699.5 |
| 89755.0 | 45697.7 | 105848.9 | 74449.1 |
| 158307.4 | 84849.5 | 141375.3 | 114261.7 |
| 845201.5 | 357338.0 | 422806.2 | 213314.7 |
| 475317.8 | 205760.1 | 349441.7 | 223912.2 |
| 633204.5 | 419047.8 | 509563.9 | 398295.0 |
| 721877.0 | 386871.0 | 586643.7 | 437791.2 |
| 251210.0 | 104468.5 | 146390.5 | 88631.0 |
| 278908.5 | 52686.5 | 360760.1 | 202064.7 |
| 1541744.0 | 1095798.8 | 1528869.9 | 1248108.1 |
| 1449656.7 | 864016.4 | 1549522.7 | 1281135.2 |
| 490527.8 | 331691.6 | 491304.8 | 452277.9 |
| 2139544.4 | 1137381.7 | 1525796.8 | 1053476.0 |
| 5233392.7 | 2751608.5 | 5917593.2 | 4680823.6 |
| 968225.8 | 430453.7 | 1501117.0 | 1177877.4 |
| 932676.7 | 532646.3 | 1368761.8 | 1096455.3 |
| 1889943.0 | 996001.3 | 2074230.4 | 1606598.7 |
| 2323556.7 | 1177962.0 | 2293423.8 | 1788897.4 |
| 1582691.3 | 899705.8 | 1834016.2 | 1414652.0 |
| 7444843.3 | 3598017.5 | 10594522.9 | 9084629.9 |
| 2916179.5 | 1251704.5 | 3746353.7 | 3078320.3 |
| 2901910.8 | 1738231.2 | 6421055.7 | 5719276.2 |
| 6052774.4 | 3445031.4 | 6493748.4 | 5623154.8 |
| 178926.4 | 101853.8 | 284480.5 | 272484.0 |
| 33224.5 | 20023.1 | 16004.3 | 14686.1 |
| 281917.5 | 196611.4 | 265057.2 | 219205.4 |
| 24449.6 | 13517.1 | 50996.9 | 48736.7 |
| 161068.1 | 107880.5 | 246833.0 | 107460.2 |
| 504295.1 | 347935.6 | 560049.9 | 394117.9 |
| 72311.5 | 46415.1 | 33532.5 | 23231.3 |

**表 12.10 续表 2 continued 2**

| 指　标 | Item | 所有者权益<br>Creditors' Equity |
|---|---|---|
| **总　计** | **Total** | **43164026.2** |
| **按登记注册类型分** | **By Status of Registration** | |
| 私营独资企业 | Solely Private-funded Enterprises | 407694.5 |
| 私营合伙企业 | Private Partnership Enterprises | 60103.0 |
| 私营有限责任公司 | Private Limited Liability Companies | 35565095.7 |
| 私营股份有限公司 | Private Share-holding Companies | 7131133.0 |
| **按轻、重工业分** | **By Light and Heavy Industries** | |
| 轻工业 | Light Industry | 13376504.7 |
| 重工业 | Heavy Industry | 29787521.5 |
| **按企业规模分** | **By Size** | |
| 大型企业 | Large | 7875484.4 |
| 中型企业 | Medium | 14302998.7 |
| 小型微型企业 | Small&Mini | 20985543.1 |
| **按行业分** | **By Sector** | |
| 煤炭开采和洗选业 | Mining and Washing of Coal | 210882.7 |
| 石油和天然气开采业 | Extraction of Petroleum and Natural Gas | 3173.5 |
| 黑色金属矿采选业 | Mining and Processing of Ferrous Metal Ores | |
| 有色金属矿采选业 | Mining and Processing of Non-Ferrous Metal Ores | |
| 非金属矿采选业 | Mining and Processing of Nonmetal Ores | 515262.4 |
| 开采辅助活动 | Mining Support Activities | |
| 其他采矿业 | Mining of Other Ores | |
| 农副食品加工业 | Processing of Food from Agricultural Products | 2028280.1 |
| 食品制造业 | Manufacture of Foods | 857161.1 |
| 酒、饮料和精制茶制造业 | Liquor, Beverage and Refined Tea | 533861.1 |
| 烟草制品业 | Manufacture of Tobacco | |
| 纺织业 | Manufacture of Textile | 96161.8 |
| 纺织服装、鞋、帽制造业 | Manufacture of Textile Wearing Apparel, Footwear and Caps | 135280.8 |
| 皮革、毛皮、羽毛(绒)及其制品业 | Manufacture of Leather, Fur, Feather and Related Products | 158739.6 |
| 木材加工及木竹藤棕草制品业 | Processing of Timber, Manufacture of Wood, Bamboo, Rattan, Palm and Straw Products | 330767.9 |
| 家具制造业 | Manufacture of Furniture | 341500.5 |
| 造纸及纸制品业 | Manufacture of Paper and Paper Products | 483917.8 |
| 印刷业、记录媒介的复制 | Printing, Reproduction of Recording Media | 518746.4 |
| 文教、工美、体育和娱乐用品制造业 | Manufacture of Culture, Education, Handicraft, Fine Arts, Sports and Entertainment Articles | 193858.6 |
| 石油加工、炼焦及核燃料加工业 | Processing of Petroleum, Coking, Processing of Nuclear Fuel | 58565.0 |
| 化学原料及化学制品制造业 | Manufacture of Raw Chemical Materials and Chemical Products | 1498808.1 |
| 医药制造业 | Manufacture of Medicines | 2624998.4 |
| 化学纤维制造业 | Manufacture of Chemical Fibers | 587802.2 |
| 橡胶和塑料制品业 | Manufacture of Rubber and Plastics | 1636633.4 |
| 非金属矿物制品业 | Manufacture of Non-metallic Mineral Products | 4887539.5 |
| 黑色金属冶炼及压延加工业 | Smelting and Pressing of Ferrous Metals | 554522.8 |
| 有色金属冶炼及压延加工业 | Smelting and Pressing of Nonferrous Metals | 1028518.5 |
| 金属制品业 | Manufacture of Metal Products | 1593039.7 |
| 通用设备制造业 | Manufacture of General Purpose Machinery | 2299190.1 |
| 专用设备制造业 | Manufacture of Special Purpose Machinery | 2215354.7 |
| 汽车制造业 | Manufacture of Motor Vehicles | 5821146.5 |
| 铁路、船舶、航空航天和其他运输设备制造业 | Manufacture of Railway, Ship, Aviation and Other Transporting Equipment | 2979428.2 |
| 电气机械及器材制造业 | Manufacture of Electrical Machinery and Equipment | 3224817.3 |
| 通信设备、计算机及其他电子设备制造业 | Manufacture of Communication Equipment, Computers and Other Electronic Equipment | 4401644.1 |
| 仪器仪表及文化、办公用机械制造业 | Manufacture of Measuring Instruments and Machinery for Cultural Activity and Office Work | 284530.4 |
| 其他制造业 | Other Manufacture | 30259.6 |
| 废弃资源综合利用业 | Comprehensive Utilization of Waste Resources | 290067.7 |
| 金属制品、机械和设备修理业 | Repair of Metal Products, Machinery and Equipment | 41579.1 |
| 电力、热力的生产和供应业 | Production and Supply of Electric Power and Heat Power | 135468.2 |
| 燃气生产和供应业 | Production and Supply of Gas | 512918.6 |
| 水的生产和供应业 | Production and Supply of Water | 49599.8 |

单位：万元 (10 000 yuan)

| 营业收入<br>Revenue | 营业成本<br>Cost | 税金及附加<br>Tax and Extra Charges | 利润总额<br>Total After-tax Profits | 利税总额<br>Total Pre-tax Profits | 应付职工薪酬<br>Total Wages |
|---|---|---|---|---|---|
| **115286170.2** | **95220663.8** | **763458.7** | **9394381.0** | **12229749.0** | **9624148.7** |
| 1263470.3 | 1066610.5 | 11703.9 | 66503.5 | 106124.4 | 111941.2 |
| 85926.5 | 60652.8 | 1034.9 | 9372.4 | 14029.1 | 8536.1 |
| 105400586.0 | 87984897.6 | 694690.3 | 8167101.4 | 10692537.9 | 8667116.3 |
| 8536187.4 | 6108502.9 | 56029.6 | 1151403.7 | 1417057.6 | 836555.1 |
| 31914559.5 | 25471567.1 | 264071.5 | 2956041.8 | 3904997.9 | 2944868.0 |
| 83371610.7 | 69749096.7 | 499387.2 | 6438339.2 | 8324751.1 | 6679280.7 |
| 25356861.2 | 22051510.2 | 141301.0 | 1870002.8 | 2356327.6 | 1616709.8 |
| 35373408.3 | 28414212.5 | 281843.4 | 3462239.4 | 4337964.1 | 3117186.6 |
| 54555900.7 | 44754941.1 | 340314.3 | 4062138.8 | 5535457.3 | 4890252.3 |
| 229402.7 | 192426.4 | 748.3 | 23796.0 | 27027.3 | 8161.4 |
| 24363.0 | 20023.7 | 5.4 | 4102.6 | 4108.0 | 218.7 |
| 823499.1 | 588570.4 | 28996.6 | 80249.0 | 137126.1 | 65459.0 |
| 6441239.4 | 5457699.0 | 29161.3 | 433567.0 | 578909.6 | 450584.0 |
| 2251359.8 | 1773790.4 | 13544.2 | 190897.0 | 265985.8 | 230300.9 |
| 856932.6 | 589266.7 | 95125.6 | 60434.1 | 174636.0 | 70028.5 |
| 194624.4 | 157696.6 | 1466.7 | 12219.5 | 18675.1 | 31266.9 |
| 423461.1 | 308620.8 | 1392.9 | 30951.4 | 41601.2 | 81041.7 |
| 564813.2 | 482958.1 | 2200.4 | 44500.0 | 56378.7 | 84720.4 |
| 1231734.4 | 1025239.0 | 3640.4 | 82703.0 | 99453.6 | 142392.9 |
| 728015.2 | 568775.4 | 5752.8 | 59065.3 | 83797.5 | 111275.9 |
| 1819002.9 | 1552105.6 | 5299.7 | 147900.9 | 169721.2 | 135090.0 |
| 1331719.0 | 1061653.4 | 9875.1 | 125331.4 | 160536.5 | 149646.5 |
| 384758.5 | 296159.7 | 3930.1 | 39696.8 | 59426.2 | 51324.1 |
| 268311.6 | 224040.7 | 6629.1 | 23206.1 | 37941.0 | 21654.4 |
| 3813004.9 | 3000815.5 | 18026.7 | 455564.6 | 558464.2 | 231251.0 |
| 3191264.4 | 1961941.0 | 23622.3 | 458870.4 | 577737.8 | 359041.9 |
| 860791.5 | 743046.4 | 2942.9 | 69662.2 | 86436.2 | 52530.5 |
| 3764583.4 | 3091268.0 | 34923.1 | 324403.0 | 440248.8 | 346839.0 |
| 8688286.9 | 6994539.0 | 69824.0 | 669288.2 | 956701.7 | 785078.2 |
| 6943608.4 | 5681949.2 | 12312.7 | 1018341.8 | 1054884.2 | 141325.4 |
| 5273317.7 | 4603898.6 | 20562.2 | 317410.6 | 413585.3 | 178734.6 |
| 4995309.2 | 4185795.8 | 26683.2 | 384592.1 | 504900.1 | 537709.7 |
| 5033246.2 | 4088534.5 | 29015.4 | 374886.2 | 511040.4 | 510530.3 |
| 4740255.2 | 3420460.0 | 35204.1 | 683667.9 | 846863.6 | 442840.5 |
| 15996158.5 | 13605231.5 | 137543.9 | 878988.7 | 1309301.8 | 1537229.3 |
| 6910756.5 | 5908219.8 | 42972.5 | 480696.9 | 668580.1 | 769102.2 |
| 10467527.0 | 9096978.6 | 35732.4 | 747714.0 | 948980.4 | 651058.4 |
| 14820066.3 | 12755832.9 | 55792.6 | 949708.5 | 1157900.9 | 1250579.9 |
| 495130.1 | 369438.9 | 3337.2 | 40455.3 | 58442.4 | 68917.9 |
| 33595.1 | 28108.4 | 133.7 | 791.9 | 1561.8 | 5018.5 |
| 773447.5 | 632937.5 | 2800.3 | 88447.0 | 106449.5 | 49276.0 |
| 57900.6 | 51063.6 | 228.8 | 804.0 | 2738.1 | 23616.2 |
| 32232.4 | 21312.9 | 308.0 | 3093.7 | 4473.4 | 8247.0 |
| 774428.5 | 641355.3 | 3347.0 | 83633.3 | 98834.8 | 37025.7 |
| 48023.0 | 38910.5 | 377.1 | 4740.6 | 6299.7 | 5031.2 |

# 表 12.11 私营工业企业经济效益指标（2022 年）
# INDICATORS ON ECONOMIC BENEFIT OF PRIVATE INDUSTRIAL ENTERPRISES (2022)

| 指　标 | Item | 总资产贡献率 Ratio of Total Assets to Industrial Output Value |
|---|---|---|
| **总　计** | **Total** | **12.9** |
| **按轻、重工业分** | **By Light and Heavy Industries** | |
| 轻工业 | Light Industry | 14.4 |
| 重工业 | Heavy Industry | 12.3 |
| **按企业规模分** | **By Size** | |
| 大型企业 | Large | 10.9 |
| 中型企业 | Medium | 15.1 |
| 小型微型企业 | Small&Mini | 12.3 |
| **按行业分** | **By Sector** | |
| 煤炭开采和洗选业 | Mining and Washing of Coal | 9.7 |
| 石油和天然气开采业 | Extraction of Petroleum and Natural Gas | 23.0 |
| 黑色金属矿采选业 | Mining and Processing of Ferrous Metal Ores | |
| 有色金属矿采选业 | Mining and Processing of Non-Ferrous Metal Ores | |
| 非金属矿采选业 | Mining and Processing of Nonmetal Ores | 10.7 |
| 开采辅助活动 | Mining Support Activities | |
| 其他采矿业 | Mining of Other Ores | |
| 农副食品加工业 | Processing of Food from Agricultural Products | 15.8 |
| 食品制造业 | Manufacture of Foods | 16.6 |
| 酒、饮料和精制茶制造业 | Liquor, Beverage and Refined Tea | 20.0 |
| 烟草制品业 | Manufacture of Tobacco | |
| 纺织业 | Manufacture of Textile | 9.9 |
| 纺织服装、服饰业 | Manufacture of Textile Wearing Apparel, Footwear and Caps | 17.7 |
| 皮革、毛皮、羽毛及其制品和制鞋业 | Manufacture of Leather, Fur, Feather and Related Products and Footwear | 19.2 |
| 木材加工和木、竹、藤、棕、草制品业 | Processing of Timber, Manufacture of Wood, Bamboo, Rattan, Palm and Straw Products | 13.8 |
| 家具制造业 | Manufacture of Furniture | 12.8 |
| 造纸和纸制品业 | Manufacture of Paper and Paper Products | 17.6 |
| 印刷和记录媒介复制业 | Printing, Reproduction of Recording Media | 15.2 |
| 文教、工美、体育和娱乐用品制造业 | Manufacture of Culture, Education, Handicraft, Fine Arts, Sports and Entertainment Articles | 17.6 |
| 石油加工、炼焦和核燃料加工业 | Processing of Petroleum, Coking, Processing of Nuclear Fuel | 9.2 |
| 化学原料和化学制品制造业 | Manufacture of Raw Chemical Materials and Chemical Products | 19.3 |
| 医药制造业 | Manufacture of Medicines | 14.2 |
| 化学纤维制造业 | Manufacture of Chemical Fibers | 7.4 |
| 橡胶和塑料制品业 | Manufacture of Rubber and Plastics | 14.3 |
| 非金属矿物制品业 | Manufacture of Non-metallic Mineral Products | 9.4 |
| 黑色金属冶炼和压延加工业 | Smelting and Pressing of Ferrous Metals | 52.0 |
| 有色金属冶炼和压延加工业 | Smelting and Pressing of Nonferrous Metals | 18.3 |
| 金属制品业 | Manufacture of Metal Products | 14.2 |
| 通用设备制造业 | Manufacture of General Purpose Machinery | 11.4 |
| 专用设备制造业 | Manufacture of Special Purpose Machinery | 21.1 |
| 汽车制造业 | Manufacture of Motor Vehicles | 8.6 |
| 铁路、船舶、航空航天和其他运输设备制造业 | Manufacture of Railway, Ship, Aviation and Other Transporting Equipment | 10.0 |
| 电气机械和器材制造业 | Manufacture of Electrical Machinery and Equipment | 10.2 |
| 计算机、通信和其他电子设备制造业 | Manufacture of Communication Equipment, Computers and Other Electronic Equipment | 10.8 |
| 仪器仪表制造业 | Manufacture of Measuring Instruments and Machinery for Cultural Activity and Office Work | 10.6 |
| 其他制造业 | Other Manufacture | 3.5 |
| 废弃资源综合利用业 | Comprehensive Utilization of Waste Resources | 19.7 |
| 金属制品、机械和设备修理业 | Repair of Metal Products, Machinery and Equipment | 3.1 |
| 电力、热力生产和供应业 | Production and Supply of Electric Power and Heat Power | 2.4 |
| 燃气生产和供应业 | Production and Supply of Gas | 9.7 |
| 水的生产和供应业 | Production and Supply of Water | 7.9 |

单位: % (%)

| 资本保值增值率<br>Ratio of Assets Appreciation YOY | 资　产负债率<br>Asset-Liability Ratio | 流动资产周转率(次)<br>Turnover Ratio of Circulating Assets (time) | 成本费用利润率<br>Ratio of Profits to Cost | 产品销售率<br>Sales as Percentage of Output |
|---|---|---|---|---|
| **108.3** | **56.2** | **2.1** | **9.2** | **95.9** |
| 110.2 | 52.1 | 2.1 | 10.6 | 96.4 |
| 107.5 | 57.8 | 2.1 | 8.7 | 95.8 |
| 108.7 | 64.0 | 1.7 | 8.2 | 92.5 |
| 109.3 | 52.0 | 2.5 | 11.4 | 95.5 |
| 107.4 | 55.2 | 2.2 | 8.3 | 97.5 |
| 102.1 | 25.5 | 5.6 | 11.6 | 100.0 |
| 3200.0 | 82.3 | 2.8 | 20.3 | 94.6 |
| 111.9 | 61.1 | 1.5 | 11.4 | 96.8 |
| 100.1 | 46.5 | 3.8 | 7.5 | 96.4 |
| 106.3 | 48.1 | 2.8 | 9.6 | 98.4 |
| 105.9 | 40.0 | 2.2 | 8.9 | 96.5 |
| 92.4 | | | | 100.0 |
| 107.0 | 53.4 | 1.6 | 6.9 | 98.3 |
| 97.6 | 43.9 | 2.6 | 8.2 | 95.4 |
| 93.1 | 47.1 | 3.1 | 8.8 | 97.0 |
| 88.1 | 56.1 | 5.7 | 7.5 | 98.5 |
| 98.8 | 50.6 | 2.5 | 9.0 | 94.8 |
| 163.0 | 51.3 | 4.1 | 9.0 | 97.1 |
| 101.5 | 53.0 | 2.9 | 10.8 | 97.9 |
| 105.2 | 43.0 | 2.8 | 12.2 | 98.5 |
| 83.5 | 86.0 | 1.2 | 9.9 | 76.1 |
| 102.7 | 50.5 | 2.6 | 14.0 | 92.7 |
| 104.0 | 37.1 | 1.5 | 18.0 | 92.2 |
| 86.3 | 45.5 | 1.5 | 9.2 | 90.9 |
| 120.2 | 48.3 | 2.7 | 9.8 | 96.7 |
| 104.6 | 54.8 | 1.5 | 8.6 | 94.8 |
| 93.5 | 73.0 | 5.2 | 17.7 | 99.0 |
| 122.1 | 57.1 | 3.5 | 6.7 | 96.6 |
| 107.6 | 56.6 | 2.7 | 8.6 | 97.3 |
| 107.4 | 49.9 | 2.1 | 8.4 | 97.7 |
| 136.0 | 45.3 | 2.3 | 18.0 | 97.5 |
| 107.4 | 64.5 | 1.6 | 6.0 | 96.8 |
| 110.3 | 55.7 | 1.7 | 7.7 | 95.6 |
| 117.2 | 66.6 | 1.6 | 7.8 | 98.6 |
| 103.0 | 59.6 | 2.4 | 7.1 | 91.9 |
| 105.1 | 50.0 | 1.4 | 9.4 | 94.7 |
| 133.7 | 34.6 | 1.7 | 2.5 | 93.4 |
| 130.6 | 47.8 | 2.9 | 13.2 | 95.7 |
| 102.3 | 55.1 | 0.8 | 1.4 | 99.8 |
| 104.1 | 64.6 | 0.3 | 10.7 | 88.9 |
| 116.6 | 52.2 | 1.5 | 12.1 | 94.6 |
| 93.5 | 40.3 | 1.6 | 11.2 | 95.5 |

**表 12.11 续表 continued**

| 指　标 | Item | 销售利润率 Rate of Return on Sale |
|---|---|---|
| **总　计** | **Total** | **8.2** |
| **按轻、重工业分** | **By Light and Heavy Industries** | |
| 轻工业 | Light Industry | 9.3 |
| 重工业 | Heavy Industry | 7.7 |
| **按企业规模分** | **By Size** | |
| 大型企业 | Large | 7.4 |
| 中型企业 | Medium | 9.8 |
| 小型微型企业 | Small&Mini | 7.5 |
| **按行业分** | **By Sector** | |
| 煤炭开采和洗选业 | Mining and Washing of Coal | 10.4 |
| 石油和天然气开采业 | Extraction of Petroleum and Natural Gas | 16.8 |
| 黑色金属矿采选业 | Mining and Processing of Ferrous Metal Ores | |
| 有色金属矿采选业 | Mining and Processing of Non-Ferrous Metal Ores | |
| 非金属矿采选业 | Mining and Processing of Nonmetal Ores | 9.7 |
| 开采辅助活动 | Mining Support Activities | |
| 其他采矿业 | Mining of Other Ores | |
| 农副食品加工业 | Processing of Food from Agricultural Products | 6.7 |
| 食品制造业 | Manufacture of Foods | 8.5 |
| 酒、饮料和精制茶制造业 | Liquor, Beverage and Refined Tea | 7.1 |
| 烟草制品业 | Manufacture of Tobacco | |
| 纺织业 | Manufacture of Textile | 6.3 |
| 纺织服装、服饰业 | Manufacture of Textile Wearing Apparel, Footwear and Caps | 7.3 |
| 皮革、毛皮、羽毛及其制品和制鞋业 | Manufacture of Leather, Fur, Feather and Related Products and Footwear | 7.9 |
| 木材加工和木、竹、藤、棕、草制品业 | Processing of Timber, Manufacture of Wood, Bamboo, Rattan, Palm and Straw Products | 6.7 |
| 家具制造业 | Manufacture of Furniture | 8.1 |
| 造纸和纸制品业 | Manufacture of Paper and Paper Products | 8.1 |
| 印刷和记录媒介复制业 | Printing, Reproduction of Recording Media | 9.4 |
| 文教、工美、体育和娱乐用品制造业 | Manufacture of Culture, Education, Handicraft, Fine Arts, Sports and Entertainment Articles | 10.3 |
| 石油加工、炼焦和核燃料加工业 | Processing of Petroleum, Coking, Processing of Nuclear Fuel | 8.7 |
| 化学原料和化学制品制造业 | Manufacture of Raw Chemical Materials and Chemical Products | 12.0 |
| 医药制造业 | Manufacture of Medicines | 14.4 |
| 化学纤维制造业 | Manufacture of Chemical Fibers | 8.1 |
| 橡胶和塑料制品业 | Manufacture of Rubber and Plastics | 8.6 |
| 非金属矿物制品业 | Manufacture of Non-metallic Mineral Products | 7.7 |
| 黑色金属冶炼和压延加工业 | Smelting and Pressing of Ferrous Metals | 14.7 |
| 有色金属冶炼和压延加工业 | Smelting and Pressing of Nonferrous Metals | 6.0 |
| 金属制品业 | Manufacture of Metal Products | 7.7 |
| 通用设备制造业 | Manufacture of General Purpose Machinery | 7.5 |
| 专用设备制造业 | Manufacture of Special Purpose Machinery | 14.4 |
| 汽车制造业 | Manufacture of Motor Vehicles | 5.5 |
| 铁路、船舶、航空航天和其他运输设备制造业 | Manufacture of Railway, Ship, Aviation and Other Transporting Equipment | 7.0 |
| 电气机械和器材制造业 | Manufacture of Electrical Machinery and Equipment | 7.1 |
| 计算机、通信和其他电子设备制造业 | Manufacture of Communication Equipment, Computers and Other Electronic Equipment | 6.4 |
| 仪器仪表制造业 | Manufacture of Measuring Instruments and Machinery for Cultural Activity and Office Work | 8.2 |
| 其他制造业 | Other Manufacture | 2.4 |
| 废弃资源综合利用业 | Comprehensive Utilization of Waste Resources | 11.4 |
| 金属制品、机械和设备修理业 | Repair of Metal Products, Machinery and Equipment | 1.4 |
| 电力、热力生产和供应业 | Production and Supply of Electric Power and Heat Power | 9.6 |
| 燃气生产和供应业 | Production and Supply of Gas | 10.8 |
| 水的生产和供应业 | Production and Supply of Water | 9.9 |

单位: % (%)

| 流动比率<br>Current Ratio | 速动比率<br>Quick Ratio | 产权比率<br>Equity Ratio | 人均实现利税（元）<br>Per Capita Pre-tax Profits (yuan) | 从业人员人均工资（元）<br>Per Capita Wages of Employees (yuan) |
|---|---|---|---|---|
| **1.2** | **1.0** | **1.3** | **135654** | **106752** |
| 1.3 | 1.0 | 1.1 | 138800 | 104673 |
| 1.2 | 1.0 | 1.4 | 134227 | 107696 |
| 1.2 | 1.0 | 1.8 | 181033 | 124209 |
| 1.2 | 0.9 | 1.1 | 153096 | 110012 |
| 1.2 | 1.0 | 1.2 | 113425 | 100204 |
| 1.1 | 1.0 | 0.3 | 575049 | 173647 |
| 0.6 | 0.6 | 4.6 | 4108000 | 218700 |
| 0.9 | 0.8 | 1.6 | 190718 | 91042 |
| 1.2 | 0.9 | 0.9 | 133543 | 103941 |
| 1.4 | 1.0 | 0.9 | 107556 | 93126 |
| 1.5 | 0.8 | 0.7 | 220779 | 88532 |
| 1.4 | 0.7 | 1.2 | 47399 | 79358 |
| 2.2 | 1.1 | 0.8 | 42537 | 82865 |
| 1.6 | 1.2 | 0.9 | 52789 | 79326 |
| 1.0 | 0.7 | 1.3 | 98469 | 140983 |
| 1.3 | 0.9 | 1.0 | 75766 | 100611 |
| 1.1 | 0.8 | 1.1 | 147841 | 117674 |
| 1.0 | 0.9 | 1.1 | 115744 | 107892 |
| 1.5 | 1.2 | 0.8 | 83230 | 71882 |
| 1.1 | 0.9 | 6.2 | 329922 | 188299 |
| 1.2 | 0.9 | 1.0 | 305840 | 126643 |
| 1.7 | 1.4 | 0.6 | 218014 | 135488 |
| 1.3 | 1.1 | 0.8 | 214482 | 130349 |
| 1.3 | 1.0 | 0.9 | 124858 | 98366 |
| 1.2 | 1.1 | 1.2 | 125010 | 102584 |
| 1.1 | 1.0 | 2.7 | 1141650 | 152950 |
| 1.4 | 1.0 | 1.3 | 290848 | 125692 |
| 1.2 | 0.9 | 1.3 | 112100 | 119385 |
| 1.3 | 1.0 | 1.0 | 104379 | 104275 |
| 1.5 | 1.2 | 0.8 | 235305 | 123045 |
| 1.1 | 0.9 | 1.8 | 86025 | 101001 |
| 1.3 | 1.1 | 1.3 | 84921 | 97689 |
| 1.2 | 1.0 | 2.0 | 152080 | 104336 |
| 1.1 | 0.9 | 1.5 | 102496 | 110700 |
| 1.3 | 1.0 | 1.0 | 77510 | 91403 |
| 1.4 | 1.0 | 0.5 | 20023 | 64340 |
| 1.2 | 1.0 | 0.9 | 339011 | 156930 |
| 1.5 | 1.1 | 1.2 | 14336 | 123645 |
| 1.1 | 1.0 | 1.8 | 64832 | 119522 |
| 1.3 | 1.3 | 1.1 | 258730 | 96926 |
| 1.3 | 1.1 | 0.7 | 134036 | 107047 |

# 表 12.12 内资工业企业主要经济指标（2022 年）
# MAIN ECONOMIC INDICATORS OF INDUSTRIAL ENTERPRISES WITH DOMESTIC FUNDS (2022)

| 指 标 | Item | 单位数（个）Number of Enterprises (unit) |
|---|---|---|
| **总 计** | **Total** | **7197** |
| **按登记注册类型分** | **By Status of Registration** | |
| #国有企业 | State-owned | 69 |
| 集体企业 | Collective-owned | 12 |
| **按轻、重工业分** | **By Light and Heavy Industries** | |
| 轻工业 | Light Industry | 2156 |
| 重工业 | Heavy Industry | 5041 |
| **按企业规模分** | **By Size** | |
| 大型企业 | Large | 124 |
| 中型企业 | Medium | 754 |
| 小型微型企业 | Small&Mini | 6319 |
| **按行业分** | **By Sector** | |
| 煤炭开采和洗选业 | Mining and Washing of Coal | 18 |
| 石油和天然气开采业 | Extraction of Petroleum and Natural Gas | 6 |
| 黑色金属矿采选业 | Mining and Processing of Ferrous Metal Ores | |
| 有色金属矿采选业 | Mining and Processing of Non-Ferrous Metal Ores | 1 |
| 非金属矿采选业 | Mining and Processing of Nonmetal Ores | 142 |
| 开采辅助活动 | Mining Support Activities | |
| 其他采矿业 | Mining of Other Ores | |
| 农副食品加工业 | Processing of Food from Agricultural Products | 500 |
| 食品制造业 | Manufacture of Foods | 200 |
| 酒、饮料和精制茶制造业 | Liquor, Beverage and Refined Tea | 70 |
| 烟草制品业 | Manufacture of Tobacco | 3 |
| 纺织业 | Manufacture of Textile | 56 |
| 纺织服装、鞋、帽制造业 | Manufacture of Textile Wearing Apparel, Footwear and Caps | 58 |
| 皮革、毛皮、羽毛（绒）及其制品业 | Manufacture of Leather, Fur, Feather and Related Products | 58 |
| 木材加工及木竹藤棕草制品业 | Processing of Timber, Manufacture of Wood, Bamboo, Rattan, Palm and Straw Products | 99 |
| 家具制造业 | Manufacture of Furniture | 95 |
| 造纸及纸制品业 | Manufacture of Paper and Paper Products | 117 |
| 印刷业、记录媒介的复制 | Printing, Reproduction of Recording Media | 113 |
| 文教、工美、体育和娱乐用品制造业 | Manufacture of Culture, Education, Handicraft, Fine Arts, Sports and Entertainment Articles | 66 |
| 石油加工、炼焦及核燃料加工业 | Processing of Petroleum, Coking, Processing of Nuclear Fuel | 17 |
| 化学原料及化学制品制造业 | Manufacture of Raw Chemical Materials and Chemical Products | 220 |
| 医药制造业 | Manufacture of Medicines | 169 |
| 化学纤维制造业 | Manufacture of Chemical Fibers | 10 |
| 橡胶和塑料制品业 | Manufacture of Rubber and Plastics | 326 |
| 非金属矿物制品业 | Manufacture of Non-metallic Mineral Products | 767 |
| 黑色金属冶炼及压延加工业 | Smelting and Pressing of Ferrous Metals | 78 |
| 有色金属冶炼及压延加工业 | Smelting and Pressing of Nonferrous Metals | 149 |
| 金属制品业 | Manufacture of Metal Products | 403 |
| 通用设备制造业 | Manufacture of General Purpose Machinery | 413 |
| 专用设备制造业 | Manufacture of Special Purpose Machinery | 301 |
| 汽车制造业 | Manufacture of Motor Vehicles | 1003 |
| 铁路、船舶、航空航天和其他运输设备制造业 | Manufacture of Railway, Ship, Aviation and Other Transporting Equipment | 477 |
| 电气机械及器材制造业 | Manufacture of Electrical Machinery and Equipment | 317 |
| 通信设备、计算机及其他电子设备制造业 | Manufacture of Communication Equipment, Computers and Other Electronic Equipment | 461 |
| 仪器仪表及文化、办公用机械制造业 | Manufacture of Measuring Instruments and Machinery for Cultural Activity and Office Work | 99 |
| 其他制造业 | Other Manufacture | 17 |
| 废弃资源综合利用业 | Comprehensive Utilization of Waste Resources | 54 |
| 金属制品、机械和设备修理业 | Repair of Metal Products, Machinery and Equipment | 11 |
| 电力、热力的生产和供应业 | Production and Supply of Electric Power and Heat Power | 114 |
| 燃气生产和供应业 | Production and Supply of Gas | 105 |
| 水的生产和供应业 | Production and Supply of Water | 84 |

单位: 万元 (10 000 yuan)

| 从业人员平均人数(万人) Average Employment (10 000 persons) | 工业总产值 Gross Output Value | 实收资本 Paid-in Capital | #国家资本 State Capital | #外商资本 Foreign Capital |
|---|---|---|---|---|
| **131.18** | **202686069.1** | **44415763.0** | **10227493.5** | **345754.2** |
| 2.00 | 2551717.0 | 1725645.3 | 658247.3 | |
| 0.16 | 109210.1 | 6719.5 | | |
| 34.36 | 42312191.1 | 5286804.3 | 424683.4 | 11307.1 |
| 96.82 | 160373878.0 | 39128958.7 | 9802810.1 | 334447.1 |
| 33.69 | 73846168.8 | 16892860.8 | 4556480.9 | 326639.6 |
| 39.81 | 54680951.1 | 10344324.4 | 2720175.2 | 4351.4 |
| 57.67 | 74158949.2 | 17178577.8 | 2950837.4 | 14763.2 |
| 0.09 | 385303.6 | 79967.2 | 56639.2 | |
| 0.19 | 1582912.1 | 1293131.3 | 34141.6 | |
| 0.0039 | 2110.7 | 30.0 | | |
| 1.02 | 1058168.6 | 1292170.2 | 50242.1 | |
| 5.18 | 8079341.0 | 748127.7 | 36227.4 | |
| 2.91 | 2902587.4 | 310155.0 | 9657.6 | |
| 0.95 | 1088155.5 | 389707.0 | 6336.2 | 10000.0 |
| 0.40 | 2294202.0 | 264386.0 | 264186.0 | |
| 0.67 | 484331.0 | 62182.0 | 5700.0 | |
| 1.02 | 491170.3 | 63694.2 | 337.0 | 77.1 |
| 1.18 | 623962.5 | 51911.3 | 22100.0 | |
| 1.13 | 1458011.7 | 123633.0 | | |
| 1.12 | 756121.5 | 97802.5 | 200.0 | |
| 1.26 | 1953887.4 | 176018.2 | 3000.0 | |
| 1.85 | 1741895.0 | 251727.6 | 6159.6 | |
| 0.74 | 411927.7 | 40476.9 | | |
| 0.17 | 557313.9 | 99069.3 | 29618.2 | |
| 4.05 | 9404406.5 | 2133879.5 | 592590.4 | |
| 4.36 | 5649223.2 | 1220488.8 | 36061.0 | |
| 0.42 | 985939.9 | 101358.9 | 5703.0 | |
| 3.72 | 4295330.7 | 603470.5 | 3465.6 | 1230.0 |
| 9.70 | 12099043.9 | 2942912.9 | 400020.7 | |
| 1.68 | 11337141.3 | 1207297.4 | 5500.0 | 53812.7 |
| 2.64 | 13357678.5 | 1629663.3 | 408123.7 | |
| 5.56 | 5908829.8 | 718673.9 | 68522.2 | |
| 6.46 | 6709105.0 | 1536744.6 | 107207.4 | |
| 4.70 | 6263694.6 | 1128437.7 | 462002.2 | |
| 24.98 | 33304833.0 | 5690035.0 | 703911.0 | 218986.9 |
| 9.47 | 8611047.8 | 1327717.6 | 245072.7 | |
| 7.80 | 12331011.2 | 1509463.4 | 232535.6 | |
| 16.09 | 27180942.1 | 7273540.6 | 256625.3 | 276.1 |
| 2.06 | 1959509.8 | 647657.3 | 166509.6 | 57020.0 |
| 1.25 | 1118106.7 | 333161.9 | 25155.5 | |
| 0.42 | 858489.7 | 128321.9 | 1590.8 | |
| 0.30 | 103158.7 | 36074.3 | 800.0 | |
| 3.51 | 11574934.4 | 6713705.9 | 4768866.5 | 4351.4 |
| 0.92 | 3044478.0 | 478842.4 | 167306.4 | |
| 1.21 | 717762.4 | 1710125.8 | 1045379.0 | |

**表 12.12 续表 1 continued 1**

| 指 标 | Item | 资 产<br>Total Assets |
|---|---|---|
| **总 计** | **Total** | **234540784.1** |
| **按登记注册类型分** | **By Status of Registration** | |
| #国有企业 | State-owned | 6857431.3 |
| 集体企业 | Collective-owned | 69400.1 |
| **按轻、重工业分** | **By Light and Heavy Industries** | |
| 轻工业 | Light Industry | 40570079.7 |
| 重工业 | Heavy Industry | 193970704.4 |
| **按企业规模分** | **By Size** | |
| 大型企业 | Large | 91998874.7 |
| 中型企业 | Medium | 58268949.2 |
| 小型微型企业 | Small&Mini | 84272960.2 |
| **按行业分** | **By Sector** | |
| 煤炭开采和洗选业 | Mining and Washing of Coal | 446541.6 |
| 石油和天然气开采业 | Extraction of Petroleum and Natural Gas | 4025928.5 |
| 黑色金属矿采选业 | Mining and Processing of Ferrous Metal Ores | |
| 有色金属矿采选业 | Mining and Processing of Non-Ferrous Metal Ores | 2011.7 |
| 非金属矿采选业 | Mining and Processing of Nonmetal Ores | 1774205.6 |
| 开采辅助活动 | Mining Support Activities | |
| 其他采矿业 | Mining of Other Ores | |
| 农副食品加工业 | Processing of Food from Agricultural Products | 5322447.5 |
| 食品制造业 | Manufacture of Foods | 2303899.8 |
| 酒、饮料和精制茶制造业 | Liquor, Beverage and Refined Tea | 1185652.0 |
| 烟草制品业 | Manufacture of Tobacco | 1754579.8 |
| 纺织业 | Manufacture of Textile | 438173.5 |
| 纺织服装、鞋、帽制造业 | Manufacture of Textile Wearing Apparel, Footwear and Caps | 263503.2 |
| 皮革、毛皮、羽毛(绒)及其制品业 | Manufacture of Leather, Fur, Feather and Related Products | 374569.6 |
| 木材加工及木竹藤棕草制品业 | Processing of Timber, Manufacture of Wood, Bamboo, Rattan, Palm and Straw Products | 843443.6 |
| 家具制造业 | Manufacture of Furniture | 699871.2 |
| 造纸及纸制品业 | Manufacture of Paper and Paper Products | 1210512.7 |
| 印刷业、记录媒介的复制 | Printing, Reproduction of Recording Media | 1515910.4 |
| 文教、工美、体育和娱乐用品制造业 | Manufacture of Culture, Education, Handicraft, Fine Arts, Sports and Entertainment Articles | 370804.9 |
| 石油加工、炼焦及核燃料加工业 | Processing of Petroleum, Coking, Processing of Nuclear Fuel | 549789.9 |
| 化学原料及化学制品制造业 | Manufacture of Raw Chemical Materials and Chemical Products | 9676064.0 |
| 医药制造业 | Manufacture of Medicines | 7557954.5 |
| 化学纤维制造业 | Manufacture of Chemical Fibers | 1114847.1 |
| 橡胶和塑料制品业 | Manufacture of Rubber and Plastics | 3503762.3 |
| 非金属矿物制品业 | Manufacture of Non-metallic Mineral Products | 16354309.2 |
| 黑色金属冶炼及压延加工业 | Smelting and Pressing of Ferrous Metals | 6205466.7 |
| 有色金属冶炼及压延加工业 | Smelting and Pressing of Nonferrous Metals | 10712837.0 |
| 金属制品业 | Manufacture of Metal Products | 5138764.9 |
| 通用设备制造业 | Manufacture of General Purpose Machinery | 8244572.5 |
| 专用设备制造业 | Manufacture of Special Purpose Machinery | 6796382.7 |
| 汽车制造业 | Manufacture of Motor Vehicles | 42250198.3 |
| 铁路、船舶、航空航天和其他运输设备制造业 | Manufacture of Railway, Ship, Aviation and Other Transporting Equipment | 8904833.4 |
| 电气机械及器材制造业 | Manufacture of Electrical Machinery and Equipment | 16867388.2 |
| 通信设备、计算机及其他电子设备制造业 | Manufacture of Communication Equipment, Computers and Other Electronic Equipment | 27768089.2 |
| 仪器仪表及文化、办公用机械制造业 | Manufacture of Measuring Instruments and Machinery for Cultural Activity and Office Work | 3065601.1 |
| 其他制造业 | Other Manufacture | 2137783.7 |
| 废弃资源综合利用业 | Comprehensive Utilization of Waste Resources | 676662.9 |
| 金属制品、机械和设备修理业 | Repair of Metal Products, Machinery and Equipment | 121859.7 |
| 电力、热力的生产和供应业 | Production and Supply of Electric Power and Heat Power | 24012993.1 |
| 燃气生产和供应业 | Production and Supply of Gas | 2579197.0 |
| 水的生产和供应业 | Production and Supply of Water | 7769371.1 |

单位：万元 (10 000 yuan)

| #流动资产 Circulating Assets | 固定资产 Fixed Assets 原 值 Original Value | 净 值 Net Value | 负 债 Total Liabilities | #流动负债 Total Circulating Liabilities |
|---|---|---|---|---|
| **120680747.4** | **127568891.6** | **65317817.3** | **131500791.8** | **102563308.2** |
| 3026916.4 | 3174911.0 | 2018857.0 | 4071886.1 | 2213658.7 |
| 43457.9 | 27053.2 | 16623.1 | 45714.6 | 43260.2 |
| 23839970.2 | 17729986.1 | 9136174.1 | 21229346.2 | 17956857.7 |
| 96840777.2 | 109838905.5 | 56181643.2 | 110271445.6 | 84606450.5 |
| 51453171.3 | 45039375.4 | 22371042.6 | 51122475.2 | 43501397.8 |
| 29431133.0 | 32921457.6 | 16022475.9 | 33442914.2 | 25629900.6 |
| 39796443.1 | 49608058.6 | 26924108.5 | 46935402.4 | 33432009.8 |
| 161824.4 | 293509.8 | 243191.1 | 204730.5 | 144309.2 |
| 484062.6 | 6311551.5 | 2720457.5 | 1108758.0 | 997738.1 |
| 1693.1 | 1031.2 | 313.4 | 1613.1 | |
| 730752.4 | 619227.0 | 341620.2 | 1031113.3 | 766358.2 |
| 2679014.7 | 2683065.6 | 1306390.3 | 2211458.9 | 1747364.4 |
| 1180943.2 | 1345390.3 | 684790.0 | 1074880.8 | 785153.8 |
| 589162.8 | 542948.6 | 283214.3 | 438561.0 | 328829.3 |
| 1443835.0 | 580826.5 | 162577.8 | 467858.1 | 466991.8 |
| 178877.6 | 274047.0 | 157626.7 | 214760.7 | 172277.0 |
| 180847.7 | 99345.2 | 48100.7 | 119417.6 | 88017.8 |
| 234461.0 | 180152.5 | 96563.9 | 181594.5 | 148089.6 |
| 278883.3 | 919415.8 | 377273.5 | 448416.4 | 225816.6 |
| 295078.7 | 479335.9 | 208844.2 | 356762.1 | 230429.1 |
| 560515.1 | 720942.8 | 477060.3 | 603614.1 | 488022.9 |
| 719525.0 | 1035803.0 | 475151.4 | 783789.9 | 623892.5 |
| 160361.6 | 260004.5 | 110240.5 | 167636.3 | 107676.8 |
| 281968.7 | 366936.8 | 98557.9 | 413380.6 | 227764.8 |
| 4168779.7 | 6836679.2 | 3413214.5 | 4984217.3 | 4176100.5 |
| 4008097.0 | 3492757.0 | 1717508.8 | 3263027.1 | 2671456.6 |
| 585263.8 | 518989.2 | 351316.2 | 510513.5 | 463158.7 |
| 1589035.0 | 2368793.1 | 1225424.0 | 1739868.2 | 1256596.9 |
| 8321768.1 | 8598799.1 | 4684350.3 | 9698785.9 | 7741705.3 |
| 2362781.2 | 4356740.8 | 3024162.3 | 3431774.4 | 2587814.9 |
| 5481964.4 | 6713718.4 | 4011794.9 | 6931567.2 | 5314210.7 |
| 2886597.4 | 2551294.3 | 1277478.0 | 3005586.9 | 2381235.1 |
| 4772598.0 | 3517680.2 | 1834908.6 | 4183039.6 | 3350117.9 |
| 4196412.0 | 2237217.6 | 1210872.6 | 3463872.6 | 2911273.1 |
| 27677660.4 | 16229144.9 | 7151364.0 | 26394377.8 | 22806069.7 |
| 5550028.3 | 4361953.6 | 1695562.1 | 5188203.3 | 4065503.2 |
| 12611370.0 | 3600828.7 | 2100234.6 | 12236135.9 | 11054669.4 |
| 14368297.1 | 10083044.9 | 5282862.2 | 14142915.0 | 11356469.7 |
| 2142849.7 | 574523.7 | 329353.0 | 1686380.4 | 1478990.8 |
| 1197604.2 | 1087458.4 | 644587.2 | 1105673.3 | 1006028.5 |
| 348978.8 | 330095.2 | 223485.7 | 317292.9 | 242132.3 |
| 101086.7 | 30405.7 | 14540.0 | 68275.3 | 65986.0 |
| 4640780.1 | 28640173.3 | 14266142.9 | 14480150.0 | 7893678.6 |
| 1233820.4 | 1291218.5 | 807107.7 | 1399579.6 | 911545.3 |
| 2273168.2 | 3433841.8 | 2259574.0 | 3441209.7 | 1279833.1 |

**表 12.12 续表 2 continued 2**

| 指 标 | Item | 所有者权益 Creditors' Equity |
|---|---|---|
| **总 计** | **Total** | **103052555.1** |
| **按登记注册类型分** | **By Status of Registration** | |
| #国有企业 | State-owned | 2785544.1 |
| 集体企业 | Collective-owned | 23685.4 |
| **按轻、重工业分** | **By Light and Heavy Industries** | |
| 轻工业 | Light Industry | 19339858.4 |
| 重工业 | Heavy Industry | 83712696.7 |
| **按企业规模分** | **By Size** | |
| 大型企业 | Large | 40889865.8 |
| 中型企业 | Medium | 24826031.8 |
| 小型微型企业 | Small&Mini | 37336657.5 |
| **按行业分** | **By Sector** | |
| 煤炭开采和洗选业 | Mining and Washing of Coal | 241811.1 |
| 石油和天然气开采业 | Extraction of Petroleum and Natural Gas | 2917170.6 |
| 黑色金属矿采选业 | Mining and Processing of Ferrous Metal Ores | |
| 有色金属矿采选业 | Mining and Processing of Non-Ferrous Metal Ores | 398.6 |
| 非金属矿采选业 | Mining and Processing of Nonmetal Ores | 743091.7 |
| 开采辅助活动 | Mining Support Activities | |
| 其他采矿业 | Mining of Other Ores | |
| 农副食品加工业 | Processing of Food from Agricultural Products | 3110986.2 |
| 食品制造业 | Manufacture of Foods | 1229018.7 |
| 酒、饮料和精制茶制造业 | Liquor, Beverage and Refined Tea | 747090.8 |
| 烟草制品业 | Manufacture of Tobacco | 1286721.7 |
| 纺织业 | Manufacture of Textile | 223412.6 |
| 纺织服装、鞋、帽制造业 | Manufacture of Textile Wearing Apparel, Footwear and Caps | 144085.4 |
| 皮革、毛皮、羽毛(绒)及其制品业 | Manufacture of Leather, Fur, Feather and Related Products | 192974.9 |
| 木材加工及木竹藤棕草制品业 | Processing of Timber, Manufacture of Wood, Bamboo, Rattan, Palm and Straw Products | 395028.0 |
| 家具制造业 | Manufacture of Furniture | 343107.6 |
| 造纸及纸制品业 | Manufacture of Paper and Paper Products | 606898.9 |
| 印刷业、记录媒介的复制 | Printing, Reproduction of Recording Media | 731254.1 |
| 文教、工美、体育和娱乐用品制造业 | Manufacture of Culture, Education, Handicraft, Fine Arts, Sports and Entertainment Articles | 203168.0 |
| 石油加工、炼焦及核燃料加工业 | Processing of Petroleum, Coking, Processing of Nuclear Fuel | 136409.2 |
| 化学原料及化学制品制造业 | Manufacture of Raw Chemical Materials and Chemical Products | 4691844.7 |
| 医药制造业 | Manufacture of Medicines | 4294927.6 |
| 化学纤维制造业 | Manufacture of Chemical Fibers | 604333.5 |
| 橡胶和塑料制品业 | Manufacture of Rubber and Plastics | 1763891.9 |
| 非金属矿物制品业 | Manufacture of Non-metallic Mineral Products | 6655516.4 |
| 黑色金属冶炼及压延加工业 | Smelting and Pressing of Ferrous Metals | 2773691.9 |
| 有色金属冶炼及压延加工业 | Smelting and Pressing of Nonferrous Metals | 3781269.4 |
| 金属制品业 | Manufacture of Metal Products | 2133176.0 |
| 通用设备制造业 | Manufacture of General Purpose Machinery | 4061530.1 |
| 专用设备制造业 | Manufacture of Special Purpose Machinery | 3332509.4 |
| 汽车制造业 | Manufacture of Motor Vehicles | 15869281.7 |
| 铁路、船舶、航空航天和其他运输设备制造业 | Manufacture of Railway, Ship, Aviation and Other Transporting Equipment | 3716629.0 |
| 电气机械及器材制造业 | Manufacture of Electrical Machinery and Equipment | 4631251.4 |
| 通信设备、计算机及其他电子设备制造业 | Manufacture of Communication Equipment, Computers and Other Electronic Equipment | 13625172.5 |
| 仪器仪表及文化、办公用机械制造业 | Manufacture of Measuring Instruments and Machinery for Cultural Activity and Office Work | 1379220.7 |
| 其他制造业 | Other Manufacture | 1032110.6 |
| 废弃资源综合利用业 | Comprehensive Utilization of Waste Resources | 359369.5 |
| 金属制品、机械和设备修理业 | Repair of Metal Products, Machinery and Equipment | 53584.1 |
| 电力、热力的生产和供应业 | Production and Supply of Electric Power and Heat Power | 9532842.1 |
| 燃气生产和供应业 | Production and Supply of Gas | 1179615.5 |
| 水的生产和供应业 | Production and Supply of Water | 4328159.0 |

单位：万元 (10 000 yuan)

| 营业收入<br>Revenue | 营业成本<br>Cost | 税金及附加<br>Tax and Extra Charges | 利润总额<br>Total After-tax Profits | 利税总额<br>Total Pre-tax Profits | 应付职工薪酬<br>Total Wages |
|---|---|---|---|---|---|
| **214397873.3** | **177712737.8** | **2889332.4** | **16105309.5** | **23095676.4** | **16501132.4** |
| 2672658.7 | 2242008.2 | 20536.1 | 137012.4 | 219907.1 | 368507.6 |
| 86619.3 | 69543.0 | 743.0 | 6184.0 | 12706.0 | 14006.4 |
| 43728543.7 | 33379813.4 | 1622859.3 | 4108010.1 | 6880639.9 | 3875896.1 |
| 170669329.6 | 144332924.4 | 1266473.1 | 11997299.4 | 16215036.5 | 12625236.3 |
| 81772474.0 | 69054513.7 | 1957515.5 | 4915828.9 | 8372110.3 | 5443792.2 |
| 55329632.0 | 44759281.5 | 414965.0 | 5200290.3 | 6662401.7 | 4819211.9 |
| 77295767.3 | 63898942.6 | 516851.9 | 5989190.3 | 8061164.4 | 6238128.3 |
| 407436.4 | 332767.1 | 1635.4 | 50914.9 | 56660.9 | 11905.6 |
| 1571363.9 | 961819.7 | 54568.3 | 465356.3 | 586845.7 | 47835.1 |
| 2026.6 | 1387.9 | 72.0 | 198.3 | 465.4 | 233.4 |
| 1007818.8 | 738983.8 | 33987.9 | 91229.6 | 158860.0 | 83610.9 |
| 7846831.7 | 6650829.2 | 35401.7 | 577096.6 | 743941.9 | 532002.8 |
| 3033619.8 | 2385465.5 | 18675.8 | 270034.5 | 368232.8 | 300514.7 |
| 1035301.8 | 696976.7 | 102963.6 | 92004.6 | 222199.8 | 87061.7 |
| 2350018.5 | 690935.8 | 1285491.8 | 220050.3 | 1716741.5 | 143988.8 |
| 456130.4 | 382200.7 | 3516.0 | 30421.3 | 41649.9 | 56230.7 |
| 472117.8 | 350073.6 | 1539.5 | 35104.9 | 46830.2 | 89272.3 |
| 604970.8 | 517296.4 | 2796.0 | 45141.7 | 58828.7 | 93837.3 |
| 1420727.4 | 1175421.2 | 4497.6 | 104401.3 | 122902.2 | 160297.5 |
| 734811.7 | 573958.4 | 5830.5 | 59383.4 | 84267.7 | 111667.6 |
| 1967619.1 | 1680672.8 | 6058.8 | 157106.4 | 181192.2 | 149077.5 |
| 1732902.0 | 1387144.4 | 12295.5 | 161408.1 | 206318.1 | 218775.9 |
| 403732.7 | 313421.7 | 3950.1 | 40149.0 | 60131.8 | 52819.1 |
| 499618.4 | 408159.7 | 11516.2 | 43804.9 | 68807.8 | 49190.0 |
| 9676140.4 | 7512425.0 | 55882.0 | 1288908.1 | 1585964.9 | 643886.0 |
| 5458948.3 | 3140546.1 | 48539.6 | 716721.3 | 991344.9 | 639479.8 |
| 896746.9 | 770050.4 | 3226.4 | 71723.0 | 89830.4 | 56424.0 |
| 4247678.1 | 3456669.7 | 41516.7 | 400067.8 | 529214.9 | 369519.6 |
| 12197635.0 | 9885793.6 | 98331.0 | 938447.1 | 1339767.6 | 1087541.6 |
| 11197190.8 | 9580132.5 | 28947.1 | 950157.0 | 1025793.2 | 301931.4 |
| 16842076.2 | 14653080.0 | 61502.3 | 1215737.8 | 1438995.1 | 439748.8 |
| 6321056.6 | 5352217.9 | 32761.9 | 450380.1 | 598202.1 | 705025.4 |
| 6750933.4 | 5501942.5 | 42210.4 | 497682.0 | 692687.7 | 718275.4 |
| 6031278.1 | 4475169.3 | 43440.4 | 757349.2 | 957657.4 | 606462.9 |
| 37681932.2 | 32161162.8 | 523508.7 | 1502384.8 | 2854893.3 | 3103706.1 |
| 8185463.0 | 6975128.2 | 54237.5 | 546589.4 | 775371.3 | 1010743.3 |
| 15472559.7 | 13654402.4 | 50951.9 | 1034715.9 | 1309870.7 | 884264.5 |
| 28377736.1 | 24466595.5 | 115705.9 | 2099996.1 | 2461136.2 | 1870580.9 |
| 1992978.5 | 1497407.4 | 13316.4 | 154399.3 | 232926.2 | 308273.4 |
| 1148838.6 | 991764.8 | 5701.8 | 57105.4 | 81192.8 | 247861.1 |
| 841142.2 | 688058.4 | 3495.7 | 89101.3 | 110978.4 | 64042.5 |
| 103074.7 | 89364.4 | 622.8 | 1686.1 | 6972.7 | 42887.1 |
| 11422450.9 | 10249032.0 | 60285.1 | 486241.7 | 812299.2 | 854197.2 |
| 3111266.8 | 2692286.1 | 8661.6 | 306489.4 | 348519.7 | 156820.0 |
| 893699.0 | 671994.2 | 11690.5 | 95620.6 | 127181.1 | 201140.5 |

# 表 12.13 内资工业企业经济效益指标（2022 年）
## INDICATORS ON ECONOMIC BENEFIT OF INDUSTRIAL ENTERPRISES WITH DOMESTIC FUNDS (2022)

| 指 标 | Item | 总资产贡献率 Ratio of Total Assets to Industrial Output Value |
|---|---|---|
| **总 计** | **Total** | **10.2** |
| **按轻、重工业分** | **By Light and Heavy Industries** | |
| 轻工业 | Light Industry | 17.2 |
| 重工业 | Heavy Industry | 8.8 |
| **按企业规模分** | **By Size** | |
| 大型企业 | Large | 9.2 |
| 中型企业 | Medium | 12.0 |
| 小型微型企业 | Small&Mini | 10.2 |
| **按行业分** | **By Sector** | |
| 煤炭开采和洗选业 | Mining and Washing of Coal | 14.7 |
| 石油和天然气开采业 | Extraction of Petroleum and Natural Gas | 15.1 |
| 黑色金属矿采选业 | Mining and Processing of Ferrous Metal Ores | |
| 有色金属矿采选业 | Mining and Processing of Non-Ferrous Metal Ores | 23.3 |
| 非金属矿采选业 | Mining and Processing of Nonmetal Ores | 9.3 |
| 开采辅助活动 | Mining Support Activities | |
| 其他采矿业 | Mining of Other Ores | |
| 农副食品加工业 | Processing of Food from Agricultural Products | 14.2 |
| 食品制造业 | Manufacture of Foods | 16.4 |
| 酒、饮料和精制茶制造业 | Liquor, Beverage and Refined Tea | 19.1 |
| 烟草制品业 | Manufacture of Tobacco | 97.3 |
| 纺织业 | Manufacture of Textile | 10.6 |
| 纺织服装、服饰业 | Manufacture of Textile Wearing Apparel, Footwear and Caps | 18.2 |
| 皮革、毛皮、羽毛及其制品和制鞋业 | Manufacture of Leather, Fur, Feather and Related Products and Footwear | 16.2 |
| 木材加工和木、竹、藤、棕、草制品业 | Processing of Timber, Manufacture of Wood, Bamboo, Rattan, Palm and Straw Products | 15.1 |
| 家具制造业 | Manufacture of Furniture | 12.7 |
| 造纸和纸制品业 | Manufacture of Paper and Paper Products | 15.5 |
| 印刷和记录媒介复制业 | Printing, Reproduction of Recording Media | 14.2 |
| 文教、工美、体育和娱乐用品制造业 | Manufacture of Culture, Education, Handicraft, Fine Arts, Sports and Entertainment Articles | 16.4 |
| 石油加工、炼焦和核燃料加工业 | Processing of Petroleum, Coking, Processing of Nuclear Fuel | 12.9 |
| 化学原料和化学制品制造业 | Manufacture of Raw Chemical Materials and Chemical Products | 16.9 |
| 医药制造业 | Manufacture of Medicines | 13.5 |
| 化学纤维制造业 | Manufacture of Chemical Fibers | 7.5 |
| 橡胶和塑料制品业 | Manufacture of Rubber and Plastics | 15.6 |
| 非金属矿物制品业 | Manufacture of Non-metallic Mineral Products | 8.9 |
| 黑色金属冶炼和压延加工业 | Smelting and Pressing of Ferrous Metals | 17.2 |
| 有色金属冶炼和压延加工业 | Smelting and Pressing of Nonferrous Metals | 14.4 |
| 金属制品业 | Manufacture of Metal Products | 12.1 |
| 通用设备制造业 | Manufacture of General Purpose Machinery | 8.7 |
| 专用设备制造业 | Manufacture of Special Purpose Machinery | 14.2 |
| 汽车制造业 | Manufacture of Motor Vehicles | 6.8 |
| 铁路、船舶、航空航天和其他运输设备制造业 | Manufacture of Railway, Ship, Aviation and Other Transporting Equipment | 8.8 |
| 电气机械和器材制造业 | Manufacture of Electrical Machinery and Equipment | 8.0 |
| 计算机、通信和其他电子设备制造业 | Manufacture of Communication Equipment, Computers and Other Electronic Equipment | 8.9 |
| 仪器仪表制造业 | Manufacture of Measuring Instruments and Machinery for Cultural Activity and Office Work | 7.7 |
| 其他制造业 | Other Manufacture | 3.7 |
| 废弃资源综合利用业 | Comprehensive Utilization of Waste Resources | 16.9 |
| 金属制品、机械和设备修理业 | Repair of Metal Products, Machinery and Equipment | 5.8 |
| 电力、热力生产和供应业 | Production and Supply of Electric Power and Heat Power | 4.6 |
| 燃气生产和供应业 | Production and Supply of Gas | 14.2 |
| 水的生产和供应业 | Production and Supply of Water | 1.9 |

单位: % (%)

| 资本保值增值率 Ratio of Assets Appreciation YOY | 资 产 负债率 Asset-Liability Ratio | 流动资产周转率(次) Turnover Ratio of Circulating Assets (time) | 成本费用利润率 Ratio of Profits to Cost | 产品销售率 Sales as Percentage of Output |
|---|---|---|---|---|
| **108.2** | **56.1** | **1.8** | **8.5** | **97.1** |
| 107.8 | 52.3 | 1.8 | 11.1 | 98.5 |
| 108.3 | 56.9 | 1.8 | 7.8 | 96.7 |
| 107.6 | 55.6 | 1.6 | 6.8 | 97.7 |
| 110.5 | 57.4 | 1.9 | 10.8 | 95.9 |
| 107.2 | 55.7 | 1.9 | 8.6 | 97.4 |
| 443.5 | 45.9 | 2.5 | 14.3 | 99.7 |
| 119.5 | 27.5 | 3.3 | 42.9 | 99.7 |
| 66.7 | 80.2 | 1.2 | 11.5 | 96.0 |
| 107.3 | 58.1 | 1.4 | 10.5 | 97.8 |
| 101.9 | 41.6 | 2.9 | 8.1 | 96.2 |
| 106.5 | 46.7 | 2.6 | 10.1 | 98.3 |
| 107.5 | 37.0 | 1.8 | 11.3 | 96.3 |
| 109.3 | 26.7 | 1.6 | 27.1 | 100.0 |
| 98.3 | 49.0 | 2.6 | 7.4 | 96.2 |
| 97.6 | 45.3 | 2.6 | 8.3 | 95.3 |
| 95.2 | 48.5 | 2.6 | 8.3 | 96.6 |
| 93.3 | 53.2 | 5.1 | 8.3 | 98.7 |
| 98.6 | 51.0 | 2.5 | 9.0 | 94.8 |
| 155.2 | 49.9 | 3.5 | 8.8 | 96.8 |
| 99.0 | 51.7 | 2.4 | 10.6 | 98.0 |
| 104.5 | 45.2 | 2.5 | 11.7 | 98.6 |
| 96.1 | 75.2 | 1.8 | 10.1 | 82.3 |
| 109.1 | 51.5 | 2.3 | 15.8 | 96.1 |
| 101.4 | 43.2 | 1.4 | 15.9 | 93.9 |
| 86.7 | 45.8 | 1.5 | 9.1 | 90.9 |
| 127.3 | 49.7 | 2.7 | 10.8 | 96.8 |
| 104.1 | 59.3 | 1.5 | 8.6 | 94.8 |
| 95.5 | 55.3 | 4.7 | 9.8 | 99.1 |
| 120.5 | 64.7 | 3.1 | 8.0 | 96.7 |
| 108.1 | 58.5 | 2.2 | 7.9 | 98.1 |
| 105.7 | 50.7 | 1.4 | 8.3 | 98.3 |
| 133.0 | 51.0 | 1.4 | 15.2 | 97.0 |
| 107.1 | 62.5 | 1.4 | 4.4 | 96.8 |
| 110.1 | 58.3 | 1.5 | 7.4 | 95.9 |
| 111.3 | 72.5 | 1.2 | 7.3 | 105.7 |
| 107.6 | 50.9 | 2.0 | 8.2 | 93.8 |
| 108.3 | 55.0 | 0.9 | 8.7 | 97.4 |
| 133.7 | 51.7 | 1.0 | 5.2 | 93.4 |
| 121.0 | 46.9 | 2.4 | 12.1 | 95.8 |
| 102.0 | 56.0 | 1.0 | 1.7 | 99.8 |
| 104.8 | 60.3 | 2.5 | 4.5 | 99.8 |
| 113.2 | 54.3 | 2.5 | 10.9 | 98.5 |
| 107.8 | 44.3 | 0.4 | 11.7 | 97.8 |

**表 12.13 续表 continued**

| 指 标 | Item | 销售利润率 Rate of Return on Sale |
|---|---|---|
| **总 计** | **Total** | **7.5** |
| **按轻、重工业分** | **By Light and Heavy Industries** | |
| 轻工业 | Light Industry | 9.4 |
| 重工业 | Heavy Industry | 7.0 |
| **按企业规模分** | **By Size** | |
| 大型企业 | Large | 6.0 |
| 中型企业 | Medium | 9.4 |
| 小型微型企业 | Small&Mini | 7.8 |
| **按行业分** | **By Sector** | |
| 煤炭开采和洗选业 | Mining and Washing of Coal | 12.5 |
| 石油和天然气开采业 | Extraction of Petroleum and Natural Gas | 29.6 |
| 黑色金属矿采选业 | Mining and Processing of Ferrous Metal Ores | |
| 有色金属矿采选业 | Mining and Processing of Non-Ferrous Metal Ores | 9.8 |
| 非金属矿采选业 | Mining and Processing of Nonmetal Ores | 9.1 |
| 开采辅助活动 | Mining Support Activities | |
| 其他采矿业 | Mining of Other Ores | |
| 农副食品加工业 | Processing of Food from Agricultural Products | 7.4 |
| 食品制造业 | Manufacture of Foods | 8.9 |
| 酒、饮料和精制茶制造业 | Liquor, Beverage and Refined Tea | 8.9 |
| 烟草制品业 | Manufacture of Tobacco | 9.4 |
| 纺织业 | Manufacture of Textile | 6.7 |
| 纺织服装、服饰业 | Manufacture of Textile Wearing Apparel, Footwear and Caps | 7.4 |
| 皮革、毛皮、羽毛及其制品和制鞋业 | Manufacture of Leather, Fur, Feather and Related Products and Footwear | 7.5 |
| 木材加工和木、竹、藤、棕、草制品业 | Processing of Timber, Manufacture of Wood, Bamboo, Rattan, Palm and Straw Products | 7.4 |
| 家具制造业 | Manufacture of Furniture | 8.1 |
| 造纸和纸制品业 | Manufacture of Paper and Paper Products | 8.0 |
| 印刷和记录媒介复制业 | Printing, Reproduction of Recording Media | 9.3 |
| 文教、工美、体育和娱乐用品制造业 | Manufacture of Culture, Education, Handicraft, Fine Arts, Sports and Entertainment Articles | 9.9 |
| 石油加工、炼焦和核燃料加工业 | Processing of Petroleum, Coking, Processing of Nuclear Fuel | 8.8 |
| 化学原料和化学制品制造业 | Manufacture of Raw Chemical Materials and Chemical Products | 13.3 |
| 医药制造业 | Manufacture of Medicines | 13.1 |
| 化学纤维制造业 | Manufacture of Chemical Fibers | 8.0 |
| 橡胶和塑料制品业 | Manufacture of Rubber and Plastics | 9.4 |
| 非金属矿物制品业 | Manufacture of Non-metallic Mineral Products | 7.7 |
| 黑色金属冶炼和压延加工业 | Smelting and Pressing of Ferrous Metals | 8.5 |
| 有色金属冶炼和压延加工业 | Smelting and Pressing of Nonferrous Metals | 7.2 |
| 金属制品业 | Manufacture of Metal Products | 7.1 |
| 通用设备制造业 | Manufacture of General Purpose Machinery | 7.4 |
| 专用设备制造业 | Manufacture of Special Purpose Machinery | 12.6 |
| 汽车制造业 | Manufacture of Motor Vehicles | 4.0 |
| 铁路、船舶、航空航天和其他运输设备制造业 | Manufacture of Railway, Ship, Aviation and Other Transporting Equipment | 6.7 |
| 电气机械和器材制造业 | Manufacture of Electrical Machinery and Equipment | 6.7 |
| 计算机、通信和其他电子设备制造业 | Manufacture of Communication Equipment, Computers and Other Electronic Equipment | 7.4 |
| 仪器仪表制造业 | Manufacture of Measuring Instruments and Machinery for Cultural Activity and Office Work | 7.8 |
| 其他制造业 | Other Manufacture | 5.0 |
| 废弃资源综合利用业 | Comprehensive Utilization of Waste Resources | 10.6 |
| 金属制品、机械和设备修理业 | Repair of Metal Products, Machinery and Equipment | 1.6 |
| 电力、热力生产和供应业 | Production and Supply of Electric Power and Heat Power | 4.3 |
| 燃气生产和供应业 | Production and Supply of Gas | 9.9 |
| 水的生产和供应业 | Production and Supply of Water | 10.7 |

单位: % (%)

| 流动比率<br>Current Ratio | 速动比率<br>Quick Ratio | 产权比率<br>Equity Ratio | 人均实现利税（元）<br>Per Capita Pre-tax Profits (yuan) | 从业人员人均工资（元）<br>Per Capita Wages of Employees (yuan) |
|---|---|---|---|---|
| **1.2** | **1.0** | **1.3** | **176062** | **125791** |
| 1.3 | 1.1 | 1.1 | 200257 | 112806 |
| 1.1 | 1.0 | 1.3 | 167476 | 130399 |
| 1.2 | 1.0 | 1.3 | 248504 | 161585 |
| 1.2 | 0.9 | 1.4 | 167334 | 121040 |
| 1.2 | 1.0 | 1.3 | 139769 | 108160 |
| 1.1 | 1.1 | 0.9 | 651275 | 136846 |
| 0.5 | 0.5 | 0.4 | 3024978 | 246573 |
| 0.0 | 0.0 | 4.1 | 116350 | 58350 |
| 1.0 | 0.9 | 1.4 | 156512 | 82375 |
| 1.5 | 1.2 | 0.7 | 143729 | 102783 |
| 1.5 | 1.1 | 0.9 | 126410 | 103163 |
| 1.8 | 1.1 | 0.6 | 234388 | 91837 |
| 3.1 | 1.4 | 0.4 | 4324286 | 362692 |
| 1.0 | 0.5 | 1.0 | 62537 | 84430 |
| 2.1 | 1.2 | 0.8 | 45957 | 87608 |
| 1.6 | 1.1 | 0.9 | 49728 | 79321 |
| 1.2 | 0.8 | 1.1 | 108475 | 141481 |
| 1.3 | 0.9 | 1.0 | 75576 | 100150 |
| 1.2 | 0.9 | 1.0 | 143689 | 118222 |
| 1.2 | 0.9 | 1.1 | 111704 | 118449 |
| 1.5 | 1.1 | 0.8 | 81369 | 71474 |
| 1.2 | 0.8 | 3.0 | 402385 | 287661 |
| 1.0 | 0.8 | 1.1 | 391403 | 158906 |
| 1.5 | 1.2 | 0.8 | 227321 | 146636 |
| 1.3 | 1.1 | 0.8 | 211366 | 132762 |
| 1.3 | 1.0 | 1.0 | 142300 | 99360 |
| 1.1 | 0.9 | 1.5 | 138078 | 112083 |
| 0.9 | 0.7 | 1.2 | 609503 | 179401 |
| 1.0 | 0.7 | 1.8 | 544868 | 166508 |
| 1.2 | 1.0 | 1.4 | 107532 | 126735 |
| 1.4 | 1.1 | 1.0 | 107244 | 111205 |
| 1.4 | 1.2 | 1.0 | 203930 | 129145 |
| 1.2 | 1.1 | 1.7 | 114273 | 124233 |
| 1.4 | 1.1 | 1.4 | 81842 | 106686 |
| 1.1 | 1.0 | 2.6 | 167975 | 113396 |
| 1.3 | 1.0 | 1.0 | 152989 | 116279 |
| 1.5 | 1.2 | 1.2 | 113126 | 149720 |
| 1.2 | 1.0 | 1.1 | 64747 | 197656 |
| 1.4 | 1.2 | 0.9 | 264865 | 152846 |
| 1.5 | 1.2 | 1.3 | 22937 | 141076 |
| 0.6 | 0.6 | 1.5 | 231622 | 243569 |
| 1.4 | 1.3 | 1.2 | 380896 | 171388 |
| 1.8 | 1.7 | 0.8 | 104848 | 165821 |

# 表 12.14 外商投资和港澳台投资工业企业主要经济指标（2022 年）
## MAIN ECONOMIC INDICATORS OF INDUSTRIAL ENTERPRISES WITH HONG KONG, MACAO, TAIWAN AND FOREIGN FUNDS (2022)

| 指 标 | Item | 单位数（个）Number of Enterprises (unit) |
|---|---|---|
| **总 计** | **Total** | **420** |
| **按登记注册类型分** | **By Status of Registration** | |
| #港澳台投资企业 | Funded by Hong Kong, Macao and Taiwan | 125 |
| 外商投资企业 | Foreign-funded | 295 |
| **按轻、重工业分** | **By Light and Heavy Industries** | |
| 轻工业 | Light Industry | 94 |
| 重工业 | Heavy Industry | 326 |
| **按企业规模分** | **By Size** | |
| 大型企业 | Large | 55 |
| 中型企业 | Medium | 90 |
| 小型微型企业 | Small&Mini | 275 |
| **按行业分** | **By Sector** | |
| 煤炭开采和洗选业 | Mining and Washing of Coal | |
| 石油和天然气开采业 | Extraction of Petroleum and Natural Gas | |
| 黑色金属矿采选业 | Mining and Processing of Ferrous Metal Ores | |
| 有色金属矿采选业 | Mining and Processing of Non-Ferrous Metal Ores | |
| 非金属矿采选业 | Mining and Processing of Nonmetal Ores | |
| 开采辅助活动 | Mining Support Activities | |
| 其他采矿业 | Mining of Other Ores | |
| 农副食品加工业 | Processing of Food from Agricultural Products | 10 |
| 食品制造业 | Manufacture of Foods | 4 |
| 酒、饮料和精制茶制造业 | Liquor, Beverage and Refined Tea | 9 |
| 烟草制品业 | Manufacture of Tobacco | |
| 纺织业 | Manufacture of Textile | 2 |
| 纺织服装、鞋、帽制造业 | Manufacture of Textile Wearing Apparel, Footwear and Caps | 4 |
| 皮革、毛皮、羽毛（绒）及其制品业 | Manufacture of Leather, Fur, Feather and Related Products | |
| 木材加工及木竹藤棕草制品业 | Processing of Timber, Manufacture of Wood, Bamboo, Rattan, Palm and Straw Products | |
| 家具制造业 | Manufacture of Furniture | 3 |
| 造纸及纸制品业 | Manufacture of Paper and Paper Products | 14 |
| 印刷业、记录媒介的复制 | Printing, Reproduction of Recording Media | 8 |
| 文教、工美、体育和娱乐用品制造业 | Manufacture of Culture, Education, Handicraft, Fine Arts, Sports and Entertainment Articles | 3 |
| 石油加工、炼焦及核燃料加工业 | Processing of Petroleum, Coking, Processing of Nuclear Fuel | |
| 化学原料及化学制品制造业 | Manufacture of Raw Chemical Materials and Chemical Products | 26 |
| 医药制造业 | Manufacture of Medicines | 4 |
| 化学纤维制造业 | Manufacture of Chemical Fibers | |
| 橡胶和塑料制品业 | Manufacture of Rubber and Plastics | 13 |
| 非金属矿物制品业 | Manufacture of Non-metallic Mineral Products | 16 |
| 黑色金属冶炼及压延加工业 | Smelting and Pressing of Ferrous Metals | 2 |
| 有色金属冶炼及压延加工业 | Smelting and Pressing of Nonferrous Metals | 3 |
| 金属制品业 | Manufacture of Metal Products | 13 |
| 通用设备制造业 | Manufacture of General Purpose Machinery | 22 |
| 专用设备制造业 | Manufacture of Special Purpose Machinery | 13 |
| 汽车制造业 | Manufacture of Motor Vehicles | 122 |
| 铁路、船舶、航空航天和其他运输设备制造业 | Manufacture of Railway, Ship, Aviation and Other Transporting Equipment | 6 |
| 电气机械及器材制造业 | Manufacture of Electrical Machinery and Equipment | 15 |
| 通信设备、计算机及其他电子设备制造业 | Manufacture of Communication Equipment, Computers and Other Electronic Equipment | 87 |
| 仪器仪表及文化、办公用机械制造业 | Manufacture of Measuring Instruments and Machinery for Cultural Activity and Office Work | 6 |
| 其他制造业 | Other Manufacture | |
| 废弃资源综合利用业 | Comprehensive Utilization of Waste Resources | 1 |
| 金属制品、机械和设备修理业 | Repair of Metal Products, Machinery and Equipment | |
| 电力、热力的生产和供应业 | Production and Supply of Electric Power and Heat Power | 4 |
| 燃气生产和供应业 | Production and Supply of Gas | 5 |
| 水的生产和供应业 | Production and Supply of Water | 5 |

单位: 万元 (10 000 yuan)

| 从业人员平均人数(万人) Average Employment (10 000 persons) | 工业总产值 Gross Output Value | 实收资本 Paid-in Capital | #国家资本 State Capital | #外商资本 Foreign Capital |
|---|---|---|---|---|
| **23.02** | **55584518.4** | **8359684.0** | **864296.8** | **3148985.3** |
| 9.71 | 26530904.2 | 3735750.4 | 200862.0 | 349350.4 |
| 13.31 | 29053614.2 | 4623933.6 | 663434.8 | 2799634.9 |
| 3.28 | 6013323.0 | 1719149.4 | 10259.3 | 371928.7 |
| 19.74 | 49571195.4 | 6640534.6 | 854037.5 | 2777056.6 |
| 14.67 | 41718424.4 | 3849374.5 | 311112.0 | 1178903.7 |
| 5.10 | 6711134.2 | 1820257.8 | 203539.5 | 706886.3 |
| 3.25 | 7154959.8 | 2690051.7 | 349645.3 | 1263195.3 |
| 0.20 | 1475220.6 | 43741.6 | 2429.3 | 25868.4 |
| 0.23 | 216496.5 | 20457.1 | | 11487.6 |
| 0.52 | 523003.1 | 212758.5 | | 173228.5 |
| 0.08 | 2059.0 | 1920.0 | | |
| 0.06 | 41006.7 | 7148.0 | | 1330.0 |
| 0.07 | 63828.0 | 370.0 | | 100.0 |
| 0.76 | 2305278.0 | 1071910.8 | | 28155.8 |
| 0.16 | 147443.4 | 23154.6 | | 10248.5 |
| 0.33 | 138543.2 | 21863.5 | | |
| 0.26 | 1388722.7 | 728726.8 | 111341.5 | 394230.4 |
| 0.09 | 334761.9 | 50348.5 | | 5831.3 |
| 0.51 | 589766.7 | 329840.4 | 54000.0 | 189746.2 |
| 0.45 | 760196.4 | 255128.3 | 21000.0 | 67564.2 |
| 0.04 | 218489.1 | 70550.0 | | 8125.0 |
| 0.10 | 323171.7 | 52182.3 | 2712.0 | 47041.9 |
| 0.20 | 303785.4 | 145316.3 | 17933.4 | 17257.0 |
| 1.11 | 1693258.9 | 458226.2 | 136147.9 | 209771.5 |
| 0.22 | 121745.9 | 58634.3 | 15992.9 | 33542.6 |
| 4.48 | 10386245.0 | 1361198.6 | 155684.0 | 743305.0 |
| 0.30 | 416097.9 | 75313.6 | 23930.4 | 24368.2 |
| 0.61 | 735011.2 | 166777.0 | 23100.8 | 121109.9 |
| 11.55 | 32279752.3 | 2554070.7 | 167566.6 | 882649.8 |
| 0.25 | 266401.4 | 25664.4 | 4636.2 | 10325.7 |
| 0.0044 | 6711.1 | 1301.4 | | 1301.4 |
| 0.05 | 271905.9 | 224109.9 | 114909.6 | 107396.4 |
| 0.25 | 427822.2 | 162924.0 | | 35000.0 |
| 0.12 | 147794.2 | 236047.2 | 12912.2 | |

**表 12.14 续表 1 continued 1**

| 指　标 | Item | 资　产<br>Total Assets |
|---|---|---|
| **总　计** | **Total** | **40812842.8** |
| **按登记注册类型分** | **By Status of Registration** | |
| #港澳台投资企业 | Funded by Hong Kong, Macao and Taiwan | 18150377.2 |
| 外商投资企业 | Foreign-funded | 22662465.6 |
| **按轻、重工业分** | **By Light and Heavy Industries** | |
| 轻工业 | Light Industry | 6303364.3 |
| 重工业 | Heavy Industry | 34509478.5 |
| **按企业规模分** | **By Size** | |
| 大型企业 | Large | 25635811.4 |
| 中型企业 | Medium | 7134521.3 |
| 小型微型企业 | Small&Mini | 8042510.1 |
| **按行业分** | **By Sector** | |
| 煤炭开采和洗选业 | Mining and Washing of Coal | |
| 石油和天然气开采业 | Extraction of Petroleum and Natural Gas | |
| 黑色金属矿采选业 | Mining and Processing of Ferrous Metal Ores | |
| 有色金属矿采选业 | Mining and Processing of Non-Ferrous Metal Ores | |
| 非金属矿采选业 | Mining and Processing of Nonmetal Ores | |
| 开采辅助活动 | Mining Support Activities | |
| 其他采矿业 | Mining of Other Ores | |
| 农副食品加工业 | Processing of Food from Agricultural Products | 713729.8 |
| 食品制造业 | Manufacture of Foods | 164731.3 |
| 酒、饮料和精制茶制造业 | Liquor, Beverage and Refined Tea | 1198244.1 |
| 烟草制品业 | Manufacture of Tobacco | |
| 纺织业 | Manufacture of Textile | 3099.4 |
| 纺织服装、鞋、帽制造业 | Manufacture of Textile Wearing Apparel, Footwear and Caps | 14982.9 |
| 皮革、毛皮、羽毛(绒)及其制品业 | Manufacture of Leather, Fur, Feather and Related Products | |
| 木材加工及木竹藤棕草制品业 | Processing of Timber, Manufacture of Wood, Bamboo, Rattan, Palm and Straw Products | |
| 家具制造业 | Manufacture of Furniture | 40744.6 |
| 造纸及纸制品业 | Manufacture of Paper and Paper Products | 2606021.3 |
| 印刷业、记录媒介的复制 | Printing, Reproduction of Recording Media | 144510.4 |
| 文教、工美、体育和娱乐用品制造业 | Manufacture of Culture, Education, Handicraft, Fine Arts, Sports and Entertainment Articles | 103735.5 |
| 石油加工、炼焦及核燃料加工业 | Processing of Petroleum, Coking, Processing of Nuclear Fuel | |
| 化学原料及化学制品制造业 | Manufacture of Raw Chemical Materials and Chemical Products | 1735422.6 |
| 医药制造业 | Manufacture of Medicines | 368118.6 |
| 化学纤维制造业 | Manufacture of Chemical Fibers | |
| 橡胶和塑料制品业 | Manufacture of Rubber and Plastics | 608943.4 |
| 非金属矿物制品业 | Manufacture of Non-metallic Mineral Products | 918541.5 |
| 黑色金属冶炼及压延加工业 | Smelting and Pressing of Ferrous Metals | 169949.5 |
| 有色金属冶炼及压延加工业 | Smelting and Pressing of Nonferrous Metals | 218509.9 |
| 金属制品业 | Manufacture of Metal Products | 301700.9 |
| 通用设备制造业 | Manufacture of General Purpose Machinery | 1705663.4 |
| 专用设备制造业 | Manufacture of Special Purpose Machinery | 185973.1 |
| 汽车制造业 | Manufacture of Motor Vehicles | 9730433.2 |
| 铁路、船舶、航空航天和其他运输设备制造业 | Manufacture of Railway, Ship, Aviation and Other Transporting Equipment | 228644.2 |
| 电气机械及器材制造业 | Manufacture of Electrical Machinery and Equipment | 936891.4 |
| 通信设备、计算机及其他电子设备制造业 | Manufacture of Communication Equipment, Computers and Other Electronic Equipment | 16324786.7 |
| 仪器仪表及文化、办公用机械制造业 | Manufacture of Measuring Instruments and Machinery for Cultural Activity and Office Work | 217954.4 |
| 其他制造业 | Other Manufacture | |
| 废弃资源综合利用业 | Comprehensive Utilization of Waste Resources | 7342.9 |
| 金属制品、机械和设备修理业 | Repair of Metal Products, Machinery and Equipment | |
| 电力、热力的生产和供应业 | Production and Supply of Electric Power and Heat Power | 660344.3 |
| 燃气生产和供应业 | Production and Supply of Gas | 962233.5 |
| 水的生产和供应业 | Production and Supply of Water | 541590.0 |

单位：万元 (10 000 yuan)

| #流动资产 Circulating Assets | 固定资产 Fixed Assets 原 值 Original Value | 净 值 Net Value | 负 债 Total Liabilities | #流动负债 Total Circulating Liabilities |
|---|---|---|---|---|
| **25851218.0** | **22554161.8** | **10848144.8** | **25561178.6** | **21029393.4** |
| 11899989.8 | 8118354.5 | 4178771.4 | 11291139.1 | 9223070.0 |
| 13951228.2 | 14435807.3 | 6669373.4 | 14270039.5 | 11806323.4 |
| 3485576.4 | 3535105.5 | 1752591.0 | 2873514.5 | 2386425.2 |
| 22365641.6 | 19019056.3 | 9095553.8 | 22687664.1 | 18642968.2 |
| 17069604.5 | 13429447.5 | 6596228.4 | 17995862.3 | 14727666.6 |
| 4408184.1 | 4008730.6 | 1774922.2 | 3704133.5 | 3158294.6 |
| 4373429.4 | 5115983.7 | 2476994.2 | 3861182.8 | 3143432.2 |
| 522086.8 | 217135.4 | 136955.8 | 472381.6 | 462086.0 |
| 98707.8 | 126490.9 | 49831.5 | 118397.4 | 117977.1 |
| 606779.3 | 433604.1 | 159693.7 | 739896.6 | 729647.6 |
| 2013.0 | 1264.8 | 899.1 | 2655.1 | 2255.1 |
| 8294.0 | 10842.2 | 5968.9 | 10421.5 | 8576.3 |
| 22731.7 | 30162.3 | 17974.6 | 11961.5 | 11961.5 |
| 1095889.9 | 2132212.2 | 1115990.3 | 981453.3 | 554874.9 |
| 94490.2 | 104173.8 | 41497.6 | 78617.0 | 71758.6 |
| 60538.4 | 35560.8 | 21956.2 | 28938.9 | 22275.9 |
| 775568.0 | 1435215.3 | 696343.0 | 540203.7 | 436054.0 |
| 301039.5 | 66604.7 | 31659.3 | 70936.3 | 68918.1 |
| 244842.4 | 899648.7 | 252557.4 | 279428.1 | 262709.1 |
| 506970.9 | 665538.8 | 287919.0 | 348753.1 | 313144.7 |
| 85624.8 | 106759.5 | 65860.9 | 126198.0 | 122153.5 |
| 129891.5 | 155525.2 | 42945.1 | 118217.3 | 107417.0 |
| 217415.4 | 228712.8 | 70105.4 | 115144.0 | 108958.0 |
| 1119812.0 | 699468.6 | 364631.9 | 886994.2 | 761757.6 |
| 140657.9 | 55014.1 | 16957.7 | 81271.5 | 79840.3 |
| 6488233.6 | 6180667.5 | 2616390.1 | 6855644.5 | 5523185.9 |
| 157719.8 | 142265.4 | 45129.7 | 93239.5 | 93239.5 |
| 627704.4 | 311078.1 | 134628.9 | 423127.2 | 394179.7 |
| 11886847.1 | 6675193.1 | 3624605.4 | 11879101.1 | 9971931.9 |
| 184438.0 | 58185.5 | 21822.3 | 97811.9 | 84293.2 |
| 3379.0 | 5862.9 | 3460.1 | 5275.5 | 4929.7 |
| 84538.2 | 657438.3 | 400551.1 | 449827.5 | 291390.6 |
| 253866.3 | 486073.2 | 279496.2 | 497233.2 | 336088.1 |
| 131138.1 | 633463.6 | 342313.6 | 248049.1 | 87789.5 |

**表 12.14 续表 2 continued 2**

| 指　标 | Item | 所有者权益 Creditors' Equity |
|---|---|---|
| **总　计** | **Total** | **15251662.6** |
| **按登记注册类型分** | **By Status of Registration** | |
| #港澳台投资企业 | Funded by Hong Kong, Macao and Taiwan | 6859237.6 |
| 外商投资企业 | Foreign-funded | 8392425.0 |
| **按轻、重工业分** | **By Light and Heavy Industries** | |
| 轻工业 | Light Industry | 3429849.1 |
| 重工业 | Heavy Industry | 11821813.5 |
| **按企业规模分** | **By Size** | |
| 大型企业 | Large | 7639948.7 |
| 中型企业 | Medium | 3430387.6 |
| 小型微型企业 | Small&Mini | 4181326.3 |
| **按行业分** | **By Sector** | |
| 煤炭开采和洗选业 | Mining and Washing of Coal | |
| 石油和天然气开采业 | Extraction of Petroleum and Natural Gas | |
| 黑色金属矿采选业 | Mining and Processing of Ferrous Metal Ores | |
| 有色金属矿采选业 | Mining and Processing of Non-Ferrous Metal Ores | |
| 非金属矿采选业 | Mining and Processing of Nonmetal Ores | |
| 开采辅助活动 | Mining Support Activities | |
| 其他采矿业 | Mining of Other Ores | |
| 农副食品加工业 | Processing of Food from Agricultural Products | 241348.2 |
| 食品制造业 | Manufacture of Foods | 46333.9 |
| 酒、饮料和精制茶制造业 | Liquor, Beverage and Refined Tea | 458347.3 |
| 烟草制品业 | Manufacture of Tobacco | |
| 纺织业 | Manufacture of Textile | 444.3 |
| 纺织服装、鞋、帽制造业 | Manufacture of Textile Wearing Apparel, Footwear and Caps | 4561.7 |
| 皮革、毛皮、羽毛（绒）及其制品业 | Manufacture of Leather, Fur, Feather and Related Products | |
| 木材加工及木竹藤棕草制品业 | Processing of Timber, Manufacture of Wood, Bamboo, Rattan, Palm and Straw Products | |
| 家具制造业 | Manufacture of Furniture | 28783.1 |
| 造纸及纸制品业 | Manufacture of Paper and Paper Products | 1624567.9 |
| 印刷业、记录媒介的复制 | Printing, Reproduction of Recording Media | 65893.0 |
| 文教、工美、体育和娱乐用品制造业 | Manufacture of Culture, Education, Handicraft, Fine Arts, Sports and Entertainment Articles | 74796.6 |
| 石油加工、炼焦及核燃料加工业 | Processing of Petroleum, Coking, Processing of Nuclear Fuel | |
| 化学原料及化学制品制造业 | Manufacture of Raw Chemical Materials and Chemical Products | 1195218.7 |
| 医药制造业 | Manufacture of Medicines | 297182.2 |
| 化学纤维制造业 | Manufacture of Chemical Fibers | |
| 橡胶和塑料制品业 | Manufacture of Rubber and Plastics | 329515.2 |
| 非金属矿物制品业 | Manufacture of Non-metallic Mineral Products | 569788.2 |
| 黑色金属冶炼及压延加工业 | Smelting and Pressing of Ferrous Metals | 43751.5 |
| 有色金属冶炼及压延加工业 | Smelting and Pressing of Nonferrous Metals | 100292.7 |
| 金属制品业 | Manufacture of Metal Products | 186556.6 |
| 通用设备制造业 | Manufacture of General Purpose Machinery | 818669.1 |
| 专用设备制造业 | Manufacture of Special Purpose Machinery | 104701.4 |
| 汽车制造业 | Manufacture of Motor Vehicles | 2874789.0 |
| 铁路、船舶、航空航天和其他运输设备制造业 | Manufacture of Railway, Ship, Aviation and Other Transporting Equipment | 135404.5 |
| 电气机械及器材制造业 | Manufacture of Electrical Machinery and Equipment | 513764.2 |
| 通信设备、计算机及其他电子设备制造业 | Manufacture of Communication Equipment, Computers and Other Electronic Equipment | 4445685.4 |
| 仪器仪表及文化、办公用机械制造业 | Manufacture of Measuring Instruments and Machinery for Cultural Activity and Office Work | 120142.6 |
| 其他制造业 | Other Manufacture | |
| 废弃资源综合利用业 | Comprehensive Utilization of Waste Resources | 2067.4 |
| 金属制品、机械和设备修理业 | Repair of Metal Products, Machinery and Equipment | |
| 电力、热力的生产和供应业 | Production and Supply of Electric Power and Heat Power | 210516.8 |
| 燃气生产和供应业 | Production and Supply of Gas | 465000.2 |
| 水的生产和供应业 | Production and Supply of Water | 293540.9 |

单位：万元 (10 000 yuan)

| 营业收入<br>Revenue | 营业成本<br>Cost | 税金及附加<br>Tax and Extra Charges | 利润总额<br>Total After-tax Profits | 利税总额<br>Total Pre-tax Profits | 应付职工薪酬<br>Total Wages |
|---|---|---|---|---|---|
| **57354906.2** | **51808710.7** | **410457.4** | **2191456.0** | **3229463.7** | **2985323.6** |
| 27095461.5 | 24971934.3 | 167636.2 | 1090643.6 | 1535478.8 | 1281344.0 |
| 30259444.7 | 26836776.4 | 242821.2 | 1100812.4 | 1693984.9 | 1703979.6 |
| 6505923.9 | 5536319.9 | 59407.8 | 570201.1 | 765460.9 | 428841.2 |
| 50848982.3 | 46272390.8 | 351049.6 | 1621254.9 | 2464002.8 | 2556482.4 |
| 42695519.5 | 39412217.1 | 330238.8 | 1094402.3 | 1733879.8 | 1852275.9 |
| 6856707.1 | 5764035.4 | 37443.6 | 548182.4 | 734722.8 | 659703.4 |
| 7802679.6 | 6632458.2 | 42775.0 | 548871.3 | 760861.1 | 473344.3 |
| 1854062.2 | 1781203.5 | 2184.2 | 40388.5 | 48420.1 | 26314.6 |
| 224796.2 | 193453.3 | 1759.0 | 2424.7 | 11798.7 | 27533.8 |
| 842217.0 | 549517.8 | 24198.7 | 289077.2 | 328349.3 | 89907.0 |
| 1140.9 | 1233.1 |  | -203.5 | -186.4 | 231.0 |
| 41108.7 | 36664.9 | 125.5 | 17.2 | 611.1 | 6728.4 |
| 63290.8 | 50683.5 | 983.2 | 7353.4 | 9762.1 | 6889.6 |
| 2194735.0 | 1939414.5 | 17077.6 | 54224.7 | 142390.6 | 120663.0 |
| 157311.0 | 119604.5 | 1251.1 | 25486.7 | 29264.5 | 17251.0 |
| 127529.7 | 99127.6 | 1102.9 | 20639.1 | 25428.5 | 36933.4 |
| 1379162.9 | 1006333.6 | 10420.6 | 250317.5 | 319582.1 | 50063.3 |
| 224485.6 | 144150.0 | 737.2 | 55623.4 | 60286.5 | 11345.8 |
| 599488.5 | 488573.7 | 6462.7 | 9268.8 | 22918.8 | 59420.9 |
| 777280.3 | 588629.3 | 7088.7 | 120462.8 | 161218.7 | 70575.2 |
| 212671.6 | 193207.8 | 630.4 | 4177.8 | 6546.3 | 5141.0 |
| 318014.7 | 286279.9 | 669.3 | 12743.6 | 15570.0 | 15046.9 |
| 338269.5 | 295072.0 | 1861.2 | 15684.9 | 21836.0 | 21321.0 |
| 1719700.9 | 1398056.3 | 8902.4 | 167010.4 | 206315.8 | 143689.2 |
| 114089.1 | 91310.3 | 633.1 | 7734.4 | 9755.2 | 28050.7 |
| 11671196.5 | 9630452.0 | 275205.6 | 380557.8 | 898762.4 | 660369.5 |
| 418045.7 | 346480.6 | 2374.3 | 35540.9 | 46716.2 | 39867.6 |
| 697534.8 | 560923.4 | 8240.5 | 72156.7 | 99509.8 | 69492.6 |
| 32125732.0 | 30934046.7 | 30806.9 | 502814.4 | 607556.7 | 1334891.7 |
| 273641.4 | 197477.6 | 1515.9 | 41747.6 | 53763.4 | 39657.4 |
| 9087.0 | 7986.1 | 78.4 | 636.7 | 891.4 | 728.9 |
| 271975.0 | 258687.4 | 1855.1 | 5691.7 | 13741.9 | 24407.5 |
| 511802.4 | 488135.1 | 2259.6 | 35476.3 | 47281.1 | 49057.3 |
| 186536.8 | 122006.2 | 2033.3 | 34402.3 | 41372.9 | 29745.3 |

# 表 12.15 外商投资和港澳台投资工业企业经济效益指标（2022 年）
## INDICATORS ON ECONOMIC BENEFIT OF INDUSTRIAL ENTERPRISES WITH HONG KONG, MACAO, TAIWAN AND FOREIGN FUNDS (2022)

| 指 标 | Item | 总资产贡献率 Ratio of Total Assets to Industrial Output Value |
|---|---|---|
| **总 计** | **Total** | **8.1** |
| **按轻、重工业分** | **By Light and Heavy Industries** | |
| 轻工业 | Light Industry | 12.3 |
| 重工业 | Heavy Industry | 7.3 |
| **按企业规模分** | **By Size** | |
| 大型企业 | Large | 6.8 |
| 中型企业 | Medium | 10.4 |
| 小型微型企业 | Small&Mini | 9.9 |
| **按行业分** | **By Sector** | |
| 煤炭开采和洗选业 | Mining and Washing of Coal | |
| 石油和天然气开采业 | Extraction of Petroleum and Natural Gas | |
| 黑色金属矿采选业 | Mining and Processing of Ferrous Metal Ores | |
| 有色金属矿采选业 | Mining and Processing of Non-Ferrous Metal Ores | |
| 非金属矿采选业 | Mining and Processing of Nonmetal Ores | |
| 开采辅助活动 | Mining Support Activities | |
| 其他采矿业 | Mining of Other Ores | |
| 农副食品加工业 | Processing of Food from Agricultural Products | 6.7 |
| 食品制造业 | Manufacture of Foods | 6.8 |
| 酒、饮料和精制茶制造业 | Liquor, Beverage and Refined Tea | 27.0 |
| 烟草制品业 | Manufacture of Tobacco | |
| 纺织业 | Manufacture of Textile | -6.0 |
| 纺织服装、服饰业 | Manufacture of Textile Wearing Apparel, Footwear and Caps | 4.1 |
| 皮革、毛皮、羽毛及其制品和制鞋业 | Manufacture of Leather, Fur, Feather and Related Products and Footwear | |
| 木材加工和木、竹、藤、棕、草制品业 | Processing of Timber, Manufacture of Wood, Bamboo, Rattan, Palm and Straw Products | |
| 家具制造业 | Manufacture of Furniture | 24.9 |
| 造纸和纸制品业 | Manufacture of Paper and Paper Products | 5.9 |
| 印刷和记录媒介复制业 | Printing, Reproduction of Recording Media | 20.2 |
| 文教、工美、体育和娱乐用品制造业 | Manufacture of Culture, Education, Handicraft, Fine Arts, Sports and Entertainment Articles | 25.1 |
| 石油加工、炼焦和核燃料加工业 | Processing of Petroleum, Coking, Processing of Nuclear Fuel | |
| 化学原料和化学制品制造业 | Manufacture of Raw Chemical Materials and Chemical Products | 18.9 |
| 医药制造业 | Manufacture of Medicines | 16.5 |
| 化学纤维制造业 | Manufacture of Chemical Fibers | |
| 橡胶和塑料制品业 | Manufacture of Rubber and Plastics | 4.4 |
| 非金属矿物制品业 | Manufacture of Non-metallic Mineral Products | 17.4 |
| 黑色金属冶炼和压延加工业 | Smelting and Pressing of Ferrous Metals | 5.0 |
| 有色金属冶炼和压延加工业 | Smelting and Pressing of Nonferrous Metals | 7.7 |
| 金属制品业 | Manufacture of Metal Products | 7.2 |
| 通用设备制造业 | Manufacture of General Purpose Machinery | 12.0 |
| 专用设备制造业 | Manufacture of Special Purpose Machinery | 4.9 |
| 汽车制造业 | Manufacture of Motor Vehicles | 9.6 |
| 铁路、船舶、航空航天和其他运输设备制造业 | Manufacture of Railway, Ship, Aviation and Other Transporting Equipment | 20.2 |
| 电气机械和器材制造业 | Manufacture of Electrical Machinery and Equipment | 10.7 |
| 计算机、通信和其他电子设备制造业 | Manufacture of Communication Equipment, Computers and Other Electronic Equipment | 3.6 |
| 仪器仪表制造业 | Manufacture of Measuring Instruments and Machinery for Cultural Activity and Office Work | 24.7 |
| 其他制造业 | Other Manufacture | |
| 废弃资源综合利用业 | Comprehensive Utilization of Waste Resources | 12.6 |
| 金属制品、机械和设备修理业 | Repair of Metal Products, Machinery and Equipment | |
| 电力、热力生产和供应业 | Production and Supply of Electric Power and Heat Power | 4.1 |
| 燃气生产和供应业 | Production and Supply of Gas | 5.0 |
| 水的生产和供应业 | Production and Supply of Water | 8.6 |

单位: % (%)

| 资本保值增值率 Ratio of Assets Appreciation YOY | 资 产负债率 Asset-Liability Ratio | 流动资产周转率(次) Turnover Ratio of Circulating Assets (time) | 成本费用利润率 Ratio of Profits to Cost | 产品销售率 Sales as Percentage of Output |
|---|---|---|---|---|
| **100.5** | **62.6** | **2.2** | **4.0** | **98.9** |
| 95.8 | 45.6 | 1.9 | 9.5 | 97.0 |
| 101.8 | 65.7 | 2.3 | 3.4 | 99.2 |
| 99.6 | 70.2 | 2.5 | 2.7 | 99.4 |
| 100.7 | 51.9 | 1.6 | 8.9 | 97.5 |
| 101.9 | 48.0 | 1.8 | 7.7 | 97.9 |
| 89.7 | 66.2 | 3.6 | 2.2 | 100.7 |
| 56.1 | 71.9 | 2.3 | 1.1 | 95.3 |
| 76.7 | 61.8 | 1.4 | 40.5 | 95.5 |
| 120.0 | 85.7 | 0.6 | -15.1 | 98.7 |
| 100.0 | 69.6 | 5.0 | 0.0 | 99.6 |
| 107.1 | 29.4 | 2.8 | 13.4 | 98.9 |
| 98.9 | 37.7 | 2.0 | 2.6 | 95.9 |
| 90.2 | 54.4 | 1.7 | 19.6 | 105.5 |
| 84.0 | 27.9 | 2.1 | 18.9 | 81.5 |
| 93.6 | 31.1 | 1.8 | 22.5 | 98.6 |
| 199.1 | 19.3 | 0.8 | 35.2 | 79.8 |
| 95.7 | 45.9 | 2.5 | 1.6 | 99.0 |
| 105.2 | 38.0 | 1.5 | 19.2 | 89.0 |
| 120.7 | 74.3 | 2.5 | 2.1 | 94.8 |
| 107.5 | 54.1 | 2.5 | 4.3 | 91.5 |
| 104.3 | 38.2 | 1.6 | 5.0 | 102.2 |
| 102.5 | 52.0 | 1.5 | 11.1 | 100.1 |
| 99.6 | 43.7 | 0.8 | 7.6 | 93.8 |
| 97.0 | 70.5 | 1.8 | 3.6 | 99.6 |
| 102.9 | 40.8 | 2.7 | 9.6 | 98.7 |
| 103.8 | 45.2 | 1.1 | 11.9 | 93.9 |
| 107.9 | 72.8 | 2.7 | 1.6 | 99.4 |
| 107.4 | 44.9 | 1.5 | 18.5 | 101.8 |
| 100.0 | 71.8 | 2.7 | 7.6 | 100.0 |
| 99.5 | 68.1 | 3.2 | 2.0 | 100.0 |
| 105.3 | 51.7 | 2.0 | 7.0 | 100.0 |
| 101.9 | 45.8 | 1.4 | 22.6 | 100.0 |

表 12.15 续表 continued

| 指　标 | Item | 销售利润率 Rate of Return on Sale |
|---|---|---|
| **总　计** | **Total** | **3.8** |
| **按轻、重工业分** | **By Light and Heavy Industries** | |
| 轻工业 | Light Industry | 8.8 |
| 重工业 | Heavy Industry | 3.2 |
| **按企业规模分** | **By Size** | |
| 大型企业 | Large | 2.6 |
| 中型企业 | Medium | 8.0 |
| 小型微型企业 | Small&Mini | 7.0 |
| **按行业分** | **By Sector** | |
| 煤炭开采和洗选业 | Mining and Washing of Coal | |
| 石油和天然气开采业 | Extraction of Petroleum and Natural Gas | |
| 黑色金属矿采选业 | Mining and Processing of Ferrous Metal Ores | |
| 有色金属矿采选业 | Mining and Processing of Non-Ferrous Metal Ores | |
| 非金属矿采选业 | Mining and Processing of Nonmetal Ores | |
| 开采辅助活动 | Mining Support Activities | |
| 其他采矿业 | Mining of Other Ores | |
| 农副食品加工业 | Processing of Food from Agricultural Products | 2.2 |
| 食品制造业 | Manufacture of Foods | 1.1 |
| 酒、饮料和精制茶制造业 | Liquor, Beverage and Refined Tea | 34.3 |
| 烟草制品业 | Manufacture of Tobacco | |
| 纺织业 | Manufacture of Textile | -17.8 |
| 纺织服装、服饰业 | Manufacture of Textile Wearing Apparel, Footwear and Caps | |
| 皮革、毛皮、羽毛及其制品和制鞋业 | Manufacture of Leather, Fur, Feather and Related Products and Footwear | |
| 木材加工和木、竹、藤、棕、草制品业 | Processing of Timber, Manufacture of Wood, Bamboo, Rattan, Palm and Straw Products | |
| 家具制造业 | Manufacture of Furniture | 11.6 |
| 造纸和纸制品业 | Manufacture of Paper and Paper Products | 2.5 |
| 印刷和记录媒介复制业 | Printing, Reproduction of Recording Media | 16.2 |
| 文教、工美、体育和娱乐用品制造业 | Manufacture of Culture, Education, Handicraft, Fine Arts, Sports and Entertainment Articles | 16.2 |
| 石油加工、炼焦和核燃料加工业 | Processing of Petroleum, Coking, Processing of Nuclear Fuel | |
| 化学原料和化学制品制造业 | Manufacture of Raw Chemical Materials and Chemical Products | 18.2 |
| 医药制造业 | Manufacture of Medicines | 24.8 |
| 化学纤维制造业 | Manufacture of Chemical Fibers | |
| 橡胶和塑料制品业 | Manufacture of Rubber and Plastics | 1.6 |
| 非金属矿物制品业 | Manufacture of Non-metallic Mineral Products | 15.5 |
| 黑色金属冶炼和压延加工业 | Smelting and Pressing of Ferrous Metals | 2.0 |
| 有色金属冶炼和压延加工业 | Smelting and Pressing of Nonferrous Metals | 4.0 |
| 金属制品业 | Manufacture of Metal Products | 4.6 |
| 通用设备制造业 | Manufacture of General Purpose Machinery | 9.7 |
| 专用设备制造业 | Manufacture of Special Purpose Machinery | 6.8 |
| 汽车制造业 | Manufacture of Motor Vehicles | 3.3 |
| 铁路、船舶、航空航天和其他运输设备制造业 | Manufacture of Railway, Ship, Aviation and Other Transporting Equipment | 8.5 |
| 电气机械和器材制造业 | Manufacture of Electrical Machinery and Equipment | 10.3 |
| 计算机、通信和其他电子设备制造业 | Manufacture of Communication Equipment, Computers and Other Electronic Equipment | 1.6 |
| 仪器仪表制造业 | Manufacture of Measuring Instruments and Machinery for Cultural Activity and Office Work | 15.3 |
| 其他制造业 | Other Manufacture | |
| 废弃资源综合利用业 | Comprehensive Utilization of Waste Resources | 7.0 |
| 金属制品、机械和设备修理业 | Repair of Metal Products, Machinery and Equipment | |
| 电力、热力生产和供应业 | Production and Supply of Electric Power and Heat Power | 2.1 |
| 燃气生产和供应业 | Production and Supply of Gas | 6.9 |
| 水的生产和供应业 | Production and Supply of Water | 18.4 |

单位: % (%)

| 流动比率<br>Current Ratio | 速动比率<br>Quick Ratio | 产权比率<br>Equity Ratio | 人均实现利税（元）<br>Per Capita Pre-tax Profits (yuan) | 从业人员人均工资（元）<br>Per Capita Wages of Employees (yuan) |
|---|---|---|---|---|
| **1.2** | **1.0** | **1.7** | **140314** | **129706** |
| 1.5 | 1.1 | 0.8 | 233443 | 130784 |
| 1.2 | 1.0 | 1.9 | 124842 | 129527 |
| 1.2 | 1.0 | 2.4 | 118200 | 126271 |
| 1.4 | 1.1 | 1.1 | 144148 | 129430 |
| 1.4 | 1.1 | 0.9 | 234111 | 145644 |
| | | | | |
| 1.1 | 0.8 | 2.0 | 239703 | 130270 |
| 0.8 | 0.7 | 2.6 | 51523 | 120235 |
| 0.8 | 0.7 | 1.6 | 627819 | 171906 |
| 0.9 | | 6.0 | -2390 | 2962 |
| 1.0 | 0.6 | 2.3 | 9700 | 106800 |
| | | | | |
| 1.9 | 1.2 | 0.4 | 135585 | 95689 |
| 2.0 | 1.5 | 0.6 | 186864 | 158350 |
| 1.3 | 1.2 | 1.2 | 184053 | 108497 |
| 2.7 | 1.2 | 0.4 | 76362 | 110911 |
| 1.8 | 1.5 | 0.5 | 1233908 | 193295 |
| 4.4 | 3.0 | 0.2 | 648242 | 121998 |
| 0.9 | 0.5 | 0.9 | 44763 | 116056 |
| 1.6 | 1.3 | 0.6 | 355891 | 155795 |
| 0.7 | 0.4 | 2.9 | 181842 | 142806 |
| 1.2 | 1.0 | 1.2 | 163895 | 158388 |
| 2.0 | 1.6 | 0.6 | 108637 | 106075 |
| 1.5 | 1.2 | 1.1 | 185703 | 129333 |
| 1.8 | 1.1 | 0.8 | 44141 | 126926 |
| 1.2 | 1.0 | 2.4 | 200527 | 147338 |
| 1.7 | 1.4 | 0.7 | 156766 | 133784 |
| 1.6 | 1.3 | 0.8 | 162598 | 113550 |
| 1.2 | 1.0 | 2.7 | 52580 | 115525 |
| 2.2 | 1.7 | 0.8 | 214197 | 157998 |
| 0.7 | 0.5 | 2.6 | 222850 | 182225 |
| 0.3 | 0.2 | 2.1 | 305376 | 542389 |
| 0.8 | 0.7 | 1.1 | 191421 | 198613 |
| 1.5 | 1.4 | 0.9 | 344774 | 247878 |

# 表 12.16 大中型工业企业主要经济指标（2022 年）
MAIN ECONOMIC INDICATORS OF LARGE & MEDIUM-SIZED INDUSTRIAL ENTERPRISES (2022)

| 指　标 | Item | 单位数（个）Number of Enterprises (unit) | 从业人员平均人数（万人）Average Employment (10 000 persons) | 工业总产值 Gross Output Value |
|---|---|---|---|---|
| **总　计** | **Total** | **1011** | **92.73** | **176957387.6** |
| **按登记注册类型分** | **By Status of Registration** | | | |
| 内资企业 | Domestic-funded Enterprises | 868 | 73.11 | 128529888.0 |
| #国有企业 | State-owned | 18 | 1.47 | 1640769.8 |
| 集体企业 | Collective-owned | 2 | 0.09 | 46999.9 |
| 港澳台投资企业 | Funded by Hong Kong, Macao and Taiwan | 53 | 8.64 | 24259467.1 |
| 外商投资企业 | Foreign-funded | 90 | 10.98 | 24168032.5 |
| **按轻、重工业分** | **By Light and Heavy Industries** | | | |
| 轻工业 | Light Industry | 250 | 19.15 | 27065971.2 |
| 重工业 | Heavy Industry | 761 | 73.58 | 149891416.4 |

| 指　标 | Item | 固定资产净值 Net Value of Fixed Assets | 负　债 Total Liabilities | 其　中 of which #流动负债 Total Circulating Liabilities |
|---|---|---|---|---|
| **总　计** | **Total** | **46764669.1** | **106240486.0** | **86996469.3** |
| **按登记注册类型分** | **By Status of Registration** | | | |
| 内资企业 | Domestic-funded Enterprises | 38393518.5 | 84543145.3 | 69112763.2 |
| #国有企业 | State-owned | 1362296.4 | 2328813.1 | 1589234.4 |
| 集体企业 | Collective-owned | 6393.4 | 20514.1 | 20514.1 |
| 港澳台投资企业 | Funded by Hong Kong, Macao and Taiwan | 3555718.4 | 10247057.2 | 8341658.1 |
| 外商投资企业 | Foreign-funded | 4815432.2 | 11450283.5 | 9542048.0 |
| **按轻、重工业分** | **By Light and Heavy Industries** | | | |
| 轻工业 | Light Industry | 6559026.0 | 16437438.7 | 14190047.1 |
| 重工业 | Heavy Industry | 40205643.1 | 89803047.3 | 72806422.2 |

单位：万元 (10 000 yuan)

| 实收资本 Paid-in Capital | 其 中 of which #国家资本 State Capital | #外商资本 Foreign Capital | 资 产 Total Assets | #流动资产 Circulating Assets | 固定资产原 值 Original Value of Fixed Assets |
|---|---|---|---|---|---|
| **32899697.5** | **7791307.6** | **2216781.0** | **183010107.6** | **102341672.6** | **95399029.6** |
| 27231985.2 | 7276656.1 | 330991.0 | 150242874.3 | 80865897.0 | 77962116.3 |
| 1155138.4 | 359809.2 | | 3846007.5 | 1779611.6 | 2208474.0 |
| 3176.0 | | | 28064.1 | 12062.3 | 7434.8 |
| 3153686.6 | 104434.2 | 312734.2 | 16006617.4 | 10684292.0 | 6937534.2 |
| 2514025.7 | 410217.3 | 1573055.8 | 16760615.9 | 10791483.6 | 10499379.1 |
| 3758250.6 | 260880.0 | 273244.9 | 31017086.8 | 19087049.3 | 12644621.8 |
| 29141446.9 | 7530427.6 | 1943536.1 | 151993020.8 | 83254623.3 | 82754407.8 |

| 所有者权益 Creditors' Equity | 营业收入 Revenue | 营业成本 Cost | 税金及附加 Tax and Extra Charges | 利润总额 Total After-tax Profits | 利税总额 Total Pre-tax Profits | 应付职工薪 酬 Total Wages |
|---|---|---|---|---|---|---|
| **76783084.1** | **186654633.8** | **158989404.7** | **2740251.5** | **11761426.9** | **17506361.5** | **12770933.5** |
| 65713192.1 | 137103548.1 | 113814385.3 | 2372569.1 | 10118638.7 | 15037572.5 | 10259185.2 |
| 1517194.4 | 1766175.4 | 1481800.9 | 15936.4 | 75122.5 | 133676.7 | 279386.0 |
| 7550.0 | 37200.8 | 29157.1 | 45.9 | 4056.3 | 8000.7 | 5301.0 |
| 5759560.1 | 24423551.4 | 22611763.1 | 154710.2 | 921196.0 | 1306127.2 | 1151018.2 |
| 5310331.9 | 25127534.3 | 22563256.3 | 212972.2 | 721592.2 | 1162661.8 | 1360730.1 |
| 14579647.6 | 28856689.9 | 21365981.4 | 1542548.7 | 3040838.3 | 5456439.5 | 2454220.6 |
| 62203436.5 | 157797943.9 | 137623423.3 | 1197702.8 | 8720588.6 | 12049922.0 | 10316712.9 |

# 表 12.17 大中型工业企业经济效益指标（2022 年）
INDICATORS ON ECONOMIC BENEFIT OF LARGE & MEDIUM-SIZED INDUSTRIAL ENTERPRISES (2022)

| 指　标 | Item | 总资产贡献率<br>Ratio of Total Assets to Industrial Output Value |
|---|---|---|
| **总　计** | **Total** | **9.8** |
| **按登记注册类型分** | **By Status of Registration** | |
| 内资企业 | Domestic-funded Enterprises | 10.3 |
| #国有企业 | State-owned | 4.1 |
| 集体企业 | Collective-owned | 28.7 |
| 港澳台投资企业 | Funded by Hong Kong, Macao and Taiwan | 8.3 |
| 外商投资企业 | Foreign-funded | 6.9 |
| **按轻、重工业分** | **By Light and Heavy Industries** | |
| 轻工业 | Light Industry | 17.7 |
| 重工业 | Heavy Industry | 8.2 |

| 指　标 | Item | 销售利润率<br>Rate of Return on Sale |
|---|---|---|
| **总　计** | **Total** | **6.3** |
| **按登记注册类型分** | **By Status of Registration** | |
| 内资企业 | Domestic-funded Enterprises | 7.4 |
| #国有企业 | State-owned | 4.3 |
| 集体企业 | Collective-owned | 10.9 |
| 港澳台投资企业 | Funded by Hong Kong, Macao and Taiwan | 3.8 |
| 外商投资企业 | Foreign-funded | 2.9 |
| **按轻、重工业分** | **By Light and Heavy Industries** | |
| 轻工业 | Light Industry | 10.5 |
| 重工业 | Heavy Industry | 5.5 |

单位：% (%)

| 资本保值增值率<br>Ratio of Assets Appreciation YOY | 资　产负债率<br>Asset-Liability Ratio | 流动资产周转率（次）<br>Turnover Ratio of Circulating Assets (time) | 成本费用利润率<br>Ratio of Profits to Cost | 产品销售率<br>Sales as Percentage of Output |
|---|---|---|---|---|
| **107.1** | **58.1** | **1.8** | **7.0** | **97.5** |
| | | | | |
| 107.4 | 56.3 | 1.7 | 8.4 | 97.1 |
| 119.5 | 60.6 | 1.0 | 4.6 | 96.9 |
| 103.7 | 73.1 | 3.1 | 12.8 | 93.3 |
| 108.2 | 64.0 | 2.3 | 4.0 | 98.8 |
| 106.2 | 68.3 | 2.3 | 3.0 | 99.1 |
| | | | | |
| 106.0 | 53.0 | 1.5 | 12.7 | 99.9 |
| 107.4 | 59.1 | 1.9 | 6.1 | 97.0 |

| 流动比率<br>Current Ratio | 速动比率<br>Quick Ratio | 产权比率<br>Equity Ratio | 人均实现利税（元）<br>Per Capita Pre-tax Profits (yuan) |
|---|---|---|---|
| **1.2** | **1.0** | **1.4** | **188789** |
| | | | |
| 1.2 | 1.0 | 1.3 | 205684 |
| 1.1 | 0.9 | 1.5 | 90937 |
| 0.6 | 0.4 | 2.7 | 88897 |
| 1.3 | 1.1 | 1.8 | 151172 |
| 1.1 | 0.9 | 2.2 | 105889 |
| | | | |
| 1.4 | 1.1 | 1.1 | 284932 |
| 1.1 | 1.0 | 1.4 | 163766 |

# 表 12.18 规模以上工业企业主要产品产量（2021－2022 年）
## OUTPUT OF MAJOR PRODUCTS OF INDUSTRIAL ENTERPRISES ABOVE DESIGNATED SIZE (2021-2022)

| 产　品 | Products | 2021 | 2022 |
|---|---|---|---|
| 化学纤维（万吨） | Chemical Fibre (10 000 tons) | 20 | 23 |
| 纱（吨） | Yarn (ton) | 49388 | 40072 |
| 布（万米） | Cloth (10 000 m) | 25022 | 28337 |
| 印染布（万米） | Printed and Dyed Fabric (10 000 m) | 19364 | 12011 |
| 毛　线（吨） | Knitting Wool (ton) | 138 | 157 |
| 蚕　丝（吨） | Silk (ton) | 810 | 396 |
| 丝织品（蚕丝及交织机织物（含蚕丝≥ 50%)）（万米） | Silk Products (silk and mixture fabric (with content of silk ≥ 50%)) (10 000 m) | 2308 | 2434 |
| 微型计算机设备（台） | Microcomputers (units) | 107303593 | 86319196 |
| #笔记本计算机 | Laptops | 93852941 | 74112059 |
| 显示器（万台） | Display(10 000 sets) | 2586 | 2352 |
| 打印机（万台） | Marking Machine(10 000 sets) | 114 | 102 |
| 移动通信手持机（手机）（万台） | Mobile Telephones(10 000 sets) | 11158 | 7449 |
| 摩托车（万辆） | Motorcycles (10 000 units) | 438 | 449 |
| 机制纸及纸板（吨） | Machine-made Paper and Paperboard (ton) | 4331499 | 4177965 |
| 日用陶瓷制品（万件） | Household Ceramics(10 000 pcs) | 629 | 657 |
| 日用玻璃制品（吨） | Daily-use Glassware (ton) | 446575 | 476285 |
| 合成洗涤剂（吨） | Synthetic Detergents (ton) | 204169 | 142665 |
| 卷　烟（亿支） | Cigarettes (100 million pieces) | 570 | 570 |
| 白　酒（万千升） | Liquor (10 000 kiloliters) | 11 | 11 |
| 啤　酒（万千升） | Beer (10 000 kiloliters) | 80 | 81 |
| 罐　头（吨） | Canned Food (ton) | 81641 | 56405 |
| 精制食用植物油（吨） | Edible Vegetable Oil (ton) | 1202422 | 1131323 |
| 皮革鞋靴（万双） | Leather Shoes (10 000 pairs) | 3604 | 3446 |
| 服　装（万件） | Garments (10 000 pcs) | 10788 | 10295 |
| 乳制品（万吨） | Dairy Products (10 000 tons) | 27 | 25 |
| 无酒精饮料（软饮料）（吨） | Non-alcoholic Beverage (soft) (ton) | 2256899 | 2034145 |
| 焦　炭（万吨） | Coke (10 000 tons) | 286 | 313 |
| 发电量（万千瓦时） | Electricity (10 000 kwh) | 9309375 | 9978400 |
| 天然气（万立方米） | Natural Gas (10 000 cu.m) | 1395500 | 1414500 |
| 生　铁（万吨） | Pig Iron (10 000 tons) | 674 | 723 |
| 粗　钢（万吨） | Crude Steel (10 000 tons) | 899 | 975 |
| 钢　材（万吨） | Steel Products (10 000 tons) | 1310 | 1691 |

表 12.18 续表 continued

| 产 品 | Products | 2021 | 2022 |
| --- | --- | --- | --- |
| 铝 材(吨) | Aluminum Product (ton) | 2177227 | 2386422 |
| 硫 酸(吨) | Sulphuric Acid (ton) | 663754 | 934573 |
| 盐 酸(吨) | Hydrochloric Acid (ton) | 33658 | 32185 |
| 烧 碱(吨) | Caustic Soda (ton) | 365645 | 369915 |
| 精甲醇(商品量)(吨) | Fine Methyl Alcohol (commodities) (ton) | 2025149 | 1937907 |
| 涂 料(吨) | Paint (ton) | 1043007 | 782388 |
| 塑料制品(吨) | Plastics (ton) | 3139124 | 3300095 |
| 合成橡胶(吨) | Synthetic Rubber (ton) | 10674 | 9908 |
| 化学原料药(吨) | Chemical Raw Material (ton) | 8866 | 9366 |
| 中成药(吨) | Traditional Chinese Medicine (ton) | 114293 | 75299 |
| 轮胎外胎(万条) | Tire (10 000 units) | 1382 | 1143 |
| 水 泥(万吨) | Cement (10 000 tons) | 6233 | 5317 |
| 人造板(立方米) | Artificial Boards (cu.m) | 1025167 | 556306 |
| 矿山设备(吨) | Mining Equipment (ton) | 71499 | 74836 |
| 起重设备(起重机)(吨) | Hoist and Derrick (ton) | 30823 | 36152 |
| 房间空气调节器(台) | Air-conditioners (unit) | 18536161 | 19160622 |
| 发电设备(千瓦) | Generating Equipment (kw) | 3371541 | 697553 |
| 交流电动机(万千瓦) | AC Motors(10 000 kw) | 401 | 362 |
| 变压器(万千伏安) | Transformer Products (10 000 kva) | 5110 | 5387 |
| 金属切削机床(台) | Metal-cutting Machines (unit) | 12471 | 10236 |
| 汽 车(辆) | Motor Vehicles (unit) | 1998024 | 2091786 |
| #轿 车 | Cars | 395748 | 548647 |
| 内燃机(发动机)(万千瓦) | Internal Combustion Engines (10 000 kw) | 28468 | 27164 |
| 泵(台) | Industry Pumps (unit) | 428783 | 286472 |
| 风 机(台) | Air Pumps (unit) | 200775 | 224968 |
| 气体压缩机(台) | Gas Compressors (unit) | 4305015 | 4909912 |
| 轴 承(万套) | Bearings (10 000 sets) | 5377 | 5172 |
| 工业锅炉(蒸吨) | Industry Boilers (ton) | 1027 | 1014 |
| 民用钢质船舶(载重吨) | Civil Steel Ships (ton) | 334923 | 316031 |
| 合成氨(吨) | Synthetic Ammonia (ton) | 1215491 | 1304715 |
| 化肥(100%)(吨) | Chemical Fertilizer (100%) (ton) | 1589095 | 1661560 |
| #氮 肥 | Nitrogen Fertilizer | 1499986 | 1600916 |
| 配混合饲料(吨) | Mingled Forage (ton) | 6267238 | 5602908 |
| 化学农药原药(吨) | Chemical Pesticides (ton) | 1737 | 907 |

# 主要统计指标解释

## ■ 工业

指从事自然资源的开采，对采掘品和农产品进行加工和再加工的物质生产部门。具体包括：(1) 对自然资源的开采，如采矿、晒盐等（但不包括禽兽捕猎和水产捕捞）；(2) 对农副产品的加工、再加工，如粮油加工、食品加工、缫丝、纺织、制革等；(3) 对采掘品的加工、再加工，如炼铁、炼钢、化工生产、石油加工、机器制造、木材加工等，以及电力、燃气及水的生产和供应等；(4) 对工业品的修理、翻新，如机器设备的修理等。

工业统计调查单位为工业法人单位。

工业法人单位指从事工业生产经营活动的法人单位。工业法人单位应同时具备以下条件：①依法成立，有自己的名称、组织机构和场所，能够独立承担民事责任；②独立拥有（或授权）使用资产，承担负债，有权与其他单位签订合同；③具有包括资产负债表在内账户，或者能够根据需要编制账户。

## ■ 工业总产值

指工业企业在本年内生产的以货币形式表现的工业最终产品和提供工业劳务活动的总价值量。

(1) 工业总产值计算应遵循的原则

①工业生产的原则。即凡是企业在本年内生产的最终产品和提供的劳务，均应包括在内。其中的最终产品，不管是否在本年内销售，只要是本年内生产的，就应包括在内。凡不是工业生产的产品，均不得计入工业总产值。

②最终产品的原则。即企业生产的成品价值必须是本企业生产的，经检验合格不需再进行任何加工的最终产品。企业对外销售的半成品也应视为最终产品计入工业总产值。而在本企业内各车间转移的半成品和在制品只能计算其期末期初差额价值。

③“工厂法”原则。即以法人工业企业作为一个整体计算工业总产值，是其本年内生产的最终产品和提供劳务的总价值量。

(2) 工业总产值的内容

包括三部分：生产的成品价值、对外加工费收入、自制半成品在制品期末期初差额价值。

①成品价值：指企业在本年内生产，并在本年内不再进行加工，经检验合格、包装入库的已经销售和准备销售的全部工业成品（包括半成品）价值合计。成品价值中包括企业生产的自制设备及提供给本企业在建工程、其他非工业部门和生活福利部门等单位使用的成品价值，但不包括用订货者来料加工的成品（半成品）价值。

工业总产值是按现行价格计算的。成品价值按成品实物量乘以本年不含应交增值税（销项税额）的产品实际销售平均单价计算。会计核算中按成本价格转账自制设备和自产自用的成品，按成本价格计算生产成品价值。

②对外加工费收入：指企业在本年内完成的对外承做的工业品加工（包括用订货者来料加工生产）的加工费收入和对外工业品修理作业所收取的加工费收入和对内非工业部门提供的加工修理、设备安装等收入。对外加工费收入按不含应交增值税（销项税额）的价格计算。

对于以对外加工生产为主，对外加工费收入所占比重较大的企业，如果对外加工费收入出现跨年度支付的情况，为保证总产值生产口径计算的准确性，则应将对外加工费收入按实际情况调整，记录本年应实际收取的对外加工费收入。

③自制半成品在制品期末期初差额价值。为了使工业总产值与工业中间投入中的物耗价值一致，以便同口径地计算工业增加值，规定本指标的计算原则是：凡是企业会计产品成本核算中计算半成品、在制品成本，则工业总产值中必须包括自制半成品在制品期末期初差额价值。反之则不包括。

自制半成品在制品期末期初差额价值等于自制半成品在制品期末价值减去期初价值后的余额，如果期末价值小于期初价值，该指标为负值，企业在计算产值时，应按负值计算，不能作为零处理。

(3) 工业总产值计算的几种具体规定

①凡自备原材料，不论其加工繁简程度如何，一律按全价，即包括自备原材料的价值，计算工业总产值。

②凡来料加工，加工企业只收取加工费，则加工企业一律按财务上结算的加工费计算工业总产值，即不包括订货者来料的价值。一般分两种情况：a、工业企业之间的来料加工，加工企业（即承包单位）按财务

## 主要统计指标解释

上结算的加工费计算工业总产值；委托加工的企业（即发包单位）按全价计算工业总产值。b、工业企业与非工业企业之间的来料加工，当工业企业作为加工企业时一律按加工费计算工业总产值。

③自制半成品、在制品期末期初差额价值，原则上应计入工业总产值，但如果会计产品成本核算中不计算自制半成品、在制品成本，则不计入工业总产值；如果会计产品成本核算中计算自制半成品、在制品成本的，则计入工业总产值。

### 轻工业

指主要提供生活消费品和制作手工工具的工业。按其所使用的原料不同，可分为两大类：(1) 以农产品为原料的轻工业，是指直接或间接以农产品为基本原料的轻工业。主要包括食品制造、饮料制造、烟草加工、纺织、缝纫、皮革和毛皮制作、造纸以及印刷等工业；(2) 以非农产品为原料的轻工业，是指以工业品为原料的轻工业。主要包括文教体育用品、化学药品制造、合成纤维制造、日用化学制品、日用玻璃制品、日用金属制品、手工工具制造、医疗器械制造、文化和办公用机械制造等工业。

### 重工业

指为国民经济各部门提供物质技术基础的主要生产资料的工业。按其生产性质和产品用途，可以分为下列三类：(1) 采掘（伐）工业，是指对自然资源的开采，包括石油开采、煤炭开采、金属矿开采、非金属矿开采等工业；(2) 原材料工业，指向国民经济各部门提供基本材料、动力和燃料的工业。包括金属冶炼及加工、炼焦及焦炭、化学、化工原料、水泥、人造板以及电力、石油和煤炭加工等工业；(3) 加工工业，是指对工业原材料进行再加工制造的工业。包括装备国民经济各部门的机械设备制造工业、金属结构、水泥制品等工业，以及为农业提供的生产资料如化肥、农药等工业。

根据上述划分原则，修理业中以重工业产品为修理作业对象的划为重工业，反之划为轻工业。

### 国有控股企业

即原来的国有及国有控股企业，根据企业实收资本中国有经济成分的出资人的实际投资情况，或国有经济成分的出资人对企业资产的实际控制、支配程度进行分类。以下情况为国有控股：（1）在企业的全部实收资本中，国有经济成分的出资人拥有的实收资本（股本）所占企业全部实收资本（股本）的比例大于50%的国有绝对控股。（2）在企业的全部实收资本中，国有经济成分的出资人拥有的实收资本（股本）所占比例虽未大于50%，但相对大于其他任何一方经济成分的出资人所占比例的国有相对控股；或者虽不大于其他经济成分，但根据协议规定拥有企业实际控制权的国有协议控股。（3）投资双方各占50%，且未明确由谁绝对控股的企业，若其中一方为国有经济成分的，一律按国有控股处理。

本篇涉及的企业登记注册类型的解释详见综合篇。

### 出口交货值

指工业企业自营（委托）出口（包括销往香港、澳门、台湾）或交给外贸部门出口的产品价值，以及外商来样、来料加工、来件装配和补偿贸易等生产的产品价值。

### 资产总计

指企业过去的交易或者事项形成的、由企业拥有或者控制的、预期会给企业带来经济利益的资源。资产一般按流动性分为流动资产和非流动资产。其中流动资产可分为货币资金、交易性金融资产、应收票据、应收账款、预付款项、其他应收款、存货等；非流动资产可分为长期股权投资、固定资产、无形资产及其他非流动资产等。来源于会计“资产负债表”中“资产总计”项目的期末余额数。

### 流动资产合计

资产满足以下条件之一应归为流动资产：（1）预计在一个正常营业周期中变现、出售或耗用，主要包括存货、应收账款等；（2）主要为交易目的而持有；（3）预计在资产负债表日起一年内（含一年）变现；（4）自资产负债日起一年内，交换其他资产或清偿负债的能力不受限制的现金或现金等价物。包括货币资金、应收票据、应收账款、存货等项目。来源于会计“资产负债表”中“流动资产合计”项目的期末余额数。

### 负债合计

指企业过去的交易或者事项形成的，预期会导致经济利益流出企业的现时义务。包括银行贷款、借款、应付账款、应付职工工资、应付职工福利费、应交税金等企业负有偿还责任的债务。根据会计“资产负债表”

## 主要统计指标解释

中"负债合计"项目的期末余额数填报。负债一般按偿还期长短分为流动负债和非流动负债。

### ■ 所有者权益

指企业资产扣除负债后由所有者享有的剩余权益。公司的所有者权益又称股东权益。包括实收资本、资本公积、盈余公积、未分配利润等。根据会计"资产负债表"中的"所有者权益合计"项的期末数填列。

### ■ 营业收入

指企业经营主要业务和其他业务所确认的收入总额。营业收入包括"主营业务收入"和"其他业务收入"。来源于会计"利润表"中"营业收入"项目的本年累计数。

### ■ 营业成本

指企业经营主要业务和其他业务所发生的成本总额。包括企业（单位）在报告期内从事销售商品、提供劳务等日常活动发生的各种耗费。包括"主营业务成本"和"其他业务成本"。来源于会计"利润表"中"营业成本"项目的本年累计数。

### ■ 税金及附加

指企业因从事生产经营活动按税法规定应缴纳的消费税、城市维护建设税、资源税、环境保护税、教育费附加及房产税、土地使用税、车船使用税、印花税等相关税费。根据会计"利润表"中"税金及附加"项目的本年累计数填报。

### ■ 营业利润

指企业从事生产经营活动所取得的利润。根据会计"利润表"中"营业利润"项目的本年累计数填报。

### ■ 应交增值税

指企业按税法规定，以销售货物、服务、无形资产、不动产或提供加工、修理修配劳务的增值额和货物进口金额为计税依据而课征的一种流转税。计算公式为：

本年应交增值税 = 销项税额 –（进项税额 - 进项税额转出）– 出口抵减内销产品应纳税额 – 减免税款 + 出口退税

### ■ 利润总额

指企业在一定会计期间的经营成果，是生产经营过程中各种收入扣除各种耗费后的盈余，反映企业在报告期内实现的盈亏总额。来源于会计"利润表"中"利润总额"项目的本期金额数。

### ■ 利税总额

指企业利润总额、税金及附加、应交增值税之和。

### ■ 固定资产原值

指固定资产的成本，包括企业在购置、自行建造、安装、改建、扩建、技术改造某项固定资产时所发生的全部支出总额。

### ■ 固定资产净额

指固定资产原值减去累计折旧、固定资产减值准备后的金额。

### ■ 工业经济效益综合指数

是综合衡量地区工业经济效益总体水平的一种特殊相对数，是反映一定时期工业经济运行质量的主要指标。工业经济效益综合指数由总资产贡献率、资本保值增值率、资产负债率、流动资产周转率、成本费用利润率、全员劳动生产率和产品销售率的实际数值分别除以该项指标的全国标准值，并乘以各自的权数，加总后除以总权数求得。该指标可从静态水平和动态趋势上较为全面地反映各地区工业经济效益的变化情况，并可在一定程度上消除地区对比的不可比因素。

### ■ 总资产贡献率

反映企业全部资产的获利能力，是企业经营业绩和管理水平的集中体现，是评价和考核企业盈利能力的核心指标。计算公式为：

$$\text{总资产贡献率}(\%) = \frac{\text{利润总额} + \text{税金总额} + \text{利息支出}}{\text{平均资产总额}} \times 100\%$$

### ■ 资本保值增值率

反映企业净资产的变动状况，是企业发展能力的集中体现。计算公式为：

$$\text{资本保值增值率}(\%) = \frac{\text{报告期期末所有者权益}}{\text{上年同期期末所有者权益}} \times 100\%$$

# 主要统计指标解释

## 资产负债率

该指标既反映企业经营风险的大小，也反映企业利用债权人提供的资金从事经营活动的能力。计算公式为：

$$资产负债率(\%)=\frac{负债总额}{资产总额}\times 100\%$$

## 流动资产周转次数

指在一定时期内流动资产完成的周转次数，反映流动资产的周转速度。计算公式为：

$$流动资产周转次数=\frac{产品销售收入}{全部流动资产平均余额}$$

## 成本费用利润率

指在一定时期内实现的利润与成本费用之比，是反映工业生产成本及费用投入的经济效益指标，同时也是反映降低成本的经济效益的指标。计算公式为：

$$成本费用利润率(\%)=\frac{利润总额}{成本费用总额}\times 100\%$$

## 全员劳动生产率

指根据产品的价值量指标计算的平均每一就业人员在单位时间内的产品生产量。是考核企业经济活动的重要指标，是企业生产技术水平、经营管理水平、职工技术熟练程度和劳动积极性的综合表现。目前，我国的全员劳动生产率是将工业企业的增加值除以同一时期全部就业人员的平均人数来计算的。计算公式为：

$$全员劳动生产率=\frac{工业增加值}{全部从业人员平均人数}$$

## 产品销售率

指工业销售产值与同期全部工业总产值之比，反映工业产品已实现销售的程度，分析工业产销衔接情况，研究工业产品满足社会需求程度的指标。计算公式为：

$$产品销售率(\%)=\frac{现价工业销售产值}{报告期现价工业总产值}\times 100\%$$

## 销售利润率

指企业利润与销售收入的比率。计算公式为：

$$销售利润率(\%)=\frac{利润}{销售收入}\times 100\%$$

## 资本积累率

指企业所有者权益增长额与年初所有者权益的比率。计算公式为：

$$资本积累率(\%)=\frac{所有者权益增长额}{年初所有者权益}\times 100\%$$

## 流动比率

指流动资产与流动负债的比率，它表明每一元流动负债有多少流动资产作为偿还的保证，反映企业用可在短期内转变为现金的流动资产偿还到期流动负债的能力。计算公式为：

$$流动比率=\frac{流动资产}{流动负债}$$

## 速动比率

指企业速动资产与流动负债的比率。计算公式为：

$$速动比率=\frac{速动资产}{流动负债}$$

## 产权比率

指企业负债总额与所有者权益的比率，是企业财务结构稳健与否的重要标志，也称资本负债率。计算公式为：

$$产权比率=\frac{负债总额}{所有者权益}$$

## 平均用工人数

指报告期企业平均实际拥有的、参与本企业生产经营活动的人员数。

## 工业企业中大、中、小、微型的划分标准：

期末从业人员数1000人及以上，并且营业收入在40000万元及以上的工业企业为大型企业；期末从业人员数300人及以上到1000人以下，并且营业收入在2000万元及以上到4000万元以下的工业企业为中型企业；期末从业人员数20人及以上到300人以下，并且营业收入在300万元及以上到2000万元以下的工业企业为小型企业；期末从业人员数20以下，或者营业收入在300万元以下的工业企业为微型企业。

# Explanatory Notes on Main Statistical Indicators

## Industry

Refers to the material production sector which is engaged in the extraction of natural resources and processing and reprocessing of minerals and agricultural products, including (1) extraction of natural resources, such as mining, salt production (but not including hunting and fishing); (2) processing and reprocessing of farm and sideline produces, such as grain and oil processing, food processing, silk reeling, spinning and weaving and leather making; (3) processing and reprocessing of mineral products, such as steel making, iron smelting, chemicals manufacturing, petroleum processing, machine building, timber processing, and production and supply of electricity, gas and water; (4) repairing and renovating of industrial products such as the machinery.

In industrial surveys, the units of enquiry are industrial corporate units.

Industrial corporate units refer to corporate units engaging in industrial production and operation activities, which meet the following requirements: (1) They are established legally, having their own names, organizations, location, and are able to take civil liability independently; (2) They possess (or are authorized to use) assets independently, assume liabilities and are entitled to sign contracts with other units; (3) They have accounts including the balance sheets or can compile the accounts according to the need.

## Gross Industrial Output Value

Refers to the total volume of final industrial products produced and industrial services provided in this year.

(1)Principles for calculations

① Statistics on industrial production follow the principle that all products produced by the enterprises and accepted through quality check during the reference period are to be included no matter whether they are sold or not during the reference period.

② Determination of final products follows the principle that all products that are included in the calculation of gross industrial output value are the final products of the enterprise which have been accepted through quality check and require no further processing. If an enterprise has semi-finished products to sell, these intermediate products are considered as the final products of the enterprise.

Finished and semi-finished products which transfer in the workshop can only calculate the difference value between the end and the beginning.

③ Gross industrial output value is calculated following the principle of factory approach, i.e. industrial enterprise is used as the basic accounting unit in calculating the gross industrial output value. By this approach, value of the same product is not to be double-counted, and the output value of different workshops (branch factories) within the enterprise should not be added. However, this approach allows the possibility of double counting between enterprises.

(2) Content

Gross industrial output value consists of 3 components: value of the finished products during the reference period, income from processing for external parties, and value of change in semi-finished products between the end and the beginning of the reference period.

① Value of finished products during the reference period: refers to the value of all finished (semi-finished) industrial products that are produced during the reference period without the need for further processing, checked for acceptance, packed and put into the warehouse of the enterprise, including the value of own-produced equipment and the value of products provided to the projects under construction of the enterprise, and to other non-industrial or welfare units. Value of finished products does not include the value of finished products (semi-finished products) that are produced using the materials from the clients who place the orders.

Value of finished products during the reference

EXPLANATORY NOTES TO MAJOR STATISTICAL INDICATORS

period is calculated by the quantity of products produced using own materials multiplied by the average unit prices at which products are sold (excluding value-added tax). Own-produced equipment and products produced for own use are valued at cost prices as in the case of enterprise accounting.

② External processing fee income: refers to the processing fee income of the industrial product processing undertaken by the enterprise within this year (including processing and producing with the supplied materials of the ordering party);Income from processing fees charged for repairing foreign industrial products and income from processing, repairing and equipment installation provided by domestic non-industrial sectors. External processing fee income is calculated at the price excluding VAT payable (output tax).

If the income from external processing is paid beyond one year, Enterprises which the share of income from processing service is significant should adjust and record actual income from external processing this year.

③ Value of change in semi-finished products between the end and the beginning of the reference period. If the enterprise accounting excludes the cost of semi-finished products, then it should not be included in the gross industrial output value, and the reverse if otherwise.

Value of change in semi-finished products between the end and the beginning of the reference period: refers to the value of change in semi-finished products between the end and the beginning of the reference period. If the value of the end is less than the beginning, the index is negative and not dealt as zero.

(3) Method of calculation

① All products produced using own materials are to be calculated with full value in reporting the gross industrial output value irrespective of the complexity of production.

② For processing of incoming materials, the processing enterprises only charge the processing fee, then the processing enterprises will calculate the total industrial output value according to the processing fee settled financially, which does not include the value of the incoming materials from the orderer.

③ The value of change in semi-finished products should be included in the gross industrial output value if it is included in the accounting record of the enterprise, otherwise it should not be included.

## Light Industry

Refers to the industry that produces consumer goods and hand tools. It consists of two categories, depending on the materials used:

(1) Industries using farm products as raw materials. These are the branches of light industry which directly or indirectly use farm products as basic raw materials, including the manufacture of food and beverages, tobacco processing, textile, clothing, fur and leather manufacturing, paper making, printing, etc.

(2) Industries using non-farm products as raw materials. These are the branches of light industry which use manufactured goods as raw materials, including the manufacture of cultural, educational articles and sports goods, chemicals, synthetic fiber, chemical products for daily use, glass products for daily use, metal products for daily use, hand tools, medical apparatus and instruments, and the manufacture of cultural and office machinery.

## Heavy Industry

Refers to the industry which produces capital goods, and provides various sectors of the national economy with necessary material and technical basis for production. It consists of the following three branches according to the purpose of production or the use of products:

(1) Mining, quarrying and logging industry, which refers to the industry that extracts natural resources, including extraction of petroleum, coal, metal and non-metal ores.

(2) Raw materials industry refers to the industry that provides various sectors of the national economy with raw materials, fuels and power. It includes smelting and processing of metals, coking and coke chemistry, chemical materials and building materials such as cement, plywood, and power, petroleum refining and coal dressing.

(3) Manufacturing industry which refers to the industry that processes raw materials. It includes

machine-building industries which equip sectors of the national economy; industries producing metal structure and cement products; and industries producing means of agricultural production, such as chemical fertilizers and pesticides.

In accordance with the above principles of classification, the repairing trades, which are engaged primarily in repairing products of heavy industry, are classified as heavy industry while those which are engaged in repairing products of light industry are classified as light industry.

## State-holding Enterprises

Cover the original state-owned enterprises and state-holding enterprises. They are classified according to the actual investment made by the contributor of state-owned part in the paid-in capital of the enterprises, or the degree of control or dominance of the contributor on the assets of the enterprises. The following cases are regarded as state-holding: (1) Absolute state-holding in which the contributors of state-owned parts possess more than 50% of all the paid-in capital (stocks) of the enterprises; (2) Relative state-holding in which the contributors of state-owned parts possess no more than 50% of the paid-in capital (stocks) of the enterprises, but more than that of any other contributors; or Agreed state-holding in which the contributors of state-owned parts possess no more than other contributors but have actual control over the enterprises according to agreements; (3) In the case both contributors possess 50% and it is not clear which one is in absolute holding position, the enterprise is regarded as state-holding enterprise if one of the contributor has state-owned elements.

For explanation of types of registration covered in this chapter, please refer to General Survey.

## Value of Export Delivery

Refers to the value of the products exported by the industrial enterprises themselves (including those sold to Hong Kong, Macao, Taiwan) or handed over to the foreign trade department, as well as the value of the products produced by the foreign businessmen, such as samples, processing with supplied materials, assembling with supplied parts and compensation trade.

## Total Assets

Refer to all resources that are owned or controlled by enterprises through previous trades or transactions with expectation of making economic profits. Classified by the degree of liquidity, total assets include current assets and non-current assets. Current assets can be classified into monetary capital, trading financial assets, notes receivable, accounts receivable, advanced payments, other receivables and inventories. Non-current assets can be divided into long-term equity investment, fixed assets, intangible assets and other non-current assets. Data on this indicator can be obtained from the year-end figures of total assets in the Balance Sheet of accounting records.

## Total Current Assets

Refer to the assets that meet one of the following requirements: (1) expected to be cashed, sold or used in a normal operation cycle, mainly including inventory and accounts receivable; (2) be owned for trading purpose mainly; (3) expected to be cashed in one year (including one year) from the day of the Balance Sheet; (4) unlimited cash or cash equivalents that can be exchanged with other assets or being capable of settling debts during one year since the day of the Balance Sheet. Included are monetary capital, notes receivable, accounts receivable and inventories. Data on this indicator can be obtained from the year-end figures of total current assets in the Balance Sheet of accounting records.

## Total Liabilities

Refers to the current obligations of the enterprise formed in the past transactions or events that are expected to cause economic benefits to flow out of the enterprise. Including bank loans, borrowings, accounts payable, wages payable to employees, employee benefits payable, taxes payable and other debts that enterprises are responsible for repaying. According to the closing balance of the "total liabilities" item in the accounting

EXPLANATORY NOTES TO MAJOR STATISTICAL INDICATORS

"balance sheet". Liabilities are generally divided into current liabilities and non-current liabilities according to the length of the repayment period.

### Creditors' Equity

Refers to the remaining equity enjoyed by the owner after deducting liabilities of corporate assets. The company's owner's equity is also called shareholders' equity. Including paid-in capital, capital reserves, surplus reserves, undistributed profits, etc. According to the ending number of the "total owner's equity" item in the accounting "balance sheet".

### Business Revenue

Refers to the total revenue recognized by an enterprise in its principal business and other business operations. Business revenue includes " revenue from principal Business" and " revenue from other business". It comes from this year’s cumulative report of "business revenue" items from the "income statement".

### Business Cost

Refers to the total cost incurred by an enterprise in its principal business and other business operations. It includes various expenditures incurred by enterprises (units) in their daily activities of selling goods and providing labour services during the reporting period. It includes "Cost of principal business" and "Cost of other business". It comes from this year’s cumulative report of "operating cost" items from the "income statement".

### Taxes and surcharges

Refers to consumption tax, urban maintenance and construction tax, resource tax, environmental protection tax, education surcharge, property tax, land use tax, vehicle and vessel use tax, stamp tax and other relevant taxes payable by enterprises for their production and business activities according to the tax law.The current year's accumulative count is reported according to the items of "taxes and Surcharges" in the accounting "income statement".

### Profit from Business

Refers to the profits obtained by an enterprise from its production and business operations.The current year's cumulative counting is reported in accordance with the operating profit item in the accounting income statement.

### Value Added Tax Payable

Refers to a type of turnover tax levied by an enterprise on the basis of taxation regulations based on the value-added amount of sales of goods, services, intangible assets, real estate, or the provision of processing, repair and replacement services, and the amount of goods imported. It is calculated as follows:

Value added tax payable=tax on sales-(tax on purchases-transferred tax on purchases) - Tax credits-tax cut +export rebate

### Total Profits

Refers to the operation results in a certain accounting period, and it is the balance of various incomes minus various spendings in the course of operation, reflecting the total profits and losses of enterprises in reference period. Data are obtained from the amount of total profits in the profit statement of the accounting record of enterprise.

### Total Value of Profit and Tax (Pre-tax Profits)

Refers to the sum of corporate profits, taxes and surcharges, and VAT payable.

### Original value of fixed assets

Refers to the cost of fixed assets, including the total amount of expenditures incurred by an enterprise in the acquisition, self-construction, installation, alteration, expansion and technical renovation of a fixed asset.

### Net fixed assets

Refers to the original value of fixed assets minus accumulated depreciation and fixed assets impairment provision.

EXPLANATORY NOTES TO
MAJOR STATISTICAL INDICATORS

## Industrial Comprehensive Index of Economic Efficiency

Is a special kind of relative figure to comprehensively measure overall economic efficiency of regional industry, showing the quality of industrial economic efficiency of the reference period. Industrial comprehensive index of economic efficiency is calculated with 7 items of ratio of total assets to industrial output value, ratio of creditors' equity of current year to that of previous year, ratio of liabilities to assets, turnover ratio of output value, circulating funds, ratio of profits to cost, overall labor productivity, ratio of sales to products. The actual figure of every indicator above is divided by responding national standard numerical value, and the results multiply correlative weight coefficients, then the total number is divided by general weight coefficient. The index comprehensively reflects the changes of regional industrial economic efficiency in static and dynamic status, eliminating the incomparable factors at a certain extent.

## Ratio of Total Assets to Industrial Output Value

Reflects the profit-making capability of all assets of the enterprise and is a key indicator manifesting the performance and management and evaluating the profit-making potential of the enterprise. It is calculated as follows:

Ratio of Total Assets to Industrial Output (%) =

$$\frac{\text{Total profits} + \text{Total taxes} + \text{Interest payment}}{\text{average assets}} \times 100\%$$

## Capital Maintenance and Appreciation Rate

Reflects the changes of an enterprise's net assets. It epitomizes the growth capability of an enterprise. Its calculating formula is:

Capital Maintenance and appreciation rate =

$$\frac{\text{Ownership equity at the end of the reporting period}}{\text{Ownership equity at the same period of the previous year}}$$

## Ratio of Liabilities to Assets

Reflect both the operation risk and the capability of the enterprise in making use of the capital from the creditors. It is calculated as follows:

$$\text{Ratio of liabilities to assets (\%)} = \frac{\text{Total liabilities}}{\text{total assets}} \times 100\%$$

## Turnover Ratio of Circulating Funds

Refers to times of turnover of circulating funds in a given period of time, which reflects the speed of the turnover of working capital and is calculated as follows:

Turnover Ratio of Circulating Funds (%) =

$$\frac{\text{Sales Revenue of Products}}{\text{Average Balance of Total Circulating Funds}} \times 100\%$$

## Ratio of Profits to Costs

Refers to the ratio of profits realized in a given period to the total costs in the same period, which reflects the economic efficiency of input cost and is calculated as follows:

$$\text{Ratio of Profits to Cost (\%)} = \frac{\text{Total Profits}}{\text{Total Costs}} \times 100\%$$

## Overall Labor Productivity

Refers to the average output per employed person in industrial enterprises in value terms. At present, the value added and the average number of staff and workers of an industrial enterprises in a given period are used to calculate the overall labor productivity. The formula used is:

Overall Labor Productivity =

$$\frac{\text{Value Added of Industry}}{\text{Average Number of Staff and Workers}}$$

## Ratio of Sales to Products

Refers to the ratio of total sales in a given period to the gross output value in the same period, which reflects the extent of industrial output sold and is calculated as follows:

Ratio of Sales to Products (%) =

$$\frac{\text{Total Sales (at Current Prices)}}{\text{Gross Output Value (at Current Prices)}} \times 100\%$$

EXPLANATORY NOTES TO MAJOR STATISTICAL INDICATORS

## Ratio of Profits to Sales

Refers to the ratio of total profits to the sales revenue in a given period and is calculated as follows:

$$\text{Ratio of Profits to Sales (\%)} = \frac{\text{Total Profits}}{\text{Sales Revenue}} \times 100\%$$

## Ratio of Accumulated Capital to Original Capital

Refers to the ratio of the increased volume of creditors' equity to the creditors' equity at the year's beginning. The formula used is:

Ratio of Accumulated Capital to Original Capital (%) =

$$\frac{\text{Increased Volume of Creditors' Equity}}{\text{Creditors' Equity at Year's Beginning}} \times 100\%$$

## Current Ratio

Refers to the ratio of the circulating assets to the circulating liabilities, i.e. the amount of circulating assets as the guarantee to pay off each yuan of circulating liabilities, which reflects the ability of the enterprise to pay off the due circulating liabilities with the circulating assets realizable in a short period of time. The formula is:

$$\text{Current Ratio (\%)} = \frac{\text{Circulating Assets}}{\text{Circulating Liabilities}}$$

## Quick Ratio

Refers to the ratio of quick assets to circulating liabilities of the enterprise, and is calculated as the follows:

$$\text{Quick Ratio} = \frac{\text{Quick Assets}}{\text{Circulating Liabilities}}$$

## Ratio of Equity to Production

Refers to the ratio of total liabilities to creditors' equity. It is the sign of financial stability of the enterprises, and also called ratio of total liabilities to total capital. The formula is:

$$\text{Ratio of Equity to Production} = \frac{\text{Total Liabilities}}{\text{Creditors' Equity}}$$

## Annual Average Employees

Refers to the number of persons engaged in the enterprise production and operation activities in the reporting period, which are actually owned by the enterprise.

## Standards for dividing large, medium, small and micro industries in industrial enterprises:

At the end of the period, the number of employees is 1,000 or more, and the industrial enterprises with operating income of 40 million yuan or more are large enterprises; the number of employees at the end of the period is 300 or more and less than 1,000, and the operating income is 20 million or more and less than 40 million Of industrial enterprises are medium-sized enterprises; industrial enterprises with a number of employees of 20 or more and less than 300 at the end of the period, and operating income of 3 million yuan or more to less than 20 million are small enterprises; Industrial enterprises with an income of less than 3 million yuan are micro-enterprises.

# 第十三章・建筑业

CONSTRUCTION

# 简要说明

## BRIEF INTRODUCTION

本章资料包括全市按登记注册地统计的资质内建筑业基本情况、建筑企业房屋施工及竣工面积主要指标、各类建筑施工企业主要经济指标等，由市统计局固定资产投资处提供。

The data in this chapter include the general information of all the construction enterprises with the place of registration in Chongqing, the main indicators on the floor space of buildings under construction and completed of construction enterprises, as well as the main economic indicators on various construction enterprises. The data in this chapter are provided by Division of Statistics of Investment in Fixed Assets, Chongqing Municipal Bureau of Statistics.

# 表 13.1 建筑业基本情况（1985 – 2022 年）
## BASIC STATISTICS ON CONSTRUCTION INDUSTRY (1985-2022)

| 年 份 Year | 企业数（个）Number of Enterprises (unit) | 年末从业人数（万人）Number of Employed Persons at Year-end (10 000 persons) | 总产值（万元）Gross Output Value (10 000 yuan) | 房屋建筑施工面积（万平方米）Floor Space of Buildings under Construction (10 000 sq.m) | 房屋建筑竣工面积（万平方米）Floor Space of Buildings Completed (10 000 sq.m) |
|---|---|---|---|---|---|
| 1985 | 298 | 14.12 | 96201 | 684.85 | 340.18 |
| 1986 | 291 | 17.12 | 112719 | 674.54 | 345.37 |
| 1987 | 303 | 18.08 | 138515 | 740.55 | 350.79 |
| 1988 | 399 | 20.71 | 183070 | 866.76 | 372.69 |
| 1989 | 400 | 20.60 | 196510 | 853.54 | 391.35 |
| 1990 | 445 | 20.89 | 220685 | 905.58 | 450.19 |
| 1991 | 465 | 21.50 | 262155 | 915.31 | 458.23 |
| 1992 | 482 | 23.58 | 340256 | 1015.59 | 490.88 |
| 1993 | 607 | 22.47 | 426228 | 1238.22 | 537.78 |
| 1994 | 561 | 26.61 | 656959 | 1456.78 | 577.22 |
| 1995 | 556 | 28.24 | 810548 | 1678.02 | 656.38 |
| 1996 | 1473 | 64.43 | 2052964 | 4065.24 | 2276.97 |
| 1997 | 1501 | 68.98 | 2440552 | 4451.06 | 2562.73 |
| 1998 | 1655 | 80.46 | 2896198 | 5275.68 | 2837.02 |
| 1999 | 1735 | 75.49 | 3175927 | 5481.86 | 2974.82 |
| 2000 | 1785 | 73.37 | 3486579 | 6088.49 | 3083.72 |
| 2001 | 1721 | 83.99 | 4368064 | 7962.27 | 4341.38 |
| 2002 | 1778 | 82.05 | 5015839 | 8707.39 | 4711.06 |
| 2003 | 1760 | 81.80 | 5862095 | 9754.10 | 4939.62 |
| 2004 | 2442 | 86.91 | 6902774 | 10184.46 | 5167.65 |
| 2005 | 2310 | 83.10 | 7835658 | 10722.57 | 5155.18 |
| 2006 | 2455 | 86.72 | 8950918 | 11522.42 | 5309.27 |
| 2007 | 2486 | 96.97 | 11287118 | 13866.76 | 5750.65 |
| 2008 | 2483 | 105.42 | 14963195 | 15618.93 | 6485.30 |
| 2009 | 2465 | 118.88 | 19152495 | 16475.84 | 7473.16 |
| 2010 | 2467 | 139.33 | 25343196 | 19489.39 | 8292.00 |
| 2011 | 2530 | 134.84 | 33288252 | 21976.19 | 8989.56 |
| 2012 | 2575 | 138.59 | 39756696 | 26269.73 | 11601.82 |
| 2013 | 2578 | 170.45 | 47312167 | 29884.62 | 12240.32 |
| 2014 | 2591 | 167.45 | 55522069 | 32886.88 | 12815.64 |
| 2015 | 2628 | 177.17 | 62569430 | 32801.61 | 13542.58 |
| 2016 | 2736 | 181.41 | 70358133 | 32077.14 | 13751.59 |
| 2017 | 2908 | 187.28 | 76080004 | 33210.82 | 13448.18 |
| 2018 | 2968 | 196.70 | 78194241 | 35140.02 | 13780.06 |
| 2019 | 3159 | 216.18 | 82229592 | 36557.76 | 13618.26 |
| 2020 | 3465 | 216.62 | 89749662 | 38122.60 | 14050.13 |
| 2021 | 3726 | 205.54 | 99430050 | 37895.19 | 13931.83 |
| 2022 | 3914 | 195.56 | 97469574 | 34968.29 | 11769.81 |

注：1）1993 年实行一套表制度，附营建筑企业有所增加；1996 年以前口径范围包括全民、城镇集体建筑安装企业，1996-2001 年为资质等级四级以上的建筑企业（下表同）。
2）2002 年起建筑业执行新建筑资质，2002 年房屋建筑施工、竣工面积和 2003 年起所有数据不含劳务分包企业（下表同）。"

Note: a) As the system of one suit of tables was implemented in 1993, the affiliated construction enterprises increased. The statistics scope before 1996 included the whole people-owned, collective-owned construction and installation enterprises; while the statistics scope from 1996 to 2001 included the construction and installation enterprises of qualification Grade-4 and above (the same below).
b) The new grade system was carried out in construction in 2002. The data of floor space under construction and completed in 2002, and all the data since 2003 exclude the data of labor subcontractors (the same below).

# 表 13.2 建筑业企业房屋施工及竣工面积(2021 – 2022 年)
## FLOOR SPACE OF BUILDINGS UNDER CONSTRUCTION AND COMPLETED BY CONSTRUCTION ENTERPRISES (2021-2022)

| 指 标 | Item | 2021 | 2022 |
|---|---|---|---|
| **房屋建筑施工面积(万平方米)** | **Floor Space of Buildings under Construction (10 000 sq.m)** | **37895.19** | **34968.29** |
| #本年新开工面积 | Floor Space of Buildings Newly Started This Year | 13250.75 | 11113.42 |
| **房屋建筑竣工面积(万平方米)** | **Floor Space of Buildings Completed (10 000 sq.m)** | **13931.83** | **11769.81** |
| 住宅房屋 | Residential Buildings | 10223.99 | 8192.06 |
| 商业及服务用房屋 | Buildings for Business and Services | 876.24 | 875.89 |
| 办公用房 | Office Buildings | 442.24 | 368.07 |
| 科研、教育、医疗用房屋 | Buildings for Scientific Research, Education, Medical Cares | 318.97 | 372.27 |
| 文化、体育和娱乐用房 | Buildings for Culture, Sports and Entertainment | 45.57 | 58.59 |
| 厂房及建筑物 | Works and Buildings | 1417.36 | 1313.21 |
| 仓库 | Warehouses | 48.83 | 41.00 |
| 其他未列明的房屋建筑物 | Other Buildings | 558.64 | 548.71 |

# 表 13.3 建筑施工企业主要经济指标（2021－2022 年）
MAIN ECONOMIC INDICATORS ON CONSTRUCTION ENTERPRISES (2021-2022)

| 指 标 | Type | 2021 | 2022 |
|---|---|---|---|
| **企业数（个）** | **Number of Enterprises (unit)** | **3726** | **3914** |
| **年末从业人数（万人）** | **Number of Employed Persons at Year-end (10 000 persons)** | **205.54** | **195.56** |
| **总产值（万元）** | **Gross Output Value (10 000 yuan)** | **99430050** | **97469574** |
| **按登记注册类型分** | **By Status of Registration** | | |
| 内资企业 | Domestic-funded Enterprises | 99310575 | 97248155 |
| #国 有 | State-owned Enterprises | 7313768 | 10985786 |
| 其他有限责任 | Other Limited Liability Enterprises | 24925483 | 24328027 |
| 私 营 | Private Enterprises | 64716454 | 59644909 |
| **按构成分** | **By Constitution** | | |
| #建筑工程 | Construction | 90046417 | 87726583 |
| 安装工程 | Installation | 6476725 | 6539514 |
| **按行业分** | **By Sector** | | |
| #房屋和土木工程建筑业 | Construction of Buildings and Civil Engineering | 91419664 | 89753570 |
| #房屋工程建筑业 | Floor Space of Buildings under Construction (10 000 sq.m) | 68958166 | 64862828 |
| 建筑安装业 | Construction Installation | 3357655 | 3216321 |
| 建筑装饰业 | Construction Decoration | 2656495 | 2578253 |
| **按资质等级分** | **By Grade** | | |
| 施工总承包 | General Contractors of Construction | 91456156 | 89703681 |
| #一 级 | First Grade | 40892336 | 38322095 |
| 二 级 | Second Grade | 20907926 | 19312466 |
| 专业承包 | Specialized Contractors of Construction | 7973895 | 7765893 |
| #一 级 | First Grade | 2708289 | 2661982 |
| 二 级 | Second Grade | 1706874 | 1721511 |
| **竣工产值（万元）** | **Output Value of Completed Construction (10 000 yuan)** | **41216193** | **42433881** |
| **按登记注册类型分** | **By Status of Registration** | | |
| 内资企业 | Domestic-funded Enterprises | 41215693 | 42433672 |
| #国 有 | State-owned Enterprises | 1988533 | 5029501 |
| 其他有限责任 | Other Limited Liability Enterprises | 10446437 | 9580275 |
| 私 营 | Private Enterprises | 27508007 | 26409400 |
| **按行业分** | **By Sector** | | |
| #房屋和土木工程建筑业 | Construction of Buildings and Civil Engineering | 38295017 | 38387788 |
| #房屋工程建筑业 | Buildings | 31536069 | 29423778 |
| 建筑安装业 | Construction Installation | 1287438 | 1221934 |
| 建筑装饰业 | Construction Decoration | 985194 | 1044711 |
| **按资质等级分** | **By Grade** | | |
| 施工总承包 | General Contractors of Construction | 38421636 | 39812244 |
| #一 级 | First Grade | 15420092 | 15227924 |
| 二 级 | Second Grade | 9193880 | 8366119 |
| 专业承包 | Specialized Contractors of Construction | 2794557 | 2621637 |
| #一 级 | First Grade | 802674 | 849626 |
| 二 级 | Second Grade | 800290 | 743476 |
| **房屋建筑施工面积（万平方米）** | **Floor Space of Buildings under Construction (10 000 sq.m)** | **37895.19** | **34968.29** |
| **房屋建筑竣工面积（万平方米）** | **Floor Space of Buildings Completed (10 000 sq.m)** | **13931.83** | **11769.81** |
| **年末自有机械设备台数（万台）** | **Number of Machinery and Equipment Self-owned at Year-end (10 000 sets)** | **10.04** | **8.71** |
| **年末自有机械设备总功率（万千瓦）** | **Total Power of Machinery and Equipment Self-owned at Year-end (10 000 kw)** | **313.10** | **342.11** |

# 表 13.4 国有建筑施工企业主要经济指标（2021－2022 年）
## MAIN ECONOMIC INDICATORS ON STATE-OWNED CONSTRUCTION ENTERPRISES (2021-2022)

| 指　标 | Type | 2021 | 2022 |
|---|---|---|---|
| **企业数（个）** | **Number of Enterprises (unit)** | **99** | **111** |
| **年末从业人数（万人）** | **Number of Employed Persons at Year-end (10 000 persons)** | **8.22** | **9.15** |
| **总产值（万元）** | **Gross Output Value (10 000 yuan)** | **7313768** | **10985786** |
| **按构成分** | **By Constitution** | | |
| #建筑工程 | Construction | 6591441 | 10072327 |
| 安装工程 | Installation | 528624 | 578511 |
| **按行业分** | **By Sector** | | |
| #房屋和土木工程建筑业 | Construction of Buildings and Civil Engineering | 7096725 | 10724816 |
| #房屋工程建筑业 | Buildings | 1674024 | 2648841 |
| 建筑安装业 | Construction Installation | 112139 | 100495 |
| 建筑装饰业 | Construction Decoration | 75934 | 102582 |
| **按资质等级分** | **By Grade** | | |
| 施工总承包 | General Contractors of Construction | 6874217 | 10473207 |
| #一　级 | First Grade | 5534315 | 7830471 |
| 二　级 | Second Grade | 331441 | 671832 |
| 专业承包 | Specialized Contractors of Construction | 439551 | 512580 |
| #一　级 | First Grade | 297787 | 314294 |
| 二　级 | Second Grade | 69078 | 124026 |
| **竣工产值（万元）** | **Output Value of Completed Construction (10 000 yuan)** | **1988533** | **5029501** |
| **按行业分** | **By Sector** | | |
| #房屋和土木工程建筑业 | Construction of Buildings and Civil Engineering | 1979100 | 4961826 |
| #房屋工程建筑业 | Buildings | 824808 | 1175763 |
| 建筑安装业 | Construction Installation | 9433 | 32554 |
| 建筑装饰业 | Construction Decoration | | 35121 |
| **按资质等级分** | **By Grade** | | |
| 施工总承包 | General Contractors of Construction | 1901179 | 4877230 |
| #一　级 | First Grade | 1446912 | 2717430 |
| 二　级 | Second Grade | 84772 | 138234 |
| 专业承包 | Specialized Contractors of Construction | 87355 | 152271 |
| #一　级 | First Grade | 43150 | 70560 |
| 二　级 | Second Grade | 6951 | 42078 |
| **房屋建筑施工面积（万平方米）** | **Floor Space of Buildings under Construction (10 000 sq.m)** | **1374.67** | **2736.76** |
| **房屋建筑竣工面积（万平方米）** | **Floor Space of Buildings Completed (10 000 sq.m)** | **525.56** | **655.59** |
| **年末自有机械设备台数（万台）** | **Number of Machinery and Equipment Self-owned at Year-end (10 000 sets)** | **1.18** | **1.24** |
| **年末自有机械设备总功率（万千瓦）** | **Total Power of Machinery and Equipment Self-owned at Year-end (10 000 kw)** | **75.57** | **107.15** |

# 表 13.5 其他有限责任制建筑施工企业主要经济指标（2021－2022 年）
MAIN ECONOMIC INDICATORS ON OTHER CONSTRUCTION ENTERPRISES OF LIMITED LIABILITY (2021-2022)

| 指　标 | Type | 2021 | 2022 |
|---|---|---|---|
| **企业数（个）** | **Number of Enterprises (unit)** | **419** | **374** |
| **年末从业人数（万人）** | **Number of Employed Persons at Year-end (10 000 persons)** | **37.96** | **33.39** |
| **总产值（万元）** | **Gross Output Value (10 000 yuan)** | **24925483** | **24328027** |
| **按构成分** | **By Constitution** | | |
| #建筑工程 | Construction | 22873029 | 22098058 |
| 安装工程 | Installation | 1580429 | 1631691 |
| **按行业分** | **By Sector** | | |
| #房屋和土木工程建筑业 | Construction of Buildings and Civil Engineering | 23747572 | 23127494 |
| #房屋工程建筑业 | Buildings | 13987105 | 12180414 |
| 建筑安装业 | Construction Installation | 841193 | 932346 |
| 建筑装饰业 | Construction Decoration | 251683 | 216088 |
| **按资质等级分** | **By Grade** | | |
| 施工总承包 | General Contractors of Construction | 23922133 | 23447598 |
| #一　级 | First Grade | 14002658 | 11996753 |
| 二　级 | Second Grade | 2956777 | 2767857 |
| 专业承包 | Specialized Contractors of Construction | 1003350 | 880430 |
| #一　级 | First Grade | 428030 | 399608 |
| 二　级 | Second Grade | 133132 | 141251 |
| **竣工产值（万元）** | **Output Value of Completed Construction (10 000 yuan)** | **10446437** | **9580275** |
| **按行业分** | **By Sector** | | |
| #房屋和土木工程建筑业 | Construction of Buildings and Civil Engineering | 10105299 | 9294767 |
| #房屋工程建筑业 | Buildings | 6709722 | 5844048 |
| 建筑安装业 | Construction Installation | 235912 | 207137 |
| 建筑装饰业 | Construction Decoration | 80081 | 66397 |
| **按资质等级分** | **By Grade** | | |
| 施工总承包 | General Contractors of Construction | 10117235 | 9284825 |
| #一　级 | First Grade | 6703993 | 5327983 |
| 二　级 | Second Grade | 1300799 | 1011760 |
| 专业承包 | Specialized Contractors of Construction | 329202 | 295450 |
| #一　级 | First Grade | 90961 | 101665 |
| 二　级 | Second Grade | 56641 | 44540 |
| **房屋建筑施工面积（万平方米）** | **Floor Space of Buildings under Construction (10 000 sq.m)** | **12548.43** | **10302.23** |
| **房屋建筑竣工面积（万平方米）** | **Floor Space of Buildings Completed (10 000 sq.m)** | **3033.91** | **2585.91** |
| **年末自有机械设备台数（万台）** | **Number of Machinery and Equipment Self-owned at Year-end (10 000 sets)** | **2.67** | **2.54** |
| **年末自有机械设备总功率（万千瓦）** | **Total Power of Machinery and Equipment Self-owned at Year-end (10 000 kw)** | **79.78** | **124.01** |

# 表 13.6 私营建筑施工企业主要经济指标（2021 – 2022 年）
## MAIN ECONOMIC INDICATORS ON PRIVATE CONSTRUCTION ENTERPRISES (2021-2022)

| 指　标 | Type | 2021 | 2022 |
|---|---|---|---|
| **企业数（个）** | **Number of Enterprises (unit)** | **3141** | **3365** |
| **年末从业人数（万人）** | **Number of Employed Persons at Year-end (10 000 persons)** | **154.16** | **148.08** |
| **总产值（万元）** | **Gross Output Value (10 000 yuan)** | **64716454** | **59644909** |
| **按构成分** | **By Constitution** | | |
| #建筑工程 | Construction | 58288966 | 53448410 |
| 安装工程 | Installation | 4254265 | 4150913 |
| **按行业分** | **By Sector** | | |
| #房屋和土木工程建筑业 | Construction of Buildings and Civil Engineering | 58160746 | 53435233 |
| #房屋工程建筑业 | Buildings | 51118650 | 47937115 |
| 建筑安装业 | Construction Installation | 2368616 | 2143334 |
| 建筑装饰业 | Construction Decoration | 2321339 | 2254905 |
| **按资质等级分** | **By Grade** | | |
| 施工总承包 | General Contractors of Construction | 58220264 | 53303153 |
| #一　级 | First Grade | 20532481 | 17160781 |
| 二　级 | Second Grade | 16977075 | 15538748 |
| 专业承包 | Specialized Contractors of Construction | 6496190 | 6341756 |
| #一　级 | First Grade | 1981012 | 1947074 |
| 二　级 | Second Grade | 1498584 | 1426503 |
| **竣工产值（万元）** | **Output Value of Completed Construction (10 000 yuan)** | **27508007** | **26409400** |
| **按行业分** | **By Sector** | | |
| #房屋和土木工程建筑业 | Construction of Buildings and Civil Engineering | 24966029 | 22748538 |
| #房屋工程建筑业 | Buildings | 22854689 | 21136903 |
| 建筑安装业 | Construction Installation | 1015731 | 951382 |
| 建筑装饰业 | Construction Decoration | 902848 | 942006 |
| **按资质等级分** | **By Grade** | | |
| 施工总承包 | General Contractors of Construction | 25158633 | 24262729 |
| #一　级 | First Grade | 6967772 | 6808222 |
| 二　级 | Second Grade | 7524252 | 7048854 |
| 专业承包 | Specialized Contractors of Construction | 2349374 | 2146671 |
| #一　级 | First Grade | 668063 | 677191 |
| 二　级 | Second Grade | 734933 | 629822 |
| **房屋建筑施工面积（万平方米）** | **Floor Space of Buildings under Construction (10 000 sq.m)** | **22853.35** | **20898.02** |
| **房屋建筑竣工面积（万平方米）** | **Floor Space of Buildings Completed (10 000 sq.m)** | **9991.79** | **8085.13** |
| **年末自有机械设备台数（万台）** | **Number of Machinery and Equipment Self-owned at Year-end (10 000 sets)** | **5.96** | **4.71** |
| **年末自有机械设备总功率（万千瓦）** | **Total Power of Machinery and Equipment Self-owned at Year-end (10 000 kw)** | **150.05** | **106.22** |

# 表 13.7 施工总承包建筑施工企业主要经济指标（2021－2022 年）
## MAIN ECONOMIC INDICATORS ON GENERAL CONTRACTORS OF CONSTRUCTION (2021-2022)

| 指　标 | Type | 2021 | 2022 |
|---|---|---|---|
| **企业数（个）** | **Number of Enterprises (unit)** | **2607** | **2770** |
| **年末从业人数（万人）** | **Number of Employed Persons at Year-end (10 000 persons)** | **177.45** | **167.71** |
| **总产值（万元）** | **Gross Output Value (10 000 yuan)** | **91456156** | **89703681** |
| **按登记注册类型分** | **By Status of Registration** | | |
| 内资企业 | Domestic-funded Enterprises | 91337180 | 89482471 |
| #国　有 | State-owned Enterprises | 6874217 | 10473207 |
| 其他有限责任 | Other Limited Liability Enterprises | 23922133 | 23447598 |
| 私　营 | Private Enterprises | 58220264 | 53303153 |
| **按构成分** | **By Constitution** | | |
| #建筑工程 | Construction | 84819262 | 82405136 |
| 安装工程 | Installation | 4481716 | 4725218 |
| **按行业分** | **By Sector** | | |
| #房屋和土木工程建筑业 | Construction of Buildings and Civil Engineering | 88743886 | 87022383 |
| #房屋工程建筑业 | Buildings | 67192998 | 63059308 |
| 建筑安装业 | Construction Installation | 1626484 | 1681796 |
| 建筑装饰业 | Construction Decoration | 391131 | 459747 |
| **按资质等级分** | **By Grade** | | |
| #一　级 | First Grade | 40892336 | 38322095 |
| 二　级 | Second Grade | 20907926 | 19312466 |
| **竣工产值（万元）** | **Output Value of Completed Construction (10 000 yuan)** | **38421636** | **39812244** |
| **按登记注册类型分** | **By Status of Registration** | | |
| 内资企业 | Domestic-funded Enterprises | 38421636 | 39812244 |
| #国　有 | State-owned Enterprises | 1901179 | 4877230 |
| 其他有限责任 | Other Limited Liability Enterprises | 10117235 | 9284825 |
| 私　营 | Private Enterprises | 25158633 | 24262729 |
| **按行业分** | **By Sector** | | |
| #房屋和土木工程建筑业 | Construction of Buildings and Civil Engineering | 37354695 | 37499398 |
| #房屋工程建筑业 | Buildings | 30926785 | 28805116 |
| 建筑安装业 | Construction Installation | 584404 | 641439 |
| 建筑装饰业 | Construction Decoration | 125080 | 131215 |
| **按资质等级分** | **By Grade** | | |
| #一　级 | First Grade | 15420092 | 15227924 |
| 二　级 | Second Grade | 9193880 | 8366119 |
| **房屋建筑施工面积（万平方米）** | **Floor Space of Buildings under Construction (10 000 sq.m)** | **36378.17** | **33223.60** |
| **房屋建筑竣工面积（万平方米）** | **Floor Space of Buildings Completed (10 000 sq.m)** | **12729.19** | **10573.46** |
| **年末自有机械设备台数（万台）** | **Number of Machinery and Equipment Self-owned at Year-end (10 000 sets)** | **9.24** | **7.99** |
| **年末自有机械设备总功率（万千瓦）** | **Total Power of Machinery and Equipment Self-owned at Year-end (10 000 kw)** | **296.82** | **327.49** |

# 表 13.8 专业承包建筑施工企业主要经济指标（2021 － 2022 年）
## MAIN ECONOMIC INDICATORS ON SPECIALIZED CONTRACTORS OF CONSTRUCTION (2021-2022)

| 指　标 | Type | 2021 | 2022 |
|---|---|---|---|
| **企业数（个）** | **Number of Enterprises (unit)** | **1119** | **1144** |
| **年末从业人数（万人）** | **Number of Employed Persons at Year-end (10 000 persons)** | **28.09** | **27.85** |
| **总产值（万元）** | **Gross Output Value (10 000 yuan)** | **7973895** | **7765893** |
| **按登记注册类型分** | **By Status of Registration** | | |
| 内资企业 | Domestic-funded Enterprises | 7973395 | 7765684 |
| #国　有 | State-owned Enterprises | 439551 | 512580 |
| 其他有限责任 | Other Limited Liability Enterprises | 1003350 | 880430 |
| 私　营 | Private Enterprises | 6496190 | 6341756 |
| **按构成分** | **By Constitution** | | |
| #建筑工程 | Construction | 5227156 | 5321447 |
| 安装工程 | Installation | 1995009 | 1814295 |
| **按行业分** | **By Sector** | | |
| #房屋和土木工程建筑业 | Construction of Buildings and Civil Engineering | 2675778 | 2731187 |
| #房屋工程建筑业 | Buildings | 1765168 | 1803521 |
| 建筑安装业 | Construction Installation | 1731171 | 1534525 |
| 建筑装饰业 | Construction Decoration | 2265365 | 2118506 |
| **按资质等级分** | **By Grade** | | |
| #一　级 | First Grade | 2708289 | 2661982 |
| 二　级 | Second Grade | 1706874 | 1721511 |
| **竣工产值（万元）** | **Output Value of Completed Construction (10 000 yuan)** | **2794557** | **2621637** |
| **按登记注册类型分** | **By Status of Registration** | | |
| 内资企业 | Domestic-funded Enterprises | 2794057 | 2621428 |
| #国　有 | State-owned Enterprises | 87355 | 152271 |
| 其他有限责任 | Other Limited Liability Enterprises | 329202 | 295450 |
| 私　营 | Private Enterprises | 2349374 | 2146671 |
| **按行业分** | **By Sector** | | |
| #房屋和土木工程建筑业 | Construction of Buildings and Civil Engineering | 940321 | 888390 |
| #房屋工程建筑业 | Buildings | 609284 | 618662 |
| 建筑安装业 | Construction Installation | 703034 | 580495 |
| 建筑装饰业 | Construction Decoration | 860114 | 913495 |
| **按资质等级分** | **By Grade** | | |
| #一　级 | First Grade | 802674 | 849626 |
| 二　级 | Second Grade | 800290 | 743476 |
| **房屋建筑施工面积（万平方米）** | **Floor Space of Buildings under Construction (10 000 sq.m)** | **1517.02** | **1744.69** |
| **房屋建筑竣工面积（万平方米）** | **Floor Space of Buildings Completed (10 000 sq.m)** | **1202.65** | **1196.34** |
| **年末自有机械设备台数（万台）** | **Number of Machinery and Equipment Self-owned at Year-end (10 000 sets)** | **0.80** | **0.72** |
| **年末自有机械设备总功率（万千瓦）** | **Total Power of Machinery and Equipment Self-owned at Year-end (10 000 kw)** | **16.27** | **14.62** |

# 表 13.9 房屋和土木工程建筑施工企业主要经济指标（2021－2022 年）
MAIN ECONOMIC INDICATORS ON CONSTRUCTION ENTERPRISES OF BUILDINGS AND CIVIL ENGINEERING (2021-2022)

| 指　标 | Type | 2021 | 2022 |
|---|---|---|---|
| **企业数（个）** | **Number of Enterprises (unit)** | **2708** | **2878** |
| **年末从业人数（万人）** | **Number of Employed Persons at Year-end (10 000 persons)** | **184.65** | **174.95** |
| **总产值（万元）** | **Gross Output Value (10 000 yuan)** | **91419664** | **89753570** |
| **按登记注册类型分** | **By Status of Registration** | | |
| 内资企业 | Domestic-funded Enterprises | 91308244 | 89540555 |
| #国　有 | State-owned Enterprises | 7096725 | 10724816 |
| 其他有限责任 | Other Limited Liability Enterprises | 23747572 | 23127494 |
| 私　营 | Private Enterprises | 58160746 | 53435233 |
| **按构成分** | **By Constitution** | | |
| #建筑工程 | Construction | 85114030 | 82907837 |
| 安装工程 | Installation | 3996508 | 4191442 |
| **按资质等级分** | **By Grade** | | |
| 施工总承包 | General Contractors of Construction | 88743886 | 87022383 |
| #一　级 | First Grade | 40042196 | 37510039 |
| 二　级 | Second Grade | 20194385 | 18690462 |
| 专业承包 | Specialized Contractors of Construction | 2675778 | 2731187 |
| #一　级 | First Grade | 555854 | 526275 |
| 二　级 | Second Grade | 348160 | 402561 |
| **竣工产值（万元）** | **Output Value of Completed Construction (10 000 yuan)** | **38295017** | **38387788** |
| **按登记注册类型分** | **By Status of Registration** | | |
| 内资企业 | Domestic-funded Enterprises | 38295017 | 38387788 |
| #国　有 | State-owned Enterprises | 1979100 | 4961826 |
| 其他有限责任 | Other Limited Liability Enterprises | 10105299 | 9294767 |
| 私　营 | Private Enterprises | 24966029 | 22748538 |
| **按资质等级分** | **By Grade** | | |
| 施工总承包 | General Contractors of Construction | 37354695 | 37499398 |
| #一　级 | First Grade | 15024248 | 13722873 |
| 二　级 | Second Grade | 9051293 | 8202012 |
| 专业承包 | Specialized Contractors of Construction | 940321 | 888390 |
| #一　级 | First Grade | 139369 | 158885 |
| 二　级 | Second Grade | 189055 | 109088 |
| **房屋建筑施工面积（万平方米）** | **Floor Space of Buildings under Construction (10 000 sq.m)** | **36284.86** | **33160.03** |
| **房屋建筑竣工面积（万平方米）** | **Floor Space of Buildings Completed (10 000 sq.m)** | **13309.14** | **11132.21** |
| **年末自有机械设备台数（万台）** | **Number of Machinery and Equipment Self-owned at Year-end (10 000 sets)** | **9.16** | **7.94** |
| **年末自有机械设备总功率（万千瓦）** | **Total Power of Machinery and Equipment Self-owned at Year-end (10 000 kw)** | **300.75** | **329.37** |

# 表 13.10 建筑安装企业主要经济指标（2021－2022 年）
## MAIN ECONOMIC INDICATORS ON CONSTRUCTION ENTERPRISES OF INSTALLATION (2021-2022)

| 指　标 | Type | 2021 | 2022 |
|---|---|---|---|
| **企业数（个）** | **Number of Enterprises (unit)** | **379** | **388** |
| **年末从业人数（万人）** | **Number of Employed Persons at Year-end (10 000 persons)** | **7.86** | **7.84** |
| **总产值（万元）** | **Gross Output Value (10 000 yuan)** | **3357655** | **3216321** |
| **按登记注册类型分** | **By Status of Registration** | | |
| 内资企业 | Domestic-funded Enterprises | 3350100 | 3208125 |
| #国　有 | State-owned Enterprises | 112139 | 100495 |
| 其他有限责任 | Other Limited Liability Enterprises | 841193 | 932346 |
| 私　营 | Private Enterprises | 2368616 | 2143334 |
| **按构成分** | **By Constitution** | | |
| #建筑工程 | Construction | 1343215 | 1405554 |
| 安装工程 | Installation | 1909387 | 1724314 |
| **按资质等级分** | **By Grade** | | |
| 施工总承包 | General Contractors of Construction | 1626484 | 1681796 |
| #一　级 | First Grade | 335261 | 405305 |
| 二　级 | Second Grade | 439540 | 384583 |
| 专业承包 | Specialized Contractors of Construction | 1731171 | 1534525 |
| #一　级 | First Grade | 657181 | 647947 |
| 二　级 | Second Grade | 488574 | 464263 |
| **竣工产值（万元）** | **Output Value of Completed Construction (10 000 yuan)** | **1287438** | **1221934** |
| **按登记注册类型分** | **By Status of Registration** | | |
| 内资企业 | Domestic-funded Enterprises | 1287438 | 1221934 |
| #国　有 | State-owned Enterprises | 9433 | 32554 |
| 其他有限责任 | Other Limited Liability Enterprises | 235912 | 207137 |
| 私　营 | Private Enterprises | 1015731 | 951382 |
| **按资质等级分** | **By Grade** | | |
| 施工总承包 | General Contractors of Construction | 584404 | 641439 |
| #一　级 | First Grade | 64942 | 6101 |
| 二　级 | Second Grade | 91029 | 113315 |
| 专业承包 | Specialized Contractors of Construction | 703034 | 580495 |
| #一　级 | First Grade | 237873 | 227479 |
| 二　级 | Second Grade | 211301 | 230154 |
| **房屋建筑施工面积（万平方米）** | **Floor Space of Buildings under Construction (10 000 sq.m)** | **523.27** | **568.52** |
| **房屋建筑竣工面积（万平方米）** | **Floor Space of Buildings Completed (10 000 sq.m)** | **191.81** | **222.72** |
| **年末自有机械设备台数（万台）** | **Number of Machinery and Equipment Self-owned at Year-end (10 000 sets)** | **0.63** | **0.58** |
| **年末自有机械设备总功率（万千瓦）** | **Total Power of Machinery and Equipment Self-owned at Year-end (10 000 kw)** | **6.60** | **7.43** |

## 表 13.11 建筑装饰企业主要经济指标（2021－2022 年）
## MAIN ECONOMIC INDICATORS ON CONSTRUCTION ENTERPRISES OF DECORATION (2021-2022)

| 指　标 | Type | 2021 | 2022 |
|---|---|---|---|
| **企业数（个）** | **Number of Enterprises (unit)** | **403** | **429** |
| **年末从业人数（万人）** | **Number of Employed Persons at Year-end (10 000 persons)** | **4.93** | **5.15** |
| **总产值（万元）** | **Gross Output Value (10 000 yuan)** | **2656495** | **2578253** |
| **按登记注册类型分** | **By Status of Registration** | | |
| 内资企业 | Domestic-funded Enterprises | 2655995 | 2578044 |
| #国　有 | State-owned Enterprises | 75934 | 102582 |
| 其他有限责任 | Other Limited Liability Enterprises | 251683 | 216088 |
| 私　营 | Private Enterprises | 2321339 | 2254905 |
| **按构成分** | **By Constitution** | | |
| #建筑工程 | Construction | 1853851 | 1788791 |
| 安装工程 | Installation | 468283 | 475305 |
| **按资质等级分** | **By Grade** | | |
| 施工总承包 | General Contractors of Construction | 391131 | 459747 |
| #一　级 | First Grade | 21377 | 55466 |
| 二　级 | Second Grade | 205489 | 196427 |
| 专业承包 | Specialized Contractors of Construction | 2265365 | 2118506 |
| #一　级 | First Grade | 1253262 | 1221058 |
| 二　级 | Second Grade | 711274 | 730713 |
| **竣工产值（万元）** | **Output Value of Completed Construction (10 000 yuan)** | **985194** | **1044711** |
| **按登记注册类型分** | **By Status of Registration** | | |
| 内资企业 | Domestic-funded Enterprises | 984694 | 1044502 |
| #国　有 | State-owned Enterprises | | 35121 |
| 其他有限责任 | Other Limited Liability Enterprises | 80081 | 66397 |
| 私　营 | Private Enterprises | 902848 | 942006 |
| **按资质等级分** | **By Grade** | | |
| 施工总承包 | General Contractors of Construction | 125080 | 131215 |
| #一　级 | First Grade | 6208 | 10090 |
| 二　级 | Second Grade | 46440 | 50791 |
| 专业承包 | Specialized Contractors of Construction | 860114 | 913495 |
| #一　级 | First Grade | 392564 | 441272 |
| 二　级 | Second Grade | 374474 | 392168 |
| **房屋建筑施工面积（万平方米）** | **Floor Space of Buildings under Construction (10 000 sq.m)** | **254.63** | **361.51** |
| **房屋建筑竣工面积（万平方米）** | **Floor Space of Buildings Completed (10 000 sq.m)** | **58.56** | **119.53** |
| **年末自有机械设备台数（万台）** | **Number of Machinery and Equipment Self-owned at Year-end (10 000 sets)** | **0.16** | **0.12** |
| **年末自有机械设备总功率（万千瓦）** | **Total Power of Machinery and Equipment Self-owned at Year-end (10 000 kw)** | **2.72** | **2.16** |

# 表 13.12 建筑施工企业按资质等级分主要财务和经济效益指标（2022 年）
## MAIN INDICATORS ON FINANCE AND ECONOMIC BENEFIT OF CONSTRUCTION ENTERPRISES BY GRADE (2022)

单位：万元 (10 000 yuan)

| 指　标 | Item | 合　计 Total | 施工总承包 General Contractors | 专业承包 Specialized Contractors |
|---|---|---|---|---|
| 企业数（个） | Number of Enterprises (unit) | 3914 | 2770 | 1144 |
| 年末从业人数（万人） | Number of Employed Persons at Year-end (10 000 persons) | 195.56 | 167.71 | 27.85 |
| 固定资产原价 | Original Value of Fixed Assets Owned | 5537831 | 4855285 | 682547 |
| 总产值 | Gross Output Value | 97469574 | 89703681 | 7765893 |
| 实收资本 | Paid-in Capital | 10701785 | 9401688 | 1300097 |
| 资产合计 | Total Assets | 80831159 | 71889039 | 8942120 |
| #流动资产 | Current Assets | 63935808 | 56256988 | 7678820 |
| 负债合计 | Total Liabilities | 58097003 | 51705376 | 6391627 |
| 流动负债 | Current Liabilities | 51645570 | 46016439 | 5629131 |
| 非流动负债 | Non-current Liabilities | 4485076 | 3933615 | 551461 |
| 所有者权益 | Creditors' Equity | 22744869 | 20194376 | 2550493 |
| 利税总额 | Total Pre-tax Profits | 5779913 | 5365274 | 414639 |
| #利润总额 | Total Profits | 3010314 | 2837438 | 172876 |
| 营业收入 | Operating Revenue | 78183142 | 70741596 | 7441546 |
| #主营业务收入 | Revenue from Major Business | 76850549 | 69557499 | 7293051 |
| 房屋建筑施工面积（万平方米） | Floor Space of Buildings under Construction (10 000 sq.m) | 34968.29 | 33223.60 | 1744.69 |
| 房屋建筑竣工面积（万平方米） | Floor Space of Buildings Completed (10 000 sq.m) | 11769.81 | 10573.46 | 1196.34 |
| 全员劳动生产率: | Overall Labor Productivity | | | |
| 按总产值计算（元/人） | In Terms of Gross Output Value (yuan/person) | 421764 | 465244 | 202871 |
| 房屋建筑面积竣工率（%） | Rate of Floor Space of Buildings Completed (%) | 33.7 | 31.8 | 68.6 |
| 资产负债率（%） | Asset-Liability Ratio (%) | 71.9 | 71.9 | 71.5 |

# 表 13.13 建筑施工企业按行业分主要财务和经济效益指标(2022 年)
## MAIN INDICATORS ON FINANCE AND ECONOMIC BENEFIT OF CONSTRUCTION ENTERPRISES BY SECTOR (2022)

单位：万元 (10 000 yuan)

| 指 标 | Item | 合 计 Total | 房屋和土木工程建筑业 Building and Civil Engineering | 建筑安装业 Construction Installation | 建筑装饰业 Construction Decoration |
|---|---|---|---|---|---|
| 企业数(个) | Number of Enterprises (unit) | 3914 | 2878 | 388 | 429 |
| 年末从业人数(万人) | Number of Employed Persons at Year-end (10 000 persons) | 195.56 | 174.95 | ·7.84 | 5.15 |
| 固定资产原价 | Original Value of Fixed Assets Owned | 5537831 | 5016594 | 281606 | 142484 |
| 总产值 | Gross Output Value | 97469574 | 89753570 | 3216321 | 2578253 |
| 实收资本 | Paid-in Capital | 10701785 | 9452276 | 519295 | 437680 |
| 资产合计 | Total Assets | 80831159 | 71920753 | 3344354 | 2990667 |
| #流动资产 | Current Assets | 63935808 | 56036418 | 2938660 | 2607687 |
| 负债合计 | Total Liabilities | 58097003 | 51405703 | 2232544 | 2307844 |
| 流动负债 | Current Liabilities | 51645570 | 45393274 | 2102108 | 2175162 |
| 非流动负债 | Non-current Liabilities | 4485076 | 4335060 | 26008 | 60156 |
| 所有者权益 | Creditors' Equity | 22744869 | 20525763 | 1111811 | 682823 |
| 利税总额 | Total Pre-tax Profits | 5779913 | 5318013 | 248851 | 111561 |
| #利润总额 | Total Profits | 3010314 | 2801408 | 135385 | 46607 |
| 营业收入 | Operating Revenue | 78183142 | 70650142 | 3329025 | 2365820 |
| #主营业务收入 | Revenue from Major Business | 76850549 | 69478618 | 3267750 | 2292072 |
| 房屋建筑施工面积(万平方米) | Floor Space of Buildings under Construction (10 000 sq.m) | 34968.29 | 33160.03 | 568.52 | 361.51 |
| 房屋建筑竣工面积(万平方米) | Floor Space of Buildings Completed (10 000 sq.m) | 11769.81 | 11132.21 | 222.72 | 119.53 |
| 全员劳动生产率: | Overall Labor Productivity | | | | |
| 按总产值计算(元/人) | In Terms of Gross Output Value (yuan/person) | 421764 | 449893 | 372259 | 169845 |
| 房屋建筑面积竣工率(%) | Rate of Floor Space of Buildings Completed (%) | 33.7 | 33.6 | 39.2 | 33.1 |
| 资产负债率(%) | Asset-Liability Ratio (%) | 71.9 | 71.5 | 66.8 | 77.2 |

重/庆/统/计/年/鉴

# 主要统计指标解释

## ■ 建筑业统计单位

指从事房屋、构筑物建造和设备安装活动的法人企业。建筑业法人企业应具有建筑业资质并能够独立核算，同时其应具备以下条件：①依法成立，有自己的名称、组织机构和场所，能够承担民事责任；②独立拥有和使用资产，承担负债，有权与其他单位签订合同；③独立核算盈亏，能够编制资产负债表。

## ■ 建筑业总产值

是以货币形式表现的建筑业企业在一定时期内生产的建筑业产品和提供的服务的总和。建筑业总产值包括：

⑴建筑工程产值：指列入建筑工程预算内的各种工程价值。

⑵安装工程产值：指设备安装工程价值，不包括被安装设备本身的价值。

⑶其他产值：建筑业总产值中除建筑工程、安装工程以外的产值。包括房屋构筑物修理产值、非标准设备制造产值、总包企业向分包企业收取的管理费以及不能明确划分的施工活动所完成的产值。

a. 房屋构筑物修理产值：指房屋和构筑物修理所完成的产值，但不包括被修理房屋、构筑物本身价值和生产设备的修理产值。

b. 非标准设备制造产值：指加工制造没有定型的非标准生产设备的加工费和原材料价值（如化工厂、炼油厂用的各种罐、槽，矿井生产统一使用的各种漏斗、三角槽、阀门等）以及附属加工厂为本企业承建工程制作的非标准设备的价值。

## ■ 房屋建筑施工面积

指在报告期内施过工的全部房屋建筑面积，包括本期新开工的房屋面积、上期施工跨入本期继续施工的房屋面积、上期停缓建在本期恢复施工的房屋面积、本期竣工的房屋面积及本期施工后又停缓建的房屋面积。

## ■ 房屋建筑竣工面积

指在报告期内房屋建筑按照设计要求全部完工，达到了使用条件，经验收鉴定合格，正式移交使用单位的房屋建筑面积。

# Explanatory Notes on Main Statistical Indicators

## Statistical Unit in the Construction Industry

Refers to a corporate enterprise engaged in the construction of buildings and structures and in the installation of equipment. A corporate construction enterprise should have qualification certificates with independent accounting system, and should meet the following 3 requirements: a) being set up in line with relevant legal basis, having its full name, organization and location, and capable of taking civil liabilities; b) independently possessing and using its assets and assuming its liabilities, and entitled to sign contracts with other institutions; and c) making independent accounts of its profits and losses, and capable of compiling its own balance sheet.

## Gross Output Value of Construction

Refers to total of construction products and services, expressed in money terms, produced or rendered by construction and installation enterprises during a given period of time. It includes:

(1) Output value of construction projects: the value of projects covered by the project budgets;

(2) Output value of installation projects: the value of the installation of equipment, (excluding the value of the equipment to be installed);

(3) Other output values: the output value of construction industry apart from that of construction projects and installation projects. It includes: output value of repair of buildings and structures; output value of non-standard equipment manufacturing; overhead expenses received by contracted enterprises from the sub-contracted enterprises and the completed output value of construction activities for which there is no clear definition.

a. Output value of repair of buildings and structures: the value created through the repairs of buildings or structures. It does not include the value of buildings or structures being repaired and the value of the repair of production equipment;

b. Output value of manufactured non-standard equipment: the value of non-standard production equipment, including raw materials and manufacturing cost, made for the construction project (i.e., chemical plant; kettles or tanks used by refineries; various fillers, triangle tanks, valves used by mines). It also includes the output value of equipment manufactured by subsidiary workshops.

## Floor Space of Buildings Under Construction

Refers to floor space of buildings under construction during the reference period, including the floor space of buildings for which construction has newly started; buildings for which construction has started earlier and is continuing during the reference period; and buildings for which construction has been suspended earlier but has restarted during the reference period; buildings completed during the reference period; and buildings under construction but construction has subsequently been during the reference period.

## Floor Space of Buildings Completed

Refers to the floor space of buildings that are completed in the reference period in accordance with the requirements of the design, up to the standard for being put into use, and having been checked and accepted by departments concerned as qualified ones.

# 第十四章 · 运输和邮电

## TRANSPORT, POSTAL AND TELECOMMUNICATION SERVICES

# 简要说明

## BRIEF INTRODUCTION

本章反映全市交通运输业和邮电通信业情况，主要包括货物和旅客运输量、港口吞吐量、交通基础设施和运输营运工具、民用车辆和船舶、主要港口码头泊位和仓库、邮电业务、电信主要通信能力和邮电通信水平。本章资料由市统计局服务业统计处负责整理编辑。

交通运输有关资料来源于市交通局、市公安局、成都铁路局、民航重庆安全监督管理局和市统计局。邮电通信业资料来源于市邮政局和市通信管理局。

The data in this chapter show the conditions of transport, postal and telecommunication services, mainly covering the data of freight and passenger traffic, freight handled at ports, transport infrastructure and means, civil motor vehicles and transport vessels, berths and warehouses at major ports, business volume of postal and telecommunication services, main communication capacity of telecommunications and level of postal and telecommunication services. The data in this chapter are sorted and compiled by Division of Service Statistics, Chongqing Municipal Bureau of Statistics.

The data of transport are provided by Ministry of Transport of Chongqing, Chongqing Public Security Bureau, Chengdu Railway Bureau, CAAC Chongqing Safety Supervision and Administrative Bureau and Chongqing Municipal Bureau of Statistics. The data of postal and telecommunication services are provided by Post Bureau of Chongqing and Chongqing Communications Administration.

# 表 14.1 主要年份客货运输量及周转量
PASSENGER AND FREIGHT TRAFFIC AND PASSENGER-KILOMETERS AND FREIGHT TON-KILOMETERS IN MAJOR YEARS

| 年 份<br>Year | 客运量<br>（万人）<br>Passenger Traffic<br>(10 000 persons) | 旅客周转量<br>（万人公里）<br>Passenger-kilometers<br>(10 000 person-km) | 货运量<br>（万吨）<br>Freight Traffic<br>(10 000 tons) | 货物周转量<br>（万吨公里）<br>Freight ton-kilometers<br>(10 000 ton-km) |
|---|---|---|---|---|
| 1952 | 82 | | 134 | 31531 |
| 1957 | 121 | | 842 | 632103 |
| 1962 | 965 | 12619 | 808 | 147390 |
| 1965 | 1707 | 23268 | 2365 | 141406 |
| 1970 | 2136 | 27461 | 2536 | 111415 |
| 1975 | 3602 | 40180 | 3226 | 276337 |
| 1978 | 5294 | 293741 | 4816 | 1189803 |
| 1980 | 7846 | 417025 | 4469 | 1106294 |
| 1985 | 16923 | 975571 | 13513 | 2004938 |
| 1986 | 18308 | 1119673 | 14860 | 2184266 |
| 1987 | 21002 | 1160714 | 15618 | 2296505 |
| 1988 | 21119 | 1206942 | 22881 | 2470614 |
| 1989 | 22692 | 1185786 | 20764 | 2676052 |
| 1990 | 20332 | 1068775 | 15546 | 2452448 |
| 1991 | 26598 | 1176783 | 16186 | 2702591 |
| 1992 | 32924 | 1543492 | 17419 | 3005694 |
| 1993 | 34025 | 1724473 | 18841 | 3282548 |
| 1994 | 36340 | 1890785 | 21130 | 3077590 |
| 1995 | 39731 | 2104270 | 22796 | 3359847 |
| 1996 | 42370 | 2094740 | 24339 | 3150421 |
| 1997 | 46199 | 2242533 | 23979 | 2972254 |
| 1998 | 49020 | 2346281 | 25328 | 2684566 |
| 1999 | 52442 | 2434000 | 25190 | 2742000 |
| 2000 | 56969 | 2577859 | 26852 | 3063900 |
| 2001 | 59244 | 2662900 | 28212 | 3253200 |
| 2002 | 61918 | 2776900 | 29787 | 3376300 |
| 2003 | 58290 | 2526100 | 32565 | 3680300 |
| 2004 | 63495 | 2994200 | 36434 | 5180300 |
| 2005 | 60436 | 3018038 | 39200 | 6248968 |
| 2006 | 61228 | 3015761 | 42808 | 8213853 |
| 2007 | 77187 | 3938936 | 49973 | 10497955 |
| 2008 | 107191 | 4430156 | 63651 | 14864332 |
| 2009 | 114598 | 4814394 | 68491 | 16442995 |
| 2010 | 126804 | 5497718 | 81385 | 20103977 |
| 2011 | 141499 | 6808274 | 96782 | 25302835 |
| 2012 | 157800 | 7553916 | 86398 | 26480626 |
| 2013 | 66645 | 6520061 | 87115 | 22932580 |
| 2014 | 70056 | 7257895 | 97287 | 25888734 |
| 2015 | 64164 | 7895976 | 103739 | 27063382 |
| 2016 | 63702 | 8337861 | 107847 | 29670457 |
| 2017 | 63298 | 8697933 | 115346 | 33707601 |
| 2018 | 63634 | 9053806 | 128234 | 35936344 |
| 2019 | 63659 | 9979708 | 112766 | 36106278 |
| 2020 | 39797 | 6338680 | 121390 | 35246991 |
| 2021 | 35250 | 6445740 | 144254 | 38416621 |
| 2022 | 21149 | 4360457 | 135433 | 38718953 |

注：1) 1996 年起铁路数据按重庆现地域进行了调整。
2) 2013 年，据交通专项调查数据，对公路、水路客（货）运量和客（货）运周转量进行了调整。
Note: a) The data of railway have been adjusted according to present administrative divisions of Chongqing since 1996.
b) The data of freight traffic and freight ton-kilometers were adjusted according to the transport survey data in 2013.

# 表 14.2 主要年份港口吞吐量和公路线路里程
VOLUME OF FREIGHT HANDLED IN COASTAL PORTS AND LENGTH OF HIGHWAYS IN MAJOR YEARS

| 年 份<br>Year | 港口货物吞吐量（万吨）<br>Freight Handled in Coastal Ports (10 000 tons) | 进 港<br>In-port | 出 港<br>Out-port | 公路线路里程（公里）<br>Length of Highways (km) | 高速公路<br>Expressways |
|---|---|---|---|---|---|
| 1952 | 61.80 | 26.60 | 35.20 | 743 | |
| 1957 | 356.10 | 73.10 | 283.00 | 1021 | |
| 1962 | 173.50 | 93.40 | 80.10 | 6044 | |
| 1965 | 217.10 | 115.70 | 101.40 | 7221 | |
| 1970 | 267.00 | 161.00 | 106.00 | 7538 | |
| 1975 | 228.90 | 108.90 | 120.00 | 9753 | |
| 1978 | 369.80 | 184.10 | 185.70 | 15421 | |
| 1980 | 378.20 | 194.10 | 184.10 | 16811 | |
| 1985 | 438.30 | 195.40 | 242.90 | 19377 | |
| 1986 | 532.70 | 303.40 | 229.30 | 19666 | |
| 1987 | 553.70 | 292.28 | 261.42 | 19942 | |
| 1988 | 570.30 | 296.14 | 274.16 | 20609 | |
| 1989 | 651.93 | 330.74 | 321.19 | 20944 | |
| 1990 | 572.50 | 275.70 | 296.80 | 21162 | |
| 1991 | 566.10 | 262.77 | 303.33 | 21474 | |
| 1992 | 664.90 | 326.80 | 338.10 | 21804 | |
| 1993 | 687.70 | 299.50 | 388.20 | 21990 | |
| 1994 | 665.65 | 289.26 | 376.39 | 22148 | |
| 1995 | 853.00 | 390.00 | 463.00 | 22556 | |
| 1996 | 1076.00 | 492.00 | 584.00 | 26892 | 114 |
| 1997 | 2548.70 | 977.20 | 1571.50 | 27045 | 114 |
| 1998 | 2477.30 | 1186.60 | 1290.70 | 27210 | 134 |
| 1999 | 2599.84 | 1610.44 | 989.40 | 28086 | 134 |
| 2000 | 2448.00 | 1485.00 | 963.00 | 30354 | 232 |
| 2001 | 2839.87 | 1690.39 | 1149.48 | 30654 | 320 |
| 2002 | 3004.00 | 1718.41 | 1285.59 | 31060 | 399 |
| 2003 | 3243.76 | 1796.24 | 1447.52 | 31407 | 580 |
| 2004 | 4539.00 | 2337.09 | 2201.91 | 32344 | 714 |
| 2005 | 5251.30 | 2758.11 | 2493.19 | 98218 | 748 |
| 2006 | 5420.43 | 2747.65 | 2672.78 | 100299 | 778 |
| 2007 | 6433.54 | 3330.46 | 3103.08 | 104705 | 1049 |
| 2008 | 7892.80 | 4349.38 | 3543.42 | 108632 | 1165 |
| 2009 | 8611.62 | 4833.29 | 3778.33 | 110951 | 1577 |
| 2010 | 9668.42 | 5682.24 | 3986.18 | 116949 | 1861 |
| 2011 | 11605.67 | 7338.72 | 4266.95 | 118562 | 1861 |
| 2012 | 12502.40 | 7670.01 | 4832.39 | 120728 | 1909 |
| 2013 | 13676.00 | 8618.55 | 5057.34 | 122846 | 2312 |
| 2014 | 14664.78 | 8946.76 | 5718.03 | 127392 | 2401 |
| 2015 | 15680.00 | 9499.00 | 6181.00 | 140551 | 2525 |
| 2016 | 17372.00 | 10037.00 | 7335.00 | 142921 | 2818 |
| 2017 | 19722.00 | 11935.00 | 7787.00 | 147881 | 3023 |
| 2018 | 20443.70 | 11469.34 | 8974.36 | 157483 | 3096 |
| 2019 | 17126.77 | 9055.68 | 8071.09 | 174284 | 3233 |
| 2020 | 16497.81 | 8926.65 | 7571.16 | 180796 | 3402 |
| 2021 | 19804.25 | 10168.28 | 9635.97 | 184106 | 3839 |
| 2022 | 20655.00 | 10360.00 | 10296.00 | 186137 | 4002 |

注：1）2006 年起，公路线路里程包括村道，2005 年数据按同口径进行了调整。
2）2019 年起，水运港口吞吐量调整为交通运输部一套表联网直报数据（不含无营运证码头）。

Note: a)The length of highways has included village roads since 2006, and the data of 2005 has been adjusted according to the same scope.
b)Since 2019, water port throughput has been adjusted to the Ministry of Transport set of tables networking direct reporting data (excluding docks without operating licenses).

# 表 14.3 主要年份邮电通信指标
## INDICATORS OF POSTAL AND TELECOMMUNICATION SERVICES IN MAJOR YEARS

| 年份 Year | 邮政局、所(个) Number of Postal Offices (unit) | 邮电业务总量(万元) Total Business Volume of Postal and Telecommunication Services (10 000 yuan) | #电信 Telecommunication Services | 邮电业务收入(万元) Business Revenue from Postal and Telecommunication Services (10 000 yuan) | #电信 Telecommunication Services |
|---|---|---|---|---|---|
| 1952 | 1023 | 12 | | 133 | |
| 1957 | 1846 | 33 | | 874 | |
| 1962 | 1747 | 102 | | 1000 | |
| 1965 | 1751 | 245 | | 1461 | |
| 1970 | 2166 | 267 | | 1371 | |
| 1975 | 1933 | 2190 | | 1726 | |
| 1978 | 1925 | 2650 | | 2103 | |
| 1980 | 1917 | 5071 | | 2650 | |
| 1985 | 1853 | 7268 | | 5796 | |
| 1986 | 1862 | 8264 | | 6840 | |
| 1987 | 1896 | 9719 | | 7675 | |
| 1988 | 1918 | 11853 | | 10120 | |
| 1989 | 2025 | 14351 | | 11734 | |
| 1990 | 2056 | 18999 | | 14222 | |
| 1991 | 2047 | 23708 | | 20585 | |
| 1992 | 2075 | 31305 | | 27608 | |
| 1993 | 2041 | 47627 | | 41653 | |
| 1994 | 1957 | 70543 | | 71212 | |
| 1995 | 2220 | 109627 | | 157568 | |
| 1996 | 2314 | 159929 | | 167313 | |
| 1997 | 1821 | 233471 | 211458 | 223052 | 184899 |
| 1998 | 1958 | 345932 | 319375 | 264846 | 219493 |
| 1999 | 1958 | 519537 | 490494 | 401767 | 349001 |
| 2000 | 2018 | 858200 | 822824 | 544369 | 482075 |
| 2001 | 2154 | 706000 | 635041 | 663200 | 593050 |
| 2002 | 2202 | 867600 | 791573 | 770500 | 695409 |
| 2003 | 2218 | 1213062 | 1128172 | 870787 | 788000 |
| 2004 | 2121 | 1686491 | 1592416 | 1006050 | 918555 |
| 2005 | 2068 | 2101467 | 1996000 | 1121730 | 1030130 |
| 2006 | 2008 | 2761750 | 2634708 | 1197759 | 1099750 |
| 2007 | 1981 | 3658095 | 3505910 | 1315347 | 1194089 |
| 2008 | 1927 | 4247535 | 4065296 | 1518100 | 1397500 |
| 2009 | 1838 | 4898417 | 4646833 | 1633300 | 1477100 |
| 2010 | 1775 | 1997363 | 1795756 | 1790807 | 1598773 |
| 2011 | 1678 | 2426432 | 2167301 | 2023921 | 1776624 |
| 2012 | 1635 | 2771655 | 2458900 | 2311346 | 2006441 |
| 2013 | 1684 | 3298926 | 2907701 | 2573186 | 2187644 |
| 2014 | 1720 | 4180875 | 3710644 | 2696119 | 2218948 |
| 2015 | 1756 | 5523531 | 4913412 | 2824637 | 2220727 |
| 2016 | 1780 | 8875912 | 8083709 | 3219900 | 2453000 |

| 年份 Year | 营业网点(处) number of business outlets (unit) | 邮政业务总量(万元) Total Business Volume of Postal Services (10 000 yuan) | 电信业务总量(万元) Total Business Volume of Telecommunication Services (10 000 yuan) | 邮电业务收入(万元) Business Revenue from Postal and Telecommunication Services (10 000 yuan) | 其中 of which #电信 Telecommunication Services |
|---|---|---|---|---|---|
| 2017 | 6583 | 999506 | 6111920 | 3508500 | 2584000 |
| 2018 | 6790 | 1348300 | 15413072 | 3687892 | 2572892 |
| 2019 | 8834 | 1663100 | 26014863 | 3901000 | 2610000 |
| 2020 | 10164 | 2021000 | 3276938 | 4145900 | 2691400 |
| 2021 | 10644 | 1631900 | 3683339 | 4605964 | 2922064 |
| 2022 | 11066 | 1894536 | 3817443 | 5078300 | 3208700 |

注：1）邮政业务总量2001年前为1990年不变价，2001-2009年为2000年不变价口径，2010年及以后为2010年不变价口径（以下各表同）。2021年起为上一年不变价。
2）电信业务总量2001年前为1990年不变价，2001-2009年为2000年不变价口径，2010-2016年为2010年不变价口径，2017-2019年为2015年不变价口径，2020年及以后为上年不变单价（以下各表同）。
3）2017年起，邮政局所个数改为营业网点处数。

Note: a) The data of total business volume of postal services before 2001 were calculated at 1990 constant price, the data from 2001 to 2009 were calculated at 2000 constant price, while the data of 2010 and afterwards were calculated at 2010 constant price (the same for the tables below).
b) The data of total business volume of telecommunication services before 2001 were calculated at 1990 constant price, the data from 2001 to 2009 were calculated at 2000 constant price, the data from 2010 to 2016 were calculated at 2010 constant price, the data of 2017 and afterwards were calculated at 2015 constant price, the data of 2020 and afterwards were calculated at the constant price of the last year (the same for the tables below).
c) Since 2017, the number of post offices has been changed to the number of business outlets.

# 表 14.4 邮电业务主要指标(1985 – 2022 年)
## MAIN INDICATORS OF POSTAL AND TELECOMMUNICATION SERVICES (1985-2022)

| 年 份 Year | 函 件（万件） Number of Letters (10 000 pcs) | 特快专递（万件） Pieces of Express Mail Services (10 000 pcs) | 邮政部门报刊累计数（万份） Accumulated Issue of Newspapers and Magazines (10 000 copies) | 长途电话（万分钟） Long-distance Calls (10 000 minutes) | 移动电话用户（万户） Mobile Telephone Subscribers (10 000 subscribers) | 固定互联网络用户（万户） Subscribers of Internet Services (10 000 subscribers) | 本地固定电话用户年末用户（万户） Subscribers of Local Telephone at Year-end (10 000 subscribers) |
|---|---|---|---|---|---|---|---|
| 1985 | 8961 | | 32750 | | | | 3.80 |
| 1986 | 10210 | | 34696 | | | | 4.83 |
| 1987 | 11755 | 1 | 36902 | | | | 5.39 |
| 1988 | 12432 | 1 | 40591 | | | | 6.07 |
| 1989 | 11609 | 2 | 16162 | | | | 6.62 |
| 1990 | 11544 | 2 | 16037 | | 0.08 | | 7.25 |
| 1991 | 11539 | 3 | 17540 | | 0.09 | | 8.87 |
| 1992 | 13618 | 7 | 18216 | | 0.15 | | 12.63 |
| 1993 | 16013 | 22 | 18464 | | 0.59 | | 18.53 |
| 1994 | 16519 | 40 | 15491 | | 1.73 | | 29.00 |
| 1995 | 14633 | 52 | 16453 | | 3.62 | | 37.24 |
| 1996 | 14100 | 63 | 15572 | | 9.00 | 0.03 | 66.50 |
| 1997 | 12159 | 68 | 28025 | | 19.15 | 0.20 | 126.25 |
| 1998 | 12715 | 97 | 30922 | | 40.73 | 0.76 | 156.28 |
| 1999 | 13266 | 145 | 33532 | | 79.90 | 2.49 | 197.88 |
| 2000 | 11542 | 210 | 31232 | | 160.00 | 10.00 | 268.43 |
| 2001 | 13561 | 260 | 27506 | | 245.80 | 28.60 | 337.70 |
| 2002 | 18038 | 235 | 27177 | | 424.70 | 55.60 | 413.63 |
| 2003 | 20497 | 272 | 25945 | | 619.40 | 88.65 | 533.40 |
| 2004 | 18426 | 334 | 19833 | | 811.61 | 122.16 | 642.39 |
| 2005 | 12499 | 348 | 22369 | | 943.40 | 128.66 | 688.91 |
| 2006 | 9553 | 386 | 22455 | | 1064.60 | 140.60 | 725.50 |
| 2007 | 6579 | 520 | 22178 | | 1176.90 | 169.30 | 723.13 |
| 2008 | 5476 | 1608 | 23475 | | 1281.70 | 189.57 | 688.10 |
| 2009 | 5218 | 2240 | 25281 | | 1440.92 | 203.80 | 627.73 |
| 2010 | 4927 | 2829 | 24942 | | 1664.40 | 263.10 | 582.70 |
| 2011 | 6146 | 4068 | 31217 | | 1801.19 | 326.78 | 571.25 |
| 2012 | 5706 | 5498 | 32440 | | 2069.65 | 388.07 | 575.71 |
| 2013 | 5348 | 10615 | 34834 | | 2380.78 | 505.00 | 580.33 |
| 2014 | 4700 | 13886 | 35824 | | 2589.89 | 539.70 | 582.97 |
| 2015 | 3119 | 20525 | 36334 | | 2788.78 | 696.50 | 564.98 |
| 2016 | 2301 | 28383 | 41273 | | 2880.10 | 848.80 | 541.62 |
| 2017 | 1768 | 32875 | 40898 | | 3274.88 | 1074.00 | 566.80 |
| 2018 | 1492 | 45795 | 37437 | 12805412 | 3650.70 | 1273.80 | 589.00 |
| 2019 | 1459 | 55322 | 33717 | 12317975 | 3678.80 | 1372.41 | 604.19 |
| 2020 | 2246 | 73105 | 29204 | 12192146 | 3640.06 | 1424.09 | 600.09 |
| 2021 | 1489 | 97900 | 27393 | 12537314 | 3751.11 | 1536.23 | 608.00 |
| 2022 | 1301 | 109177 | 29088 | 12955619 | 3962.16 | 1660.77 | 598.73 |

注：1、1985-2007 年长途电话计量单位为（万次）；2008 年起对长途电话通话时长统计口径作了调整，同时长途电话计量单位改为通话时长计量（万分钟）；2017 年对长途电话通话时长统计口径进行了调整，长途电话（万分钟）仅包括去话通话时长，不再包括来话通话时长；2018 年数据是“固定长途电话通话时长”“国内长途去话通话时长”“国际长途去话通话时长”相加。

2、2009 年起特快专递包括快递公司数据，2008 年数据按同口径进行了调整。

Note:a) From 1985 to 2007, the data of long-distance calls was calculated at 10 000 times. From 2008 to 2016, the data of long-distance calls has been calculated by hold-on time (10 000 min). In 2017, the data of long-distance calls has been calculated just by the length of outgoing call time (10 000 min), and the length of incoming call has been not included. Since 2018, the data of long-distance calls has been calculated by adding "Fixed Long-distance Call Time" "Domestic Long-distance Call Time" and "International Long-distance Call Time".

b) Since 2009, the data of express mail services has included the data of express delivery companies and the data of 2008 has been adjusted according to the same scope.

# 表 14.5 交通基础设施和交通运输营运工具（2021 - 2022 年）
## TRANSPORT INFRASTRUCTURE AND TRANSPORT MEANS (2021-2022)

| 指　标 | Item | 2021 | 2022 |
|---|---|---|---|
| **交通基础设施** | **Transport Infrastructure** | | |
| 公路线路里程（公里） | Length of Highways (km) | 184106 | 186137 |
| **按行政等级分** | **By Administrative Level** | | |
| #国　道 | National | 8313 | 8400 |
| 省　道 | Provincial | 10679 | 10745 |
| **按技术等级分** | **By Technical Level** | | |
| 等级公路 | Expressway and Class I-IV Highways | 171559 | 175802 |
| #高速公路 | Expressway | 3839 | 4002 |
| 一级公路 | First Class | 1209 | 1268 |
| 二级公路 | Second Class | 9553 | 9616 |
| 等外公路 | Highways Below Class IV | 12548 | 10335 |
| 公路桥梁数量（座） | Number of Highway-bridges (unit) | 13525 | 16561 |
| 公路桥梁总延米（延米） | Extended Length of Highway-bridges (extended meter) | 1093057 | 1678539 |
| 铁路营运里程（公里） | Length of Railways in Operation (km) | 2394 | 2781 |
| 内河航道里程（公里） | Length of Navigable Inland Waterways (km) | 4472 | 4472 |
| #等级航道 | Standard Waterways | 1948 | 1948 |
| 与重庆正班通航点（个） | Number of Navigable Cities from Chongqing (city) | 294 | 290 |
| 国　内 | Domestic Routes | 216 | 210 |
| 国　际（地区） | International (regional) Routes | 78 | 80 |
| 交通运输营运工具 | Transport Means | | |
| 公路营运载货汽车（辆） | Business Trucks (unit) | 260300 | 243090 |
| 公路营运载客汽车（辆） | Business Buses and Cars (unit) | 15045 | 14322 |
| 运输船舶实有数（艘） | Transportation Vessels (unit) | 2616 | 2741 |
| 机动船 | Motor Vessels | 2587 | 2716 |
| 驳　船 | Barges | 29 | 25 |
| 重庆机场飞行起降架次（万架次） | Throughput of Civil Aircrafts in Chongqing Airport (10 000 flights) | 30.07 | 19.96 |

注：从 2018 年起，出租车和公交车划入城市交通载客汽车，不再算作公路营运载客汽车。
Note: Since 2018, taxies and buses are considered as city business buses and cars, not as business buses and cars.

# 表 14.6 民用车辆、船舶拥有量（2021－2022 年）
## POSSESSION OF CIVIL MOTOR VEHICLES AND TRANSPORT VESSELS (2021-2022)

| 指　标 | Item | 2021 | 2022 |
|---|---|---|---|
| **民用车辆拥有量（辆）** | **Possession of Civil Motor Vehicles (unit)** | **8370935** | **8913617** |
| #私人民用车辆拥有量 | Private Vehicles | 7682323 | 8209539 |
| #载客汽车 | Buses and Cars | 4520034 | 4802882 |
| 载货汽车 | Trucks | 290959 | 303800 |
| #汽　车 | Motor Vehicles | 5454175 | 5763997 |
| 载客汽车 | Buses and Cars | 4888483 | 5186875 |
| 载货汽车 | Trucks | 535668 | 546904 |
| 其他汽车 | Others | 30024 | 30218 |
| 摩托车 | Motorcycles | 2861980 | 3093267 |
| **民用船舶拥有量（艘）** | **Possession of Civil Transport Vessels (unit)** | **2616** | **2741** |
| #私人船舶拥有量 | Private Vessels | | |
| #机动船 | Motor Vessels | | |
| #客　船 | Passenger Vessels | | |
| 货　船 | Cargo Vessels | | |
| 驳　船 | Barges | | |
| #机动船 | Motor Vessels | 2587 | 2716 |
| #客　船 | Passenger Vessels | 342 | 352 |
| 货　船 | Cargo Vessels | 2220 | 2338 |
| #驳　船 | Barges | 29 | 25 |

## 表 14.7 客货运输量、周转量及港口吞吐量（2021 – 2022 年）
## PASSENGER AND FREIGHT TRAFFIC, PASSENGER-KILOMETERS AND FREIGHT TON-KILOMETERS AND VOLUME OF FREIGHTS HANDLED IN COASTAL PORTS (2021-2022)

| 指　标 | Item | 2021 | 2022 |
|---|---|---|---|
| **客运量总计（万人）** | **Total Passenger Traffic (10 000 persons)** | **35250.15** | **21149.01** |
| 铁　路 | Railway | 6497.06 | 4823.61 |
| 公　路 | Highway | 25647.88 | 14432.14 |
| 水　路 | Waterway | 610.14 | 377.76 |
| 民　航 | Civil Aviation | 2495.07 | 1515.50 |
| **旅客周转量总计（亿人公里）** | **Total Passenger-kilometers (100 million person-km)** | **644.57** | **436.05** |
| 铁　路 | Railway | 156.64 | 126.28 |
| 公　路 | Highway | 120.39 | 77.94 |
| 水　路 | Waterway | 2.98 | 1.25 |
| 民　航 | Civil Aviation | 364.56 | 230.56 |
| **货运量总计（万吨）** | **Total Freight Traffic (10 000 tons)** | **144254.39** | **135432.72** |
| 铁　路 | Railway | 1592.82 | 1828.08 |
| 公　路 | Highway | 121185.16 | 111914.65 |
| 水　路 | Waterway | 21461.83 | 21677.69 |
| 民　航 | Civil Aviation | 14.57 | 12.30 |
| **货物周转量总计（亿吨公里）** | **Total Freight Ton-kilometers (100 million ton-km)** | **3841.66** | **3871.90** |
| 铁　路 | Railway | 246.66 | 292.17 |
| 公　路 | Highway | 1155.84 | 1063.30 |
| 水　路 | Waterway | 2435.94 | 2513.22 |
| 民　航 | Civil Aviation | 3.22 | 3.20 |
| **港口货物吞吐量（万吨）** | **Total Cargo Handled at Ports (10 000 tons)** | **19804.25** | **20655.37** |
| #集装箱 | Containers | 1882.41 | 1844.97 |
| 进港量 | In-port | 10168.28 | 10359.86 |
| 出港量 | Out-port | 9635.97 | 10295.51 |
| **空港吞吐量** | **Throughput of Airports** | | |
| 旅　客（万人） | Passengers (10 000 persons) | 3741.63 | 2246.09 |
| 货　物（万吨） | Cargo (10 000 tons) | 47.87 | 41.58 |

注：1）2019 年起，水运港口吞吐量调整为交通运输部一套表联网直报数据（不含无营运证码头）。
　　2）机场修正了 2019 年空港吞吐量数据。
Note:a) Since 2019, water port throughput has been adjusted to the Ministry of Transport set of tables networking direct reporting data （excluding docks without operating licenses）.
　　b) The airport revised the airport throughput data in 2019.

## 表 14.8 港口码头泊位数（2021－2022 年）
## NUMBER OF BERTHS IN COASTAL PORTS (2021-2022)

| 指　标 | Item | 2021 | 2022 |
|---|---|---|---|
| **码头泊位长度（米）** | **Length of Quay Berths(m)** | **54918** | **54585** |
| 生产用 | For Productive Use | 48370 | 47067 |
| 非生产用 | For Non-productive Use | 6548 | 7518 |
| **泊位个数（个）** | **Number of Berths (unit)** | **591** | **581** |
| 生产用 | For Productive Use | 478 | 458 |
| 非生产用 | For Non-productive Use | 113 | 123 |

## 表 14.9 主要港口码头仓库（2021－2022 年）
## WAREHOUSES IN MAIN COASTAL PORTS (2021-2022)

| 指　标 | Item | 2021 | 2022 |
|---|---|---|---|
| 集装箱吞吐量（吨） | Containers Handled in Coastal Ports (ton) | 18824149 | 18449725 |
| 国际集装箱 | International Containers | 5774123 | 4772414 |
| 国内集装箱 | Domestic Containers | 13050026 | 13677311 |
| 集装箱吞吐量（TEU） | Containers Handled in Coastal Ports (TEU) | 1330638 | 1291712 |
| 国际集装箱 | International Containers | 492235 | 426934 |
| 国内集装箱 | Domestic Containers | 838403 | 864779 |

注：TEU 是“折合 20 英尺标准箱”的英文缩写。
Note: TEU is the abbreviation of "Twenty-foot Equivalent Unit".

## 表 14.10 邮电业务基本情况（2021 – 2022 年）
## BASIC CONDITIONS OF POSTAL AND TELECOMMUNICATION SERVICES (2021-2022)

| 指　标 | Item | 2021 | 2022 |
|---|---|---|---|
| 邮政营业网点（处） | Number of post business outlets | 10644 | 11066 |
| 邮电业务总量（万元） | Business Volume of Postal and Telecommunication Services (10 000 yuan) | | |
| 邮　政 | Postal Services | 1631900 | 1894536 |
| 电　信 | Telecommunication Services | 3683339 | 3817443 |
| 函　件（万件） | Number of Letters (10 000 pcs) | 1489 | 1301 |
| 包　件（万件） | Number of Parcels (10 000 pcs) | 21.2 | 32.8 |
| 特快专递（万件） | Pieces of Express Mail Services (10 000 pcs) | 97900 | 109177 |
| 邮政部门报刊累计数（万份） | Accumulated Issue of Newspapers and Magazines (10 000 copies) | 27393 | 29088 |
| 电话通话量（万分钟） | Telephone call volume (10 000 minutes) | 12537314 | 12955619 |
| 本地固定电话用户（万户） | Number of Fixed Telephone Subscribers at Year-end (10 000 subscribers) | 608.00 | 598.73 |
| 固定互联网宽带接入流量（万 GB） | Flow Accessed to Fixed Broadband Subscribers (10 000 GB) | 2384933.21 | 3847541.29 |
| 移动互联网用户接入流量（万 GB） | Flow Accessed to Mobile Internet(10 000 GB) | 543353.62 | 645971.71 |
| 移动电话年末用户（万户） | Mobile Telephone Subscribers at Year-end (10 000 subscribers) | 3751.11 | 3962.16 |
| 固定互联网络用户（万户） | Internet Subscribers (10 000 subscribers) | 1536.23 | 1660.77 |

注：1）2017 年电信业务总量为 2015 年不变价口径，2016 年为 2010 年不变价口径。
2）2017 年长途电话（万分钟）仅包括去话通话时长，2016 年包括去话和来话通话时长。
3）2018 年开始，无公用电话指标。

Note: a) The data of total business volume of telecommunication services in 2016 was calculated at 2010 constant price, and services in 2017 was calculated at 2015 constant price.
b) Since 2017, the data of long-distance calls (10 000 min) has been calculated just by the length of outgoing call time, and the length of incoming call has been not included.
c) Since 2018, the public telephones has been are cancelled.

# 表 14.11 快递业务量（1997 – 2022 年）
## BUSINESS VOLUME OF EXPRESS SERVICES (1997-2022)

| 年 份<br>Year | 快 递<br>(万件)<br>Pieces of Express Mail Services<br>(10 000 pcs) | 快递业务收入<br>(亿元)<br>Revenue from Express Service<br>(100 million yuan) |
|---|---|---|
| 1997 | 67.0 | 0.2 |
| 1998 | 98.0 | 0.3 |
| 1999 | 144.0 | 0.4 |
| 2000 | 208.0 | 0.8 |
| 2001 | 260.0 | 1.0 |
| 2002 | 229.0 | 0.7 |
| 2003 | 271.0 | 0.8 |
| 2004 | 335.0 | 0.8 |
| 2005 | 349.0 | 0.8 |
| 2006 | 385.0 | 1.1 |
| 2007 | 519.0 | 1.4 |
| 2008 | 1651.3 | 3.5 |
| 2009 | 2240.0 | 4.9 |
| 2010 | 2829.4 | 6.0 |
| 2011 | 4068.3 | 7.7 |
| 2012 | 5497.9 | 10.3 |
| 2013 | 10614.8 | 13.7 |
| 2014 | 13886.3 | 20.1 |
| 2015 | 20525.4 | 28.7 |
| 2016 | 28382.5 | 39.0 |
| 2017 | 32874.9 | 44.7 |
| 2018 | 45795.0 | 58.0 |
| 2019 | 55322.4 | 70.5 |
| 2020 | 73105.4 | 83.0 |
| 2021 | 97900.0 | 103.4 |
| 2022 | 109176.8 | 111.5 |

## 表 14.12 电信主要通信能力（2021 – 2022 年）
## MAIN COMMUNICATION CAPACITY OF TELECOMMUNICATIONS (2021-2022)

| 指　标 | Item | 2021 | 2022 |
|---|---|---|---|
| 移动电话交换机容量（万户） | Capacity of Mobile Telephone Exchanges (10 000 subscribers) | 5285 | 5285 |
| 移动电话基站数（个） | Number of Base Stations of Mobile Telephones (unit) | 254958 | 274386 |
| 光缆线路长度（万公里） | Length of Optical Cable Lines (10 000km) | 142 | 150 |

## 表 14.13 邮电通信水平（2021 – 2022 年）
## POSTAL AND TELECOMMUNICATION SERVICES AVAILABLE (2021-2022)

| 指　标 | Item | 2021 | 2022 |
|---|---|---|---|
| 平均每一邮政营业网点服务面积（平方公里） | Average Area Served by Every Post Office (sq.km) | 7.74 | 7.44 |
| 平均每一邮政营业网点服务人口（万人） | Average Population Served by Every Post Office (10 000 persons) | 0.32 | 0.29 |
| 平均每人每年发函件数（件） | Annual Average Number of Letters Mailed Per Capita (piece) | 0.44 | 0.40 |
| 平均每人每年自邮政部门订报刊数（份） | Annual Average Number of Newspapers and Magazines Subscribed from Postal Departments Per Capita (piece) | 8.02 | 9.05 |
| 电话普及率（部 / 百人） | Telephone penetration rate (set/100 person) | 135.99 | 141.98 |
| 移动电话普及率（部 / 百人） | Mobile phone penetration rate (set/100 person) | 121.20 | 123.34 |

注：人均指标按年末常住人口计算。
Note: The per capital indicators are calculated upon the permanent population at year-end.

# 主要统计指标解释

## 货（客）运量

指在一定时期内，各种运输工具实际运送的货物（旅客）数量。是反映运输业为国民经济和人民生活服务的数量指标，也是制定和检查运输生产计划，研究运输发展规模和速度的重要指标。货运按吨计算，客运按人计算。货物不论运输距离长短或货物类别，均按实际重量统计；旅客不论行程远近或票价多少，均按一人一次作为客运量统计。半价票，小孩票也按一人统计。

## 货物（旅客）周转量

指在一定时期内，由各种运输工具运送的货物（旅客）数量与其相应运输距离的乘积之总和。是反映运输业生产总成果的重要指标，也是编制和检查运输生产计划，计算运输效率、劳动生产率以及核算运输单位成本的主要基础资料。通常以吨公里和人公里为计算单位。计算货物周转量通常按发出站与到达站之间的最短距离，也就是计费距离计算。计算公式为：

货物（旅客）周转量 = ∑货物（旅客）运输量 × 运输距离

## 公路里程

指报告期末公路的实际长度。统计范围：包括城间、城乡间、乡（村）间能行驶汽车的公共道路，公路通过城镇街道的里程，公路桥梁长度、隧道长度、渡口宽度。不包括城市街道里程，断头路里程，农（林）业生产用道路里程，工（矿）企业等内部道路里程。统计原则：按已竣工验收或交付使用的实际里程计算；两条或多条公路共同经由同一路段的重复里程，只计算一次。

## 内河航道里程

指在一定时期内，能通航运输船舶及排筏的天然河流、湖泊水库、运河及通航渠道的长度。包括全年季节性通航累计三个月以上的航道，不包括仅供零散流放竹、木排的河道。两省以河为界的航道里程，双方均按一半计算，以免重复。

## 民用汽车拥有量

指报告期末，在公安交通管理部门按照《机动车注册登记工作规范》，已注册登记领有民用车辆牌照的全部汽车数量。汽车拥有量统计的主要分类：根据汽车结构分为载客汽车、载货汽车及其他汽车；根据汽车所有者不同分为个人（私人）汽车、单位汽车；根据汽车的使用性质分为营运汽车、非营运汽车和特种汽车；根据汽车大小规格不同载客汽车分为大型、中型、小型和微型，载货汽车分为重型、中型、轻型和微型。

## 邮政、电信业务总量

指以货币形式表示的邮政、电信通信企业为社会提供各类邮政、电信通信服务的总数量。计算方法为各类业务的实物量分别乘以相应的不变单价，求出各类业务的货币量加总求得。没有不变单价的业务按其业务收入直接相加。

邮电业务总量 = ∑（各类邮电业务量 × 不变单价）+ 出租代维及其他业务收入

= 邮政业务总量 + 电信业务总量

## 固定电话用户

指在电信企业营业网点办理开户登记手续并已接入固定电话网上的全部电话用户。包括普通电话用户、无线市话用户、公用电话用户、窄带综合业务数字网（N—ISDN）用户、智能网专用接入终端用户等。

## 城市电话用户

指直辖市、省辖市、地级市、县级市的市区、市郊区及县城（包括县人民政府所在地的县城关区或行政建制相当于县人民政府所在地的镇）范围内接入局用交换机的电话用户数，包括分布在农村地区的独立工矿区、林区、驻军等接入局用交换机的电话用户数。

## 农村电话用户

指按行政区划属于城市范围以外的乡（镇）、村电话用户。

## 主要统计指标解释

### ■ 移动电话用户

指在电信运营企业营业网点办理开户登记手续，通过移动电话交换机进入移动电话网，占用移动电话号码的各类电话用户。包括各类签约用户、智能网预付费用户、无线上网卡用户。

### ■ 局用交换机容量

指安装在电信企业内用于接续本地固定电话的电话交换机容量，包括接入网设备容量（安装在电信运营企业用于连接语音用户的远端节点的设备容量）。

### ■ 移动电话交换机容量

指移动电话交换机根据一定话务模型和交换机处理能力计算出来的最大同时服务用户的数量。按报告期末已割接入网正式投入使用的设备实际容量统计。

### ■ 铁路营业里程

又称营业长度，指投入客货运输营业或临时营业的线路长度。

### ■ 电气化里程

指具备了电力机车牵引条件，并已交付运营的线路里程。

### ■ 定期航班航线里程

指定期航班营运里程的总长度，以万公里为计算单位。航线里程的统计分为按重复距离计算和按不重复距离计算两种形式。“按重复距离计算”是指不同航线的相同航段距离可以重复累加；“按不重复距离计算”则不同航线相同航段只统计一次。

### ■ 管道输油（气）里程

指油、气、成品油等各类介质实际输送距离，是反映运输管线长度的指标，也是计算周转量的依据。对于有复线和备用线的地段，原则上按单线计算管输里程。双线同时输送又不能分开计量的情况下，管输里程为双线长度之和除以2。

### ■ 港口货物吞吐量

指经由水路进、出港区范围，并经过装卸的货物数量。按货物流向分为进港吞吐量和出港吞吐量，按货物的贸易性质分为内贸和外贸吞吐量。货物类别根据现行的交通行业《运输货物分类和代码》标准分类。

### ■ 民用运输船舶拥有量

指报告期末在水路运输管理部门注册登记的从事水上客、货运输活动的我国企业或私人拥有的营业性运输船舶（含我国企业或私人拥有的悬挂外国旗的船舶）数量。不包括非运输船舶及农业、渔业生产船舶。

### ■ 互联网上网人数

指过去半年内使用过互联网的6周岁及以上中国居民人数。

### ■ 长途电话交换机容量

指电信企业用于接入长途电话网的电话交换机的设备额定容量。

### ■ 互联网宽带接入端口

指用于接入互联网用户的各类实际安装运行的接入端口的数量，包括xDSL用户接入端口、LAN接入端口、其他类型接入端口等，不包括窄带拨号接入端口。

CHONGQING STATISTICALYEARBOOK

# Explanatory Notes on Main Statistical Indicators

## Freight (Passenger) Traffic

Refers to the volume of freight (passenger) transported with various means. Freight transport is calculated in tons and passenger traffic is calculated in the number of persons. Despite the type of freight and traveling distance, the freight transport is calculated in the actual weight of the goods; and despite the traveling distance and ticket price, the passenger traffic is calculated by the principle that one person can be counted only once in one travel. The passenger who travels with a half-price ticket or a child ticket is also calculated as one person. The freight (passenger) traffic provides a quantitative measure to show how the transport industry serves the national economy and people, and is also an important indicator for planning the transport industry and for studying the development scale and speed of the transport industry.

## Freight Ton-kilometers (Passenger-kilometers)

Refer to the sum of the products of the volume of transported cargo (passengers) multiplying by the transport distance. It is an important indicator to reflect the achievement of transportation industry. Normally, the shortest distance between the departure station and the destination station (i.e., the payable distance) is the basis to calculate the freight ton-kilometers. This is an important indicator to show the total results of the transport industry, to prepare and examine the transport plan and to measure the efficiency, the labour productivity and the unit cost of transport. The formula is as follows:

Freight Ton-kilometers (Passenger-Kilometers) = ∑ [Freight (Passenger) Traffic × Distance of Transportation]

## Length of Highways

Refers to the actual length of highways at the end of reference period. It covers public roads running vehicles among cities, city and rural areas, township (villages), highways passing through streets at small cities and towns, length of bridges and tunnels, width of ferry piers. It does not include the length of streets in cities, dead end highways, the length of streets built for agricultural (forest) production and inside factories (mines). It can only be calculated with the actual mileage having been completed, checked and accepted or put into operation. If two or more highways go the same section of the way, the length of the section is only calculated for once.

## Length of Navigable Inland Waterways

Refers to the length of natural rivers, lakes, reservoirs and canals that are open to navigation for ships and rafts during a given period. It includes the channels with annual seasonal navigation for more than three months other than the waterways only for scattered bamboo and wooden rafts. If two provinces share one river as the border, the length of waterways will be half divided for each province to avoid duplication.

## Possession of Civil Motor Vehicles

Refer to the total numbers of vehicles that are registered and received vehicles' license tags according to the Work Standard for Motor Vehicles Registration formulated by transport management office under department of public security at the end of reference period. They are divided into following categories according to the structure of motor vehicles: passenger vehicles, trucks and others; and private vehicles and vehicles for units use according to ownerships; working vehicles, non-working vehicles and special motor vehicles according to kind of usage; large passenger

EXPLANATORY NOTES TO MAJOR STATISTICAL INDICATORS

vehicles, medium passenger vehicles and small passenger vehicles, heavy trucks, light-heavy trucks and light trucks according to sizes of vehicles.

## Business Volume of Post and Telecommunications

Refers to the total amount of postal and telecommunication services, expressed in value terms, provided by the post and telecommunications departments for society. Business volume of post and telecommunications is the sum of each service in kind multiplying with its correspondent unit price (constant price). Business without constant price add their business revenue directly.

Business Volume of Postal and Telecommunication Services = ∑ (Transaction of Post and Telecommunication Services × Constant Price) + Income from Leasing, Maintenance and other Services = Business Volume of Postal Services + Business Volume of Telecommunication Services

## Local Telephone Subscribers

Refer to all subscribers who have gone through registration procedures in the operation points of enterprises engaged in telecommunications and are hence connected to the local telecommunications service provider through fixed line network. Included are general subscribers, wireless local telephone subscribers, public telephones subscribers, N-ISDN subscribers and intelligent network terminal subscribers.

## Urban Telephone Subscribers

Refer to subscribers telephone subscribers, located at municipalities, cities under the jurisdiction of province, cities at prefectural level, downtown and suburb of city at county level town and county towns (including country towns where county government located, and towns of county level according to the administrative organizational system), that are connected to the public line telephone network, including rural mineral area, forest area, military area.

## Rural Telephone Subscribers

Refer to telephone subscribers, located at the towns and villages outside the coverage of urban areas according to the administrative division.

## Mobile Telephone Subscribers

Refer to persons who have gone through registration procedures in the operation points of enterprises engaged in telecommunications and are hence connected with the mobile telephone communication network through the mobile telephone switchboards and occupy mobile phone numbers. Included are various types of subscriber, prepaid users for intelligent network and wireless network card users.

## Capacity of Office Telephone Exchanges

Refers to the capacity (measured in gate) of telephone exchanges installed in the offices of telecommunication service providers for communication between fixed telephones. It includes the capacity of access network equipment (capacity of equipment installed in the offices of telecommunication service providers for connecting distant nodes of voice users).

## Capacity of Mobile Telephone Exchanges

Refers to the capacity of the maximum services provided to subscribers at any one time as computed based on a certain model of calls distribution and transacting capacity of the mobile telephone exchanges. It is calculated based on the actual capacity of equipments connected to network through cutover and put into operation officially at the end of the reference period.

## Length of Railways in Operation

Refers to the total length of the trunk line for passenger and freight transportation in full operation or temporary operation.

EXPLANATORY NOTES TO
MAJOR STATISTICAL INDICATORS

## Length of Electrified Trunk Line

Refers to the length of the trunk line capable for the running of electrified locomotives and having been put into operation.

## Length of Routes with Scheduled Flights

Refers to the total length of all routes for scheduled flights, which is calculated using million kilometres as the unit. There are usually two ways to calculate the route length: duplicated calculation and non-duplicated calculation. Duplicated calculation means that the same segment of different routes can be added duplicately, while the non-duplicated calculation allows the same segment of different routes be counted once only.

## Length of Oil (Gas) Pipelines

Refers to the actual transport distance of oil, gas and oil products, an indicator reflecting the length of transportation routes and a reference to calculate the freight-kilometers. For those sections with double pipelines and alternate pipeline, the length will be calculated according to the length of single pipeline in principle. If the double pipelines perform the transportation at the same time and unable to be counted separately, the length of pipelines will be the length of double pipelines divided by 2.

## Volume of Freight Handled in Coastal Ports

Refers to the volume of cargo passing in and out of the harbour area of the major coastal ports and having been loaded and unloaded. The volume of freight handled may be classified by direction of cargo flow as in-port freight and out-port freight, or by nature of cargo as freight for domestic trade and freight for foreign trade. It can also be classified by type of freight based on the existing standard classification for transportation industry "Classification and Coding for Freight".

## Possession of Civil Transport Vessels

Refers to the total number at the end of reference period of operating transport vessels owned by Chinese enterprises or privately that are registered in the water transportation management institutions and permitted to perform cargo transport activities (including vessels with foreign flags but owned by Chinese enterprises or citizens). Non-transport vessels and vessels used for agriculture and fishery are not included.

## Internet Users

Refer to the number of Chinese citizens aged 6 and over who use the Internet in the past six months.

## Capacity of Long Distance Telephone Exchanges

Refers to the rated capacity of telephone exchanges to connect long distance telephone network by enterprises engaged in telecommunications.

## Broadband Connection Terminals

Refer to the connection terminals to internet users actually installed and put into operation, including connection terminals for XDSL, connection terminals for LAN, and other types of connection terminals. N-ISDN connection terminals are not included.

# 第十五章·国内贸易

# DOMESTIC TRADE

# 简要说明

BRIEF INTRODUCTION

本章主要内容有社会消费品零售总额，批发和零售业商品销售总额，限额以上批发零售和住宿餐饮业企业财务状况、限额以上住宿业和限额以上餐饮业基本经营情况，以及限额以上批发和零售业、住宿和餐饮业连锁经营情况。本章资料由市统计局贸易外经处提供。

The data in this chapter cover the total sales of the consumer goods, total sales of wholesale and retail trade, the financial indicators of wholesale and retail, hotel and catering enterprises above designated size, the operation of hotels and the enterprises in catering trade above designated size, and the operation of chain enterprises above designated size in wholesale, retail, hotel and catering trade. All the data in this chapter are provided by Division of Trade and External Economic Relations Statistics, Municipal Bureau of Statistics.

# 表 15.1 社会消费品零售总额(1949 - 2022 年)
TOTAL RETAIL SALES OF CONSUMER GOODS (1949-2022)

单位: 万元 (10 000 yuan)

| 年 份<br>Year | 社会消费品零售总额<br>Total Retail Sales of Consumer Goods | 年 份<br>Year | 社会消费品零售总额<br>Total Retail Sales of Consumer Goods |
|---|---|---|---|
| 1949 | 46167 | 1966 | 147697 |
| 1950 | 50695 | 1967 | 155358 |
| 1951 | 55644 | 1968 | 132702 |
| 1952 | 61973 | 1969 | 152531 |
| 1953 | 77007 | 1970 | 163612 |
| 1954 | 83302 | 1971 | 172626 |
| 1955 | 84015 | 1972 | 191113 |
| 1956 | 98852 | 1973 | 195825 |
| 1957 | 108061 | 1974 | 197474 |
| 1958 | 119981 | 1975 | 217537 |
| 1959 | 141591 | 1976 | 218022 |
| 1960 | 156655 | 1977 | 233979 |
| 1961 | 133022 | 1978 | 250188 |
| 1962 | 124248 | 1979 | 301563 |
| 1963 | 112094 | 1980 | 366349 |
| 1964 | 122995 | 1981 | 405952 |
| 1965 | 134722 | 1982 | 431269 |

**表 15.1 续表 continued**

单位: 万元 (10 000 yuan)

| 年 份<br>Year | 社会消费品零售总额<br>Total Retail Sales of Consumer Goods | 年 份<br>Year | 社会消费品零售总额<br>Total Retail Sales of Consumer Goods |
|---|---|---|---|
| 1983 | 466704 | 2003 | 10169616 |
| 1984 | 538909 | 2004 | 11762277 |
| 1985 | 690779 | 2005 | 13625978 |
| 1986 | 780787 | 2006 | 16010462 |
| 1987 | 926227 | 2007 | 19286416 |
| 1988 | 1191747 | 2008 | 24392326 |
| 1989 | 1332450 | 2009 | 28779444 |
| 1990 | 1371244 | 2010 | 35149391 |
| 1991 | 1569138 | 2011 | 43847652 |
| 1992 | 2031140 | 2012 | 51410871 |
| 1993 | 2593587 | 2013 | 59461565 |
| 1994 | 3395013 | 2014 | 67628282 |
| 1995 | 4258168 | 2015 | 76675890 |
| 1996 | 5141668 | 2016 | 87284013 |
| 1997 | 5904049 | 2017 | 97693917 |
| 1998 | 6485734 | 2018 | 107052443 |
| 1999 | 7038055 | 2019 | 116316743 |
| 2000 | 7655160 | 2020 | 117872002 |
| 2001 | 8382287 | 2021 | 139676742 |
| 2002 | 9216516 | 2022 | 139260832 |

注：1993-2019 年根据四经普调整。
Note: The data of 1993-2019 has been adjusted according to the result of the 4rd National Economic Census.

## 表 15.2 社会消费品零售总额（2021 － 2022 年）
## TOTAL RETAIL SALES OF CONSUMER GOODS (2021-2022)

单位：万元 (10 000 yuan)

| 指　标 | Item | 2021 | 2022 |
|---|---|---|---|
| **总　计** | **Total** | **139676742** | **139260832** |
| **按销售单位所在地分** | **By Location** | | |
| 城　镇 | City | 119871749 | 119101442 |
| #城　区 | County | 85460517 | 84590563 |
| 乡　村 | Under County Level | 19804993 | 20159390 |
| **按消费形态分** | **By Consumption pattern** | | |
| 餐饮收入 | From Meals | 19533200 | 19154534 |
| 商品零售 | Retail sales | 120143542 | 120106298 |

注：根据全国第四次经济普查进行调整。
Note: The data has been adjusted according to the result of the 4rd National Economic Census.

## 表 15.3 限额以上住宿和餐饮业法人企业基本经营情况（2021 － 2022 年）
## BASIC CONDITIONS OF ENTERPRISES ABOVE DESIGNATED SIZE OF HOTELS AND CATERING SERVICES (2021-2022)

| 指　标 | Item | 2021 | 2022 |
|---|---|---|---|
| 营业额(万元) | Business Revenue(10 000 yuan) | 2881926 | 2763373 |
| 客房收入 | From Hotel Rooms | 660982 | 616381 |
| 餐费收入 | From Meals | 2025269 | 1965308 |
| 商品销售收入 | From Commodities | 107277 | 99764 |
| 其他收入 | Other Income | 88398 | 81920 |
| 住宿餐饮设施 | Infrastructure of Hotels and Catering Services | | |
| 床位数(个) | Number of Beds (unit) | 233755 | 221000 |
| 餐位数(位) | Number of Catering Seats (unit) | 1066696 | 1053524 |

# 表 15.4 批发和零售业商品销售总额(2022 年)
## TOTAL SALES OF ENTERPRISES IN WHOLESALE AND RETAIL TRADES (2022)

单位:万元 (10 000 yuan)

| 指 标 | Item | 销售总额 Total Sales | 零 售 Retail |
|---|---|---|---|
| **总 计** | **Total** | **402213451** | **119921908** |
| **限额以上批发和零售法人企业** | **Enterprises above Designated Size in Wholesales and Retail Trade** | **199114926** | **39390633** |
| **按登记注册类型分** | **By Status Registration** | | |
| 内资企业 | Domestic-funded Enterprises | 183324198 | 33033354 |
| 国有企业 | State-owned Enterprises | 14508714 | 814442 |
| 集体企业 | Collective-owned Enterprises | 74431 | 24595 |
| 股份合作企业 | Cooperative Enterprises | 619953 | 31062 |
| 联营企业 | Joint-owned Enterprises | 1584227 | 7263 |
| 有限责任公司 | Limited-liability Companies | 53148198 | 6348968 |
| 股份有限公司 | Share Holding Corporation Ltd. | 12291432 | 5541783 |
| 私营企业 | Private Enterprises | 101092641 | 20262944 |
| 其他企业 | Other Enterprises | 4602 | 2296 |
| 港、澳、台商投资企业 | Enterprises Funded by Hong Kong, Macao and Taiwan | 6132864 | 1934819 |
| 外商投资企业 | Foreign-funded Enterprises | 9657864 | 4422459 |
| **按行业分** | **By Sector** | | |
| 农、林、牧、渔产品批发 | Wholesale of Farm, Forestry, Animal Husbandry and Fishery Products | 1355212 | 43614 |
| 食品、饮料及烟草制品批发 | Wholesale of Food, Beverages and Tobacco | 19443040 | 965598 |
| 纺织、服装及家电用品批发 | Wholesale of Textiles, Garments and Household Electrical Appliances | 7940203 | 159187 |
| 文化、体育用品及器材批发 | Wholesale of Cultural, Sports Appliances and Equipment | 1842692 | 141317 |
| 医药及医疗器材批发 | Wholesale of Medicines and Medical Appliances | 13789103 | 97859 |
| 矿产品、建材及化工产品批发 | Wholesale of Mineral Products, Building Materials and Chemical Products | 68984631 | 2485728 |
| 机械设备、五金交电及电子产品批发 | Wholesale of Machinery, Hardware and Electronic Products | 41990580 | 1126074 |
| 贸易经纪与代理 | Trade Broker and Agency | 1113130 | 815 |
| 其他批发 | Other Wholesale not Classified Elsewhere | 3263650 | 46112 |
| 综合零售 | Retail Trades | 7366444 | 7113282 |
| 食品、饮料及烟草制品专门零售 | Special Retail of Food, Beverages and Tobacco | 2044039 | 1649176 |
| 纺织、服装及日用品专门零售 | Special Retail of Textiles, Garments and Daily Consumer Articles | 1118610 | 1063031 |
| 文化、体育用品及器材专门零售 | Retail of Cultural, Sports Appliances and Equipment | 700694 | 356965 |
| 医药及医疗器材专门零售 | Retail of Medicines and Medical Appliances | 1607469 | 1430086 |
| 汽车、摩托车、零配件和燃料及其他动力销售 | Retail of Motor Vehicles, Motorcycles, Fuel and Parts | 18651265 | 15880282 |
| 家用电器及电子产品专门零售 | Special Retail of Household Electrical Appliances and Electronic Products | 2696747 | 2324081 |
| 五金、家具及室内装修材料专门零售 | Special Retail of Hardware, Furniture and Decoration Materials | 1178914 | 862198 |
| 货摊、无店铺及其他零售 | Stalls, Non-shop and Other Retails | 4028505 | 3645230 |

# 表 15.5 限额以上批发和零售业单位主要商品分类销售额（2021－2022 年）
## SALES OF MAIN COMMODITIES OF THE ENTERPRISES ABOVE DESIGNATED SIZE IN WHOLESALE AND RETAIL TRADES BY CATEGORY (2021-2022)

单位：亿元 (100 million yuan)

| 指　标 | Item | 销售额 Total Sales | | 零　售 Retail | |
|---|---|---|---|---|---|
| | | 2021 | 2022 | 2021 | 2022 |
| **总　计** | **Total** | **18247.43** | **20260.04** | **4212.59** | **4370.33** |
| 其中：通过互联网实现的商品销售 | Commodities Sold Over the Web | 2389.19 | 1983.57 | 526.07 | 701.45 |
| 粮油、食品类 | Grain and Oil,Food | 1470.64 | 1705.40 | 673.75 | 762.38 |
| #粮油类 | Grain and Oil | 420.23 | 475.60 | 129.38 | 153.51 |
| 肉禽蛋类 | Meat, Poultry and Eggs | 184.47 | 231.38 | 89.65 | 100.69 |
| 水产品类 | Aquatic Products | 37.19 | 47.50 | 21.58 | 22.98 |
| 蔬菜类 | Vegetables | 124.70 | 144.43 | 63.84 | 67.69 |
| 干鲜果品类 | Dried and Fresh Melons and Fruits | 204.40 | 263.69 | 71.01 | 79.57 |
| 饮料类 | Beverages | 123.40 | 143.60 | 77.58 | 89.16 |
| 烟酒类 | Tobacco and Liquor | 1036.76 | 1078.43 | 101.38 | 106.71 |
| 服装鞋帽、针、纺织品类 | Clothing, Shoes, Hats and Textiles | 681.21 | 637.07 | 264.76 | 229.91 |
| 服装类 | Clothing | 497.43 | 473.06 | 197.56 | 173.69 |
| 鞋帽类 | Shoes and Hats | 131.22 | 122.06 | 47.87 | 38.40 |
| 针纺织品类 | Knitwear and Textiles | 52.56 | 41.95 | 19.33 | 17.82 |
| 化妆品类 | Cosmetics | 163.67 | 158.26 | 43.69 | 42.71 |
| 金银珠宝类 | Gold, Silver and Jewelry | 185.53 | 164.59 | 60.92 | 52.44 |
| 日用品类 | Articles for Daily Use | 340.06 | 333.42 | 181.34 | 178.12 |
| #可穿戴智能设备 | Wearable smart devices | 4.62 | 5.04 | 1.98 | 2.29 |
| 五金、电料类 | Hardware and Electrical Materials | 98.48 | 390.35 | 29.13 | 31.27 |
| 体育、娱乐用品类 | Sports and Recreation Articles | 40.24 | 39.79 | 11.82 | 12.17 |
| #照相器材类 | Photographic Equipment | 2.36 | 1.52 | 1.84 | 1.46 |
| 书报杂志类 | Newspapers and Magazines | 55.77 | 50.94 | 27.77 | 23.79 |
| 电子出版物及音像制品类 | E-journal and Video Products | 0.86 | 0.84 | 0.82 | 0.81 |
| 家用电器和音像器材类 | Household Appliances and Video Appliances | 473.07 | 429.80 | 310.32 | 283.06 |
| #能效等级为 1 级和 2 级的商品 | Commodities with energy efficiency grades 1 and 2 | 109.33 | 96.01 | 78.56 | 68.09 |
| #智能家用电器和音像器材 | Intelligent household appliances and audio-visual equipment | 110.29 | 111.42 | 96.62 | 101.33 |
| 中西药品类 | Traditional Chinese and Western Medicines | 1069.51 | 1343.87 | 150.61 | 161.71 |
| #西　药 | Western Medicines | 856.85 | 1107.35 | 104.15 | 114.08 |
| 中草药及中成药 | Traditional Chinese Medicines | 104.91 | 115.93 | 26.20 | 25.89 |
| 文化办公用品类 | Cultural and Office Articles | 468.47 | 527.42 | 123.36 | 132.55 |
| #计算机及其配套产品 | Computer and Supporting Products | 281.87 | 338.57 | 78.38 | 83.49 |
| 家具类 | Furniture | 71.86 | 66.78 | 59.77 | 57.45 |
| 通信器材类 | Communication Appliances | 1293.88 | 1103.22 | 123.52 | 125.37 |
| #智能手机 | Intelligent mobile phone | 1125.19 | 941.91 | 92.88 | 102.74 |
| 煤炭及制品类 | Coal and Related Products | 335.54 | 433.39 | 2.96 | 0.92 |
| 木材及制品类 | Wood and Wooden Products | 54.07 | 90.08 | | |
| 石油及制品类 | Petroleum and Related Products | 1413.90 | 1749.96 | 532.05 | 569.89 |
| 化工材料及制品类 | Chemical Materials and Related Products | 1069.67 | 1297.32 | | |
| #化肥类 | Fertilizers | 228.41 | 344.46 | | |
| 金属材料类 | Metal Materials | 3276.00 | 3543.70 | | |
| 建筑及装潢材料类 | Building and Decoration Materials | 643.08 | 698.62 | 128.84 | 132.12 |
| 机电产品设备类 | Mechanical and Electrical Products | 358.57 | 488.54 | 52.99 | 56.80 |
| #农机类 | Agricultural Machinery | 7.99 | 7.00 | | |
| 汽车类 | Automobiles | 2869.23 | 3010.98 | 1192.52 | 1266.18 |
| #新能源汽车 | New energy vehicle | 161.80 | 701.29 | 82.98 | 232.41 |
| 种子饲料类 | Seed and Feedstuff | 18.37 | 28.15 | | |
| 棉麻类 | Cotton, Hemp | 37.34 | 24.04 | 0.42 | 0.15 |
| 其他类 | Others | 598.25 | 721.50 | 62.30 | 54.65 |

注：以上类值为快报数据。
Note: the above values are express data.

# 表 15.6 限额以上批发业法人企业财务状况（2022 年）
## FINANCIAL INDICATORS OF WHOLESALE ENTERPRISES ABOVE DESIGNATED SIZE (2022)

| 指 标 | Item | 法人企业数（个）Number of Enterprises (unit) | 执行《2006年企业会计准则》企业数（个）Number of Enterprises which Implemented Accounting standard for Business Enterprise in 2006 (unit) | 一、年初存货 Inventory at the Beginning of Year |
|---|---|---|---|---|
| **总 计** | **Total** | **3473** | **2033** | **6148873.0** |
| **按批发行业小类分** | **By Wholesale Sector** | | | |
| 农、林、牧、渔产品批发 | Wholesale of Farm, Forestry and Animal Husbandry Products | 71 | 43 | 106241.9 |
| 谷物、豆及薯类批发 | Wholesale of Cereal, Bean and Tubers | 15 | 12 | 45746.0 |
| 种子批发 | Wholesale of Seeds | 3 | | 1243.4 |
| 畜牧渔业饲料批发 | Wholesale of Feedstuff | 15 | 9 | 1905.9 |
| 棉、麻批发 | Wholesale of Cotton and Fiber Crops | 4 | 2 | 15563.0 |
| 林业产品批发 | Wholesale of Forestry Products | 11 | 7 | 10409.3 |
| 牲畜批发 | Wholesale of Livestock | 7 | 4 | 9332.5 |
| 渔业产品批发 | Wholesale of fishery products | 2 | 1 | 548.0 |
| 其他农牧产品批发 | Wholesale of Other Farm Products and Livestock Products | 14 | 8 | 21493.8 |
| 食品、饮料及烟草制品批发 | Wholesale of Food, Beverages and Tobacco | 593 | 374 | 691911.4 |
| 米、面制品及食用油批发 | Wholesale of Rice, Flour and Edible Oil | 97 | 52 | 150216.3 |
| 糕点、糖果及糖批发 | Wholesale of Cake, Candy and Sugar | 20 | 14 | 25725.4 |
| 果品、蔬菜批发 | Wholesale of Fruits and Vegetables | 147 | 110 | 28264.9 |
| 肉、禽、蛋、奶及水产品批发 | Wholesale of Meat, Poultry, Eggs and Aquatic Products | 97 | 60 | 55054.8 |
| 盐及调味品批发 | Wholesale of Salts and Condiments | 25 | 14 | 15807.4 |
| 营养和保健品批发 | Wholesale of Nutraceutical Products | 9 | 3 | 5978.5 |
| 酒、饮料及茶叶批发 | Wholesale of Liquor, Beverages and Tea | 89 | 43 | 50895.9 |
| 烟草制品批发 | Wholesale of Tobacco | 37 | 36 | 300137.5 |
| 其他食品批发 | Wholesale of other Food | 72 | 42 | 59830.7 |
| 纺织、服装及家庭用品批发 | Wholesale of Textiles, Garments and Household Articles | 109 | 70 | 503143.9 |
| 纺织品、针织品及原料批发 | Wholesale of Textiles, Knitwear and Raw Materials | 11 | 6 | 3509.9 |
| 服装批发 | Wholesale of Garments | 10 | 7 | 301458.2 |
| 鞋帽批发 | Wholesale of Shoes and Hats | 2 | 1 | 1081.8 |
| 化妆品及卫生用品批发 | Wholesale of Cosmetics and Sanitary Articles | 14 | 6 | 33975.6 |
| 厨具卫具及日用杂品批发 | Wholesale of Kitchenware, sanitary ware and daily necessities | 15 | 9 | 26256.5 |
| 灯具、装饰物品批发 | Wholesale of Light Fittings and Decorative Articles | 5 | 4 | 28816.7 |
| 家用视听设备批发 | Wholesale of Household Audio-visual Equipments | 5 | 4 | 8885.8 |
| 日用家电批发 | Wholesale of Household Electrical Appliances | 33 | 23 | 44809.6 |
| 其他家庭用品批发 | Wholesale of Other Household Articles | 14 | 10 | 54349.8 |
| 文化、体育用品及器材批发 | Wholesale of Cultural and Sports Articles and Equipment | 39 | 29 | 403532.1 |
| 文具用品批发 | Wholesale of Cultural Articles | 9 | 6 | 7975.3 |
| 体育用品及器材批发 | Wholesale of Sports Articles | 2 | 1 | 255.0 |
| 图书批发 | Wholesale of Books | 3 | 3 | 19459.3 |
| 首饰、工艺品及收藏品批发 | Wholesale of Jewelry, Handicrafts and Collections | 24 | 18 | 374890.4 |
| 其他文化用品批发 | Wholesale of Other Cultural Goods | 1 | 1 | 952.1 |
| 医药及医疗器材批发 | Wholesale of Medicines and Medical Appliances | 434 | 286 | 1384667.6 |
| 西药批发 | Wholesale of Western Medicines | 255 | 171 | 1228149.0 |
| 中药批发 | Wholesale of Traditional Chinese Medicines | 31 | 16 | 21247.8 |
| 动物用药品批发 | Wholesale of Animal Drugs | 4 | 3 | 6843.0 |
| 医疗用品及器材批发 | Wholesale of Medical Articles and Appliances | 144 | 96 | 128427.8 |

单位: 万元 (10 000 yuan)

二、期末资产负债 Assets and Liabilities

| 流动资产合计 Total Current Assets | 应收账款 Accounts Receivable | 存货 Inventory | 固定资产原价 Total Original Value of Fixed Assets | 房屋和构筑物 Buildings and Structures | 机器设备 Machinery and Equipments |
|---|---|---|---|---|---|
| **51444138.7** | **15409570.0** | **6904819.6** | **3527517.3** | **1208968.0** | **662524.0** |
| 455839.7 | 103273.5 | 111138.3 | 150611.9 | 63219.8 | 11174.3 |
| 86749.5 | 13360.4 | 35050.9 | 127046.7 | 51417.2 | 7521.2 |
| 12515.7 | 6118.6 | 5601.6 | 3366.0 | 3223.4 | 87.9 |
| 28332.5 | 13339.3 | 3442.9 | 578.3 | 51.2 | 116.3 |
| 70223.5 | 7279.8 | 19049.4 | 4117.9 | 506.9 | 658.0 |
| 132050.9 | 38106.6 | 14562.8 | 1596.3 | 652.1 | 230.8 |
| 31445.8 | 5395.4 | 12041.4 | 8405.6 | 5466.0 | 2038.6 |
| 2669.7 | 663.4 | 186.8 | 62.3 | | |
| 91852.1 | 19010.0 | 21202.5 | 5438.8 | 1903.0 | 521.5 |
| 5524315.4 | 1299402.7 | 736347.7 | 1105890.5 | 424664.0 | 66859.7 |
| 680971.9 | 89531.1 | 144717.0 | 330866.4 | 147809.7 | 26036.6 |
| 73772.3 | 9514.2 | 25357.5 | 10977.6 | 6740.8 | 402.7 |
| 1155104.0 | 894802.0 | 41055.3 | 32350.8 | 12140.4 | 4943.0 |
| 274395.9 | 92039.8 | 59334.4 | 83017.2 | 33172.5 | 5303.4 |
| 233876.5 | 28856.3 | 17816.5 | 36653.3 | 25312.3 | 1906.7 |
| 33294.2 | 7640.6 | 7637.7 | 991.5 | 119.2 | 274.1 |
| 308841.0 | 48566.6 | 56087.4 | 26616.0 | 1950.4 | 3894.6 |
| 2254193.5 | 89418.1 | 326914.3 | 486017.8 | 119392.2 | 14880.7 |
| 509866.1 | 39034.0 | 57427.6 | 98399.9 | 78026.5 | 9217.9 |
| 2121117.6 | 1109083.3 | 391092.2 | 40686.5 | 14061.0 | 4906.8 |
| 49488.5 | 8044.5 | 5947.5 | 3393.6 | 1782.5 | 796.4 |
| 1391151.3 | 950611.9 | 192380.5 | 10501.3 | 213.2 | 292.8 |
| 5550.1 | 2426.2 | 1224.4 | 309.6 | 32.6 | |
| 139428.3 | 49696.7 | 33300.5 | 10721.0 | 7810.3 | 1322.4 |
| 51560.5 | 8652.5 | 31658.9 | 6246.2 | 3266.0 | 294.8 |
| 65752.6 | 8693.7 | 36428.7 | 1829.0 | | |
| 22044.0 | 4124.8 | 9916.1 | 712.1 | | 20.7 |
| 229754.2 | 34592.9 | 23624.2 | 4107.5 | 743.3 | 336.0 |
| 166388.1 | 42240.1 | 56611.4 | 2866.2 | 213.1 | 1843.7 |
| 1200764.4 | 280498.9 | 363272.0 | 29456.3 | 7337.9 | 4734.2 |
| 342295.7 | 170095.6 | 10335.5 | 5233.0 | 3202.0 | 482.1 |
| 6794.7 | 5127.4 | 244.3 | 85.3 | | 11.1 |
| 38624.9 | 9922.1 | 16554.0 | 2345.4 | 1795.2 | 149.0 |
| 810325.5 | 94678.7 | 335175.4 | 20992.9 | 2340.7 | 4092.0 |
| 2723.6 | 675.1 | 962.8 | 799.7 | | |
| 9117748.6 | 4053254.7 | 1586070.8 | 327587.2 | 162142.9 | 77808.3 |
| 7791340.1 | 3375296.0 | 1419857.5 | 235654.5 | 138037.2 | 45875.8 |
| 145427.1 | 80783.2 | 21141.1 | 9246.4 | 4511.6 | 1987.7 |
| 65344.9 | 30901.6 | 5414.1 | 5594.6 | 111.1 | 380.2 |
| 1115636.5 | 566273.9 | 139658.1 | 77091.7 | 19483.0 | 29564.6 |

**表 15.6 续表 1 continued 1**

| 指 标 | Item | 二、期末资产负债 Assets and Liabilities | | |
|---|---|---|---|---|
| | | 累计折旧 Cumulative Depreciation | 本年折旧 Depreciation | 固定资产净额 Net Value of Fixed Assets |
| **总 计** | **Total** | **1418673.6** | **193635.8** | **1918293.2** |
| **按批发行业小类分** | **By Wholesale Sector** | | | |
| 农、林、牧、渔产品批发 | Wholesale of Farm, Forestry and Animal Husbandry Products | 34623.7 | 4365.1 | 100907.8 |
| 谷物、豆及薯类批发 | Wholesale of Cereal, Bean and Tubers | 28459.4 | 3308.7 | 86574.9 |
| 种子批发 | Wholesale of Seeds | 710.9 | 144.3 | 2655.1 |
| 畜牧渔业饲料批发 | Wholesale of Feedstuff | 253.6 | 47.2 | 249.2 |
| 棉、麻批发 | Wholesale of Cotton and Fiber Crops | 1577.9 | 108.0 | 207.1 |
| 林业产品批发 | Wholesale of Forestry Products | 627.6 | 121.5 | 884.7 |
| 牲畜批发 | Wholesale of Livestock | 1145.9 | 456.5 | 7059.7 |
| 渔业产品批发 | Wholesale of fishery products | 21.8 | 11.8 | 9.3 |
| 其他农牧产品批发 | Wholesale of Other Farm Products and Livestock Products | 1826.6 | 167.1 | 3267.8 |
| 食品、饮料及烟草制品批发 | Wholesale of Food, Beverages and Tobacco | 434644.0 | 48050.7 | 617895.4 |
| 米、面制品及食用油批发 | Wholesale of Rice, Flour and Edible Oil | 58576.3 | 9746.3 | 267259.7 |
| 糕点、糖果及糖批发 | Wholesale of Cake, Candy and Sugar | 4481.8 | 916.6 | 5717.0 |
| 果品、蔬菜批发 | Wholesale of Fruits and Vegetables | 7525.3 | 2026.9 | 17770.8 |
| 肉、禽、蛋、奶及水产品批发 | Wholesale of Meat, Poultry, Eggs and Aquatic Products | 18305.0 | 3345.4 | 35566.0 |
| 盐及调味品批发 | Wholesale of Salts and Condiments | 18465.0 | 3632.7 | 15720.3 |
| 营养和保健品批发 | Wholesale of Nutraceutical Products | 620.1 | 132.3 | 370.5 |
| 酒、饮料及茶叶批发 | Wholesale of Liquor, Beverages and Tea | 12513.0 | 1777.0 | 10754.9 |
| 烟草制品批发 | Wholesale of Tobacco | 284583.5 | 22770.0 | 198101.3 |
| 其他食品批发 | Wholesale of other Food | 29574.0 | 3703.5 | 66634.9 |
| 纺织、服装及家庭用品批发 | Wholesale of Textiles, Garments and Household Articles | 15590.8 | 2398.7 | 21421.8 |
| 纺织品、针织品及原料批发 | Wholesale of Textiles, Knitwear and Raw Materials | 1358.2 | 138.4 | 1516.8 |
| 服装批发 | Wholesale of Garments | 1193.9 | 291.5 | 8186.3 |
| 鞋帽批发 | Wholesale of Shoes and Hats | 163.3 | 0.8 | 7.2 |
| 化妆品及卫生用品批发 | Wholesale of Cosmetics and Sanitary Articles | 4443.4 | 685.4 | 6275.8 |
| 厨具卫具及日用杂品批发 | Wholesale of Kitchenware, sanitary ware and daily necessities | 2809.9 | 128.1 | 2402.7 |
| 灯具、装饰物品批发 | Wholesale of Light Fittings and Decorative Articles | 769.6 | 175.7 | 555.0 |
| 家用视听设备批发 | Wholesale of Household Audio-visual Equipments | 423.1 | 39.6 | 1.4 |
| 日用家电批发 | Wholesale of Household Electrical Appliances | 2502.5 | 496.0 | 1537.5 |
| 其他家庭用品批发 | Wholesale of Other Household Articles | 1926.9 | 443.2 | 939.1 |
| 文化、体育用品及器材批发 | Wholesale of Cultural and Sports Articles and Equipment | 18328.3 | 2394.1 | 10628.4 |
| 文具用品批发 | Wholesale of Cultural Articles | 1541.7 | 411.1 | 3471.5 |
| 体育用品及器材批发 | Wholesale of Sports Articles | 23.8 | 3.9 | 3.0 |
| 图书批发 | Wholesale of Books | 350.7 | 72.4 | 1931.7 |
| 首饰、工艺品及收藏品批发 | Wholesale of Jewelry, Handicrafts and Collections | 15940.4 | 1862.9 | 4894.2 |
| 其他文化用品批发 | Wholesale of Other Cultural Goods | 471.7 | 43.8 | 328.0 |
| 医药及医疗器材批发 | Wholesale of Medicines and Medical Appliances | 135466.8 | 25168.5 | 165298.3 |
| 西药批发 | Wholesale of Western Medicines | 89630.7 | 14610.7 | 128835.7 |
| 中药批发 | Wholesale of Traditional Chinese Medicines | 4697.8 | 1725.4 | 3900.2 |
| 动物用药品批发 | Wholesale of Animal Drugs | 3518.5 | 552.3 | 2076.0 |
| 医疗用品及器材批发 | Wholesale of Medical Articles and Appliances | 37619.8 | 8280.1 | 30486.4 |

单位：万元 (10 000 yuan)

| 二、期末资产负债 Assets and Liabilities | | | | | |
|---|---|---|---|---|---|
| 在建工程<br>Construction in Progress | 无形资产<br>Intangible Assets | 土地使用权<br>Land Use Rights | 资产总计<br>Total Assets | 流动负债合计<br>Total Current Liabilities | 应付账款<br>Accounts Payable |
| **725541.6** | **834877.0** | **227437.9** | **61286889.3** | **40421837.1** | **13874521.8** |
| 5491.3 | 29410.8 | 12555.1 | 743232.1 | 389164.9 | 58205.7 |
| 5332.1 | 29182.1 | 12429.8 | 241637.0 | 88134.2 | 13964.8 |
| | | | 16963.1 | 1566.4 | 236.6 |
| | | | 29503.8 | 23534.8 | 3825.1 |
| 86.6 | | | 107653.6 | 73657.8 | 242.1 |
| | 0.3 | | 175156.9 | 86635.9 | 23180.5 |
| 72.6 | | | 47440.0 | 22628.9 | 7988.6 |
| | | | 2710.3 | 2486.1 | 1397.8 |
| | 228.4 | 125.3 | 122167.4 | 90520.8 | 7370.2 |
| 59247.4 | 238421.3 | 106082.6 | 7149784.4 | 2925741.5 | 747839.6 |
| 18075.0 | 100877.8 | 53486.7 | 1319787.5 | 524183.8 | 74590.3 |
| | 1168.5 | 1162.0 | 84653.9 | 60967.1 | 7179.1 |
| 3759.2 | 230.9 | 206.1 | 1207899.0 | 485556.6 | 171487.6 |
| 3881.9 | 80213.7 | 1741.8 | 392574.4 | 176549.5 | 79375.4 |
| 157.3 | 3427.7 | 2589.9 | 398845.4 | 152322.7 | 19360.5 |
| | 109.5 | | 34381.5 | 17070.9 | 4295.2 |
| 308.2 | 1363.8 | 30.0 | 337253.6 | 192530.8 | 37433.2 |
| 31480.4 | 33390.2 | 30442.2 | 2736093.8 | 958054.8 | 147796.5 |
| 1585.4 | 17639.2 | 16423.9 | 638295.3 | 358505.3 | 206321.8 |
| 3809.5 | 623.9 | 375.8 | 2215035.2 | 1746318.4 | 1176834.5 |
| 496.0 | 1.0 | | 60636.4 | 45237.7 | 8430.0 |
| | 0.6 | | 1420012.2 | 1194874.3 | 1028126.3 |
| | | | 5709.0 | 5236.4 | 73.7 |
| 312.4 | 184.4 | | 170263.5 | 83207.8 | 49710.2 |
| | 20.1 | | 54773.4 | 50191.1 | 25622.7 |
| | | | 68705.6 | 36227.7 | 19614.9 |
| | | | 24986.4 | 17213.0 | 227.6 |
| 1471.6 | 2.5 | | 239508.0 | 205450.6 | 33501.9 |
| 1529.5 | 415.3 | 375.8 | 170440.7 | 108679.8 | 11527.2 |
| | 2302.9 | 1014.0 | 1274010.2 | 791445.0 | 369082.2 |
| | 1983.6 | 1014.0 | 394939.8 | 317637.6 | 234827.4 |
| | | | 6809.7 | 5738.4 | 1500.2 |
| | 12.4 | | 42775.2 | 54818.9 | 48831.9 |
| | 211.5 | | 826217.2 | 411177.1 | 83117.9 |
| | 95.4 | | 3268.3 | 2073.0 | 804.8 |
| 28568.5 | 63252.5 | 13936.2 | 10904652.6 | 6395375.3 | 2291886.5 |
| 27239.6 | 19494.7 | 13931.2 | 9474912.5 | 5511689.1 | 1919274.3 |
| 237.3 | 168.0 | 5.0 | 159827.2 | 115517.5 | 45707.4 |
| | 139.7 | | 83816.1 | 60356.3 | 7264.7 |
| 1091.6 | 43450.1 | | 1186096.8 | 707812.4 | 319640.1 |

**表 15.6 续表 2 continued 2**

| 指　标 | Item | 二、期末资产负债 Assets and Liabilities | | |
|---|---|---|---|---|
| | | 负债合计 Total Liabilities | 所有者权益合计 Total Owner's Equity | 实收资本 Paid-up Capital |
| **总　计** | **Total** | **43849549.5** | **17617652.8** | **6058999.5** |
| **按批发行业小类分** | **By Wholesale Sector** | | | |
| 农、林、牧、渔产品批发 | Wholesale of Farm, Forestry and Animal Husbandry Products | 454477.8 | 288561.9 | 146268.7 |
| 谷物、豆及薯类批发 | Wholesale of Cereal, Bean and Tubers | 117313.8 | 124323.2 | 23770.0 |
| 种子批发 | Wholesale of Seeds | 12420.7 | 4542.4 | 4000.0 |
| 畜牧渔业饲料批发 | Wholesale of Feedstuff | 23417.3 | 6086.5 | 3385.9 |
| 棉、麻批发 | Wholesale of Cotton and Fiber Crops | 73561.0 | 34092.6 | 10598.0 |
| 林业产品批发 | Wholesale of Forestry Products | 91903.1 | 83253.8 | 61650.5 |
| 牲畜批发 | Wholesale of Livestock | 37814.7 | 9625.3 | 4400.0 |
| 渔业产品批发 | Wholesale of fishery products | 2486.1 | 224.2 | 188.0 |
| 其他农牧产品批发 | Wholesale of Other Farm Products and Livestock Products | 95561.1 | 26413.9 | 38276.3 |
| 食品、饮料及烟草制品批发 | Wholesale of Food, Beverages and Tobacco | 3180500.5 | 3926780.3 | 545392.8 |
| 米、面制品及食用油批发 | Wholesale of Rice, Flour and Edible Oil | 628511.0 | 652231.0 | 66289.7 |
| 糕点、糖果及糖批发 | Wholesale of Cake, Candy and Sugar | 64671.4 | 19982.5 | 13128.0 |
| 果品、蔬菜批发 | Wholesale of Fruits and Vegetables | 493941.0 | 712576.4 | 72508.9 |
| 肉、禽、蛋、奶及水产品批发 | Wholesale of Meat, Poultry, Eggs and Aquatic Products | 225459.2 | 167115.2 | 51177.4 |
| 盐及调味品批发 | Wholesale of Salts and Condiments | 175160.9 | 223924.6 | 193822.1 |
| 营养和保健品批发 | Wholesale of Nutraceutical Products | 24932.9 | 8637.2 | 4095.0 |
| 酒、饮料及茶叶批发 | Wholesale of Liquor, Beverages and Tea | 218363.9 | 117320.8 | 36752.0 |
| 烟草制品批发 | Wholesale of Tobacco | 983985.7 | 1752171.8 | 48675.7 |
| 其他食品批发 | Wholesale of other Food | 365474.5 | 272820.8 | 58944.0 |
| 纺织、服装及家庭用品批发 | Wholesale of Textiles, Garments and Household Articles | 1788220.0 | 429458.5 | 63865.1 |
| 纺织品、针织品及原料批发 | Wholesale of Textiles, Knitwear and Raw Materials | 47487.7 | 13148.7 | 16286.1 |
| 服装批发 | Wholesale of Garments | 1198978.3 | 221033.9 | 4979.7 |
| 鞋帽批发 | Wholesale of Shoes and Hats | 4543.5 | 1165.5 | 908.7 |
| 化妆品及卫生用品批发 | Wholesale of Cosmetics and Sanitary Articles | 87671.8 | 82591.7 | 14300.0 |
| 厨具卫具及日用杂品批发 | Wholesale of Kitchenware, sanitary ware and daily necessities | 49899.6 | 4873.8 | 5712.5 |
| 灯具、装饰物品批发 | Wholesale of Light Fittings and Decorative Articles | 45422.7 | 23282.9 | 1000.0 |
| 家用视听设备批发 | Wholesale of Household Audio-visual Equipments | 19095.8 | 5890.6 | 1578.0 |
| 日用家电批发 | Wholesale of Household Electrical Appliances | 224079.2 | 18072.1 | 13065.2 |
| 其他家庭用品批发 | Wholesale of Other Household Articles | 111041.4 | 59399.3 | 6034.9 |
| 文化、体育用品及器材批发 | Wholesale of Cultural and Sports Articles and Equipment | 836635.0 | 460711.8 | 102744.8 |
| 文具用品批发 | Wholesale of Cultural Articles | 322980.9 | 71958.9 | 26428.0 |
| 体育用品及器材批发 | Wholesale of Sports Articles | 5740.9 | 1068.8 | 500.0 |
| 图书批发 | Wholesale of Books | 55152.0 | -12376.8 | 23077.9 |
| 首饰、工艺品及收藏品批发 | Wholesale of Jewelry, Handicrafts and Collections | 450688.2 | 398865.6 | 52308.9 |
| 其他文化用品批发 | Wholesale of Other Cultural Goods | 2073.0 | 1195.3 | 430.0 |
| 医药及医疗器材批发 | Wholesale of Medicines and Medical Appliances | 6857498.5 | 4045375.0 | 819058.2 |
| 西药批发 | Wholesale of Western Medicines | 5913402.7 | 3560927.7 | 637368.0 |
| 中药批发 | Wholesale of Traditional Chinese Medicines | 129713.2 | 30114.0 | 29778.3 |
| 动物用药品批发 | Wholesale of Animal Drugs | 60356.3 | 23459.8 | 10754.8 |
| 医疗用品及器材批发 | Wholesale of Medical Articles and Appliances | 754026.3 | 430873.5 | 141157.1 |

单位：万元 (10 000 yuan)

| 二、期末资产负债 Assets and Liabilities | 三、损益及分配 Profits and Losses | | | | |
|---|---|---|---|---|---|
| 个人资本 Personal Capital | 营业收入 Gross Sales | 主营业务收入 Main Business Income | 营业成本 Operating Cost | 税金及附加 Taxes and Surcharges | 其他业务利润 Other Business Profits |
| **854580.5** | **145747552.1** | **144292598.9** | **134488282.2** | **1219216.6** | **183566.6** |
| 3463.0 | 1258131.5 | 1237241.2 | 1197526.8 | 2541.4 | 1359.9 |
| 100.0 | 250320.7 | 242075.5 | 237782.2 | 404.5 | 1310.8 |
| | 52734.4 | 50658.9 | 49396.6 | 4.4 | |
| 313.0 | 180806.8 | 180600.7 | 171306.6 | 421.3 | |
| | 315604.1 | 315604.1 | 313525.8 | 320.0 | |
| 1800.0 | 142754.8 | 140703.3 | 129225.2 | 822.7 | |
| 1000.0 | 31802.9 | 31802.9 | 29170.2 | 25.8 | |
| | 6567.8 | 6567.8 | 6315.4 | 1.3 | |
| 250.0 | 277540.0 | 269228.0 | 260804.8 | 541.4 | 49.1 |
| 85315.7 | 17760813.3 | 17562647.3 | 14744827.8 | 1031112.8 | 55656.2 |
| 6758.6 | 2475209.6 | 2433956.7 | 2364379.7 | 4035.9 | 8800.5 |
| 3748.9 | 229254.7 | 226924.8 | 202318.2 | 362.8 | 109.6 |
| 28426.0 | 2336042.2 | 2323963.8 | 2067615.6 | 3541.3 | 637.8 |
| 17497.5 | 1066443.7 | 1061395.7 | 977618.0 | 1976.4 | 12.2 |
| 3397.1 | 328789.9 | 316879.6 | 273069.0 | 1528.7 | 9593.8 |
| 200.0 | 63718.1 | 50429.5 | 52651.6 | 341.2 | |
| 5832.4 | 851479.1 | 826702.9 | 665328.4 | 3879.9 | 124.4 |
| | 8047533.4 | 7998628.8 | 5932632.7 | 1011381.5 | 6011.9 |
| 19455.2 | 2362342.6 | 2323765.5 | 2209214.6 | 4065.1 | 30366.0 |
| 13346.0 | 7126970.8 | 7041124.3 | 6584378.5 | 9725.3 | 18149.3 |
| 2008.0 | 625799.1 | 625785.1 | 621204.9 | 534.8 | |
| 1800.0 | 4768098.6 | 4764920.1 | 4396401.5 | 6343.2 | 17241.1 |
| 500.0 | 20506.5 | 20506.5 | 18443.6 | 128.4 | |
| 1500.0 | 247705.4 | 242430.1 | 204621.5 | 1172.4 | 220.8 |
| 2150.0 | 58950.8 | 58921.0 | 48266.8 | 94.8 | 202.2 |
| | 98050.9 | 96748.3 | 80129.9 | 241.7 | 214.9 |
| 1578.0 | 35718.0 | 35710.0 | 29254.8 | 76.7 | |
| 3730.0 | 1010476.3 | 936407.2 | 974488.5 | 472.8 | 33.3 |
| 80.0 | 261665.2 | 259696.0 | 211567.0 | 660.5 | 237.0 |
| 2598.0 | 1699883.8 | 1646612.9 | 1445156.1 | 10037.4 | 1214.1 |
| 2088.0 | 594245.3 | 592864.9 | 560084.3 | 1294.2 | 25.4 |
| | 19822.6 | 19822.6 | 18574.1 | 10.0 | |
| | 32244.3 | 31489.6 | 22588.3 | 26.4 | 13.0 |
| 100.0 | 1049591.8 | 999070.5 | 840720.1 | 8699.3 | 561.2 |
| 410.0 | 3979.8 | 3365.3 | 3189.3 | 7.5 | 614.5 |
| 241438.4 | 12635560.3 | 12579301.5 | 10802236.6 | 37432.5 | 20615.0 |
| 216325.9 | 10717463.9 | 10670524.1 | 9189437.8 | 31949.7 | 19916.3 |
| 4580.0 | 271595.6 | 270236.1 | 245144.1 | 509.7 | 665.5 |
| 3007.0 | 56035.3 | 55569.2 | 47789.2 | 137.8 | |
| 17525.5 | 1590465.5 | 1582972.1 | 1319865.5 | 4835.3 | 33.2 |

**表 15.6 续表 3 continued 3**

| 指 标 | Item | 三、损益及分配 Profits and Losses 销售费用 Sales Expenses | 管理费用 Management Expenses | 研发费用 R&D expenses |
|---|---|---|---|---|
| **总 计** | **Total** | **3560113.7** | **1434777.9** | **51292.1** |
| **按批发行业小类分** | **By Wholesale Sector** | | | |
| 农、林、牧、渔产品批发 | Wholesale of Farm, Forestry and Animal Husbandry Products | 21155.9 | 21324.3 | 56.4 |
| 谷物、豆及薯类批发 | Wholesale of Cereal, Bean and Tubers | 6738.4 | 10545.2 | |
| 种子批发 | Wholesale of Seeds | 1892.1 | 1243.5 | 2.8 |
| 畜牧渔业饲料批发 | Wholesale of Feedstuff | 3933.8 | 2468.6 | |
| 棉、麻批发 | Wholesale of Cotton and Fiber Crops | 469.7 | 805.4 | 53.3 |
| 林业产品批发 | Wholesale of Forestry Products | 2604.8 | 3041.2 | 0.1 |
| 牲畜批发 | Wholesale of Livestock | 585.1 | 952.4 | |
| 渔业产品批发 | Wholesale of fishery products | 47.1 | 174.8 | 0.2 |
| 其他农牧产品批发 | Wholesale of Other Farm Products and Livestock Products | 4884.9 | 2093.2 | |
| 食品、饮料及烟草制品批发 | Wholesale of Food, Beverages and Tobacco | 552764.4 | 522779.9 | 4766.6 |
| 米、面制品及食用油批发 | Wholesale of Rice, Flour and Edible Oil | 44278.0 | 40128.7 | 490.7 |
| 糕点、糖果及糖批发 | Wholesale of Cake, Candy and Sugar | 17421.3 | 7048.3 | 0.1 |
| 果品、蔬菜批发 | Wholesale of Fruits and Vegetables | 22245.4 | 31368.5 | 38.8 |
| 肉、禽、蛋、奶及水产品批发 | Wholesale of Meat, Poultry, Eggs and Aquatic Products | 48817.8 | 19352.0 | 2.2 |
| 盐及调味品批发 | Wholesale of Salts and Condiments | 30888.7 | 10818.4 | 127.9 |
| 营养和保健品批发 | Wholesale of Nutraceutical Products | 6195.5 | 3709.5 | |
| 酒、饮料及茶叶批发 | Wholesale of Liquor, Beverages and Tea | 115129.5 | 28670.1 | 357.0 |
| 烟草制品批发 | Wholesale of Tobacco | 189582.0 | 362512.9 | 3739.5 |
| 其他食品批发 | Wholesale of other Food | 78206.2 | 19171.5 | 10.4 |
| 纺织、服装及家庭用品批发 | Wholesale of Textiles, Garments and Household Articles | 242110.4 | 72238.0 | 70.2 |
| 纺织品、针织品及原料批发 | Wholesale of Textiles, Knitwear and Raw Materials | 1569.8 | 2550.6 | 70.2 |
| 服装批发 | Wholesale of Garments | 140715.2 | 45209.6 | |
| 鞋帽批发 | Wholesale of Shoes and Hats | 444.6 | 829.0 | |
| 化妆品及卫生用品批发 | Wholesale of Cosmetics and Sanitary Articles | 43593.6 | 5367.0 | |
| 厨具卫具及日用杂品批发 | Wholesale of Kitchenware, sanitary ware and daily necessities | 4781.2 | 3486.0 | |
| 灯具、装饰物品批发 | Wholesale of Light Fittings and Decorative Articles | 6806.9 | 1226.9 | |
| 家用视听设备批发 | Wholesale of Household Audio-visual Equipments | 2713.7 | 3710.1 | |
| 日用家电批发 | Wholesale of Household Electrical Appliances | 22003.9 | 7634.4 | |
| 其他家庭用品批发 | Wholesale of Other Household Articles | 19481.5 | 2224.4 | |
| 文化、体育用品及器材批发 | Wholesale of Cultural and Sports Articles and Equipment | 97004.8 | 33435.8 | 490.5 |
| 文具用品批发 | Wholesale of Cultural Articles | 12324.7 | 11489.8 | 490.4 |
| 体育用品及器材批发 | Wholesale of Sports Articles | 1574.5 | 159.4 | |
| 图书批发 | Wholesale of Books | 7023.9 | 1587.0 | |
| 首饰、工艺品及收藏品批发 | Wholesale of Jewelry, Handicrafts and Collections | 75981.4 | 19481.9 | 0.1 |
| 其他文化用品批发 | Wholesale of Other Cultural Goods | 100.3 | 717.7 | |
| 医药及医疗器材批发 | Wholesale of Medicines and Medical Appliances | 516812.4 | 231942.9 | 6164.4 |
| 西药批发 | Wholesale of Western Medicines | 392249.0 | 152390.3 | 3043.5 |
| 中药批发 | Wholesale of Traditional Chinese Medicines | 14311.9 | 9863.9 | 301.3 |
| 动物用药品批发 | Wholesale of Animal Drugs | 5370.1 | 2118.7 | |
| 医疗用品及器材批发 | Wholesale of Medical Articles and Appliances | 104881.4 | 67570.0 | 2819.6 |

单位：万元 (10 000 yuan)

三、损益及分配 Profits and Losses

| 财务费用 Financial Expenses | | | 投资收益 Income from Investment | 营业利润 Business Profits | 营业外收入 Non-business Income |
|---|---|---|---|---|---|
| | 利息收入 Interest Income | 利息费用 Interest expenses | | | |
| **184209.5** | **302777.0** | **385511.6** | **229417.2** | **3412977.2** | **187902.5** |
| 4711.8 | 4575.1 | 991.1 | 1226.8 | 17847.4 | 4752.3 |
| 718.7 | 874.2 | 1131.7 | 302.1 | 872.9 | 4171.1 |
| 16.1 | 0.5 | 6.4 | | 184.6 | 55.8 |
| 311.7 | 12.1 | 273.0 | | 2498.9 | 112.1 |
| -64.1 | 3108.8 | -2893.5 | 219.4 | 722.4 | 2.0 |
| 993.0 | 107.2 | 514.5 | | 6385.9 | 118.1 |
| 1023.3 | | 56.2 | 45.9 | 1870.8 | 8.4 |
| 12.3 | | 10.7 | | 16.6 | 0.3 |
| 1700.8 | 472.3 | 1892.1 | 659.4 | 5295.3 | 284.5 |
| -33132.1 | 82353.9 | 28235.8 | 412.7 | 938506.4 | 10091.3 |
| -302.0 | 15001.1 | 12982.9 | -1547.8 | 32420.3 | 2560.6 |
| 606.2 | 83.1 | 523.1 | 255.3 | 1726.6 | 231.8 |
| 13429.2 | -99.7 | 7781.3 | -35.1 | 209818.3 | 1185.2 |
| 2835.4 | 9248.0 | 1592.8 | 1973.4 | 18215.6 | 626.2 |
| 725.9 | 2976.3 | 2789.2 | 1463.6 | 14700.6 | 1012.7 |
| 118.7 | 7.5 | 43.7 | | 505.7 | 60.7 |
| 1515.5 | 491.2 | 741.7 | | 27022.3 | 1817.2 |
| -53665.6 | 54449.2 | 762.4 | 402.6 | 585824.9 | 613.4 |
| 1604.6 | 197.2 | 1018.7 | -2099.3 | 48272.1 | 1983.5 |
| -4702.0 | 13223.3 | 5928.5 | 3741.0 | 234574.6 | 2676.2 |
| -480.6 | 4214.5 | 3621.7 | -200.8 | 498.0 | 47.4 |
| -9938.5 | 8212.7 | -1762.3 | 2818.4 | 199446.5 | 864.7 |
| 12.1 | -18.6 | | | 648.8 | 2.4 |
| 359.7 | 201.7 | 430.9 | 1100.9 | -4614.0 | 172.1 |
| 481.5 | 6.4 | 173.4 | 16.8 | 1531.5 | 56.1 |
| 510.3 | | 0.8 | | 8304.7 | |
| 35.8 | 78.5 | 90.2 | | -73.1 | 98.5 |
| 3063.6 | 451.5 | 3134.2 | 5.7 | -1244.1 | 87.5 |
| 1254.1 | 76.6 | 239.6 | | 30076.3 | 1347.5 |
| 1297.3 | 1619.0 | 1047.9 | 244.0 | 121139.7 | 8559.7 |
| -183.2 | 1008.8 | 245.2 | 244.0 | 10298.5 | 358.9 |
| -11.5 | | -11.5 | | -441.8 | 27.9 |
| 57.2 | -78.4 | 192.4 | | 1022.6 | 21.5 |
| 1442.3 | 679.1 | 619.8 | | 110288.0 | 8151.4 |
| -7.5 | 9.5 | 2.0 | | -27.6 | |
| 62003.0 | 53513.3 | 100068.6 | 69234.6 | 1029971.7 | 6657.7 |
| 52184.5 | 52347.5 | 91076.8 | 66945.5 | 930663.5 | 4748.9 |
| 940.0 | 44.6 | 536.3 | | 1621.2 | 101.4 |
| -35.0 | 39.3 | 508.8 | 2863.2 | 3517.2 | 217.9 |
| 8913.5 | 1081.9 | 7946.7 | -574.1 | 94169.8 | 1589.5 |

**表 15.6 续表 4 continued 4**

| 指 标 | Item | 三、损益及分配 Profits and Losses<br>营业外支出 Non-business Expenses | 利润总额 Total Profits |
|---|---|---|---|
| **总 计** | **Total** | **65454.8** | **3534566.4** |
| **按批发行业小类分** | **By Wholesale Sector** | | |
| 农、林、牧、渔产品批发 | Wholesale of Farm, Forestry and Animal Husbandry Products | 415.2 | 22184.5 |
| 谷物、豆及薯类批发 | Wholesale of Cereal, Bean and Tubers | 141.0 | 4903.0 |
| 种子批发 | Wholesale of Seeds | 45.2 | 195.2 |
| 畜牧渔业饲料批发 | Wholesale of Feedstuff | 60.6 | 2550.4 |
| 棉、麻批发 | Wholesale of Cotton and Fiber Crops | 0.6 | 723.8 |
| 林业产品批发 | Wholesale of Forestry Products | 3.3 | 6500.7 |
| 牲畜批发 | Wholesale of Livestock | 73.6 | 1805.6 |
| 渔业产品批发 | Wholesale of fishery products | 0.3 | 16.6 |
| 其他农牧产品批发 | Wholesale of Other Farm Products and Livestock Products | 90.6 | 5489.2 |
| 食品、饮料及烟草制品批发 | Wholesale of Food, Beverages and Tobacco | 12527.5 | 936377.3 |
| 米、面制品及食用油批发 | Wholesale of Rice, Flour and Edible Oil | 831.9 | 34149.0 |
| 糕点、糖果及糖批发 | Wholesale of Cake, Candy and Sugar | 617.1 | 1358.6 |
| 果品、蔬菜批发 | Wholesale of Fruits and Vegetables | 257.7 | 210745.8 |
| 肉、禽、蛋、奶及水产品批发 | Wholesale of Meat, Poultry, Eggs and Aquatic Products | 821.3 | 18312.2 |
| 盐及调味品批发 | Wholesale of Salts and Condiments | 228.7 | 15484.6 |
| 营养和保健品批发 | Wholesale of Nutraceutical Products | 324.5 | 241.9 |
| 酒、饮料及茶叶批发 | Wholesale of Liquor, Beverages and Tea | 255.3 | 28584.1 |
| 烟草制品批发 | Wholesale of Tobacco | 9003.2 | 577433.3 |
| 其他食品批发 | Wholesale of other Food | 187.8 | 50067.8 |
| 纺织、服装及家庭用品批发 | Wholesale of Textiles, Garments and Household Articles | 15901.1 | 221346.4 |
| 纺织品、针织品及原料批发 | Wholesale of Textiles, Knitwear and Raw Materials | 11.4 | 533.9 |
| 服装批发 | Wholesale of Garments | 15540.6 | 184770.6 |
| 鞋帽批发 | Wholesale of Shoes and Hats | | 651.2 |
| 化妆品及卫生用品批发 | Wholesale of Cosmetics and Sanitary Articles | 79.7 | -4521.6 |
| 厨具卫具及日用杂品批发 | Wholesale of Kitchenware, sanitary ware and daily necessities | 32.7 | 1551.7 |
| 灯具、装饰物品批发 | Wholesale of Light Fittings and Decorative Articles | 161.0 | 8143.7 |
| 家用视听设备批发 | Wholesale of Household Audio-visual Equipments | 38.0 | -12.6 |
| 日用家电批发 | Wholesale of Household Electrical Appliances | 36.3 | -1192.9 |
| 其他家庭用品批发 | Wholesale of Other Household Articles | 1.4 | 31422.4 |
| 文化、体育用品及器材批发 | Wholesale of Cultural and Sports Articles and Equipment | 500.6 | 129198.8 |
| 文具用品批发 | Wholesale of Cultural Articles | 148.5 | 10508.9 |
| 体育用品及器材批发 | Wholesale of Sports Articles | | -413.9 |
| 图书批发 | Wholesale of Books | 3.0 | 1041.1 |
| 首饰、工艺品及收藏品批发 | Wholesale of Jewelry, Handicrafts and Collections | 233.1 | 118206.3 |
| 其他文化用品批发 | Wholesale of Other Cultural Goods | 116.0 | -143.6 |
| 医药及医疗器材批发 | Wholesale of Medicines and Medical Appliances | 12007.1 | 1022270.7 |
| 西药批发 | Wholesale of Western Medicines | 10519.0 | 922541.9 |
| 中药批发 | Wholesale of Traditional Chinese Medicines | 289.0 | 1433.6 |
| 动物用药品批发 | Wholesale of Animal Drugs | 118.2 | 3616.9 |
| 医疗用品及器材批发 | Wholesale of Medical Articles and Appliances | 1080.9 | 94678.3 |

单位：万元 (10 000 yuan)

| 三、损益及分配 Profits and Losses | 四、人工成本及增值税 Labor cost and Value-added Tax | | 五、从事批发和零售业活动的从业人员平均人数（人） Annual Average Employees Engaged in wholesale and retail activities (persons) |
|---|---|---|---|
| 所得税费用 Income Tax Payable | 应付职工薪酬 Employee compensation | 应交增值税 Value-added Tax | |
| **572454.4** | **1355435.8** | **1097127.0** | **120272** |
| 1802.3 | 20717.5 | 13600.1 | 2270 |
| 520.3 | 9138.2 | 900.4 | 620 |
| 69.3 | 437.7 | 318.8 | 71 |
| 166.0 | 1819.1 | 557.1 | 200 |
| 5.2 | 935.3 | 168.4 | 113 |
| 603.1 | 4008.6 | 1004.8 | 692 |
| 28.3 | 1423.1 | | 173 |
| 0.5 | 116.5 | 5.9 | 23 |
| 409.6 | 2839.0 | 10644.7 | 378 |
| 168645.4 | 382552.4 | 327332.8 | 28687 |
| 3396.1 | 30725.3 | 7097.8 | 3401 |
| 569.1 | 8396.3 | 854.2 | 1178 |
| 28973.1 | 21733.8 | 20940.5 | 4274 |
| 2282.3 | 22807.5 | 4585.0 | 3175 |
| 1317.8 | 20610.0 | 4708.5 | 1843 |
| 149.8 | 2579.9 | 938.0 | 409 |
| 3470.5 | 35190.8 | 14928.8 | 3596 |
| 121830.0 | 205680.0 | 254600.4 | 7083 |
| 6656.7 | 34828.8 | 18679.6 | 3728 |
| 34011.3 | 54440.9 | 44520.9 | 7102 |
| 83.3 | 1818.0 | 460.5 | 281 |
| 27048.1 | 6917.1 | 32171.0 | 1240 |
| 14.1 | 554.9 | 1020.9 | 90 |
| 27.4 | 13049.2 | 8596.6 | 1396 |
| 40.9 | 3918.1 | 704.8 | 855 |
| 1888.3 | 4979.3 | 1653.6 | 284 |
| 17.9 | 2585.3 | 360.4 | 773 |
| 117.3 | 9551.3 | -4462.0 | 1432 |
| 4774.0 | 11067.7 | 4015.1 | 751 |
| 20430.7 | 75672.0 | 28590.8 | 5530 |
| 1586.8 | 8273.3 | 6824.0 | 912 |
| 2.2 | 63.0 | 3.5 | 8 |
| | 4142.2 | 13.1 | 224 |
| 18841.7 | 62527.5 | 21696.0 | 4269 |
| | 666.0 | 54.2 | 117 |
| 146745.5 | 239634.7 | 220332.0 | 23864 |
| 130826.4 | 181364.7 | 178451.7 | 18700 |
| 347.8 | 9737.7 | 3138.5 | 1378 |
| -38.0 | 2100.7 | 599.9 | 127 |
| 15609.3 | 46431.6 | 38141.9 | 3659 |

**表 15.6 续表 5 continued 5**

| 指 标 | Item | 法人企业数(个) Number of Enterprises (unit) | 执行《2006年企业会计准则》企业数(个) Number of Enterprises which Implemented Accounting standard for Business Enterprise in 2006 (unit) | 一、年初存货 Inventory at the Beginning of Year |
|---|---|---|---|---|
| 矿产品、建材及化工产品批发 | Wholesale of Mineral Products, Building Materials and Chemical Products | 1648 | 870 | 1681012.9 |
| 煤炭及制品批发 | Wholesale of Coal and Related Products | 148 | 76 | 91830.7 |
| 石油及制品批发 | Wholesale of Petroleum and Related Products | 126 | 84 | 273942.8 |
| 非金属矿及制品批发 | Wholesale of Nonmetal Mineral and Related Products | 16 | 8 | 12035.2 |
| 金属及金属矿批发 | Wholesale of Metal and Metal Mineral | 546 | 304 | 580564.4 |
| 建材批发 | Wholesale of Building Materials | 504 | 235 | 204052.0 |
| 化肥批发 | Wholesale of Fertilizers | 61 | 32 | 375875.4 |
| 农药批发 | Wholesale of Pesticides | 3 | | 343.1 |
| 农用薄膜批发 | Wholesale of Films for Agriculture | 1 | | 12.1 |
| 其他化工产品批发 | Wholesale of Other Chemical Products | 243 | 131 | 142357.2 |
| 机械设备、五金产品及电子产品批发 | Wholesale of Machinery, Hardware and Electronic Products | 467 | 296 | 1221824.6 |
| 农业机械批发 | Wholesale of Agricultural Machinery | 9 | 5 | 527.4 |
| 汽车及零配件批发 | Wholesale of Automobile Fittings | 138 | 83 | 289421.9 |
| 摩托车及零配件批发 | Wholesale of Motorcycle and Fittings | 61 | 41 | 52066.8 |
| 五金产品批发 | Wholesale of Hardware | 37 | 22 | 13596.7 |
| 电气设备批发 | Wholesale of Electric Equipment | 28 | 18 | 9219.8 |
| 计算机、软件及辅助设备批发 | Wholesale of Computers, Software and Assistant Equipment | 25 | 21 | 483216.3 |
| 通信器材批发 | Wholesale of Communication Equipment | 62 | 37 | 222552.6 |
| 广播影视设备批发 | Wholesale of Broadcast and TV Equipment | 6 | 4 | 11053.9 |
| 其他机械设备及电子产品批发 | Wholesale of Other Machinery and Electronic Products | 101 | 65 | 140169.2 |
| 贸易经纪与代理 | Trade Broker and Agency | 11 | 9 | 81724.8 |
| 贸易代理 | Trade Agency | 11 | 9 | 81724.8 |
| 其他批发业 | Other Wholesales | 101 | 56 | 74813.8 |
| 再生物资回收与批发 | Wholesale of Recycled Materials | 65 | 37 | 43860.5 |
| 宠物食品用品批发 | Pet Food and Supplies Wholesale | 2 | 2 | 10369.5 |
| 互联网批发 | Wholesale of Internet Device | 13 | 7 | 8660.2 |
| 其他未列明批发业 | Other Wholesale not Classified Elsewhere | 21 | 10 | 11923.6 |
| **按登记注册类型分** | **By Status of Registration** | | | |
| 内资企业 | Domestic-funded Enterprises | 3432 | 1998 | 5385035.6 |
| 国有企业 | State-owned Enterprises | 77 | 71 | 561384.1 |
| 集体企业 | Collective-owned Enterprises | 4 | 4 | 724.5 |
| 股份合作企业 | Cooperative Enterprises | 3 | 3 | 19373.9 |
| 联营企业 | Joint Ownership Enterprises | 3 | 3 | 33593.9 |
| 国有联营企业 | State Joint Ownership Enterprises | 3 | 3 | 33593.9 |
| 有限责任公司 | Limited Liability Corporations | 378 | 298 | 1379427.0 |
| 国有独资公司 | State Sole Funded Corporations | 70 | 64 | 439230.5 |
| 其他有限责任公司 | Other Limited Liability Corporations | 308 | 234 | 940196.5 |
| 股份有限公司 | Share-holding Corporations Ltd. | 42 | 34 | 297920.0 |
| 私营企业 | Private Enterprises | 2922 | 1585 | 3092597.1 |
| 私营独资企业 | Private-funded Enterprises | 27 | 10 | 1824.0 |
| 私营合伙企业 | Private Partnership Enterprises | 1 | 1 | |
| 私营有限责任公司 | Private Limited Liability Corporations | 2862 | 1549 | 2340490.9 |
| 私营股份有限公司 | Private Share-holding Corporations Ltd. | 32 | 25 | 750282.2 |
| 其他企业 | Other Enterprises | 3 | | 15.1 |

单位：万元 (10 000 yuan)

| 二、期末资产负债 Assets and Liabilities | | | | | |
|---|---|---|---|---|---|
| 流动资产合计 Total Current Assets | 应收账款 Accounts Receivable | 存货 Inventory | 固定资产原价 Total Original Value of Fixed Assets | 房屋和构筑物 Buildings and Structures | 机器设备 Machinery and Equipments |
| 17815059.2 | 3936235.0 | 2124060.0 | 1224401.2 | 354434.1 | 170278.7 |
| 1233399.4 | 372285.7 | 97888.2 | 94909.7 | 34440.0 | 36241.7 |
| 1255848.9 | 228064.8 | 346885.6 | 608159.8 | 96936.9 | 67361.8 |
| 121820.5 | 51648.2 | 11982.7 | 10297.4 | 6325.1 | 192.9 |
| 7874093.6 | 1393325.6 | 548132.7 | 235371.6 | 102955.6 | 25362.7 |
| 4221051.5 | 1085096.7 | 602773.9 | 133146.7 | 48648.3 | 26539.5 |
| 1243653.3 | 149090.6 | 348983.7 | 39983.5 | 28794.3 | 4942.3 |
| 2547.7 | 723.1 | 336.0 | 1499.9 | | |
| 367.3 | 28.4 | 10.8 | 50.0 | 18.0 | 5.2 |
| 1862277.0 | 655971.9 | 167066.4 | 100982.6 | 36315.9 | 9632.6 |
| 14237227.7 | 4468908.3 | 1484734.7 | 545093.4 | 163159.4 | 266215.4 |
| 8117.8 | 3191.2 | 501.1 | 1028.7 | 599.0 | 176.5 |
| 7067963.7 | 1680060.7 | 432082.4 | 383852.0 | 78264.9 | 234453.0 |
| 1263721.3 | 277799.7 | 66954.4 | 15776.6 | 3011.7 | 9874.2 |
| 146583.9 | 91606.1 | 14139.1 | 16047.6 | 1365.4 | 3778.5 |
| 117761.9 | 46112.8 | 15337.5 | 59867.1 | 46587.9 | 2499.8 |
| 2025355.8 | 740195.9 | 501453.9 | 13442.6 | 8103.4 | 3443.5 |
| 1194416.0 | 266947.6 | 279287.6 | 14050.5 | 12437.4 | 746.6 |
| 26579.4 | 8911.7 | 6685.7 | 2306.7 | 904.0 | 979.5 |
| 2386727.9 | 1354082.6 | 168293.0 | 38721.6 | 11885.7 | 10263.8 |
| 291716.6 | 15134.3 | 26331.7 | 798.0 | | 83.5 |
| 291716.6 | 15134.3 | 26331.7 | 798.0 | | 83.5 |
| 680349.5 | 143779.3 | 81772.2 | 102992.3 | 19948.9 | 60463.1 |
| 296457.2 | 94048.0 | 44209.2 | 90345.8 | 17047.2 | 57468.1 |
| 27079.1 | 6566.1 | 9475.8 | 37.3 | 9.5 | 27.8 |
| 187884.2 | 10783.3 | 13917.6 | 1133.6 | | 150.6 |
| 168929.0 | 32381.9 | 14169.6 | 11475.6 | 2892.2 | 2816.6 |
| 48239035.8 | 14508937.7 | 6041073.2 | 3145183.5 | 1171365.8 | 605090.1 |
| 3884772.2 | 317621.2 | 531959.0 | 1018546.3 | 197823.8 | 248096.5 |
| 4421.1 | 2616.5 | 953.7 | 315.5 | 3.8 | 32.2 |
| 111177.4 | 43005.7 | 19362.7 | 16979.0 | 14387.0 | |
| 494755.0 | 53085.1 | 22306.9 | 7426.5 | | |
| 494755.0 | 53085.1 | 22306.9 | 7426.5 | | |
| 15141936.5 | 4073443.4 | 1937445.5 | 737618.4 | 322243.3 | 130699.6 |
| 2891367.2 | 496159.4 | 475283.9 | 357159.4 | 143437.6 | 39044.8 |
| 12250569.3 | 3577284.0 | 1462161.6 | 380459.0 | 178805.7 | 91654.8 |
| 3580594.4 | 375703.6 | 364151.4 | 200456.4 | 120892.4 | 24084.3 |
| 25021111.4 | 9643401.5 | 3164879.8 | 1163022.3 | 516015.5 | 202177.5 |
| 162240.0 | 18354.8 | 2668.9 | 3753.8 | 1395.0 | 132.7 |
| 9609.1 | 7681.2 | | 294.0 | | |
| 20127119.9 | 6661338.1 | 2341151.3 | 1104838.2 | 480016.1 | 192949.9 |
| 4722142.4 | 2956027.4 | 821059.6 | 54136.3 | 34604.4 | 9094.9 |
| 267.8 | 60.7 | 14.2 | 819.1 | | |

**表 15.6 续表 6 continued 6**

| 指标 | Item | 二、期末资产负债 Assets and Liabilities | | |
|---|---|---|---|---|
| | | 累计折旧 Cumulative Depreciation | 本年折旧 Depreciation | 固定资产净额 Net Value of Fixed Assets |
| 矿产品、建材及化工产品批发 | Wholesale of Mineral Products, Building Materials and Chemical Products | 495740.6 | 70652.3 | 664654.3 |
| 煤炭及制品批发 | Wholesale of Coal and Related Products | 56374.3 | 4458.9 | 30157.3 |
| 石油及制品批发 | Wholesale of Petroleum and Related Products | 248405.2 | 35404.6 | 347609.7 |
| 非金属矿及制品批发 | Wholesale of Nonmetal Mineral and Related Products | 3904.6 | 575.9 | 6367.9 |
| 金属及金属矿批发 | Wholesale of Metal and Metal Mineral | 77614.2 | 13510.1 | 143727.7 |
| 建材批发 | Wholesale of Building Materials | 49099.1 | 8528.3 | 63554.3 |
| 化肥批发 | Wholesale of Fertilizers | 11381.2 | 1187.5 | 24679.6 |
| 农药批发 | Wholesale of Pesticides | 1299.1 | 583.9 | |
| 农用薄膜批发 | Wholesale of Films for Agriculture | 31.4 | 1.0 | 18.6 |
| 其他化工产品批发 | Wholesale of Other Chemical Products | 47631.5 | 6402.1 | 48539.2 |
| 机械设备、五金产品及电子产品批发 | Wholesale of Machinery, Hardware and Electronic Products | 253812.4 | 35190.2 | 267645.8 |
| 农业机械批发 | Wholesale of Agricultural Machinery | 440.7 | 38.4 | 453.9 |
| 汽车及零配件批发 | Wholesale of Automobile Fittings | 181873.8 | 25854.5 | 182888.2 |
| 摩托车及零配件批发 | Wholesale of Motorcycle and Fittings | 11408.5 | 723.8 | 4269.3 |
| 五金产品批发 | Wholesale of Hardware | 8910.0 | 1259.0 | 6091.6 |
| 电气设备批发 | Wholesale of Electric Equipment | 22565.3 | 4574.7 | 36593.7 |
| 计算机、软件及辅助设备批发 | Wholesale of Computers, Software and Assistant Equipment | 7565.0 | 430.5 | 5811.4 |
| 通信设备批发 | Wholesale of Communication Equipment | 1868.5 | 831.7 | 11576.7 |
| 广播影视设备批发 | Wholesale of Broadcast and TV Equipment | 1195.7 | 209.3 | 1110.9 |
| 其他机械设备及电子产品批发 | Wholesale of Other Machinery and Electronic Products | 17984.9 | 1268.3 | 18850.1 |
| 贸易经纪与代理 | Trade Broker and Agency | 629.5 | 56.6 | 43.9 |
| 贸易代理 | Trade Agency | 629.5 | 56.6 | 43.9 |
| 其他批发业 | Other Wholesales | 29837.5 | 5359.6 | 69797.5 |
| 再生物资回收与批发 | Wholesale of Recycled Materials | 24169.5 | 4594.0 | 63502.8 |
| 宠物食品用品批发 | Pet Food and Supplies Wholesale | 26.3 | 7.5 | 2.1 |
| 互联网批发 | Wholesale of Internet Device | 401.3 | 146.8 | 732.2 |
| 其他未列明批发业 | Other Wholesale not Classified Elsewhere | 5240.4 | 611.3 | 5560.4 |
| **按登记注册类型分** | **By Status of Registration** | | | |
| 内资企业 | Domestic-funded Enterprises | 1260533.9 | 172111.7 | 1695167.7 |
| 国有企业 | State-owned Enterprises | 486727.1 | 51188.5 | 481644.2 |
| 集体企业 | Collective-owned Enterprises | 227.3 | 34.9 | 88.0 |
| 股份合作企业 | Cooperative Enterprises | 7678.2 | 681.0 | 8995.0 |
| 联营企业 | Joint Ownership Enterprises | 937.9 | 321.4 | 6488.6 |
| 国有联营企业 | State Joint Ownership Enterprises | 937.9 | 321.4 | 6488.6 |
| 有限责任公司 | Limited Liability Corporations | 273888.6 | 32594.1 | 429946.3 |
| 国有独资公司 | State Sole Funded Corporations | 128155.5 | 13046.5 | 210698.3 |
| 其他有限责任公司 | Other Limited Liability Corporations | 145733.1 | 19547.6 | 219248.0 |
| 股份有限公司 | Share-holding Corporations Ltd. | 59472.0 | 12163.9 | 128335.8 |
| 私营企业 | Private Enterprises | 431504.5 | 75108.6 | 638973.8 |
| 私营独资企业 | Private-funded Enterprises | 1356.6 | 352.4 | 1927.9 |
| 私营合伙企业 | Private Partnership Enterprises | 16.8 | 6.9 | |
| 私营有限责任公司 | Private Limited Liability Corporations | 411931.6 | 70893.9 | 601369.0 |
| 私营股份有限公司 | Private Share-holding Corporations Ltd. | 18199.5 | 3855.4 | 35676.9 |
| 其他企业 | Other Enterprises | 98.3 | 19.3 | 696.0 |

单位：万元 (10 000 yuan)

| 二、期末资产负债 Assets and Liabilities | | | | | |
|---|---|---|---|---|---|
| 在建工程 Construction in Progress | 无形资产 Intangible Assets | 土地使用权 Land Use Rights | 资产总计 Total Assets | 流动负债合计 Total Current Liabilities | 应付账款 Accounts Payable |
| 595247.5 | 402105.4 | 80378.2 | 22169322.2 | 14380172.9 | 2293843.4 |
| 2213.7 | 15893.2 | 15801.2 | 1587549.9 | 1004617.5 | 313418.5 |
| 71664.7 | 294845.0 | 39624.3 | 2357952.2 | 1307170.8 | 38267.5 |
| 55.8 | 1647.5 | 1646.5 | 144099.0 | 90298.2 | 38012.6 |
| 432583.7 | 77535.0 | 17563.6 | 9758049.0 | 6095140.5 | 723689.1 |
| 57170.4 | 2447.0 | 1875.4 | 4636831.1 | 3361650.7 | 449401.5 |
| 14582.1 | 4456.4 | 61.7 | 1470057.6 | 1042875.7 | 41036.6 |
| | | | 3985.5 | 1094.2 | 34.7 |
| | | | 512.8 | 56.1 | 32.8 |
| 16977.1 | 5281.3 | 3805.5 | 2210285.1 | 1477269.2 | 689950.1 |
| 14655.2 | 91804.9 | 11271.2 | 15546874.5 | 13057421.3 | 6818269.5 |
| | | | 12883.7 | 5465.4 | 3999.8 |
| 9167.7 | 78722.8 | 6283.7 | 7600476.4 | 6953512.0 | 3684624.9 |
| 5082.9 | 490.0 | | 1677222.6 | 1155332.0 | 439458.6 |
| 11.7 | 168.3 | | 181314.2 | 133330.4 | 57030.0 |
| | 4636.0 | 4636.0 | 168319.8 | 103656.2 | 33204.6 |
| 13.2 | 329.4 | | 2170533.0 | 1691910.8 | 895988.3 |
| | 6048.8 | | 1256622.9 | 813840.1 | 338466.9 |
| | | | 29373.5 | 24579.7 | 4223.3 |
| 379.7 | 1409.6 | 351.5 | 2450128.4 | 2175794.7 | 1361273.1 |
| | 166.8 | | 349846.4 | 262132.0 | 49696.1 |
| | 166.8 | | 349846.4 | 262132.0 | 49696.1 |
| 18522.2 | 6788.5 | 1824.8 | 934131.7 | 474065.8 | 68864.3 |
| 13257.2 | 1411.5 | 690.3 | 507086.7 | 240676.0 | 14737.9 |
| 500.0 | 4220.4 | | 48274.9 | 38571.6 | 14343.5 |
| | | | 191837.7 | 155090.4 | 23246.6 |
| 4765.0 | 1156.6 | 1134.5 | 186932.4 | 39727.8 | 16536.3 |
| 659385.7 | 612305.5 | 217555.3 | 57035976.0 | 37808986.2 | 12719395.3 |
| 511085.6 | 173910.2 | 37142.2 | 5623134.6 | 2730742.0 | 579597.3 |
| | | | 4510.7 | 3020.0 | 1306.5 |
| 2.0 | | | 122595.9 | 88712.2 | 762.3 |
| 72.4 | 116.2 | | 1191112.4 | 613074.9 | 57726.7 |
| 72.4 | 116.2 | | 1191112.4 | 613074.9 | 57726.7 |
| 69055.5 | 181477.8 | 84827.9 | 17479833.6 | 12499924.3 | 4943615.5 |
| 38024.8 | 85135.6 | 36631.7 | 3599183.8 | 2385744.8 | 245428.6 |
| 31030.7 | 96342.2 | 48196.2 | 13880649.8 | 10114179.5 | 4698186.9 |
| 11353.1 | 44926.8 | 32001.3 | 4778718.0 | 3106777.0 | 223377.0 |
| 67817.1 | 211874.5 | 63583.9 | 27835248.8 | 18766664.4 | 6913010.0 |
| | 125.3 | 125.3 | 164794.6 | 146685.3 | 3797.0 |
| | | | 9886.3 | | |
| 51782.4 | 202683.3 | 55595.7 | 22431381.2 | 16335186.3 | 5538705.5 |
| 16034.7 | 9065.9 | 7862.9 | 5229186.7 | 2284792.8 | 1370507.5 |
| | | | 822.0 | 71.4 | |

表 15.6 续表 7 continued 7

| 指 标 | Item | 二、期末资产负债 Assets and Liabilities | | |
|---|---|---|---|---|
| | | 负债合计<br>Total Liabilities | 所有者权益合计<br>Total Owner's Equity | 实收资本<br>Paid-up Capital |
| 矿产品、建材及化工产品批发 | Wholesale of Mineral Products, Building Materials and Chemical Products | 16155485.0 | 5988449.3 | 3169923.6 |
| 煤炭及制品批发 | Wholesale of Coal and Related Products | 1109130.6 | 474762.0 | 501381.0 |
| 石油及制品批发 | Wholesale of Petroleum and Related Products | 1419634.5 | 952013.7 | 708363.7 |
| 非金属矿及制品批发 | Wholesale of Nonmetal Mineral and Related Products | 92532.0 | 51567.0 | 31442.1 |
| 金属及金属矿批发 | Wholesale of Metal and Metal Mineral | 7156478.3 | 2592555.0 | 954875.8 |
| 建材批发 | Wholesale of Building Materials | 3638426.9 | 991700.5 | 596648.0 |
| 化肥批发 | Wholesale of Fertilizers | 1125242.9 | 325732.4 | 155867.0 |
| 农药批发 | Wholesale of Pesticides | 1096.1 | 2889.4 | 506.0 |
| 农用薄膜批发 | Wholesale of Films for Agriculture | 56.1 | 456.7 | 50.0 |
| 其他化工产品批发 | Wholesale of Other Chemical Products | 1612887.6 | 596772.6 | 220790.0 |
| 机械设备、五金产品及电子产品批发 | Wholesale of Machinery, Hardware and Electronic Products | 13408663.4 | 2134287.3 | 964976.1 |
| 农业机械批发 | Wholesale of Agricultural Machinery | 6450.9 | 3849.7 | 1879.7 |
| 汽车及零配件批发 | Wholesale of Automobile Fittings | 7045023.3 | 554538.2 | 447566.2 |
| 摩托车及零配件批发 | Wholesale of Motorcycle and Fittings | 1266090.9 | 411131.7 | 110749.2 |
| 五金产品批发 | Wholesale of Hardware | 133934.8 | 47379.4 | 31858.6 |
| 电气设备批发 | Wholesale of Electric Equipment | 122429.4 | 46393.6 | 29156.3 |
| 计算机、软件及辅助设备批发 | Wholesale of Computers, Software and Assistant Equipment | 1735982.2 | 434550.8 | 146062.0 |
| 通信设备批发 | Wholesale of Communication Equipment | 833866.7 | 422696.6 | 95581.5 |
| 广播影视设备批发 | Wholesale of Broadcast and TV Equipment | 24579.7 | 4793.7 | 5192.0 |
| 其他机械设备及电子产品批发 | Wholesale of Other Machinery and Electronic Products | 2240305.5 | 208953.6 | 96930.6 |
| 贸易经纪与代理 | Trade Broker and Agency | 548164.2 | 29169.0 | 33404.0 |
| 贸易代理 | Trade Agency | 548164.2 | 29169.0 | 33404.0 |
| 其他批发业 | Other Wholesales | 619905.1 | 314859.7 | 213366.2 |
| 再生物资回收与批发 | Wholesale of Recycled Materials | 312600.9 | 191261.6 | 127357.4 |
| 宠物食品用品批发 | Pet Food and Supplies Wholesale | 38620.3 | 9654.6 | 5500.0 |
| 互联网批发 | Wholesale of Internet Device | 154887.3 | 36950.4 | 26600.0 |
| 其他未列明批发业 | Other Wholesale not Classified Elsewhere | 113796.6 | 76993.1 | 53908.8 |
| **按登记注册类型分** | **By Status of Registration** | | | |
| 内资企业 | Domestic-funded Enterprises | 41144721.5 | 16048230.9 | 5257924.1 |
| 国有企业 | State-owned Enterprises | 3458192.1 | 2673874.7 | 640642.2 |
| 集体企业 | Collective-owned Enterprises | 2990.3 | 1520.4 | 208.7 |
| 股份合作企业 | Cooperative Enterprises | 87591.3 | 35004.6 | 6271.5 |
| 联营企业 | Joint Ownership Enterprises | 701705.6 | 489406.8 | 52553.5 |
| 国有联营企业 | State Joint Ownership Enterprises | 701705.6 | 489406.8 | 52553.5 |
| 有限责任公司 | Limited Liability Corporations | 13474249.4 | 3996544.1 | 1803372.2 |
| 国有独资公司 | State Sole Funded Corporations | 2538879.6 | 1053785.2 | 612516.3 |
| 其他有限责任公司 | Other Limited Liability Corporations | 10935369.8 | 2942758.9 | 1190855.9 |
| 股份有限公司 | Share-holding Corporations Ltd. | 3433243.0 | 1080647.4 | 254194.8 |
| 私营企业 | Private Enterprises | 19986489.0 | 7770671.7 | 2500631.2 |
| 私营独资企业 | Private-funded Enterprises | 148939.3 | 15628.9 | 8311.9 |
| 私营合伙企业 | Private Partnership Enterprises | 4609.4 | | |
| 私营有限责任公司 | Private Limited Liability Corporations | 17488652.6 | 4870143.8 | 2203996.4 |
| 私营股份有限公司 | Private Share-holding Corporations Ltd. | 2344287.7 | 2884899.0 | 288322.9 |
| 其他企业 | Other Enterprises | 260.8 | 561.2 | 50.0 |

单位：万元 (10 000 yuan)

| 二、期末资产负债 Assets and Liabilities | 三、损益及分配 Profits and Losses | | | | |
|---|---|---|---|---|---|
| 个人资本<br>Personal Capital | 营业收入<br>Gross Sales | 主营业务收入<br>Main Business Income | 营业成本<br>Operating Cost | 税金及附加<br>Taxes and Surcharges | 其他业务利润<br>Other Business Profits |
| 331143.4 | 63348728.6 | 62771249.3 | 60289664.6 | 63278.6 | 12082.4 |
| 20234.3 | 4939978.6 | 4887348.4 | 4703053.7 | 8964.1 | 1950.6 |
| 32479.7 | 11081205.2 | 11060042.2 | 10767804.3 | 9673.4 | 935.8 |
| 652.9 | 185663.2 | 184570.3 | 172390.8 | 246.0 | 229.5 |
| 161590.2 | 31259627.4 | 30989750.0 | 29526903.4 | 21475.2 | 5687.5 |
| 81261.0 | 6073884.9 | 5910282.5 | 5646022.5 | 12856.3 | 447.7 |
| 5349.5 | 3404565.3 | 3372877.6 | 3333016.8 | 3680.5 | 291.7 |
| 238.0 | 87201.6 | 87200.2 | 83467.3 | 25.7 | 1.4 |
| 50.0 | 10256.7 | 10256.7 | 9762.6 | 1.5 | |
| 29287.8 | 6306345.7 | 6268921.4 | 6047243.2 | 6355.9 | 2538.2 |
| 136047.9 | 37977917.4 | 37758017.7 | 35586888.0 | 57426.7 | 65246.6 |
| 200.0 | 47541.3 | 45938.2 | 43198.9 | 615.1 | 4.3 |
| 35925.3 | 15626855.4 | 15513672.1 | 14579492.3 | 29794.9 | 21485.9 |
| 6771.1 | 3280100.9 | 3277579.9 | 3059930.7 | 3830.5 | 1376.4 |
| 26820.1 | 507005.2 | 501538.1 | 468808.1 | 654.7 | 4033.4 |
| 4451.3 | 274667.9 | 269234.2 | 244077.5 | 900.6 | 838.0 |
| 2961.0 | 5926383.7 | 5926325.2 | 5656944.1 | 6509.5 | -58.4 |
| 38357.4 | 7648271.8 | 7572892.3 | 7040980.3 | 10208.6 | 33624.4 |
| 5192.0 | 163087.8 | 158334.6 | 139193.4 | 351.1 | 3465.9 |
| 15369.7 | 4504003.4 | 4492503.1 | 4354262.7 | 4561.7 | 476.7 |
| 55.0 | 995311.0 | 985084.1 | 990697.0 | 492.4 | |
| 55.0 | 995311.0 | 985084.1 | 990697.0 | 492.4 | |
| 41173.1 | 2944235.4 | 2711320.6 | 2846906.8 | 7169.5 | 9243.1 |
| 16595.1 | 1213667.2 | 1105556.9 | 1166970.4 | 3867.0 | 1988.4 |
| | 46236.0 | 46235.2 | 38505.7 | 33.8 | 17.5 |
| 1000.0 | 1298999.3 | 1298999.3 | 1283815.4 | 572.1 | |
| 23578.0 | 385332.9 | 260529.2 | 357615.3 | 2696.6 | 7237.2 |
| 854384.5 | 135316304.1 | 133908149.9 | 124664056.5 | 1199781.5 | 177819.5 |
| 100.0 | 13585546.3 | 13456426.5 | 9897874.7 | 1027124.1 | 27195.2 |
| | 24287.8 | 24287.8 | 21693.6 | 28.7 | |
| 412.7 | 523382.9 | 523153.0 | 511980.3 | 381.7 | 200.6 |
| | 1396064.0 | 1395839.8 | 1392236.0 | 1125.6 | |
| | 1396064.0 | 1395839.8 | 1392236.0 | 1125.6 | |
| 27480.4 | 41044770.0 | 40891603.6 | 39277776.2 | 57679.1 | 25636.8 |
| | 7062877.2 | 6997802.9 | 6850421.5 | 10713.3 | 7339.0 |
| 27480.4 | 33981892.8 | 33893800.7 | 32427354.7 | 46965.8 | 18297.8 |
| 3050.0 | 4971889.1 | 4943733.8 | 4819045.6 | 6709.4 | 879.4 |
| 823341.4 | 73768224.1 | 72671602.9 | 68742022.5 | 106688.2 | 123907.5 |
| 102.0 | 181113.1 | 176539.1 | 165357.7 | 198.3 | |
| | 4829.1 | | 4819.2 | 3.5 | |
| 625842.8 | 67370712.9 | 66327986.2 | 63657870.0 | 87288.6 | 115155.8 |
| 197396.6 | 6211569.0 | 6167077.6 | 4913975.6 | 19197.8 | 8751.7 |
| | 2139.9 | 1502.5 | 1427.6 | 44.7 | |

**表 15.6 续表 8 continued 8**

| 指 标 | Item | 三、损益及分配 Profits and Losses 销售费用 Sales Expenses | 管理费用 Management Expenses | 研发费用 R&D expenses |
|---|---|---|---|---|
| 矿产品、建材及化工产品批发 | Wholesale of Mineral Products, Building Materials and Chemical Products | 609057.1 | 290733.6 | 2059.7 |
| 煤炭及制品批发 | Wholesale of Coal and Related Products | 117701.7 | 29127.5 | 64.0 |
| 石油及制品批发 | Wholesale of Petroleum and Related Products | 153633.5 | 42893.1 | -11.1 |
| 非金属矿及制品批发 | Wholesale of Nonmetal Mineral and Related Products | 4073.9 | 4302.1 | |
| 金属及金属矿批发 | Wholesale of Metal and Metal Mineral | 121836.6 | 91991.0 | 57.6 |
| 建材批发 | Wholesale of Building Materials | 90217.4 | 59205.5 | 571.9 |
| 化肥批发 | Wholesale of Fertilizers | 20901.5 | 14025.9 | 218.6 |
| 农药批发 | Wholesale of Pesticides | 1669.5 | 1310.1 | |
| 农用薄膜批发 | Wholesale of Films for Agriculture | 23.8 | 56.2 | |
| 其他化工产品批发 | Wholesale of Other Chemical Products | 98999.2 | 47822.2 | 1158.7 |
| 机械设备、五金产品及电子产品批发 | Wholesale of Machinery, Hardware and Electronic Products | 1470374.0 | 230880.9 | 36505.0 |
| 农业机械批发 | Wholesale of Agricultural Machinery | 2011.0 | 959.3 | 0.1 |
| 汽车及零配件批发 | Wholesale of Automobile Fittings | 849344.0 | 91989.7 | 31331.1 |
| 摩托车及零配件批发 | Wholesale of Motorcycle and Fittings | 72883.2 | 15936.7 | 3905.5 |
| 五金产品批发 | Wholesale of Hardware | 18036.8 | 9148.8 | 1.5 |
| 电气设备批发 | Wholesale of Electric Equipment | 14007.0 | 6551.1 | 4.8 |
| 计算机、软件及辅助设备批发 | Wholesale of Computers, Software and Assistant Equipment | 157045.5 | 23276.0 | 221.2 |
| 通信设备批发 | Wholesale of Communication Equipment | 284020.6 | 43514.1 | 499.4 |
| 广播影视设备批发 | Wholesale of Broadcast and TV Equipment | 12797.5 | 3131.4 | |
| 其他机械设备及电子产品批发 | Wholesale of Other Machinery and Electronic Products | 60228.4 | 36373.8 | 541.4 |
| 贸易经纪与代理 | Trade Broker and Agency | 5063.7 | 2454.3 | |
| 贸易代理 | Trade Agency | 5063.7 | 2454.3 | |
| 其他批发业 | Other Wholesales | 45771.0 | 28988.2 | 1179.3 |
| 再生物资回收与批发 | Wholesale of Recycled Materials | 14223.0 | 14553.3 | 0.8 |
| 宠物食品用品批发 | Pet Food and Supplies Wholesale | 9352.6 | 1999.2 | 949.0 |
| 互联网批发 | Wholesale of Internet Device | 13700.7 | 2366.9 | 18.5 |
| 其他未列明批发业 | Other Wholesale not Classified Elsewhere | 8494.7 | 10068.8 | 211.0 |
| **按登记注册类型分** | **By Status of Registration** | | | |
| 内资企业 | Domestic-funded Enterprises | 3214614.6 | 1361601.2 | 50950.1 |
| 国有企业 | State-owned Enterprises | 293681.9 | 420492.4 | 32821.7 |
| 集体企业 | Collective-owned Enterprises | 1438.3 | 878.3 | 0.1 |
| 股份合作企业 | Cooperative Enterprises | 6763.3 | 1618.0 | 3.1 |
| 联营企业 | Joint Ownership Enterprises | 219.2 | 6079.7 | |
| 国有联营企业 | State Joint Ownership Enterprises | 219.2 | 6079.7 | |
| 有限责任公司 | Limited Liability Corporations | 1093392.7 | 197465.6 | 3149.8 |
| 国有独资公司 | State Sole Funded Corporations | 67675.2 | 49816.8 | 1401.0 |
| 其他有限责任公司 | Other Limited Liability Corporations | 1025717.5 | 147648.8 | 1748.8 |
| 股份有限公司 | Share-holding Corporations Ltd. | 53266.0 | 43321.5 | 251.0 |
| 私营企业 | Private Enterprises | 1765687.6 | 691664.5 | 14724.4 |
| 私营独资企业 | Private-funded Enterprises | 1986.8 | 1774.9 | 5.4 |
| 私营合伙企业 | Private Partnership Enterprises | 0.9 | 188.3 | |
| 私营有限责任公司 | Private Limited Liability Corporations | 1576732.0 | 646486.9 | 12514.5 |
| 私营股份有限公司 | Private Share-holding Corporations Ltd. | 186967.9 | 43214.4 | 2204.5 |
| 其他企业 | Other Enterprises | 165.6 | 81.2 | |

单位：万元 (10 000 yuan)

| 三、损益及分配 Profits and Losses | | | | | |
|---|---|---|---|---|---|
| 财务费用<br>Financial<br>Expenses | 利息收入<br>Interest<br>Income | 利息费用<br>Interest<br>expenses | 投资收益<br>Income from<br>Investment | 营业利润<br>Business<br>Profits | 营业外收入<br>Non-business<br>Income |
| 188816.7 | 105126.8 | 189908.6 | 141904.4 | 434885.0 | 43388.9 |
| 12636.1 | 48729.4 | 59667.4 | -1338.6 | 76840.5 | 8975.7 |
| 15444.2 | 597.1 | 11119.7 | 38721.3 | 129986.8 | 1953.6 |
| 436.7 | 390.9 | 373.5 | 205.8 | 4149.3 | 19.1 |
| 82483.9 | 25670.3 | 55482.0 | 83381.8 | 66450.8 | 22436.3 |
| 56601.0 | 5946.6 | 44113.6 | 2599.5 | 74720.0 | 3864.6 |
| 11314.7 | 18709.5 | 11929.6 | -555.6 | 15261.9 | 3153.9 |
| 10.6 | 0.6 | 11.0 | | 718.3 | 1.4 |
| 1.0 | | | | 411.6 | |
| 9888.5 | 5082.4 | 7211.8 | 18890.2 | 66345.8 | 2984.3 |
| -43657.2 | 38467.1 | 38337.9 | 7118.1 | 634870.6 | 104792.8 |
| 83.0 | 166.6 | 143.3 | | 1839.9 | 25.5 |
| -35384.9 | 34459.9 | 11213.1 | 6602.7 | 86381.3 | 25858.1 |
| -23000.9 | -4285.9 | 2922.5 | -8221.4 | 137759.9 | 7086.8 |
| 2162.1 | 23.6 | 580.6 | 119.1 | 5926.2 | 115.4 |
| 1345.4 | -10.2 | 1497.0 | 8.3 | 7046.3 | 99.0 |
| 6859.5 | 5464.9 | 11111.0 | 3862.7 | 79294.6 | 699.5 |
| 333.5 | 1057.2 | 1100.8 | 3843.5 | 266864.1 | 59251.0 |
| 275.3 | 0.4 | 245.5 | 891.0 | 7319.0 | 1428.3 |
| 3669.8 | 1590.6 | 9524.1 | 12.2 | 42439.3 | 10229.2 |
| 2775.7 | 127.8 | 14530.3 | | -14753.9 | 483.6 |
| 2775.7 | 127.8 | 14530.3 | | -14753.9 | 483.6 |
| 6096.3 | 3770.7 | 6462.9 | 5535.6 | 15935.7 | 6500.0 |
| 3943.1 | 2171.0 | 5525.2 | 4893.0 | 15937.0 | 5830.7 |
| 424.5 | 12.8 | 182.8 | | -5098.5 | 57.6 |
| -131.7 | 673.8 | 205.4 | 404.3 | -870.7 | 111.5 |
| 1860.4 | 913.1 | 549.5 | 238.3 | 5967.9 | 500.2 |
| 172931.3 | 295181.0 | 373880.0 | 186318.9 | 3203953.7 | 165251.0 |
| -41421.1 | 109600.6 | 72905.5 | 2869.8 | 551871.7 | 6170.9 |
| 5.9 | 0.1 | -1.2 | | 242.3 | 10.2 |
| 369.7 | 212.7 | 264.7 | | 2167.4 | 18.0 |
| 20737.1 | 2156.1 | 20487.1 | 77343.2 | 55902.0 | 30.7 |
| 20737.1 | 2156.1 | 20487.1 | 77343.2 | 55902.0 | 30.7 |
| 97287.2 | 72853.9 | 107060.9 | 18809.7 | 365096.6 | 67084.9 |
| 18275.8 | 19575.4 | 28525.9 | 5266.4 | 67606.7 | 9384.2 |
| 79011.4 | 53278.5 | 78535.0 | 13543.3 | 297489.9 | 57700.7 |
| 26594.8 | 48694.4 | 71730.9 | 65939.7 | 93987.9 | 6144.2 |
| 69320.0 | 61663.2 | 101431.6 | 21356.5 | 2134302.7 | 85792.1 |
| 504.0 | 7.2 | -1840.1 | | 2325.3 | 7.5 |
| 57.8 | 0.2 | 57.7 | | -240.8 | |
| 59700.1 | 57853.4 | 90311.2 | 29076.2 | 1130799.1 | 84059.9 |
| 9058.1 | 3802.4 | 12902.8 | -7719.7 | 1001419.1 | 1724.7 |
| 37.7 | | 0.5 | | 383.1 | |

表 15.6 续表 9 continued 9

| 指 标 | Item | 三、损益及分配 Profits and Losses<br>营业外支出 Non-business Expenses | <br>利润总额 Total Profits |
|---|---|---|---|
| 矿产品、建材及化工产品批发 | Wholesale of Mineral Products, Building Materials and Chemical Products | 7835.9 | 471461.2 |
| 煤炭及制品批发 | Wholesale of Coal and Related Products | 1226.6 | 84615.2 |
| 石油及制品批发 | Wholesale of Petroleum and Related Products | 1644.6 | 130295.9 |
| 非金属矿及制品批发 | Wholesale of Nonmetal Mineral and Related Products | 594.5 | 3599.8 |
| 金属及金属矿批发 | Wholesale of Metal and Metal Mineral | 1117.8 | 88842.5 |
| 建材批发 | Wholesale of Building Materials | 1185.4 | 77303.7 |
| 化肥批发 | Wholesale of Fertilizers | 746.5 | 17669.4 |
| 农药批发 | Wholesale of Pesticides | | 719.7 |
| 农用薄膜批发 | Wholesale of Films for Agriculture | | 411.6 |
| 其他化工产品批发 | Wholesale of Other Chemical Products | 1320.5 | 68003.4 |
| 机械设备、五金产品及电子产品批发 | Wholesale of Machinery, Hardware and Electronic Products | 15590.9 | 724240.3 |
| 农业机械批发 | Wholesale of Agricultural Machinery | | 1865.4 |
| 汽车及零配件批发 | Wholesale of Automobile Fittings | 12344.7 | 99894.1 |
| 摩托车及零配件批发 | Wholesale of Motorcycle and Fittings | 1126.7 | 143720.0 |
| 五金产品批发 | Wholesale of Hardware | 136.0 | 5905.6 |
| 电气设备批发 | Wholesale of Electric Equipment | 245.9 | 6901.2 |
| 计算机、软件及辅助设备批发 | Wholesale of Computers, Software and Assistant Equipment | -9.8 | 80159.1 |
| 通信设备批发 | Wholesale of Communication Equipment | 1227.5 | 324899.0 |
| 广播影视设备批发 | Wholesale of Broadcast and TV Equipment | 65.2 | 8682.1 |
| 其他机械设备及电子产品批发 | Wholesale of Other Machinery and Electronic Products | 454.7 | 52213.8 |
| 贸易经纪与代理 | Trade Broker and Agency | 204.1 | -14474.2 |
| 贸易代理 | Trade Agency | 204.1 | -14474.2 |
| 其他批发业 | Other Wholesales | 472.4 | 21961.4 |
| 再生物资回收与批发 | Wholesale of Recycled Materials | 284.4 | 21483.3 |
| 宠物食品用品批发 | Pet Food and Supplies Wholesale | 112.3 | -5153.2 |
| 互联网批发 | Wholesale of Internet Device | 10.4 | -771.4 |
| 其他未列明批发业 | Other Wholesale not Classified Elsewhere | 65.3 | 6402.7 |
| **按登记注册类型分** | **By Status of Registration** | | |
| 内资企业 | Domestic-funded Enterprises | 64788.3 | 3303557.8 |
| 国有企业 | State-owned Enterprises | 20272.6 | 537768.2 |
| 集体企业 | Collective-owned Enterprises | | 252.5 |
| 股份合作企业 | Cooperative Enterprises | 26.0 | 2159.4 |
| 联营企业 | Joint Ownership Enterprises | 330.1 | 55602.6 |
| 国有联营企业 | State Joint Ownership Enterprises | 330.1 | 55602.6 |
| 有限责任公司 | Limited Liability Corporations | 6478.0 | 425730.3 |
| 国有独资公司 | State Sole Funded Corporations | 1057.8 | 75932.4 |
| 其他有限责任公司 | Other Limited Liability Corporations | 5420.2 | 349797.9 |
| 股份有限公司 | Share-holding Corporations Ltd. | 1451.6 | 98680.5 |
| 私营企业 | Private Enterprises | 36230.0 | 2182981.2 |
| 私营独资企业 | Private-funded Enterprises | 0.5 | 2332.3 |
| 私营合伙企业 | Private Partnership Enterprises | 0.3 | -241.1 |
| 私营有限责任公司 | Private Limited Liability Corporations | 30662.9 | 1183312.5 |
| 私营股份有限公司 | Private Share-holding Corporations Ltd. | 5566.3 | 997577.5 |
| 其他企业 | Other Enterprises | | 383.1 |

单位：万元 (10 000 yuan)

| 三、损益及分配 Profits and Losses | 四、人工成本及增值税 Labor cost and Value-added Tax | | |
|---|---|---|---|
| 所得税费用<br>Income Tax Payable | 应付职工薪酬<br>Employee compensation | 应交增值税<br>Value-added Tax | 五、从事批发和零售业活动的从业人员平均人数（人）<br>Annual Average Employees Engaged in wholesale and retail activities (persons) |
| 66751.2 | 285555.8 | 205881.1 | 28594 |
| 17753.1 | 23101.7 | 48767.5 | 2269 |
| 15547.4 | 94658.2 | 27038.6 | 7190 |
| 517.2 | 2686.9 | 1843.0 | 204 |
| 8830.9 | 61126.8 | 47061.7 | 6288 |
| 7620.6 | 52840.6 | 48807.1 | 7091 |
| 3120.7 | 14852.7 | 6321.8 | 1710 |
| 13.5 | 128.2 | 58.8 | 20 |
| 8.9 | 93.9 | 14.3 | 26 |
| 13338.9 | 36066.8 | 25968.3 | 3796 |
| 131315.2 | 270907.8 | 228517.1 | 20894 |
| 105.9 | 467.2 | 386.7 | 103 |
| 36113.4 | 89346.7 | 107164.2 | 5562 |
| 20941.3 | 31384.6 | 19178.3 | 2074 |
| 931.4 | 13136.1 | 2333.7 | 1162 |
| 650.5 | 9449.9 | 2250.9 | 1091 |
| 12038.6 | 27043.2 | 20687.7 | 1356 |
| 47654.2 | 63525.9 | 49221.4 | 5648 |
| 1268.9 | 3358.2 | 2348.6 | 440 |
| 11611.0 | 33196.0 | 24945.6 | 3458 |
| -2073.3 | 919.1 | 1025.5 | 124 |
| -2073.3 | 919.1 | 1025.5 | 124 |
| 4826.1 | 25035.6 | 27326.7 | 3207 |
| 1795.4 | 10930.7 | 21097.2 | 1726 |
|  | 5275.8 | 1012.7 | 498 |
| 678.3 | 1897.8 | 1039.1 | 269 |
| 2352.4 | 6931.3 | 4177.7 | 714 |
| 533925.8 | 1210318.3 | 1038526.9 | 111784 |
| 126241.3 | 233725.4 | 278034.7 | 8958 |
| 20.6 | 1448.6 | 307.5 | 198 |
| 329.0 | 824.5 | 621.5 | 116 |
| 185.9 | 2800.9 | 885.2 | 105 |
| 185.9 | 2800.9 | 885.2 | 105 |
| 85952.2 | 275463.1 | 217373.4 | 19383 |
| 10908.9 | 63891.1 | 38931.2 | 3702 |
| 75043.3 | 211572.0 | 178442.2 | 15681 |
| 2706.9 | 44776.3 | 22880.8 | 3611 |
| 318470.1 | 651217.4 | 518409.0 | 79347 |
| 77.4 | 1743.9 | 395.3 | 331 |
|  |  | 1.8 | 4 |
| 166764.7 | 578875.3 | 386264.4 | 72980 |
| 151628.0 | 70598.2 | 131747.5 | 6032 |
| 19.8 | 62.1 | 14.8 | 66 |

表 15.6 续表 10 continued 10

| 指 标 | Item | 法人企业数(个) Number of Enterprises (unit) | 执行《2006年企业会计准则》企业数(个) Number of Enterprises which Implemented Accounting standard for Business Enterprise in 2006 (unit) | 一、年初存货 Inventory at the Beginning of Year |
|---|---|---|---|---|
| 港、澳、台商投资企业 | Enterprises with Funds from Hong Kong, Macao and Taiwan | 17 | 13 | 539503.8 |
| 合资经营企业(港或澳、台资) | Joint-venture Enterprises | 4 | 3 | 600.7 |
| 港、澳、台商独资经营企业 | Enterprises with Sole Fund | 12 | 9 | 537749.0 |
| 港、澳、台商投资股份有限公司 | Share-holding Corporations Ltd. with Investment | 1 | 1 | 1154.1 |
| 外商投资企业 | Foreign-funded Enterprises | 24 | 22 | 224333.6 |
| 中外合资经营企业 | Joint-venture Enterprises | 4 | 2 | 28182.3 |
| 外资企业 | Enterprises with Sole Fund | 17 | 17 | 114456.1 |
| 外商投资股份有限公司 | Foreign-funded Company Ltd. | 1 | 1 | 77780.7 |
| 其他外商投资企业 | Other Foreign-funded Enterprises | 2 | 2 | 3914.5 |
| **按控股情况分** | **By Holding Entity of Share** | | | |
| 国有控股 | State-holding | 319 | 294 | 1892711.3 |
| 集体控股 | Collective-holding | 22 | 16 | 246332.8 |
| 私人控股 | Private-holding | 3096 | 1691 | 3352252.7 |
| 港澳台商控股 | Held by Corporation from Hong Kong, Macao and Taiwan | 15 | 12 | 539118.4 |
| 外商控股 | Foreign-holding | 21 | 20 | 118457.8 |
| **按经营形式分** | **By Form of Business** | | | |
| 独立门店 | Independent Store | 2350 | 1345 | 2392547.9 |
| 连锁总店(总部) | Central Shop of Chain Store (Headquarter) | 14 | 9 | 300625.9 |
| 连锁直营店 | Direct-sale of Chain Store | 7 | 5 | 2749.4 |
| 连锁加盟店 | Franchise Shop of Chain Store | 3 | 1 | 126.6 |
| 其 他 | Other | 1099 | 673 | 3452823.2 |
| **按单位规模分** | **By Size of Enterprise** | | | |
| 大 型 | Large | 65 | 57 | 2001666.9 |
| 中 型 | Medium | 897 | 641 | 2959227.9 |
| 小 型 | Small | 1820 | 982 | 887391.7 |
| 微 型 | Micro | 691 | 353 | 300586.5 |

单位：万元 (10 000 yuan)

| 二、期末资产负债 Assets and Liabilities | | | | | |
|---|---|---|---|---|---|
| 流动资产合计 Total Current Assets | | | 固定资产原价 Total Original Value of Fixed Assets | | |
| | 应收账款 Accounts Receivable | 存货 Inventory | | 房屋和构筑物 Buildings and Structures | 机器设备 Machinery and Equipments |
| 1907984.9 | 587817.8 | 628273.8 | 79958.7 | 18541.6 | 49029.6 |
| 262201.9 | 232192.2 | 14474.0 | 1453.2 | 359.8 | 560.2 |
| 1642113.9 | 354957.9 | 612291.6 | 20005.3 | 5491.3 | 2659.7 |
| 3669.1 | 667.7 | 1508.2 | 58500.2 | 12690.5 | 45809.7 |
| 1297118.0 | 312814.5 | 235472.6 | 302375.1 | 19060.6 | 8404.3 |
| 138225.7 | 53633.5 | 38141.6 | 20184.2 | 17126.2 | 2957.7 |
| 986617.4 | 227142.7 | 122391.0 | 18419.9 | 1934.4 | 5446.6 |
| 121350.2 | 1411.0 | 73817.2 | 263771.0 | | |
| 50924.7 | 30627.3 | 1122.8 | | | |
| | | | | | |
| 16542987.3 | 2751564.9 | 2389689.0 | 2117754.2 | 591736.4 | 390358.5 |
| 702874.4 | 121206.6 | 241241.7 | 26437.0 | 20874.5 | 1894.0 |
| 31252746.7 | 11691799.8 | 3522134.4 | 1284630.2 | 575997.1 | 215208.6 |
| 1649360.7 | 357503.2 | 613838.4 | 79336.8 | 18425.6 | 48920.3 |
| 1296169.6 | 487495.5 | 137916.1 | 19359.1 | 1934.4 | 6142.6 |
| | | | | | |
| 21637370.1 | 5236907.6 | 3166584.6 | 1759370.1 | 656072.5 | 486475.0 |
| 2314837.4 | 124655.6 | 312417.6 | 548715.7 | 456.0 | 1565.3 |
| -356911.1 | 13507.7 | 3214.1 | 20938.7 | 3152.9 | 193.3 |
| 20205.3 | 3837.0 | 143.6 | 12.1 | | |
| 27828637.0 | 10030662.1 | 3422459.7 | 1198480.7 | 549286.6 | 174290.4 |
| | | | | | |
| 14225356.0 | 4732141.7 | 2266574.5 | 1089957.5 | 346507.9 | 338015.1 |
| 22489649.3 | 5818309.7 | 3074743.5 | 1886275.7 | 666728.4 | 239800.6 |
| 8519267.8 | 2508102.6 | 1366970.6 | 459619.3 | 150426.9 | 78313.3 |
| 6209865.6 | 2351016.0 | 196531.0 | 91664.8 | 45304.8 | 6395.0 |

**表 15.6 续表 11 continued 11**

| 指标 | Item | 二、期末资产负债 Assets and Liabilities | | |
|---|---|---|---|---|
| | | 累计折旧 Cumulative Depreciation | 本年折旧 Depreciation | 固定资产净额 Net Value of Fixed Assets |
| 港、澳、台商投资企业 | Enterprises with Funds from Hong Kong, Macao and Taiwan | 26137.0 | 4077.6 | 53765.0 |
| 合资经营企业(港或澳、台资) | Joint-venture Enterprises | 853.0 | 364.7 | 600.1 |
| 港、澳、台商独资经营企业 | Enterprises with Sole Fund | 12464.8 | 1889.2 | 7483.9 |
| 港、澳、台商投资股份有限公司 | Share-holding Corporations Ltd. with Investment | 12819.2 | 1823.7 | 45681.0 |
| 外商投资企业 | Foreign-funded Enterprises | 132002.7 | 17446.5 | 169360.5 |
| 中外合资经营企业 | Joint-venture Enterprises | 9146.2 | 1221.2 | 11031.5 |
| 外资企业 | Enterprises with Sole Fund | 12971.2 | 968.1 | 4995.9 |
| 外商投资股份有限公司 | Foreign-funded Company Ltd. | 109885.3 | 15257.2 | 153333.1 |
| 其他外商投资企业 | Other Foreign-funded Enterprises | | | |
| **按控股情况分** | **By Holding Entity of Share** | | | |
| 国有控股 | State-holding | 891860.1 | 104379.4 | 1141614.2 |
| 集体控股 | Collective-holding | 7888.7 | 1107.1 | 18030.1 |
| 私人控股 | Private-holding | 479333.9 | 83083.4 | 700053.4 |
| 港澳台商控股 | Held by Corporation from Hong Kong, Macao and Taiwan | 26039.3 | 4051.6 | 53240.8 |
| 外商控股 | Foreign-holding | 13551.6 | 1014.3 | 5354.7 |
| **按经营形式分** | **By Form of Business** | | | |
| 独立门店 | Independent Store | 732725.8 | 104581.6 | 870938.5 |
| 连锁总店(总部) | Central Shop of Chain Store (Headquarter) | 273784.3 | 29763.2 | 273913.0 |
| 连锁直营店 | Direct-sale of Chain Store | 10601.2 | 662.2 | 7870.2 |
| 连锁加盟店 | Franchise Shop of Chain Store | 4.4 | 2.3 | 7.7 |
| 其 他 | Other | 401557.9 | 58626.5 | 765563.8 |
| **按单位规模分** | **By Size of Enterprise** | | | |
| 大 型 | Large | 503139.6 | 60958.7 | 557279.6 |
| 中 型 | Medium | 723706.8 | 95678.3 | 1082207.1 |
| 小 型 | Small | 172230.6 | 33020.5 | 218281.5 |
| 微 型 | Micro | 19596.6 | 3978.3 | 60525.0 |

单位：万元 (10 000 yuan)

| 二、期末资产负债 Assets and Liabilities | | | | | |
|---|---|---|---|---|---|
| 在建工程 Construction in Progress | 无形资产 Intangible Assets | 土地使用权 Land Use Rights | 资产总计 Total Assets | 流动负债合计 Total Current Liabilities | 应付账款 Accounts Payable |
| 12553.2 | 18425.2 | 331.2 | 2231176.4 | 1425313.6 | 668567.3 |
| | 17213.6 | 331.2 | 341100.9 | 229089.4 | 218422.5 |
| 139.6 | 564.0 | | 1827441.7 | 1168629.8 | 447396.9 |
| 12413.6 | 647.6 | | 62633.8 | 27594.4 | 2747.9 |
| 53602.7 | 204146.3 | 9551.4 | 2019736.9 | 1187537.3 | 486559.2 |
| 1905.8 | 15457.1 | 9551.4 | 179488.8 | 104354.6 | -74098.0 |
| 54.6 | 168.3 | | 1026577.6 | 761087.7 | 523981.5 |
| 51642.3 | 188520.9 | | 762745.8 | 281810.4 | 35350.0 |
| | | | 50924.7 | 40284.6 | 1325.7 |
| | | | | | |
| 632863.8 | 593958.5 | 161444.1 | 22573478.7 | 12642445.3 | 1954350.3 |
| 7372.7 | 4410.9 | 61.7 | 972400.5 | 688546.6 | 66444.1 |
| 72697.3 | 217914.1 | 65600.9 | 34429259.7 | 24865464.0 | 10659767.7 |
| 12553.2 | 1542.8 | 331.2 | 1946589.0 | 1202656.8 | 452519.9 |
| 54.6 | 17050.7 | | 1365161.4 | 1022724.4 | 741439.8 |
| | | | | | |
| 564145.9 | 378270.5 | 120325.4 | 25224668.8 | 16796178.4 | 6053710.8 |
| 69578.0 | 210327.2 | 19117.9 | 3651040.7 | 1093173.7 | 326188.7 |
| 282.4 | 2670.0 | 390.7 | -340936.9 | -3111.6 | 7797.0 |
| | | | 20421.3 | 10663.9 | 2250.3 |
| 91535.3 | 243609.3 | 87603.9 | 32731695.4 | 22524932.7 | 7484575.0 |
| | | | | | |
| 103928.5 | 369740.9 | 55617.9 | 17470830.5 | 11430698.3 | 4792537.7 |
| 595514.9 | 401167.6 | 156736.4 | 27616766.9 | 18009142.9 | 5670238.6 |
| 23131.6 | 61759.0 | 12923.2 | 9658641.6 | 5573824.3 | 1378534.0 |
| 2966.6 | 2209.5 | 2160.4 | 6540650.3 | 5408171.6 | 2033211.5 |

**表 15.6 续表 12 continued 12**

| 指 标 | Item | 二、期末资产负债 Assets and Liabilities 负债合计 Total Liabilities | 所有者权益合计 Total Owner's Equity | 实收资本 Paid-up Capital |
|---|---|---|---|---|
| 港、澳、台商投资企业 | Enterprises with Funds from Hong Kong, Macao and Taiwan | 1446337.0 | 784839.4 | 287855.6 |
| 合资经营企业(港或澳、台资) | Joint-venture Enterprises | 230901.8 | 110199.1 | 95670.0 |
| 港、澳、台商独资经营企业 | Enterprises with Sole Fund | 1187840.8 | 639600.9 | 158619.0 |
| 港、澳、台商投资股份有限公司 | Share-holding Corporations Ltd. with Investment | 27594.4 | 35039.4 | 33566.6 |
| 外商投资企业 | Foreign-funded Enterprises | 1258491.0 | 784582.5 | 513219.8 |
| 中外合资经营企业 | Joint-venture Enterprises | 104466.5 | 75022.3 | 16200.0 |
| 外资企业 | Enterprises with Sole Fund | 813718.2 | 236196.0 | 26318.4 |
| 外商投资股份有限公司 | Foreign-funded Company Ltd. | 300021.7 | 462724.1 | 470501.4 |
| 其他外商投资企业 | Other Foreign-funded Enterprises | 40284.6 | 10640.1 | 200.0 |
| **按控股情况分** | **By Holding Entity of Share** | | | |
| 国有控股 | State-holding | 14634903.3 | 8176161.0 | 2923586.7 |
| 集体控股 | Collective-holding | 758312.6 | 214087.9 | 84810.2 |
| 私人控股 | Private-holding | 26157298.5 | 8191352.0 | 2735308.6 |
| 港澳台商控股 | Held by Corporation from Hong Kong, Macao and Taiwan | 1223680.2 | 722908.8 | 227575.6 |
| 外商控股 | Foreign-holding | 1075354.9 | 313143.1 | 87718.4 |
| **按经营形式分** | **By Form of Business** | | | |
| 独立门店 | Independent Store | 18761895.7 | 6064705.7 | 3018438.7 |
| 连锁总店(总部) | Central Shop of Chain Store (Headquarter) | 1183957.1 | 2467083.6 | 525543.4 |
| 连锁直营店 | Direct-sale of Chain Store | 19997.9 | 560.3 | 2140.8 |
| 连锁加盟店 | Franchise Shop of Chain Store | 10663.8 | 9757.5 | 446.5 |
| 其 他 | Other | 23873035.0 | 9075545.7 | 2512430.1 |
| **按单位规模分** | **By Size of Enterprise** | | | |
| 大 型 | Large | 12014422.9 | 5456407.6 | 1422353.0 |
| 中 型 | Medium | 19315314.7 | 8318024.2 | 2736096.2 |
| 小 型 | Small | 6440979.2 | 3218858.0 | 1539300.3 |
| 微 型 | Micro | 6078832.7 | 624363.0 | 361250.0 |

单位：万元 (10 000 yuan)

| 二、期末资产负债 Assets and Liabilities | 三、损益及分配 Profits and Losses | | | | |
|---|---|---|---|---|---|
| 个人资本 Personal Capital | 营业收入 Gross Sales | 主营业务收入 Main Business Income | 营业成本 Operating Cost | 税金及附加 Taxes and Surcharges | 其他业务利润 Other Business Profits |
| 196.0 | 4292655.4 | 4282090.1 | 4040469.8 | 10470.1 | 1728.2 |
| 196.0 | 545534.9 | 544068.8 | 531005.9 | 325.5 | 25.4 |
| | 3689200.3 | 3681310.5 | 3453997.8 | 9936.9 | 443.9 |
| | 57920.2 | 56710.8 | 55466.1 | 207.7 | 1258.9 |
| | 6138592.6 | 6102358.9 | 5783755.9 | 8965.0 | 4018.9 |
| | 411338.3 | 405792.8 | 389178.8 | 472.8 | |
| | 3146764.5 | 3117221.6 | 2879305.0 | 5894.0 | 4018.9 |
| | 2488126.1 | 2488126.1 | 2433014.5 | 2418.4 | |
| | 92363.7 | 91218.4 | 82257.6 | 179.8 | |
| | | | | | |
| 4412.7 | 42573042.1 | 42332543.3 | 37961600.8 | 1070689.2 | 46308.9 |
| 648.7 | 2196251.9 | 2181658.7 | 2133313.3 | 2603.8 | 747.8 |
| 849519.1 | 93445253.4 | 92286645.7 | 87389458.6 | 129353.4 | 130762.8 |
| | 3754161.7 | 3743741.2 | 3515390.7 | 10351.9 | 1728.2 |
| | 3778843.0 | 3748010.0 | 3488518.8 | 6218.3 | 4018.9 |
| | | | | | |
| 449833.4 | 67815609.4 | 66943080.1 | 63839469.5 | 366550.9 | 94373.1 |
| 2530.0 | 8035427.6 | 7999110.7 | 6640964.7 | 531072.0 | 3942.5 |
| 117.6 | 145547.4 | 143980.8 | 137735.8 | 208.7 | 67.6 |
| 200.0 | 16881.7 | 16777.5 | 15952.6 | 86.0 | 104.2 |
| 401899.5 | 69734086.0 | 69189649.8 | 63854159.6 | 321299.0 | 85079.2 |
| | | | | | |
| 187691.4 | 34122664.3 | 33882817.3 | 31179040.6 | 152415.9 | 94198.8 |
| 254358.2 | 64564294.6 | 64103362.5 | 59143609.2 | 1017119.9 | 82413.7 |
| 351389.9 | 25032582.3 | 24893467.6 | 23791915.8 | 35394.6 | 6398.9 |
| 61141.0 | 22028010.9 | 21412951.5 | 20373716.6 | 14286.2 | 555.2 |

表 15.6 续表 13 continued 13

| 指 标 | Item | 三、损益及分配 Profits and Losses<br>销售费用 Sales Expenses | 管理费用 Management Expenses | 研发费用 R&D expenses |
|---|---|---|---|---|
| 港、澳、台商投资企业 | Enterprises with Funds from Hong Kong, Macao and Taiwan | 113237.7 | 26150.1 | 435.1 |
| 合资经营企业(港或澳、台资) | Joint-venture Enterprises | 4925.5 | 7807.7 | 434.1 |
| 港、澳、台商独资经营企业 | Enterprises with Sole Fund | 108312.2 | 17064.9 | 1.0 |
| 港、澳、台商投资股份有限公司 | Share-holding Corporations Ltd. with Investment | | 1277.5 | |
| 外商投资企业 | Foreign-funded Enterprises | 232261.4 | 47026.6 | -93.1 |
| 中外合资经营企业 | Joint-venture Enterprises | 8274.9 | 3296.4 | |
| 外资企业 | Enterprises with Sole Fund | 149945.7 | 28893.0 | |
| 外商投资股份有限公司 | Foreign-funded Company Ltd. | 69548.8 | 14291.2 | -93.1 |
| 其他外商投资企业 | Other Foreign-funded Enterprises | 4492.0 | 546.0 | |
| **按控股情况分** | **By Holding Entity of Share** | | | |
| 国有控股 | State-holding | 671404.1 | 602890.6 | 35759.8 |
| 集体控股 | Collective-holding | 25427.1 | 8327.9 | 3.2 |
| 私人控股 | Private-holding | 2596293.5 | 768304.0 | 15094.0 |
| 港澳台商控股 | Held by Corporation from Hong Kong, Macao and Taiwan | 108570.1 | 18563.7 | 1.0 |
| 外商控股 | Foreign-holding | 158418.9 | 36691.7 | 434.1 |
| **按经营形式分** | **By Form of Business** | | | |
| 独立门店 | Independent Store | 1894336.9 | 626319.8 | 33720.6 |
| 连锁总店(总部) | Central Shop of Chain Store (Headquarter) | 198529.1 | 236189.7 | 2958.0 |
| 连锁直营店 | Direct-sale of Chain Store | 5649.0 | 855.6 | |
| 连锁加盟店 | Franchise Shop of Chain Store | 884.8 | 112.6 | |
| 其 他 | Other | 1460713.9 | 571300.2 | 14613.5 |
| **按单位规模分** | **By Size of Enterprise** | | | |
| 大 型 | Large | 1371913.8 | 269187.5 | 33759.1 |
| 中 型 | Medium | 1586306.2 | 841759.8 | 12788.5 |
| 小 型 | Small | 501323.7 | 274689.3 | 4702.0 |
| 微 型 | Micro | 100570.0 | 49141.3 | 42.5 |

单位：万元 (10 000 yuan)

| 三、损益及分配 Profits and Losses | | | | | |
|---|---|---|---|---|---|
| 财务费用 Financial Expenses | 利息收入 Interest Income | 利息费用 Interest expenses | 投资收益 Income from Investment | 营业利润 Business Profits | 营业外收入 Non-business Income |
| 7406.9 | 6103.1 | 10524.7 | 909.8 | 98954.4 | 6436.1 |
| -369.9 | 533.3 | 88.7 | | 1491.5 | 83.3 |
| 7753.0 | 5569.8 | 10436.0 | 909.8 | 96509.9 | 6347.7 |
| 23.8 | | | | 953.0 | 5.1 |
| 3871.3 | 1492.9 | 1106.9 | 42188.5 | 110069.1 | 16215.4 |
| 2543.5 | -54.8 | 212.0 | 204.4 | 7893.9 | 195.6 |
| -485.9 | 1532.1 | 893.7 | 3671.6 | 90001.9 | 10343.9 |
| 1828.0 | | | 38312.5 | 7819.6 | 1100.7 |
| -14.3 | 15.6 | 1.2 | | 4353.7 | 4575.2 |
| | | | | | |
| 83476.3 | 204109.9 | 241736.3 | 196440.8 | 982667.2 | 37025.3 |
| 11875.9 | 15305.4 | 9997.4 | 4776.1 | 19390.1 | 1190.7 |
| 82025.9 | 75699.5 | 122445.0 | 23618.9 | 2217183.0 | 128331.5 |
| 7788.6 | 5585.5 | 10438.0 | 909.8 | 97949.5 | 6435.9 |
| -957.2 | 2076.7 | 894.9 | 3671.6 | 95787.4 | 14919.1 |
| | | | | | |
| 91288.2 | 133040.5 | 150460.7 | 16873.7 | 925264.7 | 89685.8 |
| -58716.9 | 48028.2 | 1004.1 | 38682.9 | 519272.5 | 5300.5 |
| 268.6 | 25.6 | 200.8 | | 822.4 | 67.0 |
| 23.8 | -0.9 | | | 9588.1 | 593.8 |
| 151345.8 | 121683.6 | 233846.0 | 173860.6 | 1958029.5 | 92255.4 |
| | | | | | |
| 38585.2 | 81252.1 | 93364.8 | 92749.1 | 1155031.1 | 31970.4 |
| 39759.5 | 185239.1 | 201354.8 | 133070.8 | 1942939.7 | 76667.3 |
| 85010.4 | 23735.1 | 65354.0 | 3435.8 | 254555.5 | 42255.6 |
| 20854.4 | 12550.7 | 25438.0 | 161.5 | 60450.9 | 37009.2 |

**表 15.6 续表 14 continued 14**

| 指 标 | Item | 三、损益及分配 Profits and Losses | |
|---|---|---|---|
| | | 营业外支出 Non-business Expenses | 利润总额 Total Profits |
| 港、澳、台商投资企业 | Enterprises with Funds from Hong Kong, Macao and Taiwan | 171.2 | 105219.3 |
| 合资经营企业（港或澳、台资） | Joint-venture Enterprises | 6.0 | 1568.8 |
| 港、澳、台商独资经营企业 | Enterprises with Sole Fund | 165.0 | 102692.6 |
| 港、澳、台商投资股份有限公司 | Share-holding Corporations Ltd. with Investment | 0.2 | 957.9 |
| 外商投资企业 | Foreign-funded Enterprises | 495.3 | 125789.3 |
| 中外合资经营企业 | Joint-venture Enterprises | 35.5 | 8054.0 |
| 外资企业 | Enterprises with Sole Fund | -4.2 | 100350.1 |
| 外商投资股份有限公司 | Foreign-funded Company Ltd. | 464.0 | 8456.3 |
| 其他外商投资企业 | Other Foreign-funded Enterprises | | 8928.9 |
| **按控股情况分** | **By Holding Entity of Share** | | |
| 国有控股 | State-holding | 24915.8 | 994774.1 |
| 集体控股 | Collective-holding | 431.6 | 20149.2 |
| 私人控股 | Private-holding | 39940.4 | 2304718.1 |
| 港澳台商控股 | Held by Corporation from Hong Kong, Macao and Taiwan | 171.2 | 104214.2 |
| 外商控股 | Foreign-holding | -4.2 | 110710.8 |
| **按经营形式分** | **By Form of Business** | | |
| 独立门店 | Independent Store | 23906.8 | 989099.4 |
| 连锁总店（总部） | Central Shop of Chain Store (Headquarter) | 8858.9 | 515714.1 |
| 连锁直营店 | Direct-sale of Chain Store | 53.1 | 836.3 |
| 连锁加盟店 | Franchise Shop of Chain Store | 0.9 | 10181.0 |
| 其 他 | Other | 32635.1 | 2018735.6 |
| **按单位规模分** | **By Size of Enterprise** | | |
| 大 型 | Large | 18343.9 | 1168657.7 |
| 中 型 | Medium | 38539.0 | 1978959.0 |
| 小 型 | Small | 7565.1 | 290447.3 |
| 微 型 | Micro | 1006.8 | 96502.4 |

单位：万元 (10 000 yuan)

| 三、损益及分配 Profits and Losses | 四、人工成本及增值税 Labor cost and Value-added Tax | | 五、从事批发和零售业活动的从业人员平均人数（人） Annual Average Employees Engaged in wholesale and retail activities (persons) |
|---|---|---|---|
| 所得税费用 Income Tax Payable | 应付职工薪酬 Employee compensation | 应交增值税 Value-added Tax | |
| 16690.5 | 78924.6 | 23461.3 | 4257 |
| 245.3 | 7797.4 | 179.9 | 221 |
| 16442.4 | 70787.9 | 23232.6 | 3997 |
| 2.8 | 339.3 | 48.8 | 39 |
| 21838.1 | 66192.9 | 35138.8 | 4231 |
| 821.8 | 4164.6 | 2004.0 | 407 |
| 17796.4 | 31132.4 | 30884.3 | 1458 |
| 1484.9 | 30892.3 | 1391.4 | 2364 |
| 1735.0 | 3.6 | 859.1 | 2 |
| 181306.2 | 482332.5 | 410964.5 | 25391 |
| 2774.6 | 18065.8 | 5260.3 | 1487 |
| 352076.1 | 744873.9 | 625653.5 | 87653 |
| 16609.1 | 71311.4 | 23383.3 | 4064 |
| 19688.4 | 38852.2 | 31865.4 | 1677 |
| 151937.9 | 666718.4 | 426527.6 | 63929 |
| 120931.7 | 91407.2 | 163853.2 | 5549 |
| 15.6 | 3810.9 | 783.5 | 498 |
| 1520.5 | 640.7 | 818.1 | 59 |
| 298048.7 | 592858.6 | 505144.6 | 50237 |
| 187359.6 | 471600.1 | 295267.4 | 29867 |
| 327595.9 | 660326.9 | 592399.9 | 56965 |
| 38571.0 | 205119.8 | 150047.0 | 28947 |
| 18927.9 | 18389.0 | 59412.7 | 4493 |

# 表 15.7 限额以上零售业法人企业财务状况（2022 年）
## FINANCIAL INDICATORS OF RETAIL ENTERPRISES ABOVE DESIGNATED SIZE (2022)

| 指 标 | Item | 法人企业数（个）Number of Enterprises (unit) | 执行《2006年企业会计准则》企业数（个）Number of Enterprises which Implemented Accounting standard for Business Enterprise in 2006 (unit) | 一、年初存货 Inventory at the Beginning of Year |
|---|---|---|---|---|
| **总 计** | **Total** | **3970** | **2060** | **2443723.7** |
| **按零售行业小类分** | **By Retail Sector** | | | |
| 综合零售 | Comprehensive Retails | 394 | 223 | 553538.3 |
| 百货零售 | Department Stores | 145 | 92 | 293037.4 |
| 超级市场零售 | Supermarkets | 143 | 73 | 234837.9 |
| 便利店零售 | Convenience Stores | 33 | 17 | 11343.6 |
| 其他综合零售 | Other Comprehensive Retails | 73 | 41 | 14319.4 |
| 食品、饮料及烟草制品专门零售 | Special Retail of Food, Beverages and Tobacco | 618 | 269 | 86877.6 |
| 粮油零售 | Retail of Grains and Edible Oil | 65 | 26 | 8615.6 |
| 糕点、面包零售 | Retail of Cakes and Bread | 16 | 9 | 2587.3 |
| 果品、蔬菜零售 | Retail of Fruits and Vegetables | 148 | 51 | 7124.9 |
| 肉、禽、蛋、奶及水产品零售 | Retail of Meat, Poultry, Eggs and Aquatic Products | 127 | 54 | 9158.0 |
| 营养和保健品零售 | Retail of Nutraceutical Products | 8 | 5 | 1676.6 |
| 酒、饮料及茶叶零售 | Retail of Liquor, Beverages and Tea | 101 | 54 | 32436.9 |
| 烟草制品零售 | Retail of Tobacco | 6 | 3 | 8429.3 |
| 其他食品零售 | Retail of Other Food | 147 | 67 | 16849.0 |
| 纺织、服装及日用品专门零售 | Special Retail of Textile, Garments and Daily Consumer Articles | 192 | 116 | 226720.6 |
| 纺织品及针织品零售 | Retail of Textiles and Knitwear | 17 | 13 | 8801.3 |
| 服装零售 | Retail of Garments | 71 | 43 | 114160.0 |
| 鞋帽零售 | Retail of Shoes and Hats | 13 | 11 | 36621.8 |
| 化妆品及卫生用品零售 | Retail of Cosmetics and Sanitary Articles | 22 | 14 | 12885.7 |
| 厨具卫具及日用杂品零售 | Retail of Cooking Utensils, Bathroom Articles and Daily Groceries | 23 | 10 | 18897.6 |
| 钟表、眼镜零售 | Retail of Clocks, Watches and Glasses | 14 | 9 | 28139.3 |
| 箱包零售 | Retail of Suitcases and Bags | 3 | 1 | 341.9 |
| 自行车等代步设备零售 | Retail of Bicycles | 5 | 4 | 694.7 |
| 其他日用品零售 | Retail of Other General Merchandise | 24 | 11 | 6178.3 |
| 文化、体育用品及器材专门零售 | Special Retail of Cultural and Sports Articles | 88 | 42 | 95893.9 |
| 文具用品零售 | Retail of Cultural Articles | 43 | 21 | 6494.7 |
| 体育用品及器材零售 | Retail of Sports Articles | 3 | 2 | 1704.7 |
| 图书、报刊零售 | Retail of Books, Newspapers and Magazines | 9 | 4 | 60357.7 |
| 音像制品、电子和数字出版物零售 | Wholesale of audio-visual products, electronic and digital publications | 1 | | |
| 珠宝首饰零售 | Retail of Jewelry | 13 | 7 | 22216.6 |
| 工艺美术品及收藏品零售 | Retail of Handicrafts and Collections | 12 | 5 | 2065.7 |
| 乐器零售 | Retail of Musical Instrument | 2 | | 1053.4 |
| 照相器材零售 | Retail of Photographic Equipment | 1 | | 48.0 |
| 其他文化用品零售 | Retail of Other Cultural Goods | 4 | 3 | 1953.1 |

单位：万元 (10 000 yuan)

二、期末资产负债 Assets and Liabilities

| 流动资产合计 Total Current Assets | 应收账款 Accounts Receivable | 存货 Inventory | 固定资产原价 Total Original Value of Fixed Assets | 房屋和构筑物 Buildings and Structures | 机器设备 Machinery and Equipments |
|---|---|---|---|---|---|
| **10360173.4** | **955445.0** | **2812454.5** | **4052572.2** | **1107175.2** | **417012.4** |
| 1797890.4 | 229691.3 | 523345.7 | 1013515.1 | 51850.5 | 59196.7 |
| 1039713.0 | 53121.1 | 270502.8 | 698827.1 | 8403.3 | 4261.1 |
| 618203.4 | 128305.9 | 223765.2 | 229468.9 | 10082.6 | 29840.4 |
| 82483.4 | 34729.8 | 16066.7 | 60926.4 | 19946.5 | 22964.9 |
| 57490.6 | 13534.5 | 13011.0 | 24292.7 | 13418.1 | 2130.3 |
| 539978.4 | 147785.7 | 105498.3 | 158710.8 | 51561.9 | 34579.1 |
| 52599.5 | 17061.8 | 8428.7 | 38717.7 | 4882.5 | 8618.5 |
| 24906.3 | 2458.3 | 4033.9 | 8270.7 | 985.1 | 4096.2 |
| 70845.6 | 26598.3 | 9343.5 | 23450.8 | 8509.8 | 5870.7 |
| 107199.9 | 29575.4 | 10264.2 | 25248.4 | 9172.6 | 6919.4 |
| 3607.1 | 432.2 | 1552.2 | 1041.7 | 350.4 | 44.9 |
| 155994.7 | 48461.9 | 36780.7 | 27937.9 | 11476.6 | 2087.6 |
| 24338.6 | 630.3 | 8234.0 | 647.4 | | 280.7 |
| 100486.7 | 22567.5 | 26861.1 | 33396.2 | 16184.9 | 6661.1 |
| 615501.8 | 49694.3 | 212248.1 | 211674.8 | 175754.5 | 15698.0 |
| 22119.2 | 2057.8 | 9873.8 | 4197.5 | 875.4 | 342.0 |
| 379021.5 | 25529.7 | 105502.6 | 164402.7 | 152812.6 | 1827.1 |
| 102995.2 | 2685.3 | 31343.4 | 15683.6 | 6427.2 | 8836.5 |
| 22070.5 | 5082.0 | 13045.1 | 2978.7 | 518.1 | 581.8 |
| 29987.4 | 3156.2 | 19743.9 | 2779.9 | 530.2 | 680.2 |
| 37599.5 | 6447.2 | 23796.3 | 19736.2 | 14313.7 | 3095.7 |
| 957.3 | 493.5 | 383.3 | 16.7 | | |
| 1647.1 | 262.2 | 929.4 | 192.0 | | |
| 19104.1 | 3980.4 | 7630.3 | 1687.5 | 277.3 | 334.7 |
| 775727.5 | 122437.0 | 159795.3 | 177758.7 | 141825.7 | 4899.4 |
| 61679.6 | 27158.7 | 7308.5 | 10883.8 | 3701.8 | 3300.6 |
| 3763.5 | 1263.5 | 1854.8 | 578.2 | 36.5 | 541.7 |
| 653454.9 | 87407.7 | 122544.4 | 159248.3 | 134628.9 | 448.0 |
| 14.7 | 12.5 | 2.2 | | | |
| 37725.5 | 2763.1 | 23362.0 | 3732.5 | 1332.6 | 194.5 |
| 13990.9 | 3139.9 | 2308.0 | 2881.1 | 2125.9 | 414.6 |
| 1559.3 | 210.5 | 1067.6 | 57.6 | | |
| 459.4 | 18.2 | 48.0 | | | |
| 3079.7 | 462.9 | 1299.8 | 377.2 | | |

**表 15.7 续表 1 continued 1**

| 指 标 | Item | 二、期末资产负债 Assets and Liabilities 累计折旧 Cumulative Depreciation | 本年折旧 Depreciation | 固定资产净额 Net Value of Fixed Assets |
|---|---|---|---|---|
| **总 计** | **Total** | **1658307.1** | **202636.6** | **2071570.1** |
| **按零售行业小类分** | **By Retail Sector** | | | |
| 综合零售 | Comprehensive Retails | 484987.2 | 52066.8 | 463196.0 |
| 百货零售 | Department Stores | 320035.8 | 23391.9 | 355152.7 |
| 超级市场零售 | Supermarkets | 136280.7 | 18754.4 | 61522.1 |
| 便利店零售 | Convenience Stores | 21281.9 | 7912.1 | 33583.2 |
| 其他综合零售 | Other Comprehensive Retails | 7388.8 | 2008.4 | 12938.0 |
| 食品、饮料及烟草制品专门零售 | Special Retail of Food, Beverages and Tobacco | 40316.5 | 9932.5 | 98433.8 |
| 粮油零售 | Retail of Grains and Edible Oil | 6594.2 | 1614.2 | 28535.4 |
| 糕点、面包零售 | Retail of Cakes and Bread | 5798.9 | 961.0 | 1840.1 |
| 果品、蔬菜零售 | Retail of Fruits and Vegetables | 5511.8 | 1425.5 | 16410.5 |
| 肉、禽、蛋、奶及水产品零售 | Retail of Meat, Poultry, Eggs and Aquatic Products | 5726.0 | 1641.9 | 17375.0 |
| 营养和保健品零售 | Retail of Nutraceutical Products | 300.8 | 57.6 | 731.2 |
| 酒、饮料及茶叶零售 | Retail of Liquor, Beverages and Tea | 7647.7 | 1762.7 | 11087.7 |
| 烟草制品零售 | Retail of Tobacco | 384.9 | 106.7 | 262.5 |
| 其他食品零售 | Retail of Other Food | 8352.2 | 2362.9 | 22191.4 |
| 纺织、服装及日用品专门零售 | Special Retail of Textile, Garments and Daily Consumer Articles | 54993.8 | 7583.9 | 151129.7 |
| 纺织品及针织品零售 | Retail of Textiles and Knitwear | 831.5 | 394.7 | 3287.6 |
| 服装零售 | Retail of Garments | 34852.0 | 4875.5 | 126680.6 |
| 鞋帽零售 | Retail of Shoes and Hats | 9343.6 | 1184.3 | 6231.3 |
| 化妆品及卫生用品零售 | Retail of Cosmetics and Sanitary Articles | 1285.8 | 217.0 | 755.2 |
| 厨具卫具及日用杂品零售 | Retail of Cooking Utensils, Bathroom Articles and Daily Groceries | 797.8 | 79.9 | 1223.6 |
| 钟表、眼镜零售 | Retail of Clocks, Watches and Glasses | 7005.5 | 697.1 | 12507.5 |
| 箱包零售 | Retail of Suitcases and Bags | 3.9 | 3.9 | |
| 自行车等代步设备零售 | Retail of Bicycles | 16.2 | 6.4 | 153.3 |
| 其他日用品零售 | Retail of Other General Merchandise | 857.5 | 125.1 | 290.6 |
| 文化、体育用品及器材专门零售 | Special Retail of Cultural and Sports Articles | 73262.7 | 6335.4 | 100625.0 |
| 文具用品零售 | Retail of Cultural Articles | 4315.9 | 630.1 | 4268.6 |
| 体育用品及器材零售 | Retail of Sports Articles | 216.8 | 82.8 | 334.2 |
| 图书、报刊零售 | Retail of Books, Newspapers and Magazines | 66328.6 | 5276.3 | 92587.3 |
| 音像制品、电子和数字出版物零售 | Wholesale of audio-visual products, electronic and digital publications | | | |
| 珠宝首饰零售 | Retail of Jewelry | 1562.6 | 91.2 | 1004.2 |
| 工艺美术品及收藏品零售 | Retail of Handicrafts and Collections | 486.0 | 134.0 | 2362.8 |
| 乐器零售 | Retail of Musical Instrument | 45.6 | 4.8 | 8.8 |
| 照相器材零售 | Retail of Photographic Equipment | | | |
| 其他文化用品零售 | Retail of Other Cultural Goods | 307.2 | 116.2 | 59.1 |

单位：万元 (10 000 yuan)

| 二、期末资产负债 Assets and Liabilities | | | | | |
|---|---|---|---|---|---|
| 在建工程<br>Construction in Progress | 无形资产<br>Intangible Assets | 土地使用权<br>Land Use Rights | 资产总计<br>Total Assets | 流动负债合计<br>Total Current Liabilities | 应付账款<br>Accounts Payable |
| **278851.0** | **704182.8** | **302781.2** | **16837226.6** | **11704626.1** | **2129318.8** |
| 8434.4 | 24587.8 | 19816.6 | 3808509.5 | 1934261.8 | 543338.2 |
| 1282.6 | 18496.9 | 17750.3 | 2362283.4 | 1053754.5 | 230122.0 |
| 3610.1 | 3754.6 |  | 1154206.8 | 694701.3 | 278179.1 |
| 32.1 | 2167.8 | 1907.8 | 175137.4 | 145289.5 | 21194.0 |
| 3509.6 | 168.5 | 158.5 | 116881.9 | 40516.5 | 13843.1 |
| 24484.8 | 5485.7 | 2540.1 | 811231.8 | 300242.4 | 117150.7 |
| 3052.7 | 2166.6 | 2166.6 | 93796.1 | 29494.5 | 10937.5 |
| 202.1 | 169.5 |  | 36509.7 | 21901.5 | 1633.0 |
| 1780.4 | 1280.8 | 146.0 | 100450.8 | 37957.9 | 18060.2 |
| 11582.7 | 1192.1 | 195.5 | 147885.9 | 62377.1 | 27110.4 |
|  | 21.1 |  | 5923.0 | 1905.1 | 1304.2 |
| 7353.2 | 50.3 | 30.0 | 213817.0 | 84844.6 | 43559.0 |
|  | 83.8 |  | 25061.5 | 4471.4 | 2093.1 |
| 513.7 | 521.5 | 2.0 | 187787.8 | 57290.3 | 12453.3 |
| 1002.4 | 20067.9 | 19861.0 | 862726.7 | 468177.7 | 151490.5 |
|  | 18.2 |  | 41704.4 | 41883.6 | 7796.0 |
| 9.9 | 19901.5 | 19861.0 | 560681.6 | 246566.0 | 109389.3 |
| 962.3 |  |  | 109925.3 | 91090.7 | 13084.5 |
|  |  |  | 25303.5 | 20883.5 | 6149.4 |
|  |  |  | 33479.1 | 20410.7 | 2937.3 |
| 1.0 | 148.2 |  | 68295.0 | 30043.2 | 8429.1 |
|  |  |  | 1016.4 | 1358.0 | 619.9 |
|  |  |  | 1877.9 | 1127.4 | 269.3 |
| 29.2 |  |  | 20443.5 | 14814.6 | 2815.7 |
| 157697.3 | 8690.0 | 4837.6 | 1237514.5 | 515851.5 | 148579.9 |
| 4.5 | 3408.8 |  | 97908.2 | 35696.3 | 16505.1 |
|  |  |  | 16201.7 | 7858.9 | 6506.4 |
| 157685.3 | 5181.2 | 4759.6 | 1057704.9 | 430558.0 | 107445.0 |
|  |  |  | 125.2 |  |  |
| 7.5 |  |  | 40852.6 | 26531.3 | 11262.4 |
|  | 100.0 | 78.0 | 19240.4 | 13069.5 | 6255.2 |
|  |  |  | 1597.7 | 701.1 | 134.2 |
|  |  |  | 459.4 | 459.4 | 41.4 |
|  |  |  | 3424.4 | 977.0 | 430.2 |

**表 15.7 续表 2 continued 2**

| 指　标 | Item | 二、期末资产负债 Assets and Liabilities<br>负债合计<br>Total Liabilities | 所有者<br>权益合计<br>Total Owner's Equity | 实收资本<br>Paid-up<br>Capital |
|---|---|---|---|---|
| **总　计** | **Total** | **11591194.9** | 6692505.9 | 5115131.6 |
| **按零售行业小类分** | **By Retail Sector** | | | |
| 综合零售 | Comprehensive Retails | 2952971.4 | 859348.0 | 621870.7 |
| 百货零售 | Department Stores | 1705246.7 | 658760.5 | 256899.6 |
| 超级市场零售 | Supermarkets | 1026191.0 | 131269.9 | 255576.0 |
| 便利店零售 | Convenience Stores | 174977.4 | 160.0 | 77904.3 |
| 其他综合零售 | Other Comprehensive Retails | 46556.3 | 69157.6 | 31490.8 |
| 食品、饮料及烟草制品专门零售 | Special Retail of Food, Beverages and Tobacco | 454574.1 | 356724.3 | 111463.8 |
| 粮油零售 | Retail of Grains and Edible Oil | 50104.8 | 43691.3 | 15294.0 |
| 糕点、面包零售 | Retail of Cakes and Bread | 31099.2 | 5410.5 | 1753.0 |
| 果品、蔬菜零售 | Retail of Fruits and Vegetables | 59004.0 | 42618.8 | 16355.7 |
| 肉、禽、蛋、奶及水产品零售 | Retail of Meat, Poultry, Eggs and Aquatic Products | 86112.6 | 61773.3 | 31318.6 |
| 营养和保健品零售 | Retail of Nutraceutical Products | 2988.1 | 2934.9 | 1942.5 |
| 酒、饮料及茶叶零售 | Retail of Liquor, Beverages and Tea | 96574.2 | 116472.3 | 28519.3 |
| 烟草制品零售 | Retail of Tobacco | 4800.6 | 20260.9 | 2600.0 |
| 其他食品零售 | Retail of Other Food | 123890.6 | 63562.3 | 13680.7 |
| 纺织、服装及日用品专门零售 | Special Retail of Textile, Garments and Daily Consumer Articles | 650252.2 | 214778.0 | 129994.4 |
| 纺织品及针织品零售 | Retail of Textiles and Knitwear | 33899.4 | 7753.0 | 2470.3 |
| 服装零售 | Retail of Garments | 420864.8 | 145419.7 | 104697.1 |
| 鞋帽零售 | Retail of Shoes and Hats | 92328.6 | 17596.7 | 5132.9 |
| 化妆品及卫生用品零售 | Retail of Cosmetics and Sanitary Articles | 22599.3 | 1837.0 | 1544.1 |
| 厨具卫具及日用杂品零售 | Retail of Cooking Utensils, Bathroom Articles and Daily Groceries | 23821.8 | 9657.3 | 2299.4 |
| 钟表、眼镜零售 | Retail of Clocks, Watches and Glasses | 36642.8 | 29272.0 | 10152.5 |
| 箱包零售 | Retail of Suitcases and Bags | 1260.3 | -243.9 | 810.0 |
| 自行车等代步设备零售 | Retail of Bicycles | 1110.6 | 767.3 | 518.0 |
| 其他日用品零售 | Retail of Other General Merchandise | 17724.6 | 2718.9 | 2370.1 |
| 文化、体育用品及器材专门零售 | Special Retail of Cultural and Sports Articles | 579926.4 | 656742.2 | 48722.5 |
| 文具用品零售 | Retail of Cultural Articles | 51638.1 | 46270.1 | 12414.7 |
| 体育用品及器材零售 | Retail of Sports Articles | 17911.1 | -1709.4 | 1331.8 |
| 图书、报刊零售 | Retail of Books, Newspapers and Magazines | 465275.4 | 592429.5 | 20539.9 |
| 音像制品、电子和数字出版物零售 | Wholesale of audio-visual products, electronic and digital publications | 85.2 | 40.0 | |
| 珠宝首饰零售 | Retail of Jewelry | 27720.7 | 13131.9 | 7678.0 |
| 工艺美术品及收藏品零售 | Retail of Handicrafts and Collections | 14006.2 | 5234.2 | 5990.1 |
| 乐器零售 | Retail of Musical Instrument | 1196.8 | 400.9 | 250.0 |
| 照相器材零售 | Retail of Photographic Equipment | 459.4 | | |
| 其他文化用品零售 | Retail of Other Cultural Goods | 1633.5 | 945.0 | 518.0 |

单位：万元 (10 000 yuan)

| 二、期末资产负债 Assets and Liabilities | 三、损益及分配 Profits and Losses | | | | |
|---|---|---|---|---|---|
| 个人资本 Personal Capital | 营业收入 Gross Sales | 主营业务收入 Main Business Income | 营业成本 Operating Cost | 税金及附加 Taxes and Surcharges | 其他业务利润 Other Business Profits |
| **416713.7** | **37221956.1** | **36096059.4** | **33025527.3** | **123384.1** | **370993.1** |
| 28905.4 | 5912322.9 | 5559148.1 | 4686974.9 | 40937.7 | 259127.1 |
| 9355.8 | 2534244.0 | 2339358.2 | 1901195.0 | 31902.1 | 154024.1 |
| 13037.9 | 2785125.4 | 2658506.3 | 2285949.8 | 6197.6 | 102711.1 |
| 3111.1 | 366634.0 | 340250.9 | 312466.4 | 667.6 | 2308.8 |
| 3400.6 | 226319.5 | 221032.7 | 187363.7 | 2170.4 | 83.1 |
| 34657.4 | 1907898.2 | 1893252.8 | 1634076.7 | 5933.2 | 1509.9 |
| 2446.9 | 192901.7 | 189956.8 | 172059.1 | 412.1 | 1120.6 |
| 853.0 | 72341.0 | 72176.2 | 45324.7 | 89.9 | 6.8 |
| 6875.4 | 333544.5 | 331258.3 | 292908.7 | 688.8 | -0.9 |
| 11184.2 | 413219.1 | 412383.8 | 367412.3 | 1142.9 | 31.0 |
| | 18058.5 | 17796.7 | 14337.0 | 36.8 | 197.3 |
| 6589.1 | 419858.9 | 416832.9 | 349759.3 | 1857.7 | 34.8 |
| | 56862.2 | 56743.1 | 44327.9 | 182.2 | 119.1 |
| 6708.8 | 401112.3 | 396105.0 | 347947.7 | 1522.8 | 1.2 |
| 8398.1 | 1051866.3 | 983637.3 | 788625.5 | 5339.4 | 21660.7 |
| 1010.3 | 99636.5 | 98961.8 | 82046.2 | 178.6 | |
| 2232.0 | 545548.5 | 517297.8 | 407632.1 | 2931.3 | 20366.1 |
| 232.5 | 91536.0 | 91518.5 | 59868.7 | 359.0 | |
| 292.5 | 47823.6 | 46338.5 | 36860.1 | 577.8 | 62.2 |
| 1362.6 | 71501.5 | 69253.6 | 56934.1 | 430.1 | 57.8 |
| 2199.1 | 129667.1 | 94751.7 | 89697.3 | 724.0 | 1168.2 |
| 10.0 | 2168.3 | 2168.3 | 1858.6 | 5.2 | |
| 300.0 | 6920.2 | 6920.2 | 5944.3 | 19.1 | |
| 759.1 | 57064.6 | 56426.9 | 47784.1 | 114.3 | 6.4 |
| 6402.6 | 507073.8 | 495362.6 | 351899.3 | 3866.5 | 7861.7 |
| 3199.8 | 117211.4 | 114711.5 | 100271.6 | 318.1 | 55.9 |
| 34.8 | 25377.0 | 25340.6 | 17277.2 | 88.4 | 36.4 |
| 1030.0 | 284065.1 | 275852.0 | 168872.0 | 2276.6 | 7568.3 |
| 1170.0 | 43798.4 | 43735.9 | 34799.1 | 1082.1 | 200.9 |
| 250.0 | 29928.9 | 29692.8 | 24929.8 | 94.9 | 0.2 |
| 200.0 | 2202.0 | 2202.0 | 1943.8 | 1.2 | |
| | 1561.2 | 1561.2 | 1499.6 | 0.1 | |
| 518.0 | 2929.8 | 2266.6 | 2306.2 | 5.1 | |

**表 15.7 续表 3 continued 3**

| 指 标 | Item | 三、损益及分配 Profits and Losses | | |
|---|---|---|---|---|
| | | 销售费用 Sales Expenses | 管理费用 Management Expenses | 研发费用 R&D expenses |
| **总 计** | **Total** | **2483437.1** | **883894.2** | **9757.9** |
| **按零售行业小类分** | **By Retail Sector** | | | |
| 综合零售 | Comprehensive Retails | 765764.8 | 248944.6 | 3181.3 |
| 百货零售 | Department Stores | 334200.5 | 152222.4 | 2867.3 |
| 超级市场零售 | Supermarkets | 387764.9 | 64693.7 | 307.8 |
| 便利店零售 | Convenience Stores | 31845.3 | 20905.0 | 0.1 |
| 其他综合零售 | Other Comprehensive Retails | 11954.1 | 11123.5 | 6.1 |
| 食品、饮料及烟草制品专门零售 | Special Retail of Food, Beverages and Tobacco | 102417.1 | 65031.0 | 1171.0 |
| 粮油零售 | Retail of Grains and Edible Oil | 6697.1 | 4952.4 | 26.6 |
| 糕点、面包零售 | Retail of Cakes and Bread | 22713.6 | 4092.0 | 4.4 |
| 果品、蔬菜零售 | Retail of Fruits and Vegetables | 12259.5 | 11679.9 | 15.9 |
| 肉、禽、蛋、奶及水产品零售 | Retail of Meat, Poultry, Eggs and Aquatic Products | 18549.6 | 13639.9 | 203.2 |
| 营养和保健品零售 | Retail of Nutraceutical Products | 2453.8 | 892.8 | 17.0 |
| 酒、饮料及茶叶零售 | Retail of Liquor, Beverages and Tea | 12397.4 | 13144.0 | 354.5 |
| 烟草制品零售 | Retail of Tobacco | 3417.7 | 2224.4 | |
| 其他食品零售 | Retail of Other Food | 23928.4 | 14405.6 | 549.4 |
| 纺织、服装及日用品专门零售 | Special Retail of Textile, Garments and Daily Consumer Articles | 169954.1 | 63784.7 | 18.1 |
| 纺织品及针织品零售 | Retail of Textiles and Knitwear | 13782.1 | 2643.7 | 2.7 |
| 服装零售 | Retail of Garments | 83749.2 | 41613.9 | 10.9 |
| 鞋帽零售 | Retail of Shoes and Hats | 25093.5 | 5605.7 | 0.2 |
| 化妆品及卫生用品零售 | Retail of Cosmetics and Sanitary Articles | 7021.2 | 1862.6 | 2.1 |
| 厨具卫具及日用杂品零售 | Retail of Cooking Utensils, Bathroom Articles and Daily Groceries | 8354.8 | 2576.3 | 1.1 |
| 钟表、眼镜零售 | Retail of Clocks, Watches and Glasses | 26358.3 | 6826.8 | 0.8 |
| 箱包零售 | Retail of Suitcases and Bags | 428.4 | 58.6 | |
| 自行车等代步设备零售 | Retail of Bicycles | 204.6 | 311.9 | |
| 其他日用品零售 | Retail of Other General Merchandise | 4962.0 | 2285.2 | 0.3 |
| 文化、体育用品及器材专门零售 | Special Retail of Cultural and Sports Articles | 71987.4 | 54535.9 | 60.6 |
| 文具用品零售 | Retail of Cultural Articles | 10470.9 | 5901.4 | 1.3 |
| 体育用品及器材零售 | Retail of Sports Articles | 8574.7 | 596.9 | |
| 图书、报刊零售 | Retail of Books, Newspapers and Magazines | 43467.7 | 43810.2 | 20.0 |
| 音像制品、电子和数字出版物零售 | Wholesale of audio-visual products, electronic and digital publications | | | |
| 珠宝首饰零售 | Retail of Jewelry | 6021.8 | 2334.7 | 0.4 |
| 工艺美术品及收藏品零售 | Retail of Handicrafts and Collections | 2934.0 | 1429.5 | 38.9 |
| 乐器零售 | Retail of Musical Instrument | 43.0 | 178.6 | |
| 照相器材零售 | Retail of Photographic Equipment | 0.2 | 64.7 | |
| 其他文化用品零售 | Retail of Other Cultural Goods | 475.1 | 219.9 | |

单位：万元 (10 000 yuan)

三、损益及分配 Profits and Losses

| 财务费用<br>Financial Expenses | 利息收入<br>Interest Income | 利息费用<br>Interest expenses | 投资收益<br>Income from Investment | 营业利润<br>Business Profits | 营业外收入<br>Non-business Income |
|---|---|---|---|---|---|
| **137858.6** | **16767.4** | **91857.5** | **91329.6** | **545842.4** | **76678.6** |
| 51835.9 | 9817.5 | 29548.5 | 61290.2 | 113119.7 | 13133.4 |
| 23445.7 | 8802.4 | 21913.8 | 60268.1 | 107040.4 | 4097.8 |
| 25090.6 | 755.4 | 5509.7 | -1404.4 | -7126.3 | 7809.3 |
| 2341.5 | 128.0 | 1560.8 | 51.8 | -1769.4 | 455.9 |
| 958.1 | 131.7 | 564.2 | 2374.7 | 14975.0 | 770.4 |
| 5935.6 | 234.9 | 3214.5 | 2294.1 | 86868.0 | 3321.0 |
| 529.0 | 72.3 | 306.5 | 11.2 | 5874.9 | 128.7 |
| 604.0 | 13.9 | 492.7 | | -429.0 | 441.7 |
| 789.4 | 27.2 | 310.5 | 335.5 | 12048.5 | 188.5 |
| 1571.1 | 14.1 | 1199.6 | 1797.8 | 11889.8 | 975.6 |
| 95.0 | 0.5 | 2.9 | 8.9 | 273.6 | 2.4 |
| 1120.3 | -90.5 | 463.5 | -141.3 | 39371.6 | 127.0 |
| 3.3 | 150.4 | 1.0 | | 6596.7 | 28.2 |
| 1223.5 | 47.0 | 437.8 | 282.0 | 11241.9 | 1428.9 |
| 10011.2 | 4003.3 | 10517.1 | 1101.8 | 13595.7 | 3745.6 |
| 683.6 | 4.8 | 45.6 | 22.6 | 219.5 | 18.0 |
| 7210.5 | 3957.7 | 9067.1 | -1005.4 | 2855.7 | 3379.5 |
| 199.1 | 2.4 | 151.9 | 2222.7 | -2.2 | 144.8 |
| 179.7 | 1.3 | 50.7 | 18.7 | 1202.7 | 59.6 |
| 352.9 | 12.7 | 197.5 | -124.5 | 2644.9 | 48.1 |
| 1101.7 | 24.2 | 857.9 | -32.3 | 4936.1 | 47.8 |
| 0.9 | | 0.7 | | -183.6 | 4.9 |
| 18.0 | | | | 433.3 | |
| 264.8 | 0.2 | 145.7 | | 1489.3 | 42.9 |
| -2896.7 | -4712.7 | 1326.8 | 6797.3 | 34402.9 | 335.3 |
| 273.3 | 89.5 | 244.6 | | 3077.2 | 54.7 |
| 395.3 | 0.5 | 338.7 | | -1502.0 | 3.9 |
| -3961.4 | -4842.5 | 633.5 | 6766.0 | 32935.7 | 238.3 |
| 293.9 | 41.0 | 103.5 | 8.6 | -489.6 | 7.2 |
| 96.1 | -1.3 | 6.5 | 20.5 | 425.7 | 30.1 |
| 0.4 | | | 2.2 | 34.8 | |
| 0.1 | | | | -3.7 | |
| 5.6 | 0.1 | | | -75.2 | 1.1 |

表 15.7 续表 4 continued 4

| 指 标 | Item | 三、损益及分配 Profits and Losses 营业外支出 Non-business Expenses | 利润总额 Total Profits |
|---|---|---|---|
| **总 计** | **Total** | **26271.1** | **599663.3** |
| **按零售行业小类分** | **By Retail Sector** | | |
| 综合零售 | Comprehensive Retails | 5382.4 | 120317.1 |
| 百货零售 | Department Stores | 3110.3 | 107974.3 |
| 超级市场零售 | Supermarkets | 1455.2 | -1272.2 |
| 便利店零售 | Convenience Stores | 338.4 | -1651.9 |
| 其他综合零售 | Other Comprehensive Retails | 478.5 | 15266.9 |
| 食品、饮料及烟草制品专门零售 | Special Retail of Food, Beverages and Tobacco | 2280.5 | 87882.1 |
| 粮油零售 | Retail of Grains and Edible Oil | 463.8 | 5513.3 |
| 糕点、面包零售 | Retail of Cakes and Bread | 722.7 | -710.0 |
| 果品、蔬菜零售 | Retail of Fruits and Vegetables | 43.3 | 12193.7 |
| 肉、禽、蛋、奶及水产品零售 | Retail of Meat, Poultry, Eggs and Aquatic Products | 436.6 | 12428.8 |
| 营养和保健品零售 | Retail of Nutraceutical Products | 2.4 | 273.6 |
| 酒、饮料及茶叶零售 | Retail of Liquor, Beverages and Tea | 56.3 | 39442.3 |
| 烟草制品零售 | Retail of Tobacco | | 6624.9 |
| 其他食品零售 | Retail of Other Food | 555.4 | 12115.5 |
| 纺织、服装及日用品专门零售 | Special Retail of Textile, Garments and Daily Consumer Articles | 1813.8 | 17387.1 |
| 纺织品及针织品零售 | Retail of Textiles and Knitwear | 59.8 | 177.7 |
| 服装零售 | Retail of Garments | 1541.3 | 4696.7 |
| 鞋帽零售 | Retail of Shoes and Hats | 29.9 | 2022.8 |
| 化妆品及卫生用品零售 | Retail of Cosmetics and Sanitary Articles | 60.9 | 1201.4 |
| 厨具卫具及日用杂品零售 | Retail of Cooking Utensils, Bathroom Articles and Daily Groceries | 7.4 | 2632.3 |
| 钟表、眼镜零售 | Retail of Clocks, Watches and Glasses | 111.1 | 4872.8 |
| 箱包零售 | Retail of Suitcases and Bags | | -178.7 |
| 自行车等代步设备零售 | Retail of Bicycles | | 433.3 |
| 其他日用品零售 | Retail of Other General Merchandise | 3.4 | 1528.8 |
| 文化、体育用品及器材专门零售 | Special Retail of Cultural and Sports Articles | 1204.1 | 33995.8 |
| 文具用品零售 | Retail of Cultural Articles | 527.2 | 3110.8 |
| 体育用品及器材零售 | Retail of Sports Articles | 7.3 | -1505.4 |
| 图书、报刊零售 | Retail of Books, Newspapers and Magazines | 647.0 | 32480.4 |
| 音像制品、电子和数字出版物零售 | Wholesale of audio-visual products, electronic and digital publications | | |
| 珠宝首饰零售 | Retail of Jewelry | 13.3 | -495.7 |
| 工艺美术品及收藏品零售 | Retail of Handicrafts and Collections | 9.3 | 446.5 |
| 乐器零售 | Retail of Musical Instrument | | 37.0 |
| 照相器材零售 | Retail of Photographic Equipment | | -3.7 |
| 其他文化用品零售 | Retail of Other Cultural Goods | | -74.1 |

单位: 万元 (10 000 yuan)

| 三、损益及分配 Profits and Losses | 四、人工成本及增值税 Labor cost and Value-added Tax | | 五、从事批发和零售业活动的从业人员平均人数(人) Annual Average Employees Engaged in wholesale and retail activities (persons) |
|---|---|---|---|
| 所得税费用 Income Tax Payable | 应付职工薪酬 Employee compensation | 应交增值税 Value-added Tax | |
| **63693.4** | **1428296.7** | **315129** | **186570** |
| 13197.8 | 442725.8 | 70118 | 60223 |
| 10879.7 | 215274.4 | 39666 | 21011 |
| 1983.9 | 199449.5 | 22494 | 34648 |
| -873.2 | 18781.0 | 1370 | 2661 |
| 1207.4 | 9220.9 | 6588 | 1903 |
| 11784.9 | 81865.7 | 16804 | 14767 |
| 517.6 | 5018.5 | 1504 | 1040 |
| -120.4 | 13691.0 | 589 | 2161 |
| 711.7 | 13111.0 | 2205 | 2598 |
| 1305.1 | 21210.1 | 2298 | 3308 |
| 9.6 | 1236.2 | 396 | 245 |
| 7629.1 | 10378.3 | 7400 | 1964 |
| 973.8 | 2435.2 | 1201 | 296 |
| 758.4 | 14785.4 | 1212 | 3155 |
| 3849.9 | 85555.9 | 20019 | 14141 |
| 34.8 | 8830.4 | 1477 | 1190 |
| 2032.0 | 41067.6 | 10967 | 6687 |
| 33.4 | 10937.4 | 2730 | 1698 |
| 387.9 | 3913.5 | 852 | 987 |
| 42.9 | 5450.2 | 461 | 907 |
| 1273.7 | 13089.1 | 2651 | 1986 |
| 0.2 | 215.0 | 14 | 138 |
| 13.8 | 285.5 | 100 | 56 |
| 31.2 | 1767.2 | 768 | 492 |
| 4.5 | 74343.5 | 4471 | 5377 |
| 423.8 | 6240.9 | 1494 | 1029 |
| -391.0 | 803.7 | 661 | 546 |
| -31.2 | 63291.6 | 1776 | 3044 |
| -25.4 | 2481.2 | 231 | 452 |
| 24.3 | 903.9 | 246 | 175 |
| 0.6 | 136.3 | 17 | 34 |
| | 4.4 | | 6 |
| 3.4 | 481.5 | 46 | 91 |

**表 15.7 续表 5 continued 5**

| 指 标 | Item | 法人企业数(个) Number of Enterprises (unit) | 执行《2006年企业会计准则》企业数(个) Number of Enterprises which Implemented Accounting standard for Business Enterprise in 2006 (unit) | 一、年初存货 Inventory at the Beginning of Year |
|---|---|---|---|---|
| 医药及医疗器材专门零售 | Special Retail of Medicine and Medical Appliances | 158 | 93 | 147601.1 |
| 西药零售 | Retail of Western Medicine | 123 | 75 | 140444.4 |
| 中药零售 | Retail of Tradition Chinese Medicine | 16 | 11 | 5015.1 |
| 医疗用品及器材零售 | Retail of Medical Articles and Appliances | 19 | 7 | 2141.6 |
| 汽车、摩托车、零配件和燃料及其他动力销售 | Special Retail of Automobiles, Motorcycles, Fuel and Spare Parts | 1249 | 747 | 1016790.4 |
| 汽车新车零售 | Retail of New Automobiles | 883 | 533 | 841776.1 |
| 汽车旧车零售 | Retail of Second-hand Automobiles | 14 | 7 | 1284.2 |
| 汽车零配件零售 | Retail of Automobile Fittings | 31 | 17 | 4794.1 |
| 摩托车及零配件零售 | Retail of Motorcycles and Parts | 76 | 40 | 13120.4 |
| 机动车燃料零售 | Retail of Motor Fuel | 232 | 140 | 154712.1 |
| 机动车燃气零售 | Retail of Motor Gas | 11 | 8 | 758.9 |
| 机动车充电零售 | Retail of Motor Eletricity | 2 | 2 | 344.6 |
| 家用电器及电子产品专门零售 | Special Retail of Household Electrical Appliances and Electronic Products | 458 | 236 | 122235.1 |
| 家用视听设备零售 | Retail of Household Audio and Video Appliances | 78 | 43 | 26535.8 |
| 日用家电零售 | Retail of Household Electrical Appliances | 145 | 77 | 38733.9 |
| 计算机、软件及辅助设备零售 | Retail of Computers, Software and Assistant Equipment | 129 | 69 | 16720.7 |
| 通信设备零售 | Retail of Communication Equipment | 70 | 24 | 29895.1 |
| 其他电子产品零售 | Retail of Other Electronic Products | 36 | 23 | 10349.6 |
| 五金、家具及室内装饰材料专门零售 | Special Retail of Hardware, Furniture and Decoration Materials | 434 | 184 | 40543.1 |
| 五金零售 | Retail of Hardware | 119 | 50 | 12000.9 |
| 灯具零售 | Retail of Light Fittings | 16 | 5 | 1834.4 |
| 家具零售 | Retail of Furniture | 64 | 26 | 7477.5 |
| 涂料零售 | Retail of Paint | 8 | 1 | 1230.5 |
| 卫生洁具零售 | Retail of Sanitary Ware | 12 | 3 | 1120.6 |
| 木质装饰材料零售 | Retail of Wooden Decorative Materials | 18 | 11 | 1599.4 |
| 陶瓷、石材装饰材料零售 | Retail of Ceramics and Stone Decorative Materials | 48 | 24 | 3977.9 |
| 其他室内装饰材料零售 | Retail of Other Indoor Decoration Materials | 149 | 64 | 11301.9 |
| 货摊、无店铺及其他零售业 | Stall, Non-shop and Other Retails | 379 | 150 | 153523.6 |
| 互联网零售 | E-commerce Retails | 324 | 121 | 144697.3 |
| 自动售货机零售 | Vending Machine Retails | 2 | 2 | 368.8 |
| 旧货零售 | Retail of Used Goods | 1 | 1 | |
| 生活用燃料零售 | Retail of Fuel for Daily Use | 20 | 9 | 1065.4 |
| 宠物食品用品零售 | Retail of Pet Foods and Articles | 1 | 1 | 57.7 |
| 其他未列明零售业 | Other Retails not Classified Elsewhere | 31 | 16 | 7334.4 |

单位：万元 (10 000 yuan)

| 二、期末资产负债 Assets and Liabilities | | | | | |
|---|---|---|---|---|---|
| 流动资产合计 Total Current Assets | 应收账款 Accounts Receivable | 存货 Inventory | 固定资产原价 Total Original Value of Fixed Assets | 房屋和构筑物 Buildings and Structures | 机器设备 Machinery and Equipments |
| 508296.7 | 149691.4 | 161651.6 | 82316.2 | 36097.7 | 9837.8 |
| 468991.5 | 133113.0 | 152425.1 | 73007.1 | 31493.8 | 7851.8 |
| 15883.8 | 6329.0 | 7968.8 | 5198.9 | 3011.0 | 1635.6 |
| 23421.4 | 10249.4 | 1257.7 | 4110.2 | 1592.9 | 350.4 |
| 4460418.7 | -139193.0 | 1303523.5 | 2068005.1 | 550749.1 | 174990.3 |
| 3022143.6 | 220392.7 | 981926.1 | 631610.7 | 294381.2 | 95227.4 |
| 8835.0 | 1050.0 | 1584.8 | 6913.7 | 5310.0 | 328.9 |
| 22503.5 | 9270.9 | 6944.4 | 2881.7 | 218.9 | 1279.4 |
| 46253.3 | 7923.7 | 16481.7 | 9788.7 | 1871.9 | 1244.1 |
| 669753.5 | -382018.4 | 295111.9 | 1373478.5 | 222032.3 | 67484.7 |
| 680909.9 | 1762.1 | 1000.1 | 36864.2 | 26934.8 | 2996.6 |
| 10019.9 | 2426.0 | 474.5 | 6467.6 | | 6429.2 |
| 644048.5 | 114404.5 | 146556.8 | 103375.7 | 31959.6 | 24178.2 |
| 182197.5 | 19386.4 | 37571.9 | 35981.5 | 15375.7 | 5781.3 |
| 246073.3 | 26632.8 | 48993.0 | 29377.9 | 13344.4 | 4663.5 |
| 97112.0 | 38564.2 | 19759.1 | 13260.4 | 2124.6 | 4595.8 |
| 84702.5 | 16980.0 | 29993.8 | 21939.8 | 865.2 | 8336.5 |
| 33963.2 | 12841.1 | 10239.0 | 2816.1 | 249.7 | 801.1 |
| 316215.8 | 149054.2 | 49403.9 | 116998.0 | 57428.3 | 13228.3 |
| 65261.3 | 31330.8 | 12993.5 | 22847.5 | 4759.9 | 2977.2 |
| 9178.6 | 1618.6 | 2149.2 | 1341.6 | 122.5 | 120.1 |
| 28911.8 | 5500.7 | 9472.7 | 67503.2 | 50255.2 | 5671.4 |
| 6015.8 | 2850.9 | 810.4 | 1667.3 | | 1474.5 |
| 6834.9 | 3625.6 | 2199.0 | 630.2 | | 78.2 |
| 7676.5 | 3413.1 | 2137.4 | 1001.3 | 36.0 | 53.9 |
| 59156.9 | 32865.1 | 4801.9 | 7889.4 | 461.3 | 911.0 |
| 133180.0 | 67849.4 | 14839.8 | 14117.5 | 1793.4 | 1942.0 |
| 702095.6 | 131879.6 | 150431.3 | 120217.8 | 9947.9 | 80404.6 |
| 633917.6 | 115502.2 | 140998.2 | 48713.3 | 7964.1 | 19033.9 |
| 454.9 | 26.3 | 112.0 | 1122.6 | | |
| 884.9 | 85.4 | 78.4 | 64.1 | | |
| 11556.0 | 2444.6 | 1285.4 | 9430.4 | 1368.8 | 3898.4 |
| 234.8 | 170.0 | 39.8 | 295.8 | | |
| 55047.4 | 13651.1 | 7917.5 | 60591.6 | 615.0 | 57472.3 |

**表 15.7 续表 6 continued 6**

| 指 标 | Item | 二、期末资产负债 Assets and Liabilities | | |
|---|---|---|---|---|
| | | 累计折旧 Cumulative Depreciation | 本年折旧 Depreciation | 固定资产净额 Net Value of Fixed Assets |
| 医药及医疗器材专门零售 | Special Retail of Medicine and Medical Appliances | 39347.3 | 6463.1 | 40236.3 |
| 西药零售 | Retail of Western Medicine | 37185.1 | 5924.3 | 33822.8 |
| 中药零售 | Retail of Tradition Chinese Medicine | 1037.0 | 229.0 | 3987.3 |
| 医疗用品及器材零售 | Retail of Medical Articles and Appliances | 1125.2 | 309.8 | 2426.2 |
| 汽车、摩托车、零配件和燃料及其他动力销售 | Special Retail of Automobiles, Motorcycles, Fuel and Spare Parts | 838845.5 | 95104.7 | 1049652.1 |
| 汽车新车零售 | Retail of New Automobiles | 252678.0 | 50646.2 | 337436.0 |
| 汽车旧车零售 | Retail of Second-hand Automobiles | 1808.9 | 715.3 | 4754.9 |
| 汽车零配件零售 | Retail of Automobile Fittings | 1555.6 | 273.4 | 1139.6 |
| 摩托车及零配件零售 | Retail of Motorcycles and Parts | 3007.4 | 706.3 | 3157.9 |
| 机动车燃料零售 | Retail of Motor Fuel | 559862.7 | 41488.1 | 680506.5 |
| 机动车燃气零售 | Retail of Motor Gas | 18950.8 | 660.8 | 17202.1 |
| 机动车充电零售 | Retail of Motor Eletricity | 982.1 | 614.6 | 5455.1 |
| 家用电器及电子产品专门零售 | Special Retail of Household Electrical Appliances and Electronic Products | 40027.8 | 7786.7 | 51398.8 |
| 家用视听设备零售 | Retail of Household Audio and Video Appliances | 13350.1 | 2063.2 | 17107.3 |
| 日用家电零售 | Retail of Household Electrical Appliances | 12497.0 | 3367.6 | 14425.2 |
| 计算机、软件及辅助设备零售 | Retail of Computers, Software and Assistant Equipment | 4948.4 | 903.9 | 6088.0 |
| 通信设备零售 | Retail of Communication Equipment | 8181.3 | 1225.0 | 12764.2 |
| 其他电子产品零售 | Retail of Other Electronic Products | 1051.0 | 227.0 | 1014.1 |
| 五金、家具及室内装饰材料专门零售 | Special Retail of Hardware, Furniture and Decoration Materials | 36701.8 | 5845.8 | 55268.8 |
| 五金零售 | Retail of Hardware | 3921.8 | 723.9 | 8380.6 |
| 灯具零售 | Retail of Light Fittings | 367.0 | 135.5 | 488.0 |
| 家具零售 | Retail of Furniture | 25535.2 | 3100.2 | 36564.2 |
| 涂料零售 | Retail of Paint | 621.1 | 212.6 | 989.8 |
| 卫生洁具零售 | Retail of Sanitary Ware | 264.3 | 105.4 | 5.5 |
| 木质装饰材料零售 | Retail of Wooden Decorative Materials | 418.4 | 141.6 | 171.8 |
| 陶瓷、石材装饰材料零售 | Retail of Ceramics and Stone Decorative Materials | 2074.1 | 574.8 | 3184.1 |
| 其他室内装饰材料零售 | Retail of Other Indoor Decoration Materials | 3499.9 | 851.8 | 5484.8 |
| 货摊、无店铺及其他零售业 | Stall, Non-shop and Other Retails | 49824.5 | 11517.7 | 61629.6 |
| 互联网零售 | E-commerce Retails | 17195.7 | 4666.7 | 24935.0 |
| 自动售货机零售 | Vending Machine Retails | 994.8 | 19.0 | 27.8 |
| 旧货零售 | Retail of Used Goods | 12.5 | 10.2 | |
| 生活用燃料零售 | Retail of Fuel for Daily Use | 4521.0 | 890.8 | 4098.7 |
| 宠物食品用品零售 | Retail of Pet Foods and Articles | 103.5 | 0.6 | |
| 其他未列明零售业 | Other Retails not Classified Elsewhere | 26997.0 | 5930.4 | 32568.1 |

单位：万元 (10 000 yuan)

| 二、期末资产负债 Assets and Liabilities | | | | | |
| --- | --- | --- | --- | --- | --- |
| 在建工程<br>Construction in Progress | 无形资产<br>Intangible Assets | 土地使用权<br>Land Use Rights | 资产总计<br>Total Assets | 流动负债合计<br>Total Current Liabilities | 应付账款<br>Accounts Payable |
| 1186.3 | 6231.1 | 4724.3 | 718975.4 | 478435.6 | 203465.6 |
| 34.5 | 5753.9 | 4248.5 | 643429.3 | 432773.0 | 188122.3 |
| 1151.8 | 477.2 | 475.8 | 20847.5 | 14037.5 | 7488.1 |
| | | | 54698.6 | 31625.1 | 7855.2 |
| 80353.8 | 612314.8 | 227263.2 | 7120972.3 | 6661659.1 | 571524.3 |
| 24692.3 | 86215.3 | 60636.4 | 3890456.4 | 2704143.9 | 440423.3 |
| | | | 14523.1 | 10230.0 | 2297.7 |
| | 0.8 | | 25588.6 | 18240.6 | 7863.3 |
| 82.1 | 248.1 | 20.0 | 61375.9 | 30797.9 | 8946.8 |
| 52893.0 | 498627.8 | 140924.5 | 2394402.5 | 2819893.4 | 106208.1 |
| 2630.0 | 27222.8 | 25682.3 | 718189.3 | 1075695.7 | 4478.9 |
| 56.4 | | | 16436.5 | 2657.6 | 1306.2 |
| 753.4 | 738.3 | | 798930.7 | 499254.6 | 153522.8 |
| 119.5 | | | 251507.9 | 124478.7 | 35880.9 |
| 564.5 | 2.1 | | 286840.3 | 231654.7 | 81254.0 |
| 69.4 | 709.5 | | 116756.3 | 47366.6 | 21197.9 |
| | 0.6 | | 104000.4 | 69579.9 | 3594.7 |
| | 26.1 | | 39825.8 | 26174.7 | 11595.3 |
| 512.4 | 22725.1 | 22674.7 | 577672.3 | 303986.7 | 87781.3 |
| 127.5 | 173.9 | 139.9 | 90782.8 | 45323.1 | 15379.8 |
| | | | 10718.3 | 8581.7 | 1086.4 |
| 203.8 | 22472.6 | 22470.1 | 93497.5 | 18979.2 | 4599.2 |
| | 31.7 | 31.7 | 8305.3 | 5019.6 | 1986.9 |
| 15.9 | | | 7193.6 | 3489.6 | 1222.6 |
| | | | 9104.4 | 4395.7 | 1242.6 |
| | 33.0 | 33.0 | 64535.7 | 13840.2 | 6384.1 |
| 165.2 | 13.9 | | 293534.7 | 204357.6 | 55879.7 |
| 4426.2 | 3342.1 | 1063.7 | 900693.4 | 542756.7 | 152465.5 |
| 487.0 | 1513.9 | | 769937.0 | 498953.5 | 142301.4 |
| | | | 877.8 | 309.5 | 31.6 |
| | | | 884.9 | 334.7 | |
| | 1474.8 | 1063.7 | 18172.9 | 8703.0 | 766.2 |
| | | | 372.1 | 8.1 | 2.3 |
| 3939.2 | 353.4 | | 110448.7 | 34447.9 | 9364.0 |

**表 15.7 续表 7 continued 7**

| 指 标 | Item | 二、期末资产负债 Assets and Liabilities 负债合计 Total Liabilities | 所有者权益合计 Total Owner's Equity | 实收资本 Paid-up Capital |
|---|---|---|---|---|
| 医药及医疗器材专门零售 | Special Retail of Medicine and Medical Appliances | 596783.9 | 120603.2 | 120622.5 |
| 西药零售 | Retail of Western Medicine | 533728.7 | 108347.5 | 108218.3 |
| 中药零售 | Retail of Tradition Chinese Medicine | 15187.5 | 5424.8 | 4924.7 |
| 医疗用品及器材零售 | Retail of Medical Articles and Appliances | 47867.7 | 6830.9 | 7479.5 |
| 汽车、摩托车、零配件和燃料及其他动力销售 | Special Retail of Automobiles, Motorcycles, Fuel and Spare Parts | 4768756.1 | 3797139.9 | 3152457.1 |
| 汽车新车零售 | Retail of New Automobiles | 2896678.8 | 975405.7 | 2730382.1 |
| 汽车旧车零售 | Retail of Second-hand Automobiles | 11555.5 | 2967.6 | 2280.3 |
| 汽车零配件零售 | Retail of Automobile Fittings | 19772.1 | 5816.5 | 4462.6 |
| 摩托车及零配件零售 | Retail of Motorcycles and Parts | 34244.3 | 25236.9 | 13304.6 |
| 机动车燃料零售 | Retail of Motor Fuel | 1686963.7 | 2760963.2 | 389585.5 |
| 机动车燃气零售 | Retail of Motor Gas | 112361.4 | 17493.8 | 3913.9 |
| 机动车充电零售 | Retail of Motor Eletricity | 7180.3 | 9256.2 | 8528.1 |
| 家用电器及电子产品专门零售 | Special Retail of Household Electrical Appliances and Electronic Products | 580184.5 | 216459.7 | 687704.3 |
| 家用视听设备零售 | Retail of Household Audio and Video Appliances | 168132.2 | 83375.7 | 91510.3 |
| 日用家电零售 | Retail of Household Electrical Appliances | 249693.2 | 36174.7 | 541406.5 |
| 计算机、软件及辅助设备零售 | Retail of Computers, Software and Assistant Equipment | 61407.9 | 54104.0 | 36693.4 |
| 通信设备零售 | Retail of Communication Equipment | 72808.9 | 31121.8 | 14235.4 |
| 其他电子产品零售 | Retail of Other Electronic Products | 28142.3 | 11683.5 | 3858.7 |
| 五金、家具及室内装饰材料专门零售 | Special Retail of Hardware, Furniture and Decoration Materials | 385901.5 | 190061.5 | 74237.2 |
| 五金零售 | Retail of Hardware | 60139.5 | 30380.9 | 11260.1 |
| 灯具零售 | Retail of Light Fittings | 8628.5 | 2045.0 | 879.7 |
| 家具零售 | Retail of Furniture | 68956.3 | 24321.0 | 36762.3 |
| 涂料零售 | Retail of Paint | 5189.3 | 3116.0 | 2475.0 |
| 卫生洁具零售 | Retail of Sanitary Ware | 3298.7 | 3894.9 | 1131.0 |
| 木质装饰材料零售 | Retail of Wooden Decorative Materials | 5817.5 | 3286.9 | 1512.5 |
| 陶瓷、石材装饰材料零售 | Retail of Ceramics and Stone Decorative Materials | 16234.8 | 48267.7 | 6890.5 |
| 其他室内装饰材料零售 | Retail of Other Indoor Decoration Materials | 217636.9 | 74749.1 | 13326.1 |
| 货摊、无店铺及其他零售业 | Stall, Non-shop and Other Retails | 621844.8 | 280649.1 | 168059.1 |
| 互联网零售 | E-commerce Retails | 569559.5 | 202178.0 | 122505.5 |
| 自动售货机零售 | Vending Machine Retails | 480.7 | 397.1 | 501.5 |
| 旧货零售 | Retail of Used Goods | 310.1 | 574.8 | 310.1 |
| 生活用燃料零售 | Retail of Fuel for Daily Use | 10522.7 | 7650.2 | 7247.5 |
| 宠物食品用品零售 | Retail of Pet Foods and Articles | 20.0 | 352.1 | |
| 其他未列明零售业 | Other Retails not Classified Elsewhere | 40951.8 | 69496.9 | 37494.5 |

单位：万元 (10 000 yuan)

| 二、期末资产负债 Assets and Liabilities | 三、损益及分配 Profits and Losses | | | | |
|---|---|---|---|---|---|
| 个人资本 Personal Capital | 营业收入 Gross Sales | 主营业务收入 Main Business Income | 营业成本 Operating Cost | 税金及附加 Taxes and Surcharges | 其他业务利润 Other Business Profits |
| 38251.5 | 1353703.2 | 1325187.3 | 1105519.4 | 4033.5 | 1365.7 |
| 32641.8 | 1258576.6 | 1240249.3 | 1038596.9 | 3822.3 | 1365.7 |
| 4365.7 | 18155.6 | 13902.4 | 13917.1 | 54.8 | |
| 1244.0 | 76971.0 | 71035.6 | 53005.4 | 156.4 | |
| 213981.3 | 19330930.9 | 18819511.1 | 18041982.7 | 47786.1 | 69085.8 |
| 178645.3 | 10262224.0 | 9963252.0 | 9551744.1 | 33947.3 | 60692.9 |
| 1520.1 | 64065.3 | 63924.9 | 59190.7 | 110.8 | 34.6 |
| 1751.2 | 99090.8 | 94155.8 | 88317.5 | 158.0 | -0.3 |
| 2653.2 | 313414.1 | 310908.0 | 288779.1 | 927.9 | 226.4 |
| 28313.4 | 8434731.2 | 8229913.0 | 7910463.4 | 12250.7 | 8125.0 |
| 1098.1 | 148404.8 | 148364.8 | 134997.4 | 384.7 | |
| | 9000.7 | 8992.6 | 8490.5 | 6.7 | 7.2 |
| 31845.9 | 2424871.9 | 2328502.9 | 2193105.4 | 6675.2 | 4531.4 |
| 3718.7 | 587610.8 | 580541.9 | 535113.2 | 1601.9 | 37.2 |
| 11839.5 | 861604.7 | 803031.6 | 784045.1 | 1837.2 | 1402.8 |
| 8562.9 | 373741.3 | 356559.3 | 326871.9 | 1982.1 | 19.3 |
| 6482.8 | 521203.6 | 509929.0 | 478835.6 | 952.4 | 3015.0 |
| 1242.0 | 80711.5 | 78441.1 | 68239.6 | 301.6 | 57.1 |
| 21700.1 | 1114584.2 | 1095070.2 | 956079.4 | 4678.3 | 377.6 |
| 6372.2 | 199566.4 | 197557.9 | 169754.5 | 1105.1 | 88.7 |
| 250.0 | 21678.4 | 19542.1 | 17909.8 | 77.9 | |
| 3596.5 | 335482.2 | 331428.9 | 260545.9 | 2067.1 | 288.8 |
| 2075.0 | 10895.2 | 10885.4 | 9573.7 | 26.1 | |
| 301.0 | 32816.9 | 32795.5 | 28047.6 | 29.1 | |
| 532.8 | 29605.8 | 29506.2 | 26890.9 | 159.7 | |
| 2729.4 | 71740.6 | 69664.1 | 62014.1 | 339.8 | 0.1 |
| 5843.2 | 412798.7 | 403690.1 | 381342.9 | 873.5 | |
| 32571.4 | 3618704.7 | 3596387.1 | 3267264.0 | 4134.2 | 5473.2 |
| 26630.5 | 3321344.5 | 3300172.1 | 3001247.2 | 3236.7 | 5373.5 |
| | 2546.0 | 2216.2 | 1955.7 | 0.9 | |
| | 867.8 | 867.8 | 745.9 | 3.5 | |
| 2411.2 | 67783.5 | 67394.8 | 57181.9 | 410.3 | |
| | 8854.6 | 8854.6 | 6276.1 | 0.7 | |
| 3529.7 | 217308.3 | 216881.6 | 199857.2 | 482.1 | 99.7 |

**表 15.7 续表 8 continued 8**

| 指 标 | Item | 三、损益及分配 Profits and Losses | | |
|---|---|---|---|---|
| | | 销售费用 Sales Expenses | 管理费用 Management Expenses | 研发费用 R&D expenses |
| 医药及医疗器材专门零售 | Special Retail of Medicine and Medical Appliances | 204374.9 | 62692.4 | 33.5 |
| 西药零售 | Retail of Western Medicine | 183738.4 | 59329.7 | 30.8 |
| 中药零售 | Retail of Tradition Chinese Medicine | 953.1 | 1256.2 | 2.6 |
| 医疗用品及器材零售 | Retail of Medical Articles and Appliances | 19683.4 | 2106.5 | 0.1 |
| 汽车、摩托车、零配件和燃料及其他动力销售 | Special Retail of Automobiles, Motorcycles, Fuel and Spare Parts | 794805.0 | 219449.5 | 1140.8 |
| 汽车新车零售 | Retail of New Automobiles | 422303.8 | 175901.9 | 272.8 |
| 汽车旧车零售 | Retail of Second-hand Automobiles | 2017.4 | 1329.4 | |
| 汽车零配件零售 | Retail of Automobile Fittings | 3039.1 | 4939.1 | 660.0 |
| 摩托车及零配件零售 | Retail of Motorcycles and Parts | 7334.2 | 7455.8 | 19.2 |
| 机动车燃料零售 | Retail of Motor Fuel | 352088.5 | 28325.1 | 188.8 |
| 机动车燃气零售 | Retail of Motor Gas | 7815.0 | 1189.9 | |
| 机动车充电零售 | Retail of Motor Eletricity | 207.0 | 308.3 | |
| 家用电器及电子产品专门零售 | Special Retail of Household Electrical Appliances and Electronic Products | 127447.8 | 56841.5 | 1819.3 |
| 家用视听设备零售 | Retail of Household Audio and Video Appliances | 41900.3 | 11300.9 | 55.4 |
| 日用家电零售 | Retail of Household Electrical Appliances | 45522.7 | 18093.9 | 3.4 |
| 计算机、软件及辅助设备零售 | Retail of Computers, Software and Assistant Equipment | 14889.1 | 12036.3 | 713.2 |
| 通信设备零售 | Retail of Communication Equipment | 22033.7 | 10978.6 | 126.7 |
| 其他电子产品零售 | Retail of Other Electronic Products | 3102.0 | 4431.8 | 920.6 |
| 五金、家具及室内装饰材料专门零售 | Special Retail of Hardware, Furniture and Decoration Materials | 31769.3 | 35839.9 | 38.2 |
| 五金零售 | Retail of Hardware | 7916.5 | 7094.2 | 13.1 |
| 灯具零售 | Retail of Light Fittings | 741.6 | 1362.3 | |
| 家具零售 | Retail of Furniture | 11016.7 | 15138.8 | 15.1 |
| 涂料零售 | Retail of Paint | 557.6 | 570.7 | 2.8 |
| 卫生洁具零售 | Retail of Sanitary Ware | 2317.3 | 804.8 | |
| 木质装饰材料零售 | Retail of Wooden Decorative Materials | 695.0 | 856.7 | 0.5 |
| 陶瓷、石材装饰材料零售 | Retail of Ceramics and Stone Decorative Materials | 2024.3 | 2374.4 | 0.1 |
| 其他室内装饰材料零售 | Retail of Other Indoor Decoration Materials | 6500.3 | 7638.0 | 6.6 |
| 货摊、无店铺及其他零售业 | Stall, Non-shop and Other Retails | 214916.7 | 76774.7 | 2295.1 |
| 互联网零售 | E-commerce Retails | 207058.3 | 65109.2 | 2190.3 |
| 自动售货机零售 | Vending Machine Retails | 647.5 | 234.8 | |
| 旧货零售 | Retail of Used Goods | 36.8 | 45.8 | |
| 生活用燃料零售 | Retail of Fuel for Daily Use | 2246.7 | 3905.8 | 11.2 |
| 宠物食品用品零售 | Retail of Pet Foods and Articles | 24.0 | 45.2 | 1.0 |
| 其他未列明零售业 | Other Retails not Classified Elsewhere | 4903.4 | 7433.9 | 92.6 |

单位：万元 (10 000 yuan)

三、损益及分配 Profits and Losses

| 财务费用 Financial Expenses | | | 投资收益 Income from Investment | 营业利润 Business Profits | 营业外收入 Non-business Income |
|---|---|---|---|---|---|
| | 利息收入 Interest Income | 利息费用 Interest expenses | | | |
| 6994.4 | 622.7 | 4823.4 | 246.0 | 23280.7 | 2159.6 |
| 5918.1 | 603.7 | 4072.4 | 246.0 | 20062.9 | 2095.5 |
| 258.2 | 15.9 | 55.3 | | 979.0 | 20.9 |
| 818.1 | 3.1 | 695.7 | | 2238.8 | 43.2 |
| 40047.6 | 5895.2 | 32655.9 | 19352.6 | 174648.0 | 46959.1 |
| 35770.4 | 654.4 | 26888.4 | 11600.6 | 18205.2 | 37099.2 |
| 399.3 | 9.2 | 346.0 | | 1020.8 | 8.1 |
| 283.2 | 4.0 | 146.4 | | 1797.3 | 35.5 |
| 611.5 | 75.4 | 159.7 | | 6652.7 | 153.0 |
| 3656.5 | 4040.2 | 2655.2 | 7673.6 | 142275.3 | 9622.8 |
| -832.9 | 1109.6 | 2460.2 | 78.4 | 4936.6 | 32.0 |
| 159.6 | 2.4 | | | -239.9 | 8.5 |
| 9940.1 | 460.6 | 2484.9 | 96.4 | 18138.1 | 1931.7 |
| 4332.1 | 90.1 | 540.1 | | -10705.7 | 68.1 |
| 2504.6 | 68.6 | 557.7 | 94.2 | 257.4 | 654.5 |
| 686.6 | 155.6 | 368.6 | 1.5 | 17752.7 | 485.3 |
| 2249.3 | 130.8 | 959.8 | | 8165.2 | 566.3 |
| 167.5 | 15.5 | 58.7 | 0.7 | 2668.5 | 157.5 |
| 5962.4 | 171.8 | 3747.8 | 20.4 | 45817.8 | 527.6 |
| 888.4 | 37.0 | 440.5 | -1.0 | 12430.9 | 307.1 |
| 98.8 | 0.1 | 21.5 | -350.3 | 1577.3 | 9.4 |
| 3372.3 | 104.1 | 2872.2 | | 10204.5 | 169.4 |
| 29.1 | 0.6 | 27.1 | | 127.1 | 7.2 |
| 152.5 | 6.1 | 59.9 | | 1369.2 | 8.7 |
| 47.0 | 2.2 | 19.6 | | 1198.2 | 3.2 |
| 440.3 | 5.7 | 71.9 | | 4585.3 | 8.4 |
| 934.0 | 16.0 | 235.1 | 371.7 | 14325.3 | 14.2 |
| 10028.1 | 274.1 | 3538.6 | 130.8 | 35971.5 | 4565.3 |
| 8774.6 | 197.0 | 2665.7 | -19.8 | 24754.8 | 3266.8 |
| 4.8 | 0.1 | | | -299.6 | 0.2 |
| 4.0 | | | | 55.8 | |
| 290.2 | 0.4 | 159.5 | | 4101.0 | 38.0 |
| 20.5 | | | | 2136.9 | |
| 934.0 | 76.6 | 713.4 | 150.6 | 5222.6 | 1260.3 |

**表 15.7 续表 9 continued 9**

| 指 标 | Item | 三、损益及分配 Profits and Losses<br>营业外支出 Non-business Expenses | 利润总额 Total Profits |
|---|---|---|---|
| 医药及医疗器材专门零售 | Special Retail of Medicine and Medical Appliances | 979.6 | 24486.2 |
| 西药零售 | Retail of Western Medicine | 931.5 | 21227.2 |
| 中药零售 | Retail of Tradition Chinese Medicine | 22.6 | 1002.5 |
| 医疗用品及器材零售 | Retail of Medical Articles and Appliances | 25.5 | 2256.5 |
| 汽车、摩托车、零配件和燃料及其他动力销售 | Special Retail of Automobiles, Motorcycles, Fuel and Spare Parts | 12120.0 | 210778.8 |
| 汽车新车零售 | Retail of New Automobiles | 5086.8 | 50225.3 |
| 汽车旧车零售 | Retail of Second-hand Automobiles | 8.4 | 1020.5 |
| 汽车零配件零售 | Retail of Automobile Fittings | 18.6 | 1813.4 |
| 摩托车及零配件零售 | Retail of Motorcycles and Parts | 28.2 | 6777.5 |
| 机动车燃料零售 | Retail of Motor Fuel | 6967.8 | 146215.1 |
| 机动车燃气零售 | Retail of Motor Gas | 10.2 | 4958.4 |
| 机动车充电零售 | Retail of Motor Eletricity | | -231.4 |
| 家用电器及电子产品专门零售 | Special Retail of Household Electrical Appliances and Electronic Products | -135.9 | 20191.0 |
| 家用视听设备零售 | Retail of Household Audio and Video Appliances | -556.4 | -10081.2 |
| 日用家电零售 | Retail of Household Electrical Appliances | 195.6 | 701.9 |
| 计算机、软件及辅助设备零售 | Retail of Computers, Software and Assistant Equipment | 20.4 | 18217.1 |
| 通信设备零售 | Retail of Communication Equipment | 26.6 | 8705.0 |
| 其他电子产品零售 | Retail of Other Electronic Products | 177.9 | 2648.2 |
| 五金、家具及室内装饰材料专门零售 | Special Retail of Hardware, Furniture and Decoration Materials | 256.9 | 46449.8 |
| 五金零售 | Retail of Hardware | 60.0 | 12574.3 |
| 灯具零售 | Retail of Light Fittings | | 1586.7 |
| 家具零售 | Retail of Furniture | 140.5 | 10735.8 |
| 涂料零售 | Retail of Paint | 2.9 | 131.4 |
| 卫生洁具零售 | Retail of Sanitary Ware | 30.3 | 1347.6 |
| 木质装饰材料零售 | Retail of Wooden Decorative Materials | 0.4 | 1201.0 |
| 陶瓷、石材装饰材料零售 | Retail of Ceramics and Stone Decorative Materials | 15.5 | 4556.2 |
| 其他室内装饰材料零售 | Retail of Other Indoor Decoration Materials | 7.3 | 14316.8 |
| 货摊、无店铺及其他零售业 | Stall, Non-shop and Other Retails | 2369.7 | 38175.4 |
| 互联网零售 | E-commerce Retails | 1173.6 | 26856.4 |
| 自动售货机零售 | Vending Machine Retails | 0.2 | -299.7 |
| 旧货零售 | Retail of Used Goods | | 55.8 |
| 生活用燃料零售 | Retail of Fuel for Daily Use | 14.1 | 4124.9 |
| 宠物食品用品零售 | Retail of Pet Foods and Articles | | 2136.9 |
| 其他未列明零售业 | Other Retails not Classified Elsewhere | 1181.8 | 5301.1 |

单位：万元 (10 000 yuan)

| 三、损益及分配 Profits and Losses | 四、人工成本及增值税 Labor cost and Value-added Tax | | |
|---|---|---|---|
| 所得税费用 Income Tax Payable | 应付职工薪酬 Employee compensation | 应交增值税 Value-added Tax | 五、从事批发和零售业活动的从业人员平均人数（人） Annual Average Employees Engaged in wholesale and retail activities (persons) |
| 2816.4 | 128927.0 | 22694 | 20655 |
| 2573.2 | 117844.6 | 21643 | 18816 |
| 16.4 | 1620.3 | 98 | 427 |
| 226.8 | 9462.1 | 953 | 1412 |
| 22369.2 | 443879.7 | 132661 | 45531 |
| 11742.9 | 245520.6 | 67032 | 28530 |
| 39.6 | 1644.4 | 314 | 301 |
| 224.1 | 4582.2 | 169 | 590 |
| 604.4 | 4546.7 | 2304 | 895 |
| 9670.2 | 182783.2 | 61303 | 14602 |
| 295.0 | 4409.0 | 1423 | 587 |
| -207.0 | 393.6 | 116 | 26 |
| 2573.2 | 71245.5 | 16138 | 12183 |
| 619.5 | 13128.3 | 4059 | 2207 |
| 642.9 | 23111.2 | 4200 | 3851 |
| 822.4 | 11970.8 | 4427 | 2030 |
| 349.1 | 18374.7 | 2620 | 3415 |
| 139.3 | 4660.5 | 833 | 680 |
| 2919.3 | 29310.0 | 9319 | 5386 |
| 580.2 | 7669.4 | 2776 | 1435 |
| 80.0 | 1008.9 | 177 | 203 |
| 639.6 | 7195.7 | 2053 | 1092 |
| 44.0 | 1117.6 | 223 | 178 |
| 23.5 | 878.9 | 217 | 187 |
| 46.6 | 1082.2 | 382 | 179 |
| 342.4 | 3195.5 | 689 | 499 |
| 1163.0 | 7161.8 | 2802 | 1613 |
| 4178.2 | 70443.6 | 22905 | 8307 |
| 3238.5 | 63402.9 | 20783 | 7101 |
|  | 379.2 | 17 | 63 |
| 2.9 | 100.8 | 1 | 20 |
| 88.8 | 2285.6 | 710 | 395 |
| 1.5 | 130.0 | 7 | 30 |
| 846.5 | 4145.1 | 1387 | 698 |

**表 15.7 续表 10 continued 10**

| 指 标 | Item | 法人企业数(个) Number of Enterprises (unit) | 执行《2006年企业会计准则》企业数(个) Number of Enterprises which Implemented Accounting standard for Business Enterprise in 2006 (unit) | 一、年初存货 Inventory at the Beginning of Year |
|---|---|---|---|---|
| **按登记注册类型分** | **By Status of Registration** | | | |
| 内资企业 | Domestic-funded Enterprises | 3911 | 2005 | 2270410.2 |
| 国有企业 | State-owned Enterprises | 17 | 15 | 24277.3 |
| 集体企业 | Collective-owned Enterprises | 6 | 4 | 625.1 |
| 股份合作企业 | Cooperative Enterprises | 7 | 6 | 261.7 |
| 联营企业 | Joint-owned Enterprises | 1 | 1 | 40.5 |
| 国有与集体联营企业 | Joint State-collective Enterprises | 1 | 1 | 40.5 |
| 有限责任公司 | Limited Liability Corporations | 235 | 181 | 397130.0 |
| 国有独资公司 | State Sole Funded Corporations | 26 | 22 | 11752.8 |
| 其他有限责任公司 | Other Limited Liability Corporations | 209 | 159 | 385377.2 |
| 股份有限公司 | Share-holding Corporations Ltd. | 36 | 33 | 406200.6 |
| 私营企业 | Private Enterprises | 3606 | 1765 | 1441750.4 |
| 私营独资企业 | Private-funded Enterprises | 189 | 87 | 30156.8 |
| 私营合伙企业 | Private Partnership Enterprises | 10 | 4 | 1599.8 |
| 私营有限责任公司 | Private Limited Liability Corporations | 3389 | 1660 | 1404467.1 |
| 私营股份有限公司 | Private Share-holding Corporations Ltd. | 18 | 14 | 5526.7 |
| 其他企业 | Other Corporations Ltd. | 3 | | 124.6 |
| 港、澳、台商投资企业 | Enterprises Funded by Hong Kong, Macao and Taiwan | 31 | 29 | 106857.3 |
| 合资经营企业(港或澳、台资) | Joint-venture Enterprises | 2 | 2 | 1583.8 |
| 港、澳、台商独资经营企业 | Enterprises with Sole Fund | 28 | 26 | 100569.4 |
| 港、澳、台商投资股份有限公司 | Share-holding Corporations Ltd. | 1 | 1 | 4704.1 |
| 外商投资企业 | Foreign-funded Enterprises | 28 | 26 | 66456.2 |
| 中外合资经营企业 | Joint-venture Enterprises | 9 | 8 | 19942.2 |
| 中外合作经营企业 | Cooperative Enterprises | 1 | 1 | 6626.6 |
| 外资企业 | Sole-proprietorship Enterprises | 16 | 16 | 33907.3 |
| 外商投资股份有限公司 | Share-holding Corporations Ltd. | 1 | 1 | 5980.1 |
| 其他外商投资企业 | Other Foreign-funded Enterprises | 1 | | |
| **按控股情况分** | **By Holding Entity of Share** | | | |
| 国有控股 | State-holding | 161 | 143 | 429748.1 |
| 集体控股 | Collective-holding | 17 | 10 | 14070.2 |
| 私人控股 | Private-holding | 3737 | 1858 | 1846456.2 |
| 港澳台商控股 | Held by Corporation from Hong Kong, Macao and Taiwan | 30 | 28 | 104741.8 |
| 外商控股 | Foreign-holding | 22 | 21 | 48582.8 |
| 其他 | Other | 2 | | 114.7 |

单位：万元 (10 000 yuan)

二、期末资产负债 Assets and Liabilities

| 流动资产合计 Total Current Assets | 应收账款 Accounts Receivable | 存货 Inventory | 固定资产原价 Total Original Value of Fixed Assets | 房屋和构筑物 Buildings and Structures | 机器设备 Machinery and Equipments |
|---|---|---|---|---|---|
| 9539454.9 | 907857.5 | 2634939.8 | 3498648.7 | 821012.6 | 341914.4 |
| -811307.6 | 10162.4 | 33233.9 | 106566.6 | 15820.9 | 11599.8 |
| 8222.2 | 2476.6 | 742.3 | 4321.9 | 244.0 | 745.2 |
| 1475.5 | 237.5 | 153.0 | 3038.6 | 61.9 | 220.8 |
| 852.6 | | 34.1 | 569.6 | | |
| 852.6 | | 34.1 | 569.6 | | |
| 2287246.5 | 242665.8 | 517924.2 | 652889.9 | 331089.0 | 54727.9 |
| 185542.7 | 43323.9 | 18532.7 | 92000.5 | 30926.3 | 6874.2 |
| 2101703.8 | 199341.9 | 499391.5 | 560889.4 | 300162.7 | 47853.7 |
| 2629413.2 | -371411.7 | 484382.6 | 1380800.7 | 94521.7 | 12928.9 |
| 5423040.4 | 1023353.0 | 1598348.0 | 1350409.9 | 379275.1 | 261640.3 |
| 82756.8 | 10139.1 | 40360.1 | 49458.6 | 25502.7 | 7302.6 |
| 7001.0 | 393.5 | 1920.9 | 1995.2 | 848.2 | 127.0 |
| 5301210.0 | 1006269.6 | 1549900.7 | 1283967.1 | 345978.2 | 249452.3 |
| 32072.6 | 6550.8 | 6166.3 | 14989.0 | 6946.0 | 4758.4 |
| 512.1 | 373.9 | 121.7 | 51.5 | | 51.5 |
| 442643.3 | 30607.4 | 103352.0 | 157451.7 | 54083.9 | 26229.0 |
| 3121.3 | 783.2 | 1747.7 | 611.5 | | |
| 430391.9 | 29098.1 | 96285.7 | 139880.3 | 39873.8 | 24381.6 |
| 9130.1 | 726.1 | 5318.6 | 16959.9 | 14210.1 | 1847.4 |
| 378075.2 | 16980.1 | 74162.7 | 396471.8 | 232078.7 | 48869.0 |
| 111600.0 | 3303.3 | 21161.7 | 232350.8 | 127967.4 | 10102.4 |
| 10824.3 | 35.8 | 2193.6 | 12490.7 | | |
| 247703.4 | 13631.8 | 43997.5 | 109298.0 | 65139.7 | 35405.9 |
| 7833.3 | 0.5 | 6809.9 | 42332.3 | 38971.6 | 3360.7 |
| 114.2 | 8.7 | | | | |
| | | | | | |
| 2729487.0 | -198236.1 | 640009.4 | 1491801.4 | 392001.5 | 65034.8 |
| 71495.2 | 8891.4 | 20114.0 | 27166.4 | 18589.3 | 2376.9 |
| 6785333.0 | 1099513.3 | 1997648.0 | 2088952.8 | 465515.9 | 284911.1 |
| 465169.9 | 29504.0 | 100206.5 | 209610.9 | 109343.6 | 24642.4 |
| 308176.2 | 15398.5 | 54354.9 | 234989.2 | 121724.9 | 39995.7 |
| 491.3 | 360.7 | 114.1 | 51.5 | | 51.5 |

**表 15.7 续表 11 continued 11**

| 指　标 | Item | 二、期末资产负债 Assets and Liabilities | | |
|---|---|---|---|---|
| | | 累计折旧<br>Cumulative Depreciation | 本年折旧<br>Depreciation | 固定资产净额<br>Net Value of Fixed Assets |
| **按登记注册类型分** | **By Status of Registration** | | | |
| 内资企业 | Domestic-funded Enterprises | 1428672.6 | 163846.4 | 1771612.7 |
| 国有企业 | State-owned Enterprises | 48497.3 | 3523.1 | 54707.5 |
| 集体企业 | Collective-owned Enterprises | 1814.1 | 100.9 | 2222.6 |
| 股份合作企业 | Cooperative Enterprises | 553.1 | 190.9 | 1577.9 |
| 联营企业 | Joint-owned Enterprises | 369.0 | 369.0 | 200.6 |
| 国有与集体联营企业 | Joint State-collective Enterprises | 369.0 | 369.0 | 200.6 |
| 有限责任公司 | Limited Liability Corporations | 279347.9 | 56083.3 | 319249.9 |
| 国有独资公司 | State Sole Funded Corporations | 36999.9 | 22546.7 | 49415.3 |
| 其他有限责任公司 | Other Limited Liability Corporations | 242348.0 | 33536.6 | 269834.6 |
| 股份有限公司 | Share-holding Corporations Ltd. | 569697.3 | 4080.7 | 733127.2 |
| 私营企业 | Private Enterprises | 528368.1 | 99492.3 | 660501.3 |
| 私营独资企业 | Private-funded Enterprises | 19462.0 | 2903.2 | 23139.3 |
| 私营合伙企业 | Private Partnership Enterprises | 601.7 | 104.1 | 960.4 |
| 私营有限责任公司 | Private Limited Liability Corporations | 503355.2 | 95568.0 | 627739.2 |
| 私营股份有限公司 | Private Share-holding Corporations Ltd. | 4949.2 | 917.0 | 8662.4 |
| 其他企业 | Other Corporations Ltd. | 25.8 | 6.2 | 25.7 |
| 港、澳、台商投资企业 | Enterprises Funded by Hong Kong, Macao and Taiwan | 85974.5 | 15277.6 | 65114.9 |
| 合资经营企业（港或澳、台资） | Joint-venture Enterprises | 78.0 | 30.7 | 533.5 |
| 港、澳、台商独资经营企业 | Enterprises with Sole Fund | 80260.7 | 14736.6 | 53257.3 |
| 港、澳、台商投资股份有限公司 | Share-holding Corporations Ltd. | 5635.8 | 510.3 | 11324.1 |
| 外商投资企业 | Foreign-funded Enterprises | 143660.0 | 23512.6 | 234842.5 |
| 中外合资经营企业 | Joint-venture Enterprises | 63314.9 | 11682.8 | 154486.2 |
| 中外合作经营企业 | Cooperative Enterprises | 11519.7 | | 871.3 |
| 外资企业 | Sole-proprietorship Enterprises | 47445.9 | 9200.9 | 58532.2 |
| 外商投资股份有限公司 | Share-holding Corporations Ltd. | 21379.5 | 2628.9 | 20952.8 |
| 其他外商投资企业 | Other Foreign-funded Enterprises | | | |
| **按控股情况分** | **By Holding Entity of Share** | | | |
| 国有控股 | State-holding | 638446.8 | 47459.0 | 737994.7 |
| 集体控股 | Collective-holding | 7778.0 | 912.3 | 19015.4 |
| 私人控股 | Private-holding | 833950.8 | 123100.7 | 1072371.5 |
| 港澳台商控股 | Held by Corporation from Hong Kong, Macao and Taiwan | 85942.7 | 16510.9 | 117305.9 |
| 外商控股 | Foreign-holding | 92163.0 | 14647.5 | 124856.9 |
| 其他 | Other | 25.8 | 6.2 | 25.7 |

单位：万元 (10 000 yuan)

| 二、期末资产负债 Assets and Liabilities | | | | | |
|---|---|---|---|---|---|
| 在建工程<br>Construction in Progress | 无形资产<br>Intangible Assets | 土地使用权<br>Land Use Rights | 资产总计<br>Total Assets | 流动负债合计<br>Total Current Liabilities | 应付账款<br>Accounts Payable |
| 272888.7 | 635324.3 | 255609.1 | 15188498.2 | 11016974.7 | 1974696.3 |
| 7013.3 | 64655.2 | 33284.2 | -689819.3 | 145908.4 | -32696.2 |
| | 1.8 | | 14699.9 | 4278.8 | 1418.4 |
| | | | 5751.8 | 911.7 | 61.1 |
| | 131.4 | | 1182.5 | 55.3 | 17.6 |
| | 131.4 | | 1182.5 | 55.3 | 17.6 |
| 182928.3 | 170846.4 | 72415.8 | 3511095.6 | 2977467.9 | 442995.4 |
| 13694.7 | 37429.8 | 4639.3 | 392543.7 | 1318230.9 | 38533.2 |
| 169233.6 | 133416.6 | 67776.5 | 3118551.9 | 1659237.0 | 404462.2 |
| 20938.6 | 282705.9 | 76218.5 | 4676946.3 | 3150377.3 | 279705.0 |
| 62008.5 | 116696.6 | 73690.6 | 7667784.6 | 4737840.8 | 1283165.0 |
| 952.8 | 2342.0 | 1905.5 | 124912.5 | 46856.8 | 11606.3 |
| | 272.0 | 272.0 | 10045.0 | 5802.9 | 165.6 |
| 57965.8 | 97335.0 | 67441.3 | 7445650.2 | 4630502.4 | 1246794.0 |
| 3089.9 | 16747.6 | 4071.8 | 87176.9 | 54678.7 | 24599.1 |
| | 287.0 | | 856.8 | 134.5 | 30.0 |
| 543.2 | 3881.2 | 3497.9 | 649627.5 | 307854.7 | 49788.5 |
| | 18.2 | | 6842.8 | 2314.4 | 41.8 |
| 542.2 | 3763.0 | 3497.9 | 605137.3 | 293234.4 | 45201.0 |
| 1.0 | 100.0 | | 37647.4 | 12305.9 | 4545.7 |
| 5419.1 | 64977.3 | 43674.2 | 999100.9 | 379796.7 | 104834.0 |
| 4092.5 | 10525.5 | 10172.3 | 475482.6 | 97341.6 | 54192.2 |
| | 1473.7 | | 26411.5 | 16979.6 | 4994.9 |
| 132.0 | 29369.6 | 29290.4 | 443731.8 | 264895.0 | 45142.3 |
| 1194.6 | 23608.5 | 4211.5 | 53360.8 | 504.6 | 504.6 |
| | | | 114.2 | 75.9 | |
| | | | | | |
| 208621.5 | 503167.3 | 149088.4 | 4891990.7 | 4855272.8 | 376366.4 |
| 174.7 | 2826.5 | 2783.8 | 111968.1 | 65115.6 | 2908.0 |
| 65288.1 | 154097.2 | 109275.4 | 10364781.9 | 6167527.4 | 1637546.9 |
| 542.2 | 3765.5 | 3500.4 | 710262.3 | 307009.7 | 56184.1 |
| 4224.5 | 40039.3 | 38133.2 | 757366.8 | 309566.1 | 56283.4 |
| | 143.3 | | 692.3 | 125.6 | 21.1 |

**表 15.7 续表 12 continued 12**

| 指 标 | Item | 二、期末资产负债 Assets and Liabilities 负债合计 Total Liabilities | 所有者权益合计 Total Owner's Equity | 实收资本 Paid-up Capital |
|---|---|---|---|---|
| **按登记注册类型分** | **By Status of Registration** | | | |
| 内资企业 | Domestic-funded Enterprises | 10525030.2 | 6105035.1 | 4627546.2 |
| 国有企业 | State-owned Enterprises | 230664.3 | 934322.8 | 31603.1 |
| 集体企业 | Collective-owned Enterprises | 4663.1 | 10036.8 | 891.5 |
| 股份合作企业 | Cooperative Enterprises | 1159.1 | 4357.5 | 3405.4 |
| 联营企业 | Joint-owned Enterprises | 55.9 | 1126.6 | 730.4 |
| 国有与集体联营企业 | Joint State-collective Enterprises | 55.9 | 1126.6 | 730.4 |
| 有限责任公司 | Limited Liability Corporations | 2102939.6 | 1411268.9 | 743243.0 |
| 国有独资公司 | State Sole Funded Corporations | 264898.2 | 127645.5 | 33378.3 |
| 其他有限责任公司 | Other Limited Liability Corporations | 1838041.4 | 1283623.4 | 709864.7 |
| 股份有限公司 | Share-holding Corporations Ltd. | 2423305.1 | 1864025.1 | 100981.2 |
| 私营企业 | Private Enterprises | 5761908.5 | 1879375.2 | 3746391.6 |
| 私营独资企业 | Private-funded Enterprises | 54763.4 | 68003.6 | 30140.2 |
| 私营合伙企业 | Private Partnership Enterprises | 6019.0 | 3761.7 | 2470.8 |
| 私营有限责任公司 | Private Limited Liability Corporations | 5642973.4 | 1778877.3 | 3688350.6 |
| 私营股份有限公司 | Private Share-holding Corporations Ltd. | 58152.7 | 28732.6 | 25430.0 |
| 其他企业 | Other Corporations Ltd. | 334.6 | 522.2 | 300.0 |
| 港、澳、台商投资企业 | Enterprises Funded by Hong Kong, Macao and Taiwan | 422150.2 | 232384.4 | 224714.4 |
| 合资经营企业(港或澳、台资) | Joint-venture Enterprises | 5079.1 | 1763.7 | 600.0 |
| 港、澳、台商独资经营企业 | Enterprises with Sole Fund | 398549.9 | 211494.5 | 218014.4 |
| 港、澳、台商投资股份有限公司 | Share-holding Corporations Ltd. | 18521.2 | 19126.2 | 6100.0 |
| 外商投资企业 | Foreign-funded Enterprises | 644014.5 | 355086.4 | 262871.0 |
| 中外合资经营企业 | Joint-venture Enterprises | 297345.1 | 178137.5 | 124877.4 |
| 中外合作经营企业 | Cooperative Enterprises | 26967.6 | -556.1 | 24250.6 |
| 外资企业 | Sole-proprietorship Enterprises | 384819.1 | 58912.7 | 113713.0 |
| 外商投资股份有限公司 | Share-holding Corporations Ltd. | -65193.2 | 118554.0 | |
| 其他外商投资企业 | Other Foreign-funded Enterprises | 75.9 | 38.3 | 30.0 |
| **按控股情况分** | **By Holding Entity of Share** | | | |
| 国有控股 | State-holding | 2771059.8 | 3584869.7 | 603091.0 |
| 集体控股 | Collective-holding | 71205.2 | 40762.9 | 14667.4 |
| 私人控股 | Private-holding | 7692461.4 | 2649948.8 | 4055201.5 |
| 港澳台商控股 | Held by Corporation from Hong Kong, Macao and Taiwan | 481189.9 | 233979.5 | 238014.4 |
| 外商控股 | Foreign-holding | 574944.0 | 182422.8 | 203857.3 |
| 其他 | Other | 325.7 | 366.6 | 200.0 |

单位：万元 (10 000 yuan)

| 二、期末资产负债 Assets and Liabilities | 三、损益及分配 Profits and Losses | | | | |
|---|---|---|---|---|---|
| 个人资本<br>Personal Capital | 营业收入<br>Gross Sales | 主营业务收入<br>Main Business Income | 营业成本<br>Operating Cost | 税金及附加<br>Taxes and Surcharges | 其他业务利润<br>Other Business Profits |
| 412871.7 | 33133474.8 | 32099955.2 | 29347980.8 | 110505.6 | 349366.2 |
| | 1075486.6 | 1056544.9 | 1029607.5 | 1204.4 | 862.1 |
| | 42235.4 | 42230.7 | 40947.5 | 68.1 | |
| 2383.5 | 22198.3 | 18515.7 | 17345.2 | 315.8 | |
| | 6485.2 | 6485.2 | 6175.9 | 8.2 | |
| | 6485.2 | 6485.2 | 6175.9 | 8.2 | |
| 12229.4 | 6072712.5 | 5890011.5 | 5423173.4 | 14925.6 | 59410.1 |
| | 396496.8 | 391581.3 | 365064.3 | 597.3 | 79.9 |
| 12229.4 | 5676215.7 | 5498430.2 | 5058109.1 | 14328.3 | 59330.2 |
| 3972.4 | 7474130.1 | 7142396.8 | 6666054.7 | 25946.5 | 176874.6 |
| 394286.4 | 18437965.5 | 17941509.2 | 16162634.8 | 68034.1 | 112219.4 |
| 9910.7 | 466448.6 | 445280.7 | 407174.0 | 2658.5 | 339.4 |
| 1570.0 | 50996.2 | 48832.7 | 45364.4 | 265.9 | 1153.8 |
| 369557.2 | 17777635.3 | 17308894.5 | 15582941.0 | 64408.9 | 110625.5 |
| 13248.5 | 142885.4 | 138501.3 | 127155.4 | 700.8 | 100.7 |
| | 2261.2 | 2261.2 | 2041.8 | 2.9 | |
| 2078.0 | 1244156.4 | 1205169.8 | 1088485.3 | 7801.7 | 11303.5 |
| | 4997.6 | 4997.6 | 4420.5 | 2.3 | |
| 60.0 | 1208148.9 | 1170027.1 | 1073537.3 | 7596.2 | 10848.7 |
| 2018.0 | 31009.9 | 30145.1 | 10527.5 | 203.2 | 454.8 |
| 1764.0 | 2844324.9 | 2790934.4 | 2589061.2 | 5076.8 | 10323.4 |
| 1764.0 | 700839.8 | 697189.0 | 634225.8 | 2313.2 | 1010.4 |
| | 28233.8 | 24608.9 | 22961.6 | 165.3 | |
| | 1801068.9 | 1763804.1 | 1632639.1 | 2218.2 | 9313.0 |
| | 311801.0 | 302951.1 | 297590.5 | 373.7 | |
| | 2381.4 | 2381.3 | 1644.2 | 6.4 | |
| | | | | | |
| 6023.3 | 11366166.8 | 11057794.2 | 10544985.5 | 18928.4 | 63062.8 |
| | 189764.0 | 188801.2 | 175943.5 | 617.9 | 28.3 |
| 410630.4 | 22239174.3 | 21504441.4 | 19239617.7 | 91851.4 | 287375.2 |
| 60.0 | 1227610.1 | 1187036.6 | 1091101.6 | 8354.6 | 10848.7 |
| | 2196979.7 | 2155724.8 | 1971837.2 | 3628.9 | 9678.1 |
| | 1351.2 | 1351.2 | 1192.0 | 2.9 | |

**表 15.7 续表 13 continued 13**

| 指 标 | Item | 三、损益及分配 Profits and Losses | | |
|---|---|---|---|---|
| | | 销售费用 Sales Expenses | 管理费用 Management Expenses | 研发费用 R&D expenses |
| **按登记注册类型分** | **By Status of Registration** | | | |
| 内资企业 | Domestic-funded Enterprises | 2206373.3 | 747696.1 | 9715.0 |
| 国有企业 | State-owned Enterprises | 27515.6 | 5675.9 | |
| 集体企业 | Collective-owned Enterprises | 558.9 | 879.7 | 0.6 |
| 股份合作企业 | Cooperative Enterprises | 1154.4 | 1070.6 | 41.2 |
| 联营企业 | Joint-owned Enterprises | 202.3 | 46.3 | |
| 国有与集体联营企业 | Joint State-collective Enterprises | 202.3 | 46.3 | |
| 有限责任公司 | Limited Liability Corporations | 483102.6 | 121467.0 | 424.2 |
| 国有独资公司 | State Sole Funded Corporations | 30491.2 | 8712.9 | 411.6 |
| 其他有限责任公司 | Other Limited Liability Corporations | 452611.4 | 112754.1 | 12.6 |
| 股份有限公司 | Share-holding Corporations Ltd. | 508325.5 | 100432.7 | 3032.0 |
| 私营企业 | Private Enterprises | 1185428.5 | 517955.9 | 6206.2 |
| 私营独资企业 | Private-funded Enterprises | 21570.7 | 11382.0 | 11.6 |
| 私营合伙企业 | Private Partnership Enterprises | 1362.6 | 1282.5 | 0.2 |
| 私营有限责任公司 | Private Limited Liability Corporations | 1154311.0 | 500711.4 | 5657.6 |
| 私营股份有限公司 | Private Share-holding Corporations Ltd. | 8184.2 | 4580.0 | 536.8 |
| 其他企业 | Other Corporations Ltd. | 85.5 | 168.0 | 10.8 |
| 港、澳、台商投资企业 | Enterprises Funded by Hong Kong, Macao and Taiwan | 91990.8 | 70910.3 | 42.9 |
| 合资经营企业(港或澳、台资) | Joint-venture Enterprises | 252.0 | 144.0 | 0.1 |
| 港、澳、台商独资经营企业 | Enterprises with Sole Fund | 77012.3 | 68012.7 | 42.8 |
| 港、澳、台商投资股份有限公司 | Share-holding Corporations Ltd. | 14726.5 | 2753.6 | |
| 外商投资企业 | Foreign-funded Enterprises | 185073.0 | 65287.8 | |
| 中外合资经营企业 | Joint-venture Enterprises | 37550.8 | 19350.3 | |
| 中外合作经营企业 | Cooperative Enterprises | 8619.7 | 943.1 | |
| 外资企业 | Sole-proprietorship Enterprises | 129631.0 | 42941.6 | |
| 外商投资股份有限公司 | Share-holding Corporations Ltd. | 9198.0 | 2052.8 | |
| 其他外商投资企业 | Other Foreign-funded Enterprises | 73.5 | | |
| **按控股情况分** | **By Holding Entity of Share** | | | |
| 国有控股 | State-holding | 597153.1 | 73579.3 | 592.0 |
| 集体控股 | Collective-holding | 6401.4 | 3947.4 | 1.6 |
| 私人控股 | Private-holding | 1637176.0 | 681249.3 | 9110.6 |
| 港澳台商控股 | Held by Corporation from Hong Kong, Macao and Taiwan | 77964.5 | 70332.9 | 42.9 |
| 外商控股 | Foreign-holding | 164656.6 | 54617.3 | |
| 其他 | Other | 78.5 | 128.4 | 10.8 |

单位：万元 (10 000 yuan)

| 三、损益及分配 Profits and Losses | | | | | |
| --- | --- | --- | --- | --- | --- |
| 财务费用 Financial Expenses | | | 投资收益 Income from Investment | 营业利润 Business Profits | 营业外收入 Non-business Income |
| | 利息收入 Interest Income | 利息费用 Interest expenses | | | |
| 118889.7 | 15105.7 | 81264.7 | 89565.9 | 580653.6 | 68182.1 |
| -271.0 | 1588.2 | 301.4 | 692.9 | 13677.0 | 271.5 |
| -12.0 | 16.6 | 3.6 | 792.0 | 584.6 | 39.0 |
| 483.7 | -0.3 | 274.8 | | 1085.6 | 0.1 |
| -13.0 | | | | 158.0 | 0.3 |
| -13.0 | | | | 158.0 | 0.3 |
| 10865.0 | -1260.4 | 12907.8 | 20115.1 | 88512.4 | 7979.4 |
| 903.2 | -190.5 | 1100.8 | 2232.5 | 1792.1 | 1429.0 |
| 9961.8 | -1069.9 | 11807.0 | 17882.6 | 86720.3 | 6550.4 |
| 18167.8 | 13937.2 | 28065.7 | 62749.2 | 202004.3 | 10874.2 |
| 89668.6 | 824.4 | 39710.8 | 5216.7 | 274590.1 | 49017.4 |
| 2002.6 | 149.7 | 997.5 | 122.1 | 24304.2 | 380.6 |
| 189.4 | 41.0 | 65.5 | -1.0 | 2396.9 | 6.2 |
| 86868.9 | 555.4 | 38189.6 | 5095.6 | 246973.7 | 47931.7 |
| 607.7 | 78.3 | 458.2 | | 915.3 | 698.9 |
| 0.6 | | 0.6 | | 41.6 | 0.2 |
| 6018.7 | 651.9 | 3019.9 | 950.7 | -17948.4 | 2817.8 |
| 22.9 | | | 0.4 | 678.9 | 0.3 |
| 5521.0 | 642.9 | 2580.1 | 944.6 | -20669.0 | 2796.8 |
| 474.8 | 9.0 | 439.8 | 5.7 | 2041.7 | 20.7 |
| 12950.2 | 1009.8 | 7572.9 | 813.0 | -16862.8 | 5678.7 |
| 7820.0 | -291.4 | 3001.3 | | 5168.6 | 603.6 |
| -329.3 | | | | -15640.9 | 629.2 |
| 5183.1 | 1301.2 | 4571.6 | 813.0 | -9069.3 | 4168.1 |
| 272.9 | | | | 2686.6 | 277.7 |
| 3.5 | | | | -7.8 | 0.1 |
| | | | | | |
| 1716.9 | 2050.3 | 10556.2 | 22152.5 | 201582.0 | 13989.2 |
| 797.4 | -45.6 | 837.1 | 1142.4 | 1015.7 | 118.2 |
| 117064.0 | 12803.0 | 70511.9 | 66277.1 | 385509.9 | 54398.8 |
| 8285.0 | 658.5 | 5275.7 | 944.6 | -25044.1 | 2843.7 |
| 9994.7 | 1301.2 | 4676.0 | 813.0 | -17262.7 | 5328.5 |
| 0.6 | | 0.6 | | 28.0 | 0.2 |

**表 15.7 续表 14 continued 14**

| 指 标 | Item | 三、损益及分配 Profits and Losses<br>营业外支出<br>Non-business Expenses | 利润总额<br>Total Profits |
|---|---|---|---|
| **按登记注册类型分** | **By Status of Registration** | | |
| 内资企业 | Domestic-funded Enterprises | 22563.0 | 626491.6 |
| 国有企业 | State-owned Enterprises | 660.1 | 13288.5 |
| 集体企业 | Collective-owned Enterprises | 3.1 | 620.5 |
| 股份合作企业 | Cooperative Enterprises | 0.1 | 1085.6 |
| 联营企业 | Joint-owned Enterprises | | 158.3 |
| 国有与集体联营企业 | Joint State-collective Enterprises | | 158.3 |
| 有限责任公司 | Limited Liability Corporations | 3322.1 | 93672.0 |
| 国有独资公司 | State Sole Funded Corporations | 489.2 | 2731.9 |
| 其他有限责任公司 | Other Limited Liability Corporations | 2832.9 | 90940.1 |
| 股份有限公司 | Share-holding Corporations Ltd. | 7389.2 | 205489.4 |
| 私营企业 | Private Enterprises | 11188.2 | 312135.7 |
| 私营独资企业 | Private-funded Enterprises | 91.3 | 24532.9 |
| 私营合伙企业 | Private Partnership Enterprises | 4.0 | 2399.1 |
| 私营有限责任公司 | Private Limited Liability Corporations | 10963.8 | 283716.5 |
| 私营股份有限公司 | Private Share-holding Corporations Ltd. | 129.1 | 1487.2 |
| 其他企业 | Other Corporations Ltd. | 0.2 | 41.6 |
| 港、澳、台商投资企业 | Enterprises Funded by Hong Kong, Macao and Taiwan | 1817.3 | -15038.8 |
| 合资经营企业（港或澳、台资） | Joint-venture Enterprises | 0.1 | 679.1 |
| 港、澳、台商独资经营企业 | Enterprises with Sole Fund | 1767.3 | -17730.4 |
| 港、澳、台商投资股份有限公司 | Share-holding Corporations Ltd. | 49.9 | 2012.5 |
| 外商投资企业 | Foreign-funded Enterprises | 1890.8 | -11789.5 |
| 中外合资经营企业 | Joint-venture Enterprises | 739.9 | 5032.3 |
| 中外合作经营企业 | Cooperative Enterprises | 153.0 | -15164.7 |
| 外资企业 | Sole-proprietorship Enterprises | 941.3 | -5842.5 |
| 外商投资股份有限公司 | Share-holding Corporations Ltd. | 56.6 | 4192.1 |
| 其他外商投资企业 | Other Foreign-funded Enterprises | | -6.7 |
| **按控股情况分** | **By Holding Entity of Share** | | |
| 国有控股 | State-holding | 7942.8 | 208912.9 |
| 集体控股 | Collective-holding | 14.8 | 1119.1 |
| 私人控股 | Private-holding | 14909.1 | 425218.4 |
| 港澳台商控股 | Held by Corporation from Hong Kong, Macao and Taiwan | 1767.2 | -22058.5 |
| 外商控股 | Foreign-holding | 1637.0 | -13570.2 |
| 其他 | Other | 0.2 | 28.0 |

单位：万元 (10 000 yuan)

| 三、损益及分配 Profits and Losses | 四、人工成本及增值税 Labor cost and Value-added Tax | | 五、从事批发和零售业活动的从业人员平均人数(人) Annual Average Employees Engaged in wholesale and retail activities (persons) |
|---|---|---|---|
| 所得税费用 Income Tax Payable | 应付职工薪酬 Employee compensation | 应交增值税 Value-added Tax | |
| 57986.8 | 1311183.8 | 292826 | 174407 |
| 1226.3 | 21721.9 | 15877 | 2133 |
| 4.8 | 702.7 | 284 | 164 |
| 38.8 | 725.7 | 121 | 157 |
| 6.1 | 106.6 | 46 | 14 |
| 6.1 | 106.6 | 46 | 14 |
| 10676.7 | 258101.6 | 52161 | 28993 |
| 345.1 | 12868.4 | 2292 | 1812 |
| 10331.6 | 245233.2 | 49869 | 27181 |
| 16341.6 | 306186.5 | 65945 | 22817 |
| 29685.6 | 723444.3 | 158366 | 120102 |
| 876.7 | 15545.4 | 3673 | 2966 |
| 227.5 | 973.6 | 1282 | 168 |
| 28352.7 | 702495.7 | 152194 | 116163 |
| 228.7 | 4429.6 | 1216 | 805 |
| 6.9 | 194.5 | 26 | 27 |
| 1935.2 | 67828.3 | 12991 | 6239 |
| 1.7 | 865.6 | 304 | 197 |
| 1629.6 | 58366.8 | 12178 | 5082 |
| 303.9 | 8595.9 | 509 | 960 |
| 3771.4 | 49284.6 | 9313 | 5924 |
| 853.0 | 17075.6 | 1458 | 2188 |
| | 4462.7 | 308 | 647 |
| 2802.4 | 23393.8 | 7070 | 2724 |
| 116.0 | 4348.1 | 404 | 364 |
| | 4.4 | 73 | 1 |
| | | | |
| 15886.5 | 326928.3 | 81164 | 25282 |
| 133.0 | 5220.4 | 1996 | 670 |
| 42458.7 | 997789.6 | 210998 | 150374 |
| 540.4 | 60071.0 | 12178 | 5251 |
| 4667.9 | 38092.9 | 8768 | 4966 |
| 3.5 | 139.9 | 26 | 18 |

**表 15.7 续表 15 continued 15**

| 指 标 | Item | 法人企业数(个) Number of Enterprises (unit) | 执行《2006年企业会计准则》企业数(个) Number of Enterprises which Implemented Accounting standard for Business Enterprise in 2006 (unit) | 一、年初存货 Inventory at the Beginning of Year |
|---|---|---|---|---|
| **按经营形式分** | **By Form of Business** | | | |
| 独立门店 | Independent Store | 3350 | 1740 | 1382705.7 |
| 连锁总店(总部) | Central Shop of Chain Stores (Headquarter) | 85 | 63 | 698993.5 |
| 连锁直营店 | Direct-sale Shop of Chain Stores | 52 | 38 | 72432.7 |
| 连锁加盟店 | Branch Shop of Chain Stores | 8 | 5 | 7778.5 |
| 其他 | Other | 475 | 214 | 281813.3 |
| **按单位规模分** | **By Size of Enterprise** | | | |
| 大型 | Large | 54 | 47 | 835127.7 |
| 中型 | Medium | 526 | 376 | 945583.6 |
| 小型 | Small | 2017 | 1035 | 486690.4 |
| 微型 | Micro | 1373 | 602 | 176322.0 |
| **按零售业态分** | **By Type of Retail Business** | | | |
| 有店铺零售 | In-store Retail | 3582 | 1922 | 2342503.1 |
| 便利店 | Convenience Store | 95 | 52 | 33777.6 |
| 超市 | Super Market | 353 | 185 | 544978.1 |
| 折扣店 | Discount Store | 12 | 9 | 10907.4 |
| 仓储会员店 | Warehouse Membership Store | 20 | 13 | 1582.0 |
| 百货店 | Department Store | 196 | 116 | 325119.4 |
| 购物中心 | Shopping Mall | 68 | 35 | 58547.7 |
| 专业店 | Specialized Store | 1993 | 1039 | 1230021.4 |
| 品牌专卖店 | Brand Store | 1061 | 601 | 809748.4 |
| 集合店 | Collection Store | 62 | 30 | 13620.6 |
| 无人值守商店 | Unattended Store | 11 | 3 | 686.9 |
| 无店铺零售 | Off-store Retail | 559 | 247 | 335295.2 |
| 网络零售 | Online Retail | 442 | 197 | 304616.6 |
| 电视/广播零售 | Television/Radio Retail | 1 | 1 | |
| 邮寄零售 | Mailing Retail | 28 | 11 | 6483.2 |
| 无人售货设备零售 | Unmanned Vending Equipment Retail | 2 | 2 | 368.8 |
| 电话零售 | Telephone Retail | 7 | 2 | 413.1 |
| 直销 | Direct Sales | 20 | 9 | 3777.6 |
| 流动货摊零售 | Mobile stall retail | 1 | 1 | 3.3 |
| 其他 | Others | 95 | 42 | 28003.1 |

注：零售业态分为有店铺零售和无店铺零售两大类，涉及多选，有的企业会同时选择多种业态。
Note:Retail formats are divided into two categories: store retailing and non store retailing, involving multiple choices. Some enterprises will choose multiple formats at the same time.

单位：万元 (10 000 yuan)

| 二、期末资产负债 Assets and Liabilities | | | | | |
|---|---|---|---|---|---|
| 流动资产合计 Total Current Assets | 应收账款 Accounts Receivable | 存货 Inventory | 固定资产原价 Total Original Value of Fixed Assets | 房屋和构筑物 Buildings and Structures | 机器设备 Machinery and Equipments |
| 5334780.6 | 371802.3 | 1557182.4 | 1868476.9 | 730830.2 | 244279.3 |
| 3096716.5 | 332479.5 | 819952.1 | 1624851.7 | 198847.5 | 24918.4 |
| -238881.2 | 19264.2 | 91895.0 | 105586.8 | 43138.8 | 38027.7 |
| 18503.2 | 691.2 | 7593.5 | 1951.2 | 61.2 | 51.3 |
| 2149054.3 | 231207.8 | 335831.5 | 451705.6 | 134297.5 | 109735.7 |
| 5439578.4 | 367498.7 | 1075074.6 | 1841434.5 | 287391.2 | 59732.2 |
| 1703485.6 | -88596.8 | 984861.6 | 1345473.8 | 484675.2 | 223399.7 |
| 2092335.6 | 498785.4 | 518014.2 | 647494.7 | 271553.0 | 110427.9 |
| 1124773.8 | 177757.7 | 234504.1 | 218169.2 | 63555.8 | 23452.6 |
| 9755308.2 | 819707.6 | 2693265.9 | 3952165.3 | 1097676.3 | 349090.4 |
| -294860.2 | -181707.9 | 39393.9 | 131011.3 | 44667.1 | 30920.7 |
| 1595180.9 | 229546.9 | 519766.4 | 938579.6 | 56348.3 | 61746.1 |
| 24764.1 | 2148.7 | 9846.6 | 1515.5 | 453.3 | 662.7 |
| 55964.8 | 2349.6 | 3392.2 | 16755.4 | 172.3 | 14967.0 |
| 1112883.7 | 68452.7 | 301608.8 | 721883.6 | 13423.6 | 8453.6 |
| 642187.6 | 34022.2 | 121021.8 | 139429.7 | 120779.8 | 6716.6 |
| 6381623.4 | 329882.6 | 1487592.0 | 2744870.6 | 683304.9 | 167495.3 |
| 1799239.6 | 255265.8 | 837066.5 | 646773.3 | 265035.2 | 103164.4 |
| 66576.2 | 10649.8 | 22103.8 | 14817.9 | 3458.4 | 4596.9 |
| 3180.2 | 1439.7 | 693.6 | 543.8 | 35.0 | |
| 2833929.9 | 285568.8 | 429360.1 | 506949.8 | 251765.8 | 108515.0 |
| 2636006 | 229649.8 | 397528 | 427473.6 | 240060.4 | 47972.3 |
| 2154 | 141.2 | | 30.1 | | 30.1 |
| 39286.7 | 8731.9 | 7115.2 | 1791.6 | 166.5 | 698.8 |
| 454.9 | 26.3 | 112 | 1122.6 | | |
| 6554.2 | 2546.6 | 481.8 | 1511.9 | | 1290.7 |
| 44849.3 | 13764.4 | 2996.3 | 25796.8 | 68.1 | 3319.1 |
| 10656 | 2436.6 | 21.7 | | | |
| 149909 | 43478.2 | 29784.8 | 81604.6 | 13505 | 61071.4 |

**表 15.7 续表 16 continued 16**

| 指 标 | Item | 二、期末资产负债 Assets and Liabilities | | |
|---|---|---|---|---|
| | | 累计折旧 Cumulative Depreciation | 本年折旧 Depreciation | 固定资产净额 Net Value of Fixed Assets |
| **按经营形式分** | **By Form of Business** | | | |
| 独立门店 | Independent Store | 642343.3 | 98071.7 | 971562.0 |
| 连锁总店(总部) | Central Shop of Chain Stores (Headquarter) | 765016.0 | 69921.9 | 810340.2 |
| 连锁直营店 | Direct-sale Shop of Chain Stores | 52482.8 | 5346.3 | 51332.1 |
| 连锁加盟店 | Branch Shop of Chain Stores | 790.1 | 52.0 | 1158.7 |
| 其他 | Other | 197674.9 | 29244.7 | 237177.1 |
| **按单位规模分** | **By Size of Enterprise** | | | |
| 大型 | Large | 853194.6 | 94559.6 | 961705.9 |
| 中型 | Medium | 586608.0 | 96652.5 | 662444.7 |
| 小型 | Small | 150179.1 | -251.1 | 348042.0 |
| 微型 | Micro | 68325.4 | 11675.6 | 99377.5 |
| **按零售业态分** | **By Type of Retail Business** | | | |
| 有店铺零售 | In-store Retail | 1617334.2 | 193047.2 | 2017901.2 |
| 便利店 | Convenience Store | 46434.1 | 11780.2 | 67611.0 |
| 超市 | Super Market | 429187.9 | 42753.2 | 450037.6 |
| 折扣店 | Discount Store | 1276.1 | 157.1 | 200.7 |
| 仓储会员店 | Warehouse Membership Store | 5383.9 | 1285.1 | 10890.2 |
| 百货店 | Department Store | 326848.8 | 26202.8 | 361884.8 |
| 购物中心 | Shopping Mall | 35785.8 | 5936.8 | 101857.2 |
| 专业店 | Specialized Store | 1078980.8 | 89295.3 | 1457174.4 |
| 品牌专卖店 | Brand Store | 274328.1 | 62837.7 | 323857.3 |
| 集合店 | Collection Store | 6758.4 | 1476.0 | 6774.0 |
| 无人值守商店 | Unattended Store | 127.4 | 21.6 | 308.4 |
| 无店铺零售 | Off-store Retail | 213659.5 | 30008.2 | 264260.0 |
| 网络零售 | Online Retail | 180275.5 | 22445.7 | 219406.8 |
| 电视/广播零售 | Television/Radio Retail | 21.6 | 2.1 | 8.5 |
| 邮寄零售 | Mailing Retail | 372.5 | 178 | 908.2 |
| 无人售货设备零售 | Unmanned Vending Equipment Retail | 994.8 | 19 | 27.8 |
| 电话零售 | Telephone Retail | 333.7 | 207.2 | 1178.2 |
| 直销 | Direct Sales | 2827.2 | 947.6 | 22932.9 |
| 流动货摊零售 | Mobile stall retail | | | |
| 其他 | Others | 34134.5 | 8007.1 | 46554.2 |

注：零售业态分为有店铺零售和无店铺零售两大类，涉及多选，有的企业会同时选择多种业态。
Note:Retail formats are divided into two categories: store retailing and non store retailing, involving multiple choices. Some enterprises will choose multiple formats at the same time.

单位：万元 (10 000 yuan)

| 二、期末资产负债 Assets and Liabilities | | | | | |
|---|---|---|---|---|---|
| 在建工程<br>Construction in Progress | 无形资产<br>Intangible Assets | 土地使用权<br>Land Use Rights | 资产总计<br>Total Assets | 流动负债合计<br>Total Current Liabilities | 应付账款<br>Accounts Payable |
| 75909.9 | 320550.3 | 183583.8 | 8052590.3 | 5733367.6 | 834545.9 |
| 179281.5 | 236202.2 | 46736.3 | 5883515.8 | 3463397.8 | 804697.0 |
| 2094.9 | 16705.9 | 14396.4 | 44598.2 | 355188.4 | 136305.0 |
| 608.9 | 2591.0 | 2591.0 | 24283.7 | 19941.5 | 4916.9 |
| 20955.8 | 128133.4 | 55473.7 | 2832238.6 | 2132730.8 | 348854.0 |
| | | | | | |
| 182031.6 | 305634.3 | 51413.8 | 8718042.6 | 5403313.2 | 949744.2 |
| 57074.8 | 300006.1 | 177282.1 | 3539254.8 | 3804533.4 | 470949.2 |
| 34863.4 | 75057.7 | 55802.1 | 3203004.8 | 1807504.5 | 445831.4 |
| 4881.2 | 23484.7 | 18283.2 | 1376924.4 | 689275.0 | 262794.0 |
| | | | | | |
| 271438.7 | 703069.2 | 302781.2 | 15949105.4 | 11082929.0 | 1917951.1 |
| 2536.5 | 81780.4 | 38923.5 | -81349.5 | 193955.3 | 35116.4 |
| 8418.5 | 24407.5 | 19778.6 | 3469206.3 | 1797495.7 | 511089.7 |
| 9.9 | 12.2 | | 35100.1 | 50069.6 | 6432.2 |
| | 5.7 | | 98927.8 | 38286.3 | 11003.8 |
| 1291.7 | 18496.9 | 17750.3 | 2485945.3 | 1110544.4 | 257375.3 |
| 1134.9 | 11070.2 | 10944.2 | 861385.4 | 496906.9 | 178863.1 |
| 235315.2 | 534522.6 | 208794.1 | 10637521.9 | 6225011.6 | 1056813.6 |
| 27866.4 | 148056.7 | 77958.8 | 2676309.0 | 3479078.6 | 332848.5 |
| 186.3 | 4176.4 | 3992.9 | 90190.7 | 59470.3 | 12701.0 |
| | 33.3 | | 3861.5 | 1648.7 | 1079.3 |
| 168461.9 | 39629.2 | 16146.1 | 3924114.7 | 1763641.1 | 489155.0 |
| 165237.5 | 37702.5 | 16124.1 | 3505650.6 | 1470700.2 | 403589.1 |
| | 2.4 | | 2164.9 | 1163.5 | 1143 |
| 7.1 | 22.9 | 22 | 187763.4 | 182890.8 | 50457.3 |
| | | | 877.8 | 309.5 | 31.6 |
| | | | 9263.5 | 6217.2 | 2072.2 |
| 4002.7 | 15.6 | | 74918.3 | 32069.6 | 8959.5 |
| | | | 10672.2 | 3376.6 | 1679.2 |
| 3224.4 | 1923.4 | | 234532.5 | 113349.5 | 37463.9 |

**表 15.7 续表 17 continued 17**

| 指 标 | Item | 二、期末资产负债 Assets and Liabilities | | |
|---|---|---|---|---|
| | | 负债合计 Total Liabilities | 所有者权益合计 Total Owner's Equity | 实收资本 Paid-up Capital |
| **按经营形式分** | **By Form of Business** | | | |
| 独立门店 | Independent Store | 5440075.4 | 3439663.5 | 4221560.0 |
| 连锁总店(总部) | Central Shop of Chain Stores (Headquarter) | 3429393.4 | 1864584.8 | 401070.2 |
| 连锁直营店 | Direct-sale Shop of Chain Stores | 533608.3 | 109732.8 | 226255.7 |
| 连锁加盟店 | Branch Shop of Chain Stores | 20635.4 | 3648.3 | 4750.0 |
| 其他 | Other | 2167482.4 | 1274876.5 | 261495.7 |
| **按单位规模分** | **By Size of Enterprise** | | | |
| 大型 | Large | 5035760.7 | 3682281.9 | 555403.3 |
| 中型 | Medium | 3365977.0 | 1442906.8 | 1032931.1 |
| 小型 | Small | 2237455.1 | 1160423.3 | 3328723.6 |
| 微型 | Micro | 952002.1 | 406893.9 | 198073.6 |
| **按零售业态分** | **By Type of Retail Business** | | | |
| 有店铺零售 | In-store Retail | 10931490.1 | 6463109.6 | 4978972.0 |
| 便利店 | Convenience Store | 261356.3 | 167352.6 | 221634.3 |
| 超市 | Super Market | 2698023.8 | 776545.9 | 436784.7 |
| 折扣店 | Discount Store | 54725.4 | -19625.3 | 12483.0 |
| 仓储会员店 | Warehouse Membership Store | 68032.7 | 28381.0 | 36919.2 |
| 百货店 | Department Store | 1811920.8 | 677873.7 | 265639.0 |
| 购物中心 | Shopping Mall | 716789.9 | 144616.9 | 138641.9 |
| 专业店 | Specialized Store | 6159368.3 | 5125810.4 | 1220988.7 |
| 品牌专卖店 | Brand Store | 2563633.0 | 906492.6 | 3108712.1 |
| 集合店 | Collection Store | 70633.9 | 17961.8 | 16947.1 |
| 无人值守商店 | Unattended Store | 2627.6 | 1096.8 | 580.0 |
| 无店铺零售 | Off-store Retail | 2081936.6 | 1845907.6 | 375236.9 |
| 网络零售 | Online Retail | 1774476.9 | 1736766.5 | 304941.5 |
| 电视/广播零售 | Television/Radio Retail | 1163.5 | 1001.4 | 1000 |
| 邮寄零售 | Mailing Retail | 184462.5 | 3118.1 | 2330.1 |
| 无人售货设备零售 | Unmanned Vending Equipment Retail | 480.7 | 397.1 | 501.5 |
| 电话零售 | Telephone Retail | 6217.2 | 3046.3 | 2643.8 |
| 直销 | Direct Sales | 35136 | 39782.3 | 15952.8 |
| 流动货摊零售 | Mobile stall retail | 3376.6 | 7295.6 | 3800 |
| 其他 | Others | 123333.5 | 109518.5 | 73190.5 |

注：零售业态分为有店铺零售和无店铺零售两大类，涉及多选，有的企业会同时选择多种业态。
Note:Retail formats are divided into two categories: store retailing and non store retailing, involving multiple choices. Some enterprises will choose multiple formats at the same time.

单位：万元 (10 000 yuan)

| 二、期末资产负债 Assets and Liabilities | 三、损益及分配 Profits and Losses | | | | |
|---|---|---|---|---|---|
| 个人资本 Personal Capital | 营业收入 Gross Sales | 主营业务收入 Main Business Income | 营业成本 Operating Cost | 税金及附加 Taxes and Surcharges | 其他业务利润 Other Business Profits |
| 336406.6 | 19342850.3 | 18836846.6 | 17315856.8 | 77336.5 | 75788.2 |
| 26261.5 | 8954815.7 | 8528592.9 | 7638318.2 | 31797.1 | 262045.7 |
| 12844.6 | 1395466.3 | 1366509.3 | 1193785.4 | 2123.0 | 7368.5 |
| 1680.0 | 16454.0 | 16238.8 | 14180.9 | 20.1 | 3.4 |
| 39521.0 | 7512369.8 | 7347871.8 | 6863386.0 | 12107.4 | 25787.3 |
| | | | | | |
| 28159.3 | 11083404.5 | 10669661.2 | 9492478.2 | 35548.6 | 272156.1 |
| 97020.3 | 12851834.0 | 12576591.3 | 11667941.9 | 34947.6 | 58883.4 |
| 237504.2 | 8037100.3 | 7938705.3 | 7148545.4 | 41908.1 | 18616.7 |
| 54029.9 | 5249617.3 | 4911101.6 | 4716561.8 | 10979.8 | 21336.9 |
| | | | | | |
| 380907.5 | 34275646.6 | 33166526.8 | 30374708.8 | 121059.1 | 369743.8 |
| 7355.6 | 1065820.3 | 1014102.4 | 926465.2 | 2432.2 | 2852.8 |
| 35347.3 | 5608683.6 | 5293051.5 | 4470944.2 | 36612.7 | 254500.7 |
| 702.0 | 55208.2 | 49934.0 | 46984.8 | 183.4 | |
| 867.6 | 153832.9 | 148436.7 | 145752.9 | 140.8 | 27.6 |
| 11832.3 | 2804937.6 | 2611712.0 | 2103044.0 | 32770.9 | 154330.0 |
| 5484.6 | 1954967.4 | 1886924.5 | 1746122.1 | 4381.6 | 22282.8 |
| 224173.9 | 19776571.6 | 19211133.7 | 17522830.1 | 67213.5 | 192123.4 |
| 134647.8 | 8781586.4 | 8499214.9 | 8050564.1 | 29250.3 | 48505.1 |
| 6247.1 | 232710.7 | 228784.5 | 196052.1 | 215.9 | 436.8 |
| 480.0 | 6816.7 | 4653.4 | 5790.4 | 15.8 | |
| 46681.3 | 6930928.6 | 6816577.2 | 6200162.7 | 10149.1 | 16245.6 |
| 34772.2 | 6335976.7 | 6227397.6 | 5656419.9 | 9541.5 | 15622.2 |
| | 4899.5 | 4899.5 | 2347.2 | 6.2 | |
| 682.4 | 256807.1 | 253629.1 | 235790 | 200.4 | 31.5 |
| | 2546 | 2216.2 | 1955.7 | 0.9 | |
| 1363.8 | 13235 | 13235 | 11519 | 28.4 | |
| 3934 | 43808.4 | 43808.4 | 39368.3 | 91.8 | 0.3 |
| | 5152.8 | 5152.8 | 5172.3 | 1.7 | |
| 10334.4 | 392514.8 | 390227.2 | 347439 | 528 | 592.1 |

**表 15.7 续表 18 continued 18**

| 指 标 | Item | 三、损益及分配 Profits and Losses 销售费用 Sales Expenses | 管理费用 Management Expenses | 研发费用 R&D expenses |
|---|---|---|---|---|
| **按经营形式分** | **By Form of Business** | | | |
| 独立门店 | Independent Store | 901174.5 | 524358.5 | 2887.0 |
| 连锁总店（总部） | Central Shop of Chain Stores (Headquarter) | 966836.5 | 198496.5 | 3355.1 |
| 连锁直营店 | Direct-sale Shop of Chain Stores | 192711.0 | 51881.0 | 0.2 |
| 连锁加盟店 | Branch Shop of Chain Stores | 1747.9 | 1306.8 | 6.5 |
| 其他 | Other | 420967.2 | 107851.4 | 3509.1 |
| **按单位规模分** | **By Size of Enterprise** | | | |
| 大型 | Large | 1224649.6 | 251256.9 | 3385.7 |
| 中型 | Medium | 670718.5 | 301068.2 | 3742.7 |
| 小型 | Small | 303149.2 | 248473.4 | 2280.9 |
| 微型 | Micro | 284919.8 | 83095.7 | 348.6 |
| **按零售业态分** | **By Type of Retail Business** | | | |
| 有店铺零售 | In-store Retail | 2291558.5 | 824371.6 | 6748.4 |
| 便利店 | Convenience Store | 76058.3 | 32487.1 | 148.6 |
| 超市 | Super Market | 733134.1 | 210808.0 | 3198.3 |
| 折扣店 | Discount Store | 10005.5 | 5915.5 | |
| 仓储会员店 | Warehouse Membership Store | 1799.9 | 11722.9 | 0.2 |
| 百货店 | Department Store | 376080.1 | 162221.0 | 2870.1 |
| 购物中心 | Shopping Mall | 149801.1 | 33805.2 | 365.3 |
| 专业店 | Specialized Store | 1249228.3 | 448278.5 | 5714.5 |
| 品牌专卖店 | Brand Store | 422857.2 | 192024.6 | 551.4 |
| 集合店 | Collection Store | 28594.4 | 9425.3 | 57.1 |
| 无人值守商店 | Unattended Store | 291.9 | 262.7 | |
| 无店铺零售 | Off-store Retail | 491872.0 | 150977.5 | 3654.4 |
| 网络零售 | Online Retail | 470443.4 | 131600.8 | 2532.5 |
| 电视 / 广播零售 | Television/Radio Retail | 2523.6 | 18.5 | |
| 邮寄零售 | Mailing Retail | 14521.9 | 2755.6 | 15.2 |
| 无人售货设备零售 | Unmanned Vending Equipment Retail | 647.5 | 234.8 | |
| 电话零售 | Telephone Retail | 482.8 | 665.7 | |
| 直销 | Direct Sales | 1819.6 | 2993 | 147.8 |
| 流动货摊零售 | Mobile stall retail | 1.4 | 12.3 | |
| 其他 | Others | 18707.6 | 18005.1 | 1122.2 |

注：零售业态分为有店铺零售和无店铺零售两大类，涉及多选，有的企业会同时选择多种业态。
Note:Retail formats are divided into two categories: store retailing and non store retailing, involving multiple choices. Some enterprises will choose multiple formats at the same time.

单位：万元 (10 000 yuan)

| 三、损益及分配 Profits and Losses | | | | | |
|---|---|---|---|---|---|
| 财务费用 Financial Expenses | | | 投资收益 Income from Investment | 营业利润 Business Profits | 营业外收入 Non-business Income |
| | 利息收入 Interest Income | 利息费用 Interest expenses | | | |
| 84253.2 | 5135.4 | 49115.0 | 22302.4 | 353308.1 | 50793.6 |
| 30134.0 | 5632.5 | 27776.3 | 68947.8 | 178005.9 | 17981.2 |
| 9992.4 | 323.0 | 3677.0 | 39.8 | -67471.0 | 2274.6 |
| 80.7 | 0.6 | 58.8 | 15.0 | -723.1 | 18.3 |
| 13398.3 | 5675.9 | 11230.4 | 24.6 | 82722.5 | 5610.9 |
| | | | | | |
| 41713.6 | 7077.8 | 27869.5 | 74991.1 | 136956.2 | 21272.3 |
| 54234.5 | 7065.5 | 35766.0 | 6578.9 | 84557.0 | 30422.8 |
| 33669.6 | -1618.4 | 19715.8 | 14790.3 | 219172.7 | 21267.3 |
| 8240.9 | 4242.5 | 8506.2 | -5030.7 | 105156.5 | 3716.2 |
| | | | | | |
| 134241.1 | 16473.7 | 89429.1 | 91170.6 | 517404.4 | 73430.2 |
| 3784.0 | 382.5 | 2448.5 | 768.5 | 8580.0 | 1318.9 |
| 44568.3 | 9074.1 | 26286.8 | 61131.6 | 115773.6 | 12245.3 |
| 402.2 | 17.1 | 438.7 | -497.3 | -6397.6 | 546.7 |
| 879.1 | 3.6 | 35.1 | | -6247.5 | 81.7 |
| 25157.8 | 8812.5 | 22790.5 | 61540.8 | 117319.6 | 4707.7 |
| 10074.3 | 3934.3 | 10801.0 | 339.5 | 9201.6 | 1347.5 |
| 56576.8 | 8841.3 | 49415.6 | 81925.1 | 487829.1 | 26565.1 |
| 36112.5 | 2325.6 | 20152.0 | 7762.2 | 18305.2 | 35632.1 |
| 908.0 | 187.6 | 599.6 | -309.2 | -2800.8 | 801.4 |
| 25.2 | 0.1 | 8.7 | | 469.6 | 0.2 |
| 12071.4 | -2879.8 | 8127.2 | 7949.2 | 55768.9 | 5989.8 |
| 10649.9 | -3106.6 | 7040.9 | 7696.7 | 48225.8 | 5585.9 |
| 0.2 | 0.1 | | | 3.8 | |
| 75.5 | 16 | 29.2 | 124.1 | 1072.7 | 117.4 |
| 4.8 | 0.1 | | | -299.6 | 0.2 |
| 44.1 | 1.9 | 23.4 | | 404.3 | 3.5 |
| 336.4 | 1.3 | 329.2 | 90.2 | -806.1 | 333 |
| -1.4 | -1.7 | | | 16.9 | 0.2 |
| 1360 | 227.1 | 1061 | 252.5 | 7779 | 416.7 |

**表 15.7 续表 19 continued 19**

| 指 标 | Item | 三、损益及分配 Profits and Losses | |
|---|---|---|---|
| | | 营业外支出 Non-business Expenses | 利润总额 Total Profits |
| **按经营形式分** | **By Form of Business** | | |
| 独立门店 | Independent Store | 13091.2 | 393807.3 |
| 连锁总店（总部） | Central Shop of Chain Stores (Headquarter) | 8378.3 | 187608.8 |
| 连锁直营店 | Direct-sale Shop of Chain Stores | 1088.2 | -66283.6 |
| 连锁加盟店 | Branch Shop of Chain Stores | 165.0 | -869.8 |
| 其他 | Other | 3548.4 | 85400.6 |
| **按单位规模分** | **By Size of Enterprise** | | |
| 大型 | Large | 8572.0 | 152850.0 |
| 中型 | Medium | 11391.7 | 103537.6 |
| 小型 | Small | 3363.7 | 237413.3 |
| 微型 | Micro | 2943.7 | 105862.4 |
| **按零售业态分** | **By Type of Retail Business** | | |
| 有店铺零售 | In-store Retail | 25776.6 | 568485.7 |
| 便利店 | Convenience Store | 656.0 | 9243 |
| 超市 | Super Market | 3625.6 | 124393 |
| 折扣店 | Discount Store | 1449.2 | -7800 |
| 仓储会员店 | Warehouse Membership Store | 324.6 | -6490.4 |
| 百货店 | Department Store | 3270.7 | 118703.0 |
| 购物中心 | Shopping Mall | 198.3 | 10350.6 |
| 专业店 | Specialized Store | 16786.4 | 501642.9 |
| 品牌专卖店 | Brand Store | 5251.1 | 48632.4 |
| 集合店 | Collection Store | 766.5 | -2765.9 |
| 无人值守商店 | Unattended Store | | 469.8 |
| 无店铺零售 | Off-store Retail | 1839.4 | 61189.5 |
| 网络零售 | Online Retail | 1776.1 | 53328.5 |
| 电视 / 广播零售 | Television/Radio Retail | | 3.8 |
| 邮寄零售 | Mailing Retail | 2 | 1188.1 |
| 无人售货设备零售 | Unmanned Vending Equipment Retail | 0.2 | -299.7 |
| 电话零售 | Telephone Retail | 0.6 | 407.2 |
| 直销 | Direct Sales | 0.9 | -474 |
| 流动货摊零售 | Mobile stall retail | | 17.2 |
| 其他 | Others | 84.5 | 8088.6 |

注：零售业态分为有店铺零售和无店铺零售两大类，涉及多选，有的企业会同时选择多种业态。
Note:Retail formats are divided into two categories: store retailing and non store retailing, involving multiple choices. Some enterprises will choose multiple formats at the same time.

单位：万元 (10 000 yuan)

| 三、损益及分配 Profits and Losses | 四、人工成本及增值税 Labor cost and Value-added Tax | | 五、从事批发和零售业活动的从业人员平均人数（人） Annual Average Employees Engaged in wholesale and retail activities (persons) |
|---|---|---|---|
| 所得税费用 Income Tax Payable | 应付职工薪酬 Employee compensation | 应交增值税 Value-added Tax | |
| 40724.3 | 623678.2 | 180210 | 94364 |
| 15302.0 | 575379.3 | 82661 | 60114 |
| -155.8 | 100250.9 | 11602 | 15203 |
| 11.8 | 1746.1 | 278 | 357 |
| 7811.1 | 127242.2 | 40378 | 16532 |
| | | | |
| 15177.3 | 735286.1 | 100284 | 79742 |
| 23377.4 | 411940.9 | 112007 | 54132 |
| 15931.6 | 237717.7 | 66959 | 41421 |
| 9207.1 | 43352.0 | 35880 | 11275 |
| | | | |
| 61465.4 | 1380650.4 | 295660 | 179611 |
| 1659.8 | 45144.5 | 2466.8 | 6264 |
| 13617.6 | 436481.3 | 60123.7 | 59281 |
| 8.3 | 4737.1 | 356.4 | 491 |
| 23.1 | 15353.7 | 489 | 1151 |
| 10646.3 | 235921.6 | 41854 | 25149 |
| -125.3 | 32915.7 | 14881 | 4319 |
| 47273.1 | 809867.8 | 182927 | 92558 |
| 10335.3 | 268370.3 | 70123 | 38332 |
| -4.8 | 18733.3 | 1872 | 2863 |
| 16.1 | 245.0 | 259 | 78 |
| 5733.3 | 219267.1 | 43549 | 23117 |
| 4627.2 | 201488.6 | 40408.5 | 20803 |
| | 16.4 | 9.9 | 2 |
| 41.7 | 1208 | 985.4 | 361 |
| | 379.2 | 16.8 | 63 |
| 52.9 | 549.1 | 219.9 | 104 |
| 137.4 | 2935.3 | 514.6 | 419 |
| -401.2 | 9.4 | 651 | 1 |
| 1101.3 | 17052.1 | 2916.4 | 2071 |

# 表 15.8 限额以上住宿业法人企业财务状况（2022 年）
## FINANCIAL INDICATORS OF ENTERPRISES ABOVE DESIGNATED SIZE OF HOTELS (2022)

| 指 标 | Item | 法人企业数（个）Number of Enterprises (unit) | 执行《2006年企业会计准则》企业数（个）Number of Enterprises which Implemented Accounting standard for Business Enterprise in 2006 (unit) | 一、年初存货 Inventory at the Beginning of Year |
|---|---|---|---|---|
| **合 计** | **Total** | **604** | **319** | **49916.1** |
| **按住宿业行业小类分** | **By Classification of Hotels** | | | |
| 旅游饭店 | Tourist Hotels | 280 | 169 | 37360.5 |
| 旅游饭店 | Tourist Hotels | 280 | 169 | 37360.5 |
| 一般旅馆 | General Hotels | 287 | 131 | 9372 |
| 经济型连锁酒店 | Economical Chain Hotels | 79 | 28 | 1244.9 |
| 其他一般旅馆 | Other General Hotels | 208 | 103 | 8127.1 |
| 民宿服务 | Homestay Services | 4 | 2 | 15.3 |
| 民宿服务 | Homestay Services | 4 | 2 | 15.3 |
| 露营地服务 | Campsite Services | 1 | | 2551.1 |
| 其他住宿业 | Other Hotels | 32 | 17 | 617.2 |
| 其他住宿业 | Other Hotel Services | 32 | 17 | 617.2 |
| **按登记注册类型分** | **By Status of Registration** | | | |
| 内资企业 | Domestic-funded Enterprises | 594 | 310 | 49268 |
| 国有企业 | State-owned Enterprises | 7 | 7 | 474.9 |
| 集体企业 | Collective-owned Enterprises | 4 | 2 | 324 |
| 有限责任公司 | Limited Liability Corporations | 84 | 68 | 24698.2 |
| 国有独资公司 | State Sole Funded Corporations | 19 | 16 | 5701.6 |
| 其他有限责任公司 | Other Limited Liability Corporations | 65 | 52 | 18996.6 |
| 股份有限公司 | Share-holding Corporations Ltd. | 3 | 2 | 102.5 |
| 私营企业 | Private Enterprises | 496 | 231 | 23668.8 |
| 私营独资企业 | Private-funded Enterprises | 38 | 17 | 408 |
| 私营合伙企业 | Private Partnership Enterprises | 3 | | 13.1 |
| 私营有限责任公司 | Private Limited Liability Corporations | 452 | 211 | 23120.7 |
| 私营股份有限公司 | Private Share-holding Corporations Ltd. | 3 | 3 | 127 |
| 港、澳、台商投资企业 | Enterprises Funded by Hong Kong, Macao and Taiwan | 3 | 3 | 123.6 |
| 与港澳台商合资经营企业 | Cooperative Enterprises | 1 | 1 | 71.4 |
| 港澳台商独资企业 | Enterprises with Sole Fund | 2 | 2 | 52.2 |
| 外商投资企业 | Foreign-funded Enterprises | 7 | 6 | 524.1 |
| 中外合资经营企业 | Joint-venture Enterprises | 1 | 1 | 123.4 |
| 外资企业 | Enterprises with Sole Fund | 5 | 4 | 377.9 |
| 其他外商投资企业 | Other Foreign-funded Enterprises | 1 | 1 | 22.8 |

单位：万元 (10 000 yuan)

| 二、期末资产负债 Assets and Liabilities | | | | | |
|---|---|---|---|---|---|
| 流动资产<br>合　计<br>Total Current Assets | 应收账款<br>Accounts Receivable | 存　货<br>Inventory | 固定资产<br>原　价<br>Total Original Value of Fixed Assets | 房屋和<br>构筑物<br>Buildings and Structures | 机器设备<br>Machinery and Equipments |
| **1278908.5** | **79059** | **44130.4** | **1530248** | **785376.3** | **154917.8** |
| 982086 | 39923.7 | 36076.1 | 1282462.4 | 657901.5 | 131948 |
| 982086 | 39923.7 | 36076.1 | 1282462.4 | 657901.5 | 131948 |
| 274802.6 | 35985.4 | 7305.9 | 167253 | 67257.6 | 19226.7 |
| 78836.4 | 13399.4 | 1029.7 | 45225 | 21071 | 2824.5 |
| 195966.2 | 22586.0 | 6276.2 | 122028.0 | 46186.6 | 16402.2 |
| 1334.6 | 496.8 | 17.5 | 2239.3 | | 13.2 |
| 1334.6 | 496.8 | 17.5 | 2239.3 | | 13.2 |
| 92.7 | 7.4 | | 1563 | 1537.9 | |
| 20592.6 | 2645.7 | 730.9 | 76730.3 | 58679.3 | 3729.9 |
| 20592.6 | 2645.7 | 730.9 | 76730.3 | 58679.3 | 3729.9 |
| 1159538 | 75515 | 43678 | 1352385 | 693819 | 131136 |
| 38676.2 | 1045.3 | 275.4 | 81549.6 | 33884.1 | 24382.1 |
| 1788.8 | 99.4 | 313.7 | 10144.6 | 7185.6 | 472.8 |
| 564024.9 | 22244.1 | 11999.9 | 667737.8 | 346518.3 | 50431.8 |
| 232034.2 | 6493.9 | 4294.6 | 232762.5 | 141332.9 | 15552.9 |
| 331990.7 | 15750.2 | 7705.3 | 434975.3 | 205185.4 | 34878.9 |
| 974.6 | 221 | 100.3 | 4369.4 | | 122.3 |
| 554073.5 | 51904.8 | 30988.8 | 588583.7 | 306230.8 | 55727.4 |
| 6318.8 | 1179.1 | 680.9 | 20474.7 | 10363.6 | 1223.3 |
| 302 | 16.6 | 9.6 | 788.7 | 747.4 | 41.3 |
| 545703.4 | 50755.3 | 30214.2 | 564630.7 | 294501.5 | 54273.8 |
| 1749.3 | -46.2 | 84.1 | 2689.6 | 618.3 | 189 |
| 2098.3 | 748.2 | 128.2 | 85178.1 | 21286.8 | 15933.7 |
| 125.2 | 142.6 | 55.4 | 39969.7 | | |
| 1973.1 | 605.6 | 72.8 | 45208.4 | 21286.8 | 15933.7 |
| 117272.2 | 2796.2 | 324.1 | 92684.8 | 70270.7 | 7847.7 |
| 36909.8 | | 27.1 | 3533 | | |
| 73758.1 | 2735.3 | 273.4 | 56088 | 38745.6 | 6309 |
| 6604.3 | 60.9 | 23.6 | 33063.8 | 31525.1 | 1538.7 |

**表 15.8 续表 1 continued 1**

| 指 标 | Item | 二、期末资产负债 Assets and Liabilities 累计折旧 Cumulative Depreciation | 本年折旧 Depreciation | 固定资产净额 Net Value of Fixed Assets |
|---|---|---|---|---|
| **合 计** | **Total** | **686509.5** | **62804** | **684060.6** |
| **按住宿业行业小类分** | **By Classification of Hotels** | | | |
| 旅游饭店 | Tourist Hotels | 599615 | 49371.5 | 553524.3 |
| 旅游饭店 | Tourist Hotels | 599615 | 49371.5 | 553524.3 |
| 一般旅馆 | General Hotels | 73025.4 | 10969 | 69351.2 |
| 经济型连锁酒店 | Economical Chain Hotels | 21058 | 2672.9 | 18753.6 |
| 其他一般旅馆 | Other General Hotels | 51967.4 | 8296.1 | 50597.6 |
| 民宿服务 | Homestay Services | 496.9 | 127.3 | 1742.4 |
| 民宿服务 | Homestay Services | 496.9 | 127.3 | 1742.4 |
| 露营地服务 | Campsite Services | 25 | 23 | 1538 |
| 其他住宿业 | Other Hotels | 13347.2 | 2313.2 | 57904.7 |
| 其他住宿业 | Other Hotel Services | 13347.2 | 2313.2 | 57904.7 |
| **按登记注册类型分** | **By Status of Registration** | | | |
| 内资企业 | Domestic-funded Enterprises | 573285 | 55719 | 619423 |
| 国有企业 | State-owned Enterprises | 44239.2 | 2984.9 | 36013.7 |
| 集体企业 | Collective-owned Enterprises | 6291.1 | 379.3 | 3853.5 |
| 有限责任公司 | Limited Liability Corporations | 268388.9 | 23776.6 | 309128.6 |
| 国有独资公司 | State Sole Funded Corporations | 75167.7 | 7943.6 | 84560.4 |
| 其他有限责任公司 | Other Limited Liability Corporations | 193221.2 | 15833 | 224568.2 |
| 股份有限公司 | Share-holding Corporations Ltd. | 3291.2 | 309.1 | 883.7 |
| 私营企业 | Private Enterprises | 251074.1 | 28269.2 | 269543.2 |
| 私营独资企业 | Private-funded Enterprises | 8371 | 924.5 | 6728.7 |
| 私营合伙企业 | Private Partnership Enterprises | 366 | 342.9 | 45.6 |
| 私营有限责任公司 | Private Limited Liability Corporations | 240649.3 | 26661.7 | 262105.4 |
| 私营股份有限公司 | Private Share-holding Corporations Ltd. | 1687.8 | 340.1 | 663.5 |
| 港、澳、台商投资企业 | Enterprises Funded by Hong Kong, Macao and Taiwan | 50992 | 4839.4 | 34186.1 |
| 与港澳台商合资经营企业 | Cooperative Enterprises | 26420.9 | 1855.5 | 13548.8 |
| 港澳台商独资企业 | Enterprises with Sole Fund | 24571.1 | 2983.9 | 20637.3 |
| 外商投资企业 | Foreign-funded Enterprises | 62233 | 2245.5 | 30451.8 |
| 中外合资经营企业 | Joint-venture Enterprises | 3164.5 | 25.6 | 368.5 |
| 外资企业 | Enterprises with Sole Fund | 46533.3 | 1413.8 | 9554.7 |
| 其他外商投资企业 | Other Foreign-funded Enterprises | 12535.2 | 806.1 | 20528.6 |

单位：万元 (10 000 yuan)

| 二、期末资产负债 Assets and Liabilities | | | | | |
|---|---|---|---|---|---|
| 在建工程<br>Construction in Progress | 无形资产<br>Intangible Assets | 土地使用权<br>Land Use Rights | 资产总计<br>Total Assets | 流动负债合计<br>Total Current Liabilities | 应付账款<br>Accounts Payable |
| **82251.3** | **153079.7** | **145114.9** | **3070906.6** | **1438822.9** | **144643.7** |
| | | | | | |
| 68936.8 | 63656.2 | 56828.8 | 2366113.8 | 1067531.9 | 94366.7 |
| 68936.8 | 63656.2 | 56828.8 | 2366113.8 | 1067531.9 | 94366.7 |
| 13314.5 | 88371.1 | 87271.4 | 593611.3 | 336324.2 | 47167.3 |
| | 824.3 | 817.6 | 127068.1 | 78320.3 | 19988.6 |
| 13314.5 | 87546.8 | 86453.8 | 466543.2 | 258003.9 | 27178.7 |
| | | | 7505.3 | 1556.9 | 497.4 |
| | | | 7505.3 | 1556.9 | 497.4 |
| | 1014.7 | 1014.7 | 3565.3 | 2994 | 1.9 |
| | 37.7 | | 100110.9 | 30415.9 | 2610.4 |
| | 37.7 | | 100110.9 | 30415.9 | 2610.4 |
| | | | | | |
| 78197 | 142561 | 135202 | 2824017 | 1332433 | 136566 |
| 5884.9 | 7108.4 | 7086 | 98023.7 | 38553.8 | 5087.5 |
| | | | 8303.7 | 1525.9 | 214.1 |
| 32579.8 | 114877.6 | 112699.2 | 1483261.8 | 626508 | 54120.2 |
| 18173.5 | 107448.9 | 107110.7 | 837554.9 | 188500.2 | 8538.9 |
| 14406.3 | 7428.7 | 5588.5 | 645706.9 | 438007.8 | 45581.3 |
| | 16.3 | | 4290.2 | 6779.2 | 2531.7 |
| 39732.7 | 20559 | 15417.2 | 1230137.7 | 659065.9 | 74612.3 |
| 1007.4 | 111.8 | 95.4 | 25583.7 | 7811.7 | 3523.8 |
| | | | 1398.3 | 322.9 | 85.3 |
| 38725.3 | 20419 | 15321.8 | 1196456.5 | 643669.1 | 70595.1 |
| | 28.2 | | 6699.2 | 7262.2 | 408.1 |
| 3.3 | 1895.1 | 1574.7 | 41627.5 | 27788.1 | 3460.4 |
| | | | | | |
| | | | 15067.1 | 20058.1 | 1027.9 |
| 3.3 | 1895.1 | 1574.7 | 26560.4 | 7730 | 2432.5 |
| 4050.6 | 8623.3 | 8337.8 | 205262 | 78602 | 4617.5 |
| 4050.6 | | | 41990.4 | 58588.9 | 2338.7 |
| | 1009.1 | 983.2 | 131630.5 | 18167.5 | 1765.3 |
| | 7614.2 | 7354.6 | 31641.1 | 1845.6 | 513.5 |

**表 15.8 续表 2 continued 2**

| 指 标 | Item | 二、期末资产负债 Assets and Liabilities | | |
|---|---|---|---|---|
| | | 负债合计 Total Liabilities | 所有者权益合计 Total Owner's Equity | 实收资本 Paid-up Capital |
| **合 计** | **Total** | **2687084.8** | **379277** | **798852.1** |
| **按住宿业行业小类分** | **By Classification of Hotels** | | | |
| 旅游饭店 | Tourist Hotels | 2146362.9 | 215049.4 | 663057.6 |
| 旅游饭店 | Tourist Hotels | 2146362.9 | 215049.4 | 663057.6 |
| 一般旅馆 | General Hotels | 489524.5 | 104243.5 | 81339 |
| 经济型连锁酒店 | Economical Chain Hotels | 94733.5 | 32214.6 | 15903.2 |
| 其他一般旅馆 | Other General Hotels | 394791.0 | 72028.9 | 65435.8 |
| 民宿服务 | Homestay Services | 2949.9 | 4555.4 | 100.0 |
| 民宿服务 | Homestay Services | 2949.9 | 4555.4 | 100.0 |
| 露营地服务 | Campsite Services | 2994 | 571.3 | |
| 其他住宿业 | Other Hotels | 45253.5 | 54857.4 | 54355.5 |
| 其他住宿业 | Other Hotel Services | 45253.5 | 54857.4 | 54355.5 |
| **按登记注册类型分** | **By Status of Registration** | | | |
| 内资企业 | Domestic-funded Enterprises | 2504897 | 314575 | 745546 |
| 国有企业 | State-owned Enterprises | 77047.5 | 20976.2 | 6806.2 |
| 集体企业 | Collective-owned Enterprises | 7298.6 | 1005.1 | 4761.9 |
| 有限责任公司 | Limited Liability Corporations | 1398771.9 | 84462.9 | 449180.2 |
| 国有独资公司 | State Sole Funded Corporations | 673487.7 | 164067.2 | 179536.9 |
| 其他有限责任公司 | Other Limited Liability Corporations | 725284.2 | -79604.3 | 269643.3 |
| 股份有限公司 | Share-holding Corporations Ltd. | 6872.2 | -2582 | 1350 |
| 私营企业 | Private Enterprises | 1014907.1 | 210712.8 | 283447.3 |
| 私营独资企业 | Private-funded Enterprises | 16181.9 | 9342.3 | 3244.6 |
| 私营合伙企业 | Private Partnership Enterprises | 322.9 | 1075.4 | 1070 |
| 私营有限责任公司 | Private Limited Liability Corporations | 991139.8 | 200858.4 | 277562.7 |
| 私营股份有限公司 | Private Share-holding Corporations Ltd. | 7262.5 | -563.3 | 1570 |
| 港、澳、台商投资企业 | Enterprises Funded by Hong Kong, Macao and Taiwan | 100715.1 | -59087.6 | 33422.9 |
| 与港澳台商合资经营企业 | Cooperative Enterprises | 53358.1 | -38291 | 11000 |
| 港澳台商独资企业 | Enterprises with Sole Fund | 47357 | -20796.6 | 22422.9 |
| 外商投资企业 | Foreign-funded Enterprises | 81472.4 | 123789.6 | 19883.6 |
| 中外合资经营企业 | Joint-venture Enterprises | 58588.9 | -16598.5 | 3000 |
| 外资企业 | Enterprises with Sole Fund | 18173.6 | 113456.9 | 16883.6 |
| 其他外商投资企业 | Other Foreign-funded Enterprises | 4709.9 | 26931.2 | |

单位：万元 (10 000 yuan)

| 二、期末资产负债 Assets and Liabilities | 三、损益及分配 Profits and Losses | | | | |
|---|---|---|---|---|---|
| 个人资本 Personal Capital | 营业收入 Gross Sales | 主营业务收入 Main Business Income | 营业成本 Operating Cost | 税金及附加 Taxes and Surcharges | 其他业务利润 Other Business Profits |
| **214413.8** | **836153.9** | **803631.1** | **486266.9** | **11563.6** | **3937.3** |
| 170525.9 | 532158.9 | 512956.4 | 307516.5 | 9054 | 2897.6 |
| 170525.9 | 532158.9 | 512956.4 | 307516.5 | 9054 | 2897.6 |
| 21110.2 | 275962.6 | 264351 | 163071.2 | 2042.1 | 1010.4 |
| 7825 | 62847.2 | 59725.3 | 35570.1 | 330.3 | 3.3 |
| 13285.2 | 213115.4 | 204625.7 | 127501.1 | 1711.8 | 1007.1 |
| | 2048.5 | 1701.0 | 1424.5 | 19.4 | |
| | 2048.5 | 1701.0 | 1424.5 | 19.4 | |
| | 421 | 373.9 | 215.1 | 0.1 | |
| 22777.7 | 25562.9 | 24248.8 | 14039.6 | 448 | 29.3 |
| 22777.7 | 25562.9 | 24248.8 | 14039.6 | 448 | 29.3 |
| 214414 | 803843 | 771494 | 467392 | 10333 | 3857 |
| | 20122.9 | 19520.4 | 7603.4 | 294.7 | 127 |
| 3561.9 | 6992.8 | 6761.1 | 4766.5 | 15.5 | 46.6 |
| 104006.5 | 212577.4 | 202955 | 118065.6 | 3821.9 | 856.2 |
| | 71026.5 | 70170.2 | 45928.4 | 1929.5 | 28.4 |
| 104006.5 | 141550.9 | 132784.8 | 72137.2 | 1892.4 | 827.8 |
| | 5068.6 | 3678.9 | 4995.7 | 7.6 | 119.9 |
| 106845.4 | 559081.2 | 538578.7 | 331960.7 | 6193.7 | 2707.2 |
| 1291.6 | 19630.4 | 18798.1 | 12825.6 | 199.8 | 53 |
| 20 | 796.1 | 796.1 | 475.3 | 8.1 | |
| 104530.3 | 533493.2 | 513823 | 316900.2 | 5982.5 | 2654.2 |
| 1003.5 | 5161.5 | 5161.5 | 1759.6 | 3.3 | |
| | 9499.4 | 9419 | 6477 | 319.2 | 80.4 |
| | 3950.3 | 3950.3 | 607.2 | 7.9 | |
| | 5549.1 | 5468.7 | 5869.8 | 311.3 | 80.4 |
| | 22811.6 | 22718 | 12398 | 911 | |
| | 3268.9 | 3184.6 | 714.8 | 74.9 | |
| | 15751.9 | 15742.6 | 9598 | 664.3 | |
| | 3790.8 | 3790.8 | 2085.2 | 171.8 | |

**表 15.8 续表 3 continued 3**

| 指 标 | Item | 三、损益及分配 Profits and Losses | | |
|---|---|---|---|---|
| | | 销售费用 Sales Expenses | 管理费用 Management Expenses | 研发费用 R&D expenses |
| **合 计** | **Total** | **166034.9** | **226344.4** | **119.1** |
| **按住宿业行业小类分** | **By Classification of Hotels** | | | |
| 旅游饭店 | Tourist Hotels | 112451.8 | 157727.4 | 68.7 |
| 旅游饭店 | Tourist Hotels | 112451.8 | 157727.4 | 68.7 |
| 一般旅馆 | General Hotels | 50667.9 | 61749 | 50.1 |
| 经济型连锁酒店 | Economical Chain Hotels | 11170 | 18176 | 23.6 |
| 其他一般旅馆 | Other General Hotels | 39497.9 | 43573.0 | 26.5 |
| 民宿服务 | Homestay Services | 170.9 | 945.1 | |
| 民宿服务 | Homestay Services | 170.9 | 945.1 | |
| 露营地服务 | Campsite Services | 8.2 | 156.3 | |
| 其他住宿业 | Other Hotels | 2736.1 | 5766.6 | 0.3 |
| 其他住宿业 | Other Hotel Services | 2736.1 | 5766.6 | 0.3 |
| **按登记注册类型分** | **By Status of Registration** | | | |
| 内资企业 | Domestic-funded Enterprises | 158322 | 213222 | 119 |
| 国有企业 | State-owned Enterprises | 4418.4 | 7628.8 | |
| 集体企业 | Collective-owned Enterprises | 1660.8 | 748.6 | |
| 有限责任公司 | Limited Liability Corporations | 49020.5 | 80279 | -1.7 |
| 国有独资公司 | State Sole Funded Corporations | 16193.9 | 29446.9 | |
| 其他有限责任公司 | Other Limited Liability Corporations | 32826.6 | 50832.1 | -1.7 |
| 股份有限公司 | Share-holding Corporations Ltd. | 217.9 | 1604.4 | |
| 私营企业 | Private Enterprises | 103004.4 | 122960.7 | 120.8 |
| 私营独资企业 | Private-funded Enterprises | 3450.2 | 1964.2 | 1.8 |
| 私营合伙企业 | Private Partnership Enterprises | 26.2 | 271.4 | |
| 私营有限责任公司 | Private Limited Liability Corporations | 97742.3 | 117699.2 | 119 |
| 私营股份有限公司 | Private Share-holding Corporations Ltd. | 1785.7 | 3025.9 | |
| 港、澳、台商投资企业 | Enterprises Funded by Hong Kong, Macao and Taiwan | 3165.8 | 6274.1 | |
| 与港澳台商合资经营企业 | Cooperative Enterprises | 2330.1 | 3332.9 | |
| 港澳台商独资企业 | Enterprises with Sole Fund | 835.7 | 2941.2 | |
| 外商投资企业 | Foreign-funded Enterprises | 4547.1 | 6848.8 | |
| 中外合资经营企业 | Joint-venture Enterprises | 3074 | 948.9 | |
| 外资企业 | Enterprises with Sole Fund | 1174.4 | 3354.1 | |
| 其他外商投资企业 | Other Foreign-funded Enterprises | 298.7 | 2545.8 | |

单位：万元 (10 000 yuan)

| 三、损益及分配 Profits and Losses | | | | | |
| --- | --- | --- | --- | --- | --- |
| 财务费用 Financial Expenses | 利息收入 Interest Income | 利息费用 Interest expenses | 投资收益 Income from Investment | 营业利润 Business Profits | 营业外收入 Non-business Income |
| **33039.5** | **1142.1** | **21005.9** | **107.2** | **-79099.2** | **6389.9** |
| 29310.2 | 907.9 | 19335.1 | -714.1 | -76233.9 | 4723.6 |
| 29310.2 | 907.9 | 19335.1 | -714.1 | -76233.9 | 4723.6 |
| 3099.9 | 209.9 | 1554.8 | 351.2 | -4202.4 | 1607.4 |
| 864.7 | 3.8 | 95 | 10.9 | -2986.2 | 358 |
| 2235.2 | 206.1 | 1459.8 | 340.3 | -1216.2 | 1249.4 |
| 13.2 | | | 461.7 | -61.0 | 3.6 |
| 13.2 | | | 461.7 | -61.0 | 3.6 |
| 23.8 | 0.4 | 23.9 | | 17.4 | 0.7 |
| 592.4 | 23.9 | 92.1 | 8.4 | 1380.7 | 54.6 |
| 592.4 | 23.9 | 92.1 | 8.4 | 1380.7 | 54.6 |
| 28394 | 1142 | 19875 | 69 | -65902 | 5958 |
| 1061.4 | 788.3 | 188.2 | 487.8 | -463.8 | 995.6 |
| 52.2 | 6.2 | 27.1 | 17.1 | -233.7 | 6.2 |
| 14121.3 | 163 | 11955.7 | -377 | -47047.7 | 1705.5 |
| 7648 | 212.8 | 5704.4 | 92.3 | -23086.9 | 797.5 |
| 6473.3 | -49.8 | 6251.3 | -469.3 | -23960.8 | 908 |
| 27.5 | 0.2 | 4.6 | | -1784.3 | 44 |
| 13131.6 | 184.3 | 7699.8 | -58.6 | -16372.3 | 3206.3 |
| 308 | 7.6 | 106.2 | | 1129.7 | 45.1 |
| 6.1 | | | | -210.4 | 2.2 |
| 12721.7 | 177.1 | 7509.7 | -58.6 | -15721.1 | 3079.6 |
| 95.8 | -0.4 | 83.9 | | -1570.5 | 79.4 |
| 4245.3 | -3 | 754.4 | | -10982 | 284.1 |
| 2437.9 | | | | -4765.7 | 56 |
| 1807.4 | -3 | 754.4 | | -6216.3 | 228.1 |
| 400.2 | 3.1 | 376.1 | 37.9 | -2215.4 | 148.2 |
| 313.3 | | 313.3 | | -1857.2 | 6 |
| 78.4 | 3.1 | 62.8 | 37.9 | 961 | 142.2 |
| 8.5 | | | | -1319.2 | |

**表 15.8 续表 4 continued 4**

| 指 标 | Item | 三、损益及分配 Profits and Losses | |
|---|---|---|---|
| | | 营业外支出 Non-business Expenses | 利润总额 Total Profits |
| **合 计** | **Total** | **1450.5** | **-74281.1** |
| **按住宿业行业小类分** | **By Classification of Hotels** | | |
| 旅游饭店 | Tourist Hotels | 838.9 | -72458.2 |
| 旅游饭店 | Tourist Hotels | 838.9 | -72458.2 |
| 一般旅馆 | General Hotels | 598.1 | -3205.4 |
| 经济型连锁酒店 | Economical Chain Hotels | 106 | -2737 |
| 其他一般旅馆 | Other General Hotels | 492.1 | -468.4 |
| 民宿服务 | Homestay Services | 0.7 | -58.1 |
| 民宿服务 | Homestay Services | 0.7 | -58.1 |
| 露营地服务 | Campsite Services | 4.3 | 13.8 |
| 其他住宿业 | Other Hotels | 8.5 | 1426.8 |
| 其他住宿业 | Other Hotel Services | 8.5 | 1426.8 |
| **按登记注册类型分** | **By Status of Registration** | | |
| 内资企业 | Domestic-funded Enterprises | 1174 | -61241 |
| 国有企业 | State-owned Enterprises | 58.5 | 473.3 |
| 集体企业 | Collective-owned Enterprises | 0.2 | -227.7 |
| 有限责任公司 | Limited Liability Corporations | 475.7 | -45821.8 |
| 国有独资公司 | State Sole Funded Corporations | 91.7 | -22381.1 |
| 其他有限责任公司 | Other Limited Liability Corporations | 384 | -23440.7 |
| 股份有限公司 | Share-holding Corporations Ltd. | | -1740.3 |
| 私营企业 | Private Enterprises | 639.6 | -13924 |
| 私营独资企业 | Private-funded Enterprises | 28.8 | 1146 |
| 私营合伙企业 | Private Partnership Enterprises | 5.6 | -213.8 |
| 私营有限责任公司 | Private Limited Liability Corporations | 603.4 | -13363.3 |
| 私营股份有限公司 | Private Share-holding Corporations Ltd. | 1.8 | -1492.9 |
| 港、澳、台商投资企业 | Enterprises Funded by Hong Kong, Macao and Taiwan | 212.1 | -10910 |
| 与港澳台商合资经营企业 | Cooperative Enterprises | | -4709.7 |
| 港澳台商独资企业 | Enterprises with Sole Fund | 212.1 | -6200.3 |
| 外商投资企业 | Foreign-funded Enterprises | 64.4 | -2130.6 |
| 中外合资经营企业 | Joint-venture Enterprises | 11.3 | -1862.5 |
| 外资企业 | Enterprises with Sole Fund | 53.1 | 1050.1 |
| 其他外商投资企业 | Other Foreign-funded Enterprises | | -1318.2 |

单位：万元 (10 000 yuan)

| 三、损益及分配 Profits and Losses | 四、人工成本及增值税 Labor cost and Value-added Tax | | |
| --- | --- | --- | --- |
| 所得税费用 Income Tax Payable | 应付职工薪酬 Employee compensation | 应交增值税 Value-added Tax | 五、从事批发和零售业活动的从业人员平均人数（人） Annual Average Employees Engaged in wholesale and retail activities (persons) |
| **3496.5** | **196738** | 15069.7 | 32073 |
| | | | |
| 1958.9 | 138093.1 | 9740.5 | 21198 |
| 1958.9 | 138093.1 | 9740.5 | 21198 |
| 1434 | 52157.3 | 4765.5 | 9697 |
| 216.4 | 14058.7 | 1424.2 | 2662 |
| 1217.6 | 38098.6 | 3341.3 | 7035 |
| 0.5 | 825.0 | 67.1 | 113 |
| 0.5 | 825.0 | 67.1 | 113 |
| 3.4 | 114.1 | 1.8 | 18 |
| 99.7 | 5548.5 | 494.8 | 1047 |
| 99.7 | 5548.5 | 494.8 | 1047 |
| | | | |
| 3135 | 183805 | 14320 | 30337 |
| 685.4 | 7834.4 | 602.1 | 762 |
| 2.3 | 1368 | 64.1 | 282 |
| 604.5 | 70888.4 | 4479.6 | 9248 |
| 286.5 | 25523.6 | 1186.9 | 2857 |
| 318 | 45364.8 | 3292.7 | 6391 |
| | 1594.2 | 37 | 257 |
| 1842.4 | 102120.4 | 9137.2 | 19788 |
| 93.8 | 3393.9 | 204 | 751 |
| 1.2 | 190.2 | 19.7 | 36 |
| 1746.4 | 97689.8 | 8710.3 | 18678 |
| 1 | 846.5 | 203.2 | 323 |
| | 4930 | 102.2 | 646 |
| | 1879.7 | 66.7 | 297 |
| | 3050.3 | 35.5 | 349 |
| 361.9 | 8002.6 | 647.5 | 1090 |
| | 1180.1 | 93.4 | 193 |
| 361.9 | 5506 | 526.7 | 679 |
| | 1316.5 | 27.4 | 218 |

**表 15.8 续表 5 continued 5**

| 指 标 | Item | 法人企业数（个）Number of Enterprises (unit) | 执行《2006年企业会计准则》企业数（个）Number of Enterprises which Implemented Accounting standard for Business Enterprise in 2006 (unit) | 一、年初存货 Inventory at the Beginning of Year |
|---|---|---|---|---|
| **按控股情况分** | **By Holding Entity of Share** | | | |
| 国有控股 | State-holding | 52 | 48 | 22809.5 |
| 集体控股 | Collective-holding | 8 | 5 | 683.8 |
| 私人控股 | Private-holding | 535 | 258 | 25898.5 |
| 港澳台商控股 | Held by Corporation from Hong Kong, Macao and Taiwan | 3 | 3 | 123.6 |
| 外商控股 | Foreign-holding | 6 | 5 | 400.7 |
| **按经营形式分** | **By Form of Business** | | | |
| 独立门店 | Independent Store | 510 | 284 | 43169 |
| 连锁总店（总部） | Central Shop of Chain Stores (Headquarter) | | | |
| 连锁直营店 | Direct-sale Shop of Chain Stores | 7 | 6 | 52 |
| 连锁加盟店 | Branch Shop of Chain Stores | 57 | 11 | 1068.3 |
| 其他 | Other | 30 | 18 | 5626.8 |
| **按单位规模分** | **By Size of Enterprise** | | | |
| 大型 | Large | | | |
| 中型 | Medium | 70 | 59 | 25748.4 |
| 小型 | Small | 439 | 221 | 19866.2 |
| 微型 | Micro | 95 | 39 | 4301.5 |
| **按星级分** | **By Star of Hotel** | | | |
| 五星 | 5-Star | 33 | 26 | 6537.5 |
| 四星 | 4-Star | 52 | 32 | 13605 |
| 三星 | 3-Star | 57 | 31 | 3946.3 |
| 二星 | 2-Star | 4 | 1 | 48.0 |
| 一星 | 1-Star | 2 | 1 | 43 |
| 其他 | Other | 456 | 228 | 25736.3 |

单位：万元 (10 000 yuan)

| 二、期末资产负债 Assets and Liabilities | | | | | |
|---|---|---|---|---|---|
| 流动资产合计 Total Current Assets | 应收账款 Accounts Receivable | 存货 Inventory | 固定资产原价 Total Original Value of Fixed Assets | 房屋和构筑物 Buildings and Structures | 机器设备 Machinery and Equipments |
| 411987.2 | 12874.5 | 9784.8 | 556953.4 | 299039.5 | 63565.8 |
| 9676.7 | 5273.7 | 652.1 | 27996.9 | 24533.6 | 734.3 |
| 774783.9 | 57366.4 | 33268.3 | 770967.8 | 370245.7 | 66836.3 |
| 2098.3 | 748.2 | 128.2 | 85178.1 | 21286.8 | 15933.7 |
| 80362.4 | 2796.2 | 297 | 89151.8 | 70270.7 | 7847.7 |
| 1008668.9 | 62257.1 | 39333.4 | 1322520.1 | 643472.5 | 147703.2 |
| 4985.5 | 977.9 | 22.5 | 968.8 | 103.2 | 154.4 |
| 57661 | 4921.7 | 604.3 | 24280.3 | 18630.4 | 1710 |
| 207593.1 | 10902.3 | 4170.2 | 182478.8 | 123170.2 | 5350.2 |
| 810596.9 | 36502.9 | 12767.2 | 889710.7 | 477500.9 | 108554.8 |
| 417743.9 | 39558.2 | 29245.1 | 602924.6 | 285724.7 | 43755.5 |
| 50567.7 | 2997.9 | 2118.1 | 37612.7 | 22150.7 | 2607.5 |
| 485826.3 | 10988.5 | 5679.8 | 645065.8 | 337822.1 | 62520.3 |
| 130848 | 6350.4 | 3054.9 | 285495.9 | 139493.5 | 19416.5 |
| 55302.9 | 8664.8 | 2575.2 | 72891.6 | 33472.9 | 12160.5 |
| 459.3 | 117.6 | 89.6 | 592.7 | 346.5 | 98.7 |
| 168.5 | 62.5 | 51 | 401.5 | 261.2 | 72 |
| 606303.5 | 52875.2 | 32679.9 | 525800.5 | 273980.1 | 60649.8 |

**表 15.8 续表 6 continued 6**

| 指 标 | Item | 二、期末资产负债 Assets and Liabilities | | |
|---|---|---|---|---|
| | | 累计折旧 Cumulative Depreciation | 本年折旧 Depreciation | 固定资产净额 Net Value of Fixed Assets |
| **按控股情况分** | **By Holding Entity of Share** | | | |
| 国有控股 | State-holding | 234596.3 | 20077.1 | 244264.2 |
| 集体控股 | Collective-holding | 16403.9 | 1130.8 | 11590.4 |
| 私人控股 | Private-holding | 325448.8 | 34536.8 | 363936.6 |
| 港澳台商控股 | Held by Corporation from Hong Kong, Macao and Taiwan | 50992 | 4839.4 | 34186.1 |
| 外商控股 | Foreign-holding | 59068.5 | 2219.9 | 30083.3 |
| **按经营形式分** | **By Form of Business** | | | |
| 独立门店 | Independent Store | 619554 | 55694.5 | 619874.9 |
| 连锁总店(总部) | Central Shop of Chain Stores (Headquarter) | | | |
| 连锁直营店 | Direct-sale Shop of Chain Stores | 829.3 | 90 | 134.1 |
| 连锁加盟店 | Branch Shop of Chain Stores | 7203.6 | 1878.4 | 16508 |
| 其他 | Other | 58922.6 | 5141.1 | 47543.6 |
| **按单位规模分** | **By Size of Enterprise** | | | |
| 大型 | Large | | | |
| 中型 | Medium | 429539.4 | 33644.3 | 372591.1 |
| 小型 | Small | 236255.2 | 27643.7 | 300271 |
| 微型 | Micro | 20714.9 | 1516 | 11198.5 |
| **按星级分** | **By Star of Hotel** | | | |
| 五星 | 5-Star | 308270.5 | 21594.2 | 248389.4 |
| 四星 | 4-Star | 123510.7 | 9692.3 | 149977 |
| 三星 | 3-Star | 37131.4 | 2519 | 29222.8 |
| 二星 | 2-Star | 222.3 | 48.5 | 370.4 |
| 一星 | 1-Star | 27.6 | 10.5 | 240.5 |
| 其他 | Other | 217347.0 | 28939.5 | 255860.5 |

单位：万元 (10 000 yuan)

| 二、期末资产负债 Assets and Liabilities | | | | | |
|---|---|---|---|---|---|
| 在建工程 Construction in Progress | 无形资产 Intangible Assets | 土地使用权 Land Use Rights | 资产总计 Total Assets | 流动负债合计 Total Current Liabilities | 应付账款 Accounts Payable |
| 36496.8 | 117006.6 | 116403.5 | 1231002 | 488545.2 | 27495.9 |
| | 139.6 | 137.2 | 30923.3 | 10035.2 | 4310.4 |
| 45751.2 | 25415.1 | 18661.7 | 1604082.2 | 892441.3 | 107098.2 |
| 3.3 | 1895.1 | 1574.7 | 41627.5 | 27788.1 | 3460.4 |
| | 8623.3 | 8337.8 | 163271.6 | 20013.1 | 2278.8 |
| 80389.7 | 138418.5 | 131273.8 | 2313887.2 | 1300690 | 123853.7 |
| | 13.6 | | 8480.7 | 11238.4 | 2136.3 |
| 1861.6 | 380.4 | | 96209.7 | 61568.5 | 8165 |
| | 14267.2 | 13841.1 | 652329 | 65326 | 10488.7 |
| 21932.6 | 42187.4 | 40167.4 | 1780164.6 | 609958.1 | 54912.1 |
| 53611.1 | 109487.7 | 103584.1 | 1191540.5 | 800232.4 | 86077.8 |
| 6707.6 | 1404.6 | 1363.4 | 99201.5 | 28632.4 | 3653.8 |
| 22916 | 43384 | 41804.2 | 1052240.8 | 507490.4 | 33832.2 |
| 8840.3 | 10600.3 | 9401.5 | 371529 | 196929 | 20014.9 |
| 1378.2 | 2729.3 | 824.4 | 125317.9 | 59417.5 | 19051.6 |
| | | | 1056.9 | 203.4 | 64.8 |
| | 20 | 15 | 941 | 19 | 15 |
| 49116.8 | 96346.1 | 93069.8 | 1519821.0 | 674763.6 | 71665.2 |

表 15.8 续表 7 continued 7

| 指 标 | Item | 二、期末资产负债 Assets and Liabilities | | |
|---|---|---|---|---|
| | | 负债合计 Total Liabilities | 所有者权益合计 Total Owner's Equity | 实收资本 Paid-up Capital |
| **按控股情况分** | **By Holding Entity of Share** | | | |
| 国有控股 | State-holding | 1142542.2 | 88459.8 | 242412.2 |
| 集体控股 | Collective-holding | 19442.5 | 11472.3 | 28591.9 |
| 私人控股 | Private-holding | 1401501.5 | 198044.4 | 477541.5 |
| 港澳台商控股 | Held by Corporation from Hong Kong, Macao and Taiwan | 100715.1 | -59087.6 | 33422.9 |
| 外商控股 | Foreign-holding | 22883.5 | 140388.1 | 16883.6 |
| **按经营形式分** | **By Form of Business** | | | |
| 独立门店 | Independent Store | 2115582.4 | 193760 | 676093.2 |
| 连锁总店(总部) | Central Shop of Chain Stores (Headquarter) | | | |
| 连锁直营店 | Direct-sale Shop of Chain Stores | 10590.4 | -2109.7 | 700 |
| 连锁加盟店 | Branch Shop of Chain Stores | 67554.5 | 28655.2 | 14804.6 |
| 其他 | Other | 493357.5 | 158971.5 | 107254.3 |
| **按单位规模分** | **By Size of Enterprise** | | | |
| 大型 | Large | | | |
| 中型 | Medium | 1505090.8 | 275073.8 | 367379.2 |
| 小型 | Small | 1088034.3 | 103506.2 | 418093.7 |
| 微型 | Micro | 93959.7 | 697 | 13379.2 |
| **按星级分** | **By Star of Hotel** | | | |
| 五星 | 5-Star | 999123.2 | 49588.8 | 198202 |
| 四星 | 4-Star | 329114 | 41301.8 | 189442.5 |
| 三星 | 3-Star | 81694.8 | 43503.1 | 38002.7 |
| 二星 | 2-Star | 290.2 | 766.7 | 397.1 |
| 一星 | 1-Star | 26.5 | 914.5 | 914.5 |
| 其他 | Other | 1276836.1 | 243202.1 | 371893.3 |

单位：万元 (10 000 yuan)

| 二、期末资产负债 Assets and Liabilities | 三、损益及分配 Profits and Losses | | | | |
|---|---|---|---|---|---|
| 个人资本 Personal Capital | 营业收入 Gross Sales | 主营业务收入 Main Business Income | 营业成本 Operating Cost | 税金及附加 Taxes and Surcharges | 其他业务利润 Other Business Profits |
| 500 | 160937.3 | 153519.2 | 90571.5 | 2921.7 | 316.3 |
| 3561.9 | 13896.7 | 13507.6 | 6746.3 | 121.9 | 46.6 |
| 210351.9 | 632277.8 | 607651.9 | 370788.9 | 7364.7 | 3494 |
| | 9499.4 | 9419 | 6477 | 319.2 | 80.4 |
| | 19542.7 | 19533.4 | 11683.2 | 836.1 | |
| 208421.9 | 711758.8 | 680352.4 | 412188.7 | 9545.8 | 3917 |
| | 10023.7 | 9978.6 | 7106.4 | 7.1 | 0.5 |
| 4967.3 | 47226.2 | 46187.2 | 23222.5 | 165.8 | 19.8 |
| 1024.6 | 67145.2 | 67112.9 | 43749.3 | 1844.9 | |
| 45268 | 342233 | 330758.3 | 181110.2 | 6116.1 | 2855.8 |
| 167781.4 | 461428.7 | 450210.3 | 282369.9 | 5195.8 | 1081.4 |
| 1364.4 | 32492.2 | 22662.5 | 22786.8 | 251.7 | 0.1 |
| 12000 | 152991.8 | 145579.4 | 75097.1 | 3652.1 | 841.3 |
| 114068.7 | 123066 | 119461.8 | 74567.8 | 1303 | 272.2 |
| 7847.1 | 101018.2 | 99712.3 | 71441.1 | 1135.5 | 1417.4 |
| 397.1 | 1655.6 | 1653.6 | 1136.9 | 3.3 | |
| 210 | 1180.6 | 1174.1 | 273.6 | 4.4 | |
| 79890.9 | 456241.7 | 436049.9 | 263750.4 | 5465.3 | 1406.4 |

**表 15.8 续表 8 continued 8**

| 指 标 | Item | 三、损益及分配 Profits and Losses | | |
|---|---|---|---|---|
| | | 销售费用 Sales Expenses | 管理费用 Management Expenses | 研发费用 R&D expenses |
| **按控股情况分** | **By Holding Entity of Share** | | | |
| 国有控股 | State-holding | 39302.9 | 59958 | -2.2 |
| 集体控股 | Collective-holding | 2495.4 | 3973.6 | |
| 私人控股 | Private-holding | 119597.7 | 150238.8 | 121.3 |
| 港澳台商控股 | Held by Corporation from Hong Kong, Macao and Taiwan | 3165.8 | 6274.1 | |
| 外商控股 | Foreign-holding | 1473.1 | 5899.9 | |
| **按经营形式分** | **By Form of Business** | | | |
| 独立门店 | Independent Store | 144921.2 | 188576.5 | 116 |
| 连锁总店（总部） | Central Shop of Chain Stores (Headquarter) | | | |
| 连锁直营店 | Direct-sale Shop of Chain Stores | 1198.2 | 2949.1 | |
| 连锁加盟店 | Branch Shop of Chain Stores | 12229.3 | 17238.1 | 0.1 |
| 其他 | Other | 7686.2 | 17580.7 | 3 |
| **按单位规模分** | **By Size of Enterprise** | | | |
| 大型 | Large | | | |
| 中型 | Medium | 81578.3 | 113433.8 | 30.3 |
| 小型 | Small | 80088.1 | 106524.8 | 31.9 |
| 微型 | Micro | 4368.5 | 6385.8 | 56.9 |
| **按星级分** | **By Star of Hotel** | | | |
| 五星 | 5-Star | 36636.3 | 54739 | -2.2 |
| 四星 | 4-Star | 24524.5 | 36892.3 | 28.9 |
| 三星 | 3-Star | 13074.6 | 15009.8 | 42.6 |
| 二星 | 2-Star | 264.0 | 114.4 | |
| 一星 | 1-Star | 17.8 | 4.9 | 0.1 |
| 其他 | Other | 91517.7 | 119584.0 | 49.7 |

单位：万元 (10 000 yuan)

三、损益及分配 Profits and Losses

| 财务费用 Financial Expenses | 利息收入 Interest Income | 利息费用 Interest expenses | 投资收益 Income from Investment | 营业利润 Business Profits | 营业外收入 Non-business Income |
|---|---|---|---|---|---|
| 12747.3 | 936.5 | 10169.2 | 1177.5 | -37999.6 | 2362.1 |
| 49.7 | 21.3 | 27.1 | 17.1 | 528 | 17.9 |
| 15910.3 | 184.2 | 9992.4 | -1125.3 | -30287.4 | 3583.6 |
| 4245.3 | -3 | 754.4 | | -10982 | 284.1 |
| 86.9 | 3.1 | 62.8 | 37.9 | -358.2 | 142.2 |
| 26566.4 | 1102.6 | 16597.2 | -625.5 | -63587.8 | 5771.9 |
| 217.2 | | | 0.5 | -1165.3 | 3.4 |
| 372.4 | 10.9 | 277 | 92.1 | -5476.7 | 351.7 |
| 5883.5 | 28.6 | 4131.7 | 640.1 | -8869.4 | 262.9 |
| 20393.8 | 974.9 | 11759 | 900.3 | -53628.4 | 3499.6 |
| 12452.7 | 120.8 | 9151.8 | -793.6 | -25096.3 | 2830.5 |
| 193 | 46.4 | 95.1 | 0.5 | -374.5 | 59.8 |
| 18028.5 | 866.4 | 13050.9 | 726.2 | -33603.3 | 1059.9 |
| 3104.5 | 119.8 | 1691.3 | 31.1 | -15109.8 | 546.9 |
| 1353.7 | -195.5 | 1208 | -923.7 | 568.4 | 285.2 |
| 57.6 | 2.1 | 47.3 | | 83.0 | 0.2 |
| 12.9 | 0.6 | | | 839 | |
| 10482.3 | 348.7 | 5008.4 | 273.6 | -31876.5 | 4497.7 |

**表 15.8 续表 9 continued 9**

| 指 标 | Item | 三、损益及分配 Profits and Losses<br>营业外支出 Non-business Expenses | 利润总额 Total Profits |
|---|---|---|---|
| **按控股情况分** | **By Holding Entity of Share** | | |
| 国有控股 | State-holding | 318.3 | -35955.8 |
| 集体控股 | Collective-holding | 0.7 | 545.2 |
| 私人控股 | Private-holding | 866.3 | -27692.4 |
| 港澳台商控股 | Held by Corporation from Hong Kong, Macao and Taiwan | 212.1 | -10910 |
| 外商控股 | Foreign-holding | 53.1 | -268.1 |
| **按经营形式分** | **By Form of Business** | | |
| 独立门店 | Independent Store | 1382.1 | -59317.5 |
| 连锁总店（总部） | Central Shop of Chain Stores (Headquarter) | | |
| 连锁直营店 | Direct-sale Shop of Chain Stores | 0.5 | -1165.2 |
| 连锁加盟店 | Branch Shop of Chain Stores | 34.6 | -5159.6 |
| 其他 | Other | 33.3 | -8638.8 |
| **按单位规模分** | **By Size of Enterprise** | | |
| 大型 | Large | | |
| 中型 | Medium | 592.6 | -50720.4 |
| 小型 | Small | 795 | -23159.1 |
| 微型 | Micro | 62.9 | -401.6 |
| **按星级分** | **By Star of Hotel** | | |
| 五星 | 5-Star | 179.4 | -32745.7 |
| 四星 | 4-Star | 142.2 | -14705.1 |
| 三星 | 3-Star | 93.9 | 759.7 |
| 二星 | 2-Star | 0.1 | 83.1 |
| 一星 | 1-Star | | 839 |
| 其他 | Other | 1034.9 | -28512.1 |

单位：万元 (10 000 yuan)

| 三、损益及分配 Profits and Losses | 四、人工成本及增值税 Labor cost and Value-added Tax | | 五、从事批发和零售业活动的从业人员平均人数(人) Annual Average Employees Engaged in wholesale and retail activities (persons) |
|---|---|---|---|
| 所得税费用 Income Tax Payable | 应付职工薪酬 Employee compensation | 应交增值税 Value-added Tax | |
| 994.6 | 57835.3 | 3521.3 | 6940 |
| 3.9 | 3813.4 | 288 | 591 |
| 2136.1 | 123336.8 | 10604.1 | 22999 |
| | 4930 | 102.2 | 646 |
| 361.9 | 6822.5 | 554.1 | 897 |
| 3308.3 | 168867.1 | 13219.7 | 27517 |
| 0.5 | 2363.9 | 52 | 370 |
| 147.1 | 9822.4 | 703.7 | 2092 |
| 40.6 | 15684.6 | 1094.3 | 2094 |
| 2362.6 | 104931.9 | 6696.9 | 14090 |
| 1024.3 | 89536.6 | 7958.5 | 16949 |
| 109.6 | 2269.5 | 414.3 | 1034 |
| 1279.9 | 42743.7 | 2812.8 | 6258 |
| 94.6 | 31074.1 | 2730.3 | 4566 |
| 372 | 14239.5 | 1306.2 | 2628 |
| 4.8 | 221.6 | 9.0 | 58 |
| 3.1 | 65.8 | 2.6 | 13 |
| 1742.1 | 108393.3 | 8208.8 | 18550 |

# 表 15.9 限额以上餐饮业法人企业财务状况（2022 年）
# FINANCIAL INDICATORS OF ENTERPRISES ABOVE DESIGNATED SIZE OF CATERING SERVICES (2022)

| 指 标 | Item | 法人企业数（个）Number of Enterprises (unit) | 执行《2006 年企业会计准则》企业数（个）Number of Enterprises which Implemented Accounting standard for Business Enterprise in 2006 (unit) | 一、年初存货 Inventory at the Beginning of Year |
|---|---|---|---|---|
| **总计** | **Total** | **1339** | 577 | 86098.2 |
| **按餐饮业行业小类分** | **By Sector** | | | |
| 正餐服务 | Dinner Services | 1284 | 545 | 78901.9 |
| 正餐服务 | Dinner Services | 1284 | 545 | 78901.9 |
| 快餐服务 | Fast Food Services | 21 | 11 | 5694.5 |
| 快餐服务 | Fast Food Services | 21 | 11 | 5694.5 |
| 饮料及冷饮服务 | Beverages and Cold Beverage Services | 12 | 9 | 525.7 |
| 咖啡馆服务 | Cafe Services | 2 | 1 | 38 |
| 其他饮料及冷饮服务 | Other Beverages and Cold Beverage Services | 10 | 8 | 487.7 |
| 餐饮配送及外卖送餐服务 | Catering delivery and delivery service | 12 | 5 | 770.5 |
| 餐饮配送服务 | Catering distribution | 6 | 3 | 616 |
| 外卖送餐服务 | Delivery service | 6 | 2 | 154.5 |
| 其他餐饮业 | Other Catering Services | 10 | 7 | 205.6 |
| 小吃服务 | Snack Services | 4 | 1 | 139.7 |
| 其他未列明餐饮业 | Other Catering Business | 6 | 6 | 65.9 |
| **按登记注册类型分** | **By Status of Registration** | | | |
| 内资企业 | Domestic-funded Enterprises | 1326 | 569 | 80696 |
| 国有企业 | State-owned Enterprises | 6 | 4 | 141.9 |
| 集体企业 | Collective-owned Enterprises | 4 | 2 | 13.4 |
| 有限责任公司 | Limited Liability Corporations | 56 | 35 | 46951.4 |
| 国有独资公司 | State Sole Funded Corporations | 7 | 5 | 44595 |
| 其他有限责任公司 | Other Limited Liability Corporations | 49 | 30 | 2356.4 |
| 股份有限公司 | Share-holding Corporations Ltd. | 2 | | 79.3 |
| 私营企业 | Private Enterprises | 1257 | 527 | 33480 |
| 私营独资企业 | Private-funded Enterprises | 246 | 115 | 2039.4 |
| 私营合伙企业 | Private Partnership Enterprises | 5 | 2 | 187.9 |
| 私营有限责任公司 | Private Limited Liability Corporations | 1004 | 408 | 30322 |
| 私营股份有限公司 | Private Share-holding Corporations Ltd. | 2 | 2 | 930.9 |

单位：万元 (10 000 yuan)

| 二、期末资产负债 Assets and Liabilities | | | | | |
|---|---|---|---|---|---|
| 流动资产合计 Total Current Assets | 应收账款 Accounts Receivable | 存货 Inventory | 固定资产原价 Total Original Value of Fixed Assets | 房屋和构筑物 Buildings and Structures | 机器设备 Machinery and Equipments |
| **851804.2** | **84848.3** | **88738.9** | **593564.4** | **214936.8** | **101916.5** |
| | | | | | |
| 746159.8 | 70950.4 | 81562.7 | 520535.1 | 192623.3 | 61221.5 |
| 746159.8 | 70950.4 | 81562.7 | 520535.1 | 192623.3 | 61221.5 |
| 87216.6 | 10783.2 | 5812.5 | 65841.1 | 20190.2 | 38033.2 |
| 87216.6 | 10783.2 | 5812.5 | 65841.1 | 20190.2 | 38033.2 |
| 10576.2 | 416 | 449.5 | 2407.9 | | 1425 |
| 1779.1 | 34.6 | 31.7 | 683.8 | | 431.8 |
| 8797.1 | 381.4 | 417.8 | 1724.1 | | 993.2 |
| 5500.1 | 2383.9 | 790.9 | 3672.2 | 1681.2 | 974.1 |
| 4310.9 | 2081.9 | 650.1 | 3496 | 1678.7 | 968.5 |
| 1189.2 | 302 | 140.8 | 176.2 | 2.5 | 5.6 |
| 2351.5 | 314.8 | 123.3 | 1108.1 | 442.1 | 262.7 |
| 1621.8 | 20.1 | 75.6 | 151.9 | 31.5 | 105.2 |
| 729.7 | 294.7 | 47.7 | 956.2 | 410.6 | 157.5 |
| | | | | | |
| 768217 | 76608 | 83380 | 529748 | 194792 | 64064 |
| 6164.7 | 1028.4 | 150.6 | 821.6 | 206.5 | 5.3 |
| 931.9 | 281.9 | 14.7 | 544.7 | 403.4 | 118 |
| 273722.9 | 4516.9 | 46878.3 | 90813.2 | 30834.8 | 13004.5 |
| 239135.4 | 1252.7 | 44360.1 | 61491.1 | 27861 | 499.6 |
| 34587.5 | 3264.2 | 2518.2 | 29322.1 | 2973.8 | 12504.9 |
| 149.5 | 6.9 | 34.8 | 139.5 | | 134.5 |
| 487224 | 70772 | 36298 | 437415 | 163347 | 50802 |
| 15407.6 | 3682.2 | 3687.5 | 44898.6 | 20310.5 | 7456.6 |
| 1909.6 | 121.9 | 207.8 | 651.8 | 52.4 | 84 |
| 448480.9 | 66707.6 | 31461.5 | 340872.3 | 142984.2 | 43260.9 |
| 21425.8 | 260 | 940.9 | 50992 | | |

**表 15.9 续表 1 continued 1**

| 指 标 | Item | 二、期末资产负债 Assets and Liabilities 累计折旧 Cumulative Depreciation | 本年折旧 Depreciation | 固定资产净额 Net Value of Fixed Assets |
|---|---|---|---|---|
| **总计** | **Total** | **236297.9** | **34260.4** | **287173** |
| **按餐饮业行业小类分** | **By Sector** | | | |
| 正餐服务 | Dinner Services | 200733.3 | 26054.6 | 258915.2 |
| 正餐服务 | Dinner Services | 200733.3 | 26054.6 | 258915.2 |
| 快餐服务 | Fast Food Services | 32104.7 | 7631.4 | 25366.8 |
| 快餐服务 | Fast Food Services | 32104.7 | 7631.4 | 25366.8 |
| 饮料及冷饮服务 | Beverages and Cold Beverage Services | 1381.8 | 303.1 | 979.9 |
| 咖啡馆服务 | Cafe Services | 581.5 | 44.9 | 89.7 |
| 其他饮料及冷饮服务 | Other Beverages and Cold Beverage Services | 800.3 | 258.2 | 890.2 |
| 餐饮配送及外卖送餐服务 | Catering delivery and delivery service | 1882.4 | 207.5 | 1755.4 |
| 餐饮配送服务 | Catering distribution | 1837.8 | 192.5 | 1633.3 |
| 外卖送餐服务 | Delivery service | 44.6 | 15 | 122.1 |
| 其他餐饮业 | Other Catering Services | 195.7 | 63.8 | 155.7 |
| 小吃服务 | Snack Services | 50.3 | 20.8 | 51.3 |
| 其他未列明餐饮业 | Other Catering Business | 145.4 | 43 | 104.4 |
| **按登记注册类型分** | **By Status of Registration** | | | |
| 内资企业 | Domestic-funded Enterprises | 204802 | 26799 | 262381 |
| 国有企业 | State-owned Enterprises | 118.6 | 104.3 | 528.4 |
| 集体企业 | Collective-owned Enterprises | 11.5 | 2.2 | 102.9 |
| 有限责任公司 | Limited Liability Corporations | 31279.2 | 3294.8 | 35986.1 |
| 国有独资公司 | State Sole Funded Corporations | 13387.1 | 1882.3 | 27362.3 |
| 其他有限责任公司 | Other Limited Liability Corporations | 17892.1 | 1412.5 | 8623.8 |
| 股份有限公司 | Share-holding Corporations Ltd. | 87.9 | 30.9 | 49.1 |
| 私营企业 | Private Enterprises | 173301 | 23366 | 225715 |
| 私营独资企业 | Private-funded Enterprises | 14335 | 2502.3 | 24100.8 |
| 私营合伙企业 | Private Partnership Enterprises | 301.2 | 58.7 | 328.7 |
| 私营有限责任公司 | Private Limited Liability Corporations | 134153.8 | 20735 | 174804 |
| 私营股份有限公司 | Private Share-holding Corporations Ltd. | 24510.8 | 69.8 | 26481.2 |

单位：万元 (10 000 yuan)

| 二、期末资产负债 Assets and Liabilities | | | | | |
|---|---|---|---|---|---|
| 在建工程<br>Construction in Progress | 无形资产<br>Intangible Assets | 土地使用权<br>Land Use Rights | 资产总计<br>Total Assets | 流动负债合计<br>Total Current Liabilities | 应付账款<br>Accounts Payable |
| **43234.2** | **239632.2** | **6919.2** | **1902838.8** | **584685.5** | **117428.1** |
| | | | | | |
| 42773.4 | 237680.1 | 6704.2 | 1704431 | 530671 | 101099 |
| 42773.4 | 237680.1 | 6704.2 | 1704431 | 530671 | 101099 |
| 460.8 | 1715.9 | | 161996.5 | 23102.3 | 12128.8 |
| 460.8 | 1715.9 | | 161996.5 | 23102.3 | 12128.8 |
| | | | 23937.8 | 24729.2 | 2368 |
| | | | 2225.3 | 3275 | 68 |
| | | | 21712.5 | 21454.2 | 2300 |
| | | | 8303.2 | 4543.1 | 1525.9 |
| | | | 6779.5 | 3450.2 | 1393.4 |
| | | | 1523.7 | 1092.9 | 132.5 |
| | 236.2 | 215 | 4170.3 | 1639.9 | 306.4 |
| | | | 1869.9 | 1243.2 | 231.9 |
| | 236.2 | 215 | 2300.4 | 396.7 | 74.5 |
| | | | | | |
| 42773 | 237982 | 6919 | 1737897 | 541250 | 107551 |
| 5 | 1.5 | | 6720.7 | 1371.4 | 727.5 |
| | 236.2 | 215 | 1463.5 | 568.6 | 253.7 |
| 20120.4 | 209083.5 | | 696947.9 | 95945.3 | 5498.1 |
| 19870.3 | 209064 | | 631764.7 | 56868.4 | 650 |
| 250.1 | 19.5 | | 65183.2 | 39076.9 | 4848.1 |
| | 1.5 | | 371.6 | 199.2 | 38.5 |
| 22648 | 28659 | 6704 | 1032208 | 443166 | 101033 |
| 2.5 | 806.2 | | 57973.4 | 7763.5 | 4238 |
| | | | 3625.8 | 1833.5 | 677.3 |
| 22645.5 | 9202 | 6704.2 | 846378.7 | 382730.5 | 92660.7 |
| | 18650.6 | | 124229.9 | 50838.2 | 3457.3 |

**表 15.9 续表 2 continued 2**

| 指 标 | Item | 二、期末资产负债 Assets and Liabilities<br>负债合计 Total Liabilities | 所有者权益合计 Total Owner's Equity | 实收资本 Paid-up Capital |
|---|---|---|---|---|
| **总计** | **Total** | **1090436.8** | **759670.6** | **433629.8** |
| **按餐饮业行业小类分** | **By Sector** | | | |
| 正餐服务 | Dinner Services | 978464.1 | 673235.4 | 372442.4 |
| 正餐服务 | Dinner Services | 978464.1 | 673235.4 | 372442.4 |
| 快餐服务 | Fast Food Services | 70509.6 | 91486.9 | 57541.5 |
| 快餐服务 | Fast Food Services | 70509.6 | 91486.9 | 57541.5 |
| 饮料及冷饮服务 | Beverages and Cold Beverage Services | 34365.5 | -10427.6 | 1330 |
| 咖啡馆服务 | Cafe Services | 3671.9 | -1446.6 | |
| 其他饮料及冷饮服务 | Other Beverages and Cold Beverage Services | 30693.6 | -8981 | 1330 |
| 餐饮配送及外卖送餐服务 | Catering delivery and delivery service | 4611.9 | 3691.3 | 1515 |
| 餐饮配送服务 | Catering distribution | 3518.9 | 3260.6 | 1100 |
| 外卖送餐服务 | Delivery service | 1093 | 430.7 | 415 |
| 其他餐饮业 | Other Catering Services | 2485.7 | 1684.6 | 800.9 |
| 小吃服务 | Snack Services | 1598.5 | 271.4 | 50 |
| 其他未列明餐饮业 | Other Catering Business | 887.2 | 1413.2 | 750.9 |
| **按登记注册类型分** | **By Status of Registration** | | | |
| 内资企业 | Domestic-funded Enterprises | 997009 | 688157 | 370476 |
| 国有企业 | State-owned Enterprises | 6300.6 | 304.5 | 1227.8 |
| 集体企业 | Collective-owned Enterprises | 568.6 | 894.9 | 30 |
| 有限责任公司 | Limited Liability Corporations | 376487 | 265501.1 | 26689 |
| 国有独资公司 | State Sole Funded Corporations | 329710.3 | 254111.6 | 7090 |
| 其他有限责任公司 | Other Limited Liability Corporations | 46776.7 | 11389.5 | 19599 |
| 股份有限公司 | Share-holding Corporations Ltd. | 309.1 | 60.8 | 2350 |
| 私营企业 | Private Enterprises | 613343 | 421210 | 340079 |
| 私营独资企业 | Private-funded Enterprises | 14911 | 41221 | 19511.6 |
| 私营合伙企业 | Private Partnership Enterprises | 1889.8 | 1736 | 692.9 |
| 私营有限责任公司 | Private Limited Liability Corporations | 527473.7 | 323092 | 319177.6 |
| 私营股份有限公司 | Private Share-holding Corporations Ltd. | 69068.8 | 55161.1 | 696.8 |

单位：万元 (10 000 yuan)

| 二、期末资产负债 Assets and Liabilities | 三、损益及分配 Profits and Losses | | | | |
|---|---|---|---|---|---|
| 个人资本 Personal Capital | 营业收入 Gross Sales | 主营业务收入 Main Business Income | 营业成本 Operating Cost | 税金及附加 Taxes and Surcharges | 其他业务利润 Other Business Profits |
| **176837.4** | **1995804.2** | **1800830.9** | **1490575** | **10197.9** | **2250.4** |
| | | | | | |
| 175062.7 | 1634604.3 | 1444370.5 | 1208719.2 | 9656.1 | 1821.7 |
| 175062.7 | 1634604.3 | 1444370.5 | 1208719.2 | 9656.1 | 1821.7 |
| 1529.7 | 262206.8 | 257913.9 | 215887.4 | 299.9 | 306.6 |
| 1529.7 | 262206.8 | 257913.9 | 215887.4 | 299.9 | 306.6 |
| | 60982.8 | 60760.7 | 39453.6 | 95.8 | 102.1 |
| | 2093.2 | 1991.9 | 434.3 | 0.2 | 101.3 |
| | 58889.6 | 58768.8 | 39019.3 | 95.6 | 0.8 |
| 200 | 29870.8 | 29722.9 | 20047.2 | 135.3 | 0.1 |
| | 24940.2 | 24940.2 | 16225 | 65.3 | 0.1 |
| 200 | 4930.6 | 4782.7 | 3822.2 | 70 | |
| 45 | 8139.5 | 8062.9 | 6467.6 | 10.8 | 19.9 |
| | 3435.4 | 3360.6 | 2972.7 | 1.9 | 19.9 |
| 45 | 4704.1 | 4702.3 | 3494.9 | 8.9 | |
| | | | | | |
| 176837 | 1712400 | 1521820 | 1257905 | 9941 | 1943 |
| | 4094.3 | 3773.1 | 2797.6 | 47.9 | 3.6 |
| | 7892.1 | 7888.1 | 7964.7 | 4.5 | |
| 5822 | 261093.3 | 106374.3 | 202954.8 | 1040.7 | |
| | 157160.6 | 5069.7 | 151865.4 | 444 | |
| 5822 | 103932.7 | 101304.6 | 51089.4 | 596.7 | |
| | 1005.6 | 642.6 | 649.1 | 8.5 | |
| 171015 | 1437751 | 1402578 | 1043050 | 8839 | 1939 |
| 12738.1 | 142608.6 | 132004.9 | 105960.3 | 744.2 | 9.3 |
| | 4318.9 | 4318.9 | 3225.7 | 18.6 | |
| 157580.5 | 1260442.6 | 1235942.4 | 912770.9 | 8026.4 | 1930.1 |
| 696.8 | 30380.7 | 30311.7 | 21093.1 | 50.1 | |

**表 15.9 续表 3 continued 3**

| 指 标 | Item | 三、损益及分配 Profits and Losses | | |
|---|---|---|---|---|
| | | 销售费用 Sales Expenses | 管理费用 Management Expenses | 研发费用 R&D expenses |
| **总计** | **Total** | **220605.6** | **155136.2** | **1163.3** |
| **按餐饮业行业小类分** | **By Sector** | | | |
| 正餐服务 | Dinner Services | 183709.8 | 137287.8 | 1153.9 |
| 正餐服务 | Dinner Services | 183709.8 | 137287.8 | 1153.9 |
| 快餐服务 | Fast Food Services | 21033.9 | 10809.1 | 2.8 |
| 快餐服务 | Fast Food Services | 21033.9 | 10809.1 | 2.8 |
| 饮料及冷饮服务 | Beverages and Cold Beverage Services | 14017.3 | 4441.6 | 0.3 |
| 咖啡馆服务 | Cafe Services | 1472.7 | 194.7 | |
| 其他饮料及冷饮服务 | Other Beverages and Cold Beverage Services | 12544.6 | 4246.9 | 0.3 |
| 餐饮配送及外卖送餐服务 | Catering delivery and delivery service | 1046 | 1919.9 | 6.3 |
| 餐饮配送服务 | Catering distribution | 811.3 | 1572.9 | 6.1 |
| 外卖送餐服务 | Delivery service | 234.7 | 347 | 0.2 |
| 其他餐饮业 | Other Catering Services | 798.6 | 677.8 | |
| 小吃服务 | Snack Services | 103.6 | 203.2 | |
| 其他未列明餐饮业 | Other Catering Business | 695 | 474.6 | |
| **按登记注册类型分** | **By Status of Registration** | | | |
| 内资企业 | Domestic-funded Enterprises | 198704 | 142200 | 1163 |
| 国有企业 | State-owned Enterprises | 726.8 | 854.7 | |
| 集体企业 | Collective-owned Enterprises | 14.6 | 34.1 | 0.4 |
| 有限责任公司 | Limited Liability Corporations | 40274.3 | 14179 | 24.3 |
| 国有独资公司 | State Sole Funded Corporations | 2603.7 | 4482.4 | |
| 其他有限责任公司 | Other Limited Liability Corporations | 37670.6 | 9696.6 | 24.3 |
| 股份有限公司 | Share-holding Corporations Ltd. | 386.1 | 103.1 | 0.1 |
| 私营企业 | Private Enterprises | 157296 | 127006 | 1138 |
| 私营独资企业 | Private-funded Enterprises | 6306.2 | 7129.5 | 54.1 |
| 私营合伙企业 | Private Partnership Enterprises | 485.1 | 241.9 | |
| 私营有限责任公司 | Private Limited Liability Corporations | 140828.1 | 113307.1 | 1078.5 |
| 私营股份有限公司 | Private Share-holding Corporations Ltd. | 9677 | 6327.2 | 5.8 |

单位: 万元 (10 000 yuan)

| 三、损益及分配 Profits and Losses | | | | | |
|---|---|---|---|---|---|
| 财务费用 Financial Expenses | 利息收入 Interest Income | 利息费用 Interest expenses | 投资收益 Income from Investment | 营业利润 Business Profits | 营业外收入 Non-business Income |
| **17713.1** | **1948.3** | **13654.8** | **64.5** | **81284.5** | **7396.3** |
| 15777.5 | 1611.6 | 12430.9 | 59.1 | 61965.9 | 6298.2 |
| 15777.5 | 1611.6 | 12430.9 | 59.1 | 61965.9 | 6298.2 |
| 1361.6 | 305.5 | 1077.4 | 5.4 | 15438.5 | 846.8 |
| 1361.6 | 305.5 | 1077.4 | 5.4 | 15438.5 | 846.8 |
| 428.3 | 28.3 | 142.4 | | 2955.3 | 97.2 |
| 31.6 | 28.9 | 60.5 | | -40.4 | 8.7 |
| 396.7 | -0.6 | 81.9 | | 2995.7 | 88.5 |
| 109.3 | 2.9 | 4.1 | | 750.2 | 152.8 |
| 35.8 | 2.9 | 3.9 | | 367 | 151.4 |
| 73.5 | | 0.2 | | 383.2 | 1.4 |
| 36.4 | | | | 174.6 | 1.3 |
| 28.5 | | | | 145.1 | |
| 7.9 | | | | 29.5 | 1.3 |
| | | | | | |
| 16128 | 1646 | 12607 | 187 | 64390 | 6456 |
| 145.6 | 1.9 | 144.2 | | -474.9 | 50.3 |
| 5 | 3.6 | | | -142.6 | |
| 4250.4 | 39.6 | 4141.2 | | -2038.3 | 2400 |
| 3620.1 | 28.5 | 3643.9 | | -5188.6 | 1933.2 |
| 630.3 | 11.1 | 497.3 | | 3150.3 | 466.8 |
| 1 | | | | -135.3 | 6.4 |
| 11725 | 1601 | 8322 | 187 | 67174 | 3999 |
| 861.3 | 49.8 | 219.3 | 1.2 | 16904.8 | 420.7 |
| 13.4 | | 5.8 | | 646.4 | 3.2 |
| 9815.5 | 1468.3 | 7080.1 | 186.1 | 49128.2 | 3523.5 |
| 1034.9 | 82.9 | 1016.3 | | 494.3 | 51.4 |

表 15.9 续表 4 continued 4

| 指 标 | Item | 三、损益及分配 Profits and Losses | |
|---|---|---|---|
| | | 营业外支出 Non-business Expenses | 利润总额 Total Profits |
| **总计** | **Total** | **2839.5** | **88155.2** |
| **按餐饮业行业小类分** | **By Sector** | | |
| 正餐服务 | Dinner Services | 1202.7 | 69428.2 |
| 正餐服务 | Dinner Services | 1202.7 | 69428.2 |
| 快餐服务 | Fast Food Services | 1542 | 14690.4 |
| 快餐服务 | Fast Food Services | 1542 | 14690.4 |
| 饮料及冷饮服务 | Beverages and Cold Beverage Services | 92.6 | 2959.9 |
| 咖啡馆服务 | Cafe Services | 0.4 | -32.1 |
| 其他饮料及冷饮服务 | Other Beverages and Cold Beverage Services | 92.2 | 2992 |
| 餐饮配送及外卖送餐服务 | Catering delivery and delivery service | 0.2 | 902.8 |
| 餐饮配送服务 | Catering distribution | | 518.4 |
| 外卖送餐服务 | Delivery service | 0.2 | 384.4 |
| 其他餐饮业 | Other Catering Services | 2 | 173.9 |
| 小吃服务 | Snack Services | 2 | 143.1 |
| 其他未列明餐饮业 | Other Catering Business | | 30.8 |
| **按登记注册类型分** | **By Status of Registration** | | |
| 内资企业 | Domestic-funded Enterprises | 1224 | 71935 |
| 国有企业 | State-owned Enterprises | 12.6 | -437.2 |
| 集体企业 | Collective-owned Enterprises | | -142.6 |
| 有限责任公司 | Limited Liability Corporations | 296.2 | 2587.3 |
| 国有独资公司 | State Sole Funded Corporations | 33.9 | -767.5 |
| 其他有限责任公司 | Other Limited Liability Corporations | 262.3 | 3354.8 |
| 股份有限公司 | Share-holding Corporations Ltd. | 43.6 | -172.5 |
| 私营企业 | Private Enterprises | 871 | 70093 |
| 私营独资企业 | Private-funded Enterprises | 49.2 | 17287.8 |
| 私营合伙企业 | Private Partnership Enterprises | | 649.6 |
| 私营有限责任公司 | Private Limited Liability Corporations | 815.2 | 51617 |
| 私营股份有限公司 | Private Share-holding Corporations Ltd. | 7 | 538.7 |

单位: 万元 (10 000 yuan)

| 三、损益及分配 Profits and Losses | 四、人工成本及增值税 Labor cost and Value-added Tax | | 五、从事批发和零售业活动的从业人员平均人数(人) Annual Average Employees Engaged in wholesale and retail activities (persons) |
|---|---|---|---|
| 所得税费用 Income Tax Payable | 应付职工薪酬 Employee compensation | 应交增值税 Value-added Tax | |
| **7226.6** | **276246.5** | **14733.8** | **61426** |
| | | | |
| 5217.7 | 203821.7 | 14066.3 | 47667 |
| 5217.7 | 203821.7 | 14066.3 | 47667 |
| 2058.1 | 52937.6 | 292.3 | 10871 |
| 2058.1 | 52937.6 | 292.3 | 10871 |
| -116.1 | 11527 | 213.3 | 1491 |
| 1 | 495.8 | 4.2 | 107 |
| -117.1 | 11031.2 | 209.1 | 1384 |
| 38.4 | 6108.6 | 156 | 1061 |
| 33.2 | 4387.9 | 7.5 | 658 |
| 5.2 | 1720.7 | 148.5 | 403 |
| 28.5 | 1851.6 | 5.9 | 336 |
| 26 | 746.4 | 1.7 | 119 |
| 2.5 | 1105.2 | 4.2 | 217 |
| | | | |
| 5209 | 216159 | 14491 | 49879 |
| 7.8 | 900.3 | 114.1 | 256 |
| 2.1 | 1544.1 | 2.4 | 314 |
| 274 | 16671.7 | 216.7 | 3221 |
| 3.4 | 1850.5 | 383.3 | 460 |
| 270.6 | 14821.2 | -166.6 | 2761 |
| 0.2 | 140.9 | 1.6 | 34 |
| 4925 | 196862 | 14156 | 46050 |
| 1118.5 | 14101 | 1380.2 | 3427 |
| 11.9 | 638.7 | 29 | 129 |
| 3767.6 | 164985.6 | 12529.2 | 36852 |
| 26.6 | 17136.3 | 217.3 | 5642 |

**表 15.9 续表 5 continued 5**

| 指 标 | Item | 法人企业数(个) Number of Enterprises (unit) | 执行《2006年企业会计准则》企业数(个) Number of Enterprises which Implemented Accounting standard for Business Enterprise in 2006 (unit) | 一、年初存货 Inventory at the Beginning of Year |
|---|---|---|---|---|
| 其他企业 | Other Enterprises | 1 | 1 | 29.5 |
| 港、澳、台商投资企业 | Enterprises Funded by Hong Kong, Macao and Taiwan | 4 | 1 | 587.4 |
| 港澳台商独资企业 | Enterprises with Sole Fund | 4 | 1 | 587.4 |
| 外商投资企业 | Foreign-funded Enterprises | 9 | 7 | 4815.1 |
| 外资企业 | Enterprises with Sole Fund | 9 | 7 | 4815.1 |
| **按控股情况分** | **By Holding Entity of Share** | | | |
| 国有控股 | State-holding | 18 | 14 | 44985.5 |
| 集体控股 | Collective-holding | 4 | 2 | 13.4 |
| 私人控股 | Private-holding | 1303 | 552 | 35667.3 |
| 港澳台商控股 | Held by Corporation from Hong Kong, Macao and Taiwan | 4 | 1 | 587.4 |
| 外商控股 | Foreign-holding | 9 | 7 | 4815.1 |
| 其他 | Other | 1 | 1 | 29.5 |
| **按经营形式分** | **By Form of Business** | | | |
| 独立门店 | Independent Store | 1196 | 512 | 57232.2 |
| 连锁总店(总部) | Central Shop of Chain Stores (Headquarter) | 31 | 19 | 8523.7 |
| 连锁直营店 | Direct-sale Shop of Chain Stores | 36 | 20 | 1850.1 |
| 连锁加盟店 | Branch Shop of Chain Stores | 6 | 3 | 487.4 |
| 其他 | Other | 70 | 23 | 18004.8 |
| **按单位规模分** | **By Size of Enterprise** | | | |
| 大型 | Large | 13 | 13 | 7493.1 |
| 中型 | Medium | 43 | 24 | 5094.3 |
| 小型 | Small | 925 | 399 | 26471.5 |
| 微型 | Micro | 358 | 141 | 47039.3 |

单位：万元 (10 000 yuan)

| 二、期末资产负债 Assets and Liabilities | | | | | |
|---|---|---|---|---|---|
| 流动资产合计 Total Current Assets | 应收账款 Accounts Receivable | 存货 Inventory | 固定资产原价 Total Original Value of Fixed Assets | 房屋和构筑物 Buildings and Structures | 机器设备 Machinery and Equipments |
| 24.1 | 2.6 | 3.6 | 14.3 | | |
| 3835.7 | 104.9 | 598 | 4369.3 | | 171 |
| 3835.7 | 104.9 | 598 | 4369.3 | | 171 |
| 79751.5 | 8135 | 4761.2 | 59447.1 | 20145 | 37681.7 |
| 79751.5 | 8135 | 4761.2 | 59447.1 | 20145 | 37681.7 |
| | | | | | |
| 246814.4 | 2344.1 | 44561 | 65166.9 | 29405.7 | 636.7 |
| 931.9 | 281.9 | 14.7 | 544.7 | 403.4 | 118 |
| 520446.6 | 73979.8 | 38800.4 | 464022.1 | 164982.7 | 63309.1 |
| 3835.7 | 104.9 | 598 | 4369.3 | | 171 |
| 79751.5 | 8135 | 4761.2 | 59447.1 | 20145 | 37681.7 |
| 24.1 | 2.6 | 3.6 | 14.3 | | |
| | | | | | |
| 495083.1 | 47061.6 | 32880.7 | 409643 | 186125.1 | 44233 |
| 136793.3 | 10478.2 | 10086.2 | 140299.6 | 25725.7 | 51263.7 |
| 26699.6 | 1898.1 | 1999.9 | 10741.5 | 570 | 2239.4 |
| 2359.4 | 348.6 | 505 | 1094.4 | 80 | 257.8 |
| 190868.8 | 25061.8 | 43267.1 | 31785.9 | 2436 | 3922.6 |
| | | | | | |
| 140430.3 | 22392.3 | 8478.1 | 129993.7 | 21640.8 | 52325.9 |
| 156866.2 | 18553 | 4272.5 | 106210.6 | 54050.7 | 7501.6 |
| 367668.8 | 37506.1 | 28790.3 | 295563.5 | 126476.2 | 37211.9 |
| 186838.9 | 6396.9 | 47198 | 61796.6 | 12769.1 | 4877.1 |

**表 15.9 续表 6 continued 6**

| 指 标 | Item | 二、期末资产负债 Assets and Liabilities 累计折旧 Cumulative Depreciation | 本年折旧 Depreciation | 固定资产净额 Net Value of Fixed Assets |
|---|---|---|---|---|
| 其他企业 | Other Enterprises | 4.1 | 0.8 | |
| 港、澳、台商投资企业 | Enterprises Funded by Hong Kong, Macao and Taiwan | 400.8 | 34 | 3955.8 |
| 港澳台商独资企业 | Enterprises with Sole Fund | 400.8 | 34 | 3955.8 |
| 外商投资企业 | Foreign-funded Enterprises | 31095 | 7427.6 | 20836 |
| 外资企业 | Enterprises with Sole Fund | 31095 | 7427.6 | 20836 |
| **按控股情况分** | **By Holding Entity of Share** | | | |
| 国有控股 | State-holding | 14141.2 | 2111.2 | 29339.4 |
| 集体控股 | Collective-holding | 11.5 | 2.2 | 102.9 |
| 私人控股 | Private-holding | 190645.3 | 24684.6 | 232938.9 |
| 港澳台商控股 | Held by Corporation from Hong Kong, Macao and Taiwan | 400.8 | 34 | 3955.8 |
| 外商控股 | Foreign-holding | 31095 | 7427.6 | 20836 |
| 其他 | Other | 4.1 | 0.8 | |
| **按经营形式分** | **By Form of Business** | | | |
| 独立门店 | Independent Store | 145808.2 | 21123.2 | 216921.2 |
| 连锁总店(总部) | Central Shop of Chain Stores (Headquarter) | 72573.6 | 9579.3 | 60151.8 |
| 连锁直营店 | Direct-sale Shop of Chain Stores | 7018.7 | 1217.2 | 3196.9 |
| 连锁加盟店 | Branch Shop of Chain Stores | 652.1 | 355.9 | 419.3 |
| 其他 | Other | 10245.3 | 1984.8 | 6483.8 |
| **按单位规模分** | **By Size of Enterprise** | | | |
| 大型 | Large | 64718.9 | 9419.3 | 57521.5 |
| 中型 | Medium | 48369.9 | 5419.8 | 56666.2 |
| 小型 | Small | 107230.5 | 16664.7 | 154392.7 |
| 微型 | Micro | 15978.6 | 2756.6 | 18592.6 |

单位：万元 (10 000 yuan)

| 二、期末资产负债 Assets and Liabilities | | | | | |
|---|---|---|---|---|---|
| 在建工程<br>Construction in Progress | 无形资产<br>Intangible Assets | 土地使用权<br>Land Use Rights | 资产总计<br>Total Assets | 流动负债合计<br>Total Current Liablities | 应付账款<br>Accounts Payable |
| | | | 185.6 | | |
| 460.8 | 1433.5 | | 23910.9 | 10123.9 | 1292.8 |
| 460.8 | 1433.5 | | 23910.9 | 101239 | 1292.8 |
| | 217.2 | | 141030.8 | 33311.4 | 8584.2 |
| | 217.2 | | 141030.8 | 33311.4 | 8584.2 |
| | | | | | |
| 20105.4 | 209067.4 | | 642860.8 | 66229.9 | 1784.6 |
| | 236.2 | 215 | 1463.5 | 568.6 | 253.7 |
| 22668 | 28677.9 | 6704.2 | 1093387.2 | 474451.7 | 105512.8 |
| 460.8 | 1433.5 | | 23910.9 | 10123.9 | 1292.8 |
| | 217.2 | | 141030.8 | 33311.4 | 8584.2 |
| | | | 185.6 | | |
| | | | | | |
| 37136.3 | 219235.6 | 6919.2 | 1179029.3 | 361544.3 | 69322.1 |
| 460.8 | 20315.5 | | 358971.6 | 129965.2 | 19412.3 |
| 206 | 45.1 | | 35469.5 | 30487.7 | 7235.3 |
| | | | 5639.6 | 3323.6 | 377.3 |
| 5431.1 | 36 | | 323728.8 | 59364.7 | 21081.1 |
| | | | | | |
| 460.8 | 20281.2 | | 340286.2 | 137103.3 | 35404.1 |
| 5082.3 | 3010.4 | 1965.4 | 273274.2 | 131406.9 | 26433.3 |
| 37423.8 | 215851.8 | 4476 | 953604.2 | 301290.6 | 52457 |
| 267.3 | 488.8 | 477.8 | 335674.2 | 14884.7 | 3133.7 |

表 15.9 续表 7 continued 7

| 指 标 | Item | 二、期末资产负债 Assets and Liabilities | | |
|---|---|---|---|---|
| | | 负债合计 Total Liabilities | 所有者权益合计 Total Owner's Equity | 实收资本 Paid-up Capital |
| 其他企业 | Other Enterprises | 0.4 | 185.2 | 100 |
| 港、澳、台商投资企业 | Enterprises Funded by Hong Kong, Macao and Taiwan | 18565.5 | 5345.4 | 3776.6 |
| 港澳台商独资企业 | Enterprises with Sole Fund | 18565.5 | 5345.4 | 3776.6 |
| 外商投资企业 | Foreign-funded Enterprises | 74862.3 | 66168.6 | 59377.5 |
| 外资企业 | Enterprises with Sole Fund | 74862.3 | 66168.6 | 59377.5 |
| **按控股情况分** | **By Holding Entity of Share** | | | |
| 国有控股 | State-holding | 344322.7 | 250479.7 | 8978.4 |
| 集体控股 | Collective-holding | 568.6 | 894.9 | 30 |
| 私人控股 | Private-holding | 652117.3 | 436596.8 | 361367.3 |
| 港澳台商控股 | Held by Corporation from Hong Kong, Macao and Taiwan | 18565.5 | 5345.4 | 3776.6 |
| 外商控股 | Foreign-holding | 74862.3 | 66168.6 | 59377.5 |
| 其他 | Other | 0.4 | 185.2 | 100 |
| **按经营形式分** | **By Form of Business** | | | |
| 独立门店 | Independent Store | 613650.5 | 553833.7 | 302587.3 |
| 连锁总店(总部) | Central Shop of Chain Stores (Headquarter) | 203793.4 | 155178.3 | 76343.4 |
| 连锁直营店 | Direct-sale Shop of Chain Stores | 33241.4 | 2173.1 | 20577 |
| 连锁加盟店 | Branch Shop of Chain Stores | 5009.4 | 630.2 | 1585.1 |
| 其他 | Other | 234742.1 | 47855.3 | 32537 |
| **按单位规模分** | **By Size of Enterprise** | | | |
| 大型 | Large | 202067.3 | 138219 | 78033.7 |
| 中型 | Medium | 204695.1 | 68579.1 | 72500.4 |
| 小型 | Small | 436820.4 | 516728.8 | 267964.6 |
| 微型 | Micro | 246854 | 36143.7 | 15131.1 |

单位：万元 (10 000 yuan)

| 二、期末资产负债 Assets and Liabilities | 三、损益及分配 Profits and Losses | | | | |
|---|---|---|---|---|---|
| 个人资本 Personal Capital | 营业收入 Gross Sales | 主营业务收入 Main Business Income | 营业成本 Operating Cost | 税金及附加 Taxes and Surcharges | 其他业务利润 Other Business Profits |
| | 563.6 | 563.6 | 489 | 0.4 | |
| | 45768.7 | 45768.7 | 27885.6 | 18.1 | |
| | 45768.7 | 45768.7 | 27885.6 | 18.1 | |
| | 237635.8 | 233242.6 | 204784.2 | 238.5 | 307.4 |
| | 237635.8 | 233242.6 | 204784.2 | 238.5 | 307.4 |
| | | | | | |
| | 169927.9 | 17515.8 | 160183.6 | 559.6 | 3.6 |
| | 7892.1 | 7888.1 | 7964.7 | 4.5 | |
| 176837.4 | 1534016.1 | 1495852.1 | 1089267.9 | 9376.8 | 1939.4 |
| | 45768.7 | 45768.7 | 27885.6 | 18.1 | |
| | 237635.8 | 233242.6 | 204784.2 | 238.5 | 307.4 |
| | 563.6 | 563.6 | 489 | 0.4 | |
| | | | | | |
| 163882.8 | 1151732.3 | 1119050.3 | 844496 | 8358 | 1921.4 |
| 8389.7 | 395819.3 | 386317.2 | 287258.5 | 900.8 | 307.2 |
| 3042.6 | 98388.8 | 97618.8 | 59575.8 | 455.3 | 21.3 |
| 245 | 14678.6 | 14588.7 | 7767.3 | 24.9 | |
| 1277.3 | 335185.2 | 183255.9 | 291477.4 | 458.9 | 0.5 |
| | | | | | |
| 9480 | 523133.4 | 522788.8 | 421465.9 | 791.9 | 306.6 |
| 5862.6 | 245677.7 | 245021.1 | 153992.3 | 1686.2 | 27.3 |
| 154745.9 | 949897.4 | 934680 | 679049.8 | 6628 | 1760.7 |
| 6748.9 | 277095.7 | 98341 | 236067 | 1091.8 | 155.8 |

**表 15.9 续表 8 continued 8**

| 指 标 | Item | 三、损益及分配 Profits and Losses | | |
|---|---|---|---|---|
| | | 销售费用 Sales Expenses | 管理费用 Management Expenses | 研发费用 R&D expenses |
| 其他企业 | Other Enterprises | 5.8 | 23.4 | 0.1 |
| 港、澳、台商投资企业 | Enterprises Funded by Hong Kong, Macao and Taiwan | 12517.2 | 4116.5 | |
| 港澳台商独资企业 | Enterprises with Sole Fund | 12517.2 | 4116.5 | |
| 外商投资企业 | Foreign-funded Enterprises | 9384.4 | 8819.7 | |
| 外资企业 | Enterprises with Sole Fund | 9384.4 | 8819.7 | |
| **按控股情况分** | **By Holding Entity of Share** | | | |
| 国有控股 | State-holding | 4497.6 | 6367.4 | 0.1 |
| 集体控股 | Collective-holding | 14.6 | 34.1 | 0.4 |
| 私人控股 | Private-holding | 194186 | 135775.1 | 1162.7 |
| 港澳台商控股 | Held by Corporation from Hong Kong, Macao and Taiwan | 12517.2 | 4116.5 | |
| 外商控股 | Foreign-holding | 9384.4 | 8819.7 | |
| 其他 | Other | 5.8 | 23.4 | 0.1 |
| **按经营形式分** | **By Form of Business** | | | |
| 独立门店 | Independent Store | 102704 | 104531.3 | 493.8 |
| 连锁总店(总部) | Central Shop of Chain Stores (Headquarter) | 70162.9 | 25449.6 | 467.5 |
| 连锁直营店 | Direct-sale Shop of Chain Stores | 29846.2 | 6543.1 | 173 |
| 连锁加盟店 | Branch Shop of Chain Stores | 6247.8 | 1540.7 | 0.3 |
| 其他 | Other | 11644.7 | 17071.5 | 28.7 |
| **按单位规模分** | **By Size of Enterprise** | | | |
| 大型 | Large | 55750.4 | 23896.8 | 626.2 |
| 中型 | Medium | 52818.2 | 31019.3 | 172.6 |
| 小型 | Small | 100577 | 89574.5 | 298 |
| 微型 | Micro | 11460 | 10645.6 | 66.5 |

单位：万元 (10 000 yuan)

| 三、损益及分配 Profits and Losses | | | | | |
|---|---|---|---|---|---|
| 财务费用<br>Financial Expenses | | | 投资收益<br>Income from Investment | 营业利润<br>Business Profits | 营业外收入<br>Non-business Income |
| | 利息收入<br>Interest Income | 利息费用<br>Interest expenses | | | |
| 0.4 | | 0.4 | | 7.2 | |
| 553.1 | 0.5 | 0.2 | | 678.1 | 244 |
| 553.1 | 0.5 | 0.2 | | 678.1 | 244 |
| 1032.5 | 301.7 | 1047.3 | -122.8 | 16216.6 | 696.8 |
| 1032.5 | 301.7 | 1047.3 | -122.8 | 16216.6 | 696.8 |
| | | | | | |
| 3785.4 | 34.2 | 3795.4 | | -4460.7 | 1990.1 |
| 5 | 3.6 | | | -142.6 | |
| 12336.7 | 1608.3 | 8811.5 | 187.3 | 68985.9 | 4465.4 |
| 553.1 | 0.5 | 0.2 | | 678.1 | 244 |
| 1032.5 | 301.7 | 1047.3 | -122.8 | 16216.6 | 696.8 |
| 0.4 | | 0.4 | | 7.2 | |
| | | | | | |
| 10042.7 | 1537.5 | 7085.6 | 136.9 | 63165.7 | 3099.9 |
| 3298.7 | 386.1 | 2561.7 | 0.1 | 16916.8 | 1445 |
| 478.5 | 2.1 | 278.3 | -122.8 | 1035.6 | 203.9 |
| 111.4 | -0.6 | 103.3 | | -941 | 68.4 |
| 3781.8 | 23.2 | 3625.9 | 50.3 | 1107.4 | 2579.1 |
| | | | | | |
| 3148.8 | 205.8 | 2376.5 | -64.4 | 22448 | 1499.1 |
| 4137.5 | 1176.5 | 4814.5 | 14.9 | -5257.7 | 1765.5 |
| 6116.6 | 501.4 | 2750.9 | 106.9 | 54408.9 | 2195.3 |
| 4310.2 | 64.6 | 3712.9 | 7.1 | 9685.3 | 1936.4 |

表 15.9 续表 9 continued 9

| 指 标 | Item | 三、损益及分配 Profits and Losses 营业外支出 Non-business Expenses | 利润总额 Total Profits |
|---|---|---|---|
| 其他企业 | Other Enterprises | | 7.2 |
| 港、澳、台商投资企业 | Enterprises Funded by Hong Kong, Macao and Taiwan | 703.8 | 218.3 |
| 港澳台商独资企业 | Enterprises with Sole Fund | 703.8 | 218.3 |
| 外商投资企业 | Foreign-funded Enterprises | 911.9 | 16001.6 |
| 外资企业 | Enterprises with Sole Fund | 911.9 | 16001.6 |
| **按控股情况分** | **By Holding Entity of Share** | | |
| 国有控股 | State-holding | 60.8 | -9.6 |
| 集体控股 | Collective-holding | | -142.6 |
| 私人控股 | Private-holding | 1163 | 72080.3 |
| 港澳台商控股 | Held by Corporation from Hong Kong, Macao and Taiwan | 703.8 | 218.3 |
| 外商控股 | Foreign-holding | 911.9 | 16001.6 |
| 其他 | Other | | 7.2 |
| **按经营形式分** | **By Form of Business** | | |
| 独立门店 | Independent Store | 550.8 | 68028.7 |
| 连锁总店（总部） | Central Shop of Chain Stores (Headquarter) | 1790.9 | 16570.9 |
| 连锁直营店 | Direct-sale Shop of Chain Stores | 381.3 | 858.1 |
| 连锁加盟店 | Branch Shop of Chain Stores | 0.7 | -873.3 |
| 其他 | Other | 115.8 | 3570.8 |
| **按单位规模分** | **By Size of Enterprise** | | |
| 大型 | Large | 1669.1 | 22278.1 |
| 中型 | Medium | 375.4 | -3867.6 |
| 小型 | Small | 734.7 | 55732.7 |
| 微型 | Micro | 60.3 | 14012 |

单位：万元 (10 000 yuan)

| 三、损益及分配 Profits and Losses | 四、人工成本及增值税 Labor cost and Value-added Tax | | |
|---|---|---|---|
| 所得税费用<br>Income Tax Payable | 应付职工薪酬<br>Employee compensation | 应交增值税<br>Value-added Tax | 五、从事批发和零售业活动的从业人员平均人数（人）<br>Annual Average Employees Engaged in wholesale and retail activities (persons) |
| 0.4 | 40.3 | 0.7 | 4 |
| 11.6 | 10376.5 | 206.9 | 3100 |
| 11.6 | 10376.5 | 206.9 | 3100 |
| 2005.9 | 49711.1 | 35.7 | 8447 |
| 2005.9 | 49711.1 | 35.7 | 8447 |
| | | | |
| 133.5 | 3666.9 | 577.8 | 870 |
| 2.1 | 1544.1 | 2.4 | 314 |
| 5073.1 | 210907.6 | 13910.3 | 48691 |
| 11.6 | 10376.5 | 206.9 | 3100 |
| 2005.9 | 49711.1 | 35.7 | 8447 |
| 0.4 | 40.3 | 0.7 | 4 |
| | | | |
| 4747.5 | 142040.6 | 13041.8 | 32357 |
| 2098 | 84169.1 | -262.4 | 17979 |
| -41.7 | 19718.4 | 512.6 | 4599 |
| 17.9 | 2949.5 | 119.8 | 526 |
| 404.9 | 27368.9 | 1322 | 5965 |
| | | | |
| 2494.1 | 103153 | -403.1 | 22034 |
| 454.8 | 43254 | 2719.5 | 8969 |
| 3187 | 121494.7 | 11119.7 | 26974 |
| 1090.7 | 8344.8 | 1297.7 | 3449 |

# 表 15.10 按行业和业态分连锁零售企业基本情况 (2022 年)
## BASIC CONDITIONS OF CHAIN RETAIL ENTERPRISES BY SECTOR AND BUSINESS CATEGORIES (2022)

| 指 标 | Item | 总店数（个）Number of Head Stores (unit) | 门店总数（个）Number of Stores (unit) | 年末从业人数（人）Engaged Persons at Year-end (persons) | 年末零售营业面积（平方米）Operating Area of Retail Enterprises at Year-end (sq.m) | 商品销售额（万元）Total Sales of Commodities (10 000 yuan) | 商品购进总额（万元）Purchases Value (10 000 yuan) | 统一配送商品购进额（万元）Centralized Purchase and Delivery (10 000 yuan) |
|---|---|---|---|---|---|---|---|---|
| **总 计** | **Total** | **45** | **5267** | **52669** | **3953086** | **6643157** | **5660316** | **5479293** |
| **按行业分** | **By Sector** | | | | | | | |
| #综合零售 | Integrated Retail | 17 | 952 | 36411 | 3509252 | 5490042 | 4774735 | 4629792 |
| 食品、饮料及烟草制品专门零售 | Retail of Food, Beverages and Tobacco | 3 | 581 | 1720 | 19392 | 75002 | 50200 | 50200 |
| 纺织、服装及日用品专门零售 | Special Retail of Textiles, Garments and Daily Consumer Articles | 4 | 200 | 1007 | 27936 | 43965 | 15624 | 15624 |
| 文化、体育用品及器材专门零售 | Retail of Cultural, Sports Appliances and Equipments | 3 | 168 | 2463 | 43436 | 185926 | 189568 | 187802 |
| 医药及医疗器材专门零售 | Retail of Medicines and Medical Appliances | 15 | 3322 | 10776 | 341999 | 823500 | 607729 | 573413 |
| 汽车、摩托车、燃料及零配件专门零售 | Retail of Motor Vehicles, Motorcycles,Fuel and Parts | 1 | 13 | 15 | 1050 | 2494 | 1980 | 1980 |
| 家用电器及电子产品专门零售 | Special Retail of Household Electrical Appliances and Electronic Products | 2 | 31 | 277 | 10021 | 22228 | 20482 | 20482 |
| 五金、家具及室内装修材料专门零售 | Special Retail of Hardware, Furniture and Decoration Materials | | | | | | | |
| 无店铺及其他零售 | Non-shop and Other Retails | | | | | | | |
| **按业态分** | **By Business Categories** | | | | | | | |
| 便利店 | Convenience Store | | | | | | | |
| 折扣店 | Discount Store | | | | | | | |
| 超 市 | Super Market | 6 | 132 | 2200 | 95020 | 170669 | 137058 | 44795 |
| 大型超市 | Hyper Market | | | | | | | |
| 仓储会员店 | Warehouse Club | 4 | 139 | 2420 | 97512 | 253996 | 223245 | 189254 |
| 百货店 | Department Store | 2 | 178 | 15787 | 1111118 | 1489348 | 1026373 | 1007684 |
| 专业店 | Specialty Store | 21 | 3114 | 23959 | 2316603 | 3832975 | 3496193 | 3461905 |
| #加油站 | Gas Station | | | | | | | |
| 专卖店 | Franchised Store | 8 | 1205 | 6706 | 317564 | 844834 | 748460 | 746667 |
| 集合店 | Collection Store | 4 | 499 | 1597 | 15269 | 51334 | 28988 | 28988 |
| 无人值守店 | Unattended Store | | | | | | | |
| 其 他 | Other Store | | | | | | | |

注：数据为初步数据。
Note:Data is preliminary.

## 表 15.11 按行业分连锁餐饮企业基本情况 (2022 年 )
BASIC CONDITIONS OF CHAIN CATERING ENTERPRISES BY SECTOR (2022)

| 指 标 | Item | 总店数（个） Number of Head Stores (unit) | 门店总数（个） Number of Stores (unit) | 年末从业人员（人） Engaged Persons at Year-end ( persons) | 年末餐饮营业面积（平方米） Operating Area of Catering Enterprises at Year-end(sq.m) | 餐位数（位） Number of Dining-seats ( unit) | 营业额（万元） Business Revenue (10 000 yuan) | 商品购进总额（万元） Total Purchases Value(10 000 yuan) | 统一配送商品购进额（万元） Centralized Purchase and Delivery (10 000 yuan) |
|---|---|---|---|---|---|---|---|---|---|
| **总 计** | **Total** | **8** | **1182** | **27776** | **500772** | **130602** | **722504** | **246530** | **154166** |
| 正餐服务业 | Restaurant | 5 | 383 | 19368 | 357213 | 63829 | 386337 | 146857 | 54493 |
| 快餐服务业 | Fast Food | 3 | 799 | 8408 | 143559 | 66773 | 336167 | 99673 | 99673 |
| 饮料及冷饮服务业 | Beverages and Cold rinks | | | | | | | | |
| 其他餐饮服务业 | Others | | | | | | | | |

## 表 15.12 批发和零售业连锁经营情况（2021 － 2022 年）
OPERATION OF CHAIN ENTERPRISES IN WHOLESALE AND RETAIL TRADES (2021-2022)

| 指 标 | Item | 合 计 Total | | #直营店 Regular Chain | |
|---|---|---|---|---|---|
| | | 2021 | 2022 | 2021 | 2022 |
| 门店总数（个） | Number of Stores(unit) | 6994 | 6956 | 5207 | 5366 |
| 年末从业人员数（人） | Engaged Persons at Year-end(person) | 67873 | 60996 | 64465 | 58041 |
| 年末零售营业面积（平方米） | Business Area of Catering Services at Year-end (sq.m) | 4831504 | 4486380 | 4636010 | 4323625 |
| 连锁门店商品购进额 ( 万元 ) | Total Purchases Value of Chain Retail Stores(10000 yuan) | 8157538 | 8937303 | 7941791 | 8735313 |
| #统一配送商品购进额 | Centralized Purchase and Delivery | 7001236 | 6709160 | 6873797 | 6587209 |
| #自有配送中心配送商品购进额 | Purchases of Self-owned Delivery Center | 4510829 | 5161333 | 4416346 | 5060932 |
| 非自有配送中心配送商品购进额 | Purchases of Non-self-owned Delivery Center | 1926709 | 1299009 | 1924693 | 1297720 |
| 连锁门店商品销售额 ( 万元 ) | Total Sales (Wholesale & Retail)of Chain Retail Stores(10 000 yuan) | 10013472 | 10126365 | 9827852 | 9913063 |
| #零售额 | Retail Sales | 8077784 | 7990594 | 7920810 | 7835145 |

注：数据为初步数据。
Note:Data is preliminary.

## 表 15.13 住宿和餐饮业连锁经营情况（2021 – 2022 年）
## OPERATION OF CHAIN ENTERPRISES IN HOTELS AND CATERING SERVICES (2021-2022)

| 指 标 | Item | 合 计 Total | | 其 中 of which #直营店 Regular Chain | |
|---|---|---|---|---|---|
| | | 2021 | 2022 | 2021 | 2022 |
| 门店总数（个） | Number of Stores(unit) | 1101 | 1182 | 591 | 591 |
| 年末从业人员数（人） | Engaged Persons at Year-end(person) | 31809 | 27776 | 13734 | 11973 |
| 年末餐饮营业面积（平方米） | Business Area of Catering Enterprises at Year-end (sq.m) | 531951 | 500772 | 281295 | 271433 |
| 客房数（间） | Number of Rooms(room) | 357 | 357 | 357 | 357 |
| 床位数（个） | Number of beds(unit) | 635 | 635 | 635 | 635 |
| 餐位数（位） | Number of Dinning-seats(unit) | 136330 | 130602 | 70875 | 67730 |
| 连锁门店商品购进额（万元） | Total Purchases Value of Chain Retail Stores(10 000 yuan) | 264856 | 246530 | 155079 | 129635 |
| #统一配送商品购进额 | Centralized Purchase and Delivery | 172857 | 154166 | 137665 | 113752 |
| #自有配送中心配送商品购进额 | Purchases of Self-owned Delivery Center | 93744 | 80952 | 91769 | 80017 |
| 非自有配送中心配送商品购进额 | Purchases of Non-self-owned Delivery Center | 72743 | 70183 | 39525 | 30703 |
| 连锁门店营业额（万元） | Business Revenue of Chain Retail Stores(10 000 yuan) | 712508 | 722504 | 350311 | 339868 |
| #餐费收入 | From Meals | 694893 | 698234 | 333502 | 320827 |
| 商品销售额 | Total Sales of Commodities | 17615 | 24271 | 16809 | 19041 |

重/庆/统/计/年/鉴

# 主要统计指标解释

## 社会消费品零售总额

指企业（单位、个体户）通过交易直接售给个人、社会集团非生产、非经营用的实物商品金额，以及提供餐饮服务所取得的收入金额。个人包括城乡居民和入境人员，社会集团包括机关、社会团体、部队、学校、企事业单位、居委会或村委会等。

## 批发业

指向其他批发或零售单位（含个体经营者）及其他企事业单位、机关团体等批量销售生活用品、生产资料的活动，以及从事进出口贸易和贸易经纪与代理的活动，包括拥有货物所有权，并以本单位（公司）的名义进行交易活动，也包括不拥有货物的所有权，收取佣金的商品代理、商品代售活动；还包括各类商品批发市场中固定摊位的批发活动，以及以销售为目的的收购活动。

## 零售业

指百货商店、超级市场、专门零售商店、品牌专卖店、售货摊等主要面向最终消费者（如居民等）的销售活动，以互联网、邮政、电话、售货机等方式的销售活动，还包括在同一地点，后面加工生产，前面销售的店铺（如面包房）；谷物、种子、饲料、牲畜、矿产品、生产用原料、化工原料、农用化工产品、机械设备（乘用车、计算机及通信设备除外）等生产资料的销售不作为零售活动；多数零售商对其销售的货物拥有所有权，但有些则是充当委托人的代理人，进行委托销售或以收取佣金的方式进行销售。

## 批发和零售业商品购进、销售、库存额

指各种登记注册类型的批发和零售业企业（单位）以本企业（单位）为总体的，从国内、国外市场购进的商品总量，销售和出口的商品总量，库存的商品总量等情况。该指标可以反映商品流转过程中商品的购进、销售、库存之间的比例关系和存在的问题。

## 商品销售额

指对本单位以外的单位和个人出售的商品金额（包括售给本单位消费用的商品，含增值税）。商品销售包括（1）售给个人和社会集团消费用的商品；（2）售给农业、工业、建筑业、服务业等国民经济各行业用于生产、经营用的商品，包括售予批发和零售业作为转卖或加工后转卖的商品；（3）对国（境）外直接出口的商品。不包括：（1）未通过买卖行为付出的商品，如因机构变动移交给其他企业单位的商品、借出的商品、归还受其他单位委托代保管的商品、付出的加工原料和赠送给其他单位的样品等；（2）促销返券所销售的、不计入营业收入的商品；（3）经本单位介绍，由买卖双方直接结算，本单位只收取手续费的业务；（4）未发生所有权转移的商品预付卡销售，如加油卡；（5）汽车维修、电话卡销售等服务性经济活动；（6）购货退回的商品；（7）商品损耗和损失；（8）出售本单位自用的废旧物资；（9）期货交易商品；（10）自来水供应企业、电力企业、天然气供应企业提供的水、电、气。

## 住宿业

指有偿为顾客提供临时住宿的服务活动。不包括提供长期住宿场所的活动，如出租房屋、公寓等（列入房地产开发经营）。

## 餐饮业

指在一定场所，对食物进行现场烹饪、调制，并出售给顾客主要供现场消费的服务活动。

## 营业额

指住宿和餐饮业单位在经营活动中，因提供服务或销售商品等取得的全部收入（含增值税），收入主要来源于提供客房、餐费服务、商品销售和其他服务，如商务服务。不包括多产业法人企业附营的其他行业产业活动单位的餐费收入、商品销售收入等各项收入。

# 主要统计指标解释

## ■ 连锁总店（总部）

指负责连锁企业资源（商号、商誉、经营模式、服务标准、管理模式等等）的开发、配置、控制或使用等功能的企业核心管理机构。连锁经营是指经营同类商品或服务，使用统一商号的若干店铺，在同一总店（总部）的管理下，采取统一采购或特许经营等方式，实现规模效益的组织形式，包括直营连锁、特许连锁和自愿连锁三种形式。其中，直营连锁是指连锁店铺由连锁公司全资或控股开设，在总部的直接控制下，开展统一经营的连锁经营形式；特许连锁是指拥有注册商标、企业标志、专利、专有技术等经营资源的企业（特许人），以合同形式将其拥有的经营资源许可其他经营者（被特许人）使用，被特许人按合同约定在统一的经营模式下开展经营，并向特许人支付特许经营费用的连锁经营形式；自愿连锁是指若干个店铺或企业自愿组合起来，在不改变各自资产所有权关系的情况下，以同一个品牌形象面对消费者，以共同进货为纽带开展的连锁经营形式。

# Explanatory Notes on Main Statistical Indicators

## Total Retail Sales of Consumer Goods

Refer to the amount obtained by enterprises (units, self-employed individuals) through direct sales of non-production and non-business physical commodity to individuals, social institutions, and revenue from providing catering services. Individuals include rural and urban households, population from abroad, social institutions include government agencies, social organizations, military units, schools, institutions, neighborhood (village) committees.

## Wholesale Trade

Refers to the activities of selling wholesale commodities for daily use and capital goods to enterprises of wholesale and retail trades (including self-employed individuals) and other enterprises, institutions and government organs and organizations, and the activities of engaging in import and export and acting as a trade agent. The wholesaler may have the ownership of the commodities for wholesale and trade in the name of its own (a company), and the wholesaler can act as commission agent or commodity broker without the ownership of commodities. Also included are the wholesale activities at the fixed stalls in wholesale market and the acquisition for sales purpose.

## Retail Trade

Refers to the activities of department store, supermarket, franchised store, brand store, retail stall and on-the-spot-making-selling store selling commodities to the final consumers (residents) by any means including internet, post, telephone, sales machine. It also includes shops with sales and production located in the same places (such as bakeries). Retail trade excludes the activities of sales of capital goods such as grain, seed, feed, livestock, mineral products, raw material for production, industrial chemicals, and chemical products for agricultural use, machine and equipment (excluding vehicles, computers and communication equipment). Most retailers have the ownership of commodities to sell, but some are acting as agents or brokers to make transactions for a commission.

## Purchase, Sales and Stock of Commodities by Wholesale and Retail Trades

Refer to the total volume of commodities purchased, total volume of sales and exports, and the stock of commodities by wholesale and retail enterprises (establishments) of different status of registration from domestic and overseas markets. This indicator reflects the relationship among purchase, sales and stock of commodities in the circulation of goods and reveals the existing problems.

## Total Sales of Commodities

Refer to value of commodities sold by the establishments to other establishments and individuals (including goods sold for self-consumption, including the value-added tax). The commodities include: (1) commodities sold to residents and social groups for their consumption; (2) commodities sold to establishments in all industries for their production and operation, including agriculture, industry, construction, and catering services including commodities sold to wholesale and retail establishments for re-selling, with or without further processing; and (3) commodities for direct export to abroad. Excluded are (1) extended commodities without trading, such as goods handed over to other enterprises and institutions because of the change of organizations, lent goods, returned goods preserved for others, extended processing materials and samples donated to others, (2) goods sold by sales promotion which are not included in operating revenue, (3) goods of direct settlement between buyer and seller with handling fees introduced by others, (4) goods prepaid card without proprietary rights exchange, such as fuel card, (5) service economic activity, such as car repair and phone card sale, (6) goods returned after purchase, (7) damaged and spoiled goods, (8) waste and used goods of self-use, (9) future traded commodities, (10) water, electricity and natural gas provided by water enterprises, electricity enterprises and natural gas enterprises.

## Hotel Services

Refer to the charged accommodation services provided to customers, excluding the long term accommodation service activities such as rental housing and apartments (it is under real estate development and management).

## Catering Services

Refer to the activities of enterprises providing on-the-spot services of selling food cooked and prepared to the customer in certain sites.

## Business Revenue

Refers to revenue of hotels and catering services received from providing services or selling commodities (including added-value tax) through business activities, including income from providing hotels and catering services, from selling of commodities and from other services, such as business services. It does not include catering income, selling income of commodity and other income by attached operation holding by multi-industrial corporation.

## Chain Head Stores (headquarter)

Refer to the core leading stores responsible for development, allocation, administration and utilization of resources (name of stores, brand of stores, operation model, service standard, management way, etc.) of chain stores. Chain stores refers to the stores engaged in providing homogeneous commodities or services, with the central leadership of head store (headquarters) and guided by common policies, conduct centralized purchase and distributed selling of commodities, in order to gain better efficiency through standardized operation. The chain stores include regular chain stores, franchise chain stores and voluntary chain stores.

Regular Chain store refers to chain stores that are invested or controlled by the headquarters. They operate under direct and unified management from the headquarters.

# 第十六章·对外经济贸易和旅游业

FOREIGN ECONOMIC RELATIONS, TRADE AND TOURISM

# 简要说明

## BRIEF INTRODUCTION

本章内容包括全市进出口、利用外资、对外投资合作、旅游情况。进出口、利用外资、对外投资合作、旅游资料由市统计局贸易外经统计处分别根据重庆海关、市商务委、市文化旅游委有关资料整理。

This chapter includes the city's information of import and export, utilization of foreign capital, foreign investment and cooperation, and tourism. Import and export, utilization of foreign capital, foreign investment and cooperation, and tourism materials were sorted out by the Trade and Economic Affairs Department of the Municipal Bureau of Statistics based on relevant materials from Chongqing Customs, Municipal Commission of Commerce, and Municipal Commission of Culture and Tourism.

## 表 16.1 人民币汇率（年平均价）(1985－2022 年)
## REFERENCE EXCHANGE RATE OF RENMINBI (PERIOD AVERAGE) (1985-2022)

单位：人民币元 (RMB yuan)

| 年 份<br>Year | 100 美元<br>100 US Dollars | 100 日元<br>100 Japanese Yen | 100 港元<br>100 Hong Kong Dollars | 100 欧元<br>100 Euros |
|---|---|---|---|---|
| 1985 | 293.66 | 1.2457 | 37.57 | |
| 1986 | 345.28 | 2.0694 | 44.22 | |
| 1987 | 372.21 | 2.5799 | 47.74 | |
| 1988 | 372.21 | 2.9082 | 47.70 | |
| 1989 | 376.51 | 2.7360 | 48.28 | |
| 1990 | 478.32 | 3.3233 | 61.39 | |
| 1991 | 532.33 | 3.9602 | 68.45 | |
| 1992 | 551.46 | 4.3608 | 71.24 | |
| 1993 | 576.20 | 5.2020 | 74.41 | |
| 1994 | 861.87 | 8.4370 | 111.53 | |
| 1995 | 835.10 | 8.9225 | 107.96 | |
| 1996 | 831.42 | 7.6352 | 107.51 | |
| 1997 | 828.98 | 6.8600 | 107.09 | |
| 1998 | 827.91 | 6.3488 | 106.88 | |
| 1999 | 827.83 | 7.2932 | 106.66 | |
| 2000 | 827.84 | 7.6864 | 106.18 | |
| 2001 | 827.70 | 6.8075 | 106.08 | |
| 2002 | 827.70 | 6.6237 | 106.07 | 800.58 |
| 2003 | 827.70 | 7.1466 | 106.24 | 936.13 |
| 2004 | 827.68 | 7.6552 | 106.23 | 1029.00 |
| 2005 | 819.17 | 7.4484 | 105.30 | 1019.53 |
| 2006 | 797.18 | 6.8570 | 102.62 | 1001.90 |
| 2007 | 760.40 | 6.4632 | 97.46 | 1041.75 |
| 2008 | 694.51 | 6.7427 | 89.19 | 1022.27 |
| 2009 | 683.10 | 7.2986 | 88.12 | 952.70 |
| 2010 | 676.95 | 7.7279 | 87.13 | 897.25 |
| 2011 | 645.88 | 8.1050 | 82.97 | 900.11 |
| 2012 | 631.25 | 7.9037 | 81.38 | 810.67 |
| 2013 | 619.32 | 6.3323 | 79.85 | 822.19 |
| 2014 | 614.28 | 5.8196 | 79.22 | 816.51 |
| 2015 | 622.84 | 5.1553 | 80.34 | 691.41 |
| 2016 | 664.23 | 6.1243 | 85.58 | 734.26 |
| 2017 | 675.18 | 6.0244 | 86.64 | 763.03 |
| 2018 | 661.74 | 5.9890 | 84.43 | 780.16 |
| 2019 | 689.85 | 6.3347 | 88.05 | 772.55 |
| 2020 | 689.76 | 6.4626 | 88.93 | 787.55 |
| 2021 | 645.15 | 5.8735 | 83.00 | 762.93 |
| 2022 | 672.61 | 5.1261 | 85.89 | 707.21 |

# 表 16.2 进出口总值（1987 – 2022 年）
## TOTAL VALUE OF IMPORTS AND EXPORTS (1987-2022)

单位：万美元、万元 (USD 10 000, 10 000 yuan)

| 年份<br>Year | 进出口总值<br>Total Imports and Exports | 出口<br>Exports | 进口<br>Imports | 进出口差额<br>Balance of Imports and Exports |
|---|---|---|---|---|
| 1987 | 29681 | 17446 | 12235 | 5211 |
| 1988 | 41078 | 22171 | 18907 | 3264 |
| 1989 | 60299 | 29052 | 31247 | -2195 |
| 1990 | 68095 | 32729 | 35366 | -2637 |
| 1991 | 61950 | 39249 | 22701 | 16548 |
| 1992 | 74244 | 40867 | 33377 | 7490 |
| 1993 | 85470 | 41160 | 44310 | -3150 |
| 1994 | 123957 | 71527 | 52430 | 19097 |
| 1995 | 141859 | 84733 | 57126 | 27607 |
| 1996 | 158543 | 59365 | 99178 | -39813 |
| 1997 | 167843 | 78015 | 89828 | -11813 |
| 1998 | 103386 | 51411 | 51975 | -564 |
| 1999 | 121044 | 49039 | 72005 | -22966 |
| 2000 | 178547 | 99522 | 79025 | 20497 |
| 2001 | 183384 | 110248 | 73136 | 37112 |
| 2002 | 179401 | 109119 | 70282 | 38837 |
| 2003 | 259488 | 158509 | 100979 | 57530 |
| 2004 | 385735 | 209119 | 176616 | 32503 |
| 2005 | 429283 | 252054 | 177229 | 74825 |
| 2006 | 547013 | 335192 | 211821 | 123371 |
| 2007 | 744546 | 450772 | 293774 | 156998 |
| 2008 | 952121 | 572182 | 379939 | 192243 |
| 2009 | 770859 | 428008 | 342851 | 85157 |
| 2010 | 1242634 | 748875 | 493759 | 255116 |
| 2011 | 2921786 | 1983813 | 937973 | 1045840 |
| 2012 | 5320358 | 3857043 | 1463315 | 2393728 |
| 2013 | 6870410 | 4679749 | 2190661 | 2489088 |
| 2014（美元计价）USD | 9545024 | 6340935 | 3204089 | 3136846 |
| 2014（人民币计价）Yuan-denominated | 58632248 | 38947663 | 19684585 | 19263078 |
| 2015（美元计价）USD | 7447656 | 5518994 | 1928662 | 3590332 |
| 2015（人民币计价）Yuan-denominated | 46154929 | 34170285 | 11984644 | 22185641 |
| 2016（美元计价）USD | 6277125 | 4069415 | 2207710 | 1861705 |
| 2016（人民币计价）Yuan-denominated | 41403855 | 26779585 | 14624271 | 12155314 |
| 2017（美元计价）USD | 6660391 | 4259899 | 2400492 | 1859407 |
| 2017（人民币计价）Yuan-denominated | 45082489 | 28837099 | 16245390 | 12591709 |
| 2018（美元计价）USD | 7904012 | 5137710 | 2766302 | 2371408 |
| 2018（人民币计价）Yuan-denominated | 52226127 | 33952757 | 18273370 | 15679387 |
| 2019（美元计价）USD | 8396406 | 5379892 | 3016514 | 2363378 |
| 2019（人民币计价）Yuan-denominated | 57927807 | 37129167 | 20798640 | 16330527 |
| 2020（美元计价）USD | 9417635 | 6052869 | 3364767 | 2688102 |
| 2020（人民币计价）Yuan-denominated | 65133630 | 41874831 | 23258798 | 18616033 |
| 2021（美元计价）USD | 12383293 | 8000637 | 4382656 | 3617981 |
| 2021（人民币计价）Yuan-denominated | 80005889 | 51683270 | 28322619 | 23360651 |
| 2022（美元计价）USD | 12282956 | 7908905 | 4374051 | 3534854 |
| 2022（人民币计价）Yuan-denominated" | 81583530 | 52453186 | 29130344 | 23322842 |

## 表 16.3 利用外资基本情况(1985－2022 年)
## BASIC STATISTICS ON UTILIZATION OF FOREIGN CAPITAL (1985-2022)

单位：万美元 (USD 10 000)

| 年 份<br>Year | 新设外商投资企业数（个）<br>Number of Newly Established Foreign-invested Enterprises (unit) | 合同外资金额<br>Value of Contractual Foreign Capital | 实际使用外资额 (FDI)<br>Realized FDI Value |
|---|---|---|---|
| 1985 | | | 427 |
| 1986 | 6 | 1528 | 790 |
| 1987 | 10 | 774 | 1924 |
| 1988 | 18 | 1913 | 2069 |
| 1989 | 15 | 7141 | 756 |
| 1990 | 55 | 6245 | 332 |
| 1991 | 80 | 4252 | 977 |
| 1992 | 443 | 37919 | 10247 |
| 1993 | 681 | 72892 | 25915 |
| 1994 | 364 | 47932 | 44953 |
| 1995 | 280 | 74567 | 37926 |
| 1996 | 160 | 24232 | 21878 |
| 1997 | 229 | 46017 | 38466 |
| 1998 | 222 | 47577 | 43107 |
| 1999 | 169 | 50688 | 23893 |
| 2000 | 190 | 35716 | 24436 |
| 2001 | 172 | 44261 | 25649 |
| 2002 | 148 | 50215 | 28089 |
| 2003 | 187 | 55301 | 31112 |
| 2004 | 258 | 66315 | 40508 |
| 2005 | 208 | 80213 | 51575 |
| 2006 | 223 | 111558 | 69595 |
| 2007 | 240 | 440499 | 102857 |
| 2008 | 135 | 208757 | 245196 |
| 2009 | 161 | 244278 | 337577 |
| 2010 | 232 | 402848 | 304264 |
| 2011 | 326 | 624570 | 582575 |
| 2012 | 248 | 505724 | 352418 |
| 2013 | 192 | 382459 | 414353 |
| 2014 | 203 | 448258 | 423348 |
| 2015 | 242 | 466628 | 377183 |
| 2016 | 224 | 401022 | 279037 |
| 2017 | 238 | 383207 | 222004 |
| 2018 | 232 | 907480 | 325030 |
| 2019 | 223 | 313177 | 236529 |
| 2020 | 287 | 579291 | 210119 |
| 2021 | 351 | 469016 | 223584 |
| 2022 | 268 | 199462 | 185744 |

注：2004 年起，新签利用外资协议（合同）数、合同外资金额均不含对外借款。
Note: Foreign loans have been excluded from the number of newly signed agreements (contracts) of foreign capital utilization and the value of contractual foreign capital since 2004.

## 表 16.4 对外承包工程（1985－2022 年）
## FOREIGN CONTRACTING PROJECTS (1985-2022)

单位：万美元 (USD 10 000)

| 年 份<br>Year | 新签合同数（个）<br>Number of Newly Signed Contracts (unit) | 新签合同额<br>Value of Newly Signed Contracts | 完成营业额<br>Completed Turnover |
|---|---|---|---|
| 1985 | 9 | 2109 | 572 |
| 1986 | 18 | 1571 | 337 |
| 1987 | 15 | 1540 | 572 |
| 1988 | 13 | 2640 | 2683 |
| 1989 | 27 | 2605 | 2574 |
| 1990 | 14 | 2971 | 2189 |
| 1991 | 16 | 4329 | 2436 |
| 1992 | 19 | 3765 | 2896 |
| 1993 | 13 | 9440 | 2704 |
| 1994 | 45 | 4106 | 4132 |
| 1995 | 33 | 4032 | 3757 |
| 1996 | 35 | 6654 | 3160 |
| 1997 | 22 | 2607 | 2725 |
| 1998 | 24 | 1969 | 3203 |
| 1999 | 235 | 4591 | 3842 |
| 2000 | 231 | 9232 | 5806 |
| 2001 | 232 | 11590 | 6700 |
| 2002 | 117 | 12200 | 7959 |
| 2003 | 94 | 13450 | 8810 |
| 2004 | 81 | 14805 | 10078 |
| 2005 | 70 | 18498 | 12138 |
| 2006 | 72 | 21447 | 16050 |
| 2007 | 67 | 30714 | 20585 |
| 2008 | 55 | 86398 | 30673 |
| 2009 | 80 | 104463 | 36885 |
| 2010 | 48 | 81560 | 45074 |
| 2011 | 49 | 66797 | 43738 |
| 2012 | 42 | 107550 | 58406 |
| 2013 | 104 | 111288 | 103450 |
| 2014 | 132 | 117065 | 103488 |
| 2015 | 91 | 136003 | 120872 |
| 2016 | 105 | 275360 | 133546 |
| 2017 | 92 | 211179 | 170089 |
| 2018 | 79 | 324400 | 102619 |
| 2019 | 119 | 66904 | 100603 |
| 2020 | 58 | 48251 | 57223 |
| 2021 | 39 | 45188 | 42509 |
| 2022 | 54 | 36323 | 30883 |

注：2011 年起数据仅为对外承包工程，不再包含对外劳务合作。
Note: Due to the modification of statistics system, the data only includes the contracted projects with foreign countries and territories since 2011, and foreign labor cooperation not included.

# 表 16.5 国际旅游人数和外汇收入（1983 － 2022 年）
## NUMBER OF INTERNATIONAL TOURISTS AND FOREIGN EXCHANGE EARNINGS (1983-2022)

| 年 份<br>Year | 接待入境旅游人数（人次）<br>Number of Overseas Visitor Arrivals Received (person-time) | #外国人<br>Foreigners | #港澳台同胞<br>Chinese Compatriots from Hong Kong, Macao and Taiwan | 旅游外汇收入（万美元）<br>Foreign Exchange Earnings from Tourism (USD 10 000) | 入境旅游者人均逗留天数（天）<br>Average Staying Period of Overseas Visitors per Capita (day) |
|---|---|---|---|---|---|
| 1983 | 23032 | 18706 | 3997 | 26 | 1.3 |
| 1984 | 28094 | 21110 | 6505 | 259 | 1.7 |
| 1985 | 49508 | 40460 | 8370 | 527 | 2.1 |
| 1986 | 55152 | 44290 | 8904 | 860 | 1.7 |
| 1987 | 60894 | 52177 | 8253 | 1063 | 1.5 |
| 1988 | 64181 | 45193 | 18711 | 1281 | 1.5 |
| 1989 | 41248 | 21454 | 19595 | 1027 | 1.6 |
| 1990 | 69609 | 19913 | 49570 | 1823 | 1.3 |
| 1991 | 81745 | 29625 | 51950 | 2354 | 1.6 |
| 1992 | 141165 | 52949 | 88050 | 3997 | 1.3 |
| 1993 | 135596 | 59140 | 76025 | 4819 | 1.4 |
| 1994 | 138593 | 93408 | 44180 | 5432 | 1.5 |
| 1995 | 142892 | 93625 | 48942 | 6333 | 2.0 |
| 1996 | 161761 | 108163 | 53238 | 7090 | 2.3 |
| 1997 | 259414 | 154919 | 103720 | 10548 | 2.7 |
| 1998 | 163738 | 116288 | 47211 | 8837 | 3.2 |
| 1999 | 184936 | 133629 | 51173 | 9726 | 3.2 |
| 2000 | 266081 | 192863 | 73218 | 13837 | 3.2 |
| 2001 | 313254 | 219214 | 94040 | 16341 | 3.1 |
| 2002 | 461484 | 310934 | 150550 | 21802 | 2.7 |
| 2003 | 234521 | 181744 | 52777 | 11323 | 2.8 |
| 2004 | 434423 | 338892 | 95531 | 20308 | 2.7 |
| 2005 | 523872 | 418076 | 105796 | 26436 | 3.0 |
| 2006 | 603239 | 488249 | 114990 | 30872 | 3.2 |
| 2007 | 761676 | 622427 | 139249 | 38231 | 3.2 |
| 2008 | 871907 | 742792 | 129115 | 44977 | 3.0 |
| 2009 | 1048125 | 847967 | 200158 | 53721 | 3.0 |
| 2010 | 1370231 | 1039598 | 330633 | 70320 | 3.4 |
| 2011 | 1864016 | 1326135 | 537881 | 96806 | 3.9 |
| 2012 | 2242834 | 1526320 | 716514 | 116832 | 3.4 |
| 2013 | 2422605 | 1619340 | 803265 | 126831 | 3.1 |
| 2014 | 2637590 | 1686523 | 951067 | 135444 | 2.7 |
| 2015 | 2825339 | 1888294 | 937045 | 146857 | 2.5 |
| 2016 | 3165843 | 2084166 | 1081677 | 168682 | 2.5 |
| 2017 | 3583545 | 2174307 | 1409238 | 194759 | 2.6 |
| 2018 | 3880233 | 2201956 | 1678277 | 218989 | 2.8 |
| 2019 | 4113439 | 2349382 | 1764057 | 252483 | 2.8 |
| 2020 | 146342 | 76512 | 69830 | 10792 | 4.6 |
| 2021 | 99062 | 49035 | 50027 | 8159 | 5.1 |
| 2022 | 65501 | 42803 | 22698 | 1166 | 1.7 |

# 表 16.6 按商品类别分的进出口总值（2021－2022 年）
## TOTAL VALUE OF IMPORTS AND EXPORTS BY COMMODITY CATEGORY (2021-2022)

单位：万元 (10 000 yuan)

| 商品类别 | Categories of Commodities | 进出口总值 Total Imports and Exports | | 出　口 Exports | | 进　口 Imports | |
|---|---|---|---|---|---|---|---|
| | | 2021 | 2022 | 2021 | 2022 | 2021 | 2022 |
| **总　值** | **Total Value** | **80005889** | **81583530** | **51683270** | **52453186** | **28322619** | **29130344** |
| **按进出口商品类章分** | **By Category of Imported and Exported Goods** | | | | | | |
| 第 1 章 活动物 | Chapter 1 Live Animals | | | | | | |
| 第 2 章 肉及食用杂碎 | Chapter 2 Meat and Edible Meat Offal | 256390 | 423028 | 4634 | 1431 | 251755 | 421596 |
| 第 3 章 鱼、甲壳动物、软体动物及其他水生无脊椎动物 | Chapter 3 Fish, Crustaceans, Molluscs and Other Aquatic Invertebrates | 19560 | 146811 | 6 | 316 | 19554 | 146495 |
| 第 4 章 乳品；蛋品；天然蜂蜜；其他食用动物产品 | Chapter 4 Dairy Produce; Bards' Eggs; Natural Honey; Edible Products of Animal Origin, Not Elsewhere Specified or Included | 47695 | 63202 | 75 | 130 | 47621 | 63073 |
| 第 5 章 其他动物产品 | Chapter 5 Products of Animal Origin, not Elsewhere Specified or Included | 11906 | 14264 | 9530 | 7762 | 2376 | 6502 |
| 第 6 章 活树及其他活植物；鳞茎、根及类似品；插花及装饰用簇叶 | Chapter 6 Live Tree and Other Plants; Bulbs, Roots and the like;Cut Flowers and Omamental Foliage | 71 | 437 | 71 | 421 | | 16 |
| 第 7 章 食用蔬菜、根及块茎 | Chapter 7 Edible Vegetables and Certain Roots and Tubers | 8588 | 12877 | 7456 | 12531 | 1133 | 346 |
| 第 8 章 食用水果及坚果；甜瓜或柑橘属水果的果皮 | Chapter 8 Edible Fruits and Nuts; Peel of Citrus Fruits or Melons | 670589 | 487742 | 14897 | 15624 | 655692 | 472119 |
| 第 9 章 咖啡、茶、马黛茶及调味香料 | Chapter 9 Coffee, Tea, Mate and Spices | 13068 | 19898 | 3546 | 4884 | 9522 | 15014 |
| 第 10 章 谷物 | Chapter 10 Cereals | 17313 | 6015 | 1877 | 1448 | 15436 | 4567 |
| 第 11 章 制粉工业产品；麦芽；淀粉；菊粉；面筋 | Chapter 11 Products of The Milling Industry; Malt; Starches; Inulin;Wheat Gluten | 8497 | | 4190 | | 4307 | |
| 第 12 章 含油子仁及果实；杂项子仁及果仁；工业用或药用植物；稻草、秸秆及饲料 | Chapter 12 Oil Seeds and Oleaginous Fruits; Miscellaneous Grains, Seeds and Fruit; Industrial or Medicinal Plants; Straw and Fodder | 161835 | 197682 | 294 | 1221 | 161541 | 196461 |
| 第 13 章 虫胶；树胶、树脂及其他植物液、汁 | Chapter 13 Lacs; Gums, Resins and Other Vegetable Saps and Extracts | 2716 | | 2208 | | 508 | |
| 第 14 章 编结用植物材料；其他植物产品 | Chapter 14 Vegetable Plaiting Materials; Vegetable Products, Not Elsewhere Specified or Included | 571 | 1121 | 518 | 1068 | 53 | 54 |
| 第 15 章 动、植物或微生物油、脂及其分解产品；精制的食用油脂；动、植物蜡 | Chapter 15 Animal or Vegetable Fats and Oils and Their Cleavage Products; Prepared Edible Fats; Animal or Vegetable Waxes | 142728 | | 67 | | 142661 | |
| 第 16 章 肉、鱼、甲壳动物、软体动物及其他水生无脊椎动物、昆虫的制品 | Chapter 16 Preparations of Meat,of Fish or of Crustaceans, Molluscs or Other Aquatic Invertebrates | 10908 | 10824 | 10663 | 10824 | 245 | |
| 第 17 章 糖及糖食 | Chapter 17 Sugar and Sugar Confectionery | 1692 | 6824 | 59 | 1529 | 1633 | 5296 |
| 第 18 章 可可及可可制品 | Chapter 18 Cocoa and Cocoa Preparations | 726 | 1450 | 11 | 1 | 715 | 1449 |
| 第 19 章 谷物、粮食粉、淀粉或乳的制品；糕饼点心 | Chapter 19 Preparations of Cereals, Flour, Starch or Milk; Pastry-Cooks`Products | 62216 | 72802 | 3315 | 3269 | 58901 | 69533 |
| 第 20 章 蔬菜、水果、坚果或植物其他部分的制品 | Chapter 20 Preparations of Vegetables, Fruits, Nuts or Other Parts of Plants | 18312 | 19694 | 16764 | 17342 | 1548 | 2352 |

**表 16.6 续表 1 continued 1**

单位：万元 (10 000 yuan)

| 商品类别 | Categories of Commodities | 进出口总值 Total Imports and Exports | | 出口 Exports | | 进口 Imports | |
|---|---|---|---|---|---|---|---|
| | | 2021 | 2022 | 2021 | 2022 | 2021 | 2022 |
| 第 21 章 杂项食品 | Chapter 21 Miscellaneous Edible Preparations | 87694 | 68348 | 5027 | 5722 | 82667 | 62626 |
| 第 22 章 饮料、酒及醋 | Chapter 22 Beverages, Spirits and Vinegar | 8842 | 9570 | 1085 | 4303 | 7757 | 5267 |
| 第 23 章 食品工业的残渣及废料；配制的动物饲料 | Chapter 23 Residues and Waste from The Food Industries; Prepared Animal Fodder | 89490 | 54381 | 15688 | 21990 | 73801 | 32392 |
| 第 24 章 烟草、烟草及烟草代用品的制品；非经燃烧吸用的产品，不论是否含有尼古丁；其他供人体摄入尼古丁的含尼古丁的产品 | Chapter 24 Tobacco, Tobacco and Manufactured Tobacco Substitutes;Products for Non-combustion inhalation, Whether or Not Containing Nicotine; Other Nicotine-Containing Products Intended for Human Ingestion of Nicotine | 448 | 7220 | 448 | 7220 | | |
| 第 25 章 盐；硫黄；泥土及石料；石膏料、石灰及水泥 | Chapter 25 Salt; Sulphur; Earths and Stone; Plastering Materials, Lime and Cement | 41272 | | 15404 | | 25868 | |
| 第 26 章 矿砂、矿渣及矿灰 | Chapter 26 Ores, Slag and Ash | 1425325 | 1882151 | 3860 | 9312 | 1421464 | 1872839 |
| 第 27 章 矿物燃料、矿物油及其蒸馏产品；沥青物质；矿物蜡 | Chapter 27 Mineral Fuels, Mineral Oils and Products of Their Distillation; Bituminous Substances; Mineral Waxes | 263569 | 156953 | 763 | 760 | 262807 | 156193 |
| 第 28 章 无机化学品；贵金属、稀土金属、放射性元素及其同位素的有机及无机化合物 | Chapter 28 Inorganic Chemicals; Organic or Inorganic Compounds of Precious Metals, of Rare-Earth Metals, of Radioactive Elements or of Isotopes | 280442 | | 251484 | | 28959 | |
| 第 29 章 有机化学品 | Chapter 29 Organic Chemicals | 675620 | 1122492 | 523277 | 1019359 | 152343 | 103133 |
| 第 30 章 药品 | Chapter 30 Pharmaceutical Products | 219238 | 2006346 | 107914 | 108678 | 111325 | 1897668 |
| 第 31 章 肥料 | Chapter 31 Fertilizers | 158193 | 122462 | 158154 | 120520 | 39 | 1942 |
| 第 32 章 鞣料浸膏及染料浸膏；鞣酸及其衍生物；染料、颜料及其他着色料；油漆及清漆；油灰及其他类似胶黏剂；墨水、油墨 | Chapter 32 Tanning or Dyeing Extracts; Tannins and Their Derivatives; Dyes, Pigments and Other Colouring Matter; Paints and Varnishes; Putty and Other Mastics; Inks | 58580 | 68189 | 20339 | 17359 | 38241 | 50830 |
| 第 33 章 精油及香膏；芳香料制品及化妆盥洗品 | Chapter 33 Essential Oils and Retinoid; Perfumery, Cosmetic or Toilet Preparations | 222361 | 111559 | 5868 | 6361 | 216492 | 105198 |
| 第 34 章 肥皂、有机表面活性剂、洗涤剂、润滑剂、人造蜡、调制蜡、光洁剂、蜡烛及类似品、塑型用膏、“牙科用蜡”及牙科用熟石膏制剂 | Chapter 34 Soap,Organic Surface-Active Agents,Washing Preparations, Lubricating Preparations, Artificial Waxes, Prepared Waxes, Polishing or Scouring Preparations, Candles and Similar Articles, Modelling Pastes, "Dental Waxes" And Dental Preparations With a Basis of Plast | 48493 | | 25066 | | 23427 | |
| 第 35 章 蛋白类物质；改性淀粉；胶；酶 | Chapter 35 Albuminoidal Substances; Modified Starches; Glues; Enzymes | 28358 | 31519 | 7178 | 10032 | 21180 | 21487 |
| 第 36 章 炸药；烟火制品；引火合金；易燃材料制品 | Chapter 36 Explosives; Pyrotechnic Products; Matches; Pyrophoric Alloys; Products; Certain Combustible Preparations | 119 | 81 | 115 | 80 | 4 | |
| 第 37 章 照相及电影用品 | Chapter 37 Photographic or Cinematographic Goods | 87621 | 88447 | 25737 | 26911 | 61884 | 61536 |

表 16.6 续表 2 continued 2

单位: 万元 (10 000 yuan)

| 商品类别 | Categories of Commodities | 进出口总值 Total Imports and Exports | | 出口 Exports | | 进口 Imports | |
|---|---|---|---|---|---|---|---|
| | | 2021 | 2022 | 2021 | 2022 | 2021 | 2022 |
| 第 38 章 杂项化学产品 | Chapter 38 Miscellaneous Chemical Products | 356300 | 345796 | 270585 | 268806 | 85715 | 76990 |
| 第 39 章 塑料及其制品 | Chapter 39 Plastics and Articles Thereof | 576273 | 831733 | 366342 | 637107 | 209931 | 194627 |
| 第 40 章 橡胶及其制品 | Chapter 40 Rubber and Articles Thereof | 260019 | 264813 | 177220 | 188864 | 82799 | 75950 |
| 第 41 章 生皮(毛皮除外)及皮革 | Chapter 41 Raw Hides and Skins(Other Than Fur Skins) and Leather | 4146 | 1434 | 2032 | 1321 | 2114 | 113 |
| 第 42 章 皮革制品;鞍具及挽具;旅行用品、手提包及类似容器;动物肠线(蚕胶丝除外)制品 | Chapter 42 Articles of Leather; Saddlery and Hamess;ravel Goods, Handbags and Similar Containers; Articles of Animal Gut(Other Than Silk-Worm Gut) | 90036 | 167656 | 82986 | 150988 | 7050 | 16668 |
| 第 43 章 毛皮、人造毛皮及其制品 | Chapter 43 Fur Skins and Artificial Fur; Manufactures Thereof | 1605 | 567 | 1605 | 567 | | 0 |
| 第 44 章 木及木制品;木炭 | Chapter 44 Wood and Articles of Wood; Wood Charcoal; | 327407 | 175152 | 21876 | 28841 | 305531 | 146311 |
| 第 45 章 软木及软木制品 | Chapter 45 Cork and Articles of Cork | 120 | 65 | 119 | 62 | 2 | 4 |
| 第 46 章 稻草、秸秆、针茅或其他编结材料制品;篮筐及柳条编织品 | Chapter 46 Manufactures of Straw, of Esparto or of Other Plaiting Materials; Basket Ware and Wickerwork | 1566 | 3075 | 1566 | 3075 | | 0 |
| 第 47 章 木浆及其他纤维状纤维素浆;回收(废碎)纸及纸板 | Chapter 47 Pulp of Wood or of Other Fibrous Cellulosic Material; Waste and Scrap of Paper or Paperboard | 868422 | 787879 | 133 | 379 | 868289 | 787499 |
| 第 48 章 纸及纸板;纸浆、纸或纸板制品 | Chapter 48 Paper and Paperboard; Articles of Paper Pulp, of Paper or Paperboard | 124623 | 175682 | 83478 | 118481 | 41146 | 57202 |
| 第 49 章 书籍、报纸、印刷图画及其他印刷品;手稿、打字稿及设计图纸 | Chapter 49 Printed Books, Newspapers, Pictures and Other Products of The Printing Industry; Manuscripts, Typescripts and Plans | 121549 | 121844 | 11329 | 14978 | 110220 | 106866 |
| 第 50 章 蚕丝 | Chapter 50 Silk | 8041 | 10219 | 7993 | 10213 | 48 | 6 |
| 第 51 章 羊毛、动物细毛或粗毛;马毛纱线及其机织物 | Chapter 51 Wool, Fine or Coarse Animal Hair;Horsehair Yam and Woven Fabric | 100 | 87 | 83 | 52 | 16 | 36 |
| 第 52 章 棉花 | Chapter 52 Cotton | 5562 | 8701 | 5472 | 8333 | 90 | 368 |
| 第 53 章 其他植物纺织纤维;纸纱线及其机织物 | Chapter 53 Other Vegetable Textile Fibres; Paper Yam and Woven Fabrics of Paper Yam | 2650 | 2021 | 2638 | 1991 | 12 | 29 |
| 第 54 章 化学纤维长丝;化学纤维纺织材料制扁条及类似品 | Chapter 54 Man-Made Filaments;Flat Strips and Similar Products of Chemical Fiber Textile Materials | 91117 | 56165 | 78960 | 54936 | 12157 | 1229 |
| 第 55 章 化学纤维短纤 | Chapter 55 Man-Made Short Fibres | 27148 | 33470 | 26410 | 31738 | 737 | 1732 |
| 第 56 章 絮胎、毡呢及无纺织物;特种纱线;线、绳、索、缆及其制品 | Chapter 56 Wadding, Felt and Nonwoven; Special Yams; Twine,Cordage, Ropes and Cables and Articles Thereof | 46720 | 29447 | 26900 | 24620 | 19820 | 4828 |
| 第 57 章 地毯及纺织材料的其他铺地制品 | Chapter 57 Carpets and Other Textile Floor Coverings | 5107 | 6897 | 5098 | 6858 | 9 | 39 |
| 第 58 章 特种机织物;簇绒织物;花边;装饰毯;装饰带;刺绣品 | Chapter 58 Special Woven Fabrics; Tufted Textile Fabrics;Lace; Tapestries; Trimmings; Embroidery | 7182 | 16268 | 5296 | 13890 | 1887 | 2378 |
| 第 59 章 浸渍、涂布、包覆或层压的纺织物;工业用纺织制品 | Chapter 59 Impregnated, Coated, Covered or Laminated Textile Fabrics; Textile Articles of a Kind Suitable for Industrial Use | 25700 | 26141 | 6661 | 11020 | 19039 | 15120 |

**表 16.6 续表 3 continued 3**

单位：万元 (10 000 yuan)

| 商品类别 | Categories of Commodities | 进出口总值 Total Imports and Exports | | 出口 Exports | | 进口 Imports | |
|---|---|---|---|---|---|---|---|
| | | 2021 | 2022 | 2021 | 2022 | 2021 | 2022 |
| 第 60 章 针织物及钩编织物 | Chapter 60 Knitted or Crocheted Fabrics | 6937 | 21454 | 4175 | 17549 | 2762 | 3905 |
| 第 61 章 针织或钩编的服装及衣着附件 | Chapter 61 Articles of Apparel and Clothing Accessories, Knitted or Crocheted | 105894 | 236608 | 102929 | 229898 | 2965 | 6710 |
| 第 62 章 非针织或非钩编的服装及衣着附件 | Chapter 62 Articles of Apparel and Clothing Accessories,not Knitted or Crocheted | 71414 | | 64816 | | 6598 | |
| 第 63 章 其他纺织制成品；成套物品；旧衣着及旧纺织品；碎织物 | Chapter 63 Other Made Up Textile Articles;Sets; Worn Clothing And Worn Textile Articles; Rags Articles; Rags | 101669 | 86888 | 99259 | 86164 | 2410 | 724 |
| 第 64 章 鞋靴、护腿和类似品及其零件 | Chapter 64 Footwear, Gaiters and The Like; Parts of Such Articles | 79701 | 150695 | 74667 | 143024 | 5033 | 7670 |
| 第 65 章 帽类及其零件 | Chapter 65 Headgear and Parts Thereof | 7952 | 16508 | 7876 | 16330 | 76 | 178 |
| 第 66 章 雨伞、阳伞、手杖、鞭子、马鞭及其零件 | Chapter 66 Umbrellas, Sun Umbrellas, Walking-Sticks,Seat-Sticks, Whips, Riding-Crops And Parts Thereof | 2551 | 3888 | 2551 | 3883 | 1 | 5 |
| 第 67 章 已加工羽毛、羽绒及其制品；人造花；人发制品 | Chapter 67 Prepared Feathers and Down and Articles;Made of Feathers or of Down; Artificial Flowers; Articles of Human Hair | 60530 | 77293 | 57311 | 73360 | 3219 | 3933 |
| 第 68 章 石料、石膏、水泥、石棉、云母及类似材料的制品 | Chapter 68 Articles of Stone, Plaster, Cement,Asbestos, Mica or Similar Materials | 58136 | 71003 | 53147 | 63813 | 4989 | 7190 |
| 第 69 章 陶瓷产品 | Chapter 69 Ceramic Products | 274603 | 346282 | 257817 | 327651 | 16786 | 18631 |
| 第 70 章 玻璃及其制品 | Chapter 70 Glass and Glassware | 553520 | 546254 | 183615 | 211962 | 369905 | 334292 |
| 第71章 天然或养殖珍珠、宝石或半宝石、贵金属、包贵金属及其制品；仿首饰；硬币 | Chapter 71 Natural or Cultured Pearls, Precious or Semi-Precious Stones, Precious Metals, Metals Clad With Metal and Articles Thereof; Imitation Jewellery; Coin | 238096 | | 42423 | | 195673 | |
| 第 72 章 钢铁 | Chapter 72 Iron and Steel | 577972 | 586653 | 131377 | 213704 | 446595 | 372949 |
| 第 73 章 钢铁制品 | Chapter 73 Articles of Iron or Steel | 341863 | 456662 | 302744 | 421889 | 39119 | 34773 |
| 第 74 章 铜及其制品 | Chapter 74 Copper and Articles Thereof | 802430 | 917291 | 93804 | 107176 | 708626 | 810115 |
| 第 75 章 镍及其制品 | Chapter 75 Nickel and Articles Thereof | 17916 | 8357 | 1002 | 3029 | 16914 | 5328 |
| 第 76 章 铝及其制品 | Chapter 76 Aluminium and Articles Thereof | 340972 | 505057 | 266909 | 409464 | 74063 | 95593 |
| 第 78 章 铅及其制品 | Chapter 78 Lead and Articles Thereof | 57846 | 44508 | 57179 | 43885 | 667 | 623 |
| 第 79 章 锌及其制品 | Chapter 79 Zinc and Articles Thereof | 8503 | 15050 | 803 | 12831 | 7700 | 2219 |
| 第 80 章 锡及其制品 | Chapter 80 Tin and Articles Thereof | 5299 | 5395 | 170 | 97 | 5129 | 5298 |
| 第 81 章 其他贱金属、金属陶瓷及其制品 | Chapter 81 Other Base Metals; Cermets; Articles Thereof | 31568 | 17090 | 24900 | 14349 | 6667 | 2741 |

**表 16.6 续表 4 continued 4**

单位：万元 (10 000 yuan)

| 商品类别 | Categories of Commodities | 进出口总值 Total Imports and Exports | | 出口 Exports | | 进口 Imports | |
|---|---|---|---|---|---|---|---|
| | | 2021 | 2022 | 2021 | 2022 | 2021 | 2022 |
| 第82章 贱金属工具器具、利口器、餐匙、餐叉及其零件 | Chapter 82 Tools, Implements, Cutlery, Spoons and Forks,of Base Metal; Parts Thereof of Base Metal | 114706 | 131518 | 108082 | 126084 | 6624 | 5434 |
| 第83章 贱金属杂项制品 | Chapter 83 Miscellaneous Articles of Base Metal | 126909 | 191303 | 114400 | 178481 | 12510 | 12822 |
| 第84章 核反应堆、锅炉、机器、机械器具及零件 | Chapter 84 Nuclear Reactors, Boilers, Machinery and Mechanical Appliances; Parts Thereof | 33378426 | 29868661 | 28264118 | 25491767 | 5114308 | 4376894 |
| 第85章 电机、电气设备及其零件；录音机及放声机、电视图像、声音的录制和重放设备及其零件、附件 | Chapter 85 Electrical Machinery and Equipment and Parts Thereof; Sound Recorders and Reproducers, Television Image and Sound Recorders and Reproducers, and Parts and Accessories of Such Articles | 26918892 | 27084674 | 13063691 | 12657913 | 13855201 | 14426760 |
| 第86章 铁道及电车道机车、车辆及其零件；铁道及电车道轨道固定装置及其零件；附件；各种机械（包括电动机械）交通信号设备 | Chapter 86 Railway or Tramway Locomotives, Rolling-Stock and Parts Thereof; Railway or Tramway Track Fixtures And Fittings and Parts Thereof;Mechanical(Including Electro-Mechanical) Traffic Signalling Equipment of All Kinds | 14556 | 11014 | 14556 | 10759 | | 255 |
| 第87章 车辆及其零件、附件，但铁道及电车道车辆除外 | Chapter 87 Vehicles Other Than Railway or Tramway Rolling-Stock, and Parts and Accessories Thereof | 4467706 | 4837668 | 3608314 | 4438144 | 859392 | 399525 |
| 第88章 航空器、航天器及其零件 | Chapter 88 Aircraft, Spacecraft, and Parts Thereof | 22161 | 3422 | 17554 | 1037 | 4606 | 2386 |
| 第89章 船舶及浮动结构体 | Chapter 89 Ships, Boats and Floating Structures | 1325 | 37765 | 1325 | 37764 | | 1 |
| 第90章 光学、照相、电影、计量、检验、医疗或外科用仪器及设备、精密仪器及设备；上述物品的零件、附件 | Chapter 90 Optical, Photographic, Cinematographic, Measuring,Checking, Precision Medical or Surgical Instruments and Apparatus; Parts and Accessories Thereof | 1963292 | | 1250774 | | 712517 | |
| 第91章 钟表及其零件 | Chapter 91 Clocks and Watches and Parts Thereof | 31900 | 23166 | 10853 | 16373 | 21048 | 6793 |
| 第92章 乐器及其零件、附件 | Chapter 92 Musical Instruments; Parts and Accessories of Such Articles | 5731 | 6234 | 5230 | 5968 | 501 | 266 |
| 第93章 武器、弹药及其零件、附件 | Chapter 93 Arms and Ammunition; Parts and Accessories Thereof | 9774 | 2769 | 9774 | 2768 | | 1 |
| 第94章 家具；寝具、褥垫、弹簧床垫、软坐垫及类似的填充制品；未列名灯具及照明装置；发光标志、发光铭牌及类似品；活动房屋 | Chapter 94 Furniture; Bedding, Mattresses, Mattress Supports,Cushions and Similar Stuffed Furnishings; Lamps and Lighting Fittings, not Elsewhere Specified or Included; Illuminated Signs, Illuminated | 372865 | 543949 | 357639 | 531927 | 15226 | 12022 |
| 第95章 玩具、游戏品、运动用品及其零件、附件 | Chapter 95 Toys, Games and Sports Requisites; Parts and Accessories Thereof | 448558 | | 443342 | | 5217 | |
| 第96章 杂项制品 | Chapter 96 Miscellaneous Manufactured Articles | 44605 | 64762 | 41855 | 63449 | 2750 | 1314 |
| 第97章 艺术品、收藏品及古物 | Chapter 97 Works of Art, Collectors' Pieces and Antiques | 152646 | 237913 | 66078 | 125493 | 86569 | 112420 |

# 表 16.7 按贸易方式分的进出口总值(2021 – 2022 年)
## TOTAL VALUE OF IMPORTS AND EXPORTS BY CUSTOMS REGIME (2021-2022)

单位:万元 (10 000 yuan)

| 指 标 | Item | 进出口总值 Total Imports and Exports | | 出 口 Exports | | 进 口 Imports | |
|---|---|---|---|---|---|---|---|
| | | 2021 | 2022 | 2021 | 2022 | 2021 | 2022 |
| **总 计** | **Total** | **80005889** | **81583530** | **51683270** | **52453186** | **28322619** | **29130344** |
| 一般贸易 | Ordinary Trade | 26875550 | 29281562 | 15810043 | 19209224 | 11065507 | 10072339 |
| 国家间、国际组织间无偿援助和赠送的物资 | Donations by Foreign Countries and International Associations | 811 | | 811 | | | |
| 其他捐赠物资 | Other Donations from Abroad | 116 | 421 | 76 | 413 | 39 | 7 |
| 加工贸易 | Processing Trade | 36300238 | 35399523 | 30842807 | 28604624 | 5457430 | 6794899 |
| 来料加工贸易 | Compensation Trade | 2125354 | 4181343 | 662139 | 1082507 | 1463215 | 3098836 |
| 进料加工贸易 | Processing and Assembling Trade | 34174884 | 31218179 | 30180668 | 27522117 | 3994215 | 3696062 |
| 边境小额贸易 | Feeding Processing Trade | 1551 | | 1551 | | | |
| 对外承包工程出口货物 | Consignment Trade | 2941 | 4903 | 2941 | 4903 | | |
| 租赁贸易 | Petty Trade in Border Areas (excluding the barter trade between border residents) | 184 | 160 | 184 | 160 | | |
| 外商投资企业作为投资进口的设备、物品 | Goods Exportation for Contracted Projects with Foreign Countries | 41489 | 36093 | | | 41489 | 36093 |
| 出料加工贸易 | Leasing Trade | | 270 | | 116 | | 154 |
| 保税物流 | Imported Equipment and Materials as Investment of Foreign-funded Enterprises | 16517090 | 16591187 | 4988413 | 4603395 | 11528677 | 11987792 |
| 海关保税监管场所进出境货物 | Outward Processing Trade | 992185 | 837617 | 497523 | 262246 | 494662 | 575371 |
| 海关特殊监管区域物流货物 | Barter Trade | 15524905 | 15753570 | 4490890 | 4341149 | 11034015 | 11412421 |
| 海关特殊监管区域进口设备 | Tax-free Commodities on Foreign Exchange | 174811 | 162999 | | | 174811 | 162999 |
| 其他贸易 | Bonded Logistics | 91109 | 106180 | 36443 | 30194 | 54666 | 75985 |

# 表 16.8 按国别（地区）分的进出口总值（2021 – 2022 年）
## IMPORTS AND EXPORTS BY COUNTRIES OR REGIONS (2021-2022)

单位：万元 (10 000 yuan)

| 国 别（地区） | Country (Region) | 进出口总值 Total Imports and Exports | | 出 口 Exports | | 进 口 Imports | |
|---|---|---|---|---|---|---|---|
| | | 2021 | 2022 | 2021 | 2022 | 2021 | 2022 |
| **进出口贸易总值** | **Total Import-Export Value** | **80005889** | **81583530** | **51683270** | **52453186** | **28322619** | **29130344** |
| **亚 洲** | **Asia** | **42485017** | **43550819** | **20414322** | **22455992** | **22070695** | **21094826** |
| 巴 林 | Bahrain | 12812 | 22002 | 12625 | 21911 | 187 | 91 |
| 孟加拉国 | Bangladesh | 148261 | 163495 | 147636 | 163222 | 625 | 273 |
| 文 莱 | Brunei | 3373 | 2765 | 1420 | 2765 | 1954 | |
| 缅 甸 | Burma | 107653 | 116966 | 99025 | 111521 | 8629 | 5444 |
| 柬埔寨 | Cambodia | 81096 | 130574 | 79996 | 128638 | 1101 | 1936 |
| 朝 鲜 | DPRK | 33 | 499 | 33 | 499 | | |
| 中国香港 | Hong Kong (China) | 7313154 | 5610899 | 7298118 | 5602866 | 15036 | 8033 |
| 印 度 | India | 2126678 | 2340992 | 2029567 | 2289900 | 97111 | 51092 |
| 印度尼西亚 | Indonesia | 1326885 | 1512949 | 818101 | 1049213 | 508784 | 463736 |
| 伊 朗 | Iran | 54120 | 64386 | 54038 | 64359 | 82 | 27 |
| 伊拉克 | Iraq | 72668 | 101817 | 71900 | 101455 | 767 | 362 |
| 以色列 | Israel | 88792 | 132252 | 72672 | 106483 | 16120 | 25769 |
| 日 本 | Japan | 3418548 | 3027902 | 1498159 | 1587604 | 1920388 | 1440298 |
| 约 旦 | Jordan | 28490 | 38124 | 28487 | 38123 | 3 | 1 |
| 科威特 | Kuwait | 35113 | 76027 | 35113 | 76027 | | |
| 老 挝 | Laos | 38503 | 47537 | 38329 | 25934 | 174 | 21603 |
| 黎巴嫩 | Lebanon | 6781 | 20264 | 6781 | 20264 | | |
| 中国澳门 | Macao (China) | 5616 | 7314 | 5616 | 7165 | | 149 |
| 马来西亚 | Malaysia | 2471245 | 2419538 | 583258 | 779074 | 1887987 | 1640464 |
| 马尔代夫 | Maldives | 2236 | 4199 | 2236 | 4199 | | |
| 蒙 古 | Mongolia | 153159 | 167873 | 9092 | 13573 | 144067 | 154300 |
| 尼泊尔联邦民主共和国 | Nepal | 24046 | 28425 | 24046 | 28425 | | |
| 阿 曼 | Oman | 35463 | 28904 | 19391 | 28826 | 16071 | 78 |
| 巴基斯坦 | Pakistan | 439743 | 407073 | 436544 | 405445 | 3199 | 1628 |
| 巴勒斯坦 | Palestine | 960 | 1737 | 960 | 1737 | | |
| 菲律宾 | Philippines | 908799 | 905334 | 587696 | 747216 | 321103 | 158118 |
| 卡塔尔 | Qatar | 30998 | 32585 | 24847 | 32472 | 6151 | 113 |
| 沙特阿拉伯 | Saudi Arabia | 398903 | 748608 | 384811 | 721526 | 14091 | 27082 |
| 新加坡 | Singapore | 753817 | 814772 | 492608 | 544147 | 261209 | 270625 |
| 韩 国 | South Korea | 5192897 | 7856899 | 1416568 | 2671418 | 3776329 | 5185480 |
| 斯里兰卡 | Sri Lanka | 31660 | 18402 | 31506 | 18383 | 155 | 18 |
| 叙利亚 | Syria | 3575 | 2136 | 3575 | 2136 | | |
| 泰 国 | Thailand | 2111073 | 1850346 | 679005 | 710973 | 1432068 | 1139372 |
| 土耳其 | Turkey | 409780 | 477076 | 394792 | 453004 | 14988 | 24072 |
| 阿联酋 | UAE | 628898 | 864182 | 585054 | 856181 | 43844 | 8001 |
| 也 门 | Yemen | 7006 | 9454 | 7006 | 9454 | | |
| 越 南 | Vietnam | 5120898 | 4862418 | 1334044 | 1426085 | 3786854 | 3436333 |
| 中华人民共和国 | China | | 2073659 | | | | 2073659 |
| 中国台湾 | Taiwan (China) | 6469476 | 6251000 | 1027189 | 1462498 | 5442288 | 4788502 |
| 哈萨克斯坦 | Kazakhstan | 227733 | 255710 | 49250 | 87542 | 178483 | 168168 |
| 吉尔吉斯斯坦 | Kyrgyzstan | 1581 | 3307 | 1581 | 3307 | | |
| **非 洲** | **Africa** | **1733831** | **2463705** | **1433878** | **1774805** | **299953** | **688900** |
| 阿尔及利亚 | Algeria | 22837 | 22990 | 22837 | 22350 | | 640 |
| 安哥拉 | Angora | 27999 | 74884 | 27999 | 74884 | | |
| 贝 宁 | Benin | 11439 | 10118 | 11438 | 10118 | | |
| 布隆迪 | Burundi | 1612 | 4576 | 1612 | 4576 | | |

**表 16.8 续表 1 continued 1**

单位：万元 (10 000 yuan)

| 国 别(地区) | Country (Region) | 进出口总值 Total Imports and Exports | | 出 口 Exports | | 进 口 Imports | |
|---|---|---|---|---|---|---|---|
| | | 2021 | 2022 | 2021 | 2022 | 2021 | 2022 |
| 喀麦隆 | Cameroon | 13506 | 27032 | 13504 | 27032 | 3 | |
| 刚 果(布) | Congo | 1696 | 27759 | 1696 | 7094 | | 20665 |
| 吉布提 | Djibouti | 6235 | 25397 | 6235 | 25397 | | |
| 埃 及 | Egypt | 117648 | 72121 | 114155 | 69196 | 3493 | 2925 |
| 埃塞俄比亚 | Ethiopia | 47319 | 34955 | 18670 | 12579 | 28649 | 22376 |
| 加 蓬 | Gabon | 27305 | 21956 | 2803 | 3039 | 24502 | 18917 |
| 加 纳 | Ghana | 56045 | 64093 | 53542 | 64093 | 2503 | |
| 几内亚 | Guinea | 44040 | 194383 | 21308 | 20315 | 22733 | 174068 |
| 科特迪瓦 | Cote d'Ivoire | 58683 | 67456 | 40313 | 47139 | 18370 | 20317 |
| 肯尼亚 | Kenya | 52457 | 82327 | 52450 | 82063 | 7 | 264 |
| 利比里亚 | Liberia | 6598 | 7961 | 6598 | 7961 | | |
| 利比亚 | Libya | 24289 | 24777 | 24289 | 24777 | | |
| 马达加斯加 | Madagascar | 17827 | 22707 | 17799 | 22672 | 28 | 35 |
| 马 里 | Mali | 21781 | 25745 | 21781 | 25745 | | |
| 毛里塔尼亚 | Mauritania | 5797 | 4846 | 5797 | 4846 | | |
| 毛里求斯 | Mauritius | 7603 | 8053 | 7602 | 8048 | | 5 |
| 摩洛哥 | Morocco | 75734 | 71362 | 74650 | 67393 | 1084 | 3969 |
| 莫桑比克 | Mozambique | 123314 | 151013 | 60585 | 52782 | 62728 | 98231 |
| 纳米比亚 | Namibia | 19195 | 4651 | 17926 | 4651 | 1269 | |
| 尼日利亚 | Nigeria | 267508 | 394550 | 267257 | 394228 | 250 | 322 |
| 塞内加尔 | Senegal | 51319 | 49152 | 51319 | 49152 | | |
| 塞拉利昂 | Sierra Leone | 7229 | 31137 | 3012 | 2699 | 4217 | 28439 |
| 南 非 | South Africa | 295538 | 411358 | 224432 | 314217 | 71106 | 97141 |
| 苏 丹 | Sudan | 8619 | 7735 | 8619 | 7735 | | |
| 坦桑尼亚 | Tanzania | 41274 | 92968 | 34048 | 71218 | 7226 | 21750 |
| 多 哥 | Togo | 47575 | 37495 | 47450 | 37495 | 125 | |
| 突尼斯 | Tunisia | 29302 | 42195 | 28194 | 41451 | 1108 | 744 |
| 乌干达 | Uganda | 7121 | 8320 | 6582 | 8320 | 539 | |
| 布基纳法索 | Burkina Faso | 34352 | 25107 | 34352 | 25107 | | |
| 刚 果(金) | Democratic Republic of the Congo | 76037 | 205588 | 34882 | 43448 | 41155 | 162140 |
| 津巴布韦 | Zimbabwe | 17340 | 21990 | 17340 | 21989 | | |
| **欧 洲** | **Europe** | **15685770** | **15561163** | **12816896** | **12395055** | **2868874** | **3166109** |
| 比利时 | Belgium | 194310 | 206683 | 177080 | 189632 | 17230 | 17051 |
| 丹 麦 | Demark | 45593 | 71096 | 27950 | 40622 | 17643 | 30474 |
| 英 国 | UK | 1320157 | 1172074 | 1213115 | 1073046 | 107042 | 99027 |
| 德 国 | Germany | 5804027 | 5121374 | 5033721 | 4524347 | 770306 | 597027 |
| 法 国 | France | 1015091 | 764102 | 654956 | 615733 | 360135 | 148369 |
| 爱尔兰 | Ireland | 70179 | 1121639 | 57742 | 123710 | 12437 | 997929 |
| 意大利 | Italy | 607850 | 544767 | 483913 | 416893 | 123937 | 127874 |
| 卢森堡 | Luxembourg | 18800 | 2508 | 357 | 272 | 18443 | 2236 |
| 荷 兰 | Holland | 1421179 | 1412681 | 1353448 | 1345700 | 67731 | 66981 |
| 希 腊 | Greece | 215920 | 414666 | 215830 | 414133 | 89 | 534 |
| 葡萄牙 | Portugal | 93383 | 56899 | 85973 | 51339 | 7410 | 5559 |
| 西班牙 | Spain | 309871 | 430850 | 240976 | 398517 | 68894 | 32332 |
| 阿尔巴尼亚 | Albania | 4697 | 5649 | 4282 | 5266 | 415 | 382 |
| 奥地利 | Austria | 93451 | 213356 | 33140 | 130621 | 60310 | 82735 |
| 保加利亚 | Bulgaria | 42546 | 16933 | 12448 | 15644 | 30098 | 1289 |
| 芬 兰 | Finland | 63573 | 57553 | 30288 | 26018 | 33285 | 31535 |
| 匈牙利 | Hungary | 277896 | 190591 | 269153 | 179923 | 8743 | 10667 |
| 马耳他 | Malta | 7962 | 6238 | 2701 | 2078 | 5261 | 4161 |
| 挪 威 | Norway | 24675 | 18786 | 15631 | 12574 | 9044 | 6212 |

**表 16.8 续表 2 continued 2**

单位：万元 (10 000 yuan)

| 国 别(地区) | Country (Region) | 进出口总值 Total Imports and Exports | | 出 口 Exports | | 进 口 Imports | |
|---|---|---|---|---|---|---|---|
| | | 2021 | 2022 | 2021 | 2022 | 2021 | 2022 |
| 波 兰 | Poland | 874698 | 820508 | 842927 | 802313 | 31771 | 18194 |
| 罗马尼亚 | Romania | 137117 | 129167 | 115324 | 110865 | 21793 | 18302 |
| 瑞 典 | Sweden | 138577 | 150617 | 93672 | 99548 | 44905 | 51069 |
| 瑞 士 | Switzerland | 200238 | 438616 | 123229 | 380587 | 77009 | 58029 |
| 爱沙尼亚 | Estonia | 10505 | 15542 | 9708 | 14504 | 798 | 1038 |
| 拉脱维亚 | Latvia | 13585 | 13923 | 13436 | 13889 | 149 | 34 |
| 立陶宛 | Lithuania | 23343 | 22660 | 23310 | 22659 | 33 | 2 |
| 格鲁吉亚 | Georgia | 17251 | 30825 | 17113 | 30630 | 138 | 195 |
| 亚美尼亚 | Armenia | 1561 | 3353 | 1561 | 3284 | | 69 |
| 阿塞拜疆 | Azerbaijan | 16013 | 22432 | 16013 | 22432 | | |
| 俄罗斯联邦 | Russia | 1463116 | 1270969 | 813872 | 667745 | 649245 | 603224 |
| 乌克兰 | Ukraine | 177429 | 48541 | 108007 | 44376 | 69422 | 4165 |
| 斯洛文尼亚 | Slovenia | 25369 | 33227 | 18531 | 30271 | 6838 | 2957 |
| 克罗地亚 | Croatia | 23553 | 20911 | 23398 | 20729 | 156 | 182 |
| 捷 克 | Czech | 615704 | 494439 | 578254 | 470190 | 37450 | 24249 |
| 斯洛伐克 | Slovakia | 251876 | 139243 | 53697 | 41674 | 198180 | 97569 |
| 塞尔维亚 | Serbia | 22276 | 8722 | 22199 | 8570 | 77 | 152 |
| **拉丁美洲** | **Latin America** | **4941164** | **5493309** | **3918317** | **4162663** | **1022847** | **1330646** |
| 阿根廷 | Argentina | 164669 | 236959 | 129302 | 155389 | 35367 | 81570 |
| 伯利兹 | Belize | 2988 | 3406 | 2988 | 3406 | | |
| 多民族玻利维亚国 | Bolivia | 30636 | 32893 | 30026 | 30898 | 609 | 1995 |
| 巴 西 | Brazil | 1046599 | 1159019 | 489871 | 513951 | 556728 | 645068 |
| 智 利 | Chile | 753571 | 671383 | 592434 | 500350 | 161137 | 171033 |
| 哥伦比亚 | Columbia | 414004 | 490473 | 412883 | 481523 | 1121 | 8950 |
| 哥斯达黎加 | Costa Rica | 42465 | 62597 | 41574 | 59607 | 890 | 2990 |
| 多米尼加共和国 | Dominica | 49705 | 79271 | 49704 | 79269 | 1 | 2 |
| 厄瓜多尔 | Ecuador | 138487 | 264132 | 130233 | 179381 | 8254 | 84751 |
| 危地马拉 | Guatemala | 83462 | 112274 | 83460 | 112253 | 2 | 20 |
| 圭亚那 | Guyana | 6324 | 14972 | 4182 | 6219 | 2142 | 8752 |
| 海 地 | Haiti | 11342 | 4356 | 11338 | 4352 | 4 | 4 |
| 洪都拉斯 | Honduras | 48321 | 49156 | 48227 | 49156 | 94 | 1 |
| 牙买加 | Jamaica | 3948 | 5970 | 3132 | 5970 | 816 | |
| 墨西哥 | Mexico | 1284831 | 1364016 | 1187804 | 1258166 | 97026 | 105851 |
| 尼加拉瓜 | Nicaragua | 17376 | 13294 | 17376 | 13294 | | |
| 巴拿马 | Panama | 143331 | 143134 | 142005 | 141835 | 1327 | 1299 |
| 巴拉圭 | Paraguay | 49283 | 35642 | 49263 | 34840 | 20 | 802 |
| 秘 鲁 | Peru | 462609 | 441673 | 395546 | 394509 | 67064 | 47163 |
| 萨尔瓦多 | El Salvador | 24027 | 34940 | 24011 | 34938 | 16 | 2 |
| 乌拉圭 | Uruguay | 122669 | 154204 | 32629 | 48805 | 90040 | 105399 |
| 委内瑞拉 | Venezuela | 18343 | 96924 | 18198 | 36596 | 144 | 60328 |
| **北美洲** | **North America** | **12993036** | **12185853** | **12231936** | **10643832** | **761099** | **1542021** |
| 加拿大 | Canada | 999543 | 826613 | 804210 | 756641 | 195333 | 69972 |
| 美 国 | USA | 11993471 | 11347831 | 11427704 | 9887191 | 565767 | 1460640 |
| **大洋洲** | **Oceania** | **2161963** | **2325090** | **867920** | **1020839** | **1294043** | **1304251** |
| 澳大利亚 | Australia | 1776897 | 2029056 | 724814 | 866969 | 1052083 | 1162087 |
| 斐 济 | Fiji | 1456 | 1577 | 1456 | 1565 | | 12 |
| 新西兰 | New Zealand | 369295 | 276382 | 127710 | 134956 | 241585 | 141426 |
| 巴布亚新几内亚 | Papua New Guinea | 5703 | 7241 | 5703 | 7082 | | 159 |
| 东 盟(10国) | **ASEAN** | **12923343** | **12663198** | **4713482** | **5525566** | **8209861** | **7137632** |
| 欧 盟 | **European Union(EU)** | **12397852** | **12475830** | **10453814** | **10105482** | **1944038** | **2370348** |

# 表 16.9 主要商品出口数量和金额（2022 年）
MAIN EXPORT COMMODITIES IN VOLUME AND VALUE (2022)

单位：万元 (10 000 yuan)

| 品 名 | Name | 数 量 Volume 2022 | 金 额 Value 2022 |
|---|---|---|---|
| 出口重点商品 | Key import commodities | | |
| 农产品 | Agricultural Products | 7523 | 132404 |
| # 肉类（包括杂碎）(万千克) | #Meat (Including Chop Suety)(10 000 kg) | 85 | 5453 |
| 水产品（万千克） | Aquatic Products (10 000 kg) | 11 | 389 |
| # 食用水产品（万千克） | # Edible Aquatic Products (10 000 kg) | 11 | 389 |
| 蔬菜及食用菌（万千克） | Vegetables and Edible Fungi (10 000 kg) | 2871 | 27421 |
| # 鲜或冷藏蔬菜（万千克） | # Fresh or Frozen Vegetables (10 000 kg) | 750 | 5711 |
| 干鲜瓜果及坚果（（万千克） | Dried Fresh Fruits and Nuts (10 000 kg) | 1265 | 15620 |
| # 苹 果（万千克） | # Apples (10 000 kg) | | |
| 茶 叶（万千克） | Tea (10 000 kg) | 651 | 4128 |
| 粮 食（万千克） | Grains (10 000 kg) | 121 | 544 |
| 罐 头（万千克） | Canned Goods (10 000 kg) | 530 | 10985 |
| # 蔬菜罐头（万千克） | # Canned Vegetables (10 000 kg) | 88 | 1062 |
| 酒类及饮料 | Alcohol and Beverages | 46 | 4468 |
| # 果蔬汁（万千克） | # Fruit and Vegetable Juice (10 000 kg) | 7 | 226 |
| 啤 酒（万升） | Beer (10000 litres) | | |
| 烟草及其制品（万千克） | Tobacco and Its Products (10 000 kg) | | |
| 制盐（万千克） | Salt Production (10 000 kg) | 159 | 467 |
| 水泥及水泥熟料（万千克） | Cement and Cement Clinker (10 000 kg) | 210 | 360 |
| 钨品（万千克） | Tungsten (10 000 kg) | | 4 |
| 煤及褐煤（万千克） | Coal and Lignite (10 000 kg) | 37 | 101 |
| 成品油（万千克） | Refined Oil (10 000 kg) | 6 | 473 |
| 氧化铝（万千克） | Alumina (10 000 kg) | 17 | 121 |
| 稀土及其制品（万千克） | Rare Earth and Its Products (10 000 kg) | 21 | 1202 |
| # 稀 土（万千克） | # Rare Earth (10 000 kg) | 19 | 204 |
| 基本有机化学品（万千克） | Basic Organic Chemicals | 23491 | 871432 |
| # 柠檬酸（万千克） | # Citric Acid (10000 kg) | 17 | 146 |
| 医药材及药品（万千克） | Medicinal Materials and Medicines (10 000 kg) | 413 | 158161 |
| # 中药材（万千克） | # Chinese Herbal Medicine (10 000 kg) | 32 | 1069 |
| 中式成药（万千克） | Chinese Patent Medicine (10 000 kg) | 5 | 565 |
| 人用疫苗 | Human Vaccine | | 1 |
| 抗生素（制剂除外）（万千克） | Antibiotics (Except Preparations) (10 000 kg) | 11 | 17504 |

**表 16.9 续表 1 continued 1**

单位：万元 (10 000 yuan)

| 品 名 | Name | 数 量 Volume 2022 | 金 额 Value 2022 |
|---|---|---|---|
| 医用敷料（万千克） | Medical Dressing (10 000 kg) | 21 | 1628 |
| 肥 料（万千克） | Fertilizer (10 000 kg) | 49908 | 121401 |
| #矿物肥料及化肥（万千克） | # Mineral Fertilizer and Chemical Fertilizer (10000 kg) | 49582 | 120736 |
| #尿 素（万千克） | Urea (10 000 kg) | 1392 | 6030 |
| 硫酸铵（万千克） | Ammonium Sulfate (10 000 kg) | 38001 | 69042 |
| 磷酸氢二铵（万千克） | Diammonium Hydrogen Phosphate (10 000 kg) | 4146 | 21930 |
| 磷酸二氢铵（万千克） | Ammonium Dihydrogen Phosphate (10 000 kg) | 206 | 1152 |
| 合成有机染料（万千克） | Synthetic Organic Dye (10 000 kg) | 130 | 6853 |
| 美容化妆品及洗护用品（万千克） | Cosmetics and Toiletries (10 000 kg) | 69 | 4834 |
| 塑料制品（万千克） | Plastic Products (10 000 kg) | 5365 | 442541 |
| 橡胶轮胎（万千克） | Rubber Tyre (10 000 kg) | 5945 | 127916 |
| 新的充气橡胶轮胎（万千克） | New Pneumatic Rubber Tyre (10 000 kg) | 5852 | 125831 |
| 皮革、毛皮及其制品 | Leather, Fur and Products Thereof | 86 | 9300 |
| #裘皮服装（万千克） | Fur Clothing (10 000 kg) | | 35 |
| 箱包及类似容器（万千克） | Cases and Similar Containers (10 000 kg) | 1113 | 141713 |
| 皮革箱包及类似容器（万千克） | Leather Cases and Similar Containers (10 000 kg) | 26 | 3814 |
| 木及其制品（万千克） | Wood and Wood Products (10 000 kg) | 1975 | 28329 |
| #家用或装饰用木制品（万千克） | Household or Decorative Wood Products (10 000 kg) | 110 | 9059 |
| #胶合板及类似多层板（万千克） | Plywood and Similar Laminates (10 000 kg) | 102 | 1173 |
| 植物材料编织品（万千克） | Braid of Plant Material (10 000 kg) | 45 | 3075 |
| 纸浆、纸及其制品（万千克） | Pulp, Paper and Its Products (10 000 kg) | 2902 | 118860 |
| 纺织原料（万千克） | Textile Raw Materials (10 000 kg) | 874 | 27521 |
| #化学纤维纺织原料（万千克） | Chemical Fiber Textile Raw Materials (10 000 kg) | 862 | 20959 |
| 纺织纱线、织物及其制品 | Textile Yarns, Fabrics and Their Products | 9194 | 238677 |
| #纺织纱线（万千克） | Textile Yarn (10 000 kg) | 1074 | 50763 |
| 纺织织物 | Textile Fabric | 4244 | 57217 |
| 纺织制品 | Textile Products | 3876 | 130697 |
| 服装及衣着附件 | Clothing and Clothing Accessories | 13739 | 417900 |
| #服 装 | Clothing | 10769 | 389739 |
| 鞋 靴（万千克） | Shoes and Boots (10 000 kg) | 1218 | 130000 |
| 帽 类（万个） | Hats (10 000 units) | 1381 | 16136 |

表 16.9 续表 2 continued 2

单位: 万元 (10 000 yuan)

| 品　名 | Name | 数　量 Volume 2022 | 金　额 Value 2022 |
|---|---|---|---|
| 伞(万千克) | Umbrella (10 000 kg) | 41 | 2920 |
| 花岗岩石材及其制品(万千克) | Granite Stone and Its Products (10 000 kg) | 413 | 5127 |
| 陶瓷产品(万千克) | Ceramic Products (10 000 kg) | 6799 | 327651 |
| #日用陶瓷(万千克) | Ceramics for Daily Use (10 000 kg) | 4057 | 286505 |
| 建筑用陶瓷(万千克) | Ceramics for Construction (10 000 kg) | 2696 | 40413 |
| 玻璃及其制品 | Glass and Its Products | 14751 | 215032 |
| 珍珠、宝石及半宝石 | Pearls, Precious Stones and Semi-precious Stones | 1782 | 5059 |
| 贵金属或包贵金属的首饰(万克) | Precious Metal or Jewelry Covered With Precious Metal (10 000 grams) | 146 | 300 |
| 铁合金(万千克) | Ferroalloy (10 000 kg) | 147 | 1919 |
| 钢　材(万千克) | Steel (10 000 kg) | 21761 | 272313 |
| #钢铁棒材(万千克) | Steel Bar (10 000 kg) | 760 | 7228 |
| 角钢及型钢(万千克) | Angle and Section Steel (10 000 kg) | 1178 | 10294 |
| 钢铁板材(万千克) | Steel Sheet (10 000 kg) | 15128 | 174054 |
| 钢铁线材(万千克) | Iron and Steel Wire (10 000 kg) | 1223 | 19855 |
| 未锻轧铜及铜材(万千克) | Unwrought Copper and Copper (10 000 kg) | 1548 | 105399 |
| 未锻轧铝及铝材(万千克) | Unwrought Aluminium and Aluminium (10 000 kg) | 15268 | 377533 |
| 家具及其零件 | Furniture and Its Parts | 766 | 203768 |
| 玩　具 | Toy | 61802 | 615969 |
| 体育用品及设备 | Sporting Goods and Equipment | 800 | 53142 |
| 笔及其零件 | Pen and Its Parts | 2039 | 6787 |
| 机电产品 * | Mechanical and Electrical Products * | 860566 | 44978169 |
| #机械基础件 | Mechanical Foundation | 5634 | 99699 |
| #紧固件(万千克) | Fasteners (10 000 kg) | 1061 | 37781 |
| 轴　承(万套) | Bearing (10 000 sets) | 3374 | 22680 |
| 手用或机用工具(万千克) | Hand or Machine Tools (10 000 kg) | 2010 | 83090 |
| 农业机械 | Agricultural Machinery | 295 | 181346 |
| #拖拉机(万辆) | Tractors (10000 units) | | 726 |
| 食品加工机械(万台) | Food processing machinery (10 000 units) | 11 | 12541 |
| 包装机械(万台) | Packaging machinery (10 000 units) | 5 | 8631 |
| 印刷、装订机械及其零件 | Printing and Binding Machinery and Parts Thereof | 520 | 127703 |

**表 16.9 续表 3 continued 3**

单位：万元 (10 000 yuan)

| 品 名 | Name | 数 量 Volume 2022 | 金 额 Value 2022 |
|---|---|---|---|
| #打印机、复印机及一体机（万台） | Printers, Copiers and All-in-one Machines (10 000 units) | 90 | 101457 |
| 通用机械设备 | General Machinery and Equipment | 1681 | 221093 |
| 泵（万台） | Pumps (10 000 units) | 341 | 81072 |
| 压缩机（万台） | Compressor (10 000 units) | 79 | 45066 |
| 分离设备 | Separation Equipment | 39 | 23691 |
| 阀门及类似装置（万台） | Valves and Similar Devices (10 000 units) | 715 | 23082 |
| 纺织机械及其零件 | Textile Machinery and Its Parts | 2757 | 11639 |
| 缝制机械及其零件 | Sewing Machinery and Its Parts | 21 | 3595 |
| 机 床（万台） | Machine Tools (10 000 units) | 79 | 48536 |
| 自动数据处理设备及其零部件 | Automatic Data Processing Equipment and Its Components | 14036 | 23495042 |
| #自动数据处理设备（万台） | Automatic Data Processing Equipment (10 000 units) | 6763 | 20383568 |
| #平板电脑（万台） | Tablets (10 000 units) | 973 | 1841863 |
| 笔记本电脑（万台） | Notebook Computers (10 000 units) | 5545 | 17747299 |
| 中央处理部件（万台） | Central Processing Components (10 000 units) | 497 | 1037582 |
| 存储部件（万台） | Storage Components (10 000 units) | 555 | 198976 |
| 自动数据处理设备的零件、附件（万千克） | Automatic Data Processing Equipment Parts, Accessories (10 000 kg) | 1515 | 880881 |
| 液晶监视器（万台） | LCD Monitor (10 000 units) | 622 | 419248 |
| 3D 打印机（万台） | 3D Printers (10000 units) | | 376 |
| 电工器材 | Electrical Equipment | 32563 | 1076216 |
| #变压器（万个） | Transformer (10 000 units) | 6668 | 41193 |
| 原电池（万个） | Galvanic Cell (10 000 units) | 2979 | 1707 |
| 蓄电池（万个） | Battery (10 000 units) | 4235 | 306724 |
| #锂离子蓄电池（万个） | Lithium Ion Battery (10 000 units) | 3963 | 270550 |
| 电气控制装置 | Electrical Control Unit | 6730 | 284294 |
| #高压开关及控制装置 | High Voltage Switch and Control Device | 22 | 2657 |
| 低压开关及控制装置 | Low Voltage Switch and Control Device | 6708 | 281637 |
| 电线及电缆（万千克） | Wire and Cable (10 000 kg) | 784 | 90784 |
| 手 机（万台） | Mobile Phones (10 000 units) | 13564 | 3383818 |
| 家用电器 | Household Appliances | 991 | 135645 |
| #电 扇（万台） | Electric Fan (10 000 units) | 145 | 24056 |
| 空 调（万台） | Air Conditioner (10 000 units) | 1 | 1095 |

**表 16.9 续表 4 continued 4**

单位：万元 (10 000 yuan)

| 品 名 | Name | 数 量 Volume 2022 | 金 额 Value 2022 |
|---|---|---|---|
| 冰　箱（万台） | Refrigerators (10 000 units) | 18 | 4195 |
| 洗衣机（万台） | Washing Machine (10 000 units) | 1 | 360 |
| 吸尘器（万台） | Vacuum Cleaners (10 000 units) | 37 | 6311 |
| 微波炉（万台） | Microwave Oven (10 000 units) | 1 | 219 |
| 电视机 | TV | 4 | 3582 |
| 液晶电视机（万台） | LCD TV (10 000 units) | 4 | 3357 |
| 音视频设备及其零件 | Audio and Video Equipment and Its Parts | 1142 | 145575 |
| 电视摄像机，数字照相机及视频摄录一体机（万台） | TV Camera, Digital Camera and Video Recording Machine (10 000 units) | 906 | 51588 |
| 数字照相机（万台） | Digital Camera (10 000 units) | 7 | 1024 |
| 无线电广播接收设备（万台） | Radio Receiving Equipment (10 000 units) | 100 | 17165 |
| 音视频设备的零件 | Parts for Audio and Video Equipment | 63 | 51064 |
| 平板显示模组 | Flat Panel Display Module | 3209 | 383710 |
| #液晶平板显示模组（万个） | Liquid Crystal Display Panel (10 000 units) | 3093 | 356564 |
| 有机发光二极管显示屏（万千克） | Organic Light-emitting Diode Display (10 000 kg) | 13 | 12222 |
| 电子元件 | Electronic Components | 673001 | 4065913 |
| #印刷电路（万块） | Printed Circuit (10 000 units) | 28506 | 459268 |
| 二极管及类似半导体器件（万个） | Diode and Similar Semiconductor Devices (10 000 units) | 557102 | 196246 |
| #太阳能电池（万个） | Solar Cells (10 000 units) | 137 | 34869 |
| 集成电路（万个） | Integrated Circuits (10 000 units) | 67134 | 3283718 |
| 集装箱（万个） | Containers (10 000 units) | | 5 |
| 摩托车（万辆） | Motorcycles (10 000 units) | 362 | 1398428 |
| #内燃机摩托车（万辆） | Internal Combustion Engine Motorcycle (10 000 units) | 352 | 1317040 |
| 电动摩托车及脚踏车（万辆） | Electric Motorcycles and Bicycles (10 000 units) | 9 | 81182 |
| 自行车（万辆）(万辆） | Bicycles (10 000 units) | 5 | 6988 |
| 摩托车及自行车的零配件 | Spare Parts for Motorcycles and Bicycles | 7322 | 230848 |
| 汽车（包括底盘） | Automobile (Including Chassis) | 28 | 2187286 |
| #乘用车（万辆） | Passenger Cars (10 000 units) | 18 | 1402073 |
| 商用车 | Commercial Vehicle | 11 | 785212 |
| #客　车（十座及以上）(万辆） | Passenger Cars (10 Seats and Above) (10 000 units) | 1 | 27389 |
| 货　车（万辆） | Freight Cars (10 000 units) | 10 | 742227 |
| 专用汽车（万辆） | Special Purpose Vehicles (10 000 units) | | 1936 |
| 汽车零配件 | Auto Parts | 21214 | 825461 |

**表 16.9 续表 5 continued 5**

单位：万元 (10 000 yuan)

| 品　名 | Name | 数 量 Volume 2022 | 金 额 Value 2022 |
|---|---|---|---|
| #车用发动机(万台) | Automotive Engine (10 000 units) | 84 | 161909 |
| 汽车轮胎(万千克) | Car Tyre (10 000 kg) | 5667 | 121342 |
| 婴孩车及其零件(万千克) | Baby Carriage and Its Parts (10 000 kg) | 18 | 1555 |
| 飞机及其他航空器(万架) | Airplane and Other Aircraft (10000 units) | | 67 |
| #无人驾驶航空器(万架) | # Unmanned Aerial Aircraft (10000 units) | | 67 |
| 船　舶(万艘) | Ship and Boat | | 37296 |
| #液货船(万艘) | # Liquid Cargo Ship (10000 units) | | 35836 |
| 眼镜及其零件 | Glasses and Its Parts | 271 | 12670 |
| 计量检测分析自控仪器及器具 | Automatic Control Instruments and Instruments for Measurement, Testing and Analysis | 2303 | 454921 |
| 分析仪器(万台) | Analytical Instruments (10 000 units) | 29 | 13033 |
| 医疗仪器及器械 | Medical Instruments and Instruments | 8700 | 48994 |
| 钟表及其零件 | Clocks and Watches and Their Parts | 907 | 16373 |
| #手　表(万只) | Watches (10 000 units) | 586 | 6702 |
| 灯具、照明装置及其零件 | Lamps, Lighting Installations and Their Parts | 1840 | 296606 |
| 游戏机及其零附件 | Game Consoles and Accessories | 308 | 468893 |
| 高新技术产品 * | High-tech Products* | 615216 | 33774038 |
| #生物技术(万千克) | Biotechnology (10 000 kg) | | 408 |
| 生命科学技术 | Life Science and Technology | 1623 | 469406 |
| 光电技术 | Photoelectric Technology | 3570 | 393561 |
| 计算机与通信技术 | Computer and Communication Technology | 33534 | 28546160 |
| 电子技术 | Electronic Technology | 575343 | 4164165 |
| 计算机集成制造技术 | Computer Integrated Manufacturing Technology | 956 | 120395 |
| 材料技术(万千克) | Material Technology (10 000 kg) | 25 | 49800 |
| 航空航天技术 | Aerospace Technology | 27 | 6551 |
| 其他技术 | Other Technologies | 138 | 23592 |
| 电动载人汽车 *(万辆) | Electric Manned vehicle *(10 000 units) | 1 | 138095 |
| #纯电动客车(10 座及以上)(万辆) | Pure Electric Bus (10 Seats and above) (10 000 units) | | 3221 |
| 非插电式混合动力乘用车(万辆) | Non-plug-in Hybrid Passenger Vehicles (10 000 units) | 1 | 48648 |
| 插电式混合动力乘用车(万辆) | Plug-in Hybrid Passenger Vehicles (10 000 units) | | 1380 |
| 纯电动乘用车(万辆) | Pure Electric Passenger Cars (10 000 units) | 1 | 84847 |
| 文化产品 * | Cultural Products | 67479 | 1562790 |
| 食　品 * | Food * | 6587 | 86205 |

# 表 16.10 主要商品进口数量和金额(2022 年)
MAIN IMPORT COMMODITIES IN VOLUME AND VALUE (2022)

单位:万元 (10 000 yuan)

| 品 名 | Name | 数 量<br>Volume | 金 额<br>Value |
|---|---|---|---|
| | | 2022 | 2022 |
| **进口重点商品** | **Key import commodities** | | |
| 农产品 | Agricultural Products | 89134 | 1525860 |
| 肉类(包括杂碎)(万千克) | Meat (Including Chop Suety)(10 000 kg) | 11417 | 425886 |
| 牛肉及牛杂碎(万千克) | Beef and Entrails of Beef (10 000 kg) | 8080 | 332804 |
| 牛肉(万千克) | Beef (10 000 kg) | 7989 | 328899 |
| 猪肉及猪杂碎(万千克) | Pork and Chop Suety (10 000 kg) | 825 | 11347 |
| 猪肉(万千克) | Pork (10 000 kg) | 211 | 3214 |
| 羊肉及羊杂碎(万千克) | Mutton and Chop Suety (10,000 kg) | 1611 | 58263 |
| 羊肉(万千克) | Mutton (10 000 kg) | 1603 | 57948 |
| 禽肉及禽杂碎(万千克) | Poultry Meat and Chop Suety (10000 kg) | 855 | 20024 |
| 禽肉(万千克) | Poultry Meat (10 000 kg) | 213 | 4144 |
| 水产品(万千克) | Aquatic Products (10 000 kg) | 3291 | 146514 |
| 食用水产品(万千克) | Edible Aquatic Products (10 000 kg) | 3291 | 146514 |
| 冻鱼(万千克) | Frozen Fish (10 000 kg) | 15 | 311 |
| 乳品(万千克) | Dairy Products (10 000 kg) | 2725 | 119122 |
| 奶粉(万千克) | Milk Powder (10 000 kg) | 669 | 73037 |
| 干鲜瓜果及坚果(万千克) | Dried Fresh Fruits and Nuts (10 000 kg) | 26433 | 470680 |
| 粮食(万千克) | Grains (10 000 kg) | 41433 | 189619 |
| 谷物及谷物粉(万千克) | Cereals and Cereal Meal (10 000 kg) | 1484 | 4952 |
| 小麦(万千克) | Wheat (10 000 kg) | 67 | 385 |
| 大麦(万千克) | Barley (10 000 kg) | | |
| 稻谷及大米(万千克) | Rice(10 000 kg) | 1417 | 4567 |
| 豆类(万千克) | Rice (10 000 kg) | 39949 | 184667 |
| 大豆(万千克) | Beans (10 000 kg) | 39920 | 184338 |
| 食用油(万千克) | Soybean (10 000 kg) | 224 | 12530 |
| 食用植物油(万千克) | Edible Oil (10 000 kg) | 1 | 61 |
| 豆油(万千克) | Edible Vegetable Oil (10 000 kg) | | |
| 棕榈油(万千克) | Soybean Oil (10 000 kg) | | |
| 菜籽油及芥子油(万千克) | Palm Oil (10 000 kg) | | |
| 食糖(万千克) | Rapeseed and Mustard Oil (10 000 kg) | 540 | 3372 |
| 酒类及饮料 | Sugar (10 000 kg) | 160 | 7384 |
| 啤酒(万升) | Alcohol and Beverages | 12 | 160 |
| 葡萄酒(万升) | Beer (10000 litres) | 74 | 3407 |
| 制盐(万千克) | Grape Wine (10000 litres) | | 4 |
| 金属矿及矿砂(万千克) | Salt Production (10 000 kg) | 2246764 | 1872925 |
| 铁矿砂及其精矿(万千克) | Metallic Ore and Ore Sand (10 000 kg) | 1208087 | 950110 |
| 铜矿砂及其精矿(万千克) | Iron Ore and Concentrate (10 000 kg) | 15387 | 196564 |

**表 16.10 续表 1 continued 1**

单位：万元 (10 000 yuan)

| 品 名 | Name | 数 量 Volume 2022 | 金 额 Value 2022 |
|---|---|---|---|
| 铝矿砂及其精矿（万千克） | Copper Ore and Concentrate (10 000 kg) | 840792 | 296926 |
| 煤及褐煤（万千克） | Aluminium Ore and Concentrate (10 000 kg) | 93076 | 55231 |
| 成品油 （万千克） | Coal and Lignite (10 000 kg) | 110 | 4069 |
| 天然气（万千克） | Refined Oil (10 000 kg) | 25 | 113 |
| 液化天然气 （万千克） | Natural Gas (10 000 kg) | 25 | 113 |
| 多晶硅（万千克） | Liquefied Natural Gas (10 000 kg) | 30 | 8017 |
| 稀土（万千克） | Polysilicon (10 000 kg) | | 68 |
| 基本有机化学品（万千克） | Basic Organic Chemicals | 5607 | 83964 |
| 二甲苯（万千克） | Xylene (10 000 kg) | | |
| 乙二醇（万千克） | Ethylene Glycol (10 000 kg) | | 2 |
| 医药材及药品（万千克） | Medicinal Materials and Medicines (10 000 kg) | 425 | 1925149 |
| 中药材（万千克） | Chinese Herbal Medicine (10 000 kg) | 189 | 5472 |
| 人用疫苗（万千克） | Human Vaccine (10000 kg) | 93 | 1760305 |
| 肥料（万千克） | Fertilizer (10 000 kg) | 484 | 1942 |
| 矿物肥料及化肥（万千克） | NPK Compound Fertilizer (10 000 kg) | 484 | 1942 |
| 氯化钾（万千克） | Potassium Chloride (10000 kg) | 484 | 1942 |
| 美容化妆品及洗护用品（万千克） | Cosmetics and Toiletries (10 000 kg) | 329 | 107011 |
| 初级形状的塑料（万千克） | Plastic in Primary Shape (10 000 kg) | 8266 | 112125 |
| 塑料制品（万千克） | Plastic Products (10 000 kg) | 718 | 88420 |
| 天然及合成橡胶（包括胶乳）（万千克） | Natural and Synthetic Rubber (Including Latex) (10 000 kg) | 3804 | 49663 |
| 皮革、毛皮及其制品（万千克） | Leather, Fur and Products Thereof | 6 | 10714 |
| 牛皮革及马皮革 （万千克） | Cow and Horse leather (10 000 kg) | 1 | 101 |
| 木及其制品（万千克） | Wood and Wood Products (10 000 kg) | 83823 | 141114 |
| 原木（万千克） | Logs (10 000 kg) | 70108 | 93515 |
| 锯材（万千克） | Converted Timber (10 000 kg) | 9948 | 32900 |
| 纸浆、纸及其制品（万千克） | Pulp, Paper and Its Products (10 000 kg) | 172250 | 844701 |
| 纸浆 （万千克） | Pulp (10 000 kg) | 161578 | 787499 |
| 纺织原料（万千克） | Textile Raw Materials (10 000 kg) | 50 | 1628 |
| 纺织纱线、织物及其制品 | Textile Yarns, Fabrics and Their Products | 561 | 28767 |
| 纺织纱线（万千克） | Textile Yarn (10 000 kg) | 26 | 1036 |
| 棉纱线（万千克） | Textile Fabric | 15 | 312 |
| 合成纤维纱线（万千克） | Textile Products | 3 | 161 |
| 服装及衣着附件 | Clothing and Clothing Accessories | 45 | 17838 |
| 玻璃及其制品（万千克） | Glass and Its Products | 11931 | 334300 |
| 玻璃纤维及其制品（万千克） | Glass fiber and Its Products (10 000 kg) | 262 | 24890 |
| 珍珠、宝石及半宝石 | Pearls, Precious Stones and Semi-precious Stones | 1 | 70 |
| 钢材（万千克） | Steel (10 000 kg) | 5296 | 43163 |
| 未锻轧铜及铜材（万千克） | Unwrought Copper and Copper (10 000 kg) | 13485 | 802981 |
| 未锻轧铝及铝材（万千克） | Unwrought Aluminium and Aluminium (10 000 kg) | 1226 | 25737 |

**表 16.10 续表 2 continued 2**

单位：万元 (10 000 yuan)

| 品 名 | Name | 数 量 Volume 2022 | 金 额 Value 2022 |
|---|---|---|---|
| 机电产品 * | Mechanical and Electrical Products | 2019594 | 19814461 |
| 机械基础件 | Mechanical Foundation | 2848 | 57967 |
| 农业机械 | Agricultural Machinery | 1 | 1192 |
| 收获机械（万台） | Harvesting Machinery (10 000 units) | | 39 |
| 拖拉机（万辆） | Tractor (10000 units) | | 7 |
| 食品加工机械（万台） | Food processing machinery (10 000 units) | | 45 |
| 包装机械（万台） | Packaging machinery (10 000 units) | | 12115 |
| 印刷、装订机械及其零件 | Printing and Binding Machinery and Parts Thereof | 86 | 32085 |
| 打印机、复印机及一体机（万台） | Printers, Copiers and All-in-one Machines (10 000 units) | 1 | 5133 |
| 通用机械设备 | General Machinery and Equipment | 470 | 84827 |
| 泵（万台） | Pumps (10 000 units) | 11 | 20441 |
| 压缩机（万台） | Compressor (10 000 units) | 1 | 957 |
| 分离设备 | Separation Equipment | 59 | 18061 |
| 阀门及类似装置（万套） | Valves and Similar Devices (10 000 units) | 389 | 27842 |
| 机床（万台） | Machine Tools (10 000 units) | | 101432 |
| 自动数据处理设备及其零部件 | Automatic Data Processing Equipment and Its Components | 6166 | 2993900 |
| 自动数据处理设备（万台） | Automatic Data Processing Equipment (10 000 units) | 4 | 10619 |
| 中央处理部件（万台） | Central Processing Components (10 000 units) | 3 | 5156 |
| 存储部件（万台） | Storage Components (10 000 units) | 5741 | 2048816 |
| 自动数据处理设备的零件、附件（万千克） | Automatic Data Processing Equipment Parts, Accessories (10 000 kg) | 121 | 875243 |
| 半导体制造设备（万台） | Semiconductor Manufacturing Equipment (10 000 units) | | 600912 |
| 制造单晶柱或晶圆用的机器及装置（万台） | Machines and Devices for Manufacturing Single Crystal Columns or Wafers (10 000 units) | | 7433 |
| 制造半导体器件或集成电路用的机器及装置（万台） | Machines and Devices for Manufacturing Semiconductor Devices or Integrated Circuits (10 000 units) | | 241371 |
| 制造平板显示器用的机器及装置（万台） | Machines and Devices for Manufacturing Flat Panel Displays (10 000 units) | | 238294 |
| 电工器材 | Electrical Equipment | 31326 | 400942 |
| 变压器（万个） | Transformer (10 000 units) | 615 | 4204 |
| 蓄电池（万个） | Battery (10 000 units) | 297 | 4501 |
| 锂离子蓄电池（万个） | Lithium Ion Battery (10 000 units) | 297 | 4345 |
| 电气控制装置 | Electrical Control Unit | 27153 | 279607 |
| 电线及电缆（万千克） | Wire and Cable (10 000 kg) | 73 | 36577 |
| 家用电器 | Household Appliances | 4 | 2897 |
| 电视机（万台） | TV (10 000 units) | | |
| 液晶电视机（万台） | LCD TV (10 000 units) | | |
| 音视频设备及其零件 | Audio and Video Equipment and Its Parts | 50 | 82269 |
| 电视摄像机，数字照相机及视频摄录一体机（万台） | TV Camera, Digital Camera and Video Recording Machine (10 000 units) | 39 | 11029 |
| 音视频设备的零件（万千克） | Parts for Audio and Video Equipment | 10 | 70896 |
| 平板显示模组 | Flat Panel Display Module | 3934 | 549114 |
| 液晶平板显示模组（万个） | Liquid Crystal Display Panel (10 000 units) | 2845 | 228799 |
| 有机发光二极管（OLED）平板显示模组 | Organic Light-emitting Diode Display (10 000 kg) | 1089 | 320307 |

**表 16.10 续表 3 continued 3**

单位：万元 (10 000 yuan)

| 品 名 | Name | 数 量 Volume 2022 | 金 额 Value 2022 |
|---|---|---|---|
| 电子元件 | Electronic Components | 1967173 | 12925597 |
| 电容器（万千克） | Capacitor (10 000 kg) | 38 | 122112 |
| 印刷电路（万块） | Printed Circuit (10 000 units) | 72743 | 320144 |
| 二极管及类似半导体器件（万个） | Diode and Similar Semiconductor Devices (10 000 units) | 973184 | 209273 |
| 集成电路（万个） | Integrated Circuits (10 000 units) | 835973 | 12229342 |
| 汽车（包括底盘）（万辆） | Automobile (Including Chassis) | | 228418 |
| 乘用车（万辆） | Passenger Cars (10 000 units) | | 225166 |
| 商用车（万辆） | Commercial Vehicle (10 000 units) | | 3252 |
| 货车（万辆） | Freight Cars (10 000 units) | | 939 |
| 汽车零配件 | Auto Parts | 2009 | 201510 |
| 车用发动机（万台） | Automotive Engine (10 000 units) | | 67 |
| 汽车轮胎（万千克） | Car Tyre (10 000 kg) | 50 | 1041 |
| 飞机及其他航空器（万架） | Plane and Other Aircraft (10 000 units) | | |
| 航空器零部件 | Aircraft Parts | 2 | 3715 |
| 计量检测分析自控仪器及器具 | Automatic Control Instruments and Instruments for Measurement, Testing and Analysis | 674 | 406670 |
| 医疗仪器及器械 | Medical Instruments and Instruments | 10 | 50696 |
| 钟表及其零件 | Clocks and Watches and Their Parts | 7 | 6793 |
| 手表（万只） | Watches (10 000 units) | 7 | 6573 |
| 电动手表（万只） | Electric Watch (10 000 pieces) | 7 | 2445 |
| 机械手表（万只） | Mechanical Watch (10 000 pieces) | | 4128 |
| 高新技术产品 * | High-tech Products | 1835708 | 19571231 |
| 生物技术（万千克） | Biotechnology (10 000 kg) | 94 | 1760334 |
| 生命科学技术 | Life Science and Technology | 226 | 147314 |
| 光电技术 | Photoelectric Technology | 3034 | 446422 |
| 计算机与通信技术 | Computer and Communication Technology | 6980 | 3196068 |
| 电子技术 | Electronic Technology | 1825279 | 13044609 |
| 计算机集成制造技术 | Computer Integrated Manufacturing Technology | 86 | 910381 |
| 材料技术（万千克） | Material Technology (10 000 kg) | 9 | 26314 |
| 航空航天技术 | Aerospace Technology | 1 | 39030 |
| 其他技术 | Other Technologies | | 758 |
| 电动载人汽车 *（万辆） | Electric Manned vehicle (10 000 units) | | 42988 |
| 非插电式混合动力乘用车（万辆） | Non-plug-in Hybrid Passenger Vehicles (10 000 units) | | |
| 插电式混合动力乘用车（万辆） | Plug-in Hybrid Passenger Vehicles (10 000 units) | | 42988 |
| 纯电动乘用车（万辆） | Pure Electric Passenger Cars (10 000 units) | | |
| 文化产品 * | Cultural Products | 96 | 194536 |
| 食品 * | Food * | 87961 | 1483437 |

## 表 16.11 使用外资情况(2021 – 2022 年)
## VALUE OF FOREIGN CAPITAL ACTUALLY USED (2021-2022)

单位：万美元 (USD 10 000)

| 指 标 | Item | 2021 | 2022 |
|---|---|---|---|
| 新签利用外资协议(合同)数(个) | Number of Newly Signed Agreements (Contracts) of Foreign Capital Utilization (unit) | 351 | 268 |
| 合同外资金额 | Value of Contractual Foreign Capital | 469016 | 199462 |
| 实际使用外资金额 | Actually Utilized Value of Foreign Capital | 223583 | 185744 |

注：2004 年起，新签利用外资协议(合同)数、合同外资金额均不含对外借款。
Note: Foreign loans have been excluded from the number of newly signed agreements (contracts) of foreign capital utilization and the Value of Contractual Foreign Capital since 2004.

## 表 16.12 对外投资合作(2021 – 2022 年)
## OUTWARD INVESTMENT AND COOPERATION (2021-2022)

| 指 标 | Item | 2021 | 2022 |
|---|---|---|---|
| 对外直接投资额(万美元) | Value of Outward Direct Investment (USD 10 000) | 119215 | 106270 |
| #货币投资 | Currency Investment | 106509 | 87908 |
| 对外承包工程新签合同数(个) | Number of Newly Signed Contracts for Outward Contracting Projects (unit) | 39 | 54 |
| 对外承包工程新签合同额(万美元) | Value of Newly Signed Contracts for Outward Contracting Projects (USD 10 000) | 45188 | 36323 |
| 对外承包工程完成营业额(万美元) | Completed Turnover of Outward Contracted Projects (USD 10 000) | 42509 | 30883 |
| 对外劳务合作派出人数(人) | Number of People Dispatched for Outward Labor Service Cooperation (person) | 607 | 706 |

# 表 16.13 新设外商投资企业数、合同外资金额和实际使用外资金额（2021－2022 年）
## NUMBER OF NEWLY ESTABLISHED FOREIGN-INVESTED ENTERPRISES, VALUE OF CONTRACTUAL AND ACTUALLY UTILIZED FOREIGN CAPITAL (2021-2022)

| 指 标 | Item | 新设外商投资企业数（个）Number of Newly Established Foreign-invested Enterprises(unit) | |
|---|---|---|---|
| | | 2021 | 2022 |
| **总 计** | **Total** | **351** | **268** |
| **按投资方式分** | **By Investment Mode** | | |
| 中外合资经营企业 | Sino-foreign Joint Venture Enterprises | 150 | 136 |
| 中外合作经营企业 | Sino-Foreign Co-operative Enterprises | | |
| 外商独资经营企业 | Wholly Foreign Owned Enterprises | 185 | 112 |
| 外商投资股份有限公司 | Foreign-invested Company Limited By Shares | 1 | |
| 中外合作开发项目 | Sino-foreign Co-operative Development Projects | | |
| 合伙企业 | Partnership Enterprises | 15 | 20 |
| **按行业分** | **By Sector** | | |
| 第一产业 | Primary Industry | 11 | 3 |
| 第二产业 | Secondary Industry | 33 | 27 |
| 制造业 | Manufacturing | 28 | 20 |
| 电力、热力、燃气及水生产和供应业 | Production and Supply of Electricity, Heat, Gas and Water | 3 | 3 |
| 建筑业 | Construction | 2 | 4 |
| 第三产业 | Tertiary Industry | 307 | 238 |
| 批发和零售业 | Wholesale and Retail Trades | 85 | 58 |
| 交通运输、仓储和邮政业 | Transport, Storage, Post and Communication | 2 | 3 |
| 住宿和餐饮业 | Hotels and Catering Services | 22 | 9 |
| 信息传输、软件和信息技术服务业 | Information Transmission,Computer Services and Softwares | 45 | 45 |
| 金融业 | Financial Intermediation | 5 | 2 |
| 房地产业 | Real Estate | 10 | 2 |
| 租赁和商务服务业 | Leasing and Business Services | 74 | 60 |
| 科学研究和技术服务业 | Scientific Research, Technical Service and Geologic Prospecting | 38 | 38 |
| 水利、环境和公共设施管理业 | Management of Water Conservancy, Environment and Public Facilities | 4 | |
| 居民服务、修理和其他服务业 | Services to Households and Other Services | 3 | 4 |
| 教 育 | Education | | |
| 卫生和社会工作 | Health and Social Service | 3 | 1 |
| 文化、体育与娱乐业 | Culture, Sports and Entertainment | 15 | 16 |
| 公共管理、社会保障和社会组织 | Public Management and Social Organizations | 1 | |
| **按主要国别（地区）分** | **By Country (region)** | | |
| 中国香港 | Hong Kong (China) | 136 | 90 |
| 印度尼西亚 | Indonesia | 1 | |
| 日 本 | Japan | 5 | 7 |
| 韩 国 | South Korea | 16 | 9 |
| 中国澳门 | Macao (China) | 4 | 6 |
| 马来西亚 | Malaysia | 2 | 6 |
| 中国台湾 | Taiwan (China) | 71 | 66 |
| 泰 国 | Thailand | 3 | |
| 新加坡 | Singapore | 25 | 15 |
| 法 国 | France | 3 | |
| 瑞 典 | Sweden | 1 | |
| 瑞 士 | Switzerland | 1 | 1 |
| 英 国 | UK | 6 | 4 |
| 美 国 | USA | 12 | 16 |
| 加拿大 | Canada | 4 | 3 |
| 澳大利亚 | Australia | 3 | 2 |

单位: 万美元 (USD 10 000)

| 合同外资金额<br>Value of Contractual Foreign Capital | | 实际使用外资金额<br>Actually Utilized Value of Foreign Capital | |
|---|---|---|---|
| 2021 | 2022 | 2021 | 2022 |
| **469016** | **199462** | **223584** | **185744** |
| 92866 | 68531 | 20425 | 27802 |
| 79 | | | |
| 383202 | 134282 | 178942 | 150433 |
| -214 | 618 | | 1409 |
| -6917 | -3969 | 24215 | 6100 |
| 11490 | 205 | 22 | 1032 |
| 116339 | 88523 | 67832 | 46331 |
| 115462 | 50777 | 66996 | 46139 |
| 229 | 327 | 836 | 193 |
| 648 | 37419 | | |
| 341187 | 110734 | 155730 | 138380 |
| 114012 | 2790 | 47506 | 40641 |
| 7920 | 7019 | 5890 | 497 |
| 170 | 70 | 26 | 12 |
| 61389 | 58798 | 7918 | 26342 |
| 32508 | -29055 | 23983 | 17274 |
| -19663 | 9784 | 13834 | 9948 |
| 18592 | 47632 | 51856 | 42273 |
| 8814 | 11165 | 890 | 583 |
| 113131 | | 319 | |
| 35 | 1122 | 30 | 21 |
| 3879 | 883 | 3362 | 789 |
| 339 | 526 | 117 | |
| 61 | | | |
| 373802 | 97885 | 183970 | 135926 |
| 8 | | | |
| 263 | 11608 | 738 | 8338 |
| 795 | 1397 | 555 | 406 |
| -76 | 110 | | |
| 15 | 3026 | | |
| 5477 | 6189 | 71 | |
| 804 | | 17 | 16 |
| 53256 | 37335 | 25592 | 27306 |
| 2 | | | |
| 600 | | 310 | |
| 426 | 640 | | 828 |
| 1828 | 1374 | 20 | 31 |
| 8981 | 852 | 4216 | 1137 |
| 177 | 5032 | 7 | 34 |
| 152 | 1540 | 5 | 1 |

# 表 16.14 旅游基本情况(2021－2022 年)
## BASIC STATISTICS ON TOURISM (2021-2022)

| 项 目 | Item | 2021 | 2022 |
|---|---|---|---|
| **接待入境旅游人数(人次)** | **Number of Overseas Visitor Arrival Received (person-time)** | **99062** | **65501** |
| 外国人 | Foreigners | 49035 | 42803 |
| #亚 洲 | Asia | 24370 | 19641 |
| #日 本 | Japan | 8440 | 3224 |
| 韩 国 | South Korea | 10274 | 5538 |
| 印度尼西亚 | Indonesia | 170 | 150 |
| 马来西亚 | Malaysia | 1436 | 4903 |
| 新加坡 | Singapore | 2639 | 3554 |
| 泰 国 | Thailand | 337 | 738 |
| 欧 洲 | Europe | 7443 | 9513 |
| #英 国 | UK | 2053 | 2025 |
| 法 国 | France | 1145 | 598 |
| 德 国 | Germany | 2153 | 1337 |
| 意大利 | Italy | 670 | 1978 |
| 俄罗斯 | Russia | 638 | 612 |
| 西班牙 | Spain | 356 | 2721 |
| 美 洲 | America | 9467 | 5555 |
| #美 国 | USA | 6006 | 3569 |
| 加拿大 | Canada | 3155 | 1568 |
| 大洋洲 | Oceania | 1872 | 1107 |
| #澳大利亚 | Australia | 1498 | 906 |
| 非 洲 | Africa | 459 | 226 |
| 香港同胞 | Compatriots from Hong Kong | 15204 | 9398 |
| 澳门同胞 | Compatriots from Macao | 10284 | 1667 |
| 台湾同胞 | Compatriots from Taiwan | 24539 | 11633 |
| **来渝国际旅游者平均逗留天数(天)** | **Average Period Foreign Tourists Staying in Chongqing (day)** | **5.10** | **1.70** |
| **国际旅游收入(万美元)** | **Earnings from International Tourism (USD 10 000)** | **8159** | **1166** |
| **星级饭店数(个)** | **Number of Star-rated Hotel (unit)** | **150** | **139** |
| **年末旅行社数(个)** | **Number of Travel Agencies at Year-end (unit)** | **753** | **818** |
| 出境旅行社 | **International Travel Agencies** | 92 | 92 |
| 一般旅行社 | Domestic Travel Agencies | 661 | 726 |

# 表 16.15 星级饭店基本情况（2021－2022 年）
## BASIC STATISTICS ON STAR-RATED HOTELS (2021-2022)

| 项 目 | Item | 2021 | 2022 |
|---|---|---|---|
| **星级饭店数（个）** | **Number of Star-rated Hotels (unit)** | **150** | **139** |
| **按星级分** | **By Star Level** | | |
| #五星级 | 5-star | 28 | 27 |
| 四星级 | 4-star | 47 | 44 |
| 三星级 | 3-star | 63 | 58 |
| **按注册类型分** | **By Registration** | | |
| 内 资 | Domestic Funded | 141 | 130 |
| 外商及港澳台投资 | Foreign-funded and Funded by Hong Kong, Macao and Taiwan | 9 | 9 |
| **按饭店客房规模分** | **By Capacity** | | |
| 300 间以上 | With 300 Rooms and Above | 16 | 17 |
| 200-299 间 | With 200-299 Rooms | 20 | 16 |
| 100-199 间 | With 100-199 Rooms | 51 | 44 |
| 99 间以下 | With Less Than 100 Rooms | 63 | 62 |
| **星级饭店客房数（间）** | **Number of Rooms in Star-rated Hotels (unit)** | **22584** | **20975** |
| #五星级 | 5-star | 8170 | 8420 |
| 四星级 | 4-star | 7962 | 7246 |
| 三星级 | 3-star | 5767 | 4409 |
| **星级饭店床位数（张）** | **Number of Beds in Star-rated Hotels (unit)** | **36511** | **33961** |
| #五星级 | 5-star | 12171 | 12480 |
| 四星级 | 4-star | 13218 | 12435 |
| 三星级 | 3-star | 9877 | 7704 |

重/庆/统/计/年/鉴

# 主要统计指标解释

## 货物进出口总额

指实际进出我国关境的货物总金额。包括对外贸易实际进出口货物，来料加工装配进出口货物，国家间、联合国及国际组织无偿援助物资和赠送品，华侨、港澳台同胞和外籍华人捐赠品，租赁期满归承租人所有的租赁货物，进料加工进出口货物，边境地方贸易及边境地区小额贸易进出口货物，中外合资企业、中外合作经营企业、外商独资经营企业进出口货物和公用物品，到、离岸价格在规定限额以上的进出口货样和广告品(无商业价值、无使用价值和免费提供出口的除外)，从保税仓库提取在中国境内销售的进口货物，以及其他进出口货物。该指标可以观察一个国家在货物贸易方面的总规模。我国规定出口货物按离岸价格统计，进口货物按到岸价格统计。

## 商品收发货人所在地进、出口额

指在所在地海关注册登记的有进出口经营权的企业实际进、出口额。

## 进出口统计国别（地区）

进口货物统计原产国（地），出口货物统计最终目的国（地）。原产国指进口货物的生产、开采或加工制造的国家。对经过几个国家加工制造的进口货物，以最后一个对货物进行经济上可以视为实质性加工的国家作为该货物的原产国。原产国确实不详时，按“国别不详”统计。最终目的国指出口货物已知的消费、使用或进一步加工制造的国家。最终目的国不能确定时，按货物出口时尽可能预知的最后运往国统计。

## 商品目的地进口额和商品货源地出口额

目的地进口额指进口货物的消费、使用或最终抵运地的实际进口额；货源地出口额指出口货物的产地或原始发货地的实际出口额。

## 合同外资金额

是指外商投资企业(机构)的外方投资者认缴的注册资本、营运资金和投资者股权转让的溢折价。包括新设立企业合同外资和原有企业的增资/减资，但增资减资不对企业（项目）个数进行调整。

## 实际使用外资金额

是指合同外资金额的实际执行数，包括境外投资者实际缴付的注册资本、营运资金，以及受让境内投资者股权实际支付的交易对价。

## 外商直接投资

是指境外投资者在中国境内通过投资设立公司、合伙企业、分行（限境外银行）、分公司（限境外保险公司），单独或与境内投资者共同进行石油、天然气和煤层气等资源的勘探开发等方式进行的投资。上市公司中，单个境外投资者所占股权比例不低于10%。

## 对外直接投资

对外直接投资是境内投资者以控制国(境)外企业的经营管理权为核心的经济活动，体现在一经济体通过投资于另一经济体而实现其持久利益的目标。

## 对外直接投资额

指境内投资者在报告期内直接向其境外企业实现的投资，包括股权投资、收益再投资以及债务工具三部分。

## 对外承包工程

根据《对外承包工程管理条例》，对外承包工程是指中国的企业或者其他单位承包境外建设工程项目的活动。

## 对外劳务合作

指组织劳务人员赴其他国家或地区为国外的企业或机构工作的经营性活动。

## 入境游客

指报告期内来中国（大陆）观光游览、休闲度假、

## 主要统计指标解释

探亲访友、保健疗养、购物娱乐、学习交流、会议培训或开展经济、文化、体育、宗教等活动的外国人、港澳台同胞等游客（即入境旅游人数）。入境游客包括入境过夜游客和入境一日游客。

### ■ 国际旅游收入

指入境游客在中国（大陆）境内旅行、游览过程中用于交通、参观游览、住宿、餐饮、购物、娱乐等全部花费。

### ■ 出境人数（出境游客）

指中国（大陆）公民因公民出境前往其他国家、中国香港特别行政区、澳门特别行政区和台湾省观光、度假、探亲访友、就医疗养、购物、参加会议或从事经济、文化、体育、宗教活动的人数（即出境游客）。统计时，出境游客按每出境 1 次统计 1 人次。

### ■ 星级饭店

指设备、设施、服务符合《旅游饭店星级的划分与评定》，通过相关旅游管理部门评定，并取得星级饭店称号的饭店（含预备星级饭店）。

# Explanatory Notes on Main Statistical Indicators

## Total Import and Export of Goods

Refer to the real value of commodities imported and exported across the border of China. They include the actual imports and exports through foreign trade, imported and exported goods under the processing and assembling trades and materials, supplies and gifts as aid given gratis between governments and by the United Nations and other international organizations, and contributions donated by overseas Chinese, compatriots in Hong Kong and Macao and Chinese with foreign citizenship, leasing commodities owned by tenant at the expiration of leasing period, the imported and exported commodities processed with imported materials, commodities trading in border areas, the imported and exported commodities and articles for public use of the Sino-foreign joint ventures, cooperative enterprises and ventures with sole foreign investment. Also included is import or export of samples and advertising goods for which CIF or FOB value are beyond the permitted ceiling (excluding goods of no trading or use value and free commodities for export), imported goods sold in China from bonded warehouses and other imported or exported goods. The indicator of the total imports and exports at customs can be used to observe the total size of external trade in a country. In accordance with the stipulation of the Chinese government, imports are calculated at CIF, while exports are calculated at FOB.

## Import or Export Value by Location of China's Foreign Trade Managing Units

Refers to actual value of imports and exports carried out by corporations which have been registered by the local Customs house and are vested with right to run import export business.

## Imports and Exports by Countries (Regions)

Refers to the origin countries (regions) of imports and the destination countries (regions) of export. The origin countries refer to the countries where the imported products were produced, exploited, processed or manufactured. As for the imported products processed and manufactured by more than one country, the country where those products were actually processed from the economic point of view for the last time should be regarded as the origin country. Where the origin is unclear, it should be calculated as "Origin Unknown". The destination countries refer to the countries where the exported products will be consumed, used or further processed and manufactured. Where the final destination is unclear, it should be calculated as the last known destination.

## Import Value of Commodities by Place of Destination and Export Value of Commodities by Place of Origin in China

The former indicator refers to the value of import commodities of the places of their consumption, utilization or the places of their final destination. The latter indicator refers to the value of export commodities of the places of their origin or the places of the commodities dispatched.

## Contractual Foreign Capital Amount

Refers to the registered capital, working capital subscribed by the foreign investor of the foreign-invested enterprise (institution) and the premium and discount of the equity transfer of the investor. This includes the contractual foreign investment of newly established enterprises and the capital increase/decrease of existing enterprises, but the number of enterprises (projects) will not be adjusted for capital increase/decrease.

## Actually Used Foreign Capital Amount

Refers to the actually executed amount of the contract foreign capital amount, including the registered capital and working capital actually paid by the foreign

EXPLANATORY NOTES TO MAJOR STATISTICAL INDICATORS

investor, as well as the transaction consideration actually paid for the transfer of the equity of the domestic investor.

### Foreign Direct Investment

Refers to the investment made by foreign investors in China through the establishment of companies, partnership enterprises, branches of banks (limited to overseas banks), branches of insurance companies (limited to overseas insurance companies), and the exploration and development of resources such as oil, natural gas, and coalbed methane, either individually or jointly with domestic investors. In a listed company, the proportion of equity held by a single overseas investor shall not be less than 10%.

### Outward Direct Investment

Refers to the economic activities of domestic investors focussing on controlling the operation and management of overseas enterprises. The content of overseas direct investment mainly reflects goal of lasting interest of one economic entity by investing in another economic entity.

### Outward Direct Investment Amount

Refers to the investments made by domestic investors directly to their overseas enterprises during the reporting period, including equity investment, income reinvestment, and debt instruments.

### Overseas Contracted Projects

Refer to activities of contracting overseas construction projects by Chinese enterprises or any other units, which are stipulated *in the Regulations on Administration of Foreign Contracted Project.*

### Overseas Labour Services

Refer to operational activities of organizing labour force to go abroad providing services to foreign enterprises or agencies.

### Inbound tourists

Refer to foreigners, compatriots from Hong Kong, Macao and Taiwan who are in China (mainland) for sightseeing, leisure and vacation, visiting relatives and friends, health care, shopping and entertainment, learning exchanges, conferences and training, or conducting economic, cultural, sports, religious and other activities during the reporting period. Tourists (the number of inbound tourists). Inbound tourists include inbound overnight tourists and inbound one-day tourists.

### Foreign Exchange Earnings from International Tourism

Refer to the total expenditure of foreigners, overseas Chinese, Chinese compatriots from Hong Kong, Macao and Taiwan during their stay in the mainland of China on transportation, sighting, accommodation, food, shopping and entertainment.

### Outbound number (outbound tourists)

Refers to the number of Chinese (mainland) citizens who go to other countries, Hong Kong Special Administrative Region, Macao Special Administrative Region and Taiwan Province for sightseeing, vacation, visiting relatives and friends, medical care, shopping, attending meetings or engaging in economic, cultural, physical education and religious activities due to their outbound citizens (outbound tourists). In compiling statistics, each time of leaving is counted as one person-time.

### Star-rated Hotels

Refer to hotels whose equipment, facilities and services conform to the "Classification and Evaluation of Star Ratings for Tourist Hotels", which have been assessed by relevant tourism management departments and have obtained the title of star-rated hotels (including pre-star hotels).

# 第十七章·金融业

## FINANCIAL STATISTICS

# 简要说明

**BRIEF INTRODUCTION**

本章资料包括全市金融机构信贷收支、证券和保险业情况，由市统计局综合处根据有关部门资料整理编辑。资料分别来源于市地方金融监督管理局、中国人民银行重庆营业部、重庆证监局、国家金融监督管理总局重庆监管局。

The data in this chapter include the statistics on credit funds balance of financial institutions, securities and insurance, which are sorted and compiled by Division of Comprehensive Statistics, Chongqing Municipal Bureau of Statistics. The data are provided by Chongqing Local Financial Supervision and Administration Bureau, Chongqing Business Department of the People's Bank of China, China Securities Regulatory Commission Chongqing Bureau and Chongqing Supervision Bureau of the State Financial Regulatory Administration.

# 表 17.1 主要金融机构数(2021 - 2022 年)
## NUMBER OF MAIN FINANCIAL INSTITUTIONS (2021-2022)

单位：个 (unit)

| 指 标 | Item | 2021 | 2022 |
|---|---|---|---|
| **银行机构** | **Banks** | | |
| 法人机构 | Legal Entity | 58 | 57 |
| 市级分行 | Provincial branches | 48 | 49 |
| **保险机构** | **Insurance Institutions** | | |
| 法人机构 | Legal Entity | 4 | 4 |
| 市级分公司 | Provincial branches | 60 | 62 |
| **证券机构** | **Security Institutions** | | |
| 证券公司总部 | Security Companies | 1 | 1 |
| 证券分公司 | Branch Companies | 49 | 53 |
| 营业部 | Business Departments | 208 | 200 |

注：保险机构数不含中国出口信用保险公司重庆营业管理部。
Note：Chongqing Business Department of China Export & Credit Insurance Corporation is not included in the number of insurance institutions.

# 表 17.2 地方金融市场运行情况（2021 – 2022 年）
## OPERATION OF LOCAL FINANCIAL MARKET (2021-2022)

| 指 标 | Item | 2021 | 2022 |
|---|---|---|---|
| **融资担保行业** | **Financing Guarantee** | | |
| 单位数（个） | Unit Number (unit) | 121 | 116 |
| 实缴资本（亿元） | Paid-in capital (100 million Yuan) | 426.59 | 415.55 |
| 在保余额（亿元） | Guaranteed Balance (100 million yuan) | 3104.02 | 3254.53 |
| **小额贷款公司行业单位数** | **Small Loan Companies** | | |
| 单位数（个） | Unit Number (unit) | 273 | 260 |
| 注册资本（亿元） | Registered Capital (100 million yuan) | 1160.64 | 1187.68 |
| 贷款余额（亿元） | Balance of Loans (100 million yuan) | 2423.20 | 2376.03 |
| **上市与挂牌** | **Listed Companies** | | |
| 境内外上市公司（个） | Domestic and Overseas Listed Companies (unit) | 81 | 90 |
| 境内外上市公司市值（亿元） | Market Value of Companies Listed Overseas (100 million yuan) | 15092.00 | 12472.00 |
| 新三板挂牌数（个） | Number of Companies Listed in NEEQ Market (unit) | 84 | 79 |
| 重庆股份转让中心挂牌数（个） | Number of Companies Listed in Chongqing Share Transfer Center (unit) | 1866 | 1961 |
| **股权投资类企业** | **Equity Investment Companies** | | |
| 备案单位数（个） | Number of Units Registered (unit) | 802 | 848 |
| 注册及认缴资本（亿元） | Registered and Subscribed Capital (100 million yuan) | 3935.79 | 4541.70 |
| **金融要素市场** | **Financial Factor Market** | | |
| 单位数（个） | Unit Number (unit) | 12 | 12 |
| 交易量（亿元） | Turnover (100 million yuan) | 5161.19 | 4596.26 |

注：1）境外企业是指在其他国家和地区上市的企业。
2）股权投资类企业为按照地方口径，在市金融办备案的企业。
3）金融要素市场的交易量为当年累计交易量。

Note: a) Overseas companies refer to the companies listed in the stock market of other countries or regions.
b) Equity investment companies refer to those registered with Chongqing Financial Affairs Office according to the local statistic scope.
c) The turnover of financial factor market refers to the accumulative turnover of the year.

# 表 17.3 金融机构(含外资)存贷款年末余额(1980 – 2022 年)

## YEAR-END DEPOSIT AND LOAN BALANCE OF FINANCIAL INSTITUTIONS (INCLUDING FOREIGN-FUNDED INSTITUTIONS) (1980-2022)

单位：亿元 (100 million yuan)

| 年 份 Year | 本外币存款余额 Total Deposit Balance of RMB and Foreign Currencies | 人民币存款余额 Total Deposit Balance of RMB | #企业存款 Enterprise Deposits | #储蓄存款 Urban and Rural Saving Deposits | 本外币贷款余额 Total Loan Balance of RMB and Foreign Currencies | 人民币贷款余额 Total Loan Balance of RMB | 短期贷款 Short-term Loans | 中长期贷款 Medium & Long-term Loans |
|---|---|---|---|---|---|---|---|---|
| 1980 | | 29.15 | 11.32 | 6.22 | | 42.19 | 40.96 | 1.23 |
| 1981 | | 33.98 | 11.86 | 8.35 | | 50.29 | 47.69 | 2.21 |
| 1982 | | 38.66 | 12.44 | 10.56 | | 55.30 | 51.50 | 3.05 |
| 1983 | | 45.22 | 15.29 | 13.34 | | 63.25 | 58.14 | 4.32 |
| 1984 | | 70.86 | 25.40 | 18.39 | | 84.53 | 70.42 | 11.76 |
| 1985 | | 62.38 | 22.87 | 25.41 | | 101.56 | 84.85 | 14.89 |
| 1986 | | 84.57 | 27.94 | 34.79 | | 131.70 | 110.61 | 18.86 |
| 1987 | | 110.37 | 31.84 | 44.46 | | 163.63 | 125.85 | 22.99 |
| 1988 | | 123.47 | 38.22 | 50.50 | | 183.32 | 141.01 | 25.90 |
| 1989 | | 146.71 | 39.27 | 68.17 | | 214.41 | 167.66 | 29.65 |
| 1990 | | 198.00 | 48.51 | 92.17 | | 268.40 | 205.63 | 38.30 |
| 1991 | | 253.57 | 63.76 | 121.95 | | 336.85 | 249.51 | 58.82 |
| 1992 | | 315.70 | 83.75 | 154.45 | | 408.64 | 294.63 | 78.75 |
| 1993 | | 386.86 | 89.57 | 198.05 | | 495.71 | 357.59 | 98.88 |
| 1994 | | 518.27 | 143.26 | 285.40 | | 596.96 | 409.16 | 136.46 |
| 1995 | | 676.70 | 193.38 | 401.45 | | 755.39 | 501.66 | 185.89 |
| 1996 | 885.91 | 846.43 | 266.42 | 500.71 | 968.71 | 913.93 | 601.10 | 219.05 |
| 1997 | 1147.92 | 1098.67 | 429.42 | 580.67 | 1224.01 | 1156.13 | 873.14 | 248.06 |
| 1998 | 1359.52 | 1306.04 | 483.80 | 724.54 | 1443.65 | 1358.61 | 978.51 | 299.59 |
| 1999 | 1638.21 | 1580.80 | 544.00 | 909.10 | 1693.64 | 1611.68 | 1093.09 | 398.22 |
| 2000 | 1982.21 | 1904.71 | 645.54 | 1085.36 | 1966.40 | 1881.29 | 1246.81 | 470.70 |
| 2001 | 2377.99 | 2294.05 | 750.81 | 1317.17 | 1969.97 | 1871.98 | 1043.84 | 631.26 |
| 2002 | 2903.42 | 2821.04 | 909.43 | 1595.01 | 2338.17 | 2244.72 | 1191.70 | 754.57 |
| 2003 | 3512.82 | 3438.61 | 1098.15 | 1896.56 | 2976.67 | 2774.81 | 1378.85 | 1010.69 |
| 2004 | 4105.09 | 4039.61 | 1230.85 | 2189.73 | 3309.13 | 3246.28 | 1362.75 | 1346.91 |
| 2005 | 4784.76 | 4727.72 | 1337.05 | 2545.85 | 3779.28 | 3719.52 | 1471.86 | 1810.83 |
| 2006 | 5587.50 | 5519.75 | 1551.98 | 2949.05 | 4443.84 | 4388.28 | 1510.73 | 2392.26 |
| 2007 | 6662.36 | 6576.68 | 1997.71 | 3228.15 | 5197.08 | 5131.69 | 1597.12 | 3220.70 |
| 2008 | 8102.00 | 8021.95 | 2377.48 | 3988.96 | 6384.03 | 6320.81 | 1617.52 | 4093.50 |
| 2009 | 11084.82 | 10933.00 | 3770.43 | 4908.68 | 8856.56 | 8766.06 | 1499.85 | 6563.63 |
| 2010 | 13613.97 | 13454.98 | 4666.88 | 5839.66 | 10999.87 | 10888.15 | 1686.11 | 8705.32 |
| 2011 | 16128.87 | 15832.81 | 8254.56 | 6990.25 | 13195.16 | 13001.39 | 2529.81 | 9968.14 |
| 2012 | 19423.90 | 18934.83 | 9851.06 | 8361.64 | 15594.18 | 15131.22 | 3626.89 | 10919.76 |
| 2013 | 22789.17 | 22202.10 | 11697.54 | 9622.31 | 18005.69 | 17381.55 | 4613.86 | 12105.13 |
| 2014 | 25160.11 | 24501.54 | 12788.24 | 10774.12 | 20630.69 | 20011.50 | 5404.51 | 13615.01 |

注：2011 年起"企业存款"更名为"单位存款"。
Note:The index of "enterprise deposit" is replaced by "corporate deposit" since 2011.

| 年 份 Year | 本外币存款余额 Total Deposit Balance of RMB and Foreign Currencies | 人民币存款余额 Total Deposit Balance of RMB | #住户存款 Deposits of Households | 政府存款 Deposits of Governments | 本外币贷款余额 Total Loan Balance of RMB and Foreign Currencies | 人民币贷款余额 Total Loan Balance of RMB | 短期贷款 Short-term Loans | 中长期贷款 Medium & Long-term Loans |
|---|---|---|---|---|---|---|---|---|
| 2015 | 28778.80 | 28094.37 | 12207.28 | 4235.04 | 22955.21 | 22393.93 | 5539.43 | 15394.18 |
| 2016 | 32160.09 | 31216.45 | 13399.44 | 4743.21 | 25524.17 | 24785.19 | 5383.08 | 17657.00 |
| 2017 | 34853.53 | 33718.98 | 14367.38 | 5994.81 | 28417.46 | 27871.89 | 5517.30 | 20764.52 |
| 2018 | 36887.34 | 35651.57 | 15907.23 | 6651.16 | 32247.75 | 31425.87 | 5371.10 | 23949.57 |
| 2019 | 39483.20 | 37953.11 | 17860.40 | 6994.29 | 37105.02 | 36233.20 | 6091.24 | 27571.85 |
| 2020 | 42854.31 | 41270.20 | 20209.77 | 6823.20 | 41908.91 | 40960.64 | 6692.63 | 31492.83 |
| 2021 | 45908.04 | 44270.21 | 22239.89 | 6786.10 | 46927.61 | 46043.22 | 7597.31 | 34516.69 |
| 2022 | 49567.20 | 48218.18 | 25458.85 | 7247.37 | 50051.89 | 49365.86 | 7736.89 | 36193.43 |

## 表 17.4 金融机构（含外资）本外币信贷收支表（2021 － 2022 年）
## SOURCES AND USES OF RMB AND FOREIGN CURRENCIES CREDIT FUNDS OF FINANCIAL INSTITUTIONS (INCLUDING FOREIGN-FUNDED INSTITUTIONS) (2021-2022)

单位：亿元 (100 million yuan)

| 项　目 | Item | 2021 | 2022 |
|---|---|---|---|
| 各项存款余额 | Total Deposit Balance | 45908.04 | 49567.20 |
| 境内存款 | Domestic Deposit | 45859.33 | 49504.25 |
| 住户存款 | Deposits of Households | 22315.99 | 25539.60 |
| 活期存款 | Demand Deposits | 6678.32 | 7296.36 |
| 定期及其他存款 | Time & Other Deposits | 15637.67 | 18243.24 |
| 非金融企业存款 | Deposits of Non-financial Enterprises | 12902.55 | 12887.84 |
| 活期存款 | Demand Deposits | 4583.49 | 4321.91 |
| 定期及其他存款 | Time & Other Deposits | 8319.05 | 8565.93 |
| 机关团体存款 | Deposits of Government Departments & Organizations | 5437.50 | 6025.80 |
| 财政性存款 | Fiscal Deposits | 1350.21 | 1223.56 |
| 非银行业金融机构存款 | Deposits of Non-banking Financial Institutions | 3853.09 | 3827.45 |
| 境外存款 | Overseas Deposits | 48.70 | 62.95 |
| 各项贷款余额 | Total Loan Balance | 46927.61 | 50051.89 |
| 境内贷款 | Domestic Loans | 46880.60 | 49972.57 |
| 住户贷款 | Loans to Households | 19360.78 | 19201.10 |
| 短期贷款 | Short-term Loans | 3266.47 | 3224.53 |
| 消费贷款 | Consumption Loans | 1525.66 | 1403.53 |
| 经营贷款 | Operating Loans | 1740.80 | 1821.01 |
| 中长期贷款 | Mid & Long-term Loans | 16094.32 | 15976.57 |
| 消费贷款 | Consumption Loans | 14491.83 | 14183.77 |
| 经营贷款 | Operating Loans | 1602.49 | 1792.80 |
| 企（事）业单位贷款 | Loans to enterprises (Institutions) | 27491.81 | 30737.46 |
| 短期贷款 | Short-term Loan | 4969.83 | 4926.11 |
| 中长期贷款 | Mid & Long-term Loans | 18604.28 | 20420.83 |
| 票据融资 | Paper Financing | 2278.68 | 3485.81 |
| 融资租赁 | Financial Leases | 1601.27 | 1877.03 |
| 各项垫款 | Total Advances | 37.75 | 27.69 |
| 非银行业金融机构贷款 | Loans of Non-banking Financial Institutions | 28.01 | 34.01 |
| 境外贷款 | Overseas Loans | 47.01 | 79.33 |

注：外币折本币所用汇率为当年最后一个交易日的中间汇率。
Note: The exchange rates between foreign currencies and RMB are the middle rates on the last trading day in current year.

# 表 17.5 金融机构（含外资）人民币信贷收支表（2021－2022 年）
## SOURCES AND USES OF RMB CREDIT FUNDS OF FINANCIAL INSTITUTIONS (INCLUDING FOREIGN-FUNDED INSTITUTIONS) (2021-2022)

单位：亿元 (100 million yuan)

| 项　目 | Item | 2021 | 2022 |
|---|---|---|---|
| 各项存款余额 | Total Deposit Balance | 44270.21 | 48218.18 |
| 境内存款 | Domestic Deposit | 44236.61 | 48178.35 |
| 住户存款 | Deposits of Households | 22239.89 | 25458.85 |
| 活期存款 | Demand Deposits | 6629.76 | 7247.35 |
| 定期及其他存款 | Time & Other Deposits | 15610.14 | 18211.49 |
| 非金融企业存款 | Deposits of Non-financial Enterprises | 11358.16 | 11645.39 |
| 活期存款 | Demand Deposits | 4340.45 | 4106.48 |
| 定期及其他存款 | Time & Other Deposits | 7017.70 | 7538.91 |
| 机关团体存款 | Deposits of Government Departments & Organizations | 5435.89 | 6023.81 |
| 财政性存款 | Fiscal Deposits | 1350.21 | 1223.56 |
| 非银行业金融机构存款 | Deposits of Non-banking Financial Institutions | 3852.46 | 3826.74 |
| 境外存款 | Overseas Deposits | 33.60 | 39.83 |
| 各项贷款余额 | Total Loan Balance | 46043.22 | 49365.86 |
| 境内贷款 | Domestic Loans | 46031.06 | 49318.44 |
| 住户贷款 | Loans to Households | 19360.46 | 19200.66 |
| 短期贷款 | Short-term Loans | 3266.17 | 3224.13 |
| 消费贷款 | Consumption Loans | 1525.37 | 1403.12 |
| 经营贷款 | Operating Loans | 1740.80 | 1821.01 |
| 中长期贷款 | Mid & Long-term Loans | 16094.29 | 15976.54 |
| 消费贷款 | Consumption Loans | 14491.80 | 14183.74 |
| 经营贷款 | Operating Loans | 1602.49 | 1792.80 |
| 企（事）业单位贷款 | Loans to Enterprises and Institutions | 26642.59 | 30083.77 |
| 短期贷款 | Short-term Loan | 4303.14 | 4478.76 |
| 中长期贷款 | Mid & Long-term Loans | 18422.41 | 20216.89 |
| 票据融资 | Paper Financing | 2278.68 | 3485.81 |
| 融资租赁 | Financial Leases | 1601.27 | 1877.03 |
| 各项垫款 | Total Advances | 37.10 | 25.29 |
| 非银行业金融机构贷款 | Loans of Non-banking Financial Institutions | 28.01 | 34.01 |
| 境外贷款 | Overseas Loans | 12.16 | 47.42 |

## 表 17.6 按行业分金融机构（含外资）本外币贷款结构（2021－2022 年）
## LOAN COMPOSITION OF RMB AND FOREIGN CURRENCIES OF FINANCIAL INSTITUTIONS (INCLUDING FOREIGN-FUNDED INSTITUTIONS) BY SECTOR (2021-2022)

单位：亿元 (100 million yuan)

| 项　目 | Item | 2021 | 2022 |
|---|---|---|---|
| **贷款总计** | **Total Loans** | **45750** | **47664** |
| **按行业分** | **By Sector** | | |
| #农、林、牧、渔业 | Farming, Forestry, Animal Husbandry and Fishery | 143 | 159 |
| 采矿业 | Mining and Quarrying | 174 | 169 |
| 制造业 | Manufacturing | 3138 | 3362 |
| 电力、燃气及水的生产和供应业 | Production and Supply of Electricity, Gas & Water | 1196 | 1116 |
| 建筑业 | Construction | 1741 | 1805 |
| 批发和零售业 | Wholesale and Retail Trades | 1381 | 1407 |
| 交通运输、仓储和邮政业 | Transport, Storage and Post | 4806 | 5483 |
| 住宿和餐饮业 | Hotels and Catering Services | 80 | 81 |
| 信息传输、软件和信息技术服务业 | Information Transmission, Software and IT Services | 91 | 113 |
| 金融业 | Financial Intermediation | 1515 | 1567 |
| 房地产业 | Real Estate | 1859 | 1758 |
| 租赁和商务服务业 | Leasing and Business Services | 4750 | 5401 |
| 科学研究和技术服务业 | Scientific Research and Technology Services | 66 | 62 |
| 水利、环境和公共设施管理业 | Administration of Water Conservancy, Environment and Public Utilities | 5002 | 5451 |
| 居民服务、修理和其他服务业 | Household Services and Repairs and Other Services | 30 | 35 |
| 教　育 | Education | 106 | 122 |
| 卫生和社会工作 | Health and Social Work | 144 | 160 |
| 文化、体育和娱乐业 | Culture, Sports and Entertainment | 110 | 122 |
| 公共管理、社会保障和社会组织 | Public Administration, Social Security and Social Organization | 11 | 10 |
| 对境外贷款 | Loans Abroad | 47 | 79 |
| 个人贷款及透支 | Individual Loans and Overdraft | 19361 | 19201 |

# 表 17.7 金融机构（含外资）房地产贷款投向表（2021 － 2022 年）
LOANS TO REAL ESTATE FROM FINANCIAL INSTITUTIONS (INCLUDING FOREIGN-FUNDED INSTITUTIONS) (2021-2022)

单位：亿元 (100 million yuan)

| 项　目 | Item | 2021 | 2022 |
|---|---|---|---|
| 合　计 | **Total Loans** | **15282.4** | **14829.1** |
| 房地产开发贷款 | Loans to Real Estate Development | 2545.7 | 2526.1 |
| 地产开发贷款 | Loans to Land Development | 601.0 | 575.3 |
| #政府土地储备机构贷款 | Loans to Government Land Reserve Institutions | 14.0 | 10.8 |
| 房产开发贷款 | Loans to Housing Development | 1944.7 | 1950.8 |
| 住房开发贷款 | Loans to Residential Housing Development | 1606.3 | 1602.1 |
| #保障性住房开发贷款 | Loans to Low-income Housing Development | 600.4 | 597.1 |
| 商业用房开发贷款 | Loans to Housing for Commercial Use | 338.4 | 348.7 |
| 其他房产开发贷款 | Loans to Other Housing Development | | |
| 购房贷款 | Housing Purchase Loan | 12736.7 | 12302.9 |
| 企业购房贷款 | Enterprise Housing Purchase Loan | 116.6 | 132.9 |
| 商业用房贷款 | Loan for Housing for Commercial Use | 115.9 | 127.3 |
| 住房贷款 | Loan for Housing for Residential Use | 0.7 | 5.6 |
| 个人购房贷款 | Individual Housing Loan | 12620.0 | 12170.0 |
| 个人商业用房贷款 | Loan for Housing for Commercial Use | 245.1 | 194.1 |
| 个人住房贷款 | Loan for Housing for Residential Use | 12374.9 | 11975.9 |
| 新建房贷款 | Loan for Newly Built Housing | 9145.4 | 8670.9 |
| #抵押贷款 | Mortgage Loan | 9078.2 | 8632.6 |
| 再交易房贷款 | Loan for Second-hand Housing | 3229.5 | 3305.0 |
| 个人购买保障性住房贷款 | Individual Loan for Purchasing Low-income Housing | 6.0 | 6.5 |

# 表 17.8 金融机构（含外资）境内大中小型企业人民币贷款情况统计表（2021－2022 年）

## STATISTICS ON THE RMB LOANS TO THE DOMESTIC LARGE, MEDIUM AND SMALL ENTERPRISES FROM FINANCIAL INSTITUTIONS (INCLUDING FOREIGN-FUNDED INSTITUTIONS) (2021-2022)

单位：亿元 (100 million yuan)

| 项　目 | Item | 大型企业贷款 Large | | 中型企业贷款 Medium | | 小型企业贷款 Small | |
|---|---|---|---|---|---|---|---|
| | | 2021 | 2022 | 2021 | 2022 | 2021 | 2022 |
| **境内企业贷款合计** | **Total Loans to Domestic Enterprises** | **8385.4** | **8498.3** | **9742.3** | **10436.5** | **6097.1** | **7153.0** |
| #农、林、牧、渔业 | Farming, Forestry, Animal Husbandry and Fishery | 36.0 | 30.9 | 45.6 | 64.6 | 49.0 | 52.2 |
| 采矿业 | Mining and Quarrying | 114.7 | 96.8 | 41.2 | 45.1 | 15.0 | 20.2 |
| 制造业 | Manufacturing | 1719.5 | 1712.7 | 617.8 | 774.0 | 693.3 | 755.6 |
| 电力、燃气及水的生产和供应业 | Production and Supply of Electricity, Gas & Water | 344.0 | 296.2 | 376.1 | 372.2 | 444.3 | 412.7 |
| 建筑业 | Construction | 588.0 | 661.8 | 747.6 | 718.0 | 317.0 | 329.1 |
| 批发和零售业 | Wholesale and Retail Trades | 339.5 | 286.0 | 439.9 | 437.6 | 504.3 | 554.6 |
| 交通运输、仓储和邮政业 | Transport, Storage and Post | 2401.2 | 2559.4 | 1241.3 | 1429.6 | 1008.2 | 1291.5 |
| 住宿和餐饮业 | Hotels and Catering Services | 5.7 | 2.5 | 32.6 | 28.8 | 34.1 | 41.5 |
| 信息传输、计算机服务和软件业 | Information Transmission, Computer Services and Software | 12.8 | 19.9 | 28.6 | 35.2 | 34.7 | 44.1 |
| 金融业 | Financial Intermediation | 127.8 | 168.5 | 101.4 | 105.1 | 38.8 | 38.2 |
| 房地产业 | Real Estate | 305.3 | 238.6 | 1392.5 | 1335.0 | 85.8 | 91.0 |
| 租赁和商务服务业 | Leasing and Business Services | 1324.7 | 1389.7 | 1931.8 | 2143.2 | 1440.7 | 1818.3 |
| 科学研究和技术服务业 | Scientific Research and Technology Service | 7.4 | 6.4 | 27.0 | 16.9 | 25.6 | 30.5 |
| 水利、环境和公共设施管理业 | Administration of Water Conservancy, Environment and Public Utilities | 984.5 | 952.9 | 2649.2 | 2864.2 | 1339.7 | 1593.0 |
| 居民服务、修理和其他服务业 | Household Services and Other Services | 1.2 | 0.9 | 4.2 | 4.2 | 17.5 | 21.6 |
| 教　育 | Education | 21.5 | 20.5 | 27.7 | 26.9 | 12.9 | 11.9 |
| 卫生和社会工作 | Health and Social Work | 3.4 | 7.7 | 16.1 | 14.8 | 10.1 | 10.5 |
| 文化、体育和娱乐业 | Culture, Sports and Entertainment | 48.3 | 46.8 | 21.7 | 21.0 | 26.0 | 36.4 |
| **境内企业贷款合计** | **Total Loans to Domestic Enterprises** | **8385.4** | **8498.3** | **9742.3** | **10436.5** | **6097.1** | **7153.0** |
| 正常类贷款 | Pass Loan | 7994.3 | 8125.9 | 9279.2 | 9939.3 | 5857.0 | 6931.9 |
| 关注类贷款 | Special Mention Loan | 307.7 | 167.7 | 311.1 | 313.5 | 145.7 | 134.7 |
| 次级类贷款 | Substandard Loan | 22.1 | 115.9 | 57.6 | 87.4 | 21.2 | 37.5 |
| 可疑类贷款 | Doubtful Loan | 47.3 | 74.5 | 73.2 | 76.9 | 59.2 | 23.2 |
| 损失类贷款 | Loss Loan | 13.9 | 14.3 | 21.3 | 19.4 | 14.0 | 25.7 |
| **境内企业贷款合计** | **Total Loans to Domestic Enterprises** | **8385.4** | **8498.3** | **9742.3** | **10436.5** | **6097.1** | **7153.0** |
| 信用贷款 | Fiduciary Loan | 3183.6 | 3540.3 | 2654.1 | 3029.4 | 1263.9 | 1469.1 |
| 保证贷款 | Guaranteed Loan | 1702.9 | 1614.2 | 2856.9 | 3006.9 | 2647.2 | 3292.8 |
| 抵（质）押贷款 | Mortgage Loan | 3498.8 | 3343.8 | 4231.3 | 4400.3 | 2185.9 | 2391.1 |
| **境内企业贷款合计** | **Total Loans to Domestic Enterprises** | **8385.4** | **8498.3** | **9742.3** | **10436.5** | **6097.1** | **7153.0** |
| 国有控股企业 | State-holding Enterprise | 6718.7 | 6952.9 | 7491.0 | 8267.9 | 4418.1 | 5402.1 |
| 集体控股企业 | Collective-holding Enterprise | 37.6 | 38.5 | 120.9 | 99.2 | 24.3 | 21.5 |
| 私人控股企业 | Private-holding Enterprise | 842.0 | 797.0 | 1754.8 | 1664.5 | 1571.8 | 1655.0 |
| 港澳台商控股企业 | Hong Kong, Macao or Taiwan-holding Enterprise | 597.3 | 418.1 | 276.7 | 313.9 | 40.3 | 33.5 |
| 外商控股企业 | Foreign-holding Enterprise | 189.7 | 291.6 | 98.9 | 91.0 | 42.5 | 40.9 |

# 表 17.9 上市公司情况（1993 － 2022 年）
## STATISTICS ON LISTED COMPANIES (1993-2022)

单位：个 (unit)

| 年 份<br>Year | 全市总计<br>Total | 上交所<br>Shanghai Stock Exchange | 深交所<br>Shenzhen Stock Exchange | 仅发 A 股公司<br>A Share Only | 发 A、B 股公司<br>A & B Shares | 仅发 B 股公司<br>B Share Only | 发 A、H 股公司<br>A & H Shares |
|---|---|---|---|---|---|---|---|
| 1993 | 3 | 1 | 2 | 3 | | | |
| 1994 | 5 | 2 | 3 | 5 | | | |
| 1995 | 7 | 3 | 4 | 6 | | 1 | |
| 1996 | 11 | 4 | 7 | 10 | | 1 | |
| 1997 | 19 | 8 | 11 | 17 | 1 | 1 | |
| 1998 | 19 | 8 | 11 | 17 | 1 | 1 | |
| 1999 | 22 | 9 | 13 | 20 | 1 | 1 | |
| 2000 | 25 | 11 | 14 | 23 | 1 | 1 | |
| 2001 | 26 | 12 | 14 | 24 | 1 | 1 | |
| 2002 | 27 | 13 | 14 | 25 | 1 | 1 | |
| 2003 | 27 | 13 | 14 | 25 | 1 | 1 | |
| 2004 | 29 | 14 | 15 | 27 | 1 | 1 | |
| 2005 | 29 | 14 | 15 | 27 | 1 | 1 | |
| 2006 | 29 | 14 | 15 | 27 | 1 | 1 | |
| 2007 | 30 | 15 | 15 | 27 | 1 | 1 | 1 |
| 2008 | 31 | 15 | 16 | 28 | 1 | 1 | 1 |
| 2009 | 31 | 15 | 16 | 28 | 1 | 1 | 1 |
| 2010 | 34 | 16 | 18 | 31 | 1 | 1 | 1 |
| 2011 | 36 | 20 | 16 | 33 | 1 | 1 | 1 |
| 2012 | 37 | 19 | 18 | 34 | 1 | 1 | 1 |
| 2013 | 37 | 19 | 18 | 34 | 1 | 1 | 1 |
| 2014 | 40 | 21 | 19 | 37 | 1 | 1 | 1 |
| 2015 | 43 | 21 | 22 | 40 | 1 | 1 | 1 |
| 2016 | 44 | 22 | 22 | 41 | 1 | 1 | 1 |
| 2017 | 50 | 26 | 24 | 47 | 1 | 1 | 1 |
| 2018 | 50 | 26 | 24 | 47 | 1 | 1 | 1 |
| 2019 | 54 | 28 | 26 | 50 | 1 | 1 | 2 |
| 2020 | 57 | 29 | 28 | 53 | 1 | 1 | 2 |
| 2021 | 63 | 31 | 30 | 58 | 1 | 1 | 3 |
| 2022 | 70 | 34 | 32 | 65 | 1 | 1 | 3 |

注：本表不包括仅发 H 股的公司。
Note: Companies with H share only are not included in this table.

# 表 17.10 有价证券发行情况（1981 － 2022 年）
## ISSUANCE OF SECURITIES (1981-2022)

单位：亿元 (100 million yuan)

| 年 份<br>Year | 股票筹资额<br>Raised Capital | A 股<br>A Shares | B 股<br>B Shares |
|---|---|---|---|
| 1981 | | | |
| 1982 | | | |
| 1983 | | | |
| 1984 | | | |
| 1985 | | | |
| 1986 | | | |
| 1987 | | | |
| 1988 | | | |
| 1989 | | | |
| 1990 | | | |
| 1991 | | | |
| 1992 | | | |
| 1993 | 2.08 | 2.08 | |
| 1994 | 1.13 | 1.13 | |
| 1995 | 5.30 | 0.52 | 4.78 |
| 1996 | 10.41 | 4.56 | 5.85 |
| 1997 | 26.76 | 26.76 | |
| 1998 | 3.75 | 3.75 | |
| 1999 | 7.21 | 7.21 | |
| 2000 | 22.63 | 22.63 | |
| 2001 | 4.73 | 4.73 | |
| 2002 | 3.16 | 3.16 | |
| 2003 | 3.74 | 3.74 | |
| 2004 | 15.65 | 15.65 | |
| 2005 | | | |
| 2006 | 14.63 | 14.63 | |
| 2007 | 26.37 | 26.37 | |
| 2008 | 12.73 | 12.73 | |
| 2009 | 17.56 | 17.56 | |
| 2010 | 149.00 | 149.00 | |
| 2011 | 158.02 | 158.02 | |
| 2012 | 30.00 | 30.00 | |
| 2013 | 131.23 | 131.23 | |
| 2014 | 180.88 | 180.83 | |
| 2015 | 127.01 | 127.01 | |
| 2016 | 443.56 | 443.56 | |
| 2017 | 102.97 | 102.97 | |
| 2018 | 34.84 | 34.84 | |
| 2019 | 148.11 | 148.11 | |
| 2020 | 250.49 | 250.49 | |
| 2021 | 173.00 | 173.00 | |
| 2022 | 173.00 | 173.00 | |

注：股票发行量和筹资额均不含 H 股。
Note: The amount of issued shares and raised capital don't include H share.

## 表 17.11 保险业务基本情况（1996 － 2022 年）
BASIC STATISTICS ON INSURANCE BUSINESS (1996-2022)

单位：亿元 (100 million yuan)

| 年 份<br>Year | 保费收入<br>Premium | 财产保险<br>Property Insurance | 人身保险<br>Life Insurance | 赔款及给付<br>Claim and Payments | 财产保险<br>Property Insurance | 人身保险<br>Life Insurance |
|---|---|---|---|---|---|---|
| 1996 | 12.82 | 8.05 | 4.77 | 6.48 | 4.44 | 2.04 |
| 1997 | 19.52 | 9.03 | 10.49 | 7.18 | 4.39 | 2.79 |
| 1998 | 22.77 | 9.31 | 13.46 | 10.64 | 6.55 | 4.09 |
| 1999 | 25.39 | 10.04 | 15.35 | 8.91 | 4.96 | 3.95 |
| 2000 | 27.71 | 10.72 | 16.99 | 8.27 | 5.28 | 2.99 |
| 2001 | 33.72 | 11.32 | 22.40 | 11.25 | 5.91 | 5.34 |
| 2002 | 46.17 | 13.31 | 32.86 | 14.20 | 7.57 | 6.63 |
| 2003 | 57.93 | 15.24 | 42.69 | 14.53 | 8.56 | 5.97 |
| 2004 | 66.51 | 17.45 | 49.06 | 16.25 | 9.43 | 6.82 |
| 2005 | 73.10 | 19.46 | 53.64 | 17.59 | 10.54 | 7.05 |
| 2006 | 93.24 | 24.17 | 69.07 | 20.51 | 12.08 | 8.43 |
| 2007 | 124.68 | 33.10 | 91.58 | 35.25 | 18.44 | 16.81 |
| 2008 | 200.55 | 37.76 | 162.80 | 45.64 | 22.59 | 23.05 |
| 2009 | 244.70 | 47.05 | 197.65 | 56.63 | 28.88 | 27.75 |
| 2010 | 321.08 | 65.96 | 255.12 | 62.10 | 32.05 | 30.05 |
| 2011 | 311.81 | 81.63 | 230.19 | 73.98 | 39.31 | 34.66 |
| 2012 | 331.03 | 95.20 | 235.83 | 91.78 | 52.23 | 39.55 |
| 2013 | 359.23 | 112.52 | 246.71 | 124.60 | 62.98 | 61.62 |
| 2014 | 407.26 | 138.87 | 268.39 | 151.43 | 74.07 | 77.36 |
| 2015 | 514.58 | 155.93 | 358.65 | 220.19 | 84.65 | 135.54 |
| 2016 | 601.61 | 165.23 | 436.38 | 250.16 | 90.37 | 159.79 |
| 2017 | 744.75 | 183.87 | 560.88 | 256.83 | 96.46 | 160.37 |
| 2018 | 806.24 | 202.48 | 603.76 | 277.37 | 108.62 | 168.75 |
| 2019 | 916.46 | 220.22 | 696.24 | 278.99 | 115.95 | 163.05 |
| 2020 | 987.62 | 230.22 | 757.40 | 295.43 | 125.48 | 169.95 |
| 2021 | 965.50 | 213.70 | 751.80 | 302.20 | 147.70 | 154.50 |
| 2022 | 981.09 | 226.63 | 754.45 | 342.99 | 145.19 | 197.80 |

# 表 17.12 按险种分的保险业务指标（2021 － 2022 年）
## STATISTICS ON INSURANCE BUSINESS BY CLASSIFICATION (2021-2022)

单位：万元（10 000 yuan）

| 项 目 | Item | 保 费 Premium | | 赔款及给付 Claim and Payment | |
|---|---|---|---|---|---|
| | | 2021 | 2022 | 2021 | 2022 |
| 合 计 | **Total** | **9655001** | **9810858** | **3021719** | **3429943** |
| 财产保险 | Property Insurance | 2137496 | 2266345 | 1476637 | 1451920 |
| 企业财产保险 | Enterprise Property Insurance | 65320 | 63990 | 35784 | 26785 |
| 家庭财产保险 | Family Property Insurance | 13317 | 23526 | 5013 | 3737 |
| 机动车辆保险 | Motor Vehicle Insurance | 1574297 | 1650881 | 1116178 | 1045108 |
| 工程保险 | Engineering Insurance | 40984 | 22918 | 18510 | 12372 |
| 责任保险 | Liability Insurance | 163165 | 183660 | 79757 | 84033 |
| 信用保险 | Export Credit Insurance | 17128 | 39491 | 6131 | 16353 |
| 保证保险 | Guarantee Insurance | 126328 | 105025 | 94862 | 143452 |
| 船舶保险 | Ship Insurance | 9649 | 9286 | 6006 | 4405 |
| 货物运输保险 | Freight Transport Insurance | 19969 | 17119 | 7850 | 7481 |
| 特殊风险保险 | Special Risks Insurance | 2173 | 1709 | 366 | 475 |
| 农业保险 | Agriculture Insurance | 91506 | 123445 | 97722 | 96725 |
| 其他保险 | Other Insurances | 13659 | 25296 | 8459 | 10993 |
| 人身保险 | Life Insurance | 7517505 | 7544514 | 1545082 | 1978023 |
| 人寿保险 | Life Insurance | 5192252 | 5201540 | 621087 | 752753 |
| 健康保险 | Health Insurance | 2062845 | 2127076 | 835563 | 1150130 |
| 意外伤害保险 | Personal Accident Insurance | 262408 | 215897 | 88431 | 75141 |

重/庆/统/计/年/鉴

# 主要统计指标解释

## ■ 各项存款

金融机构资金来源的主要项目，包括住户存款、非金融企业存款、机关团体存款、财政性存款、非银行业金融机构存款和境外存款。

## ■ 各项贷款

金融机构资金运用的主要项目，包括住户贷款、非金融企业及机关团体贷款、非银行业金融机构贷款和境外贷款。

## ■ 保险公司

在中国境内的、经过保险监督管理部门批准设立，并依法登记注册的各类商业保险公司。

## ■ 保险金额

指保险人承担赔偿或者给付保险金责任的最高限额。

## ■ 保费

指投保人为取得保险人在约定范围内所承担赔偿责任而支付给保险人的费用。

## ■ 赔款

指保险人根据保险合同的规定，向被保险人支付的赔偿保险责任损失的金额。

## ■ 给付

包括死伤医疗给付和满期给付。死伤医疗给付是指保险人根据人寿保险及长期健康保险合同的规定，因被保险人在保险期内发生保险责任范围内的保险事故支付给被保险人（或受益人）的金额。满期给付是指被保险人生存期满，保险人按人寿保险合同规定支付给被保险人的满期保险金额。

## ■ 社会融资规模增量

指一定时期内实体经济从金融体系获得的资金总额。主要包括：人民币贷款、外币贷款（折合人民币）、委托贷款、信托贷款、未贴现的银行承兑汇票、企业债券、政府债券、非金融企业境内股票融资、投资性房地产、保险公司赔偿等。

## ■ 社会融资规模存量

指一定时期末（月末、季末或年末）实体经济从金融体系获得的资金余额。主要包括：人民币贷款、外币贷款（折合人民币）、委托贷款、信托贷款、未贴现的银行承兑汇票、企业债券、政府债券、非金融企业境内股票融资、投资性房地产等。

## ■ 境内上市公司数

指在统计期末其发行的股票在沪、深交易所上市的股份有限公司的数量。以股票上市日进行统计，同时发行A、B股的上市公司，按一家计算。

## ■ 股票总发行股本

也称上市公司总股本，是指统计期末上市公司在境内发行的全部股份数量合计，包括A股股本、B股股本和其他不流通的境内股本。

## ■ 股票市价总值

指统计期末根据上市公司股票价格和对应股票数量计算的股权价值合计。具体统计口径和计算方法如下：如当日无交易价格，采用最后交易日的收盘价；暂停上市股票的价格以零计算；未股改公司的非流通股以流通A股价格计算市值；仅发行B股的上市公司，其非流通股不进行股票市值计算；对当日除权股票进行市值计算时需要包含在途股份（已登记未上市）的市值。

## ■ 交易所债券发行额

指统计期内各类债券发行票面金额合计。按发行首日口径计算。

## ■ 债券成交额

指统计期内各类债券成交金额合计，包括债券现货成交金额和债券回购成交金额。

## ■ 证券投资基金只数

指统计期末基金市场上基金产品的只数。自基金合同生效日（基金成立日）纳入统计，自基金合同终止日从统计中剔除。一般根据证监会主代码（基金主合同）口径统计。

EXPLANATORY NOTES TO
MAJOR STATISTICAL INDICATORS

# Explanatory Notes on Main Statistical Indicators

## Total Deposits

Are the main items of financial sources of financial institutions, which include deposits of households, deposits of non-financial enterprises, deposits of government departments & organizations, fiscal deposits, deposits of non-banking financial institutions and overseas deposits.

## Total Loans

Are the main items of financial uses of financial institutions, which include loans to households, loans to non-financial enterprises and government departments & organizations, loans to non-banking financial institutions and overseas loans.

## Insurance Companies

Refer to commercial insurance companies of various forms registered by law and established in China with the approval of insurance regulatory agencies.

## Amount Insured

Refers to the maximum that the insurant will get for the claim of the case insured.

## Premium

Is the fee paid by the insurant to the insurer to obtain the obligation of compensation from the insurance within the agreed terms.

## Settled Claim

Is the compensation paid by the insurer to the insurant in accordance with the insurance contract.

## Payment

Includes payment for death, injury or medical treatment and payment at maturity. Payment for death, injury or medical treatment refers to the money paid to the insurant (or the beneficiary) in accordance with the life or health insurance contract when the insurant encounters accidents within the insured period covered in the contract. Payment at maturity refers to the payment to the insurant in accordance with the life insurance contract at the end of the insured period.

## Aggregate Financing to the Real Economy (Flow)

Refers to the total volume of financing provided by the financial system to the real economy over a period of time. It includes: RMB loans, foreign currency-denominated loans (RMB equivalent), credit loans, entrusted loans, undiscounted banker's acceptances, corporate bonds, government bonds, domestic equity financing of non-financial enterprises, investment real estate, premium of insurance, etc.

## Aggregate Financing to the Real Economy (Stock)

Refers to the total volume of financing provided by the financial system to the real economy at the end of a period (at the end of month, quarter or year). It includes: RMB loans, foreign currency-denominated loans (RMB equivalent), credit loans, entrusted loans, undiscounted banker's acceptances, corporate bonds, government bonds, domestic equity financing of non-financial enterprises, investment real estate, etc.

## Number of Domestic Listed Companies

Refers to the number of limited companies whose stocks issued are listed on the Shanghai or Shenzhen exchanges at the end of the statistical period. A listed company that issues both A and B shares at the same time are counted as one company by the date of listing.

## Total Issued Capital

Also known as total stock of listed companies, refers to the total number of shares issued by domestic listed companies at the end of the statistical period, including A share capital, B share capital and other non-tradable domestic equity.

## Total Market Capitalization

Refers to the total stock value according to the stock price of listed companies and the corresponding stock quantity at the end of the statistical period. Specific statistical coverage and calculation methods are as follows: if there is no trading price on the day, the closing price on the last trading day shall be adopted; the price of suspended listed shares shall be calculated at zero; the non-tradable shares of non-equity-restructured companies shall be calculated at the price of circulating A shares; the non-tradable shares of listed companies that issue only B shares shall not be calculated at the market value of their non-tradable shares on the same day. When calculating the market value of the right stock, the market value of the shares in transit (registered and unlisted) should be included.

## Value of Bonds in the Exchanges Issued

Refers to the total amount of coupon issued by various types of bonds during the statistical period. It is calculated at the coverage of the first day of issue.

## Bonds Trading Turnover

Refers to the total amount of all kinds of bonds traded during the statistical period, including the spot amount of bonds traded and the amount of bond repurchase traded.

## Number of Securities Investment Funds

Refers to the number of fund products in the fund market at the end of the period. It is counted since the effective date of the fund contract (the establishment date of the fund), and is excluded from the statistics since the termination date of the fund contract. It is generally counted at the coverage of the main code of the Securities Regulatory Commission (the main contract of the fund).

# 第十八章·教育、科技和文化业

EDUCATION, SCIENCE, TECHNOLOGY AND CULTURE

# 简要说明
BRIEF INTRODUCTION

本章资料主要包括全市教育事业、科学技术活动和文化事业的基本情况，由市统计局社会科技统计处根据调查资料和有关部门资料整理编辑。

教育部分包括各类教育的学校、教师和学生情况，由市教育委员会提供；专利资料由市知识产权局提供；商标申请注册来源于市市场监督管理局；文化部分主要包括图书馆、文物、群众艺术文化、广播电视、新闻出版等情况，资料主要来自市文化和旅游发展委员会。

The data in this chapter include the basic statistics on education, scientific & technological activities and culture undertakings. All the data are compiled by Division of Social and Technology Statistics, Chongqing Municipal Bureau of Statistics on the basis of the data from survey and related departments.

The statistics of education cover the data of schools, teachers and students of various kinds, which were provided by Chongqing Education Commission. The data of patent are provided by Chongqing Intellectual Property Office. The data of sampling supervision & check on quality of products are provided by Chongqing Administration for Market Regulation. The data of culture mainly include public libraries, cultural relics, mass arts & culture, radio and television, and press and publication, which are provided by Commission of Culture and Tourism of Chongqing.

# 表 18.1 主要年份各级各类学校数
## NUMBER OF SCHOOLS BY LEVEL AND TYPE IN MAJOR YEARS

单位：所 (unit)

| 年 份<br>Year | 普通高等学校<br>Regular Institutions of Higher Education | 普通中学<br>Regular Secondary Schools | 小 学<br>Primary Schools | 特殊教育学校<br>Special Schools | 幼儿园<br>Kindergartens |
|---|---|---|---|---|---|
| 1952 | 7 | 128 | 12920 | | |
| 1957 | 9 | 249 | 16201 | | |
| 1962 | 10 | 402 | 14148 | | |
| 1965 | 11 | 696 | 31503 | | |
| 1970 | 11 | 1700 | 21253 | | |
| 1975 | 8 | 1366 | 25465 | | |
| 1978 | 13 | 2948 | 25002 | | |
| 1980 | 16 | 1989 | 25120 | | |
| 1985 | 18 | 1788 | 22793 | 7 | 5800 |
| 1986 | 19 | 1739 | 22486 | 19 | 5230 |
| 1987 | 19 | 1759 | 22094 | 18 | 5542 |
| 1988 | 20 | 1753 | 21629 | 20 | 5009 |
| 1989 | 20 | 1751 | 20972 | 23 | 4726 |
| 1990 | 20 | 1753 | 20248 | 24 | 5232 |
| 1991 | 20 | 1762 | 19829 | 29 | 4486 |
| 1992 | 20 | 1766 | 19496 | 32 | 4814 |
| 1993 | 20 | 1746 | 18849 | 30 | 4061 |
| 1994 | 20 | 1725 | 18175 | 31 | 4094 |
| 1995 | 22 | 1638 | 19637 | 30 | 6046 |
| 1996 | 22 | 1651 | 16779 | 36 | 5538 |
| 1997 | 22 | 1606 | 16261 | 37 | 5741 |
| 1998 | 22 | 1555 | 15737 | 37 | 5412 |
| 1999 | 23 | 1552 | 15223 | 42 | 6007 |
| 2000 | 22 | 1568 | 14730 | 42 | 6659 |
| 2001 | 29 | 1607 | 13076 | 44 | 3726 |
| 2002 | 29 | 1574 | 12031 | 38 | 3477 |
| 2003 | 33 | 1564 | 10966 | 41 | 3093 |
| 2004 | 34 | 1511 | 10409 | 43 | 3408 |
| 2005 | 35 | 1414 | 9558 | 43 | 3287 |
| 2006 | 38 | 1373 | 8754 | 44 | 3376 |
| 2007 | 38 | 1361 | 7990 | 43 | 3351 |
| 2008 | 47 | 1325 | 7575 | 41 | 3582 |
| 2009 | 51 | 1304 | 7096 | 36 | 3700 |
| 2010 | 53 | 1273 | 5544 | 36 | 4105 |
| 2011 | 59 | 1259 | 5248 | 36 | 4114 |
| 2012 | 60 | 1231 | 4810 | 36 | 4401 |
| 2013 | 63 | 1200 | 4728 | 36 | 4547 |
| 2014 | 63 | 1179 | 4586 | 36 | 4669 |
| 2015 | 64 | 1167 | 4170 | 36 | 4816 |
| 2016 | 65 | 1120 | 2979 | 36 | 5109 |
| 2017 | 65 | 1118 | 2954 | 36 | 5210 |
| 2018 | 65 | 1122 | 2893 | 38 | 5607 |
| 2019 | 65 | 1127 | 2860 | 39 | 5660 |
| 2020 | 68 | 1132 | 2754 | 39 | 5704 |
| 2021 | 69 | 1123 | 2717 | 39 | 5684 |
| 2022 | 70 | 1120 | 2637 | 39 | 5667 |

注：1）2001 年起幼儿园资料按教育部对幼儿园数的认定标准统计，与以往年数不可比（下表同）。
2）2008 年学校数含"独立学院"数。

Note: a) The data of kindergartens have been calculated in accordance with the definition by Ministry of Education since 2001, not comparable with that of previous years (the same below).
b) Number of schools in 2008 includes the number of "non-university tertiary".

# 表 18.2 主要年份各级各类学校在校学生数
## NUMBER OF STUDENTS ENROLLMENT BY LEVEL AND TYPE IN MAJOR YEARS

单位：人 (person)

| 年 份<br>Year | 普通高等学校<br>Regular Institutions of Higher Education | 普通中学<br>Regular Secondary Schools | 小 学<br>Primary Schools | 特殊教育学校<br>Special Schools | 幼儿园<br>Kindergartens |
|---|---|---|---|---|---|
| 1952 | 6437 | 61345 | 1524145 | | |
| 1957 | 15211 | 181423 | 1539805 | | |
| 1962 | 21173 | 163628 | 1640036 | | |
| 1965 | 17408 | 266504 | 1967997 | | |
| 1970 | 4235 | 651232 | 2130534 | | |
| 1975 | 10194 | 963304 | 3415196 | | |
| 1978 | 16357 | 1631581 | 4035934 | | |
| 1980 | 25349 | 1323181 | 4316902 | | |
| 1985 | 39871 | 1102702 | 3857331 | 418 | 296336 |
| 1986 | 44454 | 1107545 | 3610433 | 543 | 306591 |
| 1987 | 47644 | 1122462 | 3279059 | 571 | 409209 |
| 1988 | 49981 | 1124510 | 2858642 | 669 | 389185 |
| 1989 | 48449 | 1111706 | 2581889 | 831 | 351175 |
| 1990 | 49331 | 1080755 | 2393235 | 803 | 413552 |
| 1991 | 49964 | 978204 | 2314986 | 1179 | 505799 |
| 1992 | 54121 | 868431 | 2361261 | 1966 | 549271 |
| 1993 | 63795 | 790396 | 2500362 | 1850 | 445940 |
| 1994 | 71118 | 876008 | 2595400 | 1415 | 534177 |
| 1995 | 73398 | 977079 | 2638555 | 1783 | 577162 |
| 1996 | 79929 | 1012654 | 2737051 | 1832 | 588854 |
| 1997 | 83764 | 1002915 | 2854307 | 1706 | 590464 |
| 1998 | 86913 | 1083691 | 2884385 | 2325 | 613298 |
| 1999 | 101601 | 1282599 | 2802741 | 9007 | 625666 |
| 2000 | 132512 | 1477861 | 2761308 | 21160 | 640804 |
| 2001 | 170006 | 1540317 | 2777859 | 18383 | 599282 |
| 2002 | 211221 | 1574357 | 2797557 | 17199 | 587645 |
| 2003 | 255266 | 1663728 | 2779441 | 14483 | 572538 |
| 2004 | 303913 | 1707489 | 2718999 | 15973 | 544759 |
| 2005 | 357926 | 1735166 | 2609754 | 12463 | 536266 |
| 2006 | 405118 | 1794129 | 2523824 | 12151 | 530842 |
| 2007 | 445800 | 1834364 | 2384527 | 11773 | 535457 |
| 2008 | 485013 | 1907856 | 2243916 | 12172 | 574187 |
| 2009 | 523279 | 1920158 | 2081367 | 13189 | 632170 |
| 2010 | 565868 | 1908158 | 1999407 | 14618 | 708711 |
| 2011 | 613026 | 1838917 | 1954818 | 16978 | 842846 |
| 2012 | 670174 | 1747002 | 1943177 | 13083 | 892635 |
| 2013 | 707610 | 1678976 | 1989128 | 15622 | 893338 |
| 2014 | 740534 | 1627301 | 2034165 | 13893 | 894679 |
| 2015 | 767114 | 1583562 | 2073320 | 14059 | 915616 |
| 2016 | 784631 | 1572832 | 2098191 | 16079 | 932584 |
| 2017 | 805208 | 1592207 | 2099536 | 18585 | 958667 |
| 2018 | 827945 | 1653294 | 2095361 | 21405 | 963121 |
| 2019 | 907426 | 1732325 | 2062948 | 25362 | 982526 |
| 2020 | 998650 | 1776046 | 2024671 | 27006 | 1007833 |
| 2021 | 1100122 | 1772254 | 2030863 | 27446 | 995239 |
| 2022 | 1171607 | 1750773 | 2031938 | 26605 | 961364 |

注：本章普通高等学校数据均含研究生（以下各表同）。
Note: The data of regular institutions of higher education in this chapter include postgraduates(the same applies to the following tables).

# 表 18.3 主要年份各级各类学校专任教师数
## NUMBER OF FULL-TIME TEACHERS BY LEVEL AND TYPE IN MAJOR YEARS

单位：人 (person)

| 年 份<br>Year | 普通高等学校<br>Regular Institutions of Higher Education | 普通中学<br>Regular Secondary Schools | 小 学<br>Primary Schools | 特殊教育学校<br>Special Schools | 幼儿园<br>Kindergartens |
|---|---|---|---|---|---|
| 1952 | 839 | 3385 | 41698 | | |
| 1957 | 2193 | 7940 | 52530 | | |
| 1962 | 3297 | | 55213 | | |
| 1965 | 3336 | | 78503 | | |
| 1970 | 3177 | 24970 | 73695 | | |
| 1975 | 3574 | 42893 | | | |
| 1978 | 3914 | | | | |
| 1980 | 5025 | 60953 | 125304 | | |
| 1985 | 8061 | 58886 | 119119 | 74 | 11937 |
| 1986 | 8236 | 55071 | 113724 | 101 | 12054 |
| 1987 | 8622 | 57044 | 112163 | 113 | 15090 |
| 1988 | 8823 | 60450 | 111596 | 145 | 15873 |
| 1989 | 8726 | 61938 | 109691 | 186 | 15898 |
| 1990 | 8677 | 64056 | 110580 | 186 | 17443 |
| 1991 | 8596 | 64934 | 111305 | 277 | 19313 |
| 1992 | 8696 | 65030 | 111667 | 321 | 19244 |
| 1993 | 8777 | 63555 | 113834 | 326 | 18388 |
| 1994 | 9186 | 65316 | 116603 | 360 | 19729 |
| 1995 | 9409 | 67498 | 117497 | 353 | 19948 |
| 1996 | 9400 | 69503 | 117711 | 383 | 20111 |
| 1997 | 9432 | 70661 | 119881 | 411 | 20665 |
| 1998 | 9498 | 72333 | 121062 | 400 | 20962 |
| 1999 | 9987 | 76158 | 120229 | 469 | 21088 |
| 2000 | 10449 | 81766 | 119014 | 569 | 22598 |
| 2001 | 12125 | 85030 | 118623 | 474 | 12067 |
| 2002 | 13954 | 87427 | 117543 | 510 | 11666 |
| 2003 | 16013 | 89560 | 115212 | 543 | 12141 |
| 2004 | 18214 | 92051 | 114007 | 541 | 12351 |
| 2005 | 20184 | 93997 | 114326 | 556 | 13220 |
| 2006 | 23717 | 95782 | 113724 | 584 | 13615 |
| 2007 | 26089 | 99807 | 119831 | 652 | 14270 |
| 2008 | 28398 | 103111 | 119161 | 670 | 15507 |
| 2009 | 29883 | 106544 | 117460 | 699 | 16579 |
| 2010 | 31070 | 109303 | 116057 | 715 | 19966 |
| 2011 | 33110 | 110951 | 115343 | 763 | 22807 |
| 2012 | 35744 | 112452 | 114036 | 804 | 26735 |
| 2013 | 37130 | 113880 | 115204 | 852 | 30199 |
| 2014 | 38944 | 114076 | 116360 | 878 | 32921 |
| 2015 | 39891 | 114709 | 118897 | 889 | 36979 |
| 2016 | 40583 | 115217 | 123066 | 926 | 41009 |
| 2017 | 41708 | 115645 | 125270 | 965 | 44327 |
| 2018 | 42946 | 117159 | 126513 | 995 | 47880 |
| 2019 | 45537 | 121078 | 128777 | 1050 | 50522 |
| 2020 | 49174 | 124305 | 130610 | 1072 | 52482 |
| 2021 | 52097 | 128078 | 133259 | 1120 | 61978 |
| 2022 | 55343 | 129754 | 134050 | 1152 | 62247 |

# 表 18.4 研究生基本情况（1996 － 2022 年）
## BASIC STATISTICS ON POSTGRADUATES (1996-2022)

单位：人 (person)

| 年 份<br>Year | 在校学生数<br>Total Enrollment | 招生数<br>New Enrollment | 毕业生数<br>Graduates |
|---|---|---|---|
| 1996 | 2953 | 1052 | 762 |
| 1997 | 3199 | 1108 | 847 |
| 1998 | 3726 | 1389 | 862 |
| 1999 | 5032 | 2132 | 991 |
| 2000 | 6233 | 2686 | 1084 |
| 2001 | 8358 | 3410 | 1401 |
| 2002 | 11110 | 4423 | 1616 |
| 2003 | 14763 | 6392 | 2715 |
| 2004 | 19367 | 8202 | 3426 |
| 2005 | 24363 | 9436 | 4193 |
| 2006 | 29000 | 10475 | 5492 |
| 2007 | 32145 | 11312 | 7483 |
| 2008 | 35005 | 12376 | 8925 |
| 2009 | 39080 | 14159 | 9759 |
| 2010 | 43149 | 14851 | 10347 |
| 2011 | 45213 | 15341 | 12351 |
| 2012 | 46569 | 15925 | 13844 |
| 2013 | 48210 | 16324 | 14189 |
| 2014 | 48979 | 16647 | 14915 |
| 2015 | 50534 | 17231 | 14866 |
| 2016 | 52156 | 17562 | 15378 |
| 2017 | 58349 | 22437 | 15517 |
| 2018 | 65134 | 24148 | 16510 |
| 2019 | 72562 | 25267 | 16677 |
| 2020 | 83094 | 30724 | 19309 |
| 2021 | 97402 | 33147 | 22291 |
| 2022 | 105474 | 34657 | 23141 |

# 表 18.5 主要年份文化机构数
## NUMBER OF CULTURAL INSTITUTIONS IN MAJOR YEARS

单位：个 ((unit))

| 年 份<br>Year | 艺术表演团体<br>Specialized Troupes | 文化馆、艺术馆<br>Cultural Centers and Art Centers | 图书馆<br>Libraries |
|---|---|---|---|
| 1975 | 54 | 33 | 10 |
| 1978 | 54 | 36 | 10 |
| 1980 | 55 | 35 | 21 |
| 1985 | 54 | 35 | 25 |
| 1986 | 52 | 35 | 26 |
| 1987 | 51 | 35 | 26 |
| 1988 | 45 | 35 | 27 |
| 1989 | 44 | 35 | 35 |
| 1990 | 42 | 39 | 36 |
| 1991 | 42 | 39 | 38 |
| 1992 | 42 | 39 | 38 |
| 1993 | 41 | 39 | 41 |
| 1994 | 36 | 40 | 41 |
| 1995 | 36 | 40 | 42 |
| 1996 | 39 | 46 | 42 |
| 1997 | 39 | 47 | 42 |
| 1998 | 39 | 47 | 42 |
| 1999 | 36 | 46 | 42 |
| 2000 | 35 | 44 | 42 |
| 2001 | 36 | 44 | 42 |
| 2002 | 32 | 44 | 43 |
| 2003 | 32 | 44 | 44 |
| 2004 | 29 | 44 | 44 |
| 2005 | 29 | 42 | 43 |
| 2006 | 78 | 41 | 43 |
| 2007 | 84 | 41 | 43 |
| 2008 | 177 | 41 | 43 |
| 2009 | 160 | 41 | 43 |
| 2010 | 381 | 41 | 43 |
| 2011 | 282 | 41 | 43 |
| 2012 | 244 | 41 | 43 |
| 2013 | 443 | 41 | 43 |
| 2014 | 512 | 41 | 43 |
| 2015 | 730 | 41 | 43 |
| 2016 | 770 | 41 | 43 |
| 2017 | 1283 | 41 | 43 |
| 2018 | 1571 | 41 | 43 |
| 2019 | 1646 | 41 | 43 |
| 2020 | 1265 | 41 | 43 |
| 2021 | 1286 | 41 | 43 |
| 2022 | 1190 | 41 | 43 |

注：艺术表演团体数据 2006 年起统计口径调整为含系统内、系统外两部分。
Note: The data of specialized troupes has included the units either inside or outside the public-owned system since 2006.

# 表 18.6 教育事业基本情况（2021 – 2022 年）
BASIC STATISTICS ON EDUCATION (2021-2022)

单位：人、所 (person, unit)

| 指　标 | Item | 2021 | 2022 |
|---|---|---|---|
| **学校数** | **Number of Schools** | | |
| 高等学校 | Higher Education | 74 | 75 |
| 普通高等学校 | Regular Higher Education Institutions | 69 | 70 |
| 本科院校 | HEIs Offering Degree Programs | 25 | 26 |
| #独立学院 | Independent Institutions | 1 | 1 |
| 专科院校 | Higher Vocational Colleges | 43 | 44 |
| 成人高等学校 | Adult Higher Education Institutions | 3 | 3 |
| 高中阶段学校 | Senior Secondary Education | 448 | 455 |
| 普通高中 | Regular Senior Secondary Schools | 269 | 277 |
| 中等职业学校 | Vocational Secondary Schools | 179 | 178 |
| 义务教育学校 | Compulsory Education | 3571 | 3480 |
| 普通初中 | Regular Junior Secondary Schools | 854 | 843 |
| 普通小学 | Regular Primary Schools | 2717 | 2637 |
| 特殊教育学校 | Special Education | 39 | 39 |
| 幼儿园 | Kindergartens | 5684 | 5667 |
| 专门学校 | Special School | 2 | 2 |
| 在校学生数 | Total Enrollment | | |
| 高等教育 | Higher Education | 1309071 | 1393942 |
| 研究生 | Postgraduates | 97402 | 105474 |
| 博　士 | Doctor's Degree | 8905 | 9806 |
| 硕　士 | Master's Degree | 88497 | 95668 |
| 普通本专科 | Undergraduate in Regular HEIs | 1002720 | 1066133 |
| 本　科 | Normal Courses | 506480 | 532586 |
| 专　科 | Short-cycle Courses | 488557 | 522175 |
| 成人本专科 | Undergraduate in Adult HEIs | 56626 | 61143 |
| 本　科 | Normal Courses | 21100 | 22934 |
| 专科 | Short-cycle Courses | 35526 | 38209 |
| 网络本专科 | Web-based Undergraduates | 152323 | 161192 |
| 本　科 | Normal Courses | 113628 | 126440 |
| 专　科 | Short-cycle Courses | 38695 | 34752 |
| 高中阶段教育 | Senior Secondary Education | 1124743 | 1151008 |
| 普通高中 | Regular Senior Secondary Schools | 639982 | 663252 |
| 中等职业教育 | Vocational Secondary Education | 484761 | 487756 |

**表 18.6 续表 1 continued 1**

单位：人、所 (person, unit)

| 指 标 | Item | 2021 | 2022 |
|---|---|---|---|
| 义务教育 | Compulsory Education | 3163135 | 3164210 |
| 普通初中 | Regular Junior Secondary Schools | 1132272 | 1132272 |
| 普通小学 | Regular Primary Schools | 2030863 | 2031938 |
| 特殊教育 | Special Education | 27446 | 26605 |
| 学前教育 | Pre-school Education | 995239 | 961364 |
| 工读学校 | Correctional Work-Study Schools | 53 | 42 |
| **招生数** | **New Enrollment** | | |
| 高等教育 | Higher Education | 430700 | 488229 |
| 研究生 | Postgraduates | 33147 | 34657 |
| 博 士 | Doctor's Degree | 2280 | 2521 |
| 硕 士 | Master's Degree | 30867 | 32136 |
| 普通本专科 | Undergraduate in Regular HEIs | 319123 | 350615 |
| 本 科 | Normal Courses | 140870 | 158368 |
| 专 科 | Short-cycle Courses | 175132 | 192247 |
| 成人本专科 | Undergraduate in Adult HEIs | 20608 | 28784 |
| 本 科 | Normal Courses | 7597 | 10139 |
| 专 科 | Short-cycle Courses | 13011 | 18645 |
| 网络本专科 | Web-based Undergraduates | 57822 | 74173 |
| 本 科 | Normal Courses | 48880 | 57907 |
| 专 科 | Short-cycle Courses | 8942 | 16266 |
| 高中阶段教育 | Senior Secondary Education | 399676 | 409230 |
| 普通高中 | Regular Senior Secondary Schools | 217560 | 232081 |
| 中等职业教育 | Vocational Secondary Education | 182116 | 177149 |
| 义务教育 | Compulsory Education | 693612 | 688144 |
| 普通初中 | Regular Junior Secondary Schools | 350912 | 350526 |
| 普通小学 | Regular Primary Schools | 342700 | 337618 |
| 特殊教育 | Special Education | 4599 | 4605 |
| 学前教育 | Pre-school Education | 276909 | 241359 |
| 工读学校 | Correctional Work-Study Schools | 53 | 40 |

**表 18.6 续表 2 continued 2**

单位：人、所 (person, unit)

| 指　标 | Item | 2021 | 2022 |
|---|---|---|---|
| **毕业生数** | **Graduates** | | |
| 高等教育 | Higher Education | 337467 | 373640 |
| 研究生 | Postgraduates | 22291 | 23141 |
| 博　士 | Doctor's Degree | 1359 | 1374 |
| 硕　士 | Master's Degree | 20932 | 21767 |
| 普通本专科 | Undergraduate in Regular HEIs | 215783 | 271002 |
| 本　科 | Normal Courses | 112774 | 123394 |
| 专　科 | Short-cycle Courses | 103009 | 147608 |
| 成人本专科 | Undergraduate in Adult HEIs | 31301 | 21022 |
| 本　科 | Normal Courses | 7799 | 7980 |
| 专　科 | Short-cycle Courses | 23502 | 13042 |
| 网络本专科 | Web-based Undergraduates | 68092 | 58475 |
| 本　科 | Normal Courses | 37143 | 41591 |
| 专　科 | Short-cycle Courses | 30949 | 16884 |
| 高中阶段教育 | Senior Secondary Education | 322859 | 339997 |
| 普通高中 | Regular Senior Secondary Schools | 201782 | 205272 |
| 中等职业教育 | Vocational Secondary Education | 121077 | 134725 |
| 义务教育 | Compulsory Education | 716498 | 740774 |
| 普通初中 | Regular Junior Secondary Schools | 371664 | 396746 |
| 普通小学 | Regular Primary Schools | 344834 | 344028 |
| 特殊教育 | Special Education | 4955 | 6067 |
| 学前教育 | Pre-school Education | 346822 | 339196 |
| 工读学校 | Correctional Work-Study Schools | 26 | 51 |
| 教职工数 | Teachers and Staff | | |
| 高等学校 | Higher Education | 70612 | 74493 |
| 普通高等学校 | Regular Higher Education Institutions | 70499 | 74377 |
| 本科院校 | HEIs Offering Degree Programs | 43751 | 46155 |
| #独立学院 | Independent Institutions | 732 | 781 |
| 本科层次职业学校 | Vocational School at Undergraduate Level | 958 | 1001 |
| 专科院校 | Higher Vocational Colleges | 25790 | 28222 |
| 成人高等学校 | Adult Higher Education Institutions | 113 | 116 |
| 高中阶段、义务教育学校 | Senior Secondary Education and Compulsory Education | 309929 | 313304 |
| 普通中学 | Regular Secondary Schools | 148334 | 150461 |
| 中等职业 | Vocational Secondary Schools | 24975 | 25561 |
| 普通小学 | Regular Primary Schools | 136620 | 137282 |
| 特殊教育学校 | Special Education | 1304 | 1293 |
| 幼儿园 | Pre-school Education | 114849 | 114920 |
| 工读学校 | Correctional Work-Study Schools | 28 | 29 |

**表 18.6 续表 3 continued 3**

单位：人、所 (person, unit)

| 指　标 | Item | 2021 | 2022 |
| --- | --- | --- | --- |
| **专任教师数** | **Full-time Teachers** | | |
| 高等学校 | Higher Education | 52132 | 55343 |
| 普通高等学校 | Regular Higher Education Institutions | 52097 | 33965 |
| 本科院校 | HEIs Offering Degree Programs | 32089 | 599 |
| #独立学院 | Independent Institutions | 542 | 21339 |
| 本科层次职业学校 | | 731 | 793 |
| 专科院校 | Higher Vocational Colleges | 19277 | 21339 |
| 成人高等学校 | Adult Higher Education Institutions | 35 | 39 |
| 高中阶段学校 | Senior Secondary Education | 64114 | 67088 |
| 普通高中 | Regular Senior Secondary Schools | 42322 | 44213 |
| 中等职业教育 | Vocational Secondary Schools | 21792 | 22875 |
| 义务教育 | Compulsory Education | 219015 | 219591 |
| 普通初中 | Regular Junior Secondary Schools | 85756 | 85541 |
| 普通小学 | Regular Primary Schools | 133259 | 134050 |
| 特殊教育学校 | Special Education | 1120 | 1152 |
| 幼儿园 | Kindergartens | 61978 | 62247 |
| 工读学校 | Correctional Work-Study Schools | 26 | 27 |
| **每一教师负担学生数** | **Student-Teacher Ratio** | | |
| 小学 | Primary Schools | 15.2 | 15.0 |
| 普通初中 | Regular Junior Secondary Schools | 13.2 | 13.0 |
| 普通高中 | Regular Senior Secondary Schools | 23.3 | 15.0 |
| 中职（不含技工校） | Secondary Vocational Schools (not including technical schools)" | 21.7 | 21.0 |
| 普通高等学校 | Regular Higher Education Institutions | 17.7 | 18.0 |
| **每十万人口在校学生数** | **Student Enrollment per 100 000 population** | | |
| 高等教育 | Higher Education | 3605 | 3837 |
| 高中阶段 | Senior Secondary Education | 3505 | 3583 |
| 初中阶段 | Junior Secondary Education | 3529 | 3385 |
| 小学 | Primary Education | 6329 | 6325 |
| 幼儿园 | Kindergartens | 3101 | 2993 |

## 表 18.7 各级学校入学率及升学率（2021－2022 年）
## NET ENROLLMENT RATIO AND PROMOTION RATE OF SCHOOLS BY LEVEL (2021-2022)

单位：%（%）

| 指　标 | Item | 2021 | 2022 |
|---|---|---|---|
| 小学学龄儿童入学率 | Net Enrollment Ratio of Primary Schools | 99.93 | 99.99 |
| 初中适龄人口入学率 | Net Enrollment Ratio of Junior Secondary Schools | 99.60 | 99.91 |
| 高中阶段毛入学率 | Gross Enrollment Ratio of Senior Secondary Schools | 98.61 | 98.99 |
| 高等教育毛入学率 | Gross Enrollment Ratio of Higher Education | 58.03 | 62.60 |
| 初中毕业生升学率 | Promotion Rate of Junior Secondary School Graduates | 99.46 | 99.47 |
| #升普通高中 | To Regular Senior Secondary Schools | 58.54 | 58.50 |
| 小学毕业生升学率 | Promotion Rate of Primary School Graduates | 100.00 | 100.00 |

## 表 18.8 普通高等学校分科学生数（2022 年）
## STUDENT ENROLLMENT IN REGULAR HIGHER EDUCATION INSTITUTIONS BY FIELD OF STUDY (2022)

单位：人（person）

| 项　目 | Item | 在校学生数 Total Enrollment | #本　科 Undergraduate Courses | 招生数 New Enrollment | #本　科 Undergraduate Courses | 毕业生数 Graduates | #本　科 Undergraduate Courses |
|---|---|---|---|---|---|---|---|
| **总　计** | **Total** | **638060** | **532586** | **188534** | **153877** | **145746** | **122605** |
| 哲　学 | Philosophy | 572 | 245 | 137 | 38 | 156 | 67 |
| 经济学 | Economics | 30552 | 26919 | 9370 | 7971 | 7682 | 6674 |
| 法　学 | Law | 34368 | 25889 | 9446 | 6527 | 8687 | 6134 |
| 教育学 | Education | 39760 | 21823 | 10955 | 6059 | 8418 | 4979 |
| 文　学 | Literature | 78943 | 73587 | 22360 | 20389 | 18391 | 17025 |
| 历史学 | History | 3100 | 2538 | 874 | 677 | 647 | 531 |
| 理　学 | Science | 35626 | 30048 | 9073 | 7195 | 8420 | 7061 |
| 工　学 | Engineering | 212147 | 179070 | 64225 | 52846 | 45810 | 38679 |
| 农　学 | Agriculture | 12957 | 8698 | 3929 | 2416 | 2557 | 1773 |
| 医　学 | Medicine | 28471 | 20059 | 7848 | 4960 | 6155 | 4226 |
| 管理学 | Administrators | 107244 | 92424 | 35198 | 30747 | 26480 | 23824 |
| 艺术学 | Art | 54320 | 51286 | 15119 | 14052 | 12343 | 11632 |
| 职业本科 | Vocational Undergraduate | 11372 | 11372 | 4491 | 4491 | 789 | 789 |

注：1）本表仅指研究生、普通本科学生。不含普通专科、成人本专科学生、网络本专科学生和在职人员攻读学位人员。
2）不含在渝军事院校。

Note: a) The table here above only covers the data of postgraduates and undergraduates. The data of junior college, adult undergraduates and web-based undergraduates are not included.
b) The data of military universities in Chongqing are not included.

# 表 18.9 中等职业教育学校分科学生情况（2022 年）
STUDENTS IN VOCATIONAL SECONDARY SCHOOLS BY FIELD OF STUDY (2022)

单位：人 (person)

| 项 目 | Item | 毕业生数 Graduates | 招生数 New Enrollment | 在校学生数 Total Enrollment |
|---|---|---|---|---|
| **总 计** | **Total** | **106766** | **138144** | **379710** |
| 农林类 | Agriculture and Forestry | 2244 | 2393 | 6237 |
| 资源与环境类 | Resources and Environment | 399 | 524 | 2025 |
| 能源类 | Energy | 204 | 235 | 722 |
| 土木水利工程类 | Civil and Hydraulic Engineering | 4138 | 4737 | 15486 |
| 加工制造类 | Manufacturing | 14344 | 20428 | 51792 |
| 石油化工类 | Petroleum and Chemical | 140 | 353 | 747 |
| 轻纺食品类 | Light Industry, Textile and Food | 1737 | 2740 | 6492 |
| 交通运输类 | Communication & Transportation | 14608 | 17662 | 51595 |
| 信息技术类 | Information Technologies | 22283 | 29962 | 82955 |
| 医药卫生类 | Medicine and Health | 11371 | 18642 | 46575 |
| 休闲保健类 | Leisure and Health | | | |
| 财经商贸类 | Finance and Trade | 8652 | 11143 | 32326 |
| 旅游类 | Tourism | 8674 | 7905 | 24302 |
| 文化艺术 | Culture and Arts | 3080 | 6034 | 12794 |
| 体育类 | Sports | 13091 | 11931 | 34947 |
| 教育类 | Education | | | |
| 司法类 | Judicature | 477 | 473 | 1581 |
| 社会公共事务类 | Social and Public Affairs | 556 | 2092 | 6667 |
| 其 他 | Others | 768 | 890 | 2467 |

注：本表不含技工学校。
Note: The data of vestibule schools are not included in this table.

# 表 18.10 各级学校在校女学生和女专任教师数（2021－2022 年）
## NUMBER OF FEMALE STUDENTS AND FEMALE FULL-TIME TEACHERS BY SCHOOL LEVEL (2021-2022)

单位：人 (person)

| 项　目 | Item | 2021 | 2022 |
|---|---|---|---|
| **女学生数** | **Number of Female Students** | **3123477** | **2641818** |
| 高等教育 | Higher Education | 648012 | 683495 |
| #研究生 | Postgraduate | 55590 | 59738 |
| 普通本专科学校 | Undergraduate in Regular HEIs | 497248 | 522030 |
| 高中教育阶段 | High School Education | 481659 | 822872 |
| 普通高中 | Regular High School | 325481 | 338111 |
| 中等职业教育 | Vocational Secondary Schools | 156178 | 484761 |
| 义务教育 | Compulsory Education | 1506373 | 1487177 |
| 普通初中 | Regular Junior Secondary School | 536942 | 514847 |
| 普通小学 | Regular Primary School | 969431 | 972330 |
| **女学生占学生总数的百分比 (%)** | **Percentage of Female Students to Total Students (%)** | **47.2** | **39.7** |
| 高等教育 | Higher Education | 49.5 | 49.0 |
| #研究生 | Postgraduate | 57.1 | 56.6 |
| 普通本专科学校 | Undergraduate in Regular HEIs | 49.6 | 49.0 |
| 高中教育阶段 | High School Education | 42.8 | 71.5 |
| 普通高中 | Regular High School | 50.9 | 51.0 |
| 中等职业教育 | Vocational Secondary Schools | 32.2 | 99.4 |
| 义务教育 | Compulsory Education | 47.6 | 47.7 |
| 普通初中 | Regular Junior Secondary School | 47.4 | 47.3 |
| 普通小学 | Regular Primary School | 47.7 | 47.9 |
| **女专任教师数** | **Number of Female Full-time Teachers** | **241736** | **242508** |
| 普通高等学校 | Regular Higher Education Institutions | 15078 | 15734 |
| 高中阶段学校 | High School Education | 32029 | 34017 |
| 普通高中 | Regular High School | 22071 | 23585 |
| 中等职业学校 | Vocational Secondary Schools | 9958 | 10432 |
| 义务教育学校 | Compulsory Education | 132795 | 135176 |
| 普通初中 | Regular Junior Secondary School | 46182 | 46875 |
| 普通小学 | Regular Primary School | 86613 | 88301 |
| **女专任教师占专任教师总数的百分比 (%)** | **Percentage of Female Full-time Teachers to Total Full-time Teachers(%)** | **63.5** | **64.9** |
| 普通高等学校 | Regular Higher Education Institutions | 50.1 | 47.4 |
| 高中阶段学校 | High School Education | 50.0 | 54.5 |
| 普通高中 | Regular High School | 52.2 | 53.3 |
| 中等职业学校 | Vocational Secondary Schools | 45.7 | 57.3 |
| 义务教育学校 | Compulsory Education | 60.6 | 61.6 |
| 普通初中 | Regular Junior Secondary School | 53.9 | 54.8 |
| 普通小学 | Regular Primary School | 65.0 | 65.9 |

# 表 18.11 科技奖励情况（2021 － 2022 年）
## REWARDS FOR SCIENTIFIC AND TECHNOLOGICAL RESEARCH (2021-2022)

单位：项 (item)

| 项　目 | Item | 2021 | 2022 |
|---|---|---|---|
| **科技奖励情况（项）** | **Rewards for Scientific and Technological Research** | | |
| **国家科学技术奖励** | **National Rewards for Scientific and Technological Research** | | |
| 最高科学技术奖 | Top Science and Technology Award | | |
| 自然科学奖 | Award for Natural Sciences | | |
| 一等奖 | 1st Prize | | |
| 二等奖 | 2nd Prize | | |
| 技术发明奖 | Award for Technological Invention | | |
| 一等奖 | 1st Prize | | |
| 二等奖 | 2nd Prize | | |
| 科技进步奖 | Award for Science and Technology Progress | | |
| 特　等 | Special Prize | | |
| 一等奖 | 1st Prize | | |
| 二等奖 | 2nd Prize | | |
| **国际科学技术合作奖** | **International Science and Technology Cooperation Award** | | |
| **重庆市科学技术奖励** | **Chongqing Rewards for Scientific and Technological Research** | **159** | **110** |
| 科技突出贡献奖 | Prize for The Outstanding Contribution in Science and Technology Research | 2 | |
| 自然科学奖 | Award for Natural Sciences | 29 | 24 |
| 一等奖 | 1st Prize | 6 | 7 |
| 二等奖 | 2nd Prize | 14 | 10 |
| 三等奖 | 3rd Prize | 9 | 7 |
| 技术发明奖 | Award for Technological Invention | 6 | 7 |
| 一等奖 | 1st Prize | 3 | 3 |
| 二等奖 | 2nd Prize | 2 | 3 |
| 三等奖 | 3rd Prize | 1 | 1 |
| 科技进步奖 | Award for Science and Technology Progress | 114 | 69 |
| 一等奖 | 1st Prize | 23 | 15 |
| 二等奖 | 2nd Prize | 46 | 27 |
| 三等奖 | 3rd Prize | 45 | 27 |
| 企业技术创新奖 | Award for Enterprise Technology Innovation | 7 | 10 |
| 国际科学技术合作奖 | Award for International Science and Technology Cooperation | 1 | |

注：2021 年重庆市科技奖励暂未公布数据。
Note：Data of 2021 Science and Technology awards have not been released yet.

## 表 18.12 科学技术协会活动情况（2022 年）
## ACTIVITIES OF SCIENCE AND TECHNOLOGY ASSOCIATIONS (2022)

| 指 标 | Item | 2022 |
|---|---|---|
| **国内学术会议** | **Domestic Academic Meetings** | |
| 举办次数（次） | Number of Meetings (time) | 606 |
| 参加人数（人次） | Number of Participants (person-times) | 250391 |
| 交流论文数（篇） | Number of Theses Presented (piece) | 1201 |
| **境内国际学术会议** | **International Academic Conference in Chongqing** | |
| 举办次数 | Number of Conferences | 5 |
| 参加人数（人次） | Number of Participants (person-time) | 2450 |
| 境外专家学者（人次） | Foreign Experts and Scholars (person-time) | 30 |
| 交流论文（篇） | Number of Theses Presented (piece) | 245 |
| **科普活动** | **Science Popularization Activities** | |
| 举办科普宣讲活动（次） | Number of Science Popularization Lectures (time) | 7313 |
| 宣讲活动受众人数（万人次） | Number of Audience (10 000 person-time) | 1779.38 |
| 举办青少年科学营（次） | Number of Science and Technology Summer (Winter) Camps for Teenagers (time) | 6 |
| 参加人数（人次） | Number of Participants (person-time) | 854 |
| 举办青少年科技竞赛（项） | Number of Teenagers Science and Technology Competitions (time) | 127 |
| 参加人数（万人次） | Number of Participants (10 000 person-time) | 70.44 |
| 获奖人数（人次） | Number of Prize Winners (person-time) | 13970 |

# 表 18.13 研究与试验发展（R&D）活动基本情况（2021 年）
## BASIC STATISTICS ON R&D ACTIVITIES (2021)

| 指 标 | Item | 合 计 Total | 科研机构 Research Institutes | 高等院校 Colleges & Universities |
|---|---|---|---|---|
| 有 R&D 活动的单位数（个） | Units Engaged in R&D Activities (unit) | 4223 | 34 | 135 |
| R&D 经费内部支出（万元） | Inner Expenditure of R&D Funds (10 000 yuan) | 6038410 | 411638 | 588804 |
| #基础研究 | Basic Research | 297396 | 59782 | 213281 |
| 应用研究 | Application Research | 749547 | 225061 | 308365 |
| 试验发展 | Testing Development | 4991467 | 126795 | 67158 |
| #日常性支出 | Daily Expenditure | 5552479 | 358361 | 474814 |
| #人员劳务费 | Remuneration for Personnel | 1878703 | 152927 | 152641 |
| #资产性支出 | Expenditure for Assets | 485931 | 53278 | 113991 |
| #仪器和设备 | Facilities | 376247 | 25950 | 67840 |
| #政府资金 | Funds from Government | 882944 | 255847 | 273077 |
| 企业资金 | Funds from Enterprises | 4881853 | 13103 | 217415 |
| 境外资金 | Foreign Funds | 5192 | | 476 |
| 其他资金 | Others | 268421 | 142688 | 97836 |
| R&D 人员（人） | R&D Personnel (person) | 202465 | 10557 | 38505 |
| #女 性 | Female | 51770 | 4383 | 14231 |
| #全时人员 | Full-time Employees | 128567 | 7976 | 11595 |
| #博士毕业 | With Doctor's Degree | 16222 | 859 | 13423 |
| 硕士毕业 | With Master's Degree | 29898 | 3811 | 14886 |
| 本科毕业 | With Bachelor's Degree | 88068 | 4434 | 9654 |
| R&D 人员全时当量（人年） | Full-time Personnel (person-year) | 123446 | 9502 | 14919 |
| #研究人员 | Researchers | 53792 | 6818 | 12728 |
| #基础研究 | Personnel of Basic Research | 8781 | 1989 | 6253 |
| 应用研究 | Personnel of Application Research | 17960 | 4633 | 7585 |
| 试验发展 | Personnel of Testing Development | 96706 | 2880 | 1080 |
| R&D 项目（课题）数（项） | Number of R&D Projects (Topics) | 64728 | 3360 | 37486 |
| R&D 项目（课题）人员全时当量（人年） | Number of Full-time Persons for Each R&D Project (Topic) (person-year) | 121743 | 7703 | 14920 |
| R&D 项目（课题）经费支出（万元） | Expenditure for R&D Projects (Topics) (10 000 yuan) | 7723716 | 140820 | 2378678 |
| 研究机构机构数（个） | Number of Research Institutions (unit) | 2611 | 35 | 574 |
| 研究机构 R&D 人员（人） | R&D Personnel in Research Institutions (person) | 92309 | 10557 | 8463 |
| #博士和硕士 | With Doctor's Degree and Master's Degree | 22828 | 4670 | 7277 |
| 研究机构 R&D 经费支出（万元） | Research Institutions' Expenditure for R&D (10 000 yuan) | 3498272 | 411638 | 164816 |
| 研究机构仪器设备原价（万元） | Original Price of Instruments and Equipment in Research Institutions (10 000 yuan) | 6608144 | 280695 | 484049 |
| #进 口 | Imported | 324488 | 92299 | 211609 |
| 专利申请数（件） | Number of Patent Applications (pcs) | 37548 | 947 | 8180 |
| #发明申请 | Invention Patent | 16345 | 645 | 5235 |
| 有效发明专利数（件） | Number of Effective Invention Patents (pcs) | 45343 | 2365 | 12573 |
| 专利所有权转让及许可数（件） | Number of Patent Right Transfers and Permissions (pcs) | 1193 | 52 | 513 |
| 专利所有权转让及许可收入（万元） | Income from Patent Right Transfers and Permissions (10 000 yuan) | 18944 | 3200 | 2932 |
| 形成国家或行业标准数（项） | Number of National or Industrial Standards Newly Formed (items) | 703 | 49 | 8 |
| 发表科技论文（篇） | Number of Scientific and Technical Theses Published (theses) | 47933 | 3036 | 39984 |
| 出版科技著作（种） | Scientific and Technical Works Published (kind) | 1651 | 100 | 1512 |

**表 18.13 续表 continued**

| 指　　标 | Item | 企　业 Enterprises | 其　他 Others |
|---|---|---|---|
| 有 R&D 活动的单位数（个） | Units Engaged in R&D Activities (unit) | 3767 | 287 |
| R&D 经费内部支出（万元） | Inner Expenditure of R&D Funds (10 000 yuan) | 4789320 | 248647 |
| #基础研究 | Basic Research | 8599 | 15733 |
| 应用研究 | Application Research | 133859 | 82261 |
| 试验发展 | Testing Development | 4646863 | 150653 |
| #日常性支出 | Daily Expenditure | 4527907 | 191398 |
| #人员劳务费 | Remuneration for Personnel | 1478242 | 94893 |
| #资产性支出 | Expenditure for Assets | 261414 | 57249 |
| #仪器和设备 | Facilities | 252328 | 30129 |
| #政府资金 | Funds from Government | 155984 | 198037 |
| 企业资金 | Funds from Enterprises | 4624924 | 26411 |
| 境外资金 | Foreign Funds | 4716 | |
| 其他资金 | Others | 3697 | 24200 |
| R&D 人员（人） | R&D Personnel | 145244 | 8159 |
| #女　性 | Female | 30690 | 2466 |
| #全时人员 | Full-time Employees | 103695 | 5301 |
| #博士毕业 | With Doctor's Degree | 1006 | 934 |
| 硕士毕业 | With Master's Degree | 9132 | 2069 |
| 本科毕业 | With Bachelor's Degree | 70220 | 3760 |
| R&D 人员全时当量（人年） | Full-time Personnel | 92743 | 6283 |
| #研究人员 | Researchers | 29471 | 4774 |
| #基础研究 | Personnel of Basic Research | 281 | 258 |
| 应用研究 | Personnel of Application Research | 3540 | 2202 |
| 试验发展 | Personnel of Testing Development | 88922 | 3824 |
| R&D 项目（课题）数（项） | Number of R&D Projects (Topics) | 22280 | 1602 |
| R&D 项目（课题）人员全时当量（人年） | Number of Full-time Persons for Each R&D Project (Topic) (person-year) | 93879 | 5242 |
| R&D 项目（课题）经费支出（万元） | Expenditure for R&D Projects (Topics) (10 000 yuan) | 5054551 | 149667 |
| 研究机构机构数（个） | Number of Research Institutions | 1956 | 46 |
| 研究机构 R&D 人员（人） | R&D Personnel in Research Institutions (person) | 70901 | 2388 |
| #博士和硕士 | With Doctor's Degree and Master's Degree | 9676 | 1205 |
| 研究机构 R&D 经费支出（万元） | Research Institutions' Expenditure for R&D (10 000 yuan) | 2843035 | 78783 |
| 研究机构仪器设备原价（万元） | Original Price of Instruments and Equipment in Research Institutions (10 000 yuan) | 5786148 | 57253 |
| #进　口 | Imported | 5 | 20575 |
| 专利申请数（件） | Number of Patent Applications (pcs) | 27768 | 653 |
| #发明申请 | Invention Patent | 9963 | 502 |
| 有效发明专利数（件） | Number of Effective Invention Patents (pcs) | 29798 | 607 |
| 专利所有权转让及许可数（件） | Number of Patent Right Transfers and Permissions (pcs) | 614 | 14 |
| 专利所有权转让及许可收入（万元） | Income from Patent Right Transfers and Permissions (10 000 yuan) | 12636 | 177 |
| 形成国家或行业标准数（项） | Number of National or Industrial Standards Newly Formed (items) | 604 | 42 |
| 发表科技论文（篇） | Number of Scientific and Technical Theses Published (theses) | 3514 | 1399 |
| 出版科技著作（种） | Scientific and Technical Works Published (kind) | | 39 |

# 表 18.14 大中型工业企业科技机构情况（2021 年）
SCIENTIFIC AND TECHNOLOGICAL INSTITUTIONS OF LARGE & MEDIUM-SIZED INDUSTRIAL ENTERPRISES (2021)

| 项　目 | Item | 科技机构数（个）<br>Number of Institutions (unit) | 科技机构科技活动人数（人）<br>Personnel of Institutions (person) | 科技机构经费内部支出（万元）<br>Inner Expenditure for Science and Technology (10 000 yuan) |
|---|---|---|---|---|
| **总　计** | **Total** | **635** | **51666** | **2451360** |
| **按隶属关系分** | **By Relationship** | | | |
| 中　央 | Central | 94 | 14197 | 991147 |
| 地　方 | Local | 77 | 5847 | 262954 |
| **按登记注册类型分** | **By Registration** | | | |
| 内资企业 | Domestic-funded | 579 | 44945 | 2067684 |
| 国有企业 | State-owned | 28 | 2485 | 114051 |
| 集体企业 | Collective-owned | 1 | 20 | 440 |
| 股份合作企业 | Cooperative Enterprise | 2 | 84 | 3211 |
| 联营企业 | Joint Ownership Enterprises | 1 | 43 | 2537 |
| 有限责任公司 | Limited Liability Corporations | 161 | 13034 | 618804 |
| 股份有限公司 | Share Holding Limited Corporations | 62 | 10668 | 640488 |
| 私营企业 | Private Enterprises | 324 | 18611 | 688152 |
| 其他企业 | Others | | | |
| 港、澳、台商投资企业 | Enterprises Funded by Hong Kong, Macao and Taiwan | 22 | 1720 | 59001 |
| 合资经营企业 | Joint-venture Enterprises | 7 | 326 | 8839 |
| 合作经营企业 | Cooperative Enterprises | | | |
| 独资经营企业 | Enterprises with Sole Funded from Hong Kong, Macao and Taiwan | 13 | 1230 | 44339 |
| 投资股份有限公司 | Share-holding Corporations Ltd. with Investment from Hong Kong, Macao and Taiwan | 2 | 164 | 5824 |
| 其他港澳台投资企业 | Others | | | |
| 外商投资企业 | Foreign Funded Enterprises | 34 | 5001 | 324674 |
| 中外合资经营企业 | Joint-venture Enterprises | 19 | 2761 | 256436 |
| 中外合作经营企业 | Cooperation Enterprises | | | |
| 外资企业 | Enterprises with Sole Fund | 13 | 1833 | 59748 |
| 外商投资股份有限公司 | Share-holding Corporations Ltd. with Foreign Investment | 2 | 407 | 8491 |
| 其他外商投资企业 | Others | | | |
| **按行业分** | **By Sector** | | | |
| 采矿业 | Mining | 1 | 18 | 135 |
| 煤炭开采和洗选业 | Mining and Washing of Coal | | | |
| 石油和天然气开采业 | Extraction of Petroleum and Natural Gas | | | |
| 黑色金属矿采选业 | Mining and Processing of Ferrous Metal Ores | | | |
| 有色金属矿采选业 | Mining and Processing of Non-Ferrous Metal Ores | | | |
| 非金属矿采选业 | Mining and Processing of Nonmetal Ores | 1 | 18 | 135 |
| 开采辅助活动 | Mining Support Activities | | | |
| 其他采矿业 | Mining of Other Ores | | | |
| 制造业 | Manufacture | 631 | 51533 | 2448948 |
| 农副食品加工业 | Processing of Food from Agricultural Products | 16 | 361 | 10366 |
| 食品制造业 | Manufacture of Foods | 10 | 601 | 16995 |

**表 18.14 续表 continued**

| 项　目 | Item | 科技机构数（个）Number of Institutions (unit) | 科技机构科技活动人数（人）Personnel of Institutions (person) | 科技机构经费内部支出（万元）Inner Expenditure for Science and Technology (10 000 yuan) |
|---|---|---|---|---|
| 酒、饮料和精制茶制造业 | Liquor, Beverages and Refined Tea | 4 | 519 | 13991 |
| 烟草制品业 | Manufacture of Tobacco | 2 | 130 | 10845 |
| 纺织业 | Manufacture of Textile | | | |
| 纺织服装、服饰业 | Manufacture of Textile Wearing Apparel, Footwear and Caps | 1 | 40 | 1495 |
| 皮革、毛皮、羽毛及其制品和制鞋业 | Manufacture of Leather, Fur, Feather and Related Products and Footwear | 3 | 60 | 610 |
| 木材加工和木、竹、藤、棕、草制品业 | Processing of Timber, Manufacture of Wood, Bamboo, Rattan, Palm and Straw Products | 4 | 112 | 3643 |
| 家具制造业 | Manufacture of Furniture | 3 | 145 | 2102 |
| 造纸和纸制品业 | Manufacture of Paper and Paper Products | 4 | 417 | 29087 |
| 印刷和记录媒介复制业 | Printing, Reproduction of Recording Media | 7 | 272 | 6531 |
| 文教、工美、体育和娱乐用品制造业 | Manufacture of Culture, Education, Handicraft, Fine Arts, Sports and Entertainment Articles | 4 | 295 | 2955 |
| 石油加工、炼焦和核燃料加工业 | Processing of Petroleum, Coking, Processing of Nuclear Fuel | 1 | 30 | 3631 |
| 化学原料和化学制品制造业 | Manufacture of Raw Chemical Materials and Chemical Products" | 37 | 1857 | 92339 |
| 医药制造业 | Manufacture of Medicines | 43 | 3532 | 138995 |
| 化学纤维制造业 | Manufacture of Chemical Fibers | 2 | 290 | 23322 |
| 橡胶和塑料制品业 | Manufacture of Rubber and Plastics | 8 | 258 | 14362 |
| 非金属矿物制品业 | Manufacture of Non-metallic Mineral Products | 30 | 1304 | 42957 |
| 黑色金属冶炼和压延加工业 | Smelting and Pressing of Ferrous Metals | 4 | 502 | 32007 |
| 有色金属冶炼和压延加工业 | Smelting and Pressing of Nonferrous Metals | 23 | 944 | 64254 |
| 金属制品业 | Manufacture of Metal Products | 19 | 861 | 42792 |
| 通用设备制造业 | Manufacture of General Purpose Machinery | 49 | 2991 | 107297 |
| 专用设备制造业 | Manufacture of Special Purpose Machinery | 32 | 1857 | 66721 |
| 汽车制造业 | Manufacture of Motor Vehicles | 117 | 17350 | 1003580 |
| 铁路、船舶、航空航天和其他运输设备制造业 | Manufacture of Railway, Ship, Aviation and Other Transporting Equipment | 50 | 3753 | 118078 |
| 电气机械和器材制造业 | Manufacture of Electrical Machinery and Equipment | 25 | 2774 | 154396 |
| 计算机、通信和其他电子设备制造业 | Manufacture of Communication Equipment, Computers and Other Electronic Equipment | 100 | 7733 | 326340 |
| 仪器仪表制造业 | Manufacture of Measuring Instruments and Machinery for Cultural Activity and Office Work | 19 | 1483 | 46250 |
| 其他制造业 | Other Manufacture | 13 | 1056 | 72428 |
| 废弃资源综合利用业 | Comprehensive Utilization of Waste Resources | 1 | 6 | 580 |
| 金属制品、机械和设备修理业 | Repair of Metal Products, Machinery and Equipment | | | |
| 电力、热力、燃气及水生产和供应业 | Production and Supply of Electric Power, Heat Power and Gas | 3 | 115 | 2277 |
| 电力、热力生产和供应业 | Production and Supply of Electric Power and Heat Power | 2 | 26 | 2224 |
| 燃气生产和供应业 | Production and Supply of Gas | 1 | 89 | 53 |
| 水的生产和供应业 | Production and Supply of Water | | | |

# 表 18.15 规模以上工业企业科技机构情况（2021 年）
SCIENTIFIC AND TECHNOLOGICAL INSTITUTIONS OF INDUSTRIAL ENTERPRISES ABOVE DESIGNATED SIZE (2021)

| 项 目 | Item | 科技机构数（个） Number of Institutions (unit) | 科技机构科技活动人数（人） Personnel of Institutions (person) | 科技机构经费内部支出（万元） Inner Expenditure for Science and Technology (10 000 yuan) |
|---|---|---|---|---|
| **总 计** | **Total** | **1928** | **74738** | **3197207** |
| **按隶属关系分** | **By Relationship** | | | |
| 中 央 | Central | 112 | 14620 | 1006620 |
| 地 方 | Local | 127 | 7513 | 360994 |
| **按登记注册类型分** | **By Registration** | | | |
| 内资企业 | Domestic-funded | 1834 | 66999 | 2770483 |
| 国有企业 | State-owned | 33 | 2572 | 115618 |
| 集体企业 | Collective-owned | 2 | 25 | 454 |
| 股份合作企业 | Cooperative Enterprise | 5 | 132 | 3570 |
| 联营企业 | Joint Ownership Enterprises | 1 | 43 | 2537 |
| 有限责任公司 | Limited Liability Corporations | 313 | 17101 | 794145 |
| 股份有限公司 | Share Holding Limited Corporations | 85 | 11220 | 657680 |
| 私营企业 | Private Enterprises | 1395 | 35906 | 1196479 |
| 其他企业 | Others | | | |
| 港、澳、台商投资企业 | Enterprises Funded by Hong Kong, Macao and Taiwan | 32 | 2012 | 71787 |
| 合资经营企业 | Joint-venture Enterprises | 12 | 487 | 15951 |
| 合作经营企业 | Cooperative Enterprises | | | |
| 独资经营企业 | Enterprises with Sole Funded from Hong Kong, Macao and Taiwan | 18 | 1361 | 50013 |
| 投资股份有限公司 | Share-holding Corporations Ltd. with Investment from Hong Kong, Macao and Taiwan | 2 | 164 | 5824 |
| 其他港澳台投资企业 | Others | | | |
| 外商投资企业 | Foreign Funded Enterprises | 62 | 5727 | 354936 |
| 中外合资经营企业 | Joint-venture Enterprises | 36 | 3252 | 278194 |
| 中外合作经营企业 | Cooperation Enterprises | | | |
| 外资企业 | Enterprises with Sole Fund | 24 | 2068 | 68251 |
| 外商投资股份有限公司 | Share-holding Corporations Ltd. with Foreign Investment | 2 | 407 | 8491 |
| 其他外商投资企业 | Others | | | |
| **按行业分** | **By Sector** | | | |
| 采矿业 | Mining | 11 | 92 | 1386 |
| 煤炭开采和洗选业 | Mining and Washing of Coal | 1 | 8 | 38 |
| 石油和天然气开采业 | Extraction of Petroleum and Natural Gas | | | |
| 黑色金属矿采选业 | Mining and Processing of Ferrous Metal Ores | | | |
| 有色金属矿采选业 | Mining and Processing of Non-Ferrous Metal Ores | | | |
| 非金属矿采选业 | Mining and Processing of Nonmetal Ores | 10 | 84 | 1348 |
| 开采辅助活动 | Mining Support Activities | | | |
| 其他采矿业 | Mining of Other Ores | | | |
| 制造业 | Manufacture | 1906 | 74409 | 3188204 |
| 农副食品加工业 | Processing of Food from Agricultural Products | 90 | 1099 | 35488 |
| 食品制造业 | Manufacture of Foods | 42 | 1048 | 27500 |

**表 18.15 续表 continued**

| 项 目 | Item | 科技机构数（个） Number of Institutions (unit) | 科技机构科技活动人数（人） Personnel of Institutions (person) | 科技机构经费内部支出（万元） Inner Expenditure for Science and Technology (10 000 yuan) |
|---|---|---|---|---|
| 酒、饮料和精制茶制造业 | Liquor, Beverages and Refined Tea | 17 | 744 | 19470 |
| 烟草制品业 | Manufacture of Tobacco | 3 | 142 | 10900 |
| 纺织业 | Manufacture of Textile | 13 | 186 | 4935 |
| 纺织服装、服饰业 | Manufacture of Textile Wearing Apparel, Footwear and Caps | 7 | 188 | 3945 |
| 皮革、毛皮、羽毛及其制品和制鞋业 | Manufacture of Leather, Fur, Feather and Related Products and Footwear | 8 | 91 | 1366 |
| 木材加工和木、竹、藤、棕、草制品业 | Processing of Timber, Manufacture of Wood, Bamboo, Rattan, Palm and Straw Products | 11 | 193 | 5331 |
| 家具制造业 | Manufacture of Furniture | 11 | 291 | 5163 |
| 造纸和纸制品业 | Manufacture of Paper and Paper Products | 21 | 740 | 40534 |
| 印刷和记录媒介复制业 | Printing, Reproduction of Recording Media | 34 | 732 | 21030 |
| 文教、工美、体育和娱乐用品制造业 | Manufacture of Culture, Education, Handicraft, Fine Arts, Sports and Entertainment Articles | 13 | 381 | 5581 |
| 石油加工、炼焦和核燃料加工业 | Processing of Petroleum, Coking, Processing of Nuclear Fuel | 4 | 55 | 5009 |
| 化学原料和化学制品制造业 | Manufacture of Raw Chemical Materials and Chemical Products" | 97 | 2928 | 133949 |
| 医药制造业 | Manufacture of Medicines | 95 | 4636 | 179120 |
| 化学纤维制造业 | Manufacture of Chemical Fibers | 3 | 306 | 23774 |
| 橡胶和塑料制品业 | Manufacture of Rubber and Plastics | 74 | 1236 | 44744 |
| 非金属矿物制品业 | Manufacture of Non-metallic Mineral Products | 146 | 2899 | 94912 |
| 黑色金属冶炼和压延加工业 | Smelting and Pressing of Ferrous Metals | 15 | 774 | 43639 |
| 有色金属冶炼和压延加工业 | Smelting and Pressing of Nonferrous Metals | 53 | 1506 | 94885 |
| 金属制品业 | Manufacture of Metal Products | 99 | 2070 | 77097 |
| 通用设备制造业 | Manufacture of General Purpose Machinery | 143 | 4771 | 157298 |
| 专用设备制造业 | Manufacture of Special Purpose Machinery | 117 | 3439 | 104989 |
| 汽车制造业 | Manufacture of Motor Vehicles | 312 | 21228 | 1114183 |
| 铁路、船舶、航空航天和其他运输设备制造业 | Manufacture of Railway, Ship, Aviation and Other Transporting Equipment | 131 | 5214 | 155923 |
| 电气机械和器材制造业 | Manufacture of Electrical Machinery and Equipment | 90 | 3838 | 189525 |
| 计算机、通信和其他电子设备制造业 | Manufacture of Communication Equipment, Computers and Other Electronic Equipment | 182 | 10208 | 447596 |
| 仪器仪表制造业 | Manufacture of Measuring Instruments and Machinery for Cultural Activity and Office Work | 53 | 2246 | 61850 |
| 其他制造业 | Other Manufacture | 17 | 1127 | 74558 |
| 废弃资源综合利用业 | Comprehensive Utilization of Waste Resources | 5 | 93 | 3912 |
| 金属制品、机械和设备修理业 | Repair of Metal Products, Machinery and Equipment | | | |
| 电力、热力、燃气及水生产和供应业 | Production and Supply of Electric Power, Heat Power and Gas | 11 | 237 | 7616 |
| 电力、热力生产和供应业 | Production and Supply of Electric Power and Heat Power | 7 | 129 | 7065 |
| 燃气生产和供应业 | Production and Supply of Gas | 3 | 103 | 457 |
| 水的生产和供应业 | Production and Supply of Water | 1 | 5 | 95 |

# 表 18.16 大中型工业企业 R&D 人员情况（2021 年）
STATISTICS ON R&D PERSONNEL IN LARGE & MEDIUM-SIZED INDUSTRIAL ENTERPRISES (2021)

| 项 目 | Item | R&D 人员数（人）R&D Personnel (person) | #参加项目人员 Researchers | #R&D 全时人员 Full-time Employees | R&D 人员折合全时当量（人年）Full-time Personnel (person-year) | #试验发展人员 Personnel of Testing Development |
|---|---|---|---|---|---|---|
| **总 计** | **Total** | **86281** | **80545** | **62750** | **55523** | **54050** |
| **按隶属关系分** | **By Relationship** | | | | | |
| 中 央 | Central | 19193 | 18123 | 14829 | 10634 | 10058 |
| 地 方 | Local | 9367 | 8879 | 6258 | 6999 | 6759 |
| **按登记注册类型分** | **By Registration** | | | | | |
| 内资企业 | Domestic-funded | 72476 | 68083 | 52154 | 45926 | 44529 |
| 国有企业 | State-owned | 2940 | 2772 | 2248 | 1681 | 1583 |
| 集体企业 | Collective-owned | 22 | 20 | 20 | 20 | 20 |
| 股份合作企业 | Cooperative Enterprise | 66 | 57 | 58 | 49 | 49 |
| 联营企业 | Joint Ownership Enterprises | 100 | 89 | 37 | 59 | 59 |
| 有限责任公司 | Limited Liability Corporations | 20822 | 19585 | 13528 | 13158 | 12532 |
| 股份有限公司 | Share Holding Limited Corporations | 14395 | 13675 | 11876 | 8175 | 7912 |
| 私营企业 | Private Enterprises | 34131 | 31885 | 24387 | 22784 | 22375 |
| 其他企业 | Others | | | | | |
| 港、澳、台商投资企业 | Enterprises Funded by Hong Kong, Macao and Taiwan | 6124 | 5256 | 4959 | 4291 | 4280 |
| 合资经营企业 | Joint-venture Enterprises | 1131 | 1081 | 796 | 749 | 738 |
| 合作经营企业 | Cooperative Enterprises | | | | | |
| 独资经营企业 | Enterprises with Sole Funded from Hong Kong, Macao and Taiwan | 4581 | 3793 | 3889 | 3276 | 3276 |
| 投资股份有限公司 | Share-holding Corporations Ltd. with Investment from Hong Kong, Macao and Taiwan | 261 | 239 | 192 | 157 | 157 |
| 其他港澳台投资企业 | Others | 151 | 143 | 82 | 109 | 109 |
| 外商投资企业 | Foreign Funded Enterprises | 7681 | 7206 | 5637 | 5307 | 5241 |
| 中外合资经营企业 | Joint-venture Enterprises | 4246 | 3999 | 3358 | 3181 | 3173 |
| 中外合作经营企业 | Cooperation Enterprises | 35 | 33 | 22 | 24 | 24 |
| 外资企业 | Enterprises with Sole Fund | 2801 | 2631 | 2060 | 1779 | 1721 |
| 外商投资股份有限公司 | Share-holding Corporations Ltd. with Foreign Investment | 599 | 543 | 197 | 323 | 323 |
| 其他外商投资企业 | Others | | | | | |
| **按行业分** | **By Sector** | | | | | |
| 采矿业 | Mining | 111 | 106 | 94 | 71 | 18 |
| 煤炭开采和洗选业 | Mining and Washing of Coal | | | | | |
| 石油和天然气开采业 | Extraction of Petroleum and Natural Gas | | | | | |
| 黑色金属矿采选业 | Mining and Processing of Ferrous Metal Ores | | | | | |
| 有色金属矿采选业 | Mining and Processing of Non-Ferrous Metal Ores | | | | | |
| 非金属矿采选业 | Mining and Processing of Nonmetal Ores | 111 | 106 | 94 | 71 | 18 |
| 开采辅助活动 | Mining Support Activities | | | | | |
| 其他采矿业 | Mining of Other Ores | | | | | |

**表 18.16 续表 continued**

| 项　目 | Item | R&D 人员数（人） R&D Personnel (person) | #参加项目人员 Researchers | # R&D 全时人员 Full-time Employees | R&D 人员折合全时当量（人年） Full-time Personnel (person-year) | #试验发展人员 Personnel of Testing Development |
|---|---|---|---|---|---|---|
| 制造业 | Manufacture | 85666 | 79963 | 62569 | 55133 | 53727 |
| 农副食品加工业 | Processing of Food from Agricultural Products | 648 | 596 | 362 | 374 | 360 |
| 食品制造业 | Manufacture of Foods | 841 | 788 | 537 | 479 | 450 |
| 酒、饮料和精制茶制造业 | Liquor, Beverages and Refined Tea | 724 | 661 | 280 | 370 | 354 |
| 烟草制品业 | Manufacture of Tobacco | 253 | 234 | 226 | 106 | 106 |
| 纺织业 | Manufacture of Textile | 19 | 18 | 17 | 14 | 14 |
| 纺织服装、服饰业 | Manufacture of Textile Wearing Apparel, Footwear and Caps | 153 | 145 | 118 | 110 | 110 |
| 皮革、毛皮、羽毛及其制品和制鞋业 | Manufacture of Leather, Fur, Feather and Related Products and Footwear | 174 | 164 | 114 | 118 | 118 |
| 木材加工和木、竹、藤、棕、草制品业 | Processing of Timber, Manufacture of Wood, Bamboo, Rattan, Palm and Straw Products | 464 | 421 | 245 | 296 | 296 |
| 家具制造业 | Manufacture of Furniture | 199 | 189 | 170 | 131 | 131 |
| 造纸和纸制品业 | Manufacture of Paper and Paper Products | 725 | 707 | 615 | 555 | 555 |
| 印刷和记录媒介复制业 | Printing, Reproduction of Recording Media | 474 | 434 | 328 | 344 | 344 |
| 文教、工美、体育和娱乐用品制造业 | Manufacture of Culture, Education, Handicraft, Fine Arts, Sports and Entertainment Articles | 389 | 380 | 269 | 264 | 264 |
| 石油加工、炼焦和核燃料加工业 | Processing of Petroleum, Coking, Processing of Nuclear Fuel | 102 | 96 | 72 | 47 | 23 |
| 化学原料和化学制品制造业 | Manufacture of Raw Chemical Materials and Chemical Products | 2949 | 2801 | 1684 | 1878 | 1687 |
| 医药制造业 | Manufacture of Medicines | 4337 | 4177 | 3281 | 2648 | 2555 |
| 化学纤维制造业 | Manufacture of Chemical Fibers | 292 | 291 | 263 | 197 | 186 |
| 橡胶和塑料制品业 | Manufacture of Rubber and Plastics | 704 | 672 | 482 | 522 | 522 |
| 非金属矿物制品业 | Manufacture of Non-metallic Mineral Products | 3402 | 3157 | 1841 | 2158 | 2128 |
| 黑色金属冶炼和压延加工业 | Smelting and Pressing of Ferrous Metals | 2260 | 2208 | 1457 | 1721 | 1721 |
| 有色金属冶炼和压延加工业 | Smelting and Pressing of Nonferrous Metals | 2533 | 2349 | 896 | 1124 | 1043 |
| 金属制品业 | Manufacture of Metal Products | 2145 | 1990 | 1786 | 1097 | 1047 |
| 通用设备制造业 | Manufacture of General Purpose Machinery | 4409 | 4159 | 3330 | 3158 | 3076 |
| 专用设备制造业 | Manufacture of Special Purpose Machinery | 3035 | 2878 | 2014 | 1795 | 1795 |
| 汽车制造业 | Manufacture of Motor Vehicles | 23316 | 21886 | 19226 | 14475 | 14155 |
| 铁路、船舶、航空航天和其他运输设备制造业 | Manufacture of Railway, Ship, Aviation and Other Transporting Equipment | 7550 | 7017 | 5195 | 4886 | 4653 |
| 电气机械和器材制造业 | Manufacture of Electrical Machinery and Equipment | 4639 | 4237 | 3533 | 2950 | 2942 |
| 计算机、通信和其他电子设备制造业 | Manufacture of Communication Equipment, Computers and Other Electronic Equipment | 15959 | 14526 | 11992 | 11401 | 11207 |
| 仪器仪表制造业 | Manufacture of Measuring Instruments and Machinery for Cultural Activity and Office Work | 1681 | 1549 | 1291 | 1095 | 1073 |
| 其他制造业 | Other Manufacture | 1212 | 1159 | 892 | 768 | 760 |
| 废弃资源综合利用业 | Comprehensive Utilization of Waste Resources | 78 | 74 | 53 | 54 | 54 |
| 金属制品、机械和设备修理业 | Repair of Metal Products, Machinery and Equipment | | | | | |
| 电力、热力、燃气及水生产和供应业 | Production and Supply of Electric Power, Heat Power and Gas | 504 | 476 | 87 | 319 | 304 |
| 电力、热力生产和供应业 | Production and Supply of Electric Power and Heat Power | 489 | 463 | 73 | 310 | 295 |
| 燃气生产和供应业 | Production and Supply of Gas | 15 | 13 | 14 | 9 | 9 |
| 水的生产和供应业 | Production and Supply of Water | | | | | |

# 表 18.17 规模以上工业企业 R&D 人员情况(2021 年)
STATISTICS ON R&D PERSONNEL IN INDUSTRIAL ENTERPRISES ABOVE DESIGNATED SIZE (2021)

| 项 目 | Item | R&D 人员数(人) R&D Personnel (person) | #参加项目人员 Researchers | #R&D 全时人员 Full-time Employees | R&D 人员折合全时当量(人年) Full-time Personnel (person-year) | #试验发展人员 Personnel of Testing Development |
|---|---|---|---|---|---|---|
| **总 计** | **Total** | **131478** | **122032** | **94254** | **83845** | **81314** |
| **按隶属关系分** | **By Relationship** | | | | | |
| 中 央 | Central | 20242 | 19106 | 15522 | 11280 | 10631 |
| 地 方 | Local | 11808 | 11139 | 8037 | 8476 | 8115 |
| **按登记注册类型分** | **By Registration** | | | | | |
| 内资企业 | Domestic-funded | 115874 | 107932 | 82256 | 73096 | 70650 |
| 国有企业 | State-owned | 3154 | 2964 | 2396 | 1792 | 1687 |
| 集体企业 | Collective-owned | 37 | 32 | 32 | 30 | 30 |
| 股份合作企业 | Cooperative Enterprise | 92 | 81 | 76 | 66 | 66 |
| 联营企业 | Joint Ownership Enterprises | 100 | 89 | 37 | 59 | 59 |
| 有限责任公司 | Limited Liability Corporations | 27808 | 26037 | 18503 | 17433 | 16556 |
| 股份有限公司 | Share Holding Limited Corporations | 15195 | 14413 | 12404 | 8704 | 8410 |
| 私营企业 | Private Enterprises | 69488 | 64316 | 48808 | 45012 | 43842 |
| 其他企业 | Others | | | | | |
| 港、澳、台商投资企业 | Enterprises Funded by Hong Kong, Macao and Taiwan | 6447 | 5560 | 5194 | 4492 | 4481 |
| 合资经营企业 | Joint-venture Enterprises | 1311 | 1252 | 914 | 845 | 835 |
| 合作经营企业 | Cooperative Enterprises | | | | | |
| 独资经营企业 | Enterprises with Sole Funded from Hong Kong, Macao and Taiwan | 4724 | 3926 | 4006 | 3381 | 3381 |
| 投资股份有限公司 | Share-holding Corporations Ltd. with Investment from Hong Kong, Macao and Taiwan | 261 | 239 | 192 | 157 | 157 |
| 其他港澳台投资企业 | Others | 151 | 143 | 82 | 109 | 109 |
| 外商投资企业 | Foreign Funded Enterprises | 9157 | 8540 | 6804 | 6257 | 6183 |
| 中外合资经营企业 | Joint-venture Enterprises | 5229 | 4886 | 4147 | 3827 | 3818 |
| 中外合作经营企业 | Cooperation Enterprises | 46 | 41 | 32 | 29 | 29 |
| 外资企业 | Enterprises with Sole Fund | 3270 | 3058 | 2418 | 2072 | 2006 |
| 外商投资股份有限公司 | Share-holding Corporations Ltd. with Foreign Investment | 612 | 555 | 207 | 329 | 329 |
| 其他外商投资企业 | Others | | | | | |
| **按行业分** | **By Sector** | | | | | |
| 采矿业 | Mining | 480 | 447 | 329 | 328 | 245 |
| 煤炭开采和洗选业 | Mining and Washing of Coal | | | | | |
| 石油和天然气开采业 | Extraction of Petroleum and Natural Gas | 228 | 216 | 157 | 171 | 141 |
| 黑色金属矿采选业 | Mining and Processing of Ferrous Metal Ores | | | | | |
| 有色金属矿采选业 | Mining and Processing of Non-Ferrous Metal Ores | | | | | |
| 非金属矿采选业 | Mining and Processing of Nonmetal Ores | 252 | 231 | 172 | 157 | 104 |
| 开采辅助活动 | Mining Support Activities | | | | | |
| 其他采矿业 | Mining of Other Ores | | | | | |

**表 18.17 续表 continued**

| 项　目 | Item | R&D人员数（人）R&D Personnel (person) | #参加项目人员 Researchers | #R&D全时人员 Full-time Employees | R&D人员折合全时当量（人年）Full-time Personnel (person-year) | #试验发展人员 Personnel of Testing Development |
|---|---|---|---|---|---|---|
| 制造业 | Manufacture | 130132 | 120780 | 93646 | 82990 | 80575 |
| 农副食品加工业 | Processing of Food from Agricultural Products | 2253 | 2051 | 1359 | 1355 | 1306 |
| 食品制造业 | Manufacture of Foods | 1692 | 1565 | 1077 | 974 | 917 |
| 酒、饮料和精制茶制造业 | Liquor, Beverages and Refined Tea | 1069 | 976 | 492 | 538 | 517 |
| 烟草制品业 | Manufacture of Tobacco | 259 | 239 | 231 | 108 | 108 |
| 纺织业 | Manufacture of Textile | 352 | 313 | 207 | 207 | 187 |
| 纺织服装、服饰业 | Manufacture of Textile Wearing Apparel, Footwear and Caps | 360 | 332 | 243 | 224 | 185 |
| 皮革、毛皮、羽毛及其制品和制鞋业 | Manufacture of Leather, Fur, Feather and Related Products and Footwear | 394 | 371 | 297 | 290 | 290 |
| 木材加工和木、竹、藤、棕、草制品业 | Processing of Timber, Manufacture of Wood, Bamboo, Rattan, Palm and Straw Products | 861 | 784 | 481 | 548 | 521 |
| 家具制造业 | Manufacture of Furniture | 554 | 513 | 428 | 361 | 361 |
| 造纸和纸制品业 | Manufacture of Paper and Paper Products | 1520 | 1443 | 1188 | 1116 | 1116 |
| 印刷和记录媒介复制业 | Printing, Reproduction of Recording Media | 1252 | 1126 | 843 | 829 | 801 |
| 文教、工美、体育和娱乐用品制造业 | Manufacture of Culture, Education, Handicraft, Fine Arts, Sports and Entertainment Articles | 602 | 571 | 396 | 377 | 368 |
| 石油加工、炼焦和核燃料加工业 | Processing of Petroleum, Coking, Processing of Nuclear Fuel | 182 | 168 | 125 | 105 | 82 |
| 化学原料和化学制品制造业 | Manufacture of Raw Chemical Materials and Chemical Products | 4725 | 4418 | 2901 | 2998 | 2736 |
| 医药制造业 | Manufacture of Medicines | 5924 | 5648 | 4381 | 3701 | 3585 |
| 化学纤维制造业 | Manufacture of Chemical Fibers | 335 | 332 | 298 | 215 | 204 |
| 橡胶和塑料制品业 | Manufacture of Rubber and Plastics | 2843 | 2630 | 1982 | 1864 | 1762 |
| 非金属矿物制品业 | Manufacture of Non-metallic Mineral Products | 6652 | 6119 | 4180 | 4134 | 3961 |
| 黑色金属冶炼和压延加工业 | Smelting and Pressing of Ferrous Metals | 2704 | 2620 | 1716 | 2021 | 2018 |
| 有色金属冶炼和压延加工业 | Smelting and Pressing of Nonferrous Metals | 3868 | 3580 | 1751 | 1951 | 1853 |
| 金属制品业 | Manufacture of Metal Products | 4932 | 4556 | 3663 | 2802 | 2712 |
| 通用设备制造业 | Manufacture of General Purpose Machinery | 8091 | 7538 | 5949 | 5537 | 5344 |
| 专用设备制造业 | Manufacture of Special Purpose Machinery | 6184 | 5754 | 4230 | 3621 | 3619 |
| 汽车制造业 | Manufacture of Motor Vehicles | 30800 | 28736 | 24511 | 19146 | 18766 |
| 铁路、船舶、航空航天和其他运输设备制造业 | Manufacture of Railway, Ship, Aviation and Other Transporting Equipment | 10222 | 9478 | 7017 | 6512 | 6245 |
| 电气机械和器材制造业 | Manufacture of Electrical Machinery and Equipment | 6867 | 6275 | 5109 | 4428 | 4387 |
| 计算机、通信和其他电子设备制造业 | Manufacture of Communication Equipment, Computers and Other Electronic Equipment | 20046 | 18343 | 15131 | 14003 | 13677 |
| 仪器仪表制造业 | Manufacture of Measuring Instruments and Machinery for Cultural Activity and Office Work | 2962 | 2752 | 2287 | 1990 | 1929 |
| 其他制造业 | Other Manufacture | 1316 | 1257 | 966 | 843 | 834 |
| 废弃资源综合利用业 | Comprehensive Utilization of Waste Resources | 297 | 278 | 197 | 182 | 180 |
| 金属制品、机械和设备修理业 | Repair of Metal Products, Machinery and Equipment | 14 | 14 | 10 | 10 | 5 |
| 电力、热力、燃气及水生产和供应业 | Production and Supply of Electric Power, Heat Power and Gas | 866 | 805 | 279 | 527 | 494 |
| 电力、热力生产和供应业 | Production and Supply of Electric Power and Heat Power | 747 | 696 | 214 | 451 | 426 |
| 燃气生产和供应业 | Production and Supply of Gas | 74 | 67 | 32 | 38 | 30 |
| 水的生产和供应业 | Production and Supply of Water | 45 | 42 | 33 | 38 | 38 |

# 表 18.18 大中型工业企业 R&D 活动经费支出与项目情况（2021 年）

## EXPENDITURE AND PROJECTS OF SCIENTIFIC & TECHNOLOGICAL ACTIVITIES OF LARGE & MEDIUM-SIZED INDUSTRIAL ENTERPRISES (2021)

单位：万元 (10 000 yuan)

| 项　目 | Item | 研究与发展经费内部支　出 Internal Expenses for R&D | 技术改造经费支出 Expenditure for Technical Transformation | 技术引进经费支出 Expenditure for Technical Recommendation | 购买境内技术用款 Purchases of Civil Technology |
|---|---|---|---|---|---|
| **总　计** | **Total** | **3064831** | **550204** | **214776** | **19181** |
| **按隶属关系分** | **By Relationship** | | | | |
| 中　央 | Central | 925688 | 84119 | 198606 | 185 |
| 地　方 | Local | 338466 | 325704 | 815 | 1674 |
| **按登记注册类型分** | **By Registration** | | | | |
| 内资企业 | Domestic-funded | 2548122 | 471133 | 11688 | 15483 |
| 国有企业 | State-owned | 107923 | 1900 | | 52 |
| 集体企业 | Collective-owned | 285 | 6 | | |
| 股份合作企业 | Cooperative Enterprise | 1984 | | | |
| 联营企业 | Joint Ownership Enterprises | 2663 | 1286 | | |
| 有限责任公司 | Limited Liability Corporations | 771943 | 100503 | 1849 | 10344 |
| 股份有限公司 | Share Holding Limited Corporations | 523164 | 280270 | 9756 | 4320 |
| 私营企业 | Private Enterprises | 1140161 | 87168 | 83 | 767 |
| 其他企业 | Others | | | | |
| 港、澳、台商投资企业 | Enterprises Funded by Hong Kong, Macao and Taiwan | 144840 | 6056 | | 2 |
| 合资经营企业 | Joint-venture Enterprises | 33702 | 407 | | 2 |
| 合作经营企业 | Cooperative Enterprises | | | | |
| 独资经营企业 | Enterprises with Sole Funded from Hong Kong, Macao and Taiwan | 101248 | 5613 | | |
| 投资股份有限公司 | Share-holding Corporations Ltd. with Investment from Hong Kong, Macao and Taiwan | 7220 | 36 | | |
| 其他港澳台投资企业 | Others | 2670 | | | |
| 外商投资企业 | Foreign Funded Enterprises | 371869 | 73015 | 203089 | 3696 |
| 中外合资经营企业 | Joint-venture Enterprises | 301000 | 71706 | 203089 | |
| 中外合作经营企业 | Cooperation Enterprises | 314 | | | |
| 外资企业 | Enterprises with Sole Fund | 64191 | 1309 | | 3696 |
| 外商投资股份有限公司 | Share-holding Corporations Ltd. with Foreign Investment | 6364 | | | |
| 其他外商投资企业 | Others | | | | |
| **按行业分** | **By Sector** | | | | |
| 采矿业 | Mining | 2472 | 14466 | | 434 |
| 煤炭开采和洗选业 | Mining and Washing of Coal | | | | |
| 石油和天然气开采业 | Extraction of Petroleum and Natural Gas | | | | |
| 黑色金属矿采选业 | Mining and Processing of Ferrous Metal Ores | | | | |
| 有色金属矿采选业 | Mining and Processing of Non-Ferrous Metal Ores | | | | |
| 非金属矿采选业 | Mining and Processing of Nonmetal Ores | 2472 | 14466 | | 434 |
| 开采辅助活动 | Mining Support Activities | | | | |
| 其他采矿业 | Mining of Other Ores | | | | |

**表 18.18 续表 continued**

单位：万元 (10 000 yuan)

| 项 目 | Item | 研究与发展经费内部支出 Internal Expenses for R&D | 技术改造经费支出 Expenditure for Technical Transformation | 技术引进经费支出 Expenditure for Technical Recommendation | 购买境内技术用款 Purchases of Civil Technology |
|---|---|---|---|---|---|
| 制造业 | Manufacture | 3027777 | 535273 | 214776 | 18747 |
| 农副食品加工业 | Processing of Food from Agricultural Products | 21947 | 1530 | | 1 |
| 食品制造业 | Manufacture of Foods | 16302 | 281 | | |
| 酒、饮料和精制茶制造业 | Liquor, Beverages and Refined Tea | 8035 | | | |
| 烟草制品业 | Manufacture of Tobacco | 8933 | | | |
| 纺织业 | Manufacture of Textile | 320 | | | |
| 纺织服装、服饰业 | Manufacture of Textile Wearing Apparel, Footwear and Caps | 4885 | | | |
| 皮革、毛皮、羽毛及其制品和制鞋业 | Manufacture of Leather, Fur, Feather and Related Products and Footwear | 3201 | | | |
| 木材加工和木、竹、藤、棕、草制品业 | Processing of Timber, Manufacture of Wood, Bamboo, Rattan, Palm and Straw Products | 8842 | 3949 | | 1180 |
| 家具制造业 | Manufacture of Furniture | 6401 | 355 | | |
| 造纸和纸制品业 | Manufacture of Paper and Paper Products | 24644 | | | |
| 印刷和记录媒介复制业 | Printing, Reproduction of Recording Media | 14547 | | | |
| 文教、工美、体育和娱乐用品制造业 | Manufacture of Culture, Education, Handicraft, Fine Arts, Sports and Entertainment Articles | 3997 | 36 | | |
| 石油加工、炼焦和核燃料加工业 | Processing of Petroleum, Coking, Processing of Nuclear Fuel | 6305 | | | |
| 化学原料和化学制品制造业 | Manufacture of Raw Chemical Materials and Chemical Products | 104973 | 45146 | 815 | 4395 |
| 医药制造业 | Manufacture of Medicines | 132979 | 11546 | 1034 | 8519 |
| 化学纤维制造业 | Manufacture of Chemical Fibers | 26108 | 5804 | | |
| 橡胶和塑料制品业 | Manufacture of Rubber and Plastics | 26298 | 426 | | |
| 非金属矿物制品业 | Manufacture of Non-metallic Mineral Products | 59694 | 7209 | | 96 |
| 黑色金属冶炼和压延加工业 | Smelting and Pressing of Ferrous Metals | 59001 | 243627 | | |
| 有色金属冶炼和压延加工业 | Smelting and Pressing of Nonferrous Metals | 76503 | 3736 | | |
| 金属制品业 | Manufacture of Metal Products | 84001 | 1009 | | 60 |
| 通用设备制造业 | Manufacture of General Purpose Machinery | 155601 | 7949 | 4410 | 227 |
| 专用设备制造业 | Manufacture of Special Purpose Machinery | 135094 | 1387 | | |
| 汽车制造业 | Manufacture of Motor Vehicles | 982654 | 112366 | 198678 | 942 |
| 铁路、船舶、航空航天和其他运输设备制造业 | Manufacture of Railway, Ship, Aviation and Other Transporting Equipment | 188036 | 26080 | | 34 |
| 电气机械和器材制造业 | Manufacture of Electrical Machinery and Equipment | 192116 | 19890 | 9756 | 165 |
| 计算机、通信和其他电子设备制造业 | Manufacture of Communication Equipment, Computers and Other Electronic Equipment | 559675 | 27356 | 83 | 2820 |
| 仪器仪表制造业 | Manufacture of Measuring Instruments and Machinery for Cultural Activity and Office Work | 46137 | 4596 | | 309 |
| 其他制造业 | Other Manufacture | 66168 | 10994 | | |
| 废弃资源综合利用业 | Comprehensive Utilization of Waste Resources | 4382 | | | |
| 金属制品、机械和设备修理业 | Repair of Metal Products, Machinery and Equipment | | | | |
| 电力、热力、燃气及水生产和供应业 | Production and Supply of Electric Power, Heat Power and Gas | 34582 | 464 | | |
| 电力、热力生产和供应业 | Production and Supply of Electric Power and Heat Power | 34540 | 445 | | |
| 燃气生产和供应业 | Production and Supply of Gas | 41 | | | |
| 水的生产和供应业 | Production and Supply of Water | | 19 | | |

# 表 18.19 规模以上工业企业 R&D 活动经费支出与项目情况(2021 年)
## EXPENDITURE AND PROJECTS OF SCIENTIFIC & TECHNOLOGICAL ACTIVITIES OF INDUSTRIAL ENTERPRISES ABOVE DESIGNATED SIZE (2021)

单位：万元 (10 000 yuan)

| 项　目 | Item | 研究与发展经费内部支出<br>Internal Expenses for R&D | 技术改造经费支出<br>Expenditure for Technical Transformation | 技术引进经费支出<br>Expenditure for Technical Recommendation | 购买境内技术用款<br>Purchases of Civil Technology |
|---|---|---|---|---|---|
| **总　计** | **Total** | **4245267** | **635349** | **223761** | **22645** |
| **按隶属关系分** | **By Relationship** | | | | |
| 中　央 | Central | 997223 | 86513 | 198606 | 185 |
| 地　方 | Local | 430489 | 328127 | 815 | 2189 |
| **按登记注册类型分** | **By Registration** | | | | |
| 内资企业 | Domestic-funded | 3673062 | 551870 | 11976 | 18037 |
| 国有企业 | State-owned | 111167 | 1950 | | 52 |
| 集体企业 | Collective-owned | 478 | 6 | | |
| 股份合作企业 | Cooperative Enterprise | 2154 | | | |
| 联营企业 | Joint Ownership Enterprises | 2663 | 1286 | | |
| 有限责任公司 | Limited Liability Corporations | 1021615 | 112016 | 1986 | 12437 |
| 股份有限公司 | Share Holding Limited Corporations | 540394 | 280569 | 9756 | 4320 |
| 私营企业 | Private Enterprises | 1994592 | 156043 | 233 | 1228 |
| 其他企业 | Others | | | | |
| 港、澳、台商投资企业 | Enterprises Funded by Hong Kong, Macao and Taiwan | 160250 | 8346 | | 912 |
| 合资经营企业 | Joint-venture Enterprises | 42422 | 1447 | | 912 |
| 合作经营企业 | Cooperative Enterprises | | | | |
| 独资经营企业 | Enterprises with Sole Funded from Hong Kong, Macao and Taiwan | 107939 | 6863 | | |
| 投资股份有限公司 | Share-holding Corporations Ltd. with Investment from Hong Kong, Macao and Taiwan | 7220 | 36 | | |
| 其他港澳台投资企业 | Others | 2670 | | | |
| 外商投资企业 | Foreign Funded Enterprises | 411954 | 75133 | 211785 | 3696 |
| 中外合资经营企业 | Joint-venture Enterprises | 327069 | 73824 | 211785 | |
| 中外合作经营企业 | Cooperation Enterprises | 663 | | | |
| 外资企业 | Enterprises with Sole Fund | 76836 | 1309 | | 3696 |
| 外商投资股份有限公司 | Share-holding Corporations Ltd. with Foreign Investment | 7386 | | | |
| 其他外商投资企业 | Others | | | | |
| **按行业分** | **By Sector** | | | | |
| 采矿业 | Mining | 53307 | 14953 | | 434 |
| 煤炭开采和洗选业 | Mining and Washing of Coal | | | | |
| 石油和天然气开采业 | Extraction of Petroleum and Natural Gas | 46406 | | | |
| 黑色金属矿采选业 | Mining and Processing of Ferrous Metal Ores | | | | |
| 有色金属矿采选业 | Mining and Processing of Non-Ferrous Metal Ores | | | | |
| 非金属矿采选业 | Mining and Processing of Nonmetal Ores | 6900 | 14953 | | 434 |
| 开采辅助活动 | Mining Support Activities | | | | |
| 其他采矿业 | Mining of Other Ores | | | | |

**表 18.19 续表 continued**

单位：万元 (10 000 yuan)

| 项　目 | Item | 研究与发展经费内部支出 Internal Expenses for R&D | 技术改造经费支出 Expenditure for Technical Transformation | 技术引进经费支出 Expenditure for Technical Recommendation | 购买境内技术用款 Purchases of Civil Technology |
|---|---|---|---|---|---|
| 制造业 | Manufacture | 4144287 | 617212 | 223761 | 21822 |
| 农副食品加工业 | Processing of Food from Agricultural Products | 73893 | 2649 | | 6 |
| 食品制造业 | Manufacture of Foods | 26356 | 3050 | | |
| 酒、饮料和精制茶制造业 | Liquor, Beverages and Refined Tea | 13130 | 17 | | |
| 烟草制品业 | Manufacture of Tobacco | 8983 | | | |
| 纺织业 | Manufacture of Textile | 4372 | 45 | | |
| 纺织服装、服饰业 | Manufacture of Textile Wearing Apparel, Footwear and Caps | 8142 | 42 | | |
| 皮革、毛皮、羽毛及其制品和制鞋业 | Manufacture of Leather, Fur, Feather and Related Products and Footwear | 7526 | 3 | | |
| 木材加工和木、竹、藤、棕、草制品业 | Processing of Timber, Manufacture of Wood, Bamboo, Rattan, Palm and Straw Products | 20615 | 4937 | | 1255 |
| 家具制造业 | Manufacture of Furniture | 14348 | 1811 | | |
| 造纸和纸制品业 | Manufacture of Paper and Paper Products | 41883 | 3068 | | |
| 印刷和记录媒介复制业 | Printing, Reproduction of Recording Media | 41026 | 1716 | | 2 |
| 文教、工美、体育和娱乐用品制造业 | Manufacture of Culture, Education, Handicraft, Fine Arts, Sports and Entertainment Articles | 7505 | 102 | | |
| 石油加工、炼焦和核燃料加工业 | Processing of Petroleum, Coking, Processing of Nuclear Fuel | 7823 | | | 63 |
| 化学原料和化学制品制造业 | Manufacture of Raw Chemical Materials and Chemical Products | 141833 | 48255 | 891 | 4395 |
| 医药制造业 | Manufacture of Medicines | 174598 | 14869 | 1034 | 8646 |
| 化学纤维制造业 | Manufacture of Chemical Fibers | 27500 | 5804 | | |
| 橡胶和塑料制品业 | Manufacture of Rubber and Plastics | 87925 | 10766 | 5 | 49 |
| 非金属矿物制品业 | Manufacture of Non-metallic Mineral Products | 113780 | 15964 | 146 | 121 |
| 黑色金属冶炼和压延加工业 | Smelting and Pressing of Ferrous Metals | 69715 | 243927 | | |
| 有色金属冶炼和压延加工业 | Smelting and Pressing of Nonferrous Metals | 106434 | 5999 | | 910 |
| 金属制品业 | Manufacture of Metal Products | 157811 | 3488 | | 77 |
| 通用设备制造业 | Manufacture of General Purpose Machinery | 242965 | 23442 | 4410 | 227 |
| 专用设备制造业 | Manufacture of Special Purpose Machinery | 206612 | 4329 | | |
| 汽车制造业 | Manufacture of Motor Vehicles | 1179295 | 120741 | 207436 | 1627 |
| 铁路、船舶、航空航天和其他运输设备制造业 | Manufacture of Railway, Ship, Aviation and Other Transporting Equipment | 248608 | 36501 | | 41 |
| 电气机械和器材制造业 | Manufacture of Electrical Machinery and Equipment | 248511 | 20655 | 9756 | 207 |
| 计算机、通信和其他电子设备制造业 | Manufacture of Communication Equipment, Computers and Other Electronic Equipment | 709405 | 27736 | 83 | 3887 |
| 仪器仪表制造业 | Manufacture of Measuring Instruments and Machinery for Cultural Activity and Office Work | 70272 | 5622 | | 309 |
| 其他制造业 | Other Manufacture | 70096 | 10994 | | |
| 废弃资源综合利用业 | Comprehensive Utilization of Waste Resources | 13165 | 681 | | |
| 金属制品、机械和设备修理业 | Repair of Metal Products, Machinery and Equipment | 161 | | | |
| 电力、热力、燃气及水生产和供应业 | Production and Supply of Electric Power, Heat Power and Gas | 47674 | 3184 | | 389 |
| 电力、热力生产和供应业 | Production and Supply of Electric Power and Heat Power | 44098 | 2651 | | 389 |
| 燃气生产和供应业 | Production and Supply of Gas | 2206 | | | |
| 水的生产和供应业 | Production and Supply of Water | 1370 | 532 | | |

# 表 18.20 大中型工业企业新产品开发情况（2021 年）
## NEW PRODUCTS DEVELOPMENT OF LARGE & MEDIUM-SIZED INDUSTRIAL ENTERPRISES (2021)

单位：万元 (10 000 yuan)

| 项　目 | Item | 新产品项目数（项） Projects of New Products (unit) | 新产品开发经费支出 Development Funds of New Products | 新产品销售收入 Sales Revenue of New Products | #新产品出口 Exports of New Products |
|---|---|---|---|---|---|
| **总　计** | **Total** | **9829** | **3488870** | **55489195** | **13410273** |
| **按隶属关系分** | **By Relationship** | | | | |
| 中　央 | Central | 1729 | 879089 | 12671406 | 456181 |
| 地　方 | Local | 1738 | 462791 | 9267710 | 1908159 |
| **按登记注册类型分** | **By Registration** | | | | |
| 内资企业 | Domestic-funded | 8704 | 2890398 | 42652756 | 5443426 |
| 国有企业 | State-owned | 607 | 107975 | 1082016 | 796 |
| 集体企业 | Collective-owned | 1 | 488 | 5094 | |
| 股份合作企业 | Cooperative Enterprise | 13 | 4327 | 24547 | |
| 联营企业 | Joint Ownership Enterprises | 13 | 4287 | 77079 | |
| 有限责任公司 | Limited Liability Corporations | 3065 | 892192 | 13401392 | 2295846 |
| 股份有限公司 | Share Holding Limited Corporations | 1099 | 539863 | 12369401 | 859577 |
| 私营企业 | Private Enterprises | 3906 | 1341266 | 15693228 | 2287206 |
| 其他企业 | Others | | | | |
| 港、澳、台商投资企业 | Enterprises Funded by Hong Kong, Macao and Taiwan | 339 | 210947 | 1878709 | 489058 |
| 合资经营企业 | Joint-venture Enterprises | 151 | 52257 | 397709 | 50907 |
| 合作经营企业 | Cooperative Enterprises | | | | |
| 独资经营企业 | Enterprises with Sole Funded from Hong Kong, Macao and Taiwan | 154 | 146320 | 1156093 | 427474 |
| 投资股份有限公司 | Share-holding Corporations Ltd. with Investment from Hong Kong, Macao and Taiwan | 24 | 7207 | 216480 | 10678 |
| 其他港澳台投资企业 | Others | 10 | 5162 | 108426 | |
| 外商投资企业 | Foreign Funded Enterprises | 786 | 387526 | 10957731 | 7477789 |
| 中外合资经营企业 | Joint-venture Enterprises | 451 | 306686 | 3437355 | 160904 |
| 中外合作经营企业 | Cooperation Enterprises | 8 | 1033 | 7 | |
| 外资企业 | Enterprises with Sole Fund | 237 | 68608 | 7517778 | 7316886 |
| 外商投资股份有限公司 | Share-holding Corporations Ltd. with Foreign Investment | 90 | 11200 | 2592 | |
| 其他外商投资企业 | Others | | | | |
| **按行业分** | **By Sector** | | | | |
| 采矿业 | Mining | 3 | 577 | 12764 | |
| 煤炭开采和洗选业 | Mining and Washing of Coal | | | | |
| 石油和天然气开采业 | Extraction of Petroleum and Natural Gas | | | 10204 | |
| 黑色金属矿采选业 | Mining and Processing of Ferrous Metal Ores | | | | |
| 有色金属矿采选业 | Mining and Processing of Non-Ferrous Metal Ores | | | | |
| 非金属矿采选业 | Mining and Processing of Nonmetal Ores | 3 | 577 | 2561 | |
| 开采辅助活动 | Mining Support Activities | | | | |
| 其他采矿业 | Mining of Other Ores | | | | |

**表 18.20 续表 continued**

单位：万元 (10 000 yuan)

| 项 目 | Item | 新产品项目数（项）Projects of New Products (unit) | 新产品开发经费支出 Development Funds of New Products | 新产品销售收入 Sales Revenue of New Products | #新产品出口 Exports of New Products |
|---|---|---|---|---|---|
| 制造业 | Manufacture | 9743 | 3460659 | 55473931 | 13410273 |
| 农副食品加工业 | Processing of Food from Agricultural Products | 108 | 22061 | 420005 | 3563 |
| 食品制造业 | Manufacture of Foods | 91 | 22196 | 238712 | 13198 |
| 酒、饮料和精制茶制造业 | Liquor, Beverages and Refined Tea | 67 | 14697 | 124966 | 270 |
| 烟草制品业 | Manufacture of Tobacco | 27 | 9066 | 22374 | |
| 纺织业 | Manufacture of Textile | 1 | 743 | | |
| 纺织服装、服饰业 | Manufacture of Textile Wearing Apparel, Footwear and Caps | 18 | 7610 | 42041 | 2853 |
| 皮革、毛皮、羽毛及其制品和制鞋业 | Manufacture of Leather, Fur, Feather and Related Products and Footwear | 27 | 3636 | 60532 | 2169 |
| 木材加工和木、竹、藤、棕、草制品业 | Processing of Timber, Manufacture of Wood, Bamboo, Rattan, Palm and Straw Products | 39 | 10513 | 228933 | |
| 家具制造业 | Manufacture of Furniture | 40 | 7920 | 83254 | |
| 造纸和纸制品业 | Manufacture of Paper and Paper Products | 63 | 48409 | 772808 | 13154 |
| 印刷和记录媒介复制业 | Printing, Reproduction of Recording Media | 31 | 12708 | 198817 | 12701 |
| 文教、工美、体育和娱乐用品制造业 | Manufacture of Culture, Education, Handicraft, Fine Arts, Sports and Entertainment Articles | 36 | 6306 | 61362 | 39703 |
| 石油加工、炼焦和核燃料加工业 | Processing of Petroleum, Coking, Processing of Nuclear Fuel | 16 | 3061 | 856 | |
| 化学原料和化学制品制造业 | Manufacture of Raw Chemical Materials and Chemical Products | 322 | 128103 | 2038754 | 105325 |
| 医药制造业 | Manufacture of Medicines | 714 | 140596 | 2268790 | 212508 |
| 化学纤维制造业 | Manufacture of Chemical Fibers | 20 | 25824 | 552243 | 44003 |
| 橡胶和塑料制品业 | Manufacture of Rubber and Plastics | 80 | 25828 | 366004 | |
| 非金属矿物制品业 | Manufacture of Non-metallic Mineral Products | 353 | 100337 | 1453661 | 50858 |
| 黑色金属冶炼和压延加工业 | Smelting and Pressing of Ferrous Metals | 209 | 180162 | 2635555 | |
| 有色金属冶炼和压延加工业 | Smelting and Pressing of Nonferrous Metals | 275 | 145364 | 1770931 | 1377 |
| 金属制品业 | Manufacture of Metal Products | 327 | 74798 | 619808 | 18967 |
| 通用设备制造业 | Manufacture of General Purpose Machinery | 690 | 153660 | 2429710 | 427094 |
| 专用设备制造业 | Manufacture of Special Purpose Machinery | 608 | 137684 | 920240 | 45084 |
| 汽车制造业 | Manufacture of Motor Vehicles | 2012 | 1008057 | 17052614 | 504399 |
| 铁路、船舶、航空航天和其他运输设备制造业 | Manufacture of Railway, Ship, Aviation and Other Transporting Equipment | 1014 | 202699 | 2532025 | 761466 |
| 电气机械和器材制造业 | Manufacture of Electrical Machinery and Equipment | 412 | 201012 | 3987733 | 167669 |
| 计算机、通信和其他电子设备制造业 | Manufacture of Communication Equipment, Computers and Other Electronic Equipment | 1566 | 645844 | 13809109 | 10973194 |
| 仪器仪表制造业 | Manufacture of Measuring Instruments and Machinery for Cultural Activity and Office Work | 330 | 52432 | 444337 | 4399 |
| 其他制造业 | Other Manufacture | 238 | 64928 | 267282 | 6319 |
| 废弃资源综合利用业 | Comprehensive Utilization of Waste Resources | 9 | 4407 | 70477 | |
| 金属制品、机械和设备修理业 | Repair of Metal Products, Machinery and Equipment | | | | |
| 电力、热力、燃气及水生产和供应业 | Production and Supply of Electric Power, Heat Power and Gas | 83 | 27635 | 2500 | |
| 电力、热力生产和供应业 | Production and Supply of Electric Power and Heat Power | 77 | 27557 | | |
| 燃气生产和供应业 | Production and Supply of Gas | 4 | 27 | 2500 | |
| 水的生产和供应业 | Production and Supply of Water | 2 | 51 | | |

## 表 18.21 规模以上工业企业新产品开发情况（2021 年）
NEW PRODUCTS DEVELOPMENT OF INDUSTRIAL ENTERPRISES ABOVE DESIGNATED SIZE (2021)

单位：万元 (10 000 yuan)

| 项　目 | Item | 新产品项目数（项） Projects of New Products (unit) | 新产品开发经费支出 Development Funds of New Products | 新产品销售收入 Sales Revenue of New Products | #新产品出口 Exports of New Products |
|---|---|---|---|---|---|
| **总　计** | **Total** | **19752** | **4904174** | **69951788** | **14289567** |
| **按隶属关系分** | **By Relationship** | | | | |
| 中　央 | Central | 2039 | 940247 | 13903994 | 463058 |
| 地　方 | Local | 2243 | 550726 | 9989732 | 2088535 |
| **按登记注册类型分** | **By Registration** | | | | |
| 内资企业 | Domestic-funded | 18189 | 4217936 | 55993323 | 6094539 |
| 国有企业 | State-owned | 663 | 112773 | 1108449 | 796 |
| 集体企业 | Collective-owned | 2 | 629 | 5402 | |
| 股份合作企业 | Cooperative Enterprise | 17 | 4623 | 29387 | |
| 联营企业 | Joint Ownership Enterprises | 13 | 4287 | 77079 | |
| 有限责任公司 | Limited Liability Corporations | 4536 | 1142009 | 16391601 | 2410633 |
| 股份有限公司 | Share Holding Limited Corporations | 1259 | 559178 | 12538451 | 862665 |
| 私营企业 | Private Enterprises | 11699 | 2394437 | 25842954 | 2820445 |
| 其他企业 | Others | | | | |
| 港、澳、台商投资企业 | Enterprises Funded by Hong Kong, Macao and Taiwan | 433 | 232630 | 2315915 | 631758 |
| 合资经营企业 | Joint-venture Enterprises | 214 | 63931 | 718388 | 183126 |
| 合作经营企业 | Cooperative Enterprises | | | | |
| 独资经营企业 | Enterprises with Sole Funded from Hong Kong, Macao and Taiwan | 185 | 156330 | 1272621 | 437955 |
| 投资股份有限公司 | Share-holding Corporations Ltd. with Investment from Hong Kong, Macao and Taiwan | 24 | 7207 | 216480 | 10678 |
| 其他港澳台投资企业 | Others | 10 | 5162 | 108426 | |
| 外商投资企业 | Foreign Funded Enterprises | 1130 | 453609 | 11642550 | 7563269 |
| 中外合资经营企业 | Joint-venture Enterprises | 680 | 353735 | 3942022 | 234309 |
| 中外合作经营企业 | Cooperation Enterprises | 17 | 1520 | 9668 | 537 |
| 外资企业 | Enterprises with Sole Fund | 330 | 85680 | 7674575 | 7328424 |
| 外商投资股份有限公司 | Share-holding Corporations Ltd. with Foreign Investment | 103 | 12674 | 16286 | |
| 其他外商投资企业 | Others | | | | |
| **按行业分** | **By Sector** | | | | |
| 采矿业 | Mining | 66 | 39287 | 1016801 | |
| 煤炭开采和洗选业 | Mining and Washing of Coal | | | | |
| 石油和天然气开采业 | Extraction of Petroleum and Natural Gas | 44 | 35229 | 924917 | |
| 黑色金属矿采选业 | Mining and Processing of Ferrous Metal Ores | | | | |
| 有色金属矿采选业 | Mining and Processing of Non-Ferrous Metal Ores | | | | |
| 非金属矿采选业 | Mining and Processing of Nonmetal Ores | 22 | 4058 | 91883 | |
| 开采辅助活动 | Mining Support Activities | | | | |
| 其他采矿业 | Mining of Other Ores | | | | |

**表 18.21 续表 continued**

单位：万元 (10 000 yuan)

| 项　目 | Item | 新产品项目数（项） Projects of New Products (unit) | 新产品开发经费支出 Development Funds of New Products | 新产品销售收入 Sales Revenue of New Products | #新产品出口 Exports of New Products |
|---|---|---|---|---|---|
| 制造业 | Manufacture | 19532 | 4827680 | 68931220 | 14289567 |
| 农副食品加工业 | Processing of Food from Agricultural Products | 369 | 71410 | 861322 | 11150 |
| 食品制造业 | Manufacture of Foods | 298 | 46994 | 470463 | 28993 |
| 酒、饮料和精制茶制造业 | Liquor, Beverages and Refined Tea | 99 | 23010 | 216309 | 270 |
| 烟草制品业 | Manufacture of Tobacco | 27 | 9066 | 22374 | |
| 纺织业 | Manufacture of Textile | 39 | 6364 | 62133 | 2039 |
| 纺织服装、服饰业 | Manufacture of Textile Wearing Apparel, Footwear and Caps | 30 | 10429 | 102930 | 2853 |
| 皮革、毛皮、羽毛及其制品和制鞋业 | Manufacture of Leather, Fur, Feather and Related Products and Footwear | 55 | 7385 | 76394 | 5041 |
| 木材加工和木、竹、藤、棕、草制品业 | Processing of Timber, Manufacture of Wood, Bamboo, Rattan, Palm and Straw Products | 112 | 21158 | 296750 | 87 |
| 家具制造业 | Manufacture of Furniture | 115 | 15938 | 206690 | 35 |
| 造纸和纸制品业 | Manufacture of Paper and Paper Products | 182 | 80118 | 986998 | 17651 |
| 印刷和记录媒介复制业 | Printing, Reproduction of Recording Media | 200 | 35635 | 474569 | 26126 |
| 文教、工美、体育和娱乐用品制造业 | Manufacture of Culture, Education, Handicraft, Fine Arts, Sports and Entertainment Articles | 88 | 15139 | 163305 | 40607 |
| 石油加工、炼焦和核燃料加工业 | Processing of Petroleum, Coking, Processing of Nuclear Fuel | 38 | 5203 | 21980 | |
| 化学原料和化学制品制造业 | Manufacture of Raw Chemical Materials and Chemical Products | 625 | 178859 | 2868454 | 137743 |
| 医药制造业 | Manufacture of Medicines | 1172 | 193466 | 2700428 | 299453 |
| 化学纤维制造业 | Manufacture of Chemical Fibers | 24 | 26446 | 564160 | 44003 |
| 橡胶和塑料制品业 | Manufacture of Rubber and Plastics | 514 | 88078 | 1244035 | 11448 |
| 非金属矿物制品业 | Manufacture of Non-metallic Mineral Products | 861 | 188955 | 2537771 | 52200 |
| 黑色金属冶炼和压延加工业 | Smelting and Pressing of Ferrous Metals | 307 | 227274 | 2810084 | |
| 有色金属冶炼和压延加工业 | Smelting and Pressing of Nonferrous Metals | 458 | 212870 | 2434794 | 3873 |
| 金属制品业 | Manufacture of Metal Products | 899 | 145408 | 1665774 | 151711 |
| 通用设备制造业 | Manufacture of General Purpose Machinery | 1483 | 250627 | 3397363 | 595084 |
| 专用设备制造业 | Manufacture of Special Purpose Machinery | 1444 | 218334 | 1584953 | 109695 |
| 汽车制造业 | Manufacture of Motor Vehicles | 4044 | 1242919 | 19258386 | 549620 |
| 铁路、船舶、航空航天和其他运输设备制造业 | Manufacture of Railway, Ship, Aviation and Other Transporting Equipment | 1609 | 267676 | 3137239 | 899519 |
| 电气机械和器材制造业 | Manufacture of Electrical Machinery and Equipment | 1043 | 272740 | 4890509 | 177684 |
| 计算机、通信和其他电子设备制造业 | Manufacture of Communication Equipment, Computers and Other Electronic Equipment | 2397 | 801604 | 14715418 | 11102255 |
| 仪器仪表制造业 | Manufacture of Measuring Instruments and Machinery for Cultural Activity and Office Work | 699 | 81721 | 719703 | 14066 |
| 其他制造业 | Other Manufacture | 255 | 70448 | 290882 | 6344 |
| 废弃资源综合利用业 | Comprehensive Utilization of Waste Resources | 44 | 12328 | 145745 | |
| 金属制品、机械和设备修理业 | Repair of Metal Products, Machinery and Equipment | 2 | 81 | 3306 | 19 |
| 电力、热力、燃气及水生产和供应业 | Production and Supply of Electric Power, Heat Power and Gas | 154 | 37208 | 3767 | |
| 电力、热力生产和供应业 | Production and Supply of Electric Power and Heat Power | 135 | 34988 | 309 | |
| 燃气生产和供应业 | Production and Supply of Gas | 12 | 1118 | 2500 | |
| 水的生产和供应业 | Production and Supply of Water | 7 | 1101 | 958 | |

## 表 18.22 专利授权量(2021 – 2022 年)
## APPLICATIONS GRANTED (2021-2022)

单位：件 (pcs)

| 项 目 | Item | 2021 | 2022 |
|---|---|---|---|
| **总 计** | **Total** | **76206** | **66467** |
| **按种类分** | **By Type** | | |
| 发 明 | Inventions | 9413 | 12207 |
| 实用新型 | Utility Models | 58410 | 46556 |
| 外观设计 | Designs | 8383 | 7704 |
| **按对象分** | **By Applicant** | | |
| 个 人 | Individuals | 7593 | 5311 |
| 大专院校 | Universities and Colleges | 9987 | 8878 |
| 科研单位 | Research Institutions | 1004 | 1109 |
| 工矿企业 | Industrial and Mineral Enterprises | 54856 | 49102 |
| 机关团体 | Government Agencies and Organizations | 2766 | 2067 |

## 表 18.23 新华书店系统图书发行流转及销售情况(2021 – 2022 年)
## XINHUA BOOKSTORE SYSTEM BOOK DISTRIBUTION CIRCULATION AND SALES STATISTICS (2021-2022)

单位：万册、万元 (10 000 copies, 10 000 yuan)

| 项 目 | Item | 册 数 Number of Books | | 金 额 Value | |
|---|---|---|---|---|---|
| | | 2021 | 2022 | 2021 | 2022 |
| **购 进** | **Purchases** | **50321** | **44246** | **652633** | **583934** |
| **销 售** | **Sales** | **47939** | **46241** | **618182** | **602156** |
| 零 售 | Retail | 16396 | | 192666 | |
| 区 县 | Districts and County | 14563 | | 171120 | |
| 县以下 | Below County | 1833 | 1890 | 21546 | 22839 |
| 批 发 | Wholesale | 31543 | 28997 | 425516 | 407898 |
| **库 存** | **Inventory** | **10826** | **9104** | **201961** | **193701** |

## 表 18.24 各类技术合同签订及执行情况(2022 年)
## SIGNING AND IMPLEMENTATION OF TECHNICAL CONTRACTS BY TYPE (2022)

| 项 目 | Item | 合同数（项）Number of Contracts (item) | 合同成交金额（万元）Value of Contracts (10 000 yuan) | #技术交易额（万元）Technology Transaction Value (10 000 yuan) | 技术交易额比重（%）As Percentage of Contract Value (%) |
|---|---|---|---|---|---|
| **总 计** | **Total** | **6919** | **6304852.74** | **1838601.55** | **29.16** |
| 技术开发 | Technical Development | 2349 | 568659.12 | 462397.08 | 81.31 |
| 技术转让 | Technical Transfer | 237 | 723821.93 | 721243.99 | 99.64 |
| 技术许可 | Technology licensing | 12 | 8601.25 | 8148.25 | 94.73 |
| 技术咨询 | Technical Consultation | 400 | 856516.57 | 115210.95 | 13.45 |
| 技术服务 | Technical Services | 3921 | 4147253.86 | 531601.28 | 12.82 |

## 表 18.25 新闻出版机构和人员数(2021－2022 年)
## NUMBER OF INSTITUTIONS AND PERSONS ENGAGED IN PRESS AND PUBLICATION (2021-2022)

单位：个、人 (unit, person)

| 指 标 | Item | 2021 | 2022 |
|---|---|---|---|
| **书报刊电子音像出版社** | **Books, newspapers and periodicals electronic audiovisual publishing house** | | |
| 机构数 | Institutions | 194 | 194 |
| 从业人员 | Personnel | 8747 | 8427 |
| **出版物和专项印刷厂** | **Publications and special printing houses** | | |
| 机构数 | Institutions | 95 | 106 |
| 从业人员 | Personnel | 4500 | 4500 |
| **国有书店** | **State-owned Book Stores** | | |
| 机构数 | Institutions | 44 | 21 |
| 从业人员 | Personnel | 1725 | 798 |

# 表 18.26 地震监测情况（1997 － 2022 年）
## SITUATION OF EARTHQUAKE MONITORING (1997-2022)

单位：个 (unit)

| 年 份<br>Year | 地震台数总数<br>Number of Seismic Stations | 国家级台<br>Number of National Stations | 省级台<br>Number of Provincial Stations | 市、县级台<br>Number of Municipality/ County-level Stations | 企业台<br>Number of Enterprise Stations | 强震观测点<br>Number of Strong Motion Observation Spots | 宏观观测点<br>Number of Macro-observation Spots |
|---|---|---|---|---|---|---|---|
| 1997 | 7 | 1 | | 6 | | | |
| 1998 | 7 | 1 | | 6 | | | |
| 1999 | 8 | 1 | | 7 | | | |
| 2000 | 8 | 1 | | 7 | | | |
| 2001 | 8 | 1 | | 7 | | | |
| 2002 | 8 | 1 | | 7 | | | |
| 2003 | 7 | 1 | | 6 | | | |
| 2004 | 7 | 1 | | 6 | | | |
| 2005 | 7 | 1 | | 6 | | | |
| 2006 | 7 | 1 | | 6 | | | |
| 2007 | 15 | 1 | 13 | | | 1 | |
| 2008 | 44 | 1 | 35 | | 6 | 2 | |
| 2009 | 44 | 1 | 35 | | 6 | 2 | |
| 2010 | 44 | 1 | 35 | | 6 | 2 | |
| 2011 | 44 | 1 | 35 | | 6 | 2 | |
| 2012 | 44 | 1 | 35 | | 6 | 2 | |
| 2013 | 45 | 1 | 33 | 4 | 7 | 34 | |
| 2014 | 45 | 1 | 33 | 4 | 7 | 4 | |
| 2015 | 45 | 1 | 33 | 4 | 7 | 4 | |
| 2016 | 45 | 1 | 37 | | 7 | 4 | |
| 2017 | 45 | 1 | 37 | | 7 | 4 | |
| 2018 | 45 | 1 | 37 | | 7 | 4 | |
| 2019 | 45 | 1 | 37 | | 7 | 4 | |
| 2020 | 41 | 1 | 33 | | 7 | 4 | |
| 2021 | 60 | 1 | 52 | | 7 | 49 | |
| 2022 | 441 | 72 | 362 | | 7 | 432 | |

注：2014 年的数据做了调整。
Note: the data of 2014 has been adjusted.

# 表 18.27 图书、期刊和报纸出版情况（2021 － 2022 年）
## PUBLICATION OF BOOKS, MAGAZINES AND NEWSPAPERS (2021-2022)

| 指　标 | Item | 2021 | 2022 |
|---|---|---|---|
| **图　书** | **Books Published** | | |
| 种　数（种） | Number of Publications (kind) | 5626 | 5405 |
| 总印数（万册、万张） | Printed Copies (10 000 copies) | 14316 | 14370 |
| 总印张数（万印张） | Printed Sheets (10 000 sheets) | 1078973 | 112416 |
| **期　刊** | **Magazines Published** | | |
| 种　数（种） | Number of Publications (kind) | 139 | 139 |
| 每期平均印数（万册） | Average Printed Copies Per Issue (10 000 copies) | 143.3 | 132.9 |
| 总印数（万册） | Printed Copies (10 000 copies) | 3105.54 | 3372.23 |
| 总印张数（万印张） | Printed Sheets (10 000 sheets) | 170159.79 | 18022.44 |
| **报　纸** | **Newspapers Published** | | |
| 种　数（种） | Number of Publications (kind) | 27 | 27 |
| 每期平均印数（万份） | Average Printed Copies Per Issue (10 000 copies) | 84 | 88 |
| 总印数（万份） | Printed Copies (10 000 copies) | 17028 | 16138 |
| 总印张数（万印张） | Printed Sheets (10 000 sheets) | 331643 | 31204 |

# 表 18.28 气象业务站点及观测项目情况 (1997-2022 年)

STATUS OF OPERATIONAL METEOROLOGICAL STATIONS AND THEIR OBSERVATION ITEMS (1997-2022)

单位：个 (unit)

| 年份 Year | 地面观测业务 Surface Observation Stations | 高空探测业务 Upper-air Observation Stations | 自动气象站 Automatic Weather Stations | 天气雷达观测业务 Weather Radar Observation Stations | 大气成分观测业务 Atmospheric Composition Observation Stations | 农业气象观测业务 Agro-Meteorological Observation Stations |
|---|---|---|---|---|---|---|
| 1997 | 35 | 1 | | 1 | | 13 |
| 1998 | 35 | 1 | | 1 | | 13 |
| 1999 | 35 | 1 | | 1 | | 13 |
| 2000 | 35 | 1 | | 1 | | 13 |
| 2001 | 35 | 1 | | 1 | | 13 |
| 2002 | 35 | 1 | | 1 | | 13 |
| 2003 | 35 | 1 | | 1 | | 13 |
| 2004 | 35 | 1 | 63 | 1 | | 13 |
| 2005 | 35 | 1 | 83 | 1 | | 13 |
| 2006 | 35 | 1 | 109 | 1 | | 13 |
| 2007 | 35 | 1 | 257 | 2 | | 13 |
| 2008 | 35 | 1 | 302 | 3 | | 13 |
| 2009 | 35 | 1 | 41 | 3 | | 13 |
| 2010 | 35 | 1 | 41 | 3 | | 13 |
| 2011 | 35 | 1 | 655 | 3 | | 13 |
| 2012 | 35 | 1 | 356 | 4 | 1 | 13 |
| 2013 | 35 | 1 | 1759 | 3 | | 13 |
| 2014 | 35 | 1 | 1924 | 4 | 1 | 13 |
| 2015 | 35 | 1 | 1924 | 4 | 7 | 13 |
| 2016 | 35 | 1 | 1924 | 4 | 7 | 13 |
| 2017 | 35 | 1 | 1924 | 4 | 7 | 13 |
| 2018 | 35 | 1 | 1924 | 4 | 7 | 13 |
| 2019 | 35 | 1 | 1924 | 4 | 7 | 13 |
| 2020 | 35 | 1 | 1924 | 4 | 7 | 13 |
| 2021 | 35 | 1 | 1929 | 5 | 7 | 13 |
| 2022 | 35 | 1 | 1929 | 5 | 7 | 13 |

**表 18.28 续表 continued**

单位：个 ( (unit))

| 年份 Year | 生态与农业气象试验业务 Eco- & Agro-Meteorological Observation Stations | 大 气 本底站 Atmospheric Background Stations | 闪电定位监测业务 Lightning Position Monitoring Stations | 太阳辐射观测业务 Solar Radiation Observation Stations | 紫外线观测业务 UV Observation | 酸雨观测业 务 Acid Rain Observation | 臭氧观测业 务 Ozone Observation | 卫星云图接收业务 Satellite Cloud Images Receiving Stations |
|---|---|---|---|---|---|---|---|---|
| 1997 | | | | 1 | | 4 | | 1 |
| 1998 | | | | 1 | | 4 | | 1 |
| 1999 | | | | 1 | | 4 | | 1 |
| 2000 | | | | 1 | | 4 | | 1 |
| 2001 | | | | 1 | | 4 | | 1 |
| 2002 | | | | 1 | | 4 | | 1 |
| 2003 | | | | 1 | | 4 | | 1 |
| 2004 | | | | 1 | 1 | 35 | | 1 |
| 2005 | | | 5 | 1 | 1 | 35 | | 1 |
| 2006 | | | 5 | 1 | 1 | 35 | | 1 |
| 2007 | | | 5 | 1 | 1 | 35 | | 1 |
| 2008 | | | 5 | 1 | 1 | 35 | | 1 |
| 2009 | | | 5 | 1 | 1 | 35 | | 1 |
| 2010 | | | 5 | 1 | 1 | 35 | | 1 |
| 2011 | | | 5 | 1 | 1 | 35 | | 1 |
| 2012 | 1 | | 5 | 1 | 1 | 35 | | 1 |
| 2013 | | | 5 | 1 | 1 | 35 | | 1 |
| 2014 | | | 5 | 1 | 1 | 35 | | 1 |
| 2015 | | | 5 | 14 | 7 | 35 | | 1 |
| 2016 | | | 5 | 14 | 7 | 35 | | 1 |
| 2017 | 1 | | 5 | 14 | 7 | 35 | | 1 |
| 2018 | 1 | | 5 | 14 | 7 | 35 | | 2 |
| 2019 | 1 | | 5 | 14 | 7 | 35 | | 2 |
| 2020 | 1 | | 5 | 14 | 7 | 4 | | 2 |
| 2021 | 1 | | 5 | 14 | 7 | 4 | | 2 |
| 2022 | 1 | | 5 | 14 | 7 | 4 | | 2 |

# 表 18.29 文化机构和人员数（2021 – 2022 年）
NUMBER AND PERSONNEL IN CULTURE AND CULTURAL RELICS INSTITUTIONS (2021-2022)

| 项　目 | Item | 2021 | 2022 |
|---|---|---|---|
| **机构数（个）** | **Number of Institutions (unit)** | **6646** | **6584** |
| 文化合计 | Cultural | 6447 | 6367 |
| 艺术表演团体 | Art Performance Group | 1286 | 1190 |
| 艺术表演场所 | Art Performance Places | 62 | 67 |
| 公共图书馆 | Public Libraries | 43 | 43 |
| 文化馆 | Cultural Centers | 41 | 41 |
| 文化站 | Cultural Stations | 1031 | 1031 |
| 艺术展览创作机构 | Art Exhibition and Creative Institutions | 14 | 17 |
| 艺术教育业 | Culture and Education | 2 | 2 |
| 文化科研机构 | Art Research Institutions | 1 | 1 |
| 文化市场经营机构 | Institutions of Bussiness of Culture | 3868 | 3877 |
| 文化行政主管部门 | Administrative Department of Culture | 40 | 40 |
| 其他文化机构 | Other Cultural Institutions | 59 | 58 |
| 文物合计 | Cultural Relics | 199 | 217 |
| 博物馆 | Museums | 111 | 130 |
| 文物保护管理机构 | Agencies of Cultural Relics Preservation | 38 | 38 |
| 文物科研机构 | Scientific and Research Agencies | 1 | 1 |
| 文物行政机构 | Cultural Relics Administrative Agencies | 41 | 41 |
| 其他文物机构 | Other Cultural Relics Agencies | 8 | 7 |
| **从业人员数** | **Number of Employed Persons (person)** | **66701** | **58281** |
| 文化合计 | Cultural | 63007 | 54568 |
| 艺术表演团体 | Art Performance Group | 21654 | 17442 |
| 艺术表演场所 | Art Performance Places | 1763 | 1706 |
| 公共图书馆 | Public Libraries | 1049 | 1045 |
| 文化馆 | Cultural Centers | 941 | 932 |
| 文化站 | Cultural Stations | 4034 | 4056 |
| 艺术展览创作机构 | Art Exhibition and Creative Institutions | 131 | 132 |
| 艺术教育业 | Culture and Education | 572 | 525 |
| 文化科研机构 | Art Research Institutions | 37 | 37 |
| 文化市场经营机构 | Institutions of Bussiness of Culture | 29579 | 25563 |
| 文化行政主管部门 | Administrative Department of Culture | 1704 | 1706 |
| 其他文化机构 | Other Cultural Institutions | 1543 | 1424 |
| 文物合计 | Cultural Relics | 3694 | 3713 |
| 博物馆 | Museums | 3258 | 3322 |
| 文物保护管理机构 | Agencies of Cultural Relics Preservation | 196 | 137 |
| 文物科研机构 | Scientific and Research Agencies | 156 | 179 |
| 文物行政机构 | Cultural Relics Administrative Agencies | 15 | 33 |
| 其他文物机构 | Other Cultural Relics Agencies | 69 | 42 |

# 表 18.30 公共图书馆情况（2021 － 2022 年）
## BASIC STATISTICS ON PUBLIC LIBRARIES (2021-2022)

| 项 目 | Item | 总 计 Total | | #市 级 At Municipal Level | |
|---|---|---|---|---|---|
| | | 2021 | 2022 | 2021 | 2022 |
| 总藏量（万册、件） | Total Collections (10 000 volumes) | 2340.69 | 2727.01 | 519.43 | 552.83 |
| 有效借书证数（万个） | Number of Valid Library Cards (10 000 units) | 293.43 | 305.03 | 53.90 | 60.07 |
| 图书流通情况 | Circulation of Books | | | | |
| 总流通人次（万人次） | Total Number of Circulation (10 000 person-times) | 1465.21 | 1552.09 | 222.79 | 196.58 |
| 书刊外借册次（万册次） | Number of Books Borrowed by Readers (10 000 volume-times) | 1184.27 | 1149.50 | 147.45 | 132.65 |
| 总支出（万元） | Total Expenditure (10 000 yuan) | 34751.50 | 35015.30 | 10582.10 | 10787.10 |
| #新增藏量购置费 | Purchase Expenses | 3137.40 | 2934.20 | 1095.70 | 1043.40 |
| 新增数字资源购置费 | New Digital Resource Purchase Expenses | 716.30 | 1003.00 | 397.70 | 629.00 |
| 本年新增藏量（万册） | Number of Books Purchased During Current Year (10 000 volumes) | 183.25 | 301.57 | 15.43 | 33.41 |
| 本年新增电子图书 | | 277.15 | 282.94 | 130.34 | 117.62 |
| 实际使用房屋建筑面积（万平方米） | Floor Space of Public Buildings actually used (10 000 sq.m) | 40.05 | 41.06 | 5.61 | 5.61 |
| #书 库 | Stack Rooms | 7.50 | 7.65 | 1.07 | 1.07 |
| 阅览室座席（个） | Seating Capacity of Reading Rooms (seat) | 33944 | 36878 | 2319 | 2615 |
| #少儿座席 | Child Seats | 7264 | 7888 | 605 | 901 |

注：图书总藏量的统计口径变化，不包含电子图书。
Note: due to the change of the statistic scope of the data of total collection of books.

# 表 18.31 文物业情况（2022 年）
## STATISTICS ON CULTURAL RELICS (2022)

| 项 目 | Item | 文物业 Cultural Relics | #博物馆 Museums | #文物保护管理机构 Protection and Management Agencies |
|---|---|---|---|---|
| 藏 品（件） | Number of Collections(pcs) | 814535 | 757163 | 11255 |
| #一级品 | Grade One | 1263 | 1259 | 4 |
| 经费支出（万元） | Total Expenditure(10 000 yuan) | 106847.00 | 88596.70 | 7534.80 |

## 表 18.32 群众艺术馆和文化馆(站)情况(2022 年)
MASS ART CENTERS AND CULTURAL CENTERS (2022)

| 项 目 | Item | 合 计<br>Total | 群众艺术馆<br>Mass Art Centers | 文化馆<br>Cultural Centers | 乡镇（街道）综合文化服务中心<br>Township (Subdistrict) Comprehensive Cultural Service Center |
|---|---|---|---|---|---|
| 单位数（个） | Number of Units (unit) | 41 | 1 | 40 | 1031 |
| 举办展览个数（个） | Conducting Exhibitions (unit) | 5400 | 15 | 616 | 4769 |
| 组织文艺活动次数（次） | Art Performances (time) | 26595 | 17 | 2850 | 23728 |
| 举办培训班班次（次） | Training Courses (time) | 21360 | 20 | 7444 | 13896 |

## 表 18.33 艺术表演团体演出情况(2022 年)
BASIC STATISTICS ON ART PERFORMANCE TROUPES (2022)

| 种 类 | Item | 国内演出场数（万场）<br>Number of Performances in China (10 000show) | 国内演出观众人数（万人次）<br>Number of Spectators of the Performances in China (10 000 person-times) |
|---|---|---|---|
| **总 计** | **Total** | **11.26** | **1148.58** |
| **按登记注册类型分** | **By Registration** | | |
| 国 有 | State-owned | 0.19 | 117.49 |
| 集 体 | Collective-owned | | |
| 其 他 | Others | 11.07 | 1331.09 |
| **按剧种分** | **By Art Troupes** | | |
| 话剧、儿童剧、滑稽剧团 | Drama, Plays for Children and Comedy Troupes | 0.05 | 7.13 |
| 歌舞、音乐类 | Song and Dance Troupes, Musicals | 4.53 | 447.95 |
| 京剧、昆曲类 | Peking Opera and Kunqu Opera | 0.01 | 5.32 |
| #京 剧 | Peking Opera Troupes | 0.01 | 5.32 |
| 地方戏曲类 | Local Opera Troupes | 0.09 | 30.67 |
| 杂技、魔术、马戏类 | Acrobatics, Performing Magic and Circus Troupes | 0.39 | 24.87 |
| 曲艺类 | Folk Arts | 0.24 | 27.49 |
| 综合性艺术表演团体 | Comprehensive Art Performance | 5.97 | 905.16 |

注：艺术表演团体统计口径调整为含系统内、系统外两部分。
Note: The scope of art performance troupes includes the troupes either inside or outside the public-owned system.

# 表 18.34 广播电台、电视台情况（2021 - 2022 年）
## STATISTICS ON RADIO AND TV STATIONS (2021-2022)

| 项　目 | Item | 2021 | 2022 |
|---|---|---|---|
| **广播电台情况** | **Statistics on Radio Stations** | | |
| 公共广播节目套数（套） | Number of Programs (set) | 39 | 31 |
| 广播节目综合人口覆盖率（%） | Radio Coverage of Population (%) | 99.49 | 99.55 |
| 中短波转播发射台（座） | Transmission and Relaying Stations of Medium and Short Wave Broadcast(unit) | 5 | 6 |
| 中短波广播发射功率（千瓦） | Power of Transmitters of Medium and Short Wave Broadcast (kw) | 120 | 120 |
| 调频转播发射台（座） | Number of Transmission and Relaying Stations of Frequency Modulation Broadcast (unit) | 53 | 60 |
| 调频发射功率（千瓦） | Power of Transmitters of Frequency Modulation Broadcast (kw) | 142.80 | 140.05 |
| 全年公共广播节目播出时间（小时） | Public Programs Broadcasting Hours of the Year (hour) | 208083 | 207648 |
| #新闻资讯 | News Programs | 447525 | 46155 |
| 专题服务 | Special Subject Programs | 60960 | 56650 |
| 综　艺 | General Entertainment Programs | 40365 | 38129 |
| 广播剧 | TV Play Programs | 14228 | 14141 |
| 广　告 | Advertising Programs | 13192 | 12697 |
| **电视台情况** | **Statistics on TV Stations** | | |
| 公共电视节目套数（套） | Number of Programs (unit) | 49 | 45 |
| 电视节目综合人口覆盖率（%） | TV Coverage of Population (%) | 99.56 | 99.65 |
| 有线电视覆盖用户数(万户) | Number of Cable Television Coverage Users（Ten thousand households） | 610.6 | 613.68 |
| #数字电视覆盖用户数 | Number of Digital Television Coverage Users | 545.80 | 549.17 |
| 全年公共电视节目播出时间（小时） | Public Programs Broadcasting Hours of the Year (hour) | 296198 | 298860 |
| #新闻资讯 | News Programs | 43513 | 42504 |
| 专题服务 | Special Subject Programs | 62214 | 62553 |
| 综艺益智 | General Entertainment Programs | 20256 | 19965 |
| 影视剧 | TV Play Programs | 98831 | 99802 |
| 广　告 | Advertising Programs | 32245 | 35218 |

重/庆/统/计/年/鉴

# 主要统计指标解释

## 普通高等学校

指按照国家规定的设置标准和审批程序批准举办的，通过全国普通高等学校统一招生考试，招收高中毕业生为主要培养对象，实施高等教育的全日制大学、独立设置的学院和高等专科学校、高等职业学校和其他机构。

大学、独立设置的学院主要实施本科层次以上教育，高等专科学校、高等职业学校实施专科层次教育，其他机构是承担国家普通招生计划任务不计校数的机构。包括普通高等学校分校和批准筹建的普通高等学校等。

## 成人高等学校

指按照国家规定的设置标准和审批程序批准举办的，通过全国成人高等学校统一招生考试，招收具有高中毕业或同等学力的在职从业人员为主要培养对象，利用函授、业余、脱产等多种形式对其实施高等学历教育的学校。包括职工高等学校、农民高等学校、管理干部学院、教育学院、独立函授学院、广播电视大学、其他机构等。其他机构是承担国家成人招生计划任务不计校数的机构。

## 小学学龄儿童入学率

指调查范围内已入小学学习的学龄儿童占校内外学龄儿童总数（包括智障儿童在内，但不包括盲聋哑儿童）的比重。计算公式：

$$\text{小学学龄儿童入学率} = \frac{\text{已入学的小学学龄儿童数}}{\text{校内外小学学龄儿童总数}} \times 100\%$$

## 专利

是专利权的简称，是对发明人的发明创造经审查合格后，由专利局依据专利法授予发明人和设计人对该项发明创造享有的专有权。包括发明、实用新型和外观设计。反映拥有自主知识产权的科技和设计成果情况。

## 有专利申请的企业

指在报告年内向国家知识产权局或中国以外的国家知识产权局（地区专利组织）提交专利申请，并收到《专利申请受理通知书》和缴纳相关费用的工业企业。

## 有专利授权的企业

指报告年内获得国家知识产权局或中国以外的国家知识产权局（地区专利组织）《专利授权通知书》并缴纳相关费用的工业企业。

## 拥有有效专利的企业（累计值）

指截至报告年末，有专利权处于维持状态的工业企业。

## 专利产品产值（当年价格）

工业企业在报告年度内生产的以货币形式表现的工业最终专利产品的总价值量。专利产品产值计算参照国家关于“工业总产值”的计算方法。

## 专利产品销售收入

工业企业在报告期内销售专利产品的货币收入总额。

## 新产品销售收入

指报告期企业销售新产品实现的销售收入。新产品是指采用新技术原理、新设计构思研制、生产的全新产品，或在结构、材质、工艺等某一方面比原有产品有明显改进，从而显著提高了产品性能或扩大了使用功能的产品。既包括经政府有关部门认定并在有效期内的新产品，也包括企业自行研制开发，未经政府有关部门认定，从投产之日起一年之内的新产品。

## 发明（专利）

指对产品、方法或者其改进所提出的新的技术方案。是国际通行的反映拥有自主知识产权技术的核心指标。

# 主要统计指标解释

## 实用新型（专利）

指对产品的形状、构造或者其结合所提出的适于实用的新的技术方案。反映具有一定技术含量的技术成果情况。

## 外观设计（专利）

指对产品的形状、图案、色彩或者其结合所作出的富有美感并适于工业上应用的新设计。反映拥有自主知识产权的外观设计成果情况。

## 驰名商标

是指在市场上享有较高声誉并为相关公众所熟知的注册商标，也是一种法律保护手段。

## 著名商标

著名商标的知名度介于驰名商标和普通商标之间的商标群落，是驰名商标坚实的后备力量。

## 文化市场经营机构

指经文化市场行政部门审批或已申报登记并领取相关许可证的、从事文化经营和文化服务活动的机构。

## 艺术表演团体

指由文化部门主办或实行行业管理（经文化行政部门审批或已申报登记并领取相关许可证），专门从事表演艺术等活动的各类专业艺术表演团体，含民间职业剧团。不包括群众业余文艺表演团体。

## 艺术表演场馆

指由文化部门主办或实行行业管理（经文化市场行政部门审批或已申报登记并领取相关许可证），有观众席、舞台、灯光设备，公开售票、专供文艺团体演出的文化活动场所。

## 研究与试验发展（R&D）

指在科学技术领域，为增加知识总量，以及运用这些知识去创造新的应用进行的系统的创造性的活动，包括基础研究、应用研究、试验发展三类活动。国际上通常采用 R&D 活动的规模和强度指标反映一国的科技实力和核心竞争力。

## R&D 人员

指参与研究与试验发展项目研究、管理和辅助工作的人员，包括项目(课题)组人员，企业科技行政管理人员和直接为项目(课题)活动提供服务的辅助人员。反映投入从事拥有自主知识产权的研究开发活动的人力规模。

## R&D 人员全时当量

指全时人员数加非全时人员按工作量折算为全时人员数的总和。例如：有两个全时人员和三个非全时人员(工作时间分别为 20%、30% 和 70%)，则全时当量为 2+0.2+0.3+0.7=3.2 人年。为国际上比较科技人力投入而制定的可比指标。

## R&D 经费支出合计

指调查单位用于内部开展 R&D 活动（基础研究、应用研究和试验发展）的实际支出。包括用于 R&D 项目（课题）活动的直接支出，以及间接用于 R&D 活动的管理费、服务费、与 R&D 有关的基本建设支出以及外协加工费等。不包括生产性活动支出、归还贷款支出以及与外单位合作或委托外单位进行 R&D 活动而转拨给对方的经费支出。

## R&D 经费支出中政府资金

指 R&D 经费内部支出中来自各级政府部门的各类资金，包括财政科学技术拨款、科学基金、教育等部门事业费以及政府部门预算外资金的实际支出。

## R&D 经费支出中企业资金

指 R&D 经费内部支出中来自本企业的自有资金和接受其他企业委托而获得的经费，以及科研院所、高校等事业单位从企业获得的资金的实际支出。

## R&D 项目（课题）数

指在当年立项并开展研究工作、以前年份立项仍继续进行研究的研发项目（课题）数，包括当年完成和年内研究工作已告失败的研发项目（课题），但不包括委托外单位进行的研发项目（课题）数。

## 主要统计指标解释

### R&D 项目（课题）人员全时当量

指实际参加研发项目（课题）活动人员折合的全时当量。

### R&D 项目（课题）经费支出

指调查单位内部在报告年度进行研发项目（课题）研究和试制等的实际支出。包括劳务费、其他日常支出、固定资产购建费、外协加工费等，不包括委托或与外单位合作进行项目（课题）研究而拨付给对方使用的经费。

### 广播／电视节目综合人口覆盖率

指根据国家广播电视总局制定的《广播电视人口覆盖率统计技术标准和方法》进行统计调查的，在对象区内能接收到由中央、省、地市或县通过无线、有线或卫星等各种技术方式转播的各级广播 / 电视节目的人口数占全国总人口数的百分比。

# Explanatory Notes on Main Statistical Indicators

## Regular Institutions of Higher Education

Refer to educational establishments set up according to the government evaluation and approval procedures, enrolling graduates from senior secondary schools and providing higher education courses and training for senior professionals. They include full-time universities, colleges, high professional schools, high professional vocational schools and others.

Universities and colleges are mainly providing undergraduate courses; those high professional schools and high professional vocational schools are mainly providing professional trainings; and others refer to educational establishments, which are responsible for enrolling students but not covered in the total number of schools, including: branch schools of universities and colleges, and universities and colleges that have been proved and prepared to construct.

## Institutions of Higher Learning for Adults

Refer to educational establishments, set up in line with relevant rules approved by the government, enrolling staff and workers with senior secondary school or equivalent education, and providing higher education courses in many forms of correspondence, spare time, or full time for adults. Professionals thus trained receive a qualification equivalent to graduates studying regular courses at regular universities, colleges and professional colleges. Institutions of higher learning for adults include schools of high education for staff and workers, schools of high education for peasants, colleges for management cadres, pedagogical colleges, independent correspondence colleges, Radio and TV universities and other educational establishments. Other educational establishments are responsible for enrolling adult students but not covered in the number of schools.

## Enrollment Rate of Primary School-aged Children

Refers to the proportion of school-aged children enrolled at schools to the total number of school-age children both in and outside schools (including retarded children, but excluding blind, deaf and mute children). The formula is:

Enrollment Rate of Primary School-aged Children =

$$\frac{\text{Total Primary School-aged Children at Schools}}{\text{Total Primary School-age Children Both at and Outside Schools}} \times 100\%$$

## Patent

Is an abbreviation for the patent right and refers to the exclusive right of ownership by the inventors or designers for the creation or inventions, given from the patent offices after due process of assessment and approval in accordance with the Patent Law. Patents are granted for inventions, utility models and designs. This indicator reflects the achievements of S&T and design with independent intellectual property.

## Enterprise with Patent Application

Refers to the industrial enterprise which has submitted patent application to the State Intellectual Property Office or the national intellectual property administration outside China (regional patent organization), received the "Notification of Patent Application Acceptance" and paid off the related fees within the year of report.

## Enterprise with Patent Granted

Refers to the industrial enterprise which has received the "Notification of Patent Granted" from the State Intellectual Property Office or the national intellectual property administration outside China (regional patent organization) and paid off the related fees within the year of report.

## EXPLANATORY NOTES TO MAJOR STATISTICAL INDICATORS

### Enterprise with Valid Patents (Cumulative Value)

Refers to the industrial enterprise with patents in the status of maintenance by the end of the year of report.

### Output Value of Patented Products (Current Price)

Refers to the total value of the final patented industrial products produced by the industrial enterprises in the year of report in the form of currency. Refer to the calculation method of "gross industrial output value" stipulated by the state for the calculation of the output value of patented products

### Sales Revenue of Patented Products

Refers to the total revenue of currency from the sales of the patented products by the industrial enterprises within the year of report.

### Sales Income of New Products

Refers to the sales income of new products of the enterprises at the reference period. New products refer to products developed and produced with new technologies and designs or improved in structure, material, process or other aspects so that their performance are improved or their functions expanded. New products include those affirmed by government authorities in their validity period and also those developed by enterprises without the affirmation of government authorities within one year after they are put into production.

### Patented Inventions

Refer to new technical proposals to the products or methods or their modifications. This is universal core indicator reflecting the technologies with independent intellectual property.

### Patented Utility Models

Refer to the practical and new technical proposals on the shape and structure of the product or the combination of both. This indicator reflects the condition of technological results with certain technical content.

### Designs

Refer to the aesthetics and industrially applicable new designs for the shape, pattern and colour of the product, or their combinations. This indicator reflects the appearance design achievements with independent intellectual property.

### Famous Trade Marks

Refer to trade marks publicly known with higher honors. It is also a legal protection.

### Well-known Trade Marks

Their fames are between famous trademarks and ordinary trademarks. And they are tough reserve force of famous trademarks.

### Cultural Market Operating Units

Refer to the units dealing in culture and cultural services, which registered and permitted with the relative certificate by cultural market administration.

### Arts Performance Troupes

Refer to the various professional performing arts groups, which sponsored by the cultural sectors or guided by the cultural society (approved by the cultural administration authority, or registered and permitted with the relative certificate), including non-governmental troupes. The mass amateur arts performance troupes are not included.

### Arts Performance Places

Refer to the various sites for cultural activities, which sponsored by the cultural sectors or guided by the cultural society (approved by the cultural market administration, or registered and permitted with the relative certificate), with the facility of auditorium, stage and lighting, and selling tickets in public.

EXPLANATORY NOTES TO MAJOR STATISTICAL INDICATORS

## Research and Development (R&D)

Refers to systematic and creative activities in the field of science and technology aiming at increasing the knowledge and using the knowledge for new application. R&D includes 3 categories of activities: basic research, applied research and experiments and development. The scale and intensity of R&D are widely used internationally to reflect the strength of S&T and the core competitiveness of a country in the world.

## R & D Personnel

Refer to persons engaged in research, management and supporting activities of R & D, including persons in the project teams, persons engaged in the management of S&T activities of enterprises and supporting staff providing direct service to the research projects. This indicator reflects the size of personnel engaged in R&D activities with independent intellectual property.

## Full-time Equivalent of R&D Personnel

Refers to the sum of the full-time persons and the full-time equivalent of part-time persons converted by workload. For instance, if there are 2 full-time persons and 3 part-time workers (20%, 30% and 70% of working hours respectively on R&D activities), the full-time equivalent are 2+0.2+0.3+0.7=3.2 person-years. This is an internationally comparable indicator of S&T manpower input.

## Total Expenditure of Funds on R&D

Refers to the real expenditure of surveyed units on their own R&D activities (basic research, applied research, experiments and development) including direct expenditure on R&D activities, indirect expenditure of management and services on R&D activities, expenditure on capital construction and material processing by others. Excluding the expenditure on production activities, return of loan, and fees transferred to cooperated or entrusted agencies on R&D activities.

## Expenditure of Government Funds on R&D

Refers to the expenditure of funds on R&D activities from government agencies at different levels, including appropriate funds on science and technology from financial departments, scientific funds, operating expenses from education departments and the real expenditure of extra budgetary funds from government agencies.

## Expenditure of Funds of Enterprises on R&D

Refers to the expenditure of funds on R&D activities from self-raised funds of enterprises and funds from other enterprises through entrustment, and the expenditure of funds of institutions, such as institution of scientific research and universities, from enterprises.

## Number of R&D Projects (subjects)

Refers to the number of R&D projects (subjects) set up and implemented at the reference year, and the number of R&D projects (subjects) set up in former years and under implementation, including the projects (subjects) finished and failed at the reference year, excluding the projects (subjects) implemented by others through entrustment.

## Full-time Equivalent of R&D Personnel

Refers to the full-time equivalent of persons actually engaged in R&D projects (subjects).

## Expenditure of Funds on R&D Projects (subjects)

Refers to the real expenditure of internal funds of the surveyed units on research and test of R&D projects (subjects) at the reference year, including service fee, other daily expenditure, cost for fixed assets, cost of external process; excluding expenditure of funds transferred to other cooperated or entrusted units of the projects.

## The Population Coverage Rate of Radio/ Television

Refers to the percentage of the whole country's population who can receive radio/television programmers transmitted by national, provincial, municipal or county stations through wireless, cable or satellite techniques, according to Statistical Standard and Method on Television and Radio Coverage of Population established by the State Administration of Radio and Television.

# 第十九章·卫生、体育及其他社会活动

## PUBLIC HEALTH, SPORTS AND OTHER SOCIAL ACTIVITIES

# 简要说明

## BRIEF INTRODUCTION

本章资料主要包括卫生事业、体育事业、民政事业、劳动和社会保障事业、公检法司情况、安全生产情况、火灾事故和道路交通事故等内容，由市统计局社会科技统计处根据有关部门资料整理提供。

卫生资料来自市卫生健康委员会，体育资料来源于市体育局，民政和劳动社会保障有关资料分别由市民政局、市人力资源和社会保障局提供，公检法司资料分别由市公安局、市人民检察院、市高级人民法院和市司法局提供，安全生产情况来自市应急管理局，火灾事故和道路交通事故分别由市消防总队和市公安交通管理局提供。

The data in this chapter mainly cover public health, sports, civil affairs, labor & social securities, public security, procuratorial, legal & judicial affairs, work safety, and fires & highway traffic accidents. The data are sorted and compiled by Division of Social and Technology Statistics, Chongqing Municipal Bureau of Statistics on the basis of the data provided by other related departments.

The data on public health are provided by Health Commission of Chongqing; the data on sports are provided by Chongqing Administration of Sports; the data on civil affairs and labor & social securities are provided by Chongqing Civil Affairs Bureau and Chongqing Administration of Labor and Social Security; the data on public security, procuratorial and legal affairs are provided by Chongqing Public Security Bureau, Chongqing People's Procuratorate, Higher People's Court and Chongqing Justice Bureau; the data on work safety are provided by Department of Emergency Management of Chongqing; and the data on fires & highway traffic accidents are provided by Chongqing Fire Brigade and Chongqing Bureau of Traffic Administration.

# 表 19.1 主要年份卫生事业情况
## STATISTICS ON PUBLIC HEALTH CARE IN MAJOR YEARS

| 年 份 Year | 机构数（个）Number of Institutions (unit) | #医院、卫生院 Hospitals and Health Centers | 床位数（张）Number of Beds in Health Care Institutions(bed) | 卫生技术人员（人）Medical Technical Personnel (person) | #执 业（助理）医师 Licensed (Assistant) Doctors" | #注册护士 Registered Nurses |
|---|---|---|---|---|---|---|
| 1952 | 742 | | 5031 | 19807 | | |
| 1957 | 2185 | | 10255 | 30290 | | |
| 1962 | 3591 | | 22971 | 35681 | | |
| 1965 | 3938 | | 20314 | 36762 | 10234 | |
| 1970 | 3579 | 2183 | 25038 | 39813 | 10475 | |
| 1975 | 4221 | 2286 | 37300 | 51536 | 12442 | |
| 1978 | 4789 | 2294 | 48948 | 59934 | 12870 | |
| 1980 | 4686 | 2316 | 51194 | 65441 | 12806 | |
| 1985 | 4796 | 2170 | 54054 | 76486 | 12577 | 11724 |
| 1986 | 5095 | 2140 | 54801 | 77437 | 12895 | 11921 |
| 1987 | 5136 | 2136 | 57178 | 78382 | 13201 | 12156 |
| 1988 | 5148 | 2151 | 59514 | 80153 | 21004 | 13688 |
| 1989 | 5229 | 2152 | 61912 | 81219 | 27789 | 16027 |
| 1990 | 5248 | 2154 | 62568 | 82690 | 28824 | 16929 |
| 1991 | 5326 | 2153 | 64057 | 83973 | 28652 | 17163 |
| 1992 | 5328 | 2160 | 64978 | 85204 | 28643 | 17557 |
| 1993 | 4807 | 2114 | 65859 | 84125 | 29516 | 17714 |
| 1994 | 4795 | 2590 | 66891 | 85586 | 30915 | 18298 |
| 1995 | 4801 | 2505 | 67243 | 86041 | 31169 | 18692 |
| 1996 | 4777 | 2567 | 66339 | 87542 | 30733 | 19289 |
| 1997 | 4743 | 2553 | 69591 | 88423 | 43178 | 19593 |
| 1998 | 4643 | 2438 | 65934 | 83696 | 43423 | 19804 |
| 1999 | 4552 | 2351 | 66003 | 88569 | 44453 | 20263 |
| 2000 | 4382 | 2250 | 65666 | 88619 | 44940 | 20773 |
| 2001 | 4151 | 2020 | 64981 | 86430 | 44666 | 20533 |
| 2002 | 2725 | 1717 | 61875 | 79850 | 37873 | 20729 |
| 2003 | 2705 | 1682 | 63287 | 78628 | 37122 | 20629 |
| 2004 | 2539 | 1574 | 63899 | 77516 | 36603 | 20249 |
| 2005 | 2447 | 1463 | 64674 | 78780 | 37321 | 20842 |
| 2006 | 2478 | 1450 | 68298 | 79805 | 37511 | 21269 |
| 2007 | 2410 | 1447 | 74785 | 83736 | 38739 | 23972 |
| 2008 | 2258 | 1396 | 81950 | 88746 | 39417 | 26799 |
| 2009 | 2425 | 1404 | 92689 | 97199 | 41943 | 31756 |
| 2010 | 17495 | 1449 | 103624 | 111079 | 47969 | 37611 |
| 2011 | 17660 | 1407 | 115627 | 120169 | 49585 | 42767 |
| 2012 | 17961 | 1405 | 130813 | 131658 | 51990 | 49823 |
| 2013 | 18923 | 1502 | 147436 | 142218 | 55221 | 55417 |
| 2014 | 18766 | 1510 | 160446 | 154091 | 58007 | 62662 |
| 2015 | 19805 | 1568 | 176674 | 166812 | 61013 | 69996 |
| 2016 | 19933 | 1606 | 190850 | 179346 | 64700 | 77463 |
| 2017 | 19615 | 1640 | 206080 | 191254 | 68419 | 84768 |
| 2018 | 20524 | 1684 | 220104 | 209237 | 76361 | 95104 |
| 2019 | 21058 | 1693 | 231895 | 224687 | 83307 | 103167 |
| 2020 | 20922 | 1675 | 235560 | 237726 | 88728 | 109428 |
| 2021 | 21361 | 1677 | 240741 | 246615 | 92131 | 114011 |
| 2022 | 22261 | 1667 | 250832 | 253241 | 94609 | 117336 |

注：1）2002 年起卫生统计制度变更，其指标名称和统计口径变化，与往年不可比：从 2002 年起卫生机构、床位、卫生技术人员统计范围均不含"医学院校"、"卫生学校"和"计生站"。卫生技术人员中，2002 年前为医生和护师（士），2002 年后改为执业（助理）医师和注册护士（表 18-1 至 18-5 同）。
2）2011 年卫生统计口径变化，与往年不可比：从 2010 年起卫生机构、卫生技术人员、执业（助理医师）、注册护士统计范围均含"村卫生室"和"个体办诊所"。

Note: a) Due to the changes of health care statistic system since 2002, the indicators and statistic scopes were changed, not comparable with the previous years: since 2002, the scope of the number of health care institutions, the number of beds and the number of medial technical personnel has not included the data of "medical universities", "health schools" and "family plan service stations". The indicators of "doctor" and "nurse" before 2002 have been replaced by "licensed (assistant) doctors" and "registered nurses" since 2002 (the same applies to the tables from 18-1 to 18-5).
b) Due to the change of statistic scope, the date are not comparable with the previous years. The data of "village health station" and "individual-run clinics" are included in the data of health institutions, medical technical personnel, licensed (assistant) doctors and registered nurses since 2010.

## 表 19.2 卫生事业情况（2021 － 2022 年）
## STATISTICS ON PUBLIC HEALTH CARE (2021-2022)

| 指　标 | Item | 2021 | 2022 |
|---|---|---|---|
| 执业（助理）医师数（人） | Number of Licensed (Assistant) Doctors (person) | 92131 | 94609 |
| 医院床位数（张） | Number of Beds in Hospitals (bed) | 178223 | 186135 |
| 孕产妇死亡率（1/10 万） | Mortality Rate of Pregnant Women (per 100 000 persons) | 9.79 | 7.56 |
| 新生儿死亡率（‰） | Mortality Rate of New Infants (‰ ) | 1.30 | 1.44 |
| 甲乙类传染病发病率（1/10 万） | Incidence Disease Rate of Class A and B Infections Diseases (per 100 000 persons) | 194.67 | 227.06 |
| 农村自来水普及率（%） | Rate of Access to Tap Water in Rural Area (%) | 83.1 | 89.0 |

注：农村自来水普及率来自市水利局，与往年不可比。
Note: The popularization rate of rural tap water comes from the Water Conservancy Bureau of the city, which is comparable with that of previous years.

## 表 19.3 医院、卫生院、社区诊疗情况（2022 年）
## STATISTICS ON VISITS AND INPATIENTS IN HOSPITALS, HEALTH STATIONS AND COMMUNITY HEALTH CENTERS (2022)

| 机构类别 | Type of Institution | 诊疗人次（万人次） Number of Visits (10 000 person -times) | #门　诊 急　诊 Outpatients and Emergency Treatment | 健康检查人数（万人） Medical Examination (10 000 patients) | 住院人数（万人） Number of Inpatients (10 000 patients) | 每百门急诊次的入院人数（人） Number of Inpatients per 100 Visits (person) |
|---|---|---|---|---|---|---|
| **医　院** | **Hospitals** | **8170.56** | **7912.71** | **548.56** | **503.07** | **6.43** |
| #综合医院 | General Hospitals | 5393.02 | 5251.01 | 416.41 | 341.77 | 6.58 |
| 中医医院 | Hospitals Specialized in Traditional Chinese Medicine | 1570.97 | 1494.90 | 85.89 | 99.13 | 6.72 |
| 中西医结合医院 | Hospitals of Integrated Traditional Chinese with Western Medicine | 136.81 | 131.44 | 7.52 | 13.47 | 10.46 |
| 口腔医院 | Stomatological Hospitals | 141.32 | 141.16 | 0.22 | 0.21 | 0.15 |
| 肿瘤医院 | Cancer Hospitals | 79.11 | 79.11 | 7.23 | 11.70 | 14.89 |
| 妇产（科）医院 | OB/GYN Hospitals | 53.85 | 52.80 | 0.81 | 2.17 | 4.17 |
| 儿科医院 | Children's Hospital | 382.92 | 381.95 | 5.52 | 11.36 | 2.96 |
| 精神病院 | Mental Hospitals | 125.10 | 109.70 | 2.04 | 6.61 | 6.02 |
| 传染病院 | Hospitals for Infectious Diseases | 22.58 | 22.58 | 2.14 | 1.93 | 8.74 |
| **社区卫生服务中心（站）** | **Community Health Service Center (Station)** | **2413.77** | **2264.75** | **161.27** | **166.01** | **7.40** |
| **卫生院** | **Health Centers** | **2384.35** | **2235.94** | **161.14** | **164.78** | **7.44** |
| #乡镇卫生院 | Township Health Centers | 1568.56 | 1426.90 | 160.13 | 35.93 | 2.55 |

# 表 19.4 卫生机构、床位、人员数(2022 年)
NUMBER OF HEALTH CARE INSTITUTIONS, BEDS AND PERSONNEL (2022)

| 机构类别 | Type of Institutions | 机构数(个) Health Care Institutions (unit) | 床位数(张) Beds (bed) | 人员合计(人) Total Personnel (person) | 卫生技术人员 Medical Technical Personnel | 其他技术人员 Other Technical Personnel | 管理人员 Management Personnel | 工勤人员 Logistic Workers |
|---|---|---|---|---|---|---|---|---|
| **总　计** | **Total** | **22261** | **250832** | **315904** | **253241** | **10111** | **28784** | **25388** |
| 医院、卫生院 | Total Number of Hospitals | 1667 | 232300 | 223544 | 184051 | 7512 | 22649 | 20920 |
| 医　院 | Hospitals | 857 | 186135 | 187187 | 152650 | 5997 | 19225 | 18512 |
| #综合医院 | General Hospitals | 434 | 109090 | 119433 | 99210 | 3221 | 12004 | 10808 |
| 中医医院 | Hospitals Specialized in Traditional Chinese Medicine | 138 | 33302 | 31863 | 27040 | 1058 | 2830 | 2333 |
| 中西医结合医院 | Hospitals of Integrated Traditional Chinese with Western Medicine | 55 | 6191 | 4844 | 3807 | 227 | 575 | 589 |
| 口腔医院 | Stomatological Hospitals | 28 | 376 | 2169 | 1676 | 126 | 253 | 150 |
| 肿瘤医院 | Cancer Hospitals | 4 | 2920 | 3607 | 2972 | 214 | 545 | 220 |
| 胸科医院 | Chest Hospitals | | | | | | | |
| 妇产(科)医院 | OB/GYN Hospitals | 19 | 1123 | 2144 | 1411 | 40 | 245 | 564 |
| 儿童医院 | Children's Hospital | 9 | 2835 | 5164 | 4195 | 143 | 536 | 444 |
| 精神病院 | Mental Hospitals | 44 | 21705 | 6084 | 4794 | 250 | 739 | 638 |
| 传染病院 | Hospitals for Infectious Diseases | 1 | 755 | 1147 | 932 | 46 | 167 | 61 |
| 卫生院 | Health Centers | 810 | 46165 | 36357 | 31401 | 1515 | 3424 | 2408 |
| 街道卫生院 | Urban Subdistrict Health Centers | 5 | 506 | 378 | 331 | 19 | 39 | 25 |
| 乡镇卫生院 | Township Health Centers | 805 | 45659 | 35979 | 31070 | 1496 | 3385 | 2383 |
| 门诊部 | Outpatient Department | 608 | 114 | 7538 | 6151 | 203 | 691 | 824 |
| 采供血机构 | Blood Centers | 13 | | 707 | 516 | 56 | 95 | 83 |
| 妇幼保健院(所、站) | Women and Children Care Centers | 41 | 5069 | 10969 | 8918 | 448 | 1193 | 1048 |
| 专科疾病防治院(所) | Specialized Disease Prevention & Treatment Institutions | 12 | 132 | 297 | 207 | 17 | 75 | 32 |
| 疾病预防控制中心 | CDC (Epidemic Preventation Stations) | 41 | | 3762 | 2734 | 443 | 569 | 253 |
| 医学科学研究机构 | Research Institutes of Medical Sciences | | | | | | | |
| 医学在职培训机构 | Training Institutes for Medical Staff and Workers | 4 | | 56 | 30 | 12 | 20 | 1 |
| 健康教育所(中心) | Health Care Training Centers | 7 | | 156 | 53 | 59 | 51 | 3 |
| 疗养院 | Sanatoriums | 3 | 313 | 198 | 143 | 5 | 32 | 23 |
| 社区卫生服务中心(站) | Community Health Service Centers | 638 | 12565 | 18637 | 15959 | 675 | 1893 | 1266 |
| 卫生监督所 | Health Supervision Institutes | 39 | | 1163 | 999 | 106 | 60 | 12 |
| 其他卫生机构 | Other Health Care Institutions | 88 | 313 | 3126 | 1808 | 391 | 599 | 498 |
| 村卫生室 | Village Health Stations | 9629 | | 17704 | 4603 | | | |
| 诊所、卫生所、医务室 | Clinics, Health Centers and Hygienic Centers | 9478 | 339 | 28301 | 27242 | 201 | 909 | 449 |

注:本表机构数包含个体办诊所、村卫生室。
Note: The number of institutions in this table includes individual-run clinics.

## 表 19.5 卫生机构各类人员数(2021 − 2022 年)
## NUMBER OF EMPLOYED PERSONS IN HEALTH INSTITUTIONS (2021-2022)

单位：人、% (person, %)

| 人员分类 | Type of Personnel | 人数 Personnel | | 构成 Composition | |
|---|---|---|---|---|---|
| | | 2021 | 2022 | 2021 | 2022 |
| **总 计** | **Total** | **308528** | **315904** | **100.0** | **100.0** |
| 卫生技术人员 | Medical Technical Personnel | 246615 | 253241 | 79.9 | 79.9 |
| 执业医师 | Licensed Doctors | 76152 | 94609 | 24.7 | 24.7 |
| 执业助理医师 | Licensed Assistant Doctors | 15979 | 79092 | 5.2 | 5.2 |
| 注册护士 | Registered Nurses | 114011 | 117336 | 37.0 | 37.0 |
| 药剂人员 | Pharmacists | 10527 | 10677 | 3.4 | 3.4 |
| 技 师（士） | Technical Workers | 14540 | 16017 | 4.7 | 4.7 |
| 其他人员 | Others | 14521 | 13679 | 4.7 | 4.7 |
| 其他技术人员 | Other Technical Personnel | 10570 | 10111 | 3.4 | 3.4 |
| 管理人员 | Management Personnel | 13178 | 28784 | 4.3 | 4.3 |
| 工勤人员 | Logistics Workers | 24826 | 25388 | 8.0 | 8.0 |
| 每万人口拥有卫生技术人员 | Number of Medical Technical Personnel per 10 000 Population | 76.77 | 78.81 | | |

## 表 19.6 结婚登记和离婚登记情况(2021 − 2022 年)
## STATISTICS ON MARRIAGES AND DIVORCES (2021-2022)

| 项 目 | Item | 2021 | 2022 |
|---|---|---|---|
| 登记结婚件数（件） | Registered Marriages (couple) | 196804 | 174039 |
| 内地居民 | Registered Marriages in the Mainland | 196572 | 173789 |
| 涉外及华侨、港澳台居民 | Registered Marriages with Foreigner or Citizen of Hong Kong, Macao and Taiwan | 232 | 250 |
| 登记结婚人数（人） | Registered Newly Married People (person) | 393608 | 348078 |
| 初 婚 | First Marriages | 253653 | 236418 |
| 再 婚 | Remarriages | 139955 | 111660 |
| 登记离婚件数（件） | Registered Divorces (couple) | 72395 | 71635 |
| #内地居民 | Registered Divorces in the Mainland | 72363 | 71582 |

## 表 19.7 民政事业情况（2021 – 2022 年）
## STATISTICS ON CIVIL AFFAIRS (2021-2022)

| 项　目 | Item | 2021 | 2022 |
|---|---|---|---|
| 民政经费支出（万元） | Expenditure for Civil Affairs (10 000 yuan) | 1161259.10 | 1230563.00 |
| 城市居民最低生活保障人数（万人） | Number of Persons Receiving Minimum Living Allowance in Urban Areas (10000 persons) | 23.93 | 21.8 |
| 农村居民最低生活保障人数（万人） | Number of Persons Receiving Minimum Living Allowance in Rural Areas (10000 persons) | 58.57 | 55.8 |
| 农村特困供养人数（万人） | Number of Persons Receiving Livelihood Guaranteed in Five Aspects in Rural Areas (10000person) | 9.8 | 9.7 |
| 享受城市居民最低生活保障人数占非农业人口比重（%） | Number of Persons Receiving Minimum Living Allowance in Urban Areas as Percentage to Total Non-agricultural Population (%) | 1.06 | 0.96 |
| 提供住宿的社会服务机构床位数(张) | Number of Beds in the Social Service Institutions Providing Accommodation (pcs) | 130386 | 133672 |
| 提供住宿的社会服务机构（个） | Number of Social Service Institutions Providing Accommodation (unit) | 1202 | 1255 |
| 儿童福利机构数（个） | Number of Child Welfare Institutions(unit) | 5 | 5 |
| 社区服务机构（个） | Community Service Institutions(unit) | 17785 | 18006 |
| 福利彩票销售额（万元） | Sales of Welfare Lotteries (10000 yuan) | 328301 | 341783 |

注：非农人口使用的是常住人口中的城镇人口，比往年不可比。
Note: The non-agricultural population uses the urban population among the permanent population, which is not comparable to previous years.

## 表 19.8 优抚对象基本情况（2021 – 2022 年）
## STATISTICS ON SPECIAL CARES FOR SERVICEMEN (2021-2022)

单位：人 (person)

| 项　目 | Item | 2021 | 2022 |
|---|---|---|---|
| **优抚对象** | **Residents Receiving Special Cares for Serviceman** | **180097** | **176068** |
| 享受定期抚恤金人数 | Persons Receiving Regular Pensions | 2763 | 2685 |
| 享受定期补助人数 | Persons Receiving Regular Subvention | 156640 | 152508 |
| #在乡复员军人 | Demobilized Soldiers in the Countryside | 6095 | 4788 |
| 带病回乡退伍军人 | Veterans in the Countryside | 52512 | 50274 |
| 伤残人员 | Wounded and Disabled Servicemen | 20694 | 20875 |

## 表 19.9 社会福利事业、企业单位数和工作人员数（2021－2022 年）
## NUMBER OF SOCIAL WELFARE INSTITUTIONS & ENTERPRISES AND EMPLOYED PERSONS (2021-2022)

单位：个、人 (unit, person)

| 项 目 | Item | 机 构 Number of Institutions and Enterprises | | 工作人员 Number of Personnel | |
|---|---|---|---|---|---|
| | | 2021 | 2022 | 2021 | 2022 |
| 提供住宿的社会服务机构 | Social Service Institutions Providing Accommodation | 1202 | 1255 | 15896 | 16118 |
| 救助管理站 | Salvation Management Stations | 37 | 37 | 358 | 364 |
| 殡葬事业单位 | Funeral and Interment Institutions | 112 | 115 | 2302 | 2329 |
| 福利彩票发行单位 | Welfare Lottery Issuing Units | 1 | 1 | 187 | 187 |
| 社区服务中心 | Community Service Centers | 309 | 311 | 3868 | 4099 |

## 表 19.10 提供住宿的社会服务基本情况（2022 年）
## BASIC STATISTICS ON THE SOCIAL SERVICE INSTITUTIONS PROVIDING ACCOMMODATION (2022)

| 项 目 | Item | 院 数（个） Number of Institutions (unit) | 工作人员（人） Number of Staff and Workers (person) | 床位数（张） Number of Beds (bed) | 年末在院人数（人） Number of Residents at Year-end (person) |
|---|---|---|---|---|---|
| 提供住宿的社会服务机构 | Social Service Institutions Providing Accommodation | 1255 | 16118 | 133672 | 65577 |
| 老年人与残疾人服务机构 | Service Institutions for the Old and the Disabled | 1197 | 14874 | 125079 | 61965 |
| 智障与精神疾病服务机构 | Service Institutions for the Retarded and People with Mental Diseases | 5 | 426 | 2978 | 2503 |
| 为儿童提供住宿的社会服务机构 | Social Service Institutions Providing Accommodation for Children | 5 | 282 | 2529 | 560 |
| 其他提供住宿的社会服务机构 | Other Social Service Institutions Providing Accommodation | 48 | 536 | 3086 | 549 |

## 表 19.11 社会活动参与情况（2021 – 2022 年）
PARTICIPATION IN SOCIAL ACTIVITIES (2021-2022)

单位：个、人 (unit, person)

| 指 标 | Item | 2021 | 2022 |
|---|---|---|---|
| 省级人大代表人数 | Number of Municipal Deputies of People's Congress | 849 | 867 |
| #女 性 | Female | 231 | 267 |
| 省级政协委员人数 | Number of Municipal Deputies of People's Political Consultative Conferences | 843 | 853 |
| #女 性 | Female | 202 | 202 |
| 基层地方妇联组织数 | Number of Local Women's Federation Unions | 12294 | 12297 |
| 工会基层组织数 | Number of Grassroots Trade Unions | 46100 | 43886 |
| 工会会员人数（万人） | Membership of Trade Unions | 525 | 529 |

## 表 19.12 基本养老保险情况（2021 – 2022 年）
STATISTICS ON BASIC PENSION INSURANCE (2021-2022)

单位：亿元、万人 (100 million yuan, 10 000 persons)

| 指 标 | Item | 2021 | 2022 |
|---|---|---|---|
| 城镇企业职工基本养老保险参保人数 | Number of Contributors to Urban Enterprise Basic Pension Insurance | 1236.61 | 1316.20 |
| #参保职工 | Employees | 836.94 | 904.52 |
| #企 业 | Enterprises | 605.58 | 670.47 |
| 城镇企业职工基本养老保险基金收入 | Total Revenue of Urban Enterprise Basic Pension Insurance | 1385.85 | 1412.84 |
| 城镇企业职工基本养老保险基金支出 | Expenditure of Urban Enterprise Basic Pension Insurance | 1139.41 | 1234.67 |
| 离休、退休人员年末人城镇企业数 | Number of Retires at Year-end | 399.67 | 411.68 |
| 机关事业单位社会养老保险参保人数 | Number of Contributors to Social Pension Insurance in Government and Public Institutions | 117.64 | 115.56 |
| 城乡居民社会养老保险参保人数 | Number of Urban and Rural Residents Participating in Social Pension Insurance | 1139.93 | 1140.32 |

注：机关事业单位社会养老保险参保人数含市级、区县级机关事业单位参保人数。
Note: The number of contributors to social pension insurance in government and public institutions includes the contributors from the governments and public institutions at municipal, district and county levels.

## 表 19.13 失业保险基本情况（2021 – 2022 年）
STATISTICS ON UNEMPLOYMENT INSURANCE (2021-2022)

| 指 标 | Item | 2021 | 2022 |
|---|---|---|---|
| 年末失业保险参保人数（万人） | Unemployment Insurance Contributors at Year-end (10 000 persons) | 598.30 | 614.24 |
| 企 业 | Enterprises | 525.56 | 538.36 |
| 事业单位 | Institutions | 41.45 | 34.88 |
| 其 他 | Others | 31.28 | 41.00 |
| 失业保险基金总收入（亿元） | Total Revenue of Unemployment Insurance (100 million yuan) | 28.15 | 32.57 |
| 失业保险费总收入（亿元 | Total Premium of Unemployment Insurance (100 million yuan) | 27.46 | 30.60 |
| 失业保险基金总支出（亿元） | Total Expenditure of Unemployment Insurance (100 million yuan) | 18.90 | 35.59 |
| 失业保险金总支出（亿元） | Total Payment of Unemployment Insurance (100 million yuan) | 13.17 | 16.50 |
| 失业保险基金当年末结余额（亿元） | Year-end Balance of Unemployment Insurance (100 million yuan) | 41.95 | 38.93 |
| 年末城镇登记失业人员数（万人） | Year-end Registered Urban Unemployment (10 000 persons) | 18.91 | 21.88 |
| 城镇登记失业人员再就业人数（万人） | Registered Urban Unemployment Reemployed (10 000 persons) | 23.69 | 24.46 |
| 领取失业保险人数（万人） | Actual Beneficiaries of Unemployment Insurance (10 000 persons) | 14.53 | 16.29 |
| 本年领取失业保险金人次数（万人次） | Person-times of Reception of Unemployment Insurance in Current Year (10 000 person-times) | 91.77 | 101.27 |

## 表 19.14 基本医疗保险情况（2021 – 2022 年）
STATISTICS ON BASIC MEDICAL CARE INSURANCE (2021-2022)

单位：亿元、万人 (100 million yuan, 10 000 persons)

| 指 标 | Item | 2021 | 2022 |
|---|---|---|---|
| 城镇职工基本医疗保险参保人数 | Basic Urban Workers Medical Care Insurance Contributors at Year-end | 796.00 | 808.00 |
| 在职职工 | Staff and Workers | 586.00 | 597.00 |
| 退休人员 | Retirees | 210.00 | 212.00 |
| 城镇职工基本医疗保险基金总收入 | Total Revenue of Urban Workers Basic Medical Care Insurance | 401.57 | 461.03 |
| 城镇职工基本医疗保险基金总支出 | Total Expenses of Urban Workers Basic Medical Care Insurance | 290.74 | 343.26 |

# 表 19.15 体育事业基本情况(2021－2022 年)
## STATISTICS ON MASS SPORTS (2021-2022)

| 项 目 | Item | 2021 | 2022 |
|---|---|---|---|
| 体育经费（万元） | Sports Expenditures (10 000 yuan) | 182547 | 234367 |
| 体育彩票销售额（万元） | Sales Value of Sports Lotteries (10 000 yuan) | 608756 | 719059 |
| 等级运动员（人） | Graded Athletes (person) | 2458 | |
| 国际级运动健将 | International Masters of Sports | | |
| 运动健将 | Masters of Sports | 48 | |
| 一级运动员 | First Grade Athletes | 637 | 399 |
| 二级运动员 | Second Grade Athletes | 1773 | 2162 |
| 获得全国最高水平比赛奖牌（个） | Number of Medals Won in the Domestic Top Competitions (Unit) | 31 | 33 |
| 其中：金牌 | Gold | 6 | 6 |
| 银 牌 | Silver | 12 | 9 |
| 铜 牌 | Copper | 13 | 18 |
| 获得世界三大赛奖牌（个） | Number of Medals Won in the Three Biggest World Games (Unit) | 3 | 9 |
| 其中：金牌 | Gold | 2 | 4 |
| 银 牌 | Silver | | 4 |
| 铜 牌 | Copper | 1 | 1 |
| 农民体育健身工程（个） | Community Fitness Centers (unit) | 100 | 455 |

注：体育经费包括体育事业费和体育基建支出。
Note: Sports expenditures include sports funds and expenditure for sports infrastructure.

# 表 19.16 律师、公证、调解工作基本情况（2021 – 2022 年）
## STATISTICS ON LAWYERS, NOTARIZATION AND MEDIATION (2021-2022)

| 项 目 | Item | 2021 | 2022 |
|---|---|---|---|
| 律师工作 | **Lawyers** | | |
| 律师事务所（所） | Number of Law Offices (unit) | 923 | 955 |
| 执业律师（人） | Number of Licensed Lawyers (person) | 14580 | 16069 |
| #专 职 | Full-time Lawyers | 11337 | 12427 |
| 聘请担任法律顾问单位（家） | Number of Units with Permanent Legal Advisors (unit) | 22648 | 24531 |
| 民事商事诉讼代理（件） | Agent of Civil Cases (case) | 193037 | 197402 |
| 刑事辩护（件） | Defender of Criminal Cases (case) | 20066 | 16051 |
| 行政诉讼代理（件） | Agent of Administrative Action (case) | 6069 | 5903 |
| 非诉讼法律事务（件） | Cases of Non-litigious Legal Affairs (case) | 26947 | 44030 |
| 涉外及涉港澳台法律事务(件) | Legal affairs concerning foreign affairs and Hong Kong, Macao and Taiwan (case) | 242 | 514 |
| 仲裁业务（件） | Arbitration Business (cases ) | 5943 | 6688 |
| 提供法律援助（件） | Provide legal aid (cases) | 15740 | 17296 |
| 参加社会公益事业和社会活动情况（次） | Participation in social welfare undertakings and social activities (times) | 22161 | 24288 |
| 公证工作 | **Notarization** | | |
| 公证处（个） | Number of Notary Offices (unit) | 41 | 41 |
| 公证员（人） | Public Notaries (person) | 246 | 281 |
| 公证员助理(人) | Notary Assistant (person) | 292 | 307 |
| 办理公证书（件） | Notarized Documents (case) | 271255 | 250295 |
| 人民调解工作 | **Number of People's Mediation** | | |
| 人民调解委员会（个） | Number of People's Mediation Committees (unit) | 12897 | 13050 |
| 人民调解员（人） | Number of Mediators (person) | 72455 | 68075 |
| 调解纠纷（件） | Number of Disputes Mediated (case) | 335948 | 402193 |
| 司法所建设 | **Construction of Judicial Institute** | | |
| 司法所（个） | Judicial Institute (unit) | 1034 | 1034 |
| 司法助理员（人） | Judicial Assistance (person) | 2884 | 4566 |
| 安置帮教对象（人） | Persons Resettled and Helped (person) | 29842 | 29756 |
| 基层法律服务 | **Legal Service at Grassroots Level** | | |
| 基层法律服务所（个） | Legal Service Institute at Grassroots Level (unit) | 303 | 303 |
| 基层法律工作者（人） | Grassroots Legal Service Workers (person) | 1768 | 1730 |
| 担任法律顾问（家） | Acting as Legal Adviser(times ) | 1794 | 2045 |
| 代理诉讼事务（件） | Acting litigation affairs (cases) | 33615 | 27819 |
| 代理非诉讼事务（件） | Acting for non-litigation affairs (cases) | 3444 | 3531 |
| 办理法律援助（件） | Legal Assistance Handled (case) | 7453 | 5852 |

## 表 19.17 国内外公证文书（2021 － 2022 年）
DOMESTIC AND FOREIGN-RELATED NOTARIAL DOCUMENTS (2021-2022)

单位：件、% (case, %)

| 项目 | Item | 国内公证文书 Domestic Notarial Documents 办证件数 Number of Notarial Documents Issued | | 比重 Percentage | |
|---|---|---|---|---|---|
| | | 2021 | 2022 | 2021 | 2022 |
| **办理公证总数** | **Total** | **271255** | **250295** | **100.0** | **100.0** |
| **按国内外分类** | **Classification at home and abroad** | | | | |
| 国内公证数 | Domestic Notarial Documents | 244160 | 213614 | 90.0 | 90.0 |
| 涉外公证数 | Foreign-related Notarial Documents | 25292 | 34959 | 9.3 | 9.3 |
| 涉港澳公证数 | Notarial Documents Related to Hong Kong and Macao | 550 | 505 | 0.2 | 0.2 |
| 涉台公证数 | Notarial Documents Related to Taiwan | 1253 | 1217 | 0.5 | 0.5 |
| **按内容分类** | **Categorization by content** | | | | |
| 合同（协议） | Contract (Agreement) | 11414 | 9275 | 4.2 | 4.2 |
| 继承 | Inheritance | 51982 | 39087 | 19.2 | 19.2 |
| 委托 | Consignment | 65530 | 54913 | 24.2 | 24.2 |
| 声明 | Declaration | 37122 | 29613 | 13.7 | 13.7 |
| 赠与 | Bestowal | 3998 | 1762 | 1.5 | 1.5 |
| 遗嘱 | Testament | 2542 | 2392 | 0.9 | 0.9 |
| 现成监督 | On-the-spot supervision | 1034 | 324 | 0.4 | 0.4 |
| 婚姻状况、亲属关系、收养关系 | Marital Status,Kinship Confirmation and Adoptive Relationship | 3094 | 3181 | 1.1 | 1.1 |
| 出生、生存、死亡 | Birth,Living and Death | 2546 | 3293 | 0.9 | 0.9 |
| 身份、经历、学历、学位、职务、职称 | Identity,Experience,Education Background,Degree, Post,Professional Title | 243 | 232 | 0.1 | 0.1 |
| 有无违法犯罪记录 | Illegal and Criminal Record Check | 3334 | 4292 | 1.2 | 1.2 |
| 公司章程 | Corporation Constitutions | 3 | | | |
| 保全证据 | Preservation of evidence | 8100 | 15580 | 3.0 | 3.0 |
| 证书、执照 | Certificate,License | 14228 | 19974 | 5.2 | 5.2 |
| 签名、印鉴 | Signature ,Stamp | 2934 | 2941 | 1.1 | 1.1 |
| 文本相符 | Conformity of Documentation | 6358 | 7858 | 2.3 | 2.3 |
| 赋予强制执行效力 | Executor Force | 54720 | 52511 | 20.2 | 20.2 |
| 执行证书 | Certificate of Execution | 1398 | 2280 | 0.5 | 0.5 |
| 抵押登记 | Mortgage Registration | 1 | 1 | | |
| 提存 | Drawing | 195 | 241 | 0.1 | 0.1 |
| 保管 | Storage | | | | |
| 其他 | Others | 479 | 545 | 0.2 | 0.2 |

## 表 19.18 公安机关立案的刑事案件情况（2021 － 2022 年）
## CRIMINAL CASES REGISTERED IN PUBLIC SECURITY ORGANS (2021-2022)

| 指 标 | Item | 2021 | 2022 |
|---|---|---|---|
| 刑事案件立案数（起） | Total Registered Criminal Cases (case) | 127638 | 106122 |
| 刑事案件破案率（%） | Rate of Solved Criminal Cases (%) | 31.7 | 33.7 |

## 表 19.19 检察机关审查批准、决定逮捕犯罪嫌疑人和提起公诉被告人情况（2022 年）
## ARRESTS OF CRIMINAL SUSPECTS AND DEFENDANTS UNDER PUBLIC PROSECUTION APPROVED BY PEOPLE'S PROCURATORATE (2022)

| 案件类别 | Category of Cases | 批捕、决定逮捕合计 Total of Arrests | | 决定起诉合计 Total of Public Prosecutions | |
|---|---|---|---|---|---|
| | | 件 (case) | 人 (person) | 件 (case) | 人 (person) |
| **合 计** | **Total** | **7959** | **10665** | **22943** | **32505** |
| 危害国家安全案 | Offences Against State Security | 8 | 9 | 5 | 6 |
| 危害公共安全案 | Offences Against Public Security | 83 | 87 | 5490 | 5525 |
| 破坏社会主义市场经济秩序案 | Offences Against Socialist Economic Order | 179 | 322 | 541 | 1053 |
| 侵犯公民人身、民主权利案 | Offences Against Citizens' Personal and Democratic Rights | 1118 | 1238 | 1823 | 2102 |
| 侵犯财产案 | Offences Against Properties | 2613 | 3505 | 5431 | 7935 |
| 妨害社会管理秩序案 | Offences Against Social Management of Order | 3953 | 5499 | 9413 | 15610 |
| 危害国防利益案 | Offences Against National Defense | | | 2 | 3 |
| 军人违反职责案 | Offences on Dereliction of Duty by Servicemen | | | | |
| 贪污贿赂案 | Offences on Corruption and Bribery | 2 | 2 | 215 | 245 |
| 渎职案 | Offences on Abuse and Dereliction of Duty | 3 | 3 | 23 | 26 |

# 表 19.20 人民法院刑事一审案件收结案情况（2021 – 2022 年）
FIRST TRIAL CRIMINAL CASES ACCEPTED AND SETTLED BY COURTS (2021-2022)

单位：件 (case)

| 类 别 | Category of Cases | 收 案 Accepted Cases | | 结 案 Settled Cases | |
|---|---|---|---|---|---|
| | | 2021 | 2022 | 2021 | 2022 |
| **合 计** | **Total** | **26813** | **25233** | **24820** | **23427** |
| 危害公共安全罪 | Offences against Public Security | 6736 | 5652 | 6597 | 5592 |
| 破坏社会主义市场经济秩序罪 | Offences against Socialist Economic Order | 864 | 768 | 656 | 547 |
| 侵犯公民人身权利、民主权利罪 | Offences against Citizens' Personal and Democratic Rights" | 2296 | 2130 | 1973 | 1781 |
| 侵犯财产罪 | Offences against Properties | 6959 | 5859 | 6571 | 5473 |
| 妨害社会管理秩序罪 | Offences against social Management of Order | 9677 | 10485 | 8831 | 9805 |
| 危害国防利益罪 | Offences against National Defense | 9 | 3 | 9 | 3 |
| 贪污贿赂罪 | Offences on Corruption and Bribery | 247 | 297 | 168 | 209 |
| 渎职罪 | Offences on Dereliction of Duty | 21 | 32 | 13 | 16 |
| 危害国家安全罪 | Offences against Country Safety | | | | |
| 其它 | Others | 4 | 7 | 2 | 1 |

注：收结案中含上年结转。
Note: The numbers of accepted and settled cases include the cases turned over from the previous year.

## 表 19.21 人民法院民事、行政一审案件收结案情况(2021 – 2022 年)
## FIRST TRIAL CIVIL AND ADMINISTRATIVE CASES ACCEPTED AND SETTLED BY COURTS (2021-2022)

单位：件 (case)

| 类 别 | Category of Cases | 收 案 Accepted Cases | | 结 案 Settled Cases | |
|---|---|---|---|---|---|
| | | 2021 | 2022 | 2021 | 2022 |
| **民事一审案件** | **First Trial of Civil Cases** | **666786** | **597178** | **571893** | **540457** |
| 婚姻家庭、继承纠纷 | Disputes of Marriages and Family Affairs | 64541 | 51395 | 59070 | 48269 |
| 物权纠纷 | Disputes of Inheritance | 11728 | 9175 | 9543 | 7787 |
| 合同纠纷 | Disputes of Contracts | 463899 | 417565 | 400504 | 381619 |
| 劳动争议、人事争议 | Labor Disputes and Personnel Disputes | 31341 | 29461 | 25056 | 25241 |
| 侵权责任纠纷 | Disputes of Ownership and Infringement of Right | 37443 | 33577 | 29895 | 29101 |
| 其他民事一审案件 | Other First Trial of Civil Cases | 57834 | 56005 | 47825 | 48440 |
| **行政一审案件** | **First Trial of Administrative Cases** | **10805** | **8915** | **8858** | **7766** |

注：收案中含上年结转。
Note: The number of accepted cases includes the cases turned over from the previous year.

## 表 19.22 安全生产情况(2002 – 2022 年)
## BASIC STATISTICS ON WORK SAFETY (2002-2022)

| 年 份 Year | 亿元地区生产总值生产安全事故死亡率 Mortality Rate of Work Safety Accident Per 100 Billion Yuan GDP | 煤炭生产百万吨死亡率 Mortality Rate Per 1 Million Tons of Coal Production |
|---|---|---|
| 2002 | 1.440 | 21.080 |
| 2003 | 1.410 | 17.820 |
| 2004 | 0.890 | 12.240 |
| 2005 | 0.750 | 13.730 |
| 2006 | 0.610 | 9.300 |
| 2007 | 0.470 | 7.640 |
| 2008 | 0.340 | 6.820 |
| 2009 | 0.300 | 5.440 |
| 2010 | 0.230 | 4.000 |
| 2011 | 0.170 | 3.000 |
| 2012 | 0.130 | 2.730 |
| 2013 | 0.118 | 2.390 |
| 2014 | 0.097 | 2.597 |
| 2015 | 0.080 | 1.260 |
| 2016 | 0.070 | 3.340 |
| 2017 | 0.050 | 0.286 |
| 2018 | 0.044 | 1.229 |
| 2019 | 0.044 | 0.424 |
| 2020 | 0.038 | 5.041 |
| 2021 | 0.031 | 0.000 |
| 2022 | 0.021 | 0.000 |

## 表 19.23 道路交通事故情况（2022 年）
## BASIC STATISTICS ON TRAFFIC ACCIDENTS (2022)

| 类 别 | Type | 发生数（起）<br>Number of Traffic Accidents (case) | 死亡人数（人）<br>Number of Deaths (person) | 受伤人数（人）<br>Number of Injuries (person) | 损失折款（万元）<br>Losses Converted into Cash (10 000 yuan) |
|---|---|---|---|---|---|
| **总 计** | **Total** | **4581** | **917** | **4794** | **3678.49** |
| #死亡事故 | Deaths | 874 | 917 | 373 | 1861.2 |
| 伤人事故 | Injuries | 3361 | | 4421 | 1393.15 |
| 财产损失事故 | Assets Losses | 346 | | | 424.14 |
| #机动车 | Motor Vehicles | 4213 | 842 | 4414 | 3367.1 |
| #汽 车 | Automobiles | 2920 | 585 | 2894 | 3151.16 |
| 摩托车 | Motorcycles | 1184 | 226 | 1403 | 191.06 |
| 拖拉机 | Tractors | 8 | 3 | 7 | 0.74 |
| 非机动车 | Non-motor-driven Vehicles | 242 | 28 | 288 | 35.76 |
| #自行车 | Bicycles | 36 | 4 | 40 | 15.26 |
| 行人乘车人 | Pedestrians and Passengers | 126 | 47 | 92 | 275.64 |

## 表 19.24 火灾事故情况（2022 年）
## BASIC STATISTICS ON FIRES (2022)

| 项 目 | Item | 合 计<br>Total | 按事故发生程度分 By Serious Degree of Fires | | | |
|---|---|---|---|---|---|---|
| | | | 特 大<br>Extra-Serious | 重 大<br>Serious | 较大<br>Large | 一般<br>Ordinary |
| 发 生（起） | Fires (case) | 30343 | | | 6 | 30337 |
| 死 亡（人） | Deaths (person) | 123 | | | 13 | 110 |
| 受 伤（人） | Injuries (person) | 80 | | | | 80 |
| 损失折款（万元） | Losses Converted into Cash (10 000 yuan) | 24735 | | | 7400 | 17335 |
| 平均每起事故损失（万元） | Average Loss Per Fire (10 000 yuan) | 0.82 | | | 1233 | 0.57 |

注：损失折款指直接经济损失（下表同）。
Note: The losses converted into cash refer to direct losses (the same for tables below).

# 主要统计指标解释

## 等级运动员人数

指经考核正式批准授予等级运动员称号的人数。运动员等级分为国际级运动健将、运动健将、一级运动员、二级运动员、三级运动员、少年级运动员。

## 等级裁判员人数

指经考核正式批准授予等级裁判员称号的人数。裁判员等级分为国际裁判、国家级裁判、一级裁判、二级裁判、三级裁判。

## 医疗卫生机构

指从卫生（卫生计生）行政部门取得《医疗机构执业许可证》、《计划生育技术服务许可证》，或从民政、工商行政、机构编制管理部门取得法人单位登记证书，为社会提供医疗服务、公共卫生服务或从事医学科研和医学在职培训等工作的单位。医疗卫生机构包括医院、基层医疗卫生机构、专业公共卫生机构、其他医疗卫生机构。

## 医院

包括综合医院、中医医院、中西医结合医院、民族医院、各类专科医院和护理院，不包括专科疾病防治院、妇幼保健院和疗养院，包括医学院校附属医院。

## 卫生技术人员

包括执业医师、执业助理医师、注册护士、药师（士）、检验技师（士）、影像技师、卫生监督员和见习医（药、护、技）师（士）等卫生专业人员。不包括从事管理工作的卫生技术人员（如院长、副院长、党委书记等）。

## 执业医师

指《医师执业证》“级别”为“执业医师”且实际从事医疗、预防保健工作的人员，不包括实际从事管理工作的执业医师。执业医师类别分为临床、中医、口腔和公共卫生四类。

## 执业（助理）医师

指《医师执业证》“级别”为“执业助理医师”且实际从事医疗、预防保健工作的人员，不包括实际从事管理工作的执业助理医师。执业助理医师类别分为临床、中医、口腔和公共卫生四类。

## 社会福利企业单位

指以安置城镇有一定劳动能力的盲、聋、哑和肢体残疾人员就业为目的，享受国家减免税待遇的国有或集体企业。包括福利工厂、福利商业和服务业、假肢厂和安置农场等单位。该指标主要反映我国对残疾人照顾的特殊政策。

## 城镇职工基本养老保险

1. **参保职工人数** 指报告期末按照国家法律、法规和有关政策规定参加城镇职工基本养老保险并在社保经办机构已建立缴费记录档案的职工人数，包括中断缴费但未终止养老保险关系的职工人数，不包括只登记未建立缴费记录档案的人数。

2. **离退休人员人数** 指报告期末参加城镇职工基本养老保险的离休、退休和退职人员的人数。

3. **基金收入** 指根据国家有关规定，由纳入职工基本养老保险范围的缴费单位和个人按国家规定的缴费基数和缴费比例缴纳的养老保险费，以及通过其他方式取得的形成基金来源的收入。包括单位和职工个人缴纳的基本养老保险费、基本养老保险基金利息收入、委托投资收益、上级补助收入、下级上解收入、转移收入、财政补贴和其他收入。

4. **基金支出** 指按照国家政策规定的开支范围和开支标准从职工基本养老保险基金中支付给参加职工基本养老保险的个人养老保险待遇支出，以及由于保险关系转移、上下级之间补助、上解等原因而发生的支出。其他支出包括基本养老金、医疗补助金、丧葬补助金和抚恤金、病残津贴、补助下级支出、上解上级支出、转移支出和其他支出等。

5. **基金累计结余** 指职工基本养老保险基金收支相抵后的期末累计余额。

## 主要统计指标解释

### 城乡居民基本养老保险

1. **参保人数** 指报告期末，参加城乡居民养老保险（在经办机构参保登记并已建立缴费记录以及制度实施当年已经年满60周岁并在经办机构参保登记）的人数（不包括已经办理注销登记手续的人数）。

2. **基金收入** 指根据国家有关规定，由参加城乡居民基本养老保险的个人按规定缴费的城乡居民基本养老保险费，以及通过集体补助、财政补助等其他方式取得的形成基金来源的收入。包括个人缴费收入、集体补助收入、政府补贴收入、利息收入、委托投资收益、转移收入、上级补助收入、下级上解收入和其他收入。

3. **基金支出** 指按照国家政策规定的开支范围和开支标准从城乡居民基本养老保险基金中支付给参加城乡居民基本养老保险的个人养老保险待遇支出，以及由于参保人员跨统筹地区或跨制度流动而发生的支出等。包括养老保险待遇支出、转移支出、补助下级支出、上解上级支出和其他支出。

4. **基金累计结余** 指城乡居民基本养老保险基金收支相抵后的期末累计余额。

### 离休、退休、退职人员

指正式办理了离休、退休、退职手续，并享受相应的离休、退休、退职待遇的人员。

### 失业保险

1. **参保人数** 指报告期末按照国家法律、法规和有关政策规定参加了失业保险的城镇企业、事业单位的职工及地方政府规定参加失业保险的其他人员的人数。

2. **基金收入** 指报告期内筹集的失业保险基金的总额，包括失业保险费收入、利息收入、财政补贴收入、其他收入、转移收入、上级补助收入、下级上解收入。

3. **基金支出** 指报告期内为保障失业人员基本生活、促进其再就业等支出的基金总额，包括失业保险金支出、医疗补助金支出、丧葬补助金和抚恤金支出、职业培训和职业介绍补贴支出、农民合同制工人一次性生活补助支出、其他支出、转移支出、上级补助支出、下级上解支出。

4. **基金累计结余** 指截至报告期末失业保险基金收支相抵后的累计余额。

### 基本医疗保险

1. **参保人数** 指报告期末按国家有关规定参加职工基本医疗保险和城乡居民基本医疗保险人员的合计。

2. **基金收入** 指由用人单位和个人按照国家规定的缴费基数、缴费比例或缴费标准缴纳的基本医疗保险费，财政补贴资金以及通过其他方式取得的形成基金来源的款项，包括：单位缴纳收入、个人缴纳收入、财政补贴收入、利息收入、上级补助收入、下级上解收入和其他收入。

3. **基金支出** 指按照国家政策规定的开支范围和开支标准，从基本医疗保险基金中支付给参保人员的医疗保险待遇支出，以及其他支出。包括住院费用支出、门诊费用支出、大病保险支出、生育保险与职工基本医疗保险合并实施的统筹地区生育待遇支出、补助下级支出、上解上级支出和其他支出。

4. **基金累计结余** 指基本医疗保险基金收支相抵后的期末累计结余金额。

### 律师

指依法取得律师执业证书，担任法律顾问，民事（刑事、行政）案件代理人、刑事案件辩护人、办理非诉讼业务，解答法律询问，代写法律事务文书等，为社会提供法律服务的人员。

### 公证人员

指在公证处工作的人员总称，包括公证处主任、副主任、公证员、公证员助理（助理公证员）和其他从事辅助性工作的人员。

### 公证文书

指公证处根据当事人申请，依照事实和法律，按照法定程序制作的，具有法律效力的司法证明文书。

### 调解员

指在人民调解委员会担负调解民间纠纷工作的人员，包括调解委员会的委员和调解小组的调解员。

### 调解民间纠纷

指调解委员会按照法律规定，根据自愿原则，用说服教育的方法调解民间发生的有关民事权利和义务争执的件数，包括调解成功数和调解未成功数。

# 主要统计指标解释

## 人民检察院直接立案侦查案件

指按照管辖的规定，由人民检察院直接立案侦查的贪污贿赂犯罪、渎职犯罪、国家机关工作人员利用职权实施的侵犯公民人身权利和民主权利的犯罪以及经省级人民检察院决定立案侦查的国家机关工作人员利用职权实施的其他重大犯罪案件。

## 大案

指贪污、贿赂案数额在 5 万元以上，挪用公款案数额在 10 万元以上，集体私分、巨额财产来源不明、隐瞒境外存款案数额在 50 万元以上以及按照《人民检察院直接受理的渎职、侵权重、特大案件标准（试行）》认定的案件。该指标主要反映人民检察院立案查办的职务犯罪案件中经济损失大、社会危害严重的案件。

## 要案

指县、处级以上干部的犯罪案件。该指标主要反映国家工作人员中县、处级以上干部因职务犯罪被人民检察院依法立案侦查的情况。

## 决定逮捕

指人民检察院对直接立案侦查的案件，认为需要逮捕犯罪嫌疑人时，依据法律做出的逮捕决定。该指标主要反映人民检察院对直接受理的案件行使决定逮捕权的情况。

## 批准逮捕

指人民检察院对公安机关、国家安全机关、监狱管理机关提出逮捕的犯罪嫌疑人进行审查，根据事实，依法做出逮捕决定。该指标主要反映人民检察院对提请逮捕犯罪嫌疑人进行审查后依法做出批准逮捕决定的情况。

## 决定起诉

指人民检察机关对公安机关、国家安全机关、监狱管理机关和检察机关内设机构反贪污贿赂部门移送起诉的刑事犯罪嫌疑人进行审查，根据事实，依法向人民法院提起公诉。

## 基层医疗卫生机构

包括社区卫生服务中心、社区卫生服务站、街道卫生院、乡镇卫生院、村卫生室、门诊部、诊所(医务室)。

## 专业公共卫生机构

包括疾病预防控制中心、专科疾病防治机构、妇幼保健机构（含妇幼保健计划生育服务中心）、健康教育机构、急救中心（站）、采供血机构、卫生监督机构、取得《医疗机构执业许可证》或《计划生育技术服务许可证》的计划生育技术服务机构。

## 卫生人员

指在医院、基层医疗卫生机构、专业公共卫生机构及其他医疗卫生机构工作的职工，包括卫生技术人员、乡村医生和卫生员、其他技术人员、管理人员和工勤人员。一律按支付年底工资的在岗职工统计，包括各类聘任人员(含合同工)及返聘本单位半年以上人员，不包括临时工、离退休人员、退职人员、离开本单位仍保留劳动关系人员、本单位返聘和临聘不足半年人员。

# Explanatory Notes on Main Statistical Indicators

## □ Number of Athletes in Grades

Refers to the number of athletes who have been given titles through examination. The titles of athletes include international masters of sports, masters of sports, first-grade, second-grade and third-grade sportsmen and young athletes.

## □ Number of Referees in Grades

Refers to the number of referees who have been given titles after examination. They are classified as international referees, national referees and referees of the first, second and third grades.

## □ Medical and Health Care Institutions

Refer to the units which have been qualified the Certification of Health Care Institution, certification of family planning technical service by the administration of public health (family planning), or qualified the Certification of Corporate Unit by the civil affairs, administration for industry and commerce, commission office for public sector reform, and engaging in medical health care services, public health services, or medicine research and on-job training, etc., including: hospitals, health care institutions at grass-root level, specialized public health institutions, and other medical and health care institutions.

## □ Hospitals

Include general hospitals, hospitals specialized in traditional Chinese medicine, hospitals of integrated traditional Chinese and western medicine, ethnic hospitals, specialized hospitals and nursing hospitals, excluding specialized disease prevention and treatment institutes, maternal and child health care hospitals and convalescent hospitals, including affiliated hospital of medical college.

## □ Medical Technical Personnel

Refer to the professional staff engaged in health care, including licensed doctors, licensed assistant doctors, registered nurses, pharmacists, laboratory technicians, imaging staff, health care supervisors and intern doctors, pharmacists, nurses, and technical personnel, excluding the medical technical personnel engaged in managerial job (e.g. president, vice president and secretary of the party committee etc.).

## □ Licensed Doctors

Refer to the medical workers who have obtained the licenses of qualified doctors and are employed in medical treatment, disease prevention or healthcare institutions, excluding the licensed doctors engaged in management job. The licensed doctors are divided into 4 categories: clinician, Chinese medicine physicians, dentist and public health physicians.

## □ Licensed Assistant Doctors

Refer to the medical workers who have obtained the licenses of qualified assistant doctors and are employed in medical treatment, disease prevention or healthcare institutions, excluding the licensed assistant doctors engaged in management job. The classification of licensed assistant doctors is clinician, Chinese medicine, dentist and public health.

## □ Social Welfare Enterprises

Are collective owned enterprises which employ the blind, deaf-mute, and other handicapped people who are able to work in cities and towns and enjoy exemption from state taxes, including welfare plants, welfare commercial services, artificial limb plants and farms, etc. This indicator reflects the preferential policies toward disabled persons.

## □ Basic Pension Insurance for Urban Staff and Workers

**1. Number of staff and workers covered** refers to staff and workers participating in the basic pension insurance for urban staff and workers program according to national laws, regulations and related policies at the end of the reference period, who have already had payment records in social security management agencies, including those who have interrupt payment without terminating the insurance program. Those who have registered in the program but with no payment records are not included.

**2. Number of retirees** refers to the number of retirees participating in the basic pension insurance for urban staff and workers programs by the end of the reference period.

**3. Revenue of the basic pension insurance program** refers to payments made by employers and individuals participating in the pension insurance program of staff in accordance with the basis and proportion stipulated in State regulations, and income from other sources that become the source of pension insurance fund, including the premium paid by employers and staff and workers, interest income, entrusted investment income, subsidies from higher level agencies, income as transfer from subordinate agencies, transferred income, government financial subsidies and other income.

**4. Expenditure of basic pension insurance program** refer to personal pension insurance payment made on pensions subsidies to those covered in pension insurance programs of staff according to related national policies on scope and standard of expenditure, also included are expenditure which arises due to shift of the insurance relationship or adjustment of funds among agencies, transfer to agencies at higher level. Other expenditure includes: basic pension insurance, medical fees, funeral subsidies, compensation payments, disability allowance, expenses on subsidies to lower subordinates, expenses as transfer to agencies at higher level, transferred expenditure and other expenditure.

**5. Balance of basic pension insurance program** refers to the balance of staff basic pension insurance funds at the end of the reference period after deducting expenses from revenue.

## Basic Pension Insurance for Urban and Rural Residents

**1. Number of participants** refers to people participating in the basic pension insurance for urban and rural residents program who registered with the participation and established payment records, and who were 60 years old or above when the system was established and registered with the participation. Those who cancelled their registration are not included.

**2. Revenue of the insurance program** refers to the revenue from the payments made, in accordance with related regulations of the government, by individuals participating in the basic pension insurance for urban and rural residents programme and from the subsidies contributed by collective subsidies, public finance and other sources. It includes the payment by individual participants, collective subsidies, government subsidies, interest income, entrusted investment income, transferred income, subsidies from higher levels, contributions from lower levels, and income from other sources.

**3. Expenditure of the insurance program** refers to payment made to those covered in the basic pension insurance for urban and rural residents according to related national policies on scope and standard of expenditure. Also included are expenditures which arise due to movement of participants among different locations or system. It includes the payment to the individual participants, transferred expenditures, expenses on subsidies to lower subordinates, expenses as transfer to agencies at higher level, and other expenditures.

**4. Balance of insurance program** refers to the balance of basic pension insurance funds for urban and rural residents at the end of the reference period after deducting expenses from revenue.

**Retired or Resigned Personnel** refers to people who have formally gone through the formalities for their retirement or quitting work and enjoy the corresponding treatments.

## Unemployment Insurance

**1. Number of people covered** refers to staff and workers in urban enterprises or institutions who have participated in the unemployment insurance program according to relevant policies and regulations, and other people who have participated according to local government regulations at the end of the reference period.

**2. Revenue of the unemployment insurance program** refers to the total unemployment insurance funds raised in the reference period, including unemployment insurance premium, interest income, financial subsidies, other incomes, transferred income, subsidies from higher level agencies and income as transfer from subordinate agencies.

**3. Expenditure of the unemployment insurance program** refers to total expenses during the reference period to guarantee the basic livelihood of unemployed people, and to encourage their re-employment. Included are unemployment relief, medical fees, funeral subsidies, compensation payments, training expenses, job placement expenses, one-time subsistence allowance for contracted migrant workers, other expenditures, transferred expenditure, expenses as transfer to higher level agencies and subsidies to lower level agencies.

**4. Balance of the unemployment insurance program** refers to the balance of revenue of the program after deducting expenses at the end of the reference period.

## Basic Medical Care Insurance

**1. Number of people participating in the insurance program** refers to the total number of basic medical insurance for employees and the basic medical insurance for urban and

EXPLANATORY NOTES TO MAJOR STATISTICAL INDICATORS

rural residents participating in the basic medical care insurance program according to related regulations at the end of the reference period.

**2. Revenue of the insurance program** refers to payments made by employers and individuals participating in the medical care insurance program in accordance with the basis and proportion stipulated in State regulations, government subsidies and income from other sources that become the source of medical insurance fund, including payment by employers and individuals, financial subsidies, interest income, subsidies from higher level agencies, income as transfer from subordinate agencies, and other incomes.

**3. Expenditure of the insurance program** refers to medical care payment made to people covered in basic medical care insurance program within the scope and standards of expenditure according to related national policies, and other expenses, including combined regional maternity expenditure of medical expenses of hospital inpatients, medical expenses for outpatients patients, serious illness insurance expenditure, maternity insurance, basic medical insurance for staff and workers, and other expenditure.

**4. Balance of the basic medical care insurance program** refers to the balance of medical care insurance funds at the end of the reference period after deducting expenses from revenue.

## Lawyers

Are certified legal workers according to law, and who are employed by legal counseling firms to act as legal advisers, agents in criminal or civil lawsuits, or defenders in criminal lawsuits, or to handle non-litigious legal affairs, to advise on matters of law or to write legal papers for others, and provide service to the public.

## Notary Personnel

Refers to people working for notary offices including: directors, deputy director, notaries, assistant notaries, and other people providing assistance.

## Notary Documents

Refer to the judicatory notary documents drawn up by the request of the party and are in accordance with facts and laws and following certain legal proceedings.

## Mediators

Refer to workers on people mediation committees responsible for mediating in civil disputes and cases of slight infraction of the law. They include members of the mediation committees and mediators of mediation groups.

## Mediation of Civil Disputes

Refers to number of cases made by mediation committees in mediating in civil disputes concerning civil rights and duties through persuasion and education in accordance with the provisions of law on a voluntary basis, so as to solve disputes by helping the parties involved come to an agreement and understanding, including those unsuccessful ones.

## Cases Registered and Handled Directly by People's Procuratorate Offices

Refer to those serious criminal cases that, according to the functional jurisdiction, are registered and handled by the People's Procuratorate Offices, including the ones on bribery and corruption, the ones on abuse and dereliction of duty, offenses against citizens' personal and democratic rights by government officials abusing their powers; and that are registered and handled by the provincial Procuratorate offices in relation to other major crimes committed by government officials by abusing their powers.

## Large Cases

Refer to cases involving a corruption or bribery of over 50,000 yuan, or a misappropriation of over 100,000 yuan, Cases of collectively illegal possession of public funds, unstated sources of large properties, or disguised overseas savings deposits involving 500,000 yuan, or a case that has been defined by Standard on Serious and Large Cases of Misconduct and Tortious that Directly Accepted by People's Procurators Office (trial). This indicator mainly reflects number of accepted cases of job-related criminals that caused serious economic losses or extremely harmful to the society.

## Key Cases

Refer to cases committed by government officials with a ranking of division director or county administrator. This indicator mainly reflects the recorded and spied on cases by the people's procurators offices toward government official with a ranking of division director or county administrator.

EXPLANATORY NOTES TO MAJOR STATISTICAL INDICATORS

## Decision on Arrest

Refers to decision made by the people's procuratorate office, in accordance with laws, to arrest the suspect(s) in the cases that are accepted and to be investigated by the procurators office. This indicator mainly reflects the implementation of the decision on arrest by people's procuratorate office.

## Approval for Arrest

Refers to the decision made by people's procuratorate office, in accordance with the law and relevant facts, to approve the arrest of the suspect(s) as proposed by the public security departments, state security departments or prisons authority. This indicator reflects approved arrests made by people's procuratorate offices that are proposed by related departments.

## Decision on Prosecution

Refers to the decision made by procurators office, in accordance with laws and relevant facts, to institute proceedings to the people court against the suspect(s) of criminal cases handed over by the public security departments, state security departments or authority of prisons, or by the anti-corruption departments within the procurators office.

## Health Care Institutions at Grass-root Level

Include community health service centers, community health service stations, urban health centers, township health centers, village clinics, outpatient departments and clinics (health centers).

## Specialized Public Health Institutions

Include centers for disease control and prevention, specialized disease prevention and treatment institutions, women and children care agencies(including women and children health care family planning service center), health education institutions, first aid centers, blood gathering and supplying institutions, health supervision and inspection agencies, and family planning technical service centers that obtained the Certification of Health Care Institution or certification of family planning technical service centers.

## Health Care Employees

Refer to all employees engaged in the health care institutions, such as hospitals, health care institutions at grass-root level, specialized public health institutions, and other medical and health care institutions, including medical technical personnel, village doctors and assistants, other technical personnel, managerial and service staff. The data is based on the year end payroll, including personnel hired (including contract labor) and re-employed after retirement by the institution for over half a year and excluding temporary workers, retired personnel, resigned personnel, personnel who have left the institution but kept the contract relation and personnel who are re-employed after retirement or temporarily employed for less than half a year.

# 第二十章·区　县

## DISTRICTS, COUNTIES

# 简要说明

## BRIEF INTRODUCTION

本章资料包括按“主城区都市区（中心城区、主城新区）、渝东北三峡库区城镇群、渝东南武陵山区城镇群”三个分组的全市38个区县（自治县）的主要经济社会统计资料。

“中心城区”包括渝中区、大渡口区、江北区、沙坪坝区、九龙坡区、南岸区、北碚区、渝北区、巴南区，即主城九区；“主城新区”包括涪陵区、长寿区、江津区、合川区、永川区、南川区、綦江区、大足区、璧山区、铜梁区、潼南区和荣昌区；“渝东北三峡库区城镇群”包括万州区、开州区、梁平区、城口县、丰都县、垫江县、忠县、云阳县、奉节县、巫山县和巫溪县。“渝东南武陵山区城镇群”包括黔江区、武隆区、石柱县、秀山县、酉阳县和彭水县。

为便于排版，对资料中各区县名称均采用简称，即：石柱土家族自治县、秀山土家族苗族自治县、酉阳土家族苗族自治县、彭水苗族土家族自治县统一简称为：石柱县、秀山县、酉阳县、彭水县。

本章资料分别由市统计局人口和就业处、核算处、工业处、服务业处、固定资产投资处、贸易外经处、社会科技处、能源资源统计处、普查中心、综合处和国家统计局重庆调查总队根据有关专业统计资料、各区县统计局资料和市级有关部门的区县资料整理编辑。

This chapter includes the main economic and social indicators of 38 districts and counties (autonomous counties) grouped by the “The city proper of Chongqing (The central urban area of Chongqing and The new area of Chongqing city proper), The city cluster of three gorges reservoir area in northeast Chongqing, The city cluster of Wuling mountain area in southeast Chongqing”.

The central urban area of Chongqing covers the 9 central urban districts, namely Yuzhong, Dadukou, Jiangbei, Shapingba, Jiulongpo, Nan’an, Beibei, Yubei and Banan. The new area of Chongqing city proper covers 12 districts and counties of Fuling, Changshou, Jiangjin, Hechuan, Yongchuan, Nanchuan, Qijiang, Dazu, Bishan, Tongliang, Tongnan, and Rongchang. The “Three Gorges Reservoir Urban Group of Northeast Chongqing” covers 11 districts and counties of Wanzhou, Kaizhou, Liangping, Chengkou, Fengdu, Dianjiang, Zahongxian, Yunyang, Fengjie, Wushan and Wuxi. The “Wuling Mountain Urban Group of Southeast Chongqing” covers 6 districts and counties of Qianjiang, Wulong, Shizhu, Xiushan Youyang and Pengshui.

For the convenience of layout, shorter terms are used for the name of some districts and counties. Shizhu Tujia Autonomous County, Xiushan Tujia&Miao Autonomous County, Youyang Tujia&Miao Autonomous County and Pengshui Miao&Tujia Autonomous County are uniformly called as Shizhu County, Xiushan County, Youyang County and Pengshui County.

The data in this chapter are prepared and compiled by Division of Population and Employment Statistics, Division of National Economic Accounting, Division of Industry Statistics, Division of Service Statistics, Division of Statistics of Investment in Fixed Assets, Division of Trade and Foreign Economic Relations Statistics, Division of Social and Technology Statistics, Division of Energy and Natural Resources Statistics, Census Center, Division of Comprehensive Statistics of Chongqing Municipal Bureau of Statistics as well as the NBS Survey Office in Chongqing on the basis of the data provided by the related divisions of Municipal Bureau of Statistics, the statistical bureaus of districts and counties and the related municipal departments.

# 表 20.1 各区县户数和人口（2022 年）
## HOUSEHOLDS AND POPULATION BY REGION (2022)

| 区 县 | Region | 年末总户数（户籍统计）（万户）Year-end Households (registration statistics) (10 000 households) | 年末总人口（户籍统计）（万人）Year-end Population (registration statistics) (10 000 persons) | #城镇人口 Non-agricultural | #女 性 Female | 按年龄组分 By Age 0-17 岁 Aged 0-17 | 18-35 岁 Aged 18-35 | 35-59 岁 Aged 35-59 | 60 岁及以上 Aged 60 and Over |
|---|---|---|---|---|---|---|---|---|---|
| **全 市** | **Total** | **1292.06** | **3413.80** | **1710.71** | **1669.88** | **605.81** | **702.15** | **1380.17** | **725.67** |
| 主城都市区 | The city proper of Chongqing | 783.88 | 1967.43 | 1200.71 | 978.36 | 344.03 | 359.59 | 814.10 | 449.71 |
| 中心城区 | The central urban area of Chongqing | 313.37 | 740.98 | 626.93 | 377.43 | 140.24 | 124.36 | 303.14 | 173.24 |
| 主城新区 | The new area of Chongqing city proper | 470.51 | 1226.45 | 573.78 | 600.93 | 203.79 | 235.23 | 510.96 | 276.47 |
| 渝东北三峡库区城镇群 | The city cluster of three gorges reservoir area in northeast Chongqing | 384.65 | 1073.50 | 388.52 | 515.04 | 186.79 | 247.29 | 426.18 | 213.24 |
| 渝东南武陵山区城镇群 | The city cluster of Wuling mountain area in southeast Chongqing | 123.53 | 372.87 | 121.48 | 176.48 | 74.99 | 95.27 | 139.89 | 62.72 |
| 万州区 | Wanzhou District | 68.81 | 170.82 | 71.10 | 84.21 | 25.43 | 32.92 | 73.50 | 38.97 |
| 黔江区 | Qianjiang District | 20.38 | 55.50 | 22.95 | 26.25 | 11.09 | 14.01 | 21.53 | 8.87 |
| 涪陵区 | Fuling District | 44.31 | 112.48 | 51.57 | 55.35 | 18.87 | 20.89 | 50.14 | 22.58 |
| 渝中区 | Yuzhong District | 20.56 | 49.05 | 49.05 | 25.19 | 5.92 | 6.85 | 18.80 | 17.48 |
| 大渡口区 | Dadukou District | 13.19 | 29.14 | 29.14 | 14.96 | 5.54 | 4.77 | 11.86 | 6.97 |
| 江北区 | Jiangbei District | 28.04 | 65.42 | 63.86 | 33.51 | 11.11 | 10.57 | 26.89 | 16.85 |
| 沙坪坝区 | Shapingba District | 38.80 | 95.77 | 87.22 | 49.05 | 20.27 | 16.20 | 37.76 | 21.54 |
| 九龙坡区 | Jiulongpo District | 42.73 | 100.72 | 85.75 | 51.59 | 19.52 | 16.39 | 41.37 | 23.44 |
| 南岸区 | Nan'an District | 32.60 | 80.86 | 76.01 | 41.57 | 16.88 | 13.32 | 32.67 | 17.99 |
| 北碚区 | Beibei District | 27.91 | 65.83 | 48.56 | 33.40 | 9.96 | 10.23 | 28.09 | 17.55 |
| 渝北区 | Yubei District | 66.93 | 156.58 | 125.21 | 79.25 | 34.34 | 29.41 | 66.10 | 26.73 |
| 巴南区 | Ba'nan District | 42.61 | 97.61 | 62.13 | 48.91 | 16.70 | 16.62 | 39.60 | 24.69 |
| 长寿区 | Changshou District | 38.16 | 86.93 | 38.18 | 42.99 | 12.09 | 16.60 | 37.85 | 20.39 |
| 江津区 | Jiangjin District | 62.07 | 146.39 | 70.20 | 71.87 | 22.87 | 26.53 | 60.64 | 36.35 |
| 合川区 | Hechuan District | 57.69 | 147.92 | 72.61 | 71.96 | 21.69 | 26.80 | 62.50 | 36.93 |
| 永川区 | Yongchuan District | 41.34 | 113.55 | 52.31 | 56.46 | 21.41 | 20.29 | 47.28 | 24.57 |
| 南川区 | Nanchuan District | 25.16 | 67.89 | 29.40 | 33.45 | 11.71 | 13.06 | 28.83 | 14.29 |
| 綦江区 | Qijiang District | 45.27 | 116.66 | 59.41 | 57.40 | 17.94 | 23.36 | 47.41 | 27.95 |
| #綦江区（不含万盛） | Qijiang District (excluding Wansheng) | 34.88 | 90.68 | 41.19 | 44.32 | 14.14 | 18.40 | 36.45 | 21.69 |
| 大足区 | Dazu District | 32.62 | 106.76 | 51.36 | 51.55 | 21.86 | 22.26 | 42.17 | 20.47 |
| 璧山区 | Bishan District | 26.28 | 65.57 | 34.87 | 32.69 | 10.85 | 12.18 | 27.66 | 14.88 |
| 铜梁区 | Tongliang District | 32.38 | 84.16 | 40.30 | 41.16 | 14.34 | 15.51 | 35.03 | 19.28 |
| 潼南区 | Tongnan District | 33.82 | 94.18 | 30.84 | 44.67 | 16.27 | 21.42 | 35.84 | 20.65 |
| 荣昌区 | Rongchang District | 31.41 | 83.96 | 42.73 | 41.38 | 13.89 | 16.33 | 35.61 | 18.13 |
| 开州区 | Kaizhou District | 56.62 | 166.03 | 63.85 | 79.25 | 31.70 | 40.76 | 63.47 | 30.10 |
| 梁平区 | Liangping District | 32.02 | 91.17 | 37.75 | 43.74 | 15.46 | 19.59 | 37.70 | 18.42 |
| 武隆区 | Wulong District | 13.91 | 40.44 | 11.87 | 19.37 | 6.99 | 8.68 | 16.52 | 8.25 |
| 城口县 | Chengkou County | 8.79 | 24.90 | 7.10 | 11.76 | 5.14 | 5.74 | 9.48 | 4.54 |
| 丰都县 | Fengdu County | 27.30 | 79.64 | 24.66 | 38.25 | 12.80 | 18.78 | 32.44 | 15.62 |
| 垫江县 | Dianjiang County | 33.22 | 94.80 | 40.77 | 45.60 | 16.59 | 22.53 | 37.36 | 18.32 |
| 忠 县 | Zhongxian County | 34.15 | 95.29 | 33.08 | 45.62 | 16.63 | 19.31 | 38.39 | 20.96 |
| 云阳县 | Yunyang County | 45.45 | 131.57 | 46.18 | 62.63 | 23.22 | 33.16 | 50.11 | 25.08 |
| 奉节县 | Fengjie County | 35.94 | 103.84 | 28.14 | 49.13 | 18.27 | 27.11 | 38.93 | 19.53 |
| 巫山县 | Wushan County | 23.11 | 62.21 | 16.81 | 29.57 | 11.42 | 15.02 | 24.56 | 11.21 |
| 巫溪县 | Wuxi County | 19.24 | 53.23 | 19.08 | 25.28 | 10.13 | 12.37 | 20.24 | 10.49 |
| 石柱县 | Shizhu County | 19.13 | 54.41 | 16.27 | 26.30 | 9.56 | 13.69 | 21.02 | 10.14 |
| 秀山县 | Xiushan County | 21.41 | 67.40 | 22.00 | 32.12 | 14.19 | 18.12 | 24.57 | 10.52 |
| 酉阳县 | Youyang County | 26.26 | 85.19 | 27.83 | 39.95 | 18.90 | 22.20 | 30.60 | 13.49 |
| 彭水县 | Pengshui County | 22.44 | 69.93 | 20.56 | 32.49 | 14.26 | 18.57 | 25.65 | 11.45 |

**表 20.1 续表 continued**

| 区 县 | Region | 出生（户籍统计） Birth (registration statistics) 人数（万人） Population (10 000 persons) | 出生率（‰） Birth Rate (‰) | 死亡（户籍统计） Mortality (registration statistics) 人数（万人） Population (10 000 persons) | 死亡率（‰） Mortality Rate (‰) | 自然增长（户籍统计） Natural Growth (registration statistics) 人数（万人） Population (10 000 persons) | 自然增长率（‰） Natural Growth Rate (‰) | 常住人口（万人） Resident Population (10 000 persons) | 城镇化率（%） Urban Rate (%) |
|---|---|---|---|---|---|---|---|---|---|
| **全 市** | **Total** | **20.84** | **6.10** | **24.37** | **7.14** | **-3.53** | **-1.04** | **3213.34** | **70.96** |
| 主城都市区 | The city proper of Chongqing | 11.84 | 6.02 | 13.88 | 7.07 | -2.04 | -1.05 | 2122.72 | 79.80 |
| 中心城区 | The central urban area of Chongqing | 5.19 | 7.06 | 3.55 | 4.83 | 1.64 | 2.23 | 1047.76 | 93.30 |
| 主城新区 | The new area of Chongqing city proper | 6.65 | 5.40 | 10.33 | 8.40 | -3.68 | -3.00 | 1074.96 | 66.65 |
| 渝东北三峡库区城镇群 | The city cluster of three gorges reservoir area in northeast Chongqing | 6.20 | 5.76 | 7.95 | 7.38 | -1.75 | -1.62 | 804.14 | 54.51 |
| 渝东南武陵山区城镇群 | The city cluster of Wuling mountain area in southeast Chongqing | 2.80 | 7.51 | 2.54 | 6.81 | 0.26 | 0.70 | 286.48 | 51.68 |
| 万州区 | Wanzhou District | 0.83 | 4.84 | 1.19 | 6.96 | -0.36 | -2.12 | 156.43 | 70.00 |
| 黔江区 | Qianjiang District | 0.43 | 7.73 | 0.34 | 6.22 | 0.09 | 1.51 | 49.24 | 60.89 |
| 涪陵区 | Fuling District | 0.56 | 4.93 | 0.93 | 8.29 | -0.37 | -3.36 | 111.52 | 73.36 |
| 渝中区 | Yuzhong District | 0.23 | 4.65 | 0.21 | 4.32 | 0.02 | 0.33 | 57.77 | 100.00 |
| 大渡口区 | Dadukou District | 0.19 | 6.62 | 0.16 | 5.66 | 0.03 | 0.96 | 43.56 | 97.80 |
| 江北区 | Jiangbei District | 0.45 | 6.96 | 0.22 | 3.42 | 0.23 | 3.54 | 94.54 | 99.40 |
| 沙坪坝区 | Shapingba District | 0.69 | 7.29 | 0.33 | 3.45 | 0.36 | 3.84 | 148.56 | 97.10 |
| 九龙坡区 | Jiulongpo District | 0.67 | 6.65 | 0.41 | 4.11 | 0.26 | 2.54 | 153.56 | 94.18 |
| 南岸区 | Nan'an District | 0.59 | 7.36 | 0.38 | 4.73 | 0.21 | 2.63 | 120.80 | 96.93 |
| 北碚区 | Beibei District | 0.38 | 5.77 | 0.59 | 8.99 | -0.21 | -3.22 | 84.00 | 87.57 |
| 渝北区 | Yubei District | 1.35 | 8.77 | 0.58 | 3.74 | 0.77 | 5.03 | 225.42 | 90.00 |
| 巴南区 | Ba'nan District | 0.64 | 6.58 | 0.67 | 6.92 | -0.03 | -0.34 | 119.55 | 84.31 |
| 长寿区 | Changshou District | 0.43 | 4.96 | 0.59 | 6.72 | -0.16 | -1.76 | 68.75 | 71.27 |
| 江津区 | Jiangjin District | 0.72 | 4.92 | 1.44 | 9.81 | -0.72 | -4.89 | 135.38 | 62.00 |
| 合川区 | Hechuan District | 0.68 | 4.54 | 1.43 | 9.59 | -0.75 | -5.05 | 123.40 | 65.00 |
| 永川区 | Yongchuan District | 0.63 | 5.52 | 0.91 | 7.98 | -0.28 | -2.46 | 114.68 | 71.64 |
| 南川区 | Nanchuan District | 0.38 | 5.60 | 0.52 | 7.71 | -0.14 | -2.11 | 57.12 | 62.24 |
| 綦江区 | Qijiang District | 0.64 | 5.49 | 1.01 | 8.63 | -0.37 | -3.14 | 100.66 | 69.01 |
| #綦江区（不含万盛） | Qijiang District (excluding Wansheng) | 0.50 | 5.49 | 0.81 | 8.86 | -0.31 | -3.37 | 77.00 | 65.71 |
| 大足区 | Dazu District | 0.72 | 6.70 | 0.84 | 7.84 | -0.12 | -1.14 | 83.44 | 62.63 |
| 璧山区 | Bishan District | 0.39 | 5.97 | 0.54 | 8.24 | -0.15 | -2.27 | 76.30 | 72.75 |
| 铜梁区 | Tongliang District | 0.44 | 5.18 | 0.71 | 8.41 | -0.27 | -3.23 | 68.80 | 63.92 |
| 潼南区 | Tongnan District | 0.61 | 6.41 | 0.73 | 7.75 | -0.12 | -1.34 | 68.11 | 60.51 |
| 荣昌区 | Rongchang District | 0.45 | 5.39 | 0.68 | 8.08 | -0.23 | -2.69 | 66.80 | 61.84 |
| 开州区 | Kaizhou District | 1.02 | 6.15 | 1.23 | 7.40 | -0.21 | -1.25 | 119.95 | 52.61 |
| 梁平区 | Liangping District | 0.49 | 5.35 | 0.74 | 8.07 | -0.25 | -2.72 | 64.30 | 51.96 |
| 武隆区 | Wulong District | 0.24 | 5.88 | 0.35 | 8.60 | -0.11 | -2.72 | 35.76 | 51.31 |
| 城口县 | Chengkou County | 0.16 | 6.57 | 0.18 | 7.05 | -0.02 | -0.48 | 19.85 | 42.27 |
| 丰都县 | Fengdu County | 0.39 | 4.92 | 0.68 | 8.55 | -0.29 | -3.63 | 55.30 | 51.03 |
| 垫江县 | Dianjiang County | 0.52 | 5.47 | 0.71 | 7.51 | -0.19 | -2.04 | 64.61 | 51.06 |
| 忠 县 | Zhongxian County | 0.46 | 4.79 | 0.80 | 8.31 | -0.34 | -3.52 | 71.53 | 50.72 |
| 云阳县 | Yunyang County | 0.88 | 6.66 | 0.91 | 6.86 | -0.03 | -0.20 | 92.62 | 54.84 |
| 奉节县 | Fengjie County | 0.72 | 6.92 | 0.71 | 6.83 | 0.01 | 0.09 | 74.42 | 51.59 |
| 巫山县 | Wushan County | 0.41 | 6.49 | 0.42 | 6.74 | -0.01 | -0.25 | 46.35 | 45.70 |
| 巫溪县 | Wuxi County | 0.32 | 6.09 | 0.38 | 7.20 | -0.06 | -1.11 | 38.78 | 41.44 |
| 石柱县 | Shizhu County | 0.36 | 6.63 | 0.39 | 7.09 | -0.03 | -0.46 | 38.69 | 59.06 |
| 秀山县 | Xiushan County | 0.55 | 8.16 | 0.44 | 6.58 | 0.11 | 1.58 | 49.74 | 47.69 |
| 酉阳县 | Youyang County | 0.66 | 7.77 | 0.54 | 6.32 | 0.12 | 1.45 | 60.67 | 44.01 |
| 彭水县 | Pengshui County | 0.56 | 8.01 | 0.48 | 6.86 | 0.08 | 1.15 | 52.38 | 50.52 |

# 表 20.2 各区县生产总值（2022 年）
## GROSS DOMESTIC PRODUCT BY REGION (2022)

（上年 =100）(preceding year=100)

| 区 县 | Region | 地区生产总值（万元）Gross Domestic Product (10000 yuan) | 第一产业 Primary Industry | 第二产业 Secondary Industry | 第三产业 Tertiary Industry | 人均地区生产总值（元）Per Capita GDP (yuan) |
|---|---|---|---|---|---|---|
| **全 市** | **Total** | **291290300** | **20120500** | **116938600** | **154231200** | **90663** |
| 主城都市区 | The city proper of Chongqing | 223524200 | 11096400 | 92322600 | 120105200 | 105402 |
| 中心城区 | The central urban area of Chongqing | 113564700 | 1290700 | 36706400 | 75567600 | 108844 |
| 主城新区 | The new area of Chongqing city proper | 109959500 | 9805700 | 55616200 | 44537600 | 102070 |
| 渝东北三峡库区城镇群 | The city cluster of three gorges reservoir area in northeast Chongqing | 51528700 | 6769300 | 19444600 | 25314800 | 63941 |
| 渝东南武陵山区城镇群 | The city cluster of Wuling mountain area in southeast Chongqing | 16286800 | 2254800 | 5171600 | 8860400 | 56881 |
| 万州区 | Wanzhou District | 11184349 | 1149736 | 3253057 | 6781556 | 71397 |
| 黔江区 | Qianjiang District | 2816670 | 358014 | 1043298 | 1415358 | 57424 |
| 涪陵区 | Fuling District | 15043670 | 924490 | 8699578 | 5419602 | 134655 |
| 渝中区 | Yuzhong District | 15609116 | 0 | 1267086 | 14342030 | 267738 |
| 大渡口区 | Dadukou District | 3388933 | 12329 | 1818071 | 1558533 | 78831 |
| 江北区 | Jiangbei District | 16027557 | 12655 | 4057373 | 11957529 | 170970 |
| 沙坪坝区 | Shapingba District | 11067267 | 54004 | 3332502 | 7680761 | 74552 |
| 九龙坡区 | Jiulongpo District | 17639398 | 77868 | 6171476 | 11390054 | 115117 |
| 南岸区 | Nan'an District | 9221301 | 45657 | 3322202 | 5853442 | 76462 |
| 北碚区 | Beibei District | 7420092 | 194289 | 3931103 | 3294700 | 88445 |
| 渝北区 | Yubei District | 22971141 | 315886 | 8216399 | 14438856 | 103010 |
| 巴南区 | Ba'nan District | 10219927 | 577944 | 4590083 | 5051900 | 85763 |
| 长寿区 | Changshou District | 9186302 | 644181 | 5650539 | 2891582 | 133164 |
| 江津区 | Jiangjin District | 13300177 | 1335071 | 7524700 | 4440406 | 97918 |
| 合川区 | Hechuan District | 10002845 | 1122653 | 3237221 | 5642971 | 80782 |
| 永川区 | Yongchuan District | 12028369 | 878445 | 6494338 | 4655586 | 104777 |
| 南川区 | Nanchuan District | 4214187 | 659913 | 1619974 | 1934300 | 73655 |
| 綦江区 | Qijiang District | 7707869 | 836603 | 3487456 | 3383810 | 76338 |
| #綦江区（不含万盛） | Qijiang District (excluding Wansheng) | 5313098 | 701431 | 2333259 | 2278408 | 68711 |
| 大足区 | Dazu District | 8172059 | 734797 | 3849327 | 3587935 | 97822 |
| 璧山区 | Bishan District | 9209495 | 428072 | 4505232 | 4276191 | 121066 |
| 铜梁区 | Tongliang District | 7336347 | 668803 | 3848745 | 2818799 | 106525 |
| 潼南区 | Tongnan District | 5585064 | 910525 | 2331620 | 2342919 | 81445 |
| 荣昌区 | Rongchang District | 8173028 | 662142 | 4367550 | 3143336 | 122168 |
| 开州区 | Kaizhou District | 6620342 | 925244 | 2549503 | 3145595 | 55073 |
| 梁平区 | Liangping District | 5771578 | 662467 | 2798351 | 2310760 | 89593 |
| 武隆区 | Wulong District | 2659424 | 324294 | 1094089 | 1241041 | 74483 |
| 城口县 | Chengkou County | 663069 | 133934 | 155973 | 373162 | 33446 |
| 丰都县 | Fengdu County | 3911704 | 552144 | 1550349 | 1809211 | 70545 |
| 垫江县 | Dianjiang County | 5306113 | 650889 | 2296995 | 2358229 | 81884 |
| 忠 县 | Zhongxian County | 5080952 | 600786 | 2271455 | 2208711 | 70726 |
| 云阳县 | Yunyang County | 5576907 | 741846 | 2207998 | 2627063 | 60060 |
| 奉节县 | Fengjie County | 3952465 | 690983 | 1397371 | 1864111 | 53000 |
| 巫山县 | Wushan County | 2222393 | 384505 | 665558 | 1172330 | 47912 |
| 巫溪县 | Wuxi County | 1238761 | 276856 | 297770 | 664135 | 31869 |
| 石柱县 | Shizhu County | 2090654 | 375181 | 594405 | 1121068 | 53959 |
| 秀山县 | Xiushan County | 3582099 | 347990 | 1100371 | 2133738 | 72096 |
| 酉阳县 | Youyang County | 2316612 | 428708 | 337970 | 1549934 | 38168 |
| 彭水县 | Pengshui County | 2821343 | 420605 | 1001396 | 1399342 | 53791 |

**表 20.2 续表 continued**

（上年 =100）(preceding year=100)

| 区 县 | Region | 地区生产总值指数（可比价）Indices of GDP (constant prices) | 第一产业 Primary Industry | 第二产业 Secondary Industry | 第三产业 Tertiary Industry | 人均地区生产总值指数 Indices of Per Capita GDP |
|---|---|---|---|---|---|---|
| **全 市** | **Total** | **102.6** | **104.0** | **103.3** | **101.9** | **102.5** |
| 主城都市区 | The city proper of Chongqing | 102.3 | 103.4 | 102.7 | 101.8 | 102.1 |
| 中心城区 | The central urban area of Chongqing | 101.7 | 103.8 | 101.4 | 101.6 | 101.1 |
| 主城新区 | The new area of Chongqing city proper | 103.0 | 103.3 | 103.6 | 102.3 | 103.2 |
| 渝东北三峡库区城镇群 | The city cluster of three gorges reservoir area in northeast Chongqing | 104.1 | 105.0 | 105.9 | 102.6 | 104.3 |
| 渝东南武陵山区城镇群 | The city cluster of Wuling mountain area in southeast Chongqing | 103.2 | 104.3 | 103.6 | 102.6 | 103.2 |
| 万州区 | Wanzhou District | 103.5 | 105.9 | 107.3 | 101.5 | 103.7 |
| 黔江区 | Qianjiang District | 103.2 | 105.5 | 104.7 | 101.5 | 102.7 |
| 涪陵区 | Fuling District | 102.6 | 103.7 | 102.2 | 103.1 | 102.8 |
| 渝中区 | Yuzhong District | 101.9 |  | 101.3 | 101.9 | 102.7 |
| 大渡口区 | Dadukou District | 104.7 | 106.7 | 111.9 | 97.3 | 103.2 |
| 江北区 | Jiangbei District | 103.7 | 103.7 | 112.6 | 101.0 | 102.7 |
| 沙坪坝区 | Shapingba District | 101.9 | 101.7 | 97.6 | 103.8 | 101.7 |
| 九龙坡区 | Jiulongpo District | 102.7 | 101.6 | 104.5 | 101.8 | 102.5 |
| 南岸区 | Nan'an District | 100.1 | 101.1 | 100.7 | 99.7 | 99.7 |
| 北碚区 | Beibei District | 99.1 | 101.9 | 92.0 | 109.5 | 98.8 |
| 渝北区 | Yubei District | 100.3 | 104.8 | 97.5 | 101.9 | 99.0 |
| 巴南区 | Ba'nan District | 102.0 | 104.5 | 104.8 | 99.4 | 101.3 |
| 长寿区 | Changshou District | 102.6 | 103.0 | 102.4 | 102.9 | 103.0 |
| 江津区 | Jiangjin District | 103.2 | 103.9 | 104.2 | 101.5 | 103.5 |
| 合川区 | Hechuan District | 102.6 | 103.6 | 102.8 | 102.2 | 103.0 |
| 永川区 | Yongchuan District | 103.5 | 103.7 | 105.4 | 100.8 | 103.6 |
| 南川区 | Nanchuan District | 103.4 | 102.6 | 103.5 | 103.7 | 103.6 |
| 綦江区 | Qijiang District | 103.0 | 103.0 | 104.8 | 101.3 | 103.3 |
| #綦江区（不含万盛） | Qijiang District (excluding Wansheng) | 103.0 | 103.2 | 104.9 | 101.2 | 103.4 |
| 大足区 | Dazu District | 103.3 | 103.6 | 104.6 | 101.9 | 103.4 |
| 璧山区 | Bishan District | 103.6 | 103.9 | 104.8 | 102.1 | 103.2 |
| 铜梁区 | Tongliang District | 103.0 | 102.1 | 104.0 | 101.8 | 102.9 |
| 潼南区 | Tongnan District | 103.0 | 105.1 | 104.1 | 101.1 | 103.6 |
| 荣昌区 | Rongchang District | 102.7 | 100.6 | 100.9 | 105.7 | 102.8 |
| 开州区 | Kaizhou District | 104.4 | 104.8 | 104.0 | 104.7 | 104.7 |
| 梁平区 | Liangping District | 104.2 | 106.1 | 105.9 | 101.7 | 104.3 |
| 武隆区 | Wulong District | 102.5 | 102.4 | 104.1 | 101.3 | 102.5 |
| 城口县 | Chengkou County | 103.9 | 102.0 | 110.8 | 102.2 | 103.7 |
| 丰都县 | Fengdu County | 104.0 | 104.3 | 105.4 | 102.7 | 104.3 |
| 垫江县 | Dianjiang County | 104.3 | 104.1 | 106.3 | 102.7 | 104.6 |
| 忠 县 | Zhongxian County | 104.1 | 103.7 | 107.5 | 101.0 | 104.5 |
| 云阳县 | Yunyang County | 104.7 | 106.3 | 106.9 | 102.6 | 104.9 |
| 奉节县 | Fengjie County | 104.5 | 104.7 | 102.3 | 106.1 | 104.6 |
| 巫山县 | Wushan County | 104.1 | 106.3 | 104.2 | 103.4 | 104.0 |
| 巫溪县 | Wuxi County | 102.7 | 103.7 | 105.2 | 101.3 | 102.9 |
| 石柱县 | Shizhu County | 104.0 | 105.6 | 106.4 | 102.3 | 104.3 |
| 秀山县 | Xiushan County | 103.5 | 103.1 | 105.2 | 102.8 | 103.5 |
| 酉阳县 | Youyang County | 102.3 | 103.7 | 102.6 | 101.9 | 102.4 |
| 彭水县 | Pengshui County | 103.5 | 105.5 | 99.3 | 105.9 | 104.0 |

# 表 20.3 各区县农业和农村经济(2022 年)
AGRICULTURE AND RURAL ECONOMY BY REGION (2022)

| 区 县 | Region | 农林牧渔业总产值(万元) Gross Output Value (10 000 yuan) | 农 业 Farming | 林 业 Forestry | 牧 业 Animal Husbandry | 渔 业 Fishery | 农林牧渔服务业 Farming, Forestry, Animal Husbandry and Fishery Services | 农林牧渔业总产值指数(可比价)(上年=100) Indices of Gross Output (constant prices) (preceding year=100) |
|---|---|---|---|---|---|---|---|---|
| **全 市** | **Total** | **30684459** | **18817834** | **1764195** | **8009449** | **1369934** | **723047** | **104.6** |
| 主城都市区 | The city proper of Chongqing | 16389884 | 10263575 | 760758 | 4094133 | 930994 | 340424 | |
| 中心城区 | The central urban area of Chongqing | 1792239 | 1345967 | 73250 | 189738 | 106912 | 76373 | |
| 主城新区 | The new area of Chongqing city proper | 14597645 | 8917608 | 687509 | 3904395 | 824081 | 264051 | |
| 渝东北三峡库区城镇群 | The city cluster of three gorges reservoir area in northeast Chongqing | 10546878 | 6274263 | 710114 | 2895734 | 369526 | 297241 | |
| 渝东南武陵山区城镇群 | The city cluster of Wuling mountain area in southeast Chongqing | 3747697 | 2279995 | 293323 | 1019582 | 69414 | 85383 | |
| 万州区 | Wanzhou District | 1698076 | 1139711 | 96597 | 366669 | 61688 | 33412 | 106.4 |
| 黔江区 | Qianjiang District | 598504 | 341841 | 50022 | 183802 | 9286 | 13553 | 106.0 |
| 涪陵区 | Fuling District | 1395841 | 994462 | 73578 | 238013 | 57296 | 32492 | 104.1 |
| 渝中区 | Yuzhong District | | | | | | | |
| 大渡口区 | Dadukou District | 17977 | 11749 | 3254 | 1014 | 467 | 1494 | 106.9 |
| 江北区 | Jiangbei District | 18412 | 10276 | 6006 | 1028 | 552 | 551 | 104.1 |
| 沙坪坝区 | Shapingba District | 86372 | 55557 | 1369 | 4607 | 9101 | 15737 | 102.7 |
| 九龙坡区 | Jiulongpo District | 108549 | 78826 | 2133 | 7391 | 12696 | 7504 | 101.9 |
| 南岸区 | Nan'an District | 60567 | 52824 | 1868 | 1432 | 2378 | 2065 | 101.6 |
| 北碚区 | Beibei District | 260337 | 220294 | 4246 | 20064 | 7651 | 8081 | 102.3 |
| 渝北区 | Yubei District | 446967 | 330827 | 31514 | 46016 | 18061 | 20550 | 105.4 |
| 巴南区 | Ba'nan District | 793059 | 585613 | 22860 | 108187 | 56007 | 20392 | 105.1 |
| 长寿区 | Changshou District | 982745 | 507670 | 19824 | 326272 | 106942 | 22038 | 103.4 |
| 江津区 | Jiangjin District | 1897378 | 1354835 | 58120 | 387478 | 67529 | 29417 | 104.3 |
| 合川区 | Hechuan District | 1691275 | 910203 | 60510 | 563788 | 129495 | 27280 | 104.1 |
| 永川区 | Yongchuan District | 1283740 | 760008 | 54685 | 351267 | 100223 | 17558 | 104.1 |
| 南川区 | Nanchuan District | 985959 | 606469 | 79996 | 246455 | 28917 | 24122 | 103.0 |
| 綦江区 | Qijiang District | 1289671 | 920065 | 91143 | 233856 | 26985 | 17622 | 103.4 |
| #綦江区(不含万盛) | Qijiang District (excluding Wansheng) | 1085334 | 782485 | 55455 | 208163 | 23502 | 15730 | 103.6 |
| 大足区 | Dazu District | 1071108 | 616479 | 77109 | 295816 | 68632 | 13072 | 104.1 |
| 璧山区 | Bishan District | 655087 | 348504 | 7787 | 260294 | 30109 | 8392 | 104.3 |
| 铜梁区 | Tongliang District | 1022296 | 468030 | 33594 | 394520 | 98994 | 27158 | 102.6 |
| 潼南区 | Tongnan District | 1314593 | 910355 | 83933 | 225553 | 80489 | 14263 | 105.5 |
| 荣昌区 | Rongchang District | 1007952 | 520528 | 47230 | 381085 | 28473 | 30636 | 101.0 |
| 开州区 | Kaizhou District | 1443525 | 844572 | 76286 | 395716 | 90481 | 36470 | 105.3 |
| 梁平区 | Liangping District | 1014256 | 595464 | 50682 | 302576 | 47494 | 18040 | 106.7 |
| 武隆区 | Wulong District | 546616 | 351368 | 26601 | 132132 | 14888 | 21627 | 102.9 |
| 城口县 | Chengkou County | 219930 | 107475 | 26417 | 77980 | 2230 | 5828 | 102.7 |
| 丰都县 | Fengdu County | 869001 | 420109 | 103582 | 290584 | 36358 | 18368 | 104.9 |
| 垫江县 | Dianjiang County | 1025009 | 656838 | 31102 | 258611 | 40014 | 38444 | 104.5 |
| 忠 县 | Zhongxian County | 931789 | 539237 | 52775 | 278497 | 43799 | 17480 | 104.1 |
| 云阳县 | Yunyang County | 1217856 | 628529 | 82361 | 396548 | 33000 | 77417 | 107.2 |
| 奉节县 | Fengjie County | 1063865 | 752235 | 30777 | 245483 | 8584 | 26787 | 105.4 |
| 巫山县 | Wushan County | 620386 | 342776 | 99027 | 157358 | 2744 | 18481 | 107.1 |
| 巫溪县 | Wuxi County | 443185 | 247318 | 60508 | 125711 | 3134 | 6514 | 104.0 |
| 石柱县 | Shizhu County | 590461 | 430406 | 29490 | 103645 | 19815 | 7106 | 106.0 |
| 秀山县 | Xiushan County | 581368 | 323771 | 41614 | 178626 | 15754 | 21602 | 103.7 |
| 酉阳县 | Youyang County | 720064 | 390621 | 93479 | 217857 | 7551 | 10557 | 104.2 |
| 彭水县 | Pengshui County | 710684 | 441989 | 52118 | 203520 | 2120 | 10938 | 106.1 |

表 20.3 续表 1 continued 1

| 区 县 | Region | 农作物播种面积（公顷）Sown Areas of Farm Crops (hectare) | #粮 食 Grain | 农用化肥施用量（折纯）（吨）Consumption of Chemical Fertilizer (net) (ton) | 农药使用量（吨）Consumption of Chemical Pesticides (ton) | 粮食产量（吨）Output of Grain (ton) | 油料产量（吨）Output of Oil-bearing Crops (ton) |
|---|---|---|---|---|---|---|---|
| **全 市** | **Total** | **3479024** | **2046710** | **887412.50** | **15975.33** | **10728378** | **708492** |
| 主城都市区 | The city proper of Chongqing | 1560482 | 877027 | 410201.04 | 7870.38 | 5233452 | 292662 |
| 中心城区 | The central urban area of Chongqing | 139420 | 74988 | 39431.74 | 577.21 | 396084 | 6670 |
| 主城新区 | The new area of Chongqing city proper | 1421062 | 802039 | 370769.30 | 7293.17 | 4837368 | 285993 |
| 渝东北三峡库区城镇群 | The city cluster of three gorges reservoir area in northeast Chongqing | 1271954 | 806949 | 321932.35 | 5588.99 | 3882470 | 268135 |
| 渝东南武陵山区城镇群 | The city cluster of Wuling mountain area in southeast Chongqing | 646587 | 362735 | 155279.11 | 2515.96 | 1612456 | 147694 |
| 万州区 | Wanzhou District | 171860 | 100639 | 37763 | 1066 | 490133 | 21976 |
| 黔江区 | Qianjiang District | 81170 | 49334 | 23123 | 579 | 231312 | 21034 |
| 涪陵区 | Fuling District | 182634 | 94016 | 38310 | 1261 | 443924 | 6600 |
| 渝中区 | Yuzhong District | | | | | | |
| 大渡口区 | Dadukou District | 936 | 220 | 835 | 8 | 981 | 118 |
| 江北区 | Jiangbei District | 873 | 505 | 326 | 6 | 2297 | 21 |
| 沙坪坝区 | Shapingba District | 5527 | 2640 | 2398 | 26 | 10792 | 241 |
| 九龙坡区 | Jiulongpo District | 6986 | 2690 | 1783 | 98 | 11294 | 1289 |
| 南岸区 | Nan'an District | 866 | 372 | 1155 | 8 | 1982 | 6 |
| 北碚区 | Beibei District | 18689 | 9209 | 7631 | 180 | 43761 | 1012 |
| 渝北区 | Yubei District | 38569 | 21019 | 11478 | 80 | 109817 | 2723 |
| 巴南区 | Ba'nan District | 66974 | 38334 | 13826 | 173 | 215162 | 1261 |
| 长寿区 | Changshou District | 84424 | 61322 | 19825 | 260 | 324404 | 13054 |
| 江津区 | Jiangjin District | 152745 | 97290 | 46868 | 1016 | 627585 | 20274 |
| 合川区 | Hechuan District | 177457 | 113721 | 28932 | 522 | 683865 | 32459 |
| 永川区 | Yongchuan District | 109397 | 66900 | 51430 | 1634 | 476305 | 26574 |
| 南川区 | Nanchuan District | 91278 | 49396 | 32203 | 371 | 306545 | 17864 |
| 綦江区 | Qijiang District | 119455 | 70246 | 37067 | 432 | 397526 | 16201 |
| #綦江区（不含万盛） | Qijiang District (excluding Wansheng) | 100076 | 59044 | 29440 | 294 | 347336 | 14604 |
| 大足区 | Dazu District | 115657 | 63248 | 26477 | 501 | 412028 | 50522 |
| 璧山区 | Bishan District | 57775 | 27697 | 8945 | 105 | 166315 | 6118 |
| 铜梁区 | Tongliang District | 92832 | 56347 | 34691 | 386 | 347483 | 16420 |
| 潼南区 | Tongnan District | 155922 | 56748 | 32460 | 345 | 368129 | 53480 |
| 荣昌区 | Rongchang District | 81486 | 45112 | 13560 | 460 | 283258 | 26426 |
| 开州区 | Kaizhou District | 175643 | 116519 | 50735 | 670 | 568744 | 39458 |
| 梁平区 | Liangping District | 101098 | 66907 | 42363 | 1178 | 354985 | 19943 |
| 武隆区 | Wulong District | 89980 | 49233 | 16217 | 274 | 188180 | 11119 |
| 城口县 | Chengkou County | 42457 | 25498 | 5331 | 38 | 89624 | 4034 |
| 丰都县 | Fengdu County | 108357 | 68411 | 25437 | 289 | 328079 | 20265 |
| 垫江县 | Dianjiang County | 106852 | 65898 | 33909 | 445 | 404044 | 23115 |
| 忠 县 | Zhongxian County | 113427 | 76466 | 31121 | 552 | 402031 | 39651 |
| 云阳县 | Yunyang County | 137116 | 91069 | 25389 | 543 | 403254 | 36677 |
| 奉节县 | Fengjie County | 133750 | 80109 | 26938 | 617 | 399079 | 29504 |
| 巫山县 | Wushan County | 88944 | 55748 | 17665 | 128 | 206887 | 19711 |
| 巫溪县 | Wuxi County | 92451 | 59686 | 25281 | 63 | 235609 | 13801 |
| 石柱县 | Shizhu County | 83024 | 45531 | 24011 | 574 | 221137 | 7010 |
| 秀山县 | Xiushan County | 114669 | 52604 | 26813 | 430 | 294000 | 38383 |
| 酉阳县 | Youyang County | 147938 | 85370 | 26204 | 251 | 366814 | 35101 |
| 彭水县 | Pengshui County | 129806 | 80662 | 38911 | 408 | 311013 | 35047 |

**表 20.3 续表 2 continued 2**

| 区 县 | Region | 甘蔗产量（吨）Output of Sugarcane (ton) | 烟叶产量（吨）Output of Tobacco (ton) | 茶叶产量（吨）Output of Tea (ton) | 水果产量（吨）Output of Fruits (ton) | 蔬菜产量（吨）Output of Vegetables (ton) | 猪肉产量（吨）Output of Pork (ton) |
|---|---|---|---|---|---|---|---|
| **全 市** | **Total** | **83243** | **55235** | **53027** | **5932844** | **22723637** | **1499649** |
| 主城都市区 | The city proper of Chongqing | 53645 | 2078 | 27791 | 2140848 | 13559448 | 629360 |
| 中心城区 | The central urban area of Chongqing | | 474 | 4263 | 199320 | 1225426 | 26727 |
| 主城新区 | The new area of Chongqing city proper | 53645 | 1604 | 23529 | 1941528 | 12334022 | 602633 |
| 渝东北三峡库区城镇群 | The city cluster of three gorges reservoir area in northeast Chongqing | 29341 | 21260 | 8020 | 3395196 | 6242877 | 620672 |
| 渝东南武陵山区城镇群 | The city cluster of Wuling mountain area in southeast Chongqing | 257 | 31897 | 17216 | 396799 | 2921312 | 249617 |
| 万州区 | Wanzhou District | 470 | 1380 | 2537 | 617768 | 1310269 | 86969 |
| 黔江区 | Qianjiang District | | 4208 | 501 | 74598 | 272034 | 61400 |
| 涪陵区 | Fuling District | 254 | 604 | 865 | 225299 | 2559105 | 56627 |
| 渝中区 | Yuzhong District | | | | | | |
| 大渡口区 | Dadukou District | | | | 2328 | 16631 | 40 |
| 江北区 | Jiangbei District | | | 3 | 1340 | 6419 | 131 |
| 沙坪坝区 | Shapingba District | | | | 6494 | 41885 | 329 |
| 九龙坡区 | Jiulongpo District | | | | 13908 | 68434 | 1147 |
| 南岸区 | Nan'an District | | | | 3939 | 10102 | 196 |
| 北碚区 | Beibei District | | | 39 | 24247 | 193472 | 2639 |
| 渝北区 | Yubei District | | 68 | 15 | 73835 | 312537 | 5887 |
| 巴南区 | Ba'nan District | | 406 | 4205 | 73229 | 575946 | 16358 |
| 长寿区 | Changshou District | 4000 | | 47 | 238930 | 390312 | 46419 |
| 江津区 | Jiangjin District | 27934 | 198 | 1884 | 274571 | 1107662 | 64761 |
| 合川区 | Hechuan District | 684 | 99 | 199 | 175581 | 1072632 | 89685 |
| 永川区 | Yongchuan District | 41 | | 8699 | 150465 | 756988 | 32665 |
| 南川区 | Nanchuan District | | | 4537 | 69302 | 546447 | 51080 |
| 綦江区 | Qijiang District | 346 | 677 | 1673 | 67780 | 851376 | 48649 |
| #綦江区（不含万盛） | Qijiang District (excluding Wansheng) | 346 | 570 | 938 | 56395 | 641825 | 43891 |
| 大足区 | Dazu District | 5348 | 26 | 693 | 77157 | 490588 | 44898 |
| 璧山区 | Bishan District | 59 | | 904 | 181440 | 851397 | 17243 |
| 铜梁区 | Tongliang District | 679 | | 155 | 75534 | 799943 | 39108 |
| 潼南区 | Tongnan District | 4206 | | 183 | 370564 | 2282352 | 61332 |
| 荣昌区 | Rongchang District | 10093 | | 3691 | 34906 | 625222 | 50166 |
| 开州区 | Kaizhou District | 15033 | 208 | 851 | 626253 | 641573 | 89010 |
| 梁平区 | Liangping District | 1844 | 61 | 286 | 222457 | 707304 | 53288 |
| 武隆区 | Wulong District | 118 | 4184 | 827 | 71128 | 698344 | 39345 |
| 城口县 | Chengkou County | | 38 | 717 | 6918 | 70737 | 11021 |
| 丰都县 | Fengdu County | 1922 | 2614 | 185 | 95919 | 567536 | 44214 |
| 垫江县 | Dianjiang County | 4905 | 440 | 166 | 143472 | 853369 | 54925 |
| 忠 县 | Zhongxian County | 3906 | | 732 | 515270 | 389747 | 55951 |
| 云阳县 | Yunyang County | 1261 | 453 | 357 | 409008 | 605055 | 76545 |
| 奉节县 | Fengjie County | | 4655 | 614 | 513096 | 479040 | 57055 |
| 巫山县 | Wushan County | | 6910 | 586 | 186384 | 308829 | 45690 |
| 巫溪县 | Wuxi County | | 4501 | 989 | 58652 | 309418 | 46004 |
| 石柱县 | Shizhu County | 18 | 3545 | 102 | 41480 | 515375 | 21453 |
| 秀山县 | Xiushan County | | 156 | 12675 | 104041 | 462187 | 27516 |
| 酉阳县 | Youyang County | | 11234 | 2800 | 74649 | 495582 | 52012 |
| 彭水县 | Pengshui County | 121 | 8570 | 310 | 30904 | 477790 | 47891 |

# 表 20.4 各区县工业（2022 年）
## INDUSTRY BY REGION (2022)

| 区 县 | Region | 工业企业资产总计（万元） Total Assets of Industrial Enterprises (10 000 yuan) | 主营业务收入（万元） Revenue from Principal Business (10 000 yuan) | 利润总额（万元） Total Profits (10 000 yuan) |
|---|---|---|---|---|
| **全 市** | **Total** | **275353627** | **264172780** | **18296765** |
| 主城都市区 | The city proper of Chongqing | 244346889 | 241651806 | 16128893 |
| 中心城区 | The central urban area of Chongqing | 134524652 | 131129399 | 5704142 |
| 主城新区 | The new area of Chongqing city proper | 109822237 | 110522407 | 10424751 |
| 渝东北三峡库区城镇群 | The city cluster of three gorges reservoir area in northeast Chongqing | 21827002 | 17726159 | 1537899 |
| 渝东南武陵山区城镇群 | The city cluster of Wuling mountain area in southeast Chongqing | 9179736 | 4794815 | 629974 |
| 万州区 | Wanzhou District | 7596711 | 4841551 | 425029 |
| 黔江区 | Qianjiang District | 2415378 | 1357815 | 118124 |
| 涪陵区 | Fuling District | 19619916 | 21768776 | 3463568 |
| 渝中区 | Yuzhong District | 354276 | 215424 | 5592 |
| 大渡口区 | Dadukou District | 4850920 | 3870300 | 581534 |
| 江北区 | Jiangbei District | 21841983 | 16801775 | 189750 |
| 沙坪坝区 | Shapingba District | 14549205 | 25724616 | 437969 |
| 九龙坡区 | Jiulongpo District | 18848800 | 17273571 | 1178329 |
| 南岸区 | Nan'an District | 10336510 | 9548288 | 626669 |
| 北碚区 | Beibei District | 19376726 | 9279608 | 818830 |
| 渝北区 | Yubei District | 35656887 | 38884204 | 969903 |
| 巴南区 | Ba'nan District | 8709344 | 9531613 | 895566 |
| 长寿区 | Changshou District | 15853563 | 14540635 | 1140772 |
| 江津区 | Jiangjin District | 17788401 | 17742162 | 1395418 |
| 合川区 | Hechuan District | 7090373 | 4080462 | 174995 |
| 永川区 | Yongchuan District | 12417671 | 16234821 | 1869840 |
| 南川区 | Nanchuan District | 3114503 | 2585690 | 147065 |
| 綦江区 | Qijiang District | 5647755 | 5293920 | 346984 |
| #綦江区（不含万盛） | Qijiang District (excluding Wansheng) | 2900188 | 2477156 | 92307 |
| 大足区 | Dazu District | 5330688 | 4233458 | 274992 |
| 璧山区 | Bishan District | 11317938 | 11208070 | 707094 |
| 铜梁区 | Tongliang District | 5088787 | 7158523 | 405014 |
| 潼南区 | Tongnan District | 2079667 | 1296412 | 77411 |
| 荣昌区 | Rongchang District | 4472976 | 4379479 | 421598 |
| 开州区 | Kaizhou District | 1974443 | 2774918 | 111437 |
| 梁平区 | Liangping District | 1658769 | 1719203 | 123762 |
| 武隆区 | Wulong District | 1460649 | 529465 | 71553 |
| 城口县 | Chengkou County | 452912 | 133124 | -1869 |
| 丰都县 | Fengdu County | 1635817 | 1054135 | 75502 |
| 垫江县 | Dianjiang County | 1772201 | 2133908 | 267160 |
| 忠 县 | Zhongxian County | 2212406 | 1905747 | 253741 |
| 云阳县 | Yunyang County | 1613427 | 2291098 | 228133 |
| 奉节县 | Fengjie County | 1612896 | 571057 | 51812 |
| 巫山县 | Wushan County | 533758 | 183268 | 11734 |
| 巫溪县 | Wuxi County | 763662 | 118152 | -8543 |
| 石柱县 | Shizhu County | 1337721 | 811632 | 146910 |
| 秀山县 | Xiushan County | 1245618 | 1306253 | 182823 |
| 酉阳县 | Youyang County | 720449 | 267471 | 3727 |
| 彭水县 | Pengshui County | 1999920 | 522178 | 106838 |

**表 20.4 续表 continued**

| 区 县 | Region | 总资产贡献率（%）<br>Ratio of Total Assets to Industrial Output Value (%) | 资产负债率（%）<br>Asset-liability Ratio (%) | 产品销售率（%）<br>Sales as Percentage of Output (%) | 全员劳动生产率（元/人年）<br>Overall Labor Productivity (yuan/person-year) |
|---|---|---|---|---|---|
| **全 市** | **Total** | **9.9** | **57.0** | **97.5** | **457817** |
| 主城都市区 | The city proper of Chongqing | 9.7 | 57.3 | 97.6 | 449455 |
| 中心城区 | The central urban area of Chongqing | 7.0 | 60.1 | 98.4 | 385628 |
| 主城新区 | The new area of Chongqing city proper | 13.1 | 53.8 | 97.0 | 500741 |
| 渝东北三峡库区城镇群 | The city cluster of three gorges reservoir area in northeast Chongqing | 10.0 | 52.8 | 95.2 | 500106 |
| 渝东南武陵山区城镇群 | The city cluster of Wuling mountain area in southeast Chongqing | 14.8 | 60.7 | 97.7 | 677435 |
| 万州区 | Wanzhou District | 7.8 | 54.8 | 95.7 | 430468 |
| 黔江区 | Qianjiang District | 25.3 | 57.8 | 98.1 | 1372387 |
| 涪陵区 | Fuling District | 22.9 | 47.4 | 96.5 | 1055424 |
| 渝中区 | Yuzhong District | 3.5 | 52.8 | 100.0 | 551409 |
| 大渡口区 | Dadukou District | 15.6 | 55.0 | 98.1 | 368920 |
| 江北区 | Jiangbei District | 4.4 | 64.1 | 98.9 | 517398 |
| 沙坪坝区 | Shapingba District | 4.2 | 70.5 | 100.1 | 246533 |
| 九龙坡区 | Jiulongpo District | 8.1 | 52.2 | 97.4 | 485815 |
| 南岸区 | Nan'an District | 13.0 | 65.1 | 107.1 | 464342 |
| 北碚区 | Beibei District | 5.7 | 42.6 | 98.6 | 372348 |
| 渝北区 | Yubei District | 5.1 | 68.0 | 97.2 | 352631 |
| 巴南区 | Ba'nan District | 14.3 | 53.6 | 90.1 | 434625 |
| 长寿区 | Changshou District | 9.6 | 49.5 | 98.8 | 810389 |
| 江津区 | Jiangjin District | 11.4 | 54.6 | 96.1 | 510025 |
| 合川区 | Hechuan District | 5.1 | 61.2 | 93.9 | 370303 |
| 永川区 | Yongchuan District | 18.8 | 49.7 | 98.7 | 520710 |
| 南川区 | Nanchuan District | 9.4 | 63.1 | 96.8 | 524221 |
| 綦江区 | Qijiang District | 10.1 | 67.0 | 96.4 | 417264 |
| #綦江区（不含万盛） | Qijiang District (excluding Wansheng) | 6.6 | 70.1 | 97.8 | 384861 |
| 大足区 | Dazu District | 7.3 | 51.7 | 97.6 | 347946 |
| 璧山区 | Bishan District | 8.6 | 66.7 | 97.9 | 318444 |
| 铜梁区 | Tongliang District | 11.8 | 54.8 | 95.2 | 389368 |
| 潼南区 | Tongnan District | 5.8 | 55.5 | 95.5 | 567454 |
| 荣昌区 | Rongchang District | 15.2 | 39.1 | 96.9 | 426399 |
| 开州区 | Kaizhou District | 10.0 | 56.2 | 99.1 | 416249 |
| 梁平区 | Liangping District | 9.8 | 40.7 | 97.7 | 672569 |
| 武隆区 | Wulong District | 8.6 | 65.4 | 97.4 | 596225 |
| 城口县 | Chengkou County | 1.5 | 64.8 | 102.5 | 366081 |
| 丰都县 | Fengdu County | 6.6 | 49.5 | 72.8 | 505247 |
| 垫江县 | Dianjiang County | 19.8 | 39.9 | 97.6 | 478798 |
| 忠 县 | Zhongxian County | 13.9 | 53.8 | 97.1 | 841933 |
| 云阳县 | Yunyang County | 20.9 | 43.3 | 96.5 | 636043 |
| 奉节县 | Fengjie County | 5.3 | 58.5 | 98.6 | 378072 |
| 巫山县 | Wushan County | 4.3 | 62.8 | 96.0 | 264461 |
| 巫溪县 | Wuxi County | -0.1 | 79.7 | 93.2 | 258165 |
| 石柱县 | Shizhu County | 15.0 | 66.0 | 97.8 | 492827 |
| 秀山县 | Xiushan County | 18.8 | 50.5 | 100.5 | 463286 |
| 酉阳县 | Youyang County | 2.7 | 74.1 | 88.7 | 340231 |
| 彭水县 | Pengshui County | 8.1 | 58.9 | 95.5 | 719094 |

# 表 20.5 各区县建筑业（2022 年）
CONSTRUCTION BY REGION (2022)

| 区 县 | Region | 企业数（个）Number of Construction Enterprises (unit) | 年末从业人数（万人）Number of Employed Persons at Year-end (10 000 persons) | 总产值（万元）Gross Output Value (10 000 yuan) | 房屋建筑施工面积（万平方米）Floor Space under Construction (10 000 sq.m) | 房屋建筑竣工面积（万平方米）Floor Space Completed (10 000 sq.m) | #住 宅 Residential Buildings |
|---|---|---|---|---|---|---|---|
| **全 市** | **Total** | **3914** | **195.56** | **97469574** | **34968.29** | **11769.81** | **8192.06** |
| 主城都市区 | The city proper of Chongqing | 2647 | 128.25 | 68919318 | 29594.89 | 9107.25 | 6417.06 |
| 中心城区 | The central urban area of Chongqing | 1326 | 48.43 | 36852744 | 19239.40 | 4129.44 | 2777.76 |
| 主城新区 | The new area of Chongqing city proper | 1321 | 79.81 | 32066574 | 10355.48 | 4977.81 | 3639.30 |
| 渝东北三峡库区城镇群 | The city cluster of three gorges reservoir area in northeast Chongqing | 966 | 61.12 | 25833661 | 4962.20 | 2407.68 | 1668.98 |
| 渝东南武陵山区城镇群 | The city cluster of Wuling mountain area in southeast Chongqing | 301 | 6.20 | 2716596 | 411.20 | 254.88 | 106.01 |
| 万州区 | Wanzhou District | 218 | 5.69 | 2383646 | 919.72 | 128.65 | 106.91 |
| 黔江区 | Qianjiang District | 80 | 0.93 | 335805 | 62.30 | 26.66 | 6.69 |
| 涪陵区 | Fuling District | 183 | 11.24 | 5252569 | 945.09 | 353.35 | 251.83 |
| 渝中区 | Yuzhong District | 153 | 8.41 | 5106666 | 2966.42 | 654.41 | 377.52 |
| 大渡口区 | Dadukou District | 65 | 0.91 | 3014805 | 1628.03 | 232.96 | 132.92 |
| 江北区 | Jiangbei District | 80 | 2.16 | 1334155 | 401.91 | 158.98 | 92.03 |
| 沙坪坝区 | Shapingba District | 152 | 4.00 | 2884613 | 1157.12 | 292.35 | 205.34 |
| 九龙坡区 | Jiulongpo District | 220 | 5.74 | 4376060 | 2234.28 | 440.20 | 299.63 |
| 南岸区 | Nan'an District | 111 | 2.81 | 4103263 | 2642.09 | 646.95 | 472.73 |
| 北碚区 | Beibei District | 95 | 3.39 | 1739858 | 414.18 | 251.75 | 185.63 |
| 渝北区 | Yubei District | 324 | 14.18 | 9970574 | 5717.38 | 806.68 | 466.76 |
| 巴南区 | Ba'nan District | 126 | 6.83 | 4322751 | 2077.99 | 645.16 | 545.20 |
| 长寿区 | Changshou District | 56 | 2.42 | 3152334 | 2048.04 | 653.72 | 631.01 |
| 江津区 | Jiangjin District | 103 | 15.05 | 5345706 | 2224.59 | 1082.18 | 859.07 |
| 合川区 | Hechuan District | 156 | 7.29 | 3155681 | 910.45 | 481.10 | 357.17 |
| 永川区 | Yongchuan District | 150 | 10.75 | 4581947 | 1231.18 | 710.74 | 460.49 |
| 南川区 | Nanchuan District | 64 | 1.24 | 535739 | 104.15 | 19.06 | 8.97 |
| 綦江区 | Qijiang District | 183 | 3.63 | 871625 | 186.96 | 111.64 | 53.66 |
| #綦江区（不含万盛） | Qijiang District (excluding Wansheng) | 145 | 3.08 | 610121 | 162.97 | 96.66 | 43.74 |
| 大足区 | Dazu District | 88 | 6.58 | 1465174 | 309.05 | 165.52 | 123.56 |
| 璧山区 | Bishan District | 79 | 4.04 | 1855254 | 571.81 | 367.68 | 209.40 |
| 铜梁区 | Tongliang District | 125 | 8.03 | 3434260 | 975.55 | 643.46 | 444.10 |
| 潼南区 | Tongnan District | 73 | 6.24 | 1341779 | 323.53 | 159.56 | 115.90 |
| 荣昌区 | Rongchang District | 61 | 3.30 | 1074505 | 525.08 | 229.80 | 124.14 |
| 开州区 | Kaizhou District | 80 | 9.87 | 5594277 | 1021.96 | 607.78 | 495.42 |
| 梁平区 | Liangping District | 56 | 5.71 | 1857590 | 25.60 | 8.80 | 6.34 |
| 武隆区 | Wulong District | 43 | 0.36 | 178293 | 22.88 | 18.10 | 6.06 |
| 城口县 | Chengkou County | 29 | 0.23 | 90022 | 0.99 | 0.44 | 0.04 |
| 丰都县 | Fengdu County | 69 | 6.62 | 2249958 | 206.34 | 135.44 | 96.88 |
| 垫江县 | Dianjiang County | 126 | 8.72 | 3618595 | 947.73 | 705.48 | 525.24 |
| 忠 县 | Zhongxian County | 64 | 4.45 | 1555699 | 150.68 | 51.14 | 38.32 |
| 云阳县 | Yunyang County | 101 | 7.39 | 3758835 | 575.73 | 217.72 | 84.47 |
| 奉节县 | Fengjie County | 90 | 9.71 | 3540304 | 599.72 | 471.18 | 283.73 |
| 巫山县 | Wushan County | 53 | 1.38 | 808983 | 392.88 | 35.32 | 24.77 |
| 巫溪县 | Wuxi County | 80 | 1.34 | 375752 | 120.87 | 45.72 | 6.86 |
| 石柱县 | Shizhu County | 48 | 0.72 | 237633 | 66.82 | 38.65 | 13.72 |
| 秀山县 | Xiushan County | 38 | 2.44 | 1356768 | 155.02 | 111.27 | 40.04 |
| 酉阳县 | Youyang County | 36 | 0.77 | 286264 | 43.11 | 30.40 | 17.02 |
| 彭水县 | Pengshui County | 56 | 0.98 | 321834 | 61.06 | 29.80 | 22.48 |

注：本表数据不包括劳务分包企业。
Note:The data in this table exclude construction enterprises of labor subcontracting.

# 表 20.6 各区县总承包建筑业企业主要经济指标（2022 年）
## MAIN ECONOMIC INDICATORS ON CONSTRUCTION ENTERPRISES OF GENERAL CONTRACTING BY REGION (2022)

| 区 县 | Region | 企业数（个）Number of Enterprises (unit) | 年末从业人数（万人）Number of Employed Persons at Year-end (10 000 persons) | 总产值（万元）Gross Output Value (10 000 yuan) | 利税总额（万元）Total Pre-tax Profits (10 000 yuan) | 按总产值计算的劳动生产率（元/人）Overall Labor Productivity by Gross Output Value (yuan/person) |
|---|---|---|---|---|---|---|
| **全 市** | **Total** | **2770** | **167.71** | **89703681** | **5365274** | **465244** |
| 主城都市区 | The city proper of Chongqing | 1636 | 103.11 | 61972102 | 2905986 | 524210 |
| 中心城区 | The central urban area of Chongqing | 656 | 38.78 | 32607682 | 1114361 | 691134 |
| 主城新区 | The new area of Chongqing city proper | 980 | 64.34 | 29364421 | 1791625 | 710487 |
| 渝东北三峡库区城镇群 | The city cluster of three gorges reservoir area in northeast Chongqing | 868 | 58.72 | 25126270 | 1946062 | 371910 |
| 渝东南武陵山区城镇群 | The city cluster of Wuling mountain area in southeast Chongqing | 266 | 5.88 | 2605309 | 513226 | 370599 |
| 万州区 | Wanzhou District | 166 | 4.65 | 2127275 | 77327 | 377176 |
| 黔江区 | Qianjiang District | 65 | 0.87 | 315675 | 24706 | 322118 |
| 涪陵区 | Fuling District | 105 | 10.16 | 4830869 | 140695 | 423760 |
| 渝中区 | Yuzhong District | 52 | 7.56 | 4539500 | 122192 | 550242 |
| 大渡口区 | Dadukou District | 31 | 0.78 | 2902263 | 108298 | 866347 |
| 江北区 | Jiangbei District | 39 | 1.33 | 941488 | 16977 | 592131 |
| 沙坪坝区 | Shapingba District | 58 | 2.53 | 2351651 | 74833 | 948246 |
| 九龙坡区 | Jiulongpo District | 113 | 4.59 | 3725789 | 165324 | 614817 |
| 南岸区 | Nan'an District | 59 | 2.37 | 3725316 | 264859 | 1031944 |
| 北碚区 | Beibei District | 64 | 2.84 | 1405541 | 48666 | 465411 |
| 渝北区 | Yubei District | 160 | 10.73 | 8902763 | 267755 | 705449 |
| 巴南区 | Ba'nan District | 80 | 6.05 | 4113371 | 45456 | 663447 |
| 长寿区 | Changshou District | 49 | 2.29 | 3121757 | 93039 | 1300732 |
| 江津区 | Jiangjin District | 68 | 6.52 | 4338384 | 152732 | 731599 |
| 合川区 | Hechuan District | 97 | 6.04 | 2810745 | 110483 | 393111 |
| 永川区 | Yongchuan District | 126 | 9.64 | 4403455 | 286836 | 388312 |
| 南川区 | Nanchuan District | 56 | 1.14 | 509454 | 27879 | 428113 |
| 綦江区 | Qijiang District | 122 | 2.74 | 720604 | 66474 | 223790 |
| #綦江区（不含万盛） | Qijiang District (excluding Wansheng) | 88 | 2.20 | 460530 | 58733 | 176448 |
| 大足区 | Dazu District | 77 | 6.02 | 1351785 | 245204 | 198500 |
| 璧山区 | Bishan District | 70 | 3.93 | 1791952 | 171809 | 419661 |
| 铜梁区 | Tongliang District | 93 | 6.70 | 3151366 | 261439 | 452133 |
| 潼南区 | Tongnan District | 65 | 6.15 | 1283421 | 174184 | 187635 |
| 荣昌区 | Rongchang District | 52 | 3.01 | 1050630 | 60851 | 296788 |
| 开州区 | Kaizhou District | 79 | 9.76 | 5574264 | 386982 | 503547 |
| 梁平区 | Liangping District | 50 | 5.08 | 1762266 | 201678 | 369448 |
| 武隆区 | Wulong District | 40 | 0.35 | 167078 | 11452 | 428404 |
| 城口县 | Chengkou County | 28 | 0.23 | 90022 | 6014 | 321508 |
| 丰都县 | Fengdu County | 57 | 6.51 | 2181973 | 207842 | 275850 |
| 垫江县 | Dianjiang County | 121 | 8.59 | 3551159 | 193901 | 317351 |
| 忠 县 | Zhongxian County | 60 | 4.41 | 1534954 | 72603 | 341861 |
| 云阳县 | Yunyang County | 97 | 7.33 | 3712178 | 287487 | 438792 |
| 奉节县 | Fengjie County | 84 | 9.49 | 3433036 | 426063 | 321145 |
| 巫山县 | Wushan County | 52 | 1.37 | 800834 | 45839 | 488313 |
| 巫溪县 | Wuxi County | 74 | 1.31 | 358310 | 40325 | 252331 |
| 石柱县 | Shizhu County | 47 | 0.71 | 235866 | 11257 | 245694 |
| 秀山县 | Xiushan County | 36 | 2.43 | 1343398 | 423659 | 461649 |
| 酉阳县 | Youyang County | 34 | 0.71 | 280221 | 23451 | 363923 |
| 彭水县 | Pengshui County | 44 | 0.80 | 263072 | 18701 | 260467 |

# 表 20.7 各区县专业承包建筑业企业主要经济指标（2022 年）
# MAIN ECONOMIC INDICATORS ON CONSTRUCTION ENTERPRISES OF SPECIALIZED CONTRACTING BY REGION (2022)

| 区　县 | Region | 企业数（个） Number of Enterprises (unit) | 年末从业人数（万人） Number of Employed Persons at Year-end (10 000 persons) | 总产值（万元） Gross Output Value (10 000 yuan) | 利税总额（万元） Total Pre-tax Profits (10 000 yuan) | 按总产值计算的劳动生产率（元/人） Overall Labor Productivity by Gross Output Value (yuan/person) |
|---|---|---|---|---|---|---|
| **全　市** | **Total** | **1144** | **27.85** | **7765893** | **414639** | **202871** |
| 主城都市区 | The city proper of Chongqing | 1011 | 25.14 | 6947216 | 361170 | 197028 |
| 中心城区 | The central urban area of Chongqing | 670 | 9.65 | 4245063 | 211917 | 219270 |
| 主城新区 | The new area of Chongqing city proper | 341 | 15.48 | 2702153 | 149254 | 169947 |
| 渝东北三峡库区城镇群 | The city cluster of three gorges reservoir area in northeast Chongqing | 98 | 2.39 | 707390 | 45971 | 264940 |
| 渝东南武陵山区城镇群 | The city cluster of Wuling mountain area in southeast Chongqing | 35 | 0.32 | 111287 | 7498 | 317963 |
| 万州区 | Wanzhou District | 52 | 1.04 | 256372 | 9451 | 237381 |
| 黔江区 | Qianjiang District | 15 | 0.05 | 20130 | -955 | 335503 |
| 涪陵区 | Fuling District | 78 | 1.08 | 421701 | 19014 | 348513 |
| 渝中区 | Yuzhong District | 101 | 0.85 | 567167 | 22055 | 59639 |
| 大渡口区 | Dadukou District | 34 | 0.13 | 112542 | 3683 | 416823 |
| 江北区 | Jiangbei District | 41 | 0.83 | 392667 | 8936 | 409029 |
| 沙坪坝区 | Shapingba District | 94 | 1.48 | 532962 | 25797 | 328989 |
| 九龙坡区 | Jiulongpo District | 107 | 1.15 | 650271 | 39837 | 359266 |
| 南岸区 | Nan'an District | 52 | 0.44 | 377947 | 19426 | 804143 |
| 北碚区 | Beibei District | 31 | 0.55 | 334317 | 20288 | 642916 |
| 渝北区 | Yubei District | 164 | 3.45 | 1067811 | 60596 | 313141 |
| 巴南区 | Ba'nan District | 46 | 0.77 | 209380 | 11300 | 265038 |
| 长寿区 | Changshou District | 7 | 0.13 | 30578 | 2475 | 145608 |
| 江津区 | Jiangjin District | 35 | 8.53 | 1007322 | 21541 | 117267 |
| 合川区 | Hechuan District | 59 | 1.25 | 344936 | 14560 | 265335 |
| 永川区 | Yongchuan District | 24 | 1.11 | 178492 | 14062 | 159367 |
| 南川区 | Nanchuan District | 8 | 0.11 | 26285 | 1605 | 238955 |
| 綦江区 | Qijiang District | 61 | 0.89 | 151021 | 11590 | 157314 |
| #綦江区（不含万盛） | Qijiang District (excluding Wansheng) | 57 | 0.88 | 149591 | 10856 | 157464 |
| 大足区 | Dazu District | 11 | 0.56 | 113390 | 23007 | 202481 |
| 璧山区 | Bishan District | 9 | 0.11 | 63303 | 5183 | 575478 |
| 铜梁区 | Tongliang District | 32 | 1.33 | 282894 | 25450 | 211115 |
| 潼南区 | Tongnan District | 8 | 0.09 | 58358 | 8623 | 583582 |
| 荣昌区 | Rongchang District | 9 | 0.29 | 23875 | 2143 | 82328 |
| 开州区 | Kaizhou District | 1 | 0.10 | 20014 | 2428 | 200138 |
| 梁平区 | Liangping District | 6 | 0.64 | 95324 | 13091 | 146652 |
| 武隆区 | Wulong District | 3 | 0.02 | 11215 | 1080 | 560760 |
| 城口县 | Chengkou County | 1 | 0.00 | 0 | 0 | #DIV/0! |
| 丰都县 | Fengdu County | 12 | 0.11 | 67985 | 4026 | 261479 |
| 垫江县 | Dianjiang County | 5 | 0.13 | 67436 | 5728 | 396683 |
| 忠　县 | Zhongxian County | 4 | 0.03 | 20745 | 823 | 414898 |
| 云阳县 | Yunyang County | 4 | 0.06 | 46657 | 3193 | 777612 |
| 奉节县 | Fengjie County | 6 | 0.23 | 107268 | 5157 | 412570 |
| 巫山县 | Wushan County | 1 | 0.01 | 8149 | 1167 | 814880 |
| 巫溪县 | Wuxi County | 6 | 0.04 | 17442 | 908 | 436055 |
| 石柱县 | Shizhu County | 1 | 0.01 | 1766 | 192 | 176640 |
| 秀山县 | Xiushan County | 2 | 0.01 | 13370 | 4346 | 668500 |
| 酉阳县 | Youyang County | 2 | 0.05 | 6043 | 417 | 120864 |
| 彭水县 | Pengshui County | 12 | 0.18 | 58762 | 2418 | 309275 |

# 表 20.8 各区县公路交通运输业（2022 年）
## HIGHWAY TRANSPORTATION BY REGION (2022)

| 区 县 | Region | 公路里程（公里）Length of Highways (km) | #等级公路 Expressway and Class I-IV Highways | 高速公路 Expressway |
|---|---|---|---|---|
| **全 市** | **Total** | **186137** | **175802** | **4002** |
| 主城都市区 | The city proper of Chongqing | 73734 | 70558 | 2410 |
| 中心城区 | The central urban area of Chongqing | 13317 | 12733 | 694 |
| 主城新区 | The new area of Chongqing city proper | 60417 | 57826 | 1717 |
| 渝东北三峡库区城镇群 | The city cluster of three gorges reservoir area in northeast Chongqing | 75049 | 69644 | 962 |
| 渝东南武陵山区城镇群 | The city cluster of Wuling mountain area in southeast Chongqing | 37354 | 35601 | 629 |
| 万州区 | Wanzhou District | 7603 | 7600 | 218 |
| 黔江区 | Qianjiang District | 6588 | 6588 | 133 |
| 涪陵区 | Fuling District | 6586 | 6519 | 174 |
| 渝中区 | Yuzhong District | | | |
| 大渡口区 | Dadukou District | 147 | 147 | 5 |
| 江北区 | Jiangbei District | 421 | 421 | 55 |
| 沙坪坝区 | Shapingba District | 1409 | 1396 | 65 |
| 九龙坡区 | Jiulongpo District | 1651 | 1605 | 53 |
| 南岸区 | Nan'an District | 591 | 538 | 38 |
| 北碚区 | Beibei District | 1804 | 1755 | 63 |
| 渝北区 | Yubei District | 3495 | 3495 | 207 |
| 巴南区 | Ba'nan District | 3799 | 3375 | 208 |
| 长寿区 | Changshou District | 3813 | 3813 | 107 |
| 江津区 | Jiangjin District | 6647 | 6144 | 191 |
| 合川区 | Hechuan District | 6370 | 5542 | 194 |
| 永川区 | Yongchuan District | 5162 | 5100 | 134 |
| 南川区 | Nanchuan District | 4827 | 4680 | 141 |
| 綦江区 | Qijiang District | 7233 | 7233 | 213 |
| #綦江区（不含万盛） | Qijiang District (excluding Wansheng) | 5657 | 5657 | 161 |
| 大足区 | Dazu District | 3901 | 3901 | 125 |
| 璧山区 | Bishan District | 2833 | 2074 | 107 |
| 铜梁区 | Tongliang District | 4682 | 4514 | 98 |
| 潼南区 | Tongnan District | 5578 | 5570 | 151 |
| 荣昌区 | Rongchang District | 2788 | 2736 | 82 |
| 开州区 | Kaizhou District | 8373 | 5538 | 135 |
| 梁平区 | Liangping District | 5147 | 4132 | 93 |
| 武隆区 | Wulong District | 5435 | 5361 | 88 |
| 城口县 | Chengkou County | 4537 | 4517 | 37 |
| 丰都县 | Fengdu County | 7418 | 6897 | 64 |
| 垫江县 | Dianjiang County | 4510 | 4486 | 76 |
| 忠 县 | Zhongxian County | 6617 | 6612 | 110 |
| 云阳县 | Yunyang County | 7796 | 7568 | 73 |
| 奉节县 | Fengjie County | 9356 | 9309 | 77 |
| 巫山县 | Wushan County | 6255 | 6011 | 57 |
| 巫溪县 | Wuxi County | 7438 | 6974 | 24 |
| 石柱县 | Shizhu County | 5785 | 5737 | 147 |
| 秀山县 | Xiushan County | 4845 | 4557 | 79 |
| 酉阳县 | Youyang County | 6293 | 6073 | 100 |
| 彭水县 | Pengshui County | 8407 | 7284 | 83 |

注：1）2006 年起，公路里程包括村道。
2）渝中区公路归为市政道路，不属于本表统计范围。
Note: a) The length of highways has included village roads since 2006.
b) The highways in Yuzhong District are municipal roads, not included in the statistic scope of this table.

# 表 20.9 各区县(自治县)固定资产投资较上年增长情况(2022 年)
## GROWTH RATE OF THE INVESTMENT IN FIXED ASSETS BY REGION COMPARED WITH THE LAST YEAR (2022)

| 区 县 | Region | 全社会固定资产投资增长情况 Growth Rate of Total Investment in Fixed Assets (%) | #工 业 Industry | #基础设施投资 Investment in Infrastructure Construction | 房地产开发投资 Real Estate Development |
|---|---|---|---|---|---|
| **全 市** | **Total** | **0.7** | **10.4** | **9.0** | **-20.4** |
| 主城都市区 | The city proper of Chongqing | -2.0 | 7.8 | 9.5 | -21.1 |
| 中心城区 | The central urban area of Chongqing | -7.1 | -1.1 | 15.0 | -26.1 |
| 主城新区 | The new area of Chongqing city proper | 5.3 | 11.5 | 2.5 | -7.4 |
| 渝东北三峡库区城镇群 | The city cluster of three gorges reservoir area in northeast Chongqing | 9.5 | 25.4 | 8.0 | -14.5 |
| 渝东南武陵山区城镇群 | The city cluster of Wuling mountain area in southeast Chongqing | 8.3 | 18.5 | 7.6 | -22.3 |
| 万州区 | Wanzhou District | 3.1 | 10.7 | 16.1 | -30.5 |
| 黔江区 | Qianjiang District | 13.6 | 18.7 | -3.2 | -6.5 |
| 涪陵区 | Fuling District | 2.3 | 11.0 | -7.0 | 0.0 |
| 渝中区 | Yuzhong District | 1.0 | -100.0 | 26.5 | 3.0 |
| 大渡口区 | Dadukou District | 1.6 | 3.6 | 43.0 | -5.4 |
| 江北区 | Jiangbei District | 0.1 | 25.0 | 43.2 | -15.0 |
| 沙坪坝区 | Shapingba District | 1.2 | 26.1 | 33.0 | -11.2 |
| 九龙坡区 | Jiulongpo District | 1.1 | -3.2 | 49.4 | -22.7 |
| 南岸区 | Nan'an District | -3.8 | -4.3 | 17.6 | -28.0 |
| 北碚区 | Beibei District | -23.5 | -3.9 | -19.4 | -42.1 |
| 渝北区 | Yubei District | -7.4 | -2.5 | -11.6 | -32.6 |
| 巴南区 | Ba'nan District | 1.1 | 12.8 | 43.1 | -31.4 |
| 长寿区 | Changshou District | 5.2 | -0.9 | 46.3 | -42.1 |
| 江津区 | Jiangjin District | 5.5 | 14.2 | 41.8 | -7.6 |
| 合川区 | Hechuan District | 4.8 | 2.1 | -7.5 | -16.1 |
| 永川区 | Yongchuan District | 10.4 | 8.1 | 12.5 | -2.2 |
| 南川区 | Nanchuan District | 7.5 | 13.3 | 0.4 | 5.4 |
| 綦江区 | Qijiang District | 11.4 | 36.5 | 19.5 | -13.3 |
| #綦江区(不含万盛) | Qijiang District (excluding Wansheng) | 15.2 | 30.3 | 15.3 | -2.7 |
| 大足区 | Dazu District | 8.2 | 13.9 | 1.1 | 2.1 |
| 璧山区 | Bishan District | 4.9 | 13.8 | 7.0 | -11.7 |
| 铜梁区 | Tongliang District | 3.2 | 13.6 | -25.2 | -16.7 |
| 潼南区 | Tongnan District | 12.3 | 21.8 | -29.9 | 10.7 |
| 荣昌区 | Rongchang District | 3.2 | 5.7 | -3.6 | -17.0 |
| 开州区 | Kaizhou District | 12.1 | 14.2 | 38.4 | -17.1 |
| 梁平区 | Liangping District | 12.8 | 27.3 | 13.1 | -30.1 |
| 武隆区 | Wulong District | 11.7 | 3.6 | 67.5 | -17.8 |
| 城口县 | Chengkou County | 9.3 | 53.2 | 50.1 | -43.4 |
| 丰都县 | Fengdu County | 10.2 | 29.8 | -3.9 | 2.7 |
| 垫江县 | Dianjiang County | 14.2 | 21.3 | -17.1 | -7.8 |
| 忠 县 | Zhongxian County | 11.5 | 2.1 | 25.2 | -6.6 |
| 云阳县 | Yunyang County | 17.7 | 103.6 | -3.1 | -21.6 |
| 奉节县 | Fengjie County | 10.0 | 25.1 | 16.7 | 4.3 |
| 巫山县 | Wushan County | -2.7 | 1.0 | -14.2 | -8.6 |
| 巫溪县 | Wuxi County | 3.2 | 38.4 | -1.6 | -22.5 |
| 石柱县 | Shizhu County | 10.0 | 86.4 | 13.2 | -19.6 |
| 秀山县 | Xiushan County | 0.6 | 5.9 | 13.1 | -37.8 |
| 酉阳县 | Youyang County | 11.6 | 6.4 | 4.1 | -10.4 |
| 彭水县 | Pengshui County | 10.1 | 35.0 | -33.0 | -17.5 |

表 20.9 续表 1 continued 1

| 区 县 | Region | 房地产开发（万元）Real Estate Development | #住宅 Residential Buildings | 房屋施工面积（万平方米）Floor Space of Buildings under Construction (10 000 sq.m) | #住宅 Residential Buildings | 房屋新开工面积（万平方米）Floor Space of Buildings Started This Year (10 000 sq.m) | #住宅 Residential Buildings |
|---|---|---|---|---|---|---|---|
| **全 市** | **Total** | **32168663** | **24110429** | **22646.90** | **14984.24** | **2222.44** | **1537.53** |
| 主城都市区 | The city proper of Chongqing | 27510406 | 20389913 | 18782.74 | 12319.42 | 1755.37 | 1202.21 |
| 中心城区 | The central urban area of Chongqing | 20155193 | 14436168 | 12307.49 | 7730.28 | 1221.39 | 800.68 |
| 主城新区 | The new area of Chongqing city proper | 7355213 | 5953745 | 6475.25 | 4589.14 | 533.98 | 401.53 |
| 渝东北三峡库区城镇群 | The city cluster of three gorges reservoir area in northeast Chongqing | 3527863 | 2788034 | 2747.81 | 1883.23 | 329.37 | 231.82 |
| 渝东南武陵山区城镇群 | The city cluster of Wuling mountain area in southeast Chongqing | 1130394 | 932482 | 1116.35 | 781.59 | 137.70 | 103.51 |
| 万州区 | Wanzhou District | 459736 | 323365 | 627.71 | 397.74 | 81.63 | 53.85 |
| 黔江区 | Qianjiang District | 157072 | 133985 | 164.50 | 108.32 | 7.73 | 6.61 |
| 涪陵区 | Fuling District | 1031172 | 669511 | 465.25 | 286.16 | 17.87 | 8.16 |
| 渝中区 | Yuzhong District | 606803 | 290975 | 387.41 | 150.42 | 3.90 | 2.92 |
| 大渡口区 | Dadukou District | 1538557 | 1333747 | 719.03 | 468.98 | 34.32 | 28.66 |
| 江北区 | Jiangbei District | 1507351 | 1031241 | 913.83 | 417.70 | 86.43 | 35.95 |
| 沙坪坝区 | Shapingba District | 2888539 | 2023146 | 1462.07 | 984.14 | 168.53 | 133.88 |
| 九龙坡区 | Jiulongpo District | 2065393 | 1292734 | 1011.31 | 613.97 | 153.27 | 83.62 |
| 南岸区 | Nan'an District | 1232889 | 814314 | 1033.28 | 600.32 | 213.41 | 134.18 |
| 北碚区 | Beibei District | 1637855 | 1224479 | 952.95 | 686.25 | 119.11 | 78.84 |
| 渝北区 | Yubei District | 6078878 | 4683619 | 3896.30 | 2423.45 | 364.99 | 262.37 |
| 巴南区 | Ba'nan District | 2598928 | 1741913 | 1931.31 | 1385.03 | 77.44 | 40.26 |
| 长寿区 | Changshou District | 194678 | 121044 | 202.58 | 121.52 | 14.34 | 10.40 |
| 江津区 | Jiangjin District | 1425454 | 1162437 | 1094.67 | 762.09 | 103.39 | 56.00 |
| 合川区 | Hechuan District | 544163 | 451495 | 633.66 | 450.09 | 27.58 | 23.93 |
| 永川区 | Yongchuan District | 972980 | 801153 | 505.42 | 391.23 | 65.77 | 54.88 |
| 南川区 | Nanchuan District | 558326 | 521647 | 433.13 | 306.02 | 65.93 | 58.00 |
| 綦江区 | Qijiang District | 307189 | 237574 | 548.73 | 379.24 | 9.36 | 4.15 |
| #綦江区（不含万盛） | Qijiang District (excluding Wansheng) | 210786 | 159007 | 467.51 | 322.35 | 5.58 | 1.38 |
| 大足区 | Dazu District | 156426 | 132918 | 403.08 | 320.03 | 39.53 | 30.39 |
| 璧山区 | Bishan District | 1112395 | 964100 | 986.75 | 700.78 | 109.04 | 88.72 |
| 铜梁区 | Tongliang District | 598243 | 502114 | 351.35 | 230.38 | 28.98 | 20.57 |
| 潼南区 | Tongnan District | 217201 | 189962 | 557.65 | 387.82 | 15.35 | 11.94 |
| 荣昌区 | Rongchang District | 236986 | 199790 | 292.98 | 253.79 | 36.84 | 34.40 |
| 开州区 | Kaizhou District | 406445 | 347429 | 181.66 | 131.86 | 69.17 | 47.25 |
| 梁平区 | Liangping District | 150211 | 117398 | 252.31 | 182.23 | 28.93 | 23.92 |
| 武隆区 | Wulong District | 249135 | 188637 | 228.06 | 147.32 | 22.01 | 14.34 |
| 城口县 | Chengkou County | 60776 | 46186 | 105.19 | 60.86 | 15.55 | 8.62 |
| 丰都县 | Fengdu County | 560941 | 449153 | 248.25 | 177.63 | 15.59 | 10.87 |
| 垫江县 | Dianjiang County | 326603 | 282226 | 350.03 | 251.32 | 46.39 | 36.86 |
| 忠 县 | Zhongxian County | 469703 | 358762 | 306.85 | 198.54 | 7.96 | 3.91 |
| 云阳县 | Yunyang County | 401730 | 358359 | 191.93 | 139.66 | 19.50 | 16.12 |
| 奉节县 | Fengjie County | 171377 | 146292 | 201.23 | 139.35 | 18.79 | 16.13 |
| 巫山县 | Wushan County | 373043 | 238782 | 175.06 | 123.74 | 21.04 | 10.97 |
| 巫溪县 | Wuxi County | 147298 | 120082 | 107.59 | 80.31 | 4.80 | 3.30 |
| 石柱县 | Shizhu County | 221786 | 188437 | 177.72 | 125.66 | 18.20 | 14.44 |
| 秀山县 | Xiushan County | 273012 | 234144 | 258.82 | 197.24 | 52.75 | 42.86 |
| 酉阳县 | Youyang County | 84203 | 70324 | 97.77 | 63.52 | 6.87 | 4.31 |
| 彭水县 | Pengshui County | 145186 | 116955 | 189.48 | 139.53 | 30.14 | 20.95 |

**表 20.9 续表 2 continued 2**

| 区 县 | Region | 房屋竣工面积（万平方米）Floor Space of Buildings Completed (10 000 sq.m) | #住宅 Residential Buildings | 商品房销售面积（万平方米）Floor Space of Commercialized Buildings Sold (10 000 sq.m) | #住宅 Residential Buildings | 商品房销售额（万元）Total Sale of Commercialized Buildings Sold (10 000 yuan) | #住宅 Residential Buildings |
|---|---|---|---|---|---|---|---|
| **全 市** | **Total** | **2792.57** | **1914.99** | **4142.92** | **2723.02** | **29548733** | **23216880** |
| 主城都市区 | The city proper of Chongqing | 2202.91 | 1491.57 | 3231.07 | 2019.73 | 24771429 | 19201744 |
| 中心城区 | The central urban area of Chongqing | 1498.68 | 995.01 | 1940.41 | 979.81 | 17309064 | 12786260 |
| 主城新区 | The new area of Chongqing city proper | 704.24 | 496.56 | 1290.66 | 1039.92 | 7462365 | 6415484 |
| 渝东北三峡库区城镇群 | The city cluster of three gorges reservoir area in northeast Chongqing | 474.28 | 338.25 | 672.15 | 517.16 | 3590323 | 2990563 |
| 渝东南武陵山区城镇群 | The city cluster of Wuling mountain area in southeast Chongqing | 115.37 | 85.17 | 239.70 | 186.13 | 1186981 | 1024573 |
| 万州区 | Wanzhou District | 148.19 | 91.06 | 92.98 | 54.78 | 467796 | 339978 |
| 黔江区 | Qianjiang District | 9.62 | 7.57 | 36.72 | 20.43 | 125698 | 91787 |
| 涪陵区 | Fuling District | 91.90 | 55.15 | 89.49 | 53.44 | 468994 | 329285 |
| 渝中区 | Yuzhong District | 13.73 | 9.16 | 42.62 | 14.66 | 781782 | 388252 |
| 大渡口区 | Dadukou District | 52.43 | 30.17 | 160.96 | 91.68 | 1226874 | 1006037 |
| 江北区 | Jiangbei District | 124.50 | 87.58 | 91.82 | 40.21 | 1276792 | 716799 |
| 沙坪坝区 | Shapingba District | 385.11 | 258.57 | 250.01 | 118.48 | 2185045 | 1736192 |
| 九龙坡区 | Jiulongpo District | 158.48 | 117.24 | 208.19 | 129.30 | 2025819 | 1624870 |
| 南岸区 | Nan'an District | 99.14 | 61.82 | 149.45 | 101.50 | 1447759 | 1217821 |
| 北碚区 | Beibei District | 108.60 | 80.67 | 169.79 | 132.61 | 1657090 | 1480666 |
| 渝北区 | Yubei District | 379.27 | 223.22 | 585.46 | 264.37 | 5135234 | 3709351 |
| 巴南区 | Ba'nan District | 177.42 | 126.60 | 282.10 | 87.01 | 1572669 | 906272 |
| 长寿区 | Changshou District | 33.67 | 24.78 | 27.91 | 19.39 | 142196 | 97536 |
| 江津区 | Jiangjin District | 142.06 | 91.05 | 202.65 | 168.25 | 1310565 | 1124766 |
| 合川区 | Hechuan District | 86.15 | 63.12 | 118.51 | 83.70 | 576713 | 481392 |
| 永川区 | Yongchuan District | 45.33 | 33.51 | 235.23 | 211.36 | 1218538 | 1150716 |
| 南川区 | Nanchuan District | 66.03 | 44.45 | 99.48 | 93.91 | 500708 | 480495 |
| 綦江区 | Qijiang District | 15.46 | 7.69 | 58.87 | 41.50 | 256725 | 206194 |
| #綦江区（不含万盛） | Qijiang District (excluding Wansheng) | 14.34 | 6.57 | 47.51 | 30.74 | 190670 | 143000 |
| 大足区 | Dazu District | 62.90 | 48.20 | 46.82 | 41.15 | 252441 | 229048 |
| 璧山区 | Bishan District | 92.64 | 71.74 | 247.07 | 202.04 | 1790387 | 1560923 |
| 铜梁区 | Tongliang District | 14.98 | 13.54 | 72.26 | 40.63 | 437795 | 282732 |
| 潼南区 | Tongnan District | 19.73 | 14.52 | 41.48 | 38.23 | 221115 | 207736 |
| 荣昌区 | Rongchang District | 33.40 | 28.82 | 50.88 | 46.34 | 286188 | 264661 |
| 开州区 | Kaizhou District | 28.47 | 25.28 | 121.76 | 76.94 | 690520 | 538376 |
| 梁平区 | Liangping District | 39.99 | 26.72 | 49.23 | 39.53 | 269001 | 234032 |
| 武隆区 | Wulong District | 6.47 | 4.06 | 29.99 | 21.88 | 191125 | 162414 |
| 城口县 | Chengkou County | 28.11 | 16.45 | 14.62 | 11.61 | 95775 | 80252 |
| 丰都县 | Fengdu County | 8.74 | 7.19 | 68.79 | 57.75 | 336072 | 273306 |
| 垫江县 | Dianjiang County | 65.73 | 47.61 | 86.52 | 75.38 | 463162 | 413416 |
| 忠 县 | Zhongxian County | 20.89 | 15.39 | 41.68 | 37.74 | 191723 | 173210 |
| 云阳县 | Yunyang County | 23.22 | 23.02 | 106.07 | 93.38 | 636202 | 557368 |
| 奉节县 | Fengjie County | 45.47 | 36.12 | 22.11 | 21.73 | 154486 | 152725 |
| 巫山县 | Wushan County | 65.23 | 49.42 | 38.03 | 26.35 | 168865 | 126620 |
| 巫溪县 | Wuxi County | 0.22 | 0.00 | 30.37 | 21.96 | 116721 | 101280 |
| 石柱县 | Shizhu County | 44.27 | 31.17 | 53.70 | 34.14 | 238976 | 188420 |
| 秀山县 | Xiushan County | 3.94 | 3.38 | 70.06 | 66.62 | 372563 | 348333 |
| 酉阳县 | Youyang County | 10.47 | 10.23 | 12.46 | 10.72 | 80514 | 74687 |
| 彭水县 | Pengshui County | 40.61 | 28.76 | 36.77 | 32.34 | 178105 | 158932 |

# 表 20.10 各区县社会消费品零售总额（2022 年）
## TOTAL RETAIL SALES OF CONSUMER GOODS BY REGION (2022)

| 区 县 | Region | 社会消费品零售总额（亿元）Total Retail Sales of Consumer Goods (100 million yuan) | 社会消费品零售总额指数（上年 =100）Index of Total Retail Sales of Consumer Goods (preceding year=100) |
|---|---|---|---|
| **全 市** | **Total** | **13926.08** | **99.7** |
| 主城都市区 | The city proper of Chongqing | 10361.75 | 99.2 |
| 中心城区 | The central urban area of Chongqing | 6010.98 | 97.9 |
| 主城新区 | The new area of Chongqing city proper | 4350.77 | 101.0 |
| 渝东北三峡库区城镇群 | The city cluster of three gorges reservoir area in northeast Chongqing | 2674.04 | 101.3 |
| 渝东南武陵山区城镇群 | The city cluster of Wuling mountain area in southeast Chongqing | 890.29 | 101.2 |
| 万州区 | Wanzhou District | 438.01 | 99.1 |
| 黔江区 | Qianjiang District | 156.06 | 101.5 |
| 涪陵区 | Fuling District | 580.02 | 100.7 |
| 渝中区 | Yuzhong District | 1309.55 | 96.7 |
| 大渡口区 | Dadukou District | 76.34 | 100.6 |
| 江北区 | Jiangbei District | 799.56 | 104.0 |
| 沙坪坝区 | Shapingba District | 553.08 | 96.7 |
| 九龙坡区 | Jiulongpo District | 862.14 | 97.0 |
| 南岸区 | Nan'an District | 585.33 | 96.6 |
| 北碚区 | Beibei District | 201.14 | 97.0 |
| 渝北区 | Yubei District | 1043.02 | 97.4 |
| 巴南区 | Ba'nan District | 473.48 | 97.3 |
| 长寿区 | Changshou District | 580.02 | 100.7 |
| 江津区 | Jiangjin District | 310.04 | 100.6 |
| 合川区 | Hechuan District | 416.06 | 101.9 |
| 永川区 | Yongchuan District | 346.29 | 99.2 |
| 南川区 | Nanchuan District | 509.02 | 100.7 |
| 綦江区 | Qijiang District | 359.39 | 100.7 |
| #綦江区（不含万盛） | Qijiang District (excluding Wansheng) | 234.81 | 100.8 |
| 大足区 | Dazu District | 310.61 | 101.8 |
| 璧山区 | Bishan District | 347.49 | 101.6 |
| 铜梁区 | Tongliang District | 280.18 | 101.3 |
| 潼南区 | Tongnan District | 308.56 | 101.6 |
| 荣昌区 | Rongchang District | 289.73 | 100.7 |
| 开州区 | Kaizhou District | 387.12 | 101.8 |
| 梁平区 | Liangping District | 309.90 | 101.9 |
| 武隆区 | Wulong District | 138.22 | 101.0 |
| 城口县 | Chengkou County | 26.58 | 98.4 |
| 丰都县 | Fengdu County | 232.56 | 102.4 |
| 垫江县 | Dianjiang County | 277.72 | 102.2 |
| 忠 县 | Zhongxian County | 254.24 | 101.1 |
| 云阳县 | Yunyang County | 394.32 | 102.0 |
| 奉节县 | Fengjie County | 122.62 | 101.6 |
| 巫山县 | Wushan County | 117.51 | 101.4 |
| 巫溪县 | Wuxi County | 65.70 | 101.4 |
| 石柱县 | Shizhu County | 98.49 | 101.1 |
| 秀山县 | Xiushan County | 238.94 | 100.9 |
| 酉阳县 | Youyang County | 99.34 | 100.2 |
| 彭水县 | Pengshui County | 143.34 | 102.5 |

注：根据四经普调整。
Note: The data has been adjusted according to the result of the 4rd National Economic Census.

# 表 20.11 各区县财政收支(2022 年)
## GOVERNMENT REVENUE AND EXPENDITURE BY REGION (2022)

单位：万元 (10 000 yuan)

| 地 区 | Region | 区县级一般公共预算收入 General Public Budgetary Revenue at District (county) Level | #增值税（含其他税收收入科目） Value-added Tax | #增值税 Value-added Tax | #企业所得税 Corporate Income Tax | #个人所得税 Individual Income Tax |
|---|---|---|---|---|---|---|
| **全 市** | **Total** | **14231034** | **2082395** | **2070482** | **1337335** | **414782** |
| 主城都市区 | The city proper of Chongqing | 10536537 | 1450799 | 1439256 | 1116872 | 296993 |
| 中心城区 | The central urban area of Chongqing | 5450774 | 876269 | 864874 | 640896 | 218944 |
| 主城新区 | The new area of Chongqing city proper | 5085763 | 574530 | 574382 | 475976 | 78049 |
| 渝东北三峡库区城镇群 | The city cluster of three gorges reservoir area in northeast Chongqing | 2614079 | 425604 | 425291 | 153069 | 71069 |
| 渝东南武陵山区城镇群 | The city cluster of Wuling mountain area in southeast Chongqing | 1080418 | 205992 | 205935 | 67394 | 46720 |
| 万州区 | Wanzhou District | 715431 | 162931 | 162867 | 60585 | 19647 |
| 黔江区 | Qianjiang District | 259088 | 68984 | 68957 | 11586 | 13602 |
| 涪陵区 | Fuling District | 600288 | 131181 | 131162 | 144065 | 16593 |
| 渝中区 | Yuzhong District | 407575 | 98531 | 92460 | 55814 | 32174 |
| 大渡口区 | Dadukou District | 184079 | 41232 | 41205 | 22894 | 4971 |
| 江北区 | Jiangbei District | 671933 | 186041 | 181398 | 106325 | 29397 |
| 沙坪坝区 | Shapingba District | 402987 | 52747 | 52694 | 24791 | 12671 |
| 九龙坡区 | Jiulongpo District | 561038 | 87039 | 86571 | 25192 | 15834 |
| 南岸区 | Nan'an District | 568019 | 110612 | 110610 | 54934 | 19967 |
| 北碚区 | Beibei District | 253493 | 33959 | 33946 | 11455 | 9257 |
| 渝北区 | Yubei District | 589551 | 86355 | 86283 | 63235 | 26972 |
| 巴南区 | Ba'nan District | 403948 | 41050 | 41014 | 31400 | 6710 |
| 长寿区 | Changshou District | 504474 | 54762 | 54764 | 60288 | 9449 |
| 江津区 | Jiangjin District | 676453 | 95526 | 95437 | 49925 | 8395 |
| 合川区 | Hechuan District | 531695 | 48605 | 48598 | 26801 | 5938 |
| 永川区 | Yongchuan District | 420629 | 95272 | 95284 | 74399 | 6361 |
| 南川区 | Nanchuan District | 227215 | 6034 | 6031 | 14941 | 2685 |
| 綦江区 | Qijiang District | 289217 | 32832 | 32829 | 12667 | 3940 |
| #綦江区（不含万盛） | Qijiang District (excluding Wansheng) | 212368 | 21976 | 21975 | 7117 | 2234 |
| 大足区 | Dazu District | 429830 | 19485 | 19485 | 12025 | 3147 |
| 璧山区 | Bishan District | 435598 | 16437 | 16434 | 35883 | 11266 |
| 铜梁区 | Tongliang District | 401676 | 23857 | 23843 | 18349 | 4062 |
| 潼南区 | Tongnan District | 300332 | 17954 | 17936 | 8474 | 2808 |
| 荣昌区 | Rongchang District | 268356 | 32585 | 32579 | 18159 | 3405 |
| 开州区 | Kaizhou District | 306009 | 50914 | 50825 | 11830 | 5584 |
| 梁平区 | Liangping District | 301094 | 26800 | 26799 | 8891 | 3202 |
| 武隆区 | Wulong District | 203228 | 21662 | 21661 | 13399 | 12817 |
| 城口县 | Chengkou County | 61983 | 8603 | 8598 | 1861 | 1294 |
| 丰都县 | Fengdu County | 251883 | 25945 | 25938 | 10159 | 2881 |
| 垫江县 | Dianjiang County | 210634 | 51019 | 51019 | 16592 | 8126 |
| 忠 县 | Zhongxian County | 225660 | 45720 | 45725 | 12208 | 17993 |
| 云阳县 | Yunyang County | 181430 | 29516 | 29506 | 13667 | 3567 |
| 奉节县 | Fengjie County | 169309 | 9622 | 9558 | 7534 | 3279 |
| 巫山县 | Wushan County | 102211 | 3210 | 3210 | 5025 | 3925 |
| 巫溪县 | Wuxi County | 88435 | 11324 | 11246 | 4717 | 1571 |
| 石柱县 | Shizhu County | 129279 | 28003 | 28002 | 12324 | 2270 |
| 秀山县 | Xiushan County | 170465 | 34882 | 34872 | 13837 | 7847 |
| 酉阳县 | Youyang County | 150858 | 21379 | 21369 | 4112 | 6053 |
| 彭水县 | Pengshui County | 167500 | 31082 | 31074 | 12136 | 4131 |

**表 20.11 续表 continued**

单位：万元 (10 000 yuan)

| 地 区 | Region | 区县级一般公共预算支出 General Public Budgetary Expenditure at District (county) Level | #农林水支出 Expenditure for Agriculture, Forestry and Water Conservancy | #教育支出 Expenditure for Education | #卫生健康支出 Expenditure for Public Health and Family Planning | #社会保障和就业支出 Expenditure for Social Security and Employment Effort | #文化旅游体育与传媒支出 Expenditure for Culture, Sport and Media |
|---|---|---|---|---|---|---|---|
| **全 市** | **Total** | **32830797** | **3547179** | **6732920** | **2965986** | **4453376** | **445825** |
| 主城都市区 | The city proper of Chongqing | 21150157 | 1528037 | 4171733 | 2023386 | 2754640 | 280573 |
| 中心城区 | The central urban area of Chongqing | 10151870 | 310229 | 2018256 | 1000557 | 1210898 | 119037 |
| 主城新区 | The new area of Chongqing city proper | 10998287 | 1217808 | 2153477 | 1022829 | 1543742 | 161536 |
| 渝东北三峡库区城镇群 | The city cluster of three gorges reservoir area in northeast Chongqing | 8049822 | 1300316 | 1766692 | 670030 | 1230852 | 93916 |
| 渝东南武陵山区城镇群 | The city cluster of Wuling mountain area in southeast Chongqing | 3630818 | 718826 | 794495 | 272570 | 467884 | 71336 |
| 万州区 | Wanzhou District | 1521387 | 184359 | 278655 | 137248 | 216673 | 21587 |
| 黔江区 | Qianjiang District | 644827 | 125180 | 144970 | 67461 | 78017 | 7373 |
| 涪陵区 | Fuling District | 1206603 | 124899 | 214492 | 90777 | 147772 | 15692 |
| 渝中区 | Yuzhong District | 768648 | 472 | 151874 | 65937 | 140529 | 10010 |
| 大渡口区 | Dadukou District | 384745 | 8683 | 92122 | 34562 | 41251 | 6679 |
| 江北区 | Jiangbei District | 988425 | 9235 | 186576 | 116352 | 105311 | 11642 |
| 沙坪坝区 | Shapingba District | 907230 | 19570 | 225417 | 69592 | 163869 | 15282 |
| 九龙坡区 | Jiulongpo District | 953159 | 18954 | 255429 | 117646 | 151442 | 16634 |
| 南岸区 | Nan'an District | 910071 | 36997 | 182617 | 98878 | 104949 | 6455 |
| 北碚区 | Beibei District | 647903 | 50433 | 129400 | 66137 | 99081 | 12238 |
| 渝北区 | Yubei District | 1142435 | 98663 | 276236 | 143052 | 151397 | 15584 |
| 巴南区 | Ba'nan District | 816390 | 56600 | 168824 | 91301 | 118319 | 17829 |
| 长寿区 | Changshou District | 911869 | 73108 | 157902 | 76890 | 112555 | 9841 |
| 江津区 | Jiangjin District | 1160398 | 126686 | 252055 | 142116 | 191730 | 19389 |
| 合川区 | Hechuan District | 919118 | 118003 | 194041 | 100842 | 158908 | 17651 |
| 永川区 | Yongchuan District | 1054295 | 107485 | 232799 | 91789 | 128315 | 12817 |
| 南川区 | Nanchuan District | 631592 | 77622 | 117348 | 55187 | 85389 | 7127 |
| 綦江区 | Qijiang District | 1034479 | 103126 | 192267 | 86022 | 209044 | 12887 |
| #綦江区（不含万盛） | Qijiang District (excluding Wansheng) | 711223 | 79106 | 145786 | 64016 | 130374 | 7252 |
| 大足区 | Dazu District | 1005629 | 116815 | 173027 | 92622 | 119980 | 21270 |
| 璧山区 | Bishan District | 678926 | 74750 | 124322 | 57783 | 76988 | 15191 |
| 铜梁区 | Tongliang District | 815975 | 81344 | 140893 | 85852 | 115844 | 13231 |
| 潼南区 | Tongnan District | 750256 | 110024 | 154376 | 52352 | 95687 | 9191 |
| 荣昌区 | Rongchang District | 829147 | 103946 | 199955 | 90597 | 101530 | 7249 |
| 开州区 | Kaizhou District | 902832 | 138308 | 238261 | 85673 | 180016 | 8375 |
| 梁平区 | Liangping District | 695828 | 99748 | 167885 | 56522 | 92125 | 10433 |
| 武隆区 | Wulong District | 467450 | 100023 | 87051 | 31626 | 56205 | 9220 |
| 城口县 | Chengkou County | 367257 | 82015 | 61069 | 20203 | 40705 | 3266 |
| 丰都县 | Fengdu County | 652237 | 119049 | 141380 | 51307 | 89390 | 10513 |
| 垫江县 | Dianjiang County | 652138 | 89653 | 147723 | 53861 | 99130 | 6237 |
| 忠 县 | Zhongxian County | 714303 | 109712 | 155539 | 54375 | 100111 | 9301 |
| 云阳县 | Yunyang County | 828511 | 124139 | 199596 | 80091 | 146894 | 8226 |
| 奉节县 | Fengjie County | 669368 | 123069 | 167923 | 54862 | 112245 | 6066 |
| 巫山县 | Wushan County | 547746 | 108959 | 108759 | 40865 | 83938 | 5625 |
| 巫溪县 | Wuxi County | 498215 | 121305 | 99902 | 35023 | 69625 | 4287 |
| 石柱县 | Shizhu County | 561425 | 89011 | 112452 | 41140 | 70716 | 26491 |
| 秀山县 | Xiushan County | 617658 | 99370 | 140064 | 47806 | 80454 | 11157 |
| 酉阳县 | Youyang County | 637905 | 146647 | 161003 | 49520 | 105406 | 8596 |
| 彭水县 | Pengshui County | 701553 | 158595 | 148955 | 35017 | 77086 | 8499 |

# 表 20.12 各区县金融机构存贷款、人民生活和社会福利（2022 年）
## DEPOSIT AND LOAN OF FINANCIAL INSTITUTIONS,PEOPLE'S LIVELIHOOD AND SOCIAL WELFARE BY REGION (2022)

| 区 县 | Region | 金融机构人民币存款余额（亿元）Total Deposit Balance of RMB of Financial Institutions (100 million yuan) | #住户存款 Saving Deposits of Residents | 金融机构人民币贷款余额（亿元）Total Loan Balance of RMB of Financial Institutions (100 million yuan) |
|---|---|---|---|---|
| **全 市** | **Total** | **48218.18** | **25458.85** | **49365.86** |
| 主城都市区 | The city proper of Chongqing | 39434.33 | 18674.19 | 43199.47 |
| 中心城区 | The central urban area of Chongqing | 29731.92 | 11250.97 | 35455.71 |
| 主城新区 | The new area of Chongqing city proper | 9702.41 | 7423.22 | 7743.76 |
| 渝东北三峡库区城镇群 | The city cluster of three gorges reservoir area in northeast Chongqing | 6499.46 | 5338.62 | 3987.07 |
| 渝东南武陵山区城镇群 | The city cluster of Wuling mountain area in southeast Chongqing | 1789.56 | 1443.97 | 1964.15 |
| 万州区 | Wanzhou District | 1747.86 | 1340.03 | 930.84 |
| 黔江区 | Qianjiang District | 325.75 | 255.34 | 425.20 |
| 涪陵区 | Fuling District | 1127.82 | 726.95 | 916.06 |
| 渝中区 | Yuzhong District | 5617.02 | 1263.62 | 6672.31 |
| 大渡口区 | Dadukou District | 736.73 | 430.19 | 858.53 |
| 江北区 | Jiangbei District | 7677.32 | 1282.73 | 10820.77 |
| 沙坪坝区 | Shapingba District | 2300.57 | 1387.71 | 2206.47 |
| 九龙坡区 | Jiulongpo District | 2650.63 | 1581.02 | 2347.24 |
| 南岸区 | Nan'an District | 2009.17 | 1196.02 | 2225.89 |
| 北碚区 | Beibei District | 1037.66 | 741.64 | 771.95 |
| 渝北区 | Yubei District | 6459.45 | 2516.01 | 8438.23 |
| 巴南区 | Ba'nan District | 1243.40 | 852.02 | 1114.32 |
| 长寿区 | Changshou District | 743.53 | 593.15 | 526.79 |
| 江津区 | Jiangjin District | 1356.81 | 1041.19 | 1048.44 |
| 合川区 | Hechuan District | 1087.56 | 912.03 | 781.04 |
| 永川区 | Yongchuan District | 1049.17 | 748.19 | 835.37 |
| 南川区 | Nanchuan District | 476.95 | 360.09 | 523.13 |
| 綦江区 | Qijiang District | 816.84 | 654.99 | 583.26 |
| #綦江区（不含万盛） | Qijiang District (excluding Wansheng) | 630.89 | 504.59 | 456.21 |
| 大足区 | Dazu District | 552.30 | 459.16 | 535.53 |
| 璧山区 | Bishan District | 768.68 | 549.39 | 670.87 |
| 铜梁区 | Tongliang District | 681.05 | 547.36 | 458.77 |
| 潼南区 | Tongnan District | 479.60 | 405.75 | 403.41 |
| 荣昌区 | Rongchang District | 562.10 | 424.97 | 461.09 |
| 开州区 | Kaizhou District | 933.56 | 786.27 | 490.85 |
| 梁平区 | Liangping District | 572.84 | 489.09 | 316.37 |
| 武隆区 | Wulong District | 248.26 | 192.68 | 297.51 |
| 城口县 | Chengkou County | 157.53 | 97.53 | 118.74 |
| 丰都县 | Fengdu County | 456.33 | 395.50 | 278.58 |
| 垫江县 | Dianjiang County | 488.99 | 421.75 | 316.61 |
| 忠 县 | Zhongxian County | 601.29 | 515.72 | 364.44 |
| 云阳县 | Yunyang County | 638.80 | 541.49 | 335.90 |
| 奉节县 | Fengjie County | 403.56 | 334.49 | 375.29 |
| 巫山县 | Wushan County | 256.27 | 220.07 | 274.10 |
| 巫溪县 | Wuxi County | 242.43 | 196.68 | 185.36 |
| 石柱县 | Shizhu County | 317.14 | 264.60 | 292.84 |
| 秀山县 | Xiushan County | 285.17 | 221.58 | 364.12 |
| 酉阳县 | Youyang County | 334.84 | 275.86 | 289.45 |
| 彭水县 | Pengshui County | 278.40 | 233.92 | 295.02 |

**表 20.12 续表 continued**

| 区 县 | Region | 城市居民最低生活保障人数（人）Number of Persons Receiving Minimum Living Allowance in Rural Areas (person) | 提供住宿的社会服务机构（个）Residential Social Welfare Institutions (unit) | 提供住宿的社会服务机构床位数（张）Social Services Institutions with Accommodation |
|---|---|---|---|---|
| **全 市** | **Total** | **218011** | **1255** | **133672** |
| 主城都市区 | The city proper of Chongqing | 108958 | 770 | 79218 |
| 中心城区 | The central urban area of Chongqing | 42285 | 309 | 32717 |
| 主城新区 | The new area of Chongqing city proper | 66673 | 461 | 46501 |
| 渝东北三峡库区城镇群 | The city cluster of three gorges reservoir area in northeast Chongqing | 77034 | 433 | 41476 |
| 渝东南武陵山区城镇群 | The city cluster of Wuling mountain area in southeast Chongqing | 30911 | 33 | 5435 |
| 万州区 | Wanzhou District | 17168 | 40 | 6327 |
| 黔江区 | Qianjiang District | 4821 | 6 | 1406 |
| 涪陵区 | Fuling District | 8444 | 16 | 2778 |
| 渝中区 | Yuzhong District | 9389 | 25 | 1941 |
| 大渡口区 | Dadukou District | 1769 | 33 | 2400 |
| 江北区 | Jiangbei District | 3974 | 11 | 1006 |
| 沙坪坝区 | Shapingba District | 5075 | 64 | 7388 |
| 九龙坡区 | Jiulongpo District | 6810 | 36 | 3972 |
| 南岸区 | Nan'an District | 6513 | 32 | 3980 |
| 北碚区 | Beibei District | 3136 | 29 | 2737 |
| 渝北区 | Yubei District | 1996 | 28 | 2892 |
| 巴南区 | Ba'nan District | 3623 | 51 | 6401 |
| 长寿区 | Changshou District | 4045 | 36 | 3104 |
| 江津区 | Jiangjin District | 7083 | 78 | 7640 |
| 合川区 | Hechuan District | 11186 | 64 | 6860 |
| 永川区 | Yongchuan District | 4691 | 34 | 2982 |
| 南川区 | Nanchuan District | 2766 | 14 | 1080 |
| 綦江区 | Qijiang District | 10025 | 41 | 4334 |
| #綦江区（不含万盛） | Qijiang District (excluding Wansheng) | 6824 | 32 | 3842 |
| 大足区 | Dazu District | 6435 | 47 | 5407 |
| 璧山区 | Bishan District | 1689 | 12 | 2197 |
| 铜梁区 | Tongliang District | 2629 | 53 | 4301 |
| 潼南区 | Tongnan District | 1938 | 33 | 3248 |
| 荣昌区 | Rongchang District | 5742 | 33 | 2570 |
| 开州区 | Kaizhou District | 15207 | 24 | 3663 |
| 梁平区 | Liangping District | 2551 | 32 | 3071 |
| 武隆区 | Wulong District | 2644 | 12 | 1504 |
| 城口县 | Chengkou County | 1346 | 30 | 1752 |
| 丰都县 | Fengdu County | 4030 | 52 | 3487 |
| 垫江县 | Dianjiang County | 3425 | 72 | 4603 |
| 忠 县 | Zhongxian County | 3062 | 116 | 10623 |
| 云阳县 | Yunyang County | 8876 | 33 | 3637 |
| 奉节县 | Fengjie County | 11658 | 20 | 2330 |
| 巫山县 | Wushan County | 7186 | 4 | 828 |
| 巫溪县 | Wuxi County | 2525 | 10 | 1155 |
| 石柱县 | Shizhu County | 3169 | 6 | 568 |
| 秀山县 | Xiushan County | 10012 | 4 | 1220 |
| 酉阳县 | Youyang County | 5957 | 2 | 193 |
| 彭水县 | Pengshui County | 4308 | 3 | 544 |

# 表 20.13 各区县居民收支情况（2022 年）
## PER CAPITA INCOME AND EXPENDITURE OF HOUSEHOLDS BY REGION (2022)

| 区 县 | Region | 全体居民人均可支配收入（元）Per Capita Annual Disposable Income | 城镇常住居民人均可支配收入（元）Per Capita Disposable Income of Urban Residents (yuan) | 农村常住居民人均可支配收入（元）Per Capita Disposable Income of Rural Residents (yuan) | 全体居民人均生活消费支出（元）Per Capita Annual Living Expenditure (yuan) | 城镇常住居民人均生活消费支出（元）Per Capita Living Expenditure of Urban Residents (yuan) | 农村常住居民人均生活消费支出（元）Per Capita Living Expenditure of Rural Residents (yuan) |
|---|---|---|---|---|---|---|---|
| **全 市** | **Total** | **35666** | **45509** | **19313** | **25371** | **30574** | **16727** |
| 主城都市区 | The city proper of Chongqing | | | | | | |
| 中心城区 | The central urban area of Chongqing | | | | | | |
| 主城新区 | The new area of Chongqing city proper | | | | | | |
| 渝东北三峡库区城镇群 | The city cluster of three gorges reservoir area in northeast Chongqing | | | | | | |
| 渝东南武陵山区城镇群 | The city cluster of Wuling mountain area in southeast Chongqing | | | | | | |
| 万州区 | Wanzhou District | 40718 | 49423 | 20746 | 28205 | 33206 | 16732 |
| 黔江区 | Qianjiang District | 32463 | 42809 | 16767 | 21223 | 26599 | 13068 |
| 涪陵区 | Fuling District | 40963 | 48550 | 20748 | 30489 | 35910 | 16044 |
| 渝中区 | Yuzhong District | 53433 | 53433 | | 38773 | 38773 | |
| 大渡口区 | Dadukou District | 48163 | 48648 | 26787 | 31785 | 32008 | 21949 |
| 江北区 | Jiangbei District | 52608 | 52788 | 27470 | 31571 | 31696 | 14033 |
| 沙坪坝区 | Shapingba District | 48846 | 49521 | 27028 | 36811 | 37330 | 20025 |
| 九龙坡区 | Jiulongpo District | 50265 | 51696 | 27740 | 33710 | 34478 | 21619 |
| 南岸区 | Nan'an District | 49357 | 50014 | 28800 | 33090 | 33553 | 18613 |
| 北碚区 | Beibei District | 46178 | 49170 | 25632 | 33995 | 35908 | 20859 |
| 渝北区 | Yubei District | 48647 | 51373 | 24920 | 34667 | 36343 | 20079 |
| 巴南区 | Ba'nan District | 46895 | 50972 | 25645 | 36503 | 39896 | 18823 |
| 长寿区 | Changshou District | 37795 | 44703 | 21170 | 27824 | 32722 | 16036 |
| 江津区 | Jiangjin District | 39113 | 47734 | 25537 | 28024 | 34196 | 18304 |
| 合川区 | Hechuan District | 37391 | 44990 | 23691 | 29119 | 35075 | 18383 |
| 永川区 | Yongchuan District | 41262 | 47732 | 25315 | 26244 | 29493 | 18235 |
| 南川区 | Nanchuan District | 34454 | 43264 | 20284 | 22454 | 26578 | 15821 |
| 綦江区 | Qijiang District | | | | | | |
| #綦江区（不含万盛） | Qijiang District (excluding Wansheng) | 33179 | 40172 | 20165 | 23095 | 27073 | 15693 |
| 万盛经开区 | Wansheng Economic Development District | 31432 | 34518 | 19513 | 20395 | 21594 | 15761 |
| 大足区 | Dazu District | 36317 | 44790 | 22760 | 24824 | 30250 | 16144 |
| 璧山区 | Bishan District | 42408 | 49070 | 25393 | 24824 | 27950 | 16842 |
| 铜梁区 | Tongliang District | 39030 | 47581 | 24561 | 23302 | 28138 | 15120 |
| 潼南区 | Tongnan District | 34320 | 43339 | 21069 | 21877 | 27061 | 14261 |
| 荣昌区 | Rongchang District | 36749 | 45429 | 23267 | 23296 | 27894 | 16153 |
| 开州区 | Kaizhou District | 30762 | 41344 | 19478 | 22764 | 29346 | 15744 |
| 梁平区 | Liangping District | 34000 | 45673 | 21808 | 20987 | 25182 | 16605 |
| 武隆区 | Wulong District | 32523 | 46360 | 18412 | 22100 | 28992 | 15071 |
| 城口县 | Chengkou County | 22200 | 34526 | 13359 | 15914 | 23474 | 10490 |
| 丰都县 | Fengdu County | 30324 | 41728 | 18829 | 19510 | 25742 | 13227 |
| 垫江县 | Dianjiang County | 33936 | 45713 | 22039 | 22839 | 28832 | 16785 |
| 忠 县 | Zhongxian County | 33831 | 46618 | 21039 | 22750 | 29630 | 15867 |
| 云阳县 | Yunyang County | 27572 | 36504 | 17073 | 18762 | 23046 | 13727 |
| 奉节县 | Fengjie County | 26636 | 36841 | 16033 | 18208 | 22330 | 13924 |
| 巫山县 | Wushan County | 25735 | 39667 | 14484 | 18673 | 25910 | 12828 |
| 巫溪县 | Wuxi County | 20918 | 32117 | 13163 | 15182 | 20170 | 11728 |
| 石柱县 | Shizhu County | 31591 | 40872 | 18323 | 17587 | 20631 | 13237 |
| 秀山县 | Xiushan County | 28337 | 42421 | 15873 | 17654 | 22797 | 13102 |
| 酉阳县 | Youyang County | 22259 | 33298 | 13789 | 16882 | 23275 | 11977 |
| 彭水县 | Pengshui County | 26519 | 37220 | 15882 | 18633 | 23828 | 13468 |

# 表 20.14 各区县教育和文化(2022 年)
## EDUCATION AND CULTURE BY REGION (2022)

| 区 县 | Region | 普通中学 Regular Secondary Schools 学校数(个) Number of Schools (unit) | 专任教师数(人) Full-time Teachers (person) | 在校学生数(人) Total Enrollment (person) | 小 学 Primary Schools 学校数(个) Number of Schools (unit) | 专任教师数(人) Full-time Teachers (person) | 在校学生数(人) Total Enrollment (person) |
|---|---|---|---|---|---|---|---|
| **全 市** | **Total** | **1120** | **129754** | **1750773** | **2637** | **134050** | **2031938** |
| 主城都市区 | The city proper of Chongqing | 611 | 75810 | 1006186 | 1431 | 80532 | 1277990 |
| 中心城区 | The central urban area of Chongqing | 255 | 32924 | 411777 | 473 | 37807 | 653237 |
| 主城新区 | The new area of Chongqing city proper | 356 | 42886 | 594409 | 958 | 42725 | 624753 |
| 渝东北三峡库区城镇群 | The city cluster of three gorges reservoir area in northeast Chongqing | 333 | 36263 | 514547 | 840 | 35971 | 513695 |
| 渝东南武陵山区城镇群 | The city cluster of Wuling mountain area in southeast Chongqing | 176 | 17681 | 230040 | 366 | 17547 | 240253 |
| 万州区 | Wanzhou District | 63 | 5744 | 84881 | 90 | 4902 | 85236 |
| 黔江区 | Qianjiang District | 27 | 2977 | 36275 | 51 | 2631 | 40600 |
| 涪陵区 | Fuling District | 46 | 4438 | 63715 | 90 | 4368 | 58078 |
| 渝中区 | Yuzhong District | 12 | 2512 | 22552 | 31 | 2425 | 33050 |
| 大渡口区 | Dadukou District | 9 | 1158 | 16690 | 21 | 1545 | 29785 |
| 江北区 | Jiangbei District | 26 | 3382 | 45679 | 38 | 3139 | 54019 |
| 沙坪坝区 | Shapingba District | 37 | 4130 | 52911 | 70 | 5378 | 98657 |
| 九龙坡区 | Jiulongpo District | 35 | 5491 | 66937 | 54 | 5667 | 98816 |
| 南岸区 | Nan'an District | 27 | 3491 | 45253 | 45 | 4191 | 77124 |
| 北碚区 | Beibei District | 18 | 2931 | 37816 | 55 | 2489 | 41540 |
| 渝北区 | Yubei District | 51 | 6353 | 79618 | 89 | 8802 | 148081 |
| 巴南区 | Ba'nan District | 40 | 3476 | 44321 | 70 | 4171 | 72165 |
| 长寿区 | Changshou District | 29 | 3112 | 30864 | 34 | 2888 | 32656 |
| 江津区 | Jiangjin District | 46 | 5050 | 71509 | 101 | 4547 | 75519 |
| 合川区 | Hechuan District | 34 | 4300 | 62020 | 106 | 4310 | 59958 |
| 永川区 | Yongchuan District | 35 | 4189 | 64267 | 111 | 4236 | 71437 |
| 南川区 | Nanchuan District | 17 | 2295 | 36148 | 57 | 2768 | 35548 |
| 綦江区 | Qijiang District | 37 | 4033 | 48806 | 84 | 4294 | 56919 |
| #綦江区(不含万盛) | Qijiang District (excluding Wansheng) | 28 | 3114 | 38146 | 61 | 3305 | 42887 |
| 大足区 | Dazu District | 33 | 4262 | 60418 | 91 | 4409 | 65594 |
| 璧山区 | Bishan District | 16 | 2369 | 33571 | 40 | 2296 | 42161 |
| 铜梁区 | Tongliang District | 21 | 3352 | 45564 | 61 | 2781 | 41505 |
| 潼南区 | Tongnan District | 21 | 2818 | 38237 | 73 | 2859 | 44794 |
| 荣昌区 | Rongchang District | 21 | 2668 | 39290 | 110 | 2969 | 40584 |
| 开州区 | Kaizhou District | 30 | 3060 | 44443 | 65 | 3197 | 40935 |
| 梁平区 | Liangping District | 8 | 1089 | 15103 | 42 | 1185 | 16364 |
| 武隆区 | Wulong District | 44 | 3285 | 38817 | 51 | 2603 | 32376 |
| 城口县 | Chengkou County | 16 | 3249 | 43735 | 56 | 3317 | 41791 |
| 丰都县 | Fengdu County | 11 | 1400 | 19364 | 54 | 1680 | 18398 |
| 垫江县 | Dianjiang County | 26 | 3578 | 55809 | 100 | 3398 | 41768 |
| 忠 县 | Zhongxian County | 68 | 5996 | 84031 | 78 | 5374 | 95055 |
| 云阳县 | Yunyang County | 40 | 4507 | 60176 | 102 | 4115 | 61274 |
| 奉节县 | Fengjie County | 30 | 3146 | 47063 | 94 | 3807 | 48232 |
| 巫山县 | Wushan County | 22 | 2537 | 31785 | 82 | 2496 | 33617 |
| 巫溪县 | Wuxi County | 19 | 1957 | 28157 | 77 | 2500 | 31025 |
| 石柱县 | Shizhu County | 20 | 2289 | 29919 | 46 | 2215 | 26437 |
| 秀山县 | Xiushan County | 25 | 2639 | 33857 | 55 | 3178 | 45619 |
| 酉阳县 | Youyang County | 38 | 3628 | 53059 | 89 | 3934 | 54968 |
| 彭水县 | Pengshui County | 22 | 2863 | 38113 | 74 | 2986 | 40253 |

**表 20.14 续表 continued**

| 区 县 | Region | 广播覆盖率（%） Radio Coverage of Population (%) | 电视覆盖率（%） Television Coverage of Population (%) | 公共图书馆（个） Number of Public Libraries (unit) | 公共图书馆藏 书（万册） Number of Books in Public Libraries (10 000 volumes) |
|---|---|---|---|---|---|
| **全 市** | **Total** | **99.55** | **99.66** | **43** | **2727.01** |
| 主城都市区 | The city proper of Chongqing | 99.85 | 99.75 | 26 | 2291.22 |
| 中心城区 | The central urban area of Chongqing | 100.00 | 100.00 | 11 | 1278.17 |
| 主城新区 | The new area of Chongqing city proper | 99.77 | 99.60 | 15 | 1013.05 |
| 渝东北三峡库区城镇群 | The city cluster of three gorges reservoir area in northeast Chongqing | 99.16 | 99.52 | 11 | 318.05 |
| 渝东南武陵山区城镇群 | The city cluster of Wuling mountain area in southeast Chongqing | 99.05 | 99.56 | 6 | 117.74 |
| 万州区 | Wanzhou District | 100.00 | 99.66 | 1 | 33.51 |
| 黔江区 | Qianjiang District | 99.01 | 99.21 | 1 | 34.29 |
| 涪陵区 | Fuling District | 99.97 | 99.16 | 2 | 189.43 |
| 渝中区 | Yuzhong District | 100.00 | 100.00 | 2 | 192.67 |
| 大渡口区 | Dadukou District | 100.00 | 100.00 | 1 | 41.15 |
| 江北区 | Jiangbei District | 100.00 | 100.00 | 1 | 76.60 |
| 沙坪坝区 | Shapingba District | 100.00 | 100.00 | 2 | 521.26 |
| 九龙坡区 | Jiulongpo District | 100.00 | 100.00 | 1 | 119.91 |
| 南岸区 | Nan'an District | 100.00 | 100.00 | 1 | 51.15 |
| 北碚区 | Beibei District | 100.00 | 100.00 | 1 | 76.69 |
| 渝北区 | Yubei District | 100.00 | 100.00 | 1 | 119.61 |
| 巴南区 | Ba'nan District | 100.00 | 100.00 | 1 | 79.13 |
| 长寿区 | Changshou District | 100.00 | 100.00 | 1 | 79.87 |
| 江津区 | Jiangjin District | 100.00 | 99.98 | 1 | 142.14 |
| 合川区 | Hechuan District | 99.33 | 99.28 | 1 | 91.86 |
| 永川区 | Yongchuan District | 100.00 | 100.00 | 1 | 118.88 |
| 南川区 | Nanchuan District | 98.35 | 97.48 | 1 | 43.85 |
| 綦江区 | Qijiang District | 99.77 | 99.76 | 2 | 87.51 |
| #綦江区（不含万盛） | Qijiang District (excluding Wansheng) | 99.91 | 99.90 | 1 | 66.35 |
| 大足区 | Dazu District | 99.98 | 99.90 | 2 | 49.87 |
| 璧山区 | Bishan District | 99.98 | 99.20 | 1 | 44.85 |
| 铜梁区 | Tongliang District | 100.00 | 100.00 | 1 | 55.82 |
| 潼南区 | Tongnan District | 99.57 | 99.77 | 1 | 52.97 |
| 荣昌区 | Rongchang District | 100.00 | 100.00 | 1 | 56.00 |
| 开州区 | Kaizhou District | 99.71 | 99.91 | 1 | 21.69 |
| 梁平区 | Liangping District | 99.47 | 99.28 | 1 | 25.96 |
| 武隆区 | Wulong District | 100.00 | 100.00 | 1 | 16.24 |
| 城口县 | Chengkou County | 95.34 | 97.01 | 1 | 19.51 |
| 丰都县 | Fengdu County | 99.34 | 99.93 | 1 | 18.25 |
| 垫江县 | Dianjiang County | 100.00 | 100.00 | 1 | 50.59 |
| 忠 县 | Zhongxian County | 96.82 | 99.69 | 1 | 87.15 |
| 云阳县 | Yunyang County | 99.65 | 99.67 | 1 | 14.52 |
| 奉节县 | Fengjie County | 99.42 | 99.42 | 1 | 15.11 |
| 巫山县 | Wushan County | 98.28 | 99.22 | 1 | 23.22 |
| 巫溪县 | Wuxi County | 97.79 | 97.79 | 1 | 8.54 |
| 石柱县 | Shizhu County | 100.00 | 100.00 | 1 | 16.15 |
| 秀山县 | Xiushan County | 98.00 | 99.97 | 1 | 26.21 |
| 酉阳县 | Youyang County | 99.30 | 99.99 | 1 | 11.19 |
| 彭水县 | Pengshui County | 98.52 | 98.33 | 1 | 13.66 |

# 表 20.15 各区县卫生（2022 年）
## PUBLIC HEALTH CARE BY REGION (2022)

| 区 县 | Region | 卫生机构数（个）Number of Health Care Institutions (unit) | 卫生机构床位数（张）Hospital Beds in Health Care Institutions (bed) | 卫生技术人员（人）Medical Technical Personnel (person) | #执 业（助理）医师 Licensed (assistant) Doctors | #注册护士 Registered Nurses |
|---|---|---|---|---|---|---|
| **全 市** | **Total** | **22261** | **250832** | **253241** | **94609** | **117336** |
| 主城都市区 | The city proper of Chongqing | 12788 | 152347 | 169484 | 63199 | 80213 |
| 中心城区 | The central urban area of Chongqing | 5456 | 74996 | 96659 | 35287 | 47069 |
| 主城新区 | The new area of Chongqing city proper | 7332 | 77351 | 72825 | 27912 | 33144 |
| 渝东北三峡库区城镇群 | The city cluster of three gorges reservoir area in northeast Chongqing | 6265 | 64320 | 52364 | 20049 | 22690 |
| 渝东南武陵山区城镇群 | The city cluster of Wuling mountain area in southeast Chongqing | 2367 | 25575 | 19779 | 7131 | 8669 |
| 万州区 | Wanzhou District | 1279 | 12716 | 13375 | 5169 | 5971 |
| 黔江区 | Qianjiang District | 317 | 4814 | 4206 | 1415 | 1979 |
| 涪陵区 | Fuling District | 653 | 7874 | 8449 | 3257 | 3648 |
| 渝中区 | Yuzhong District | 413 | 16595 | 23165 | 7523 | 12122 |
| 大渡口区 | Dadukou District | 274 | 3063 | 3599 | 1357 | 1702 |
| 江北区 | Jiangbei District | 548 | 9473 | 12578 | 4474 | 6355 |
| 沙坪坝区 | Shapingba District | 618 | 9700 | 11382 | 4329 | 5431 |
| 九龙坡区 | Jiulongpo District | 748 | 10527 | 12081 | 4281 | 5791 |
| 南岸区 | Nan'an District | 669 | 5313 | 8592 | 3360 | 4054 |
| 北碚区 | Beibei District | 435 | 5239 | 6076 | 2336 | 2669 |
| 渝北区 | Yubei District | 940 | 7014 | 11224 | 4471 | 5149 |
| 巴南区 | Ba'nan District | 811 | 8072 | 7962 | 3156 | 3796 |
| 长寿区 | Changshou District | 462 | 6163 | 5087 | 1878 | 2363 |
| 江津区 | Jiangjin District | 613 | 9933 | 8158 | 3504 | 3473 |
| 合川区 | Hechuan District | 848 | 7896 | 8137 | 3213 | 3741 |
| 永川区 | Yongchuan District | 759 | 9878 | 8584 | 2997 | 4137 |
| 南川区 | Nanchuan District | 465 | 4745 | 4560 | 1603 | 2193 |
| 綦江区 | Qijiang District | 527 | 6957 | 5364 | 1830 | 2544 |
| #綦江区（不含万盛） | Qijiang District (excluding Wansheng) | 395 | 4354 | 3404 | 1282 | 1514 |
| 大足区 | Dazu District | 716 | 5885 | 5100 | 2016 | 2231 |
| 璧山区 | Bishan District | 530 | 4738 | 5010 | 1951 | 2441 |
| 铜梁区 | Tongliang District | 881 | 4387 | 4979 | 1982 | 2285 |
| 潼南区 | Tongnan District | 430 | 4211 | 3946 | 1549 | 1577 |
| 荣昌区 | Rongchang District | 448 | 4684 | 5451 | 2132 | 2511 |
| 开州区 | Kaizhou District | 582 | 4905 | 4015 | 1640 | 1767 |
| 梁平区 | Liangping District | 182 | 1555 | 1406 | 483 | 564 |
| 武隆区 | Wulong District | 492 | 5237 | 3594 | 1245 | 1578 |
| 城口县 | Chengkou County | 439 | 5188 | 4424 | 1727 | 1904 |
| 丰都县 | Fengdu County | 349 | 3022 | 2062 | 801 | 800 |
| 垫江县 | Dianjiang County | 600 | 5973 | 4277 | 1603 | 1914 |
| 忠 县 | Zhongxian County | 777 | 9726 | 7188 | 2887 | 3129 |
| 云阳县 | Yunyang County | 708 | 8593 | 5753 | 2333 | 2347 |
| 奉节县 | Fengjie County | 568 | 6154 | 4754 | 1648 | 2287 |
| 巫山县 | Wushan County | 418 | 4106 | 3055 | 1009 | 1296 |
| 巫溪县 | Wuxi County | 363 | 2382 | 2055 | 749 | 711 |
| 石柱县 | Shizhu County | 363 | 3894 | 2789 | 1128 | 1229 |
| 秀山县 | Xiushan County | 359 | 3844 | 3487 | 1152 | 1640 |
| 酉阳县 | Youyang County | 395 | 4067 | 2866 | 1080 | 1097 |
| 彭水县 | Pengshui County | 441 | 3719 | 2837 | 1111 | 1146 |

注：卫生机构数含个体诊所。
Note: The number of health care institutions include individual-run clinics.

# 表 20.16 各区县对外经济贸易（2022 年）
## FOREIGN ECONOMIC RELATIONS AND TRADE BY REGION (2022)

| 区 县 | Region | 进出口总值（亿元） Total Imports and Exports (100 million yuan) | 出 口 Exports | 进 口 Imports |
|---|---|---|---|---|
| **全 市** | **Total** | **8158.35** | **5245.32** | **2913.03** |
| 主城都市区 | The city proper of Chongqing | 8033.84 | 5193.44 | 2840.40 |
| 中心城区 | The central urban area of Chongqing | 7148.76 | 4684.76 | 2464.00 |
| 主城新区 | The new area of Chongqing city proper | 885.08 | 508.68 | 376.40 |
| 渝东北三峡库区城镇群 | The city cluster of three gorges reservoir area in northeast Chongqing | 66.38 | 27.24 | 39.14 |
| 渝东南武陵山区城镇群 | The city cluster of Wuling mountain area in southeast Chongqing | 58.13 | 24.64 | 33.49 |
| 万州区 | Wanzhou District | 51.94 | 15.16 | 36.78 |
| 黔江区 | Qianjiang District | 1.72 | 1.28 | 0.44 |
| 涪陵区 | Fuling District | 218.55 | 122.03 | 96.53 |
| 渝中区 | Yuzhong District | 103.13 | 47.45 | 55.68 |
| 大渡口区 | Dadukou District | 40.98 | 21.87 | 19.11 |
| 江北区 | Jiangbei District | 955.27 | 359.24 | 596.03 |
| 沙坪坝区 | Shapingba District | 3488.46 | 2421.14 | 1067.31 |
| 九龙坡区 | Jiulongpo District | 174.09 | 153.21 | 20.88 |
| 南岸区 | Nan'an District | 99.08 | 75.98 | 23.10 |
| 北碚区 | Beibei District | 241.01 | 115.18 | 125.83 |
| 渝北区 | Yubei District | 1923.36 | 1401.68 | 521.68 |
| 巴南区 | Ba'nan District | 123.39 | 89.00 | 34.39 |
| 长寿区 | Changshou District | 131.33 | 65.65 | 65.68 |
| 江津区 | Jiangjin District | 262.73 | 142.89 | 119.85 |
| 合川区 | Hechuan District | 23.24 | 21.83 | 1.40 |
| 永川区 | Yongchuan District | 84.18 | 52.92 | 31.26 |
| 南川区 | Nanchuan District | 24.04 | 0.70 | 23.34 |
| 綦江区 | Qijiang District | 7.53 | 4.26 | 3.27 |
| #綦江区（不含万盛） | Qijiang District (excluding Wansheng) | | | |
| 大足区 | Dazu District | 22.75 | 9.61 | 13.14 |
| 璧山区 | Bishan District | 53.05 | 42.14 | 10.91 |
| 铜梁区 | Tongliang District | 14.50 | 13.27 | 1.23 |
| 潼南区 | Tongnan District | 21.14 | 19.19 | 1.95 |
| 荣昌区 | Rongchang District | 22.04 | 14.19 | 7.85 |
| 开州区 | Kaizhou District | 3.39 | 2.58 | 0.81 |
| 梁平区 | Liangping District | 2.25 | 1.53 | 0.72 |
| 武隆区 | Wulong District | 0.81 | 0.81 | |
| 城口县 | Chengkou County | | | |
| 丰都县 | Fengdu County | 1.35 | 0.66 | 0.69 |
| 垫江县 | Dianjiang County | 3.05 | 2.99 | 0.06 |
| 忠 县 | Zhongxian County | 0.96 | 0.96 | |
| 云阳县 | Yunyang County | 2.52 | 2.50 | 0.02 |
| 奉节县 | Fengjie County | 0.52 | 0.47 | 0.06 |
| 巫山县 | Wushan County | 0.39 | 0.39 | 0.00 |
| 巫溪县 | Wuxi County | | | 0.00 |
| 石柱县 | Shizhu County | 33.20 | 0.29 | 32.91 |
| 秀山县 | Xiushan County | 0.74 | 0.59 | 0.14 |
| 酉阳县 | Youyang County | 21.65 | 21.65 | |
| 彭水县 | Pengshui County | 0.03 | 0.03 | |

注：进出口数据来源于重庆海关。
Note: The data of import and export are provided by Chongqing Commerce Commission.

# 表 20.17 各区县规模以上工业能源消费总量(2022 年)
## ENERGY CONSUMPTION OF ENTERPRISES ABOVE DESIGNATED SIZE BY REGION (2022)

| 区 县 | Region | 规模以上工业能源消费总量(万吨标准煤) Energy Consumption of Enterprises above Designated Size by Region (10 000 tons of standard coal) |
|---|---|---|
| 全 市 | **Total** | **4650.78** |
| 主城都市区 | The city proper of Chongqing | 3661.78 |
| 中心城区 | The central urban area of Chongqing | 430.28 |
| 主城新区 | The new area of Chongqing city proper | 3231.51 |
| 渝东北三峡库区城镇群 | The city cluster of three gorges reservoir area in northeast Chongqing | 810.81 |
| 渝东南武陵山区城镇群 | The city cluster of Wuling mountain area in southeast Chongqing | 178.19 |
| 万州区 | Wanzhou District | 340.89 |
| 黔江区 | Qianjiang District | 37.06 |
| 涪陵区 | Fuling District | 541.25 |
| 渝中区 | Yuzhong District | 1.75 |
| 大渡口区 | Dadukou District | 34.01 |
| 江北区 | Jiangbei District | 33.01 |
| 沙坪坝区 | Shapingba District | 32.06 |
| 九龙坡区 | Jiulongpo District | 85.88 |
| 南岸区 | Nan'an District | 20.00 |
| 北碚区 | Beibei District | 96.25 |
| 渝北区 | Yubei District | 77.44 |
| 巴南区 | Ba'nan District | 49.88 |
| 长寿区 | Changshou District | 1081.76 |
| 江津区 | Jiangjin District | 406.34 |
| 合川区 | Hechuan District | 290.21 |
| 永川区 | Yongchuan District | 118.57 |
| 南川区 | Nanchuan District | 125.35 |
| 綦江区 | Qijiang District | 443.81 |
| #綦江区(不含万盛) | Qijiang District (excluding Wansheng) | 289.80 |
| 大足区 | Dazu District | 32.74 |
| 璧山区 | Bishan District | 44.68 |
| 铜梁区 | Tongliang District | 55.98 |
| 潼南区 | Tongnan District | 50.33 |
| 荣昌区 | Rongchang District | 40.50 |
| 开州区 | Kaizhou District | 84.32 |
| 梁平区 | Liangping District | 23.90 |
| 武隆区 | Wulong District | 10.12 |
| 城口县 | Chengkou County | 1.06 |
| 丰都县 | Fengdu County | 131.24 |
| 垫江县 | Dianjiang County | 33.75 |
| 忠 县 | Zhongxian County | 71.71 |
| 云阳县 | Yunyang County | 12.45 |
| 奉节县 | Fengjie County | 108.06 |
| 巫山县 | Wushan County | 1.95 |
| 巫溪县 | Wuxi County | 1.46 |
| 石柱县 | Shizhu County | 68.17 |
| 秀山县 | Xiushan County | 31.82 |
| 酉阳县 | Youyang County | 14.59 |
| 彭水县 | Pengshui County | 16.44 |

# 表 20.18 各区县法人单位数、产业活动单位数（2022 年）
## NUMBER OF CORPORATE UNITS AND ESTABLISHMENTS BY REGION (2022)

| 区 县 | Region | 法人单位（个）Number of Corporate Units (unit) | #企 业 Enterprises | 产业活动单位（个）Number of Establishments (unit) |
|---|---|---|---|---|
| **全 市** | **Total** | **782071** | **705046** | **843111** |
| 主城都市区 | The city proper of Chongqing | 552342 | 512929 | 596467 |
| 中心城区 | The central urban area of Chongqing | 325411 | 311772 | 352101 |
| 主城新区 | The new area of Chongqing city proper | 226931 | 201157 | 244366 |
| 渝东北三峡库区城镇群 | The city cluster of three gorges reservoir area in northeast Chongqing | 164530 | 137321 | 176462 |
| 渝东南武陵山区城镇群 | The city cluster of Wuling mountainarea in southeast Chongqing | 65199 | 54796 | 70182 |
| 万州区 | Wanzhou District | 27210 | 24354 | 29722 |
| 黔江区 | Qianjiang District | 10467 | 8814 | 11467 |
| 涪陵区 | Fuling District | 23266 | 20557 | 25774 |
| 渝中区 | Yuzhong District | 23462 | 22104 | 26542 |
| 大渡口区 | Dadukou District | 11167 | 10510 | 12158 |
| 江北区 | Jiangbei District | 38076 | 36887 | 41424 |
| 沙坪坝区 | Shapingba District | 34460 | 33015 | 37650 |
| 九龙坡区 | Jiulongpo District | 78395 | 76754 | 82224 |
| 南岸区 | Nan'an District | 28837 | 27463 | 31372 |
| 北碚区 | Beibei District | 17277 | 15760 | 19228 |
| 渝北区 | Yubei District | 65589 | 62975 | 71556 |
| 巴南区 | Ba'nan District | 28148 | 26304 | 29947 |
| 长寿区 | Changshou District | 15159 | 13603 | 16657 |
| 江津区 | Jiangjin District | 29841 | 27414 | 31806 |
| 合川区 | Hechuan District | 16511 | 14317 | 18090 |
| 永川区 | Yongchuan District | 18477 | 16421 | 20139 |
| 南川区 | Nanchuan District | 16882 | 14398 | 17978 |
| 綦江区 | Qijiang District | 22988 | 20466 | 24701 |
| #綦江区（不含万盛） | Qijiang District (excluding Wansheng) | 13010 | 11407 | 13980 |
| 大足区 | Dazu District | 18266 | 15614 | 19345 |
| 璧山区 | Bishan District | 18402 | 16774 | 19624 |
| 铜梁区 | Tongliang District | 14981 | 12933 | 16213 |
| 潼南区 | Tongnan District | 18485 | 16582 | 19396 |
| 荣昌区 | Rongchang District | 13673 | 12078 | 14643 |
| 开州区 | Kaizhou District | 22606 | 19419 | 23849 |
| 梁平区 | Liangping District | 11382 | 9427 | 12052 |
| 武隆区 | Wulong District | 8500 | 6967 | 9026 |
| 城口县 | Chengkou County | 6679 | 5365 | 7082 |
| 丰都县 | Fengdu County | 11329 | 8658 | 12177 |
| 垫江县 | Dianjiang County | 14694 | 12700 | 15601 |
| 忠 县 | Zhongxian County | 13843 | 11999 | 15115 |
| 云阳县 | Yunyang County | 22998 | 19974 | 24556 |
| 奉节县 | Fengjie County | 16876 | 12738 | 17599 |
| 巫山县 | Wushan County | 8898 | 6472 | 10029 |
| 巫溪县 | Wuxi County | 8015 | 6215 | 8680 |
| 石柱县 | Shizhu County | 9676 | 8152 | 10374 |
| 秀山县 | Xiushan County | 13620 | 12000 | 14674 |
| 酉阳县 | Youyang County | 12432 | 10169 | 13460 |
| 彭水县 | Pengshui County | 10504 | 8694 | 11181 |

# 第二十一章·三峡工程重庆库区移民

## RESERVOIR AREA OF THREE GORGES PROJECT IN CHONGQING

# 简要说明

## BRIEF INTRODUCTION

本章资料包括三峡工程重庆库区经济和社会发展情况、移民工程投资完成情况，由市统计局综合处根据市水利局资料整理编辑。

库区指库区15区县，包括万州区、涪陵区、渝北区、巴南区、长寿区、江津区、开州区、武隆区、丰都县、忠县、云阳县、奉节县、巫山县、巫溪县、石柱县。重点库区指8个重点移民区县，包括万州区、涪陵区、开州区、丰都县、忠县、云阳县、奉节县、巫山县。

This chapter includes the economic and social development of the reservoir area of Three Gorges Project in Chongqing, the statistics on the completed investment in Three Gorges Resettlement. The data here are provided by Ministry of Water Resources of Chongqing and sorted and compiled by Division of Comprehensive Statistics of Chongqing Municipal Bureau of Statistics.

The Reservoir Area refers to 15 districts and counties, namely Wanzhou, Fuling, Yubei, Ba'nan, Changshou, Jiangjin, Fengdu, Kaizhou, Wulong, Zhongxian, Yunyang, Fengjie, Wushan, Wuxi and Shizhu. The Key Reservoir Area refers to 8 key districts and counties of migration, namely Wanzhou, Fuling, Fengdu, Zhongxian, Kaixian, Yunyang, Fengjie and Wushan.

# 表 21.1 三峡工程重庆库区经济和社会发展情况（2021 – 2022 年）
## ECONOMIC AND SOCIAL DEVELOPMENT OF THE RESERVOIR AREA OF THREE GORGES PROJECT IN CHONGQING (2021-2022)

| 指 标 | Item | 2021 | | 2022 | |
|---|---|---|---|---|---|
| | | 库区合计 Total of Reservoir Area | 重点库区 Key Area | 库区合计 Total of Reservoir Area | 重点库区 Key Area |
| **地区生产总值（亿元）** | **Gross Domestic (100 million yuan)** | **10957.16** | **5064.41** | **11525.92** | **5359.28** |
| 第一产业 | Primary Industry | 937.26 | 568.23 | 981.91 | 596.96 |
| 第二产业 | Secondary Industry | 4733.85 | 2112.63 | 5056.30 | 2259.50 |
| 第三产业 | Tertiary Industry | 5286.05 | 2383.55 | 5487.71 | 2502.82 |
| **人 口** | **Population** | | | | |
| 户籍总户数（万户） | Total Number of Households (10 000 households) | 594.66 | 335.12 | 597.74 | 335.69 |
| 户籍人口（万人） | Total Household Population (10 000 persons) | 1559.39 | 927.37 | 1557.47 | 921.88 |
| 城 镇 | Urban | 672.75 | 335.47 | 678.33 | 335.39 |
| 乡 村 | Rural | 886.64 | 591.90 | 879.14 | 586.49 |
| 男 性 | Male | 800.94 | 480.69 | 799.49 | 477.87 |
| 女 性 | Female | 758.45 | 446.68 | 757.98 | 444.01 |
| 年末常住人口（万人） | Year-end Permanent Residents (10 000 persons) | 1389.52 | 731.25 | 1390.45 | 728.12 |
| 城镇化率（%） | Urbanization Rate (%) | 65.67 | 58.24 | 66.39 | 58.96 |
| **居民收入** | **Wages and Income** | | | | |
| 城镇常住居民人均可支配收入（元） | Per Capita Disposable Income of Urban Residents | 44309 | 42239 | 46597 | 44209 |
| 农村常住居民人均可支配收入（元） | Per Capita Disposable Income of Rural Residents | 18462 | 17509 | 19885 | 18758 |
| **财 政（亿元）** | **Government Finance (100 million yuan)** | | | | |
| 区县级一般公共预算收入 | General Public Budgetary Income at District (County) Level | 529.1 | 252.8 | 514.5 | 255.1 |
| 区县级一般公共预算支出 | General Public Budgetary Expenditure at District (County) Level | 1252.2 | 683.0 | 1259.9 | 704.3 |

注：第七次全国人口普查后国家对历史年份人口和就业数据进行了修订。
Note:After the 7th national population census, the country revised the population and employment data in historical years.

**表 21.1 续表 1 continued 1**

| 指 标 | Item | 2021 | | 2022 | |
|---|---|---|---|---|---|
| | | 库区合计 Total of Reservoir Area | 重点库区 Key Area | 库区合计 Total of Reservoir Area | 重点库区 Key Area |
| **农 业** | **Agriculture** | | | | |
| 蔬菜总播种面积（万亩） | Sown Areas of Vegetables (10 000 mu) | 586 | 368 | 598 | 375 |
| 蔬菜总产量（万吨） | Gross Output of Vegetables (10 000 tons) | 1033 | 656 | 1077 | 686 |
| 猪 肉（万吨） | Pork (10 000 tons) | 71 | 48 | 75 | 51 |
| 禽 肉（万吨） | Meat of Poultry (10 000 tons) | 13 | 8 | 14 | 8 |
| 猪出栏量（万头） | Slaughtered Hogs (10 000 heads) | 902 | 610 | 951 | 648 |
| 禽出栏量（万只） | Slaughtered Poultry (10 000 heads) | 8757 | 5214 | 8938 | 5382 |
| 禽蛋产量（万吨） | Output of Poultry Eggs (10 000 tons) | 25 | 13 | 27 | 14 |
| 粮食播种面积（万亩） | Sown Areas of Grain (10 000 mu) | 1560 | 1009 | 1583 | 1024 |
| #夏 粮 | Grain Crops Harvested in Summer | 334 | 225 | 335 | 225 |
| 秋 粮 | Grain Crops Harvested in Autumn | 1226 | 784 | 1248 | 799 |
| #水 稻 | Rice | 427 | 265 | 426 | 264 |
| 玉 米 | Corn | 359 | 219 | 362 | 221 |
| 薯 类 | Tubers | 577 | 394 | 591 | 403 |
| 粮食总产量（万吨） | Gross Output of Grain (10 000 tons) | 526 | 330 | 516 | 324 |
| #夏 粮 | Grain Crops Harvested in Summer | 74 | 51 | 75 | 52 |
| 秋 粮 | Grain Crops Harvested in Autumn | 452 | 279 | 442 | 273 |
| #水 稻 | Rice | 206 | 123 | 202 | 121 |
| 玉 米 | Corn | 133 | 80 | 134 | 80 |
| 薯 类 | Tubers | 159 | 108 | 151 | 103 |
| **工 业（规模以上）** | **Industry (above Designated Size)** | | | | |
| 企业数（个） | Number of Enterprises (unit) | 2683 | 1019 | 2815 | 1077 |
| 工业总产值（万元） | Gross Output Value of Industry (10 000 yuan) | 113131970 | 36325118 | 117038857 | 37364226 |
| 出口交货值（万元） | Sales of Exported Products (10 000 yuan) | 16458572 | 806250 | 17712182 | 958312 |
| 资产总计（万元） | Total Assets (10 000 yuan) | 112176286 | 32804170 | 118369602 | 36799374 |
| 主营业务收入（万元） | Revenue from Principal Business (10 000 yuan) | 114301204 | 33965966 | 117548412 | 35390549 |
| 利润总额（万元） | Total After-tax Profits (10 000 yuan) | 9689756 | 4415001 | 9232535 | 4620957 |

**表 21.1 续表 2 continued 2**

| 指　标 | Item | 2021 | | 2022 | |
|---|---|---|---|---|---|
| | | 库区合计 Total of Reservoir Area | 重点库区 Key Area | 库区合计 Total of Reservoir Area | 重点库区 Key Area |
| 利税总额（万元） | Total Pre-tax Profits (10 000 yuan) | 12954165 | 5654197 | 12659020 | 5971206 |
| 全部从业人员平均数(万人) | Average Employment (10 000 persons) | 57.9 | 15.9 | 58.2 | 16.3 |
| 总资产贡献率（%） | Ratio of Total Assets to Industrial Output Value (%) | 12.0 | 17.7 | 11.1 | 16.7 |
| 资本保值增值率（%） | Ratio of Assets Appreciation YOY (%) | 109.6 | 115.2 | 104.7 | 106.7 |
| 资产负债率（%） | Asset-Liability Ratio (%) | 57.1 | 48.6 | 57.0 | 50.4 |
| 流动资产周转率（次） | Turnover Ratio of Circulating Assets (time) | 2.0 | 2.4 | 2.0 | 2.2 |
| 成本费用利润率（%） | Ratio of Profits to Cost (%) | 9.2 | 15.2 | 8.6 | 15.1 |
| 全员劳动生产率（元/人年） | Overall Labor Productivity (yuan/person-year) | 494174 | 669757 | 546401 | 737207 |
| 产品销售率（%） | Sales as Percentage of Output (%) | 98.1 | 97.3 | 96.1 | 95.6 |
| **国内贸易** | **Domestic Trade** | | | | |
| 社会消费品零售总额(万元) | Total Retail Sales (10 000 yuan) | 50728614 | 25000158 | 50714054 | 25263982 |
| 限额以上法人企业数（个） | Number of Corporate Enterprises above Designated Size (unit) | 3413 | 1885 | 3716 | 2130 |
| 批发业 | Wholesale | 1205 | 520 | 1290 | 575 |
| 零售业 | Retail | 1494 | 896 | 1612 | 1024 |
| 住宿业 | Hotel | 223 | 115 | 245 | 134 |
| 餐饮业 | Catering | 491 | 354 | 569 | 397 |
| **教　育** | **Education** | | | | |
| 学校数（所） | Number of Schools (unit) | | | | |
| #普通高等学校 | Regular Institutions of Higher Education | 24 | 9 | 24 | 8 |
| 普通中学 | Regular Secondary Schools | 552 | 339 | 555 | 339 |
| 小　学 | Primary Schools | 1180 | 706 | 1158 | 687 |
| 专任教师数（人） | Number of Full-time Teachers (person) | | | | |
| #普通高等学校 | Regular Institutions of Higher Education | 15966 | 5782 | 17264 | 5905 |
| 普通中学 | Regular Secondary Schools | 56118 | 33005 | 56868 | 33231 |
| 小　学 | Primary Schools | 58104 | 31864 | 57866 | 31063 |
| 在校学生数（人） | Student Enrollment (person) | | | | |
| 普通高等学校 | Regular Institutions of Higher Education | 343799 | 135068 | 135433 | 45058 |
| 普通中学 | Regular Secondary Schools | 781590 | 477871 | 770029 | 466277 |
| 小　学 | Primary Schools | 864840 | 472863 | 859917 | 455636 |
| **卫　生** | **Public Health** | | | | |
| 卫生机构数（个） | Number of Health Institutions (unit) | 9212 | 5292 | 9396 | 5495 |
| 卫生机构床位数（张） | Number of Hospital Beds (bed) | 94684 | 53311 | 100859 | 60379 |
| 卫生技术人员（人） | Medical Technological Personnel (person) | 86601 | 47245 | 89782 | 50445 |

## 表 21.2 三峡移民工程后续工作专项资金完成投资情况(2022 年底止)
## COMPREHENSIVE STATISTICS ON THE COMPLETED INVESTMENT IN THE FOLLOW-ON WORK OF THREE GORGES RESETTLEMENT (END OF 2022)

单位：亿元 (100 million yuan)

| 区 县 | Region | 三峡后续工作专项资金累计计划投资 Total Planned Investment in the Follow-on Work of Three Gorges Resettlement | 截至 2022 年 12 月底三峡后续工作专项资金累计完成投资 Investment in the Follow-on Work of Three Gorges Resettlement by the End of December 2020 | 三峡后续工作专项资金本期完成投资 Completed Investment in This Term | | | |
|---|---|---|---|---|---|---|---|
| | | | | 合计 Total | 移民安稳致富和促进库区经济社会发展 Stabilization of Resettlers and the Economic and Social Development of Resoir Areas | 库区生态环境建设与保护 Construction and Protection of the Ecological Environment of the Resevoir Areas. | 地质灾害防治 Geological Hazard Control |
| 重庆市合计 | Total of Chongqing | 680.03 | 664.97 | 18.49 | 10.79 | 5.94 | 1.45 |
| 库区合计 | Total of Reservoir Area | 641.16 | 627.35 | 16.50 | 9.44 | 5.87 | 0.96 |
| 渝北区 | Yubei | 6.89 | 6.89 | 0.02 | 0.02 | | |
| 巴南区 | Ba'nan | 11.16 | 10.23 | 0.81 | 0.44 | 0.37 | |
| 江津区 | Jiangjin | 5.67 | 5.45 | 0.54 | 0.52 | 0.02 | |
| 长寿区 | Changshou | 18.25 | 18.21 | 0.04 | 0.01 | 0.03 | |
| 武隆区 | Wulong | 20.04 | 19.84 | 0.11 | 0.11 | | |
| 巫溪县 | Wuxi | 5.59 | 5.59 | 0.08 | | 0.08 | |
| 石柱县 | Shizhu | 10.23 | 9.98 | 0.12 | 0.07 | 0.04 | 0.01 |
| 万州区 | Wanzhou | 129.15 | 126.66 | 0.49 | | | 0.45 |
| 涪陵区 | Fuling | 80.11 | 78.42 | 2.56 | 1.90 | 0.50 | 0.14 |
| 开州区 | Kaixian | 74.78 | 73.71 | 3.15 | 2.03 | 0.92 | 0.03 |
| 丰都县 | Fengdu | 44.09 | 43.31 | 1.35 | 0.49 | 0.71 | 0.15 |
| 忠 县 | Zhongxian | 50.24 | 49.09 | | | | |
| 云阳县 | Yunyang | 71.61 | 70.37 | 2.74 | 1.94 | 0.69 | 0.11 |
| 奉节县 | Fengjie | 60.55 | 57.31 | 4.48 | 1.91 | 2.51 | 0.06 |
| 巫山县 | Wushan | 52.80 | 52.29 | 0.01 | | | 0.01 |

# 第二十二章·基本单位名录库

# STATISTICS ON BASIC UNITS

# 简要说明
## BRIEF INTRODUCTION

本章资料包括按行业分的法人、产业活动单位数，按机构类型和登记注册类型分的法人、产业活动单位数，按区县、行业分的法人单位数和企业法人单位数，按区县、登记注册类型分的法人单位数和企业法人单位数。

This chapter includes the number of legal persons and industrial activity units by industry, the number of legal persons and industrial activity units by institution type and registration type, the number of legal person units and enterprise legal person units by district, county and industry, and the number of districts, counties and registrations The number of registered legal entities and the number of corporate legal entities.

# 表 22.1 按行业分组的法人单位数和产业活动单位数（2022 年）
## NUMBER OF CORPORATE UNITS AND ESTABLISHMENTS BY SECTOR (2022)

单位：个 (unit)

| 指 标 | Item | 法人单位 Corporate Units | 产业活动单位 Establishments |
|---|---|---|---|
| **总 计** | **Total** | **782071** | **843111** |
| **按三次产业分组** | **By Strata of Industry** | | |
| 第一产业 | Primary Industry | 88054 | 88460 |
| 第二产业 | Secondary Industry | 105061 | 110534 |
| 第三产业 | Tertiary Industry | 588956 | 644117 |
| **按国民经济行业分组** | **By Sector** | | |
| **农、林、牧、渔业** | **Agriculture, Forestry, Animal Husbandry and Fishery** | **94654** | **95136** |
| 农 业 | Farming | 48132 | 48331 |
| 林 业 | Forestry | 3500 | 3523 |
| 畜牧业 | Animal Husbandry | 25775 | 25900 |
| 渔 业 | Fishery | 10647 | 10706 |
| 农、林、牧、渔专业及辅助性活动 | Services of Farming, Forestry, Animal Husbandry and Fishery | 6600 | 6676 |
| **采矿业** | **Mining** | **1393** | **1523** |
| 煤炭开采和洗选业 | Mining and Washing of Coal | 167 | 210 |
| 石油和天然气开采业 | Extraction of Petroleum and Natural Gas | 17 | 30 |
| 黑色金属矿采选业 | Mining and Processing of Ferrous Metal Ores | 72 | 78 |
| 有色金属矿采选业 | Mining and Processing of Non-ferrous Metal Ores | 21 | 20 |
| 非金属矿采选业 | Mining and Processing of Non-metal Ores | 1050 | 1107 |
| 开采专业及辅助性活动 | Support Activities for Mining | 39 | 48 |
| 其他采矿业 | Mining of Other Ores | 27 | 30 |
| **制造业** | **Manufacture** | **68144** | **69499** |
| 农副食品加工业 | Processing of Food from Agricultural Products | 4991 | 5079 |
| 食品制造业 | Manufacture of Foods | 2268 | 2322 |
| 酒、饮料和精制茶制造业 | Manufacture of Liquor, Beverages and Refined Tea | 2037 | 2088 |
| 烟草制品业 | Manufacture of Tobacco | 7 | 11 |
| 纺织业 | Manufacture of Textile | 1368 | 1399 |
| 纺织服装、服饰业 | Manufacture of Textile, Wearing Apparel and Accessories | 2013 | 2037 |
| 皮革、毛皮、羽毛及其制品和制鞋业 | Manufacture of Leather, Fur, Feather and Related Products and Footwear | 842 | 852 |
| 木材加工和木、竹、藤、棕、草制品业 | Processing of Timber, Manufacture of Wood, Bamboo, Rattan, Palm and Straw Products | 2992 | 3019 |
| 家具制造业 | Manufacture of Furniture | 2369 | 2392 |
| 造纸和纸制品业 | Manufacture of Paper and Paper Products | 975 | 990 |
| 印刷和记录媒介复制业 | Printing, Reproduction of Recording Media | 1579 | 1623 |
| 文教、工美、体育和娱乐用品制造业 | Manufacture of Articles for Culture, Education, Arts and Crafts, Sport and Entertainment Activities | 1335 | 1364 |
| 石油、煤炭及其他燃料加工业 | Manufacture of Raw Chemical Materials and Chemical Products | 189 | 199 |
| 化学原料和化学制品制造业 | Manufacture of Medicines | 1708 | 1764 |
| 医药制造业 | Manufacture of Chemical Fibres | 593 | 614 |
| 化学纤维制造业 | Manufacture of Rubber and Plastics Products | 48 | 48 |
| 橡胶和塑料制品业 | Manufacture of Non-metallic Mineral Products | 2516 | 2553 |
| 非金属矿物制品业 | Smelting and Pressing of Ferrous Metals | 7024 | 7196 |
| 黑色金属冶炼和压延加工业 | Smelting and Pressing of Non-ferrous Metals | 461 | 478 |
| 有色金属冶炼和压延加工业 | Manufacture of Metal Products | 618 | 627 |

**表 22.1 续表 1 continued 1**

单位：个 (unit)

| 指 标 | Item | 法人单位<br>Corporate Units | 产业活动单位<br>Establishments |
|---|---|---|---|
| 金属制品业 | Manufacture of General Purpose Machinery | 6995 | 7105 |
| 通用设备制造业 | Manufacture of Special Purpose Machinery | 5824 | 5923 |
| 专用设备制造业 | Manufacture of Automobiles | 4387 | 4471 |
| 汽车制造业 | Manufacture of Railway ,Ship, Aerospace and Other Transport Equipment | 5129 | 5239 |
| 铁路、船舶、航空航天和其他运输设备制造业 | Manufacture of Electrical Machinery and Apparatus | 2696 | 2731 |
| 电气机械和器材制造业 | Manufacture of Computers, Communication and Other Electronic Equipment | 2007 | 2056 |
| 计算机、通信和其他电子设备制造业 | Manufacture of Measuring Instruments and Machinery | 2269 | 2292 |
| 仪器仪表制造业 | Other Manufacture | 924 | 944 |
| 其他制造业 | Utilization of Waste Resources | 434 | 440 |
| 废弃资源综合利用业 | Repair of Metal Products, Machinery and Equipment | 502 | 544 |
| 金属制品、机械和设备修理业 | Manufacture of Metal Products, Machinery and Equipment Maintenance | 1044 | 1099 |
| **电力、热力、燃气及水生产和供应业** | **Production and Supply of Electric Power, Gas and Water** | **2611** | **3477** |
| 电力、热力生产和供应业 | Production and Supply of Electric Power and Heat Power | 1461 | 1747 |
| 燃气生产和供应业 | Production and Supply of Gas | 305 | 426 |
| 水的生产和供应业 | Production and Supply of Water | 845 | 1304 |
| **建筑业** | **Construction** | **33996** | **37182** |
| 房屋建筑业 | Construction of Housing | 6991 | 8233 |
| 土木工程建筑业 | Civil Engineering Construction | 6107 | 6927 |
| 建筑安装业 | Architectural Installation | 3815 | 4151 |
| 建筑装饰、装修和其他建筑业 | Architectural Decoration and Other Construction | 17083 | 17871 |
| **批发和零售业** | **Wholesale and Retail Trade** | **232551** | **253302** |
| 批发业 | Wholesale Trade | 97873 | 101936 |
| 零售业 | Retail Trade | 134678 | 151366 |
| **交通运输、仓储和邮政业** | **Transport, Storage and Postal Services** | **18325** | **22134** |
| 铁路运输业 | Transport Via Railway | 45 | 69 |
| 道路运输业 | Transport Via Road | 11284 | 12204 |
| 水上运输业 | Water Transport | 464 | 499 |
| 航空运输业 | Air Transport | 94 | 112 |
| 管道运输业 | Transport Via Pipeline | 8 | 11 |
| 多式联运和运输代理业 | Loading, Unloading, Portage and Transport Agency | 3816 | 4088 |
| 装卸搬运和仓储业 | Storage | 1833 | 1951 |
| 邮政业 | Post | 781 | 3200 |
| **住宿和餐饮业** | **Hotels and Catering Services** | **28535** | **30941** |
| 住宿业 | Hotels | 6938 | 7336 |
| 餐饮业 | Catering Services | 21597 | 23605 |
| **信息传输、软件和信息技术服务业** | **Information Transmission, Software and Information Technology** | **38830** | **40725** |
| 电信、广播电视和卫星传输服务 | Telecommunication, Radio, Television and Satellite Transmission Services | 853 | 1562 |
| 互联网和相关服务 | Internet and Related Services | 5517 | 5683 |
| 软件和信息技术服务业 | Software and Information Technology Services | 32460 | 33480 |
| **金融业** | **Financial Intermediation** | **2273** | **8705** |

**表 22.1 续表 2 continued 2**

单位：个 (unit)

| 指 标 | Item | 法人单位 Corporate Units | 产业活动单位 Establishments |
|---|---|---|---|
| 货币金融服务 | Money Finance Services | 1171 | 5809 |
| 资本市场服务 | Capital Market Services | 612 | 887 |
| 保险业 | Insurance | 301 | 1746 |
| 其他金融业 | Other Finance | 189 | 263 |
| **房地产业** | **Real Estate** | **23373** | **27335** |
| 房地产业 | Real Estate | 23373 | 27335 |
| **租赁和商务服务业** | **Leasing and Business Services** | **98099** | **103167** |
| 租赁业 | Leasing | 16008 | 16520 |
| 商务服务业 | Business Services | 82091 | 86647 |
| **科学研究和技术服务业** | **Scientific Research and Technical Services** | **34579** | **37263** |
| 研究和试验发展 | Research and Experimental Development | 2282 | 2350 |
| 专业技术服务业 | Professional Technical Services | 19840 | 22005 |
| 科技推广和应用服务业 | Services of Science and Technology Application and Promotion | 12457 | 12908 |
| **水利、环境和公共设施管理业** | **Water Conservancy, Environment and Public Facilities Management** | **7815** | **8286** |
| 水利管理业 | Management of Water Conservancy | 261 | 343 |
| 生态保护和环境治理业 | Ecological Protection and Environmental Governance | 1220 | 1283 |
| 公共设施管理业 | Management of Public Facilities | 3732 | 3927 |
| 土地管理业 | Management of Land | 2602 | 2733 |
| **居民服务、修理和其他服务业** | **Services to Households, Repair and Other Services** | **20329** | **21371** |
| 居民服务业 | Resident Services | 9990 | 10521 |
| 机动车、电子产品和日用产品修理业 | Vehicles, Electronic Products and Commodities Maintenance Services | 7221 | 7592 |
| 其他服务业 | Other Services | 3118 | 3258 |
| **教 育** | **Education** | **18750** | **19892** |
| 教 育 | Education | 18750 | 19892 |
| **卫生和社会工作** | **Health and Social Work** | **7704** | **9120** |
| 卫 生 | Health | 5015 | 6251 |
| 社会工作 | Social Work | 2689 | 2869 |
| **文化、体育和娱乐业** | **Culture, Sports and Entertainment** | **20373** | **21070** |
| 新闻和出版业 | Journalism and Publishing Activities | 231 | 241 |
| 广播、电视、电影和录音制作业 | Broadcasting, Movies, Televisions and Audiovisual Activities | 3134 | 3287 |
| 文化艺术业 | Cultural and Art Activities | 6166 | 6365 |
| 体 育 | Sports | 2514 | 2652 |
| 娱乐业 | Entertainment | 8328 | 8525 |
| **公共管理、社会保障和社会组织** | **Public Administration, Social Security and Social Organizations** | **29737** | **32983** |
| 中国共产党机关 | Organs of CPC | 461 | 472 |
| 国家机构 | Government Agencies | 9962 | 13052 |
| 人民政协、民主党派 | People's Political Consultative Conference and Democratic Parties | 166 | 172 |
| 社会保障 | Social Security | 312 | 402 |
| 群众团体、社会团体和其他成员组织 | Non-governmental Organizations, Social Organizations and Other Organizations | 7806 | 7850 |
| 基层群众自治组织及其他组织 | Grass Roots Self-governing Organizations | 11030 | 11035 |

# 表 22.2 按机构类型和登记注册类型分的法人单位数、产业活动单位数（2022 年）

## NUMBER OF CORPORATE UNITS AND ESTABLISHMENTS BY INSTITUTIONAL TYPE AND STATUS OF REGISTRATION (2022)

单位：个 (unit)

| 指 标 | Item | 法人单位 Corporate Units | 产业活动单位 Establishments |
|---|---|---|---|
| **总 计** | **Total** | **782071** | **843111** |
| **按机构类型分组** | **By Institutional Type** | | |
| 企 业 | Enterprises | 705046 | 761807 |
| 事业单位 | Public Institutions | 16393 | 18409 |
| 机 关 | Governmental Agencies | 3449 | 5480 |
| 社会团体 | Social Organizations | 7372 | 7388 |
| 民办非企业 | Private Non-enterprise | 8735 | 8755 |
| 其他组织机构 | Others | 41076 | 41272 |
| **按登记注册类型分组** | **By Status of Registration** | | |
| 内 资 | Domestic-funded Enterprises | 779225 | 837225 |
| 国 有 | State-owned | 22412 | 27460 |
| 集 体 | Collective-owned | 4995 | 5532 |
| 股份合作 | Cooperative Share-holding | 569 | 688 |
| 联 营 | Joint Ownership | 458 | 504 |
| 国有联营 | State Joint Ownership | 26 | 28 |
| 集体联营 | Collective Joint Ownership | 162 | 179 |
| 国有与集体联营 | Joint State-collective Ownership | 23 | 31 |
| 其他联营 | Other Joint Ownership | 247 | 266 |
| 有限责任公司 | Limited-liability Corporations | 10116 | 16043 |
| 国有独资公司 | Solely State-owned | 1726 | 3505 |
| 其他有限责任公司 | Other Limited-liability Corporations | 8390 | 12538 |
| 股份有限公司 | Share-holding Limited Companies | 1330 | 7692 |
| 私 营 | Private | 700412 | 740206 |
| 私营独资 | Solely Private-funded Enterprises | 161530 | 163711 |
| 私营合伙 | Private Partnership Enterprises | 8662 | 8855 |
| 私营有限责任公司 | Private Limited Liability Corporations | 528502 | 564512 |
| 私营股份有限公司 | Private Share-holding Limited Companies | 1718 | 3128 |
| 其 他 | Others | 38933 | 39100 |
| 港、澳、台商投资 | Enterprises with Funds from Hong Kong, Macao and Taiwan | 1275 | 2438 |
| 合资经营 | Joint-venture Enterprises | 246 | 456 |
| 合作经营 | Cooperative Enterprises | 13 | 21 |
| 独资经营 | Solely-funded Enterprises | 960 | 1853 |
| 投资股份有限公司 | Share-holding Limited Companies | 32 | 74 |
| 外商投资 | Foreign-funded Enterprises | 1571 | 3448 |
| 中外合资经营 | Joint-venture Enterprises | 440 | 728 |
| 中外合作经营 | Cooperative Enterprises | 13 | 27 |
| 外资企业 | Solely-funded Enterprises | 998 | 2278 |
| 外商投资股份有限公司 | Share-holding Limited Companies | 74 | 366 |

# 表 22.3 按行业分组的企业法人单位数和产业活动单位数(2022 年)
## NUMBER OF CORPORATE UNITS AND ESTABLISHMENTS BY SECTOR (2022)

单位：个 (unit)

| 指 标 | Item | 法人单位 Corporate Units | 产业活动单位 Establishments |
|---|---|---|---|
| **总 计** | **Total** | **705046** | **761807** |
| **按三次产业分组** | **By Strata of Industry** | | |
| 第一产业 | Primary Industry | 68240 | 68579 |
| 第二产业 | Secondary Industry | 104676 | 110142 |
| 第三产业 | Tertiary Industry | 532130 | 583086 |
| **按国民经济行业分组** | **By Sector** | | |
| **农、林、牧、渔业** | **Agriculture, Forestry, Animal Husbandry and Fishery** | **73198** | **73603** |
| 农 业 | Farming | 34551 | 34720 |
| 林 业 | Forestry | 2930 | 2945 |
| 畜牧业 | Animal Husbandry | 21329 | 21427 |
| 渔 业 | Fishery | 9430 | 9487 |
| 农、林、牧、渔专业及辅助性活动 | Services of Farming, Forestry, Animal Husbandry and Fishery | 4958 | 5024 |
| **采矿业** | **Mining** | **1393** | **1523** |
| 煤炭开采和洗选业 | Mining and Washing of Coal | 167 | 210 |
| 石油和天然气开采业 | Extraction of Petroleum and Natural Gas | 17 | 30 |
| 黑色金属矿采选业 | Mining and Processing of Ferrous Metal Ores | 72 | 78 |
| 有色金属矿采选业 | Mining and Processing of Non-ferrous Metal Ores | 21 | 20 |
| 非金属矿采选业 | Mining and Processing of Non-metal Ores | 1050 | 1107 |
| 开采专业及辅助性活动 | Support Activities for Mining | 39 | 48 |
| 其他采矿业 | Mining of Other Ores | 27 | 30 |
| **制造业** | **Manufacture** | **67767** | **69118** |
| 农副食品加工业 | Processing of Food from Agricultural Products | 4723 | 4810 |
| 食品制造业 | Manufacture of Foods | 2258 | 2311 |
| 酒、饮料和精制茶制造业 | Manufacture of Liquor, Beverages and Refined Tea | 2020 | 2071 |
| 烟草制品业 | Manufacture of Tobacco | 7 | 11 |
| 纺织业 | Manufacture of Textile | 1367 | 1397 |
| 纺织服装、服饰业 | Manufacture of Textile, Wearing Apparel and Accessories | 2013 | 2037 |
| 皮革、毛皮、羽毛及其制品和制鞋业 | Manufacture of Leather, Fur, Feather and Related Products and Footwear | 842 | 852 |
| 木材加工和木、竹、藤、棕、草制品业 | Processing of Timber, Manufacture of Wood, Bamboo, Rattan, Palm and Straw Products | 2950 | 2977 |
| 家具制造业 | Manufacture of Furniture | 2367 | 2390 |
| 造纸和纸制品业 | Manufacture of Paper and Paper Products | 975 | 990 |
| 印刷和记录媒介复制业 | Printing, Reproduction of Recording Media | 1579 | 1623 |
| 文教、工美、体育和娱乐用品制造业 | Manufacture of Articles for Culture, Education, Arts and Crafts, Sport and Entertainment Activities | 1327 | 1356 |
| 石油、煤炭及其他燃料加工业 | Petroleum Refining,Coking and Nuclear Fuel Processing | 189 | 199 |
| 化学原料和化学制品制造业 | Manufacture of Raw Chemical Materials and Chemical Products | 1699 | 1754 |
| 医药制造业 | Manufacture of Medicines | 581 | 602 |
| 化学纤维制造业 | Manufacture of Chemical Fibres | 48 | 48 |
| 橡胶和塑料制品业 | Manufacture of Rubber and Plastics Products | 2516 | 2553 |

表 22.3 续表 1 continued 1

单位：个 (unit)

| 指 标 | Item | 法人单位 Corporate Units | 产业活动单位 Establishments |
|---|---|---|---|
| 非金属矿物制品业 | Manufacture of Non-metallic Mineral Products | 7022 | 7194 |
| 黑色金属冶炼和压延加工业 | Smelting and Pressing of Ferrous Metals | 461 | 478 |
| 有色金属冶炼和压延加工业 | Smelting and Pressing of Non-ferrous Metals | 618 | 627 |
| 金属制品业 | Manufacture of Metal Products | 6994 | 7104 |
| 通用设备制造业 | Manufacture of General Purpose Machinery | 5824 | 5923 |
| 专用设备制造业 | Manufacture of Special Purpose Machinery | 4385 | 4469 |
| 汽车制造业 | Manufacture of Automobiles | 5129 | 5239 |
| 铁路、船舶、航空航天和其他运输设备制造业 | Manufacture of Railway ,Ship, Aerospace and Other Transport Equipment | 2696 | 2731 |
| 电气机械和器材制造业 | Manufacture of Electrical Machinery and Apparatus | 2007 | 2056 |
| 计算机、通信和其他电子设备制造业 | Manufacture of Computers, Communication and Other Electronic Equipment | 2268 | 2291 |
| 仪器仪表制造业 | Manufacture of Measuring Instruments and Machinery | 924 | 944 |
| 其他制造业 | Other Manufacture | 433 | 439 |
| 废弃资源综合利用业 | Utilization of Waste Resources | 502 | 544 |
| 金属制品、机械和设备修理业 | Manufacture of Metal Products, Machinery and Equipment Maintenance | 1043 | 1098 |
| **电力、热力、燃气及水生产和供应业** | **Production and Supply of Electric Power,Gas and Water** | **2602** | **3465** |
| 电力、热力生产和供应业 | Production and Supply of Electric Power and Heat Power | 1459 | 1745 |
| 燃气生产和供应业 | Production and Supply of Gas | 304 | 425 |
| 水的生产和供应业 | Production and Supply of Water | 839 | 1295 |
| **建筑业** | **Construction** | **33996** | **37182** |
| 房屋建筑业 | Construction of Housing | 6991 | 8233 |
| 土木工程建筑业 | Civil Engineering Construction | 6107 | 6927 |
| 建筑安装业 | Architectural Installation | 3815 | 4151 |
| 建筑装饰、装修和其他建筑业 | Architectural Decoration and Other Construction | 17083 | 17871 |
| **批发和零售业** | **Wholesale and Retail Trade** | **227553** | **248251** |
| 批发业 | Wholesale Trade | 94882 | 98918 |
| 零售业 | Retail Trade | 132671 | 149333 |
| **交通运输、仓储和邮政业** | **Transport, Storage and Postal Services** | **18280** | **22061** |
| 铁路运输业 | Transport Via Railway | 44 | 68 |
| 道路运输业 | Transport Via Road | 11256 | 12148 |
| 水上运输业 | Water Transport | 462 | 497 |
| 航空运输业 | Air Transport | 94 | 112 |
| 管道运输业 | Transport Via Pipeline | 8 | 11 |
| 多式联运和运输代理业 | Loading, Unloading, Portage and Transport Agency | 3814 | 4086 |
| 装卸搬运和仓储业 | Storage | 1823 | 1941 |
| 邮政业 | Post | 779 | 3198 |
| **住宿和餐饮业** | **Hotels and Catering Services** | **28449** | **30838** |
| 住宿业 | Hotels | 6895 | 7281 |
| 餐饮业 | Catering Services | 21554 | 23557 |

**表 22.3 续表 2 continued 2**

单位：个 (unit)

| 指 标 | Item | 法人单位 Corporate Units | 产业活动单位 Establishments |
|---|---|---|---|
| **信息传输、软件和信息技术服务业** | **Information Transmission, Software and Information Technology** | **38774** | **40665** |
| 电信、广播电视和卫星传输服务 | Telecommunication, Radio, Television and Satellite Transmission Services | 851 | 1559 |
| 互联网和相关服务 | Internet and Related Services | 5500 | 5664 |
| 软件和信息技术服务业 | Software and Information Technology Services | 32423 | 33442 |
| **金融业** | **Financial Intermediation** | **2241** | **8663** |
| 货币金融服务 | Money Finance Services | 1150 | 5778 |
| 资本市场服务 | Capital Market Services | 608 | 883 |
| 保险业 | Insurance | 299 | 1744 |
| 其他金融业 | Other Finance | 184 | 258 |
| **房地产业** | **Real Estate** | **23265** | **27225** |
| 房地产业 | Real Estate | 23265 | 27225 |
| **租赁和商务服务业** | **Leasing and Business Services** | **95261** | **100258** |
| 租赁业 | Leasing | 15889 | 16401 |
| 商务服务业 | Business Services | 79372 | 83857 |
| **科学研究和技术服务业** | **Scientific Research and Technical Services** | **33057** | **35619** |
| 研究和试验发展 | Research and Experimental Development | 2139 | 2203 |
| 专业技术服务业 | Professional Technical Services | 19269 | 21402 |
| 科技推广和应用服务业 | Services of Science and Technology Application and Promotion | 11649 | 12014 |
| **水利、环境和公共设施管理业** | **Water Conservancy, Environment and Public Facilities Management** | **7449** | **7860** |
| 水利管理业 | Management of Water Conservancy | 195 | 243 |
| 生态保护和环境治理业 | Ecological Protection and Environmental Governance | 1171 | 1233 |
| 公共设施管理业 | Management of Public Facilities | 3546 | 3718 |
| 土地管理业 | Management of Land | 2537 | 2666 |
| **居民服务、修理和其他服务业** | **Services to Households, Repair and Other Services** | **19983** | **21016** |
| 居民服务业 | Resident Services | 9752 | 10279 |
| 机动车、电子产品和日用产品修理业 | Vehicles, Electronic Products and Commodities Maintenance Services | 7212 | 7583 |
| 其他服务业 | Other Services | 3019 | 3154 |
| **教 育** | **Education** | **8644** | **9550** |
| 教 育 | Education | 8644 | 9550 |
| **卫生和社会工作** | **Health and Social Work** | **4464** | **5654** |
| 卫 生 | Health | 3474 | 4575 |
| 社会工作 | Social Work | 990 | 1079 |
| **文化、体育和娱乐业** | **Culture, Sports and Entertainment** | **18670** | **19256** |
| 新闻和出版业 | Journalism and Publishing Activities | 181 | 191 |
| 广播、电视、电影和录音制作业 | Broadcasting, Movies, Televisions and Audiovisual Activities | 3081 | 3231 |
| 文化艺术业 | Cultural and Art Activities | 5138 | 5241 |
| 体 育 | Sports | 2260 | 2396 |
| 娱乐业 | Entertainment | 8010 | 8197 |

# 表 22.4 按登记注册类型分组的企业法人单位数和产业活动单位数(2022 年)
# NUMBER OF ENTERPRISES AS CORPORATE UNITS AND ESTABLISHMENTS BY STATUS OF REGISTRATION (2022)

单位：个 (unit)

| 指 标 | Item | 法人单位 Corporate Units | 产业活动单位 Establishments |
|---|---|---|---|
| **总 计** | **Total** | **705046** | **761807** |
| 内 资 | Domestic-funded Enterprises | 702201 | 755923 |
| 国 有 | State-owned | 852 | 1938 |
| 集 体 | Collective-owned | 1514 | 1945 |
| 股份合作 | Cooperative Share-holding | 445 | 563 |
| 联 营 | Joint Ownership | 81 | 112 |
| 国有联营 | State Joint Ownership | 11 | 13 |
| 集体联营 | Collective Joint Ownership | 38 | 49 |
| 国有与集体联营 | Joint State-collective Ownership | 6 | 11 |
| 其他联营 | Other Joint Ownership | 26 | 39 |
| 有限责任公司 | Limited-liability Corporations | 9361 | 15289 |
| 国有独资公司 | Solely State-owned | 1689 | 3468 |
| 其他有限责任公司 | Other Limited-liability Corporations | 7672 | 11821 |
| 股份有限公司 | Share-holding Limited Companies | 1309 | 7671 |
| 私 营 | Private | 688638 | 728403 |
| 私营独资 | Solely Private-funded Enterprises | 155741 | 157914 |
| 私营合伙 | Private Partnership Enterprises | 4940 | 5118 |
| 私营有限责任公司 | Private Limited Liability Corporations | 526281 | 562285 |
| 私营股份有限公司 | Private Share-holding Limited Companies | 1676 | 3086 |
| 其 他 | Others | 1 | 2 |
| 港、澳、台商投资 | Enterprises with Funds from Hong Kong, Macao and Taiwan | 1275 | 2437 |
| 合资经营 | Joint-venture Enterprises | 246 | 455 |
| 合作经营 | Cooperative Enterprises | 13 | 21 |
| 独资经营 | Solely-funded Enterprises | 960 | 1853 |
| 投资股份有限公司 | Share-holding Limited Companies | 32 | 74 |
| 外商投资 | Foreign-funded Enterprises | 1570 | 3447 |
| 中外合资经营 | Joint-venture Enterprises | 440 | 728 |
| 中外合作经营 | Cooperative Enterprises | 12 | 26 |
| 外资企业 | Solely-funded Enterprises | 998 | 2278 |
| 外商投资股份有限公司 | Share-holding Limited Companies | 74 | 366 |

# 表 22.5 按行业、区县分组的法人单位数 (2022 年 )
## NUMBER OF CORPORATE UNITS BY SECTOR AND REGION (2022)

单位：个 (unit)

| 指 标 | Item | 全 市 Total | 万州区 Wanzhou District | 黔江区 Qianjiang District | 涪陵区 Fuling District | 渝中区 Yuzhong District |
|---|---|---|---|---|---|---|
| **总 计** | **Total** | **782071** | **27210** | **10467** | **23266** | **23462** |
| **按三次产业分组** | **By Strata of Industry** | | | | | |
| 第一产业 | Primary Industry | 88054 | 4011 | 1845 | 2622 | |
| 第二产业 | Secondary Industry | 105061 | 3727 | 967 | 2761 | 976 |
| 第三产业 | Tertiary Industry | 588956 | 19472 | 7655 | 17883 | 22486 |
| **按国民经济行业分组** | **By Sector** | | | | | |
| **农、林、牧、渔业** | **Agriculture, Forestry, Animal Husbandry and Fishery** | **94654** | **4354** | **1947** | **3197** | |
| 农 业 | Farming | 48132 | 2539 | 882 | 1469 | |
| 林 业 | Forestry | 3500 | 160 | 101 | 80 | |
| 畜牧业 | Animal Husbandry | 25775 | 783 | 772 | 668 | |
| 渔 业 | Fishery | 10647 | 529 | 90 | 405 | |
| 农、林、牧、渔专业及辅助性活动 | Services of Farming, Forestry, Animal Husbandry and Fishery | 6600 | 343 | 102 | 575 | |
| **采矿业** | **Mining** | **1393** | **51** | **35** | **34** | |
| 煤炭开采和洗选业 | Mining and Washing of Coal | 167 | 1 | 3 | 2 | |
| 石油和天然气开采业 | Extraction of Petroleum and Natural Gas | 17 | | | 2 | |
| 黑色金属矿采选业 | Mining and Processing of Ferrous Metal Ores | 72 | 1 | | | |
| 有色金属矿采选业 | Mining and Processing of Non-ferrous Metal Ores | 21 | | | | |
| 非金属矿采选业 | Mining and Processing of Non-metal Ores | 1050 | 41 | 32 | 28 | |
| 开采专业及辅助性活动 | Support Activities for Mining | 39 | 5 | | 1 | |
| 其他采矿业 | Mining of Other Ores | 27 | 3 | | 1 | |
| **制造业** | **Manufacture** | **68144** | **1711** | **497** | **1657** | **112** |
| 农副食品加工业 | Processing of Food from Agricultural Products | 4991 | 121 | 67 | 265 | 3 |
| 食品制造业 | Manufacture of Foods | 2268 | 41 | 26 | 57 | 1 |
| 酒、饮料和精制茶制造业 | Manufacture of Liquor, Beverages and Refined Tea | 2037 | 70 | 37 | 59 | |
| 烟草制品业 | Manufacture of Tobacco | 7 | | 1 | 1 | |
| 纺织业 | Manufacture of Textile | 1368 | 55 | 20 | 34 | |
| 纺织服装、服饰业 | Manufacture of Textile, Wearing Apparel and Accessories | 2013 | 90 | 14 | 32 | 8 |
| 皮革、毛皮、羽毛及其制品和制鞋业 | Manufacture of Leather, Fur, Feather and Related Products and Footwear | 842 | 15 | 3 | 10 | |
| 木材加工和木、竹、藤、棕、草制品业 | Processing of Timber, Manufacture of Wood, Bamboo, Rattan, Palm and Straw Products | 2992 | 86 | 22 | 49 | |
| 家具制造业 | Manufacture of Furniture | 2369 | 106 | 22 | 48 | 1 |
| 造纸和纸制品业 | Manufacture of Paper and Paper Products | 975 | 12 | 3 | 19 | 2 |
| 印刷和记录媒介复制业 | Printing, Reproduction of Recording Media | 1579 | 60 | 19 | 44 | 24 |
| 文教、工美、体育和娱乐用品制造业 | Manufacture of Articles for Culture, Education, Arts and Crafts, Sport and Entertainment Activities | 1335 | 36 | 21 | 30 | 7 |
| 石油、煤炭及其他燃料加工业 | Petroleum Refining,Coking and Nuclear Fuel Processing | 189 | 8 | | 7 | |
| 化学原料和化学制品制造业 | Manufacture of Raw Chemical Materials and Chemical Products | 1708 | 43 | 11 | 75 | 1 |
| 医药制造业 | Manufacture of Medicines | 593 | 22 | 6 | 16 | |
| 化学纤维制造业 | Manufacture of Chemical Fibres | 48 | | | 6 | 1 |
| 橡胶和塑料制品业 | Manufacture of Rubber and Plastics Products | 2516 | 62 | 11 | 81 | 3 |
| 非金属矿物制品业 | Manufacture of Non-metallic Mineral Products | 7024 | 215 | 105 | 235 | 3 |
| 黑色金属冶炼和压延加工业 | Smelting and Pressing of Ferrous Metals | 461 | 7 | 10 | 18 | |

表 22.5 续表 1 continued 1

| 指 标 | Item | 大渡口区 Dadukou District | 江北区 Jiangbei District | 沙坪坝区 Shapingba District | 九龙坡区 Jiulongpo District | 南岸区 Nan'an District |
|---|---|---|---|---|---|---|
| **总 计** | **Total** | **11167** | **38076** | **34460** | **78395** | **28837** |
| **按三次产业分组** | **By Strata of Industry** | | | | | |
| 第一产业 | Primary Industry | 113 | 135 | 232 | 682 | 203 |
| 第二产业 | Secondary Industry | 1731 | 2771 | 4586 | 9134 | 2807 |
| 第三产业 | Tertiary Industry | 9323 | 35170 | 29642 | 68579 | 25827 |
| **按国民经济行业分组** | **By Sector** | | | | | |
| **农、林、牧、渔业** | **Agriculture, Forestry, Animal Husbandry and Fishery** | **129** | **160** | **266** | **743** | **229** |
| 农 业 | Farming | 107 | 106 | 168 | 439 | 161 |
| 林 业 | Forestry | 2 | 6 | 33 | 86 | 20 |
| 畜牧业 | Animal Husbandry | 3 | 14 | 9 | 40 | 7 |
| 渔 业 | Fishery | 1 | 9 | 22 | 117 | 15 |
| 农、林、牧、渔专业及辅助性活动 | Services of Farming, Forestry, Animal Husbandry and Fishery | 16 | 25 | 34 | 61 | 26 |
| **采矿业** | **Mining** | **3** | **3** | **1** | **9** | **3** |
| 煤炭开采和洗选业 | Mining and Washing of Coal | | | | 1 | |
| 石油和天然气开采业 | Extraction of Petroleum and Natural Gas | | | | | |
| 黑色金属矿采选业 | Mining and Processing of Ferrous Metal Ores | 2 | | | 1 | |
| 有色金属矿采选业 | Mining and Processing of Non-ferrous Metal Ores | | | | | |
| 非金属矿采选业 | Mining and Processing of Non-metal Ores | 1 | 3 | 1 | 6 | 3 |
| 开采专业及辅助性活动 | Support Activities for Mining | | | | 1 | |
| 其他采矿业 | Mining of Other Ores | | | | | |
| **制造业** | **Manufacture** | **1118** | **1008** | **2949** | **5382** | **1225** |
| 农副食品加工业 | Processing of Food from Agricultural Products | 31 | 22 | 39 | 86 | 32 |
| 食品制造业 | Manufacture of Foods | 24 | 29 | 43 | 106 | 26 |
| 酒、饮料和精制茶制造业 | Manufacture of Liquor, Beverages and Refined Tea | 3 | 9 | 22 | 26 | 10 |
| 烟草制品业 | Manufacture of Tobacco | | | | | 2 |
| 纺织业 | Manufacture of Textile | 8 | 13 | 134 | 33 | 23 |
| 纺织服装、服饰业 | Manufacture of Textile, Wearing Apparel and Accessories | 7 | 26 | 9 | 50 | 43 |
| 皮革、毛皮、羽毛及其制品和制鞋业 | Manufacture of Leather, Fur, Feather and Related Products and Footwear | 4 | 3 | 4 | 8 | 10 |
| 木材加工和木、竹、藤、棕、草制品业 | Processing of Timber, Manufacture of Wood, Bamboo, Rattan, Palm and Straw Products | 33 | 8 | 76 | 196 | 24 |
| 家具制造业 | Manufacture of Furniture | 35 | 11 | 100 | 222 | 57 |
| 造纸和纸制品业 | Manufacture of Paper and Paper Products | 20 | 18 | 72 | 89 | 16 |
| 印刷和记录媒介复制业 | Printing, Reproduction of Recording Media | 28 | 70 | 94 | 145 | 57 |
| 文教、工美、体育和娱乐用品制造业 | Manufacture of Articles for Culture, Education, Arts and Crafts, Sport and Entertainment Activities | 17 | 13 | 53 | 56 | 15 |
| 石油、煤炭及其他燃料加工业 | Petroleum Refining,Coking and Nuclear Fuel Processing | 3 | | 7 | 13 | 2 |
| 化学原料和化学制品制造业 | Manufacture of Raw Chemical Materials and Chemical Products | 21 | 32 | 81 | 114 | 34 |
| 医药制造业 | Manufacture of Medicines | 3 | 19 | 13 | 33 | 21 |
| 化学纤维制造业 | Manufacture of Chemical Fibres | | 1 | | | 1 |
| 橡胶和塑料制品业 | Manufacture of Rubber and Plastics Products | 33 | 37 | 124 | 216 | 80 |
| 非金属矿物制品业 | Manufacture of Non-metallic Mineral Products | 63 | 47 | 207 | 485 | 67 |
| 黑色金属冶炼和压延加工业 | Smelting and Pressing of Ferrous Metals | 16 | 11 | 13 | 35 | 4 |

单位：个 (unit)

| 北碚区 Beibei District | 渝北区 Yubei District | 巴南区 Ba'nan District | 长寿区 Changshou District | 江津区 Jiangjin District | 合川区 Hechuan District | 永川区 Yongchuan District | 南川区 Nanchuan District | 綦江区 Qijiang District | 綦江区（不含万盛）Qijiang District (excluding Wansheng) | 大足区 Dazu District | 璧山区 Bishan District | 铜梁区 Tongliang District |
|---|---|---|---|---|---|---|---|---|---|---|---|---|
| **17277** | **65589** | **28148** | **15159** | **29841** | **16511** | **18477** | **16882** | **22988** | **13010** | **18266** | **18402** | **14981** |
| 893 | 1469 | 3633 | 2477 | 4794 | 2024 | 2204 | 4610 | 3678 | 2744 | 3497 | 1966 | 2263 |
| 3865 | 5920 | 5031 | 1990 | 6451 | 3113 | 3187 | 2121 | 2938 | 1769 | 4359 | 4789 | 3194 |
| 12519 | 58200 | 19484 | 10692 | 18596 | 11374 | 13086 | 10151 | 16372 | 8497 | 10410 | 11647 | 9524 |
| 963 | 1624 | 3731 | 2601 | 5221 | 2193 | 2338 | 4817 | 3828 | 2842 | 3643 | 2050 | 2370 |
| 655 | 934 | 2317 | 1429 | 2853 | 1001 | 1245 | 2433 | 1436 | 1098 | 1314 | 1419 | 1014 |
| 34 | 86 | 363 | 63 | 175 | 100 | 95 | 281 | 134 | 59 | 140 | 270 | 96 |
| 93 | 289 | 192 | 543 | 894 | 422 | 379 | 1331 | 1751 | 1337 | 1042 | 146 | 448 |
| 111 | 160 | 761 | 442 | 872 | 501 | 485 | 565 | 357 | 250 | 1001 | 131 | 705 |
| 70 | 155 | 98 | 124 | 427 | 169 | 134 | 207 | 150 | 98 | 146 | 84 | 107 |
| 22 | 6 | 12 | 24 | 39 | 81 | 83 | 50 | 80 | 54 | 40 | 11 | 53 |
| 3 |  | 1 | 1 |  | 17 | 28 | 11 | 9 | 3 | 5 |  | 5 |
|  |  |  | 2 |  | 2 | 2 | 1 | 1 | 1 |  |  | 1 |
|  | 1 |  |  |  |  | 1 |  | 3 | 3 |  |  |  |
|  |  |  |  |  |  |  | 2 |  |  | 1 |  |  |
| 18 | 1 | 10 | 18 | 39 | 59 | 49 | 35 | 64 | 45 | 32 | 10 | 47 |
|  | 2 |  | 1 |  | 2 | 3 | 1 | 2 | 1 | 2 | 1 |  |
| 1 | 2 | 1 | 2 |  | 1 |  |  | 1 | 1 |  |  |  |
| **2989** | **3212** | **3702** | **1233** | **5035** | **2082** | **2155** | **1510** | **1640** | **1101** | **3710** | **3958** | **2356** |
| 22 | 84 | 96 | 94 | 271 | 162 | 117 | 136 | 96 | 54 | 101 | 47 | 118 |
| 33 | 118 | 77 | 47 | 263 | 134 | 80 | 45 | 65 | 32 | 71 | 68 | 49 |
| 12 | 38 | 24 | 27 | 73 | 57 | 73 | 102 | 89 | 58 | 32 | 24 | 35 |
| 36 | 25 | 61 | 22 | 40 | 39 | 13 | 67 | 21 | 15 | 29 | 34 | 53 |
| 13 | 91 | 333 | 11 | 38 | 57 | 27 | 32 | 10 | 6 | 19 | 35 | 89 |
| 8 | 9 | 21 | 3 | 11 | 22 | 14 | 15 | 9 | 7 | 13 | 221 | 83 |
| 36 | 47 | 150 | 57 | 163 | 49 | 129 | 68 | 69 | 44 | 102 | 49 | 100 |
| 34 | 48 | 165 | 53 | 207 | 81 | 81 | 85 | 36 | 20 | 65 | 84 | 79 |
| 59 | 36 | 76 | 16 | 51 | 24 | 68 | 15 | 15 | 12 | 28 | 84 | 50 |
| 47 | 147 | 82 | 29 | 68 | 40 | 42 | 25 | 24 | 14 | 17 | 177 | 24 |
| 41 | 53 | 62 | 14 | 43 | 45 | 32 | 34 | 32 | 20 | 98 | 20 | 27 |
| 3 | 11 | 2 | 4 | 12 | 3 | 10 | 5 | 12 | 6 | 7 | 4 | 1 |
| 52 | 73 | 85 | 121 | 146 | 46 | 61 | 57 | 41 | 20 | 54 | 45 | 52 |
| 30 | 23 | 43 | 22 | 12 | 22 | 7 | 15 | 15 | 6 | 11 | 13 | 16 |
| 3 | 3 | 3 | 5 | 5 | 1 | 3 |  | 2 | 1 | 2 | 4 |  |
| 116 | 66 | 129 | 66 | 249 | 89 | 86 | 36 | 40 | 22 | 138 | 300 | 143 |
| 175 | 146 | 243 | 144 | 395 | 325 | 294 | 275 | 273 | 184 | 222 | 157 | 201 |
| 8 | 20 | 16 | 18 | 52 | 12 | 14 | 5 | 10 | 5 | 59 | 8 | 3 |

表 22.5 续表 2 continued 2

| 指 标 | Item | 潼南区 Tongnan District | 荣昌区 Rongchang District | 开州区 Kaizhou District | 梁平区 Liangping District | 武隆区 Wulong District | 城口县 Chengkou County |
|---|---|---|---|---|---|---|---|
| **总 计** | **Total** | **18485** | **13673** | **22606** | **11382** | **8500** | **6679** |
| **按三次产业分组** | **By Strata of Industry** | | | | | | |
| 第一产业 | Primary Industry | 1089 | 1017 | 3800 | 2249 | 2071 | 1573 |
| 第二产业 | Secondary Industry | 2273 | 2357 | 2946 | 1647 | 821 | 503 |
| 第三产业 | Tertiary Industry | 15123 | 10299 | 15860 | 7486 | 5608 | 4603 |
| **按国民经济行业分组** | **By Sector** | | | | | | |
| **农、林、牧、渔业** | **Agriculture, Forestry, Animal Husbandry and Fishery** | **1187** | **1146** | **4122** | **2404** | **2116** | **1638** |
| 农 业 | Farming | 594 | 564 | 1822 | 1200 | 1091 | 652 |
| 林 业 | Forestry | 17 | 44 | 123 | 135 | 59 | 22 |
| 畜牧业 | Animal Husbandry | 212 | 251 | 1488 | 514 | 833 | 868 |
| 渔 业 | Fishery | 266 | 158 | 367 | 400 | 88 | 31 |
| 农、林、牧、渔专业及辅助性活动 | Services of Farming, Forestry, Animal Husbandry and Fishery | 98 | 129 | 322 | 155 | 45 | 65 |
| **采矿业** | **Mining** | **121** | **30** | **48** | **34** | **25** | **23** |
| 煤炭开采和洗选业 | Mining and Washing of Coal | | 15 | 6 | 8 | 1 | 1 |
| 石油和天然气开采业 | Extraction of Petroleum and Natural Gas | 3 | | | | | |
| 黑色金属矿采选业 | Mining and Processing of Ferrous Metal Ores | | 1 | | | | 5 |
| 有色金属矿采选业 | Mining and Processing of Non-ferrous Metal Ores | | | | | 1 | 1 |
| 非金属矿采选业 | Mining and Processing of Non-metal Ores | 116 | 14 | 41 | 24 | 23 | 16 |
| 开采专业及辅助性活动 | Support Activities for Mining | 2 | | 1 | 1 | | |
| 其他采矿业 | Mining of Other Ores | | | | 1 | | |
| **制造业** | **Manufacture** | **1600** | **1692** | **1999** | **1324** | **410** | **242** |
| 农副食品加工业 | Processing of Food from Agricultural Products | 222 | 213 | 198 | 147 | 109 | 58 |
| 食品制造业 | Manufacture of Foods | 36 | 79 | 65 | 38 | 19 | 15 |
| 酒、饮料和精制茶制造业 | Manufacture of Liquor, Beverages and Refined Tea | 38 | 51 | 148 | 77 | 30 | 38 |
| 烟草制品业 | Manufacture of Tobacco | | | 1 | | | |
| 纺织业 | Manufacture of Textile | 40 | 39 | 97 | 25 | 8 | 9 |
| 纺织服装、服饰业 | Manufacture of Textile, Wearing Apparel and Accessories | 65 | 50 | 225 | 74 | 6 | 2 |
| 皮革、毛皮、羽毛及其制品和制鞋业 | Manufacture of Leather, Fur, Feather and Related Products and Footwear | 34 | 14 | 65 | 23 | 3 | 2 |
| 木材加工和木、竹、藤、棕、草制品业 | Processing of Timber, Manufacture of Wood, Bamboo, Rattan, Palm and Straw Products | 197 | 45 | 135 | 158 | 19 | 19 |
| 家具制造业 | Manufacture of Furniture | 49 | 44 | 127 | 60 | 4 | 4 |
| 造纸和纸制品业 | Manufacture of Paper and Paper Products | 22 | 17 | 19 | 59 | 2 | 1 |
| 印刷和记录媒介复制业 | Printing, Reproduction of Recording Media | 32 | 35 | 33 | 24 | 20 | 4 |
| 文教、工美、体育和娱乐用品制造业 | Manufacture of Articles for Culture, Education, Arts and Crafts, Sport and Entertainment Activities | 18 | 104 | 36 | 72 | 4 | 10 |
| 石油、煤炭及其他燃料加工业 | Petroleum Refining,Coking and Nuclear Fuel Processing | 7 | 3 | 7 | 6 | 2 | 1 |
| 化学原料和化学制品制造业 | Manufacture of Raw Chemical Materials and Chemical Products | 63 | 52 | 44 | 32 | 8 | 7 |
| 医药制造业 | Manufacture of Medicines | 13 | 43 | 20 | 5 | 7 | 3 |
| 化学纤维制造业 | Manufacture of Chemical Fibres | | | | | | |
| 橡胶和塑料制品业 | Manufacture of Rubber and Plastics Products | 40 | 77 | 43 | 47 | 10 | |
| 非金属矿物制品业 | Manufacture of Non-metallic Mineral Products | 214 | 236 | 251 | 155 | 95 | 30 |
| 黑色金属冶炼和压延加工业 | Smelting and Pressing of Ferrous Metals | 5 | 12 | 6 | 5 | 1 | 10 |

单位：个 (unit)

| 丰都县 Fengdu County | 垫江县 Dianjiang County | 忠 县 Zhongxian County | 云阳县 Yunyang County | 奉节县 Fengjie County | 巫山县 Wushan County | 巫溪县 Wuxi County | 石柱县 Shizhu County | 秀山县 Xiushan County | 酉阳县 Youyang County | 彭水县 Pengshui County |
|---|---|---|---|---|---|---|---|---|---|---|
| **11329** | **14694** | **13843** | **22998** | **16876** | **8898** | **8015** | **9676** | **13620** | **12432** | **10504** |
| 2735 | 1835 | 2335 | 4823 | 5723 | 2638 | 2584 | 2331 | 3036 | 1984 | 2880 |
| 1300 | 3134 | 1394 | 4451 | 1529 | 765 | 779 | 965 | 1331 | 1342 | 1106 |
| 7294 | 9725 | 10114 | 13724 | 9624 | 5495 | 4652 | 6380 | 9253 | 9106 | 6518 |
| **2884** | **2048** | **2631** | **5726** | **5990** | **2745** | **2702** | **2475** | **3155** | **2309** | **2972** |
| 1067 | 1093 | 1477 | 2653 | 3822 | 1781 | 1306 | 1191 | 1706 | 913 | 1279 |
| 56 | 53 | 40 | 71 | 126 | 65 | 50 | 85 | 81 | 72 | 76 |
| 1363 | 441 | 558 | 1675 | 1609 | 696 | 1135 | 896 | 1074 | 910 | 1426 |
| 249 | 248 | 260 | 424 | 166 | 96 | 93 | 159 | 175 | 89 | 99 |
| 149 | 213 | 296 | 903 | 267 | 107 | 118 | 144 | 119 | 325 | 92 |
| **30** | **18** | **33** | **26** | **53** | **45** | **31** | **34** | **88** | **40** | **74** |
| 2 | 4 |  | 5 | 16 | 13 | 1 | 2 | 2 |  | 4 |
|  | 1 | 1 |  |  |  |  |  |  | 1 |  |
|  |  | 2 |  | 1 | 1 |  | 1 | 46 |  | 6 |
|  |  | 1 |  |  | 1 | 1 | 3 | 2 | 3 | 5 |
| 28 | 12 | 24 | 20 | 30 | 29 | 28 | 26 | 38 | 33 | 51 |
|  | 1 | 3 | 1 | 3 |  |  | 2 |  | 1 | 3 |
|  |  | 2 |  | 3 | 1 | 1 |  |  | 2 | 5 |
| **748** | **1681** | **872** | **3699** | **1066** | **362** | **366** | **588** | **775** | **956** | **523** |
| 178 | 188 | 171 | 842 | 232 | 48 | 48 | 74 | 83 | 88 | 82 |
| 27 | 47 | 43 | 252 | 70 | 24 | 16 | 23 | 33 | 43 | 35 |
| 41 | 53 | 65 | 175 | 47 | 37 | 37 | 37 | 62 | 239 | 40 |
|  |  |  |  | 1 |  |  |  |  |  | 1 |
| 16 | 60 | 25 | 186 | 15 | 10 | 10 | 18 | 13 | 19 | 18 |
| 27 | 34 | 66 | 210 | 39 | 35 | 19 | 18 | 30 | 69 | 10 |
| 10 | 44 | 10 | 51 | 16 | 16 | 9 | 15 | 13 | 23 | 8 |
| 49 | 159 | 59 | 338 | 71 | 19 | 37 | 36 | 58 | 51 | 29 |
| 24 | 131 | 31 | 119 | 41 | 6 | 11 | 22 | 30 | 26 | 20 |
| 5 | 17 | 5 | 13 | 11 | 2 | 3 | 7 | 5 | 4 | 10 |
| 17 | 28 | 31 | 20 | 22 | 13 | 8 | 5 | 7 | 12 | 5 |
| 11 | 33 | 12 | 146 | 33 | 11 | 19 | 13 | 23 | 29 | 12 |
| 4 | 6 | 2 | 10 | 12 | 4 | 3 | 1 | 1 | 1 | 5 |
| 22 | 56 | 19 | 48 | 15 | 7 | 6 | 17 | 25 | 23 | 19 |
| 12 | 14 | 5 | 31 | 26 | 3 | 6 | 16 | 13 | 8 | 6 |
| 1 | 2 | 1 | 1 |  |  | 1 |  |  | 1 | 1 |
| 13 | 60 | 14 | 40 | 21 | 3 | 5 | 8 | 17 | 8 | 5 |
| 137 | 239 | 100 | 409 | 184 | 54 | 75 | 108 | 142 | 168 | 150 |
| 8 | 10 | 4 | 24 |  | 1 |  | 3 | 26 | 7 |  |

**表 22.5 续表 3 continued 3**

| 指 标 | Item | 全 市 Total | 万州区 Wanzhou District | 黔江区 Qianjiang District | 涪陵区 Fuling District | 渝中区 Yuzhong District |
|---|---|---|---|---|---|---|
| 有色金属冶炼和压延加工业 | Smelting and Pressing of Non-ferrous Metals | 618 | 16 | 7 | 24 | |
| 金属制品业 | Manufacture of Metal Products | 6995 | 265 | 50 | 177 | 10 |
| 通用设备制造业 | Manufacture of General Purpose Machinery | 5824 | 76 | 9 | 35 | 10 |
| 专用设备制造业 | Manufacture of Special Purpose Machinery | 4387 | 43 | 6 | 36 | 13 |
| 汽车制造业 | Manufacture of Automobiles | 5129 | 44 | | 61 | |
| 铁路、船舶、航空航天和其他运输设备制造业 | Manufacture of Railway ,Ship, Aerospace and Other Transport Equipment | 2696 | 17 | 1 | 73 | 2 |
| 电气机械和器材制造业 | Manufacture of Electrical Machinery and Apparatus | 2007 | 62 | 10 | 32 | 6 |
| 计算机、通信和其他电子设备制造业 | Manufacture of Computers, Communication and Other Electronic Equipment | 2269 | 55 | 6 | 30 | 6 |
| 仪器仪表制造业 | Manufacture of Measuring Instruments and Machinery | 924 | 10 | | 9 | 6 |
| 其他制造业 | Other Manufacture | 434 | 7 | 1 | 10 | 1 |
| 废弃资源综合利用业 | Utilization of Waste Resources | 502 | 25 | 2 | 19 | |
| 金属制品、机械和设备修理业 | Manufacture of Metal Products, Machinery and Equipment Maintenance | 1044 | 42 | 7 | 65 | 4 |
| **电力、热力、燃气及水生产和供应业** | **Production and Supply of Electric Power, Gas and Water** | **2611** | **101** | **33** | **152** | **6** |
| 电力、热力生产和供应业 | Production and Supply of Electric Power and Heat Power | 1461 | 82 | 18 | 94 | 1 |
| 燃气生产和供应业 | Production and Supply of Gas | 305 | 7 | 5 | 32 | 1 |
| 水的生产和供应业 | Production and Supply of Water | 845 | 12 | 10 | 26 | 4 |
| **建筑业** | **Construction** | **33996** | **1911** | **409** | **984** | **862** |
| 房屋建筑业 | Construction of Housing | 6991 | 348 | 92 | 222 | 138 |
| 土木工程建筑业 | Civil Engineering Construction | 6107 | 215 | 76 | 141 | 124 |
| 建筑安装业 | Architectural Installation | 3815 | 135 | 43 | 129 | 144 |
| 建筑装饰、装修和其他建筑业 | Architectural Decoration and Other Construction | 17083 | 1213 | 198 | 492 | 456 |
| **批发和零售业** | **Wholesale and Retail Trade** | **232551** | **8554** | **3097** | **6984** | **7495** |
| 批发业 | Wholesale Trade | 97873 | 3513 | 901 | 3342 | 3855 |
| 零售业 | Retail Trade | 134678 | 5041 | 2196 | 3642 | 3640 |
| **交通运输、仓储和邮政业** | **Transport, Storage and Postal Services** | **18325** | **769** | **266** | **1002** | **392** |
| 铁路运输业 | Transport Via Railway | 45 | 2 | | 3 | 3 |
| 道路运输业 | Transport Via Road | 11284 | 468 | 184 | 586 | 193 |
| 水上运输业 | Water Transport | 464 | 62 | 1 | 77 | 15 |
| 航空运输业 | Air Transport | 94 | 2 | 1 | 1 | 6 |
| 管道运输业 | Transport Via Pipeline | 8 | | | 1 | |
| 多式联运和运输代理业 | Loading, Unloading, Portage and Transport Agency | 3816 | 128 | 32 | 203 | 127 |
| 装卸搬运和仓储业 | Storage | 1833 | 77 | 21 | 111 | 21 |
| 邮政业 | Post | 781 | 30 | 27 | 20 | 27 |
| **住宿和餐饮业** | **Hotels and Catering Services** | **28535** | **857** | **411** | **848** | **1441** |
| 住宿业 | Hotels | 6938 | 135 | 90 | 146 | 766 |
| 餐饮业 | Catering Services | 21597 | 722 | 321 | 702 | 675 |
| **信息传输、软件和信息技术服务业** | **Information Transmission, Software and Information Technology** | **38830** | **847** | **253** | **806** | **2237** |
| 电信、广播电视和卫星传输服务 | Telecommunication, Radio, Television and Satellite Transmission Services | 853 | 23 | 28 | 22 | 32 |
| 互联网和相关服务 | Internet and Related Services | 5517 | 143 | 60 | 142 | 264 |
| 软件和信息技术服务业 | Software and Information Technology Services | 32460 | 681 | 165 | 642 | 1941 |

单位：个 (unit)

| 大渡口区 Dadukou District | 江北区 Jiangbei District | 沙坪坝区 Shapingba District | 九龙坡区 Jiulongpo District | 南岸区 Nan'an District | 北碚区 Beibei District | 渝北区 Yubei District | 巴南区 Ba'nan District | 长寿区 Changshou District | 江津区 Jiangjin District | 合川区 Hechuan District | 永川区 Yongchuan District | 南川区 Nanchuan District |
|---|---|---|---|---|---|---|---|---|---|---|---|---|
| 6 | 1 | 23 | 96 | 4 | 16 | 15 | 13 | 8 | 38 | 14 | 18 | 34 |
| 139 | 63 | 239 | 586 | 107 | 207 | 223 | 387 | 114 | 503 | 169 | 196 | 170 |
| 193 | 92 | 412 | 762 | 99 | 555 | 310 | 528 | 68 | 805 | 137 | 211 | 91 |
| 101 | 78 | 238 | 528 | 94 | 251 | 401 | 202 | 42 | 383 | 106 | 120 | 48 |
| 78 | 185 | 352 | 508 | 84 | 320 | 540 | 306 | 80 | 537 | 184 | 152 | 47 |
| 127 | 32 | 286 | 321 | 55 | 304 | 65 | 289 | 14 | 248 | 79 | 34 | 19 |
| 49 | 51 | 104 | 240 | 65 | 137 | 128 | 150 | 22 | 186 | 48 | 51 | 22 |
| 22 | 34 | 83 | 167 | 93 | 103 | 183 | 59 | 36 | 83 | 60 | 145 | 23 |
| 12 | 31 | 33 | 92 | 28 | 305 | 101 | 31 | 9 | 58 | 22 | 17 | 2 |
| 6 | 7 | 13 | 44 | 11 | 14 | 27 | 18 | 9 | 20 | 20 | 13 | 11 |
| 7 | 12 | 13 | 26 | 6 | 8 | 19 | 7 | 37 | 34 | 14 | 25 | 9 |
| 29 | 53 | 62 | 99 | 55 | 41 | 162 | 44 | 41 | 41 | 21 | 22 | 17 |
| **10** | **32** | **27** | **38** | **23** | **25** | **98** | **54** | **60** | **179** | **76** | **60** | **101** |
| 4 | 15 | 8 | 15 | 13 | 8 | 53 | 21 | 37 | 72 | 20 | 29 | 67 |
| 1 | 4 | 2 | 5 | 2 | 2 | 18 | 8 | 5 | 11 | 19 | 13 | 18 |
| 5 | 13 | 17 | 18 | 8 | 15 | 27 | 25 | 18 | 96 | 37 | 18 | 16 |
| **629** | **1781** | **1671** | **3805** | **1611** | **870** | **2768** | **1307** | **715** | **1239** | **897** | **914** | **478** |
| 120 | 188 | 196 | 558 | 200 | 130 | 424 | 223 | 146 | 372 | 247 | 220 | 98 |
| 62 | 258 | 249 | 495 | 214 | 202 | 438 | 264 | 134 | 252 | 151 | 134 | 98 |
| 94 | 276 | 189 | 551 | 317 | 65 | 494 | 159 | 94 | 101 | 72 | 84 | 54 |
| 353 | 1059 | 1037 | 2201 | 880 | 473 | 1412 | 661 | 341 | 514 | 427 | 476 | 228 |
| **4221** | **10480** | **10524** | **34944** | **9014** | **4282** | **17381** | **8016** | **4581** | **8084** | **4125** | **5596** | **3718** |
| 2675 | 4598 | 4108 | 18511 | 4096 | 1400 | 6315 | 2889 | 1755 | 4609 | 1802 | 1964 | 1289 |
| 1546 | 5882 | 6416 | 16433 | 4918 | 2882 | 11066 | 5127 | 2826 | 3475 | 2323 | 3632 | 2429 |
| **269** | **1050** | **1124** | **1519** | **497** | **360** | **1508** | **784** | **559** | **900** | **357** | **349** | **240** |
| 1 | 7 | 1 | 7 | 1 |  | 4 | 1 | 1 | 1 | 1 | 1 |  |
| 172 | 608 | 661 | 881 | 341 | 215 | 735 | 495 | 409 | 608 | 226 | 214 | 145 |
| 5 | 32 | 6 | 5 | 11 | 8 | 11 | 4 | 5 | 23 | 24 | 4 |  |
|  | 2 | 6 | 5 | 2 | 1 | 39 | 4 |  | 2 | 3 | 2 | 1 |
|  |  | 1 | 1 | 1 | 1 |  | 1 |  |  |  | 1 |  |
| 28 | 255 | 280 | 404 | 64 | 94 | 458 | 147 | 71 | 155 | 35 | 64 | 67 |
| 46 | 113 | 119 | 172 | 46 | 30 | 178 | 107 | 61 | 90 | 52 | 44 | 13 |
| 17 | 33 | 50 | 44 | 31 | 11 | 83 | 25 | 12 | 21 | 16 | 19 | 14 |
| **222** | **1651** | **1018** | **1261** | **976** | **404** | **2084** | **687** | **499** | **782** | **400** | **562** | **1183** |
| 46 | 436 | 336 | 242 | 308 | 84 | 581 | 143 | 59 | 159 | 74 | 90 | 238 |
| 176 | 1215 | 682 | 1019 | 668 | 320 | 1503 | 544 | 440 | 623 | 326 | 472 | 945 |
| **584** | **4217** | **3225** | **6470** | **2536** | **958** | **6855** | **1300** | **420** | **561** | **525** | **626** | **282** |
| 23 | 71 | 37 | 112 | 39 | 16 | 112 | 17 | 14 | 17 | 28 | 17 | 11 |
| 63 | 498 | 350 | 691 | 374 | 138 | 802 | 205 | 78 | 96 | 102 | 184 | 56 |
| 498 | 3648 | 2838 | 5667 | 2123 | 804 | 5941 | 1078 | 328 | 448 | 395 | 425 | 215 |

**表 22.5 续表 4 continued 4**

| 指 标 | Item | 綦江区 Qijiang District | 綦江区（不含万盛） Qijiang District (excluding Wansheng) | 大足区 Dazu District | 璧山区 Bishan District |
|---|---|---|---|---|---|
| 有色金属冶炼和压延加工业 | Smelting and Pressing of Non-ferrous Metals | 55 | 47 | 41 | 15 |
| 金属制品业 | Manufacture of Metal Products | 155 | 107 | 864 | 293 |
| 通用设备制造业 | Manufacture of General Purpose Machinery | 148 | 117 | 281 | 420 |
| 专用设备制造业 | Manufacture of Special Purpose Machinery | 91 | 59 | 355 | 497 |
| 汽车制造业 | Manufacture of Automobiles | 157 | 134 | 476 | 572 |
| 铁路、船舶、航空航天和其他运输设备制造业 | Manufacture of Railway ,Ship, Aerospace and Other Transport Equipment | 65 | 49 | 377 | 160 |
| 电气机械和器材制造业 | Manufacture of Electrical Machinery and Apparatus | 31 | 20 | 86 | 110 |
| 计算机、通信和其他电子设备制造业 | Manufacture of Computers, Communication and Other Electronic Equipment | 32 | 15 | 70 | 401 |
| 仪器仪表制造业 | Manufacture of Measuring Instruments and Machinery | 2 | 1 | 17 | 60 |
| 其他制造业 | Other Manufacture | 13 | 7 | 17 | 16 |
| 废弃资源综合利用业 | Utilization of Waste Resources | 19 | 11 | 49 | 7 |
| 金属制品、机械和设备修理业 | Manufacture of Metal Products, Machinery and Equipment Maintenance | 13 | 8 | 9 | 33 |
| **电力、热力、燃气及水生产和供应业** | **Production and Supply of Electric Power, Gas and Water** | **161** | **118** | **32** | **34** |
| 电力、热力生产和供应业 | Production and Supply of Electric Power and Heat Power | 73 | 45 | 6 | 8 |
| 燃气生产和供应业 | Production and Supply of Gas | 20 | 16 | 5 | 8 |
| 水的生产和供应业 | Production and Supply of Water | 68 | 57 | 21 | 18 |
| **建筑业** | **Construction** | **1072** | **505** | **588** | **820** |
| 房屋建筑业 | Construction of Housing | 357 | 165 | 156 | 110 |
| 土木工程建筑业 | Civil Engineering Construction | 218 | 94 | 86 | 222 |
| 建筑安装业 | Architectural Installation | 79 | 45 | 61 | 57 |
| 建筑装饰、装修和其他建筑业 | Architectural Decoration and Other Construction | 418 | 201 | 285 | 431 |
| **批发和零售业** | **Wholesale and Retail Trade** | **5939** | **3266** | **4236** | **4329** |
| 批发业 | Wholesale Trade | 2106 | 1224 | 1317 | 1470 |
| 零售业 | Retail Trade | 3833 | 2042 | 2919 | 2859 |
| **交通运输、仓储和邮政业** | **Transport, Storage and Postal Services** | **1418** | **353** | **325** | **553** |
| 铁路运输业 | Transport Via Railway | 3 | | | |
| 道路运输业 | Transport Via Road | 1185 | 240 | 215 | 426 |
| 水上运输业 | Water Transport | | | 2 | |
| 航空运输业 | Air Transport | 3 | | 1 | |
| 管道运输业 | Transport Via Pipeline | | | | |
| 多式联运和运输代理业 | Loading, Unloading, Portage and Transport Agency | 123 | 58 | 47 | 64 |
| 装卸搬运和仓储业 | Storage | 89 | 46 | 39 | 41 |
| 邮政业 | Post | 15 | 9 | 21 | 22 |
| **住宿和餐饮业** | **Hotels and Catering Services** | **1734** | **893** | **633** | **372** |
| 住宿业 | Hotels | 541 | 294 | 99 | 68 |
| 餐饮业 | Catering Services | 1193 | 599 | 534 | 304 |
| **信息传输、软件和信息技术服务业** | **Information Transmission, Software and Information Technology** | **459** | **194** | **248** | **680** |
| 电信、广播电视和卫星传输服务 | Telecommunication, Radio, Television and Satellite Transmission Services | 18 | 9 | 9 | 11 |
| 互联网和相关服务 | Internet and Related Services | 81 | 40 | 69 | 101 |
| 软件和信息技术服务业 | Software and Information Technology Services | 360 | 145 | 170 | 568 |

单位：个 (unit)

| 铜梁区 Tongliang District | 潼南区 Tongnan District | 荣昌区 Rongchang District | 开州区 Kaizhou District | 梁平区 Liangping District | 武隆区 Wulong District | 城口县 Chengkou County | 丰都县 Fengdu County | 垫江县 Dianjiang County | 忠县 Zhongxian County | 云阳县 Yunyang County | 奉节县 Fengjie County | 巫山县 Wushan County |
|---|---|---|---|---|---|---|---|---|---|---|---|---|
| 25 | 24 | 4 | 26 | 1 | | 4 | 14 | 15 | 6 | 17 | 1 | 2 |
| 237 | 167 | 131 | 210 | 148 | 27 | 9 | 51 | 208 | 79 | 508 | 58 | 23 |
| 203 | 54 | 81 | 26 | 31 | 8 | 4 | 13 | 32 | 20 | 42 | 10 | 5 |
| 202 | 53 | 148 | 49 | 33 | 6 | 5 | 25 | 57 | 13 | 45 | 51 | 6 |
| 238 | 25 | 54 | 22 | 10 | 9 | | 2 | 24 | 7 | 12 | 2 | 2 |
| 70 | 5 | 7 | 1 | 8 | 3 | | 8 | 8 | 3 | 10 | 2 | |
| 81 | 36 | 55 | 49 | 21 | 3 | 2 | 8 | 27 | 22 | 44 | 14 | 6 |
| 114 | 89 | 62 | 50 | 34 | 2 | | 6 | 54 | 35 | 54 | 29 | 4 |
| 14 | 2 | 11 | 8 | | | | 3 | 6 | 1 | 4 | 9 | 11 |
| 14 | 10 | 10 | 6 | 14 | | 2 | 4 | 21 | 7 | 14 | 10 | 2 |
| 23 | 12 | 6 | 15 | 7 | 4 | 1 | 4 | 34 | 7 | 16 | 8 | 3 |
| 12 | 28 | 9 | 17 | 10 | 1 | 2 | 8 | 14 | 9 | 18 | 16 | 5 |
| **36** | **44** | **42** | **134** | **27** | **121** | **52** | **139** | **31** | **87** | **123** | **75** | **59** |
| 21 | 7 | 5 | 61 | 5 | 104 | 47 | 50 | 12 | 35 | 101 | 53 | 48 |
| 4 | 8 | 11 | 14 | 7 | 7 | 3 | 11 | 8 | 12 | 8 | 5 | 1 |
| 11 | 29 | 26 | 59 | 15 | 10 | 2 | 78 | 11 | 40 | 14 | 17 | 10 |
| **761** | **538** | **602** | **783** | **273** | **266** | **188** | **391** | **1419** | **414** | **622** | **354** | **304** |
| 132 | 151 | 170 | 174 | 78 | 113 | 63 | 112 | 395 | 115 | 178 | 86 | 168 |
| 169 | 101 | 107 | 177 | 50 | 49 | 37 | 69 | 646 | 60 | 164 | 87 | 27 |
| 67 | 53 | 48 | 47 | 34 | 15 | 7 | 30 | 50 | 43 | 40 | 55 | 20 |
| 393 | 233 | 277 | 385 | 111 | 89 | 81 | 180 | 328 | 196 | 240 | 126 | 89 |
| **3797** | **7514** | **4395** | **6696** | **3609** | **1896** | **1328** | **2946** | **3509** | **3750** | **6176** | **3720** | **2244** |
| 1083 | 4183 | 1808 | 2054 | 1066 | 735 | 191 | 1052 | 1461 | 1482 | 2306 | 1619 | 726 |
| 2714 | 3331 | 2587 | 4642 | 2543 | 1161 | 1137 | 1894 | 2048 | 2268 | 3870 | 2101 | 1518 |
| **208** | **563** | **299** | **254** | **135** | **145** | **65** | **233** | **282** | **286** | **322** | **271** | **168** |
| | | | | | 1 | | | 1 | 1 | 3 | 2 | |
| 149 | 306 | 208 | 149 | 93 | 97 | 45 | 122 | 152 | 158 | 117 | 120 | 77 |
| 1 | 8 | 1 | 4 | | 3 | 1 | 25 | | 21 | 44 | 28 | 22 |
| 1 | 2 | 2 | | 1 | 2 | | | | 1 | 1 | | 1 |
| | | | | | | | | | | 1 | | |
| 28 | 187 | 54 | 45 | 19 | 18 | 4 | 51 | 80 | 65 | 98 | 76 | 39 |
| 16 | 37 | 24 | 36 | 9 | 13 | 2 | 22 | 34 | 28 | 37 | 30 | 13 |
| 13 | 23 | 10 | 20 | 13 | 11 | 13 | 13 | 15 | 12 | 21 | 15 | 16 |
| **517** | **480** | **256** | **1328** | **548** | **813** | **1421** | **472** | **393** | **416** | **581** | **414** | **386** |
| 65 | 89 | 49 | 298 | 45 | 254 | 115 | 175 | 44 | 47 | 119 | 108 | 162 |
| 452 | 391 | 207 | 1030 | 503 | 559 | 1306 | 297 | 349 | 369 | 462 | 306 | 224 |
| **258** | **474** | **504** | **534** | **148** | **100** | **48** | **163** | **573** | **339** | **220** | **271** | **111** |
| 8 | 11 | 9 | 20 | 6 | 9 | 12 | 9 | 8 | 10 | 17 | 14 | 7 |
| 70 | 60 | 98 | 114 | 22 | 24 | 11 | 38 | 101 | 46 | 65 | 67 | 47 |
| 180 | 403 | 397 | 400 | 120 | 67 | 25 | 116 | 464 | 283 | 138 | 190 | 57 |

**表 22.5 续表 5 continued 5**

单位：个 (unit)

| 指 标 | Item | 巫溪县 Wuxi County | 石柱县 Shizhu County | 秀山县 Xiushan County | 酉阳县 Youyang County | 彭水县 Pengshui County |
|---|---|---|---|---|---|---|
| 有色金属冶炼和压延加工业 | Smelting and Pressing of Non-ferrous Metals | 1 | 11 | 9 | 10 | 4 |
| 金属制品业 | Manufacture of Metal Products | 31 | 55 | 47 | 48 | 41 |
| 通用设备制造业 | Manufacture of General Purpose Machinery | 1 | 15 | 22 | 11 | 4 |
| 专用设备制造业 | Manufacture of Special Purpose Machinery | 5 | 26 | 13 | 15 | 2 |
| 汽车制造业 | Manufacture of Automobiles | 1 | 7 | 29 | 1 | 1 |
| 铁路、船舶、航空航天和其他运输设备制造业 | Manufacture of Railway ,Ship, Aerospace and Other Transport Equipment | | 1 | 2 | | |
| 电气机械和器材制造业 | Manufacture of Electrical Machinery and Apparatus | 5 | 20 | 16 | 4 | 4 |
| 计算机、通信和其他电子设备制造业 | Manufacture of Computers, Communication and Other Electronic Equipment | 2 | 15 | 21 | 5 | 2 |
| 仪器仪表制造业 | Manufacture of Measuring Instruments and Machinery | | 3 | 5 | | 2 |
| 其他制造业 | Other Manufacture | 2 | 3 | 10 | 25 | 2 |
| 废弃资源综合利用业 | Utilization of Waste Resources | 4 | 6 | 7 | 7 | |
| 金属制品、机械和设备修理业 | Manufacture of Metal Products, Machinery and Equipment Maintenance | 1 | 5 | 13 | 11 | 5 |
| **电力、热力、燃气及水生产和供应业** | **Production and Supply of Electric Power, Gas and Water** | **138** | **62** | **25** | **81** | **33** |
| 电力、热力生产和供应业 | Production and Supply of Electric Power and Heat Power | 121 | 51 | 18 | 55 | 23 |
| 燃气生产和供应业 | Production and Supply of Gas | 2 | 3 | 3 | 7 | 5 |
| 水的生产和供应业 | Production and Supply of Water | 15 | 8 | 4 | 19 | 5 |
| **建筑业** | **Construction** | **245** | **288** | **456** | **277** | **484** |
| 房屋建筑业 | Construction of Housing | 82 | 62 | 57 | 71 | 239 |
| 土木工程建筑业 | Civil Engineering Construction | 43 | 58 | 137 | 43 | 50 |
| 建筑安装业 | Architectural Installation | 12 | 15 | 26 | 29 | 26 |
| 建筑装饰、装修和其他建筑业 | Architectural Decoration and Other Construction | 108 | 153 | 236 | 134 | 169 |
| **批发和零售业** | **Wholesale and Retail Trade** | **1775** | **2348** | **4456** | **4105** | **2687** |
| 批发业 | Wholesale Trade | 537 | 859 | 1543 | 1660 | 993 |
| 零售业 | Retail Trade | 1238 | 1489 | 2913 | 2445 | 1694 |
| **交通运输、仓储和邮政业** | **Transport, Storage and Postal Services** | **73** | **173** | **228** | **149** | **230** |
| 铁路运输业 | Transport Via Railway | | | | | |
| 道路运输业 | Transport Via Road | 38 | 112 | 115 | 92 | 167 |
| 水上运输业 | Water Transport | 2 | 7 | | | 2 |
| 航空运输业 | Air Transport | | | 2 | | |
| 管道运输业 | Transport Via Pipeline | | | | | |
| 多式联运和运输代理业 | Loading, Unloading, Portage and Transport Agency | 21 | 27 | 83 | 34 | 41 |
| 装卸搬运和仓储业 | Storage | 6 | 12 | 23 | 11 | 10 |
| 邮政业 | Post | 6 | 15 | 5 | 12 | 10 |
| **住宿和餐饮业** | **Hotels and Catering Services** | **535** | **734** | **452** | **382** | **382** |
| 住宿业 | Hotels | 100 | 386 | 55 | 111 | 75 |
| 餐饮业 | Catering Services | 435 | 348 | 397 | 271 | 307 |
| **信息传输、软件和信息技术服务业** | **Information Transmission, Software and Information Technology** | **97** | **142** | **307** | **244** | **208** |
| 电信、广播电视和卫星传输服务 | Telecommunication, Radio, Television and Satellite Transmission Services | 11 | 9 | 5 | 14 | 17 |
| 互联网和相关服务 | Internet and Related Services | 37 | 64 | 44 | 62 | 50 |
| 软件和信息技术服务业 | Software and Information Technology Services | 49 | 69 | 258 | 168 | 141 |

**表 22.5 续表 6 continued 6**

单位：个 (unit)

| 指 标 | Item | 全 市 Total | 万州区 Wanzhou District | 黔江区 Qianjiang District | 涪陵区 Fuling District | 渝中区 Yuzhong District |
|---|---|---|---|---|---|---|
| **金融业** | **Financial Intermediation** | **2273** | **50** | **37** | **75** | **161** |
| 货币金融服务 | Money Finance Services | 1171 | 28 | 22 | 34 | 80 |
| 资本市场服务 | Capital Market Services | 612 | 3 | 6 | 10 | 34 |
| 保险业 | Insurance | 301 | 18 | 8 | 26 | 41 |
| 其他金融业 | Other Finance | 189 | 1 | 1 | 5 | 6 |
| **房地产业** | **Real Estate** | **23373** | **579** | **231** | **522** | **1109** |
| 房地产业 | Real Estate | 23373 | 579 | 231 | 522 | 1109 |
| **租赁和商务服务业** | **Leasing and Business Services** | **98099** | **2757** | **1370** | **2896** | **5020** |
| 租赁业 | Leasing | 16008 | 639 | 289 | 535 | 203 |
| 商务服务业 | Business Services | 82091 | 2118 | 1081 | 2361 | 4817 |
| **科学研究和技术服务业** | **Scientific Research and Technical Services** | **34579** | **817** | **387** | **887** | **1326** |
| 研究和试验发展 | Research and Experimental Development | 2282 | 38 | 19 | 34 | 87 |
| 专业技术服务业 | Professional Technical Services | 19840 | 537 | 308 | 565 | 777 |
| 科技推广和应用服务业 | Services of Science and Technology Application and Promotion | 12457 | 242 | 60 | 288 | 462 |
| **水利、环境和公共设施管理业** | **Water Conservancy, Environment and Public Facilities Management** | **7815** | **186** | **73** | **317** | **167** |
| 水利管理业 | Management of Water Conservancy | 261 | 8 | 5 | 8 | 6 |
| 生态保护和环境治理业 | Ecological Protection and Environmental Governance | 1220 | 33 | 10 | 50 | 26 |
| 公共设施管理业 | Management of Public Facilities | 3732 | 85 | 46 | 168 | 70 |
| 土地管理业 | Management of Land | 2602 | 60 | 12 | 91 | 65 |
| **居民服务、修理和其他服务业** | **Services to Households, Repair and Other Services** | **20329** | **855** | **308** | **605** | **701** |
| 居民服务业 | Resident Services | 9990 | 478 | 155 | 260 | 373 |
| 机动车、电子产品和日用产品修理业 | Vehicles, Electronic Products and Commodities Maintenance Services | 7221 | 273 | 107 | 244 | 165 |
| 其他服务业 | Other Services | 3118 | 104 | 46 | 101 | 163 |
| **教 育** | **Education** | **18750** | **643** | **325** | **583** | **511** |
| 教 育 | Education | 18750 | 643 | 325 | 583 | 511 |
| **卫生和社会工作** | **Health and Social Work** | **7704** | **247** | **96** | **161** | **273** |
| 卫 生 | Health | 5015 | 127 | 56 | 108 | 189 |
| 社会工作 | Social Work | 2689 | 120 | 40 | 53 | 84 |
| **文化、体育和娱乐业** | **Culture, Sports and Entertainment** | **20373** | **645** | **203** | **438** | **917** |
| 新闻和出版业 | Journalism and Publishing Activities | 231 | 3 | | 6 | 31 |
| 广播、电视、电影和录音制作业 | Broadcasting, Movies, Televisions and Audiovisual Activities | 3134 | 63 | 32 | 72 | 214 |
| 文化艺术业 | Cultural and Art Activities | 6166 | 227 | 42 | 178 | 298 |
| 体 育 | Sports | 2514 | 74 | 31 | 58 | 84 |
| 娱乐业 | Entertainment | 8328 | 278 | 98 | 124 | 290 |
| **公共管理、社会保障和社会组织** | **Public Administration, Social Security and Social Organizations** | **29737** | **1276** | **489** | **1118** | **732** |
| 中国共产党机关 | Organs of CPC | 461 | 12 | 3 | 9 | 36 |
| 国家机构 | Government Agencies | 9962 | 434 | 139 | 384 | 258 |
| 人民政协、民主党派 | People's Political Consultative Conference and Democratic Parties | 166 | 6 | 4 | 6 | 16 |
| 社会保障 | Social Security | 312 | 22 | 1 | 8 | 10 |
| 群众团体、社会团体和其他成员组织 | Non-governmental Organizations, Social Organizations and Other Organizations | 7806 | 201 | 122 | 289 | 334 |
| 基层群众自治组织及其他组织 | Grass Roots Self-governing Organizations | 11030 | 601 | 220 | 422 | 78 |

表 22.5 续表 7 continued 7

| 指 标 | Item | 大渡口区 Dadukou District | 江北区 Jiangbei District | 沙坪坝区 Shapingba District | 九龙坡区 Jiulongpo District | 南岸区 Nan'an District |
|---|---|---|---|---|---|---|
| **金融业** | **Financial Intermediation** | **43** | **311** | **49** | **112** | **112** |
| 货币金融服务 | Money Finance Services | 23 | 131 | 31 | 65 | 47 |
| 资本市场服务 | Capital Market Services | 17 | 111 | 4 | 21 | 45 |
| 保险业 | Insurance | 1 | 35 | 7 | 14 | 10 |
| 其他金融业 | Other Finance | 2 | 34 | 7 | 12 | 10 |
| **房地产业** | **Real Estate** | **501** | **1752** | **1421** | **2425** | **1429** |
| 房地产业 | Real Estate | 501 | 1752 | 1421 | 2425 | 1429 |
| **租赁和商务服务业** | **Leasing and Business Services** | 1421 | 7354 | 5385 | 11018 | 5375 |
| 租赁业 | Leasing | 276 | 556 | 628 | 1631 | 558 |
| 商务服务业 | Business Services | 1145 | 6798 | 4757 | 9387 | 4817 |
| **科学研究和技术服务业** | **Scientific Research and Technical Services** | **428** | **2797** | **1935** | **4004** | **1667** |
| 研究和试验发展 | Research and Experimental Development | 57 | 119 | 136 | 353 | 195 |
| 专业技术服务业 | Professional Technical Services | 250 | 1839 | 1300 | 2193 | 1088 |
| 科技推广和应用服务业 | Services of Science and Technology Application and Promotion | 121 | 839 | 499 | 1458 | 384 |
| **水利、环境和公共设施管理业** | **Water Conservancy, Environment and Public Facilities Management** | **130** | **320** | **282** | **730** | **232** |
| 水利管理业 | Management of Water Conservancy | 1 | 6 | 8 | 12 | 4 |
| 生态保护和环境治理业 | Ecological Protection and Environmental Governance | 52 | 88 | 60 | 124 | 60 |
| 公共设施管理业 | Management of Public Facilities | 58 | 138 | 142 | 351 | 150 |
| 土地管理业 | Management of Land | 19 | 88 | 72 | 243 | 18 |
| **居民服务、修理和其他服务业** | **Services to Households, Repair and Other Services** | **327** | **1577** | **1113** | **1824** | **1143** |
| 居民服务业 | Resident Services | 137 | 986 | 519 | 749 | 567 |
| 机动车、电子产品和日用产品修理业 | Vehicles, Electronic Products and Commodities Maintenance Services | 137 | 326 | 361 | 784 | 377 |
| 其他服务业 | Other Services | 53 | 265 | 233 | 291 | 199 |
| **教 育** | **Education** | **319** | **983** | **1314** | **1259** | **881** |
| 教 育 | Education | 319 | 983 | 1314 | 1259 | 881 |
| **卫生和社会工作** | **Health and Social Work** | **162** | 321 | 378 | 432 | 337 |
| 卫 生 | Health | 121 | 250 | 225 | 304 | 165 |
| 社会工作 | Social Work | 41 | 71 | 153 | 128 | 172 |
| **文化、体育和娱乐业** | **Culture, Sports and Entertainment** | **273** | **1726** | **1149** | **1773** | **1016** |
| 新闻和出版业 | Journalism and Publishing Activities | 1 | 29 | 9 | 26 | 12 |
| 广播、电视、电影和录音制作业 | Broadcasting, Movies, Televisions and Audiovisual Activities | 43 | 255 | 187 | 507 | 144 |
| 文化艺术业 | Cultural and Art Activities | 79 | 406 | 350 | 442 | 347 |
| 体 育 | Sports | 47 | 225 | 150 | 211 | 135 |
| 娱乐业 | Entertainment | 103 | 811 | 453 | 587 | 378 |
| **公共管理、社会保障和社会组织** | **Public Administration, Social Security and Social Organizations** | **378** | **553** | **629** | **647** | **531** |
| 中国共产党机关 | Organs of CPC | 20 | 43 | 13 | 9 | 9 |
| 国家机构 | Government Agencies | 163 | 161 | 215 | 239 | 222 |
| 人民政协、民主党派 | People's Political Consultative Conference and Democratic Parties | 8 | 8 | 8 | 8 | 8 |
| 社会保障 | Social Security | 4 | 5 | 10 | 11 | 3 |
| 群众团体、社会团体和其他成员组织 | Non-governmental Organizations, Social Organizations and Other Organizations | 89 | 214 | 215 | 227 | 145 |
| 基层群众自治组织及其他组织 | Grass Roots Self-governing Organizations | 94 | 122 | 168 | 153 | 144 |

单位：个 (unit)

| 北碚区 Beibei District | 渝北区 Yubei District | 巴南区 Ba'nan District | 长寿区 Changshou District | 江津区 Jiangjin District | 合川区 Hechuan District | 永川区 Yongchuan District | 南川区 Nanchuan District | 綦江区 Qijiang District | 綦江区（不含万盛） Qijiang District (excluding Wansheng) | 大足区 Dazu District | 璧山区 Bishan District | 铜梁区 Tongliang District |
|---|---|---|---|---|---|---|---|---|---|---|---|---|
| **56** | **574** | **54** | **31** | **33** | **31** | **36** | **22** | **45** | **24** | **30** | **38** | **37** |
| 30 | 272 | 33 | 16 | 17 | 22 | 22 | 14 | 21 | 12 | 18 | 19 | 17 |
| 16 | 239 | 10 | 8 | 5 | 4 | 3 | 4 | 3 | 2 | 6 | 10 | 5 |
| 5 | 29 | 9 | 4 | 7 | 4 | 10 | 1 | 16 | 8 | 2 | 5 | 5 |
| 5 | 34 | 2 | 3 | 4 | 1 | 1 | 3 | 5 | 2 | 4 | 4 | 10 |
| **695** | **2995** | **1012** | **365** | **769** | **626** | **638** | **384** | **471** | **210** | **374** | **714** | **551** |
| 695 | 2995 | 1012 | 365 | 769 | 626 | 638 | 384 | 471 | 210 | 374 | 714 | 551 |
| 2111 | 12315 | 2759 | 1521 | 2745 | 1842 | 1812 | 1518 | 1935 | 1059 | 1539 | 1871 | 1319 |
| 373 | 1466 | 616 | 305 | 718 | 298 | 374 | 367 | 397 | 219 | 251 | 482 | 248 |
| 1738 | 10849 | 2143 | 1216 | 2027 | 1544 | 1438 | 1151 | 1538 | 840 | 1288 | 1389 | 1071 |
| **1098** | **5847** | **1185** | **517** | **1198** | **506** | **663** | **406** | **805** | **451** | **391** | **642** | **310** |
| 148 | 413 | 59 | 34 | 52 | 22 | 41 | 15 | 45 | 27 | 23 | 63 | 21 |
| 504 | 3317 | 788 | 281 | 529 | 290 | 402 | 245 | 338 | 157 | 231 | 311 | 174 |
| 446 | 2117 | 338 | 202 | 617 | 194 | 220 | 146 | 422 | 267 | 137 | 268 | 115 |
| **228** | **1024** | **196** | **167** | **250** | **165** | **193** | **162** | **308** | **167** | **195** | **213** | **115** |
| 4 | 28 | 8 | 6 | 19 | 2 | 5 | 1 | 17 | 10 | 7 | 5 | 1 |
| 29 | 147 | 37 | 30 | 35 | 24 | 42 | 16 | 44 | 19 | 18 | 39 | 22 |
| 115 | 349 | 104 | 81 | 132 | 95 | 105 | 111 | 148 | 76 | 94 | 94 | 61 |
| 80 | 500 | 47 | 50 | 64 | 44 | 41 | 34 | 99 | 62 | 76 | 75 | 31 |
| **475** | **2034** | **726** | **414** | **537** | **448** | **407** | **466** | **720** | **368** | **399** | **361** | **325** |
| 246 | 941 | 312 | 197 | 255 | 223 | 199 | 225 | 342 | 184 | 210 | 167 | 185 |
| 151 | 790 | 311 | 161 | 231 | 145 | 141 | 188 | 269 | 123 | 148 | 137 | 103 |
| 78 | 303 | 103 | 56 | 51 | 80 | 67 | 53 | 109 | 61 | 41 | 57 | 37 |
| **503** | **1636** | **721** | **364** | **671** | **570** | **557** | **316** | **419** | **268** | **490** | **428** | **423** |
| 503 | 1636 | 721 | 364 | 671 | 570 | 557 | 316 | 419 | 268 | 490 | 428 | 423 |
| 170 | 693 | 376 | 171 | 325 | 258 | 149 | 201 | 239 | 140 | 179 | 159 | 234 |
| 116 | 619 | 261 | 115 | 155 | 144 | 103 | 90 | 135 | 79 | 81 | 130 | 133 |
| 54 | 74 | 115 | 56 | 170 | 114 | 46 | 111 | 104 | 61 | 98 | 29 | 101 |
| **492** | **1847** | **755** | **250** | **517** | **447** | **521** | **274** | **427** | **232** | **376** | **334** | **398** |
| 10 | 48 | 5 |  | 6 | 3 | 4 |  | 5 | 1 | 2 | 3 |  |
| 84 | 420 | 66 | 15 | 83 | 31 | 44 | 20 | 54 | 29 | 48 | 37 | 30 |
| 184 | 483 | 190 | 65 | 115 | 82 | 129 | 99 | 120 | 69 | 131 | 91 | 115 |
| 49 | 328 | 90 | 33 | 77 | 42 | 57 | 57 | 65 | 23 | 49 | 51 | 54 |
| 165 | 568 | 404 | 137 | 236 | 289 | 287 | 98 | 183 | 110 | 146 | 152 | 199 |
| **576** | **1088** | **771** | **667** | **756** | **882** | **818** | **754** | **1288** | **765** | **838** | **835** | **913** |
| 13 | 16 | 14 | 12 | 9 | 14 | 9 | 9 | 18 | 11 | 9 | 17 | 14 |
| 159 | 374 | 282 | 235 | 212 | 207 | 288 | 259 | 480 | 200 | 344 | 206 | 370 |
| 7 | 9 | 10 | 6 | 7 | 6 | 7 | 2 | 7 | 6 | 3 | 2 | 1 |
| 2 | 9 | 14 | 7 | 13 | 2 | 7 | 5 | 6 | 1 | 9 | 4 | 2 |
| 208 | 293 | 151 | 138 | 218 | 247 | 245 | 235 | 309 | 197 | 173 | 327 | 193 |
| 187 | 387 | 300 | 269 | 297 | 406 | 262 | 244 | 468 | 350 | 300 | 279 | 333 |

表 22.5 续表 8 continued 8

| 指 标 | Item | 潼南区 Tongnan District | 荣昌区 Rongchang District | 开州区 Kaizhou District | 梁平区 Liangping District | 武隆区 Wulong District | 城口县 Chengkou County |
|---|---|---|---|---|---|---|---|
| **金融业** | **Financial Intermediation** | **31** | **25** | **22** | **21** | **18** | **13** |
| 货币金融服务 | Money Finance Services | 13 | 14 | 19 | 17 | 12 | 10 |
| 资本市场服务 | Capital Market Services | 8 | 4 | | | 2 | 1 |
| 保险业 | Insurance | 7 | 4 | 3 | 2 | 2 | 1 |
| 其他金融业 | Other Finance | 3 | 3 | | 2 | 2 | 1 |
| **房地产业** | **Real Estate** | **450** | **365** | **580** | **171** | **158** | **51** |
| 房地产业 | Real Estate | 450 | 365 | 580 | 171 | 158 | 51 |
| **租赁和商务服务业** | **Leasing and Business Services** | **2526** | **1754** | **1993** | **577** | **640** | **407** |
| 租赁业 | Leasing | 647 | 297 | 572 | 135 | 201 | 96 |
| 商务服务业 | Business Services | 1879 | 1457 | 1421 | 442 | 439 | 311 |
| **科学研究和技术服务业** | **Scientific Research and Technical Services** | **786** | **756** | **613** | **227** | **236** | **106** |
| 研究和试验发展 | Research and Experimental Development | 27 | 90 | 17 | 10 | 10 | 3 |
| 专业技术服务业 | Professional Technical Services | 480 | 313 | 292 | 94 | 166 | 67 |
| 科技推广和应用服务业 | Services of Science and Technology Application and Promotion | 279 | 353 | 304 | 123 | 60 | 36 |
| **水利、环境和公共设施管理业** | **Water Conservancy, Environment and Public Facilities Management** | **145** | **104** | **258** | **99** | **89** | **65** |
| 水利管理业 | Management of Water Conservancy | 2 | 2 | 13 | 4 | 5 | 2 |
| 生态保护和环境治理业 | Ecological Protection and Environmental Governance | 13 | 33 | 22 | 16 | 4 | 3 |
| 公共设施管理业 | Management of Public Facilities | 71 | 55 | 133 | 48 | 52 | 22 |
| 土地管理业 | Management of Land | 59 | 14 | 90 | 31 | 28 | 38 |
| **居民服务、修理和其他服务业** | **Services to Households, Repair and Other Services** | **292** | **304** | **654** | **284** | **86** | **165** |
| 居民服务业 | Resident Services | 136 | 138 | 357 | 151 | 46 | 91 |
| 机动车、电子产品和日用产品修理业 | Vehicles, Electronic Products and Commodities Maintenance Services | 126 | 99 | 218 | 95 | 21 | 59 |
| 其他服务业 | Other Services | 30 | 67 | 79 | 38 | 19 | 15 |
| **教 育** | **Education** | **335** | **359** | **638** | **268** | **152** | **104** |
| 教 育 | Education | 335 | 359 | 638 | 268 | 152 | 104 |
| **卫生和社会工作** | **Health and Social Work** | **114** | **121** | **228** | **142** | **69** | **84** |
| 卫 生 | Health | 72 | 61 | 176 | 69 | 55 | 53 |
| 社会工作 | Social Work | 42 | 60 | 52 | 73 | 14 | 31 |
| **文化、体育和娱乐业** | **Culture, Sports and Entertainment** | **479** | **287** | **523** | **311** | **457** | **134** |
| 新闻和出版业 | Journalism and Publishing Activities | 1 | | 2 | | 5 | |
| 广播、电视、电影和录音制作业 | Broadcasting, Movies, Televisions and Audiovisual Activities | 40 | 32 | 68 | 27 | 114 | 6 |
| 文化艺术业 | Cultural and Art Activities | 45 | 114 | 246 | 144 | 109 | 43 |
| 体 育 | Sports | 42 | 35 | 54 | 50 | 15 | 41 |
| 娱乐业 | Entertainment | 351 | 106 | 153 | 90 | 214 | 44 |
| **公共管理、社会保障和社会组织** | **Public Administration, Social Security and Social Organizations** | **806** | **632** | **1199** | **780** | **703** | **545** |
| 中国共产党机关 | Organs of CPC | 8 | 11 | 8 | 15 | 26 | 10 |
| 国家机构 | Government Agencies | 315 | 275 | 392 | 282 | 319 | 217 |
| 人民政协、民主党派 | People's Political Consultative Conference and Democratic Parties | 2 | 4 | 3 | 2 | 1 | 1 |
| 社会保障 | Social Security | 13 | 8 | 19 | 11 | 2 | 10 |
| 群众团体、社会团体和其他成员组织 | Non-governmental Organizations, Social Organizations and Other Organizations | 177 | 183 | 250 | 128 | 142 | 103 |
| 基层群众自治组织及其他组织 | Grass Roots Self-governing Organizations | 291 | 151 | 527 | 342 | 213 | 204 |

单位：个 (unit)

| 丰都县 Fengdu County | 垫江县 Dianjiang County | 忠 县 Zhongxian County | 云阳县 Yunyang County | 奉节县 Fengjie County | 巫山县 Wushan County | 巫溪县 Wuxi County | 石柱县 Shizhu County | 秀山县 Xiushan County | 酉阳县 Youyang County | 彭水县 Pengshui County |
|---|---|---|---|---|---|---|---|---|---|---|
| **15** | **19** | **21** | **23** | **23** | **23** | **10** | **22** | **18** | **19** | **13** |
| 11 | 13 | 14 | 13 | 15 | 10 | 6 | 13 | 11 | 9 | 9 |
| 1 | 4 | 3 | 5 | 4 | 4 | 1 | 2 | 1 | 8 | |
| | | 3 | 5 | 1 | 4 | 1 | 3 | 4 | 1 | 3 |
| 3 | 2 | 1 | | 3 | 5 | 2 | 4 | 2 | 1 | 1 |
| **182** | **300** | **207** | **261** | **192** | **174** | **89** | **158** | **167** | **138** | **167** |
| 182 | 300 | 207 | 261 | 192 | 174 | 89 | 158 | 167 | 138 | 167 |
| **913** | **1724** | **2340** | **2212** | **1475** | **613** | **483** | **827** | **1406** | **1358** | **968** |
| 170 | 375 | 289 | 563 | 284 | 124 | 143 | 212 | 326 | 197 | 167 |
| 743 | 1349 | 2051 | 1649 | 1191 | 489 | 340 | 615 | 1080 | 1161 | 801 |
| **257** | **564** | **396** | **413** | **477** | **295** | **148** | **201** | **364** | **672** | **252** |
| 11 | 27 | 26 | 8 | 23 | 4 | 1 | 7 | 13 | 24 | 7 |
| 143 | 333 | 227 | 195 | 223 | 183 | 73 | 123 | 233 | 277 | 151 |
| 103 | 204 | 143 | 210 | 231 | 108 | 74 | 71 | 118 | 371 | 94 |
| **140** | **165** | **95** | **233** | **123** | **103** | **91** | **134** | **136** | **119** | **63** |
| 8 | 4 | 5 | 16 | 5 | 2 | 7 | 8 | 7 | 4 | 6 |
| 16 | 24 | 10 | 11 | 19 | 8 | 10 | 14 | 20 | 8 | 3 |
| 79 | 104 | 42 | 74 | 53 | 49 | 25 | 89 | 42 | 52 | 45 |
| 37 | 33 | 38 | 132 | 46 | 44 | 49 | 23 | 67 | 55 | 9 |
| **215** | **288** | **255** | **357** | **298** | **124** | **160** | **208** | **440** | **191** | 243 |
| 119 | 136 | 147 | 169 | 146 | 44 | 70 | 114 | 191 | 84 | 125 |
| 74 | 93 | 85 | 146 | 107 | 43 | 77 | 67 | 193 | 85 | 84 |
| 22 | 59 | 23 | 42 | 45 | 37 | 13 | 27 | 56 | 22 | 34 |
| **252** | **313** | **336** | **325** | **285** | **203** | **216** | **225** | **325** | **286** | **212** |
| 252 | 313 | 336 | 325 | 285 | 203 | 216 | 225 | 325 | 286 | 212 |
| 140 | 203 | 190 | 188 | 133 | 71 | 91 | 86 | 80 | 108 | 95 |
| 99 | 106 | 79 | 121 | 74 | 57 | 68 | 61 | 59 | 97 | 81 |
| 41 | 97 | 111 | 67 | 59 | 14 | 23 | 25 | 21 | 11 | 14 |
| **416** | **447** | **372** | **402** | **251** | **191** | **148** | **325** | **222** | **397** | **233** |
| 2 | | 4 | | 5 | 3 | | 3 | | 2 | 1 |
| 28 | 35 | 46 | 51 | 33 | 40 | 18 | 58 | 25 | 38 | 26 |
| 232 | 226 | 194 | 130 | 88 | 75 | 59 | 139 | 40 | 47 | 62 |
| 16 | 25 | 24 | 46 | 32 | 15 | 39 | 29 | 27 | 35 | 22 |
| 138 | 161 | 104 | 175 | 93 | 58 | 32 | 96 | 130 | 275 | 122 |
| **793** | **717** | **803** | **1089** | **1405** | **677** | **617** | **646** | **520** | **601** | **665** |
| 6 | 7 | 4 | 10 | 6 | 12 | 8 | 5 | 7 | 7 | 3 |
| 257 | 222 | 309 | 338 | 414 | 198 | 145 | 271 | 105 | 146 | 126 |
| 1 | 1 | 3 | 1 | 1 | 1 | 1 | 1 | 2 | 1 | 1 |
| 13 | 17 | 3 | 27 | 7 | 15 | 4 | 1 | 4 | 2 | 2 |
| 183 | 172 | 116 | 257 | 589 | 128 | 134 | 131 | 135 | 168 | 237 |
| 333 | 298 | 368 | 456 | 388 | 323 | 325 | 237 | 267 | 277 | 296 |

# 表 22.6 按区县、登记注册类型分组的法人单位数（2022 年）
## NUMBER OF CORPORATE UNITS BY STATUS OF REGISTRATION AND REGION (2022)

| 区 县 | Item | 总 计 Total | 内 资 Domestic-funded Enterprises | 国 有 State-owned | 集 体 Collective-owned | 股份合作 Cooperative Share-holding | 联 营 Joint Ownership |
|---|---|---|---|---|---|---|---|
| **全 市** | **Total** | **782071** | **779225** | **22412** | **4995** | **569** | **458** |
| 万州区 | Wanzhou District | 27210 | 27167 | 910 | 93 | 7 | 36 |
| 黔江区 | Qianjiang District | 10467 | 10455 | 319 | 27 | 5 | 5 |
| 涪陵区 | Fuling District | 23266 | 23183 | 696 | 132 | 3 | 41 |
| 渝中区 | Yuzhong District | 23462 | 23141 | 667 | 108 | 51 | 11 |
| 大渡口区 | Dadukou District | 11167 | 11122 | 370 | 61 | 6 | 2 |
| 江北区 | Jiangbei District | 38076 | 37783 | 407 | 33 | 14 | |
| 沙坪坝区 | Shapingba District | 34460 | 34289 | 635 | 162 | 18 | 7 |
| 九龙坡区 | Jiulongpo District | 78395 | 78158 | 546 | 160 | 68 | 18 |
| 南岸区 | Nan'an District | 28837 | 28704 | 552 | 34 | 52 | 6 |
| 北碚区 | Beibei District | 17277 | 17152 | 459 | 86 | 10 | 7 |
| 渝北区 | Yubei District | 65589 | 64969 | 971 | 106 | 100 | 15 |
| 巴南区 | Ba'nan District | 28148 | 28054 | 679 | 68 | 20 | 7 |
| 长寿区 | Changshou District | 15159 | 15080 | 543 | 66 | 7 | 6 |
| 江津区 | Jiangjin District | 29841 | 29751 | 725 | 241 | 19 | 16 |
| 合川区 | Hechuan District | 16511 | 16458 | 643 | 272 | 9 | 6 |
| 永川区 | Yongchuan District | 18477 | 18413 | 635 | 53 | 14 | 4 |
| 南川区 | Nanchuan District | 16882 | 16858 | 702 | 93 | 10 | 8 |
| 綦江区 | Qijiang District | 22988 | 22949 | 1083 | 212 | 20 | 31 |
| #綦江区（不含万盛） | Qijiang District (excluding Wansheng) | 13010 | 12990 | 515 | 156 | 8 | 21 |
| 大足区 | Dazu District | 18266 | 18239 | 761 | 414 | 13 | 4 |
| 璧山区 | Bishan District | 18402 | 18337 | 418 | 246 | 23 | 25 |
| 铜梁区 | Tongliang District | 14981 | 14948 | 714 | 73 | 2 | 9 |
| 潼南区 | Tongnan District | 18485 | 18465 | 550 | 56 | 8 | 7 |
| 荣昌区 | Rongchang District | 13673 | 13639 | 533 | 85 | 3 | 4 |
| 开州区 | Kaizhou District | 22606 | 22590 | 814 | 126 | 5 | 13 |
| 梁平区 | Liangping District | 11382 | 11374 | 587 | 170 | 7 | 1 |
| 武隆区 | Wulong District | 8500 | 8494 | 546 | 50 | 6 | 5 |
| 城口县 | Chengkou County | 6679 | 6676 | 485 | 122 | 9 | |
| 丰都县 | Fengdu County | 11329 | 11325 | 546 | 112 | 2 | 10 |
| 垫江县 | Dianjiang County | 14694 | 14681 | 506 | 93 | 24 | 27 |
| 忠 县 | Zhongxian County | 13843 | 13825 | 612 | 215 | 11 | 17 |
| 云阳县 | Yunyang County | 22998 | 22985 | 678 | 155 | 1 | 69 |
| 奉节县 | Fengjie County | 16876 | 16861 | 667 | 780 | 5 | 10 |
| 巫山县 | Wushan County | 8898 | 8891 | 550 | 29 | 2 | 3 |
| 巫溪县 | Wuxi County | 8015 | 8010 | 400 | 109 | 3 | 8 |
| 石柱县 | Shizhu County | 9676 | 9670 | 513 | 32 | 8 | 12 |
| 秀山县 | Xiushan County | 13620 | 13615 | 292 | 6 | | 1 |
| 酉阳县 | Youyang County | 12432 | 12423 | 363 | 41 | 1 | 6 |
| 彭水县 | Pengshui County | 10504 | 10491 | 335 | 74 | 3 | 1 |

单位：个 (unit)

| 国有联营 State Joint Ownership | 集体联营 Collective Joint Ownership | 国有与集体联营 Joint State-collective Ownership | 其他联营 Other Joint Ownership | 有限责任公司 Limited-liability Corporations | 国有独资公司 State Sole Funded | 其他有限责任公司 Other Limited-liability Corporations | 股份有限公司 Share-holding Limited Companies | 私营 Private |
|---|---|---|---|---|---|---|---|---|
| **26** | **162** | **23** | **247** | **10116** | **1726** | **8390** | **1330** | **700412** |
| 1 | 23 | 3 | 9 | 362 | 61 | 301 | 41 | 24243 |
|  | 2 | 1 | 2 | 116 | 17 | 99 | 32 | 8889 |
| 1 | 21 | 5 | 14 | 328 | 63 | 265 | 44 | 20474 |
|  | 4 | 1 | 6 | 708 | 153 | 555 | 79 | 21432 |
|  | 1 |  | 1 | 212 | 31 | 181 | 24 | 10325 |
|  |  |  |  | 576 | 94 | 482 | 60 | 36546 |
| 1 | 1 |  | 5 | 541 | 48 | 493 | 52 | 32607 |
| 1 | 4 | 5 | 8 | 714 | 60 | 654 | 98 | 76208 |
| 1 | 1 |  | 4 | 738 | 63 | 675 | 72 | 27011 |
|  | 1 | 2 | 4 | 549 | 47 | 502 | 29 | 15339 |
| 7 | 4 | 1 | 3 | 1294 | 162 | 1132 | 185 | 61601 |
| 1 |  |  | 6 | 341 | 45 | 296 | 38 | 26095 |
| 2 | 2 |  | 2 | 190 | 51 | 139 | 35 | 13454 |
| 3 | 5 | 1 | 7 | 292 | 64 | 228 | 48 | 27155 |
|  | 3 |  | 3 | 148 | 22 | 126 | 26 | 14326 |
|  | 2 | 1 | 1 | 165 | 26 | 139 | 23 | 16467 |
|  | 3 | 1 | 4 | 118 | 34 | 84 | 17 | 14390 |
|  | 5 |  | 26 | 361 | 73 | 288 | 55 | 20070 |
|  |  |  | 21 | 178 | 30 | 148 | 25 | 11250 |
|  | 4 |  |  | 156 | 30 | 126 | 38 | 15645 |
|  | 13 |  | 12 | 190 | 29 | 161 | 23 | 16693 |
|  | 7 |  | 2 | 87 | 33 | 54 | 15 | 12992 |
| 1 | 1 |  | 5 | 82 | 26 | 56 | 22 | 16714 |
| 1 |  | 1 | 2 | 85 | 29 | 56 | 13 | 12237 |
|  | 1 |  | 12 | 191 | 33 | 158 | 21 | 19577 |
|  |  |  | 1 | 91 | 24 | 67 | 16 | 9387 |
|  | 1 |  | 4 | 109 | 40 | 69 | 13 | 6959 |
|  |  |  |  | 52 | 19 | 33 | 12 | 5294 |
| 1 | 1 |  | 8 | 93 | 42 | 51 | 18 | 8708 |
|  | 22 |  | 5 | 144 | 21 | 123 | 22 | 12733 |
|  | 10 | 1 | 6 | 103 | 30 | 73 | 18 | 12010 |
|  | 5 |  | 64 | 186 | 31 | 155 | 27 | 20006 |
| 2 | 5 |  | 3 | 150 | 24 | 126 | 33 | 12734 |
| 1 | 1 |  | 1 | 75 | 31 | 44 | 13 | 6483 |
|  | 4 |  | 4 | 68 | 23 | 45 | 13 | 6256 |
|  | 1 |  | 11 | 82 | 33 | 49 | 19 | 8178 |
| 1 |  |  |  | 92 | 53 | 39 | 11 | 12190 |
|  | 4 |  | 2 | 248 | 38 | 210 | 9 | 10175 |
| 1 |  |  |  | 79 | 23 | 56 | 16 | 8809 |

**表 22.6 续表 continued**

单位：个 (unit)

| 区　县 | Item | 私营独资 Solely Private-funded Enterprises | 私营合伙 Private Partnership Enterprises | 私营有限责任公司 Private Limited Liability Corporations | 私营股份有限公司 Private Share-holding Limited Companies | 其他内资 Other Domestic Funded | 港澳台商投资 Enterprises with Funds from Hong Kong, Macao and Taiwan | 外商投资 Foreign Funded |
|---|---|---|---|---|---|---|---|---|
| **全　市** | **Total** | **161530** | **8662** | **528502** | **1718** | **38933** | **1275** | **1571** |
| 万州区 | Wanzhou District | 7737 | 261 | 16214 | 31 | 1475 | 17 | 26 |
| 黔江区 | Qianjiang District | 2948 | 186 | 5725 | 30 | 1062 | 6 | 6 |
| 涪陵区 | Fuling District | 5862 | 129 | 14428 | 55 | 1465 | 32 | 51 |
| 渝中区 | Yuzhong District | 687 | 245 | 20428 | 72 | 85 | 167 | 154 |
| 大渡口区 | Dadukou District | 787 | 79 | 9442 | 17 | 122 | 22 | 23 |
| 江北区 | Jiangbei District | 1619 | 540 | 34290 | 97 | 147 | 103 | 190 |
| 沙坪坝区 | Shapingba District | 1190 | 381 | 30963 | 73 | 267 | 92 | 79 |
| 九龙坡区 | Jiulongpo District | 2694 | 884 | 72469 | 161 | 346 | 100 | 137 |
| 南岸区 | Nan'an District | 1189 | 260 | 25465 | 97 | 239 | 64 | 69 |
| 北碚区 | Beibei District | 2585 | 202 | 12504 | 48 | 673 | 49 | 76 |
| 渝北区 | Yubei District | 3658 | 1267 | 56402 | 274 | 697 | 252 | 368 |
| 巴南区 | Ba'nan District | 4208 | 219 | 21601 | 67 | 806 | 51 | 43 |
| 长寿区 | Changshou District | 4461 | 187 | 8782 | 24 | 779 | 28 | 51 |
| 江津区 | Jiangjin District | 5833 | 218 | 21051 | 53 | 1255 | 52 | 38 |
| 合川区 | Hechuan District | 3237 | 143 | 10912 | 34 | 1028 | 17 | 36 |
| 永川区 | Yongchuan District | 4098 | 273 | 12047 | 49 | 1052 | 22 | 42 |
| 南川区 | Nanchuan District | 6450 | 148 | 7754 | 38 | 1520 | 14 | 10 |
| 綦江区 | Qijiang District | 8037 | 103 | 11879 | 51 | 1117 | 18 | 21 |
| #綦江区（不含万盛） | Qijiang District (excluding Wansheng) | 5177 | 48 | 5991 | 34 | 837 | 9 | 11 |
| 大足区 | Dazu District | 6349 | 99 | 9146 | 51 | 1208 | 13 | 14 |
| 璧山区 | Bishan District | 1745 | 488 | 14392 | 68 | 719 | 28 | 37 |
| 铜梁区 | Tongliang District | 4230 | 83 | 8636 | 43 | 1056 | 15 | 18 |
| 潼南区 | Tongnan District | 7483 | 108 | 9096 | 27 | 1026 | 12 | 8 |
| 荣昌区 | Rongchang District | 2990 | 197 | 9006 | 44 | 679 | 13 | 21 |
| 开州区 | Kaizhou District | 9727 | 233 | 9587 | 30 | 1843 | 10 | 6 |
| 梁平区 | Liangping District | 5718 | 42 | 3615 | 12 | 1115 | 4 | 4 |
| 武隆区 | Wulong District | 2934 | 189 | 3830 | 6 | 806 | 6 | |
| 城口县 | Chengkou County | 3589 | 23 | 1679 | 3 | 702 | 2 | 1 |
| 丰都县 | Fengdu County | 3835 | 153 | 4707 | 13 | 1836 | 3 | 1 |
| 垫江县 | Dianjiang County | 4297 | 137 | 8280 | 19 | 1132 | 5 | 8 |
| 忠　县 | Zhongxian County | 5382 | 152 | 6458 | 18 | 839 | 10 | 8 |
| 云阳县 | Yunyang County | 10450 | 125 | 9408 | 23 | 1863 | 8 | 5 |
| 奉节县 | Fengjie County | 3923 | 187 | 8613 | 11 | 2482 | 9 | 6 |
| 巫山县 | Wushan County | 2591 | 103 | 3778 | 11 | 1736 | 5 | 2 |
| 巫溪县 | Wuxi County | 2606 | 80 | 3565 | 5 | 1153 | 4 | 1 |
| 石柱县 | Shizhu County | 3241 | 55 | 4873 | 9 | 826 | 5 | 1 |
| 秀山县 | Xiushan County | 4875 | 202 | 7097 | 16 | 1023 | 2 | 3 |
| 酉阳县 | Youyang County | 4625 | 206 | 5317 | 27 | 1580 | 6 | 3 |
| 彭水县 | Pengshui County | 3660 | 75 | 5063 | 11 | 1174 | 9 | 4 |

# 表 22.7 按行业、区县分组的企业法人单位数（2022 年）
## NUMBER OF ENTERPRISES AS CORPORATE UNITS BY SECTOR AND REGION (2022)

单位：个 (unit)

| 指　标 | Item | 全　市 Total | 万州区 Wanzhou District | 黔江区 Qianjiang District | 涪陵区 Fuling District | 渝中区 Yuzhong District |
|---|---|---|---|---|---|---|
| **总　计** | **Total** | **705046** | **24354** | **8814** | **20557** | **22104** |
| **按三次产业分组** | **By Strata of Industry** | | | | | |
| 第一产业 | Primary Industry | 68240 | 3413 | 1124 | 2310 | |
| 第二产业 | Secondary Industry | 104676 | 3725 | 957 | 2697 | 976 |
| 第三产业 | Tertiary Industry | 532130 | 17216 | 6733 | 15550 | 21128 |
| **按国民经济行业分组** | **By Sector** | | | | | |
| **农、林、牧、渔业** | **Agriculture, Forestry, Animal Husbandry and Fishery** | **73198** | **3637** | **1206** | **2562** | |
| 农　业 | Farming | 34551 | 2068 | 478 | 1196 | |
| 林　业 | Forestry | 2930 | 146 | 83 | 79 | |
| 畜牧业 | Animal Husbandry | 21329 | 695 | 506 | 638 | |
| 渔　业 | Fishery | 9430 | 504 | 57 | 397 | |
| 农、林、牧、渔专业及辅助性活动 | Services of Farming, Forestry, Animal Husbandry and Fishery | 4958 | 224 | 82 | 252 | |
| **采矿业** | **Mining** | **1393** | **51** | **35** | **34** | |
| 煤炭开采和洗选业 | Mining and Washing of Coal | 167 | 1 | 3 | 2 | |
| 石油和天然气开采业 | Extraction of Petroleum and Natural Gas | 17 | | | 2 | |
| 黑色金属矿采选业 | Mining and Processing of Ferrous Metal Ores | 72 | 1 | | | |
| 有色金属矿采选业 | Mining and Processing of Non-ferrous Metal Ores | 21 | | | | |
| 非金属矿采选业 | Mining and Processing of Non-metal Ores | 1050 | 41 | 32 | 28 | |
| 开采专业及辅助性活动 | Support Activities for Mining | 39 | 5 | | 1 | |
| 其他采矿业 | Mining of Other Ores | 27 | 3 | | 1 | |
| **制造业** | **Manufacture** | **67767** | **1709** | **487** | **1593** | **112** |
| 农副食品加工业 | Processing of Food from Agricultural Products | 4723 | 119 | 61 | 202 | 3 |
| 食品制造业 | Manufacture of Foods | 2258 | 41 | 26 | 56 | 1 |
| 酒、饮料和精制茶制造业 | Manufacture of Liquor, Beverages and Refined Tea | 2020 | 70 | 35 | 59 | |
| 烟草制品业 | Manufacture of Tobacco | 7 | | 1 | 1 | |
| 纺织业 | Manufacture of Textile | 1367 | 55 | 20 | 34 | |
| 纺织服装、服饰业 | Manufacture of Textile, Wearing Apparel and Accessories | 2013 | 90 | 14 | 32 | 8 |
| 皮革、毛皮、羽毛及其制品和制鞋业 | Manufacture of Leather, Fur, Feather and Related Products and Footwear | 842 | 15 | 3 | 10 | |
| 木材加工和木、竹、藤、棕、草制品业 | Processing of Timber, Manufacture of Wood, Bamboo, Rattan, Palm and Straw Products | 2950 | 86 | 22 | 49 | |
| 家具制造业 | Manufacture of Furniture | 2367 | 106 | 22 | 48 | 1 |
| 造纸和纸制品业 | Manufacture of Paper and Paper Products | 975 | 12 | 3 | 19 | 2 |
| 印刷和记录媒介复制业 | Printing, Reproduction of Recording Media | 1579 | 60 | 19 | 44 | 24 |
| 文教、工美、体育和娱乐用品制造业 | Manufacture of Articles for Culture, Education, Arts and Crafts, Sport and Entertainment Activities | 1327 | 36 | 21 | 30 | 7 |
| 石油、煤炭及其他燃料加工业 | Petroleum Refining,Coking and Nuclear Fuel Processing | 189 | 8 | | 7 | |
| 化学原料和化学制品制造业 | Manufacture of Raw Chemical Materials and Chemical Products | 1699 | 43 | 11 | 75 | 1 |
| 医药制造业 | Manufacture of Medicines | 581 | 22 | 5 | 16 | |
| 化学纤维制造业 | Manufacture of Chemical Fibres | 48 | | | 6 | 1 |
| 橡胶和塑料制品业 | Manufacture of Rubber and Plastics Products | 2516 | 62 | 11 | 81 | 3 |

表 22.7 续表 1 continued 1

| 指 标 | Item | 大渡口区 Dadukou District | 江北区 Jiangbei District | 沙坪坝区 Shapingba District | 九龙坡区 Jiulongpo District | 南岸区 Nan'an District |
|---|---|---|---|---|---|---|
| **总 计** | **Total** | **10510** | **36887** | **33015** | **76754** | **27463** |
| **按三次产业分组** | **By Strata of Industry** | | | | | |
| 第一产业 | Primary Industry | 100 | 120 | 170 | 556 | 167 |
| 第二产业 | Secondary Industry | 1731 | 2770 | 4586 | 9134 | 2806 |
| 第三产业 | Tertiary Industry | 8679 | 33997 | 28259 | 67064 | 24490 |
| **按国民经济行业分组** | **By Sector** | | | | | |
| **农、林、牧、渔业** | **Agriculture, Forestry, Animal Husbandry and Fishery** | **116** | **144** | **200** | **615** | **190** |
| 农 业 | Farming | 95 | 95 | 120 | 349 | 132 |
| 林 业 | Forestry | 2 | 6 | 29 | 83 | 18 |
| 畜牧业 | Animal Husbandry | 2 | 12 | 7 | 27 | 6 |
| 渔 业 | Fishery | 1 | 7 | 14 | 97 | 11 |
| 农、林、牧、渔专业及辅助性活动 | Services of Farming, Forestry, Animal Husbandry and Fishery | 16 | 24 | 30 | 59 | 23 |
| **采矿业** | **Mining** | **3** | **3** | **1** | **9** | **3** |
| 煤炭开采和洗选业 | Mining and Washing of Coal | | | | 1 | |
| 石油和天然气开采业 | Extraction of Petroleum and Natural Gas | | | | | |
| 黑色金属矿采选业 | Mining and Processing of Ferrous Metal Ores | 2 | | | 1 | |
| 有色金属矿采选业 | Mining and Processing of Non-ferrous Metal Ores | | | | | |
| 非金属矿采选业 | Mining and Processing of Non-metal Ores | 1 | 3 | 1 | 6 | 3 |
| 开采专业及辅助性活动 | Support Activities for Mining | | | | 1 | |
| 其他采矿业 | Mining of Other Ores | | | | | |
| **制造业** | **Manufacture** | **1118** | **1007** | **2949** | **5382** | **1224** |
| 农副食品加工业 | Processing of Food from Agricultural Products | 31 | 22 | 39 | 86 | 31 |
| 食品制造业 | Manufacture of Foods | 24 | 29 | 43 | 106 | 26 |
| 酒、饮料和精制茶制造业 | Manufacture of Liquor, Beverages and Refined Tea | 3 | 9 | 22 | 26 | 10 |
| 烟草制品业 | Manufacture of Tobacco | | | | | 2 |
| 纺织业 | Manufacture of Textile | 8 | 13 | 134 | 33 | 23 |
| 纺织服装、服饰业 | Manufacture of Textile, Wearing Apparel and Accessories | 7 | 26 | 9 | 50 | 43 |
| 皮革、毛皮、羽毛及其制品和制鞋业 | Manufacture of Leather, Fur, Feather and Related Products and Footwear | 4 | 3 | 4 | 8 | 10 |
| 木材加工和木、竹、藤、棕、草制品业 | Processing of Timber, Manufacture of Wood, Bamboo, Rattan, Palm and Straw Products | 33 | 8 | 76 | 196 | 24 |
| 家具制造业 | Manufacture of Furniture | 35 | 11 | 100 | 222 | 57 |
| 造纸和纸制品业 | Manufacture of Paper and Paper Products | 20 | 18 | 72 | 89 | 16 |
| 印刷和记录媒介复制业 | Printing, Reproduction of Recording Media | 28 | 70 | 94 | 145 | 57 |
| 文教、工美、体育和娱乐用品制造业 | Manufacture of Articles for Culture, Education, Arts and Crafts, Sport and Entertainment Activities | 17 | 12 | 53 | 56 | 15 |
| 石油、煤炭及其他燃料加工业 | Petroleum Refining,Coking and Nuclear Fuel Processing | 3 | | 7 | 13 | 2 |
| 化学原料和化学制品制造业 | Manufacture of Raw Chemical Materials and Chemical Products | 21 | 32 | 81 | 114 | 34 |
| 医药制造业 | Manufacture of Medicines | 3 | 19 | 13 | 33 | 21 |
| 化学纤维制造业 | Manufacture of Chemical Fibres | | 1 | | | 1 |
| 橡胶和塑料制品业 | Manufacture of Rubber and Plastics Products | 33 | 37 | 124 | 216 | 80 |

单位：个 (unit)

| 北碚区 Beibei District | 渝北区 Yubei District | 巴南区 Ba'nan District | 长寿区 Changshou District | 江津区 Jiangjin District | 合川区 Hechuan District | 永川区 Yongchuan District | 南川区 Nanchuan District | 綦江区 Qijiang District | 綦江区（不含万盛） Qijiang District (excluding Wansheng) | 大足区 Dazu District | 璧山区 Bishan District | 铜梁区 Tongliang District |
|---|---|---|---|---|---|---|---|---|---|---|---|---|
| **15760** | **62975** | **26304** | **13603** | **27414** | **14317** | **16421** | **14398** | **20466** | **11407** | **15614** | **16774** | **12933** |
| 654 | 1196 | 3207 | 2098 | 3976 | 1585 | 1550 | 3490 | 3233 | 2396 | 2700 | 1586 | 1673 |
| 3863 | 5911 | 5030 | 1989 | 6425 | 3108 | 3179 | 2108 | 2933 | 1765 | 4354 | 4786 | 3188 |
| 11243 | 55868 | 18067 | 9516 | 17013 | 9624 | 11692 | 8800 | 14300 | 7246 | 8560 | 10402 | 8072 |
| **708** | **1322** | **3287** | **2192** | **4348** | **1671** | **1638** | **3645** | **3351** | **2473** | **2790** | **1655** | **1753** |
| 465 | 718 | 1981 | 1131 | 2225 | 679 | 886 | 1659 | 1124 | 844 | 828 | 1126 | 607 |
| 26 | 79 | 346 | 60 | 154 | 96 | 71 | 202 | 125 | 53 | 122 | 245 | 74 |
| 68 | 261 | 166 | 493 | 802 | 351 | 171 | 1117 | 1644 | 1258 | 865 | 97 | 372 |
| 95 | 138 | 714 | 414 | 795 | 459 | 422 | 512 | 340 | 241 | 885 | 118 | 620 |
| 54 | 126 | 80 | 94 | 372 | 86 | 88 | 155 | 118 | 77 | 90 | 69 | 80 |
| **22** | **6** | **12** | **24** | **39** | **81** | **83** | **50** | **80** | **54** | **40** | **11** | **53** |
| 3 |  | 1 | 1 |  | 17 | 28 | 11 | 9 | 3 | 5 |  | 5 |
|  |  |  | 2 |  | 2 | 2 | 1 | 1 | 1 |  |  | 1 |
|  | 1 |  |  |  |  | 1 |  | 3 | 3 |  |  |  |
|  |  |  |  |  |  |  | 2 |  |  | 1 |  |  |
| 18 | 1 | 10 | 18 | 39 | 59 | 49 | 35 | 64 | 45 | 32 | 10 | 47 |
|  | 2 |  | 1 |  | 2 | 3 | 1 | 2 | 1 | 2 | 1 |  |
| 1 | 2 | 1 | 2 |  | 1 |  |  | 1 | 1 |  |  |  |
| **2987** | **3205** | **3701** | **1232** | **5008** | **2077** | **2147** | **1498** | **1636** | **1098** | **3706** | **3955** | **2350** |
| 21 | 79 | 95 | 93 | 256 | 162 | 114 | 131 | 94 | 52 | 100 | 46 | 118 |
| 33 | 118 | 77 | 47 | 262 | 134 | 80 | 45 | 64 | 31 | 71 | 67 | 49 |
| 12 | 38 | 24 | 27 | 72 | 57 | 73 | 99 | 89 | 58 | 32 | 24 | 35 |
| 36 | 25 | 61 | 22 | 40 | 39 | 13 | 66 | 21 | 15 | 29 | 34 | 53 |
| 13 | 91 | 333 | 11 | 38 | 57 | 27 | 32 | 10 | 6 | 19 | 35 | 89 |
| 8 | 9 | 21 | 3 | 11 | 22 | 14 | 15 | 9 | 7 | 13 | 221 | 83 |
| 36 | 45 | 150 | 57 | 161 | 45 | 125 | 65 | 68 | 44 | 101 | 48 | 94 |
| 34 | 48 | 165 | 53 | 206 | 81 | 81 | 85 | 36 | 20 | 65 | 84 | 79 |
| 59 | 36 | 76 | 16 | 51 | 24 | 68 | 15 | 15 | 12 | 28 | 84 | 50 |
| 47 | 147 | 82 | 29 | 68 | 40 | 42 | 25 | 24 | 14 | 17 | 177 | 24 |
| 40 | 53 | 62 | 14 | 43 | 45 | 32 | 34 | 32 | 20 | 97 | 20 | 27 |
| 3 | 11 | 2 | 4 | 12 | 3 | 10 | 5 | 12 | 6 | 7 | 4 | 1 |
| 52 | 73 | 85 | 121 | 140 | 46 | 60 | 57 | 41 | 20 | 53 | 45 | 52 |
| 30 | 23 | 43 | 22 | 12 | 22 | 7 | 15 | 15 | 6 | 11 | 13 | 16 |
| 3 | 3 | 3 | 5 | 5 | 1 | 3 |  | 2 | 1 | 2 | 4 |  |
| 116 | 66 | 129 | 66 | 249 | 89 | 86 | 36 | 40 | 22 | 138 | 300 | 143 |

**表 22.7 续表 2 continued 2**

| 指 标 | Item | 潼南区 Tongnan District | 荣昌区 Rongchang District | 开州区 Kaizhou District | 梁平区 Liangping District | 武隆区 Wulong District | 城口县 Chengkou County |
|---|---|---|---|---|---|---|---|
| **总 计** | **Total** | **16582** | **12078** | **19419** | **9427** | **6967** | **5365** |
| **按三次产业分组** | **By Strata of Industry** | | | | | | |
| 第一产业 | Primary Industry | 977 | 681 | 2759 | 1744 | 1687 | 1160 |
| 第二产业 | Secondary Industry | 2255 | 2348 | 2939 | 1640 | 810 | 499 |
| 第三产业 | Tertiary Industry | 13350 | 9049 | 13721 | 6043 | 4470 | 3706 |
| **按国民经济行业分组** | **By Sector** | | | | | | |
| **农、林、牧、渔业** | **Agriculture, Forestry, Animal Husbandry and Fishery** | **1050** | **764** | **2961** | **1848** | **1727** | **1213** |
| 农 业 | Farming | 514 | 362 | 1072 | 886 | 837 | 398 |
| 林 业 | Forestry | 16 | 36 | 99 | 90 | 44 | 17 |
| 畜牧业 | Animal Husbandry | 199 | 174 | 1270 | 417 | 731 | 718 |
| 渔 业 | Fishery | 248 | 109 | 318 | 351 | 75 | 27 |
| 农、林、牧、渔专业及辅助性活动 | Services of Farming, Forestry, Animal Husbandry and Fishery | 73 | 83 | 202 | 104 | 40 | 53 |
| **采矿业** | **Mining** | **121** | **30** | **48** | **34** | **25** | **23** |
| 煤炭开采和洗选业 | Mining and Washing of Coal | | 15 | 6 | 8 | 1 | 1 |
| 石油和天然气开采业 | Extraction of Petroleum and Natural Gas | 3 | | | | | |
| 黑色金属矿采选业 | Mining and Processing of Ferrous Metal Ores | | 1 | | | | 5 |
| 有色金属矿采选业 | Mining and Processing of Non-ferrous Metal Ores | | | | | 1 | 1 |
| 非金属矿采选业 | Mining and Processing of Non-metal Ores | 116 | 14 | 41 | 24 | 23 | 16 |
| 开采专业及辅助性活动 | Support Activities for Mining | 2 | | 1 | 1 | | |
| 其他采矿业 | Mining of Other Ores | | | | 1 | | |
| **制造业** | **Manufacture** | **1583** | **1683** | **1992** | **1318** | **399** | **238** |
| 农副食品加工业 | Processing of Food from Agricultural Products | 207 | 210 | 193 | 146 | 101 | 56 |
| 食品制造业 | Manufacture of Foods | 36 | 79 | 65 | 38 | 19 | 15 |
| 酒、饮料和精制茶制造业 | Manufacture of Liquor, Beverages and Refined Tea | 38 | 51 | 147 | 76 | 30 | 36 |
| 烟草制品业 | Manufacture of Tobacco | | | 1 | | | |
| 纺织业 | Manufacture of Textile | 40 | 39 | 97 | 25 | 8 | 9 |
| 纺织服装、服饰业 | Manufacture of Textile, Wearing Apparel and Accessories | 65 | 50 | 225 | 74 | 6 | 2 |
| 皮革、毛皮、羽毛及其制品和制鞋业 | Manufacture of Leather, Fur, Feather and Related Products and Footwear | 34 | 14 | 65 | 23 | 3 | 2 |
| 木材加工和木、竹、藤、棕、草制品业 | Processing of Timber, Manufacture of Wood, Bamboo, Rattan, Palm and Straw Products | 196 | 43 | 134 | 155 | 18 | 19 |
| 家具制造业 | Manufacture of Furniture | 49 | 43 | 127 | 60 | 4 | 4 |
| 造纸和纸制品业 | Manufacture of Paper and Paper Products | 22 | 17 | 19 | 59 | 2 | 1 |
| 印刷和记录媒介复制业 | Printing, Reproduction of Recording Media | 32 | 35 | 33 | 24 | 20 | 4 |
| 文教、工美、体育和娱乐用品制造业 | Manufacture of Articles for Culture, Education, Arts and Crafts, Sport and Entertainment Activities | 18 | 103 | 36 | 71 | 3 | 10 |
| 石油、煤炭及其他燃料加工业 | Petroleum Refining,Coking and Nuclear Fuel Processing | 7 | 3 | 7 | 6 | 2 | 1 |
| 化学原料和化学制品制造业 | Manufacture of Raw Chemical Materials and Chemical Products | 63 | 52 | 44 | 32 | 8 | 7 |
| 医药制造业 | Manufacture of Medicines | 12 | 43 | 20 | 5 | 6 | 3 |
| 化学纤维制造业 | Manufacture of Chemical Fibres | | | | | | |
| 橡胶和塑料制品业 | Manufacture of Rubber and Plastics Products | 40 | 77 | 43 | 47 | 10 | |

单位：个 (unit)

| 丰都县 Fengdu County | 垫江县 Dianjiang County | 忠 县 Zhongxian County | 云阳县 Yunyang County | 奉节县 Fengjie County | 巫山县 Wushan County | 巫溪县 Wuxi County | 石柱县 Shizhu County | 秀山县 Xiushan County | 酉阳县 Youyang County | 彭水县 Pengshui County |
|---|---|---|---|---|---|---|---|---|---|---|
| **8658** | **12700** | **11999** | **19974** | **12738** | **6472** | **6215** | **8152** | **12000** | **10169** | **8694** |
| 1667 | 1229 | 2038 | 4085 | 3914 | 1571 | 1868 | 1874 | 2365 | 1624 | 2089 |
| 1241 | 3121 | 1389 | 4441 | 1488 | 751 | 770 | 960 | 1326 | 1338 | 1104 |
| 5750 | 8350 | 8572 | 11448 | 7336 | 4150 | 3577 | 5318 | 8309 | 7207 | 5501 |
| **1776** | **1384** | **2313** | **4916** | **4157** | **1661** | **1956** | **1993** | **2445** | **1828** | **2176** |
| 503 | 629 | 1240 | 2165 | 2680 | 944 | 864 | 859 | 1194 | 691 | 751 |
| 34 | 45 | 33 | 62 | 88 | 50 | 28 | 74 | 55 | 54 | 59 |
| 938 | 353 | 514 | 1479 | 1039 | 508 | 907 | 802 | 963 | 803 | 1214 |
| 192 | 202 | 251 | 379 | 107 | 69 | 69 | 139 | 153 | 76 | 65 |
| 109 | 155 | 275 | 831 | 243 | 90 | 88 | 119 | 80 | 204 | 87 |
| **30** | **18** | **33** | **26** | **53** | **45** | **31** | **34** | **88** | **40** | **74** |
| 2 | 4 |  | 5 | 16 | 13 | 1 | 2 | 2 |  | 4 |
|  | 1 | 1 |  |  |  |  |  |  | 1 |  |
|  |  | 2 |  | 1 | 1 |  | 1 | 46 |  | 6 |
|  |  | 1 |  |  | 1 | 1 | 3 | 2 | 3 | 5 |
| 28 | 12 | 24 | 20 | 30 | 29 | 28 | 26 | 38 | 33 | 51 |
|  | 1 | 3 | 1 | 3 |  |  | 2 |  | 1 | 3 |
|  |  | 2 |  | 3 | 1 | 1 |  |  | 2 | 5 |
| **691** | **1668** | **867** | **3689** | **1025** | **348** | **357** | **583** | **770** | **952** | **521** |
| 133 | 177 | 168 | 836 | 192 | 39 | 43 | 71 | 83 | 85 | 80 |
| 24 | 46 | 43 | 252 | 70 | 23 | 15 | 23 | 33 | 43 | 35 |
| 39 | 53 | 64 | 175 | 47 | 36 | 36 | 37 | 61 | 238 | 40 |
|  |  |  |  | 1 |  |  |  |  |  | 1 |
| 16 | 60 | 25 | 186 | 15 | 10 | 10 | 18 | 13 | 19 | 18 |
| 27 | 34 | 66 | 210 | 39 | 35 | 19 | 18 | 30 | 69 | 10 |
| 10 | 44 | 10 | 51 | 16 | 16 | 9 | 15 | 13 | 23 | 8 |
| 47 | 159 | 59 | 335 | 70 | 16 | 37 | 36 | 57 | 51 | 29 |
| 24 | 131 | 31 | 119 | 41 | 6 | 11 | 22 | 30 | 26 | 20 |
| 5 | 17 | 5 | 13 | 11 | 2 | 3 | 7 | 5 | 4 | 10 |
| 17 | 28 | 31 | 20 | 22 | 13 | 8 | 5 | 7 | 12 | 5 |
| 11 | 33 | 12 | 146 | 33 | 11 | 17 | 13 | 23 | 29 | 12 |
| 4 | 6 | 2 | 10 | 12 | 4 | 3 | 1 | 1 | 1 | 5 |
| 22 | 56 | 19 | 48 | 15 | 7 | 6 | 17 | 24 | 23 | 19 |
| 9 | 13 | 4 | 30 | 26 | 3 | 6 | 15 | 11 | 8 | 6 |
| 1 | 2 | 1 | 1 |  |  | 1 |  |  | 1 | 1 |
| 13 | 60 | 14 | 40 | 21 | 3 | 5 | 8 | 17 | 8 | 5 |

**表 22.7 续表 3 continued 3**

| 指　标 | Item | 全　市 Total | 万州区 Wanzhou District | 黔江区 Qianjiang District | 涪陵区 Fuling District | 渝中区 Yuzhong District |
|---|---|---|---|---|---|---|
| 非金属矿物制品业 | Manufacture of Non-metallic Mineral Products | 7022 | 215 | 105 | 235 | 3 |
| 黑色金属冶炼和压延加工业 | Smelting and Pressing of Ferrous Metals | 461 | 7 | 10 | 18 | |
| 有色金属冶炼和压延加工业 | Smelting and Pressing of Non-ferrous Metals | 618 | 16 | 7 | 24 | |
| 金属制品业 | Manufacture of Metal Products | 6994 | 265 | 49 | 177 | 10 |
| 通用设备制造业 | Manufacture of General Purpose Machinery | 5824 | 76 | 9 | 35 | 10 |
| 专用设备制造业 | Manufacture of Special Purpose Machinery | 4385 | 43 | 6 | 36 | 13 |
| 汽车制造业 | Manufacture of Automobiles | 5129 | 44 | | 61 | |
| 铁路、船舶、航空航天和其他运输设备制造业 | Manufacture of Railway ,Ship, Aerospace and Other Transport Equipment | 2696 | 17 | 1 | 73 | 2 |
| 电气机械和器材制造业 | Manufacture of Electrical Machinery and Apparatus | 2007 | 62 | 10 | 32 | 6 |
| 计算机、通信和其他电子设备制造业 | Manufacture of Computers, Communication and Other Electronic Equipment | 2268 | 55 | 6 | 30 | 6 |
| 仪器仪表制造业 | Manufacture of Measuring Instruments and Machinery | 924 | 10 | | 9 | 6 |
| 其他制造业 | Other Manufacture | 433 | 7 | 1 | 10 | 1 |
| 废弃资源综合利用业 | Utilization of Waste Resources | 502 | 25 | 2 | 19 | |
| 金属制品、机械和设备修理业 | Manufacture of Metal Products, Machinery and Equipment Maintenance | 1043 | 42 | 7 | 65 | 4 |
| **电力、热力、燃气及水生产和供应业** | **Production and Supply of Electric Power, Gas and Water** | **2602** | **101** | **33** | **152** | **6** |
| 电力、热力生产和供应业 | Production and Supply of Electric Power and Heat Power | 1459 | 82 | 18 | 94 | 1 |
| 燃气生产和供应业 | Production and Supply of Gas | 304 | 7 | 5 | 32 | 1 |
| 水的生产和供应业 | Production and Supply of Water | 839 | 12 | 10 | 26 | 4 |
| **建筑业** | **Construction** | **33996** | **1911** | **409** | **984** | **862** |
| 房屋建筑业 | Construction of Housing | 6991 | 348 | 92 | 222 | 138 |
| 土木工程建筑业 | Civil Engineering Construction | 6107 | 215 | 76 | 141 | 124 |
| 建筑安装业 | Architectural Installation | 3815 | 135 | 43 | 129 | 144 |
| 建筑装饰、装修和其他建筑业 | Architectural Decoration and Other Construction | 17083 | 1213 | 198 | 492 | 456 |
| **批发和零售业** | **Wholesale and Retail Trade** | **227553** | **8401** | **3016** | **6678** | **7495** |
| 批发业 | Wholesale Trade | 94882 | 3419 | 855 | 3091 | 3855 |
| 零售业 | Retail Trade | 132671 | 4982 | 2161 | 3587 | 3640 |
| **交通运输、仓储和邮政业** | **Transport, Storage and Postal Services** | **18280** | **767** | **264** | **1000** | **392** |
| 铁路运输业 | Transport Via Railway | 44 | 2 | | 3 | 3 |
| 道路运输业 | Transport Via Road | 11256 | 466 | 182 | 584 | 193 |
| 水上运输业 | Water Transport | 462 | 62 | 1 | 77 | 15 |
| 航空运输业 | Air Transport | 94 | 2 | 1 | 1 | 6 |
| 管道运输业 | Transport Via Pipeline | 8 | | | 1 | |
| 多式联运和运输代理业 | Loading, Unloading, Portage and Transport Agency | 3814 | 128 | 32 | 203 | 127 |
| 装卸搬运和仓储业 | Storage | 1823 | 77 | 21 | 111 | 21 |
| 邮政业 | Post | 779 | 30 | 27 | 20 | 27 |
| **住宿和餐饮业** | **Hotels and Catering Services** | **28449** | **857** | **407** | **847** | **1441** |
| 住宿业 | Hotels | 6895 | 135 | 88 | 145 | 766 |
| 餐饮业 | Catering Services | 21554 | 722 | 319 | 702 | 675 |

单位：个 (unit)

| 大渡口区 Dadukou District | 江北区 Jiangbei District | 沙坪坝区 Shapingba District | 九龙坡区 Jiulongpo District | 南岸区 Nan'an District | 北碚区 Beibei District | 渝北区 Yubei District | 巴南区 Ba'nan District | 长寿区 Changshou District | 江津区 Jiangjin District | 合川区 Hechuan District | 永川区 Yongchuan District | 南川区 Nanchuan District |
|---|---|---|---|---|---|---|---|---|---|---|---|---|
| 63 | 47 | 207 | 485 | 67 | 175 | 146 | 243 | 144 | 395 | 325 | 294 | 275 |
| 16 | 11 | 13 | 35 | 4 | 8 | 20 | 16 | 18 | 52 | 12 | 14 | 5 |
| 6 | 1 | 23 | 96 | 4 | 16 | 15 | 13 | 8 | 38 | 14 | 18 | 34 |
| 139 | 63 | 239 | 586 | 107 | 207 | 223 | 387 | 114 | 503 | 169 | 196 | 170 |
| 193 | 92 | 412 | 762 | 99 | 555 | 310 | 528 | 68 | 805 | 137 | 211 | 91 |
| 101 | 78 | 238 | 528 | 94 | 251 | 401 | 202 | 42 | 383 | 105 | 120 | 48 |
| 78 | 185 | 352 | 508 | 84 | 320 | 540 | 306 | 80 | 537 | 184 | 152 | 47 |
| 127 | 32 | 286 | 321 | 55 | 304 | 65 | 289 | 14 | 248 | 79 | 34 | 19 |
| 49 | 51 | 104 | 240 | 65 | 137 | 128 | 150 | 22 | 186 | 48 | 51 | 22 |
| 22 | 34 | 83 | 167 | 93 | 103 | 183 | 59 | 36 | 83 | 60 | 145 | 23 |
| 12 | 31 | 33 | 92 | 28 | 305 | 101 | 31 | 9 | 58 | 22 | 17 | 2 |
| 6 | 7 | 13 | 44 | 11 | 14 | 27 | 18 | 9 | 20 | 20 | 13 | 11 |
| 7 | 12 | 13 | 26 | 6 | 8 | 19 | 7 | 37 | 34 | 14 | 25 | 9 |
| 29 | 53 | 62 | 99 | 55 | 41 | 162 | 44 | 41 | 40 | 21 | 22 | 17 |
| **10** | **32** | **27** | **38** | **23** | **25** | **96** | **54** | **60** | **179** | **76** | **60** | **100** |
| 4 | 15 | 8 | 15 | 13 | 8 | 52 | 21 | 37 | 72 | 20 | 29 | 67 |
| 1 | 4 | 2 | 5 | 2 | 2 | 18 | 8 | 5 | 11 | 19 | 13 | 18 |
| 5 | 13 | 17 | 18 | 8 | 15 | 26 | 25 | 18 | 96 | 37 | 18 | 15 |
| **629** | **1781** | **1671** | **3805** | **1611** | **870** | **2768** | **1307** | **715** | **1239** | **897** | **914** | **478** |
| 120 | 188 | 196 | 558 | 200 | 130 | 424 | 223 | 146 | 372 | 247 | 220 | 98 |
| 62 | 258 | 249 | 495 | 214 | 202 | 438 | 264 | 134 | 252 | 151 | 134 | 98 |
| 94 | 276 | 189 | 551 | 317 | 65 | 494 | 159 | 94 | 101 | 72 | 84 | 54 |
| 353 | 1059 | 1037 | 2201 | 880 | 473 | 1412 | 661 | 341 | 514 | 427 | 476 | 228 |
| **4213** | **10477** | **10514** | **34902** | **8972** | **4074** | **17365** | **7981** | **4546** | **8048** | **4066** | **5569** | **3665** |
| 2674 | 4598 | 4101 | 18489 | 4069 | 1374 | 6309 | 2875 | 1738 | 4587 | 1754 | 1942 | 1250 |
| 1539 | 5879 | 6413 | 16413 | 4903 | 2700 | 11056 | 5106 | 2808 | 3461 | 2312 | 3627 | 2415 |
| **268** | **1049** | **1120** | **1518** | **496** | **360** | **1503** | **784** | **557** | **897** | **357** | **349** | **240** |
| 1 | 7 | 1 | 7 | 1 |  | 4 | 1 | 1 | 1 | 1 | 1 |  |
| 172 | 607 | 657 | 881 | 341 | 215 | 733 | 495 | 407 | 606 | 226 | 214 | 145 |
| 5 | 32 | 6 | 5 | 11 | 8 | 10 | 4 | 5 | 23 | 24 | 4 |  |
|  | 2 | 6 | 5 | 2 | 1 | 39 | 4 |  | 2 | 3 | 2 | 1 |
|  |  | 1 | 1 | 1 | 1 |  | 1 |  |  |  | 1 |  |
| 28 | 255 | 280 | 404 | 64 | 94 | 457 | 147 | 71 | 155 | 35 | 64 | 67 |
| 45 | 113 | 119 | 171 | 45 | 30 | 177 | 107 | 61 | 89 | 52 | 44 | 13 |
| 17 | 33 | 50 | 44 | 31 | 11 | 83 | 25 | 12 | 21 | 16 | 19 | 14 |
| **222** | **1651** | **1017** | **1261** | **976** | **400** | **2084** | **685** | **498** | **782** | **399** | **561** | **1179** |
| 46 | 436 | 335 | 242 | 308 | 82 | 581 | 143 | 58 | 159 | 73 | 89 | 237 |
| 176 | 1215 | 682 | 1019 | 668 | 318 | 1503 | 542 | 440 | 623 | 326 | 472 | 942 |

**表 22.7 续表 4 continued 4**

| 指 标 | Item | 綦江区 Qijiang District | 綦江区(不含万盛) Qijiang District (excluding Wansheng) | 大足区 Dazu District | 璧山区 Bishan District |
|---|---|---|---|---|---|
| 非金属矿物制品业 | Manufacture of Non-metallic Mineral Products | 273 | 184 | 222 | 157 |
| 黑色金属冶炼和压延加工业 | Smelting and Pressing of Ferrous Metals | 10 | 5 | 59 | 8 |
| 有色金属冶炼和压延加工业 | Smelting and Pressing of Non-ferrous Metals | 55 | 47 | 41 | 15 |
| 金属制品业 | Manufacture of Metal Products | 155 | 107 | 864 | 293 |
| 通用设备制造业 | Manufacture of General Purpose Machinery | 148 | 117 | 281 | 420 |
| 专用设备制造业 | Manufacture of Special Purpose Machinery | 91 | 59 | 355 | 497 |
| 汽车制造业 | Manufacture of Automobiles | 157 | 134 | 476 | 572 |
| 铁路、船舶、航空航天和其他运输设备制造业 | Manufacture of Railway ,Ship, Aerospace and Other Transport Equipment | 65 | 49 | 377 | 160 |
| 电气机械和器材制造业 | Manufacture of Electrical Machinery and Apparatus | 31 | 20 | 86 | 110 |
| 计算机、通信和其他电子设备制造业 | Manufacture of Computers, Communication and Other Electronic Equipment | 32 | 15 | 70 | 401 |
| 仪器仪表制造业 | Manufacture of Measuring Instruments and Machinery | 2 | 1 | 17 | 60 |
| 其他制造业 | Other Manufacture | 13 | 7 | 17 | 16 |
| 废弃资源综合利用业 | Utilization of Waste Resources | 19 | 11 | 49 | 7 |
| 金属制品、机械和设备修理业 | Manufacture of Metal Products, Machinery and Equipment Maintenance | 13 | 8 | 9 | 33 |
| **电力、热力、燃气及水生产和供应业** | **Production and Supply of Electric Power, Gas and Water** | **160** | **117** | **31** | **34** |
| 电力、热力生产和供应业 | Production and Supply of Electric Power and Heat Power | 73 | 45 | 6 | 8 |
| 燃气生产和供应业 | Production and Supply of Gas | 20 | 16 | 5 | 8 |
| 水的生产和供应业 | Production and Supply of Water | 67 | 56 | 20 | 18 |
| **建筑业** | **Construction** | **1072** | **505** | **588** | **820** |
| 房屋建筑业 | Construction of Housing | 357 | 165 | 156 | 110 |
| 土木工程建筑业 | Civil Engineering Construction | 218 | 94 | 86 | 222 |
| 建筑安装业 | Architectural Installation | 79 | 45 | 61 | 57 |
| 建筑装饰、装修和其他建筑业 | Architectural Decoration and Other Construction | 418 | 201 | 285 | 431 |
| **批发和零售业** | **Wholesale and Retail Trade** | 5815 | 3187 | 4193 | 4300 |
| 批发业 | Wholesale Trade | 2040 | 1171 | 1286 | 1450 |
| 零售业 | Retail Trade | 3775 | 2016 | 2907 | 2850 |
| **交通运输、仓储和邮政业** | **Transport, Storage and Postal Services** | **1416** | **353** | **324** | **553** |
| 铁路运输业 | Transport Via Railway | 3 | | | |
| 道路运输业 | Transport Via Road | 1183 | 240 | 214 | 426 |
| 水上运输业 | Water Transport | | | 2 | |
| 航空运输业 | Air Transport | 3 | | 1 | |
| 管道运输业 | Transport Via Pipeline | | | | |
| 多式联运和运输代理业 | Loading, Unloading, Portage and Transport Agency | 123 | 58 | 47 | 64 |
| 装卸搬运和仓储业 | Storage | 89 | 46 | 39 | 41 |
| 邮政业 | Post | 15 | 9 | 21 | 22 |
| **住宿和餐饮业** | **Hotels and Catering Services** | **1730** | **892** | **632** | **369** |
| 住宿业 | Hotels | 539 | 293 | 99 | 68 |
| 餐饮业 | Catering Services | 1191 | 599 | 533 | 301 |

单位：个 (unit)

| 铜梁区 Tongliang District | 潼南区 Tongnan District | 荣昌区 Rongchang District | 开州区 Kaizhou District | 梁平区 Liangping District | 武隆区 Wulong District | 城口县 Chengkou County | 丰都县 Fengdu County | 垫江县 Dianjiang County | 忠县 Zhongxian County | 云阳县 Yunyang County | 奉节县 Fengjie County | 巫山县 Wushan County |
|---|---|---|---|---|---|---|---|---|---|---|---|---|
| 201 | 214 | 236 | 251 | 155 | 95 | 30 | 135 | 239 | 100 | 409 | 184 | 54 |
| 3 | 5 | 12 | 6 | 5 | 1 | 10 | 8 | 10 | 4 | 24 | | 1 |
| 25 | 24 | 4 | 26 | 1 | | 4 | 14 | 15 | 6 | 17 | 1 | 2 |
| 237 | 167 | 131 | 210 | 148 | 27 | 9 | 51 | 208 | 79 | 508 | 58 | 23 |
| 203 | 54 | 81 | 26 | 31 | 8 | 4 | 13 | 32 | 20 | 42 | 10 | 5 |
| 202 | 53 | 147 | 49 | 33 | 6 | 5 | 25 | 57 | 13 | 45 | 51 | 6 |
| 238 | 25 | 54 | 22 | 10 | 9 | | 2 | 24 | 7 | 12 | 2 | 2 |
| 70 | 5 | 7 | 1 | 8 | 3 | | 8 | 8 | 3 | 10 | 2 | |
| 81 | 36 | 55 | 49 | 21 | 3 | 2 | 8 | 27 | 22 | 44 | 14 | 6 |
| 114 | 89 | 62 | 50 | 34 | 2 | | 6 | 54 | 35 | 54 | 29 | 4 |
| 14 | 2 | 11 | 8 | | | | 3 | 6 | 1 | 4 | 9 | 11 |
| 14 | 10 | 9 | 6 | 14 | | 2 | 4 | 21 | 7 | 14 | 10 | 2 |
| 23 | 12 | 6 | 15 | 7 | 4 | 1 | 4 | 34 | 7 | 16 | 8 | 3 |
| 12 | 28 | 9 | 17 | 10 | 1 | 2 | 8 | 14 | 9 | 18 | 16 | 5 |
| **36** | **43** | **42** | **134** | **26** | **121** | **52** | **137** | **31** | **87** | **123** | **75** | **59** |
| 21 | 7 | 5 | 61 | 4 | 104 | 47 | 50 | 12 | 35 | 101 | 53 | 48 |
| 4 | 8 | 11 | 14 | 7 | 7 | 3 | 10 | 8 | 12 | 8 | 5 | 1 |
| 11 | 28 | 26 | 59 | 15 | 10 | 2 | 77 | 11 | 40 | 14 | 17 | 10 |
| **761** | **538** | **602** | **783** | **273** | **266** | **188** | **391** | **1419** | **414** | **622** | **354** | **304** |
| 132 | 151 | 170 | 174 | 78 | 113 | 63 | 112 | 395 | 115 | 178 | 86 | 168 |
| 169 | 101 | 107 | 177 | 50 | 49 | 37 | 69 | 646 | 60 | 164 | 87 | 27 |
| 67 | 53 | 48 | 47 | 34 | 15 | 7 | 30 | 50 | 43 | 40 | 55 | 20 |
| 393 | 233 | 277 | 385 | 111 | 89 | 81 | 180 | 328 | 196 | 240 | 126 | 89 |
| 3760 | 6974 | 4306 | 6562 | 3415 | 1725 | 1283 | 2646 | 3382 | 3619 | 5614 | 3523 | 1963 |
| 1060 | 3855 | 1740 | 1984 | 954 | 619 | 173 | 840 | 1358 | 1399 | 1978 | 1472 | 609 |
| 2700 | 3119 | 2566 | 4578 | 2461 | 1106 | 1110 | 1806 | 2024 | 2220 | 3636 | 2051 | 1354 |
| **208** | **561** | **297** | **253** | **135** | **145** | **64** | **232** | **281** | **285** | **320** | **269** | **167** |
| | | | | | 1 | | | 1 | 1 | 3 | 1 | |
| 149 | 306 | 208 | 149 | 93 | 97 | 44 | 122 | 152 | 157 | 116 | 119 | 77 |
| 1 | 8 | 1 | 4 | | 3 | 1 | 25 | | 21 | 43 | 28 | 22 |
| 1 | 2 | 2 | | 1 | 2 | | | | 1 | 1 | | 1 |
| | | | | | | | | | | 1 | | |
| 28 | 187 | 54 | 45 | 19 | 18 | 4 | 51 | 80 | 65 | 98 | 76 | 38 |
| 16 | 36 | 22 | 36 | 9 | 13 | 2 | 21 | 33 | 28 | 37 | 30 | 13 |
| 13 | 22 | 10 | 19 | 13 | 11 | 13 | 13 | 15 | 12 | 21 | 15 | 16 |
| **517** | **480** | **256** | **1321** | **548** | **812** | **1418** | **471** | **389** | **415** | **579** | **413** | **367** |
| 65 | 89 | 49 | 294 | 45 | 254 | 114 | 175 | 43 | 46 | 119 | 108 | 148 |
| 452 | 391 | 207 | 1027 | 503 | 558 | 1304 | 296 | 346 | 369 | 460 | 305 | 219 |

表 22.7 续表 5 continued 5

单位：个 (unit)

| 指 标 | Item | 巫溪县 Wuxi County | 石柱县 Shizhu County | 秀山县 Xiushan County | 酉阳县 Youyang County | 彭水县 Pengshui County |
|---|---|---|---|---|---|---|
| 非金属矿物制品业 | Manufacture of Non-metallic Mineral Products | 75 | 108 | 142 | 168 | 150 |
| 黑色金属冶炼和压延加工业 | Smelting and Pressing of Ferrous Metals | | 3 | 26 | 7 | |
| 有色金属冶炼和压延加工业 | Smelting and Pressing of Non-ferrous Metals | 1 | 11 | 9 | 10 | 4 |
| 金属制品业 | Manufacture of Metal Products | 31 | 55 | 47 | 48 | 41 |
| 通用设备制造业 | Manufacture of General Purpose Machinery | 1 | 15 | 22 | 11 | 4 |
| 专用设备制造业 | Manufacture of Special Purpose Machinery | 5 | 26 | 13 | 15 | 2 |
| 汽车制造业 | Manufacture of Automobiles | 1 | 7 | 29 | 1 | 1 |
| 铁路、船舶、航空航天和其他运输设备制造业 | Manufacture of Railway ,Ship, Aerospace and Other Transport Equipment | | 1 | 2 | | |
| 电气机械和器材制造业 | Manufacture of Electrical Machinery and Apparatus | 5 | 20 | 16 | 4 | 4 |
| 计算机、通信和其他电子设备制造业 | Manufacture of Computers, Communication and Other Electronic Equipment | 2 | 14 | 21 | 5 | 2 |
| 仪器仪表制造业 | Manufacture of Measuring Instruments and Machinery | | 3 | 5 | | 2 |
| 其他制造业 | Other Manufacture | 2 | 3 | 10 | 25 | 2 |
| 废弃资源综合利用业 | Utilization of Waste Resources | 4 | 6 | 7 | 7 | |
| 金属制品、机械和设备修理业 | Manufacture of Metal Products, Machinery and Equipment Maintenance | 1 | 5 | 13 | 11 | 5 |
| **电力、热力、燃气及水生产和供应业** | **Production and Supply of Electric Power, Gas and Water** | **138** | **62** | **25** | **81** | **33** |
| 电力、热力生产和供应业 | Production and Supply of Electric Power and Heat Power | 121 | 51 | 18 | 55 | 23 |
| 燃气生产和供应业 | Production and Supply of Gas | 2 | 3 | 3 | 7 | 5 |
| 水的生产和供应业 | Production and Supply of Water | 15 | 8 | 4 | 19 | 5 |
| **建筑业** | **Construction** | **245** | **288** | **456** | **277** | **484** |
| 房屋建筑业 | Construction of Housing | 82 | 62 | 57 | 71 | 239 |
| 土木工程建筑业 | Civil Engineering Construction | 43 | 58 | 137 | 43 | 50 |
| 建筑安装业 | Architectural Installation | 12 | 15 | 26 | 29 | 26 |
| 建筑装饰、装修和其他建筑业 | Architectural Decoration and Other Construction | 108 | 153 | 236 | 134 | 169 |
| **批发和零售业** | **Wholesale and Retail Trade** | **1712** | **2265** | **4430** | **3470** | **2614** |
| 批发业 | Wholesale Trade | 491 | 796 | 1525 | 1306 | 967 |
| 零售业 | Retail Trade | 1221 | 1469 | 2905 | 2164 | 1647 |
| **交通运输、仓储和邮政业** | **Transport, Storage and Postal Services** | **72** | **172** | **227** | **149** | **229** |
| 铁路运输业 | Transport Via Railway | | | | | |
| 道路运输业 | Transport Via Road | 37 | 111 | 114 | 92 | 166 |
| 水上运输业 | Water Transport | 2 | 7 | | | 2 |
| 航空运输业 | Air Transport | | | 2 | | |
| 管道运输业 | Transport Via Pipeline | | | | | |
| 多式联运和运输代理业 | Loading, Unloading, Portage and Transport Agency | 21 | 27 | 83 | 34 | 41 |
| 装卸搬运和仓储业 | Storage | 6 | 12 | 23 | 11 | 10 |
| 邮政业 | Post | 6 | 15 | 5 | 12 | 10 |
| **住宿和餐饮业** | **Hotels and Catering Services** | **531** | **728** | **449** | **376** | **381** |
| 住宿业 | Hotels | 98 | 382 | 55 | 107 | 75 |
| 餐饮业 | Catering Services | 433 | 346 | 394 | 269 | 306 |

表 22.7 续表 6 continued 6

单位：个 (unit)

| 指 标 | Item | 全 市 Total | 万州区 Wanzhou District | 黔江区 Qianjiang District | 涪陵区 Fuling District | 渝中区 Yuzhong District |
|---|---|---|---|---|---|---|
| **信息传输、软件和信息技术服务业** | **Information Transmission, Software and Information Technology** | **38774** | **847** | **251** | **806** | **2236** |
| 电信、广播电视和卫星传输服务 | Telecommunication, Radio, Television and Satellite Transmission Services | 851 | 23 | 28 | 22 | 32 |
| 互联网和相关服务 | Internet and Related Services | 5500 | 143 | 60 | 142 | 264 |
| 软件和信息技术服务业 | Software and Information Technology Services | 32423 | 681 | 163 | 642 | 1940 |
| **金融业** | **Financial Intermediation** | **2241** | **49** | **36** | **74** | **159** |
| 货币金融服务 | Money Finance Services | 1150 | 27 | 21 | 33 | 80 |
| 资本市场服务 | Capital Market Services | 608 | 3 | 6 | 10 | 32 |
| 保险业 | Insurance | 299 | 18 | 8 | 26 | 41 |
| 其他金融业 | Other Finance | 184 | 1 | 1 | 5 | 6 |
| **房地产业** | **Real Estate** | **23265** | **579** | **231** | **522** | **1055** |
| 房地产业 | Real Estate | 23265 | 579 | 231 | 522 | 1055 |
| **租赁和商务服务业** | **Leasing and Business Services** | **95261** | **2685** | **1344** | **2836** | **4887** |
| 租赁业 | Leasing | 15889 | 639 | 288 | 533 | 203 |
| 商务服务业 | Business Services | 79372 | 2046 | 1056 | 2303 | 4684 |
| **科学研究和技术服务业** | **Scientific Research and Technical Services** | **33057** | **734** | **376** | **847** | **1298** |
| 研究和试验发展 | Research and Experimental Development | 2139 | 30 | 19 | 31 | 78 |
| 专业技术服务业 | Professional Technical Services | 19269 | 503 | 302 | 550 | 763 |
| 科技推广和应用服务业 | Services of Science and Technology Application and Promotion | 11649 | 201 | 55 | 266 | 457 |
| **水利、环境和公共设施管理业** | **Water Conservancy, Environment and Public Facilities Management** | **7449** | **180** | **70** | **311** | **155** |
| 水利管理业 | Management of Water Conservancy | 195 | 6 | 5 | 8 | 6 |
| 生态保护和环境治理业 | Ecological Protection and Environmental Governance | 1171 | 33 | 9 | 50 | 26 |
| 公共设施管理业 | Management of Public Facilities | 3546 | 82 | 44 | 164 | 62 |
| 土地管理业 | Management of Land | 2537 | 59 | 12 | 89 | 61 |
| **居民服务、修理和其他服务业** | **Services to Households, Repair and Other Services** | **19983** | **849** | **303** | **596** | **674** |
| 居民服务业 | Resident Services | 9752 | 472 | 152 | 255 | 351 |
| 机动车、电子产品和日用产品修理业 | Vehicles, Electronic Products and Commodities Maintenance Services | 7212 | 273 | 107 | 243 | 163 |
| 其他服务业 | Other Services | 3019 | 104 | 44 | 98 | 160 |
| **教育** | **Education** | **8644** | **280** | **137** | **215** | **284** |
| 教育 | Education | 8644 | 280 | 137 | 215 | 284 |
| **卫生和社会工作** | **Health and Social Work** | **4464** | **136** | **26** | **87** | **188** |
| 卫生 | Health | 3474 | 95 | 17 | 63 | 156 |
| 社会工作 | Social Work | 990 | 41 | 9 | 24 | 32 |
| **文化、体育和娱乐业** | **Culture, Sports and Entertainment** | **18670** | **581** | **183** | **413** | **860** |
| 新闻和出版业 | Journalism and Publishing Activities | 181 | 2 |  | 4 | 21 |
| 广播、电视、电影和录音制作业 | Broadcasting, Movies, Televisions and Audiovisual Activities | 3081 | 61 | 31 | 68 | 210 |
| 文化艺术业 | Cultural and Art Activities | 5138 | 178 | 37 | 164 | 268 |
| 体 育 | Sports | 2260 | 66 | 20 | 55 | 72 |
| 娱乐业 | Entertainment | 8010 | 274 | 95 | 122 | 289 |

表 22.7 续表 7 continued 7

| 指　标 | Item | 大渡口区 Dadukou District | 江北区 Jiangbei District | 沙坪坝区 Shapingba District | 九龙坡区 Jiulongpo District | 南岸区 Nan'an District |
|---|---|---|---|---|---|---|
| **信息传输、软件和信息技术服务业** | **Information Transmission, Software and Information Technology** | **583** | **4214** | **3221** | **6464** | **2533** |
| 电信、广播电视和卫星传输服务 | Telecommunication, Radio, Television and Satellite Transmission Services | 23 | 71 | 37 | 111 | 39 |
| 互联网和相关服务 | Internet and Related Services | 63 | 497 | 350 | 689 | 374 |
| 软件和信息技术服务业 | Software and Information Technology Services | 497 | 3646 | 2834 | 5664 | 2120 |
| **金融业** | **Financial Intermediation** | **43** | **309** | **49** | **112** | **112** |
| 货币金融服务 | Money Finance Services | 23 | 131 | 31 | 65 | 47 |
| 资本市场服务 | Capital Market Services | 17 | 110 | 4 | 21 | 45 |
| 保险业 | Insurance | 1 | 35 | 7 | 14 | 10 |
| 其他金融业 | Other Finance | 2 | 33 | 7 | 12 | 10 |
| **房地产业** | **Real Estate** | **497** | **1748** | **1410** | **2421** | **1422** |
| 房地产业 | Real Estate | 497 | 1748 | 1410 | 2421 | 1422 |
| **租赁和商务服务业** | **Leasing and Business Services** | **1400** | **7213** | **5319** | **10923** | **5309** |
| 租赁业 | Leasing | 276 | 556 | 628 | 1628 | 558 |
| 商务服务业 | Business Services | 1124 | 6657 | 4691 | 9295 | 4751 |
| **科学研究和技术服务业** | **Scientific Research and Technical Services** | **420** | **2761** | **1909** | **3978** | **1640** |
| 研究和试验发展 | Research and Experimental Development | 56 | 108 | 129 | 347 | 188 |
| 专业技术服务业 | Professional Technical Services | 247 | 1824 | 1288 | 2183 | 1072 |
| 科技推广和应用服务业 | Services of Science and Technology Application and Promotion | 117 | 829 | 492 | 1448 | 380 |
| **水利、环境和公共设施管理业** | **Water Conservancy, Environment and Public Facilities Management** | **121** | **315** | **267** | **722** | **215** |
| 水利管理业 | Management of Water Conservancy | | 6 | 5 | 12 | 4 |
| 生态保护和环境治理业 | Ecological Protection and Environmental Governance | 52 | 88 | 60 | 123 | 58 |
| 公共设施管理业 | Management of Public Facilities | 50 | 133 | 132 | 345 | 137 |
| 土地管理业 | Management of Land | 19 | 88 | 70 | 242 | 16 |
| **居民服务、修理和其他服务业** | **Services to Households, Repair and Other Services** | **321** | **1559** | **1101** | **1812** | **1106** |
| 居民服务业 | Resident Services | 132 | 973 | 508 | 741 | 535 |
| 机动车、电子产品和日用产品修理业 | Vehicles, Electronic Products and Commodities Maintenance Services | 137 | 325 | 360 | 784 | 377 |
| 其他服务业 | Other Services | 52 | 261 | 233 | 287 | 194 |
| **教育** | **Education** | **191** | **676** | **878** | **770** | **549** |
| 教育 | Education | 191 | 676 | 878 | 770 | 549 |
| **卫生和社会工作** | **Health and Social Work** | **104** | **251** | **254** | **298** | **158** |
| 卫生 | Health | 84 | 219 | 177 | 244 | 134 |
| 社会工作 | Social Work | 20 | 32 | 77 | 54 | 24 |
| **文化、体育和娱乐业** | **Culture, Sports and Entertainment** | **251** | **1697** | **1108** | **1724** | **924** |
| 新闻和出版业 | Journalism and Publishing Activities | | 26 | 8 | 24 | 10 |
| 广播、电视、电影和录音制作业 | Broadcasting, Movies, Televisions and Audiovisual Activities | 42 | 253 | 183 | 500 | 140 |
| 文化艺术业 | Cultural and Art Activities | 70 | 390 | 331 | 418 | 281 |
| 体　育 | Sports | 39 | 218 | 139 | 202 | 122 |
| 娱乐业 | Entertainment | 100 | 810 | 447 | 580 | 371 |

单位：个 (unit)

| 北碚区 Beibei District | 渝北区 Yubei District | 巴南区 Ba'nan District | 长寿区 Changshou District | 江津区 Jiangjin District | 合川区 Hechuan District | 永川区 Yongchuan District | 南川区 Nanchuan District | 綦江区 Qijiang District | 綦江区（不含万盛）Qijiang District (excluding Wansheng) | 大足区 Dazu District | 璧山区 Bishan District | 铜梁区 Tongliang District |
|---|---|---|---|---|---|---|---|---|---|---|---|---|
| **958** | **6846** | **1299** | **419** | **559** | **523** | **626** | **282** | **455** | **192** | **248** | **680** | **257** |
| 16 | 112 | 17 | 13 | 17 | 28 | 17 | 11 | 18 | 9 | 9 | 11 | 8 |
| 138 | 801 | 205 | 78 | 94 | 102 | 184 | 56 | 79 | 39 | 69 | 101 | 69 |
| 804 | 5933 | 1077 | 328 | 448 | 393 | 425 | 215 | 358 | 144 | 170 | 568 | 180 |
| **56** | **567** | **54** | **30** | **32** | **30** | **35** | **21** | **45** | **24** | **30** | **38** | **37** |
| 30 | 267 | 33 | 15 | 16 | 21 | 21 | 13 | 21 | 12 | 18 | 19 | 17 |
| 16 | 239 | 10 | 8 | 5 | 4 | 3 | 4 | 3 | 2 | 6 | 10 | 5 |
| 5 | 28 | 9 | 4 | 7 | 4 | 10 | 1 | 16 | 8 | 2 | 5 | 5 |
| 5 | 33 | 2 | 3 | 4 | 1 | 1 | 3 | 5 | 2 | 4 | 4 | 10 |
| **694** | **2989** | **1011** | **364** | **769** | **626** | **636** | **384** | **471** | **210** | **367** | **712** | **551** |
| 694 | 2989 | 1011 | 364 | 769 | 626 | 636 | 384 | 471 | 210 | 367 | 712 | 551 |
| **2073** | **12034** | **2733** | **1452** | **2692** | **1731** | **1761** | **1478** | **1887** | **1036** | **1195** | **1837** | **1295** |
| 372 | 1465 | 614 | 299 | 716 | 291 | 355 | 364 | 396 | 219 | 247 | 475 | 247 |
| 1701 | 10569 | 2119 | 1153 | 1976 | 1440 | 1406 | 1114 | 1491 | 817 | 948 | 1362 | 1048 |
| **1055** | **5755** | **1153** | **484** | **1158** | **464** | **633** | **328** | **692** | **374** | **363** | **615** | **282** |
| 138 | 385 | 56 | 32 | 51 | 20 | 39 | 9 | 40 | 24 | 22 | 61 | 19 |
| 489 | 3279 | 780 | 270 | 518 | 262 | 391 | 198 | 303 | 138 | 219 | 303 | 162 |
| 428 | 2091 | 317 | 182 | 589 | 182 | 203 | 121 | 349 | 212 | 122 | 251 | 101 |
| **221** | **1002** | **186** | **155** | **226** | **160** | **187** | **153** | **296** | **164** | **188** | **201** | **108** |
| 4 | 24 | 7 | 2 | 6 | 2 | 5 | 1 | 16 | 10 | 5 | 4 | 1 |
| 29 | 143 | 34 | 29 | 33 | 24 | 42 | 15 | 41 | 19 | 18 | 37 | 18 |
| 109 | 343 | 98 | 78 | 126 | 93 | 99 | 103 | 143 | 74 | 90 | 88 | 58 |
| 79 | 492 | 47 | 46 | 61 | 41 | 41 | 34 | 96 | 61 | 75 | 72 | 31 |
| **461** | **2009** | **721** | **400** | **530** | **438** | **405** | **454** | **717** | **368** | **381** | **354** | **325** |
| 242 | 932 | 309 | 189 | 251 | 217 | 197 | 214 | 339 | 184 | 195 | 161 | 185 |
| 151 | 790 | 311 | 161 | 231 | 145 | 141 | 188 | 269 | 123 | 148 | 137 | 103 |
| 68 | 287 | 101 | 50 | 48 | 76 | 67 | 52 | 109 | 61 | 38 | 56 | 37 |
| **244** | **1043** | **346** | **153** | **265** | **167** | **254** | **133** | **159** | **89** | **163** | **223** | **175** |
| 244 | 1043 | 346 | 153 | 265 | 167 | 254 | 133 | 159 | 89 | 163 | 223 | 175 |
| **105** | **594** | **272** | **105** | **167** | **140** | **80** | **83** | **109** | **62** | **51** | **122** | **132** |
| 91 | 552 | 224 | 86 | 107 | 96 | 56 | 41 | 79 | 48 | 44 | 108 | 99 |
| 14 | 42 | 48 | 19 | 60 | 44 | 24 | 42 | 30 | 14 | 7 | 14 | 33 |
| **447** | **1787** | **718** | **217** | **476** | **414** | **483** | **227** | **375** | **209** | **324** | **295** | **333** |
| 9 | 38 | 4 |  | 3 | 1 | 3 |  | 5 | 1 | 1 | 3 |  |
| 83 | 417 | 66 | 15 | 82 | 29 | 43 | 19 | 54 | 29 | 48 | 37 | 30 |
| 151 | 449 | 165 | 39 | 86 | 70 | 108 | 66 | 86 | 51 | 93 | 65 | 80 |
| 41 | 320 | 81 | 28 | 70 | 33 | 56 | 45 | 54 | 20 | 43 | 44 | 43 |
| 163 | 563 | 402 | 135 | 235 | 281 | 273 | 97 | 176 | 108 | 139 | 146 | 180 |

**表 22.7 续表 8 continued 8**

| 指　标 | Item | 潼南区 Tongnan District | 荣昌区 Rongchang District | 开州区 Kaizhou District | 梁平区 Liangping District | 武隆区 Wulong District | 城口县 Chengkou County |
|---|---|---|---|---|---|---|---|
| **信息传输、软件和信息技术服务业** | **Information Transmission, Software and Information Technology** | **473** | **502** | **534** | **148** | **99** | **47** |
| 电信、广播电视和卫星传输服务 | Telecommunication, Radio, Television and Satellite Transmission Services | 11 | 9 | 20 | 6 | 9 | 12 |
| 互联网和相关服务 | Internet and Related Services | 59 | 96 | 114 | 22 | 24 | 10 |
| 软件和信息技术服务业 | Software and Information Technology Services | 403 | 397 | 400 | 120 | 66 | 25 |
| **金融业** | **Financial Intermediation** | **31** | **25** | **22** | **19** | **17** | **12** |
| 货币金融服务 | Money Finance Services | 13 | 14 | 19 | 16 | 11 | 9 |
| 资本市场服务 | Capital Market Services | 8 | 4 | | | 2 | 1 |
| 保险业 | Insurance | 7 | 4 | 3 | 2 | 2 | 1 |
| 其他金融业 | Other Finance | 3 | 3 | | 1 | 2 | 1 |
| **房地产业** | **Real Estate** | **450** | **363** | **580** | **171** | **158** | **51** |
| 房地产业 | Real Estate | 450 | 363 | 580 | 171 | 158 | 51 |
| **租赁和商务服务业** | **Leasing and Business Services** | **2496** | **1702** | **1910** | **554** | **605** | **331** |
| 租赁业 | Leasing | 637 | 292 | 571 | 134 | 200 | 96 |
| 商务服务业 | Business Services | 1859 | 1410 | 1339 | 420 | 405 | 235 |
| **科学研究和技术服务业** | **Scientific Research and Technical Services** | **768** | **716** | **571** | **175** | **192** | **66** |
| 研究和试验发展 | Research and Experimental Development | 25 | 85 | 17 | 9 | 8 | 2 |
| 专业技术服务业 | Professional Technical Services | 469 | 298 | 280 | 79 | 139 | 53 |
| 科技推广和应用服务业 | Services of Science and Technology Application and Promotion | 274 | 333 | 274 | 87 | 45 | 11 |
| **水利、环境和公共设施管理业** | **Water Conservancy, Environment and Public Facilities Management** | **137** | **100** | **227** | **94** | **87** | **59** |
| 水利管理业 | Management of Water Conservancy | 1 | 1 | 7 | 2 | 5 | 1 |
| 生态保护和环境治理业 | Ecological Protection and Environmental Governance | 13 | 33 | 20 | 14 | 3 | 2 |
| 公共设施管理业 | Management of Public Facilities | 68 | 54 | 110 | 47 | 52 | 20 |
| 土地管理业 | Management of Land | 55 | 12 | 90 | 31 | 27 | 36 |
| **居民服务、修理和其他服务业** | **Services to Households, Repair and Other Services** | **288** | **302** | **647** | **283** | **82** | **162** |
| 居民服务业 | Resident Services | 133 | 137 | 352 | 150 | 43 | 89 |
| 机动车、电子产品和日用产品修理业 | Vehicles, Electronic Products and Commodities Maintenance Services | 126 | 98 | 218 | 95 | 21 | 59 |
| 其他服务业 | Other Services | 29 | 67 | 77 | 38 | 18 | 14 |
| **教育** | **Education** | **112** | **98** | **247** | **85** | **71** | **37** |
| 教育 | Education | 112 | 98 | 247 | 85 | 71 | 37 |
| **卫生和社会工作** | **Health and Social Work** | **45** | **50** | **155** | **32** | **23** | **22** |
| 卫生 | Health | 39 | 31 | 120 | 26 | 16 | 19 |
| 社会工作 | Social Work | 6 | 19 | 35 | 6 | 7 | 3 |
| **文化、体育和娱乐业** | **Culture, Sports and Entertainment** | **432** | **240** | **472** | **269** | **413** | **99** |
| 新闻和出版业 | Journalism and Publishing Activities | | | 2 | | 5 | |
| 广播、电视、电影和录音制作业 | Broadcasting, Movies, Televisions and Audiovisual Activities | 39 | 32 | 67 | 27 | 113 | 5 |
| 文化艺术业 | Cultural and Art Activities | 33 | 84 | 203 | 109 | 80 | 17 |
| 体　育 | Sports | 36 | 24 | 50 | 44 | 14 | 40 |
| 娱乐业 | Entertainment | 324 | 100 | 150 | 89 | 201 | 37 |

单位：个 (unit)

| 丰都县 Fengdu County | 垫江县 Dianjiang County | 忠县 Zhongxian County | 云阳县 Yunyang County | 奉节县 Fengjie County | 巫山县 Wushan County | 巫溪县 Wuxi County | 石柱县 Shizhu County | 秀山县 Xiushan County | 酉阳县 Youyang County | 彭水县 Pengshui County |
|---|---|---|---|---|---|---|---|---|---|---|
| **163** | **570** | **338** | **219** | **270** | **110** | **95** | **141** | **306** | **244** | **208** |
| 9 | 8 | 10 | 17 | 14 | 7 | 11 | 9 | 5 | 14 | 17 |
| 38 | 101 | 46 | 64 | 67 | 47 | 36 | 63 | 43 | 62 | 50 |
| 116 | 461 | 282 | 138 | 189 | 56 | 48 | 69 | 258 | 168 | 141 |
| **13** | **19** | **19** | **22** | **23** | **23** | **9** | **19** | **18** | **19** | **13** |
| 10 | 13 | 12 | 12 | 15 | 10 | 6 | 12 | 11 | 9 | 9 |
| 1 | 4 | 3 | 5 | 4 | 4 |  | 2 | 1 | 8 |  |
|  |  | 3 | 5 | 1 | 4 | 1 | 2 | 4 | 1 | 3 |
| 2 | 2 | 1 |  | 3 | 5 | 2 | 3 | 2 | 1 | 1 |
| **182** | **300** | **207** | **261** | **191** | **174** | **89** | **158** | **166** | **138** | **167** |
| 182 | 300 | 207 | 261 | 191 | 174 | 89 | 158 | 166 | 138 | 167 |
| **877** | **1671** | **2176** | **2125** | **1205** | **595** | **467** | **800** | **1384** | **1332** | **947** |
| 169 | 365 | 287 | 536 | 284 | 124 | 143 | 212 | 326 | 197 | 166 |
| 708 | 1306 | 1889 | 1589 | 921 | 471 | 324 | 588 | 1058 | 1135 | 781 |
| **221** | **529** | **362** | **368** | **453** | **241** | **107** | **175** | **352** | **575** | **241** |
| 10 | 27 | 24 | 7 | 20 | 3 | 1 | 5 | 13 | 19 | 6 |
| 129 | 322 | 219 | 184 | 213 | 164 | 65 | 112 | 226 | 266 | 145 |
| 82 | 180 | 119 | 177 | 220 | 74 | 41 | 58 | 113 | 290 | 90 |
| **134** | **161** | **89** | **216** | **110** | **97** | **76** | **123** | **125** | **114** | **61** |
| 8 | 3 | 3 | 15 | 4 | 1 | 2 | 3 | 1 | 4 | 5 |
| 15 | 23 | 9 | 11 | 10 | 7 | 6 | 13 | 19 | 8 | 3 |
| 74 | 102 | 41 | 63 | 50 | 46 | 23 | 85 | 40 | 50 | 44 |
| 37 | 33 | 36 | 127 | 46 | 43 | 45 | 22 | 65 | 52 | 9 |
| **210** | **271** | **250** | **350** | **292** | **113** | **155** | **203** | **437** | **182** | **240** |
| 118 | 121 | 143 | 167 | 141 | 41 | 66 | 111 | 189 | 78 | 123 |
| 74 | 92 | 85 | 146 | 107 | 43 | 77 | 67 | 193 | 83 | 84 |
| 18 | 58 | 22 | 37 | 44 | 29 | 12 | 25 | 55 | 21 | 33 |
| **46** | **100** | **82** | **86** | **57** | **26** | **23** | **74** | **80** | **67** | **48** |
| 46 | 100 | 82 | 86 | 57 | 26 | 23 | 74 | 80 | 67 | 48 |
| **82** | **93** | **113** | **89** | **57** | **31** | **47** | **36** | **34** | **55** | **38** |
| 57 | 70 | 45 | 61 | 40 | 26 | 28 | 17 | 25 | 49 | 33 |
| 25 | 23 | 68 | 28 | 17 | 5 | 19 | 19 | 9 | 6 | 5 |
| **356** | **414** | **330** | **349** | **211** | **148** | **105** | **298** | **208** | **270** | **219** |
| 1 |  | 3 |  | 3 | 2 |  | 1 |  | 1 | 1 |
| 27 | 35 | 45 | 49 | 33 | 39 | 17 | 56 | 24 | 36 | 26 |
| 197 | 202 | 162 | 86 | 52 | 38 | 21 | 129 | 34 | 40 | 56 |
| 14 | 23 | 17 | 43 | 30 | 15 | 36 | 20 | 26 | 21 | 16 |
| 117 | 154 | 103 | 171 | 93 | 54 | 31 | 92 | 124 | 172 | 120 |

# 表 22.8 按区县、登记注册类型分组的企业法人单位数（2022 年）
## NUMBER OF ENTERPRISES AS CORPORATE UNITS BY STATUS OF REGISTRATION AND REGION (2022)

| 区 县 | Item | 总 计<br>Total | 内资<br>Domestic-funded Enterprises | 国 有<br>State-owned | 集 体<br>Collective-owned | 股份合作<br>Cooperative Share-holding | 联营<br>Joint Ownership |
|---|---|---|---|---|---|---|---|
| **全 市** | **Total** | **705046** | **702201** | **852** | **1514** | **445** | **81** |
| 万州区 | Wanzhou District | 24354 | 24311 | 36 | 43 | 6 | 5 |
| 黔江区 | Qianjiang District | 8814 | 8802 | 18 | 10 | 2 | 1 |
| 涪陵区 | Fuling District | 20557 | 20474 | 13 | 53 | 1 | 5 |
| 渝中区 | Yuzhong District | 22104 | 21783 | 44 | 72 | 51 | 2 |
| 大渡口区 | Dadukou District | 10510 | 10465 | 10 | 41 | 6 | 1 |
| 江北区 | Jiangbei District | 36887 | 36594 | 12 | 27 | 14 | |
| 沙坪坝区 | Shapingba District | 33015 | 32844 | 52 | 114 | 17 | 1 |
| 九龙坡区 | Jiulongpo District | 76754 | 76517 | 39 | 147 | 68 | 6 |
| 南岸区 | Nan'an District | 27463 | 27330 | 51 | 16 | 52 | |
| 北碚区 | Beibei District | 15760 | 15636 | 33 | 73 | 10 | 1 |
| 渝北区 | Yubei District | 62975 | 62355 | 113 | 16 | 33 | 3 |
| 巴南区 | Ba'nan District | 26304 | 26210 | 29 | 48 | 19 | 1 |
| 长寿区 | Changshou District | 13603 | 13524 | 29 | 21 | 7 | 4 |
| 江津区 | Jiangjin District | 27414 | 27324 | 31 | 118 | 17 | 4 |
| 合川区 | Hechuan District | 14317 | 14264 | 22 | 54 | 9 | |
| 永川区 | Yongchuan District | 16421 | 16357 | 15 | 29 | 12 | 1 |
| 南川区 | Nanchuan District | 14398 | 14374 | 12 | 47 | 9 | 1 |
| 綦江区 | Qijiang District | 20466 | 20427 | 22 | 145 | 20 | 5 |
| #綦江区（不含万盛） | Qijiang District (excluding Wansheng) | 11407 | 11387 | 7 | 120 | 8 | |
| 大足区 | Dazu District | 15614 | 15587 | 11 | 26 | 11 | |
| 璧山区 | Bishan District | 16774 | 16709 | 15 | 55 | 22 | 2 |
| 铜梁区 | Tongliang District | 12933 | 12900 | 17 | 38 | 2 | |
| 潼南区 | Tongnan District | 16582 | 16562 | 9 | 13 | 7 | 1 |
| 荣昌区 | Rongchang District | 12078 | 12044 | 16 | 27 | 3 | 1 |
| 开州区 | Kaizhou District | 19419 | 19403 | 10 | 26 | 4 | 1 |
| 梁平区 | Liangping District | 9427 | 9419 | 12 | 14 | 2 | 1 |
| 武隆区 | Wulong District | 6967 | 6961 | 14 | 10 | | |
| 城口县 | Chengkou County | 5365 | 5362 | 23 | 8 | 2 | |
| 丰都县 | Fengdu County | 8658 | 8654 | 19 | 47 | 1 | 1 |
| 垫江县 | Dianjiang County | 12700 | 12687 | 12 | 33 | 23 | 14 |
| 忠 县 | Zhongxian County | 11999 | 11981 | 16 | 53 | | 2 |
| 云阳县 | Yunyang County | 19974 | 19961 | 8 | 3 | | 2 |
| 奉节县 | Fengjie County | 12738 | 12723 | 9 | 22 | 4 | 2 |
| 巫山县 | Wushan County | 6472 | 6465 | 22 | 11 | | 1 |
| 巫溪县 | Wuxi County | 6215 | 6210 | 7 | 13 | 1 | 1 |
| 石柱县 | Shizhu County | 8152 | 8146 | 19 | 17 | 6 | 9 |
| 秀山县 | Xiushan County | 12000 | 11995 | 8 | 5 | | 1 |
| 酉阳县 | Youyang County | 10169 | 10160 | 17 | 14 | 1 | 1 |
| 彭水县 | Pengshui County | 8694 | 8681 | 7 | 5 | 3 | |

单位：个 (unit)

| 国有联营 State Joint Ownership | 集体联营 Collective Joint Ownership | 国有与集体联营 Joint State-collective Ownership | 其他联营 Other Joint Ownership | 有限责任公司 Limited-liability Corporations | | | 股份有限公司 Share-holding Limited Companies | 私营 Private |
|---|---|---|---|---|---|---|---|---|
| | | | | | 国有独资公司 State Sole Funded | 其他有限责任公司 Other Limited-liability Corporations | | |
| **11** | **38** | **6** | **26** | **9361** | **1689** | **7672** | **1309** | **688638** |
| 1 | 3 | | 1 | 358 | 60 | 298 | 41 | 23822 |
| | | 1 | | 116 | 17 | 99 | 31 | 8624 |
| 1 | | 2 | 2 | 321 | 63 | 258 | 43 | 20038 |
| | | | 2 | 547 | 125 | 422 | 79 | 20988 |
| | | | 1 | 208 | 31 | 177 | 23 | 10176 |
| | | | | 574 | 94 | 480 | 60 | 35907 |
| | | | 1 | 431 | 48 | 383 | 52 | 32177 |
| 1 | 1 | 1 | 3 | 703 | 58 | 645 | 98 | 75456 |
| | | | | 598 | 62 | 536 | 71 | 26542 |
| | 1 | | | 322 | 47 | 275 | 27 | 15170 |
| 2 | 1 | | | 1281 | 161 | 1120 | 184 | 60725 |
| 1 | | | | 309 | 45 | 264 | 38 | 25766 |
| 1 | 2 | | 1 | 190 | 51 | 139 | 35 | 13238 |
| 1 | 3 | | | 288 | 63 | 225 | 47 | 26818 |
| | | | | 142 | 22 | 120 | 26 | 14011 |
| | | 1 | | 164 | 26 | 138 | 23 | 16113 |
| | 1 | | | 117 | 34 | 83 | 17 | 14171 |
| | 5 | | | 358 | 73 | 285 | 55 | 19822 |
| | | | | 175 | 30 | 145 | 25 | 11052 |
| | | | | 156 | 30 | 126 | 29 | 15354 |
| | 1 | | 1 | 181 | 28 | 153 | 23 | 16411 |
| | | | | 87 | 33 | 54 | 15 | 12741 |
| 1 | | | | 81 | 26 | 55 | 20 | 16431 |
| | | | 1 | 83 | 28 | 55 | 13 | 11901 |
| | | | 1 | 191 | 33 | 158 | 21 | 19150 |
| | | | 1 | 91 | 24 | 67 | 16 | 9283 |
| | | | | 108 | 40 | 68 | 13 | 6816 |
| | | | | 52 | 19 | 33 | 12 | 5265 |
| 1 | | | | 93 | 42 | 51 | 18 | 8475 |
| | 13 | | 1 | 138 | 21 | 117 | 22 | 12445 |
| | 1 | 1 | | 103 | 30 | 73 | 17 | 11790 |
| | 2 | | | 179 | 31 | 148 | 27 | 19742 |
| | 1 | | 1 | 149 | 24 | 125 | 33 | 12504 |
| | | | 1 | 75 | 31 | 44 | 12 | 6344 |
| | 1 | | | 66 | 22 | 44 | 13 | 6109 |
| | 1 | | 8 | 82 | 33 | 49 | 19 | 7994 |
| 1 | | | | 92 | 53 | 39 | 11 | 11878 |
| | 1 | | | 248 | 38 | 210 | 9 | 9870 |
| | | | | 79 | 23 | 56 | 16 | 8571 |

**表 22.8 续表 continued**

单位：个 (unit)

| 区 县 | Item | 私营独资 Solely Private-funded Enterprises | 私营合伙 Private Partnership Enterprises | 私营有限责任公司 Private Limited Liability Corporations | 私营股份有限公司 Private Share-holding Limited Companies | 其他内资 Other Domestic Funded | 港澳台商投资 Enterprises with Funds from Hong Kong, Macao and Taiwan | 外商投资 Foreign Funded |
|---|---|---|---|---|---|---|---|---|
| **全 市** | **Total** | **155741** | **4940** | **526281** | **1676** | **1** | **1275** | **1570** |
| 万州区 | Wanzhou District | 7521 | 71 | 16201 | 29 | | 17 | 26 |
| 黔江区 | Qianjiang District | 2854 | 65 | 5679 | 26 | | 6 | 6 |
| 涪陵区 | Fuling District | 5764 | 91 | 14128 | 55 | | 32 | 51 |
| 渝中区 | Yuzhong District | 554 | 146 | 20217 | 71 | | 167 | 154 |
| 大渡口区 | Dadukou District | 704 | 64 | 9391 | 17 | | 22 | 23 |
| 江北区 | Jiangbei District | 1169 | 356 | 34285 | 97 | | 103 | 190 |
| 沙坪坝区 | Shapingba District | 1043 | 213 | 30853 | 68 | | 92 | 79 |
| 九龙坡区 | Jiulongpo District | 2548 | 434 | 72315 | 159 | | 100 | 137 |
| 南岸区 | Nan'an District | 1058 | 174 | 25214 | 96 | | 64 | 69 |
| 北碚区 | Beibei District | 2477 | 173 | 12473 | 47 | | 49 | 75 |
| 渝北区 | Yubei District | 3399 | 756 | 56300 | 270 | | 252 | 368 |
| 巴南区 | Ba'nan District | 4094 | 96 | 21512 | 64 | | 51 | 43 |
| 长寿区 | Changshou District | 4350 | 89 | 8776 | 23 | | 28 | 51 |
| 江津区 | Jiangjin District | 5718 | 149 | 20898 | 53 | 1 | 52 | 38 |
| 合川区 | Hechuan District | 3055 | 88 | 10837 | 31 | | 17 | 36 |
| 永川区 | Yongchuan District | 3949 | 87 | 12029 | 48 | | 22 | 42 |
| 南川区 | Nanchuan District | 6336 | 84 | 7715 | 36 | | 14 | 10 |
| 綦江区 | Qijiang District | 7912 | 88 | 11772 | 50 | | 18 | 21 |
| #綦江区（不含万盛） | Qijiang District (excluding Wansheng) | 5092 | 38 | 5889 | 33 | | 9 | 11 |
| 大足区 | Dazu District | 6125 | 74 | 9106 | 49 | | 13 | 14 |
| 璧山区 | Bishan District | 1615 | 365 | 14363 | 68 | | 28 | 37 |
| 铜梁区 | Tongliang District | 4005 | 68 | 8626 | 42 | | 15 | 18 |
| 潼南区 | Tongnan District | 7300 | 95 | 9009 | 27 | | 12 | 8 |
| 荣昌区 | Rongchang District | 2809 | 105 | 8945 | 42 | | 13 | 21 |
| 开州区 | Kaizhou District | 9351 | 200 | 9569 | 30 | | 10 | 6 |
| 梁平区 | Liangping District | 5632 | 29 | 3610 | 12 | | 4 | 4 |
| 武隆区 | Wulong District | 2895 | 96 | 3819 | 6 | | 6 | |
| 城口县 | Chengkou County | 3574 | 18 | 1670 | 3 | | 2 | 1 |
| 丰都县 | Fengdu County | 3719 | 44 | 4699 | 13 | | 3 | 1 |
| 垫江县 | Dianjiang County | 4059 | 98 | 8269 | 19 | | 5 | 8 |
| 忠 县 | Zhongxian County | 5242 | 101 | 6430 | 17 | | 10 | 8 |
| 云阳县 | Yunyang County | 10287 | 56 | 9377 | 22 | | 8 | 5 |
| 奉节县 | Fengjie County | 3822 | 71 | 8600 | 11 | | 9 | 6 |
| 巫山县 | Wushan County | 2536 | 27 | 3770 | 11 | | 5 | 2 |
| 巫溪县 | Wuxi County | 2521 | 36 | 3548 | 4 | | 4 | 1 |
| 石柱县 | Shizhu County | 3109 | 28 | 4850 | 7 | | 5 | 1 |
| 秀山县 | Xiushan County | 4704 | 88 | 7071 | 15 | | 2 | 3 |
| 酉阳县 | Youyang County | 4478 | 56 | 5309 | 27 | | 6 | 3 |
| 彭水县 | Pengshui County | 3453 | 61 | 5046 | 11 | | 9 | 4 |

# 附 录

# APPENDIX

# 简要说明

## BRIEF INTRODUCTION

本章中全国数据摘自《中国统计摘要2023》，部分数据为初步统计数，正式统计数据以《中国统计年鉴2023》为准。

The data of the whole nation in this table are extracted from China Statistical Summary2023, and some of the data are primary statistics. See China Statistical Yearbook2023 for the official data (the same applies to the following tables).

# 附录 1: 重庆市国民经济主要指标占全国的比重(2022 年)
## APPENDIX I: CHONGQING'S MAIN INDICATORS OF NATIONAL ECONOMY AS PERCENTAGE OF WHOLE NATION (2022)

| 指 标 | Item | 全 国<br>Whole Nation | 重 庆<br>Chongqing | 重庆占全国的比重(%)<br>Chongqing as Percentage of Whole Nation (%) |
|---|---|---|---|---|
| 土地面积(万平方公里) | Land Area (10 000 sq. km) | 960 | 8.24 | 0.86 |
| 年末户籍总人口(万人) | Year-end Population (10 000 persons) | 141175 | 3413.80 | 2.42 |
| 年末就业人员数(万人) | Year-end Employment (10 000 persons) | 73351 | 1644.37 | 2.24 |
| 国内(地区)生产总值(亿元) | Gross Domestic Product (100 million yuan) | 1210207.2 | 29129.03 | 2.41 |
| 第一产业 | Primary Industry | 88345.1 | 2012.05 | 2.28 |
| 第二产业 | Secondary Industry | 483164.5 | 11693.86 | 2.42 |
| 第三产业 | Tertiary Industry | 638697.6 | 15423.12 | 2.41 |
| 主要农业产品产量(万吨) | Output of Major Agricultural and Industrial Products (10 000 tons) | | | |
| 粮 食 | Gain | 68653 | 1072.84 | 1.56 |
| 油 料 | Oil-bearing Crops | 3654 | 70.85 | 1.94 |
| 城镇常住居民人均可支配收入(元) | Per Capita Disposable Income of Urban Residents(yuan) | 49283 | 45509 | |
| 农村常住居民人均可支配收入(元) | Per Capita Disposable Income of Rural Residents(yuan) | 20133 | 19313 | |
| 邮政业务总量(亿元) | Total Business Volume of Postal Services (100 million yuan) | 14316.7 | 189.45 | 1.32 |
| 电信业务总量(亿元) | Total Business Volume of Telecommunication Services (101 million yuan) | 17497.5 | 381.74 | 2.18 |
| 社会消费品零售总额(亿元) | Retail Sales of Consumer Goods (100 million yuan) | 439733 | 13926.08 | 3.17 |
| 房地产开发投资(亿元) | Real Estate Development (100 million yuan) | 128074.6 | 3216.87 | 2.51 |
| 金融机构人民币各项存款余额(亿元) | Deposit Balance of RMB of Financial Institutions (100 million yuan) | 2584998 | 48218.18 | 1.87 |
| 金融机构人民币各项贷款余额(亿元) | Loan Balance of RMB of Financial Institutions (100 million yuan) | 2139853 | 49365.86 | 2.31 |
| 货物进出口总额(亿元) | Total Imports and Exports (100 million Yuan) | 420678.2 | 8158.35 | 1.94 |
| 出口额 | Exports | 239654.0 | 5245.32 | 2.19 |
| 进口额 | Imports | 181024.2 | 2913.03 | 1.61 |
| 建筑业总产值(亿元) | Gross Output Value of Construction (100 million yuan) | 307935 | 9746.96 | 3.17 |
| 在校学生数(万人) | Student Enrollment (10 000 persons) | | | |
| #普通、职业高等学校 | Ordinary and vocational colleges and universities | 3659 | 106.61 | 2.91 |
| 普通小学 | Primary Schools | 10732 | 203.19 | 1.89 |
| 执业(助理)医师(万人) | Licensed (Assistant) Doctors (10 000 persons) | 444 | 9.46 | 2.13 |
| 医院床位数(万张) | Number of Beds in Hospitals and Health Centers (10 000 units) | 766 | 25.08 | 3.27 |

## 附录 2: 全国国民经济与社会发展速度指标

## APPENDIX II: INDICATORS ON THE GROWTH RATE OF NATIONAL ECONOMIC AND SOCIAL DEVELOPMENT

| 指 标 | Item | 2022 年 | 2022 年为下列各年 % 2022 as Percentage of the Following Years (%) | | | | 平均每年增长（%） Average Annual Growth Rate (%) | | |
|---|---|---|---|---|---|---|---|---|---|
| | | | 1978 | 1990 | 2000 | 2021 | 1979-2022 | 1991-2022 | 2001-2022 |
| **人 口** | **Population** | | | | | | | | |
| 年末总人口（万人） | Year-end Population (10 000 persons) | 141175 | 146.7 | 123.5 | 111.4 | 99.9 | 0.9 | 0.7 | 0.5 |
| 城镇人口 | Urban Population | 92071 | 533.9 | 304.9 | 200.6 | 100.7 | 3.9 | 3.5 | 3.2 |
| 乡村人口 | Rural Population | 49104 | 62.1 | 58.4 | 60.7 | 98.5 | -1.1 | -1.7 | -2.2 |
| **就业和失业** | **Employment and Unemployment** | | | | | | | | |
| 就业人员数（万人） | Employment (10 000 persons) | 73351 | 182.7 | 113.3 | 101.8 | 98.3 | 1.4 | 0.4 | 0.1 |
| #城镇就业人员 | Employment in Urban Areas | 45931 | 482.8 | 269.5 | 198.4 | 98.2 | 3.6 | 3.1 | 3.2 |
| 城镇登记失业人员（万人） | Registered Unemployment in Urban Areas (10 000 persons) | 1203 | 227.0 | 313.9 | 202.2 | 115.7 | 1.9 | 3.6 | 3.3 |
| **国民经济核算** | **National Accounting** | | | | | | | | |
| 国内生产总值（亿元） | Gross Domestic Product (100 million yuan) | 1210207.2 | 4480.1 | 1589.0 | 589.3 | 103.0 | 9.0 | 9.0 | 8.4 |
| 第一产业 | Primary Industry | 88345.1 | 659.0 | 345.6 | 239.3 | 104.1 | 4.4 | 4.0 | 4.0 |
| 第二产业 | Secondary Industry | 483164.5 | 6768.3 | 2235.6 | 631.0 | 103.8 | 10.1 | 10.2 | 8.7 |
| 第三产业 | Tertiary Industry | 638697.6 | 6439.7 | 1781.1 | 671.8 | 102.3 | 9.9 | 9.4 | 9.0 |
| **财 政** | **Government Finance** | | | | | | | | |
| 一般公共预算收入（亿元） | General Public Budget Revenue (100 million yuan) | 203703.48 | | | | | | | |
| 一般公共预算支出（亿元） | General Public Budget Expenditure (100 million yuan) | 260609.17 | | | | | | | |
| **能 源** | **Energy** | | | | | | | | |
| 一次能源生产总量（万吨标准煤） | Total Energy Output (10 000 ton of standard coal) | 466000 | 743.0 | 448.8 | 336.6 | 109.2 | 4.7 | 4.8 | 5.7 |
| 能源消费总量（万吨标准煤） | Total Consumption of Energy (10 000 ton of standard coal) | 541000 | 947.0 | 548.3 | 368.2 | 102.9 | 5.2 | 5.5 | 6.1 |
| **固定资产投资** | **Investment in Fixed Assets** | | | | | | | | |
| 全社会固定资产投资总额（亿元） | Total Investment in Fixed Assets (100 million yuan) | | | | | | | | |
| #房地产开发 | Real Estate Development | 128074.6 | | | | | | | |
| **对外贸易和实际利用外资** | **Foreign Trade and Foreign Capital Actually Utilized** | | | | | | | | |
| 货物进出口总额（亿元） | Total Imports and Exports (100 million Yuan) | 420678.2 | 118500.9 | 7566.0 | 1071.2 | 107.6 | 17.5 | 14.5 | 11.4 |
| 出口额 | Exports | 239654.0 | 142949.0 | 8026.4 | 1161.4 | 110.3 | 18.0 | 14.7 | 11.8 |
| 进口额 | Imports | 181024.2 | 96602.9 | 7032.0 | 971.2 | 104.3 | 16.9 | 14.2 | 10.9 |
| 外商直接投资（亿美元） | Foreign Direct Investment (USD 100 million) | 1891.3 | | 5423.9 | 464.5 | 109.0 | | 13.3 | 7.2 |

注：国内生产总值按可比价格计算，固定资产投资总额平均每年增长速度按累计法计算，一般公共预算收入和支出按可比口径计算，其他价值量指标按当年价格计算。

Note: GDP, general public budget revenue and expenditure are calculated on the basis of comparable price, the average growth rate of investment in fixed assets is calculated on the basis of accumulative method, and other value and index indicators are calculated at current price.

**附录 2 续表 continued**

| 指 标 | Item | 2022 年 | 2022 年为下列各年 % 2022 as Percentage of the Following Years (%) | | | | 平均每年增长（%） Average Annual Growth Rate (%) | | |
|---|---|---|---|---|---|---|---|---|---|
| | | | 1978 年 | 1990 年 | 2000 年 | 2021 年 | 1979-2022 | 1991-2022 | 2001-2022 |
| **主要产品产量** | **Output of Major Products** | | | | | | | | |
| 粮 食（万吨） | Gain（10 000 tons) | 68652.8 | 225.3 | 153.8 | 148.5 | 100.5 | 1.9 | 1.4 | 1.8 |
| 棉 花（万吨） | Cotton（10 000 tons) | 598.0 | 276.0 | 132.7 | 135.4 | 104.3 | 2.3 | 0.9 | 1.4 |
| 油 料（万吨） | Oil-bearing Crops（10 000 tons) | 3654.2 | 700.3 | 226.5 | 123.7 | 101.1 | 4.5 | 2.6 | 1.0 |
| 肉 类（万吨） | Meat（10 000 tons) | 9328.4 | 989.2 | 326.5 | 155.1 | 103.8 | 5.3 | 3.8 | 2.0 |
| 原 煤（亿吨） | Coal（100 million tons) | 45.6 | 737.7 | 422.1 | 329.4 | 110.5 | 4.6 | 4.6 | 5.6 |
| 原 油（万吨） | Oil（10 000 tons) | 20472.2 | 196.8 | 148.0 | 125.6 | 102.9 | 1.6 | 1.2 | 1.0 |
| 水 泥（万吨） | Cement（10 000 tons) | 212951.3 | 3264.1 | 1015.5 | 356.7 | 89.6 | 8.2 | 7.5 | 6.0 |
| 粗 钢（万吨） | Steel（10 000 tons) | 101795.9 | 3203.1 | 1534.2 | 792.2 | 98.3 | 8.2 | 8.9 | 9.9 |
| 发电量（亿千瓦时） | Electricity（100 million kwh) | 88487.1 | 3449.1 | 1424.5 | 652.8 | 103.7 | 8.4 | 8.7 | 8.9 |
| **建筑业** | **Construction** | | | | | | | | |
| 建筑业总产值（亿元） | Gross Output Value of Construction (100 million yuan) | 307935 | | | | | | | |
| **运 输** | **Transportation** | | | | | | | | |
| 客运量（万人） | Passenger Traffic (10 000 persons) | 558738 | 220.0 | 72.3 | 37.8 | 67.3 | 1.8 | -1.0 | -4.3 |
| 货运量（万吨） | Freight Traffic (10 000 tons) | 5152571 | 1613.0 | 530.9 | 379.2 | 97.2 | 6.5 | 5.4 | 6.2 |
| **邮电通信业** | **Telecommunications and Postal Services** | | | | | | | | |
| 移动电话用户（万户） | Mobile Telephone Subscribers (10 000 subscribers) | 168344 | | 9189602.6 | 1991.5 | 102.5 | | 42.9 | 14.6 |
| 固定电话用户（万户） | Fixed Telephone Subscribers (10 000 subscribers) | 17941 | 9318.1 | 2619.1 | 123.9 | 99.3 | 10.9 | 10.7 | 1.0 |
| **国内贸易** | **Domestic Trade** | | | | | | | | |
| 社会消费品零售总额（亿元） | Retail Sales of Consumer Goods(100 million yuan) | 439733 | 28213.3 | 5297.9 | 1143.7 | 99.8 | 13.7 | 13.2 | 11.7 |
| **科技、教育、卫生** | **Science & Technology, Education and Health** | | | | | | | | |
| 研究与试验发展经费支出(亿元） | Expenditure on R&D (100 million yuan) | 30870 | | | 3446.5 | 110.4 | | | 17.5 |
| 技术市场成交额（亿元） | Contract Value of Technology Market (100 million yuan) | 47791 | | | 7343.4 | 128.1 | | | 21.6 |
| **在校学生数(万人）** | **Student Enrollment (10 000 persons)** | | | | | | | | |
| #普通、职业高等学校 | Ordinary and vocational colleges and universities | 3659.4 | 4275.0 | 1773.8 | 658.1 | 104.7 | 8.9 | 9.4 | 8.9 |
| 普通高中 | Regular Senior Secondary Schools | 2713.9 | 174.7 | 378.3 | 225.9 | 104.2 | 1.3 | 4.2 | 3.8 |
| 初 中 | Secondary Schools | 5120.6 | 102.5 | 130.7 | 81.8 | 102.0 | 0.1 | 0.8 | -0.9 |
| 普通小学 | Primary Schools | 10732.1 | 73.4 | 87.7 | 82.5 | 99.6 | -0.7 | -0.4 | -0.9 |
| 医院数（万个） | Number of Hospitals(unit) | 3.7 | 398.1 | 257.4 | 226.7 | 101.2 | 3.2 | 3.0 | 3.8 |
| 医院床位数(万张） | Number of Beds in Hospitals (10 000 bed) | 766.3 | 696.6 | 410.0 | 353.7 | 103.4 | 4.5 | 4.5 | 5.9 |
| 执业(助理)医师（万人） | Number of Licensed (Assistant) Doctors (10 000 person) | 443.5 | 453.4 | 251.5 | 213.6 | 103.4 | 3.5 | 2.9 | 3.5 |

# 附录 3：全国各省（自治区、直辖市）国民经济主要指标（2022 年）

## APPENDIX III: MAIN INDICATORS OF NATIONAL ECONOMY BY PROVINCE, MUNICIPALITY AND AUTONOMOUS REGION (2022)

| 地 区 | Region | 年末常住人口（万人）Resident Population at Year-end (10 000 persons) | 地区生产总值（亿元）Gross Domestic Product (100 million yuan) | 第一产业 Primary Industry | 第二产业 Secondary Industry |
|---|---|---|---|---|---|
| **东部地区** | **Eastern Region** | | | | |
| 北 京 | Beijing | 2184 | 41610.9 | 111.5 | 6605.1 |
| 天 津 | Tianjin | 1363 | 16311.3 | 273.1 | 6038.9 |
| 河 北 | Hebei | 7420 | 42370.4 | 4410.3 | 17050.1 |
| 辽 宁 | Liaoning | 4197 | 28975.1 | 2597.6 | 11755.8 |
| 上 海 | Shanghai | 2475 | 44652.8 | 97.0 | 11458.4 |
| 江 苏 | Jiangsu | 8515 | 122875.6 | 4959.4 | 55888.7 |
| 浙 江 | Zhejiang | 6577 | 77715.4 | 2324.8 | 33205.2 |
| 福 建 | Fujian | 4188 | 53109.9 | 3076.2 | 25078.2 |
| 山 东 | Shandong | 10163 | 87435.1 | 6298.6 | 35014.2 |
| 广 东 | Guangdong | 12657 | 129118.6 | 5340.4 | 52843.5 |
| 海 南 | Hainan | 1027 | 6818.2 | 1417.8 | 1310.9 |
| **中部地区** | **Central Region** | | | | |
| 山 西 | Shanxi | 3481 | 25642.6 | 1340.4 | 13840.8 |
| 吉 林 | Jilin | 2348 | 13070.2 | 1689.1 | 4628.3 |
| 黑龙江 | Heilongjiang | 3099 | 15901.0 | 3609.8 | 4648.9 |
| 安 徽 | Anhui | 6127 | 45045.0 | 3513.7 | 18588.0 |
| 江 西 | Jiangxi | 4528 | 32074.7 | 2451.5 | 14359.6 |
| 河 南 | Henan | 9872 | 61345.1 | 5817.8 | 25465.0 |
| 湖 北 | Hubei | 5844 | 53734.9 | 4986.7 | 21240.6 |
| 湖 南 | Hunan | 6604 | 48670.4 | 4602.7 | 19182.6 |
| **西部地区** | **Western Region** | | | | |
| 重 庆 | Chongqing | 3213 | 29129.0 | 2012.1 | 11693.9 |
| 四 川 | Sichuan | 8374 | 56749.8 | 5964.3 | 21157.1 |
| 贵 州 | Guizhou | 3856 | 20164.6 | 2861.2 | 7113.0 |
| 云 南 | Yunnan | 4693 | 28954.2 | 4012.2 | 10471.2 |
| 西 藏 | Tibet | 364 | 2132.6 | 180.2 | 804.7 |
| 陕 西 | Shaanxi | 3956 | 32772.7 | 2575.3 | 15933.1 |
| 甘 肃 | Gansu | 2492 | 11201.6 | 1515.3 | 3945.0 |
| 青 海 | Qinghai | 595 | 3610.1 | 380.2 | 1585.7 |
| 宁 夏 | Ningxia | 728 | 5069.6 | 407.5 | 2449.1 |
| 新 疆 | Xinjiang | 2587 | 17741.3 | 2509.3 | 7271.1 |
| 内蒙古 | Inner Mongolia | 2401 | 23158.6 | 2653.7 | 11241.8 |
| 广 西 | Guangxi | 5047 | 26300.9 | 4269.8 | 8938.6 |

注：1) 本表绝对数按当年价计算。
2) 本表各省、市固定资产投资数据不含跨区投资和农户投资。
3) 本表交通数据均不含民航数据。

| 第三产业 Tertiary Industry | 地区生产总值指数（上年=100） Indices of Gross Domestic Product (Preceding Year=100) | 人均地区生产总值（元） Per Capita GDP (yuan) | 人均地区生产总值指数（上年=100） Indices of Per Capita GDP (Preceding Year=100) | 农林牧渔业总产值（亿元） Gross Output Value of Farming, Forestry, Animal Husbandry and Fishery (100 million yuan) | #农 业 Farming | #林 业 Forestry | #牧 业 Animal Husbandry | #渔 业 Fishery |
|---|---|---|---|---|---|---|---|---|
| 34894.3 | 100.7 | 190313 | 100.8 | 268.2 | 129.8 | 86.5 | 42.3 | 3.9 |
| 9999.3 | 101.0 | 119235 | 101.8 | 521.4 | 276.8 | 8.9 | 147.2 | 70.5 |
| 20910.0 | 103.8 | 56995 | 104.1 | 7667.4 | 4035.7 | 266.6 | 2391.7 | 342.3 |
| 14621.7 | 102.1 | 68775 | 102.8 | 5180.0 | 2258.3 | 161.7 | 1694.6 | 881.3 |
| 33097.4 | 99.8 | 179907 | 100.0 | 273.5 | 149.3 | 8.3 | 46.4 | 51.2 |
| 62027.5 | 102.8 | 144390 | 102.5 | 8733.8 | 4685.7 | 185.6 | 1294.2 | 1856.9 |
| 42185.4 | 103.1 | 118496 | 102.2 | 3752.3 | 1769.8 | 183.0 | 405.7 | 1261.2 |
| 24955.5 | 104.7 | 126829 | 104.3 | 5502.6 | 2065.7 | 429.9 | 1066.3 | 1740.7 |
| 46122.3 | 103.9 | 86003 | 103.9 | 12130.7 | 6206.5 | 227.3 | 3003.5 | 1729.7 |
| 70934.7 | 101.9 | 101905 | 101.7 | 8892.3 | 4308.2 | 549.2 | 1680.2 | 1898.2 |
| 4089.5 | 100.2 | 66602 | 99.5 | 2272.0 | 1236.8 | 118.7 | 340.5 | 466.6 |
| | | | | | | | | |
| 10461.3 | 104.4 | 73675 | 104.5 | 2211.6 | 1288.4 | 174.5 | 615.8 | 9.1 |
| 6752.8 | 98.1 | 55347 | 99.2 | 3217.9 | 1512.7 | 69.5 | 1482.6 | 61.6 |
| 7642.2 | 102.7 | 51096 | 103.9 | 6718.2 | 4320.5 | 212.3 | 1842.8 | 147.9 |
| 22943.3 | 103.5 | 73603 | 103.3 | 6278.0 | 2937.0 | 473.3 | 1812.5 | 660.3 |
| 15263.7 | 104.7 | 70923 | 104.6 | 4223.8 | 1916.7 | 416.9 | 1094.4 | 553.2 |
| 30062.2 | 103.1 | 62106 | 103.5 | 10952.2 | 6948.3 | 149.5 | 2832.3 | 147.4 |
| 27507.6 | 104.3 | 92059 | 103.4 | 8939.3 | 4193.1 | 311.2 | 2128.2 | 1584.3 |
| 24885.1 | 104.5 | 73598 | 104.8 | 8160.1 | 3973.2 | 477.4 | 2466.9 | 617.8 |
| | | | | | | | | |
| 15423.1 | 102.6 | 90663 | 102.5 | 3068.4 | 1881.8 | 176.4 | 800.9 | 137.0 |
| 29628.4 | 102.9 | 67777 | 102.9 | 9859.8 | 5528.8 | 438.2 | 3281.7 | 343.1 |
| 10190.4 | 101.2 | 52321 | 101.2 | 4908.7 | 3313.7 | 340.0 | 941.4 | 79.6 |
| 14470.8 | 104.3 | 61716 | 104.7 | 6635.8 | 3629.9 | 492.2 | 2192.3 | 119.9 |
| 1147.8 | 101.1 | 58438 | 101.4 | 278.6 | 121.0 | 7.0 | 143.4 | 0.2 |
| 14264.2 | 104.3 | 82864 | 104.3 | 4601.9 | 3310.4 | 86.1 | 925.4 | 36.2 |
| 5741.2 | 104.5 | 44968 | 104.7 | 2680.7 | 1806.4 | 36.4 | 662.2 | 1.7 |
| 1644.2 | 102.3 | 60724 | 102.1 | 566.2 | 238.3 | 13.1 | 302.3 | 4.3 |
| 2213.0 | 104.0 | 69781 | 103.5 | 845.9 | 455.6 | 11.5 | 323.5 | 22.8 |
| 7961.0 | 103.2 | 68552 | 103.3 | 5469.0 | 3754.0 | 53.5 | 1305.3 | 32.1 |
| 9263.1 | 104.2 | 96474 | 104.2 | 4316.8 | 2208.5 | 107.5 | 1876.3 | 31.3 |
| 13092.5 | 102.9 | 52164 | 102.6 | 6938.5 | 3977.7 | 548.5 | 1509.5 | 575.8 |

Note:a) The values in this table are calculated at current prices.
b) The data of investment in fixed assets in this table excludes trans-regional investment and investment of rural households.
c) The civil aviation data are not include in traffic data of this table.

**附录 3 续表 1 continued 1**

| 地 区 | Region | 农林牧渔业总产值指数（可比价）（上年=100）Indices of Gross Output Value of Farming, Forestry, Animal Husbandry and Fishery (Preceding Year=100) | 粮食产量（万吨）Grain Output (10 000 tons) | 油料产量（万吨）Oil-bearing Crops Output (10 000 tons) | 肉类产量（万吨）Meat Output (10 000 tons) | #猪 肉 Pork | #牛 肉 Beef | #羊 肉 Lamb |
|---|---|---|---|---|---|---|---|---|
| **东部地区** | **Eastern Region** | | | | | | | |
| 北 京 | Beijing | -2.0 | 45.4 | 0.9 | 4.3 | 2.8 | 0.4 | 0.2 |
| 天 津 | Tianjin | 2.9 | 256.2 | 0.4 | 29.5 | 16.7 | 2.9 | 1.0 |
| 河 北 | Hebei | 4.6 | 3865.1 | 115.4 | 478.8 | 273.4 | 58.1 | 36.9 |
| 辽 宁 | Liaoning | 3.2 | 2484.5 | 113.4 | 446.2 | 242.6 | 32.3 | 6.7 |
| 上 海 | Shanghai | -1.1 | 95.6 | 0.3 | 9.5 | 8.3 | 0.0 | 0.2 |
| 江 苏 | Jiangsu | 3.9 | 3769.1 | 96.3 | 318.1 | 179.4 | 2.9 | 7.2 |
| 浙 江 | Zhejiang | 3.4 | 621.0 | 33.0 | 108.5 | 71.4 | 1.5 | 2.4 |
| 福 建 | Fujian | 3.9 | 508.7 | 23.6 | 296.3 | 128.1 | 2.7 | 2.3 |
| 山 东 | Shandong | 4.8 | 5543.8 | 274.0 | 844.5 | 368.4 | 60.4 | 33.7 |
| 广 东 | Guangdong | 4.8 | 1291.5 | 117.4 | 481.0 | 279.8 | 4.5 | 2.0 |
| 海 南 | Hainan | 3.5 | 146.6 | 7.5 | 69.2 | 33.9 | 2.0 | 1.1 |
| **中部地区** | **Central Region** | | | | | | | |
| 山 西 | Shanxi | 5.0 | 1464.3 | 15.0 | 143.2 | 92.4 | 9.1 | 11.2 |
| 吉 林 | Jilin | 4.1 | 4080.8 | 81.6 | 291.0 | 150.1 | 44.3 | 8.3 |
| 黑龙江 | Heilongjiang | 2.5 | 7763.1 | 14.3 | 312.5 | 191.8 | 52.7 | 15.2 |
| 安 徽 | Anhui | 4.5 | 4100.1 | 173.4 | 475.3 | 248.3 | 11.7 | 22.5 |
| 江 西 | Jiangxi | 4.3 | 2151.9 | 137.5 | 359.9 | 249.9 | 17.1 | 3.1 |
| 河 南 | Henan | 5.1 | 6789.4 | 684.0 | 660.0 | 434.9 | 36.7 | 29.0 |
| 湖 北 | Hubei | 4.4 | 2741.1 | 374.2 | 441.2 | 331.7 | 16.3 | 10.5 |
| 湖 南 | Hunan | 3.8 | 3018.0 | 277.0 | 580.9 | 457.9 | 21.6 | 18.2 |
| **西部地区** | **Western Region** | | | | | | | |
| 重 庆 | Chongqing | 4.5 | 1072.8 | 70.8 | 205.3 | 150.0 | 8.0 | 6.9 |
| 四 川 | Sichuan | 4.5 | 3510.5 | 433.8 | 685.7 | 478.0 | 38.6 | 27.4 |
| 贵 州 | Guizhou | 4.2 | 1114.6 | 105.6 | 241.0 | 178.8 | 22.8 | 4.7 |
| 云 南 | Yunnan | 5.5 | 1958.0 | 63.5 | 521.6 | 393.2 | 43.6 | 21.7 |
| 西 藏 | Tibet | 4.8 | 107.3 | 4.7 | 28.6 | 1.8 | 21.4 | 5.1 |
| 陕 西 | Shaanxi | 4.6 | 1297.9 | 56.3 | 132.1 | 101.6 | 8.9 | 10.2 |
| 甘 肃 | Gansu | 5.9 | 1265.0 | 61.3 | 142.6 | 67.9 | 27.2 | 36.5 |
| 青 海 | Qinghai | 4.6 | 107.3 | 30.9 | 41.0 | 6.3 | 21.9 | 12.4 |
| 宁 夏 | Ningxia | 4.9 | 375.8 | 4.5 | 36.8 | 9.0 | 12.5 | 12.5 |
| 新 疆 | Xinjiang | 5.8 | 1813.5 | 37.2 | 204.7 | 57.0 | 49.4 | 60.7 |
| 内蒙古 | Inner Mongolia | 4.9 | 3900.6 | 170.0 | 284.1 | 73.7 | 71.9 | 110.2 |
| 广 西 | Guangxi | 5.0 | 1393.1 | 76.5 | 454.9 | 262.7 | 14.9 | 4.3 |

| 奶类产量<br>（万吨）<br>Diary Output<br>(10 000 tons) | 水泥产量<br>（万吨）<br>Cement Output<br>(10 000 tons) | 钢材产量<br>（万吨）<br>Steel Output<br>(10 000 tons) | 汽车产量<br>（万辆）<br>Motor Vehicle<br>Output (10 000 units) | 微型计算机设备<br>（万台）<br>Micro Computers<br>(10 000 units) | 发电量<br>（亿千瓦时）<br>Electricity<br>Production<br>(100 million KWH) |
|---|---|---|---|---|---|
| 26.2 | 203.4 | 184.3 | 87.1 | 858.6 | 467.1 |
| 51.1 | 529.5 | 5543.7 | 60.3 | 0.1 | 764.9 |
| 549.3 | 10033.9 | 32169.2 | 90.6 | | 3792.9 |
| 135.1 | 3910.9 | 7727.5 | 76.6 | 49.4 | 2256.8 |
| 30.2 | 369.6 | 1920.9 | 302.5 | 2760.7 | 955.0 |
| 68.8 | 14235.7 | 14882.2 | 94.4 | 3330.5 | 6077.3 |
| 19.7 | 12953.7 | 2934.8 | 124.9 | 129.6 | 4349.9 |
| 22.1 | 9692.9 | 3505.5 | 33.9 | 1185.3 | 3088.8 |
| 304.5 | 13522.5 | 10529.1 | 101.9 | 0.7 | 6203.6 |
| 19.9 | 15226.4 | 5627.4 | 415.4 | 6948.8 | 6365.7 |
| 0.3 | 1626.4 | | 2.2 | | 405.7 |
| | | | | | |
| 143.1 | 4844.6 | 6354.6 | 16.5 | 3.6 | 4298.8 |
| 29.4 | 1731.4 | 1532.0 | 215.6 | | 1056.9 |
| 501.9 | 1881.1 | 999.7 | 8.3 | | 1217.6 |
| 50.7 | 14218.7 | 3963.0 | 174.7 | 2950.2 | 3298.8 |
| 7.9 | 8997.2 | 3457.0 | 41.4 | 4946.6 | 1725.0 |
| 217.8 | 11488.4 | 4158.0 | 55.3 | 97.2 | 3429.8 |
| 9.2 | 11056.2 | 3911.1 | 189.6 | 1336.2 | 3108.7 |
| 7.2 | 9998.4 | 3038.3 | 26.3 | 208.2 | 1768.1 |
| | | | | | |
| 3.2 | 5321.1 | 1690.6 | 203.8 | 8631.9 | 997.8 |
| 70.8 | 13070.1 | 3583.0 | 72.5 | 9221.2 | 4846.2 |
| 3.7 | 6428.1 | 607.3 | 4.6 | 0.1 | 2299.0 |
| 70.2 | 9693.7 | 2550.7 | 2.2 | 571.0 | 4016.6 |
| 57.8 | 792.7 | | | | 128.2 |
| 170.5 | 6529.8 | 2010.5 | 133.8 | 8.4 | 2852.1 |
| 92.7 | 4047.8 | 1091.6 | | | 1954.1 |
| 35.3 | 978.5 | 120.6 | | | 998.1 |
| 342.5 | 1667.5 | 578.5 | | | 2235.1 |
| 231.5 | 3877.5 | 1324.7 | 1.4 | | 4793.4 |
| 740.8 | 3597.0 | 3041.9 | 5.4 | | 6619.2 |
| 13.1 | 10426.5 | 4995.6 | 177.0 | 179.7 | 2115.9 |

**附录 3 续表 2 continued 2**

| 地 区 | Region | 客运量（万人）Passenger Throughput (10 000 persons) | 旅客周转量（亿人公里）Passenger Turnover Volume (100 million person·km) | 货运量（万吨）Cargo Throughput (10 000 tons) | 货物周转量（亿吨公里）Cargo Turnover Volume (100 million tons·km) |
|---|---|---|---|---|---|
| **东部地区** | **Eastern Region** | | | | |
| 北 京 | Beijing | 25055 | 89 | 18918 | 1017 |
| 天 津 | Tianjin | 8295 | 98 | 52898 | 2666 |
| 河 北 | Hebei | 8410 | 382 | 232136 | 14234 |
| 辽 宁 | Liaoning | 17579 | 269 | 166281 | 4611 |
| 上 海 | Shanghai | 7397 | 76 | 141059 | 32370 |
| 江 苏 | Jiangsu | 47077 | 621 | 279143 | 11829 |
| 浙 江 | Zhejiang | 32659 | 491 | 321583 | 13545 |
| 福 建 | Fujian | 16567 | 260 | 169091 | 11340 |
| 山 东 | Shandong | 17536 | 415 | 334165 | 14273 |
| 广 东 | Guangdong | 42329 | 723 | 351809 | 28078 |
| 海 南 | Hainan | 6688 | 60 | 30007 | 9964 |
| **中部地区** | **Central Region** | | | | |
| 山 西 | Shanxi | 6274 | 119 | 211540 | 6473 |
| 吉 林 | Jilin | 7417 | 122 | 46467 | 1874 |
| 黑龙江 | Heilongjiang | 9203 | 126 | 52119 | 1852 |
| 安 徽 | Anhui | 14672 | 484 | 394061 | 11282 |
| 江 西 | Jiangxi | 16217 | 456 | 196926 | 5120 |
| 河 南 | Henan | 26828 | 640 | 259983 | 11751 |
| 湖 北 | Hubei | 26050 | 475 | 209475 | 7544 |
| 湖 南 | Hunan | 38244 | 687 | 213251 | 2932 |
| **西部地区** | **Western Region** | | | | |
| 重 庆 | Chongqing | 19634 | 207 | 135491 | 3880 |
| 四 川 | Sichuan | 40221 | 393 | 186423 | 3202 |
| 贵 州 | Guizhou | 20323 | 320 | 94999 | 1417 |
| 云 南 | Yunnan | 16698 | 248 | 145857 | 2000 |
| 西 藏 | Tibet | 630 | 22 | 4024 | 130 |
| 陕 西 | Shaanxi | 13372 | 279 | 164723 | 4369 |
| 甘 肃 | Gansu | 8013 | 209 | 72945 | 3681 |
| 青 海 | Qinghai | 1118 | 43 | 18467 | 703 |
| 宁 夏 | Ningxia | 2701 | 37 | 48623 | 874 |
| 新 疆 | Xinjiang | 12149 | 193 | 88293 | 2503 |
| 内蒙古 | Inner Mongolia | 3557 | 89 | 211615 | 5221 |
| 广 西 | Guangxi | 20654 | 378 | 213331 | 5173 |

| 固定资产投资增速（%）<br>Growth Rate of Investment in Fixed Assets (%) | #房地产开发投资（亿元）<br>Investment in Real Estate Development (100 million yuan) | 商品房销售面积（万平方米）<br>Housing Floor Space of Sales (10 000 sq. m) | 商品房销售额（亿元）<br>Total Sales of Commercialized Buildings (100 million yuan) | 建筑业总产值（亿元）<br>Total Output Value of Construction (100 million yuan) |
|---|---|---|---|---|
| 3.6 | 4178.5 | 1040 | 3977 | 13866.1 |
| -9.9 | 2127.9 | 974 | 1516 | 4751.3 |
| 7.9 | 4092.1 | 4616 | 3702 | 6951.3 |
| 3.6 | 2362.0 | 2182 | 1815 | 3936.9 |
| -1.0 | 4979.5 | 1853 | 7468 | 9273.9 |
| 3.8 | 12406.9 | 12115 | 14812 | 40660.0 |
| 9.1 | 12939.5 | 6815 | 12660 | 23861.1 |
| 7.5 | 5133.6 | 5452 | 5872 | 16851.0 |
| 6.1 | 9180.2 | 11686 | 9808 | 17559.6 |
| -2.6 | 14963.0 | 10591 | 15870 | 22956.5 |
| -4.2 | 1158.4 | 644 | 1098 | 467.2 |
| | | | | |
| 5.9 | 1764.2 | 2257 | 1515 | 6145.5 |
| -2.4 | 1014.8 | 1001 | 696 | 2100.7 |
| 0.6 | 628.6 | 926 | 569 | 1414.5 |
| 9.0 | 6203.5 | 6757 | 5160 | 11702.6 |
| 8.6 | 2209.3 | 6703 | 4905 | 10694.8 |
| 6.7 | 5684.8 | 9260 | 5679 | 13414.4 |
| 15.0 | 5933.9 | 6084 | 5203 | 21155.0 |
| 6.6 | 4858.3 | 6653 | 4239 | 14481.0 |
| | | | | |
| 0.7 | 3216.9 | 4143 | 2955 | 9747.0 |
| 6.0 | 7215.8 | 9321 | 7600 | 17845.6 |
| -5.1 | 1814.3 | 2908 | 1686 | 4260.2 |
| 7.5 | 3152.0 | 2938 | 1999 | 8168.6 |
| -18.0 | 60.7 | 60 | 51 | 203.8 |
| 8.1 | 4254.8 | 3309 | 3270 | 10067.9 |
| 10.1 | 1481.7 | 1470 | 835 | 2477.7 |
| -7.6 | 296.2 | 204 | 145 | 566.5 |
| 10.2 | 420.0 | 716 | 502 | 725.8 |
| 7.6 | 1158.9 | 1516 | 883 | 3101.5 |
| 17.6 | 978.3 | 1381 | 868 | 1332.8 |
| 0.1 | 2206.3 | 4193 | 2295 | 7194.3 |

附录 3 续表 3 continued 3

| 地 区 | Region | 社会消费品零售总额（亿元）Total Retail Sales of Consumer Goods (100 million yuan) | 进出口总额（亿美元）Total Imports and Exports (USD 100 million) | #出 口 Export | 一般公共预算收入（亿元）General Public Budget Revenue (100 million yuan) |
|---|---|---|---|---|---|
| **东部地区** | **Eastern Region** | | | | |
| 北 京 | Beijing | 13794.2 | 5465.0 | 881.7 | 5714.4 |
| 天 津 | Tianjin | 3572.0 | 1267.6 | 571.8 | 1846.6 |
| 河 北 | Hebei | 13720.1 | 843.2 | 510.5 | 4084.0 |
| 辽 宁 | Liaoning | 9526.2 | 1187.5 | 538.2 | 2524.3 |
| 上 海 | Shanghai | 16442.1 | 6272.4 | 2563.7 | 7608.2 |
| 江 苏 | Jiangsu | 42752.1 | 8177.5 | 5225.9 | 9258.9 |
| 浙 江 | Zhejiang | 30467.2 | 7034.4 | 5158.0 | 8039.4 |
| 福 建 | Fujian | 21050.1 | 2975.0 | 1820.4 | 3339.1 |
| 山 东 | Shandong | 33236.2 | 4994.3 | 3047.7 | 7104.0 |
| 广 东 | Guangdong | 44882.9 | 12470.4 | 7999.6 | 13279.7 |
| 海 南 | Hainan | 2268.4 | 300.9 | 107.4 | 832.4 |
| **中部地区** | **Central Region** | | | | |
| 山 西 | Shanxi | 7562.7 | 277.3 | 181.8 | 3453.9 |
| 吉 林 | Jilin | 3807.7 | 233.8 | 75.2 | 851.0 |
| 黑龙江 | Heilongjiang | 5210.0 | 396.9 | 81.3 | 1290.6 |
| 安 徽 | Anhui | 21518.4 | 1131.3 | 714.2 | 3589.1 |
| 江 西 | Jiangxi | 12853.5 | 1006.7 | 763.8 | 2948.3 |
| 河 南 | Henan | 24407.4 | 1279.0 | 787.6 | 4261.6 |
| 湖 北 | Hubei | 22164.8 | 927.3 | 632.2 | 3280.7 |
| 湖 南 | Hunan | 19050.7 | 1054.3 | 769.9 | 3101.8 |
| **西部地区** | **Western Region** | | | | |
| 重 庆 | Chongqing | 13926.1 | 1228.3 | 790.9 | 2103.4 |
| 四 川 | Sichuan | 24104.6 | 1511.7 | 931.5 | 4882.2 |
| 贵 州 | Guizhou | 8507.1 | 119.1 | 77.8 | 1886.4 |
| 云 南 | Yunnan | 10838.8 | 500.4 | 241.4 | 1949.3 |
| 西 藏 | Tibet | 726.5 | 6.9 | 6.5 | 179.7 |
| 陕 西 | Shaanxi | 10401.6 | 726.4 | 452.2 | 3311.6 |
| 甘 肃 | Gansu | 3922.2 | 88.3 | 19.1 | 907.6 |
| 青 海 | Qinghai | 842.1 | 6.5 | 4.0 | 329.1 |
| 宁 夏 | Ningxia | 1338.4 | 38.6 | 29.6 | 460.1 |
| 新 疆 | Xinjiang | 3240.5 | 366.8 | 311.1 | 1889.2 |
| 内蒙古 | Inner Mongolia | 4971.4 | 227.7 | 94.3 | 2824.4 |
| 广 西 | Guangxi | 8539.1 | 980.5 | 546.8 | 1687.7 |

| 一般公共预算支出（亿元）General Public Budget Expenditure (100 million yuan) | 全体居民人均可支配收入（元）Per Capita Disposable Income of Urban Residents(yuan) | 城镇常住居民人均可支配收入（元）Per Capita Disposable Income of Urban Residents(yuan) | 农村常住居民人均可支配收入（元）Per Capita Disposable Income of Rural Residents(yuan) | 居民消费价格指数（上年=100）General Consumer Price Index (preceding year=100) | 农产品生产者价格指数（上年=100）Producer Price Index of Farm Products (Preceding Year=100) |
|---|---|---|---|---|---|
| 7469.2 | 77414.5 | 84023.1 | 34753.8 | 101.8 | 102.7 |
| 2740.1 | 48976.1 | 53003.2 | 29017.8 | 101.9 | 98.4 |
| 9336.5 | 30867.0 | 41277.7 | 19364.2 | 101.8 | 103.5 |
| 6253.0 | 36088.8 | 44002.6 | 19908.0 | 102.0 | 103.6 |
| 9393.2 | 79609.8 | 84034.0 | 39729.4 | 102.5 | 102.6 |
| 14903.2 | 49861.7 | 60178.1 | 28486.5 | 102.2 | 100.1 |
| 12017.7 | 60302.5 | 71267.9 | 37565.0 | 102.2 | 101.5 |
| 5702.9 | 43117.7 | 53817.1 | 24986.6 | 101.9 | 100.8 |
| 12131.5 | 37560.1 | 49049.7 | 22109.9 | 101.7 | 100.6 |
| 18509.9 | 47064.6 | 56905.3 | 23597.8 | 102.2 | 100.1 |
| 2095.5 | 30956.6 | 40117.5 | 19117.4 | 101.6 | 106.8 |
| 5872.7 | 29178.2 | 39532.0 | 16322.7 | 102.1 | 104.0 |
| 4044.0 | 27974.5 | 35470.9 | 18134.5 | 102.1 | 100.7 |
| 5452.0 | 28345.5 | 35042.1 | 18577.4 | 101.9 | 102.5 |
| 8378.9 | 32745.2 | 45133.2 | 19574.9 | 102.0 | 102.8 |
| 7288.3 | 32418.7 | 43696.5 | 19936.0 | 102.0 | 97.5 |
| 10644.6 | 28222.4 | 38483.7 | 18697.3 | 101.5 | 97.2 |
| 8626.0 | 32913.6 | 42625.8 | 19709.5 | 102.1 | 100.6 |
| 9005.3 | 34036.0 | 47301.2 | 19546.3 | 101.8 | 103.6 |
| 4892.8 | 35665.9 | 45508.9 | 19312.7 | 102.1 | 98.7 |
| 11914.7 | 30679.2 | 43233.3 | 18672.4 | 102.0 | 99.1 |
| 5849.2 | 25508.2 | 41085.7 | 13706.7 | 101.6 | 95.9 |
| 6699.7 | 26936.8 | 42167.9 | 15146.9 | 101.6 | 96.7 |
| 2593.8 | 26674.8 | 48752.9 | 18209.5 | 101.5 | |
| 6766.3 | 30115.8 | 42431.3 | 15704.3 | 102.1 | 104.4 |
| 4263.5 | 23273.1 | 37572.4 | 12165.2 | 101.9 | 100.2 |
| 1975.1 | 27000.0 | 38735.8 | 14456.2 | 102.4 | 98.4 |
| 1583.5 | 29599.3 | 40193.7 | 16430.3 | 102.3 | 98.3 |
| 6857.3 | 27062.7 | 38410.2 | 16549.9 | 101.8 | 99.6 |
| 5885.1 | 35920.6 | 46295.4 | 19640.9 | 101.8 | 100.8 |
| 5893.9 | 27980.7 | 39703.0 | 17432.7 | 101.9 | 100.8 |

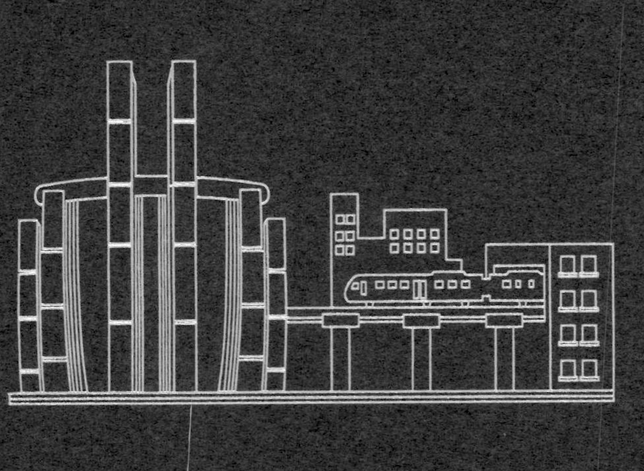